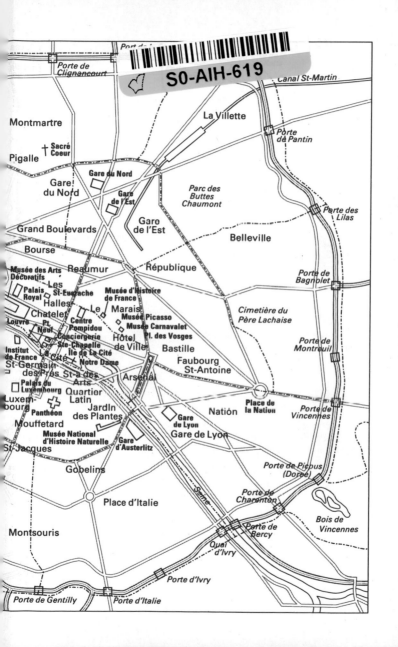

Paris

Guide Bleu

Paris

PRENTICE HALL

NEW YORK • LONDON • TORONTO • SYDNEY • TOKYO • SINGAPORE

Published by Prentice Hall
A Division of Simon & Schuster Inc.
15 Columbus Circle
New York, 10023

Originally published in France by Hachette Guides Bleus 1988
Revised edition 1990
Copyright © 1988, 1990, 1991 by Hachette Guides Bleus

Maps © Hachette and TCI 1988, 1990, 1991

Color maps © George Philip Ltd., 1989, 1991

Additional maps by Euromap Limited, Pangbourne, Berkshire

English translation © 1991 Harrap Books Ltd

Published in Great Britain by Harrap Books Ltd 1991

First American Edition 1991

Production by Book Production Consultants Ltd, Cambridge, UK

Phototypeset by Witwell Ltd, Southport

Printed and bound in England by Clays Ltd., St Ives Plc.

While every care has been taken in the compilation of this guide, the
publishers cannot be held responsible for any changes to the
information listed.

Library of Congress Cataloging-in-Publication Data

Guide Bleu Paris. English.
    Guide Bleu Paris.
      1632 p. ca
    Translation of: Guide Bleu Paris.
    ISBN 0-13-650144-3
    1. Paris (France)-Description-1975-Guidebooks. I. Title
DC708. G7613 1991
914.4'36104839-dc20
                                                    89-48039
                                                    CIP

Contents

How to use this guide

TO PLAN YOUR STAY IN PARIS

Consult the maps: 'What to see in Paris' (1): The Center (pp. 4–5) and 'What to see in Paris' (2): Away from the Center (pp. 10–11).

Glance through the 'Ideas – Discoveries' section (p. 27).

TO KNOW THE CAPITAL BETTER

Read 'Paris in History' (p. 48), 'Architecture in Paris' (p. 73), 'Paris Today' (p. 116), 'The Museums of Paris' (p. 1105).

TO VISIT PARIS

Open the guide at the descriptive sections for Districts and Monuments (p. 135) and for Museums (p. 1105).

Consult the color maps (between pp. 804 and 805) and the Métro map inside cover.

TO KNOW MORE ABOUT PARTICULAR SUBJECTS

Consult the Thematic 'Inset' Index (p. 1539).

TO FIND A DISTRICT, STREET, MONUMENT, MUSEUM OR PERSON

Consult the General Index (p. 1591) or Index of People (p. 1552).

TO FIND PRACTICAL INFORMATION

Consult the section entitled 'Practical Paris' (p. 15).

Symbols and abbreviations

Reference to color maps, e.g., 10–A3: the page number (10) is followed by the coordinates (A3).

In maps of museums and galleries the floor level in brackets is for the benefit of U.S. readers.

*noteworthy
**of great interest
***of exceptional interest

This symbol precedes an important monument or street on your walk through the district; in museums it indicates the most interesting exhibits or rooms.

The arrow indicates that the subject is dealt with elsewhere (→alphabetic entry or inset). Inserts are indicated by the symbol ▷.

The following additional symbols are used in this volume:

- ⚓ Church, abbey
- ☐ Civic building of interest
- ▣ Museum
- ⚶ Park, garden, forest
- ⚵ Zoological gardens, nature reserve
- ⚶ Panorama, viewpoint

Abbreviations

alt.	altitude	**m**	metre/s
Apr.	April	**Mar.**	March
approx.	approximately	**ml/s**	mile/s
arch.	architect	**mm**	millimetre
Aug.	August	**min.**	minute
Ave.	avenue	**Mon.**	Monday
Bd/Boul.	boulevard	**Nov.**	November
bldg	building	**Oct.**	October
c.	circa/century	**p./pp**	page/s
cm	centimetre	**pl.**	place/plan
cuis.	cuisine	**pop.**	population
d.	died	**r.**	right
Dec.	December	**rm/s**	room/s
E	East	**S**	South
Feb.	February	**St/Ste**	Saint
Fri.	Friday	**Sat.**	Saturday
ft	feet	**Sept.**	September
h.	hour/s	**sq. (ml/ft)**	square (mile/foot)
ha	hectare/s	**Sun.**	Sunday
hab.	inhabitants	**tel.**	Telephone
in	inch/es	**t**	ton
it.	itinerary	**Thurs.**	Thursday
Jan.	January	**Tues.**	Tuesday
Jul.	July	**V**	see
kg	kilogram	**vol.**	volume
km	kilometre	**W**	West
kWh	Kilowatt-hour	**Wed.**	Wednesday
l.	left	**yd/s**	yard/s

What to see in Paris

1 - The Center

For the museums → What to see in the museums of Paris.

ARSENAL*. The area around the Arsenal, one of the most important libraries in Paris after the Bibliothèque Nationale, is surprisingly tranquil. A pleasant walk on the banks of the basin that shelters the Paris marina.

BASTILLE. Linked to the history of the Revolution, the Place de la Bastille is still the setting for many demonstrations. The district is full of changes with the building of the Nouvel Opéra.

BEAUBOURG**. One of the oldest parts of Paris, this has become a cultural mecca snce the creation of the Pompidou Center.

BIBLIOTHÈQUE NATIONALE**. Impressive for its great collections and for the grandeur of the building.

BOURSE**. A district completely dedicated to money, where the Palais de la Bourse is the temple.

THE BRIDGES OF PARIS***. Major elements in the urban development of Paris, from both the utilitarian and the architectural viewpoints.

CHÂTELET*. Geographically, this is the center of Paris. A little further on, go to see the Church of Saint-Germain-l'Auxerrois, a major Gothic monument.

ILE DE LA CITÉ***. Old medieval fragments can still be found in the shadow of the cathedral. The Place Dauphine is one of the most charming squares in Paris.

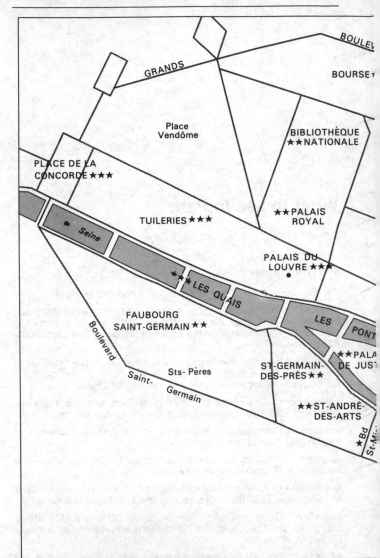

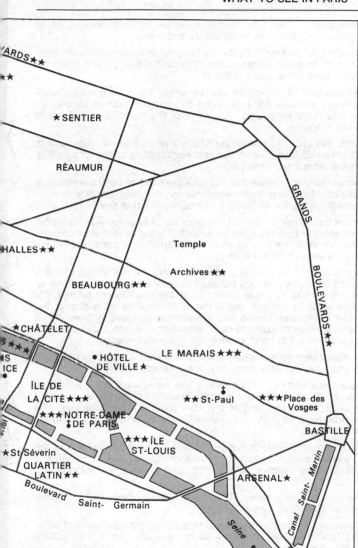

Paris —The Center

CONCORDE***.   The most beautiful square in Paris, because of its harmonious layout, its architecture and vistas.

GRANDS BOULEVARDS**.   Brilliantly lit by neon signs and the illuminations of its great theaters, the Grands Boulevards still mark the boundaries of the heart of Paris.

LES HALLES**.   A composite district where the huge complex comprising the Forum des Halles and an important cultural center, lies next to medieval streets. Do not miss the magnificent Church of Saint-Eustache.

HÔTEL DE VILLE*.   This building has recovered a certain dignity, with its whitened façades and the vast surrounding space for strolling, that isolates it from the traffic.

LATIN QUARTER**.   Since the Middle Ages this has been the students' district. It has many churches, some very fine. See the Gallo-Roman remains at the Cluny baths (→Sorbonne/What to see in Paris (2)).

PALAIS DU LOUVRE***.   One of the most beautiful palaces in the world, its history has always been inextricably linked to that of its country. The Grand Louvre project and the construction of the glass pyramid are the insignia of the 20th c.

THE MARAIS***.   The museum district where the restoration of many *hôtels* is being vigorously pursued: the Hôtel Salé and the setting up of the Picasso museum within it, is the most recent project; the Hôtel de Sully remains one of the most beautiful in the district; the Hôtel Carnavalet, turned into a historical museum by the Ville de Paris, is a superb example of Renaissance and 17th-c. civil architecture. See the first royal square, the Place des Vosges.

NOTRE-DAME***.   The cathedral of cathedrals, the 'parish of history in France', perfect in its harmony, scene of memorable events.

PALAIS DE JUSTICE**.   This building was not always in the service of the law. The Conciergerie, with its memories of the Revolution, is an important surviving part of the royal palace of the Capetians. The former royal chapel, the Sainte-Chapelle, is a jewel of Gothic architecture.

PALAIS-ROYAL**.   This district, dominated by the palace, seat of the Conseil d'Etat, is a place of seductive charm. Walk in its gardens bordered by galleries, and in the main courtyard, where Buren's columns stand.

THE QUAYS OF THE SEINE***.   The romantic walk of Paris, with the most remarkable views over the city.

RÉAUMUR*.   A district given over to clothing manufacture and printing. In the Rue Réaumur there are unusual late 19th- and early 20th-c. façades.

SAINT-ANDRÉ-DES-ARTS**.   Many narrow streets have kept their medieval layout. See the fine 17th-c. *hôtel* in the charming Cour de Rohan.

FAUBOURG SAINT-GERMAIN**. This large district seems to present all the facets of Parisian life. Art galleries and antique shops are concentrated around the Rue des Saints-Pères; the aristocratic mansions around the Rue de Grenelle and the Palais Bourbon hum with political activity; commerce and the religious life share the Sèvres-Babylone district.

SAINT-GERMAIN-DES-PRÉS**. The enduring mythology of the district is maintained by the famous cafés close to the Church of Saint-Germain-des-Prés. The little streets around the Saint-Germain market and the Rue de Buci recall some of the atmosphere of old fairs. Along the Seine see and admire the elegance of the Hôtel de la Monnaie (the Mint) and the Palais de l'Institut.

ILE SAINT-LOUIS***. There is a village atmosphere about this island. The façades of the *hôtel* along the quays, suffused with light, are particularly beautiful.

CANAL SAINT-MARTIN**. The place to go to find industrial Paris, characteristic of the beginning of the 20th c.

SENTIER*. A world apart, entirely devoted to the clothing industry.

TUILERIES***. Beyond the garden with its *fin-de-siècle* charm, around the Place Vendôme and the Rue de la Paix, is the luxury jewelry center of Paris and the ostentation of its rich clientèle. The atmosphere is more authentically Parisian around the Place de Marché-Saint-Honoré and the majestic Church of Saint-Roch.

What to see in Paris

2 - Away from the Center

For the museums →What to see in the museums of Paris.

ARC DE TRIOMPHE***. This, with the Eiffel Tower, is Paris's most famous monument. The Place de l'Etoile is a fine example of a setting planned specifically for a great monument.

AUTEUIL*. An extraordinary open-air museum of contemporary architecture: buildings by Guimard, Le Corbusier and Mallet-Stevens.

BATIGNOLLES. The Square des Batignolles is one of the most picturesque in Paris.

BELLEVILLE AND MÉNILMONTANT*. A typically Parisian *quartier* which has retained its 1930s appearance. Belleville is now the site for a remarkable urban and architectural experiment.

BOIS DE BOULOGNE*. The Parc de Bagatelle, the Jardin d'Acclimatation and the Musée des Arts et Traditions Populaires are some, but not all, of the attractions of this magnificent wood.

PARC DES BUTTES-CHAUMONT**. One of the most pleasant and least expected parks in Paris. Its picturesqueness lies in its irregular, wild terrain, with ruins and rocks.

CATACOMBS*. The Catacombs hold all the human bones taken, from the 18th c. onwards, from cemeteries considered to be dangerous to health. This descent into the world of the dead holds some surprises.

CHAILLOT**. The monumental Palais de Chaillot and the Palais d'Art

Moderne will attract those interested in the colossal architecture of the late 1930s.

CHAMPS-ELYSÉES***. The luxury buildings that border the upper section of the avenue will interest those who like modern architecture. The lower part, alongside the gardens, remains one of the most beautiful walks in Paris.

CHARONNE. This district has long retained its country-town atmosphere to be found around the Rue Saint-Blaise.

CHERCHE-MIDI. A residential district with a number of 18th-c. *hôtels*.

CLIGNANCOURT-LA-CHAPELLE. A working-class suburb that reveals another reality of Parisian life – that of the immigrant workers and the transitory population.

LA DÉFENSE*. The Tête-Défense project, with the building of the Grande Arche, constituted the final, monumental touch to the creation of this suburb, a veritable town of skyscrapers created in the early 1960s.

DENFERT-ROCHEREAU. The Place Denfert-Rochereau, where the famous Lion de Belfort stands, is one of the great intersections of the Left Bank. Go to see the charming Rue Daguerre with its traditional market.

LES EGOUTS (THE SEWERS). This visit, previously made by boat, is now done on foot; the circuit is of some 220 yards/200m.

EIFFEL TOWER***. The symbol of Paris, its fantastic metal frame dramatized by new floodlighting, tends to make the visitor forget the admirable Classical building nearby of the Ecole Militaire.

AVENUE FOCH AND DAUPHINE DISTRICT*. Famed as 'the most beautiful avenue in the world', the Ave. Foch compels admiration by its width, its lawns and trees and its vistas. Around the Ave. Victor-Hugo the Dauphine district is characterized by luxury apartment buildings and private mansions.

FRANCOIS-Ier. The prestige of this worldly and luxurious district derives in part from the presence of one of Paris's best concert halls, the Théâtre des Champs-Elysées.

GARE DE LYON-BERCY. The Palais Omnisports and the new Ministry of Finance building are the two most spectacular developments in a huge project that will entirely change the district.

GARE DU NORD AND GARE DE L'EST. The Paris of the Second Empire is epitomized here with *passages*, covered markets and long perspectives at the end of which the railway station supplants the church.

GOBELINS*. A village charm can still be found at the beginning of the Ave. des Gobelins, in the small streets around the factory.

GRENELLE*. Contrasting with the steel and glass towers of the Front de Seine, the old village of Grenelle retains country workers' modest dwellings, along with some fine Restoration houses.

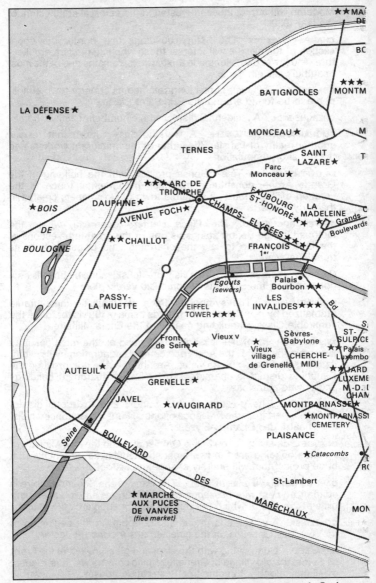

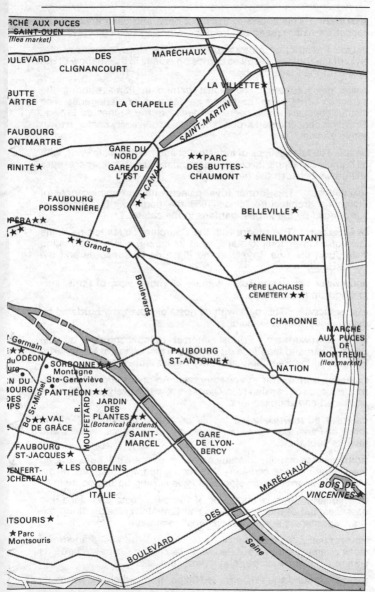

Away from the Center

INVALIDES*. This is one of the most open and quiet areas of the capital. Its vistas spread out from the imposing Hôtel des Invalides.

ITALIE. A district of contrasts, in which the sleepy provincial life-style of the Butte-aux-Cailles carries on quietly in the shadow of the towers of the Place d'Italie.

JARDIN DES PLANTES**. The oldest garden in Paris, offering the attraction of its maze, its alpine garden and its menageries. The district conceals small, secret gardens like the Arènes de Lutèce. Activity is concentrated around the Jussieu university center, a town within a town.

JAVEL. The last vestiges of industrialist and *misérabiliste* Paris, with its humble dwellings, its cul-de-sacs and narrow streets where grass still grows between the paving stones.

LUXEMBOURG*. This former royal palace with its reminiscences of Florentine architecture, since 1958 the home of the Senate, is surrounded by the largest gardens in the capital.

LA MADELEINE*. The square with the Church of La Madeleine in the style of a Greek temple standing in its center, offers an arresting vista down the Rue Royale to the Place de la Concorde and the Palais Bourbon.

BOULEVARDS DES MARÉCHAUX. A more all-round view of Paris, surprising with its contrasts.

PARC MONCEAU*. This park with its nostalgic charm, is bordered by ostentatious 19th-c. mansions.

BUTTE MONTMARTRE**. Tourist interest is concentrated on the Sacre-Coeur and the Place du Tertre; the real village of Montmartre lies around the Rue Lepic and the Rue des Abbesses.

FAUBOURG MONTMARTRE ET POISSONNIÈRE. An under-appreciated district, a mecca of Parisian Neo-Classicism, with a lively population of craftsmen and shopkeepers.

CIMETIÈRE DU MONTPARNASSE*. This cemetery, the smallest of the three in Paris, contains the graves of many artists, writers and famous publishers.

MONTPARNASSE DISTRICT*. Many artists' studios are still here, around the station and the cemetery. The contemporary creations of the Maine-Montparnasse development have sprung up beside them.

MONTSOURIS*. This is a district of narrow streets and dead-end passages, full of artists' studios. The Cité Universitaire, along the Boul. Jourdan, is a truly international community.

MOUFFETARD**. The district of La Mouffe has the appearance of a small village in the heart of Paris with its church (Saint-Médard), its square (La Contrescarpe) and its market stalls.

NATION. Around the Place de la Nation, from which the spacious

Cours de Vincennes opens out, are many interesting examples of 19th- and 20th-c. architecture.

NOTRE-DAME-DES-CHAMPS. This essentially residential district is ringed by educational establishments, particularly alongside the Observatoire gardens.

ODÉON*. The streets around the fine Neo-Classical building of the Théâtre de l'Odéon have preserved an air of distinction inherited from the *Ancien Régime*, with elegant boutiques and long-established bookshops.

OPÉRA**. The Palais Garnier, recognized as the best example of Napoléon III architecture, today overlooks one of the most hectic intersections of the capital.

PANTHÉON**. This temple for the great is considered the highest expression of Neo-Classical architecture in Paris.

PASSY-LA MUETTE. The descendant of the former village of Passy, where Parisians came to take the waters, this district retains a countrified atmosphere.

CIMETIÈRE DU PÈRE-LACHAISE**. One of the largest of Parisian cemeteries, containing a considerable part of French 19th-c. funerary statuary.

PLAISANCE. A district that has been undergoing complete renovation since the beginning of the 20th c. Some of its buildings were designed by Ricardo Bofill.

LES PUCES*. Surrealists, intellectuals and artists have all contributed to the fame of this strange market, a social and ethnic microcosm where antique objects and furniture are to be found, but also new and second-hand goods.

FAUBOURG SAINT-ANTOINE*. This old district, traditionally devoted to wood manufacturers, is now taken over by young painters and other creative artists, a fad that the opening of the Nouvel Opéra will no doubt encourage.

FAUBOURG SAINT-HONORÉ**. One of the more elegant districts of Paris, with the Rue du Faubourg Saint-Honoré, where 18th-c. mansions abound, among them the Elysée Palace, official residence of the head of state.

SAINT-JACQUES*. Dominated by the Observatoire, one of the great world centers of astronomical research, the *faubourg* preserves some parts of its old countryside within artists' colonies. Many religious communities still live here. The most famous, the Abbaye de Port-Royal, has been converted into a hospital.

SAINT-LAZARE*. This is the busiest district in Paris, the station, the big department stores, insurance companies and travel agencies all attract considerable crowds. The district has buildings characteristic of the metal frame method of construction.

SAINT-MARCEL. A student quarter, less touristy than the Latin Quarter, it contains the largest university hospital group of France, the Pitié-Salpêtrière.

SAINT-SULPICE. Around the church with its astonishing architecture, a network of little, secret streets leads to the Luxembourg garden. There are still several 18th-c. mansions in the Rue Saint-Sulpice.

SORBONNE. Over the centuries the Sorbonne has played an important political rôle. Today it is the seat of the Université de Paris-IV, Paris-III and the Ecole des Chartres.

TERNES. There are many beautiful buildings by Haussmann in this district, typical of the 19th-c. bourgeoisie.

TRINITÉ*. A relatively new and unknown district containing many examples of 19th-c. architecture, from the Restoration to the Second Empire.

VAL-DE-GRÂCE. The Val-de-Grâce is one of the most remarkable 17th-c. architectural ensembles to be seen in Paris. In the Rue Saint-Jacques the Institut des Jeunes Sourds (Institute for the Young Deaf) and the Church of Saint-Jacques-du-Haut-Pas preserve the memory of the religious establishments that were once numerous in the street.

VAUGIRARD*. This large district has kept many of its original village aspects, but also has many interesting examples of contemporary architecture.

LA VILLETTE*. This part of the capital around the site of the former abattoirs, has now been opened up to pedestrians and, through the Parc de la Villette and the Cité de Sciences et de l'Industrie, to leisure and cultural activities.

BOIS DE VINCENNES*. The largest promenade in Paris, with its château and its zoological and floral gardens.

Practical Paris

Emergencies

Ambulances: (*Samu*), tel. 45–67–50–50.
Doctors: (*S.O.S. Médecins*), tel. 43–77–77–77 or 47–07–77–77.
24-hour pharmacy: 84 Ave. des Champs-Elysées – 75008.

Daily information

Weather: *Météo*, tel. 43–69–00–00.
Post: On weekdays, post offices in Paris are open from 8am to 7pm; Saturday, 8am to 12 noon.

Post offices open until 11.30pm: 71 Ave. des Champs-Elysées – 75008; 59 Rue du Louvre – 75001.

Telegrams by telephone: 44–44–11–11.
Speaking clock: tel. 36–99.
Alarm service: tel. 46–88–71–11.
Directory enquiries: tel. 12.
Administrative information: CIRA, tel. 43–46–13–46 (9am – 6pm).
Banks: open daily except Sat., Sun. and public holidays.
Bureaux de change generally open Sat. am. Banks close at noon on days preceding public holidays.

Bureaux de change open daily inc. Suns and public holidays:
- Gare de Lyon, tel. 43–41–52–70 (7am – 11pm).
- Gare du Nord, tel. 42–80–11–50 (6.30am – 10pm).
- Gare de l'Est, tel. 42–06–51–97 (7am – 9pm).
- Gare Saint-Lazare, tel. 43–87–72–51 (7am – 9pm).

- Gare d'Austerlitz, tel. 45-84-91-40 (7.30 – 11.30am/1 – 9pm Mon. to Sat; 7am – 9pm Sun. and public holidays).

- 117 Ave. des Champs-Elysées, tel. 47-23-27-22 (daily except Sun. 9am – 8pm).

- Porte Maillot, 47-58-22-05 (Mon. – Fri., 9.30am – 12.20pm/2 – 4.20pm).

Lost property:
Central office: 39*bis* Rue de Dantzig – 75015, tel. 45-31-14-80.
Property lost in the sewers: 1 Place Mazas, tel. 43-43-16-19.

General information

Paris Town Hall – Hôtel de Ville: reception hall, 29 Rue de Rivoli, tel. 42-76-42-42.

Office du Tourisme de Paris: Central Office, 127 Ave. des Champs-Elysées – 75008, tel. 47-23-61-73.

- Gare de Lyon office, tel. 43-43-33-24.
- Gare d'Austerlitz office, tel. 45-84-91-70.
- Gare du Nord office, tel. 45-26-94-82.
- Gare de l'Est office, tel. 46-07-17-73.
- Eiffel Tower office, tel. 45-51-22-15 (in season, 11am – 6pm).

Cultural, sports and leisure information

Information loisirs 24h/24: in French, tel. 47-20-94-94; in English, tel. 47-20-88-98; in German, tel. 47-20-57-58.

Allo spectacles: all about exhibitions, films, plays and concerts, in Paris and Ile de France, tel. 42-81-26-20.

Allo sports: all about sport in Paris, tel. 42-76-54-54 (Mon., Thurs., 10.30am – 5pm; Fri. 10.30am – 4.30pm).

The weeklies: *Une semaine de Paris Pariscope*, *L'Officiel des Spectacles*, *7 à Paris*, published Wed., on sale in kiosks, give programmes for all theaters, shows, cinemas, concerts, exhibitions etc., and useful addresses for leisure activities.

Tourism

Panoramic coach tours: with commentaries in several languages.
- Cityrama, 4 Place des Pyramides – 75001, tel. 42-60-30-14.
- Paris-Vision, 214 Rue de Rivoli – 75001, tel. 42-60-31-25.

Boat trips: cruises on the Seine with commentaries in various languages:

- Bateaux-Mouches, tel. 42-25-96-10; also lunch/tea/dinner cruises, tel. 42-25-96-10;

- Bateaux Parisiens-Vedettes Tour Eiffel, tel. 45-51-33-08; also lunch/dinner cruises, tel. 47-05-09-85;

- Vedettes du Pont-Neuf, tel. 46-38-98-38.
- Vedettes Paris-Ile-de-France, tel. 47-05-71-29;
- Nautic Croisières (groups only), tel. 46-21-48-15.

Cruises with commentary on the canals of Paris and the Seine:
- Canauxrama, tel. 46-24-86-16;
- Neptour, tel. 47-72-32-32;
- Paris Canal, tel. 48-74-75-30. (Apr. - Nov.);
- La Patache, tel. 48-74-75-30.

Guided tours for children: Paris-Basket, 42-77-23-31.

Helicopter trips:
- Helicap, tel. 45-57-75-51;
- Heli-France, tel. 45-57-53-67;
- Heli-Promenade, tel. 46-34-16-18.

Guide-interpreters:
- Amicale Inter-Guides, tel. 42-68-01-04;
- Association des Guides-interprètes et conférenciers (lecturers), tel. 47-82-24-91;
- Club National des Guides et Courriers, tel. 42-80-01-27;
-Troismil, tel. 45-63-99-11.

Guide-lecturers (selection):
- Association des Conférenciers Officiels, tel. 45-66-24-91;
- Evasion Loisir Acceuil, tel. 42-06-96-30;
- Paris Passion, tel. 42-33-08-95;
- Caisse Nationale des Monuments Historiques, tel. 48-87-24-14;
- Les Amis de l'histoire-Clio, tel. 47-34-36-63.
- Ecoute du Passé, tel. 43-44-49-86.

Transport

Métro, RAPT enquiries, tel. 43-46-14-14.
Railway, SNCF enquiries, tel. 45 82 50-50.
Airlines: reservations Air France, tel. 45-35-61-61.
- reservations Air Inter, tel. 45-39-25-25;
- Orly airport, tel. 48-84-52-52;
- Charles-de-Gaulle airport, tel. 48-62-12-12;
- Le Bourget airport, tel. 48-62-12-12.
Roads: state of, tel. 48-58-33-33.
Motorway traffic information, tel. 47-05-90-01.
Car rental:
- Autorent, tel. 45-55-53-49;
- Avis Train + Car, tel. 46-09-92-12;
- Budget, 05-10-00-01;
- Europcar, tel. 30-43-82-82;

– Hertz, tel. 47–88–51–51;
– Inter Touring Service, tel. 45–88–52–37 (also cars for the handicapped);

– Mattéi, tel. 43–46–11–50;
– TT Auto-Service, tel. 46–51–51–70.
Luxury car rental: max. 4 passengers + chauffeur-guide-interpreter: Aristo's, tel. 47–37–53–70.

Chauffeur-driven cars: Executive Car-Carey Limousine, tel. 42–65–54–20.

Bicycle rental: Paris-Vélo, tel. 43–37–59–22.

Markets

Saint-Ouen flea market (Sat., Sun., Mon., 7am – 7.30pm).
Bric-à-brac, Porte de Vanves (Sat., Sun., 7am – 7.30pm).
Book markets: Quai du Louvre, Quai de la Mégisserie, Quai des Grands-Augustins, Quai de Conti, Quai Malaquais.

Stamps and postcards: under the trees of the Ave. Gabriel (Thurs., Sat., Sun., from 10am).

Flowers: Place Louis-Lépine and Quai de la Corse (Mon. – Sat., 8am – 7.30pm).

Bird market: Place Louis-Lépine and Quai de la Corse (Sun., 8am – 7pm) and Quai de la Mégisserie (shops open daily).

Auction rooms

Nouveau Drouot, 9 Rue Drouot – 75009, 42–46–17–11 (daily exc. Sun., 11am – 6pm).

Principal annual exhibitions

Jan.: sailing boats:Salon International de la Navigation de Plaisance (Centre National de l'Industrie et Techniques – CNIT – La Défense).

Feb.: Salon du Tourisme.

Mar.: household arts, agriculture, sound: Salon des Arts Ménagers, Salon de l'Agriculture (Parc des Expositions), Salon du Son.

Sept.: computers and office equipment: Salon de l'Informatique et du Matériel de Bureau (SICOB, at the CNIT, La Défense).

Oct.: automobile: Salon de l'Automobile (Parc des Expositions).

Nov.: children's exhibition: Salon de l'Enfance (CNIT, La Défense).

Maps of Paris

Districts and Monuments

Museums

The Journey

Some formalities

ENTRY DOCUMENTS. A valid passport is needed to enter France. A British Visitor's Passport (valid for one year and obtainable from Post Offices in the UK) is also acceptable. Nationals of EEC countries do not require a visa so long as their stay does not exceed three months. A visa is required for other visitors.

Documents for motorists: a valid driving licence is required, also a vehicle registration certificate (logbook), a national identity plate or sticker to be displayed at the back of the vehicle, and an international green card (as proof of third-party insurance).

ANIMALS.Domestic pets must have a certificate of good health and of vaccination against rabies – authenticated by a veterinary surgeon from the country of origin. All animals will be quarantined for six months on their return to the UK.

CURRENCY. The monetary unit is the frank (f or F), which consists of 100 centimes (c). There are banknotes for denominations of 20f, 50f, 100f and 500f, and coins of 5c, 10c, 20c, 50c, ½f, 1f, 5f and 10f.

There are no restrictions on the amount of foreign currency that can be taken into France but at present you cannot take out more than 12,000f. Check with your bank or travel agent before your holiday.

BANKING HOURS: see Practical Information, page 15.

CUSTOMS. The same regulations apply as for other EEC countries. Check the current position at the time of travel. Pick up a leaflet at the airport or railway station or on board ship or consult your travel agent.

For more details on what can be taken in or out of France, write to the French Government Tourist Office, 178 Piccadilly, London, W1.

ELECTRICITY. Generally 220 volts/50Hz AC but check before using any electrical appliance.

EMERGENCY NUMBERS. Ambulance: 43-78-26-26. Fire: 418. Police: 417. (See also Practical Information, page 15).

HEALTH INSURANCE. Visitors from the UK and Ireland, as members of EEC countries, are able to claim a refund of up to 75% of medical expenses incurred while in France. Check with your local Health Authority before your journey and obtain the necessary form (E111).

All travellers are advised to take out insurance against accident/theft before their journey.

LOST PROPERTY: see Practical Information, page 15.

TIME. France follows Central European Time: one hour ahead of Greenwich Mean Time in Winter and two hours ahead in Summer, and six hours ahead of Eastern Standard Time: New York 6am, London 11am, Paris 12 noon. From September to March clocks are put forward one hour.

The French use a 24-hour clock.

HOTEL ACCOMMODATION. A list of hotels can be obtained from the French Government Tourist Office, 178 Piccadilly, London W1 (tel. 071-491 7622). Alternatively, the Paris Tourist Office, 127 Champs Elysees, 75001 Paris, will provide information. There is also an accommodation bureau at Paris Nord station.

The journey by air

There are frequent scheduled flights to Paris from the UK as well as various charter flights. British Airways and Air France operate services from Heathrow and Gatwick, and there are also flights from Stansted (Air France and Air UK). In addition, Air Lingus and Air France operate services from Dublin to Paris.

There are also direct flights from the USA and Canada (Pan Am), TWA, Canadian Airlines, etc).

Paris has two airports: Charles de Gaulle and Orly.

Information and reservations:

Air UK,
Heathrow Airport,
Hounslow,
Middlesex, (Tel. 081-745 7017/0345 666 777)

Air France,
158 New Bond Street,

London, W1 (Tel. 071-499 9511)
also at 119 Avenue des Champs Elysées,
75384 Paris Cedex 08 (Tel. 42-99-23-64)

British Airways,
75 Regent Street,
London, W1 (Tel. 071-897 4000)

Air Canada,
Heathrow Airport,
Hounslow (Tel 081-759 2636)
and 140 Regent Street,
London, W1 (Tel. 071 439 7941)

Canadian Airlines International Ltd.,
62 Trafalgar Square,
London WC1 071-930 5664)

Pan American Airways (Pan Am),
193 Piccadilly,
London, W1 (Tel. 071-409-0688)

Pan American World Airways (Pan Am),
Pan Am Building,
4th Floor,
200 Park Avenue,
New York, NY 10166 (Tel. 212-687-2600)

Transworld Airlines (TWA),
200 Piccadilly,
London, W1 (Tel. 071-439 0807)
and at 100 South Bedford Road,
Mount Kisco,
New York, NY (Tel. 212-298-213)

The journey by ship/train

There are fast train services from London's Victoria station to Dover
Western Docks and from the same station to Folkestone and
Newhaven, connecting with ships and hovercraft to the French
ports and onward train services to Paris.

Typical journey times:
London to Paris via Calais or Boulogne: 7½ hours
London to Paris via Dieppe: 9½ hours
London to Paris via Boulogne by Hoverspeed: 5½ hours
On arrival at Calais, Dieppe or Boulogne waiting trains will take you
on to Paris (the train journey – included in above times – is approx. 3
hours).

Bargain rail fares are available for young people under 26 and for
senior citizens of 60 plus.

Information and reservations:

Ship/hovercraft

Hoverspeed Ltd.,
Maybrook House,
Queen's Gardens,
Dover,
Kent CT17 9UG (Tel. 0304-240241/0304 240202)

P & O European Ferries,
127 Regent Street,
London W1R (Tel. 071-734 4431)
(Dover office: Tel. 0304 223000)

Sealink, UK
Platform 2, Victoria Station,
London, SW1 (Tel. 071-828 1948/630 1373/387 1234)

Rail

International Rail Centre (Platform 2),
Victoria Station,
London SW1V 1JY (Tel. 071-834 2345)
(or the Travel Centre at Liverpool Street Station)

French Railways,
179 Piccadilly,
London W1 (Tel. 071-409 1224)

Eurotrain,
52 Grosvenor Gardens,
London, SW1W 0AG (Tel. 071-730-3402)
(This company specializes in discount rail travel for people under 26 years.)

The journey by coach

Journey by coach to the Continent is arranged by the following company:

Euroways (Eurolines) Express Coaches Ltd.,
52 Grosvenor Gardens,
London, SW1 (Tel. 071-730 8325)

See also package holidays.

Book at the above address or at:
The Coach Centre,
13 Regent Street, London, SW1.

Victoria Coach Station,
Buckingham Palace Road, London, SW1

A London/Paris coach service is also operated by Hoverspeed Ltd, Dover (address given above).

Package holidays

Most of the major travel companies – Thomas Cook, Thomson Holidays, Cosmos, Horizon, etc. have package deals (air/rail/coach) including trips to Paris. Consult your travel agent for details.

In addition, there are a number of firms who specialize in holidays in Paris. These include:

Paris Travel Service Ltd.,
54 Ebury Street,
London, SW1W (Tel. 071-730 3422)

Time Off,
Chester Close,
Chester Street,
London, SW1 (Tel. 071-235 8070)

The journey by car

The French Government Tourist Office, 178 Piccadilly, London W1V (Tel. 071-499 6911) and any of the automobile associations will be glad to assist the motorist in planning his or her route to Paris. (Sealink also offer services to the motorist in association with the AA).

Car rental – see Practical Information, p.17.

Ideas – Discoveries

Bird's eye view of Paris

Paris is also a landscape, albeit an urban one, made up of many architectural and other details, set against a vast horizon. This aspect of Paris, that is so often ignored, is best seen from several high vantage points: from the third level of the Eiffel Tower, from the Butte Montmartre and the top of the Sacré-Coeur, and from the top floor of the Montparnasse Tower. More accessible, though partial, views should not be disregarded, such as those from the top of the Arc de Triomphe looking straight down the Champs-Elysées towards the Place de la Concorde or in the opposite direction towards La Défense; from the roof of La Samaritaine, the store with a terrace overlooking the Seine and the entire Left Bank, and from the tower of Notre-Dame with its view of the Latin Quarter and the Seine.

Have a drink in the bar of the Hôtel Concorde-Lafayette (3 Place du Général-Koenig, 17th arr.) while enjoying a view of the Bois de Boulogne and the Place Charles-de-Gaulle-Etoile.

There are also a few (expensive) restaurants where you can lunch or dine with views of Paris spread out at your feet. These are: the Ciel de Paris, on the 56th Floor of the Montparnasse Tower (33 Av. du Maine, 15th arr., tel: 45-38-52-35); the Jules Verne (with a dinner-show) on the second level of the Eiffel Tower (tel: 45-55-61-44); Morot-Gaudry (8 Rue de la Cavalerie, 15th arr., tel: 45-67-06-85), and the Tour d'Argent, behind Notre-Dame and overlooking the Ile Saint-Louis (15 and 17 Quai de la Tournelle, 5th arr., tel: 43-54-23-31).

For a quick bird's-eye view two companies offer helicopter flights over the French capital: Hélicop (tel: 45–57–75–51) and Héli-France (tel: 45–57–53–67).

Paris by night

Why waste time sleeping? Paris never sleeps, and from dusk to dawn the capital is always ready to entertain.

For art lovers the doors of the Beaubourg Pompidou Center remain open until 10 pm, as, on Wednesdays, do those of the Musée Picasso. The Musée d'Orsay usually closes earlier, but remains open until 9:45 pm on Thursdays.

Walks in the summer? Long after midnight you can stroll along the Champs-Elysées, through Saint-Germain-des-Prés, Les Halles, or Montparnasse. Cinemas? Some have a late show from midnight to 2 am. If you want a drink you can have a few nightcaps until 2 am, at Les Fouquets (99 Ave. des Champs-Elysées, 8th arr.), or at La Closerie des Lilas (171 Boul. du Montparnasse, 6th arr.); Les Deux Magots (170 Boul. Saint-Germain, 6th arr.) or La Coupole (102 Boul. du Montparnasse, 14th arr.). If you still feel in the mood, Harry's New York Bar (5 Rue Danou, 2nd arr.), La Taverne de Rubens (12 Rue Saint-Denis, 1st arr.), Le Trappiste (4 Rue Saint-Denis, 1st arr.) and Le Sélect (99 Boul. du Montparnasse, 6th arr.) stay open until 3 am. Or have another meal, since some restaurants remain open all night: La Tour de Montlhéry (5 Rue des Prouvaires), 1st arr., Au Pied de Cochon (6 Rue Coquillière, 1st arr.), La Maison d'Alsace (39 Ave. des Champs-Elysées, 8th arr.), La Brasserie des Champs-Elysées (65 Ave. des Champs-Elysées, 8th arr.) and Le Grand Café (4 Boul. des Capucines, 9th arr.).

An urgent letter? The main Post Office (48 Rue du Louvre, 1st arr.) never closes! Forgotten something? The drugstores (133 Ave. des Champs-Elysées, 8th arr.; 1 Ave. Matignon, 8th arr.; 149 Boul. Saint-Germain, 6th arr.) are open until 2 am, and the As Eco supermarket in the quartier de l'Horloge, near Beaubourg, is open twenty-four hours a day.

The lights of Paris

Jump into a taxi one evening, and for the price of two cinema tickets give yourself a treat by seeing the lights of Paris, while the traffic is still moving and the floodlit public buildings can be seen to advantage.

A round trip from the Hôtel de Ville will go past all the principal floodlit sites in the capital. On weekdays the lights are not switched off until midnight, and on Saturdays and on the eve of public holidays, not until 1am. Go along the *quais* on the Right Bank with their lovely view of the slumbering Ile Saint-Louis. Cross the Seine by the Pont Sully and follow the Left Bank as far as the Quai Malaquais, then pass by the Cathedral of Notre-Dame and the old houses along the Quai de Montebello. Once beyond the Ile de la Cité the Louvre can be seen on the far side of the river, facing La Monnaie (the Mint), the Institut and the Ecole des Beaux-Arts. Cross by the Pont du Carrousel. Within the confines of the Louvre itself, the Arc de Triomphe du Carrousel stands at one end of the famous view which stretches to La Défense. Follow the Ave. de l'Opera as far as the luxurious Palais Garnier, then turn into the Rue de la Paix which sweeps down to the Place Vendôme with its brilliantly laid-out 17th-century houses, among the most noble in Paris. The Rue des Capucines rejoins the Grands Boulevards which take you to the Church of La Madeleine. The Rue Royale, regally decorated during Christmas and the New Year, runs into the Place de la Concorde. Drive right up the Champs-Elysées to the Arc de Triomphe and then turn down the Ave. Kléber to the Place du Trocadéro. Pass the Palais de Chaillot via the Avenue du Président-Wilson and follow the Ave. Albert-de-Mun to the Place de Varsovie. The floodlit gardens of the Eiffel Tower and the Trocadéro face each other on either side of the Pont d'Iéna. To return to the Hôtel de Ville take the road along the Right Bank; the view of the *quais* to the north of the Ile de la Cité and of the Conciergerie is magnificent.

Ethnic Paris

Paris is more than just the capital of France; it is a multicultural, international city. The places where foreigners live and meet are scattered throughout the capital and are constantly changing. If you live in Paris you soon pick up the clues to these changes, and catch up again.

Japanese Paris

The main centre of the 25,000 Japanese who live in Paris is in the 1st arrondissement. Books and newspapers may be bought at Tokyo-Do (4 Rue Sainte-Anne, 1st arr.) or at Junku (262 Rue Saint-Honoré, 1st arr.). At Le Carrefour du Japon (12 Rue Sainte-Anne, 1st arr.) you can rent books and video-casettes, enroll for cookery courses and play various Japanese games.

The many popular restaurants should not be overlooked: Ogura (20 Rue de la Michodière, 2nd arr.), Foujita (41 Rue Saint-Roch, 1st arr.), Ko (10 Rue du Marché-Saint-Honoré, 1st arr.), or Kinugawa (9 Rue du Mont-Thabor, 1st arr.). There are even Japanese fast-food restaurants: Iguma (11 Rue Gaillon, 2nd arr.) and Okamé (235 Rue du Faubourg-Saint-Honoré); the latter also provides a catering service. A luxury cake shop has just opened: Toraya (10 Rue Saint-Florentin, 1st arr.), the Parisian branch of an institution which, as connoisseurs are aware, has existed in Japan for over a thousand years. Japanese residents in Paris have their own department store as well – Daïmaru – with a vast counter for both fresh and frozen food, Japanese rice and beer, and a wealth of domestic appliances (Palais des Congrès, Place de la Porte-Maillot, 17th arr.). There are also food shops like Kioko (176 Rue Saint-Jacques, 5th arr.). The best shop for kimonos in Paris is Kimonoya (11 Rue du Pont-Louis-Philippe, 4th arr.). Paris also has its own Zen temple (17 Rue des Cinq-Diamants, 13th arr.).

In the evening you may either have a Japanese massage at Carita's (11 Rue du Faubourg-Saint-Honoré, 8th arr.), or visit a 'hara-oke' bar like the Hanagura (13 Rue Monsieur-le-Prince, 6th arr.) and join the fans to catch up with the Japanese 'top-twenty' on video.

A few galleries specialize in Japanese prints, lacquer, ivory and calligraphy. These include the top Parisian print-seller, Huguette Berès (25 Quai Voltaire, 7th arr.); Janette Ostier (26 Place des Vosges, 3rd arr.) for calligraphy, and the gallery at 50 Rue Sainte-Anne (1st arr.) for vases.

Another famous, and conspicuous, reminder of the attraction of Japan for Parisians is the Pagode. Today it has been converted into a cinema and is in a small garden in the 17th arr. (57 bis Rue de Babylone). This authentic pagoda was bought in Japan by the owner of the Bon Marché store and re-erected in Paris at the end of the 19th c. as a present for his wife; her soirées were the talk of Paris. But it is in the Musée d'Ennery (59 Ave. Foch, 16th arr.) that one of the finest collections of Japanese art in Paris is to be seen.

Russian Paris

Successive waves of exiles account for the 60,000 Russians now living in Paris. There are the White Russian aristocrats who escaped the Revolution, former Red Army men and, lately, dissident Jews and intellectuals. The White Russians were convinced that they would soon return home, but meanwhile made themselves reasonably comfortable and gradually settled in the French capital.

Those who still go to Mass meet under the five onion domes of the Byzantine Cathedral of Alexandre-Nevski (12 Rue Daru, 8th arr.), erected in 1860, the gift of Tsar Alexander II, or in the Church of Saint-Serge (93 Rue de Crimée, 19th arr.). Every Sunday afternoon, concerts of Slav music are arranged at the Conservatoire Rachmaninov (26 Ave. de New York, 16th arr.), where most of the professors are of Russian origin.

They get their reading matter from Editeurs Réunis (11 Rue de la Montagne-Sainte-Geneviève, 5th arr.), La Maison du Livre Etranger (9 and 12 Rue de l'Eperon, 6th arr.), the Librairie Sialsky (2 Rue Pierre-le-Grand, 8th arr.), and the Bibliothèque Tourgueniev (11

Rue de Valence, 5th arr.), rather than from Le Globe which is the official Soviet bookshop (2 Rue de Buci, 6th arr.).

The emigrés buy their blinis, borscht, black bread and piroshkis at Daru's (19 Rue Daru, 8th arr.), Soukhanoff's (5 Rue Isabey, 16th arr.) or Au Régal (4 Rue Nicolo, 16th arr.). They take tea at the Petit Boulé (16 Ave. de La Motte-Picquet, 7th arr.), and dine at the Samovar (14 Rue Sauval, 1st arr.), La Toison d'Or (29 Rue Castagnary, 15th arr.), La Ville de Pétrograd (13 Rue Daru, 8th arr.), at Dominique (19 Rue Bréa, 6th arr.), Le Tchaïka (9 Rue de L'Eperon, 6th arr.), or the Café Pouchkine (5 Rue Marie-Stuart, 2nd arr.). Then there are nightclubs like Raspoutine (58 Rue Bassano, 8th arr.) and L'Etoile de Moscou (6 Rue Arsène-Houssaye, 8th arr.), or the Cosmos cinema (76 *bis* Rue de Rennes, 6th arr.), where Russian films are shown.

A touch of nostalgia is supplied by a few antique dealers or dealers specializing in icons. Saint-Pétersbourg (106 Rue de Miromesnil, 8th arr.) and Nikolenko (220 Boul. Saint-Germain, 7th arr.) sell antiques and antiquarian books. Artel (25 Rue Bonaparte, 6th arr.); sells icons.

Asian Paris

Nearly 200,000 Asian refugees – Cambodians, Laotians, Vietnamese and, predominantly, Chinese – live in the Paris region. They swiftly made their main base in the newly created 13th arrondissement, an area of skyscrapers between the Porte d'Ivry and the Porte d'Italie. Cheap restaurants, shops and businesses of all kinds, from green-grocers and supermarkets to small factories, have turned this area into a city-within-a-city providing a peaceful and almost completely independent existence.

Beyond this central district stretches a network of small supermarket chains catering to the rest of Paris, the best-known being the Thanh Binh (29 Place Maubert and 18 Rue Lagrange, 5th arr.).

Finally, a number of Chinese restaurants stand out from the many recently opened establishments, many of which are not authentic Chinese. Eat Chinese at Le Pays du Sourire (32 Rue de Bièvre, 16th arr.), La Belle de Chine (29 Rue Copernic, 16th arr.) or at Ling Nam (10 Rue de Mazagran, 10th arr.). For Sino-Vietnamese cuisine try Vi Foc (33 Rue de Longchamp, 16th arr.); for Indochinese, the Coin des Gourmets (5 Rue Dante, 5th arr.). The cuisine of all the SE Asian countries can be found within the complex of restaurants at Nioulaville (32–34 Rue de l'Orillon, 11th arr.).

Polish Paris

Is Paris the second capital of Poland? Ever since the great wave of emigration in 1831, Paris has been part of Polish history, and many famous Poles have become part of the international fabric of Paris, giving their names to streets, squares, monuments and other works. 'Polonia', as the Polish colony in Paris is called, is some 10,000 strong and not only keeps alive the memory of the Polish past but also close contact with current events in Poland.

For long the headquarters of the colony's élite has been the Hôtel Lambert (1 and 3 Quai d'Anjou), one of the loveliest buildings on the Ile Saint-Louis. Clustered around it are the main historical buildings connected with the exiles: the Bibliothèque Polonaise, the Musée Adam Mickiewicz (6 Quai d'Orléans) and the Librairie Libella (12 Rue Saint-Louis-en-l'Ile.). There is another Polish bookshop in Saint-Germain-des-Prés, Ksiegarnia Polska (125 Boul. Saint-Germain, 6th arr.).

The Church of the Assumption (262 Rue Saint-Honoré, 1st arr.) has been the Polish parish church in Paris since 1814. It was also the departure point for trucks laden with supplies for the dissident group Solidarity, in Poland. The Polish colony eats at Le Relais de Varsovie (13 Rue François-Miron, 4th arr.) and Chez Dolowski (16 Rue Charlemagne, 4th arr.), which also has a grocery store and catering service.

The place least frequented by Polish exiles, of course, is the official Institut Polonais (31 Rue Jean-Goujon, 8th arr.).

Department stores

The French call them 'Cathedrals of Commerce'. The idea of gathering all the goods one needs to buy in a single space, with prices marked and free entry for all, was introduced in the late 19th c. Paris in which traffic flowed freely and crowds were able to keep on the move, unlike today. The wide streets laid out by Baron Haussmann during the Second Empire and the invention of the omnibus freed traffic and allowed people to look beyond the restricted horizon of the local corner shop for their domestic needs.

Originally the first big stores were converted galleries and arcades but soon developed an architectural style of their own using iron and glass. Thus there came into being the Belle Jardinière, the Deux Magots, the Petit Chaperon Rouge, La Lampe Merveilleuse, Le Coin de la Rue, the Grands Magasins Du-fayel, Au Gagne-petit. . . . Today, six monuments remain from this age of extravagance: Le Printemps and the Galeries Lafayette (Grands Boulevards), La Samaritaine and Le Bazar de L'Hôtel de Ville (Rue de Rivoli) and two smaller ones, Bon Marché on the Left Bank and Les Trois Quartiers (La Madeleine).

Nowadays, and it was probably just the same a century ago, half of those who enter these stores leave without making a purchase, since there are so many things to do. In such comfortable and even rather heady surroundings, time can be whiled away day-dreaming, eating, seeing the latest styles, or simply strolling around. Some of these establishments are historic monuments and worth a visit on that score alone. Because the department stores are well aware that they will increase their turnover if they do not function as mere sales outlets, they mount all sorts of attractive merchandising promotions, from genuine archeological and cultural exhibitions to fashion shows and events such as the traditional Christmas displays, the special 'weeks' and the annual sales, those moments of madness which are some of the high points of life in Paris.

La Samaritaine

Pont-Neuf and 75 Rue de Rivoli, 1st arr.

This store is often criticized for what are its great attractions, its old-fashioned atmosphere and deliberate feeling for the past, with its spaciousness and unhurried service. Its four buildings stand proudly between the Seine and the Rue de Rivoli and are undoubtedly the vestiges of a vanished age. Although they have been modified several times, they still preserve a fine architectural ensemble that includes Frantz Jourdain's façade to Store no. 2, a thirties façade overlooking the Seine. The main shopping hall of Store no. 2 is crowned by murals and stained glass that has recently been restored. The roof of the main building has a cafeteria on one of the finest terraces in Paris, which looks straight down onto the Seine.

Do not miss the magnificent confectionary department with its own bar, the all-embracing perfumery department, the well-stocked, lively haberdashery, the gleaming bathroom fittings, the functional working clothes, the impressive range of bedroom furnishings and one of the last invisible menders in Paris.

Bon Marché

38 Rue de Sèvres and 135 Rue du Bac, 7th arr.

Founded in the middle of the 19th c. by Aristide Boucicaut, originator of 'La Semaine du Blanc', today it is the sole surviving department store on the Left Bank. The main building has three lofty shopping halls with fine wrought-iron staircases and balustrades. The stained glass in the magnificent 2nd-floor glass roof (Square Boucicaut side) has recently been restored and there are some fine awnings on the Rue de Babylone.

Don't miss the carpet department which carries the widest range of carpets of any department store in Paris, the largest and finest grocery department in Paris with an excellent wine and spirits section, the fashionable women's clothes and the amazing antiques department.

Le Bazar de l'Hôtel de Ville

52–64 Rue de Rivoli, 4th arr.

Known as the Bazar Napoléon before 1870, this is the very antithesis of La Samaritaine – confined space, noise, clutter – because the Bazar de l'Hôtel de Ville is obsessed by the idea of being a modern store. So the interior is in a permanent state of modernization and redecoration in an attempt to disguise its old-fashioned origins. This is a pity. The store has managed to make itself the great place for the 'do-it-yourself' enthusiast who does not want to hire an expert.

Do not miss the incredible basement, in which it is easy to get lost, devoted to hardware and tools, the garden centre and the cutlery department and household cleaning items.

Le Printemps

64 Boulevard Haussmann, 9th arr.

Parisian shoppers are not enough for this Right Bank department store which makes every effort to draw in customers from overseas. Paul Sédille's fine façade with its famous statues and turrets has unfortunately been dwarfed recently by new storeys added to a nearby building. The fine 1930s stained-glass dome was removed in the 1970s to the new building.

Do not miss the many fashion departments, the book department (which is the largest in any store), the perfumery department, children's toys, wedding presents and tableware and the two restaurants – one beneath the stained glass of the dome, the other on the terrace with its spectacular view.

Les Galeries Lafayette

40 Boulevard Haussmann, 9th arr.

Its founder, Théophile Bader, dreamed of creating an Oriental bazaar. All that remains today is the façade of Les Chandelles on the Rue de la Chaussée-d'Antin, designed in the early 1900s by the architect Ferdinand Chanut, directly inspired by the Orient. The main building contains the largest shopping hall in Paris, but it has unfortunately lost its grand staircase. The floral design of the balustrades are attributed to Louis Majorelle. There is a fine stained-glass dome on the top floor.

This is the best department store for fashion wear, so do visit the clothes departments on two floors where all the principal manufacturers and designers are represented. There is also a wide variety of shoes, men's and children's clothes, perfumery (under the dome) and carpets.

Markets

Each district, each village of Paris, has its own street market. There are more of them now than there were in the 19th c. – nearly a hundred all told. Most of them are open every day except Monday, providing a non-stop spectacle and supplying the demanding Parisian housewife with a flow of fresh produce. Sometimes there is room for a leisurely stroll as in the markets in the Rue Mouffetard (5th arr.), the Rue de Buci (6th arr.), the Boul. de Belleville with its range of exotic produce (11th arr.), the Rue Poncelet (17th arr.), or the Rue Lepic (18th arr.).

Unfortunately the covered markets, survivors of the earliest use of cast iron in building, have often been converted to other uses. Some, however, retain their original purpose; these include the Marché des Enfants Rouges (39 Rue de Bretagne, 3rd arr.), the Marché Saint-Quentin, heavily restored (85 *bis* Boul. Magenta, 10th arr.), the Marché Aligre between the Rue Aligre and the Rue de Cotte (12th arr.), the Marché des Batignolles (96 Rue Lemercier, 17th arr.) and the Marché Secrétan (46 Rue Bouret and 33 Ave. Secrétain, 11th arr.).

Paris also has three large flower markets, open every day except Monday. They are in the heart of the Ile de la Cité (Place Louis-Lépine, 4th arr.), on the E side of the Madeleine (Place de la Madeleine, 8th arr.) and on the central island in the Place des Ternes (17th arr.).

▲▲ Gardens

With 22 sq. ft/2m.² of open space per inhabitant, Paris is one of the most deprived capital cities in Europe in this respect. Nor is this lack of parkland compensated for in the quality of the few parks and gardens there are. The two largest open spaces – the Bois de Boulogne and the Bois de Vincennes – contain little to please the eye, while the state of some historic gardens, such as those of the Tuileries, which are State responsibilities, has for many years been quite deplorable. There are exceptions among the famous parks such as the Luxembourg Garden, for which the Senate is responsible, or smaller, less well known gardens, which provide many opportunities for walks, rest and recreation.

1st arrondissement

The Square du Vert-Galant (Place du Pont-Neuf) is completely unpretentious, but its position at water-level on the west tip of the Ile de la Cité, between the two arms of the Seine, makes it very special. In the summer it is a place to stop and cool off between the Right and Left Banks.

The Jardin du Palais-Royal (Place du Palais-Royal and Rue de Beaujolais): ever since Louis-Philippe brought its hectic and licentious night-life to an abrupt end, the garden has become a sleepy backwater. Even today, ringed by its drowsy shops, it is the most peaceful spot in the heart of Paris, since the row over Buren's columns died down.

3rd arrondissement

The Square Georges-Gain (Rue Payenne) is a tiny fresh green space in the heart of the Marais, squeezed between the Hôtel Peletier and the Musée Carnavalet for which it harbors a few homeless statues.

5th arrondissement

The Jardin des Plantes (Place Valhubert, Rue Geoffroy-Saint-Hilaire, Rue Cuvier and Rue Buffon) was once Louis XIII's Royal Physic Garden, later redesigned and run for fifty years by Buffon. This vast garden (some 57 acres/23 ha) in extent has for centuries been the chief propagation centre for exotic plant species. It contains botanical gardens, tropical greenhouses and trees several centuries old.

The Square des Arènes de Lutèce (51 Rue Monge) is a restful, unassuming little neighborhood square beside the Roman arena, with a gnarled eighty-year-old Verzy beech (a rarity).

The Square Viviani (Quai de Montebello) is the garden of the Church of Saint-Julien-le-Pauvre. This little square faces Notre-Dame and houses a number of ancient trees, among them the oldest in Paris, a locust tree or false acacia, genus *Robinia*, planted in 1601 by Robin.

6th arrondissement

The Luxembourg Garden (Boul. Saint-Michel and Rue Vaugirard) is huge (some 55 acres/22 ha) and admirably maintained by the Senate. It is an example of the classic French garden with its massive fountain, terrace and walks lined with box and yew hedges; it also has a small part along the Rue Guynemer landscaped in the English style.

The Square Laurent-Prache (Rue de l'Abbaye) opens onto the Place Saint-Germain-des-Prés and is one of the few peaceful and, in summer, cool refuges in the area.

The courtyard of the Ecole des Beaux-Arts (14 Rue Bonaparte or 17

Quai Malaquais) is within a stone's throw of the Latin Quarter. An Italian atmosphere lingers in the tiny, cool Cour du Mûrier.

7th arrondissement

Musée Rodin (77 Rue de Varenne): the garden around the 18th-c. house in which Rodin once lived was restored at the turn of the century; rose bushes were planted and the sculptor's works stand in various parts of the garden with none of the usual formality of a museum.

8th arrondissement

Parc Monceau (Boul. de Courcelles and Boul. Malesherbes): the Folie-Monceau consists of about (20 acres/8 ha) laid out in the English style with gloomy mock ruins, Gothic remains, fragments of Greek temples, a Chinese pagoda, an Egyptian pyramid, and genuine Romantic fantasies. It also contains the tree with the widest girth in Paris, a splendid Oriental plane tree, 23¼ft/7.10m round the trunk.

13th arrondissement

The square René-le-Gall (corner of Rue Croulebarbe and Rue Corvisart): This peaceful and almost melancholy garden, close to the Gobelins, is laid out in the Neo-Antique style of the 1930s and is planted with the ash and sycamore that grew on the banks of the Bièvre, which once flowed here.

14th arrondissement

The Parc Montsouris (Boul. Jourdan and Rue Gazan) comprises some 40 acres/16 ha, prettily laid out in the English style around an artificial lake on the southern limits of Paris.

15th arrondissement

The Parc Georges-Brassens (Rue des Morillons) has been recently laid out on the site of the Vaugirard slaughter-houses and is a sad example of what some modern landscape gardeners can do in the way of parks, which grow less green, and more dusty and barren, cluttered with garish garden furniture. It does have a garden inspired by those in Andalusia, containing over 70 varieties of aromatic plants, but arranged and catalogued unimaginatively.

16th arrondissement

Municipal Flower Garden (3 Ave. de la Porte-d'Auteuil): on the site of Louis XV's nursery-garden and flanked by large, colorful flower-beds stands a splendid and all-too-rare collection of late 19th-c. greenhouses sheltering specimens of mature plants from both temperate and tropical zones. The large palm-house is a calm and restful place.

There is a peaceful little country garden surrounding the house where Balzac once lived (47 Rue Raymouard), when Passy was a rural suburb.

18th arrondissement

Musée de Montmartre (17 Rue Saint-Vincent): a tranquil little half-overgrown garden lies at the foot of the pretty Parisian house containing the Musée Montmartre.

19th arrondissement

The Jardin des Buttes-Chaumont (Rue Botzaria and Rue Manin), laid out at the end of the 19th c., consists of nearly 60 acres/24 ha on the slopes of Belleville. Built on the site of a gypsum quarry it has been made to look like a mysterious, tortured landscape of ravines, cliffs and rocks with an artificial lake. There is a magnificent view of Paris.

Street art

Painting walls is coming back into fashion. Today few specimens survive of an advertising technique common at the beginning of the 20th c. and which was brutally suppressed during the Nazi occupation by the Law of 1943, although one that did survive may be seen at 2 Rue du Petit-Pont (5th arr.). However, since 1979 and with a new law color has returned to the walls of Paris. At first it was all a joke with *trompe-l'oeil*, caricature, distorted perspectives, until two forms came to dominate – the work of art and the commercial advertisement.

This revival does not have the range of the 'street art' of some American or Mexican towns, but a few Parisian examples are worth the visit if you are in the neighborhood. The ideal wall for this 'art' is the bare, exposed gable-end or side wall of a block which can be seen from the far end of the street.

Among the best-known painted walls are those covered in trompe-l'oeil. Fabio Rieti's include *Imaginary Windows* (a ventilation shaft turned into an apartment block near Beaubourg, on the corner of the Place Edmond-Michelet and the Rue Aubry-Le-Boucher, 4th arr.), *The False Façade* (corner of the Rue de Penthièvre and the Ave. Delcassé, 8th arr.), *The Staircase* (corner of the Rue Pierre-Lescot and the Rue Etienne-Marcel, 1st arr.) and *Portrait of Johann Sebastian Bach* (53 Rue de Clisson, 13th arr.). Those by André Mendard: *La Grande Prairie* (corner of the Boul. de Strasbourg and the Rue de Metz, 10th arr.), and the big wall at the junction of the Rue Beautreillis and the Rue Neuve-Saint-Pierre; Pierre François de Gorse's landscape (corner of the Rue de Bretagne and the Rue de Belleyme, 3rd arr.); *The Messenger,* an abstract painting by Juan-Luis Cousino (23 Rue de l'Amiral-Roussin, 15th arr.); *The Plane Tree* by Zanko (corner of the Rue de Strasbourg and the Rue du Château-d'eau, 10th arr.), and *La Butte Montmartre autrefois* by Arditi (corner of the Rue du Mont-Cenis and the Rue Duc, 18th arr.)

There are other decorated walls at 67 Rue de la Tombe-Issoire (14th arr.), at the junctions of the Rue de Mogador, the Rue de la Victoire and the Rue Joubert (9th arr.), at the corner of the Rue Damrémont and the Rue Vauvenargues (18th arr.), and at the junction of the Boul. Saint-Germain and the Rue Grégoire-de-Tours (6th arr.).

Advertising agencies have taken up the baton and launched out into this more permanent form of promotion. In Paris the most spectacular achievements have been the advertisements for Les Petits-Beurre Lu (75 *bis* Rue d'Auteuil, 16th arr.), those for the Paris airport shops by Pierre Combert (125 Ave. Général-Leclerc, 14th arr.) and the chimpanzee eating *petits-suisses* (cream cheeses) on the corner of the Rue du Renard and the Rue du Cloître-Saint-Merri (4th arr.).

Historic commercial buildings

Somewhat belatedly after so many of them have vanished in recent years, the Historic Monuments Commission has recognized the artistic worth of the architecture and ornamentation of many business premises – shops, cafés and restaurants. A certain number have survived intact and have been protected by law since 1984. It would be a shame not to pause for a moment to admire these minor masterpieces of late 19th-c. craftsmanship with their imitations of academic genre painting and local street scenes, their tiles, their Art Nouveau sculpted woodworks and glass-covered painted cloth, or those of the early 20th c. showing the influence of Art Deco and the dominance of the architect over the decorator in marble, glass and metal shopfronts.

Hundreds of these creations still survive and they can be found almost everywhere as you stroll through the streets of Paris.

1st arrondissement

15 Rue Montamartre (excellent little café); 3 Rue Etienne-Marcel (restaurant); 33 Rue du Pont-Neuf (restaurant); 24 Rue de la Grande-Truanderie (Restaurant Pharamond, with marquetry by Panzani on the 1st floor); corner of the Rue Saint-Denis and the Rue de la Cossonnerie (café); 3 Rue Montorgueil (Restaurant L'Escargot); 17 Rue de Beaujolais (Restaurant Le Grand Véfour, under the arches of the garden of the Palais-Royal, with French Restoration painted and gilded ceiling and Second Empire paintings on silk under glass).

2nd arrondissement

143 Rue Saint-Denis (café); 71 Rue Sainte-Anne (interior of pharmacy); 42 Rue des Petits-Champs (grocer); 51 Rue Montorgueil (confectioner – recently spoiled by alterations).

3rd arrondissement

Corner of the Rue de Poitou and the Rue de Saintonge (bakery).

4th arrondissement

80 Rue François-Miron (café), 23 Rue des Frances-Bourgeois (bakery); corner of the Rue des Frances-Bourgeois and the Rue de Sévigné (bakery); corner of the Rue Malher and the Rue des Rosiers (bakery); 63 Rue Rambuteau (interior of dairy); 32 Rue Vieille-du-Temple (fine but small horseshoe-shape bistro bar); 8 Rue Jean-du-Bellay (pharmacy); 12 Rue Jean-du-Bellay (restaurant); 5 Rue de la Bastille (Brasserie Bofinger, stained-glass roof, faience tiles in lavatories, marquetry by Panzani).

5th arrondissement

16 Rue des Fossés-Saint-Jacques (bakery); 18 Rue des Fossés-Saint-Jacques (restaurant in a former shop); corner of the Quai Montebello and the Rue du Haut-Pavé (Restaurant La Bouteille d'Or); 200 Rue Saint-Jacques (butcher); corner of the Rue Saint-Jacques and the Rue Roger-Collard (grocer); 49 Rue des Ecoles (brasserie Le Balzar).

6th arrondissement

13 Rue de l'Ancienne-Comédie (Restaurant Le Procope; corner of the Rue Mabillon and the Rue Guisarde (restaurant); corner of the Rue de Seine and the Rue Jacques-Callot (interior décor of the Café La Palette); 115 Boul. Saint-Germain (wooden shop-front); corner of the Rue Vaugirard and the Rue Madame (former butcher shop-front); 59 Boul. Montparnasse (restaurant with 1900 décor).

7th arrondissement

30 Rue des Saints-Pères (confectioner); 79 Rue du Bac (impressive wooden shop-front); 41 Ave. La Bourdonnais (former dairy); 54 Ave. La Bourdonnais (pharmacy); 41 Rue de Bourgogne (dairy); 64 Rue Saint-Dominique (bakery); 112 Rue Saint-Dominique (bakery).

8th arrondissement

9 Place de la Madeleine (Restaurant Lucas-Carton, with carved wood motifs by Planel and bronzes by Galli); 57 Boul. Haussmann (dry-cleaners); 1 Rue Chauveau-Lagarde (remains of an Empire shop-front); 109 Boul. Haussmann (stationer).

9th arrondissement

7 Rue du Faubourg-Montmartre (Restaurant Chartier, one of the last 'Bouillons' built at the end of the 19th c.); 24 Rue du Faubourg-Montmartre (interior decoration from a fishmonger); corner of the Rue du Faubourg-Montmartre and the Rue de Provence (one of the finest old shop premises in Paris; a superb grocer-confectioner with a décor of painted cloth under glass and period fixtures); 18 Rue Vignon (confectioner: the restrained marble shop-front is an example of the classicism of Art-Deco); 12 Boul. des Capucines (Café de la Paix, decorated inside by Garnier, architect of the Paris Opéra); 25 Rue Le Peletier (Restaurant Petit Riche).

10th arrondissement

23 Rue de Dunkerque (1925 décor of the Brasserie Terminus Nord); corner of the Rue du Faubourg-Poissonnière and the Rue des Messageries (restaurant).

11th arrondissement

Corner of the Rue Saint-Sabin and the Rue Amelot (butcher); corner of the Boul. Beaumarchais and the Rue du Pasteur-Wagner (bakery); corner of the Rue de la Roquette and the Rue de la Folie-Régnault (bakery).

12th arrondissement

174 Rue du Faubourg-Saint-Antoine (grocer-confectioner); 19 Rue Montgallet (bakery); 10 Rue Théophile-Roussel (former dairy); corner of the Rue Théophile-Roussel and the Rue Antoine-Vollon (bar and restaurant); Gare de Lyon (Restaurant Le Train Bleu and station refreshment room).

14th arrondissement

10 *bis* Rue Roger (small, painted wooden shop-front of a former bookseller); 105 Rue Vercingétorix (remarkable bakery, the sole survivor of the total refurbishment of the street).

15th arrondissement

10 Rue Lecourbe (dairy); 34 Rue du Laos (restaurant); 53 Rue Amiral-Roussin (café interior).

16th arrondissement

5 Rue Mesnil (splendid little neighborhood bar); 25 Rue de la Pompe (former florist, recently converted to a restaurant); 16 Ave. Victor-Hugo (1925 décor of the Restaurant-bar Prunier Traktir with black marble, onyx and glass paste decorations).

18th arrondissement

128 Rue Lamarc (bakery); 22 Boul. de Clichy (Le Pigalle, a bar in the 1960s style); 44 Rue Damrémont (cake shop); corner of the Rue Marcadet and the Rue Carpeaux (bakery).

Luxury hotels

Why not explore one or two of the luxury hotels of Paris, those museums of the high life and extravagance, which are as much a part of the history of the French capital as the department stores or the Champs-Elysées? After all, you need not take a room for the night to sense the atmosphere of these places.

In fact you can breakfast at the Crillon (10 Place de la Concorde, 8th arr.), at the Bristol (112 Rue du Faubourg-Saint-Honoré, 8th arr.), at the Ritz (15 Place Vendôme, 1st arr.), at the Prince de Galles (33 Ave. George-V, 8th arr.), at the Plaza Athénée (25 Ave. Montaigne, 8th arr.), or at the George V (31 Ave. George-V, 8th arr).

Acquiring a tan

A suntan in Paris of all places? Well, why not? Summers are sunny and sometimes very hot. At that time of the year the city looks its best and it is pleasant to lie in the sun for an hour or two and acquire that mark of the well-heeled – a Parisian tan.

There are, in fact, far more places than you think where you can sunbathe, though each year they grow ever more crowded, with ever more scantily clad bodies.

Obviously they include the open-air swimming-pools, although these are usually overcrowded. They are the Piscine Keller (8 Rue de l'Ingénieur-Keller, 12th arr.), the Piscine Molitor (2–8 Ave. de la Porte-Molitor, 16th arr.), the Piscine Roger-Le-Gall (34 Boul. Carnot, 12th arr.), the Piscine Georges-Hermant (4 Rue David-d'Angers, 19th arr.), the Piscine de la Butte-aux-Cailles (5 Place Paul-Verlaine, 13th arr.), the pool at the Hôtel Nikko (61 Quai de Grenelle, 15th arr.), and the Piscine Deligny (Quai Anatole-France, 7th arr.), the last of the dozen 'floating' swimming-baths which existed near the Seine at the turn of the century. It was the most fashionable pool in the days when George Sand and Gustave Flaubert went there to take a dip.

However, the quays along the Seine have now become the fashionable place to acquire a tan. Most sunbathers head for the 'urban beaches' where every square metre between the Pont d'Austerlitz and the Pont de Solférino is filled on sunny days. The quays and the tips of the two islands (Ile de la Cité and Ile Saint-Louis) and the Right Bank of the Seine between the Pont des Arts and the Pont Royal are among the most popular places in Paris for this activity.

Jogging

Parisians keep up a fast pace all day long, but for those who want to go even faster, there are places in the capital where devotees of jogging can endure the vigors of their daily exercise in greater freedom.

The parks are obviously the ideal spots: the Bois de Boulogne on the edge of the city and the Bois de Vincennes on the W provide hundreds of acres and many different routes, although these may be very crowded on weekdays. The civic authorities provide a list of danger-free areas, which have clearly marked exercise stops. Each Sunday morning exercise sessions are available with qualified instructors for all levels of ability (tel: 42–76–54–54.).

Central Paris offers plenty of open spaces to jog or exercise. One of the most popular is the 1 mile/2km run in the Luxembourg Gardens (6th arr.), with a similar run around the Jardin des Plantes (5th arr). The Parc Montsouris (14th arr). provides 1½ miles/2.5km, some of it quite hilly, in pleasant surroundings. This course is favored by students from the nearby Cité Universitaire. The Parc des Buttes-Chaumont (19th arr.) has a fine run of just over a mile with hills to tackle and a couple of slopes 500 yards long. Lastly, the quays along the Seine still have a few clear lengths of a mile or so, particularly between the Pont d'Alma and the Pont des Arts and between the Pont de Tolbiac and the Pont de Sully.

Where to drink

There is always time for a drink in Paris, hence certain places – cafés, tea-rooms or brasseries – have become institutions, almost shrines, places for a chance encounter or for a rendez-vous.

Some of them still maintain standards set in an earlier, more gracious period – although in recent years some have fallen off – unaffected by the changing fashions of the last few decades.

Bistros for the wine lover

Le Rubis (10 Rue du Marché-Saint-Honoré, 1st arr.): all types of Beaujolais in a crowded bar; La Taverne Henri IV (13 Place du Pont-Neuf, 1st arr.): with two cellar levels below this, it is one of the best and most pleasantly situated small bistros in Paris; Chez Clovis (corner of the Rue Berger and the Rue des Prouvaires, 1st arr.): has a stunning semi-circular bar; La Cloche des Halles (corner of the Rue Coquillière and the Rue du Coq-Héron, 1st arr.): Beaujolais and Loire wines; Au Duc de Richelieu (110 Rue de Richelieu, 2nd arr.): specializes in Beaujolais; Au Franc-Pinot (corner of the Rue des Deux-Ponts and the Quai de Bourbon, 4th arr.): Loire wines and some Bordeaux; Café de la Nouvelle Mairie (19 Rue des Fossés-Saint-Jacques, 5th arr.): top quality Loire wines; Le Sauvignon (80 Rue des Saints-Pères, 7th arr.): regional wines in a tiny bistro; Cave-dégustation (9 Rue du Chabrol, 10th arr.): regional wines; Le Savoyard (39 Rue Popincourt, 11th arr.): wines from the Savoy region; Le Baron Rouge (1 Rue Théophile-Roussel, 12th arr.): close to the Marché Aligre; Le Rallye (6 Rue Daguerre, 14th arr.): a wide selection of regional wines; Aux Négociants (23 Rue Lambert, 18th arr.): Beaujolais and Loire wines, one of the last remaining Montmartre bistros.

Tea-rooms

Angelina (226 Rue de Rivoli, 1st arr.): opposite the Tuileries, they line up for the famous Mont-Blanc – meringues with chestnut cream Chantilly – and to drink tea or hot chocolate surrounded by Lorrant-Heilbronn's landscape paintings; Verlet (256 Rue Saint-Honoré, 1st arr.): tiny shop and tea-room, but famous in Paris for every type of coffee; La Mosquée de Paris (39 Rue Geoffroy-Saint-Hilaire, 5th arr.): mint-tea and Loukoums (Turkish delight). La Pagode (57 *bis* Rue de Babylone, 7th arr.): a tiny tea-room in a peaceful garden at the foot of a genuine pagoda; Ladurée (16 Rue Royale, 8th arr.): between the Madeleine and the Place de la Concorde, with the best macaroons in Paris; Aux Délices (39 Rue de Villiers, 17th arr.): tea-rooms with quality cakes up to pre-war standard.

Good beer guide

Le Trappiste (4 Rue Saint-Denis, 1st arr.); La Taverne de Rubens (12 Rue Saint-Denis, 1st arr.); Le Gobelet d'Argent (Il Rue du Cygne, 1st arr.): British beers; Académie de la Bière (88 *bis* Boul. de Port-Royal, 5th arr.): over a hundred different beers, particularly those from small breweries in N France; Pub Saint-Germain (17 Rue de L'Ancienne-Comédie, 6th arr.): a 'shrine' with over three hundred beers from all over the world, of which about twenty are on tap; La Taverne de Nesles (32 Rue Dauphine, 6th arr.): a few hundred beers from all over the world; Au Général La Fayette (52 Rue La Fayette, 9th arr.): about a hundred different beers served in the *Belle Epoque* décor of the most attractive tavern in Paris; L'Abbaye de Leffe (75 Ave. de Saint-Ouen, 17th arr.): a portrait of the Queen of the Belgians looks down on all the greatest Belgian brews.

Remembrance of things past

Those who have known Paris in the past bemoan the fact that the capital is changing all too quickly and is becoming dull and ordinary, that the 'vie parisienne' is fading away, that even when the places have survived, often their atmosphere has disappeared.

If you look carefully, and especially if you get off the beaten track, you may still get a flavour of the Paris of the 1950s, perhaps even of pre-war Paris. There are places where, either by chance or deliberate effort, the old atmosphere is alive. The danger now is not of physical extinction, but that they will be turned into crowded places of pilgrimage. And so, without actually listing the places whose existence is most precarious – the least known and best-preserved – one can suggest a tour of discovery that is enough to stir the echoes of the past and stimulate the desire for more.

First stroll down the 'passages' which have not yet been refurbished: the Passage Choiseul (between the Rue des Petits-Champs and the Rue Saint-Augustin), the Passage Jouffroy (between the Rue de la Grange-Batelière and the Boul. Montmartre), the Passage des Panoramas (between the Boul. Montmartre and the Rue Saint-Marc), and the finest and best-preserved of them all, the Passage Vero-Dodat (between the Rue Jean-Jacques-Rousseau and the Rue du Bouloi).

Go shopping in La Samaritaine, the most old-fashioned of the Parisian department stores, or in those superb shops where the service has somehow kept its pre-war standards: the Epicerie-confiserie Des Familles (corner of the Rue du Faubourg-Montmartre and the Rue de Provence, 9th arr.), the Epicerie Tetrel (42 Rue des Petits-Champs, 2nd arr.), the Confiserie Tanrade (18 Rue Vignon, 9th arr.) the Teinturier Parfait(57 Boul. Haussmann, 8th arr.).

Take tea at Ladurée (16 Rue Royal, 8th arr.), in the tea-room of the department store, Les Trois Quartiers (17 Boul. de la Madeleine, 1st arr.) or at Délices (39 Ave. de Villiers, 17th arr.), where the pastries are of the same high standard as fifty years ago.

Drink a glass of fine wine at the Savoyard (39 Rue Popincourt, 11th arr.), at La Tartine (24 Rue de Rivoli, 4th arr.), or at Aux Négociants (23 Rue Lambert, 18th arr.), or a beer at Général La Fayette (52 Rue La Fayette, 9th arr.).

And finally, lunch or dine in one of those restaurants which seem timeless. In summer there is the terrace of the Petit Saint-Benoît, a few steps away from the Place Saint-Germain (4 Rue Saint-Benoît, 6th arr.), or the pavement outside La Cité Berryer, a tiny fragment of nostalgic village life in the heart of Paris a few yards away from the Place de la Madeleine and the Place de la Concorde (25 Rue Royal, 8th arr.). There is the bustle and the late 19th-c. décor of the former 'Bouillon', Chartier, dating from the heyday of the *Belle Epoque*, which still has the cheapest bill-of-fare in Paris (7 Rue du Faubourg-Montmartre, 9th arr.). There are the paintings as well as the menu from the turn of the century at Le Petit Riche (25 Rue Le Peletier, 9th arr.); La Petite Normande (24 Rue de la Grande-Truanderie, 1st arr.) is one of the few market restaurants to survive the disappearance of Les Halles, while there is a bohemian Latin Quarter atmosphere in the luxurious brasserie Le Balzar (49 Rue des Ecoles, 5th arr.). Or try one or two of the neighborhood restaurants that still exist: Le Dauphin (167 Rue Saint-Honoré), Les Arts (73 Rue de Seine, 6th arr.), Le Champagne (21 Rue Joubert, 9th arr.), Au Pied du Fouet (45

Rue de Babylone, 7th arr.), and Le Pot-au-feu (34 Rue Vignon, 9th arr.), where at any hour of the day you can be sure of getting a pot-au-feu.

Eric Conan

Paris in History

From prehistory to the Norman invasions

The destiny of Paris and its choice as capital were determined by two factors, one geographical, the other political, and both must be studied in order to understand how the little town of the Parisii tribe grew into a great city. Time and again Paris was chosen as capital – first in the time of the Barbarian invasions by the Roman Emperor Julian the Apostate, then in AD 508 by Clovis. After the short Carolingian reign, the Capetians made Paris the head city – *caput* – of their kingdom and, from the thirteenth century onwards, the permanent seat of France's government. This designation as capital, certainly the origin of Paris's fortune and later grandeur, confirmed the importance of an exceptional geographical position, that had been recognized in prehistory, as shown by the traces of inhabitation dating from the Paleolithic and Neolithic eras. Thus Paris flourished, thanks to its location on the river.

A Quaternary site

The immense river of the Quaternary period had formed the basin of a large meander, still recognizable today in the line of hills that runs from Charonne to Ménilmontant, Belleville, Montmartre and Chaillot. When the rise in temperature occurred, the river changed course, and the water level fell allowing the emergence, beyond the marshy area of the old river bed (the 'Marais': marsh, as its name shows, is part of it), of a platform of gravelly land (the first four arrondissements less their outer fringe) and a string of small islets.

In early times, these islets formed a natural ford across the river, situated as they are precisely on the most favorable route between northern and southern Gaul, which followed the valley of the pass at La Chapelle, between the hills of Belleville and Montmartre. Coming from Rouen or Senlis it was easy to cross the Seine to reach the flood-proof plateau of the Left Bank, that is, the Montague Sainte-Geneviève, and continue towards what is now Orléans.

Because of this natural ford, the central isle soon grew into a large defensive stronghold with a population located at the hub of overland and river traffic. The river traffic was made easy by the calm and easily navigable course of the Seine and the convenient network of its tributaries – the Oise, the Marne, the Aube, the Yonne and the Loing – and consequently increased. The boatmen formed a powerful corporation, the *Nautes,* playing an important economic and, later, political role.

The site had many advantages: it had broad access to the neighboring regions outside the copiously irrigated area of the Paris basin; it was close to fertile lands that were able to produce enough food for a large town; it had quarries of stone and plaster that could be used for building houses; it stood at the centre of the communication routes in every direction; it was quite close to the sea, and could benefit from its fish and greater commercial trade; and it was centrally positioned in northern France. Conversely there were drawbacks: Paris was right on the invasion routes and, being poorly defended to the east, was vulnerable. As it grew and spread beyond the secure precincts of the Ile de la Cité it became a tempting and easy prey. Paris has been besieged, taken and occupied several times in the course of history, and its fate has very often influenced the outcome of European conflicts.

Traces of human settlement bear witness to man's appearance on the Parisian site as far back as the Lower and Middle Paleolithic periods and, after an interruption, to the Neolithic (4th and 3rd millennia), as seen on the site of the Louvre and at Villejuif. The culture of the Bronze Age took firm root here: gallery tombs at Argenteuil, Meudon and Conflans-Sainte-Honorine, and caches of foundry work like that at Thiais, bear witness to frequent trading with distant regions, from Great Britain to the Mediterranean. During the Second Iron Age the Celtic populations, particularly the Quarisii or Parisii, came from Germany. They no doubt settled in the middle of the 3rd century, in the place named, before their arrival, Lucotecia (Lutetia). Prosperous and independent, despite the close proximity of the powerful Senons (at Sens), the Parisii struck gold pieces of remarkable originality. Then came the Gallic Wars. Caesar, in his memoirs, *Commentarii*, mentions the city of the Parisii in 53–52 BC. In answer to an appeal from the Gallic chieftain Vercingetorix, the Parisii rose against the Roman invaders and sent a contingent of 8,000 men. At the same time they destroyed their town, Paris, and their bridges before the arrival of Caesar's lieutenant Labenius, who defeated their chief Camulogene, probably on the plain of Grenelle.

The Gallo-Roman town

After the Roman conquest the town was split into two parts: the rebuilt Gallic town on the Ile de la Cité and, on the plateau of the Left Bank, a new Roman city like those which were then springing up throughout Gaul. Recent excavations by the Direction des Antiquités in the Paris region have provided a more exact knowledge of the topography and extent of the new city. Its boundaries were some distance from the river and its flood-prone banks, on top of the plateau which provided a vast empty space for construction along the route to Orléans. This, then, became the central axis, the *cardo*, now the Rue Saint-Jacques, extending the route from the north (Rue Saint-Martin, on the Right Bank). Two long straight roads, at right angles (*decumani*), followed approximately the lines of the Rue Soufflot and the Rue des Ecoles. The forum was at the crossroads of the Rue Soufflot and the Rue Saint-Jacques. The building of an underground garage has allowed an appraisal of the city's layout (public square, temple and basilica) as it was at the start of the 2nd century. Nearby there was a bath-house *(Thermes du Midi*, Rue Gay-Lussac) and a residential district (on the site of the Luxembourg Gardens, where numerous remains have been found).

At one side, backing on to the sloping ground and facing the Bièvre river, there stood a dual-purpose building used both as a theatre and a circus, a composite building of a specifically Gallo-Roman type, but unusually large; the *Arènes de Lutèce* in the Rue Monge. The cemetery was close to the Val-de-Grâce. Later, the town spread down the slope towards the N. A theatre was built (Rue Racine), as were the *Thermes de l'Est* (Rue du Collège de France) and in particular the large *Thermes du Nord*, constructed at the end of the 2nd, or the beginning of the 3rd century, a grandiose edifice, two rooms of which may be seen – one of which is roofed with a massive vault – at the Musée de Cluny, at the intersection of the Boul. Saint-Michel and Boul. Saint-Germain. The water was brought to these bath-houses from Arceuil by an aquaduct 9.4ml/15km long, crossing the Bièvre Valley. It is probable that the administrative headquarters were at the Ile de la Cité, which would explain the purpose of the vast civil building, the massive foundations of which have been discovered beneath the parvis of Notre-Dame. The marshy Right Bank doubtless accommodated only the river port. A shrine, overlooking a number of villas, stood on the hill to the N, on the *mons Mercurii*. Under the Caesars, the Flavians and the Antonines, Lutetia was a prosperous, mercantile town of average size, with perhaps 8000 inhabitants.

During the Barbaric invasions, half of the country was overrun, including Lutetia. In the middle of the 3rd century the town was devastated by fire, traces of which have been found on the remaining fragments of buildings. The Ile de la Cité once again served as a defensive stronghold, with blocks of stone torn from monuments and tombs to make a massive enceinte or enclosing wall along the river bank. Many traces of this first defensive wall of Paris have been discovered. As in other towns in France, excavations have brought up carved stones, drums of columns, capitals and architraves, making it possible to imagine the richness of the destroyed buildings.

Nevertheless, while the city walls, which enclosed only about 22 acres/9 ha, gave shelter several times to the population, it does not seem that the Left Bank was totally abandoned, the forum itself having been fortified, as Michel Fleury has proved. So life went on in partly-reconstructed buildings, and houses were even put up on the Right Bank on the mound of Saint-Gervais, a flood-proof hillock on the edge of the river. Lutetia now became an important strategic base for the maintenance of the Roman Empire. Responsible for its defence, the Caesars twice stayed in the town, which was in effect a large fortress. The first Caesar, Julian the Apostate, came in 358 and again in the winter of 359–360, when he was proclaimed Emperor. He devoted a few lines in his memoirs to the evocation of his 'dear Lutetia', a 'town blessed by God'. After him came Valentinian I in 365 and 366. Julian's writings seem to confirm the belief that they lived in the palace of the Cité. Christianity came to the Roman town at the time of the Emperor Decius, as is proved by the martyrdom of the first bishop, St Denis, in 250. He became the patron saint of France. A large Christian cemetery was developed outside the town, in the Saint-Marcel district, where numerous tombs have been found. It was at about this time that the name of Paris supplanted that of Lutetia.

The Merovingian capital

In the 5th century, the Paris region formed an independent Gallo-Roman state, isolated amidst the turmoil of the invasions. That of Attila's Huns is the most deeply memorable. In 451 with the help of a shepherdess from Nanterre named Geneviève, the future patron saint of Paris, the Bishop of Paris, St Marcel, roused his compatriots' courage so that they resisted the Huns and the town was saved from a siege. But definitive victory belonged to the Franks. Vanquishing the Roman Syagrius at Soissons in 486, Clovis made himself the master of Gaul and became the first Christian king of the Franks. Once he had defeated the Visigoths at Vouillé he decided, in 508, to make Paris the seat of his kingdom, and he died there three years later.

His successors placed a pre-eminent value on Paris, as seen from the importance given to it in the sharing out of territory among the dynasty on the death of kings, and from the grandeur of the churches they built there. Clovis built the basilica of the Saints-Apôtres, which he chose as his tomb; the bodies of St Clotilde and St Geneviève were later interred there and St Geneviève's name remained attached to the abbey that stood at the top of the Montagne Sainte-Geneviève on the site of the Rue Clovis. For his burial Childebert I, son of Clovis, who ruled Paris for forty-seven years, built the church of Sainte-Croix-Saint-Vincent which is today Saint-Germain-des-Prés, where other Merovingian sovereigns, Chilpéric and Clotaire II, were also to lie.

King Dagobert, however, preferred to be buried in the basilica that St Geneviève had built to the N of Paris over the tomb of St Denis, thus preceding most of the Frankish kings. Early historians of Paris, like Gregory of Tours, draw attention also to the beauty of the first cathedral church, dedicated to St Etienne. Recent digs have revealed a building that was immense for the period, the largest in Merovingian Gaul, a church with five naves, 118 ft/36m wide, and superbly decorated; its construction, according to Michel Fleury, should be attributed to Childebert I.

Beside it was a baptistery and a second church, dedicated, even at this early date, to Notre-Dame. At the other end of the island stood the royal palace. The town spread to both banks of the river, as shown by the number of the first churches dedicated, fifteen in all. The itinerant royal court moved around the villas of the Paris region: Reuilly, Clichy, Chelles, Rueil and Garges-lès-Gonesse.

Decline under the Carolingians

From the beginning of the Merovingian decline in the 7th century Paris ceased to play the dominant role and the seat of political power moved NE to Austrasia; this change was accentuated with the accession of a new dynasty, the Carolingians, whose origins and properties were in the Rhineland, although Pepin the Short occasionally stayed in Paris between 751–68. Charlemagne chose Rome and Aix-la-Chapelle as the capitals of the Empire, and resided only rarely in Paris. The Abbey of Saint-Denis, one of the richest of the monasteries, still provided a link with the new dynasty, since Charles Martel and Pépin the Short (Le Bref) were buried there, and Pépin and Charlemagne rebuilt the basilica. However, Paris, poorly defended, weakened by the division of territory and abandoned by the last of the now helpless Carolingians, was to fall prey to the Norse pirates. Sailing up the Seine, they pillaged and burnt the town several times (845, 856, 861). The great siege of 885–886 is celebrated for the energetic defence of the Cité by Bishop Gozlin, who built up the ramparts and erected wooden towers at the ends of the bridges, and by Eudes, Count of Paris and Duke of France, who was soon to wear the crown (887–98). The town was saved, but the suburbs were destroyed. The ultimate ruin of the Roman town on the Left Bank dates from this siege. Paris then withdrew into the Ile de la Cité and remained there for a century. In 987 it was taken over by the first of the Capetians, Hugh Capet, who was elected by the nobility in preference to the Carolingians.

Medieval Paris

The city of the first Capetians

With the coming of the Capetians, dukes of France and counts of Paris, the Paris region became the center of power once again. Paris itself strengthened its position, even though the sovereign sometimes chose to stay in other towns, like Laon and particularly Orléans. It rose through trading, mostly on the Right Bank ('Outre-Grand-pont'), the lowness of which, along the concave curve of the meander, provided convenient natural harbors; first the cove of the Strand, then the Port de l'Ecole, at the northern extremity of the Pont-Neuf. The Right Bank was also where the great land routes met, cloth from the north arriving by the Rue Saint-Denis, corn by the Rue Saint-Honoré, and fish from the North Sea by the Rue des Poissoniers. Together with the Lendit fair a market was established between Saint-Laurent and Saint-Martin-des-Champs. The size of the city soon necessitated the removal of the market from the Ile de la Cité to a more open space. In about 1137 Louis VI, le Gros (the Fat), built Les Halles on the site of Les Champeaux – the little fields – an area favoured by its location at the intersection of consignments by river and road. The Paris Halles were to remain there for eight and a half centuries. The *anneau de marais,* the land that was the former bed of the Seine, was than drained and cultivated (Marais Sainte-Opportune to the E, Couture l'Evêque to the W) and vegetables and cereals were grown. Bridges were thrown across the drainage ditch to ensure better communication with neighboring villages that also helped to supply the city. Between 1150–1210 Philippe-Auguste built the first town wall around the Right Bank. Nothing remains of it now. It enclosed a few small hills, out of reach of the Seine's flood-waters, Saint-Gervais, the parishes of Saint-Merri and Saint-Jacques-la-Boucherie. The neighboring parish, Saint-Germain-L'Auxerrois, no doubt had its own enceinte. In the 12th century new parishes grew up outside the city gates, Saint-Paul on the Melun road, Saint-Nicolas-des-Champs on the road to Senlis and Saints-Innocents on that to Rouen.

The Cité, densely built and populated with its fourteen parishes, remained the seat of power, both royal and episcopal. In 1163 Bishop Maurice de Sully laid the foundation stone of the cathedral of Notre-Dame on the site of the two Merovingian churches and, to the S of it, built the first episcopal palace. The Kings, Hugh Capet, Robert the Pious, Henri I, Philippe I, Louis VI (the Fat) and Louis VII (the Young) frequently stayed in the Cité palace, which was renovated by Robert and Louis VI, Robert trying to offer a more pleasant residence to his new wife, the Provençal Constance

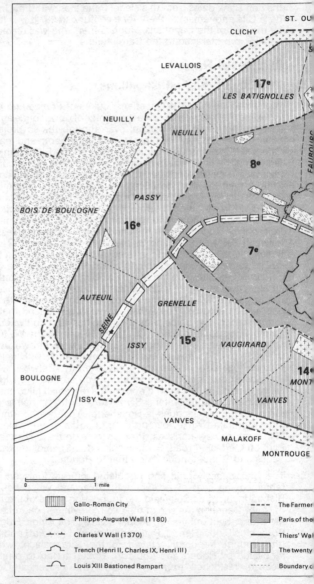

The Growth of Paris

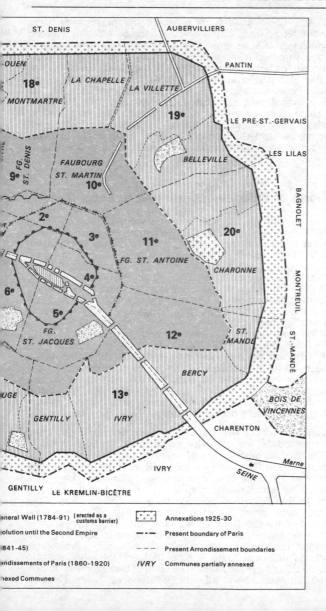

ST. DENIS AUBERVILLIERS

PANTIN

-OUEN

18e

LA CHAPELLE LA VILLETTE

MONTMARTRE

19e

LE PRÉ-ST.-GERVAIS

FG. ST. DENIS

FAUBOURG ST. MARTIN

9e

LES LILAS

BELLEVILLE

10e

BAGNOLET

2e

3e

11e

20e

FG. ST. ANTOINE

CHARONNE

MONTREUIL

6e

4e

5e

FG. ST. JACQUES

12e

ST. MANDÉ

ST.-MANDÉ

BERCY

UGE

13e

BOIS DE VINCENNES

GENTILLY IVRY

CHARENTON

Marne

IVRY SEINE

GENTILLY LE KREMLIN-BICÊTRE

neral Wall (1784-91) (erected as a customs barrier)   Annexations 1925-30

olution until the Second Empire   ---- Present boundary of Paris

841-45)   --- Present Arrondissement boundaries

ndissements of Paris (1860-1920)   *IVRY* Communes partially annexed

hexed Communes

d'Arles, and Louis anxious to reinforce the palace's defences against the feudal lords of the Ile-de-France by erecting a strong keep which was later destroyed under Louis XVI. The accesses to the bridge were also reinforced: Grand Châtelet on the Right Bank at the end of the large bridge rebuilt near the palace, along the line of the Rue Saint-Denis, and Petit Châtelet on the Left Bank at the end of the Petit-Pont, along the line of the Rue Saint-Jacques. The Left Bank was almost abandoned. The slopes of the Montagne Sainte-Geneviève were given over to cultivation – the *clos* – mainly controlled by the great abbeys, Sainte-Geneviève and Saint-Victor. Further on, at Saint-Germain-des-Prés, an important agricultural centre formed around the monastery buildings of the Benedictine monks.

The works of Philippe Auguste and St Louis IX

The town spread far beyond its first enceinte. The new king, Philippe II (Philippe Auguste) envisaged a more extensive defensive system capable of resisting the assaults of the king of England. On his orders the burghers, in 1190, built a deep rampart of stone, flanked by round towers, to enclose the new parishes and the market at Les Champeaux, culminating on the W side with the fortress of the Louvre, which would also serve as a royal residence. An important new departure was that the new defensive wall also enclosed the Left Bank. A decisive change had begun: a trading centre had been set up at the head of the Petit-Pont. Besides, the area of the *clos*, formerly the wine-growers' ground, had begun to attract others, the students. Previously, they had attended the cathedral schools in the cloister of Notre-Dame, in the Cité, which had acquired a great reputation, but the teachers soon sought to get away from the tutelage of the bishop and to create new, independent schools, with teaching close to that of the famous Saint-Victor schools. It was on the Left Bank that the new teaching centres were set up, and the student population settled.

After bitter differences with the king and the bishop, masters and students placed themselves under the patronage of Pope Innocent II and founded an organization of defence, the *Universitas,* which was recognized in 1209–1210. As a symbol of its independence the University of Paris, in 1252, received the right to its own seal. Survival of the scholars was assured by private foundations and colleges (that of Robert de Sorbon, the theological college of the *Sorbonne,* dates from the long reign of St Louis) that were established on the Left Bank, as were the convents of the recently-founded new religious orders which were seeking to become part of the world of teaching, like the Jacobins (Dominicans), whose great convent was built close to the Rue Soufflot, and the Franciscans in the Rue de L'Ecole-de-Médecine. The fame of the university quickly attracted students from all of Christendom, who grouped themselves according to their origins into 'Nations'. On an international level the university secured the intellectual reputation of Paris, already growing in the 12th century with the teachings of Guillaume de Champeaux and Peter Abélard.

Philippe Auguste often stayed in his capital, taking a personal interest in its development. He paved a number of important streets, ordered the collection of rain water from the Pré-Saint-Gervais and Bellemont to feed public fountains, and ordered the expulsion of the Jews in 1182. The immense fame of St Louis (Louis IX), his grandson, added further to Paris' reputation. The palace of the Cité was his favorite residence and he built several extra wings there to house his family and servants and, in particular, the Sainte-Chapelle, a miracle of Gothic architecture, with its celebrated stained-glass windows. It was intended to serve as the palace chapel and to house the relic of the Crown of Thorns that the king had acquired (1246–1248). In the same period the construction of Notre-Dame cathedral was proceeding (the main works, with the façades of the transept, were finished in 1250). During his reign, the Gothic style also made its mark on the choir of Saint-Germain-des-Prés and the refectory of Saint-Martin-des-Champs. Enclosed buildings, *halles,* now provided cover for the markets and commerce at Les Champeaux. As the king most often held court in Paris, princes and dignitaries built themselves *hôtels,* generally in the available open space close to the city wall. These princely constructions were in natural stone, while houses were timber-framed and presented a high triangular gable to the street, as can be seen on miniatures in medieval manuscripts. The pronounced corbelling of the upper storeys overhung the stone-faced ground floor, used as shops or workshops. In the city, houses lined the streets, as well as the bridges and quays, hiding the Seine from passersby. Beyond the city gates they pressed together along the roads leading to the great built-up suburban areas.

The Hundred Years War

The cruel king Philippe the Fair (1285–1314) continued the work of his grandfather St Louis; he altered the palace of the Cité and in particular built the notorious Conciergerie prison. It is difficult for historians to estimate the population of medieval Paris, but it seems reasonable to suggest a figure of about 8000 in 1328. The political, financial and mercantile importance of the town was growing. The Right Bank, especially, saw a considerable extension; in 1350 four-fifths of Parisian taxpayers lived there and the *Prévôt des Marchands* (Provost of the Merchants), in 1356, initiated the building of a new enceinte for the city on that bank, which was to be continued by Charles V (builder of the Bastille), after the failure of the revolt led by Etienne Marcel. This wall, strengthened by square towers, followed the line of the great boulevards of today.

The name of Etienne Marcel evokes the first Parisian revolution. The vicissitudes of the Hundred Years War with the English (1337–1453), the captivity of the Second Valois king Jean II ('the Good') and the depredations of both English and French soldiers caused an explosion of popular discontent which helped the ambition of the provost of the merchants, Marcel, the signal of the first break between sovereign and capital. This was to leave the king feeling insecure and made him leave the palace of the Cité, bloodied by the riot, preferring from then on the residences of the eastern periphery, the Hôtel Saint-Paul and later the Hôtel des Tournelles, from which it was easier to escape. Because of this, the eastern districts, where the intimate members of the brilliant court of the Valois lived, took on an aristocratic lustre which they only finally lost during the Revolution of 1789. The English occupation, the misfortunes of war and the economic crisis brought utter ruin to the city, especially when John, Duke of Bedford repelled Joan of Arc's army during the siege of 1429. Recovery was slow and Charles VII, barely having re-entered his 'good city' in 1436, left again in haste to take up residence once more in the Loire Valley.

However, the central machine of royal government had had its seat there since the reigns of Philippe Auguste, St Louis and Philippe the Fair: the *Parlement*, the *Chambre des Comptes*, the Treasury, the Archives and the Mint. Anxious to keep control of the city, the king granted no communal charter to Paris, but did concede to its inhabitants the individual privilege of *bourgeois du roi* (burghers of the king) and bestowed favors on the guild of river traders who thereby, with other corporations (the butchers, mercers and drapers) became a political power, obtaining a commercial tribunal, exemption from taxes and finally a governing body, the *Parloir des Bourgeois* (the burghers' assembly). In 1258, St Louis had taken away the royal provostship from the burghers to confer it on to one of his agents, Etienne Boileau. Five years later the Hanse elected the first municipal government to be composed of a *prévôt des marchands*, Evrard de Valenciennes, assisted by four counselors. So, in the 13th century the Parisian system of dual authority, State and City, came into being.

Classical Paris

City of the Renaissance

Economic expansion only got under way again just before 1450, and provincial immigration just before 1500. Now the monarchs began to take a growing interest in the city, echoing the new preoccupation with town planning which had emerged in Italy a century earlier with the Renaissance, the intention being to link the beautiful to the useful for the enjoyment of the citizen. Under Louis XII, called 'the Father of the People', the first architectural ordinance was imposed on the reconstruction of the houses on the new Notre-

Dame bridge: they were to have uniform façades built in brick and stone. This style also left its mark on the new *Chambre de Comptes*. Yet traditional architecture still retained the Flamboyant Gothic style in such eminent works as the churches of Saint-Séverin and Saint-Etienne-du-Mont, the Hôtel de Sens and the Hôtel de Cluny.

Louis XII had lived mainly at Blois, but in 1528 François I officially fixed his residence in Paris. As a result he decided to modify, then to rebuild, the Louvre fortress, an operation begun by Lescot in 1546 and only finished for Henri II. François had the first *quai* built of stone, ordered the demolition of the gates of the old city walls, laid down the line of the main streets and commanded the municipality to build a town hall worthy of the grandeur of the capital.

Paris, which was to seem to Charles V as great as a whole world, was enjoying enormous intellectual renown. To the traditional teaching of the University, oriented above all towards theology and the liberal arts, François I added modern teaching in humanism and the exact sciences: the Collège de France.

The new style of art made progress in the royal buildings (the Fontaine des Innocents, the church of Saint-Etienne, the Tuileries Palace), echoing the sophisticated splendour of the royal entries into Paris. Land under cultivation within the city walls, as at Sainte-Catherine, was taken over for the building of handsome mansions, such as the Hôtel Carnavalet.

The war with the Empire continued and defences needed to be strengthened, so Charles V's walls were reinforced by bastions capable of withstanding the latest artillery.

Soon, to the foreign war was added a religious civil war. In Paris, the first to adopt the ideas of the Reformation were the princes, the intellectuals and the rich merchants. The common people of Paris, traditionally faithful to the outward show of Catholicism (relics, processions and ritual) were inflamed by certain iconoclast outrages to demand sanctions, thereby justifying the intolerant policies of the Faculty of Theology, which were supported by Henri II. His consort Catherine de' Medici maneuvred for a time, allowing an armed conflict to develop between the two camps that was the generator of the first religious wars. She then brutally intervened against the Protestants by ordering the Massacre of St Bartholomew (1572). This was to make Parisians even more hostile to her son, Henri III, when he tried to return to more moderate policies. The Catholic League found its firmest support and its most fervent apologists in the capital. It rose against the king in the days of the barricades of 1588. Henri III fled, then returned to lay siege to the city, before being assassinated at Saint-Cloud by the monk Jacques Clément. His cousin Henri de Bourbon, now Henri IV (le Grand), continued to harass the city, which reached the depths of misery, its suburbs in ruins, its population starving and its houses abandoned.

Town planning in the 17th century

As a Protestant, Henri IV, in 1590, was refused entry into his own capital. When he abjured his faith in 1594, remarking cynically, 'Paris is well worth a mass', the gates opened before him. Building works were at once put in hand to reduce unemployment, embellish the city and serve the glory of the king. Work was recommenced at the Louvre and at the Tuileries, thereafter joined to one another by the Grande and Petite Galeries. The Pont-Neuf bridge, begun by Henri III, was completed, and for the first time passersby had an unrestricted view of the river. The bridge was built together with the triangular Place Dauphine, the materials were ordered to be brick and stone, and at its apex Marie de'Medici erected the equestrian statue of her husband. At the same time a street was laid following the line of the bridge on the Left Bank: the Rue Dauphine, which led to the village of Saint-Germain. On the land of the Hôtel des Tournelles, left untended since the accidental death of Henri II during a tourney in 1559, Henri IV ordered the laying out of a magnificent public square, the Place Royale, now the Place des Vosges, designed for equestrian jousts and flanked by high, uniform houses for all the aristocracy to reside. The north-east sector within the ramparts was sold off as building plots by the Grand Prior of the Temple and there was a further project for a planned public square, the Place de France, which came to nothing. The first planning regulations were drawn up by the Duc de Sully, who vigorously conducted the king's policies for Paris, in concert with the *prévôt des marchands*, François Miron, and trade and industry prospered.

In 1610 a religious fanatic, Ravaillac, helped by an obstruction in the Rue Feronnière which held up the king's coach, assassinated Henri IV. However the work set in hand by the king continued, on the initiative of private promoters who bought up large tracts of open land, laid out new streets and resold the plots bordering them. Louis le Barbier created a new district on the Left Bank on the site of the former Pré-aux-Clercs between the Rue de l'Université and the *quai*, while Christophe Marie created the Ile Saint-Louis on two muddy islets in the Seine, where the architect Louis le Vau was to build a circle of ostentatious mansions including the Hôtel Lambert and the Hôtel Lanzun. To the W Cardinal Richelieu demolished Charles V's rampart because it was preventing the extension of the garden of his palace (the future Palais-Royal), and replaced it with a fortified wall named 'des Fossés Jaunes' (because of the color of the bricks) enclosing other newly-built districts – Villeneuve, Montmartre and the first Faubourg Saint-Honoré (1633–1636). The mansions of government personnel were constructed around the home of this powerful cardinal-minister, including the Hôtel La Vrillière, now the Banque de France.

The town was being extended in all directions, while the ring of rural villages saw the proliferation of country houses for the Parisian wealthy, and of religious foundations that sprang up everywhere in the Catholic renewal of the Counter-Reformation. Sixty convents were opened in Paris between 1600 and 1639, concerned especially with helping the poor and teaching the Ursulines and the Order of the Visitation. . . . Most were to be found in the Faubourg Saint-Honoré, the Marais and the Faubourg Saint-Jacques. The last came to look like a holy town, greatly favoured by the pious Spanish queen, Anne of Austria. It was she who caused the immense Val-de-Grâce to be built on a large open space to commemorate the birth of the heir to the throne, Louis XIX. Domes which were Italian in inspiration crowned a number of these churches and chapels, suddenly giving an ultramontane look to the Left Bank. During this period attention was focused on the training of the clergy and on the formation of all pastoral types of society (seminaries; the Oratory and Saint-Sulpice institutions; the founding of the Jesuits). Through the tireless work of St Vincent-de-Paul, hospitals and charitable foundations multiplied without, however, succeeding in stemming the spread of poverty or in teaching the masses to read and write. It was in this climate of theological and spiritual renewal that the Jansenist movement emerged (Angélique Arnauld and the Abbé de Saint-Cyran), while Paris, formerly the suffragan bishopric of Sens in the tradition of Gallo-Roman political geography, at last acceded to the rank of archbishopric in 1622.

The revolt among the nobility known as the Fronde caused a terrible economic crisis which aggravated the people's distress. Throughout Louis XIV's reign deaths outnumbered births, the population growth in Paris resulting only from continual provincial immigration. The scale of poverty was so great that it led to the creation in 1656 of the Hôpital Général.

The monarchy felt the same fear of the Parisian populace as had Charles V and Henri III; after the revolts of 1648–1649 the Sun King left the city. It was Colbert, the wealthy middle-class merchant appointed Controller-General of Finance and Superintendent of Buildings in 1664, who was to mastermind Louis XIV's rule in Paris, after the king had made his home at Versailles in 1677, before making it the seat of government in 1682.

In the early glorious years of Louis' reign, the security of the city seemed sufficiently assured by the ring of fortifications built by Vauban, on the French frontiers, for the ramparts to be taken down (1670) and replaced by a promenade planted with trees, the *nouveau cours*. In place of the fortified gates, triumphal arches in the Antique style were built, celebrating the victories of the young king – the Porte Saint-Denis and the Porte Saint-Martin. The *cours* was to be continued on the Left Bank along a broken line that went from the Boul. de l'Hôpital to the Boul. des Invalides.

Following the example of Cardinal Mazarin (1602–1661), who had ordered the executors of his will to build a college for students from the newly-annexed provinces (the Palais de l'Institut), Colbert established on the Left Bank, which alone had the necessary space, the great establishments of the reign: the Hôpital de la Salpétrière, the Observatoire and finally the Hôtel Royal des Invalides for disabled ex-servicemen (*mutilés de guerre*), for which the architect Hardouin-Mansart built an exceptional church with a perfect dome, standing like a royal memorial in the still-deserted plain.

The difficult problem of the completion of the Louvre arose at the very time when the king was no longer hiding his intention of leaving the capital for good. Contradictory projects were put forward by the Italian Bernini, whom the king had summoned, François Mansart, Louis le Vau and many others. The final solution, a theatrical colonnade facing the city, was the brain-child of a doctor of medicine, Perrault. In front of the Tuileries Palace, which Le Vau had greatly altered, Le Nôtre laid out a new, carefully planned garden, bordered by terraces. Following the example of the Place des Vosges, Louis XIV created two new royal squares with statues of himself, and whose geographical positions are a good illustration of how the development of Paris was pushing westwards: the Place des Victoires and the Place Vendôme, both flanked by buildings with uniform façades based on the Versailles formula, which abolished the concept of juxtaposed residences, keeping only the notion of urban decor. But all these extravagant building projects increased the country's penury.

While the Marais was entering a period of decline and obsolescence the western districts of the two banks, the Faubourg Saint-Germain and the Faubourg Saint-Honoré, joined by the new Pont-Royal, saw a decisive new upsurge in development and the construction of large, aristocratic houses which, for the first time, created an almost exclusively residential area. Simultaneously Colbert brought in State industries and incumbents who enjoyed State privileges, which were to create the beginnings of a fixed working population in the city. Paris had now become a metropolis, the inhabitants in 1715 probably numbering some 500,000.

The Age of Enlightenment

The creation of Versailles as a seat of politics had not deprived Paris of its intellectual pre-eminence. On the contrary, it had made of the city an irreverent force opposed to the court and receptive to the new thinking. It took a short-lived revenge on the death of Louis XIV with the brief stay of the young Louis XV, at Vincennes and the Tuileries, but the king soon returned to Versailles (1722). During his reign there was an upsurge of the independence and brilliance of the *Cité des Lettres et des Arts,* its attraction now enhanced by the climate of opposition to old-established values. This was the era of the philosophers, the encyclopedists, the triumph of the salons, the Faubourg Saint-Honoré and the opulent middle classes (Mme Geoffrin). But it was also a time of economic expansion, with a sharp increase in population (650,000 inhabitants in 1789) and a huge increase in private building, which the laying down of boundaries in 1724 was unable to restrict. The most remarkable aspect of these new houses was the desire, for the first time, for comfort (separate apartments, lavatories, corridors, the development of common parts, courtyards, staircases). The first half of the century left the field open to the ideas and enterprise of private individuals.

On the other hand, from 1748 to 1947 onwards, Louis XV took more interest in Paris and set important works in hand, the most original being the Place Louis-XV, the present-day Place de la Concorde. It was a space opening wide on to the river, the copses of the Champs-Elysées and the terraces of the Tuileries gardens; set away from the traffic. This esplanade, the remarkable creation of Jacques-Ange Gabriel, was made for strolling and public festivities.

Other large-scale projects followed, the construction of major buildings, the surrounding districts regulated by legislation and designed to a set scale: the new church of Sainte-Geneviève and its square, the new Odéon theatre and the district facing it, the Ecole Militaire and the esplanade of the Champ-de-Mars. The more the century advanced, the more the theme of 'City and Citizen' aroused the interest of philosophers, architects, art connoisseurs and administrators. The creation of the post of *Lieutenant de Police* in 1667 by Colbert, with the nomination of Nicolas de la Reynie, placed in the hands of one man total responsibility – highways, supplies, public health and police – for the administration of a large town. His 18th-century successors, like D'Argenson and Sartine, turned out to be excellent municipal ministers.

Buildings were no longer considered for themselves, but for their function and social significance. Not only churches and palaces, but markets, water supply, sewers, abattoirs and theaters were given more serious thought, collaboration and the drawing up of building programmes took place and foreshadowed modern town planning. This bore its first fruits under Louis XVI with precise and strict legislation on the height of new houses, proportional to the width of the thoroughfares on which they would stand (1783).

The building of a sixth wall, the *mur d'octroi*, by the rapacious farmers general (*fermiers généraux* – members of the corporations entitled to farm taxes) which was to put an end to tax evasion by making commercial traffic pass through the gates of entry designed by Ledoux, made the people even more discontented. The cemetery of Saints-Innocents, long condemned as a source of infection and epidemics, was replaced by a market. New bridges were thrown across the Seine by the engineer Perronet (the Pont de la Concorde, the Pont de Neuilly). Administrative buildings, like the Ecole de Médecine, the Ecole de Droit, the Hôtel de la Monnaie, the Mont-de-Piété, the Théâtre Français and the Palais de Justice, were made more splendid. The architect Verniquet drew up the first accurate plan of Paris, essential for the consideration of changes to be made to the old town to demolish certain buildings and improve the flow of traffic.

As a result, building plots rose in value and were quickly exploited by their owners. Low houses and vacant lots in the new districts gave way to high, stone-built buildings to rent, changing the appearance of the city. The Duc d'Orléans did not blush to follow the bankers' example in splitting off the sides of his garden at the Palais-Royal to put up such buildings, constructed as a peristyle.

The Revolution of 1789

The city was going through a phase of great expansion and change at the outbreak of the Revolution, and public opinion played a large part. The debate on constitutional reform was occupying the delegates to the Estates General at Versailles when they were rudely interrupted by the people of Paris. Stricken by the economic crisis and the price of bread, their political sensibilities aroused by the writings of the philosophers and the ferment of ideas stirring in cafés, political clubs and newspapers, and still resentful of the king who had deserted them, the Parisians suddenly turned on the very symbol of hostile absolutism: the Bastille. July 14 irremediably overturned the process of reform. It brought in its wake the return to Paris of the humiliated Louis XVI, the proclamation of Bailly, the first mayor, then the bloody procession of October 5 and 6 when the king and his family were brought back to the Tuileries as prisoners of the Revolution. At this point the real power was in the hands of the political clubs: the Jacobins (from Dominican) and the Cordeliers (from Franciscan), the names of the convents in which they had installed themselves after the clergy had been dispossessed of all they owned by the Revolution. The clubs were to batter away at monarchial power, constitutional or otherwise, and bit by bit establish the dictatorship of a small group determined to impose the principles of the new order: Liberty, Equality and Fraternity. Opinion in the provinces, or rather in the Departments created in 1790, encouraged by the fraternal Fête de la Fédération celebrated on July 14, 1790, on the Champ-de-Mars, was expressed by the group known as the *Girondins* which, discredited by the poor handling of the frontier wars, was finally removed from power by Robespierre in June 1793.

Parisians, onlookers at the guillotine when they were not themselves victims of it, sorely tried by harshly-imposed food rationing and the collapse of the paper money (the *assignats*), lived through the two years of the Terror under the Committee of Public Safety, which was principally concerned with saving the nation from foreign invasions and combating the pro-royal revolt of the western Departments. The monarchy had not survived the taking of the Tuileries on August 10, 1792, and Robespierre's dictatorship succumbed to reaction and lassitude on 9 Thermidor, Year II (July

27 1794). Compromise regimes followed, the Thermidorian Convention and the Directory, but political power was no longer in Parisian hands and it was the star of a soldier, Bonaparte, that was to guide the new destiny of France.

The Revolution left no enduring monument in Paris, unless it is, as Michelet has said, the great open space of the Champ-de-Mars, the setting for so many national celebrations. Much thought was devoted to changing and opening up the Cité (the *Plan des Artistes),* but little was actually done. Changes came about in a disorderly fashion through the confiscation of the assets of the Church and the *émigrés,* the sale of which against paper money (*assignats*) quickly made the speculators' fortunes.

This operation freed an eighth of the land in Paris. While few of the *émigrés'* houses were destroyed, some convents and churches were razed, but only to make way for unplanned developments and, paradoxically, this wasted opportunity resulted in a sharp reduction of open space.

During the Revolution building did not entirely stop. During these years districts were built up and large buildings for rental erected, as in the Rue de la Chaussée d'Antin in the Odéon district; their Louis XVI style is particularly restrained and severe. After the Thermidorian interlude, Directoire Neo-Classicism became less severe and interior decoration much richer, with harsher colours. Because of the inferior materials no interiors have survived. Private *hôtels* again began to be built. A whiff of Egyptomania, following Bonaparte's expedition, was added to the preponderant influences of Antiquity, as in the house in the Place du Caire.

The 19th and 20th centuries

The capital of the Napoleonic Empire

Napoleon chose Paris as the capital of his great empire: then, in 1809, he made Rome his second capital, in the manner of Charlemagne uniting the Eternal City to Aix-la-Chapelle. This twinning, presaging that of 1956, was a political gesture: Paris remained the uncontested metropolis of Imperial Europe, to which Napoleon dreamt of gathering the artistic and intellectual riches, and even the records, of all the annexed countries. Paris, an object of conquest for the young Corsican, had been the scene of his political emergence, with the crushing of the reactionary uprising before Saint-Roch on the 13 Vendémiaire and the *coup d'état* of the 18 Brumaire at the Orangery of Saint-Cloud. The city came to be associated with Imperial pomp – the coronation, the marriage with Marie-Louise, the baptism of the King of Rome – as well as with military glories – reviews and processions, the 'Te Deum' of victories. . . .

In his passion for reorganization, Napoleon took a personal interest in Paris and its problems, taking up the ideas formulated under the *ancien régime*. Through the intermediary of the Préfet de la Seine, he directed the planning of its streets and services. He wanted large, Roman-style monuments: the Pont d'Iéna, the Arc de Triomphe du Carrousel, the colossal Arc de Triomphe of the Place de l'Etoile (only to be completed under Louis-Philippe), the Madeleine, the Bourse and a series of fountains. The modernization of urban services looked to the future: supplies were assured by a network of markets, with a central market at Les Halles, by abattoirs, by reserve granaries and the wine market; a water supply by the digging of the Canal de l'Ourcq. To all this he added the construction of *quais*, the laying of sewers, the numbering of houses and the creation of cemeteries on the outskirts of the city.

However, the Emperor lacked the time to open up the new thoroughfares suggested in the *Plan des Artistes*. Only the bold WE opening of the Right Bank was begun with the laying out of the Rue de Rivoli leading from the Place de la Concorde, for which Fontaine, Napoleon's favourite architect, in collaboration with Percier, designed the unusual arcaded façades and the roof lines. The creation of new districts on the hill of Chaillot and on the plain of the Left Bank remained in the project portfolio, otherwise there would have been the Palais du Roi de Rome and a vast collection of administrative buildings (the University, the Archives, etc.).

From the time of the Consulate the population had recovered the losses suffered under the Revolution, and at the first census of 1801 had reached the level of 546,856. Immigration from the provinces, halted by earlier events, now resumed, helping to form a new workforce, attracted by the creation of textile (cotton processings) and luxury industries.

With the fall of the Empire foreign armies entered Paris twice, before and after the Hundred Days and Waterloo. Cossacks and English troops bivouacked in the Champs-Elysées in 1814 and 1815. Twice, through the intervention of Fouché and Talleyrand, Louis XVIII returned to his '*bonne ville*', greeted by a population weary with war, but in whom nostalgia for the military glory of the Empire was to remain alive and well. Louis XVIII, and then Charles X, installed themselves in the Tuileries Palace; neither was concerned with changing the face of Paris, but there was a surge of private building, financed by the rising Banque de France. New, airy and well-planned districts, in some of which English influence made itself felt, with buildings for rent and houses surrounded by gardens, were laid out to the W: François I, Beaujon, Europe, Saint-Georges. A pleasing Classicism, drawing frequently on Antiquity for its inspiration, gave them a unity of style which is still perceptible, in spite of demolitions.

The brilliant society of high finance and the closed aristocratic world of the Faubourg Saint-Germain (the latter hostile to the rise of the moneyed middle class which flourished under Louis-Philippe), was a privileged society fully described by Balzac in his *Comédie Humaine.* It contrasted starkly to the modest bourgeoisie of functionaires and shopkeepers and the impoverished working class crammed into the central districts described by Eugène Sue and Victor Hugo. There were 1000 inhabitants per hectare (some 400 per acre) in the Grève, Saint-Merri and in the Cité. Harbours of alcoholism, tuberculosis, prostitution and crime, these districts were the source of devastating epedimics: in 1832 cholera claimed 44,000 victims. In 1848, 65% of Parisians were too poor to pay tax and 80% of the dead went to a common grave. As a result these central districts were, with the eastern suburbs and notably the Faubourg Saint-Antoine, the centre of opposition to the régime. It was here that the barricades of the revolution of 1830 were raised, the 'July Monarchy' riots (the Rue Transnonnain, of sinister memory, was part of the Rue Beaubourg), then those of the 1848 revolution. The only street of any size laid out by Louis-Philippe's government was the unambitious Rue Rambuteau; it was named after a Prefect of the Seine whose modernization programme for Les Halles was barely outlined when the monarchy fell.

In 1841 Thiers secured agreement to the building of a fortified outer wall, once more made necessary by the political insecurity of Europe. It was built through the suburban communes, with seventeen advance forts, a few of which, like Champigny, still survive. Finally, France entered the age of the railway. The first Gare Saint-Lazare, the point of departure for Saint-Germain-en-Laye and Versailles, was inaugurated in 1837. The law of 1842 provided for six lines leaving the capital to cross the country, the famous *Réseau en étoile.* The first omnibuses had appeared in 1828.

The Paris of Haussmann

At the outbreak of the revolution of 1848 the works commenced by Raubuteau were interrupted, but the provisional government, instantly faced with the danger of unemployment, was quick to secure the work for the Ateliers Nationaux (national workshops). The sites opened by the Second Republic were taken over at once by the President-Prince, Louis-Napoléon Bonaparte, nephew of Napoleon I, soon to become Napoléon II. He had his own ideas, matured in his contact with England during the long years of exile, on modern town planning, on the proper arrangements for a great capital and on a social policy for housing. He managed to surround himself with men of action who made up a general staff of exceptional quality. The Prefect of the Seine, Haussmann, directed the overall programme, its planning, execution and finance; Belgrand was the hydraulic engineer and Alphand the landscape architect.

Thanks to the wealth of the ruling classes and to economic forces then in a phase of strong expansion, they achieved this immense programme with astonishing rapidity. Steam had arrived. This was a world of engineers – men of action of Saint-Simonian inspiration – exploiting the resources of metallurgy not only to build railroads but to construct great frameworks for the new stations (the Gare de l'Est and the Gare du Nord) as well as the steel-framed pavilions – the 'umbrellas', all glass and iron, desired by the emperor – that Victor Altard built at the Halles Centrales.

Haussmann cut and sliced into old Paris to open a new road network; first the main axial crossing formed vertically by the Boul. de Sebastopol, the Boul. du Palais and the Boul. Saint-Michel, and horizontally by the extension of the Rue Saint-Honoré as far as the Rue Saint-Antoine, then a series of oblique streets linking the crossings with strategic points of Parisian topography, as the Rue de Turbigo joined the ancient site of Saints-Eustache to the Place de la Republique, where an army barracks maintained military control over these traditionally revolutionary districts.

The Cité was almost entirely razed. In this desert in front of Notre-Dame, were built the new Hôtel-Dieu and the barracks of the Municipal Guard, now the Préfecture de Police. The Louvre Palace was doubled in size and linked by a second gallery to the Tuileries, the Imperial residence.

The new districts were opened up by other thoroughfares (the Boul. Malesherbes and the Boul. Haussmann), the old *secteurs* of the Left Bank more slowly (the Rue des Ecoles, the start of the Boul. Saint-Germain); some new streets served the stations (the Boul. Magenta, the Boul. de Strasbourg, the Rue de Ronnes).

Public highways were asphalted, provided with pavements and sometimes planted with trees. On the building land made available by expropriation, the price of which rocketed, buildings in natural stone with carved decoration were built alongside opulent apartment buildings for the well-to-do bourgeoisie Zola described in his novels.

To bring water to Paris, Belgrand canalized the rivers Dhuis and Vanne, the length of the sewer system rose from 93 to 311 miles/150 to 500km, making use of the course of the Bièvre to carry waste water away to the Seine at Asnières. Finally Alphand created large parks on the periphery, one to the E, the Bois de Vincennes, the other to the W, the Bois de Boulogne, and a series of green open spaces and squares cleverly contrived on unbuilt land like the Parc Montsouris and the Parc Buttes-Chaumont, and on the former domain of the Orléans family (the Parc Monceau).

Paris, the intellectual and artistic centre of the world and the site of industrial exhibitions visited by sovereigns, attained, at the end of the Second Empire, one of the summits of its influence. In 1860 the communes between the old city and Thiers' outer wall were annexed, while between 1851 and 1871 the population almost doubled, and banking, credit and commerce prospered. But the war of 1870 brutally shattered this euphoria and brought in its wake a series of disasters that for a time paralysed the entire city.

From the Commune to the Great War

Military defeat brought the immediate fall of the Imperial régime. The provisional government, which had installed a bourgeois republic, failed to save the city from the humiliation of surrender. The working population, much of which had become Parisian when the Suburban Communes were annexed in 1860, reacted against this political abandonment and when Thiers belatedly tried to take away their guns which they might have used for the wrong purposes, the insurrection exploded (March 18, 1871) and rapidly subdued Paris. The *Commune*, which took its name from the glorious hours of the Paris of 1792, set itself up as a revolutionary government. Its few weeks of existence were a unique experience of socialism applied to a city under siege. Karl Marx made a penetrating study of this. The government of the Republic, having withdrawn to Versailles, wore down – under the eye of the Prussians – the resistance of the Communards and cruelly repressed the uprising.

The city was entered by the *Versailles* (the regular troops) and was still smoking from the fires lit by the rebels at the Palais des Tuileries and the Cours des Comptes, the Palais de Justice, the Palais Royale and the Hôtel de Ville, where the city archives and the registers of all its population were completely destroyed. Thus humbled, at the same time Paris lost the political power that had ensured her supremacy since 1789. In 1871 it was the provinces that triumphed and held political power during the Third Republic, notably through the radical socialist political élite from the Midi.

After the ruin and the slaughter, recovery was slow. Haussmann's programme was cautiously restarted with the prolongation of the Boul. Saint-Germain and the completion of the Opéra. Immigration, especially from the North, Brittany and the Auvergne, once again brought a spectacular increase in the population. The two-million mark was reached after the census of 1876, then rapidly passed 2,714,000 in 1901 and 2,888,000 in 1911. The population in the arrondissements of the city center was stagnating or diminishing, but in the outer suburbs, it was increasing, those former villages that new streets now linked to Haussmann's urban system. Town planning became less extravagant and elitist. The taste for spectacular and symbolic monuments had not diminished, as can be seen in the Sacré-Coeur, the old Trocadéro, the Eiffel Tower, the Grand and Petit Palais, monuments often erected to mark world exhibitions when the French economy was happy to show off its recovery from the ruinous war, and the young republic to show its strength to the monarchies that were still very much in the majority in Europe. But now the authorities were eager to bestow public amenities on the entire population: the extension of the water supply and sewerage systems, the distribution of gas and electricity, the clearance of household rubbish in special containers to which the prefect Poubelle had the misfortune to give his name. The building of *lycées* (schools) – along the lines of the Jules Ferry legislation – and of hospitals, was intensified. The triumph of all these egalitarian services was incontestably owed to the Metropolitan Railway which, in 1900,'brought in the new century'.

This was the *Belle Epoque*. Society, self-assured, was to know a few years of euphoria. Art Nouveau symbolized this almost aggressive search for modernity. Guimard's expression of it, especially the apartment block in metal, faience and glass brick, the Castel Berenger, was the most thoughtful and homogenous, while most contemporary building plunged into a whirlwind of eclecticism, masking important advances in structural techniques. The insatiable appetite for construction even changed the legislation: due to the decree of 1902 the new buildings were vast blocks topped by immense roofs, sprouting overhangs and multi-coloured bay windows in which any excuse served to gain more space, horizontally or vertically. Luxury apartment buildings began to supplant private mansions now that the use of elevators raised the value of the upper levels. The Boul. Raspail, the Champ-de-Mars, Passy, Auteuil and the quays of the western districts all saw the rise of these tall cliffs of sculpted stone, which shielded the life of the society described by Marcel Proust.

The two World Wars

The war of 1914 brutally interrupted the modernization of the city. For four years, with all building at a standstill, it suffered privation and anguish from the approach of the front-line which even forced the government to evacuate for a time to Bordeaux (September-December 1914), then came the Zeppelin raids, the bombs, and the shells of 'Big Bertha', the German cannon positioned at Crépu-en-Laonnois.

The victory parade of July 14, 1919 marked the end of the nightmare, but the beginning of the hard post-war years. In the midst of the economic and political crisis in which Paris strove to regain a dominant role (the uprising of the Ligues patriots against the parliamentary Left on February 6, 1934; the procession in support of the Popular Front on July 14, 1935), the authorities were powerless to begin any large development programme. A few rare and important road-works were carried out, such as the Boulevard Haussmann; others, like the extension of the Rue Etienne-Marcel, abandoned. The Metro was extended to the inner suburbs. Social housing got under way under the policy of the *HLM (habitations à loyers modérés)*. The great exhibitions were still used as occasions for the building of new Palais des Beaux-Arts, as in the Colonial

Exhibition of 1931 at the Porte Dorée and the Exhibition of Arts and Techniques at the Trocadéro in 1937. However, building was uncoordinated, no new open spaces were added to those provided by Haussmann and the conversion of the former area of military fortifications into green belt was abandoned in favour of groups of municipal housing blocks.

Old housing stock, left untended for generations because of the unfortunate rent policy, became a breeding-ground for tuberculosis; its eradication was sought only through the destruction of these officially designated 'insalubrious' properties. Meanwhile Le Corbusier dreamt his dream (the *Plan Voisin*) of a new Paris composed of huge blocks, isolated and uniform, standing at the historic centre of the Right Bank. Thanks to the brothers Perret, concrete made its first appearance in Paris in the Théâtre des Champs-Elysées, the Mobilier National, the Musée des Travaux Publics and the buildings of the Rue Raynouard. With this new material the construction of large apartment blocks was possible and to a large extent they transformed the area of the Portes.

In June 1940 the new German invasion led to the occupation of the capital by the enemy army. Once again, and for four years, the scourge of hardships and bombings by British and American planes fell upon Paris. The German presence was an added ordeal. The first signs of resistance occurred as early as November 11, 1940 with the student procession to the tomb of the Unknown Soldier. The *armée de l'ombre* was organized and spread, in spite of imprisonments (prisons were the Santé, the Cherche-Midi and Fresnes, the camps, Drancy and Romainville), torture in the Gestapo headquarters in the Rue des Saussaies, the Avenue Foch and the Rue Lauriston, the death trains to Germany and the executions. In May 1943 the National Council of the Resistance held its first meeting in the Rue du Four, headed by Jean Moulin, a month before his arrest in the Lyon region.

With the Allied landings and offensive in Normandy, the Resistance intervened to hasten the liberation of the capital; on August 15, 1944, the public services were already on strike, on August 19 the CNR and the Parisian Committee of Liberation hoisted the tricolor at the Hôtel de Ville, while 1,200 policemen shut themselves inside the Préfecture and were attacked by German troops. Street fighting and barricades multiplied during the days following until the entry into Paris of the tanks of Leclerc's division on August 24 and 25. At the Gare Montparnasse the German commandant of 'Gross Paris', General von Cheltitz, pressed by the Swedish consul, Raoul Nordling, refused to carry out Hitler's orders to 'blow up Paris' and surrendered. On August 26 General de Gaulle was bowing before the tomb of the Unknown Soldier, going on foot down the Champs-Elysées and attending a service of celebration and deliverance at Notre-Dame, disturbed by the last fusillades of rooftop machine-gunners. On April 2, 1945 the City received the Croix de la

Libération with the following citation: '. . .Capital faithful to itself and to France, has shown under enemy occupation and oppression, and in spite of the voices of surrender and betrayal, its unshakeable resolution to fight and conquer. . .'.

Jean-Pierre Babelon

Architecture in Paris

For more than two thousand years, men have been building on this patch of land. Styles and construction methods have succeeded one another, often standing side by side as the city and the life and work of its inhabitants developed. Parts of the city have, at times, been ruthlessly destroyed, obliterating traces of the past, but each age has nevertheless left its own testimony in its monuments, which make up a remarkable manual of architecture, from the Gallo-Roman period to the dynamic present day: twenty centuries spent in providing the best possible buildings for all the activities of man.

The Gallo-Roman period

In the early centuries of our age, Lutetia was just a small provincial settlement on the Seine, and its monuments bore no comparison with the great cities of Antiquity. We have, however, preserved two buildings characteristic of Roman genius, the arenas and the Palais des Thermes. Their still-impressive remains and the less obvious traces of other rediscovered monuments are enough to show, in the context of a small provincial town, the characteristics of that Roman 'genius' that was simply a sense of organization: the taste for public buildings, monuments, logic; architecture in the service of the public good.

Then night fell on Paris. From the time of the invasions of the Frankish, Merovingian and Carolingian periods, nothing tangible remains apart from a few small columns and capitals, and we need to skip over seven centuries – the only interruption in the architectural history of Paris that has occurred. Then comes the next monument, the bell-tower of Saint-Germain-des-Prés, built around 1000 AD. This is the symbol and prime example of Parisian Romanesque architecture, which otherwise consists only of a few vestiges or parts of buildings, in particular the chapel of Saint-Aignan, the last of the numerous little churches of the Cité to survive.

The long, great Parisian Middle Ages

Early Gothic architecture

The fact that Paris retains from the 10th century only modest relics of the art which created Cluny, Vézelay and Saint-Trophime is due to demolitions and reconstructions, but also because the Ile-de-France, cradle of Gothic art, was the first region to reject the Romanesque in favour of a more ambitious form of architecture. From 1130 to 1135, even before the Abbey church of Saint-Denis at Suger, intersecting ribs appeared in the vaulting of the choir of Saint-Martin-des-Champs, the clumsily-moulded ribs falling back on to capitals that were still Romanesque in inspiration. But the formula was soon refined and at Saint-Pierre-de-Montmartre there is a crossing which is already delicate, elegant, vigorous and in every way worthy of the name of Gothic. By now the new technique was tried and tested and in the following years the choir of Saint-Germain-des-Prés, with its beautiful double ambulatory, was built. And on April 21, 1163, a memorable day in the history of the monuments of Paris, Pope Alexander III consecrated this apse, at the same time laying the first stone of Notre-Dame-de-Paris.

The cathedral

On the site of a Gallo-Roman temple and of the later small churches of Saint-Etienne and Notre-Dame, a place where prayers had been offered up for a thousand years, the bishop, Maurice de Sully, then his successor Eudes, directed the building of the new shrine.

Last of the Early Gothic cathedrals (Laon, Noyon, Soissons, Sens, Senlis), and first of the great classically harmonious cathedrals (Chartres, Reims, Amiens, Beauvais, Strasbourg), Notre-Dame-de-Paris truly stands at the turning-point in the evolution of Gothic art through its conception and structure: sexpartite rib vaults, but resting on uniform pillars; five naves but, against all the rules, only three doors on the façade; tribunes to accommodate the greatest possible number of worshippers, but a strong attempt, still unsuccessful, to increase the lighting in the clerestory. The principal interest of this building lies in the sometimes indecisive pursuit of an ideal that was not yet completely defined.

But today we see an almost naked structure which our imaginations must clothe with all the monumental arts of the period. The painted decoration of the cathedral has entirely disappeared. Of the original stained glass there remain only scraps, all its goldwork has been completely destroyed and only a few pieces of carved decoration survive. Finally, in the early 19th century, Viollet-le-Duc restored it, adding the gargoyles and, to some tastes, was deplorably thorough.

The influence of Notre-Dame

New in conception, marvellously executed, imposing in its proportions, Notre-Dame could not fail to influence architecture throughout the bishopric, where the country churches being built, tried modestly to imitate it. Two of these are now within the boundaries of the capital: Saint-Denis-de-la-Chapelle, of which the nave where Joan of Arc prayed, survives, and Saint-Germain-Charonne (largely rebuilt later), which still has a bay with its fine capital decorated with vine leaves, ferns and trefoil.

In Paris itself, still in line of descent from the cathedral, the choir of Saint-Germain-des-Prés was provided with flying buttresses, Saint-Pierre-de-Montmartre was enlarged and, especially, close to the cathedral, the Church of Saint-Julien-le-Pauvre was built; this, by a miracle to which Paris is unaccustomed, has kept its surroundings and its atmosphere, as well as two fine carved capitals. Besides these parish churches, the presence should be noted in late medieval Paris of monasteries, of which there are a few remains. Of the former Abbey of Sainte-Geneviève, the Lycée Henri IV has kept the kitchens, the refectory (now a chapel) and the bell-tower of the abbey church. Outside the city walls stood the Priory of Saint-Martin-des-Champs, with an enceinte (outer wall) of which two towers remain.

These are the shrines of the little town loved by the king, Philippe Auguste, who paved its streets and sought to defend it with a fortified wall, the first of those concentric circles which were to punctuate the growth of Paris. Considerable parts of this six-foot thick (two metres) wall still stand, notably in the Rue des Jardins-Saint-Paul. And, to support this enceinte at its most vulnerable point, he built a keep, the great round tower of the Louvre, of which all of the surviving lower part was recently uncovered.

The Golden Age of Gothic

This early Parisian Gothic art, sober and still a little heavy, was to blossom under St Louis and to become more ornate, more florid, more daring, and to evoke the spirit of Reims Cathedral as it is known today. One building symbolizes and illustrates this period: the Sainte-Chapelle.

Here is the perfect example of a palatine chapel of the period.

Composed of two storeys, corresponding to the social segregation of the royal family and its servants, its restricted proportions allowed Gothic architecture, now in full possession of its powers, to reach the level of virtuosity, resolving with discreet elegance those problems of weight, of the interplay of forces and of lighting which it was its conscious aim to conquer; given the difficulty of the site chosen the victory could only be triumphant. Was Pierre de Montreuil the creator of the Sainte-Chapelle? It is probable, and it is him we find again at Notre-Dame, where the progressive construction of side-chapels now required the lengthening of the transepts. These were now provided with new façades with wide windows, richly ornamented to which, nevertheless, Viollet-le-Duc brought his own additions.

Pierre de Montreuil is found again in the two great monasteries which stood outside the walls of Paris at the time: Saint-Germain-des-Prés and Saint-Martin-des-Champs. For the former, he was commissioned to rebuild the monastery buildings around the old church; but the irresponsibility, first of the monks, then of the town planners, has left pitifully few remains: the gable end of the refectory and the remnants of the admirable Lady Chapel, the door of which is in the Cluny Museum. On the other hand, there is still the beautiful refectory of Saint-Martin-des-Champs, a large rectangular room with two naves, still dominated by the lector's throne, which opened on to the now-vanished cloisters by a doorway where flowers and vine and ivy leaves carved in the soft stone are the last memories of the green countryside that then surrounded it. Many churches of the period have disappeared. The front door of Saint-Pierre-des-Boeufs survives, re-erected close to Saint-Séverin.

Parisian art of the 14th century

The 14th c. seems to mark a pause: architecture, in full control of its resources, its techniques stabilized, seems somewhat to have lost its inventiveness and freshness of inspiration.

New churches grew larger: the nave of Saint-Martin-des-Champs, the choir of Saint-Germain-l'Auxerrois. Despite 19th- century restorations and alterations Saint-Leu-Gilles and the Chapel of Saint-Jean de Beauvais have clearly retained the slightly austere character of this impeccable style. But special mention must be made of an exceptional building, used for nearly two centuries now as a fire station: the Bernadine refectory. In spite of the regrettable internal arrangements the austere elegance of Cistercian architecture is still there to be seen and admired.

So far civil architecture has not been mentioned. Nothing remains of the abodes of the late Middle Ages, from that of the king to that of the artisan, and it is not until the 14th century that the homes of men are found among the monuments preserved: an ecclesiastical abode, a lordly mansion, two royal palaces.

The Abbot of Ourscamp built himself, in the Marais, a Paris residence of which a fine, low, vaulted room remains (46 Rue François-Miron). All that is left of the numerous mansions built in Paris by the feudal aristocracy of the 14th century is the postern of the Hôtel de Clisson, built around 1380, with its two corbelled turrets on the side of the Rue des Archives. As for the royal palace, this was still on the Ile de la Cité, the seat of both temporal and spiritual powers, and on the very site of the Roman governor's palace. Retaining the Sainte-Chapelle, Philippe the Fair rebuilt the living quarters, of which the famous towers of the Conciergerie still stand, much restored in the 19th century, and the great rooms of the ground floor. This is the majestic and austere home of an autocratic king, in which the severity of line is only slightly attenuated by the elegance of a few sculptures. But as the palace was becoming little by little the domain of the lawyers, Charles V ordered his architect Raymond du Temple to partially reconstruct the Louvre palace, the lower part of which has recently been uncovered: this has been the great Parisian archeological revelation of recent years.

The rise of statuary art

Sculpture in the Paris of the period kept its monumental character while asserting its personality and even individuality. The Virgin of the door of the cloister of Notre-Dame, integral to, and inseparable from the architecture, was followed by those kept at Saint-Germain-des-Prés and in the cathedral. These are individual, personalized statues with the graceful 'Gothic sway', with its swirling drapery. Also in Notre-Dame, the bas-reliefs on the choir screen depict religious scenes, with an anecdotal care that shows the influence of ecclesiastical theater of the time.

Royal building

Charles V was one of Paris's great builders. Like Philippe Auguste, he had provided it with a new enceinte, flanked by a fortress, the Bastille. Of this building, which is supremely important for the history of architecture, as well as the history of Paris and of France, only a few scanty remains survive in the corridors of the Métro. Of the Hôtel Saint-Paul, the residence of the sovereign, there is only a reminder provided by street name plates. On the other hand, the château that was his favourite home, Vincennes, has been preserved almost intact; a keep surrounded by a rectangular enceinte, where the king hoped to gather all the great of his kingdom within his sight: a premonition of Versailles.

When the Holy Roman Emperor made his state visit to Paris in 1378,

Charles V, his nephew, took him to the Louvre, to Vincennes and to the Hôtel Saint-Paul, with its gardens and its menagerie. Little by little the emphasis moved, to the detriment of ecclesiastical buildings, to palaces and homes. Previously used entirely for religious purposes, architecture increasingly assumed its secure role.

Riches of Parisian Flamboyant art

Paris is one of the places rich in the Gothic architecture of the 15th century often called 'Flamboyant'. Moreover, the style lasted abnormally long in the capital – until the beginning of the 17th century. The success of the formula in the 15th century is enough to explain this survival, along with the conservative mentality of the clergy and the traditionalism of the corporations.

To begin with, there were seven churches. The growth of the city and its population necessitated the building of new shrines and the reconstruction or enlargement of those that were too small. Many have been preserved: Saint-Laurent, Saint-Médard, Saint-Germain-de-Charonne, Saint-Nicolas-des-Champs, Saint-Germain-l'Auxerrois, Saint-Séverin and Saint-Merri, as well as later churches which will be discussed further on, and in which the long-victorious tradition of modernism will be seen. The Gothic, in Paris, lasted five centuries.

There is no need to describe these buildings individually; it is better for the reader to go out and discover them. In all of them there is, both in plan and structure, a certain simplification by comparison with the churches of the great age of Gothic: less concern with height, fewer vertical and horizontal divisions, more concern with circulation and lighting and above all a taste for decoration, no longer only as a medium for teaching, that is, a Bible in images, but decoration that was gratuitous, anecdotal and almost secure – decoration for its own sake.

Here we will only point out certain particularities: the external frieze of the apse of Saint-Laurent, a representational band of animals and picturesque human figures; the decorated pendants of Saint-Nicolas-des-Champs; the porch of Saint-Germain-l'Auxerrois, with its carved keystones and its celebrated statue of St Mary the Egyptian, carrying her three loaves; again at Saint-Germain-l'Auxerrois, a whole series of anecdotal sculptures, as if in flight on the pinnacles and gargoyles in which parables turn into medieval stories; finally, at Saint-Séverin, more carvings, other gargoyles, the famous ambulatory with its twisted column and stained-glass windows of the period in which the art of glass painting evolved towards a pictorial technique and a secular inspiration. In all these churches intelligence of conception, elegance, and virtuosity somewhat for its own sake, are all far removed from evangelical simplicity.

This pursuit of the Flamboyant style continued throughout the 16th century. The Saint-Jacques tower was raised between 1509 and 1523 and its four storeys remained as impervious to Renaissance art as did the Church of Saint-Merri, rebuilt between 1520 and 1522. In the latter, the intricate vaulting of the crossing, the tracery of the windows and the carving of the doors show the persistence of a style which effortlessly scorns the divisions of art historians.

But the most startling example of this anomaly (we will speak of its façade later), is the Church of Saint-Gervais, constructed over the period 1494–1656. This is a purely Gothic building and of an even stricter Gothicism than the preceding buildings: here the Flamboyant style appears to be left behind, and there is a return to an almost classical Gothic, with simplified lines, purified ornamentation, and free of proscribed decoration, with the exception of the wonderful crown of hanging keystones in the Chapel of the Virgin.

All these churches had their own cemeteries, usually surrounded by galleries of ossuaries, where bones were piled up. Saint-Séverin has kept its ossuaries, constructed in the 15th century, but unfortunately altered in the 19th, a restoration which has given them an historically false, though quite picturesque, romantic look.

The charnel-house leads directly into the 15th-century cloister, the Cloître des Billettes, the last surviving Parisian building of this sort with its four galleries of six bays each, the vaults of which are ribbed, with decorated keystones. Of the Franciscan convent the refectory remains, restored at last in our own time.

The architecture of lords and peasants

In the 15th century there were as many civil constructions going up as religious ones, or even more so. They have been greatly decimated, but some notable examples remain, as much of aristocratic mansions as of more modest homes. Three great lordly residences have been preserved, in whole or in part: the Hôtel de Bourgogne, the Hôtel de Sens and the Hôtel de Cluny. The house owned by the Dukes of Burgundy to the north of Les Halles had a quadrangular tower added by Jean the Fearless , at the beginning of the century, and in the tympanum of the gate the emblems that the duke opposed to the gnarled club of Orléans can still be seen: two wood-planes and a plumb-line. This gate gives on to a spiral staircase, the central column of which branches out at the top storey to form the ribs of the vault: Gothic formulae seem more and more empty of meaning and to be used entirely at the whim of the decorator.

Prelates too built their baronial halls in Paris, among them the Archbishop of Sens, who much preferred to live in the capital. The construction of the Hôtel de Sens was begun in 1475; this hapless building has suffered from the outrageously excessive zeal of 19th-

and 20th-century restorers, to the point where only its silhouette, still picturesque with its gables and turrets, can be considered as authentic, while the detail of its construction and above all of its decoration is to be regarded with some doubt everywhere.

The third Flamboyant residence of Paris is the best preserved. This *hôtel* was built from 1485 to 1498 for the abbots of Cluny; all the buildings have been kept, with the chapel and even the courtyard's enclosing wall. The building has changed little and, though the internal arrangement has been modified, it is possible to reconstruct its main lines by studying the façades. A country house, but with a defensive aspect, the Hôtel de Cluny proclaims its regard for comfort by its situation, between courtyard and garden, its large windows, the space given over to common areas and the number of fireplaces. The charming chapel itself, beside the garden, is arranged so as to be accessible from the apartments. The carved decoration, though altered in the 19th century, emphasizes that this is a house for relaxation, comfortable, at times sumptuous, and well protected.

While the *grands seigneurs* and prelates lived in more or less isolated mansions, the bourgeoisie, artisans and shopkeepers shared narrow houses. The surface area of each related to the social status of its occupant. A number of houses in the Rue Parcheminerie, the Rue François-Miron and the Rue Xavier-Privas must go back to the 15th century, but the dating of them is difficult; some, like the house of Nicolas Flamel, have undergone hideous restorations. But their external arrangements can be seen fairly well; they have not changed much since earlier times: a ground floor built of stone, most often occupied by workshops with a display of goods, with a door which, when it gave on to an interior courtyard, became a carriage-door; above, corbelled upper storeys, the wooden structure of which was left uncovered, but which in the following period tended to be hidden under a render (plaster was now to take its place in Parisian architecture, and was to be used for a long time). At the top, the house culminated in a triangular gable (*pignon*), a sign of affluence that was to pass into popular proverbial language ('*avoir pignon sur rue*'), but which the municipality was soon to prohibit, making compulsory roof-lines running parallel to the line of the street. The houses were pressed one against the other along narrow streets, on bridges, on river banks, and Paris knew no open spaces other than crossroads and church squares.

Renaissance architecture was to be, above all, a quest for space and light.

Towards a new spirit
A late Renaissance

The characteristic traits of that artistic revolution, the Renaissance, which began in Italy, the influence of Antiquity, of individualism, the pre-eminence of secular art, appeared late in Parisian architecture, by comparison with other privileged regions, like the Loire Valley. Not only did religious architecture stick to its traditional formulae, but civil architecture, though always more ready to adopt new ideas, did not find its new impulse until the middle of the century.

This persistence of the spirit of the Middle Ages meant that religious architecture in Paris, contrary to other regions, hung on to its pre-eminence and vitality. Numbers of churches were built in Paris throughout the 16th century. Some of them were purely Gothic. In others, new doctrines gradually gained ground. Saint-Etienne-du-Mont, except for its façade, was built from 1492 to 1586. In plan and elevation it is still Flamboyant Gothic in style, with its flowing traceries and many-ribbed vaults with hanging keystones. But there are differences which announce new times: the great arcades of the nave gave up the pointed arches for the semicircular ones dear to Antiquity; they are surmounted by balustraded triforiums (arcaded wall passages) communicating with the rood-loft, the last left in Paris. Built from 1525 to 1535, it is still medieval in character, with the liernes (tertiary ribs) and tiercerons (secondary ribs) of its vault. But its general design and above all its decoration herald new ideas: the two Fames of the corner-stones, with their flowing hair and uncovered breasts, introduce the spirit of the Renaissance into this medieval environment for the first time in Paris.

Stranger still, perhaps, is the case of Saint-Eustache, built from 1532 to 1640, again with the exception of the façade. There also, the plan and elevation are traditional Gothic, the nave with aisles, the choir and transept with ribbed vaults and lit by pointed equilateral windows. But the pillars and colonnettes are replaced by columns in the classical style, and pilasters, standing free or superimposed, that look curiously like a Gothic body dressed in Renaissance elements.

This happens in alterations to and enlargements of earlier churches – faithfulness to Gothic structures, but a leaning towards new ornamentation. At Saint-Germain-l'Auxerrois the ambulatory and its chapels were finished in a traditional style pushed to the point of exuberance in the vault of the Chapel of the Virgin, but the Renaissance influence appeared in the side door, where a pediment is carried on two pilasters. In 1544, the church was given an admirable rood-screen with figures of the Evangelists in low relief by Jean Goujon, fragments of which are at the Louvre. At Saint-Nicolas-des-Champs the choir was rebuilt rather as at Saint-Eustache, the structure Gothic but with new proportions and a new outline. Here too there is a side door with pilasters and pediment.

Religious architecture of the time gave the impression of being in a state of divorce: the builder was faithful to well-tried formulae, while the decorator showed his awareness of the new art forms.

Public and private life

For its part, civil architecture had great difficulty in getting away from medieval precepts. Construction techniques, especially in houses of medium size, were slow to evolve. In the Rue des Francs-Bourgeois and the Rue Hautville pepper-pot turrets continued to be built at the corners, and in basements intersecting rib-vaults with rows of columns were still used: innovation was to come from the upper classes. The creation of the first administrative building is noteworthy. In 1532 the municipality ordered the construction of its Hôtel de Ville by Dominique de Cortone and Pierre Chambiges; for a long period this set the style for the genre. Set on fire during the Commune and subsequently destroyed, only a few architectural fragments of the building are left.

The Renaissance in Paris really began with the Hôtel Carnavalet, which saw the inauguration of a formula that was to enjoy a rich and long future. The Florentines of the same period built their palaces at the corner of two streets, at the edge of the traffic, leaving open access to the inner courtyard. This was utterly contrary to the lifestyle of a French aristocrat. Pierre Lescot (ca.1510–78), commissioned in 1544 to build the Hôtel de Ligneris, which is now called Carnavalet, repeated the same formula in the courtyard and garden as at the Hôtel de Cluny. He surrounded the courtyard on the other three sides with low wings; the one bordering on the street provided the building with both privacy and protection; behind the house was a garden, also giving no outside access and closed to public view. The main building was reserved for the master of the house and its arrangements were simple: large communicating rooms, lit by wide windows divided into four by mullion crosses. At the base of the roof there were dormer windows with pediments. The building was more remarkable for its plan than for its structure, but the decoration was to provide a dazzling additional element.

Traditionally, and probably correctly, the sculpted decoration is attributed to Jean Goujon (c.1510–68). Although it reveals the work of several hands, one is struck by the coherence and harmony of this decorative plan, and its complete integration into the architectural style.

Of the numerous other private residences built in Paris at this time, little remains. One should, however, see the *hôtel* built in the Rue Scipion by the financier Sardini; the arcaded façade, decorated with terracotta medallions, remains the only surviving example in Paris of this then-popular type of decoration. Of the great Hôtel de la Reine, now the Hôtel de Soissons, built by Jean Bullant for Catherine de' Medici, only the strange Doric column on the side of the Bourse de Commerce stands, and the Ecole des Beaux-Arts retains some vestiges of the Hôtel Legendre. Beside the Carnavalet stands the Arc de Nazareth, of the same period, with its peculiar brackets. But the most famous monument of the time was a fountain.

For Henri II's ceremonial entry into Paris, Jean Goujon rebuilt the Fontaine des Innocents, on the site of the Cimetié des Innocents, in the style of an Italian loggia, open to the street. At the end of the 18th century it was moved and reassembled to a symmetrical plan, but kept its Classical arrangement in the form of a triumphal arch and Goujon's admirable bas-reliefs of nymphs with rippling drapery, in which he symbolized a fluidity which was what the fountain most lacked. With this small monument the taste for Classicism and the new secular, almost sensual art, established themselves in the streets of Paris.

This taste for the Classical orders was to be more and more evident in the buildings of the end of the century, though its expression posed problems for architects that they were not always capable of resolving fully, as, for example, in the Hôtel Lamoignon.

The royal castle becomes a palace

During this time an exceptional piece of building work was in hand, at the home of the king, the Louvre. It will be remembered that around Philippe Auguste's big tower Charles V had re-erected a square of buildings. François I began by pulling down the central tower then, twenty years later, using Pierre Lescot and Jean Goujon, he decided to rebuild the quadrilateral to the same plan and on the SW corner of the present-day Cour Carrée. The king died soon afterwards and it was Henri II who, deciding to quadruple the surface area of the palace, adopted the plan that gave rise to the *cour* as it is today.

At that time, Pierre Lescot built the wing that has kept his name, in which the art of the second Renaissance is found in full flower, purified and structured, blending charm and nobility. Jean Goujon's delicate and slender bas-reliefs, their relief almost imperceptible on the lower storeys, more accentuated and theatrical on the attic storey, is integrated into Lescot's architectural framework with such precision that one wonders about the detail of so perfect a collaboration. In the interior it was Goujon who created the astonishing classical conception of the caryatides in the Salle des Caryatides of 1551.

As this first section of the Louvre was being finished, Catherine de' Medici was building for herself, further to the west, an elongated palace, the Tuileries, at right angles to the Seine which, beyond its gardens, closed off the view. Twice destroyed, by the war in 1871 and by politics in 1884, only scattered fragments of it remain. Catherine, remembering perhaps the long covered passage that linked the Uffizi to the Pitti Palace, had the Tuileries joined to the Louvre by a gallery almost 500 metres long, built along the bank of the Seine. In so doing, she was initiating the gigantic building programme of a truly royal city, which would take three centuries to complete.

The last of the Valois kings had little time for building. But their cousin, the Cardinal Charles de Bourbon, Abbot of Saint-Germain-des-Prés, betrayed his hopes of the crown by erecting a new abbot's palace and made it into a revolutionary building, in which the Classical orders were reduced to the bare minimum, where there was scarcely any sculpted decoration but, on the other hand, where there was colour. With this building, blue slate, white stone and red brick made a forceful entry into Parisian architecture.

The vigor and clarity of the 17th century
The dawning of Classical architecture

When after ten years of civil war Henri IV set the builders back to work, the spirit of architecture had changed: Classicism was abandoned, the elegance of sculpted bas-reliefs judged to be superfluous. From this time on architecture was to rely more on the choice, contrast and arrangement of materials and on the art of the stone-cutter rather than on the virtuosity of the decorator.

Henri IV, a man who liked the open air, wished to cut deep into the tissue of the city to bring space to it and improve the flow of its traffic. His predecessor had undertaken the linking of the two banks of the Seine by a large bridge, the Pont-Neuf; Henri completed it.

The king wanted royal squares, and the finest of them was laid out in the Marais. A little later the statue of Louis XIII was placed there and it became a customary formula; Henri IV's creation, a geometrical general plan with uniform houses surrounding the statue of the king, was now given a name: a *place royale*. But insensitive municipal officials have rebaptized the square that carried his name, the Place des Vosges. The other building complex of this reign, the Place Dauphine, has greatly suffered. Of the triangle it formed, the apex of which ran towards the tip of the Ile de la Cité, only two sides survive, rebuilt and altered. But the two houses at the entrance, on the Pont Neuf, still have their slate roofs, arcades and stone quoins at the corners, which set off the red of the brick. The Hôpital Saint-Louis is also a kind of *place*, an austere quadrilateral surrounded by four L-shaped buildings of in the same style.

Henri IV may be considered the first royal town planner, before Louis XIV and the two Napoleons. Even private enterprises followed his conception, as is the case with the development of the Ile Saint-Louis, carried out at the same time as the building of the Pont Marie, one of the prettiest bridges in Paris.

Henri IV's appetite for monuments was to lead him into carrying on the work on the Louvre: the western part of the S wing of the Cour Carrée was finished and the Galerie du Bord de l'Eau, until then at ground-floor level only, was given its two upper storeys. This unfortunate gallery was restored, altered and partially reconstructed during the Second Empire. However, by looking at the Barbet-le-Jouy gate, the style of the architect, Androuet du Cerceau, can be analysed: ringed columns, vermiculated bossages, broken pediments, a well-ordered but heavy decorative style. The elegance of the Renaissance had passed and the balanced majesty of Classical art had not yet arrived.

The style already changed considerably with Jacques Lemercier, commissioned by Louis XIII to carry on the work on the Cour Carrée. He completed the northern half of the W wing, repeating Lescot's design, and built part of the N façade, erecting between the two the Pavillon de l'Horloge, an elegant construction, four storeys high, topped by a dome, and of which the well-balanced arrangements included carefully placed sculptures. A new work programme was later carried out by Le Vau from 1659 to 1664. Relying heavily on Lescot's designs, he succeeded in completing the building of the quadrilateral, but without the second storey, and these wings were to remain as empty boxes until Napoleonic times. To this programme belongs the beautiful Cour du Sphynx, which presents a wholly Louis XIV breadth of conception, equilibrium and majestic harmony.

A French palace for Italian tastes

We must go back a little to speak of the Palais du Luxembourg, built for Marie de' Medici. The queen, who was tired of the Louvre, wanted a home to remind her of the Florence of her youth so Salomon de Brosse built this new palace with its front courtyard, the entrance to which was marked by an unusual pavilion topped by a dome. But this dome does not make the Luxembourg in the least like an Italian palace, and little more than the bossages recall the Pitti Palace. The plan of the house is that followed by Lescot in the Hôtel Carnavalet, executed in a majestic style in which the use of pilasters, columns and bossages sets off a discreet sculpted decoration; only a few pieces of gilded woodwork survive from its interior decoration.

The palace had been built far from the center, to the S of the built-up area of the city, so that it should have the benefit of gardens. But to give these an Italian look, with fountains and cascades, water was needed. The Florentine engineer, Tomas Francini, was employed for this. He built an aqueduct which provided the park with grottoes and fountains, from which the nymphaeum still survives, now called the Fontaine Medici. It has been moved from its original position and rebuilt, but its decorative detail still remains. This fountain, more than the palace itself, evokes the Italian Baroque.

The Cardinal patrons

In Paris, the building of a palace was an assertion of power: after Marie de' Medici's came those of Richelieu and Mazarin. Of the first, built by Lemercier and which was famous under the name of Palais-Cardinal before becoming the Palais-Royal, only a low gallery decorated with anchors and the prows of ships remains.

Not far away, Cardinal Mazarin built a house which, after alterations, has become the Bibliothèque Nationale. Having acquired the Hôtel Tubeuf, which still survives, the cardinal called on François Mansart to add a building with two superimposed galleries. The gallery, indeed, was now making its appearance in most great Parisian houses. Originating in Mantua in the 15th century, used in the 16th century in the Loire châteaux and at Fontainebleau, by the beginning of the *grand siècle* it was becoming an essential element of the Parisian *hôtel* as an exhibition and receiving room. At the Palais Mazarin the two galleries were intended to display the cardinal's ostentatious collections: the upper one has its original decoration, by the artist Romanelli, whose decorations for the summer apartments of Anne of Austria are still at the Louvre.

The example of the two ministers was followed by a number of *grands seigneurs* and dignitaries, who built themselves *hôtels*, mostly in the Marais, many of which survive. With these the pattern for great houses was set for more than a century, built between courtyard and garden, with access from the street barred by a gate flanked by buildings, the roof in slate and suitably sloped for the rainy Parisian climate. The façades, in which the mixture of bricks and stone was soon abandoned, were of natural stone, or sometimes of rubble-stone faced with plaster, an architecture using pediments and the Classical orders in compositions that were more or less imposing, according to the social status of the owners.

The beginning of the great heritage of Parisian *hôtels*

The Rue Saint-Antoine was the main access to Paris from the E, and it was only later that the construction of Versailles was to give more importance to the W. Noble residences were therefore built along it: the Hôtel de Mayenne, unfortunately disfigured in the 19th century; the Hôtel Sully, the work of Jean Androuet du Cerceau, which has kept its general arrangement intact (entry porch framed by pavilions, courtyards, main building, garden with, at the end, an orangery giving on to the Place des Vosges); not far away the Arsenal has preserved the interesting apartments of the Maréchale de La Meilleraye, in the joyously elaborate and colorful decorative style of the period, with a ceiling by Simon Vouet.

However, it was in the Marais, which was to be the residential district of the aristocracy throughout the 17th century, that the greatest houses were built. Certain of them deserve particular mention.

At the Hôtel de Chalons-Luxembourg, note the fine gate with its coat of arms surmounted by a lion's head; the Hôtel de Saint-Aignan, the work of Le Muet, has a grandiose arrangement of Corinthian pilasters and an interesting staircase. At the Hôtel de Beauvais the architect Lepautre made clever use of an awkwardly-shaped plot of land to produce a house of theatrical aspect, with a large Corinthian staircase decorated by Desjardins. The Hôtel Lamoignon was extended by a wing on to the street, terminating with a watch tower carried on elegant pendentives. The Hôtel de Vigny, by Le Vau, still has some interior decorations of the period.

But the two most beautiful *hôtels* in the Marais belonging to the first half of the 17th century were known by surnames. The Hôtel Aubert de Fontenay, called Salé (now the Musée Picasso), was built in 1656. Its façade, flanked by sphinxes, is surmounted by an imposing curvilinear pediment, while inside is perhaps the finest staircase in Paris. The medieval spiral and the small staircase with parallel flights of stairs, stringer upon stringer, were beginning to be replaced by the majestic staircases that turned this utilitarian construction into one of the most sumptuous features of the house.

The Hôtel Amelot de Bisseuil, called the Hôtel des Ambassadeurs de Hollande, has two decorated courtyards surrounded by buildings embellished with cherubs, inside which, in a setting of period decoration, are a pretty gallery by Michel Corneille and an Italian-style bed-chamber, the only one of its kind to survive in Paris.

François Mansart, uncompromising and misunderstood

The buildings of François Mansart, the first great protagonist of French classicism and the greatest architect of the time, should be considered separately. They are: the two Hôtels de Guénégaud, one in the Rue des Francs-Bourgeois, the other in the Rue des Archives, the Hôtel Bouthillier de Carigny, occupied, deplorably, by a fire station; the Hôtel Colbert de Villacerf, in which four Corinthian pilasters support a curvilinear pediment, and the remodelling of the Hôtel Carnavalet, where the low wing beside the courtyard was raised. Finally, Mansart succeeded Le Vau at the Hôtel d'Aumont, where the flawless façades on to the courtyards are decorated with triglyphs, garlands and human busts.

These different buildings display the characteristics of the architect: severity, elegance, symmetry and logic, all expressed with a certain cool restraint.

A new district

Building was also going on on the Ile Saint-Louis, not for the great families, who disdained to leave the Marais, but for parliamentarians and the *nouveaux-riches*. Several of these residences are to be found along the quays of the island and the two most important, both built by Le Vau, are the Hôtel Lambert and the Hôtel Lauzun.

Here the traditional plan, with the house placed between courtyard and garden, underwent modifications to accommodate the shape and restricted size of the plots. In both *hôtels* the house is arranged around the courtyard with, in the case of Lambert, the main façade at the back, its lower part left open to form a covered vestibule, a formula which was quickly abandoned, only to reappear in the 18th century.

But it is above all for their interior decoration that the two *hôtels* are justly celebrated. While the paintings of the famous Cabinet des Muses of the Hôtel Lambert have been dispersed, the gallery has been preserved, with its Baroque illusionistic ceiling by Lebrun and the painted and sculpted decoration, in which Lebrun and an Opstal recounted the story of Hercules, with a sense of pomp that foreshadowed Vaux-le-Vicomte and Versailles. There is no gallery at the Hôtel Lauzun (home of the commander of the French at the Battle of the Boyne), but a series of rooms that are among the most perfect examples of the decorative stye of the first half of the century: gilded paneling in which are set inlaid landscapes, sculpted overdoors and painted ceilings together make a glowing ensemble, a trifle heavy in places, in others lacking a sense of balance and proportion, but full of invention and imagination.

Religious architecture

The Parisian *hôtel* of the period was a formula of great originality, destined to spread throughout Europe, but religious architecture, which had only progressed away from Gothic structures with great difficulty, found its new style in Italian formulae adapted to the climate of France and to French tastes. Three centuries passed before this French Baroque, long disdained and given the name of 'Jesuit', obtained recognition and the science of its construction, its harmonious proportions and the richness of its decoration were appreciated. Certain earlier churches were either adapted to the new aesthetic style, or it was used in the continuation of their construction. The changeover to prevailing tastes was most marked at Saint-Etienne-du-Mont, where Pierre Biard completed the rood-screen with two side doors, contrasting in their linear sobriety with the florid style of the central part. Then Claude Guérin built the façade, and the amusing superimposition of orders and pediments demonstrating the hesitations of a style that had not yet managed to find its strengths. At the same time, arcaded galleries were built behind the church, with stained-glass windows which deserve to be better known. Laurent La Hire gave the church one of the finest pulpits in Paris. Saint-Gervais, too, was given its façade, possibly designed by Salomon de Brosse and Clément II Métezau. Here the separation of styles is very apparent; on to this purely Gothic church was grafted an arrangement totally different in inspiration, a superimposition of Classical orders in which the horizontals counterbalance the upward thrust of the columns. The side chapels, built at the same period to keep privileged Parisians away from the common people, display interesting contemporary decoration.

Of the Couvent des Filles du Calvaire, raised by Marie de' Medici beside the Luxembourg, a chapel and a cloister survive. The exterior of the church of the Oratory, by Lemercier, affects an architectural whimsicality designed to charm the sophisticated parishioners for whom it was intended.

This was the time of the appearance of the dome in Parisian religious architecture: the first, unknown and not visible, is that of the Chapelle des Petits-Augustins, lost today among the buildings of the Ecole des Beaux-Arts. Then came the dome of the Couvent des Carmes (White Friars), shyly sitting on top of this rather austere monastery. There is another dome, this time tall and elegant, at Saint-Paul-Saint-Louis, a theatrical and grandiose work built for the Jesuits by father Martellange and Father Derrand. Its façade recalls that of Saint-Gervais, but more animated and decorative, evoking more the Italy of Borromini than the France of Mansart. The interior decoration, full of emphasis and panache, is the enthusiastic interpretation of the spirit of the Counter-Reformation.

At the church of the Couvent de la Visitation, Italian and French influences are fused together by the genius of the architect François Mansart who, in fact, never went to Italy. A large cupola, with a lantern, placed on a square mass, dominates the portal, in which the rather stiff elegance of the Hôtel d'Aumont appears again. At this time, Richelieu commissioned Lemercier to rebuild the old Sorbonne, of which the church remains, and in which for the first time a type of façade appeared, often to be reproduced: an elevation on two storeys, three bays at ground level, only one above, the disproportion softened by scrolled buttresses. Above this façade rises the dome, but Lemercier was unable to avoid the hiatus caused by the difference in plan of the two storeys; the arrangement can be discerned only from a distance.

The Val-de-Grâce is a group of monastic buildings of great distinction; it was begun by François Mansart and continued by Lemercier and others to his designs. The church has a single nave giving directly on to side chapels, a plan Italian in inspiration found at the time in monastery churches not bound by the exigencies of parish services. While, as at the Sorbonne, the dome is ill-assorted with the façade, it is seen from outside the choir in all its elegance, with lanterns and sculpted groups by Buyster serving as finials. The monastic buildings, restrained but dignified, are arranged around a cloister with arched arcades which open on to gardens through an imposing façade which already has more of the worldliness of 18th-century convents than of great Gothic abbeys.

It is no surprise to find greater austerity in the buildings of the Jansenists, an austerity which may appear, to the jaded eye, a refreshing quality. The Port-Royal convent in Paris, built by Lepautre in 1646–1648, has retained its simple cloister, the wooden balusters of its staircases, its chapter-house and the chapel that Mère Angélique Arnauld found too luxurious, and where the ghost of Pascal seems still to hover.

Louis XIV and Paris

There is no doubt that the great king always mistrusted this unpredictable capital: he removed his home from it altogether, preferring instead to create for himself the world of Versailles. Nor is there any doubt that he was one of the sovereigns who, by his own will or that of his ministers, most changed the look of Paris.

The eternal building-works at the Louvre

Once again the Louvre had to be tackled. The first work put in hand was on the Galerie d'Apollon where, for the first time in Paris, all the flamboyant decorative arts were brought together under the direction of the great Charles Lebrun (1619–90). At the same time, Le Vau continued the building of the Cour Carrée, following the style of his predecessors. But the régime wanted the palace to have a monumental façade which would proclaim the glory of the reign in the midst of the Parisian townscape: following the rejection of Bernini's proposals, this was to be Claude Perrault's colonnade, the assertion of the originality of the French style and its independence from Italian architecture. The moat planned for this façade was created only in 1967. It was a phase of building that included important alterations, in particular on the edge of the Seine, where the new and pretty façade that faces the Institut was raised. But this fine élan was short-lived and did not reach fruition. Work ceased in 1680 for lack of money, leaving the interior arrangements unfinished; the sculptures for the façades were not completed, and even the roofing of the internal wings of the courtyard was left open to the rain for a century and a half. The king's government had wished to give a brilliant exterior to what in theory was the royal residence, but did not trouble to make it habitable, since the king no longer spent his time there.

A monument for a college

At the same time Le Vau had, in 1663, begun the construction, on the other side of the Seine, of the Collège Marazin, but its popular name was the Collège des Quatre Nations. In his will Mazarin had left money and instructions for this College to be built. Sited on the river, its chapel is surmounted by a dome (the famous cupola) and is enclosed by two quadrant wings while behind, the college buildings, ostentatious or austere according to their intended purpose, are arranged around three courtyards. Mazarin had wished to give the lie to the accusations of avarice made against him, by endowing Paris with one of its outstanding monuments. But it is to the will and pleasure of Louis XIV that the finest Parisian building of the century is owed.

The glory of the Invalides

Until this time ex-soldiers who were retired for reasons of age or disablement led precarious and often poverty-stricken lives, their main hope being to be taken in by the convents. In 1670 the king decided to build a refuge for them in Paris, and entrusted the task to Libéral Bruant (c.1635–97).

Bruant's conception was a strong, sober group of buildings which, naturally, showed something of the barracks and something of the convent: a large, square courtyard bordered by arcades, at the back of which was to be the chapel, all concealed behind a façade 690ft/ 210m long, with a triumphal portal. But protocol forbade that the king should use the same entrance as his subjects. Besides, the building, while imposing and comfortable enough for the old soldiers for whom it was intended lacked the magnificence necessary to proclaim the glory of the royal planner. Finally, it was wished to make the new building the point of departure for the urban planning of the whole district. For all these reasons, J. Hardouin-Mansart's services were called upon and he gave his genius free rein.

It was no doubt he who had already built the soldiers' church, on Bruant's plans. In 1676 the idea came to him of adding an adjoining second church in the form of a Greek cross, surmounted by a dome, and to create a new façade for it, which he intended, in imitation of St Peter's in Rome, to enclose with two quadrant wings. These wings were never built, and their absences felt in the façade's composition which is a little disproportionate in relation to the dome. The dome is the crowning glory of the Invalides and J. Hardouin-Mansart's masterpiece. Not only does it crown the south façade without giving the uncomfortable feeling of disproportion experienced at the Sorbonne and the Val-de-Grâce, but from the other side it makes an admirable composition with Bruant's façade, which was not conceived in relation to it. It is one of the few strokes of genius to be admired in the Parisian landscape.

Today the approaches to the monument have been cleared of the inopportune buildings erected by the military, and the moat and the garden of the Intendant have been created, or restored, according to the original plans.

A monastery for the sick

If the Invalides convent was glorious, the Salpêtrière asylum was utilitarian. Intended for the sick, vagabonds, prostitutes and convicts, it was less a hospital than a place of relegation. Louis Le Vau, then Libéral Bruant, erected the sober buildings, dominated by a chapel whose eight naves radiating from the centre allowed the segregation of the different categories of inmates.

The observatory

A fine observatory to house the astronomers was built by Claude Perrault who, however, gave more thought to the proportions and decoration of the building than to the needs of the scientists working there. The architecture of the time did not take account of the functional. It sought to charm and, especially, to surprise and impress, as can still be seen in the triumphal gates erected at the points of entry to the capital. Of these, the Porte Saint-Denis and the Porte Saint-Martin remain, in the form of triumphal arches, but in which all the decoration serves to magnify the glory of Louis XIV in terms of suitably adapted mythology.

New royal palaces

It was on the private initiative of a court official that the Place des Victoires was created, a circular *place* surrounding a monument by Deschamps: this disappeared in the Revolution (the figures from the base are at Sceaux). The layout of the *place* was disturbed in the 19th century by the cutting of the Rue Etienne Marcel, but the new statue is worthy of its predecessor and the surviving façades of the buildings retain their elegance and charm.

J. Hardouin-Mansart appears again in the Place Vendôme. Louvois had at first intended a series of public buildings here which would have constituted a kind of prestige administrative city. Problems with the royal treasury caused the project to be abandoned and it was decided to sell the land off as building plots, but also to build the façades in order to safeguard architectural unity. As with the Ile Saint-Louis a century earlier, this new district attracted not the conservatively-minded aristocracy, who remained attached to their chosen territory, but those with more recent and sometimes dubious fortunes. To the chapter of public architecture in the Paris of the *Grand Siècle* should be added mention of the Pont Royal, the work of Jacques Gabriel and the friar Angelo Romano, which retained its elegant lines, a few fountains, and some traces of decoration in the Rue de l'Ancienne Comédie that remind us that the Comédie-Française began its life there.

The courtier in his home

In their plan and dispositions the Parisian *hôtels* of Louis XIV's reign were similar to those of the first half of the century: a courtyard and a garden, a gate enclosed by outbuildings, reception rooms and other more private apartments. A certain reduction of area can be observed, the result no doubt of land speculation and, because of that, a more judicious use of available space. As to the architecture and decoration, even more than in the preceding period these showed the social rank or pretensions of the owners.

The Marais continued to be the traditional residential district and fine houses were still being built there. Mention must be made of the Hôtel du Grand Veneur, with its magnificent staircase; the Hôtel Le Peletier de Saint-Fargeau, by Pierre Bullet, who adorned the façade on the garden side with a pediment by Laurent Magnier; the Hôtel Barbes, with its arcaded courtyard; the Hôtel Amelot de Chaillou, by P. Bullet; the Hôtel du Lude or du Châtillon; the Hôtel Presty, with its fine oval stair-well; the splendid Louis XIV gate of the Hôtel d'Aubray, where the drama of the poisons was played out. Special mention must be made of two architects' residences: the charming house that Libéral Bruant built for himself in the Rue de la Perle and the imposing Hôtel de Sagonne, symbol of the social and financial success of J. Hardouin-Mansart, where the admirable painted ceilings by Lafosse and Mignard may still be seen.

But new residences were also tending to move away from the Marais, particularly towards the W; the building of the Place Vendôme is an example. Among these were the Hôtel de Sémonville, which still has a ceiling with painted beams, the Hôtel Moreau and its fine stair-well and the Hôtel de Saint-Roman. More modest dwellings were built around the Halles, like the first large *maison de rapport,* as the new apartment buildings erected for the express purpose of renting were called, in the Rue de la Ferronnerie. Still further to the W, near to the future Place Vendôme, came people with different ideas, like the composer Lully, whose house survives in the Rue Sainte-Anne: this is not a mansion between its courtyard and its garden, but simply a town house, set on the street.

On the Left Bank, new houses were built at the foot and on the side of the Montagne Sainte-Geneviève, like the Hôtel de Laffémas, the Hôtel de Bacq with its fine porte-cochère, and the imposing residence built by Boffrand for Lebrun: its garden façade is of such balance and harmony that it has been said to have been conceived according to the Golden Section.

Churches still being built

Religious architecture unquestionably was taking second place; the art of building was now in the service of ambition or of utilitarian needs. That does not mean, however, that religious architecture in Paris during Louis XIV's reign was negligible.

The growth of the city once again encouraged the creation of new parishes and the rebuilding of churches that had become too small for them. But it is a fact that the four buildings begun in the second half of the century remained unfinished for lack of funds. This was the case with Saint-Roch, commenced in 1653 on Lemercier's design, and of Saint-Sulpice, the rebuilding of which had been undertaken in 1645: the building work, having begun in the choir, stopped at the crossing.

Le Vau turns up again at Saint-Louis-en-l'Ile, only the choir of which was erected (from 1664 to 1679), with decoration very much in the image of that worldly parish. Finally, to replace a medieval church, the construction of Saint-Nicolas-du-Chardonnet was started in 1656.

The finances of the religious orders, however, seem to have been healthier, and the building continued of convent chapels, now hard to distinguish from churches, following their reconsecration to parish use: Saint-Jacques-du-Haut-Pas, to which the architect Gittard succeeded in giving the Jansenist flavour desired by its founder, Mme de Longueville, and which has admirable stonework inside; L'Assomption, which because of a wrong interpretation, no doubt, of the plans sent from Rome by the architect Errand, was provided with a cupola out of proportion with the building; Saint-Thomas-d'Aquin, by Pierre Bullet, of which the harmony of proportion and the elegance went unrecognized for quite some time.

These churches were, of course, accompanied by convent buildings, yet retained much nobility. The abbey buildings of Saint-Germain-des-Prés were largely rebuilt in this manner, but unfortunately road-building in the 19th century permitted the survival only of part of the cloister and, on the *place*, of a pretty house with a wrought-iron balcony. At the Schola Cantorum there is a pleasant façade overlooking a courtyard and a few decorative fragments of the convent of the English Benedictines. Some architectural remains keep alive the memory of the Carmelite monastery in the Rue Saint-Jacques and of the convent of the Recollect nuns in the Rue du Bac.

But in religious art, the period is at least as important for its decorative works as for building. The clergy, showing its distaste for medieval architecture, did not shrink from subjecting Gothic churches to transformations which would have been unthinkable earlier. Many of these changes have subsequently been eliminated, and we are beginning to regret their loss. Such is the case with the new decoration of the choir of Notre-Dame, carried out from 1699 to 1714 by Robert de Cotte. The covering of the pillars of the choir with marble and stucco was destroyed by Viollet-le-Duc in the name of unity of style, and of the admirable stalls, masterpieces of 18th-century wood carving, there is only a part, along with the famous statues of Coysevox and Costou.

Carved woodwork in the period played an important part in church decoration. The stalls and churchwardens' pews at Saint-Gervais and at Saint-Germain-l'Auxerrois are worthy of note, as are the *boiseries* that accompany Van Loo's great paintings at Notre-Dame-des-Victoires, one of the rare groups of religious pictures to have remained in the place for which it was conceived.

A chapter should be devoted to the funerary sculpture of the period. It is curious to observe how, in the century which saw the disappearance of the custom of erecting large tombs for deceased kings at Saint-Denis – proclamations of contemporary sculpture – the churches of Paris were receiving tombs in a quantity and of a quality never equalled, for *grands seigneurs*, army generals, ministers, ecclesiastics and ordinary bourgeoisie. The reader may discover them at Saint-Germain-des-Prés (King Casimir of Poland, and the Castellan brothers), at Saint-Nicolas-du-Chardonnet (the mother of Lebrun), at the Invalides (Turenne), at the Institut (Mazarin), at Saint-Eustache (Colbert) and finally, at Saint-Roch, a veritable museum of 17th- and 18th-century funerary sculpture. In this way, while walking, little by little, beyond the modern streets and the cars, the eyes and mind of the visitor will be opened to the re-emerging of this 17th-century city, bound by a political and religious order, conventional and sumptuous, hiding the misery of a large part of its population behind a superb façade, which succeeded for a long time in ensuring that it was either forgotten or unrecognized.

From the luxuriant to the austere: the 18th century

La Régence: revolution in style

Louis XIV died on September 1, 1715 and the change of régime reinforced and helped to develop the stylistic evolution, which had begun in the previous decade. The Classical orders, symbols of pomp and majesty, were cast aside: the curve took the place of the straight line and ornamentation, often with no thought for its suitability, reigned supreme. Financial speculation put money into the hands of a new class and stimulated a wave of building as new houses in the new style were built for the new rich.

It is hard today to picture what these great houses must have looked like, newly built and decorated in the airy Rococo style which influenced architecture, interior decoration and furniture design. If only for their exteriors, mention should be made of the Hôtels Chenizot, de Brienne, de Charolais, d'Estrées and de Gournay; the Hôtels Séguier, Pidoux and du Président Hénault for their balconies, and the Hôtels de Clermont Tonnerre and Gouffier de Thoix for their porticoes. The Hôtel Dodun had a fine staircase; the Hôtels de Seignelay and de Longueil are outstanding for their paneled reception rooms; the Hôtel de Brancas for its parquet floors; the Hôtel de Mailly for its ceiling, and last, for its overall décor, the famous Galerie Dorée which Robert de Cotte conceived for the Hôtel La Vrillière.

Paneling is perhaps the essential element in these new precepts for a Parisian town house. What began as no more than a simple form of insulation to protect rooms from damp and cold became a dazzling medium for the sculptor's chisel to cut with the delicacy of a goldsmith, swirling mouldings from soft wood, using the panels as frames from a series of widely differing designs. These deliberately asymmetrical designs of diminishing depth were often painted with different shades of goldleaf, that imparted a glittering warmth to the finished panel. Attention should be drawn once again to those admirable panels by Lange and Hardouin in the Salon des Ambassadeurs in the Elysée Palace.

For the first time a number of the houses mentioned stood in the Faubourg Saint-Germain. This was the road to Versailles and developers, attracted by the cheapness of land that was still used for market-gardens, laid the foundations of what was to become the aristocratic district of the 18th century. It encompassed a loose network of alleys and gardens and provided a refined way of life for the privileged few.

Despite this new development it was still in the Marais that two *hôtels* were built of which the architecture and interior decoration, dating from 1704 to about 1740, are a demonstration of the evolution of stylistic formulae from the end of the Louis XIV style to the high point of the Louis XV style.

Indian summer in the Marais

Commissioned by the Prince de Soubise to transform the old Hôtel de Guise in the Rue des Archives, the architect Delamir's solution was to move the façade to the Rue des Francs-Bourgeois, setting it behind a colonnaded forecourt. In the Marais, with its narrow building plots, he blended space with architecture and created a sense of surprise, magnificently enhancing with its subtle interplay of columns, balustrades and statues, the façade of the building which now houses the French national archives. These were the years (1704–05) when the Louis XIV style matured and became more human without losing its sense of sobriety.

Nearby, Delamir was soon commissioned to build another *hôtel* for Cardinal de Rohan, for which he designed an imposing garden façade still very much in the Louis XIV style, with a simple entrance façade onto the forecourt. The stables were set in a courtyard on one side of the house and derive their elegance from their proportions and the outlines of their roofs, on which Robert Le Lorrain's dramatic bas-relief *Les Chevaux du Soleil* (Horses of the Sun), set like a jewel against a dark cloth, was a trumpet call in the melancholy harmony of the last years of Louis XIV's reign. Delamir, however, was independent and at that time official architecture was firmly in the hands of the Mansart clan. The designer of these two great horses was vilified and harshly criticized. On the death of the Prince de Soubise in 1712, Delamir was dismissed and replaced by Boffrand, who set about decorating the interior.

The prince's apartments occupied the ground floor. They suffered greatly from 19th-century alterations, although an attempt has been made to restore what has survived. However, on the first floor, in the princess' apartments, the dazzling decorations have been preserved. Created approximately between the years 1730 and 1740, the *tour de force* is the oval drawing-room, in which Natoire tells the story of Cupid and Psyche in a setting of stucco and gilded paneling which may well exemplify the high point of Rococo before it succumbed to extravagances and extremes. The surviving interior décor of the Hôtel de Rohan includes, besides the staircase, the Cabinet des Singes, with monkeys dressed as fashionable Parisians, painted by Huet between 1745 and 1752, where the sculptor's work yields pride of place to the painter, who conjures up all the period's fascination with the exotic, with exploration and adventure, in a lighthearted, festive spirit.

Thus the building and decoration of these two *hôtels* was begun when the canons of architecture were still those of Versailles, touched with the ardour of the *Régence,* and completed in the age of Louis XV, when architecture, apart from some minor extravagances, was perhaps the most original in French history. Restrained but refined, balanced and harmonious, little enamoured of the Classical orders, but knowing how to use stone to its full advantage in both building and sculpture, the age has left a series of town houses which, despite the disfigurement that they have suffered during well-intentioned alterations, comprise an impressive and undervalued inheritance.

The new (1740) façade of the Hôtel d'Albret was the last major work to be undertaken in the Marais at this time.

The Left Bank and the Right Bank

The vast majority of building developments were still taking place in the Faubourg Saint-Germain. Among them were the Hôtel Biron, by Gabriel and Aubert, now the Musée Rodin, which still retains its gardens and even some of its paneling; the Hôtel de Lassay by Lassurance and Aubert, formerly no more than a single-storey building in which five paneled reception rooms survive; the Hôtel de Noirmoutiers by Courtonne and Lassurance; the Hôtel Matignon, again by Courtonne, with the original decoration in two reception rooms, one on the ground floor, the other on the first, showing pastoral scenes painted by a youthful Fragonard; the Hôtels d'Avaray, de Roquelaure, de Lesdiguières, Chanac de Pompadour, and the Hôtel de Chalais with its superbly proportioned state drawing-room. It is impossible to mention all the buildings and permission to visit them is often hard to obtain.

However, contemporaneously another district had been developed. This was the Faubourg Saint-Honoré with open country on either side, a continuation of the old Rue Saint-Honoré, running first through market-gardens and then farmland. The first house in this new district is known today as the Elysée Palace, built by Mollet in 1718. This was gradually joined by others which have often been less well preserved than those in the Faubourg Saint-German. Among those which remain are the Circle Interallié and the British Embassy.

Returning towards the centre of Paris, one comes upon the town houses in the Place Vendôme, mostly erected in the 18th century behind façades by Mansart. The Crédit Foncier scrupulously maintains the Hôtels d'Evreux, Desvieux and Castagné which it occupies, while the Royal Chancery – the present Ministry of Justice – has remained ensconced for the past two and a half centuries among the paneling carved for a *fermier général*.

One might imagine, scanning these incomplete lists, that every nobleman, royal official or wealthy citizen had a mansion to himself. In practice, many of these houses were subdivided and a fashionable address might conceal a tiny attic room or a garret in the kitchen wing. This led to the widespread building of the *maison de rapport,* the equivalent of the modern block of apartments, consisting of a number of identical lodgings under one roof. Among the earliest of these are the houses within the precincts of Saint-Gervais, Rue François-Miron, their balconies bearing a stylized elm tree. While these new, uniform façades – which are also to be found in the Rue de la Parcheminerie, the Rue de la Harpe and the Rue Saint-Martin – were lending a fresh look to the Parisian street, the street fountains and shop-signs were receiving a facelift. In the case of the former, it is interesting to compare the typically Rococo style of the Maubuée fountain (1733) with the famous Fontaine des

Quatre Saisons begun in the following year. Bouchardon's inspiration is pure Louis XVI, although it was another forty years before that monarch was to come to the throne.

Furthermore, it was only in such minor works as these that the royal power made itself felt upon the Parisian townscape during this period. During the first half of the century the only public buildings worth mentioning are the Bibliothéque Royale, erected to complete the Hôtel Mazarin, the lecture theatre at the Ecole de Médecine in the Rue de la Bûcherie and some insignificant alterations to the Louvre. Only at the end of the reign was there a return to the days of major public works.

The resumption of church building

On the other hand, the age of Louis XV, characterized as licentious if not downright blasphemous, saw a great deal of work in the realm of religious architecture. However, it was less the laying of new foundations than the continuation of work begun in the previous age upon such shrines as the Oratoire, Notre-Dames-des-Victoires, Saint-Thomas-d'Aquin and Saint-Louis-en-l'Ile, which were finished in more or less their original architectural style, but with more up-to-date interiors.

Two churches stand out by their striving after novelty, the one, Saint-Roch, in its ground-plan, the other, Saint-Sulpice, in its elevation. At Saint-Roch, work was completed (from 1701–1760) by making the original ground-plan more complex. A Lady Chapel was grafted onto the original ambulatory and given, in its turn, an ambulatory of its own. This led into the dimly-lit Blessed Sacrement chapel, at the E end of which there was a further chapel of the Crucifixion by Boullée. It was like a succession of contrived stagesets seemingly wishing to give to the church the same mysterious room arrangements of small apartment houses of the period.

Oppenord resumed work at Saint-Sulpice in 1719 and it is interesting to observe the on-site activities of an architect better known as a draughtsman. In any case building was strictly by 17th-century rules and it is only in the details of the interior décor, that one discerns Oppenord, the decorator who played an important part in the development of the *Régence* style. All was changed when, in (1732), the Italian Servadoni was commissioned to put up the façade. This strange character, with his appreciation of Gothic art, yearned for a return to façades with twin towers. Very Baroque in design, these stood at either end of a massive pediment which overhung a pair of superimposed Classical portals. However, the pediment was destroyed by lightning; nobody liked the twin towers, and new ones were built.

Renovation and alteration

Furthermore, the clergy strove to adapt to contemporary taste Gothic churches whose style they could not appreciate. They did not hesitate at Saint-Germain-l'Auxerrois to convert the piers of the chancel into fluted columns in the Classical style with heightened capitals. These alterations have often been branded as vandalism regardless of their elegance, in fact that they show evidence of changing tastes. This is certainly the case, again at Saint-Germain-l'Auxerrois, with the fine wrought-iron chancel railings, but more especially at Saint-Merri, in the dramatic stucco and marble decorations with which Michel-Ange Slodtz covered the whole of the chancel, evidence of his skill at adaptation and his long-neglected feeling for the decorative. Other churches were provided with contemporary furnishings which, within the sober settings of the older churches, add an occasional touch of the sometimes unruly display of the 18th century. There is, for example, the Rococo pulpit in the Eglise des Blancs-Manteaux, the impressive series of sculptured funeral monuments in Saint-Roch or, at Saint-Sulpice, the tomb of Languet de Gergy, on which Death and the Angel of the Resurrection, the one as high-flown as the other, do battle for the soul of this parish priest.

Monastic renewal

In Paris this irreligious age also produced plenty of religious houses. Their buildings, less well known than those of the Middle Ages, have suffered severely; nonetheless, an attempt can be made to list those which have survived. The biggest project concerned the ancient Abbey of Sainte-Geneviève, a large proportion of which was rebuilt during the reign of Louis XV. Of this reconstruction there remain a monumental staircase capped by a dome supported on pillars representing the 'sacred tree', the palm, the galleries of the former library, unfortunately converted into dormitories, the muniment (records) room with its Corinthian pilasters, and the small room housing the collection of coins and medals with its delicately carved paneling.

Not far away building was started on the convent of the Holy Ghost Fathers (Pères du Saint-Esprit); today the majestic refectory still survives. It is next door to the tiny Community of Saint-Aure, which conceals a charming Louis XV façade overlooking the forecourt.

The Hôpital Saint-Antoine, successor to the Abbey of Saint-Antoine-des-Champs, was to preserve a noble two-storey façade capped by a pediment, while the Ministère des Ancients Combattants has kept the majestic external arrangement of the Couvent de Pentemont in the Rue de Bellechasse. In the same district the War Department has preserved the cloister gallery and two staircases, all that remains of the novice-house of the Jacobins. Their existence is, however, virtually unknown. A delightful side-door, the work of Desmaisons, survives from the Theatines' convent.

Although these scattered remnants are sometimes hard to visit, they nonetheless help one to grasp the spirit behind 18th-century monastic buildings, the grandeur of their proportions, the sense of mass which they incorporate, the sobriety of their interior décor which blends so well with their architecture. This inspiration has often been characterized as profane, but this is not always true.

Neo-Classicism
A gentle passing

It is a commonplace that the Louis XVI style made its appearance long before the death of Louis XV and that it was less an abrupt change of direction than a gradual development, with many pauses and retrograde movements. In Paris its advent was particularly precocious since, by 1734, the Fontaine des Quatre Saisons had formalized these new concepts. However, by contrast, forty years later many private town houses still remained faithful to the graceful and flowery simplicity of the Louis XV style. And yet it was during the reign of Louis XV, Louis le Bien-Aimé, and through his most famous architect, Ange-Jacques Gabriel, that those two monumental buildings, which are symbols of the Louis XVI style – the Ecole Militaire (1751) and the Place de la Concorde (1754) – were built in Paris.

Louis XV's Invalides

Louis XV, like his great-grandfather, wished to leave Paris a monument to his own glory, a glory associated with feats of arms. Louis XIV had been concerned for his disabled soldiers (invalides): Louis XV wished to help those who were to become his officers and he chose the market-gardens on the Left Bank as the site of his new institution.

To view the Ecole Militaire from the Place de Fontenoy, its natural approach, is to admire in particular the skilful handling of mass, displayed in the composition of the whole, rising gradually from the jutting wings to culminate in the central dome. This allocation of mass and voids, of horizontal and vertical lines, the visual effect of the main staircase and the chapel, show how the Louis XVI style was to draw its strength and beauty not from its decorative elements but from the distribution of its architectural elements.

Folies for an Age of Unreason

The French *folie* is a class of building typical of an age of elegance, which attracts in spite of its vague aura of decadence. Unlike the

English 'folly', this was a small pleasure house, its refinement matched by its small scale, which derived its name not from foolishness but from its rustic setting – from the Latin word *folia,* meaning leaves, foliage. Although the *folie* erected by Ledoux for the dancer, Mlle Guimard, has vanished, in the heart of the old villages swallowed up by the city, Beaudouin's Pavillon Carré at Ménilmontant can still be seen; also the Château des Brouillards in Montmartre, the Hôtel Pascher at Auteuil, and especially the Bagatelle park. This was created in sixty-three days by Bélanger and, despite 19th-century alterations, its *folie* has preserved part of its original proportions and interior decoration and thus continues to deserve its motto – *parva sed apta.* It was always associated with love and gallantry. The new school of landscape gardening used decorative buildings which are more like the English 'folly' in appearance, as in the case of *La Naumachie* in the Parc Meudon. They foreshadow Romanticism.

Classicism in church architecture

Like the Baroque Movement before it, Neo-Classicism in its hey-day felt itself bound to alter a number of churches on an even more radical but less successful scale. In Saint-Nicolas-des-Champs and Saint-Médard the pillars in the choir were paradoxically transformed into Doric columns, while to Saint-Médard was added a side-chapel reminiscent of Ledoux's work. The crypt below the choir of Saint-Leu-Saint-Gilles was also Doric, but the period's most interesting addition is undoubtedly the Chapel of the Souls in Purgatory in Sainte-Marguerite, decorated by Brunetti. *Trompel'oeil* painting, the common secular decoration of the Louis XVI style, now forcefully invaded the religious sphere.

Only one parish church was built at this time with the intention of serving the expanding Faubourg Saint-Honoré, but it was fundamental to the development of the style. This was Saint-Philippe-du-Roule, built by Chalgrin (1774–84) on the site of the parish church of Roule, to a new ground-plan inspired by the antiquarian tendencies of the age and in direct imitation of the Roman basilica. It comprised a nave, but no transept, flanked by side-aisles and ending in a decorated semi-circular domed apse, with no ambulatory and narrower than the nave. The ceiling was not vaulted, but flat and decorated. This 'basilical design', in which an agreeable antiquarian flavour blended with an ease of construction which kept building costs down, was to remain popular until at least the middle of the 19th century.

The tide of building continued to flow strongly so far as monastic architecture was concerned and resulted in such fine buildings as the Chapelle du Saint-Esprit, again the work of Chalgrin; a staircase by Antoine in Saint-Martin-des-Champs; the doorway of the Capuchin novice house which still stands with its massive Doric columns in the Boul. de Port-Royal. This order had its house in the Rue Caumartin, erected by Brongniart (1780–82) but the monastic buildings have been defaced by successive expansions of the Lycée Condorcet and practically nothing survives of the famous cloister with its Doric columns, the archeologist's treatment of an essentially Christian architectural form. The chapel of the order became the Church of Saint-Louis-d'Antin and in its severity, its dim light and lack of ornament, is typical of Neo-Classicism taken to extremes in religious architecture . . . and yet it has its grandeur.

Crowning the heights

However, the greatest undertaking in monastic architecture of the time was the rebuilding of the abbey-church of Sainte-Geneviève, now known as the Panthéon.

As with the Ecole Militaire and the Place de la Concorde, it was Louis XV who initiated the building of a monument which today typifies the Louis XVI style. The decision was made to rebuild the venerable but decaying abbey-church, to set it on the brow of the hill in front of the abbey buildings and to entrust the scheme to Soufflot. He was an architect who not only admired the Greek monuments which he had seen in northern Italy, but was equally interested in mediaeval architecture, and here aimed to combine 'the lightness of Gothic buildings with the purity of Greek architecture', a lofty idea which made no sense architecturally, since it is impossible to reconcile the static concept of the vertical thrust of Greek architecture with the dynamism of Gothic architecture where the balance of forces thrust at an angle and in opposite directions. However, Langier, the leading Neo-Classical critic, called it 'the first example of perfect architecture'. Soufflot wagered his life on the solution of this problem and lost.

The transformation of the church into the Panthéon and the alterations made by Soufflot's successors have weakened the original concept. It must be remembered that the entire building had been conceived as a setting for the tomb of St Geneviève, placed under the dome in the middle of the church, visible from nearly every part of the building and strongly lit: hence the Greek cross ground-plan and the simple groups of columns which, employed as boldly as Gothic pillars, supported the massive dome at the transept. Hence, too, the windows to give the interior a triumphant brightness. To replace the columns by massive pillars, to block off the windows to achieve a dim religious light and, above all, to remove the central point of interest, have done much to emasculate the structure and particularly its interior, which was its most striking element. Nevertheless, the upper portions with their galleries and the domes supported on pendentives, are overwhelming, as is the breadth of the building and its harmonious proportions.

The exciseman's wall

Towards the end of the reign the innovative and visionary Ledoux was commissioned to undertake the most functional piece of architecture imaginable – to surround Paris with a new wall, not defensive this time, but bureaucratic and intended to ease the collection of tolls on goods brought into the city. The architect of the salt works at Arc-et-Senans magnified his commissions to such an extent that, instead of the simple toll-gates envisaged, with equally simple toll-houses for the excisemen, Soufflot produced as many triumphal archways, each one different, in which he demonstrated his highly original and personalized interpretation of Classical themes. The scheme was never completed, either then or later. The French Revolution not only suppressed the tolls, but many of the buildings which were its symbols, and 19th-century vandalism did the rest. Of Ledoux's forty-five toll-houses only four survive – in the Parc Monceau, in the Place Denfert-Rochereau, at La Nation and at La Villette.

Development declines with the French Revolution

The city wall was not completed when the French Revolution broke out. Building developments slowed down considerably without coming to a complete standstill and near the Luxembourg, in the Marais and to the N of the boulevards, there are still a number of buildings in the typical decorative style of the period.

Revolutionary fêtes needed settings. These were generally temporary, but sometimes permanent structures were produced, for example David's two fine semi-circular sets of stone seats in the Tuileries gardens. It was David, too, who had the famous Horses of Marly moved to the entrance to the Champs-Elysées.

Once the Reign of Terror was over, building started again, but slowly. Financial affairs were in chaos and the political future was too uncertain to encourage developers.

Napoleon's Paris
The town-planning Emperor

Never before had there been a ruler who had conceived quite such grandiose plans. Napoleon not only wanted to provide the city with monuments, but these, in his opinion, should be combined with town-planning projects: the opening up of large vistas, the creation of an administrative district around the Champ-de-Mars and the demolition of the slums. If the realization of these projects did not come up to the level of their conception, the reason could be found in the wars that interrupted his reign and in the economic spirit of an Emperor who was reluctant to finance sumptuous projects by taxation Also it lay as much in the interest he took (even more pronounced towards the end of his reign) in public works: construction of quays, demolition of the houses built on bridges, digging of drains, providing pavements, institution of street numbering, cutting of the Canal de l'Ourcq and building markets and slaughter-houses. Considerable municipal work, more imposing than anything carried out during the whole of the preceding two centuries, got under way. But this, to a great extent, has disappeared. However, the Marché Saint-Germain has been preserved, but for how long? One of the Emperor's greatest town-planning projects was the *voie triomphale* (the triumphal way), the Rue de Rivoli, running the length of the Tuileries, which he intended to have lined with identical arcaded buildings to give a truly monumental effect.

At the same time new bridges were built over the Seine. Among these were the Pont d'Iéna in stone, classic and of beautiful design, and another, the Passerelle des Arts. This, which was rebuilt with modifications in 1980, was the first of its kind in France.

The fashion for columns

The Rue de Rivoli was linked to the Place Vendôme by the new Rue de Castiglione, for which a suitable central embellishment was sought to replace the old monument of Louis XIV. However, the fashion was for columns, and Republican France and then Imperial France had endlessly embroidered on the theme. Of all the projects offered for various commemorations, in the towns or on various sites, the only one to be realized was the Colonne Vendôme, modelled on Trajan's column. The absurdity of introducing this large vertical object into a background of horizontal lines was ignored.

Napoleon wanted to endow the capital with prestigious monuments. Ancient Rome was largely used as a model with colonnades adapted to all purposes.

On the site where the *Ancien Régime* had started to construct the church of La Madeleine, Vignon erected the Temple de la Gloire. It was built in the style of an ancient temple as a kind of commemorative military monument, unfinished until Louis-Phillipe's reign. Symmetrically, on the other side of the Concorde, Poyer put up the new façade of the Chambre des Députés, a simple covering applied to the old walls of the Palais-Bourbon. This made it possible to re-establish symmetry with the Pont de la Concorde. Even more paradoxically, it was decided to give the new Bourse the appearance of an old temple. Brongniart began this project in 1808. There were also more columns erected on the façade of the Théâtre des Variétés.

Water for the Parisians

Since his consulship, Bonaparte had wanted to increase the water supply – which was very inadequate – to the public fountains, and to construct others. For this it was necessary to dig the Canal de l'Ourcq, which had to supply a whole new series of fountains whose style, often original, showed the artistic trends of the period. The Fontaine de Mars and the Fontaine de la Paix recall the art of Classical Antiquity, while the Colonne du Châtelet, that of Egypt. There was also the Fontaine de la Rue de Sevrès, which is a copy of the Renaissance fountain which now backs on to the Fontaine Médicis. And the new techniques now used at Creusot allowed the casting of bronze lions on the façade of the Institute (today in Boulogne) and of the Place du Château-d'Eau (now at La Villette).

The permanent building site at the Louvre

The Emperor also decided finally to complete the group of palace buildings formed by the Louvre and the Tuileries, and though he did more work there than any of the earlier rulers, he was still unable to finish the task. Thanks to him the Cour Carrée was at last completed. This was carried out discreetly by Percier and Fontaine, who knew better than to interfere with the work of their predecessors. Then, after having cleared a large part of the Cour du Carrousel, the problem of completing the double palace was attacked. But there Napoleon had to overcome the obstinacy of his architects, who, disturbed by the dissimilarity of the axes of the Cour Carrée and the Tuileries, wanted to conceal the anomaly by the construction of a central building. The Emperor, a born town-planner, finally managed to enforce a sensible solution which was to leave the space between the two palaces open and to build only the wing which would enclose an immense rectangle along the length of the Rue de Rivoli. However, so much time had been lost in discussion that, when the Empire fell, the long wing stopped at the *guichets de Rohan* (Rohan Gates). In revenge, the Emperor took advantage of the open space by endowing the Palais des Tuileries with a triumphal entrance.

A triumphal arch as portal

At the time the Arc du Carrousel was no more than a majestic gate to the Palais des Tuileries. It was a kind of miracle that, although the palace has disappeared, the isolated arch has lost none of its proportions and elegance. On the contrary it unexpectedly opened up an exceptional view of the Champs-Elysées. A copy of a Roman arch, faced with colored marble, it is an elegant pastiche whose decoration, completely contemporary, bears witness to the often unrecognized vitality of the sculptors of the period. The chariot-group on the top, modified during restoration, reappeared in all its glory in 1985.

The Arc de Triomphe

If these few words, without further qualification, now mean to the whole world the Arc de Triomphe de l'Etoile, it is due to Napoleon. In fact he did at first contemplate placing it at the Bastille, that is to say at the E exit of Paris on the Route des Victoires. Champagny (the minister)and Chalgrin (the architect), urged him to construct it on the Etoile hill, in view of the Tuileries Palace, copying the Gloriette at Schönbrunn. It was Chalgrin who must take credit for adopting the idea of a solid edifice with a single arch, unbacked by columns, creating a mass which is in scale with the landscape. Subsequent governments completed and decorated the monument.

Funerary architecture

The Empire completed the organization of the three great cemeteries begun during the Revolution. But the most astonishing project in this field was the development of the catacombs, with much funereal decoration, inscriptions written on the walls and the creation of the bones themselves into a mural décor.

Private architecture

Few mansions were built, but many were renovated for the new masters. There still remain the Hôtel Bourienne, dating from the consulship, and the Beauharnais from the First Empire, which show the elegance and slightly affected style of the time. This was a logical development and an intensification of the style of Louis XVI. Of the work by Caroline Murat at the Elysée, there remain the staircase, the Salon du Conseil des Ministres and the famous Boudoir d'Argent.

Hereditary monarchy and bourgeois monarchy

Defence and representation of the monarchy

The Bourbons – both in construction and décor – made use of the two themes which were the basis of their government: monarchy and religion.

One of the tasks considered to be the most urgent was the re-establishment of the royal statues in the Paris squares. The Place Vendôme had a column which no one dared remove. There was reluctance to reinstall in the Concorde an effigy of Louis XV, a much discredited sovereign. But the Pont-Neuf received a new Henri IV, the Place des Victoires a Louis XIV, and the Place des Vosges a Louis XIII, the first two being extremely honorable and the third somewhat doubtful. The completion of the Louvre was also part of this idealistic plan. It was only at the end that the Pavillon de Rohan was constructed, but situated inside the palace. Fontaine developed the Galerie Charles X which has kept intact its pompous but perfectly balanced décor.

The extolling of religious sentiment

It was normal that the Restoration should have its effect on the construction of new churches necessitated by the growth of the capital. Some were built in the coldest Neo-Classical style: Saint-Pierre-du-Gros-Caillou, Notre-Dame-de-Bonne-Nouvell, Saint-Denis-du-Saint-Sacrement.

The most interesting is Saint-Vincent-de-Paul by Lepère and Hittorff. It is based on the plan of a basilica, but surmounted by two belfries, with a large staircase built high up as in some Romanesque churches. The interior is richly though conventionally decorated and the effect is completely harmonious. More 'triumphal' décor can be found at Notre-Dame-de-Lorette and in the Chapelle des Lazaristes, whose little-known interior has about it an air of Spanish inspiration.

Finally, especially characteristic of the politics of the Restoration, was the building of a chapel known as *expiatoire* (sacrificial). It was erected on the site where Louis XVI and Marie-Antoinette were buried, to plans drawn up by Fontaine. This elegant monument, with its entrance cloister and dim lighting, is a perfect expression of contemplative meditation.

Various projects

The monumental history of the Restoration in Paris still remains to be written and told by those who know where it is to be found. Many unspoiled examples of the time are still unappreciated, such as the pulpit in Saint-Germain-des-Prés, the fountain in the Place Gaillon, the Atelier and Gymnase theaters, the staircase in the Bibliothèque Mazarine, the Debauve et Gallais shop, Rue Saint-Pères, or the décor of the Véfour restaurant. Examples abound and vary in both style and interest. This is quite contrary to earlier written records and customarily held opinions.

A new column

Louis-Philippe, in his turn, found himself faced with the necessity of putting up commemorative monuments, but, in so doing, tried to pay universal homage. Above all he wanted to honour those to whom he owed his throne. For this reason he erected a hollow metal column at the Bastille which was surmounted by the famous statue of the Génie de la Liberté. Like many projects of his reign, the monument lacks grandeur. Parliamentarianism could also be seen exercising its rights by transforming the Palais-Bourbon and the Luxembourg to adapt to their new rôles. To this is owed the admirable décor of the two palaces by Delacroix.

The legend of the Eagle

Thus pacified (or so it seemed), the Republicans turned to flattering the Bonapartists by finishing the monuments begun by the Emperor. The Madeleine was completed and, most importantly, the Arc de Triomphe. Its success was assured by the decoration in high-relief on the main façades. These showed colossal groups, including Rude's *La Marseillaise*, facing the Champs Elysées.

Napoleon was remounted on the column of Vendôme, this time in frock-coat and small hat; and when the Emperor's body was brought to Paris, Visconti prepared a grandiose red granite tomb for it at the Invalides, where the sarcophagus was watched over by Pradier's *victoires*. Thus, in self-defence, did Louis-Philippe carve the name of his successor in stone.

The memory of the old monarchy

Balm had to be poured on the embittered hearts of the partisans of traditional monarchy. As for them, they perched the statues of Philippe Auguste and St Louis on top of the columns of the Nation. But in revenge, the 'roi-citoyen' (citizen king) did not replace the royal statue on the Place de la Concorde, but found a conciliatory solution: the obelisk.

The Gothic renaissance

The ever-increasing interest of the millions brought up on Gothic architecture gave rise to two new elements in this period – pastiche and restoration. As far as the first is concerned, Sainte-Clothilde is the prototype. It is a slightly dry building, a little skimped but which shows an understanding of the weaknesses of medieval architecture.

As regards the country, the necessary restoration of Gothic monuments was resumed under Viollet-le-Duc. He was a sensitive man who gravitated towards an idealized Gothic architecture with all the constraints it imposes on its monuments. Allied to this was his profound knowledge of medieval art and a faculty of inventive pastiche which at times arouses admiration. His restoration and modification of Notre-Dame, though sometimes questionable, is a milestone in the history of Parisian architecture.

Innovative architecture

Certain architects found new formulae adapted to the use of the buildings they were commissioned to design. Charged with the conversion of the old Couvent des Augustins into the Ecole des Beaux-Arts, Duban used parts of it very successfully together with the remains of the Musée de Lenoir, without ever interfering with its proportions or its décor. And Labrouste (1801–75) commissioned to build the Library of Sainte-Geneviève, succeeded, by harmonizing slender cast-iron pillars with stone and glass, in creating a building which today is still proof of rationality.

The Haussmann Revolution

Until he came to power, Napoléon III had practically never lived in France. On his succession he was painfully affected by contemporary Paris which was still medieval in many aspects and hideously insanitary. This modern sovereign, strongly in favour of scientific and social progress, wanted an airy, clean Paris where the ruling class could find accommodation worthy of its status. At the same time he took into account that the network of the Parisian streets was ideally set out for rioting and that this topography had been the direct cause of the successive downfalls of Charles X and Louis-Philippe. Therefore, what was needed was a town which favoured strategic operations. To preside over this upheaval, the Emperor Napoléon III found an ideal planner in Haussmann. During the course of sixteen years he implemented an enormous scheme of demolition, development and construction.

The pickaxe assault on Paris

It was Napoléon III and Haussmann who, together, drew the *grandes voies* (main routes) on the map of the town with a red pencil. Thus they razed to the ground the pockets of insanitary houses, levelled out the hills, ripped open the old districts, and laid out a new framework for the capital. It was an operation of financial magnitude unimaginable today, whose usefulness and necessity has to be recognized, even if the manner of its achievement is questionable. A considerable number of historic monuments, old houses and picturesque streets were sacrificed. One of the most heartrending examples of this wholesale destruction was the Ile de la Cité. This should have been designated a 'conservation area' but, deplorably, three-quarters of it were destroyed. To make way for the alignment of the new routes, the heart of Saint-Leu-Saint-Gilles was reduced, while Saint-Laurent, which was lengthened, was given a new façade which is, at least, not without charm.

At last a healthy city

Arbitrarily and politically supervised, the new Paris of Haussmann was at least finally provided with public utilities, or what would now be called amenities, like other capital cities. London, in particular, had long benefited from such amenities: water supply, drains, pavements in most places, markets, schools and high schools, hospitals and new green spaces. Thanks to an impressively broad conception and an execution of astonishing rapidity, the capital, in this sector, made an advance which it would retain for a long time.

The masons set to work

This clearance of land and creation of infrastructure allowed a campaign of construction – of a magnitude never before conceived – to get under way immediately. The campaign was, to a large extent, devoted to the residential areas, those 'Haussmannian' buildings which went up along the length of the new routes. These buildings, with their well-finished stone façades, had some relief work and were covered with decoration graded according to the height of the storeys, low-relief below, and high-relief towards the upper storeys.

It was the end of cohabitation of the various social classes under the same roof, and working families were pushed out towards the edge of the city or the suburbs, something which weighed heavily in the future class struggle. The buildings were reserved for the middle class. But this class included categories which, whether out of jealousy or ignorance, distributed themselves on the various floors, from the bottom to the top, according to the importance or their social position of their income. The appearance of the elevator in 1867 gradually upset this social order. Private mansions also began to be built, the most famous being that of the Mme de Paiva on the Champs-Elysées.

Old and new churches

During the Second Empire, however, a considerable number of public buildings were erected largely for political reasons. The conservative and traditional population were offered churches, designed as pastiches of the Romanesque style (Saint-Honoré-d'Eylau), the Gothic (Saint-Jean-Baptiste at Belleville), the Renaissance (la Trinité) and the Classical style (Saint-François-Xavier). There were buildings which, though far from indifferent, would have been preferable had they shown the innovative tendencies seen in Saint-Pierre-de-Montrouge; also especially in Saint-Eugène and Saint-Augustin, where cast iron and iron reign, though in a concealed fashion.

The palace of the reign

It is perhaps at the Palais du Luxembourg, in the Salle des Conférences, that the best decorative collection of the period can be admired in all its sumptuousness and flashy luxuriousness. But above all, the reign must be credited with the completion of the Louvre-Tuileries complex of buildings, four centuries after Catherine de'Medici. Reverting to the plan so skilfully drawn up by Visconti, Lefuel built two majestic wings on either side of the central space. These have been long criticized and are only now beginning to be appreciated for their solidity and slightly redundant harmony (Cour Napoléon, façade on the Place du Palais-Royal). They have been refurbished inside and out. A detailed study of the complex still remains to be done.

The masterpiece of the 19th century

However, it was Charles Garnier who endowed Paris with the exceptional monument of the period: the Opéra. It was skilfully lavish in conception, as much in plan as in elevation, and of a volume which, similar to that of a cathedral, had rigorously defined interior distribution. More than that, it has an astonishing decorative style, the symbol of a rich, joyful class which was oblivious in its pursuit of pleasure.

Tradition and innovation

The other monuments of the period symbolize well the academic and original tendencies of their creators. While Joseph-Louis Duc transformed – and often disfigured – the Palais de Justice in a stiff, pompous style where classicism had one last airing of well-worn clichés, Labrouste constructed a reading room at the Bibliothèque Nationale more audacious than that which he designed at Sainte-Geneviève. And while Ballu created a frigid domed building for the Tribunal de Commerce, Hittorff put up that masterpiece of logic and harmony – the Gare du Nord. At the same time, Baltard was building the Pavillons des Halles with which we are now reproached by our children for having destroyed (one of the pavilions was transferred to Nogent-sur Marne).

In one construction, as in all the others, can be seen the desire for good building, a taste for monumental architecture and a generosity of proportion. This was the hallmark of the last period, when a changing Paris was the fruit of a collective plan and single will.

Paris of the Exhibitions
The importance of international exhibitions

From now on no single authoritative will was to assert itself in urban development except in a temporary form. This was seen during the Paris Exhibitions of 1878, 1889, 1900, 1925, 1931 and 1937. The first three are interesting for the architectural history of Paris, in the sense that those of 1878 and 1889 confirm an innovative tendency in form and technique, while that of 1900 marked a backward step in the use of stucco and papier-mâché.

After the demolition of the old Trocadéro, only the Pavillon de Suède (remounted at Courbevoie) remained from the Exhibition of 1878. But the Exhibition of 1889 left us the Tour Eiffel. It is not only a masterpiece of technique but also governed by technique. Its form is created by the solution to the mathematical problem that its construction presented. As far as the Exhibition of 1900 is concerned, it has not, as one might imagine, left us a legacy of Art Nouveau buildings, but either entirely traditional buildings, both in concept and execution, like the Petit Palais, or buildings with a new structure, in metal. However, this metal skeleton remains carefully hidden beneath a cladding of conventional stone, like the Grand Palais or the Gare d'Orsay or, as with the Pont Alexandre-III, covered with redundant decoration which is now beginning to charm public taste.

Reconstruction and academic classicism

At the same time the bourgeois Republic marked its construction and reconstruction with an eclecticism in which dying academic classicism took refuge; the reconstruction of the Hotel de Ville, with its characteristic interior décor, the building of the Sacré-Coeur and that of the Sorbonne, and the Salle des Fêtes in the Elysée are perhaps more significant for social history than for architecture.

New research

It is in the private sector that the desire for originality and logic can be found. The enlargement of the big shops permitted some architects to experiment with ideas that allowed the maximum amount of light, display and ease of circulation. This was sometimes carried out in an audacious manner like that of Frantz Jourdain at La Samaritaine. And in religious architecture, alongside the dubious pastiches, buildings like Notre-Dame-du-Travail, were given a structure entirely made of metal.

Art Nouveau

But it was also in the area of private architecture that one of the most astonishing architectural and decorative styles of French history flowered. This, during that period, was known as the 'modern style'. In Paris, its two representatives were Lavriotte, designer of several buildings, and especially Hector Guimard, the best of the French Art Nouveau architects, creator of the synagogue in the Rue Pavée, the Castel Béranger apartment building and the entrances to the Métro. His work, long decried, is today at last recognized and preserved. This new Baroque style with its naturalist tendencies, rendered in modern materials, shocked our grandfathers and amused our fathers; today it enchants us.

The arrival of concrete

Where iron denoted suppleness, elegance, slenderness and fluidity of curve, concrete replied with rigidity, sobriety and exultation of the straight line. This new material, known for a long time but equally long disdained, whose astonishing possibilities only revealed themselves little by little, was first 'launched' by Anatole de Badot at Saint-Jean in Montmartre. Then August Perret used it, first in the famous building on the Rue Franklin, then for the Théâtre des Champs-Elysées, built in 1912, but looking as though it were built about twenty years later.

The indecisive period between two wars

The hesitation, incapacity and carelessness that characterized French politics between 1918 and 1939 seems equally characteristic of its architecture. The use of an increasing number of new materials, the current of research which manifested itself in the 1925 Paris Exhibition and the need for new public buildings were unfortunately insufficient incentives to provide the capital with architecture of a high standard. Doubtless the principal reason for this was the gulf between public sector building and nearly all innovative architects.

Religious architecture

That was the reason why the numerous churches built during the period are either banal in style, or often completely without any style. A most remarkable exception is the Eglise du Saint-Esprit, whose concrete structure is clad in a resolutely contemporary decoration.

Museum architecture

If the Colonial Exhibition of 1931 was responsible for the redevelopment of the Porte Dorée where the museum now called Musée des Arts Africains et Océaniens is sited, the International Exhibition of 1937 should have given Paris a new group of museums, as the result of the new scientific research work on museums called *muséologique*.

But nothing was done, and an enlightened use of the buildings was lost in a welter of circumstantial argument.

The demolition of the Trocadéro having already been agreed, the resulting site ought to have provided the Paris townscape with some completely original architecture. Instead of that, a group of buildings of indifferent character was allowed to be constructed. In the Musée d'Art Moderne the two buildings joined by a colonnade give a more elegant impression, but the interior distribution of space is poor. The only museum worthy of the name, the Musée de Travaux Publics, was begun by Auguste Perret. It was eventually rescued from ostracism. Perret was unable to finish it and the building has been used for other purposes ever since. To make up for this he was able to complete the construction of the Mobilier National.

School and university architecture

It is perhaps in this field that the greatest successes were seen between the two World Wars. When the administration finally realized that it was not necessary for a school to look either like a barracks or a prison, architects were able to design school buildings which were airy, colourful and decorated. The same care can be seen in the creation of the new university buildings, and also in the Cité Universitaire, where Le Corbusier built the Pavillon Suisse, that forceful architectural statement which carried considerable influence.

Parisian architecture between the wars can be defined as a permanent conflict. On the one hand there were original architects such as Perret, Le Corbusier, Sauvage (tiered building in the Rue Vavin and Mallet-Stevens), who sought a new ethos by using new materials. And on the other there were the traditionalists such as Roux-Spitz who tried to reassure their clients by giving a 'modern' look to Classical buildings which still reigned supreme in the eyes of those on whom commissions depended.

Georges Poisson

Paris Today

Post-war Paris to the 1950s

As the French economy gradually recovered in the immediate post-war period the country reorganized itself. Soon the pull of the capital began to make itself felt again as people returned to be reunited with their families and friends but especially to look for work. As no new building had yet begun the newcomers moved into the old apartment blocks. Since the 1920s the population of Paris had been falling because many people were moving to the suburbs. It experienced a short period of increase, culminating at around 2,850,000 inhabitants in the 1954 census. Most accommodations were old, badly maintained and poorly equipped – only 16% of apartments had a bathroom in 1954 and some had only a lavatory in the 'kitchen' part, not even partitioned off – so this influx worsened housing conditions which were already bad.

The situation called for new urban planning and building. The first important projects of the 1950s involved sparsely populated areas, the industrial quarters and sectors around the old Paris fortifications, other parts of which had been replaced in the 1930s by housing projects (US) offering cheap accommodation. The pace of construction and the transformation of Paris was soon speeded up with economic growth.

The 1950s to the 1970s: the renovation of Paris

From the late 1950s to the early 1970s a great deal of renovation took place. With the economy growing fast, the population of Paris and its environs rose considerably and, with it, the demand for housing. The climate was therefore right for development on a huge scale which was concentrated mostly outside Paris.

The growth of Paris

Controlling the rate of growth of Paris was a major preoccupation for politicians and civic authorities, who had to adapt their laws to deal with it. The district of the Région de Paris was created in 1961 under the authority of a prefect (*préfet*) to ensure the control and coordination of an increasingly rapid urban development (1.2 million extra inhabitants from 1954 to 1962). In 1964 the Region was divided into new administrative areas taking into account the changes taking place: Paris became a department, the only commune-department in France, surrounded by seven others. Three of these make up the '*petite couronne*' – Hauts-de-Seine, Seine-Saint-Denis, Val-de-Marne; four others form the '*grande couronne*' – Essonne, Yvelines, Val d'Oise and Seine-et-Marne – the whole area covering about 4,633 sq. miles/12,000 sq. kilometres, of which only 105 sq. kilometres represent the capital itself.

In 1965 the main regional scheme which outlined the future of the agglomeration of Paris was published. To direct its development growth centers were planned around existing towns and, more importantly, in new towns. Of equal importance was the modernization of the region with new facilities especially in the field of transport. A regional network of fast rail services was planned, with emphasis on the new towns, as well as a system of motorways and fast roads.

The city rebuilt

As elsewhere, a vast rebuilding scheme based on the modern concepts dominant among town planners, architects and the responsible administrators and politicians got underway. These concepts had been proclaimed and discussed many times since the inter-war period, in particular in the Athens Charter, the architect Le Corbusier being one of their most famous advocates. They are based on the belief that technological progress must bring an improvement in urban life and needs the separation of different functions – housing, services and industry – logically organized: the development of graded transportation systems with differences being made between fast traffic and local services; the improvement of housing conditions measured by standards of hygiene.

Paris's guiding urban plan, finalized in the 1960s, could not completely embrace these ideas, which would have led to large-scale demolitions. It did, however, draw inspiration from these ideas and positively states the aim of adapting the city to the modern world. Excluding historical sections, the traditional urban Paris of roads lined with houses and apartment buildings is doomed. The demo-lition and modernization of almost a third of the city was proposed; most of the old inner suburbs were involved and also districts in the very center, Les Halles and the surrounding area, about 400,000 homes – most of them very uncomfortable – housing a million inhabitants. The new buildings were to be apartment blocks and skyscrapers, far taller than the buildings they replaced. In the sections which were not to be completely rebuilt the construction of high blocks of apartments set back from existing façades was favoured for the sake of improved sanitation.

For about 20 years these ambitious concepts have governed the transformation of Paris and entailed considerable rebuilding – 230,000 homes were built from 1954 to 1975 – and many important schemes were completed: the ring road (finished in 1973); the Georges Pompidou motorway along the Right Bank of the Seine and the first stages in the setting up of a regional express network.

City in turmoil

Redevelopment is far from achieving its early aims but it has already hideously scarred the face of Paris and, in numerous places, broken the appearance of balanced unity which has been given to it over past centuries. The worst affected areas are undoubtedly those with the tower blocks: Montparnasse where the highest office tower in Paris reaches 673 ft, the Front de Seine, on the bank of the river (15th arr.), Italie (13th arr.), Place des Fetes, the Flandré-Riquet district (19th arr.), Saint-Blaise (20th arr.); many outer districts, and in particular, La Défense. The many smaller-scale projects, in the south and east of Paris especially (13th, 14th, 15th, 19th and 20th arr.) have completely changed the traditional appearance of these districts. In many ways, indeed, the characteristics of the redeveloped areas contrast sharply with the older parts of the city, because of their discontinuous, unaligned and stylized oblong shapes of enormous dimensions and height and their repetitive appearance almost devoid of decorative material and color.

In general, the monuments associated with this period are large public investments; they grew from the planning and architectural theories already mentioned, but differed greatly in their conception and appearance. What they have in common is their large size and the search for the maximum economic use of the new materials – concrete, glass and metal. Among the examples most often mentio-ned are: the Palais de l'UNESCO (architects: Breuer, Nervi, Zehrfuss, 1958); its height is in proportion to the immediate neighborhood of the Ecole Militaire and Invalides; the Maison de la Radio (architects: Bernard, Lhuillier, Niermans brothers, Sibelle, 1963); the Faculté des Sciences de Jussieu (architects: Albert, Cassan, Coulon, Seassal, 1965–71); the Maison de l'Iran in the Cité Universitaire (architects: Parent, Foroughi, Ghiai, 1968); the Palais des Congrès of the Porte Maillot (architects: Gillet, Guibout, Maloletenko, 1972); the headquarters of the French Communist Party (architect: Niemeyer, 1972); the block consisting of the Montparnasse station and tower (architects: Arretche, Beaudouin, Cassan, Dubuisson, Hyom de Marien, Lopez, 1963–73); the new stadium of the Parc des Princes (architect: Taillebert 1972) and the Sheraton-Montparnasse Hotel (architect: Dufau, 1974).

The old heritage rediscovered

The time when all this renovation was taking place coincided with important decisions affecting Paris's early heritage. In 1959 André Malraux, Minister of Culture, launched a clean-up, trying it out on major public buildings first. The work was then extended to all districts. Paris lost its sombre grimy look and its façades rediscovered the clear tones of their original paint and stonework. Melraux's new legislation was drawn up largely to protect the most precious of the historic sections. In Paris this applies mainly to the Marais, where much of that part of the heritage built during the 16th and 17th centuries is found; not only the great mansions but also the modest houses surrounding them are progressively being restored. The historic quarters in the center are causing increasing concern, particularly on the Left Bank (Saint-Germain, Latin Quarter). Public pressure in the Marais or around the Rue de Bièvre in the 5th arr. and, even more so, private enterprise, have given rise to numerous refurbishment projects.

The 1970s to the 1990s: the modernization and development of Paris

The turning-point in urban policy

The 1970s saw the passing of the policy of radical renovation, which sought to revolutionize the city on a grand scale, and the birth of a policy anxious to reconcile new building to the existing urban framework.

This great change can only be explained if it is considered in the context of the time, marked by a series of questionings, re-examinations, even crises. The western nations experienced a slowing-down of their rate of economic growth primarily because of the oil crisis, and the pressure for construction in great urban centers slackened off. The continuation of the policy of district planning, begun at the beginning of the 1960s, was questioned. Indeed the population of the Ile-de-France stabilized at a level well below that envisaged by the experts – 10 million inhabitants in 1975. Numerous businesses – especially large industrial enterprises – had relocated to the provinces. Commitment to further operations of the same type, involving smaller concerns, appeared less justified and perhaps financially risky.

In Paris itself, the population declined sharply, as did economic activity, most of the urban development taking place outside the capital, especially in new towns.

In the city itself, the numerous renewal and construction schemes which were and are under way have not brought all the anticipated results: the trend of a declining and aging population, started in the 1960s, accelerated – 2.3 million inhabitants in 1975. Housing costs rose rapidly and the social diversity characteristic of Paris diminished, while at the same time in certain quarters there are still old, dilapidated buildings housing low-income families, mostly immigrant workers.

The effects in urban and architectural terms of this renovation are arousing increasingly unanimous opposition, as indeed are the planned super highways that would require demolitions and damage to the landscape. This is still the major concern of ecological associations which get increasing support.

This was also a time of endless discussions and important changes for development projects. In 1970 work on the new Villette abattoir, begun in 1962, ran into enormous financial difficulties and grounded to a halt; permission to pull down the old Gare d'Orsay was granted, but refusal to authorize the construction of a hotel in its place stopped the project. The site for the Georges-Pompidou Center was decided on in 1971 and, despite opposition, demolition of the Baltard Pavilions of Les Halles market went ahead (only one has been re-erected, at Nogent-sur-Marne). The plan for a major N-S road following the course of the Saint-Martin canal was abandoned. Soon after his election in 1974 as President of the Republic, Valéry Giscard d'Estaing took two major decisions: to drop the express-way planned for the Left Bank of the Seine and to cancel a building project for the International Business Centre, intended for the site of Les Halles; this led to a rethink of the whole development plan.

Even before these decisions, work had begun in 1973–1974 on the legislation that was to provide the new planning policy for Paris; approved in 1977 these regulations expressed the determination to maintain the capital's diversity and the mixed nature of its functions – homes, activities of all kinds – proper care of the architectural and historical heritage and preservation of the landscape. Among the proposed lines of action the most important priorities were the construction of housing in order to slow down depopulation; control of office building, preferably to be confined near to main public transportation junctions; creation of modern workshops for craftsmen and light industry; cancellation of the plan for a network of super highways with priority given to public transportation. There was a return to the traditional style of Paris building.

Once again, new buildings as a general rule had to be aligned with existing façades. The planned extensions were for the most part given up; authorized heights were reduced – 81ft/25m in the center, 101ft/31m on the periphery, 120ft/37m in certain areas close to recently erected blocks, to be in proportion to existing buildings. In addition the regulations have been amended to favour alignment with neighboring buildings, to ensure better integration into the urban landscape.

A mayor in Paris

The introduction of these new concepts was to have the benefit of a new administrative framework. Since the *Ancien Régime*, central government had mistrusted Paris; the revolutionary periods serving only to strengthen this feeling. The status accorded by Napoleon I, which was one of tutelage, had been perpetuated; the elected municipal council had no real power, as it was in the hands of two prefects appointed by the Government: the Prefect of Paris and the Prefect of Police. The capital's constitution, adopted by Parliament in December 1975, brought her closer into line with other French communes. The municipal council which elects the mayor is formed by 109 councillors elected by universal suffrage in the twenty arrondissements. However, it has no power over the police, who remain under a prefect. The election took place in 1977 and Paris again had a mayor – Jacques Chirac – after centuries of almost uninterrupted administration under the power of the state.

At the regional level changes were made too. The Regional Council of the Ile-de-France, locally elected, was introduced in 1976, with the prefect retaining executive power and administrative authority.

The revision of town planning

In 1978 and 1979 the municipality of Paris reviewed those most important renovation projects which were still under way, trying to adapt them to the newest ideas. The sections affected were those earmarked for high-rise buildings and tower blocks, some of them already partially renovated (Rues de l'Ouest and Vercingetorix, Belleville, Pere-Lachaise, Saint-Blaise. . .).

The 1980s were marked by a sharp slowing down in the pace of construction. However, a whole series of initiatives on the part of municipalities aimed at the creation of new residential areas was started, based on the newly redefined town-planning principles. The emphasis of the Programme Plan for the east of Paris, adopted in 1983, is on altering the balance in favour of that still under-privileged part of the capital which offers much scope for development and improvement.

From 1983 the amount of intervention has lessened; reconstruction and maintenance are sometimes closely associated in the rehabilitation of old buildings. Above all, they make use of sites previously occupied by warehouses, goods stations, industrial premises, usually dilapidated, rather than trying to remodel inhabited areas. This is especially so with the big building schemes launched during the 1980s which, in the 1990s, will lead to the transformation of important Parisian sites: to the SW the old Citroën land; to the SE various places along the Seine, the districts of Berry and Tolbiac; to the NE the approaches to La Villette and a number of canals.

The picture presented by the new concept, which represents a return to the city, is extremely diverse. Some constructions remain similar in treatment to those of the previous period, but a reduction of scale and a return to the principles of alignment of façades with the street ensures better integration with existing buildings. Meanwhile, interesting and diverse designs abound, some of great simplicity – in imitation of certain older buildings – others with a more or less complicated play on the wide range of shapes, materials and specifications allowed by modern techniques. Acknowledgement of existing surroundings and of the architectural history of Paris is reappearing alongside innovations. Altogether these developments reflect a renewed concern for architecture and decoration, and illustrate the range of interpretation possible under the building regulations, much stricter though they are than before.

The most publicized of these creations sometimes grouped together under the label of 'new Parisian architecture' mostly concern council apartment developments and communal facilities. The public sector shares the aspirations of many architects to break with the previous poverty of expression, and to propose an urban architecture adapted to its environment, worthy of the historical city of Paris.

No attempt will be made here to draw up a long and arbitrary balance-sheet of all these building schemes which will soon be obsolete. However, it is possible to mention some areas with a number of interesting buildings. First, there are the ambitious schemes revised at the end of the 1970s or launched afterwards, among which are the former Citroën land between the Rue Balard and the quays of the Seine, and the southern part of the Rue Saint-Charles and the Ave. Félix-Faure (15th arr.). The sector of the Rue Vercingétorix, the Rue de l'Ouest and the Rue Raymond-Losserand (14th arr.); the approaches to the Rue des Amandiers and those of the Rue Saint-Blaise and the Rue Vitruve (20th arr.). Note that these last examples, especially the Saint-Blaise sector, juxtapose different conceptions, allowing the recent evolution of Parisian town planning to be retraced by means of a sort of exhibition of buildings. A number of operations on a smaller scale equally deserve mention, for example, the Rue des Hautes-Formes (13th arr.); the Rue Mathis (19th arr.); the Rue de la Mare and the Rue des Cascades, the Rue des Prairies, the Rue Saint-Fargeau and the Passage Gambetta (20th arr.).

Improvements in public transportation: the problem of the car

One of the major changes of policy defined in the mid 1970s was the abandonment of the planned network of super highways. From now on building schemes were to aim principally at local improvements linked to neighboring operations. The most important started at the end of the 1980s, and involved certain major urban routes – the widening of the Rue de Flandre, improvement of the Left Bank quays in the W. – and especially the SE section of the city, a district in a state of complete transformation with an overhead bridge for the Métro built above the existing Pont de Bercy, and the building of a new bridge between the Gare de Lyon and the Gare d'Austerlitz.

But the vast parking lot that Paris and the Region has become with more than 3 million vehicles, and the increase in the daily number of car journeys, pose acute problems in such an ancient city, so crowded and busy. The creation of infrastructures and garages, the development of paid parking, the improvement in the management of the street network have been unable to solve the enormous difficulties of traffic and parking particularly during peak hours. Due to the priority given to public transport – by which most journeys are made – a growing demand for fast, efficient modes of transportation has been satisfied.

In this field the most spectacular development is unquestionably the setting up of the RER (Regional Express Network). Conceived in the early 1960s, progressively put into operation from 1969, this fast Metro network has been established by linking some existing lines under the very heart of Paris, and, a major innovation, combining the services of the RATP and the SNCF. The new links and the underground stations have led to impressive works; forming connections between the different networks – Métro, train and RER. These stations – Chatelet-les Halles; Auber; Charles de Gaulle-Etoile; Gare de Lyon; Gare du Nord; Nation – make it far easier to travel between the different sectors of Paris and most of the Région. Lines A (E–W) and B (N–S) join together in the vast station of Chatelet-les Halles, the central hub of the network, where the even juxtaposed platforms are designed to receive, subsequently, a South-East-North connection, line D. A new connecting station came into service in 1988 at Saint-Michel and it is now possible to change trains between line B and line C which follows the Seine on the Left Bank.

Other measures favored the use of public transport: the improved circulation of buses by specially created lanes; the modernization of the Métro and its extension into the suburbs, and the introduction in 1975 of the 'orange card', a system of geographically zoned season tickets for all public transportation.

Paris is, of course, the convergence point of the national and international rail networks. The advent of the high speed train (TGV) to the Gare de Lyon combined with the completion of the RER, and the difficulties of coping with the heavy flow of travellers, called for the remodelling on a huge scale of this station and its run-down surroundings. Access to the trains had been improved by the creation of a huge passage under the tracks, emerging at a new square onto the Rue de Chalon with offices and housing surrounding the refurbished station. The decision to build the TGV Atlantique has led to plans for a major transformation of the Gare Montparnasse and the immediate vicinity. This operation will call for the erection of a TGV station, offices, shops and a paved garden above the tracks; this should be completed at the beginning of the 1990s.

A series of exceptional buildings

It was not so much the building projects and conservation of the countryside, or the partly underground transport infrastructures that spectacularly marked the end of the 1970s and the beginning of the 1980s, but the creation of a series of vast facilities programmes. Amazingly ambitious in their extent and architectures these projects have done much to reinforce the attraction of Paris nationally and internationally.

The Halles and Plateau Beaubourg scheme was a major opportunity to revitalize the heart of Paris, the decline of which was proclaimed as being beyond remedy. Decided on in 1960 and making possible the transfer of the wholesale food market to Rungis in 1969, this was an opportunity without parallel since the beginning of the century: 37 acres/15 ha to be remodelled at the very crossroads of the historical routes that shaped the city. It posed important questions for the future of the old city center and the choice of planning and architecture for the end of the 20th century. Countless ideas and schemes were proposed, many plans drawn up, decisions taken and modified, debates and heated discussions on the preparation and implementation of the operation, all clearly showing how concern for Paris went way beyond national frontiers, and the near impossibility with such a huge planning problem of finding an answer that would attract wide support.

Political and administrative changes have also had a direct influence on the project's development, some major decisions having been taken by the highest state officials and, after the coming into effect of the new statute of Paris, by those of the city. In what amounts to a key period for Paris town planning, the Halles operation has taken in one concept after another over a period of 15 years.

The old market zone was the center chosen for important developments: the RER central station – used by a million travellers each day – and a vast underground commercial complex of which the first part, the Forum, looks onto a central open-air well, surrounded by stained glass, and the second, monumental in style, comprises public sporting (gymnasium, swimming-pool), social and cultural facilities (auditorium, the Paris video-cassette library. . . .) At ground level three groups of buildings border the Forum, on the E side: glass pavilions with metal frames house some of the facilities, the other more traditional structures are given over to housing, hotels and offices. A garden covers these underground developments, allowing a clear view of the Church of Saint-Eustache. The Plateau Beaubourg has been unused since the 1930s, and was chosen for a complex of new dwellings and shops, incorporating on the Rue Saint-Martin, some protected old façades and, most importantly, the spectacular Centre National d'Art et de Culture Georges Pompidou, a gigantic contemporary art exhibition culture center.

Motor vehicles have been diverted underground and a huge pedestrian precinct installed above ground, conforming with the 1960s' principle of separating the traffic. The streets and squares now restricted to pedestrians – particular the lively Piazza Beaubourg – are those most frequented by Parisians and visitors.

The Halles and Beaubourg have, from the start, played an integral rôle in the revival of the Right Bank center which is undoubtedly now the principal place in Paris for happenings. All around refurbishment is going on rapidly, extending to the Palais Royal and the W fringe of the Marais district.

The decision taken in 1969 by the then President of the Republic Georges Pompidou, to create the center to which his name was later given, was to become a major achievement. International prizewinners, its architects (Piano and Rogers) wanted to change the image of cultural institutions, and so created their huge and spectacular transparent building of synthetic glass, steel beams and colored plastic which show all the interior functions from the outside. Today, Beaubourg (nickname of the Georges Pompidou Center) has more visitors than even the Eiffel Tower in France, and is one of the busiest tourist attractions in the world. The Paris tradition of erecting monuments for important public amenities has now been revived. Since the end of the 19th century, this tradition had been expressed mainly through international exhibitions which have given Paris the Eiffel Tower (1889), the Grand and the Petit Palais (1900), the Palais de Chaillot and the Palais de Tokyo (1937).

Valéry Giscard d'Estaing's seven-year term (1974–1981) saw,

besides the completion of the Pompidou Center inaugurated in 1977, the launching of several new projects:

— The conversion of the former Gare d'Orsay into a museum devoted to the art and civilization of the end of the 19th and the beginning of the 20th c. (architects, Bardon, Colboc, Philippon; architect for interior arrangement, Aulenti);

— the creation at La Villette of the Musée des Sciences et des Techniques in the huge sales hall of the former abattoirs, entirely readapted for the purpose (architect, Fainsilbier), and of a large park;

— the creation of the Institut de Monde Arabe, initially envisaged in the 15th arrondissement;

— outside Paris, the construction of a building to complete, at La Défense, the long perspective that stretches as far as the Arc de Triomphe and the Louvre.

On his election as Mayor, Jacques Chirac put in hard work on the Palais Omnisports de Bercy. This pyramid-shaped building, with its sloping, grass-covered façades (architects, Andrault, Parat), filled the need, in 1984, for a large-scale hall in Paris for artistic and sporting displays.

The presidency of François Mitterrand has seen the completion of existing projects, some modified or resdesigned, but also the launching of a series of new projects:

— The Musée d'Orsay was inaugurated in 1986;

— opened at La Villette in 1985 and 1986: Le Zénith, a pop and rock concert hall (architects, Chaix, Morel); the Grande Halle, a huge metal structure of the Second Empire, restored and transformed into an exhibition center (architects, Robert et Reichen); the Cité des Sciences et de l'Industrie and its Géode, a hemispherical cinema auditorium. This great cultural and recreational complex will further receive the Cité de la Musique (architect, De Portzamparc). The Parc de la Villette (architect, Tschumi), which surrounds these facilities, is conceived as a vast open space with attractions, galleries, and reference points, the 'folies':

— the project of the Institut du Monde Arabe has been completely rethought. A resolutely contemporary structure of steel and glass (architects, Nouvel, Soria, Lezenes, Architecture Studio) has replaced the first, more traditional design; the building, on the banks of the Seine opposite the prow of the Ile Saint-Louis, was inaugurated in 1987;

— the new Ministry of Finance at Bercy, created to house the offices formerly in the Louvre, has recently been put into service. The project chosen (architect, Chemetov) is of an immense building-cum-bridge 118ft/360m in length, the only one in Paris that spans the quay and has its foundation in the bed of the Seine;

— the Grand Louvre consists of the extension of the museum on to the Louvre Palace, and of a big reorganization made possible by the creation of new underground spaces beneath the Cour Carrée and the Cour Napoléon. The architect (I.M.Pei) has created a new main entrance marked by a glass pyramid 69ft/21m high. This idea aroused lively argument between 'ancients and moderns', which has been well overshadowed by the success achieved since its opening in 1989. Although outside Paris, mention must be made of the Grande Arche (architect. O Van Spreckelsen), which symbolically completes the prospect of Paris, repeating the theme of the Louvre's triumphal arch.

— The Opéra de la Bastille (architect, Ott) had its inaugural concert on 14 July 1989; its purpose is to give Paris a modern concert hall for the opera, the Palais Garnier being devoted to dance.

In the 1990s the Bibliothèque de France will provide Paris with a new, major, monumental group of buildings, at the Sud de la Seine, on the Left Bank, on the Quai de la Gare. The proposal chosen (architect, Perrault) places a large rectangular terrace along the river; four tall towers, containing offices and book reserve stocks, will stand over a sunken central garden, around which will be public reception areas and reading rooms. All these projects have, of course, aroused much architectural comment, but also more general criticism of the favouritism shown to Paris, at the expense of the provinces, and of the determination of politicians to leave their mark on Paris with major works. But debates, criticisms and analyses aside, there is a discernible common view on what is being done. The purpose is to proclaim the role of Paris as the source of life and culture, to increase its influence – and with it that of France – by adding to the traditional assets of a great historic city those of a modern, creative one as well.

Heritage and landscape

Protection and appreciation of the heritage and landscape have been strengthened, perhaps in reaction to the effects of renovation. The classification or listing of ancient monuments has been extended to include more recent works; the heritage of the 19th c., long ignored or despised, has been totally re-evaluated; some 20th c., works have also been taken into account. This extension has involved some new, less prestigious constructions: markets, schools, stations and entrances to Métro stations, decorated shop fronts and, simultaneously, many areas outside the historical center.

Interest is growing in old apartment buildings in the historical quarters of the center, as well as in the numerous sectors created in the 19th c., particularly to the W. The resurfacing and repainting of façades and the cleaning and renovation of middle- or working-class apartment blocks, often uncovered the quality of the traditional urban landscape of Paris, its overall homogeneity and, at the same time, the diversity and richness of its details.

The most important buildings have been magnificently restored: among the Classical works, the Hôtel des Invalides, its gardens and esplanade, and several hôtels of the Marais (which has become one of the most sought-after districts of Paris), in particular the Hôtel Salé which houses the Musée Picasso. Among 19th-c. constructions, as well as the Gare d'Orsay and the Grande Halle of La Villette, there is the Châtelet theater, now called the Théâtre Musical de Paris, and the Eiffel Tower, the night-time look of which is now entirely changed thanks to a new system of illumination.

A long-term programme has been initiated to restore their former attraction to the picturesque sections of the Seine and canals. Work proceeds gradually as the activities which occupy their banks, warehousing, transport and parking, spread. Many projects have already been completed in the very center of Paris: the garden of the Quai Saint-Bernard with its open-air exhibition of contemporary sculpture; the Promenade of the Port de la Tourelle; reconstruction of the Pont des Arts preserving its original character; the garden and marina of the dock in the Arsenal district. In the NE of Paris, the banks of La Villette's canals have been partly converted into a tree-lined mall which will be extended towards the Place de Stalingrad, to connect with a vast pedestrian precinct, arranged around the rotunda built by Ledoux.

An important scheme for the creation of large gardens has also been started. The Parc Georges-Brassens has replaced the old slaughter-houses of Vaugirard; open green spaces have been laid out at Les Halles and on the hill of Belleville. The early 1980s will see the opening of three new parks: at La Villette and on the banks of the Seine, to the W on the site of the old Citroën plant and, to the E, at Bercy.

Population and the economy

The population and economic trends in Paris, which began in the early 1960s, have carried on beyond the 1970s but with a notable change in rhythm. Depopulation continues but at a markedly slower rate. There were 2,176,000 inhabitants in Paris in 1982. Its population registers a higher proportion of people living alone, the elderly and the wealthier classes. Although they have been going on for several decades, these trends have now slowed down.

Demographic and sociological developments vary from district to district. Some, like the Marais, the outskirts of Les Halles and, more recently, the Bastille, change quite rapidly; the numerous restorations are accompanied by a marked decline in the number of inhabitants and a strong influx of professionals and executives. The shifts are not so marked in the east of the city where large-scale construction continues; the population is more stable, younger and contains a higher proportion of lower-paid workers and middle-management executives. The traditional divide between middle-class west and working-class east still exists in some ways but the difference is now less obvious and its nature somewhat changed; for example, everywhere the decline of industry throughout the region has reduced the number of factory workers. Unquestionably the imaginary line between the two parts of the city has moved eastwards and become more complex, particularly in the center.

The variety of types of employment in Paris has decreased as in all the other great cities of the West; the nature of them has changed, with a reduction in the production sector and a growth in the services sector. Manufacturing has declined sharply and several sectors of the economy have experienced difficulties: textiles, leather, printing, metalwork – moreover, the buildings and land (frequently dilapidated) occupied by these enterprises have often been transformed into housing or offices. Some cores of activity combining manufacture and commerce are, nevertheless, still genuinely go-ahead, such as the jewellery trade in the Temple district, the ready-to-wear clothing industry around the Rue du Sentier and especially the Rue de Turenne. Starting in the 1980s, new workshop buildings (Rue de l'Evangile, Boul. Davout, for example) have provided craftsmen and small industrial enterprises with modern premises.

Conversely, the services sector has expanded; in 1982 it provided 80% of the 1,800,000 jobs in Paris. However, the control of office development has undoubtedly prevented even sharper growth. New office buildings have been spread between the major development zones, in particular near the Gare de Lyon and the Gare Montparnasse. The biggest operation of this sort will take shape in the 1990s, to the south-east of Paris, near the new Ministry of Finance at Bercy and, especially, at Tolbiac, on the Left Bank, where a very large services center is planned.

The charm of Paris owes a lot to the liveliness, variety and attractiveness of its shops. New shopping complexes have been created in the center (Halles, Champs-Elysées) and on the outskirts, but commercial activity goes on and is developed along the many streets whose lively bustle is part and parcel of the image of Paris.

Paris has also asserted its international rôle of cultural and economic capital by taking its place in the front rank of the world's cities for tourism and exchanges, thanks to the development of a whole range of facilities for visitors – hotels, conference and congress rooms and exhibition centers – among them the new exhibition park of Paris-Nord, opened by the Paris Chamber of Commerce at Villepinte, near Charles de Gaulle airport.

The political capital

The increase in its economic and cultural potential has clearly helped to reinforce the political pre-eminence of Paris. As the capital, Paris remains the mirror, the symbol and, sometimes, the catalyst of the evolution of France.

City of government, Paris is also a national and international meeting-place, and therefore the site of many ceremonies. Since World War II it has seen the advent of the Fifth Republic in 1958, the ceremonial investitures of Presidents, the national funerals of General de Gaulle in 1969 and of Georges Pompidou in 1974, and other State occasions.

Symbolic city, Paris has known many crises because it echoes the concerns of France and the world and, more directly, the events which occur in the city itself. Thus, Paris, in the early 1960s, experienced a tragic time during the war in Algeria; it played a part in the events of May 1968 and, in the 1980s has had its share of suffering from indiscriminate terrorism.

A new municipal organization

For a long time Paris was governed directly by the central authority because it is the capital city. That now seems long ago, so much has the situation changed by the return in 1977 to municipal government.

In 1982 the movement for decentralization of power to local communities was considerably accelerated with the transfer of a whole range of State functions. Regional executive power, exercised until then by the Prefect, is now entrusted to the President of the Regional Council, an assembly which from now on will be elected by universal suffrage (the first election under the new procedures took place in 1986). The power of the communes has also been increased; they are now chiefly responsible for town planning and construction.

The law PLM – Paris, Lyons, Marseilles – has given to the three largest French cities special statutes creating councils for their arrondissements. Paris councillors, the number of whom has been raised to 163, are still elected in the 20 arrondissements and afterwards choose the Mayor of Paris; but, simultaneously, councillors for the arrondissement local councils are elected. In each one the elected assembly selects a mayor from among the Paris councillors. The power of arrondissement councils is, however, limited to local services and of advising on matters concerning the arrondissement. All major decisions rest with the Mayor of Paris.

During the 45 years which have passed since the end of the last war, Paris has undergone important changes in its image, its substance and the part it plays. In these changes, two distinctly contrasting, though overlapping, periods can be seen. First, impelled by the economic expansion of the 1960s, there was a period of radical change. Symbolically, and perhaps over-simplifying, this was the time of high-rise apartments, super highways and large-scale infrastructural schemes. Then, during crisis and economic uncertainty, a period followed of growing respect for the city's character, variety and appearance. It was an era of architectural diversity, integration with the older districts and of great, mainly cultural, public projects.

At the end of the 1980s a new period began. Respect for the existing city remains a priority, but the necessity for some modernization is making itself felt; this expresses itself through large building projects in the cultural field, but also in the major planning operations; it is often justified by international competition between cities and by the prospect of the single European market of 1992.

In their different ways, both these periods have been ambitious for Paris, and had some common objectives: to cherish the city's heritage, to accept necessary changes, to adapt to modern times, to maintain the close integration of living quarters and all forms of activity, to develop international prestige. The contrast between the methods used clearly shows the changing attitudes, and highlights the never-ending search for the difficult but necessary balance, between modernity and tradition, between the intense activity, innovation and exceptional heritage which go to make up the power and the legend of Paris.

Nathan Starkman

Districts and Monuments

☐ The Arc de Triomphe***

8th, 16th, 17th arr./Map ref. 8–C1
Métro: Charles-de Gaulle Etoile (RER)
Bus: 22, 30, 31, 52, 73, 92
Parking: Ave. des Champs-Elysées
Taxis: 1 Ave. Victor-Hugo. Tel: 45–01–85–24; 1 Ave. de Wagram. Tel: 43–80–01–99.

Along with the Eiffel Tower, this is the capital's most famous monument. Its construction, by order of Napoleon I, set in motion the redevelopment of the Place de l'Etoile under the Second Empire, now renamed in honour of Charles de Gaulle.

Historical background

In the 18th c. the steep road that led from Paris to the open area of the Etoile was levelled by Royal Decree (1768), and at the same time an avenue (the future Champs-Elysées) was created from the Palais de Tuileries out to Neuilly. At the instigation of the Marquis de Marigny, the circular esplanade of the Etoile was laid out as a public promenade with, on the S side, the grassed-over amphitheaters of the Chaillot promenade which still existed in 1854. The Etoile had become the most majestic gateway to Paris. On the eve of the Revolution the Parisian tax boundaries were extended from the Rue de Chaillot (Quentin-Bauchart) to the Place de l'Etoile. The architect, Claude-Nicolas Ledoux, designed the twin buildings of the Etoile city gates in the purest Neo-Classical style. Situated slightly in front of the Arc de Triomphe on the Paris side, for a long time they marked the boundary between Paris and Neuilly, but were destroyed when the suburban communes were annexed in 1860. Four of the 46 city gates designed by Ledoux still survive.

The original idea of a triumphal arch dates from 1806. Napoleon (letter to Champigny of February 18) wished to see it erected 'at the entry to the boulevards near the place where the Bastille was', but the site turned out to be unsuitable. Finally it was decided to put up the arch near 'the side of the Chaillot hill by the Etoile'. The foundation stone was laid on August 15. The chosen architect, Chalgrin, had to submit various designs. For the marriage of Napoleon to Marie-Louise on April 2, 1810 a full-scale wood and canvas model of the arch was made. After the fall of the Empire little progress was made until October 9, 1823 when Louis XVIII had the arch completed, dedicating it to his victorious armies returning from Spain. With some difficulty the architect Huyot was persuaded to carry out the task. Finally, the July revolution and the fiat of Louis-Philippe restored the arch to its original purpose. In 1832 Blouet was commissioned to complete the construction 'in the spirit of Chalgrin' which he did in 1836, adorning the façades with colossal groups of figures in high relief.

The Place de l'Etoile and the Arc de Triomphe

The Place de l'Etoile

The Etoile, as it looks today, was laid out after the building of the Arc de Triomphe, to a general plan established by the Prefect Haussmann's decree, dated August 13, 1854. This added broad new roads to the five existing ones, so that now there are 12 avenues radiating like the points of a star from the *place*, hence its name.

The *Hôtels* of the Marshals

The great mansions surrounding the *place* were built by Hittorff and Rohault de Fleury. Haussmann would have preferred more grandiose buildings in keeping with the Arc de Triomphe, but Hittorff had the backing of Napoléon III, who saw a way of adding to his uncle's glory by scaling down the houses to make the arch seem even more monumental. The building of these private *hôtels* (1860–68) resulted in the creation of the Rue Circulaire (Rue de Tilsit and Rue de Presbourg) giving access to the houses, which had no access to the *place* itself.

The layout of this round *place* complements the refined proportions and silhouettes of the colossal façades in keeping with the majesty of the surroundings, but without impairing the architectural power and symbolism of the Arc de Triomphe.

The Arc de Triomphe

Open daily except Tues. and public holidays 10 am–6 pm.

Inside the arch is a small museum full of documents and souvenirs of the arch's construction (→Museums), but probably of greater interest is the magnificent view* from the platform at the top of the arch, which overlooks the 12 symmetrical avenues radiating from the *place* and allows you to realize the magnitude of the project. This monument, built to Chalgrin's plan between 1806 and 1836, is a superb example of the architecture of the Second Empire, because of its grandeur and size (163ft/49.54m at its highest point, 147ft/44.82m wide, the ceiling of the arch 96ft/29.19m high). It also presents the most important collection of sculpture from the first half of the 19th c. The main façades are decorated with four colossal groups in high-relief, one of them being Rude's masterpiece: the *Departure of the Army in 1792* or *La Marseillaise* (facing E on the r. side of the Champs-Elysées). The other groups are: facing E on the l., Cortot's *Triumph of Napoleon* (1810); on the W side (opposite the Ave. de la Grande-Armée) on the r., the *Resistance of the French* in 1814 and, on the l., the *Peace of 1815*, both by Etex. These four high-reliefs are owed to Louis-Philippe who went far beyond Napoleon's original idea. Above these groups and the side arches are six bas-reliefs depicting to the E, the *Funeral of Marceau* by Lemarie, and the *Battle of Aboukir* by Seurre the Elder; to the S the *Battle of Jemmapes* by Marochetti, showing the young Louis-Philippe, who was then a Republican general; to the W, the *Crossing of the Arcole* by Feuchères, and *The Taking of Alexandria* by Chaponnière; to the N, the *Battle of Austerlitz* by Gechter. On the four tympana of the main archway Pradier has sculpted figures of Fame; the tympana of the side arches have sculptures by Bra (N side) and Valois (S side). The frieze (440ft/135m) under the pediment shows, on the E side and on half the periphery, the *Departure of the French Armies*; on the other side to the W, the *Return of the French Armies*. This huge composition with figures 6½ft/2m high, was executed by Rude, Brun, Jacquet, Laitié, Caillouette and Seurre the Elder. The attic storey is decorated with shields engraved with the names of the 172 most important battles of the Republic and the Empire including those in which the French were not victorious; on the interior walls 128 feats of arms of the same period are inscribed, and below the side arches are the names of 660 generals who took part in these actions, with those who died in battle underlined.

The Tomb of the Unknown Soldier

Beneath the central arch, facing the Champs-Elysées, lies the Tomb of the Unknown Soldier under a large slab with, at its foot, a bronze plaque representing the 'Shaef' shoulder-flash. The inscription reads: 'Ici repose un soldat français mort pour la patrie, 1914–1918' ('Here lies a French soldier who died for his country'). Its flame has been relit every evening since November 11, 1923. Visitors may attend this ceremony at 6 pm.

▷ A gigantic altar for the nation

The Arc de Triomphe, originally only one of many monuments erected to the glory of the armies of the Republic and the Empire, has become over the years a national symbol. When Napoleon's ashes were brought from St Helena on December 15, 1840, the cortège passed beneath the arch; and it was under the 'arch beyond measure' that he had celebrated in verse, that Victor Hugo, who died on May 22, 1885, received posthumous homage. But it was not until July 14, 1919 that the arch played for the first time 'the glorious role originally intended for it' (M. Poëte), when the traditional parade of soldiers passed under its immense vault, celebrating their victory. When the body of an unknown soldier, killed in action, was buried under the Arc on January 28, 1921, the monument took on even greater patriotic significance. It was here, on August 26, 1944, the day after the liberation of Paris, that General de Gaulle came to bow before the tomb before proceeding on foot down the Champs-Elysées. On the eve of this day of victory the Arc witnessed the last of the fighting.

Today the Tomb of the Unknown Soldier is the focal point of ceremonial occasions, but it is through innumerable daily visits that the people really pay homage here.

The Arsenal district*

4th arr./Map 18–D3
Métro: Sully-Morland
Bus: 67, 86, 87
Parking: Between the Boul. Bourdon and the Boul. de la Bastille
Taxis: 23 Boul. Morland. Tel: 42-77-59-88

Over half the triangle enclosed by the Seine, the Arsenal canal-basin and the Boul. Henri-IV is occupied by government offices, but it is the Arsenal itself that is the focus of attention. Behind its austere façade lie magnificent interiors and a library containing a priceless collection of medieval manuscripts.

Although it stands in the heart of Paris, there is surprisingly little activity around the Arsenal. Behind the great barracks of the Garde

Républicaine, the quiet little streets with few or no shops in them, seem to have been forgotten in the noise and confusion of the French capital. Close to the historic district of the Marais, several of these centuries-old houses have noteworthy façades – 13 and 17 Rue de la Cerisaie, for example. The Arsenal canal-basin has been turned into the Paris yacht marina. It provides a pleasant, almost maritime setting for a stroll.

Tour of the district

30 mins.

The Arsenal**

1 Rue de Sully tel: (42-72-19-09). Library open daily except Sun. 10 am-5 pm; closed Sept. 1-15. To visit the state rooms: Write to CNMHS, Hotel de Sully, 62 Rue Saint-Antoine.

The library inside this forbidding building is second in size only to the Bibliothèque Nationale. On the terrace outside the entrance is a statue by Ipoustéguy in honour of Rimbaud, erected in 1985.

The Royal Arsenal was housed c.1380 in the Tour de Billy, a bastion in Charles V's city wall near the river. On July 19, 1538 the tower was destroyed by lightning. It was packed with arms and munitions and the ensuing explosion demolished a large number of houses and even blew out the stained-glass windows in the Abbey of Saint-Victor on the other side of the Seine. During the reign of Louis XIV the manufacture of small arms and gunpowder and the casting of cannon were confined to the Left Bank and the Arsenal became primarily a weapon- and ammunition-store as well as the sculptor's workshop in which the large bronze statues for Versailles were cast. Under Louis XIII it became a court of justice which condemned Fouquet (1661-64) and investigated the notorious poisoning scandal (1680-83) involving the Marquise de Brinvilliers, executed in 1676. The Grand Master of the Artillery, a position always occupied by a high ranking member of the French aristocracy, was held, during the reign of Henri IV, by Maximilien de Béthune, Duc de Sully. He was also the Surintendant des Finances (Chancellor of the Exchequer) and in his time the Arsenal became the seat of governmental power. Sully rebuilt it and used it to receive King Henri IV whenever he came to discuss his private affairs or those of his kingdom. Antoine-René de Voyer, Marquis de Paulmy d'Argenson, gave the building its cultural purpose. A diplomat and sometime Minister of War, he was above all a scholar, unusually fascinated by the Middle Ages and its illuminated manuscripts. In 1785 the Comte d'Artois (the future Charles X) purchased his collection, adding to it part of the famous library of the Duc de la Vallière and that of the Prince de Soubise. During the French Revolution the collection was augmented by the archives of the Bastille and books seized from monastic libraries. In Year V of the One and Indivisible Republic (1797) it became the Bibliothèque Nationale de l'Arsenal.

On April 14, 1824, Charles Nodier was appointed Librarian and remained in office for the next 20 years. His house was soon the meeting place for painters and poets, including Alfred de Musset, Alexandre Dumas, Victor Hugo, Sainte-Beuve, et al. A famous engraving by Johannot depicts the librarian's drawing-room. A few years before his death in 1905 one of Nodier's successors, the poet José Maria de Heredia, was host to writers such as Régnier, Louÿs, Mallarmé, Barrès and Verlaine, in the Salon des Parnassiens, which he had founded.

The building itself was erected in 1594 for the then Grand Master of the Artillery, Sully, and improved between 1718 and 1745 by Germain Boffrand, who doubled the size of Henri IV's original building by constructing a second wing along what is now the Boul. Morland. The façade attributed to Philippe Delorme and the interiors commissioned by the Maréchal de La Meilleraye for his wife survived these 19th-c alterations.

The Library houses 14,000 manuscripts, a million printed books and about 120,000 prints. Its most precious possession is an incomparable collection of illuminated manuscripts; the archives of the Bastille, and an almost complete collection of French dramatic works – some 250,000 items in all – from the beginning of French theater. Among its treasures are St Louis' Psalter, the manuscript of Renaud de Montauban, the Terence of the Dukes and the Hours of the Master of the Flowers, a large number of incunabula (books printed pre-1500), many rare book-bindings and numerous historical curios and documents. The latter include the warrant committing the Man in the Iron Mask to prison, as well as his death certificate, mementoes of the notorious prisoner Latude, manuscripts by Conrart, the first Secretary of the Académie Française, Dangeau's diary and the letters of Henri IV to the Marquise de Verneuil. There is a special department devoted to the stage, including the Rondel, Jouvet, Craig and Baty collections.

The State Rooms: On the first floor facing the entrance to the library and between busts of Henri IV and of Sully, are Mme de La Meilleraye's apartments**decorated at the time of her marriage in 1637. The painted ceiling is attributed to Simon Vouet. Above the alcove are Silence, The Four Quarters of the Earth, The Siege of La Rochelle and The Entry of Henri IV into Paris. The lower panels are magnificently decorated with foliage and wildfowl. These decorations are remarkable examples of the Louis XIII-Mazarin style, comparable to those in the Hôtel Lauzun. A second room, Madame's oratory, contains paintings of great women in history, including Joan of Arc and Mary Queen of Scots with the features of Mme de La Meilleraye. The paneling in the music room is a fine example of the decorative Louis XV style. The overdoors are painted in grisaille with Bouchardon's *Four Seasons*. Various artistic and archeological curios are on display, together with Louis XV and Louis XVI furniture, woodwork and paneling and a clock by Julien Le Roy.

The Celestines Barracks

This building, situated on the Boul. Henri IV to the r. of the Arsenal, was erected in the 19th c. in the Louis XIII style as the headquarters of the Garde Républicaine. It occupies the site of the old monastic buildings of a Celestine convent, which in turn had replaced the Carmelite convent when that order, taking advantage of the generosity of Charles V, who lived in the Hôtel Saint-Pol, moved to the Place Maubert in 1313. In 1370 the king rebuilt their church at his own expense. Later a fine Renaissance cloister was erected and Louis XIII had a chapel built for the House of Orléans, which was not demolished until 1849. Inside is the riding school, a metal structure from 1893. Return to the front of the Arsenal.

Boulevard Morland

The street was built over what was once an arm of the Seine. No. 17 is an enormous office block housing the Préfecture de la Seine, known as the Centre Morland. The barracks of the Garde Republicaine stand at the junction with the Rue Schombert (no. 4), a brick and cast-iron building designed by the architect J. Bouvard erected in 1883. Turn l. down the Rue Mornay.

The Arsenal canal-basin

This wet-dock fills part of what was once the moat round the Bastille (the wall on the Boul. Bourdon side is very old). It forms the S end of the Canal Saint-Martin, which actually runs underneath the Pl. de la Bastille. Alterations have transformed it into a marina with moorings for 200–300 small craft. On the E side of the basin there are terraced gardens with children's playgrounds; over 1,000 sq. yds./9000m² in area, with a bronze statue of Henri Arnold (1983). Access is by the cast-iron footbridge (1895). Opposite, at no. 36 Boul. de la Bastille, stands what was once a power-station, known as the Usine Contrescarpe (1910–15) built by the engineer, L. Perissé.

The Auteuil* district

Although the district is now built-up and completely integrated into the French capital, it has never lost its original village atmosphere. The Rue d'Auteuil remains an ordinary high street and the little square in front of the parish church still looks as though it might be set in the provinces. The row of tiny houses, each with its own garden, still stands around the old cemetery in the Rue Claude-Lorrain.

However, what is so special about Auteuil is its little hamlets, havens of greenery (Hameau Boileau, Hameau de Boulainvilliers, Villa de la Réunion, Villa Montmorency), half-way houses between the Bois de Boulogne and the built-up areas of Paris itself. Even though people no longer come to take the waters at Passy or to spend the summer in a country house in Auteuil, these hamlets are still redolent of those days. During the 19th c. the land was divided into building-plots, great care always being taken to keep a peaceful belt of green around these middle-class homes. Far from the bustle of Paris which surrounds them, some preserve a few architectural *folies*, like the miniature château in the Hameau Boileau or Gide's house at Villa Montmorency.

Furthermore, the Auteuil district is in itself an extraordinary open-air museum of modern architecture. The most famous Art Nouveau architect of the first half of the 20th c., Hector Guimard, worked here, and in the district are some rare Parisian examples of inter-war modernist architecture by Le Corbusier and Mallet-Stevens.

Historical background

The encounter between the Gauls under Camulogenus and the Roman legions of Labienus in a clearing in the great forest to the W of Lutetia is set by some historians roughly on the site of present-day Auteuil. In about the year 1100, the Norman Abbey of Bec exchanged its rich lands at Auteuil for the Norman estates of the Parisian Abbey of Sainte-Geneviève and, until the French Revolution, the Abbots of Sainte-Geneviève were the feudal lords of Auteuil where they built a parish church which also served Passy, Longchamp and Boulogne. Although looted by the troops of Charles the Bad, King of Navarre, in 1358 during his War with the Dauphin, and by the English during the Hundred Years' War, as well as by rebellious peasants and brigands who throughout the centuries found safe refuge in the neighboring forests, Auteuil, despite it all, remained a sedate village producing a wine that had carried the name of Auteuil as far afield as Denmark.

In 1343 the hamlet of Boulogne was split off, as was Passy 300 years later. Nonetheless, Auteuil gained in importance because of its position on the Seine as a dock for passenger barges, and on the road to Versailles. Having hot springs said to cure the 'languid humours', it also became a holiday resort and spa.

It was fashionable to go to Auteuil to escape the summer heat in the countryside. After the poet Boileau, Molière made it a retreat where he could rest and forget his bitterness at being neglected by his wife and his king. Thereafter, Auteuil never looked back. Racine came to the village to write his comedy, *Les Plaideurs*, in the house which many years later Mme Récamier was to make her home. Louis XV himself had a pleasure-house here. Maurice Quentin de La Tour, Hubert Robert, Ampère, Volney, Mme Helvétius, Turgot, Benjamin Franklin, Chateaubriand, Marie-Joseph Chénier, Baron Gérard, the painter Gros, Carpeaux and Gavarni were all regular visitors, as were the men who made the French Revolution and those who created the Empire and the Republic that succeeded it. Proust was born in a house where 96 Rue Le Fontaine now stands, near the N. Boileau. In 1860 Auteuil was incorporated into Paris, and this prosperous village became one of the richest districts of the French capital.

Tour of the district

Two walks are suggested, taking in all the treasures of this extensive district.

From the municipal Flower Garden to the Rue Boileau

16th arr.
Métro: Porte d'Auteuil
Bus: 52, PC
Parking: Porte d'Auteuil, Ave. du Général-Sarrail
Taxis: 114 Boul. Excelmans. Tel: 46-51-14-61
Auteuil Market: Wed., Sat. 7.30–1.30

Municipal Flower Garden*

3 Ave. de la Porte-d'Auteuil (open daily 10–5 pm: admission free for children under six).

Once the site of Louis XV's nursery-gardens, this is one of the loveliest oases in Paris, a relatively unfrequented mass of flowers. The four stone statues decorating the iron railings at the entrance come from the Pavillon de Madame (the Comtesse de Provence) at Versailles. The palm house and the collections of hothouse plants are open to visitors throughout the year; especially flourishing are azaleas in spring and chrysanthemums in autumn. Many of the plants are now grown at Rungis.

The principal hothouse was designed by Jean-Camille Formigé and measures over 325ft/99m long by 39ft/12m wide and 25ft/7.75m high with the central dome above the palm house rising to a height of over 50ft/15.75m. The simplicity of the metal framework, uncluttered by supporting struts, gives the complex an airy open feel. The principal hothouse was erected by the engineers Schwartz and Meurer between 1895 and 1898. Outside the main entrance there is a bas-relief of a bacchic orgy by Jules Dalou (1891).

Not far away, on the other side of the boulevard, in the Rue Nungesser-et-Coli, stands an apartment building (no. 22) designed by Roux-Spitz in 1931 and another (no. 24), by Le Corbusier, built a year later. The latter was designed with no interior walls, one room running into another, an innovation that few people understood.

The Poets' Garden

Ave. du Général-Sarrail.Open 9 am–5 pm.

The Poets' Garden was created in 1954 but since the 1970s it has been isolated from the Municipal Flower Garden by the new circular-road. It contains Rodin's bust of Victor Hugo as well as the monument to Joachim Gasquet by Guénot (1928) and Dejean's bust of Théophile Gautier (1933). Other poets are commemorated by quotations from their poems carved on blocks of stone set amid their favorite flowers.

The Boul. de Montmorency (on the N side of the Place de la Porte d'Auteuil, at no. 67) is the mansion that belonged to the Goncourt brothers. Jules died there in 1870 aged 40 and Edmond in 1896 aged 74. In this barn they entertained Zola, Daudet, Maupassant, Huysmans, Janin, Murger and Gautier. The house was purchased by the Paris municipal authorities in 1932.

Rue d'Auteuil

This was once the village main street lined on both sides with the country houses of wealthy Parisians. Notice the entrance to Porte d'Auteuil Métro station, which is typical of Guimard's style (→inset). Nos. 63–73 stand on the site of the Château du Coq, which belonged to Samuel Bernard in 1717. He left it to one of his mistresses, Mme de Fontaine. In 1761 Louis XV purchased it to use as his love-nest.

The 18th-c. mansion which stood at no. 59 was burned down in 1871 and rebuilt at the end of the century. It has witnessed many important events in French history. Between 1750 and 1772 it was owned by Maurice Quentin de La Tour, who sold it to Mme

Helvétius. She was nicknamed 'Our Lady of Auteuil' and it was here that she entertained all the intellectual lions of the day. She died in 1800 and was buried in the garden, her body later being moved to the local cemetery. She was a charming old lady by the time that Turgot, himself aged 81, and later Benjamin Franklin, at almost the same age, proposed to her. Condorcet wrote his treatise *La Justice Prévotale* here, moved by a popular demonstration at which the red flag was unfurled for the first time. A few years later, Bonaparte, not yet known as Napoleon, stayed in the house which, from 1854, belonged to one of his great-nephews. Prince Pierre Bonaparte became notorious in January 1870 when he murdered Victor Noir, a journalist with whom he had quarrelled.

No. 40 was for many years the Auberge du Mouton Blanc, the late 17th-c. equivalent of the Brasserie Lipp. Among its regular customers were Molière and his friends. Nos. 43–47 comprise a beautiful 18th-c. *hôtel* of which the façade survives, split by balconies and balustrades. Marshal de Saxe's mistress, Marie de Verrières, lived and held her famous salon here. No. 16, is the 17th-c. Hôtel Pusher, rebuilt in 1806, which still has its fine façade with four massive pilasters and triangular pediment. A little further on at no. 11 *bis*, the central block and the forecourt of the Lycée Jean-Baptist-Say are all that remain of the late 17th-c. Château du Ternaux.

Place d'Auteuil

Until 1867 this was known as the Place du Chancelier-d'Auguesseau, a fact still commemorated in the middle of the square by the chancellor's grave topped with a stone obelisk. The square was once the churchyard.

In 1319 King Philippe V le Long (the Tall) laid the foundation stone of the Church of Notre-Dame, the first church to be built in the village of Auteuil, a foundation of the Abbey of Sainte-Geneviève. Over the centuries it was frequently enlarged and altered and was finally rebuilt (1877–92) by Vaudremer in the prevailing fashion of the day, as a Romano-Byzantine pastiche. On the other side of the square, facing the church, is a huge parochial and cultural centre. The very fine Ave. Théophile-Gautier runs off the square. François Mauriac lived and died at no. 38. Rue Mirabeau via the Rue Wilhelm runs alongside the garden of the Institution Sainte-Perrine, built on what was the vast property of the Abbey of Sainte-Geneviève.

Avenue de Versailles

Follow the Ave. de Versailles for a very short distance along the Seine to see its interesting apartment buildings. J. Ginsberg designed no. 25 (1932) and no. 42 (1934), and nos. 54 and 56 have interiors by V. Vasarely. No. 123 stands on the site of the mansion that once belonged to Hortense Schneider, the famous Offenbach singer; no. 127 typifies the work of Bassompierre, Sirvin and Rutte; while no. 142 by Guimard marks the high-point of Art Nouveau architecture and has a most unusual staircase. Turn r. down the Ave. de la Villa-de-la-Réunion: at no. 8 in this peaceful private road you will see the Hôtel Deron Levent begun by Guimard in 1905.

Rue Chardon-Lagache

On the r. at no. 42 stands the Hôtel Jassedé* (1983), a masterpiece of Guimard's pre–Art Nouveau period, decorated with tiles by Müller. The furniture (now dispersed) included some of Guimard's earliest designs. The building suffered from later alterations and has recently been restored. It stands only a few yards from the Hôtel Deron-Levent so that it is possible to compare works by the same architect in two very different styles.

Boulevard Exelmans

This boulevard splits Auteuil in two. Carpeau had a house and studio at no. 39. The latter was frequently enlarged, especially by Guimard as a young man, who added a second storey and left his mark on the façade. At the SE end of the boulevard is another of Guimard's buildings, the convent school of the Sacré-Coeur (7 Ave. de la Frillère), finished in 1895. Its sloping cast-iron columns are developed from a design by Viollet-le-Duc, and their ornamentation is the earliest example of Art Nouveau influence in the work of Guimard. The building was threatened with demolition, but was saved at the last moment and converted into apartments. Next door is the Auteuil Cemetery (57 Rue Claude-Lorrain) containing the graves of Hubert Robert (d. 1808), Gavarni (d. 1866), Gounod (d. 1893) and Mme Helvétius (d. 1800).

Rue Boileau*

Runs from the Boul. Exelmans to the Rue Molitor.

This is a really typical Auteuil street. For many years it marked the boundary of the abbey-lands of Sainte-Geneviève. Walk down it and you may admire not only examples of Art Nouveau architecture, but also some interesting contemporary buildings. At no. 67 stood the aerodynamic laboratory which the engineer Eiffel established in 1909 at nos. 56–58. Since 1977 the street has acquired a somewhat exotic appearance thanks to the Vietnamese Embassy which mingles brick, glass and tiles in a futuristic version of traditional Vietnamese styles. No. 40 is a strange Art Nouveau mansion, now the Algerian Embassy, by Richard and Audiger (1907), inspired by

N. African architecture and faced with earthenware tiles by Gentil and Bourdet. At no. 38 the Hameau Boileau begins. Boileau owned a large estate here, where he lived for many years and entertained his friends, who built their own country houses nearby. No. 34 is the first private house which Guimard built in 1891 for M. Roszé, on the site of the painter Hubert Robert's house. Rue Molitor: Constant Lemaire was the architect (1906) of no. 31, on the l., a house in the rustic style which is reminiscent of Art Nouveau and of buildings in Belgium and northern France. Many different materials are used and the building has rounded windows. Rue Michel-Ange: Pierre Brossolette was born at no. 77 *bis* in 1903 in this street which runs along the side of the Ecole Normale Israélite. A plaque at no. 6 commemorates Marshal Joffre who lived in the house from 1909–1919. We now reach the Place Jean-Lorrain where the open-air cafés give it a festive air.

From the Maison de Radio France to the Rue Mallet-Stevens

16th arr./Map ref. 13–A3
Métro: Passy or Bir-Hakeim, both some distance away; RER: Kennedy-Radio-France
Bus: 22, 52, 70, 72
Parking: Avenue du Président-Kennedy
Taxis: Place du Docteur-Hayem. Tel: 42-24-99-99
Lafontaine Market: Tues, Thurs. 7.30–1.30

The Maison de Radio-France*

116 Ave. du Président-Kennedy (conducted tours only: book one month in advance). For information write to the Service Acceuil Animation, Maison de Radio-France, 116 Ave. du Président-Kennedy, or tel: 42-30-21-80 Mon.-Fri. For public concerts tel: 42-30-22-22 (tickets at the door or from ticket agencies).

The Maison de Radio-France, generally called the Maison de la Radio, was built between 1952 and 1963 to a design by the architect, Henri Bernard. Externally it looks like a circular crown nearly 575ft/175m in diameter and 120ft/36m high, dominated by a square central tower nearly 230ft/70m high. Its foundations comprise 756 piles sunk over 55ft/17m deep, and the overall volume of the buildings is 16 million cubic ft/450,000m³. Two techniques, widely used later, were tested here – the use of precast facing panels and of very large aluminium frames in which the window glass was set and which made possible the creation of a large number of different window patterns. Because it is a functional and designed to such high architectural standards, the Maison will stand as a monument typifying 20th-c. architecture, even if it seems a pity that the architect was not allowed to raise the central tower to the full height planned, so that it is out of proportion with the rest of the building.

After a reorganization of its services, the Maison de Radio-France has 62 studios in all, two of which are equipped for television broadcasts (the main television center is situated at Buttes-Chaumont). The outer circle provides soundproofing for the entire building and contains the main entrance hall, rest rooms for performers, news broadcasting studios and about 1000 offices. The entrance hall contains *La Forêt*, by the sculptor Stahly, while the four lounges for performers, with their extensive views, are decorated respectively with mosaics by Bazaine and Singier and tapestries by Manessier and Soulanges.

Within this outer circle there is an inner circular crown on a lower level which houses 20 studios, all completely soundproofed, three public rooms and an auditorium seating 1000, decorated with two large metal bas-reliefs by Louis Leyques, and a 100-pipe organ by Gonzales. Studio 103 is a concert hall which can hold a full symphony orchestra and an audience of 500. It is decorated with a tapestry by Roger Bezombes. Studio 102 provides an 800-seat theater in which all types of performance can be staged. Last, there is Studio 105, a concert and recital hall seating 200 that has an entrance lobby decorated with a fresco by Georges Mathieu. Visitors pass along a gallery that encircles and looks down into all the studios. The O.R.T.F also houses an interesting Musée de la Radio et de la Télévision (→Museums) that shows the history of telecommunications from Chappe's visual telegraph to satellite TV.

The third and central circle houses the sound archives (250,000 tapes), a library (65,000 works) and the record library (1 million discs). It encircles the central node in which the CDM (routing matrix) is housed. This accepts signals from the studios inside the Maison de la Radio and from outside sources, and channels them to the 200 transmitters in France for broadcasting as radio programs. Last, there is the 21-storey, 230ft/70m tower, housing the archives and known as the Mémoire du Siècle.

Nuclear fallout shelters have been built in the basements which house, among other things, a huge thermodynamic power station that produces over 2000hp and pumps water from a depth of 1800ft/550m at 27°C. By using heat-exchangers this water can provide hot or cold air without the use of fuel.

Ancillary departments include a post office (Paris 120), a bank, a bookshop, a SNCF/Air France travel agency and several bars, restaurants, etc.

Rue La Fontaine**

Running from the Place du Docteur-Hayem, behind the Maison de la Radio, this road takes its name, not from the famous author of the fables, but from the highly reputed thermal spring. It is one of the most interesting streets in Auteuil and it is no exaggeration to say that it and the little roads leading off it make up a museum of the work of the Art Nouveau architect Hector Guimard.

No. 14 is the celebrated apartment block, Castel Béranger, erected by Guimard between 1894 and 1898, perhaps his major work; because of its exuberance of line it was called 'cockeyed' at the time (→inset). Other apartment buildings designed by Guimard stand at nos. 8 and 10 Rue Agar and at nos. 17, 19 and 21 Rue La Fontaine. No. 40 was built as a Foundation to offer apprenticeships to the orphans of Auteuil (*orphelins-apprentis*); it shows the influence of many styles – Neo-Gothic for the chapel (1927) with lofty pinnacles, rose-windows and a spire, but functional for its other buildings. Guimard also designed no. 11 Rue François-Millet (1909), and the Hôtel Mezzara (1911) at no. 60. This has an almost Louis XV refinement with interiors by the architect. Permission to view the Hôtel Messara may be obtained from the Recteur of the Université de Paris. No. 65, the Studio Building, is a monumental group of buildings erected by Henri Sauvage (1928) exclusively as artists' studios. It was one of his last works, notable for the way in which the cold tones of Gentil and Bourdet's facing-tiles harmonize with the building. No. 85 was designed by Ernest Herscher 1905 and is an interesting example of Art Nouveau architecture. Herscher cared more for engraving than architecture, and designed few buildings, but another by him in the Rue Scheffer is just as noteworthy. The Villa Montmorency (12 Rue Poussin) stands where the Comtesse de Boufflers, the Prince de Conti's mistress, had a vast estate. André Gide lived in the Allée des Sycomores and the philosopher, Henri Bergson, in the Ave. des Tilleuls.

Avenue Mozart

Running from the Rue La Fontaine to the Rue Henri-Heine.

No. 122 is the mansion Hector Guimard built for himself with a studio for his wife, who was an artist. Finished in 1912, it demonstrates how Guimard was more concerned with surface decoration than with structure, and the way in which this architect enlivened his façades with bow-windows, corbels, etc. On the other side of the Villa Flore, is no. 120, a narrow house from Guimard's Art Déco period. Rue Henri-Heine is a fairly new street and in 1910 consisted of only one building. No. 30 is now a school by P. Abraham (1930); and no. 18 an Art Déco apartment block erected by Guimard in 1926, one of the last examples of Art Nouveau in a more severe style than its predecessors. The architect owned the building and kept an apartment here. It was his last residence in France before he departed for good to the USA in 1939.

Cross the Rue Jasmin where no. 10 marks the entrance to the Sq. Jasmin. No. 3 is a private house built by Guimard in 1922. Although unassuming, experimental methods were used to put it up in a few days, from prefabricated parts.

The Rue du Docteur-Blanche displays different styles by other architects. No. 19 was the property of the famous psychotherapist Dr Blanche, who died here in 1893. His son, the painter Jacques-Emile Blanche (d. 1942) also lived here.

To the l. at nos. 8 and 10 Sq. du Docteur-Blanche, is the L-shaped building, the Villas La Roche and Jeanneret* built by Le Corbusier in 1923. These two villas stand on *pilotis* (stilts) leaving the ground-floor open, with windows along their entire length. Their style is extremely spare and far ahead of their time; inside, ramps take the place of stairs. They now house the Fondation Le Corbusier, a documentation center for his work. (→Museums). On the r. pass the end of the Rue de l'Yvette in which the Musée Henri-Bouchard is located (→Museums). Mallet-Stevens built no. 9 in 1927.

Rue Mallet-Stevens*

The street is named after one of the boldest and most original architects (d. 1944) of the first half of the 20th c., who applied the principles of Cubism to architecture (→inset). Nos. 4, 6, 7, 10 and 12 are examples of his work. Like Le Corbusier or André Lurçat, Mallet-Stevens moved away from the exuberant undulations of Art Nouveau to severity and geometric shapes. These houses – mostly white and tiered – generally belong to artists. The Rue de L'Assomption has changed both in appearance and atmosphere in recent years with the erection of contemporary blocks of luxury apartments surrounded by ponds and gardens. No. 88, the Church of Notre-Dame-de-l'Assomption, was once the chapel of the Missionaires de la Miséricorde. This street leads back to the Maison de Radio-France.

▷ Hector Guimard, architect and designer (1868–1942)

Auteuil offers an ideal introduction to the work of Hector Guimard, for it was here that he developed the essence of his style.

His earliest work (34 Rue Boileau; 42 Rue Chardon-Lagache; 1 ter Rue Molitor; 7 Ave. de La Frillière, and 39 Boul. Exelmans) reveal him as the rival of Viollet-le-Duc, enraptured by color, complexity and mass but, as yet, showing no obvious spark of his true genius. This only burst forth with the completion in 1898 of the Castel Béranger, a transitional and intensely personal work, that brought Guimard into the limelight.

Except for the apartment buildings in the Ave. de Versailles, to find examples of his most exciting and personal work you have to go to the W suburbs of Paris, to Normandy and to Lille.

Here he devoted himself to building country houses at Garches, Sèvres, Le Vésinet, Hermanville, Cabourg, Auvers-sur-Oise and Villemoisson. Most of the buildings that he designed between 1899 and 1905 have either been demolished or altered beyond recognition, their aggressive originality running counter to the ideas of the 1950s and '60s. This is especially true of the extraordinary Salle Humbert de Romans, 60 Rue Saint-Didier (→Ave. Foch and the Dauphine district). His imaginative, original entrances for the Paris Métro, metal arches in extreme Art Nouveau shapes, are a direct result of his investigation into the practicalities of standardization of building parts (1899–1904). Porte Dauphine is a charming summer house, its stained glass evoking dragonfly wings (→Ave. Foch and the Dauphine district).

Mockery and then neglect made Guimard swiftly revise his style to make it more 'French', thus giving birth (1905–14) to those little gems, the Hôtels Guimard (Ave. Mozart) and Mezzara (Rue La Fontaine) as well as the apartment buildings on the Rue Agar and the Rue François-Millet.

This change can be seen in his furniture (displayed in the Musée des Arts Décoratifs, the Petit Palais and the Musée d'Orsay) and in his wrought ironwork, a field in which Guimard was an absolute master.

During the interwar years he tried to take his place in the Art Déco movement but his buildings in this style (120 Ave. Mozart, 18 Rue Henri-Heine, 3 Sq. Jasmin and 36–38 Rue Greuze) were badly received. It was a bitterly disappointed architect who left France in 1939 with his wife to settle in New York, where he died in obscurity.

▷ Castel Béranger: Apartments at moderate rents

To really appreciate this housing complex – three apartment blocks standing round a courtyard – it must be placed in the context of its period (1894–98). In those days the Rue La Fontaine was far from being the middle-class thoroughfare it is today. Far from it – the locality was undeveloped, the street unlit and unpaved. Small factories, workshops, sheds and warehouses stretched along it all interlocking with the water-borne traffic on the nearby Seine. The Paris had yet to be built and this was a genuine working-class suburb, distant from the city center and only barely affected by urban expansion. First and foremost the Castel Béranger is a modestly priced apartment building no matter how much its lavish decoration would seem to contradict this. The apparent contradiction is clarified when the cheapness of most of the building materials – gritstone, metal, glass bricks – is taken into account. By economizing on materials and using the site to its full advantage,

Guimard was able to spend more money on external decoration. But even here we should not be misled: the stained glass, balconies, sandstone tiling, mosaics and ironwork were all mass-produced in large quantities, which meant that individually their unit-price was little more than that of stock items.

Guimard designed everything – wallpaper, doorknobs, kitchen stoves – even the stair rods and fireplaces, and some of the furniture. To create all this (and it occupied him fully from 1895 to 1898) he had the advantage of an understanding client, Mme Fournier, a widow who, after her husband's death, gave Guimard a free hand. Her trust was not misplaced. The rents were moderate, but within five years Mme Fournier had recovered her investment.

Guimard was no loser, either; first a prize in the first Concours de Façades de la Ville de Paris, then the publication of a deluxe edition of his designs, an exhibition and a lecture, all of which were reviewed in the arts pages of Le Figaro. The apartment block was the turning point in his career. It made him famous and became, as it were, the manifesto of the Art Nouveau movement. Making his home there was like living in an advertisement for his own work.

▷ Le Corbusier and Mallet-Stevens in Auteuil

Auteuil had been the melting-pot of contemporary architecture during the Art Nouveau period and remained so for the Art Déco movement. Fringed by woodland, the district did not change during the 1920s and looked as it had 40 years before, so it is not surprising to find, within a few hundred yards of each other, the first important buildings erected by Le Corbusier in Paris, the Villas La Roche and Jeanneret (8 and 10 Sq du Docteur-Blanche: 1923) and the famous street which Mallet-Stevens divided into building plots between 1926 and 1927.

Up to that time the careers of these two architects had proceeded along very similar lines. Le Corbusier had built only a few villas in his home town of La Chaux-de-Fonds in French Switzerland, having spent much of his available time from 1907–1910 in the studios of the most avant-garde architects of the day such as Hoffmann, Perret, Behrens, Gropius and Mies Van der Rohe. Having completed his first work in France (the Atelier Ozenfant and a villa at Vaucresson, 1922) and his famous exhibition pavilion of the Esprit Nouveau at the Paris Arts Décoratifs exhibition of 1925, he designed these two villas as a kind of manifesto for a remarkably carefully planned and economical style of architecture.

Mallet-Stevens came to building comparatively late and his first villa – and earliest masterpiece – the Villa de Noailles at Hyères, dates from 1923. Having made his name with the Pavillon du Tourisme at the Arts Décoratifs exhibition, he undertook the important task of dividing the street which now bears his name, Impasse Mallet-

Stevens, into building plots. The most ambitious houses erected there were those for himself and his wife, and for the Martell brothers, sculptors with whom he frequently collaborated.

▷ Auteuil's markets

On the open space beside the Rue d'Auteuil, the Rue Donizetti and the Rue La Fontaine: Wed. and Sat., 7am–1.30pm. Rue Gros and Rue La Fontaine: Tues. and Fri., 7am–1.30pm. Place de la Porte-Molitor: Tues. and Fri., 7am–1.30pm. Ave. de Versailles (between Rue Le Marois and Rue Gadin: Tues., Thurs. and Sun., 7am–1.30pm).

▣ Museums to visit

Musée de Radio-France (116 Ave. du Président-Kennedy): history of sound broadcasting and display of recording studios of the Maison de la Radio.

Musée Henri Bouchard (25 Rue de l'Yvette): the sculptor Henri Bouchard's studio.

Fondation Le Corbusier (8–10 Square du Docteur-Blanche): temporary exhibitions of modern architecture in the two adjoining villas, La Roche and Jeanneret built by Le Corbusier.

L'autobus (the bus)

The bus, a fairly rapid form of transport despite the traffic, is undoubtedly one of the best ways to see Paris. Convenient and pleasant, it manages to take visitors from one place to another while giving them an opportunity to enjoy the city's atmosphere. But the bus can also be used simply for a pleasure trip, to discover the more remote tourist areas of the town.

The history of the bus

Parisian transport has always been an individual business. It used to be possible to get from one point to another along the town's narrow, muddy streets only on foot, by horse or by mule.

In 1662, on the initiative of the philosopher Pascal, the first vehicles designed for passenger transport appeared. Nicknamed the *carosses à cinq sols* (the coaches with five floors) these carriages were heavy and uncomfortable and could carry only eight people. Their success was somewhat ephemeral, since the venture collapsed in 1680. It was almost 150 years later before a second attempt was made. In 1828 the first omnibus company was set up in Paris (named after a hatter, N. Omnes, who had a shop where the vehicles stopped). Identical to the horse-drawn public carriages, the omnibuses carried a maximum of 20 travellers and announced their passage with the sound of a trumpet. This new means of transport, very popular with Parisians, developed rapidly. A number of companies were set up (the Gazelles, the Dames Réunies, the Hirondelles Parisiennes) each seeking to exploit the most well-travelled routes.

In 1855, the municipality of Paris combined the companies under the Compagnie Générale de Omnibus, for more regular and efficient service. Most of the routes that were used then correspond to today's bus routes. The vehicles were modernized: *une impériale* (or open platform) was installed under the roof of the omnibus. In 1856 the *chemin de fer americain* (American railway) was inaugurated. This strange vehicle was pulled by horses, but ran on rails from Boulogne to the Place de la Concorde, where the wheels were changed so that it could cross Paris like an ordinary horse-drawn carriage.

Until 1890 the only public transport in Paris was by horse-drawn trams or omnibuses. At that time these used about 14,000 horses. The arrival of the electric tramway and the *autobus* altered this situation completely. In 1905 an experimental automobile was put in service between Montmartre and Saint-Germain-des-Prés. This was a public horsedrawn carriage now fitted with a motor and rubber tyres. The bus, swift and easy to handle, replaced the tram, which disappeared for ever in 1937.

Today, the bus system, after a considerable drop in popularity in the 1970s, is rapidly expanding; in 1984 more than 755 million journeys were recorded, compared with only 500 million in 1973.

How to travel

The number of tickets required depends on the length of the journey: one ticket for one or two sectors, two beyond that. You can also buy a *carnet* (book) of ten tickets, each valid for one journey. Children under four travel free, those from four to ten for half-price.

A Formule 1 ticket allows unlimited travel for one day on all bus routes, Métro and RER. The Paris-Visite ticket is a short-term season ticket (2, 4, or 7 days) which also allows unlimited travel on all systems. Tickets are on sale in all Métro stations, except the Paris-Visite tickets, which can only be obtained from the major stations (Saint-Michel, Charles-de-Gaulle, Odéon, Bastille, Invalides, Châtelet, etc.).

Timetables

Most buses run from 6.30am to 9pm. Some buses run until 12.30am, while others run all night. A minimum service is available on certain routes on Sundays. Information can be found on bus shelters or in RATP information bureau.

General Information

Tickets and maps are available at all the RATP ticket offices in the Métro stations.

For all information on fares and routes tel: 43–46–14–14. The tourist brochure, *Paris Patchwork*, about discovering Paris by bus is available in the RATP offices: 53 *bis*, Quai des Grands-Augustins (6th arr.) and Place de la Madeleine, Marché aux fleurs (8th arr.).

Tour of Paris by bus

Departure: Place Charles-de-Gaulle-Etoile/1½hrs. to the Opéra; 2½hrs. to Montmartre.

This suggested route will give some insight into the extremely varied life of Paris. By crossing the effervescent district of the Champs-Elysées, the elegant residential Faubourg Saint-Germain and the youthfully cosmopolitan Latin Quarter, visitors will find themselves at the very heart of historical Paris. Return through the luxurious commercial Opéra district, via the Place de Clichy (very lively) in the evening to reach Montmartre. This district has kept the character of an old village set a little apart from the bustle of Paris. To avoid the traffic, make this trip in the morning or early afternoon.

From the Arc de Triomphe to the Musée d'Orsay

Catch the 73 bus opposite no. 135 Ave. Champs-Elyseés, which is 50m down on the r. side.

The Champs-Elysées

The avenue, laid out by Le Nôtre in 1670, was very fashionable during the Second Empire when it was the home of elegant society. Today the avenue has been overrun by cinemas, cafés and shopping arcades, but it is still a focal point for Parisian life. Beyond the roundabout to the S are the Grand Palais and the Petit Palais, built in a slightly pompous style for the International Exhibition of 1900. From here there is a very fine view of Les Invalides.

Place de la Concorde

The avenue runs into the Place de la Concorde, designed by Gabriel, who also built the *hôtels* with their remarkable colonnade (1757–1770) situated to the N. At the center stands the obelisk, given to Louis-Philippe by the Viceroy of Egypt in 1831. To the E the Jardin des Tuileries opens out, bordered by the pavilions of the Jeu de Paume and the Orangerie.

The Pont de la Concorde leads to the Palais-Bourbon, seat of the

Assemblée Nationale, whose Neo-Classical façade was erected during the Empire period. Leave the bus at the terminus, Rue de Solferino, in front of the Hôtel de Salm. Built in the Louis XVI style, it was reconstructed after a fire in 1871.

From the Musée d'Orsay to the Tour Eiffel

Take bus 69, which follows the quay on the r.: the bus stop is in front of the Musée d'Orsay (the Seine side).

▣ The Musée d'Orsay

The museum, which was inaugurated in 1986, is devoted to art of the second half of the 19th c. It occupies the old Gare d'Orsay, built by Laloux (1898–1900) for the International Exhibition. The 69 bus goes through the Saint-Germain district, which was very fashionable in the 18th c. Here there are beautiful mansions built between 1680 and 1730, now occupied by ministries or embassies.

After a detour via the Boul. Saint-Germain and the Rue du Bac, the bus goes through the narrow Rue de Grenelle, which is lined with fine houses, and then crosses the Esplanade des Invalides.

The Esplanade des Invalides

The Hôtel des Invalides, which lies to the S, was built by Libéral Bruant (1670–76) for soldiers wounded during the reign of Louis XIV, so that they would not have to beg in the streets. At the end, the Cupola of the Dôme des Invalides, the work of J. H. Mansart (1708), is visible. To the N there is a view of the Grand Palais. The bus stops at the Champ-de-Mars near the Eiffel Tower. This was designed by Gustave Eiffel for the International Exhibition of 1889. It offers a beautiful view of the Palais de Chaillot beyond the Seine and of the Ecole Militaire.

From the Tour Eiffel to the Ile Saint-Louis

Take the 87 bus, which stops opposite the 69 bus, but goes in the opposite direction. The bus travels along the Champ-de-Mars, the Ave. Duquesne and the Boul. des Invalides to the Rue de Sèvres, an important and busy shopping center which leads into Saint-Germain-des-Prés. The Romanesque church has been altered several times. It is one of the oldest in the capital.

The Latin Quarter

The Boul. Saint-Germain then crosses the Quartier Latin. At the corner of the Boul. Saint-Michel, on the N side, is the Musée de Cluny. This private *hôtel* was built at the end of the 15th c. on the ruins of the *Thermes gallo-romains* (Gallo-Roman Baths). From there the Boul. crosses the Place Maubert and passes the Church of Saint-Nicholas-du-Chardonnet (completed in the 17th c.) Leave the bus on the Ile Saint-Louis after it has crossed the Sully bridge (Pont-de-Sully-Quai-de Bethune stop).

From the Ile Saint-Louis to the Place Saint-Michel

Return to the Right Bank by recrossing the bridge and take the 24 bus. Quai Saint-Bernard opposite the Institut du Monde Arabe. The Quai de la Tournelle runs parallel to the Ile Saint-Louis, whose mostly 17th c. buildings have beautiful façades. On the other side of the quay small streets fan out, such as the Rue de Bièvre which dates from the Middle Ages.

Notre-Dame

Notre-Dame Cathedral, immediately recognizable by its high towers, was constructed on the Ile de la Cité between 1163 and 1330. It is a Gothic masterpiece, remarkable for the audacity of the flying buttresses of its apse. At the W end of the island is the Palais de Justice, much altered in the 19th c. Leave the bus after the Place Saint-Michel (Saint-Michel or Pont-Neuf stops) to catch the 27 bus which leaves from the same stop.

From the Place Saint-Michel to the Opéra

As it travels along the quays the bus passes the Pont-Neuf, the Hôtel de la Monnaie, built by D.- J. Antoine in 1771 in the typically sober style of the Louis XVI period, and the Palais de l'Institut, dominated by the dome of the Académie Française. Constructed in the second half of the 17th c., its recessed semicircular façade shows an Italian influence. The Pont du Carrousel leads to the Palais du Louvre.

The Louvre

The Louvre, once a royal palace, has become the greatest museum in Paris. Beginning in 1988 a huge glass pyramid has been built in the Cour Napoléon III. This symbol of modernism faces the Arc du Carrousel which commemorates the victories won by Napoleon in 1805. The gates of the Louvre lead out on to the Place Colette, which is dominated by the Théâtre de la Comédie-Française, and on to the Ave. de l'Opera with its fashionable shops. The Théâtre de l'Opéra hides the view of the avenue. The building is the work of

Charles Garnier (1861-75) and symbolizes the ostentation and eclecticism of the Second Empire.

From the Opéra to Montmartre

Bus 27 continues towards Montmartre, terminating at the Gare Saint-Lazare (58 Rue de l'Arcade). It goes through the district where most of the large department stores are. Go towards the station and take bus 80 in the Rue de Rome to the l. of the station. The bus goes to the Place de Clichy, a popular meeting place that is particularly lively in the evenings. The Rue Caulaincourt goes under the Montmartre cemetery then round the hill and deep into a busy section of Montmartre, unfamiliar to tourists, to the Place Jules-Joffrin terminus. From there the Montmartre bus goes to the foot of the basilica of the Sacré-Cœur, which was built in thanksgiving for prayers answered during the 1870 siege of Paris. There is a superb view of Paris and the suburbs.

Passing the tourist haunt of the Place du Tertre and the famous Cabaret du Lapin Agile, which was highly fashionable at the beginning of the 20th c., the bus arrives in the Place Pigalle. Return to the center of Paris by Métro bus 67 (to the Louvre) or 30 (to the Etoile and the Trocadéro).

Some bus routes

Bus 20 links the Place de la Bastille to the Opéra, going through the Place de la République and along the Grands Boulevards.

Bus 27 goes from the Luxembourg (7 Rue Gay-Lussac) to the Opéra, along the Boul. Saint-Michel and the Quai de Conti and across the courtyard to the Louvre.

Bus 29 goes through the Marais district between Beaubourg (35 Rue Rambuteau) and the Bastille.

Bus 42 goes round the Place de l'Opéra (9 Rue Scribe) to the Eiffel Tower, passing through the Place de la Concorde, along the Champs-Elysées and across the Place de l'Alma.

The 58 departs from the Hôtel de Ville (10 Rue Saint-Martin), crosses the Latin Quarter via the Rue Mazarine, the Odéon and the Luxembourg, and then rejoins Montparnasse (for a tour of Montparnasse, bus stop at 40 Ave. du Maine).

Bus 63 goes from the Latin Quarter to Passy: Odéon (opposite 25 Rue de l'Ecole-de-Médecine), Saint-Sulpice, Boul. Saint-Germain, Quai d'Orsay, Invalides, Place du Trocadéro, Porte de La Muette (terminus).

Bus 73 goes down the Champs-Elysées from the Arc de Triomphe (135 Ave. des Champs-Elysées), passes by the Place de la Concorde and stops at the Musée d'Orsay.

Bus 82 leaves the Luxembourg (Place Edmond-Rostand), crosses Montparnasse, skirts the Dôme de Invalides and the Ecole Militaire, goes along the Champ-de-Mars (Eiffel Tower) and crosses the Seine by the Pont d'Iéna to reach the Place du Trocadéro.

Bus 83 (double-decker bus) from the Champs-Elysées to the Observatoire: Rond-Point des Champs-Elysées, Quai d'Orsay, Boul. Saint-Germain, the Boul. Raspail and the Rue d'Assas, Boul. de Port-Royal (for the Observatoire, the bus stop at 134, Boul. de Port-Royal).

Bus 95 goes from the Gare Montparnasse (22 Place Raoul-Dautry) to Montmartre: Rue de Rennes, Saint-Germain-des-Prés, Pont du Carrousel, Opéra, Saint-Lazare, Place de Clichy, Rue Caulaincourt.

Some itineraries

The quays

Take the bus 72 at the Pont Mirabeau on the Right Bank (69 Ave. de Versailles) or walk from the Jardin du Trocadéro (opposite 58 Ave. de New York). Follow the Seine as far as the Hôtel de Ville terminus.

From there, cross the Ile de la Cité to the Right Bank where bus 24 (15 Quai des Grands-Augustins) rejoins the Place de la Concorde.

A tour round Paris

The 'petite ceinture' (PC) circles Paris (→ Boulevard des Maréchaux). It stops at all the Paris Portes.

From the Luxembourg to the Marché aux Puces de Saint-Ouen (Saint-Ouen flea market)

Take bus 85 (31 Boul. Saint-Michel) which crosses Paris in a N–S direction, over the Ile de la Cité, by the Louvre and along the Faubourg Montmartre. Get off at the Michelet-Rosiers stop, Ave. de la Porte-de-Clignancourt.

From the Pont Neuf to La Villette

Catch bus 75 (1 Rue de la Monnaie), at the corner of the Samaritaine store which goes to the Cité de la Villette via the Saint-Martin canal and the Buttes-Chaumont. Get off at the terminus, Porte de Pantin.

Belleville and Ménilmontant

Bus 96, which leaves from Saint-Germain-des-Prés (147 Boul. Saint-Germain), goes through the Marais and along the Rue de Ménilmontant as far as the Porte des Lilas (terminus).

From the Eiffel Tower to Père-Lachaise

Bus 69 departs from the Champ-de-Mars (Ave. Joseph-Bouvard), goes along the Rue Saint-Dominique, past the Louvre and the Bastille to reach Père-Lachaise cemetery.

The Bastille district

4th, 11th, 12th arr./Map ref. 18–D2
Métro: Bastille
Bus: 20, 29, 65, 69, 76, 86, 87, 91
Parking: Place de la Bastille between Boul. de la Bastille and the Boul. Bourdon
Taxis: 6 Place de la Bastille. Tel: 43–45–10–00
Market: Boul. Richard-Lenoir, from the Rue Amelot to the Rue Saint-Sabin, Thurs., Sun. 7am–1.30pm.

Steeped in revolutionary history, the Place de la Bastille is still the scene of numerous political and trade union demonstrations. Of a slightly less aggressive nature are the groups of motorcyclists from the Paris area who gather there every Friday evening.

Today the Place de la Bastille is a large, busy and sprawling crossroads. It still marks the border between the heart of Paris and the suburbs. In fact, the atmosphere of the district on the W of the square is considerably different from that on the E. On one side there is the Marais, with its stately, discreet houses. On the other are the busier and more boisterous suburbs. The building of the vast new Opera House has radically altered the balance and appearance of the square to the SE. The atmosphere and character of this traditionally working-class neighbourhood has been transformed by the intrusion of this monumental cultural institution.

The history of the Bastille

The old route from the citadel to the present site of the square used to form part of the old Roman way to Meaux. The Abbaye Saint-

Antoine was also on this route, so it was natural that the gate in the Philippe Auguste perimeter wall that guarded the road should be called Porte Saint-Antoine. The abbey was financed by the rich Parisian landowners who had established themselves in great houses on both sides of the road to Meaux. In the 14th c. when Etienne Marcel, the *prévôt des marchands* (provost marshal) fortified the city, the Porte Saint-Antoine was flanked by two large towers. Later, Charles V strengthened Etienne Marcel's fortifications even more. The work was directed by Hugues Aubriot, who put up huge blockhouses where the boundary wall crossed the road to the Abbaye Saint-Antoine. Since it was close to the Hôtel Saint-Pol, the Porte Saint-Antoine was also reinforced by two additional towers. One of these was situated on the rising ground where no. 1 Rue Saint-Antoine now stands. The group of fortifications to the E of the town formed a solid fortress. This was the Bastille which, until its destruction, underwent few alterations. During the English occupation, the garrison was captured. It was commanded by a certain John Falstolf, who was to be immortalized by Shakespeare in the character of Falstaff. Some years later, on August 4 and again on September 22, 1464, Louis XI turned the cannons of the Bastille on the men of the *Téméraire*. But it was this king who turned the Bastille into a State prison. Cardinal de la Balue and Guillaume de Haraucourt were among the first prisoners. After them came Philippe de Commynes and Jacques d'Armagnac. History, however, relates that the Bastille's first prisoner was Hugues Aubriot, who had worked on its construction.

A famous prison

The Wars of Religion sent numerous prisoners to the Bastille, among others the famous potter, Bernard Palissy, then over 78 years old. He died two years later in 1590. In 1601 Maxmilien de Béthune, Duc de Sully, already Grand Master of the Artillery at the Arsenal, became commander of the Bastille. Under Richelieu, the old fortress became a state prison for whoever dared oppose royal power. An order simply bearing the king's seal could send a miscreant behind the high walls for an unspecified length of time. At the beginning of 1649, having received no reinforcements, the governor, Du Tremblay, surrendered to the rabble with his 25 soldiers. He then handed the Bastille over to La Grande Mademoiselle, who, in order to protect Condé, turned the cannons on what is now the Faubourg Saint-Antoine.

Fouquet was closely guarded there by d'Artagnan. A nobleman called Rohan, who had the idea of surrendering the town of Quilleboeuf in Normandy to the Dutch, was also imprisoned there. He had a servant with him, an adventurer known as the Man in the Iron Mask; his mask was, in fact, made of velvet. The scant attention paid to the Man in the Iron Mask during his imprisonment indicates that he was not anyone of great importance.

During the 18th c. the Bastille had some famous residents: Voltaire (twice), Marmontel, Lally-Tollendal, the Marquis de Sade, the celebrated Latude and many more. Some prisoners who had contacts and sufficient money could even invite guests if they wished. Some of them kept open house and were renowned for their fine hospitality. One of the towers was even known as the Tour de la Liberté. But the unknown and less fortunate could lie forgotten in the dungeons where they might drown in the flood waters of the Seine. By 1784 the Bastille was scarcely used and there was talk of its being demolished. But it remained there, the symbol of royal high-handedness, where a simple sealed order could incarcerate anyone who fell out of favor with the monarch. For this reason the Bastille became a target for destruction during the revolutionary days of July 1789. At the end of November all that remained of it were a few sections of wall.

Pierre François Palloy, the contractor who directed the demolition, was a good businessman. He had models and reproductions of the Bastille made from the stones of the fortress, which he sent to the mayors of the revolutionary communes. Napoleon had the idea of erecting a huge fountain in the new square in the form of an elephant. During the Restoration, the plaster model of the elephant was placed at the side of the present Gare de Vincennes. Victor Hugo made it famous in *Les Misérables*, by having Gavroche shelter inside the model. The plaster cast was demolished in 1846, but the pedestal, by the architect Alavoine, still remains. It now supports the Bastille column.

Tour of the district

30 mins.

The Place de la Bastille is one vast crossroads from which radiate numerous arterial roads.

▷ July 14, 1789

For several days troops had been mustering around Paris, increasing the tension among the citizens. On July 11 the popular minister, Necker, returned and the people of Paris reacted immediately by obtaining arms and organizing themselves. On the morning of July 14, the mob made its way to the Invalides and then to the Arsenal to steal arms from the military depôts. Soon after the rioters marched on the Bastille, but were stopped at the walls by the Swiss guard. At above five in the afternoon, the assailants returned accompanied by French guards who had rejoined the insurrection. With the general confusion and the impossibility of knowing where everyone was, Launay, governor of the fortress, which was garrisoned with only 32 Swiss guards and 82 *invalides* (wounded soliders), would have been wise to surrender. Instead the Bastille was overrun and its defenders massacred. The seven people (among whom was a madman) still imprisoned there received a triumphant ovation. This highly symbolic feat, so easily accomplished, had an immediate effect everywhere, which showed how popular political initiative in the capital could affect the whole country.

The remains of the fortress

A line of stones – in front of no. 5 in the Place de la Bastille, and more noticeably in front of no. 49 Boul. Henri-IV, shows traces of the old towers and fortified walls of the Bastille. The fortress was situated where the houses now stand and the square marks the old site of the bastion which extended in a point towards the Faubourg (see map of the Bastille on a marble plaque affixed to no. 3 Place de la Bastille). On the platform in the Métro station (line 5, Pantin direction) there is an inscription marking the old outer boundary of the Bastille's eastern moat. It is also known that some fragments of the Tour de la Liberté were taken to the Square Henri-Galli by the Pont Sully, and that the Bastille clock, which stopped on July 14 1789, suffered many misfortunes before it was finally recovered and put on display in the Restaurant du Carillon de la Bastille.

The Bastille or July column*

Entrance fee. Open daily except Tues., 10am– 4, 5 or 6pm, depending on the season.

The column stands in the center of the square. On March 9 1833, the Chambre des Députés decreed that a monument should be erected to commemorate the victims of the July Revolution. In 1840 the bodies were transferred to its underground vaults. The dead of the 1848 revolution were then also brought to the vaults. The column is 154ft (47m) high, 169ft (51.50m): if the Genie de la Liberté which surmounts it is included - a gilded bronze figure, designed by Dumont - it weighs 174 tonnes. A staircase of 238 steps leads to the upper gallery from where there is a magnificent view. The pedestal is the work of Alavoine. The column rests on a circular base of white marble, upon which is a square plinth. The sides are decorated with 24 symbolic bronze medallions. On the W face, a bronze lion by Barye symbolizes the July insurrection. On the E side are the arms of Paris. The shaft of the bronze column, is divided into five drums which bear the names of the victims in gold letters.

Boulevard Richard-Lenoir

Situated to the N of the square, the old Boul. de la Reine-Hortense now bears the names of the engineers Richard and Lenoir, who set up the district's first cotton factories. This lovely boulevard, under which flows the Saint-Martin canal, used to be known for its ham fairs (in autumn and on Palm Sundays) and scrap iron markets (in spring).

The *foire à la ferraille* (scrap iron fair), founded in 1222 with a charter by Philippe Auguste, was originally held in the square in front of Notre-Dame. During the 19th c. its location changed several times. It is now one of the main secondhand markets where knickknacks and all kinds of antiques can be found alongside the scrap iron. When it began to disrupt the traffic, this traditional event was transferred to Nogent-sur-Marne and the Ile de Chatou.

The Bastille Opéra*

To the SE, between the Rue de Lyon and the Rue de Charenton lay the old Gare de Vincennes or Gare de la Bastille. These buildings were demolished in 1985 to make way for a gigantic construction site for a new opera house.

The Bastille not only forms the link between two important events in the history of Paris, but also between two of the city's distinct geographical areas. It is where crowds gather at festivals or assemble to demonstrate. So it was natural that the Bastille should seem the perfect symbolic choice for the new 'popular Opéra', designed to replace the Opéra Garnier (→see Opéra). Plans for the new Opéra were announced on March 8, 1982, and an international competition was launched in February 1983. The design problem was draconian. Fitting such large volumes into a site shaped like an elongated triangle presented a considerable challenge. The building had to house not only a large hall with 2700 seats and five movable stages (as well as others 53ft/16m below them) to permit quick changes of scenery; but a rehearsal theater, a modular hall of 600 to 1300 seats, scenery and set scenery workshop, shops and a *Maison de l'Opéra* containing library, record and video libraries. There were 756 responses to the Mission-Opéra competition. A design by Carlos Ott, who was among those who paid most scrupulous attention to the stipulations of the competition and to the constraints of the site, won the competition in 1983. Unlike others, who redrew the open space of the Place de la Bastille, he designed his scheme as an architectural entity. His design, despite its height (92ft/28m), took into account the existing urban structure by leaving the Rue de Lyon and its groups of houses untouched. In this scheme, the architect tackled each of the major sections separately by using simple forms: semicylinders, parallelepipeds (three-dimensional forms based on a parallelogram) and porticoes.

The façade is transparent in order to establish a *dialogue entre l'intérieur et l'extérieur* (rapport between interior and exterior). The political upheavals of March 1986 postponed the project. However, construction was resumed, except on the scenery workshop, which was abandoned indefinitely. The large hall containing 2700 seats *à la vocation musicale, chorégraphique et lyrique* (devoted to music, choreography and opera) has been constructed complete with its complex scenic mechanisms. However, only the shell of the modular hall will be built.

The Opera House was inaugurated by a concert on July 14 1989.

The viaduct

A little further away in the Rue de Lyon the viaduct of the old Vincennes railway can be seen. It stretches along the Ave. Daumesnil as far as the Gare de Reuilly. It was built in the mid-19th c. when trains were unable to run underground because, not being electric, they gave off too much smoke. As space is limited in this populous district, the viaduct will surely be re-used. It has been suggested that the area under the viaduct could be used for housing and shops. A long terraced garden and a path for cyclists will be built on the site of the disused tracks.

The Batignolles district

17th arr./Map ref. 3–B2; 4–C2
Métro: Villiers
Bus: 31, 30
Taxis: 17th arr. town hall. Tel: 43–87–00–00.
Parking: FNAC, 22, Ave. de Wagram: Métro Brochant. Tel: 46–27–00–00.
Markets: 96, Rue Lemercier (open daily 8am–12.30pm and 4–7.30pm, Sun. 8am–12.30pm); Rues Navier, Lantiez and des Spinettes (Tues. and Fri. 7am–1.30pm).

In this district of Paris there was no open country, no woods, no vines, only arid land which for many years had been used for military manoeuvres. During the Restoration a certain social class began to build two- or three-storey houses here. They were largely pensioners, semi-retired officers on half pay, businessmen, Polish and Russian exiles, and officials.

Today it is one of the few districts that has kept its character and its own way of life. It is home to a social group that is not usually associated with Parisian buildings dating from the 17th c. These people do not belong to the aristocracy from around the Parc Monceau, nor to the bourgeoisie of the Ternes, but to a petite bourgeoisie which has scarcely changed in 150 years.

The parish church of Batignolles still seems to mark the center of a big village, with its square, market, town hall and public gardens. Behind the church, the Square des Batignolles, one of the most picturesque in Paris, borders the railway cutting where the sight of passing trains still continues to fascinate small boys. A little further on, the Rue Lemercier, which lies in a populous and busy area, is the site of one of the last great covered markets built in the 19th c. Beyond the boisterous and colourful Ave. de Clichy, the roads which lead to the Square des Epinettes are less attractive. Nonetheless, the charming Cité des Fleurs with its gardens and trees has miraculously preserved its rustic character.

Tour of the district

1 hr.

Rue de Lévis

This was an ancient Roman road which followed the route from Paris to Argenteuil. It passed by the Château de Monceaux, home of the Lévis. (In the 17th c. a Maréchal Duc de Lévis side by side with the Duc de Lévis Mirepois defended Canada against the English). In the 19th c. it was a popular working-class street. At no. 8 important political gatherings were held in the meeting rooms. As many as 5000 people would sometimes come to hear Ledru-Rollin, Barbès, Blanqui, Gambetta, Louise Michel (who lived at 88 Boul. des Batignolles) or Victor Hugo. Today the political clamour is silenced and the Rue de Lévis is essentially commercial. Shops line this extremely lively street, a pedestrian precinct with a permanent and picturesque market. The Rue Cardinet, like the Rue Legendre, which runs parallel to it, extends a long way to the NE. Beyond the Pont Cardinet are the workshops and the SNCF cargo stations, which occupy the vast areas bounded by the railway tracks, the Boul. Berthier and the Ave. de Clichy. It is better to follow the Rue Legendre. No. 27 was designed by J. Sauvage in 1928. In the Rue Boursault, nos. 62 and 68 are fine examples of Art Nouveau architecture. No. 62, designed by R. Simonet (1901), was re-faced in sandstone by Bigot. It is without doubt the first example of the integration of a bow window with a façade. The adjoining house is also unusual; it is one of the narrowest in Paris. Rejoin the Rue Legendre near the Church of Sainte-Marie-des-Batignolles (1828) and the Square des Batignolles (→ inset). Avenue de Clichy. This tree-shaded avenue, with its many shops, was portrayed many times by artists between the two World Wars. Marcoussis and Fontanarosa, among others, had their studios here. Turn r. towards La Fourche crossroads where the Ave. de Saint-Ouen branches off.

The Church of Saint-Michel-des-Batignolles

12 bis, Rue Saint-Jean (closed noon–2pm; tel: 43–87–33–94).

The present church, begun in 1913 by Bernard Haubold, was consecrated in 1942 before it had been completed. It is built of concrete, with a brick covering which is unusual for Paris. The ground plan consists of three parallel naves separated by two narrow side aisles; each nave has uncovered roof timbers; the arches bordering the naves and the rows of columns supporting the arches give the interior a picturesque effect. On top of the bell-tower stands St Michael, designed by Emmanuel Frémiet; at the end of the l. side-aisle is the *Naissance de la Vierge* (Birth of the Virgin), by Jeronimo Jacinto de Espinosa (mid-17th c.).

Return to the avenue, which leads to Clichy. Cross the Rue Brochant along which runs the Batignolles market.

The Epinette district

This densely populated district extends N as far as the Ave. de Clichy and the Rue Guy-Moquet. Continue along the Cité des Fleurs (→inset). At the crossing with the Rue Jonquière is the Church of Saint-Joseph-des-Epinettes (40 Rue Pouchet). This church was constructed in 1910, but in the Neo-Byzantine style. Its underground chapel with accordion-like concrete folds gives it the dated air of revival-style architecture. Take the Rue Jonquière in the direction of the Square des Epinettes (→inset).

▷ The green spaces of the 17th arrondissement

Although the Park Monceau is the district's largest and most famous garden, there are other oases of green. These are the garden squares and private driveways of pretty houses. The leafy shade of their trees – some of them over 100 years old – give the district a delightful relaxed air.

 The Square des Batignolles, Place Charles-Fillion, is one of the largest and most picturesque of the 24 garden squares of Paris. It was designed by Alphand on the orders of Haussmann. It is 16,650m^2 in area and has the charm of an English garden, with its grotto, waterfall, stream and miniature lake.

Cité des Fleurs, which was built in 1847, lies between the Ave. de Clichy and the Rue de la Jonquière. To help create a peaceful country atmosphere an ordinance decreed that each house should have three fruit trees in its front garden. The Square des Epinettes was laid out in the late 19th c. The Rue Maria-Deraismes was redeveloped in 1980 and children's play areas added. It is decorated with a sculpture by Dalou and a statue of the feminist, Maria Deraismes (1829–94), by Barrias. Since 1954 the Square de l'Amérique Latin, Porte Champerret, has been popular with children because of its play areas. To round out this 'green walk', visit the Villa des Ternes (→Ternes) at no. 96 Ave. des Ternes, which comprises charming houses surrounded by gardens.

▷ **The Batignolles poets**

Paul Verlaine's family was one of the many petite bourgeoisie who settled here after 1915. The future poet of the *Poèmes Saturniens* and *Fêtes Galantes* spent his childhood at 45 Rue Lemercier, then at 25 Rue Jean-Leclaine, and went to the Lycée Chaptal. Stephane Mallarmé lived at 89 Boul. des Batignolles. Here, for several years, he used to gather his friends and disciples together for his famous 'Tuesdays', lectures whose influence on contemporary poetry was considerable. Finally, 52 Rue Nollet was where Max Jacob lived.

The Beaubourg district**

3rd, 4th arr./Map ref. 17–B1, B2
Métro: Hôtel-de-Ville, Châtelet (RER), Rambuteau
Bus: 21, 38, 47, 58, 67, 70, 72, 74, 75, 76, 81, 85, 96
Parking: Rue Lobau, Rue Beaubourg
Taxis: Place du Châtelet, opposite 12 Ave. Victoria. Tel. 42–33–20–99

The avant-garde architecture and brilliant colors of the Pompidou Center should not make us forget that it has been built in one of the oldest districts of Paris, which still has very fine 17th and 18th c. buildings and, in the Rue Montmorency, what is believed to be the capital's oldest house. In the narrow streets for pedestrians only that have been recently refurbished around the Saint-Merri church, there are still façades of great elegance, often built on medieval foundations. But these historical surroundings are not frozen in the past. The Horloge district, an entirely new housing development, has been built in a pedestrian-only area.

The success of the development is not entirely certain, but it is an interesting experiment. A little further, in the Rue Beauborg and the Rue Etienne-Marcel, there are several luggage and hat shops and woollen goods wholesalers.

The picturesqueness of the district and the proximity of the Pompidou Center have attracted art galleries and fashion boutiques. The success of the whole venture shows in the throngs of tourists, sandwich sellers and postcard vendors. The crowds are thickest in the streets leading to the Pompidou Center and the piazza in front of it, where the casual stroller who can tolerate the crush can while away an hour or two listening to street musicians or watching jugglers, magicians, fire eaters and fakirs.

History of the district

In the 11th c. the *Beau Bourg* was a charming village surrounded by vineyards where the Parisian bourgeoisie came to take the country air. The construction of Philippe-Auguste's perimeter wall brought it within Paris and the Rue Beaubourg was its main street. The development of the district began between the Rue Saint-Martin and the Rue du Temple and in particular around the Saint-Merri church. The residents were mostly clothing workers, but there were also carters, carpenters, coopers, and others. The Rue Saint-Martin, a broad winding street, attracted troubadours, poets and musicians. From the 13th c., monasteries and charitable institutions were established to the E of the Rue Beaubourg and the great families traditionally associated with the district, like the Montmorencys and the Beauvilliers, built fine *hôtels* here. When the new Saint-Merri church was built in the 16th c., the medieval houses gradually gave way to the private mansions, or *hôtels*, of the new nobility, who lived here in peace until the French Revolution.

The construction of the Rue Rambuteau and the extension of the Rue Beaubourg, begun during the July Monarchy and continued under the Second Empire, greatly changed the district which, despite these developments, was gradually abandoned. In 1934 many of its large houses were demolished. Today, having been included in the development plan for the Halles district, it is enjoying a new lease of life, especially in the cultural sense, thanks to the Pompidou Center.

Tour of the district

1½ hrs.

Rue Saint-Martin

From the Rue de Rivoli to the Rue Rambuteau.

This is the second oldest street in Paris, after the Rue Saint-Jacques. In the city's early history it was only a track that ran parallel to the Roman road leading from Senlis to Orléans. Later it became the pilgrims' way to St Martin's tomb in Tours, running along the route originally taken by St James of Compostela. It has also been called the Rue Royale-Saint-Martin and, during the Revolution, the Rue de la Fraternité.

This street, stretching from the Pont Notré-Dame to the Porte Saint-Martin, is a pedestrian mall from the Rue de Rivoli as far as the Rue Rambuteau. In this area the Beaubourg Center has inspired changes: the resurfacing, repainting and restoring of buildings, the opening of many art galleries, and the disappearance of prostitution.

A sculpture by J. Lipchitz (1931), *Le Champ de Voyelles,* marks the crossroads of the Rue des Lombards and the Rue de la Verrerie (→below) Gérard de Nerval, who lived and died in the district, spent his childhood at no. 72 (→Châtelet).

⚓ Church of Saint-Merri**

78 Rue Saint-Martin, or 76 Rue de la Verrerie. 9am–7pm. Tel: 42–71–93-93

History of the building

This shrine dates back to the 7th c. In about 700, St Médéric, the Abbot of Saint-Martin d'Autun, was buried here with great ceremony. In the 9th c. his name, contracted to Merri, was given to a chapel built on the site of a shrine dedicated to Saint-Pierre-aux-Bois. The church was rebuilt in 1220 (the choir stood on the site of the present transept) and again in the 16th c. in the Flamboyant Gothic style. Work began on the nave, which was finished in 1520; the choir, completed in 1552, was given a rood screen. The Gothic tower, to the r., was finished in the style of the 16th c. in 1612. In the 18th c., the interior décor was changed to reflect contemporary taste, and the rood loft and choir-screen demolished. It is one of the most interesting examples of conversion of a Gothic structure to the Baroque style (→inset), and it gives us an idea of how the choir of Notre-Dame looked in the 18th c. On the site of the former

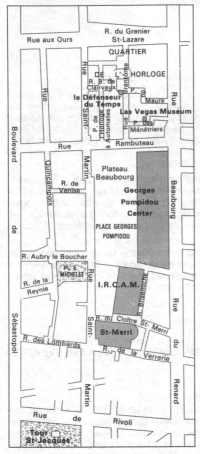

The Beaubourg district

charnelhouses (r. side of the church), Boffrand built a hugh chapel in 1742, decorated in 1748 by Paul-Ambroise Slodtz. Finally, in 1752, it was decided to redecorate the choir and the work was done by Michel-Ange Slodtz; at the same time part of the 16th-c. stained-glass was replaced by clear glass. A gate in the Classical style was also planned, but funds were not available.

The church was closed in 1793 and became first a saltpeter factory, then the Temple du Commerce. (It had been the parish church of the Lombard money lenders.) Restoration was carried out in the 19th c.; the statues on the façade that had been destroyed in the Revolution were replaced in 1842. At that time and later, at the beginning of the Third Republic, the City of Paris had the chapels around the choir decorated by various artists, including Chassériau.

The exterior

Though partly mutilated, the façade retains a richness of decoration with many pinnacles, blind arcades and sculpted friezes. The statues of the central door was remade in 1842 by Brun and Desprez; the statuettes under the coving were copied from those of the S door of the transept of Notre-Dame. To the l. of the façade is a small turret surmounted by a bell-tower that houses the oldest bell in Paris: *La Merry* (1331).

The interior

A jewel of the Flamboyant Gothic style, this church still has its rich furnishings.

The nave. On the organ-chest*, built in 1647 by the master joiner Germain Pilon, two large figures of angels support the side turrets. The gallery was remade in 1755 by the Slodtz brothers. Saint-Saëns was organist at Saint-Merri in 1853. Norbert Dufourcq is the present incumbent, but the instrument is now almost unplayable and its restoration is being considered. The pulpit, by the Slodtz brothers (mid-18th c.) is supported by two carved palm trees. Until the Revolution it was surmounted by a figure symbolizing Religion, now replaced by a colored plaster angel. Fragments of stained-glass windows depict, on the r., starting near to the organ: St Nicholas, St Agnes, St Francis of Assisi, St Anne, St Joachim and the Virgin, and on the l., St Mary Magdalene, Christ's Miracles, St John the Baptist.

On the r. is a double side-aisle and the communion chapel. In the embrasures of the arcades opening on to the communion chapel are depicted four episodes from the life of St Bruno (French school, 17th c.). The communion chapel was built as an annex by Boffrand in 1744, with three bays lit by oval lanterns. On the walls to l. and r. are two bas-reliefs by Paul-Ambroise Slodtz (1758). Above the altar is *The Pilgrims at Emmaus* by C. Coypel (18th c.); to the r., *St Charles Borromeo giving Communion to the Plague-stricken* by Colson (1819); to the l. *The Vision of St John Chrysostom* by Péron (1819).

In the r. arm of the transept, to the l. of the door that opens on to the Rue de la Verrerie, is a painting, *Christ and the Woman of Samaria*, attributed to Noël Coypel (17th c.). Above the altar, *St Peter*, by Vien (1754).

The choir. The two small altars at the entrance to the choir were each decorated with a painting commissioned from Carle Van Loo in 1753: on the r., *The Virgin and the Infant Jesus*; the one on the l. was stolen in 1970 and replaced by a painting of 1818 by Ménageot. The choir, Gothic in structure, was altered in 1752 by Michel-Ange Slodtz: the pillars and arcades were covered with applied marble stucco; the paving is colored marble. At the end of the apse is a large *Christ in Glory* in gilt wood by Slodtz. The stained-glass windows in the first three bays are 16th c.; those of the apse are by Lavergna (1866). Most of the chapels were decorated with murals in the 19th c. The first commissions, given during the July Monarchy, were for the chapels on the N side, those on the S side having been decorated after 1870. In the 2nd chapel: *The Life of St Joseph,* by Lafon (1870), 3rd chapel: *The Life of St Denis,* by Henri Lévy (1878). 5th chapel: *The Life of St Francis Xavier,* by Glaize (1878), was, at the end of the chapel on the l., *St Peter at Prayer* (early 17th c.) and on the r., *Crucifixion of St Peter* (18th c.), and between the two paintings, a *Virgin* sculpted by Vassé (18th c.). 6th chapel: *The Life of St James,* by Matout (1872–77); 7th chapel (axial), to the l., *Annunication,* and to the r., a *Pietà* by Collin du Vermont (18th c.); 9th chapel: decorations by Henri Lehmann; 10th chapel: *The Life of St Philomena,* by Amaury-Duval; 11th chapel: *The Life of St Mary the Egyptian,* by Chassériau; 12th chapel: *The Life of St Vincent de Paul,* by Lepaulle; 13th chapel: *The Life of St Marie de l'Incarnation,* by S. Cornu; l.-hand arm of the transept, on the back wall, *Découverte de la Profanation des Saintes Hosties* (Discovery of the Profanation of the Host, at Saint-Merri in 1723), by Clément Belle (18th c.). Above the altar, *St Merri delivering the Prisoners**, by Simon Vouet (17th c.).

L.-hand side-aisle and its chapels. 1st chapel: *Holy Family* after Raphael. 3rd chapel: on the altar, *Pietà* attributed to Nicolas Legendre. 5th chapel: entrance to the crypt rebuilt in 1515, restored in the 19th c.; the roof is a ribbed vault supported on a central pillar.

Rue Saint-Martin, continued

Almost opposite the church, there is a 17th c. bas-relief on the wall of no. 89, the Maison de l'Annonciation; the staircase dates from the same period. No. 113 is the house where the chemist Marcelin Berthelot lived. Turn around and walk along the N side of the church.

Rue du Cloître-Saint-Merri

Built over the gardens of the cloisters, this street is now completely renovated and has some pretty balconies. The N wall of the Saint-Merri church has rich Flamboyant Gothic decoration and picturesque gargoyles. To the l. there is a view of the Pompidou Center (→ Museums). Parts of the Center occupied by the IRCAM (The Institute for Musical Acoustic Research and Coordination), are underground beneath the Place Igor-Stravinsky and its fountain*. The latter, the largest fountain built in Paris since the one at the Trocadéro in 1937, is decorated with animated sculptures by Jean Tinguely and Niki de Saint-Phalle that celebrate the composer and his works.

The Rue de la Verrerie. Continue along the S side of the church which is on this street; the transept, however, is hidden by the beautiful presbytery* (1730). Another entrance to the church, at no. 76, has an 18th-c. portal. Opposite are several old houses at nos. 79, 85, 87, 91 and 93. Eugène Labiche died in no. 67.

Rue des Lombards

As the name suggests, this street was once the realm of Lombard money changers and Italian bankers, and tradition has it that Boccaccio was born here in 1313. At no. 10 is the Théâtre Le Tintamare. The buildings on this street have also been renovated and certain mansions show to advantage: at no. 14, a mediocre façade, but three remarkable floors of medieval cellars; note also the façades of nos. 17 and 22; at no. 62, a large vaulted hall is certainly the last trace of the church of Saint-Agnes; the house at no. 67 retains fine vaulted cellars.

The Rue Nicolas-Flamel, with its steep slope, shows how much levelling had to be done for the laying out of the Rue de Rivoli.

Rue Quincampois*

In the 18th c. the Rue Quincampois was a very elegant street. Finely dressed ladies and high financiers crowded around the doors of the Hôtel de Beaufort, no. 65 today. There, in 1716, the Scots financier John Law founded his Banque Générale authorized by Philippe, Duc d'Orléans. Speculation was rife, fortunes were made overnight and a hunchback made himself 150,000 livres by letting people use his hump as a desk to sign away their money. By 1720 John Law and thousands of others were ruined. Today, after the refurbishing and restoration of its *hôtels*, the tall balconied façades, the *portes-cochères* with their ostentatious sculpture and ironworks, the ornamental keystones in the arches, make this one of the most interesting streets to visit.

At nos. 2-4, a large Gothic house, altered in the 17th c. At no. 12, a fine example of Louis XIII architecture with chamfered bossages; 17th and 18th c. (wrought ironwork). The house at no. 13 probably dates from the last years of the 16th c. No. 14 retains a very beautiful façade (wrought ironwork) and a *porte-cochère* with a sculpted motif of musical instruments. At no. 22, the fine gate of the *marchandes-lingères* (linen drapers, 1716), originally in the Place Sainte-Opportune, has recently been reused in the reconstruction of the building. Cross the Rue de La Reynie and the Rue Aubry-le-Boucher, greatly shortened and widened when the district was rebuilt; they are in effect a western extension of the Beaubourg Center's piazza.

Rue Quincampois*, continued

After no. 27 comes the sham façade built by Fabio Rieli to hide the ventilation vent of the street underpass; 'animated' *trompe-l'oeil* windows have been painted on the concrete. Nothing remains of the Passage Jabach, where the celebrated financier and art-lover of that name had his mansion; his collection of pictures, bought by Colbert, remains one of the treasures of the Louvre. The beautiful house at no. 36 is said to have belonged to relatives of the Poquelin-Molière family; it still has its painted ceilings and vaulted cellars with thick, round pillars with geometric capitals, but unfortunately these are not on display to the public. At no. 58, the Hôtel de Sémonville has exceptionally tall and wide windows, as well as painted ceilings (ca. 1660). Note also nos. 60 and 62. The Rue Quincampois ends at the Rue aux Ours ('street of goose roasters', from a corruption of the word for geese, 'oies'), which is given over to wholesale trading. At nos. 82–84, landmark remains of the Théâtre Molière, founded in 1791.

Rue de Venise

Turn back to this street which emerges at the piazza in front of the transparent façade of the Beaubourg Center. At the corner of the Rue Saint-Martin, a bas-relief depicts a boat in full sail on one side and water birds on the other. The Fontaine Maubuée (18th c.) has been rebuilt here; it and its predecessors (from 1320 onwards) stood on the site now occupied by the center.

▣ Le Centre Georges-Pompidou (Pompidou Center)**

Commonly known as the Beaubourg Center, this museum was conceived by President Pompidou in 1969, with construction continuing from 1972 until the official inauguration on January 31, 1977. The design competition attracted 681 proposals, nearly 500 of them from outside France. The winning design was proposed by Renzo Piano and Richard Rogers, in association with Gianfrancò Franchini, John Young and Ove Arup & Partners.

The building occupies well over a million sq ft/103,000m², but only 650,000 sq ft/60,000m² are used. It is 545ft/166m long, 197ft/60m wide and 138ft/42m high. After the initial shock, you come to accept this enormous vessel, all funnels, which seems to have berthed at the wrong port. The funnels are there because one of the overriding ideas was to place outside the building everything that, inside, would hamper the use of space,which was to be as vast and flexible as possible. The result is that the escalators are presented like architectural gangways, and the technical services ducts look like drapes hung at practicable windows on a stage. The superstructure is composed of long-span beams resting, without any intermediate support, on the two vertical service sections reserved, on the W side, for circulation, and on the E for the air-conditioning, heating and electrical supply ducts.

Enter the building to appreciate how flexibly it adapts to the many activities that it offers (→Museums). There is no fee for taking the escalators up to the top floor, from which there is a superb view*.

Horloge district

The district is distinguished by the modern façades along the N side of the public square. Contained within the Rue du Grenier-Saint-Lazare, the Rue Beaubourg, the Rue Rambuteau and the Rue Saint-Martin, this was a place of artisans' workshops where hats, haberdashery and fancy trimmings (*frivolités*) were made. Fifteen years ago it was completely run-down, but the area has been renovated on the initiative of its inhabitants. Only the façades of the Rue Saint-Martin and four buildings in the Rue Beaubourg (1903–20) were kept. Now a pedestrian and shopping precinct, its modern buildings harmonize with the traditional urban architecture, and no traffic is allowed inside the area. At the entry to the Rue Rambuteau stands a sculpture by Ossip Zadkine (1964) depicting *The Flight of Prometheous* after he had stolen fire from heaven. Farther into the district, no. 8 Rue Bernard-de-Clairvaux, used to be the Museé des Automates (Robot Museum), now closed. Since 1979, it has displayed a large clock with mechanical figures, the work of Jacques Monestier. Its life-size Jack, the 'Defender of Time', does victorious combat, every hour, with one of the three monsters from earth, sea and air: at noon and 6pm he does battle with all three at once.

Rue Saint-Martin

From the Rue Rambuteau to the Rue Réaumur.

Return to this street and follow it northwards. Beyond the Rue Rambuteau, the renovated 18th-c. façades conceal the new Horloge district. At no. 141, note the fine staircase of the Hôtel Moreau, at no. 147, the courtyard and staircase; at no. 160, note the masks and ornamental carvings of the arches and the wrought ironwork of the handsome façade (1740); at no. 159, the Passage Molière is being restored. At no. 168, the house where Gérard de Nerval was born (b. 1808) stands on the site of the Chapelle Saint-Julien-des-Menestriers (1331–35), which was there until the Revolution.

You come out into the Rue du Grenier-Saint-Lazare, which offers a curious contrast between the modernism of its S side (Horloge district) and the old houses (Louis XIII and Louis XIV) of its N side. Follow the Rue Saint-Martin, which has interesting 16th and 17th c. houses, to arrive in front of the ancient Abbey of Saint-Martin-des-Champs** (→District of the Rue Réaumur).

Rue de Montmorency

This very old street takes its name from the aristocratic Montmorency family, who had a house at no. 5 that Fouquet is said to have occupied. Théophile de Via (1590–1626), the ardent Huguenot and dedicated libertine, is supposed to have sought refuge here. This tranquil little street has changed greatly over the last few years.

At no. 51, a pseudo-Gothic restaurant occupies the over-restored house of Nicolas and Pernelle Flamel. This house, built in 1407, was badly spoiled in the 18th c. A recent restoration has revealed pillars with carved images. It is now considered to be the oldest house in Paris, followed by no. 3 Rue Volta, which lost the title in 1978. Nicolas Flamel, writer and leading figure at the Université, had a great reputation with his students, who added to his many qualities by claiming that he possessed the philosopher's stone. His house was always open to all the poverty-stricken, from whom he asked nothing in return, except that they pray for the dead.

Rue Beaubourg

This street marks the boundary with the Marais for all streets W of the Rue Beaubourg (→Marais district).

The Beaubourg Center has attracted numerous nearby galleries of contemporary art (→inset). The street as it is today, extended by the Rue du Renard as far as the Hôtel de Ville, was laid out in the mid-19th c., then widened in 1910. It was renamed in order to erase the painful memory of the events to which its first name, the 'Rue Transnonain', referred. It is hard to imagine that this wide, well-lit street was the scene of the massacres carried out by Bugeaud's men, and of the savage battles of April 13 and 14, 1834 which took place in front of the *hôtel* of the archbishops of Reims, on the site of the present no. 62. At no. 37, there is a building awarded the first prize for architecture in 1903 by the City of Paris; at no. 71 stands the hostel building (1910) for the employees of the Félix Potin shop on the Boul. de Sébastopol (architect: P. Auscher).

Rue Rambuteau. Cross this street, one of the few created under Louis-Philippe. Much shortened by the changes at Les Halles, it is still very animated between the Rue Beaubourg and the Rue des Archives, thanks to its colorful market; most of its houses date from the Louis-Philippe period but are, with the exception of nos. 50–56, rather disfigured. Rue du Renard. This is an extension of the Rue Beaubourg. No. 12, formerly the Syndicat de l'Epicerie building, today houses a theater (pretty auditorium) and is a fine example of modern architecture. It was built in 1901 by Fr. Barbaud and Bautain and decorated by Rispal; note the motto on the façade: '*Un pour tous et tous pour un*' ('One for all and all for one').

▷ Vandalism or embellishment?

In the 17th and 18th c., some Parisian churches underwent major modifications, which produced a few masterpieces, but destroyed many others: the art of the Middle Ages no longer suited the tastes of the day, Neo-Gothic art did not yet exist, and the liturgy had new needs. So, as early as 1654, the choir of the Church of Saint-Laurent was decked out in heavy Corinthian decorations and Saint-Séverin was covered in marble. At the command of Louis XIV, the architect Robert de Cotte completely altered the choir of Notre-Dame: the new decorations were sumptuous, but the disappearance of the 12th-c. high altar, some funerary monuments, the pews and the rood-screen, is regrettable. 'Embellishments' continued in the second half of the 18th c. At Saint-Germain d'Auxerrois, Saint-Nicolas-des-Champs and at Saint-Médard, the columns, especially those marking the ends of their choirs, were fluted, in accordance with the contemporary return to the Classical style. The choir of Saint-Merri was completely altered in 1752 by the Slodtz brothers. Added to these upheavals were the destruction of several rood-screens and the replacement of stained by clear glass. Sometimes, to make room for platforms carrying statues during religious processions, there was no hesitation in even chipping away at Gothic doorways, as at Notre-Dame and Saint-Germain-l'Auxerrois.

▷ The galleries of the Beaubourg district

The creation of the Pompidou Center caused certain galleries to move from the Left Bank to the district between the Halles and the Marais. Since the late 1970s many more have opened. Often tucked at the back of a courtyard or on an upper floor, they are remarkable for the generous space they provide for exhibitions, and for the sophistication of their architecture. Their efforts have allowed the Parisian public to become more familiar with the work of previously little-exhibited foreign artists. The only thing that they have in common is the desire to present living, and generally young, artists. None can be described in a word; to try to do so would only diminish a constantly envolving story.

▷ Contemporary art galleries

Bama: 40 Rue Quincampoix, 75004. Tel: 42-77-38-87
Galerie Beaubourg: 23 Rue du Renard, 75004. Tel: 42-71-20-50
Bellint: 28 *bis* Boul. Sébastopol, 75004. Tel: 42-78-01-91
Alain Blondel: 4 Rue Aubry-le-Boucher, 75004. Tel: 42-78-66-67
Gilbert Brownstone: 17 Rue Saint-Gilles, 75003. Tel: 42-78-43-21

Farideh Cadot: 77 Rue des Archives, 75003. Tel: 42-78-08-36
Chantal Crousel et Ghislaine Hussenot: 5 *bis* Rue des Haudriettes, 75003. Tel: 48-87-60-81
Liliane et Michel Durand-Dessert: 3 Rue des Haudriettes, 75003. Tel: 42-77-63-60.
Jean Fournier: 44 Rue Quincampoix, 75004. Tel: 42-77-32-31

Galerie de France: 50–52 Rue de la Verrerie, 75004. Tel: 42–74–38–00
Gillespie-Laage-Salomon: 57 Rue du Temple, 75004. Tel: 42–78–11–71.

Yvon Lambert: 5 Rue du Grenier-Saint-Lazare, 75004. Tel: 42–71–04–25 and 108 Rue Vieille-du-Temple, 75003. Tel: 42–71–09–33.

Baudoin-Lebon: 34 Rue des Archives, 75004. Tel: 42–72–09–10.

Ghislain Mollet-Vieville: 26 Rue Beaubourg, 75003. Tel: 42–78–72–31 (by appointment).

Françoise Palluel: 91 Rue Quincampoix, 75004. Tel: 42–71–84–15.
Regards: 11 Rue des Blancs-Manteaux, 75004. Tel: 42–77–19–61.
Daniel Templon: 30 Rue Beaubourg, 75003. Tel: 42–72–14–10 and 1 Impasse Beaubourg, 75003.

Galerie Charles Cartwright: 38 Rue des Archives, 75004. Tel: 48–04–86–86.

Photographic galleries

Michèle Chomette: 24 Rue Beaubourg, 75004l. Tel: 42–78–05–62.
Agathe Gaillard: Rue du Pont-Louis-Philippe, 75004. Tel: 42–77–38–24.

Samia Saouma: 2 Impasse des Bourdonnais, 75001. Tel: 42–36–44–56.
Zabriskie: 37 Rue Quincampoix, 75004. Tel: 42–72–35–47.

Belleville and Ménilmontant*

Belleville has none of the picturesque qualities of the famous heights of Montmartre. On this hilltop (the highest after Montmartre) everything is far more basic, from the age-old poverty of the courtyards where the street singer's song still echoes, to the titanic task of rebuilding or rehabilitating the blocks of apartments. Standing a little apart from the rest of the French capital, Belleville has preserved its 1930s look and you can still see steep little streets with uneven sidewalks and decaying house fronts. This is a traditionally working-class Parisian district, slightly altered by the influx of foreign workers from Africa and South East Asia. Crowded and busy, Belleville is still highly typical of the true face of Paris.

Obsolete urban design and old, decaying housing have made the rehabilitation of Belleville essential. For some years now the hill has been the scene of an experiment in urban design and architecture which has been interesting to observe.

History of Belleville and Ménilmontant

Although Belleville was only formed into a commune in the 18th c., this hill, 420ft/128m high, was populated during the Middle Ages and, in the 15th c., developed into a real village. Around it stretched the estates of the nobility and the Church. On the Paris side at the bottom of the hill, were the homes of the men who worked in the nearby quarries and small local workshops. On the other side, the hamlet of Mesnil-Montant adjoined the village of Belleville on the next hilltop. Vines and fruit trees were grown on the slopes. At their foot were taverns and wineshops and the hovels of the men who worked in the nearby suburbs.

Populous, unruly and desperately poor, Belleville was quick to join any uprising. When, in 1860, the Commune was incorporated into Paris, the authorities sought to break it up by dividing it between the 19th and 20th arrondissements. This simply aggravated popular discontent and soon the whole district was united in opposition to the policies of Napoléon III. In 1870 Belleville paid a heavy price when the Commune was suppressed in a week of bloodshed; it was the last district of Paris to surrender to Government forces.

Tour of the district

From the Rue de Belleville to the Rue de Ménilmontant

20th arr.
Métro: Belleville
Bus: 26
Parking: 81–83 Rue du Faubourg-du-Temple
Taxis: 122 Boul. de la Villette. Tel: 46–07–00–00
45 mins.

Boulevard de Belleville

This boulevard was made in the 19th c. to ease the flow of traffic through a densely populated and chaotic, unplanned district. Today it is a busy and cosmopolitan thoroughfare. Its broad pavements are the site, on Tues. and Fri., of one of the largest open-air markets in Paris, famous for its Asian produce (→inset). On the other side of the road junction, along the Boul. de la Villette, are Chinese restaurants and shops stocking Asian goods.

Rue de Belleville

Turn r. along the steep and winding Rue de Belleville, which follows the line of the old road that led to the village of Belleville. The end of the road was once lined by dancehalls, taverns and drinking dens known as *courtilles*. Thus, every Shrove Tuesday night until 1830, the *Descente de la Courtille* took place and a stream of fantastically decorated floats and rowdy, masked and drunken revellers poured down the Rue de Belleville, led by the master of ceremonies, Mylord l'Arsouille (Blackguard).

Although the N side of the street has been completely rebuilt, the S side preserves its old houses with their tiny courtyards – a typical example being no. 40.

Rue Jouye-Rouve (on the r).

This narrow, uneven street seems very quiet after the hubbub of the Rue de Belleville. The buildings which line it are mostly former workshops or lodging houses. On the l., at nos. 13–15, is an amusing entrance to a modern block of apartments in which the different numbers are held by two carnival characters. Go through the archway and climb the steps to see the wooded slope behind the building. A little further on stands no. 27, the unpretentious Hôtel de Belleville, with an enamelled sign, small balconies and pots of geraniums, all of which seem to have wandered off a prewar film set. Now go along the Rue Julien-Lacroix, which leads into Nouveau Belleville, with the Parc de Belleville in the center.

▲▲▲ The Parc de Belleville

This park of over 11 acres/ 45,000m2, planted with 1200 trees and shrubs, is nearly finished and will provide a much needed open space for this section of Paris. Its picturesque quality is the result of its integration with the landscape of the hillside, replacing dilapidated blocks of buildings which were demolished, gypsum quarries and wasteland on the steep slope. Climb to the top of the park at the Rue Piat, to be rewarded by a magnificent view* over Paris. Walk down the hill again and turn l. along the Rue Julien-Lacroix as far as the Place Maurice-Chevalier. The Place Maurice-Chevalier lies in the heart of the Ménilmontant district. This tree shaded square, in front of the Church of Notre-Dame-de-la-Croix, still retains some of the attractions of an old village in the provinces.

▲ The Church of Notre-Dame-de-la-Croix

Built between 1860 and 1869 in the Neo-Romanesque style after the design of the architect Héret, the church is the last of a succession of shrines on the same site, the earliest having been erected in the 15th c. by the monks of Sainte-Croix de la Bretonnerie. When the later chapels became too small, the building of the present church was authorized after a petition was presented by discontented parishioners. No sooner was it finished than the Commune secularized it to use for rallies and even meetings of a women's committee. Notre-Dame-de-la-Croix is the third longest church in Paris, exceeded only by Notre-Dame and Saint-Sulpice; its bell tower is over 250ft/78m tall. The organ is by the famous builder, Cavaillé-Coll, and has never been altered since it was installed at the end of the 19th c. The Place de Ménilmontant runs alongside the S transept of the church.

Rue de Ménilmontant

Go back a short distance to the Rue de Ménilmontant to see on your l. the picturesque Rue des Cascades. Its names refers to Ménilmontant's once numerous brooks and waterfalls. No. 119 is the extremely elegant Pavillon de l'Asile des Petits-Orphelins, an orphanage built by Baudoin in 1770 in the Neo-Classical style. Further up the Rue des Cascades, at no. 145, the Saint-Simoniens set up a community in 1831. Go back down the Rue de Ménilmontant and when you reach the Boul. de Belleville you will have a spectacular view of the steeply sloping Rue de Ménilmontant and Rue Oberkampf. On the l., before the Boul. de Belleville, take a look at the Cité du Labyrinthe, a maze of tiny courtyards and narrow passageways, typical of the network of old buildings which once comprised this district.

Rue des Amandiers

Nearby, the visitor who is interested in contemporary architecture and urban planning can see the completely reconstructed area of the Rue des Amandiers. The block of houses standing between this street and the Rue de Tlemcen is especially noteworthy. On the corner of the Rue Elisa-Borey and the Rue Soleillet notice the apartment block decorated with painted tiles and wrought ironwork, erected in 1985 by the architect Zublena.

The upper end of the Rue de Belleville

20th arr.
Métro: Jourdain
Bus: 60
Taxis: 5 Rue Lassus. Tel: 42–08–42–66.
45 mins.

The old village of Belleville was separated from that of La Villette by two hills, the Butte de Caumont and the Butte de Beauregard, over which the Rues Pelleport, Haxo and Pixérécourt were laid. The Butte de Beauregard was riddled with quarries from which gypsum was extracted of such good quality that it became an important export. The quarries stopped being worked just before the Franco-Prussian War in 1870; in some places they are over 80ft/25m deep with two or three levels of galleries.

♦ The Church of Saint-Jean-Baptiste-de-Bastille

139 Rue de Belleville (open daily 9am–7pm; Sun. 1–3pm). Tel: 42-08-54-54

The present building was erected in the Neo-Gothic style by the architects Lassus and Truchy (1854–59) to replace the old parish church belonging to the commune of Belleville. The tympana of the three doorways were carved by Perey (1858). The stained glass is by Martel (1863–65) and Steinheil (1865). On the r. side of the transept hang *The Marriage of the Virgin, The Nativity* and *The Death of St Joseph* by J.-B. Leloir (1870–74) and on the l. side *St John the Baptist Preaching in the Desert, The Baptism of Christ* and *The Beheading of St John the Baptist* by Maillot (1870–77).

Rue des Fêtes back along the Rue de Belleville leads to the square of the same name. No trace is now left of the old Place Sainte-Geneviève (which was renamed the Place des Fêtes because of all the bars and dancehalls around it) since it is covered with apartment blocks either erected since 1970 or in the course of construction. On the other side of the Rue de Belleville the Rues Olivier-Métra, Frédérick-Lemaître or Pixerécourt have changed far less, but the Rue Pelleport is now monotonously modern.

The Belleville Cemetery

Entrance at 40 Rue du Télégraphe.

The Rue de Belleville continues to climb towards the Belleville Cemetery, opened in 1808 on part of the Château de Ménilmontant's grounds, on land 420ft/128m above sea level. Among the memorials, there is a pyramid erected in memory of the 35 guards shot in the Rue Haxo on May 26, 1871, and the tomb of Louis Gaumont (d. 1946), father of the French film industry. To the r. of the gateway a tablet commemorates Chappe's successful experiments with his signal telegraph made when the estate was owned by the Saint-Fargeau family.

Rue Haxo

This street is associated with one of the best-known incidents of the Commune. At no. 85, on May 26, 1871, 59 hostages – eight Jesuits, three lay priests, four civilians and 35 guards from Paris – were taken from the Grande-Roquette prison, and shot in front of the wall of a courtyard now occupied by apartment blocks. Deputy Eugène

Varlin, tried to stop the execution, but the Communards would not listen to him, driven to desperation by the terrible massacre of thousands of their fellows by troops of the Versailles Government. Later, Varlin himself was executed by the same government. The Church of Notre-Dame-des-Otages, at no. 81, was erected (1936–38) by the architect Barbier in memory of this tragedy.

Place Saint-Fargeau

Set on a slope, this forms a lively crossroads where the beautiful Ave. Gambetta that runs alongside the Père-Lachaise cemetery cuts across several streets: the Rue Saint-Fargeau which follows the line of the old country lane running from Ménilmontant to Rosny, the Rue Darcy which runs alongside the Ménilmontant and La Dhuis reservoirs (with a capacity of some 30 million gal/1400 million m²) built by Belgrand in 1864 on what had been the estates of the Le Peletier de Saint-Fargeau family.

One autumn day in 1776, J.-J. Rousseau was returning from his usual walk through the neighbouring woods, fields and vineyards when he was knocked over by a hound belonging to the Marquis de Le Peletier de Saint-Fargeau. He never recovered from the accident and died two years later.

The Rue du Groupe-Manouchian preserves the memory of the Armenian poet and his 22 companions, members of the Resistance, executed by the Germans in 1944. Their names appeared on the red poster which was plastered 'like a splash of blood' across the walls of Paris in 1943.

Below the Rue Haxo and the Rue du Groupe-Manouchian, the steep and twisting Rue du Surmelin and Rue de la Dhuis are lined by the occasional block of luxury apartments and by country cottages so typical of this district.

▣ Museum to visit

Musée Edith Piaf (→inset), 5 Rue Crespin-du-Crast: devoted to a survey of the singer's life.

▷ The Great Eastern Paris Plan

Although half the population of the city live in the districts to the E. of Paris their environmental, urban planning and traffic control needs have been neglected for a long time. For some years they have been the focus of a rebuilding program, since three-quarters of the land available for development within the city is concentrated here.

Besides improving the living conditions in these districts, the Great Eastern Paris Plan also aims to shift certain institutions and activities to this eastern sector. The Opéra-Bastille, the Cité des Sciences de la Villette, the Ministère des Finances or the Palais Omnisport de Bercy are as much a part of the plan as the construction of Nouveau Belleville. This plan revolves round the new park and the rehabilitation of the entire district as far as the Boul. de Belleville. More than 1400 apartments have been built in blocks none of which is more than five storeys high. The tower blocks of the 1960s have been rejected in favour of smaller buildings which create or re-create the atmosphere of a village.

▷ Markets

On the pavements of the Boul. de Belleville: Tues. and Fri., 7am–1.30pm.

Boul. de Ménilmontant, between the Rue des Panoyaux and the Rue de Tlemcen: Tues. and Fri., 7am–1.30pm.

Boul. Mortier, between the Ave. de la Porte de Ménilmontant and the Rue Maurice-Bertaux: Thurs. and Sun., 7am–1.30pm.

On the pavements of the Rue des Pyrénées, between the Rue de l'Ermitage and the Rue de Ménilmontant: Thurs. and Sun., 7am–1.30pm.

Rue du Télégraph, to the r. of the Belleville Cemetery: Wed. and Sat. 7am–1.30pm.

The Bibliothèque Nationale district**

2nd arr./Map ref. 10–D3 and → Palais-Royal district
Métro: Pyramides, Palais-Royal, Bourse
Bus: 29, 39, 48, 67
Parking: Rue des Pyramides, Place de la Bourse
Taxis: Palais-Royal Métro station. Tel: 42-60-61-40

The complex of buildings occupied by the Bibliothèque Nationale has for long been a headache for successive architects who have had to enlarge or alter them. This worthy monument, the Bibliothèque Nationale, as it now stands, retains substantial 17th and 18th c. architectural fragments but in fact its most remarkable alterations were made in the 19th c. During the Second Empire the architect Labrouste (1801–75) developed a highly innovative and rational system in which structural metal is shown openly in columns and vaulting for the Reading-Room and the stack. The 19th c. also left the district with several examples of its most original item of urban architecture: the covered gallery.

A beautiful example is the graceful Galerie Vivienne, behind the library, with fashionable *maisons de couture* and elegant shops. Its neighbour, the Galerie Colbert, is more cultural and serves as a window display for the activities of the Bibliothèque Nationale. Outside its main entrance, in the small Square Louvois, it seems only natural to find the national sound-archive between the Rue Rameau and the Rue Lulli. Stroll through the little streets which leads to the Ave. de l'Opéra. During the day they are crowded with workers from the offices which have taken over the district. By night they are deserted except around the theaters in the Rue de la Michaudière or the Rue Monsigny or the shady bars in the Rue Sainte-Anne.

☐ The Bibliothèque Nationale*

88 Rue de Richelieu

Formerly the Bibliothèque Royale, the Bibliothèque Nationale occupies an area bounded by the Rue de Richelieu, the Rue Colbert, the Rue Vivienne and the Rue des Petits-Champs and, with its stock of 12 million volumes, is one of the richest in the world. The holdings are supplemented by priceless collections of incunabula (books printed before 1500), manuscripts, prints, coins, medals, maps and plans, musical scores, recordings of music, other archival materials, films, photographs and theatrical costumes. The Bibliothèque Nationale is an outstanding storehouse of multimedia communication materials, in some respects a global memory bank.

History of the Bibliothèque Nationale

Royal Inheritance

The oldest royal French library was without doubt that of Charles V, assembled in one of the towers of the Louvre and numbering 973 works when Gilles Malet catalogued it in 1373. It lacked funds after the death of Charles V and, when Charles VI died, the collection was sold to the Duke of Bedford, who took it to England where it was dispersed. The Valois kings re-established the Royal Library on the banks of the Loire. Louis XII, a soldier and book-lover, combined the library of the Château of Blois with that of the House of Orléans and added the Sforza and Visconti libraries. His son, François I, as befitted a 'Renaissance man', established a library at Fontainebleau where he had moved Louis XII's books: together they formed a substantial collection. However, under the direction first of

Guillaume Budé and then of Pierre du Châtel, it was enriched by the acquisition of Greek, Latin and oriental manuscripts. In 1537 the king issued instructions from Montpellier that all printers must deposit copies of every book they printed in the Royal Library, thus instituting the copyright deposit system.

After the death of François I, the library followed his successors. Charles IX transferred it to Paris and then, in 1604, Henri IV housed it in the Cordeliers' convent in the Rue de la Harpe. At this time, the library acquired 800 manuscripts from Catherine de' Medici as well as the second Bible of Charles the Bald which had for centuries been kept in Saint-Denis. During the reign of Louis XIII the collection of copies of historic and diplomatic documents assembled by Loménie de Brienne was added to it, while under his son, Louis XIV, it began to assume the shape it would one day take as the Bibliothèque Nationale.

The Royal Library in the Palais Mazarin

Colbert had moved the overflow from the Louvre to two houses which he owned in the Rue Vivienne. They stood next to the town house of the Surintendant des Finances, Tubeuf, and the Hôtel de Chevry. Both the latter were owned by Mazarin, who in 1654 had had them enlarged by Mansart adding two galleries. The Hôtel Tubeuf stood on the Rue des Petits-Champs, and the Hôtel de Chevry stood at the corner of that street and the Rue de Richelieu. Throughout the reign of Louis XIV the library continued to expand, adding 9000 manuscripts that had belonged to the Dupuy brothers, sometime 'keepers' of the Library, and the libraries of Gaston d'Orléans, Fouquet, the Duc de Béthune, Marolles, and a collection of manuscripts presented by the Emperor of China. In 1692 the Library, or at least part of it, was opened to the public subject to certain conditions. Later the financier, John Law, acquired all the buildings (1719–20) and set up his Banque Royale in them. Its failure led to the confiscation of the property by the Regent, Philippe d'Orléans, who had encouraged it at the beginning, and, in 1724, to the establishment of the Royal Library in that portion of the Hôtel de Nevers fronting the Rue de Richelieu. The architect Robert de Cotte was commissioned to adapt the rooms to their new use. Mansart's two galleries running parallel with the Rue de Richelieu were lengthened and the new buildings were known as the Upper and Lower Galleries. After the death of the Marquise de Lambert, who owned the N section of the Hôtel de Nevers, beyond the Rue Colbert, Robert de Cotte's son, Jules-Robert, extended the tall block on the E side of the main courtyard *Cour d'honneur*, at a right-angles as the N wing along the Rue Colbert. Into it was moved the Cabinet des Médailles et des Antiques (Department of Medals and Antiques) which was then housed in the Arcade de Nevers overlooking the Rue Colbert. Throughout the 18th c. the Library grew richer acquiring books and documents bequeathed by Hozier, the libraries of Louvois, Delamare, Brossard and especially of Colbert, and a collection that had once belonged to the Abbey of Saint-Martial at Limoges. Cataloguing began and in 1720 the Library was opened to scholars.

The seal is set in the 19th century

During the 18th c. the collections expanded so fast that by 1780 anxiety was being expressed about how to enlarge the building. The architect Boullée suggested roofing over the *Cour d'honneur* to create a vast circular room lit from above. The financial problems that beset the closing years of the *Ancien Régime* thwarted his plans. In 1786 the area within the rectangle formed by the Rue des Petits-Champs, the Rue de Richelieu, the Rue Colbert and the Rue Vivienne was occupied by the Bourse, the Bibliothèque du Roi (Royal Library), the Loterie Royale and still by a few private houses. After the French Revolution libraries confiscated from Royalists who had fled the country, and from religious houses, coupled with the enforcement of the legal deposit system, unleashed a flood of books which only grew larger as methods of printing improved. Not until 1833 did the Library regain possession of all the spaces that had once been the Palais Mazarin. From then on, the wildest and most varied schemes were considered for rebuilding or moving the Library. In the end, the architect Labrouste radically altered the original buildings (1857–73). The rotunda on the corner of the Rue de Richelieu, the main bookstore and the reading room were opened in 1867 and the entrance facing the Square Louvois finished in 1873. In 1881 the architect Pascal erected the buildings which form the corners of the Rue Colbert and the Rue Vivienne. All that remains of Robert de Cotte's buildings is the central façade overlooking the principal courtyard.

Extensions in the 20th century

The most spectacular enlargement took place in the Rue Montbauron at Versailles in 1934 when an eight-storey building was erected by the architect Roux-Spitz, containing nearly 25 mls/40km shelving to house part of the periodicals collection.

The construction of the Bibliothèque de France, to be completed in 1995, has begun on the banks of the Seine to house the surplus from the Bibliothèque Nationale. The design chosen is that of Dominique Perrault.

Tour of the Bibliothèque Nationale (National Library)

Organized tours by the CNMHS. Tel: 48-87-24-14
Access to the Galeries Mazarine and Mansart during temporary exhibitions.

As well as its administrative and technical services, the Bibliothèque Nationale comprises 12 other departments.

Le Département des Imprimés (Department of Printed Books)

It houses 12 million volumes, almost the entire production of printed matter in France since the time of François I, thanks to the copyright registration which brings in 40,000 works each year, not including foreign works. The department has a Reading Room, a Catalog Room and reserve collections of more rare works.

Through a window at the entrance of the library you can see the large Reading Room of the Département des Imprimés (Department of Printed Books, 360 seats). Built in 1863 by Labrouste, this room is one of the most remarkable achievements in the architectural use of iron, with its nine ceramic domes, each one lit by a central bull's eye, supported by 16 graceful iron columns. Universally admired, the Reading Room is famous as a model of rational and functional architecture.

Le Département des Manuscrits (Department of Manuscripts)

This department has a rich collection of 250,000 specimens. In addition to manuscripts from the time before the invention of printing, there are documents which are interesting for their age, rarity, intrinsic value, binding or illustrations, as well as correspondence of every kind. Through bequests, donations and by acquisitions, the library has managed to obtain the manuscripts of Hugo, Proust, Roger Martin du Gard and Pierre and Marie Curie. These are classified according to language.

Le Cabinet des Estampes (Print Room)

This was created by Louis XIV in 1667. He acquired 184,000 prints from the collection of Michel de Marolles; they were already classified by artist and subject matter, which makes this the oldest and richest collection of etchings in the world: 12 million engravings, 2 million photographs, posters, postcards and a valuable collection of small prints that resemble playing-cards. The sheer range of this department was made possible because copyright registration has ensured the acquisition of two copies of each engraving since the early 17th c.

Le Département des Cartes et Plans (Department of Maps and Plans)

This department, founded in 1828, has the largest collection of old maps in the world, some dating from the 13th c.

Le Département de la Musique (Music and Record Library)

This collection is housed in a modern building on the corner of the Rue de Richelieu and the Square Louvois. The musical section of the Bibliothèque Nationale stores works by early composers as well as 1,400,000 musical stores, 360,000 records and 16,000 tapes.

Le Département des Médailles, des Monnaies et des Antiques (Department of Medals, Coins and Antiques)

This section evolved from the Cabinet du Roi (King's Cabinet) which assembled a collection of coins, medals, cameos and *objets d'art* from ancient times and the Middle Ages. During the Revolution the confiscation of religious treasures, in particular those of Sainte-Chapelle and Saint-Denis, considerably enriched this department. The registration of copyright of official coins and medals at the Mint or by French editors, the bequests, donations and foreign exchanges have all enriched this department. All coins discovered in France have to be submitted to this department (→ Museums: Cabinet des Médailles).

Mansart and Mazarine Galleries

These are built one above the other in a building designed by François Mansart (1644–45). The Galerie Mansart on the ground floor once housed the Cardinal's own collections. The gallery above (Galerie Mazarine) was a library. Today these galleries are for temporary exhibitions organized by the library.

Almost all the interior decoration of the Galerie Mansart* (situated just beyond the Coypel room) has disappeared. It was decorated with stucco and grisailles by Grimaldi, and paintings of monuments, but the gallery was wrecked, first in the 18th c. by the construction of the Bourse, and then in the 19th c. by the Cabinet des Estampes (Print Room). Finally it was restored and arranged specifically as an exhibition room.

The Galerie Mazarine** has retained its ceilings with their sunken painted panels of mythological subjects by Romanelli, and also its window frames and the niches opposite, which are decorated with landscape paintings by Grimaldi.

Tour of the district

45 mins.

This district is characterized by the enlargements, modifications and renovations carried out in the Rue de Richelieu, the Rue des Petits-Champs, the Rue de Louvois, Rue Colbert and Rue Vivienne, and also in the Galerie Colbert which has recently been restored.

Square Louvois

This square is situated in front of the main entrance to the Bibliothèque Nationale, for which it is a kind of verdant antechamber. The Opéra stood here until the Duc de Berry, on his way to watch his mistress dance, was assassinated (1820). The Archbishop of Paris gave him the Last Rites on the 'unholy' ground on condition that the building, erected a century earlier by Brongniart, be demolished. It was replaced by a garden where, in 1844, Hector Martin Visconti the Younger erected the monumental Louvois fountain decorated with Jean Baptiste Klagmann's statues depicting the rivers (Seine, Loire, Saone and Garonne).

Take the Rue Colbert which runs alongside the N section of the Bibliothèque Nationale.

Rue Vivienne

Because of its privileged location beside the library many aristocrats chose to live here during the 17th c.; during the 18th c. it became a center for finance and in the 19th c. for luxury commerce. Today its appearance has greatly changed. Set in the axis of the Palais-Royal built by Richelieu between 1634 and 1639, it was inhabited by the political aristocracy. In 1649, President Tubeuf sold his mansion in Rue des Petits-Champs to Mazarin and, in 1650, had a new *hôtel* built by the architect Pierre Le Muet at nos. 12–16.

To the r., behind the park bordering the street, one can see the wing built by F. Mansart for Mazarin's collections (→Galeries Mansart and Mazarine). The Bibliothèque du Roi (King's Library), the future Bibliothèque Nationale (→ above) was installed in 1666 at no. 6, Place de la Galerie Vivienne. In the 18th c. the political habitués were ousted by the financial crowd who had, till then, been living in the Marais. No. 1 was allocated to the Bourse des Valeurs from 1724 to 1793.

For the remainder of the Rue Vivienne →district of La Bourse.

La Galerie Vivienne

Completed in 1823 this arcade rivalled the Galerie Colbert. It has three entrances at 6 Rue Vivienne, 5 Rue de la Banque and 4 Rue des Petits Champs. No. 13 has preserved the monumental stairway of the ancient mansion where Vidocq lived. Vidocq was a convict and the head of a police brigade made up of former convicts. Today it is brought to life by clothing shops and fashion designers. One exits by 4 Rue des Petits-Champs. The Rue des Petits-Champs was opened in 1634 to form the perpendicular axis to the Rue de Richelieu; it leads to the Ave. de l'Opéra (→below).

The Colbert Arcade

6 Rue des Petits-Champs (open Mon.-Sat. 10am-6pm).

Built in 1826 on the site of a mansion by Le Vau, it has just been completely restored in almost exactly the same style as the Bibliothèque Nationale for which it is an important annex, open to the public.

The section which opens on to the Rue des Petit-Champs is occupied by the Boutique Colbert which sells postcards, posters, publications and various objects copied from the collection at the Bibliothèque Nationale. Inside, under the entrance porch, is a painting portraying Colbert promoting commerce.

As well as the Grand Café Colbert with its décor now restored so that it looks as it did in 1900, this charming arcade houses two museums: the Musée Charles-Cros (→ Museums) which shows the history of the phonograph, and a Dramatic Arts museum (window displays only) showing costumes, sketches of scenery and props, posters, photographs, etc. Of noble proportions, this arcade is broken by a rotunda 49ft/15m in diameter, its character and delicate polychrome decoration showing a Pompeian influence. It was once the glory of the gallery because of the candelabra perched high up in a bronze coconut tree. Displayed all round are temporary exhibitions of prints and photographs. Beyond that is a curved aisle which allows you to walk from the Palais-Royal to its neighbouring Galerie Vivienne almost without having to step outside. At 8 Rue des Petits-Champs, behind a gate, can be seen the brick and stone façade of the Hôtel Tubeuf, typical of the Louis XIII style, built in 1633 by Le Muet. The Rue Chabanais to the r. is composed almost entirely of 18th-c. houses with *portes-cochères* (carriage entrances, wrought ironwork). The architect, Eugène Viollet-le-Duc, was born at no. 1 in 1814. No. 12 was occupied by le Chabanais and had a worldwide reputation as a brothel until it was closed around 1947.

Rue Sainte-Anne

Cross this road, which was named after Anne of Austria, where there are still a few lovely mansions: note no. 34, the 18th-c. Hôtel de Laborde de Sérincourt*; no. 46 where Bossuet died on April 12, 1704; no. 47 retains the façade of the Hôtel Lulli, built by Daniel Gittard in 1671, which looks on to no. 45, Rue de Petits-Champs. Commissioned as the residence for the superintendent of the King's music, this mansion is more like an apartment block than a suburban mansion with courtyard and garden. The ground floor with arches and colossal pilasters is a forerunner of the Place des Victoires and Place Louis-le-Grand, known today as the Place Vendôme.

Rue des Moulins

Take a little stroll along this street where there have been no windmills since 1868. Nos. 4, 6, 8 and 9 are a collection of 18th-c. mansions. From 1759 to 1789 the Baron d'Holbach held a salon at no. 8 where famous literary men used to meet. No. 10 is a 17th-c. mansion which belonged to the composer Lully.

Passage Choiseul

The entrance to this alley is at no. 4, Rue des Petits-Champs. It was opened in 1825 and is equally remarkable for its other entrance in the Rue Saint-Augustin, cut through the beautiful façade of a mansion built by Lepauvre in 1655, and for its inner Ionic gallery which supported a monumental clock. The memory of the Parnassians (Sully Prudhomme, François Coppée, Barbey d'Aurevilly, Lecomte de Lisle, Heredia) is evoked at no. 23, the bookshop, Percepied. The satirical writer Céline spent his childhood here and describes it in *Mort à Credit*.

Rue de Méhul

This very short street opens to the r. of the Rue des Petits-Champs and ends in a square in the center of which the Salle Ventadour was originally erected (1826–29, architect Hervé). It housed the Opéra-Comique and the Théâtre de la Renaissance, which saw the triumph of *Ruy Blas* on November 8, 1838, then later gave refuge to the Italians and to the Opéra after the fire in 1873 at the Salle Le Peletier. Today the building which occupies almost all the square belongs to the social services section of the Banque de France. Rue des Petits-Champs (→ below): beautiful façades at nos. 55 and 61. At no. 57 Jean-Jacques Rousseau found a garret in which he lived at the beginning of his relationship with Thérèse Levasseur. In 1804 Mme.

Hugo, the poet's mother, settled into no. 76 with her children. Take the Ave. de l'Opéra on the r., then the Rue Gaillon which leads to the Place Gaillon.

Place Gaillon

The Gaillon fountain is in this square, built by Louis Visconti in 1827, and the Restaurant Drouant where the members of the jury for the Prix Goncourt gather to vote for the best book of the year. There are several beautiful 18th-c. mansions, especially nos. 3 and 5.

▣ Museums to visit

Cabinet des Médailles et des Antiques* (58 Rue de Richelieu): medals, jewellery and art objects from Antiquity to the 18th c.

Musée Charles-Cros (Galerie Colbert, Rue des Petits-Champs): history of the phonograph and mechanical musical instruments.

🌲 The Bois de Boulogne*

16th arr./Map ref. 7–A3
Métro: Porte de Maillot (also: Porte Dauphine, Porte d'Auteuil)
Bus: 22, 32, 43, 52, 63, 123, 144, 244 and PC
Railway (SNCF): Petite Ceinture line; stations: Neuilly-Porte Maillot, Foch-Porte Dauphine, Henri-Martin, Passy-la Muette, Auteuil

The Bois de Boulogne, situated on the western outskirts of Paris, is a magnificent park of 2132 acres/863ha, crossed by several roads and numerous footpaths. It stretches from the edge of the former fortifications of the Seine, between Neuilly to the N and Boulogne to the S; an integral part of the City of Paris, the whole of the Bois is in the 16th arrondissement.

History of the Bois de Boulogne

The Bois de Boulogne is what remains of the immense Forêt du Rouvre, or Forêt de Rouvray from the common name of its oak trees, *chênes rouvres*, which spread out to the NW of Paris and covered the surrounding hills. Philippe IV the Fair built a church at the Hameau des Menus to commemorate a pilgrimage to Notre-

Dame de Boulogne. The church disappeared, but the name survived.

In 1460, after the Hundred Years War, Louis XI ordered Olivier le Daim to oversee the restoration of the woods. Two roads were thrust through them, one from Passy to Boulogne, the other from Passy to the Neuilly ferry. In 1531, François I built himself the Château de Madrid at the crossroads of the present 'Porte' of the same name, but the Bois still had a sufficiently bad reputation as the haunt of robbers and other lowlife for his son Henri II to try to protect it with a high wall with eight gates, which Louis XIV later opened to the public. During the reign of Henri IV, 15,000 mulberry trees were planted. Louis XIV drew up the first regulations for the conservation and replanting of the woodlands. Beyond this, to adapt the woods for the hunt, he cut a number of straight pathways radiating from the central points.

In the 18th c., fine houses appeared around the Bois: the Château de la Muette and the Château de Neuilly, the Folie Saint-James, the Bagatelle and the Ranelagh. Unfortunately, during the Revolution the Bois was almost totally destroyed, Bagatelle alone escaping. It was not until the Second Empire that the Bois de Boulogne again became a popular place for walking and riding. In 1848 it became the property of the State and in 1852 Napoléon III ceded it to the Ville de Paris, stipulating that the city lay it out as a public promenade and maintain it; 59m/95km of roadways were built, the Bois was extended as far as the Seine, and its outer wall was removed. In 1852 and 1855 the landscape was entirely changed. Winding paths were added to the earlier, rectilinear paths, of which only the Allée de la Reine-Marguerite and the Ave. de Longchamp survive. It was during this period that the Upper Lake and Lower Lake (with its two islands) were created, with the waterfall between them. Then, from 1855 to 1858, the Longchamp racetrack was constructed. Three rivers were also created: from the Lower Lake they flow to the ponds at the Porte de Neuilly, the Saint-James pool and the waterfall at the Longchamp intersection. The forest received particular attention, with more than 400,000 trees planted. Flower-beds were dug at the most popular places, and large areas for games and sports created, as well as pavilions, chalets and unpretentious shelters for walkers. Concessions were granted to societies such as the Jardin d'Acclimatation and the Pré Catelan. The work, which took nearly six years, was closely supervised by Napoléon III and the Empress Eugénie (→ inset).

More recently, the building of the Boulevard Périphérique has necessitated a tunnel under the Upper Lake and the crossing of a part of the municipal Flower Garden. Today the Bois de Boulogne has once again acquired a bad reputation, especially at night. In the early morning, though, innumerable *sportifs* jogging along the paths, who have replaced Constantin Guys' elegant ladies, lend reassurance.

Tour of the Bois de Boulogne

3 hrs.

We suggest visiting the principal sites of the Bois by a circular 6¼m/ 10km route, most of it by car. It includes those roads that have been closed to traffic for cyclists, walkers and riders, thereby creating a circuit for sportsmen and those seeking healthy exercise, between the Porte de Boulogne and the Route de l'Hippodrome.

Arriving by the Ave. Foch, the main entrance to the Bois, you pass the Porte Dauphine. To go to the lake, leave the car near the Porte Dauphine and go on foot to the Route de Suresnes.

The Route de Suresnes

Pass, on the r., the Pavillon Dauphine (café-restaurant) and come out at the crossroads – the Carrefour du Bout-des-Lacs – where you will find the Pavillon Royal (café-restaurant, open Feb.–Nov.).

The Lower Lake or Grand Lac

Boats for hire.

The road running round the Lower Lake is bordered to the E by the lawns of the former Château de la Muette where, in 1783, the first manned flight took place in Montgolfier's balloon, with Pilâtre de Rozier and D'Arlandes (see plaque); to the W the path runs beside the lawns of the Croix-Catelan, with the courts, grounds and buildings of the Racing-Club, one of the principal sports complexes of Paris. The Lower Lake, with a surface area of nearly 7 acres/11ha, has two islands, joined by a bridge.

The Chalet des l'Iles (café-restaurant), on the larger of the two islands, is a genuine Swiss chalet erected by the builder Seiler near Berne, dismantled and re-erected here during the Second Empire, evidence of the infatuation of the Empress Eugénie with this kind of building.

Four other chalets, now vanished, were erected in the Bois; they came from a factory set up by Seiler in the suburb of La Villette. The one that survives on the lake was converted to a restaurant and closed to the public whenever the Imperial family visited it.

The Kiosque de l'Empereur, at the S end of the lake, was one of the first of Davioud's buildings, dating from about 1857. It is reached via the Chalet de l'Ile's landing-stage, on the perimeter route, to the E of the lake. Built for the exclusive use of the Imperial couple, it too is in the style of a Swiss chalet, with ornamental wooden fretwork and carving. The first floor, octagonal in shape and made of wood and glass, rests on a substructure in decorative red and yellow brick. The floor and ceiling are in oak, walnut and maple marquetry with,

as their central motif, the intertwined monograms of the Emperor and his wife. The domed roof is surmounted by a lead spike carrying a weathervane representing the coat of arms of the city of Paris. Restored with careful concern for authenticity 1985–86 by the Service des Espaces Verts de la Ville de Paris, the chalet has contributed greatly to the rehabilitation of the Bois undertaken in recent years.

The Upper Lake or Petit Lac

Pedal-boats (pédalos) for hire.

To the S of the Grand Lac, this approximately 2-acre 3-ha stretch of water was drained to allow work on the Boulevard Périphérique to proceed, then recreated above the tunnel carrying the boulevard beneath it. To the S, the Butte Montmartre is the main entry to the Auteuil racetrack, which is reserved for steeplechase events. Not far off you can see the fine greenhouses of the Municipal Flower Garden (→ Auteuil). Go by car along the Route de l'Hippodrome, which leads (1m/1.6km) to the racecourse and the Longchamp intersection.

The Longchamp crossroads

This is situated near the artificial Grande Cascade, the waterfall created in the Second Empire to provide a picturesque scene evocative of Switzerland. For this purpose 5,232 cu. yds/4000m³ of rock were brought here from the forest of Fontainebleau, and enormous hydraulic works were required to bring water from the Longchamp pond to this artificial cascade, 33ft/10m high. On a pathway behind this pool a monument was erected in memory of 35 young people shot here by German troops on August 16, 1944. The surrounding trees still bear traces of the bullets. Nearby is the Chalet de la Grande Cascade (restaurant).

The Longchamp racecourse

The routes des Tribunes, which runs round the racecourse to the N and the W, can be reached on foot. You pass in front of the pretty Château de Longchamp, where the conferences of the Centre International de l'Enfance (International Childhood Center) are held, and whose grounds contain the remains two towers and a gable of Longchamp Abbey (→ inset).

The racecourse, opened by Napoléon III in 1857, is devoted to the *Sociéte d'Encouragement's* flat races, and every summer the Grand Prix de Paris is run here. Years ago, during the Fête Nationale National Holiday, a ceremonial review of the garrison of Paris took place here. The tiers of seating, rebuilt in 1966, can accommodate

12,000 spectators, and in the reception hall there are bureaux de change, tourist offices, a panoramic restaurant with a view over the course and closed-circuit color television. Return to the Longchamp intersection. Leave the Route des Moulins, also closed to traffic, which leads to the polo ground, near which may be seen a stele with an inscription commemorating one of the first world records for speed in aviation, set on November 10, 1906 by the Brazilian flier Santos-Dumont. To the NE of the polo ground, between the terrace of Bagatelle and the Seine, stretch the vast sports grounds created in 1856, the Allée du Bord de l'Eau and the Paris-Ouest camping site.

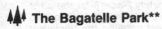 The Bagatelle Park**

Métro: Pont-de Neuilly. Bus: 43, 244. Entrance fee. Open 8.30am–6.20pm, depending on the season. Tel: 47–47–47–10.

The park can be reached by car from the Longchamp intersection by the Sèvres-Neuilly road. This beautiful 59 acres/24ha park set in the woods and walled on all sides, was bought by the Ville de Paris in 1905 from Sir Henry Murray Scott.

There are frequent flower shows, painting and sculpture exhibitions, and concerts (in the Trianon and Orangerie). The elegant little domed château (not open to the public) is in the course of restoration. Bagatelle was built under the Regency. The first use of its as a home was granted to a councillor of the Cour des Aides in 1716 and later, in 1720, to the Maréchal d'Estrées. In the 18th c. the little château had a somewhat romantic history, in which both the Regent and Louis XV play a part. The Comte d'Artois bought the property in 1775 and made a bet with his sister-in-law, Marie-Antoinette, that he would build a new palace in two months. The architect, Bélanger, won the wager for him in 63 days. The half moon of the front part of the building contained a round salon decorated in the Pompeian style with small private rooms off it. Bagatelle was once occupied by Napoleon, who dreamt of making it a palace for the King of Rome, later it reverted to the Comte d'Artois, who gave it to the Duc de Berry. It was acquired in 1835 by Lord Seymour, Duke of Hertford, who raised the attic storey, enlarged the windows and placed a balustrade round the roof; he also built the *Orangerie,* stables and outhouses (now the *restaurant-salon de thé*), and the gardener's lodge on the side of the woods. It was inherited, along with the family fortune and rich collections, by his adoptive, reputedly natural, son, Sir Richard Wallace (→ inset), who laid out the two terraces we see today and commissioned the architect Léon de Sanges to build the Trianon and the two gatehouses. On his death he left the property to his wife, who hardly ever used it. Her secretary, and heir, Sir Henry Murray Scott, sold it to the City of Paris in 1905 for the sum of 6 million francs.

Jean-Claude-Nicolas Forestier who, among other things, designed the Champ-de-Mars and was Conservateur des Parcs et Jardins de la Ville, wanted to make the Bagatelle gardens a collection of open-air plants, perennials and climbers. A friend of Monet, he drew his inspiration from the Impressionists, grouping flowers by species and accentuating the effects of mass. The rose garden* remains his major work; situated opposite the Orangerie, it offers a fine view of the Seine valley and Mont-Valérien. There are 8000 rose bushes of 700 varieties, with new varieties added each year at the time of the Concours Internationale de la Rose (early June). The park has other fine collections of plants: in April the spring bulb-plants (S section) and the rhododendrons (N section); in June, roses and irises (SW section); in summer, superb acquatic plants N section; in autumn, dahlias and the colors of the tree foliage; in winter, the winter-flowering trees and shrubs, and snowdrops.

The Pré Catelan

This enclosure, situated to the SE of the park, can be reached by the Route de la Reine-Marguerite. Its name is associated with a sad legend (→ inset). Besides the Restaurant du Pré Catelan there is the Jardin La Fontaine (1954) and the Jardin Shakespeare (1953), with representations of the witches' heath from *Macbeth,* the pool where Ophelia drowned, the Forest of Arden from *As You Like It,* the Mediterranean terraces of *The Tempest* and the Greek forest of *A Midsummer Night's Dream.* In the midst of these surrounding is an open-air theater. Further on, at the Carrefour de la Croix-Catelan, a stone pyramid of the 18th c.

The Allée de Longchamp. Follow this lane towards the Porte Maillot. On the l. is the Société Hippique de l'Etrier (private club: clay pigeon shooting; skating rink). More to the N, between the Porte de Madrid and the Jardin d'Acclimatation, the pool known as the Mare de Saint-James is surrounded by charming woods.

At the point where the Allée de Longchamp rejoins the road that runs from the Porte Maillot to the Jardin de l'Acclimatation, at the junction of two roads, are the Mare d'Armenonville and the Pavillon d'Armenonville (banquets; receptions).

The Jardin d'Acclimatation (Children's Amusement Park)

Main entrance: Porte des Sablons. Open daily 9am-7.30pm. Tel: 46-24-10-80.

Created by the Société d'Acclimatation and opened to the public in 1860, the garden occupies the NW corner of the Bois. Originally a zoological garden, it has become as amusement park for children (open-air circus, games, merry-go-rounds etc.), while still keeping some animals (lions, bears, monkeys, deer, birds, fish etc.), some of which are tame and allowed to roam about. A little train brings visitors from near the Porte Maillot to the main entrance. Near the entrance is a floral clock 26ft/8m in diameter. On the site of the former palmhouse of the Jardin d'Acclimatation on the Route Mahatma-Gandhi is the Musée des Arts et Traditions Populaires (→ Museums), in a tall modern building. Also on this road, on part of the site of the Jardin d'Acclimatation, stands the Bowling de Paris, where competitions are held (several restaurants). At the W end of the Jardin, on the road from La Muette to Neuilly, is the Centre Hippique du Bois de Boulogne, set up in 1966 by the Société d'Equitation de Paris and the Groupe Hippique du Touring-Club de France (show-ring for 1000 spectators); opposite is the Boule du Lac Saint-James.

▷ The Emperor-gardener

Napoléon III invented the public garden for Paris, motivated by his philanthropy and concern for public health; before him only the aristocracy had gardens in the capital, sometimes opened to the public according to the whim of their owners. He gave Paris the suburban woods of Boulogne and Vincennes, the urban parks of the Buttes-Chaumont and Montsouris, and public squares, so that each district should have the benefit of a garden.

We know that the Emperor had acquired a taste for English landscaped gardens during his exile in London, and he took a personal interest in the design of certain places, particularly the Bois de Boulogne. It was to serve Napoléon III's objectives that Haussmann created the Service Municipal des Parcs et Plantations, under the direction of the civil engineer Alphand, assisted by the horticulturalist Barillet-Deschamps and the architect Davioud. The service was founded simultaneously with the creation of the Bois de Boulogne, and in 20 years provided Paris with 4532 acres/1834ha of green spaces – broadly speaking, the parks we still have today.

▷ The trees of the Bois de Boulogne

Be sure to see the trees at Bagatelle, the Pré Catelan and the Jardin Fleuriste Municipale (→Auteuil), which is on the edge of the Bois.

 The doyen of all the trees is a yew, 210 years old, in the Parc de Bagatelle, closely followed by several 200-year-old oaks (Rond-Royal, Racing-Club de France), the most imposing being the one at the Pré Catelan (21ft 8in/6.60m in circumference). Among the oldest trees are also a copper beech (200 years old, Pré Catelan) and several cedars of Lebanon (Parc de Bagatelle, 200 years old, and on the shores of the Lower Lake and the Ile des Cédres).

Lovers of curiosities will be able to see the strange fruiting of the cucumber tree (Pré Catelan, Aug.–Sept.), the bizarre flowering of the *arbre aux pochettes* (Parc de Bagatelle, May–June) and the monkey puzzle tree, with its branches closely covered in stiff, sharp leaves.

For further information: *Les Arbres Remarquables des Promenades et Parcs de Paris* (Unusual trees on walks and in Paris parks), obtainable from the Direction des Parcs, Jardins et Espaces Verts, 3 Ave. Porte-d'Auteuil, 75016.

▷ The former Abbey of Longchamp

In 1256, St Isabelle, the sister of St Louis, founded a cloistered order of nuns at an abbey, the Order of Our Lady of Humility. It was set up at the place called 'Longchamp', between the present-day Longchamp intersection and the Seine. Isabelle of France died there in 1269. But with the passing of the centuries the monastery became fashionable and, in the 18th c., the church was a meeting place for high society, which came in droves during the last three days of Holy Week to hear the Matins and Lauds (*Tenebrae*) sung by a singer from the Opéra who had renounced the world, Mlle Le Maure. One said that one was going '*aux Ténèbres*'. The nuns were expelled during the Revolution and the monastery closed. The buildings were put up for sale, but found no buyer and were demolished in 1795.

▷ The Wallace Collection

A rich and generous patron, Sir Richard Wallace, acquired great popularity by subsidizing ambulances during the war of 1870, and by building in Paris 100 fountains which still bear his name. His collection, most of which was inherited from the Duke of Hertford, comprised art objects of the 17th and 18th c. It was especially famous for its clocks and furniture, mostly of royal origin, and by the greatest French cabinet-makers (Riesner, Weisweiler, Oeben and Boulle). The paintings were French (Watteau, Boucher and Fragonard), Flemish, English, Italian and Spanish: these, the decorative *objets d'art*, the arms and armour, all bear witness to the sure taste of a wise collector. On Wallace's death the collection became the property of Lady Wallace, who bequeathed the part of it kept in England to the British nation, along with their home: this makes up the famous Wallace Collection, at Hertford House, Manchester Square in London. The pieces kept at Bagatelle and in Paris she left to her secretary and lover Sir Murray Scott. In his lifetime Bagatelle was sold to the City of Paris and on his death in 1912 the entire contents of the house in the Rue Lafitte were bought by the antiquarian Jacques Seligmann.

▷ The Legend of the Croix-Catelan

It's hard to imagine that this peaceful place, less crowded than the rest of the Bois, was the scene of a bloody drama in the 14th c. Even if this event is pure fiction, and the origin of the name is in fact that of Théophile Catelan, Louis XV's Captain of the Hunt, the tale may be true, since vagabonds and brigands once haunted the forest, robbing and killing.

The then king of France, Philippe the Fair, a great lover of romances, sent to Aix-en-Provence for the best of the troubadours, Arnault Catelan, who brought with him a casket of gifts. Convinced that the troubadour's baggage contained precious objects, the Captain of the Guard, sent by the king to protect him, killed the unfortunate Arnault. In fact, the casket contained only a few perfumes from Provence and some liqueurs. The criminal shared the booty with his confederates: they were betrayed by the delicious fragrances with which they sprayed themselves, and which the king recognized, and were condemned to be burnt alive over a slow fire. At the exact spot of the murder an expiatory monument in the form of a pyramid was raised.

▣ Museums to visit

Musées des Arts et Traditions Populaires (6 Route du Mahatma-Gandhi): French ethnography and popular arts.

Musée en Herbe (Jardin d'Acclimatation): exhibitions and artistic activities for children.

The Bourse district**

2nd arr./Map ref. 11–A2, A3→ Palais-Royal district.
Métro: Bourse.
Bus: 20, 29, 39, 48, 67, 74, 85.
Parking: Pl. de la Bourse.
Taxis: at the Métro Richelieu-Drouot. Tel. 42-46-00-00.

The atmosphere in any financial center is a mixture of feverish excitement and a certain professional chill. The district of La Bourse is no exception to this rule as far as the uninitiated are concerned. The Palais de la Bourse (Stock Exchange), or Palais Brongniart, as it is called after its architect, is the heart of the district. This temple dedicated to the god of money testifies to the prosperous state of industry and art in France during the 19th c. It has retained all its majesty, even if it looks a little strange today next to that other hive of activity on the same square, the Agence France-Presse.

During the week, to get a sense of the atmosphere, you need only mix with the crowds moving restlessly in the neighboring streets. As the architect Claude Nicolas Ledoux remarked, 'the man who starts a business matter in the morning can complete it just as well at the theater as at the Bourse'. The profusion of terraces and cafés, nightspots (especially on the Boulevard Montmartre), and various galleries gives this part of Paris its uniqueness. Peace returns to the Bourse at the end of each week. Action moves S to the Place des Victoires where shops sell luxury goods, and N to the great boulevards, traditional places for Sunday strolls.

History of the district

The heart of the district, represented by the Palais de la Bourse, (Stock Exchange) started to beat to the rhythm of financial fluctuations as early as the beginning of the 19th c. This creation *ex nihilo* coincides, in fact, with the beginnings of capitalism and of the Industrial Revolution and the intensification of business activity.

Having become the financial center of Paris, the surrounding area is dedicated solely to money and there are many banks and financial establishments located between the Boulevard des Italiens in the N and the Rue de Rivoli in the S. The symbols of this power are reflected even in the place-names. The Rue de la Banque links the Palais de la Bourse to the Banque de France, the latter being close to the Ministry of Finance. The Palais is also called the Bourse des Valeurs, not to be confused with the Bourse du Commerce to the E of the Place des Deux-Ecus.

Tour of the district

45 mins

☐ The Palais de la Bourse

Open daily except weekends and public holidays, tours every half hour from 11.00 a.m.–1 p.m. during quotation time. Meet at 4 Place de la Bourse at 1.30 p.m. For further information tel. 42-33-99-83.

In 1720, after the bankruptcy of John Law, it was forbidden for anyone, except accredited brokers, to negotiate on paper in a public place. Four years later a Council ruling regulated the organization of the Stock Market and defined the profession of stockbroker by conferring on the Bourse what had before been the privilege of the Commune of Parisian tradesmen. But it was not until the reign of Napoleon I that Paris was given its 'temple' of commerce. In 1826, the Bourse left its temporary residences in Rue Vivienne, the Louvre and the Palais-Royal, and settled permanently into the vast Vespasian temple which Brongniart had begun in 1808 and to which he gave his name.

The exterior

Erected on the site of the old convent, for repentant sinners, Les Filles-Saint-Thomas, this building in the Imperial Roman style, surrounded by a grandiose peristyle of Corinthian columns, is a fine example of Neo–Classicism in Europe. The addition of two wings at the N and S, in 1903, gave the Bourse a cruciform appearance. The entrance steps on the W and E are flanked by four allegorical statues of women seated on high pedestals; to the r. of the main façade, *Commerce* by Dumont (1852) and, opposite, *Justice* by Duret (1851); by the newer façade, *Agriculture* and to its l., *Industry* by Seurre and Pradier (1851).

The interior

The large room known as the Salle de la Corbeille is on the ground floor. It is lit by a glass roof in the center of the ceiling and all round are paintings in grisaille by Meynier and A. Pujol (1826). The recent modernization of the Bourse removed the stockbrokers' central enclosure, focal point of the exchange. Since then the floor, at the heart of the dealing area, is frantic with professionals who throw themselves into their operations as feverishly as ever despite the increase in computerization. Take the Rue de la Bourse (opened in 1833), and note no 2. in the style of a Florentine palace, which is a former salesroom.

Rue des Colonnes

Formerly the Passage des Colonnes. Opened in 1791, it ran between the Rue Feydeau and the Rue des Filles-Saint-Thomas making it easier to reach the Théâtre Feydeau (19–21 Rue Feydeau). Its row of arches in the Directoire style with Egyptian motifs was broken up when, on converting it to a street in 1798, the Rue de la Bourse was cut through it.

Rue Richelieu

From the Bourse to the Boul. Montmartre.

No. 87 is the modern building of the headquarters of the Assurances Générales de France (architect J. Belmont). Among the numerous 19th-c. buildings no. 104 was erected in 1834 by Visconti. At the beginning of the 19th c., no. 112 was Frascati's famous gambling house.

For the S section where literary and historical associations are more numerous →Palais-Royal district.

In the adjoining streets are two buildings dating from the 1930s. No. 24 Rue Feydeau, on the r., with its accordion-style façade allowing maximum light (1932, architect F. Colin); no. 10 Rue Saint-Marc is an office block built by H. Sauvage in 1929. The singer Malibran was born in 1808 at no. 31.

Rue Vivienne

Situated in the axis of the Palais-Royal (→Bibliothèque Nationale), it was extended to the N, after the demolition of the Convent of Les Filles-Saint-Thomas in 1809, as far as the Rue Feydeau, then between 1824 and 1830, up to the Boulevard Montmartre, and cut across in 1864 by the Rue du 4-Septembre. There you will find numerous shops specializing in numismatics and heraldry. Come out at the Place de la Bourse where a post office stands on the N side (architects: J. Debat-Ponson and M. Roux-Spitz).

Rue de la Banque

Situated to the S of the Place de la Bourse, this road owes its name to the Banque de France in front of which it starts (→below). The architect Victor Baltard greatly contributed to its present-day appearance. At no. 12, the Church of the Petits-Pères was built in the reign of Louis XIII in memory of La Rochelle. At no. 8, Baltard built the town hall for the 2nd arrondissement (1850) against the sides of the church of Notre Dame-des-Victoires, and opposite from nos. 9 to 13 he converted the old Hôtel du Timbre (1844) which is now occupied by the tax administration offices.

⚭ The Basilica of Notre-Dame-des-Victoires**

Place des Petits-Pères. Tel. 42-60-96-71.

The Passage des Petits-Pères starts opposite the Galerie Vivienne (→Bibliothèque Nationale district) and leads to the square of the same name. The square is still called after the 'Petits-Pères' (little fathers) which was the familiar name given to the discalced (shoeless) Hermits of St Augustine; their convent was here before the Revolution.

The only building that was not demolished in 1859 is the basilica. The dedication refers to the capture of La Rochelle from the Huguenots. Although begun in 1629, the church was not finished until 1740, after many interruptions. The choir with its beautifully carved stalls was built by Pierre le Muet from 1629 to 1632; the transept and the last bay of the nave, erected between 1642 and 1666, were the work of Libéral Bruant; the edifice was completed and given its vault by Sylvain Cartault between 1737 and 1740.

The interior

The church has a nave with four very deep barrel-vaulted bays; the arches along the nave open onto connecting chapels similar to the Gesù church in Rome; the transverse arms between the nave and the chancel are not very prominent and the choir is very deep. The walls and columns are covered with numerous ex-votos. The organ case and the pulpit date from 1740. The r. wall of the transept forms the chapel consecrated to the Très Saint et Immaculé Coeur de Marie (The Holy and Immaculate Heart of Mary); the annual pilgrimage to the Virgin first made here in 1836 by the Abbé Desfriche des Genettes always attracts an enormous crowd. On display in the choir are seven works* by Carle Van Loo painted specifically for that location; from r to l: *The Baptism of St Augustine* (1755), *The Consecration of St Augustine* (1754), *The Death of St Augustine* (1748), *The Vow of Louis XIII at the Siege of La Rochelle* (1746), *The Translation of the Relics of St Augustine* (1748), *The Disputation of St Augustine with the Donatists* (1753) and *The Preaching of St Augustine* (1755). The vigor of these compositions and the variety of facial expressions make this collection one of the masterpieces of 18th-c. religious art. In the second chapel to the r see the tomb of the composer, Jean-Baptiste Lully, with the figures of *Poésie* (Poetry) and *Musique* (Music) are by Pierre Cotton (1687); his bust is by Gaspard Collignon (and not Coysevox).

▷ The Revolution's destructions

Parisian churches and their works of art were choice targets for the vandalism of the Revolution and it is now rare to see complete sets of ecclesiastical furnishings in their original places. As early as 1792, religious objects in gold, silver and other precious metals were sent to the Mint for melting; the bells got the same treatment. The Revolutionaries also attacked the buildings and many statues, inside and outside, were either completely destroyed or decapitated.

The vigilance of some particular individuals saved a few from wholesale destruction: in 1977, the heads of the Kings of Judah, which decorated Notre-Dame, were found in the basement of a Parisian bank (Musée de Cluny). Other works of art had a happier destiny: as early as June 1791, Alexandre Lenoir collected some hundreds of these art objects and deposited them at the Petits-Augustins which became, in 1795, the Musée des Monuments Français (French Monuments). Unfortunately, after the dispersal of the contents of this museum in 1816, sculptures and paintings were not always returned to their place of origin and were often distributed arbitrarily to other churches and museums. The Basilica of Notre-Dame-des-Victoires is fortunate to have preserved the seven paintings by Carle Van Loo in the choir.

Rue du Vide-Gousset

Pickpocket Street.

This short street connects the Place des Petits-Pères to the Place des Victoires. At the beginning of the 19th c, it led from the Bourse then located at the Church of Notre-Dame-des-Victoires, to the Banque de France; its name recalls the unpleasant art that was practised there. At nos. 2 and 4 (and no. 1 Rue Aboukir) a *hôtel* built for Nicolas de Rambouillet in 1634, also known as the Hôtel de Clerambault: note the balcony at no. 2.

Place des Victoires**

This was one of the first royal squares to be designed as a setting for a reigning king's statue. In 1685 Jules Hardouin-Mansart cleared it to make room for the statue of Louis XIV, commissioned by Marshal de la Feuillade in 1679 after the victory at Nimègue, and paid for out of his own pocket. An astute courtier, he wished to show publicly his admiration and gratitude for his sovereign. A work commissioned by an important courtier, this is the archetype of a royal square designed like a room in the open air to show to advantage a statue of the king, with the proportions of the statue determining the size of the square. To this end no street entering the square on one side was aligned with a street on the other so that on approaching it, the effigy of the king would always stand out against the façades. Moreover, the ground-floor arches of the buildings were closed, rather than being used as arcades, so that people walking would always be in a good position to see the statue. The uniform façades of the buildings round the square were decorated with pilasters. Throughout history this square has been repeatedly remodelled. Hardouin-Mansart's work, emphasizing regularity and harmony, which became a model for numerous squares throughout France, was mutilated during the reconstruction of most of the surrounding buildings. The opening of the Rue Etienne-Marcel (1883) gave access to a square whose originality lay in the fact that it was closed, or at least appeared to be so. Turning your back on the Rue Etienne-Marcel, you can once again see the work of Jules Hardouin-Mansart.

Originally residential, this square was inhabited by some famous people, among them the art patron Crozat, the rich financier Samuel Bernard and the Marquis de Marigny. Since then, the luxury shops around have lent it its ostentatious décor.

▷ The royal squares

The royal squares served as show places for the statues of reigning monarchs. At the beginning of the 18th c, these were closed off and sheltered by houses, but were eventually opened up to neighbouring districts and became open crossroads revealing new perspectives.

Under the reign of Henri IV, Paris saw the birth of the Place de Vosges, Place Dauphine and the beginnings of a Place de France. It was only at the succession of Louis XIV that two new projects were completed: the Place des Victoires and Place Vendôme. The last royal square to be built was the Place de la Concorde during the reign of Louis XV.

▷ The statue of Louis XIV

The original statue was completely different from the one there today. The first, by Martin Desjardins, represented the king life-size, dressed in coronation robes and being crowned with the laurels of victory by La Victoire; the statue rested on a pedestal decorated with six bas-reliefs and flanked by figures of four chained men representing Holland, Spain, Austria and Prussia. Four lanterns burned night and day at the corners of the square as if to emphasize the sacredness of this triumphant place. During the Revolution, in 1792, the statue was melted down but the figures on the plinth are still preserved in the Parc de Sceaux. A mock-antique statue representing Général Desaix, in the nude, replaced that of Louis XIV. In 1815 this was melted down to be used for the statue of Henri IV on the Pont-Neuf. The present equestrian statue of Louix XIV by Bosio, was erected in 1822.

Rue Croix-des-Petits-Champs

The odd-numbered side of the street, S of the square, has become the headquarters for the Banque de France which has altered the street's architectural aspect by taking up such a large block between the Rue de la Vrillière, Rue Croix-des-Petits-Champs, Rue de Valois and Rue du Colonel Driant. This street's name refers to the stone cross erected, about 1418, on the corner with the Rue du Bouloi. No. 43, Hôtel Portalis, notable for its two towers with squinch arches, was built around 1685. No. 39 is the main entrance to the Banque de France. See also the early façade of the Banque de France (rebuilt 1870–1875) at nos. 1 and 3 Rue de la Vrillière.

☐ The Banque de France*

This is the central bank and, as such, is responsible for the issue of currency. Since 1811 the bank has occupied the Hôtel de Toulouse (formerly the Hôtel de la Vrillière) which has been completely restored; the only original remaining part is the corner on the Rue Radziwill. Inside, the Galerie Dorée (visiting is limited to cultural associations), measuring 160 ft by 23 ft (50m by 7m), is one of the first of those sumptuously decorated 17th-c. arcades, other examples of which include those at the Palais de Luxembourg, Versailles, the Hôtel Lambert and the Bibliothèque Nationale.

It was for the very rich Secretary of State, Louis Phelypeaux de la Vrillière, that François Mansart (uncle of J. H. –Mansart) built, near the Palais Cardinal, that mansion with its distinctive long gallery to house his great collection of paintings (1635–38). Large historical paintings, similar to those in the Galerie Farnèse were framed in the wood paneling on the first floor, beneath the barrel vault painted by François Pernier. In 1713, the house was sold to the Comte de Toulouse, legitimate son of Louis XIV and Mme de Montespan. The mansion, now known as the Hôtel de Toulouse, was altered by Robert de Cotte (1713–19) who transformed it into another palace. The paintings under the vault were left untouched, but the gallery was stripped down and embellished by sumptuous moulded panelings designed by the sculptor, Vassé (1719). The spaces between the doors were decorated by slightly projecting pilasters, the niches facing the windows were mirrored, and the entrance door and the monumental chimney at either end were crowned by marine divinities – an allusion to the Comte de Toulouse's position as Admiral of France. The collection of great paintings, which had been added to by a few others, was removed to the piers. This magnificent mansion was gradually destroyed, first during the Revolution, then when it was allocated to the Imprimerie Nationale (State Press) and finally when it was purchased by the Banque de France. It was rebuilt during the 19th c., as was the Galerie Dorée, which was reconstructed with the help of copies of paintings scattered throughout various museums. Only those sculptures of Vassé in wood and stucco evoking *La Chasse* (The Hunt) and *La Peche* (Fishing) were reused. The Banque de France owns many 18th-c. works of art, never seen by the public, notably *La Fête à Saint-Cloud* painted by Fragonard (c. 1775) for the apartments of the Duc de Penthièvre, son of the Comte de Toulouse.

The Galerie Verot-Dodat

The Rue Croix-des-Petits-Champs crosses the Rue du Bouloi. In the 19th c. this district was the center for lithographic printing houses, especially on the Rue du Bouloi, Rue Coquillière, Rue du Coq-Héron and Rue J. J. Rousseau.

No. 2 Rue du Bouloi is the entrance to the arcade created in 1822 by two pork butchers, Vero and Dodat, who by using gas lighting (which was still a novelty) made a fortune as soon as the arcade opened because they were able to charge high rents. Its success was also due to the splendour of the shop fronts which exploited the contrast of dark wood with shining brass and bronze. These small shops gave the gallery a luxurious appearance, with checkerboard tiling and stained-glass skylights. The great tragedienne Rachel was living on the third floor of no. 38 when the Théâtre–Français opened in 1836. Note at no. 24, the shop of the antiquarian Robert Capia (open 6.30 a.m. - 10.00 p.m.), who specialises in antique dolls. The shop has maintained the same policy since the time of Charles X (no dogs, no gramophones, no parrots . . .). Rue Jean-Jacques Rousseau. This is a rather complicated street, truncated by the Place des Deux-Ecus. In this first and oldest section, you will see some beautiful, tall façades (nos. 3, 13, 14, 19 and 20) and some interesting houses on the opposite side (even numbers: 2, 4, 6 and 12). Retrace your steps to the Rue Saint-Honoré.

The Oratoire*

In 1616, the Carmelite Oratorian Congregation had a chapel built on the site of the Hôtel de Bouchage, the house of Gabrielle d'Estrées in the 16th c., where Chatel had attempted to assassinate Henry VI, for which he was drawn and quartered at the Place de Grève. Louis XIII planned to integrate this fashionable chapel with the Palais du Louvre in order to enlarge it, but he did not have the time to fulfill his ambition. The Oratoire, built by Métezeau the younger from Le Mercier's design, became a temple of eloquence. The court flocked to listen to Bossuet, Massillon, Bourdaloue and Malebranche.

The present façade dates from the 19th c. During the Revolution it was an arms depot, after that a warehouse for storing costumes from the Opéra, then finally the Temple de l'Oratoire was given by Napoleon (1811) to the Calvinists. Inside, are the remains of a funeral monument to Cardinal de Bérulle and a ceiling painted by Simon Vouet.

From the arches of the Rue de Rivoli the E end or chevet of the church can be seen with the statue of Admiral de Coligny by Crauk, (1889). It was not exactly on this spot that the famous Protestant leader was assassinated during the massacre of St Bartholomew (night of August 24, 1572) but a little further on at no 144 Rue de Rivoli (the plaque is wrong) in a house which was demolished only in 1852. Sophie Arnould, the singer and actress, was born here in 1740.

🌲 Parc des Buttes-Chaumont**

19th arr.
Métro: Buttes Chaumont, Botzaris.
Bus: 26, 60, 75.
Parking: Garage Chambon, 89-90 Rue de la Villette.
Taxis: 10 Ave. Laumière. Tel. 42-06-00-00. Near Métro Station Botzaris. Tel. 42-05-00-00.

The Parc des Buttes-Chaumont, covering 9.3 acres/230,000m², is situated in the middle of the once popular district of Belleville, and is certainly one of the most pleasant and unexpected parks of the capital. Napoléon III commanded Haussmann to make this park like the one at Montsouris in the S, to give the working class the clean air found in green spaces. The bare hills (*monts chauves,* bald mountains, hence the name Chaumont) were laid out by the engineer Darcel (1866–67), and the landscape gardener Barillet-Deschamps, working under Alphand (chief organizer of the Parisian walks created during the Second Empire). From 272ft./83m to 371ft/101m in altitude, these form the most western promontory of the hills in Belleville.

It was one of the most highly praised works in the provision of green spaces and earned Alphand the name of 'engineer-artist'.

The history of the park

These hills, so pleasing today, were, in the Middle Ages, quarries and rubbish dumps. The Montfaucon gallows at the bottom made them one of the most sinister places in Paris, an area that François Villon knew well. Like the author of *La Ballade des Pendus,* the misfits of the time made their transitory homes in these vast chalk quarries and rocky crevices. The Buttes served in 1814 as the battlefield during the 'Battle of Paris', between the National Guard and the Cossacks and, in 1871, were instrumental in delaying the advance of the Versailles on March 26 and 27.

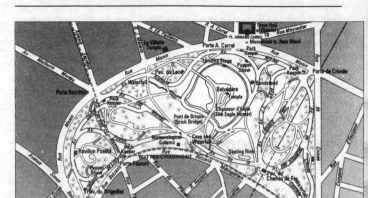

Visit to the park

30 mins.

The creators of the park, inspired by the style of Hubert Roberts, cleverly exploited the natural variety of levels afforded by the hills, transforming the ruins and rocks of this wild piece of land into the beautiful park of today.

There are six entrance gates to the park, the main one at Place Armand–Carrel.

The lake: boat trips to the Chemin des Aiguilles

The lake has a surface area of approx. 2 ha. A mass of steep rocks 164ft./50m high soars from the middle of the lake, forming the island, the most picturesque spot in the park.

The island

Two bridges, one called Pont de Brique (Brick Bridge) or Pont des Suicidés (Suicide Bridge), the other La Passerelle (the Footbridge) lead to the island, which is crowned with a reproduction of the temple called the Sibyl after that at Tivoli. From this little temple there are beautiful views of Montmartre (where the Communards from Buttes-Chaumont were bombarded by the Versaillés) and of Saint-Denis.

The Chemin des Aiguilles

The Chemin des Aiguilles, a staircase of 200 steps cut into the rock, leads to the landing stage for the boats: restaurant, puppet show, various attractions. Of the two artificial streams flowing into the lake, one cascades 105ft/32m into a grotto with a 66ft/20m arch decorated with artificial stalactites. All the way along the Rue Botzaris, the park is enclosed by a stone balustrade (also currently being restored) from where the view over Montmartre and Saint-Denis is magnificent.

▷ 'Picturesqueness' at the Parc Chaumont

The term 'picturesque' is used to describe 18th and 19th c. gardens whose designs ran counter to the prevailing Classical design of French gardens and where asymmetry and irregularity were employed to simulate a natural effect, often embellished by some exotic piece of architecture. For the engineer Darcel, instructed by Napoleon III to design the capital's new gardens, the picturesque was that which is essentially natural. In this respect the site for the future Parc des Buttes-Chaumont greatly interested him: 'This piece of land with its very steep slopes dominating Paris and the plains of Saint-Denis, is naturally very picturesque.' However, to perfect the wildness of nature, rich soil and artificial rocks were added, preserving 'the real precipices'. To blend in with this walk, the architect Davioud created other buildings in the same architectural style. One, at the topmost point of the park, is a small temple similar to that at Ile de Reuilly in the Bois de Vincennes. The model for this is the temple of the Sybil in Tivoli, which had already inspired the small garden gazebos popular in the 18th c

In *Le Paysan de Paris,* Aragon gives a mythical dimension to the Parc des Buttes-Chaumont, which he refers to as a 'legendary Paradise' or 'apartment of dreams'.

The Catacombs*

14th arr./Map ref. 22–D3
Métro: Denfert-Rochereau. Bus: 38, 68, 216.
Parking (open-air) on the central reservation between Place
Denfert-Rochereau and Place Saint-Jacques.
Taxis: Place Denfert-Rochereau. Tel. 43-54-00-00.

The catacombs that are open to the public are in the 14th arrondissement, in the area bounded by the Rue Rémy-Dumoncel, the Rue Hallé, the Rue d'Alembert and the Ave. René-Coty. They cover some 13,000 sq. yds/11,000m², a mere seven per cent of Paris's former underground quarries.

The history of the Catacombs

The Parisian catacombs, unlike those of Rome, which claim pre-Christian origins, date back only to the end of the 18th c. For over 500 years Paris had a cemetery, the Cimetière des Innocents, which served as the burial-ground for the remains of generations of the deceased from Paris's 20 parishes. However, it eventually became a breeding ground for infectious diseases. From 1725 onwards the inhabitants of the district around the cemetery campaigned for parliamentary action, but it was not until 1785 that the Conseil d'Etat consented to the closing and evacuation of the cemetery. The site chosen for the deposition of the remains was a place called 'La Tombe-Issoire', in part of a former stone-quarry, under the Montsouris plain. The transfer of the bones from the cemetery to the catacombs, which took place at night for 15 months, was considered so successful as a public health measure that the administration decided to go even further and between 1787 and 1814 a number of Parisian graveyards, especially those belonging to churches, were forbidden to perform burials. This historic timing means that many of the victims of the revolutionary days (August 28–29, 1788; April 28, 1789; August 10, 1792; the September 1792 prison massacres) were interred in the new ossuary. This must have included the corpses formerly buried at Errancis (the land to the E of the Parc Monceau which was used as a burial ground in 1794), among them probably the remains of Louis XVI's sister Mme Elisabeth, Danton, Desmoulins, Lavoisier and Robespierre. Ever since, any human remains found in Parisian ground have been laid to rest in the catacombs, but it is impossible to identify specific people with particular remains. Just before the 1789 Revolution the Comte d'Artois (later Charles X) threw parties for his Court in this macabre setting, with music, dancing and plenty of wine. The ossuary is divided off from neighboring quarries by thick masonry walls between pillars of the original stone, which were left by the quarries to prevent the roof from caving in and which cut the enclosed space into numerous meanders of some 87yds/80m in length. It's reckoned that the bones of 6 million people are gathered in these catacombs. The pillars bear inscriptions, mainly in French and Latin, but also in Greek, Italian and Swedish. Some of these inscriptions indicate the provenance of the remains, but the majority express religious or philosophical sentiments.

The catacombs have been open to the public since the 19th c. when visitors were given a candle or a tinderbox before descending, and had to follow a large black line painted on the gallery wall (still visible in many of the galleries). Today it is advisable to take a flashlight.

Tour of the Catacombs

Entrance: eastern gatehouse of the former Place d' Enfer tollgate, 1 Place Denfert-Rochereau.
Open Tues.-Fri. 2–4 p.m. Sat–Sun. 9–11 a.m. and 2–4 p.m. Groups welcome (maximum 30 people). Tel. 43-22-47-63. Guided tour, Tues. 2.45 p.m., lasts about 1 hour. Bring a flashlight.

No deviation from the marked itinerary is allowed, though the route is sometimes changed, and there is no entry beyond the grills which separate the catacombs from the former quarries.

A 90–step stairway at the back of the former tollhouse (built by the architect Claude-Nicolas Ledoux) leads down into the kingdom of the dead.

At the entrances to the galleries proper (66ft/20m below ground level) two rooms are devoted to a display of the work of the photographer Nadar (1861). The tour begins in the galleries laid out at the end of the 18th c.

Beyond the galleries which run under Ave. Général-Leclerc and Ave. René-Coty are the foundations of the Arcueil aqueduct (1612-13).

The quarries of Paris

The ancient city of Lutetia was able to develop as it did principally because of the local abundance of high-quality building materials. The sedimentary rock of the Paris Basin offered coarse limestone, gypsum (the chief ingredient in 'plaster of Paris'), clay, sand and gravel. From the Roman conquest to the 12th c., palaces, churches and religious houses were built with stone quarried from what is today the Jardin des Plantes on the W bank of the Bièvre. After the 12th c., quarries in the suburbs of Saint-Germain, Saint-Michel, Saint-Jacques, Montparnasse and Montsouris were in use, as well as those of the Oise.

By 1792 there were 18 quarries in Paris, with some 100miles/160km of underground galleries extending beneath one tenth (2100 acres/850h) of the city's surface area. Mining continued until 1813, but a large number of cave-ins (the result of abandoning old works without filling them in) caused Louis XVI's Conseil d'Etat to initiate a general inspection in 1777, whose task it was to record and map the existing quarries.

The Parisian quarries were basically laid out as follows: coarse limestone was quarried from the Left Bank in the 13th, 14th, 15th and the N of the 5th and 6th arrondissements, as well as from some quarries in the 16th arrondissement (Chaillot) and the 12th arrondissement (Daumesnil); gypsum in the 18th, 19th and 20th arrondissements; sand in the 15th (Grenelle), 7th, 12th (Bercy) and 13th arrondissements; and clay in the 15th arrondissement (Vaugirard).

In 1813 all underground excavations were forbidden – but this did not mean an end to the use of the existing quarries. During the 1848 Revolution the rebels took refuge in the quarry at Montmartre where they were massacred by Cavaignac's troops. During the Commune the quarries to the S provided access to and communication with the strongholds of Vanves, Montrouge and Ivry. The Resistance fighters used them during World War II, which is why they were called 'the Underground' by the British.

Today, 95% of Paris's quarries have been filled in or reinforced, so that there is no danger of accidental collapse.

L'Atelier (the Workshop)

At street level in the Rue Hallé, turning sharply at an angle (W - E) you come to a former quarry, now shored up: L'Atelier. A few metres further, carved out of the rock, is a relief representing the fortress of Port-Mahon, chief stronghold of the Balearics, which was seized by Richelieu in 1757. This relief was sculpted between 1777 and 1782, by Decure, one of the shoring workmen and a veteran of Louis XV's armies, who had been imprisoned in this fortress. While working on a stairway to improve access to the catacombs, he died, buried when the walls caved-in. Continuing the tour, you come to a well nicknamed the 'quarries' footbath'. Originally intended to provide drinking-water for thirsty quarriers, the well more often gave them an unexpected footbath, since the clarity of the underground water rendered it virtually invisible.

The ossuary

The doorway to the ossuary has been cut from one wall of the gallery beneath the Rue Hallé, in a fairly large room with two supporting masonry pillars. On the lintel, cut into the rock itself, is a line from Jacques Delille (famous for his French translation of Virgil): 'Stop, for this is the Kingdom of Death'. To the l. a monument commemorates the historical circumstances that led to the creation of the catacombs. Pass through the doorway and through a sort of hallway to reach the galleries that contain the remains from the Parisian cemeteries of Saint-Laurent, Saint-Jacques-du-Haut-Pas, Saint-Jean-de-la-Trinité, Saint-Leu, from the leper hospital in the Rue de Douai, the Carmelite monastery in the Place Maubert, the Cimetière des Innocents, and from the cemeteries of Saint-Landry, Saint-Nicholas-des-Champs, Saint-Etienne-des-Grès, and others.

The bones are stacked between the pillars and against the walls, forming a flat, even wall of bones above which there are various macabre ornamental arrangements, such as strings of skulls and crossed tibias. Behind these façades the remains are piled up indiscriminately. While visiting this section of the catacombs, you can also see a spring, known as the Fountain of the Samaritan woman (see John IV); it forms a circular basin surrounded by steps. A little further on there is a stone altar, a copy of a magnificent tomb found in 1807 between Vienne and Valence on the banks of the Rhône. The altar is in a room called the crypt of Sacellum (Mass has for many years been celebrated there on the first Sunday after All Souls' Day, November 2). This leads to another crypt, supported by two stone pillars, which houses a monument in the form of an ancient cup on a pedestal, known as the sepulchral lamp.

Next comes the so-called tomb of Gilbert, named after the lines taken from his poem on the Last Judgement, which are carved on the stone beneath. However, the sarcophagus is not the poet's esting place, but only an old part of the foundation which has been made to look like a tomb.

his leads to the remains of the Revolution's early protagonists from graveyards of the Hôtel de Brienne, Place de Grèvé, Rue Meslee, Faubourg Saint-Antoine, the Tuileries, etc. Notice the gravestone of Françoise Gellain, Dame Legros, who helped Latude escape from the Bastille. On the way to the exit from the ossuary there is a spacious crypt to the l. called the Crypt of the Passion, in the middle of which stands a supporting pillar decorated with skulls and tibia known as Le Tonneau. An inspection gallery under the Rue Rémy-Dumoncel leads the visitor back to daylight. There one can see two remarkable examples of subsidence, 37ft./11.3m and 36ft./11m deep; emptied and shored up, these sinkholes demonstrate the danger they could pose for roadworks or buildings above. A short way further on, the exit stairway leads into a little property belonging to the City of Paris, at 36 Rue Rémy-Dumoncel. This 84-step staircase climbs 57ft./17.5m and was constructed in one of the former wells down which the remains were lowered to the galleries (the Crypt of the Passion, mentioned above, is another such former well).

▷ **A concert at the Catacombs**

There is a circular hall with excellent accoustics near the entry to the ossuary. On April 2, 1897 from midnight to 2 a.m. this was the venue for an exceptional clandestine concert, arranged by a group of aesthetes, to which several journalists received this bizarre invitation: 'The pleasure of your company is requested at a sacred and secular concert to be held on Friday April 2, 1897 in the ossuary of the catacombs of Paris to be played by a gathering of eminent musical artists.

'A word of advice: Enter at no. 92 Rue Dareau, near Rue Hallé, from 11 p.m. onwards. To avoid attracting a crowd of curious onlookers, please do not ask your carriages to stop at the door.'

At 11 p.m. nearly 100 people gathered in the Rotonde des Tibias (Tibia Rotunda). At half-past midnight, the orchestra's candles were lit and for two hours the 45-piece orchestra played music in keeping with the venue: Chopin's *Marche Funèbre*, Saint-Saëns' *Danse Macabre*, a specially written piece by Xavier Leroux, a musician who was playing that night but who is now completely unknown, even to musicologists, called *Choral et Marche Funèbre des Perses* (inspired by an opera by Ferdinando Paër, whose music Napoleon admired more than anyone else's), and the Funeral March from Beethoven's *Eroica Symphony*.

Further information: *Paris* by Seân Jannet (Batsford); *Historic Paris* by Paul Blanchard (Letts Guides); *Sam White's Paris* by Sam White

(New English Library); *The Companion Guide to Paris* by Vincent Cronin (Collins); *The Seine* by Anthony Glyn (Weidenfeld).

The Chaillot district**

16th arr./Map ref. 7–B3, 13–B1
Métro: Trocadéro. Bus: 22, 30, 32, 63.
Parking: Ave. Georges–Mandel.
Taxis: Place du Trocadéro, 1 Ave. d'Eylau. Tel. 47-27-00-00.
Market: Ave. du Président–Wilson, between Place d'Iéna and Rue Debrousse. (Wed. and Sat. 7 a.m. – 1.30 p.m.)

This vast luxurious district stretches serenely along the length of the Right Bank, across the river from the tightly packed 15th arrondissement, and not far from the vibrant Champs–Elysées. Here the streets are mostly lined with well-to-do buildings and private mansions, an island of calm and quiet and a favorite location for foreign countries' legations and consulates.

It is a popular place for strolling because of its greenery and the richness of its 20th-c. architecture. At the end of Ave. Kléber, near the Ave. Président–Wilson, stands the monumental Palais de Chaillot, and the Palais d'Art Moderne, rare examples of the 1930s Colossal style, which is now coming back into favor.

The history of the district

Some time before the 7th c. a shanty town grew up on the hill, which was known as Nigeon, and would later form part of the village of Chaillot. A manor that overlooked the Seine there was given by Queen Anne to the religious brotherhood of Minims known popularly in the district as 'les Bonhommes' ('the Gentlemen'). Where the Palais de Chaillot now stands, Catherine de' Medici had built a country house, which in the 17th c. fell into the hands of Marshal Bassompierre, who was as famous for his love affairs as for his courage. When he left it, bound for the Bastille, where he spent 12 years, he first gallantly burned 6,000 love letters, the last traces of the *vie galante* he had led there. His heirs sold the château in 1651 to the ex-queen of England, Henrietta Maria, widow of Charles I, who founded the famous Convent of the Visitation there. The nuns were irreverently called 'Bassompierre's girlfriends'. It was here that the French divine Bossuet preached the Queen's funeral oration. Louise de La Vallière came here twice seeking solace, after Louis

XIV had tired of her naïveté, and before she took refuge in a Carmelite monastery. The Bonhommes' house stood to the W.

When Napoleon's son (the King of Rome) was born, the Emperor ordered a palace to be built for him which, in the words of its architects Percier and Fontaine, was to be the world's 'biggest and most extraordinary' palace. It was to stand on the hill, stretching as far as the Bois de Boulogne. The scheme foundered with the Emperor's downfall, but not before Henrietta Maria's existing château had been razed to the ground. All that remained of Napoleon's dream palace were a couple of ramparts which were used later in the building of the Trocadéro Palace in 1878. As a result of Haussmann's roadworkings, the hill was considerably levelled.

Tour of the district

1½ hrs.

Place du Trocadéro

Originally called the Place du Roi-de-Rome when it was established in 1869, this square became known as the Place du Trocadéro in 1877. It sits on top of the Chaillot hill which dominates the Right Bank. The former Palais de Chaillot was a single building that blocked the wonderful view across the river which the new Palais de Chaillot (1935–37) frames, its central opening offering a superb SE vista towards the Eiffel Tower, the Champ-de-Mars and the Ecole Militaire.

High on a pedestal in the center of the Place stands an equestrian statue of Marshal Foch, the work of Robert Wlérick and Raymond Martin. It was unveiled on November 11, 1951 to commemorate the 33rd anniversary of the 1918 Armistice, and the centenary of the Marshal's birthday (1851–1929). To the W, between Ave. Georges-Mandel and Ave. Paul-Doumer, the *Place* is dominated by the high terrace of the Passy cemetery. Set against the supporting wall is the monument erected 'To the glory of the French army of 1914–1918', which was inaugurated in May 1956. Its sheer size has aroused much criticism of its creator, Paul Landowski.

Passy Cemetery

Entrance: 2 Ave. Paul-Doumer.

The cemetery has a surface area of 20,400 sq. yds./17,060m², and contains 261 plots held in perpetuity. Since 1874 it has been Paris's most stylish cemetery. The entrance, rebuilt in 1934, is decorated with bas-reliefs by Janthial. It is difficult to recommend an exact route round the cemetery, since the pathways are not identified by name; however, since there are relatively few points of interest, a quick visit is easily possible. Begin on the r.

Renée Vivien (Pauline Tarn, d. 1909), lesbian poetess who translated Greek works. The Dupont sepulchre (name of the founder of 'Cafés Dupont'), with a bronze group, including a Mercury with a caducens. Marie Bashkirtseff's (d.1884) orthodox chapel dominates this part of the cemetery. She died at 24, leaving behind a diary which brought her posthumous fame. The next chapel is a columned rotunda, whose crypt is visible; it belongs to the Talleyrand–Périgord family. Maurice Paleologuse (d.1944), for a long time ambassador to the Russian Emperor Nicholas II; he left a great deal of interesting historical documents. Henri Farman (d.1958) a French aviation pioneer, represented here with a carving of a joy–stick. Opposite, the Curpilowski sepulchre which has a group in stone by Dunikowski, known as L'Accolade. Jean Giraudoux (d.1944), one of the greatest writers of the 20th c. Georges Mandel (d.1944), assassinated by French militia in the forest of Fontainebleau. The tomb, with pyramid, of the Comte de Las Cases; he went with Napoleon to Saint Helena, and stayed there nearly two years. Each evening he wrote up that day's conversations with Napoleon; this journal became Le Mémorial de Sainte-Hélène. Charles Luizet, Prefect of Police of Paris, who took up his post on August 20, 1944 in a Préfecture besieged by the Germans; he died in 1947, having just been named Governor General of French Equatorial Africa. General Huntziger (d.1941), Minister of War in the Vichy Government, who suffered the humiliation of having to sign the French surrender on June 22, (1940) at Rethondes, in the same railway carriage used by Foch 22 years earlier. The famous actress Réjane (d.1920). Jean Chiappe (d.1940), former Prefect of Police who died in a mysterious plane crash over the Mediterranean. The tomb of the painter Edouard Manet (d.1883), with a bust by Leenhoff. His sister-in-law, Berthe Morisot (d.1895), also a painter, lies next to him. Marinoni (d.1904): inventor of the rotary printing press he was director of the Petit Journal. The beautiful chapel of the Cognacq–Jay family, who established the Samaritaine chain of department stores, gave Paris a museum, and launched the idea of reduced admission fees for large families. The aviator Costes (d.1973) has an unusual monument on which the many dangerous flights he undertook are retraced across two hemispheres. Opposite in the third row the grave of the popular actor, Fernandel (d.1971). Bordering the pathway, a bust of Octave Mirabeau (d.1917). Jane Henriot, actress of the Comédie Française, who was burned alive in the fire of March 8, 1900; statue by Dourgon. The composer André Messager (d.1929). The composer Gabriel Fauré (d.1924); tombstone in pink granite. The composer Claude Debussy (d.1918) lies buried in a very solitary grave, well to the side under a hillock of myrtle; his name appears only on the back of the funerary stele.

Other personalities who are buried at Passy, but who do not appear

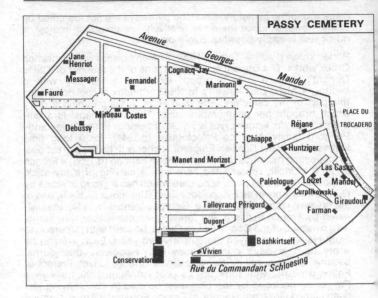

PASSY CEMETERY

Jane Henriot
Messager
Fauré
Fernandel
Cognacq-Jay
Marinoni
Mirbeau Costes
Debussy
Manet and Morizot
Chiappe
Réjane
Huntziger
Paléologue
Lozet
Las Cases
Mandel
Curplikowski
Giraudoux
Talleyrand Périgord
Farman
Dupont
Bashkirtseff
Vivien
Conservation

PLACE DU TROCADERO

Avenue Georges Mandel

Rue du Commandant Schloesing

on the reference map: the sculptor L. Barrias (d.1905), bust by Allar; the actress Julia Bartet, known as 'La Divine' (d.1941); the humorist Tristan Bernard (d.1947); the playwrights Henry Bernstein (d.1953) and Edouard Bourdet (d.1945); the chapel of the Carnot family (the blood-soaked clothing that President Sadi Carnot was wearing when he was assassinated at Lyons in 1894 is preserved here in a coffer); the painter T. Chartran (d.1907), bust by Carlès; the writer Francis de Croisset (d.1937); the painter Dagnan–Bouveret (d.1919); the industrialist and philanthropist Benjamin Delessert (d.1847), whose son Gabriel, buried with him, was Prefect of Police. The sculptor Frémiet (d.1910), whose statue of Joan of Arc stands in the Place des Pyramides; the historian and government minister Georges Hanotaux (d.1944); the playwright Paul Herview (d.1915); the singer Rosine Laborde (d.1907), statue by Landowski; Lefuel (d.1880) architect of the Louvre under Napoléon III; the poetress Rosemonde Gérard, wife of Edmond Rostand and mother of Maurice and Jean Rostand; Alexandre Millerand (d.1943), President of the French Republic; the decorator Ruhlmann who lies in a tomb of very modern design; the actress Marie Ventura; the art-critic Weisweiler.

Palais de Chaillot*

Built for the 1937 Paris Exhibition by the architects Carlu, Boileau, and Azéma on the site, and on some of the foundations, of the former Palais du Trocadéro, the Palais de Chaillot's main feature is the pair of huge curved wings, each of which stretches out 213 yds./ 195m. These do not meet in the center, but each wing ends in an immense pavilion. This creates a center space between the two main pavilions, laid out as a vast terrace immediately below which is a theater, which offers a superb view. The Palais houses an exceptional collection of 1930s architecture, sculpture and painting. The descent towards the Seine is particularly splendid. In its present form the Chaillot hill is now probably nearer Napoleon's dream and the original design of Percier and Fontaine than the 1878 Palais du Trocadéro.

The Palais du Trocadéro was originally only 'temporary', built by Davioud and Bourdais for the 1878 Exhibition. It was a huge building which comprised two wings, joined by a central rotunda (190 ft./58m in diameter and 164 ft./50m high), flanked by two square minarets (230 ft./70m high), and surrounded by two storeys of aroaded galleries. The wings survived, incorporated with the wings of the present Palais de Chaillot. But already in 1878 the Palais du Trocadéro could boast a concert hall with seating for 5000 spectators, the Musée de Sculpture Comparée set up by Viollet-le-Duc (forerunner of the Musée des Monuments Français), and the Musée d'Ethnographie, founded by Doctor Henry, which was to become the Musée de l'Homme.

The entrance pavilions

The façade of the Palais de Chaillot is faced with gold-colored limestone from Massangis (Yonne) and the two main pavilions bear inscriptions in gold letters on both sides by the poet Paul Valéry. The main entrances (approached from the Place du Trocadéro) are surmounted by monumental bronze sculptures depicting *Les Connaissances Humaines* (Human Knowledge) by Delamarre to the l. and *Les Elements* (The Elements) by Sarrebezolles to the r. The pavilion at the head of the Passy (r.-hand) wing, in whose entrance hall stands an Amerindian totem pole 52 ft./16m high, houses the Musée de l'Homme (Museum of Mankind) and the Musée de la Marine (Marine Museum); and has above the doors, a bas-relief by the Martel Brothers. The pavilion at the head of the Paris (l.-hand) wing which houses the Musée des Monuments Français (Museum of French Monuments), also has a bas-relief above its doors by Hairon and Quinquad. Two monumental stairways, one from each pavilion, lead to the theater. The Paris wing also houses the Cinémathèque and the Musée du Cinéma. The rear-facing façades, along the Rue Franklin and the Ave. du Président-Wilson, are windowless, but are decorated with bas-reliefs sculpted (on the

Paris side) by Abbal, Costa, Bertola, Delbarre, Veziem, Collamarini, and Martin; and (on the Passy side) by Yencesse, Joffre, Zwobada, Saunpique, Sartorio, Contesse, and Arnold. The monument to Paul Adam (1862-1920) by Landowski (1931) is set against the far end of the Paris wing.

The parvis and terrace

In contrast to the sober, pure vertical lines of the two pavilions, the central parvis (enclosed courtyard) between them is decorated along the sides with ornamental pools and statues in gilded bronze by Gimond, Pryas, Couturier, Cornet, Niclausse and others. On the terrace in front of the Paris wing stands Bouchard's bronze *Apollo*; in front of the Passy wing, also in bronze, Pommier's *Hercules.*

Paul Valéry's funerary vigil and other official funeral ceremonies took place on this terrace (July 24-25, 1945). The parvis and terrace are popular with peddlers and hawkers of exotic arts and crafts as well as with roller skaters and skateboarders. Most striking is the superb view* down over the main ornamental pool with its fountains, the river, the Eiffel Tower, the Champ-de-Mars and the Ecole Militaire beyond.

The Théâtre de Chaillot

From both sides of the parvis two huge stairways lead down to the terrace. At the foot of the steps are two stone statues by Wlérick and Lejeune. Beneath the terrace is the façade of the Théâtre de Chaillot with nine high rectangular bays (decorated in bas-relief by Auricoste, Navarre, Grange, Michelet and Belmondo) between unadorned buttresses. The construction of this underground theater posed considerable technical problems which were fortunately solved without disrupting the balance of the architecture as a whole. The third and sixth Plenary Sessions of the UN General Assembly were held here in 1948, and 1951-52.

Jean Vilar's Théâtre National Populaire (TNP) was post-war France's most adventurous theatrical project. Huge audiences (up to 2500) applauded *El Cid, Ruy Blas, Le Prince de Hombourg.* Jean Vilar's style of production, which reduced sets and props to the bare essentials, concentrating instead on effective costumes and lighting, contributed to the theater's success. The theater also had a team of young, keen and dynamic actors and actresses with whom the public could identify, including the renowned Gérard Philipe and Jeanne Moreau. When in 1963 Jean Vilar resigned in protest against the government's inadequate support, Georges Wilson took over as director, to be followed by Jack Lang. The latter decided to break open the great hall, preferring mobile structures such as a revolving stage to give the actors unrestricted freedom of movement. When the TNP became the Théâtre National de Chaillot, it was left to André-Louis Perinetti to inaugurate the new structures –

not that he ever fully exploited them. When Antoine Vitez took over as director of the theater in 1981, he too tried to create a new relationship between stage and the auditorium. Soon, however, he gave up and asked set designer Yannis Kokkos to restore the theater to the conventional arrangements with tiers of seats facing the stage. In 1966 an experimental theater seating 520 was set up under the name Salle Gémier.

The theater's interior has changed considerably since it was first designed by the Nierman brothers. However, the hall, the galleries, the foyers and stairways, in all their original grandeur, are still clad entirely in marble and polished stone whose richness accentuates the architecture's sober lines. These spaces also house an important collection of contemporary painting including works by, for the entrances: Maurice Denis and his group; for the stairways: Billotey, Narbonne, Souverbie, and Marchand; for one of the Vestibules des Quatre-Colonnes: Brianchon Chapelain-Midy, Oudot and Planson; and for the other: Boussingault, Céria, Dufrène and Luc-Albert Moreau; for the smokers' bar: Othon Friesz and Raoul Dufy; for the dress circle: de Waroquier and Charlemagne; for the stalls Vuillard, Roussel and Bonnard; and finally Jaulmes for the main foyer – a huge 289 ft./88m gallery with high windows looking out onto the Champ-de-Mars – with décor by Sue and light fixtures by R. Subes.

The main ornamental pool

The long, rectangular pool lies at the foot of the terrace, opposite the theater entrance and on line with the Iéna Bridge. The pool, whose illuminated fountains are especially beautiful at night, is framed by sloping lawns, and surrounded by several stone and bronze-gilt statues. At the upper end there is *Homme* (Man) by (Traverse) and *Femme* (Woman) by Bacque, *Taureau* (Bull) by Jouve, and *Chevaux* (Horses) by Guyot. Two decorative groups in stone by Pierre Poisson and Drivier stand at the lower end.

The Trocadero Gardens

The gardens (which cover 25 acres/10h.) were transformed and restored by R. Lardat after the 1937 Exhibition. Embellished by pools and streams, the gardens are cut diagonally by two sections of the Ave. des Nations Unies which pass through them: one is an extension of the Ave. d'Iéna, the other of the Boul. Delessert – both leading down to the Pont d'Iéna. Underground passageways connect the gardens between these avenues. In the NE section of the gardens, at the foot of the Paris wing, is the underground Trocadéro Aquarium (open daily 10am – 5.30pm. Tel. 42-23-62-95), also renovated in 1937, which exhibits a collection of freshwater fishes from the rivers of France. In the W part of the gardens, at the foot of the rocky escarpments, is a fragment from Philippe de l'Ormes' western façade of the Tuileries, placed here in 1883; there is also a dormer window from the old 11th-c. Hôtel de Ville and the monument to Admiral Grasse (1772–88) by P. Landowski. Turn l. along the Ave. de New York, then l. again on the Ave. Albert-de-Mun.

Avenue d'Iéna

As far as the Place d'Iéna.

This wide arterial road follows approximately the same path as an ancient roadway that ran through the village of Chaillot, where Henri IV and the beautiful Gabrielle d'Estrées had a summer house. Today it is an extremely cosmopolitan avenue.

The large mansion at no 2 was built between 1884 and 1887 by the architect Brune for Jules Grévy, President of the Republic. Subsequently it became the residence of the US Ambassador before being replaced by an apartment block in 1973. At no 4, the Iranian Embassy occupies what in its day (1898) was considered to be a modern-style building, designed by Xavier Schoellkopf; the Classical façade it has today dates from the eve of World War I, at which time the house belonged to the Comte de Cambacérès. No 10 is the former mansion of Prince Roland Bonaparte, built by Janty between 1892 and 1899; today it houses the Centre Français du Commerce Extérieur, having been renovated for that purpose in 1929 by Roux-Spitz. In the prince's time, it housed a scientific library of 100,000 volumes, as well as a collection of Napoleonic memorabilia. Marie Bonaparte (Princess George of Greece), a renowned psychoanalyst, was born in this house.

Place d'Iéna

In the center of the Place d'Iéna stands an equestrian statue of Washington in bronze by David C. French and Edward G. Poitier, donated by the Société des Filles de la Révolution (Daughters of the Revolution) in 1900.

To the SW of the Place d'Iéna, on the corner of the Ave. d'Iéna and the Ave. du President-Wilson, stands the circular entry to the Palais du Conseil Economique et Social (the seat of the Economic and Social Council). It was built by Auguste Perret (d.1952) between 1937 and 1938 for the Musée des Travaux Publics (Museum of Public Works). It is one of this great architect's most successful buildings, at once classical and original, with fluted concrete columns and a brilliantly curved flying staircase made of concrete inside. The shape of the entrance exactly follows the semi-circular form of the amphitheater it houses. Between 1960 and 1962 another 196 ft./60m long wing was added along the Ave. du Président-Wilson in the same style by the architect Vimont, for the headquarters of the Union Européenne Occidentale (Western

European Union). On the third side of the triangular island, you can still see a stone and brick building which was once the Dépôt des Phares et Balises (beacons and lighthouses warehouse); this building is typical of its architect, Léonce Raynaud. The Musée Guimet (→Museums) stands on the corner of Ave. d'Iéna and the Rue Boissière.

Avenue du Président-Wilson

On this street, formerly the Ave. du Trocadéro, once stood the Manutention Militaire (military storehouse) which replaced the Savonnerie ('soapworks' – an allusion to the building's original use) carpet manufactory, forerunner of the famous Gobelins. Nos. 11–12 were once the site of property owned by Mme de Pompadour, later occupied by the singer Sophie Arnould, and demolished in 1865. Also near here at the end of the 18th c. Tallien had his elegant 'rustic' cottage where fashionable beauties and dandies – the *Merveilleuses* – dressed in fashionable exaggerated clothes and powdered wigs, led the high life. Nothing remains of this, save the beautiful cedar on the corner of no. 12; planted in 1788, it graced the former Polish Embassy and the places evoked by Anatole France in *Le Lys rouge*. No 34 was the home of Laure Haymann, whom Proust used as the model for his Odette.

▣ The Palais d'Art Moderne*

11–13 Ave. du Président-Wilson.

This museum comprises two buildings, the Palais d'Art Moderne de la Ville de Paris (the Palais de New-York) to the E and the Palais de Tokyo to the W, which were built for the 1937 Exhibition and cover 5 acres/2ha. running from the Seine up to the Ave. du Président-Wilson, a slope of 39 ft./12m (→Museums).

The original modernist plans of Le Corbusier and Mallet-Stevens were rejected in favor of the more traditional academic designs of Dondel, Aubert, Viart and Dastugue. Those who prefer post-modern architecture will like this building's atavistic Greco-Roman style and more than one visitor will be seduced by the high colonnade of white stone which links the two wings, forming a portico round the large central patio. Of similar inspiration there are the monumental sculpted bronze doors, notably those on the Alma Rotunda, surmounted by a very beautiful statue of the City of Paris by Dideron. Equally attractive, but sadly dilapidated at present while awaiting its planned restoration, is the Cour des Musées (Museum Courtyard). With its vast central pool, its four reclining figures by Drivier, Dejean and Guénot, its walls decorated with bas-reliefs by Janniot, Gaumont and Baudry on the themes of 'The Muses and Legend', the courtyard is like a great open-air exhibition. Antoine Bourdelle's immense allegorical group on the terrace wall dominates the space. The sculpture was erected in 1948 by the Association des Français Libres (Free French Association) to the memory of Free French volunteers killed between 1940 and 1945. Two other bronzes by Bourdelle, *La Force* (strength) and *La Victoire* (Victory) stand on either side of the peristyle.

The Palais Galliera

The Palais Galliera stands in the Square Brignolles-Galliera, entered from Ave. Président-Wilson, opposite the Palais d'Art Moderne. The building is in Italian Renaissance style, built by Léon Ginain between 1878 and 1894 to house the collections that the Italian Duchesse de Galliera planned to donate to the City of Paris. The central pavilion has three large arcades with statues representing *Painting* by Chapu, *Architecture* by Thomas, and *Sculpture* by Cavalier; this is flanked by two colonnaded wings, forming porticoes, also adorned with statues. The building houses the Musée de la Mode et du Costume (→ Museums), which has over 400 complete costumes. These are shown in temporary thematic exhibitions. The entrance is on the Ave. Pierre-Ier-de-Serbie.

Rue Georges-Bizet

Via the Ave. Pierre-Ier-de Serbie

At the beginning of the 19th c. this street was known as Rue des Blanchisseuses (washerwomen) because it led right down to the river.

At no 5 is the Greek Orthodox Church which was commissioned by a rich Greek national, who presented it to the Greek state (which still owns it) and built by the architect Vaudremer in 1895. The Byzantine style paintings are by Lameire. Covering the half-house of the apse and protected by an inconostasis, is the *Pantocrator* (Christ in Glory).

✝ The Church of Saint-Pierre-de-Chaillot

35 Ave. Marceau

(Closed 1-3; Sunday closed 1-4. Tel. 47-20-12-33).

Today's church, designed by Emile Blois and built between 1933 and 1937, replaced an older one that had a choir dating back to the 17th c. and an 18th-c. nave. The new building is in the form of a Greek cross, its façade flanked by a bell-tower and, is a free interpretation of the Romanesque, which takes full advantage of the opportunities offered by working in concrete. The partition-wall of the entrance is decorated with a huge relief showing episodes from the *Life of St Peter* by Jean Bouchard; this, too, echoes Romanesque. The church's interior has an austere grandeur, the result of the architect's skilful handling of space. The high pillars at the crossing of the transept are decorated with frescoes by Nicolas Untersteller; the stained-glass windows and polychrome stonework on the altars are by the Mauméjean brothers. The *Stations of the Cross,* and the bas-reliefs on the high altar and pulpit are by Bouchard. On leaving the church, turn l. into the busy Rue de Chaillot, then r. into the Rue Georges-Bizet.

Place des Etats-Unis

This square is bordered by private mansions *(hôtels particuliers),* most of them now converted to diplomatic use as embassies and consulates. The large house at no. 13 was commissioned by the banker Bischoffsheim from the architect Sanson. He even had a painted ceiling by Solimena brought from Palermo for its ballroom. Between the wars, his granddaughter Vicomtesse Marie-Laure de Noailles held her famous literary and artistic gatherings here. The Place des Etats-Unis boasts several 'American' monuments: a monument by Boucher to the American volunteers who died for France in World War I; Bertholdi's bronze group, *La Fayette and Washington* (1895); a bust of Myron T. Herrick, former US Ambassador to France; a statue of the American surgeon Horace Weiss by Bouthée (1910); and, finally, a statue of General Pershing. Follow the Rue Galilée to the r. from the NE corner of the Place des Etats-Unis. The house at no. 30 was designed by Paul Sédille, the architect of the Printemps department stores. The two caryatids supporting the porch were sculpted in 1895 by Allar; the poem inscribed on the lintel refers to their strongly contrasting expressions.

■ **The Ave. d'Iéna** (final stretch). The small museum at no. 60 *bis* (open Mon. – Fri. 9am – 1pm, 2–5pm. Tel. 47-20-65-40), organized by the French Football Federation, houses a collection of souvenirs commemorating the French national team's greatest moments. The Ave. d'Iéna crosses the Place de l'Uruguay. At no. 51 Rodolphe Kahn's former mansion is now occupied by the Centre Culturel Portugais. Further on, at no. 7 on the Rue Lapérouse, there is an aluminium and glass building constructed in 1951 (architects, Gravereau and Lopez with a façade by the engineer Jean Prouté), the headquarters of the Federation Nationale du Batiment et des Travaux Publics. Glass has also been extensively used at no. 29 on the façade of the main office of the Compagnie Bancaire (M. Herbert, 1978).

The Ave. Marceau via the Rue de Presbourg (heading E.) is a wide street that forms a direct link between the Place Charles-de-Gaulle-Etoile and the Place de l'Alma. The Danish Embassy, inaugurated in 1967, stands at no. 77. Designed by architects Preben Hansen and Bernard Zehrfuss, its unusual method of construction allows the building's concrete skeleton to remain visible.

Avenue Kléber

Originally called the Ave. du Roi-de-Rome. It runs between the Place Général-de-Gaulle-Etoile and the Place du Trocadéro. Two former mansions bear witness to the long tradition of luxurious style and rich quality of this well-to-do and cosmopolitan district. The contrast between the two buildings also highlights the contradictory currents in early 20th c. architecture.

The former Hôtel Mercédès stands on the corner of the Rue de Presbourg. This modernist building was erected in 1903 by the architect Georges Chedanne. The façades are embellished by curved bow windows surmounted by galleries. On the keystones of the ground-level bays, the sculptors Gasq and Boutry have depicted couples driving or reading maps, while the corbels above feature figures of women swathed in scarves and men in driving goggles and helmets. All these enjoyable little scenes form a unique iconographic ensemble on the history of the car. By contrast the former Hôtel Majestic at no. 19 by Sibien (1908) is an example of conservative architecture, the opulence of whose sculpted decoration only highlights its stylistic obsolescence. Yet its outwardly academic appearance concedes the use of what were at the time up-to-the-minute techniques (such as floors of reinforced concrete), and its roof garden offered a unique panorama of the city. Built on the site of the Hôtel de Castille, where Queen Isabelle II lived between 1868 and 1904, the Hôtel Majestic, acquired by the State in 1939, is used today as an international conference center.

Other celebrities who have had connections with the Ave. Kléber include: Aristide Briand who died at no. 52 (March 7, 1932), and the great Lithuanian poet O. V. Milosz (1877-1939) who lived at no. 73. Not far off, at 44 Rue Hamelin, Marcel Proust lived from 1919 until his death in 1922.

Other places of interest on the outskirts of the district are the Arc de Triomphe, Ave. des Champs-Elysées and Ave. Foch.

▷ Art collectors and connoisseurs of the 16th arrondissement

There may be no shops or boutiques offering works of art for sale in Chaillot but, partly due to a certain tradition and partly because of the concentration of wealth here, it has always been home to a number of famous collectors. Since such people are notoriously discreet about their wealth, the list that follows is inevitably incomplete, and focuses on the past rather than the present.

The Goncourt brothers (Jules and Edmond), who lived in a small mansion on the Boul. de Montmorency at Auteuil, were largely responsible for re-establishing the reputation of 18th-c. art, and opened up the mysteries of the Far East to their contemporaries. The novelist Adolphe d'Ennery collected items from China and Japan, which are now on display in the pleasant museum of exotic art at 59 Ave. Foch. The aims of the industrialist Emile Guimet from Lyons were much more scientific, and his collection forms the basis of the famous museum named after him, at 6 Place d'Iéna. The miller and manufacturer of various kinds of pastry dough, Camille Groult, had an outstanding collection of 18th-c. French and English paintings in a mansion on the Ave. Malakoff which no longer exists. The huge mansion at 51 Ave. d'Iéna, which today houses the Centre Culturel Portugais, was where Calouste Gulbenkian (the famous 'Mister 1%') had his collection of paintings and sculpture. This is now on show at the museum he established in Lisbon. The most famous collector, however, is surely the couturier Jacques Doucet. His elegant mansion at 19 Rue Spontini (sadly, no longer there) housed a collection of 18th-c. art. When this came up for auction in 1912 it was regarded as 'the sale of the century'. Also worth mentioning are Jules Strauss' Impressionist collection; Georges Pauilhac's collection of weaponry, now in the Musée de l'Armée; the Marmotan family, father and son, whose museum is dedicated to the art of the First Empire. The last is a good example of how these collections betray their origins in the enthusiasm of amateurs who spent their wealth out of enlightened curiosity.

▣ Museums to visit

Musee Guimet (6 Place d'Iéna): Asian art.

Musée d'Art Moderne de la Ville de Paris (11 Ave. du Président-Wilson): modern and contemporary art.

Musée de la Mode et du Costume (10 Ave. Pierre-Ier-de-Serbie): costumes and accessories from the 18th c. to the present day.

Musée des Monuments Français (Palais de Chaillot, Place du Trocadéro): casts of sculpture from the 11th to 19th c.

Musée de l'Homme (Palais de Chaillot, Place du Trocadéro): anthropology, prehistory, and ethnography.

Musée de la Marine (Palais de Chaillot, Place du Trocadéro): maritime history, and models of boats from the 18th c. to the present day.

Musée du Cinéma (Palais de Chaillot, Ave. Albert-de-Mun): history of cinema, displays of studios, costumes and sets.

Musée des Matériaux (Place du Trocadéro): architectural and building materials.

Musée du Football (60 bis Ave. d'Iéna): memorabilia and photographs of the French National football team.

The Champs-Elysées***

8th arr./Map ref. 8-C2, D2; 9-A2, B2, B-3
Métro: Concorde.
Bus: 24, 42, 52, 72, 73, 84, 94
Parking: Place de la Concorde
Taxis: 258 Rue de Rivoli. Tel. 42-61-67-60.

The urban planning of the Champs-Elysées (Elysian Fields) is of recent date. Its development began in the Second Empire, and entailed a significant extension of the capital to the W.

The upper section, lined with luxury apartment blocks, cinemas, offices, shopping arcades, fast food places and famous bars, draws a disparate population of business people, tourists and young suburbanites who have momentarily abandoned the Grands Boulevards. The eastern section, where huge gardens surround the Place de la Concorde, has retained its original character. While the sumptuous carriages of Swann's friends (Proust's novel) no longer descend the wide tree-lined alleys, these 'carriage rides' nevertheless remain among the finest promenades in Paris.

History of the Champs-Elysées

The Champs-Elysées was laid out expressly to embellish and extend the royal view from the Tuileries. As early as 1616 Marie de'Medici had ordered the planting of three avenues of trees, the Cours-la-Reine. A decree of 1667 ordered the planting of a promenade, or Grand-Cour, extending on from the Tuileries gardens. This was to be carried out under the direction of André Le Nôtre, who had planned to create a large intersection from which the Grand-Cour, the Cours-la-Reine and a new thoroughfare to be laid across the Faubourg Saint-Honoré would all radiate. The line of the Grand-Cours, renamed the Champs-Elysées in 1709, was extended in the 18th c. beyond the Rond-Point as far as the Etoile hill.

At the instigation of the Duc d'Antin, the Superintendant of Buildings, the hill was levelled in 1710 to give easier access to carriages. In 1772 the Marquis de Marigny, also a Superintendant of Buildings, widened the avenue and extended it to the Neuilly Bridge built by Perronet. In 1777, a colonel of the Swiss Guard noted the presence of cabarets, cafés and shacks in a report and commented, 'Several individuals have cows grazing in the Champs-Elysées, their number is considerable, they may be a nuisance to the promenade'. In 1800 the Champs-Elysées had only six houses, the oldest of which was the Hôtel de Massa (1784), and the area was still relatively wild and little frequented.

It was mostly during the Second Empire that the district was filled with fine private houses and *hôtels* for visiting financiers and business people. With the addition of fountains, asphalted pavements and gaslight, came cafés, restaurants and theaters, and with them the Champs-Elysées became the symbol of gracious living, and a popular rendezvous.

On July 14, 1919 the French and Allied armies marched in procession down the triumphal way of the Champs-Elysées, as did General de Gaulle on August 26, 1944, at the head of Leclerc's division to the adulation of a liberated populace.

Tour of the district

1 hr.

From the Place de la Concorde, continue along the r.-hand side of the Champs-Elysées.

The gardens of the Champs-Elysées**

These gardens, laid out by Hittorff in 1838, have scarcely changed in 150 years. The paths, one of which is named after Marcel Proust, the lawns and the flowerbeds of today look almost as they did when the young Proust, accompanied by his maid, and with as much hope as apprehension, went on his way to his rendezvous with Marie de Bernadaki, who was unaware that she would one day serve as the model for Gilberte in Proust's great novel.

On either side of the avenue are the pavilions built by Hittorff: on the l., the Restaurant Ledoyen, which has been there since the days of Louis XVI, and on the r. the Etoile, Gabriel-Potel and Chabot pavilions; the latter was home to the Alcazar d'Eté, during the *Belle Époque* of the Parisian *'caf' conc' (café-concert)* at the beginning of the Third Republic, home to Thérésa, Paulus and many other famous entertainers. The building was enlarged by Formigé. Near the Palais de l'Elysée* (→ Faubourg Saint-Honoré) the monument to Alphonse Daudet, erected in 1902, stands in a garden setting. In 1984 five bronze stelae, sculpted by Jean-Clos, were placed in the garden in homage to the Resistance fighter, Jean Moulin.

The Espace Pierre-Cardin has a place in the forefront of Parisian cultural life. Originally it was a simple *café chantant* opened in 1830. A hundred years later the City of Paris decided to erect a building on the site comprising a restaurant and the Théâtre des Ambassadeurs, where Cocteau's *Parents Terribles* was created, the play in which his favourite actor, Jean Marais, made his début. The fountains, from the Napoléon III period, are by Duret.

Further on the gardens are bounded by the Ave. Gabriel, which is lined by the American Embassy*, the gardens of the British Embassy (→Faubourg Saint-Honoré) and those of the Elysée Palace, enclosed by the Grille du Coq; between the two is a building in stone, glass and aluminium put up in 1978.

At the intersection with the Ave. de Marigny the open-air stamp market Bourse aux Timbres is held (Thurs., Sat., Sun., and public holidays). The Hôtel de Rothschild (23 Ave. de Marigny) has become the Résidence Marigny, the property of the State, reserved for distinguished foreign guests.

The Théâtre Marigny

In 1883 Charles Garnier, the architect of the Opéra, built a 'panorama' (a theater in which the performance space surrounded the audience), in the Carré Marigny on the site of a little theater that Offenbach had directed from 1855 to 1858. In 1896 the panorama was converted into a music-hall, and then in 1925 into the Théâtre Marigny as it is today. The theater was most famous from 1946 to 1956, when the newly created Renaud-Barrault company was in residence there.

Return to the Place Georges-Clemenceau where, on a rock to the r., is a statue of Clemenceau (F. Cogné, 1932).

Avenue Winston-Churchill

At the beginning of the century this avenue was called the Place Nicolas-II and led to the Pont Alexandre-III (→Bridges of Paris) which was built to commemorate the Franco-Russian alliance. The opening of this remarkable vista* on to the esplanade and dome of the Invalides was part of the large-scale public works undertaken at the time of the Universal Exhibition of 1900, along with the two palaces built at different points on the avenue.

▣ The Petit Palais** (on the l)

Designed by Charles Girault and built between 1897 and 1900 to house a retrospective of French art as part of the Universal Exhibition, it now houses the collections of the City of Paris Museums.

This building, like its neighbor, bears witness to the return to academicism following the apotheosis of iron architecture at the Universal Exhibition of 1889. Its galleries are arranged around a semicircular courtyard. The main façade, facing the Grand Palais, has a certain grandeur, with its Ionic colonnade framing a great porch crowned by a dome which echoes that of the Invalides. The iron-work entrance door beneath the porch has a massive richly sculpted stone frame. At the foot of the steps, on the l., is *Les Quatres Saisons* (The Four Seasons), by Convers; on the r., *La Seine et les affluents* (The Seine and its Tributaries), by Ferrary, larger than life groups; the striking vaulting of the doorway, in which flowers, fruits and animals are interlaced, is crowned by *La Villede Paris protégeant les Arts* (The City of Paris protecting the Arts), by Injalbert; above the pediment, on the l. is a painting and on the r. a sculpture, both by R. de Saint–Marceaux. The sculpted decoration continues in the bas-reliefs above the windows behind the colonnade with *Les Arts* and *Les Industries Diverses,* by Fagel and Hughes. The side pavilions have, on the Champs-Elysées side, *Venus* and on the Seine side, *Juno,* both by A. Moncel. Finally, decorating the door of the rear-facing façade, in the broken pediment, are *Trois Parques* (Three Fates), *Jour* (Day) and *Nuit* (Night), by H. Lemaire; and above the pediment, *Histoire* and *Archélogie,* by Desvergnes

◼ The Grand Palais** (to the r).

Facing the Petit Palais, the Grand Palais, also built between 1897 and 1900, was to be 'the monument consecrated by the Republic to the glory of French art'. In the stylistic schizophrenia of its architectures, the building is perfectly representative of its period, its great iron-built hall a riot of Art Nouveau in clashing with the Classical stone dressing of the façades. The façade on the Ave. Winston-Churchill is by Deglane.

Above the corner pavilions, colossal bronze quadrigae by Récipon. Behind the colonnade, a glass mosaic on a red background depicts *Les Grandes Epoques de l'Art* (Great Eras of Art), by G. Martin after E. Fournier. The façade on the Ave. Général-Eisenhower was built by Louvet above a monumental portal, a bas-relief by Theunissen, *Les Arts et les Sciences,* paying homage to the new century, *Nuit* (Night), by Sicard, and *L'Aurore* (Dawn), by Soulès. Opposite this doorway, a marble fountain known as the *Miroir d'Eau* (Water Mirror) decorated with figures of women and children, by R. Larche, offers a typical specimen of decoration in the modern style. On the Ave. Franklin-Roosevelt is a façade by Thomas with on either side of the central porch, two equestrian groups by Falquière and Peter. Behind the colonnade, a polychrome stoneware frieze (a kind of sandstone used in pottery) represents *Le Défilé des arts à travers les ages* (The march of the arts through the ages), executed at Sèvres from the cartoons of Joseph Blanc. The great hall and its cupola (architects Daydé and Pillé) may be seen during temporary exhibitions (FIAC, Salon du Livre, Salon des Antiquaries etc.); entrance Ave. W.-Churchill. The remainder of the buildings are occupied by the Galeries Nationales du Grand Palais (→Museums), the Palais de la Découverte (→Museums) and the Faculté des Lettres et Sciences Humaines de Paris.

The Théâtre du Rond-Pont

Beneath the trees, between the Ave. de Selves and the Ave. Franklin-Roosevelt, the former 'panorama' set up by Dairond, which became the Palais des Glaces skating rink in about 1834, has housed the Renaud-Barrault Theater Company since 1980. After leaving the Comédie-Française the two actors installed their company in the Théâtre Marigny, then at the Odéon and the Elysée-Montmartre. They later spent some time at the then disused Gare d'Orsay, where they built a portable wooden stage now transferred to this location.

The Rond-Point des Champs-Elysées

Originally laid out in 1670, the Rond-Point was truly finished only in 1815. The shopping arcades on the NW corner face the former Hôtel Lehon, now occupied by the daily newspaper *Jours de France;* the building has recently been enlarged by a wing on to the Champs-Elysées. The luminous fountains in glass tiles were created by Max Ingrand (1958).

Avenue Matignon

Having crossed the Rond-Point, walk up this avenue and back again. It is lined with galleries of contemporary art (Art Curial and Bernheim-Jeune among others), and leads to the Faubourg Saint-Honoré. The poet Heinrich Heine (1797-1856) died in a house on the site of no. 3. No. 17 was built for *Time and Life* by P. Dufau. No. 20, with a stone-and-glass façade, was built by Mazzacconi. Tradition has it that Marie-Antoinette's lover Axel von Fersen lived in a *hôtel* where no. 19 now stands: the Louis XVI boudoir of the *hôtel* is preserved at the Musée Carnavalet. Finally no. 25 is the Hôtel de la Vaupalière*, built in 1761 by Colignon for his own use.

The Ave. Franklin-Roosevelt. Cross this street but do not continue on it. It is difficult to believe today that when it was laid out by the Duc d'Antin the avenue had a very sinister reputation. Since the end of the 19th c. luxury shops have replaced the more or less disreputable pleasure-gardens. The great photographer Nadar died at no. 49 and Réjane, the actress, lived at no. 25.

Avenue des Champs-Elysées*

Between the Rond-Point and the Arc de Triomphe the avenue is lined with luxury shops, large cafés, cinemas and the offices of airlines, industrial companies and banks.

At no. 15 the Duc de Morny, the lover of the Comtesse Lehon, wife of the Belgian ambassador, had a small *hôtel* that was popularly known as 'la niche à Fidèle'.

The Hôtel de la Paiva*

25 Ave. des Champs-Elysées

Built by Manguin, this *hôtel* is now the headquarters of the Travellers Club. It is a remarkable example of the Neo-Renaissance decorative style of the Second Empire and a last reminder of the great era of the Champs-Elysées. Numerous artists such as P. Baudry (who decorated the ceiling of the great salon), Legrain, Dalou, Carrier-Belleuse and Barbedienne contributed to the sumptuous onyx and gilded bronze décor.

The Marquise de Paiva y Araujo by marriage, Thérèse Lachman, from humble Polish origins, made a dazzling career as an adventuress. By her second marriage she became the Comtesse de Donnersmarch (related to the Bismarcks) and was accused of espionage. Most people thought she was a spy. The soirées at the Hôtel de Paive were glittering Parisian events; the Goncourts, Emile de Girardin, Sainte-Beuve, Théophile Gautier and Arsène Houssaye were all in attendance.

Avenue des Champs-Elysées*, continued

At nos. 52-60 large office buildings have replaced the Hôtel de Massa, which was removed, stone by stone, in 1928, to no. 38 Faubourg Saint-Jacques and is now the headquarters of the Société des Gens de Lettres. The *hôtel,* a fine example of Louis XVI architecture, was famous for the entertainments given there by the Italian ambassador, the Conte Marescalchi. Charles Dickens, who stayed in Paris in 1855 (living at no. 49) and Thomas Jefferson, who as American ambassador inhabited the pavilion on the corner of the Rue de Berri (the present no. 52); plaque from 1785 to 1789, both knew the real Champs-Elysées.

There are some buildings for those interested in modern architecture. At no. 68, the Guerlain building, designed in 1913 by C. Ménès, the architect of great *hôtels* and transatlantic passenger liners, gives the bow window its place on one of the capital's smartest avenues. Note the façade of no. 116 *bis*: its accordion-like structure, deliberately modernist (architect, J. Desbouis: 1929), was intended as a radio station. At no. 103, the building of Crédit Commercial de

France (formerly the Elysée-Palace Hôtel) and Hôtel Kléber-Colombes (the former Hôtel Mercédès), situated higher up, at no. 9, are examples of the art of G. Chédanne (1861-1940): combining the modern style with *rocaille* arabesques. This architect owes his reputation to the Parisien Libérè building (→ Rue Réamur) which, it is now known, was not his work.

Today the Champs-Elysées has become, like the Opéra district, center of business: tourism; ready-to-wear fashion; car showrooms (Citroën at no. 42, Renault at nos. 51-63, Volvo at no. 125, Chrysler at no. 136, Fiat at no. 140, Alfa-Romeo at no. 150, Peugeot at no. 154) and airline companies (Varigan at nos. 27-33, Aeroflot at no. 38, Alitalia at no. 73, Japan Airlines at no. 75, Aeroliñas Argentinas at no. 77, British Airways* at no. 91, Air Afrique at no. 104, Air France at nos. 118-121). But the avenue has links with aviation other than commercial ones: two pioneers of French aviation Santos-Dumont and Henry de la Vaulx, lived at no. 150 and no. 122 respectively.

The Maison de l'Iran at nos. 65-67, with its craft work, jewels and wonderful caviar, the Centre Japonais du Commerce Extérieur and the Maison d'Extrême-Orient at no. 100 have all chosen the Champs-Elysées to display their riches. The Paris Tourism Office is at no. 127, while the Maison du Danemark at no. 142, has under the same roof the Danish national tourism office, a travel agency, Danish Railways, the Association of Danish Students and two renowned restaurants.

Elsewhere, the office buildings house newspapers and the headquarters of businesses and film companies, while the ground floor is occupied by cinemas, expensive ready-to-wear clothes shops and big cafés, some of which, like Le Fouquet, are frequented by journalists and film people.

The Lido cabaret attracts an international clientèle. There are shopping arcades such as the Arcades des Champs-Elysées, Les Champs and Point-Show. The Drugstore Matignon and the Drugstore Publicis are also worth mentioning; the latter, after a fire, was rebuilt in 1975 by P. Dufau. The Champs Elysées end at the Place Charles-de-Gaulle, in front of the Arc de Triomphe***.

▣ Museums to visit

Musée du Petit Palais (Ave. Winston-Churchill): paintings and *objets d'art* from antiquity to the present day.

Galeries Nationales du Grand Palais (Ave. du Général-Eisenhower): exhibition hall.

Palais de la Découverte (Ave. Franklin-D.-Roosevelt): the experimental study of the sciences; experiments for all ages, from children to adults.

Musée de l'Arc de Triomphe (Place de l'Etoile): engravings, documents and souvenirs relating to the Arc de Triomphe.

▷ # The gardens of the Champs-Elysées

In the early years of the 19th c. at the time when the Restaurant Ledoyen was just a modest inn, a few eating places and cafés – the Aurore and the Café de la Réunion most famous among them – shared a mixed and noisy clientèle. The project of making the gardens into a fashionable park, suitably enhanced with fountains, and at the same time a center for public entertainment, goes back to the July Monarchy. After completing his alterations to the Place de la Concorde Hittorff found himself entrusted, from 1838, with making the desired changes to the gardens. Besides the four pavilions (Ledoyen, L'Horloge, L'Alcazar d'Eté and Les Ambassadeurs) he built a 'panorama' and a circus where Franconi produced his famous equestrian spectacles. Later, the Champs-Elysées gardens were the setting for the World Fair of 1855. The Palais de l'Industrie, a long, rectangular steel-framed building, was built as a response to the challenge of the Crystal Palace, erected in 1851 in Hyde Park, London, while the round panorama building and a 1300 yds/1200m arcade on the quay served as annexes. This temple of commerce and industry was torn down to give way to the two new giants – the Grand Palais and the Petit Palais – of the Exhibition of 1900.

Charonne

20th arr.
Métro: Porte de Bagnolet.
Bus: 76, 101, PC.
Parking: Porte de Bagnolet Bus Station, between the access roads to autoroute A3.
Taxis: 6 Place de la Porte de Bagnolet. Tel. 43-60-60-79.

Until its absorption by the town of Paris under the Second Empire, the last village of Paris, Charonne, far from the noise and bustle of the capital, retained much of the rural character described by J. J. Rousseau in his *Confessions* and in *Les Rêveries d'un promeneur solitaire*. Street names such as Rue des Haies (hedges), Rue des Prairies (meadows), Rue des Maraîchers (market-gardeners) and Rue du Clos (enclosure), show that the fields adjoining the village were devoted to growing fruit and vegetables. For a long time this agrarian tradition distinguished Charonne from the neighboring district of Belleville or Ménilmontant, where work was primarily artisanal, later industrial. That is why it was a sought-after place for rich Parisians to stay, who had country houses built there at great expense during the 18th c.

With its annexation by Paris in 1860, the last fields disappeared under the onslaught of property developers but, well sheltered behind Père-Lachaise Cemetery, the village did not suffer too badly from the upheavals felt by the center of the capital in this period. Of course, the country byways and small houses with built-on workshops have now given way to big apartment blocks, but walking up the almost untouched Rue Saint-Blaise will give you the striking impression of being in a little village in the Ile-de-France, to which the threatening tower blocks nearby add a certain nostalgic charm.

Tour of the district

1 hr.

From the Place de la Porte-de-Bagnolet follow the Rue George-Chavez and take the small stairway on the r. that leads to the Rue Irénée-Blanc.

Rue Irénée-Blanc

This is an area developed by La Campagne à Paris (Countryside in Paris), an inexpensive housing estate started in 1907 and completed 20 years later. All these villas surrounded by flowers and luxuriant vegetation suggest some smart remote suburb, rather than a capital city.

Place Édith-Piaf

To reach this square, take the Rue du Capitaine-Ferber on the l. In the shaded central area the small electricity substation, an early 19th-c. building of brick and metal, survives with its glazed ceramic frieze intact.

Cross the square and follow the Rue de Pelleport.

Rue de Bagnolet

From no. 21 to no. 9 and on the opposite side of the street are several interesting examples of Post-Modern architecture. The return to Classical forms: arches, pediments, cornices, etc., is set off here through the use of unusual materials: ceramic, glass, brick and metal.

On the far side lies the Square de la Fondation Debrousse, at the end of which you can see the new buildings used for medical treatment. This was once the site of the Château de Bagnolet, acquired and embellished by Mlle. de Blois, daughter of Louis XIV and Mme. de Montespan, wife of the Regent, Philippe d'Orléans. The only remains of the chateau are some wrought-iron railings and the elegant little Pavilion de l'Ermitage* at no. 148 (1723). With Neo-Classicism clearly emerging through its graceful Rococo, this building shows what the area was like in the 18th c. During the Revolution the Ermitage belonged to Baron de Batz, who tried unsuccessfully to help Louis XVI to escape.

Place Saint-Blaise

On the l. you can see the Church of Saint-le-Cyril built on a square ground-plan and covered with a flattened cupola by the architect Bocquerel in 1935. On the r. is the Church of Saint-Germain-de-Charonne.

⚱ The Church of Saint-Germain-de-Charonne

Open 9am – noon, 2–7pm. Tel. 43-71-42-04.

Standing on the side of a hill, reached by a stairway of 31 steps, this is probably one of the most interesting and attractive churches in Paris. The former church of the commune of Charonne, it was annexed to Paris in 1859.

A church was certainly built here during the 11th c. Tradition has it that St. Germain, Bishop of Auxerre, met St Geneviève, still a young girl, in Charonne, about A.D. 430. The church was completely rebuilt at the end of the 13th c., and given a bell-tower. In the first half of the 15th c. it was again rebuilt. After a fire in the 17th c., the façade was repaired in 1737 and a new doorway made on the S side. It was repeatedly restored in the 19th c.

Interior: The ground plan of the church is irregular. Inside, the sculpted bunches of grapes on the pillars symbolize the vineyards of Charonne. The original stained glass was replaced by Adeline Hébert-Stevens, Pauline Peugnez and Paul Bondy. On entering, at the back of the church, note the painting of *St Germain blessing St. Geneviève*, a late–18th c. work attributed to Suvée.

In the 17th and 18th c., the church was famous for its concerts, which at the time were exceptional for a country church. During the Commune, this area saw bloody fights between the Fedérés (insurgents of the Commune) and the Versaillais (those faithful to the National Assembly), on May 27, 1871. Ten years later, during excavations, workmen discovered the bodies of those massacred by the Versaillais.

Rue Saint-Blaise

Before visiting Charonne cemetery follow this street from the other side of the square as far as Rue Vitruve; it continues to Montreuil. This is the heart of what is left of the old village of Charonne of which the Rue Saint-Blaise was the main street. It is still lined by little old houses (18th c.), cleverly restored, which hide beautiful courtyards (note no. 23) and small gardens.

Continuing down the Rue Vitruve on the l. is no. 55, an old country house from the beginning of the 19th c. A little further on, at no. 68, the kindergarten is a remarkably successful example of contemporary architecture.

Return to the Place Saint-Blaise via the Rue Saint-Blaise which on this side offers views* towards Charonne church, its steps and shady terraces, and the rustic presbytery, which look as if they belong in a country village.

Charonne Cemetery

As at Saint-Pierre-de-Montmartre, the charming cemetery at Charonne surrounds the church. Walk around, in the shadows to find tombs from another era as well as some more recent ones: that of the Bauer family, Henry and Gérard (son and grandson of Alexandre Dumas), of Pierre Blanchard (d.1963), Josette Clotis-Malraux (d.1944) and of Gauthier and Vincent Malraux, who died in 1961; also the tomb of Robert Brasillach (d.1945). Note also the grave of Magloire Begue who called himself 'secretary to Robespierre and lover of roses'.

Cross the cemetery and follow on the l. the Chemin du Parc de Charonne.

Take the Rue Stendhal (r.). Notice at the end the Villa Stendhal on the r., the wall painted with a colored fresco.

Follow on the l. the picturesque Rue Charles-Renouvier which has a viaduct crossing the Rue des Pyrénées.

Rue des Pyrénées

This street crosses the whole of the 20th arrondissement, from the Rue de Belleville to the Cours de Vincennes. Note at no. 190 the Jouye-Rouve-Taniès dispensary built in the early 1900s by Louis Bonnier, an unusual charity for the time. Follow r., Rue des Rondeaux, around the edge of Père-Lachaise cemetery, then the Ave. du Père-Lachaise.

At one side of the Place Gambetta is the *hôtel de ville* (Town Hall) of the 20th arrondissement, a severe edifice built between 1867 and

1877. Its banqueting room was decorated by the academic painter Léon Glaize. Nearby, the Tenon Hospital is a short way beyond the charming Square Edouard-Vaillant.

A little further on, on the l., in the Rue de la Chine, stands a building put up in 1909 by Henri Sauvage and Charles Sarazin.

‡ The Church of Saint-Jean-Bosco

79, Rue Alexandre-Dumas.Open 9am – noon, 2–7pm. Tel. 43-70-29-27

Anyone interested in 1930s architecture should visit the Church of Saint-Jean-Bosco, though it is a little out of the way.

The church was built between 1933 and 1937 by the Salesian Fathers who follow the teaching of St. Francis de Sales (architect Rotter). The building is typical of the domestic architecture of the mid-1920s, especially in the decoration of the panels below the ceiling cornice, which recall the drawing-rooms and bedrooms of the period.

At the far end of the r.-hand aisle, a chapel houses a shrine containing the effigy and relics of Dom Bosco (1815–88), founder of the Salesian order, who was canonized in 1934. He stayed in Paris for two months in 1883. The church is at the same time a national shrine, a parish church and the headquarters of the charitable foundation of Sainte-Anne-de-Charonne, founded by the Abbé Planchat, which the Salesians took over in 1919.

> Markets

On the Boul. Charonne, between the Rue de Charonne and the Rue Alexandre-Dumas: Wed., Sat., 7am – 1.30pm.

Rue Belgrand, Rue de la Chine and Place Edith-Piaf: Wed., Sat., 7am – 1.30pm.

Place de la Réunion, between Ave. de la Porte-de-Ménilmontant and Rue Maurice-Bertaux: Thurs., Sun., 7am – 1.30pm.

Boul. Davout, between Ave. de la Porte-de-Montreuil and 94 Boul. Davout: Tue., Fri., 7am – 1.30pm.

Flea Market, Marché aux Puces, Porte de Montreuil, Ave. de la Porte-de-Montreuil: Sat., Sun., Mon., 7am–7.30pm.

The district of the Châtelet and Saint-Germain-l'Auxerrois*

1st and 4th arr./Map ref. 17–B1, B2
Métro: Châtelet.
Bus: 21, 38, 47, 58, 69, 70, 72, 74, 75, 76, 81, 85.
Parking: Rue du Louvre, Place de l'Hôtel-de-Ville.
Taxis: Place du Châtelet. Tel. 42-33-20-99.

Sightseers who cross the daunting crossroads of the Place du Châtelet, throbbing with traffic, or that part of the Rue de Rivoli favored by the cut-price clothing trade, will find it hard to believe that they are in one of the oldest districts of Paris. The quiet little streets behind the Théâtre Musical de Paris (Paris Music Hall), prove that this is true, however, and allow the curious to rediscover half-hidden fragments of old Paris, dating back to the Middle Ages and the Renaissance. These narrow streets have preserved many remarkable buildings, but not the familiar customs of former times; nowadays, on summer evenings it is rare to see the musicians in their tuxedoes rushing out of the theater and into the nearest bar during the intermission.

Placed squarely on the route between the Louvre and Notre-Dame or the Beaubourg Center, Châtelet is the area through which the greatest number of tourists pass.

The history of the Châtelet

The name Châtelet comes from the fortress gateway leading to the Cité, the Grand Châtelet, which Louis VI Le Gros (The Fat) had built in 1130 to control access to the Grand-Pont and to the Île de la Cité. The Grand Châtelet replaced the wooden tower erected by Charles le Chauve (The Bald) against the Norse attacks two centuries earlier. The military importance of this new fortress declined after Philippe Auguste constructed a new defensive wall a little further away. From 1250 to 1357 the Grand Châtelet, the plan of which can be seen on the front of the Chambre des Notaires, situated between the Rue Saint-Denis and the Boul. de Sébastopol, served as the seat of the Paris Municipal Town Council. The goldsmiths, bankers and the very powerful Guild of Butchers were based in this neighborhood.

Turned into a prison and enlarged between the 16th and 18th centuries, the Grand Châtelet was demolished between 1802 and

1806 to make way for the present Place du Châtelet. Continuously inhabited and built over from ancient times, the surrounding area suffered much from the urban transformations of the 19th c.

Tour of the district

1 hr.

Place du Châtelet

This square is the geographical center of Paris, the junction of its main N-S and E-W axes, at the hub of the capital's traffic. From the square there is a fine view* of the Palais de Justice and its towers across the Seine.

In the center of the square stands the Fontaine du Châtelet, also called the Palm Fountain, built in 1806 by Bralle to commemorate Napoleon's victories, with bas-reliefs and a statue by Boizot. In 1856 it was moved to a new base sculpted by Jacquemart, decorated with sphinxes and an inscription indicating the site of the Parloir aux Bourgeois (Burghers' Parlor), forerunner of the Paris Municipal Council. On either side of the square stand two famous theaters, both built by Davioud in 1862. The Théâtre du Châtelet (now the Théâtre Musical de Paris), which has the second largest auditorium in Paris (originally 3000 seats) originally put on spectacular plays with dazzling sets – *Around the World in Eighty Days* was a major success.

In 1874 the Colonne Concerts replaced drama as the theater's chief attraction. Opposite, the Théâtre de la Ville, formerly the Théâtre Sarah-Bernhardt, was bought by the great actress in 1899 when it was the Théâtre des Nations. There she performed *L'Aiglon* in March 1900, the play which Edmond Rostand wrote for her, and which became one of the peaks of her long career. She later re-created *La Dame aux Camélias, Tosca,* and others.

Aged 66, with one leg amputated, she again played *Daniel,* by L. Verneuil, and Racine's *Athalie,* retaining her 'golden voice' to the end of her life. Although the façade is unchanged, the interior of the theater was entirely rebuilt in 1968. In the restaurant, a plaque on a wide pillar recalls that Gérard de Nerval, the mystical poet, was found hanged (1855) on a railing in Rue Vieille-Lanterne, on the site of the present stage. Sarah Bernhardt's dressing-room has been preserved near the foyer.

Take the Rue Adolphe Adam to see how the Théâtre de la Ville was extended at the rear (E side) with iron panels and stonework after its original construction. In 1982 it was badly damaged by fire only two years after it was reopened.

The Tour Saint-Jacques

Visits by appointment.

Dominating the Square Saint-Jacques, which stretches between the Rue de Rivoli and the Ave. Victoria, this tower is the sole remnant of the venerable 16th-c. Church of Saint-Jacques-de-la-Boucherie. There has probably been a church on this site since Carolingian times. Starting point for pilgrims to Santiago de Compostela in Spain, at the crossroads of the major N-S roadway and river route, it marked one of the vital centers of the growing city. The church was demolished in 1797; only the belfry, built between 1508 and 1522 by Jean and Didier de Félin, was left. It flanked the S side of the church and illustrates the vitality of the Flamboyant Gothic style in 16th-c. Paris. After 1836 it was used as a shot tower until Ballu restored it in 1858. Since 1891 it has been a meteorological station for the Observatory at Montsouris.

At the top of the NW corner a graceful bell-turret bears the colossal statue of St James the Greater; at the other corners are figures of an eagle, a winged lion and a winged bull: symbols of three of the Evangelists. The original statues were worn away by time, so were brought down to the square below and reproduced exactly by Chenillon. At ground-level under the keystone of the arch a statue of the 17th-c. philosopher Pascal by Cavelier, has an inscription stating that he verified, from this tower, the experiments into the weight of air that he had carried out at Puy-le-Dôme in 1648. Nineteen other statues by Bonnassieux, Pascal-Dantan the Elder, Desprez and others, stand in the niches. A plaque was put on the base by the Society of Friends of St. James of Compostela.

In 1959 in the Square Saint-Jacques a stele was erected to the memory of Gérard de Nerval, near the spot where he was found hanged in 1855: a replica of the bronze medallion made from life by Jehan du Seigneur in 1851.

Take the Ave. Victoria which commemorates the British Queen's visit to Paris in 1854, and leads to the Hôtel de Ville.

Return towards the Place du Châtelet along the Ave. Victoria as far as the Rue des Lavandières-Sainte-Opportune.

Rue des Lavandières-Sainte-Opportune

By 1244 this street already bore its name, which it owes to the washerwomen who walked down it to the water-troughs on the banks of the Seine. The name also recalls the ancient collegiate church of Sainte-Opportune. No. 13 is an 18th-c. house which still has a shield carved with the emblem of the Guild of Goldsmiths. Notice the dormer windows at no. 25.

Take the Rue des Deux-Boules: No. 3 is a mansion called Des Deux-Boules (Two Balls), built in the 18th c. in a sober style. The concave sides and splayed *porte-cochère* allowed carriages to maneuver easily despite the narrowness of the street.

Go l. by Rue Bertin-Poirée. Take the Rue Saint-Germain-l'Auxerrois which preserves several fine 18th-c. houses, recognizable by their wrought-iron balconies. Note at no. 18, at the corner of the Rue Bertin-Poirée, the iron gate of a wine-merchant.

A little further down, on the r., the Rue des Orfèvres is still lined with 17th and 18th c. houses. At no. 9 the former house of the Warders of the Goldsmiths' Guild, and at no. 8 the façade of the old Chapel of Saint Eloi*, built in 1566 by Philibert Delorme. No. 10 is another fine 18th-c. building which belonged to the Guild of Goldsmiths.

Go back to the l., down the Rue des Bourdonnais, then to the Quai de la Mégisserie.

Cross the Rue du Pont-Neuf, which was widened and modernized when Baltard was constructing Les Halles, and has consequently lost much of its character.

Rue de la Monnaie

This street takes its name from the Monnaie (Mint) which was transferred to the Quai Conti in 1774; like the preceding streets, it dates from the 13th c.

Part of this area is occupied by the great mass of the four buildings of La Samaritaine department store, named after the pump known as 'The Samaritan' which was installed during the reign of Henri IV under one of the arches of the Pont-Neuf to supply water to the center of Paris. The store's founders, Ernest Cognacq and his wife Louise Jay, are also known for their important collection of paintings (→Museums).

Rue de Rivoli*

This street is nothing but a series of ready-to-wear boutiques. Follow it in the direction of the Louvre. In 1848 the Rue de Rivoli was lengthened between the Rue de Rohan and the Rue de Sévigné by cutting through a succession of small streets. It has had several evocative names: Rue des Mauvaises-Paroles (broken promises); R de la Vieille-Harengerie (old herring-market); de la Vieille-Monnaie (old Mint); and des Coquilles (shells). This section, uninteresting architecturally, is much livelier than that along the side of the Louvre.

Take the Rue de l'Arbre-Sec on the l. In the courtyard of no. 15 you will find the Renaissance door of the Church of Saint-Germain-l'Auxerrois.

The Rue des Prêtres-Saint-Germain-l'Auxerrois is the old medieval passageway of the cloister along the S side of the church. The oldest houses are no. 19 (ironwork), no. 17 (where the *Journal des Débats* was based 1800-1940), and no. 15.

Place du Louvre

This is flanked on one side by the monumental colonnade serving as entrance to the Palais du Louvre. Opposite, the old façade of the Church of Saint-Germain-l'Auxerrois is now balanced by the buildings of the Mairie (Town Hall) of the 1st arrondissement (architect Hittorff, 1859-60), Neo-Renaissance in style. The Neo-Gothic belfry has an amazing peal of 35 bells playing *Le Tambourin* by Rameau, *La Marche* by Turenne and an old French song by Chapuis. One clock face shows the time, another the day of the week, and the month; and the third the phase of the moon. Statues of Saints Germain, Denis, and Landry.

☩ The Church of Saint-Germain-l'Auxerrois**

2 Place du Louvre.
Open 8am-12.30pm and 3-6pm. Tel. 42-60-13-96.

The church of the Louvre and parish church of the kings of France, full of historical associations, this church remains, despite mutilations, a major Gothic monument.

History of the building

The origins of this church are undoubtedly Merovingian but the church has been rebuilt many times and of the original Romanesque building, only the 12th-c. tower remains. In the 13th c., it became necessary to build a larger church: the central porch, choir and Chapel of the Virgin date from this period. In the 15th c. a large part of the church was reconstructed including the nave and doorway. Work continued in the 16th c. with construction of the rood-screen designed by Pierre Lescot, and sculpted by Jean Goujon. On the night of August 24, 1572, from the bell-tower of Saint-Germain the signal was given for the St. Bartholomew's Day massacre. With the installation of the Valois Court in the Louvre, Saint-Germain became the 'royal parish' and sovereigns came here often to hear Mass. From the 17th c. until the Revolution the church was frequented by many illustrious figures, some of whom were buried here; among these are many artists who lived at the Louvre (the architects Le Vau, de Cotte, Gabriel and Soufflot; the sculptors Desjardins, Coysevox, Coustou and Vassé; the painters Coypel, Desportes, Restout, Boucher, Van Loo and Chardin; the goldsmith Claude Ballin, the engraver Silvestre, the poet Malherbe and many others).

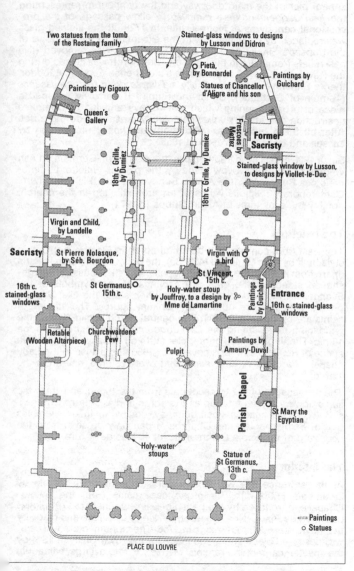

Two statues from the tomb of the Rostaing family

Stained-glass windows to designs by Lusson and Didron

Pietà, by Bonnardel

Paintings by Guichard

Paintings by Gigoux

Statues of Chancellor d'Aligre and his son

Queen's Gallery

Frescoes by Mottez

Former Sacristy

18th c. Grille, by Dumiez

18th c. Grille, by Dumiez

Stained-glass window by Lusson, to designs by Viollet-le-Duc

Virgin and Child, by Landelle

Sacristy

St Pierre Nolasque, by Séb. Bourdon

Virgin with a bird

St Vincent, 15th c.

16th c. stained-glass windows

St Germanus, 15th c.

Holy-water stoup by Jouffroy, to a design by Mme de Lamartine

Paintings by Guichard

Entrance

16th c. stained-glass windows

Retable (Wooden Altarpiece)

Churchwardens' Pew

Pulpit

Paintings by Amaury-Duval

Parish Chapel

St Mary the Egyptian

Holy-water stoups

Statue of St Germanus, 13th c.

⇨ Paintings
○ Statues

PLACE DU LOUVRE

The Church of Saint-Germain-l'Auxerrois

The 18th c. was an unfortunate period for the church: in 1710 the central pier of the main doorway and the tympanum representing the *Last Judgement* were removed to allow passage of the processional canopy as at Notre-Dame. In 1728 all the stained glass was replaced by clear glass, with the exception of the windows of the transept. Finally, in 1754, the rood-screen was removed (five bas-reliefs from it are in the Louvre). The church was closed during the Revolution in 1793 and became a storehouse for animal fodder, then a printing-works, and finally a *Temple de la Reconnaissance* (Temple of Gratitude). Under the Empire it narrowly escaped a piece of urban planning which would have entailed its complete destruction and in 1831 it was completely ransacked during a riot. After all these indignities, restoration was finally undertaken by Lassus and Baltard from 1838 to 1855.

Since 1926 artists have traditionally attended Saint-Germain on Ash Wednesday, to fulfil a vow made by the painter Willette. L'Aumonerie des Beaux-Arts (the Artists' Benevolent Fund) is based here. Contemporary religious works of art are exhibited in the church, notably the sculptures of Albert Dubos (d.1974).

The exterior

The west front consists of a beautiful porch in Flamboyant Gothic style built by Jean Gaussel (1435-39), the only Gothic porch in Paris apart from that of the Sainte-Chapelle. On the voussoir, wedge-shaped stones of the arch are carvings of the Symbols of the Evangelists, the *Adoration of the Shepherds* and the *Last Supper;* on the pendants are human and animal figures. The statues of saints are by Desprez (1841). The central porch is mid-13th c.; the tympanum representing the *Last Judgement* was destroyed in the 18th c. The Virgin on the center pier (19th c.) replaced the primitive statue of St. Germain, rediscovered in 1950 and placed in the Lady chapel. The other statues, somewhat over-restored, date from the 13th c.

The two façades of the transept date from the 15th c. and show the same flowery ornamentation as the porch and west front. On the l. side (N) of the apse, a small doorway, created in 1570, resembles that of Saint-Nicolas-des-Champs: it can only be seen from the courtyard of the École Communale; at 15 Rue de l'Arbre-Sec.

The interior

At the entrance are two holy-water stoups in white marble by Lerambert (17th c.). The organ case came from the Sainte-Chapelle, purchased by the parish of Saint-Germain in 1791; it was designed by Pierre-Noël Rousset, the king's architect, and made by the master carpenter Lavergne in 1756. The monumental royal pew* was designed by Le Brun, and made for the royal family in 1684 by the master carpenter François Mercier; it has a large baldaquin canopy, its draperies scattered with fleurs-de-lys and held up by angels, is supported by fluted columns. The 17th-c. pulpit is even more massive.

The S side-aisle and chapels. . The Chapel of the Virgin (Lady Chapel), fills the second bay. The altar and the retable are by Lassus, with the *Tree of Jesse* designed by Viollet-le-Duc. Above is a stone Virgin of the Champagne School (early 14th c.); the murals, painted by Amaury-Duval (19th c.) depict the *Coronation of the Virgin*. There are two stone statues in this chapel: one of St. Germain (13th c.) formerly on the center pier of the main door and rediscovered in 1950 in the crypt; the other of St Mary the Egyptian* (late 15th c.) with her long hair, which comes originally from the porch, where it is now replaced by a cast. The windows of the chapel are by Maréchal 1847.

Right transept. The rose window and two others have retained their beautiful early 16th c. stained glass*: in the rose window, the Eternal Father is surrounded by angels, martyrs and confessors; adjacent windows show *Doubting Thomas* and *The Ascension, The Assumption* and *The Coronation of the Virgin*. The murals were painted by Guichard (19th c.); the white marble water-stoup is by Jouffroy (1844), designed by Mme de Lamartine.

The chancel. This is the oldest part of the church. In the 18th c. it underwent alterations; the pillars are now fluted columns; the rood-screen sculpted by Jean Goujon was destroyed. The choir is enclosed by beautiful incised iron grilles* by Dumiez (1767). To the l. of the entrance to the choir is a seated wooden statue of St Germanus of Auxerre* (late 15th c.), a rare example of Gothic art still in place in a Parisian church. To the r., St Vincent, second patron of the church, in stone (late 15th c.). Stained glass by Thévenot (1839–40) and by Lusson (1868).

The ambulatory and chapels. Above a door just past the S transept is the *Virgin with a Bird** in polychrome wood (late 15th c.). 3rd chapel: stained-glass window by Lusson from a cartoon by Viollet-le-Duc, representing the 12 apostles. To the l. of the old sacristy door: frescoes by Mottez. 4th chapel: marble statues of a father and his son, both called Étienne d'Aligre, both Chancellors of France (d.1635 and 1677), by Laurent Magnier; murals by Guichard (1843–45) showing the life of St Landry. 5th chapel: marble *Pietà* by Bonnardel (1859). 7th chapel: marble statues of Tristan (d.1591) and Charles de Rostaing (d.1660) originally in the old Church of the Feuillants (Cistercians) reformed by J. de la Barrière. 8th chapel: on the walls, *St. Germain Blessing St Geneviève* and *St. Geneviève encouraging of the inhabitants of Paris,* by Jean Gigoux (1840). Between the 8th and 9th chapels, the Queen's pew where Queen Marie-Amélie, wife of Louis-Philippe, sat during Mass. 12th chapel: *Virgin and Child* by Landelle 1857. 13th chapel: on the r., *St. Peter Nolasco Receiving his Habit from Our Lady of Ransom* (the order he founded) by Sébastien Bourdon (17th c.) This chapel gives access to the sacristy where a large 16th c. Flemish triptych* is temporarily on show before being restored: the center panel is carved with scenes from the *Life of the Virgin,* while the two side-panels are painted.

The l. transept. Fine stained glass* (16th c.): the rose window shows the Holy Ghost, the four surrounding lights, incidents from the *Passion, Miracles of Christ,* and male and female saints.

The l. side-aisle and chapels. 4th chapel: Flemish retable* in carved wood (1519), representing the *Tree of Jesse* and scenes from the *Life and Passion of Christ.* The stained glass in these chapels is by Maréchal (1847).

It is possible to return to the Place du Châtelet via the Quai de la Mégisserie (→Quais), down one side of which run bookstalls and on the other picturesque flower stalls and pet shops.

▷ La Samaritaine

The Samaritaine department store buildings, which cover several blocks, offer a real anthology of industrial and commercial architecture from 1900 to 1930. The shop in the Rue du Pont-Neuf that Ernest Cognacq opened in 1869 was instantly successful; 3 years later, in 1900, an entirely new department store was built by the architect Frantz Jourdain. The building, with a metal frame and large glass panels, was quite revolutionary since it allowed its structure of riveted iron, considered a crude material, to be visible throughout. As it continued to expand at an extraordinary rate the store had to be extended once more along the Seine. Between 1926 and 1928 Henri Sauvage and F. Jourdain built the monumental façade along the Quai du Louvre which remains one of the better examples of Art Deco. But the most remarkable of these buildings, at the corner of the Rue de Rivoli and the Rue Boucher, was constructed by the same architects in 1930. Although it took nine months to demolish the old buildings and erect the new one, trade continued without any interruption.

Today, La Samaritaine is still the biggest department store in Paris. A recent renovation program has cleverly restored 'youth' to the big 'glass house', the painted and sculptured frieze round it, and to the fine Art-Nouveau ironwork of the staircase to their original appearance. On the 9th floor a terrace (open from Easter to October), with an orientation plan, provides a panoramic view of the riverside and the whole of Paris.

Rue du Cherche-Midi district

6th arr./Map ref. 16–C3.
Métro: Sèvres–Babylone.
Bus: 39, 63, 68, 70, 83, 84, 87, 94.
Parking: Rue Velpeau.
Taxis: Place Alphonse–Deville Hôtel Lutetia. (Tel. 45-48-84-75).
Market: Boul. Raspail, between Rue du Cherche–Midi and Rue de Rennes (Tues. and Fri. 7am–1.30pm)

In the 18th c. the Rue du Cherche–Midi was a beautiful road lined with convents and large private houses and enlived by numerous craftsmen's workshops. The charming façades along this short road are a reminder of a bygone age when high–class commerce was conducted in an atmosphere of calm elegance. Between the crossroads of the Croix–Rouge and the Boul. Raspail, fashion boutiques rub shoulders with the famous Poilâne bakery. Beyond the Boul. Raspail, there are numerous book shops and antique shops. The Rue Saint–Placide, with its many *'dégriffé'* (cheap clothes shops selling designer garments with the labels removed) and stalls on the sidewalks, adds vitality to this residential quarter.

Tour of the district

1 hr.

Carrefour de la Croix-Rouge

This crossroads has been called Croix Rouge since the 15th c. Many people were punished at the pillory which stood here in the 18th c. A huge street barricade was erected in 1871. Today it forms a kind of meeting point between Saint–Germain–des–Prés, the Saint–Germain district and the busy Rue de Sèvres.

Rue du Cherche-Midi

As far as the Boul. Raspail.

This has been the way to Vaugirard since 1388. It is a long, beautiful street whose unusual name has a controversial origin. It may have come from a shop sign on which was painted a sundial and people *qui cherchaient midi à quatorze heures,* ('looking for noon at two o'clock'), a reference to a French proverb about 'looking for something where it is not' or 'looking for trouble where there is none'. Or, more likely, it is a corruption of a local saying 'la Chasse au midi': (the original name of the street was Rue du Chassé Midi), for the street which begins near the Hôtel de la Chasse, goes south toward the Midi. No. 19 has a medallion in bas-relief of an astronomer tracing a sundial, but this is of a more recent date than the name of the street. In the 17th c. the outstandingly beautiful mansions at nos. 9, 11, 13 and 15 formed a magnificent group, which was later destroyed. In 1719 nos. 13 and 11 belonged to an extraordinary woman, the Comtesse de Verrue (1670-1719), daughter of the Duc de Luyne and Anne de Rohan, who owned many properties in the district. The Comtesse's various adventures made news at the time. Opposite, at no. 8, is the headquarters of the Poilâne bakery, which has done a great deal to safeguard and expand the manufacture of traditional French bread. Its bread, baked in wood-fired ovens, is the most famous and highly praised in Paris. The magnificent Hôtel de Marcilly at no. 18 has two 18th-c. façades and a pediment in relief in the style of Bourchardon.

Boulevard Raspail

From the Rue du Cherche-Midi to the Rue de Rennes.

At no. 56, on the corner, a beautiful modern building now replaces the old military prison of the Cherche-Midi, where the first Dreyfus trial took place in 1894. Estienne d'Orves, as well as many other members of the Resistance, was interned here before being shot by the Germans. The prison has been replaced by the Maison des Sciences de l'Homme (1968, architects Lods, Depondt, Malizard and Beauclair) which is constructed entirely in metal and glass. It was designed to encourage communication among researchers from different branches of science, by providing a center for seminars and the establishment of inter-disciplinary scientific teams. It has numerous institutes and laboratories attached to the CNRS and the Ecole Pratique des Hautes Etudes. Follow the boulevard towards the Rue de Rennes. On the r. is one of the façades of the Hotel de Croy. At no. 78, on the corner of the Rue de Rennes, the old Crédit Municipal or *mont-de-piété* (pawnshop) now houses the Bibliothèque André-Malraux. This public library specializes in the cinema and houses the Adrienne Munnier bequest from the library in the Rue de l'Odéon.

To continue along the Boul. Raspail (→ Vaugirard).

Rue du Regard

First r. on the Rue de Rennes.

Three hundred years ago Louis XIII used to hunt in this neighborhood. In 1667 the street acquired its present name from the *regard de fontaine* (fountain inspection grid) located there. Since 1667 the odd-numbered houses include several beautiful 18th-c.

mansions whose gardens, and sometimes even the buildings themselves, have been cut by the Boul. Raspail. The fountain is at the corner of Rue de Vaugirard. It was built in 1810 and moved in 1855 to the back of the Medici fountain (→Jardin du Luxembourg). The Hôtel de Beaune at no. 7 and the Hôtel de Croy at no. 5 were built by Bailly in the early 18th c. Note the portals, pediments and wrought ironwork. Chateaubriand lived at no. 7 in 1824. The Marquis de Dreux Brézé lived at no. 1, before Dr. Récamier, who moved in after him, entertained the cream of fashionable Parisian society ('Le Tout Paris') from the world of politics, literature and the arts.

Rue du Cherche-Midi, continued

As far as the Rue Saint-Placide.

Follow this street towards Montparnasse. No. 40 is an early 18th-c. mansion which, in 1779, belonged to the Duc de Rochambeau, a hero of the American War of Independence and victor over the English at Yorktown. It was here, too, that the French branch of the Society of Cincinnati was formed; probably the first old soldiers' association in the world. No. 44 is the house where the Abbé Grégoire died. He was a member of the constitutional convention and he engineered the vote abolishing slavery in France and founded the Conservatoire des Arts et Métiers. In 1768 Marat, who succeeded Danton as Minister of Justice, lived there. It was he who read out to Louis XVI his death sentence.

Rue Saint-Placide

This street has been much changed during the last few years. The proximity of the large Bon Marché shops (→Saint-Germain and Sèvres-Babylone) devoted to ready-to-wear clothing and constant markdowns, adds greatly to the liveliness of the area. In 1810 the poet Hégésippe Moreau was born at no. 9, and J. K. Huysmans (author of *A. Rebours*), died at no. 31 in 1907. Nos. 36–38 were built by Davioud.

Rue du Cherche-Midi, continued

To the end.

Glance into the courtyards and note the ornamental pediments, sculpted garlands and ironwork of the even-numbered houses. No. 72 is a fine building. There is a fountain representing Jupiter in the courtyard of no. 86. No. 81 is a 17th-c. mansion. The great house at no. 83 belonged to the Comte de Clermont-Tonnerre, who was cut down on his doorstep on August 10, 1792. At nos. 85–87 is the little Hôtel de Montmorency, built in 1743; its façades* on the Rues du

Cherche-Midi and Ferrandi are registered as ancient monuments. The neighboring mansion, no. 89, is the Hôtel de Montmorency-Bours, built in 1756 and confiscated during the Revolution. During the Empire it was the property of Maréchal Lefebvre, made famous by his wife. Today it is the Mali embassy; a statue of Napoleon I stands at the foot of a beautiful staircase. No. 95 is an 18th-c. mansion whose façades giving on to the road and garden are also in the registery of ancient monuments; note the portal, wrought ironwork and decorated pediment. At no. 98 *bis*, behind a new façade, is a very attractive courtyard.

▣ Museum to visit

Musée Hébert (85 Rue du Cherche-Midi): Works by Ernest Hébert.

The Ile de la Cité***

1st arr./Map ref. 17-A2, B2.
Métro: Pont-Neuf, Cité.
Bus: 21, 24, 38, 81, 85, 96.
Parking: Rue Harlay, Parvis Notre-Dame.
Taxis: Place du Châtelet. Tel. 42-33-20-99; 29 Quai Saint-Michel. Tel. 43-29-63-66.

At the height of its power in the Middle Ages, the Ile de la Cité was the true center of Paris, whose influence, symbolized by its glorious palace and brilliant cathedral, radiated throughout the entire country. Today, apart from the Sainte-Chapelle, that bright jewel enshrined within the precincts of the Palais de Justice, and several halls in the Conciergerie, all the central part of the island wears the face given to it in the 19th c.

The W end of the island, turned toward the open sea like the prow of a ship, looks out over one of the finest views of Paris. In the interior, however, not even the triangle of the Place Dauphine was spared the upheavals of the 19th c. The monumental façade of the Palais de Justice has destroyed its architectural harmony. Chestnut trees hide the façade today, though, and the charming Place Dauphine has retained the character of a village on holiday, much loved by artists and writers.

Not quite so much harm was done to the rest of the island in the 19th c. Even if much of the restoration of the period was of dubious architectural merit, it is to this that we owe the rescue of Notre-

Dame from imminent ruin and the preservation of the great monument to this day almost intact. It is to this century, as well, that we owe the creation of the Place du Parvis, which allows a full appreciation of the cathedral's façade.

In the shadow of the cathedral some fragments of old medieval urban life can still be found, though the little streets and quays which offer marvellous glimpses of the Seine, the Ile Saint-Louis and the chevet (E end of Notre-Dame) have in fact changed greatly from the squalid places they were in the Middle Ages. Costly renovations and electronic entry systems have helped erase the memory of the quarter's reputation for crime. Along with the Place Dauphine, this is the only part of the island that is still residential, but the real life of the district has disappeared, chased away by busloads of tourists and souvenir sellers.

With a Préfecture, a Palais de Justice, a Tribunal de Commerce and a hospital, the Ile de la Cité is essentially an administrative district. During the day it is amusing to see lawyers in their robes running across the Boul. du Palais for a cup of coffee in a bistro opposite the Palais. The rhythm is slower and more calm in the Place Louis-Lépine. Impassive florists are undisturbed by police sirens and the ambulance bells of the Hôtel-Dieu. All the activity of the island seems concentrated in front of Notre-Dame, where tourists from every corner of the world seem to have come together to enjoy the improvised concerts of Andean flutes or African percussion.

The history of the Ile de la Cité

The island owes its development to its position at a natural crossroads: the Ile de la Cité, which lies on the Seine, an extremely important transport route, it also lies at a point where the river is easy to cross.

The island was the center of the ancient town of Lutetia, first inhabited by the Celtic tribe known as the Parisii, a Gaulish fishing people. The city was taken by Labenius' Roman legions in 52 BC, and remained in Roman hands until the 5th c. AD, though in 276 the surrounding barbarian tribes compelled the sparse population on the banks of the Seine to resettle on the island.

About 360 Lutetia was renamed Paris after the original inhabitants. Until the 10th c. the town suffered frequent Viking attacks - four in 20 years at one point. These left such terrible memories that, until the 16th c., the prayer could still be heard in Parisian churches 'A furore normannorum, libera nos, Domine.' (From the fury of the Norsemen, deliver us, O Lord). But in fighting off the Norsemen, the Counts of Paris - Count Eudes and Hugues le Grand in particular - acquired such glory that the son of the latter, Hugh Capet, was able to lay claim to the crown in 987 and, having defeated the Carol-

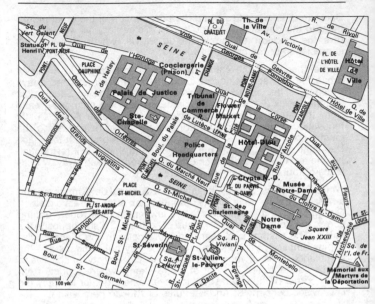

L'Ile de la Cité

ingian Charles de Lorraine and his vassals, to become the first Capetian monarch.

The island underwent the first of many modifications under the first Bourbon king, Henry IV, who enlarged its west end to create the Place Dauphine. Subsequently, the work of Haussmann in the 19th c. caused the almost complete disappearance of the medieval city.

Tour of the island

Place Dauphine

This is one of the most charming squares in Paris. It was laid out in 1607 by Henri IV, and named in honour of the Dauphin, the future Louis XIII. It was intended to provide the bankers and merchants with a suitably enclosed space near the palace where they could carry on their negotiations. The ground on which the Pont Neuf and the Place Dauphine were built formerly consisted of three small islands separated by a sandy arm of the Seine: the Ile aux Juifs, the Ile des Passeurs de Vaches and the Ilot (little island) de la

Gourdaine. On the orders of Philippe IV, Jacques de Molay, Grand Master of the Knights Templar, was burnt at the stake here in 1314, with many others of the order. In 1607 the Président de Harlay was authorized to link the islands and build on them. This created a lovely triangular *place* with room for 32 houses of more or less uniform design, of brick and white stone. This was the second royal garden square created in the 17th c. (the first was the Place Royale, the present Place des Vosges). All the houses had two storeys with arcades all along the ground floor and terracotta tiled roofs. The square was enclosed, with only two passages giving access to it. The one which still remains faces the point and is framed between two beautiful Louis XIII houses. The owners, not being constrained by the restrictions in force at the Place Royale, did not respect the uniformity of the houses, which was soon spoiled. In 1874, Duc Louis demolished the houses that enclosed the *place* to the E so that his façade of the palace could be seen to greater advantage (1857–68).

During her youth, the Place Dauphine was the whole universe for Manon Philipon, the future revolutionary. She lived at no. 37, where she married, becoming Mme Roland de la Platière (there is an erroneous inscription at no. 41 Quai de l'Horloge). The French author and librettist of *Carmen*, Ludovic Halévy, died at no. 26 in 1908. Since 1789, the house had belonged to the Bréguet family, to which he was related.

Although it was drastically disfigured by severe restoration, the Place Dauphine, often recalled by Gérard de Nerval in *La Main enchantée* and Anatole France in *Les Dieux ont soif* (*The Gods will have Blood*), remains one of the most agreeable in Paris. At ground level new, attractive restaurants are always opening; there are several art galleries, as well as the Flinker bookshop, a favorite of Thomas Mann's. While these bring life to the quays, the quays themselves never seem to get overcrowded. A large parking lot has been built under the square and the main road has been replaced by a triangular lawn; on the E side the slope in the land has been corrected in such a way that an embankment and a screen of trees seem to have restored the square to its original design as an enclosed space.

Square de Vert-Galant

This square, whose name was Henri IV's nickname (the Gay Spark) forms the E point of the Ile de la Cité. It is reached by crossing the Pont-Neuf (bridges). Leave by the steps behind the equestrian statue of Henri IV to reach the shady square. There is a magnificent view of the Louvre and La Monnaie (the Mint) as well as of the dome of the Institute. This is also the departure point for the *vedettes* (boats) from the Pont Neuf.

Quai de l'Horloge*

The quay goes along past the old towers of the first palace of the kings of France (Palais de Justice). No. 1 is the entrance to the Conciergerie**, notorious for the famous and infamous people who were imprisoned there.

Boulevard du Palais

This boulevard, which crosses from one side of the island to the other, has on its r. the Palais de Justice*, which encloses the Sainte-Chapelle***. It also passes the forbidding façade of the Tribunal de Commerce (Law Courts), built by Bailly (1860–65); its dome (141ft/42m high), inspired by the one in Brescia, stands out against a view of the Boulevard Sébastapol. Four monumental statues represent La Fermeté (Steadfastness, L. Eude), La Loi (The Law, E. Robert), La Justice (J. Chevalier), and La Prudence (J. Samson). The four figures on the attic storey are by Carrier–Belleuse. Inside, the great main stairway is a fine example of Second Empire ostentation.

The Rue de Lutèce separates the Tribunal de Commerce from the buildings of the Préfecture de Police. The construction of an underground parking lot has created an important archeological dig in this sector of the city, historically, one of the most important in the capital. Beneath medieval cellars, the Roman city has lain buried for more than 1,000 years.

The Marché aux fleurs*

(Place Louis Lépine, Mon.–Sat. 8am–7pm; access by the Quai de Corse) is one of the most famous and one of the last flower markets in Paris; on Sun. it becomes the Marché aux oiseaux (bird market). The square is named after a popular prefect who gave the Paris police their whistles and truncheons.

Place du Parvis–Notre-Dame*

Haussmann's road works did away with the tangled network of lanes and culs-de-sac that extended from the palace to the cathedral. Together with the leper-houses which hid the façade of the cathedral, 22 churches in its shadow and numerous taverns were razed. In the Rue aux Fèves (which goes through the large courtyard of the barracks of the Préfecture de Police) was the Pomme de Pin, a tavern whose regular customers included Molière, Mignard, Lully, La Fontaine, Boileau, Racine and many others.

The Place du Parvis is the heart of the Cité, itself at the heart of Paris. It is the theoretical starting point of all of the national highways which link Paris to the other cities of France. Consequently, it is from this point that distances are calculated: it is the

'Kilomètre zéro'. This symbolic center has been marked by a bronze plaque decorated with the arms of the Ville de Paris and the four points of the compass. In August 1944, the square was the scene of bitter fighting between the French and the Nazis in the final struggle for the liberation of Paris.

For the Cathedral*** →Notre-Dame de Paris.

The Hôtel-Dieu

The Hôtel-Dieu lies on the N side of the *parvis* or square. It is the hospital for the center of Paris, designed in Neo-Florentine style by the architect Diet (1866-78) to replace an old orphanage, the Hospice des Enfants Trouvés, which Boffrand built in 1747. The old Hôtel-Dieu, which was built at the same time as Notre-Dame (12th c.), stretched to both banks of the river. It was completely demolished to make way for Haussmann's plans, and re-erected on the other side of the courtyard on the site of the present Square Charlemagne. A statue of Charlemagne with Roland and Oliver by Louis and Charles Rochet (1877) stands in the square. It is a work of *haute archéologie* in which Durandal's sword, preserved in Madrid, is scrupulously reproduced.

The Préfecture de Police (on the W side of the courtyard) took over the old barracks of the Cité. It was here that the Paris police rallied to the Resistance, when they locked themselves in and resisted the German forces' attacks of August 19 and 26, 1944. A monument in the Cour de 19-Août recalls this tragic and decisive battle.

The Crypte du Parvis Notre-Dame

Entrance on the Rue de la Cité side, daily 10am-6:30pm, April 1 - Sept. 30.; 10am-5:30pm, Oct. - March 30.

In this crypt, which is more than 263ft./80m long, the remains of the square's ancient substructure can be seen in the sequence of archeological strata. There are Roman walls, fragments of hypocaust halls, remains from the height of the Roman Empire and from the Gaul of the Parisii, and part of the first wall round the Cité (3rd c.), foundations of a great brick and stone building, the present annex of the crypt; foundations of the Merovingian Cathedral of Saint-Etienne; and tombs from the old Hôtel-Dieu, as well as the foundations of the Hospice des Enfants Trouvés, built by Boffrand during the Regency.

Cross the Rue d'Arcole, site of the former Rue du Chevet de Saint-Landry and Rue de Saint-Pierre-aux-boeufs.

The old district of Notre-Dame

The area bounded by the Rue d'Arcole, the cathedral and the extreme point of the Cité was once occupied by the Cloître de

Notre-Dame. Episcopal schools were founded here, creating a veritable city within the city. The Ecole de Notre-Dame, the first in the kingdom, had such celebrated teachers as Guillame de Champeaux, Abélard, Maurice de Sully, St Dominic and St Bonaventure. The schools disappeared when the University was built at the foot of the Sainte-Geneviève hill. The monastery then became a center of learning for both ecclesiastical and secular students in the service of the chapter. The canons occupied 46 separate houses. Other little churches encircled the cathedral: Saint-Denis-du-Pas, Saint-Michel and Saint-Jean-le-Rond; this last was the old circular baptistry built on to the walls of Notre-Dame. One November morning in 1717 the abandoned child of Mme Tencin was found on the steps of Saint-Jean-le-Rond. He was baptized Jean le Rond and grew up to be the famous philosopher, mathematician, and contributor to the *Encyclopédie*, d'Alembert (1717–83).

The Rue du Cloître-Notre-Dame was originally enclosed by the monastery. The Musée de Notre-Dame is at no. 10 (→ Museums).

Rue Massillon

To the l. of the Rue du Cloître-Notre-Dame

No. 8 is the Hôtel de Gaillon (18th c.), the home of the Maîtrise de la Cathédrale (choir school) which has been in existence since 1455. No. 6 is a 17th-c. mansion. At the corner of the Rue Massillon and the Rue Chanoinesse, a plaque indicates the site of the house where Joachim du Bellay died. The *Gallo-Roman* enceinte (perimeter wall) of the Cité whose remains were discovered in 1898, crossed in front of this house.

Rue Chanoinesse

This street also formed part of the Cloître. No. 12 is the Hôtel du Grand Chantre: the house was renovated in the 17th c., but the façade which faces the Rue des Chantres, has been preserved in its original state (also another façade at 1-, Rue des Ursins). Bichat, founder of modern histology, died at no. 14 in 1802. Racine, the dramatist, lived at no. 16 (the same building as 7 Rue des Ursins). Lacordaire, theologian and preacher, at no. 17. Nos. 22 and 24 are the last of the canons' houses to have kept their unusual staircases, decorative ironwork and boundary stones. No. 26, a 17th-c. mansion, is linked to no. 19 Rue des Ursins by a passage whose entrance is paved with tombstones which may have come from one of the Cité churches.

In the area bordered by the Rue Chanoinesse, the Rue des Chantres and the Seine once stood the house of Canon Fulbert, the vengeful uncle of the ill-fated Héloïse (→ inset).

Rue de la Colombe

This road has had the same name since 1223. Originally it was very narrow, and was enlarged only in the 19th c. The only even-numbered house that remains is no. 4. At no. 6 traces of the Gallo-Roman perimeter wall of Lutetia can be seen; nos. 3, 5 and 7 are old houses. In the 18th c. the painter Raguenet had a house in the street and a studio, producing views of Paris that are on view today in the Carnavalet. A bistro called La Colombe has replaced the Saint-Nicholas tavern which was established here in 1250. Its archway and doors have been preserved.

Rue des Ursins

In the 14th c. this street was named the Rue de Port-Saint-Landry, then later Rue d'Enfer (and in between, Rue Inferior, so-called because of its position in relation to the river). There are still some very old houses here. Juvénal des Ursins, *Prévôt des marchands* (provost marshal), whose magistral portrait by Jean Fouquet the painter and miniaturist, now hangs in the Louvre, had a mansion here. Racine lived at no. 8, a 17th-c. building at the end of the courtyard. A shed in the courtyard of no. 10 has some remains of the Saint-Aignan chapel (not visible) founded in 1118 where St Bernard preached modesty, good manners and diligence, to his students. A beautiful statue of the Virgin which came from the chapel is on display in the transept of Notre-Dame. Rue des Chantres. A magnificent mansion stands at the corner of this street and the Quai aux Fleurs. The street was once entirely occupied by the garages of the Préfecture de Police. The Rue des Chantres turns back towards the Rue Chanoinesse and the Rue du Cloître-Notre Dame which goes to the eastern end of the Ile de la Cité.

The Quai aux Fleurs

From here there is a beautiful view of the Ile Saint-Louis, the church of Saint-Gervais-Saint-Protais and the Hôtel de Ville. The poet Edmond Fleg lived at no. 51 from 1908 until his death in 1951. The poet Edmond Haraucourt died at no. 5 in 1941. Katherine Mansfield came to Francis Carco's house at no. 13.

The Square Jean-XXIII

This square, formerly the Square d'Archevêché, was created by the Préfet de Paris, Rambuteau, on a vacant site where the archbishop's palace stood in the 17th c. Pillaged by the rioters of 1831, it was demolished soon after. The Gothic-style Fontaine de la Vierge by Vigouroux has adorned the center of the square since 1845. From here there is a very fine view of the chevet (E wall) of Notre-Dame.

The Square de l'Ile-de-France

This square occupies the eastern extremity of the island and was used as a promenade by the canons. It became a public garden in 1914 when the Morgue was removed. The Mémorial des Martyrs de la Déportation* can be seen here (open daily 10am-noon, 2-5pm; free admission). A moving work in a spare style by the architect Henri Pingusson, it was unveiled by General de Gaulle in 1962.

▣ Museum to visit

Musée de Notre-Dame (10 Rue du Cloître-Notre-Dame): history of the cathedral.

▷ Vanished churches

Of some 300 churches which were in existence in Paris in the 18th c., only about 60 remain - that is, less than a quarter. Their destruction began in the Ile de la Cité in the late 18th c. with the razing of Saint-Christophe, Sainte-Geneviève-des-Ardents and Saint-Jean-le-Rond. The vandalism of the Revolution and 19th-c. land speculations dealt equally serious blows to Paris's architectural heritage: from 1790 to 1861 almost 100 churches and chapels were demolished. The Ile de la Cité, which could still count a score or so of little sanctuaries to its name, was particularly affected by the loss of Saint-Pierre-des-Arcis, Saint-Germain-le-Vieux, Saint-Germain-du-Pas, Saint-Landry, Saint-Pierre-aux-Boeufs, Sainte-Madeleine and Sainte-Marine.

The Cité was not the only district of Paris to see its churches disappear: on the Right Bank, Saint-Jean-en-Grève, Sainte-Opportune, Saints-Innocents and Saint-Sauveur, all vanished, though Saint-Jacques-de-la-Boucherie's tower was saved; and on the Left Bank, Saint-Côme, Saint-Benoît, Saint-Jean-de-Latran and Saint-Hyppolite no longer appear on Paris maps.

▷ Abélard and Héloïse

Héloise lodged at her uncle Fulbert's house with what would be called today his assistant professor, the theologian, Peter Abélard. Abélard refuted official teaching, championing the conceptualist against the universalist position in medieval thought. He took 3000 students with him to the slopes of the Sainte-Geneviève hill to teach his new philosophy, officially condemned by the Church. Moreover, the young and brilliant theologian was in love with Héloïse, and they became lovers, then married in secret. Fulbert went mad with fury and paid some thugs to castrate Abélard. The lovers separated and retreated from the world, she to a convent, he to a monastery. Their great love has been perpetuated in their famous correspondence, and in the hymns (really love letters to her) that Héloïse asked Abélard to write for her nuns, such as *David's Lament for Jonathan*. Abélard died in 1142 at the priory of Saint-Marcel near Chalon-sur-Saône. Héloïse, who became the abbess of the convent of the Paracletes, survived him by 22 years. Their remains, separated three times, were finally reunited in the Père-Lachaise cemetery.

Clignancourt and La Chapelle

18th arr. 5–A1, B1; 6–C2, D2.
Métro: Jules–Joffrin.
Bus: 31, 60, 80, 85.
Parking: 50 Rue Custine; 65–67 Rue Ordener.
Taxis: Place Jules–Joffrin. Tel. 46-06-00-00. Place de la Chapelle. Tel. 42-08-00-00.

A working-class suburb of Paris before its incorporation within the city limits in 1860, the Clignancourt-la Chapelle district has not changed its character. Its history is not inscribed in monuments as it is in other parts of the city; rather it is the district's inhabitants who hand it down to us. Leaving the middle-class district to the W, at the foot of the Butte Montmartre, to the E and towards the city limits, lies one of the poorest parts of Paris. The working class, who in the late 19th c. lived not far from the fortifications on these mostly unpaved streets, have given way to a largely immigrant population. The district's monuments are therefore those which some innovative architects put up in the early 20th c. in the hope of arousing some interest in public housing.

The points of interest referred to in the tour below are often far apart, so it is not possible to give a convenient route. But it is possible to discover by following these streets at random past the spice shops and Afro-Caribbean hairdressers, a side of the city that could be called the reverse of picture-postcard Paris.

Tour of the district

1½ hrs.

Place Jules-Joffrin

This square, which was laid out in 1858, marks a sort of boundary between the Grandes-Carrières district to the W, Clignancourt to the E and the Butte-Montmartre to the S. The town hall of the 18th arrondissement, inaugurated in 1892, was built in the Neo-Renaissance style by the architect Varollier. Despite its classical layout, it has one of the most beautiful stained-glass-covered courtyards of the 19th c. The great flight of stairs and fine metal columns which support the trusses recall the virtuosity of the Grand Palais staircase. Opposite is the Church of Notre-Dame-de-Clignancourt (1859–96).

At 7 Rue de Trétaigne (to the SW of the Place Jules-Joffrin) the architects Henri Sauvage and Charles Sarazin constructed in 1903 the Société Anonyme des Logements à Bon Marché (Anonymous Society for Low-Priced Housing), a building in which concrete was used without decoration for the first time. This project fore-shadowed the HLM (Habitation a Loyer Modéré – Low-Rent Hous-ing), large buildings constructed for people with low incomes.

At 63 Rue du Mont Cenis to the S at the corner of the Rue Marcadet, an 18th-c. house with a 15th-c. corner tower is one of the last traces of old Montmartre (today very much restored).

The Square de Clignancourt (to the NE) opened in 1913, has a bandstand in the middle.

At no. 29 Rue Baudelique (to the NE) the Conservatoire Municipal of the 18th arrondissement (opened in 1985), is a good example of modern architecture. The simple severity of the façade is enlivened by colored decoration. The architect is Claude Charpentier, the ceramist, Philippe Hebrecht and the sculptor, Denis Muguet.

The Grandes-Carrières district

This district extends to the NE of the Rue Ordener and owes its name to the plaster quarries, mined since time immemorial, which constituted the principal resources of Montmartre. Because of frequent cases of subsidence, working them was eventually forbidden, and in 1860 they were filled in to avoid further risk.

Rue Ordener. This interminable road, colorless but lively, boasts at no. 159 the shop-front of an early 20th-c. bakery decorated with the sign 'Benoist' under glass. At no. 189 three large buildings contain a group of no fewer than 187 artists' studios called 'Montmartre aux Artistes', built in 1934 by the architect Adolphe Thiers.

Rue Championnet. Most notable here is the Church of Saint-Geneviève-des-Grandes-Carrières, the old Chapelle des Oeuvres in the Rue Championinet, erected in the parish in 1907. At no. 104 (and at 1 Rue Gustave-Rouanet) is a very large brick group of school buildings by the architect Bois.

Rue Belliard. This street, further still to the N, runs along the old Ceinture railway. No. 188 is an important example of early 20th-c.

architecture in Paris, the house which the architect Henri Deneux designed for himself in 1913, using reinforced concrete, protected and disguised by colored ceramic tiles forming a geometric pattern of Oriental inspiration.

Clignancourt

Situated to the E of the Place Jules-Joffrin, this district is crossed by two large thoroughfares: the Rue de Clignancourt and the Boul. Barbès. Until the 1860 union with Paris, Clignancourt was an old hamlet of Montmartre, which from 1969 until the Revolution was dependent on the Abbé of Montmartre. Today the district is largely inhabited by immigrants, many from the former French colonies in North Africa.

The Boul. Ornano leads to the Porte de Clignancourt. At no. 43 the cinema, Ornano 43, built in 1933 by Gridaine, has retained its nostalgic façade although it has now become a supermarket. It is representative of the cinema architecture of the period which was often inspired by the style of ocean liners.

In Rue des Amiraux, between the Rue des Poissonniers and the Rue de Clignancourt, the architect Henri Sauvage created his most accomplished work at no. 13 in 1922. This tiered building** is covered in white ceramic tiles. The tiered system allows each apartment to receive the same amount of sun; this and the installation of a swimming-pool inside the building (always open) were revolutionary in public housing.

Not far away a garden square with a wall painted by Paul de Gobert was recently opened, level with 52 Rue Boinod.

Boulevard Barbès

This boulevard is full of shops and always very busy. Passersby come and go, some looking, some buying, others not, but everybody always 'shopping'. A walk between Marcardet-Poissoniers and Barbès-Rochechouart Métro stations reveals this new face of the city.

The streets which open up towards the W all lead to the Butte Montmartre. The block of houses between nos. 7 and 17 in the Boul. Barbès was once occupied by the old Dufayel shops*, designed by Rives (1895). Its most interesting façade is on the Rue de Clignancourt (nos. 22-34). The sculpted pediment by J. Dalou represents 'Progress leading Trade and Industry'. In the niches the caryatids by the sculptor Falguière are still visible.

La Goutte-d'Or district to the E

The rich vineyards that once covered this region and gave it its name are long forgotten. To be precise, the district now covers Rue de la Goutte-d'Or, Rue de Chartres, Rue Polonceau, Rue de la Charbonnière and Rue Caplat. And it is in these streets, especially during Ramadan, that you can meet the Maghribs, the immigrants of Paris. Despite their reputation for poverty, you have only to notice the numerous traders, restaurateurs and café owners to realize that all is not misery here. Yet if something seems strange, it may be that, more than the boutiques selling oriental cloth and clothing, more than the scents of spices, *merguez* (sausages) and mint tea, more than the piercing music that drifts from the windows – what is most striking is the number of luggage shops: this is largely a milieu of immigrants and people in transit. On summer evenings the dice- and card-players gathered on the sidewalks, the music of '*là-bas*' ('back home'), the furtive comings and goings and the inevitable 'loulous' poured into their leather jeans, create a strange atmosphere. And what the outsider does not see, but senses, is another reality: the immigrant worker, tossed from one job to another, the absent family, the seedy hotel room, the overcrowded lodgings.

The sector of La Goutte-d'Or is currently the object of a campaign of renovation and rehabilitation designed to make the area cleaner and safer, including the construction at the corner of the Rue Polonceau and the Rue de la Goutte-d'Or, of a *centre polyvalent d'animation* (multi-purpose community center). Between the Rue Saint-Matthieu, the Rue Saint-Luc and the Rue Saint-Bruno stands the huge Church of Saint-Bernard-de-la-Chapelle.

⚑ The Church of Saint-Bernard-de-la-Chapelle

11 Rue Affre. Open 9.15am-noon, 5-7pm; closed Sun. am. Tel. 42-64-52-12.

This church, built between 1858 and 1861 from plans by Auguste-Joseph Magne, is a 15th-c. Gothic pastiche. It was decorated during the Second Empire by the painters Bonnegrâce, Dauban, Claudius Jacquand and Robert Fleury. In the two arms of the transept there are two stone bas-reliefs by Geoffrey Dechaume. There are stained-glass windows by Gsell, Laurent and Oudinot.

Barbès-Rouchechouart station

At the junction of the Boul. Rochechouart, Boul. Barbès, Boul. de la Chapelle and Boul. Magenta, is the Barbès-Rochechouart elevated Métro station, a focal point for passersby and illicit street vendors. This station, opened in 1903, is part of the Etoile-Nation line and was constructed in stone, iron and glass by Jean-Camille Formigé.

Beside it, the Tati shops, which occupy most of the buildings between the Boul. Barbès and the Rue de Clignancourt, have become a veritable *phénomène de société* attracting an ever-greater crowd for ever-lower prices.

From the other side of the crossroads at the corner of the Boul. Magenta and the Boul. de la Chapelle, the Louxor-Pathe Cinema* is a real curiosity. Constructed in 1921 by the architect Ripey, its Neo-Egyptian mosaic décor is by Tibéri.

Boulevard de la Chapelle

Immediately S of the boulevard lies the group of buildings which form the Hôpital Lariboisière, the largest of its kind in the whole of Paris. Built between 1846 and 1854 (architect Gauthier) thanks to a legacy from the Comtesse de Lariboisière interred in the chapel in 1851, it has been greatly enlarged and modernized during the last few years.

At 37 *bis*, the Théâtre des Bouffes du Nord, left empty for a long time, is now one of the most important places in Paris for avant-garde theater.

The Chapelle district

To the N of the boulevard, dominated by the Métro viaduct, the Rue Marx-Dormoy and the Rue de la Chapelle which continues from it once formed the main street of the old Village de la Chapelle called the Chapelle-Sainte-Geneviève (before 1829) and the Chapelle-Saint-Denis (until 1860). Some old single-storey houses with mansard roofs remain from that time. This was the route taken by royal processions going to or coming from Saint-Denis. Joan of Arc and her officers, the Duc d'Alencon, Duc de Bourbon, Duc Dunois and the Duc La Hire, were billeted here in this village in the days that preceded the attack on Paris. Joan of Arc was, a few days later, wounded in front of the Porte Saint-Honoré.

⚓ The Church of Saint-Denis-de-la-Chapelle

16 Rue de la Chapelle. Open 7.30am-noon, 2-7pm. Tei. 46-07-54-31.

The church stands beside the new basilica of Saint-Jeanne-d'Arc. This old church, whose origins are thought to go back to Merovingian times, was wholly dedicated to St Geneviève. A statue of Joan of Arc by Charpentier (1890) stands in front of the church. The façade was renovated in the 18th c, but the nave and the side-aisles (early 13th c.) with timbered roofs and cornices with leaf motifs look today much as they did to Joan of Arc when she came to pray during the night of September 7, 1429. The choir and the chapels date only from the 19th c.

⚰ The basilica of Sainte-Jeanne-d'Arc

Open Sun.

In 1919 the decision was taken to build this monumental basilica near the old sanctuary to fulfil a vow made in 1914. The Archbishop of Paris laid the first stone of the new building in 1932. The massive façade, which was inspired by medieval military architecture, dwarfs the small Classical portal of the church. The first part of the nave, which communicates with the N side-aisle of the church through several doors, is covered with a dome which remained unfinished until 1935, when construction ceased. This bay now serves as the narthex of the new basilica, built by the architect Pierre Isnard and consecrated in 1964. The building (10,750 sq.ft./1000m²) in area has a visible concrete structure in spare style and gives the impression of being a balanced and harmonious space. Under the basilica a crypt and meeting rooms cover a similar area.

For visitors interested in 19th-c. architecture, a final detour to see the Marché de la Chapelle not far from here (8 Rue de la Guadeloupe) is well worthwhile. It is a covered market with a metal structure (1885, architect August Magne), and one of the last of its kind still in existence.

▷ The arrondissements of Paris

The Directory replaced the 48 revolutionary divisions of the city with 12 municipal districts, which were retained until 1860. *'Etre marié à la mairie du 13 arrondissement'* (to get married in the town hall of the 13th arrondissement) was the current euphemism for common-law marriage.

The city limits of Paris changed on January 1, 1860 with the annexation of 11 communes contained between the *mur d'octroi* or *mur des Fermiers généraux* (the *octroi* was a tariff imposed on certain goods entering the city and the *Fermiers* were the tax collectors): this wall was the limit of the municipal tax authority and the military boundary of Paris and its suburbs: Auteuil, Passy, Les Batignolles, Montmartre, La Chapelle, La Villette, Belleville, Charonne, Bercy, Vaugirard, Grenelle and small areas of other districts.

The Buttes-Chaumont and Montsouris parks were created within this new periphery. The area of Paris grew from 8118 acres/3288ha to 7088 acres/17,500ha. The boundaries and the numbering of the 12 old districts were modified and the 20 new districts were each divided into four. Their names and boundaries have remained unchanged to the present day.

▷ Markets

Boul. Ornano (between the Rue du Mont-Cenis and the Rue Ordener): Tues., Fri. and Sun. 7am-1pm.

Boul. de la Chapelle (opposite the Hôpital Lariboisière): Thurs. and Sat. 7.30am-1pm.

Rue Ordener (between the Rue Montcalm and the Rue Championnet): Wed. and Sun. 7.30-1pm.

Rue Duhesme and Rue du Poteau: daily street markets. Marché de la Chapelle (Rue de l'Olive): Mon.-Sun. 8am-1pm; 3.30-7.30pm; Sun. 8am-1pm.

Place de la Concorde***

8th arr./Map ref. 9–B3
Métro: Concorde
Bus: 24, 42, 52, 72, 73, 84, 94
Parking: Place de la Concorde
Taxis: 258 Rue de Rivoli, (Métro: Concorde). Tel. 42-61-67-60.

The harmonious layout of the Place de la Concorde, its elegant architecture and the magnificent views from its center make it one of the most beautiful squares in Paris. However, because it has served as a major crossroads ever since the opening up of the Rue de Rivoli in the early 19th c., it has always suffered from ghastly traffic jams. It was a concern for economy that caused Louis XV to choose this marshy spot outside the town, which in any case belonged to him. J. A. Gabriel designed the original square whose creation followed the expansion of the capital to the W and was inaugurated in 1763. Unlike former royal squares (Dauphine, Royale, Victoires, Louis-le-Grand) it is a large open octagon, nearly 21 acres/87,000m² in area, with only two large mansions on the N side of the square. More than a piece of urban design, the square is really an urban landscape on the principles of formal French gardens. However, the equestrian statue of Louis XV (the Well Beloved as he was called) which marks the intersection of the two perpendicular axes, conforms to the traditional scheme. Commissioned by Parisian alderman Bouchardon, it was finished by Pigalle (the model is in the Louvre). The statue stood in the middle of the Place Louis-XV until 1792; at that time, the square, renamed Place de la Revolution, became the scene of bloody executions. Rather optimistically named Place de la Concorde after the final decree of the Convention (1795), it again became Place Louis-XV in 1814, then Place Louis-XVI in 1823 (there is a plaque on the wall of the Hôtel de Crillon at the corner of the Rue Boissy d'Anglas) and the Place de la Charte for a short time in 1830. It regained its current name under the July Monarchy. Louis-Philippe wished to dispel the aura of sacredness of the place where both a king and a theoretician of the Revolution had been guillotined. He also had the square embellished with statues, fountains and an obelisk so strange and so redolent of history that there was not the slightest risk of arousing any passion. The square as it is today was planned by the July Monarchy. Its architect, Hittorff (1792–1867), the second great designer of the square in 1835, respected and did not damage the work of his predecessor, Gabriel.

A tour of the square

The Obelisk of Luxor

After the statue of Louis XV and that of Liberty during the Revolution, the 3,300-year-old Obelisk of Luxor was chosen by Hittorff to be the centerpiece of the Place de la Concorde. It is a monolith of pink syenite, 75 ft./22.86m high, weighing about 507,000lb./230t, on a pedestal of Breton granite. Its four faces are covered with hieroglyphics celebrating the epic deeds of Rameses II. It came from the Temple of Rameses II at Thebes (Upper Egypt, 13th c. BC) and was given to Louis-Philippe by Mohammed Ali (who also gave Cleopatra's Needle to the city of London) in 1831, having previously been offered to Charles X by Mehmet Ali in 1829.

The fountains

On either side of the obelisk are two great fountains (floodlit on some evenings) nearly 30 ft./9m high. They are copies of those in St Peter's Square, Rome. They were built between 1836 and 1846, and designed by Hittorff. They comprise three basins superimposed one above the other, the lower pool measuring 52 ft./16.5m in diameter. The emblematic figures represent in the N fountain, *Navigation Fluviale* (River Navigation), with a Triton and a Nereid by Antoine Moine; and in the S fountain, *Navigation maritime* (Ocean Navigation), with the *Pêche des Perles* (Pearl-fishing), by Valois, which inspired a poem by Baudelaire. The fountain on the site is built of the guillotine which decapitated Louis XVI. Hittorff designed the lamps.

Statues of the great towns of France

Around the square are statues representing the eight great towns of France on massive stone pedestals constructed by Gabriel. These marked the access to the dry moat, where flowerbeds have now been planted. The statues erected during Louis-Philippe's reign include *Lyons* and *Marseille* by Petitot; *Bordeaux* and *Nantes* by Caillonette and, best of all, *Rouen* and *Brest* by Cortot and *Lille* and *Strasbourg* by Pradier. Juliette Drouet was Pradier's model for Strasbourg. Between 1870 and 1914 this statue became a kind of focal point for patriotic pilgrimage. Marie-Antoinette d'Ensignies, wife of a Prefect of Police of Lille, modelled for the statue of *Lille*.

The Jardin des Tuileries, whose Terrasse des Feuillants and Terrasse du Bord de l'Eau are visible, lies along the E side of the square.

To the S the Pont de la Concorde (→ Bridges) has a very fine view of the river, the palace, the Sacré-Coeur and the Chaillot hill. It was constructed in 1790 by Perronet, partly with stone from the Bastille. On this side the balustrades follow the line of the moat which was filled in in 1854. The trees of the Cours-la-Reine can be seen from here (→ Quai de la Conference).

The Marly Horses**

The W side of the square opens on to the Ave. des Champs-Elysées whose entrance has been guarded since 1795 by the famous *Chevaux de Marly*, originally sculpted by Guillaume Coustou for a drinking-trough in Marly, Louis VIX's château near Versailles. In 1745 they replaced the equestrian statues of *La Renommée* and *Mercure* by Antoine Coysevox, which were transferred to the Jardin des Tuileries. Badly eroded over the years, Coustou's horses were restored and in 1984 housed in the Louvre. They were replaced by a couple of replicas and at the same time another pair were made and returned to their original home in Marly. They represent the famed Numidian horses first mastered in Africa.

Gabriel's Palaces*

Between 1757 and 1770 Gabriel built two majestic palaces. On the N side of the Place de la Concorde, their Corinthian colonnades are surmounted by pediments carved on the E side by Slodtz and on the W by Coustou the Younger (replicas). Then to the r. was the Garde-meuble de la Couronne (royal furniture store); the Crown Jewels mysteriously disappeared when it was broken into in 1792. Since 1789 it has been the Ministère de la Marine (entrance at 2 Rue Royale). Marie-Antoinette had a small apartment here which she used when she visited Paris incognito. The Bureau de Presse of the Ministère de la Marine now occupies her bedroom. On the other side of the Rue Royale is the Hôtel de Coislin,* where the Chateau-briands lived from 1805 to 1807 before they set up home in the Vallee-aux-Loups. Nos. 6 and 8, hôtels de Lambot de Fougères and de Pastoret, once reserved for developers and contractors who grew rich building the Place Louis-XV, are today shared by the Automobile Club and the Hôtel Crillon.

In 1788 the Hôtel d'Aumont at no. 10 belonged to Crillon, who regained possession of it in 1814. In 1904 the Duchesse de Polignac, the last of the line, died and the mansion became part of the hotel trade. Under the gallery, on the Rue Royale side, a plaque in both English and French recalls *'les traités d'amitie, de commerce et d'alliance signés en cet hôtel le 6 fevrier 1778 et par lesquels la France avant tout autre nation, reconnaissait l'indépendence des Etats-Unis'* (the treaties of friendship, commerce and alliance signed in this *hôtel* on February, 6 1778 by which France, first among all other nations, recognizes the independence of the United States). On the Rue Boissy-d'Anglas side another plaque commemorates the Pact of the Société des Nations, drawn up in this house by President Wilson and the Allied delegates from February to April 1919.

Hôtel de La Vrillière*

Corner of the Rue Saint-Florentin and Rue de Rivoli.

This mansion was constructed by Chalgrin in the 18th c. from plans by Gabriel, for the secretary of the king's household, Phelypeaux de La Vrillière, Comte de Saint-Florentin. It is the only house built according to Gabriel's designs, as all his other work was for the Crown. Originally symmetrical buildings were to have framed the principal buildings. The hotel was inhabited by the Duc de Fitz-James and then by Talleyrand, who died there in 1838. His niece, the beautiful Princesse de Lieven, held her famous salon here between 1846 and 1857. The house, which has an extraordinary ceiling*, is occupied today by the cultural services and the Consulate of the United States Embassy.

No. 7 Rue Saint-Florentin was built in 1761 by Letellier and occupied in the 19th c. by a prince of the Galitzine family and Ferdinand de Lesseps.

The United States Embassy

Corner of the Place de la Concorde and Rue Boissy-d'Anglas.

This embassy was built between the years 1921 to 1933 on the site of the Hôtel Grimod de la Reynière. This original mansion was built some time after 1770 by Nicolas Barré, and lived in, in the late 18th c., by Balthasar Grimod de la Reynière, gastronome and wit. It was occupied by the Russian Embassy and later by the Turkish Embassy.

Rue Royale*

This luxurious street, running between Gabriel's two palaces, has rural and modest origins. Before the creation of the Place Louis-XV it was only a path which crossed the swamps at Gourdes along the Louis XIII boundary. But while the square was being laid out, Gabriel opened out the road and flanked it as far as the Rue Saint-Honoré with great mansions, all built on an identical model, creating a superb view of both the future Madeleine and the Palais-Bourbon. The bridge which was to extend the axis of the road was not built until the Revolution.

Odd numbers: Philippe de Girard, the unrecognized inventor of the flax spinning machine, lived at no. 1. No. 3 is the famous restaurant, Maxim's, founded in 1891 by Maxime Gaillard in a mansion which had belonged to the Duc de Richelieu, Louis XVIII's minister and Governor of Odessa. The café with its lemon and cashew nut trees was frequented by the great courtiers of the 1890s, the Prince of Wales (the future Edward VII), Prince Orloff, Prince Galitzine and Marquis de Dion, among others. No. 9, partly occupied by the Jansen antique shop (founded in 1881), was where the Duc de La Rochefoucauld-Liancourt died in 1827. The Galerie Royale is at no. 11. Jean-Baptiste Suard, the Academician, who was the only person to stay with Louis XVI on the day of his execution, lived at no. 13.

Even numbers: The Ministère de la Marine is at no. 2. No. 6, which was inhabited by Mme de Staël shortly before her death, has two beautiful rooms, both in the registry of historic monuments. No. 8 is the architect Jacques-Ange Gabriel's own house; some original paneling still remains. The undoubtedly oldest shop in the street is no. 10, the florist Lachaume. Alphonse Allais, the humorist writer, lived at no. 24.

▷ An obelisk's journey

Le Luxor, the ship specially built to carry this solar symbol, which formerly stood in front of the Pylon of the Temple of Amun at Thebes, took two years and 25 days to reach Toulon. It continued all the way up to the Pont de la Concorde where its cargo waited another three years before its final installation.

The ingenuity shown by the engineer Apollinaire Lebas in bringing his boat safely to its destination is depicted on the granite pedestal. After it had been unloaded in Paris in 1835, the obelisk was pulled on to a ramp situated downstream from the Pont de la Concorde; Two hundred artillerymen were requisitioned for the purpose. A year later, when the base was ready, the long haul resumed. On August 16 the monolith was hoisted to the level of its pedestal by four winches manned by 120 artillerymen. The whole operation finally reached a successful conclusion when the obelisk was successfully set up straight, at last, on October 25, 1836, but only after a small box containing some medallions with Louis-Philippe's effigy on them had been carefully deposited in a cavity. Two hundred thousand spectators came to applaud the event.

▷ **The square in history**

During the Revolution of 1789, the guillotine stood at the side of the Jardins des Champs-Elysées for the execution of Louis XVI, and was moved to the side of the Tuileries for the execution of Charlotte Corday, Marie-Antoinette, the Girondins, Danton, Philippe Egalité, Mme du Barry, Manon Roland, Camille Desmoulins, Saint-Just and Fabre d'Eglantine. The guillotine, transferred for a time to the Place du Trône-Renversé (now the Place de la Nation), was returned to the Place de la Revolution for the execution of Robespierre and his companions (10, 11, 12 Thermidor 1794; Thermidor was the eleventh month in the French Republican calendar – July-Aug.).

These gory moments should not make one forget that the square was also the scene of many celebrations from the First to the Second Empire. It was also the site of the Industrial Exhibition in 1834. Temporary pavilions and a replica of the obelisk of Luxor were erected there. For the Fête de l'Empereur in 1866, the square was lit with electricity for the first time.

La Défense*

2km W from Paris.
Information: EPAP, Tour Fiat, La Défense, 6 Place de la Coupole.
Tel. 47-96-24-24.
Trains: SNCF: La Défense; RER: La Défense.
Bus: 73.

The great arch known as the Tête-Défense (completed 1989), is situated at the end of the Esplanade – the last monumental touch in the development of this suburb, so well linked to the capital that it has practically become the 21st arrondissement.

In 1958 a decision was taken to create here a veritable city of skyscrapers. La Défense was to become one of the rare examples of the application of the principles espoused in the Charter of Athens (an international architectural manifesto of 1943), with its largely high-rise buildings and the abolition of traditional streets. Many remarkable buildings were erected here, such as the Palais du CNIT (National Center for Industry and Technology), to the extent that this giant building site is now considered a laboratory of contemporary architecture.

More than 100,000 people come daily into La Défense to work, but only 20,000 live here. The new Centre Commercial des Quatre Temps with its 200 shops and cinemas, and the construction of new housing should, in time, restabilize the life of the district. Today La Défense swarms with activity by day but in the evenings and on weekends, the *parvis*, deserted and windy, seems unreal. Brave the winds, for La Defénse is worth a visit to gauge the full effect of this vertical city where, slowly and by fits and starts, the pattern of urban life in the 21st c. is being revealed.

The history of La Défense

The birth of a town

Until the 18th c. only windmills crowned the Chantecoq hill. Between 1765 and 1770 the Marquis de Marigny, brother of Mme de Pompadour, created a roundabout at the junction of several roads on the summit, along the axis of the Ave. de Neuilly, which it extended. This crossroads did not take the name of Rond-point de la Défense until after the siege of Paris in 1871. From 1855 to 1870 it was graced by a statue of Napoleon, now in the courtyard of the Invalides; later, from 1872 until 1964, it was replaced by a bronze group by Barrias, symbolizing *La Défense de Paris* (The Defence of Paris).

Situated at the far end of the long vista from the Arc de Triomphe at the Etoile, the site forms an architectural framework worthy of its monumentality. In the 18th c. a project was dreamed up to create a triumphal way in front of the entrance to the Croix-de-Noailles in the forest of Saint-Germain-en-Laye. However, between the two World Wars, many projects remained unfinished. In 1955, with the improved French economic situation, an ambitious piece of urban renewal was undertaken, whose development was entrusted, in 1956, to the Etablissement Public pour l'Aménagement de La Défense (EPAD), an organization favoring mixed business and residential development.

A difficult process

EPAD's program, the most ambitious city planning project undertaken in Paris, called for the restructuring of a rundown urban zone and the remodelling of transport routes; the creation of a district designed to decongest a Paris that was saturated with offices; and finally the construction of housing. In 1957 the first stage of the project, the remarkable concrete Palais du CNIT, was begun. In 1961 the Réseau Express Régional (RER) was begun on a site near the Pont de Neuilly to assure a rapid Métro link between La Défense and the Etoile, as well as with the business district of the Opéra. The massive plan, adopted in 1964, separated automobile traffic from pedestrians (the Ave. de La Défense, later Ave. du Général-de-Gaulle, the W exit of Paris, was, during the 1950s, the busiest in the suburb). This separation was effected by building an elevated pedestrian mall covering the future highway A14 (Pont de Neuilly-Orgeval) and two other roads serving the district. To either side of this central mall, some 30 towers providing 3.2 million sq.ft./300,000m² of office space were to be built carefully matched in height (328 ft./100m maximum), with the exception of the main building in the area opposite the Palais du CNIT at a height of 656 ft./200m.

The development

After a difficult start, the completion of the RER link in 1970 between La Défense and the Opéra made the offices a more commercial proposition. Because of particularly favorable economic conditions, companies wishing to enlarge their premises began to seek office space in La Défense, the first being Esso in 1962. Demand increased, resulting in increased construction, reaching a total of 13 million sq.ft./1.5 million m² of office space. The constraints of the overall plan were abandoned and during the summer of 1972 the GAN Tower's concrete core rose to a height of 42 storeys, dwarfing the Arc de Triomphe and interfering with one of the world's unique views, that from the Champs-Elysées W through the Arc over the suburbs of the city.

The limitations of the project

The unfavorable reaction which greeted the eruption of this vertical object in the Parisian skyline provoked a government decision in 1974 to limit the volume of construction, thereby calling into question the future of some of the projects.

Over and above the controversy surrounding the value of its architecture La Défense has been hit by an economic crisis. The towers are prohibitively expensive to maintain, and employees and their firms were naturally reluctant to install themselves in large open-plan offices without privacy, neon-lit, badly soundproofed and poorly ventilated. EPAD, placed in a critical financial situation, turned towards the construction of energy-efficient buildings that took account of the complaints of office employees. This gave birth to a new generation of towers, more slender and elongated in form and with broken up, less monolithic façades. In addition, sculptures and plants were introduced into this universe of steel and concrete.

Measures to restart the project, including a budgetary grant designed to cover the operational deficit, were taken by the Government in 1978. In the longer term, the construction of the A14 highway beneath La Défense, the extension of the No. 1 Métro line (Vincennes–Neuilly) and the opening of the new Défense–Cergy–Pontoise rail link would provide better transport services for the area, increasing the attractiveness.

Among the companies installed there are: Roussel–Uclaf and IBM–France, Esso, Fiat, Les Assurances Générales de France, BP, the Crédit Lyonnais, Technip, C. & A., Unilever, Westinghouse, Pétroles d'Aquitaine and EDF–GDF.

Tour of La Défense

1½ hrs.

The district of La Défense, which covers 395 acres/160h, is

enclosed by a one-way circular boulevard (Boul. Circulaire), to which are linked the service roads giving access to the numerous underground parking lots.

The Roussel-Hoechst Tower *D11*

The tower, which is situated to the l. of the Pont de Neuilly, dominates the Bellini quarter, where a house once stood in which the composer of *Norma* died in 1835.

The attractive blue-green tower, which houses the central offices of the Société Nobel-Bozel, was constructed in 1966 by J. de Mailly and the engineer J. Prouvé, and was the first skyscraper to be built in the Paris area. Its structure is similar to that perfected by Mies van der Rohe in his buildings in Chicago and New York: a weight-bearing core of concrete whose non-load-bearing curtain walls are supported by a supple envelope of glass and steel with rounded corners.

The Assur Tower *D1*

Located symmetrically to the r., the Louis-Blanc district is dominated by this unusual tower (architect Pierre Dufau), shaped like a three-pointed star. It is 492 ft./150m high, its 39 floors clad in aluminium and tinted glass and houses the offices of the Union des Assurance de Paris. Behind it rise two large buildings (architects Binoux and Folliason) containing shops, a hotel and other amenities situated around a central square (sculptures by Lartigue).

Further N, on the banks of the Seine, is the Neptune Tower also by Binoux and Folliason in aluminum and glass.

The circular boulevard swings round to the l. of the GAN, Manhattan (1965), EDF-GDF, Aquitaine, Europe and Septentrion Towers (→below).

The Place de la Coupole is reached by the Rue Albert-Gleizes on the l.

The Fiat Tower* *D6*

This tower, built in 1976, rising 587 ft./178m with 1.1 million sq.ft./102,500m^2 of office space, is the tallest and largest building in La Défense. Its French architects, R. Saubot and F. Julien, worked in collaboration with L. Skidmore, N.A. Owings and J. O. Merrill of New York, designers of a series of skyscrapers, the earliest and most famous being the Lever House on Park Ave. (1952). Here they abandoned the curtain-wall for exterior load-bearing walls. The high quality of their cladding in polished black African granite and the elaborate filigree of the aluminium frames enclosing the grey tinted window panes, places the building stylistically in the purist tradition of Mies van der Rohe. Another refinement of detail: the width of the windows increases towards the top to compensate for the slight narrowing necessary for wind-bracing, thus avoiding a tapered effect.

The tower's superstructure comprises 46 levels, four below ground; the ground floor contains conference rooms and a shopping gallery. The building is served by 23 elevators. On the 26th storey EPAD has put models and maps of La Défense on display (very fine view of the district). There is direct access to public transport from inside the building.

The Fiat's twin, the Elf Tower (designed by the same architects 11 years later), bears witness to the economic and social upheavals suffered by La Défense. With an equal square footage area, the Elf Tower's maintenance costs are less than half those of the Fiat Tower. Furthermore, the narrowness of the newer building has allowed the creation of individual offices each with its own window, as the employees wished.

Place de la Défense

The Place de la Défense, on the site of the old crossroads, covers the clover-leaf intersections, the parking lot (1200 spaces), and the bus station.

It forms the central section of the pedestrian axis, 1ml/1.5km long, which crosses La Défense. This is extended to the W by the *parvis* and to the E by the esplanade, which leads to the Pont Neuilly. The design of this central mall is by E. Aillaud. The architect suggested the construction of a low administrative building to the N of the square, the Maison de la Défense, and to the W a blind arcade to create a caesura between the square and the *parvis*. The square is dominated by a huge red 'stabile' by Calder (1976) – his last work, and a sculpture by Miro.

The Grande Arche**

1 April to 30 Sept.: Mon. – Fri.: 9am-6pm; Sun. 9.30am-midnight
1 Oct. to 31 Mar.: Mon.-Sat.: 10am-6pm; Sun.: 10am-midnight
Tel. 47-78-13-33

An architectural and technical tour de force, the Grande Arche today forms part of the historical prospect of Paris, which begins in the courtyard of the Louvre Palace, and is marked out by the Tuileries, the Concorde, and the Arc de Triomphe. The Grande Arche is conceived as a huge hollow cube, clad completely in glass and white marble. It impresses by its enormity; it weighs more than

300,000 tons and its central void, as wide as the Champs-Elysées (230ft/70m), could take Notre-Dame and its spire (330ft/100m). Access is by two monumental flights of steps. Beneath the arch, several external elevators take visitors directly to the rooftop belvedere, which gives a superb view* over Paris. The design of the Grande Arche, chosen by François Mitterrand in 1983, is by the Danish architect Otto von Spreckelsen (d. 1987). The arch was inaugurated in the summer of 1989 and today houses in its two 'legs' the Ministêre de l'Equipment and offices of international companies. The Foundation for the Rights of Man occupies the space beneath the belvedere.

Centre National des Industries et des Techniques (CNIT)* A1–2

The *parvis* forms the ceiling of the RER, a vast hall lined with boutiques (architect, H. Vicariot; 1970). It is flanked by the Centre National des Industries et des Techniques (architects, Zehrfuss, Camelot and de Mailly).

Its construction from 1957 to 1959 was a great technical achievement. Its concrete vault, like an inverted shell, is the largest in the world, with a span of 754ft./230m. It is formed by two superimposed vaults, with three points of support, each at the apex of a triangle, connected by strong steel cables.

The glass façade, embedded in an aluminium framework, is designed to adjust to the vault's variations in volume due to changes in temperature. Some important exhibitions have been held at the CNIT but since 1985 it has been largely abandoned. Its adaptation was entrusted to the architects Andrault Parat, who retained only the vault, trebling the useable surfaces to make a large international business center, with 60 member states (whose flags fly on the *parvis*), a conference center and a European information and communications center.

The Elysées-La Defense building D7

To the S of the *parvis* stands the Elysées-La Défense building, headquarters of the French branch of the First National City Bank (architect, B. Sanbot, F. Julien, W. Overcash), which moved here from the Champs-Elysées in 1982. The scooped-out façade reduces the building's weight and allows the maximum amount of natural light to enter. In front stand two monumental figures, a polyester sculpture by J. Miró (1978). S of this building is the Centre Commercial les Quatre Saizons with 200 shops, restaurants, cinemas and two department stores (architects, A. T. F. A).

The Esplanade

The esplanade, which descends towards the Seine, is 1968 ft./600m long. The landscape architect Dan Kiley originally proposed the planting of four rows of plane trees. This proved problematic since the trees are unable to grow in open ground, so the vista is dotted with sculptures and fountains. There is an ornamental copper fountain* close to the Place de la Défense, designed by Y. Agam; the wall in front of the Esso building was sculpted by V. Guirro; and the ornamental ponds and ventilation shafts of the A14 highway were decorated by J. Leclerq. J. Dubuffet has created a site-specific sculpture to complete the project.

From the esplanade, pedestrian walks lead to places with idyllic names (Place des Corolles, Place les Reflets, Place des l'Iris, etc.), and to the groups of buildings built above the parking lot infra-structure reached by access roads branching off the circular boulevard.

Boieldieu district *D8*

To the S of the esplanade.

Situated within the Place de la Défense, the N 13 and the Ave. Jean-Moulin, this district contains two office blocks (architects J. M. Delb, M. Chesneau and J. Vérola). To the W is the Winterthur Tower and adjoining it to the E the Franklin Tower. The higher of the two reaches 360 ft./110m and the façades are in aluminium and anodized with bronze. Behind, the housing is dominated by Défense 2000 (architects Proux, de Monès and Srot), a 45-storey apartment block, with flared crossbeams.

Villon district *D9*

To the E of the esplanade.

This district, named after the famous Cubist painter Jacques Villon, encompasses the Atlantique Tower and the Crédit Lyonnais Tower (architects Dubuisson and Jausserand; 1972). These 25-storey towers have weight-bearing concrete pillars moulded with dark glazed porcelain. The windows are fitted into a black aluminium framework. Separated by the Place de la Pyramide with its white marble sculpture by J. Silva (*Dame Lune*) the 36-storey Generale Tower (architect, J. de Mailly); 1972 presents a decorative façade with windows encased by cruciform buckles in aluminium-colored bronze. To the S of the Villon group of houses, the Eve apartment block (architects Hourlier and Gury) is a white 28-storey tower with an elliptical plan.

The Michelet district has recently seen the construction of the triangular PFA building, architect J. Willerwal; (1985). Situated on a

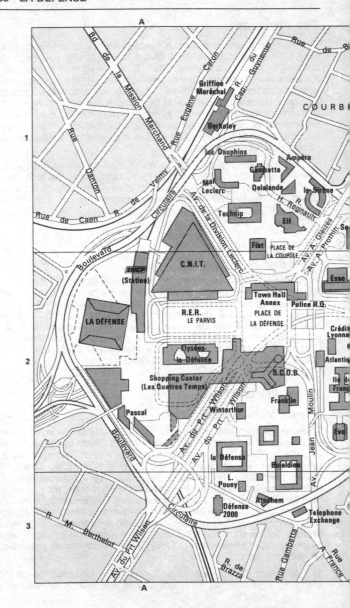

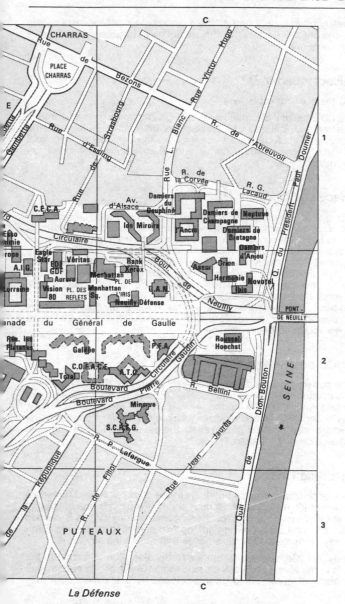

La Défense

rectangular piece of land on the outskirts of La Défense, it is known as the *batiment-phare* (lighthouse building) because of the way its windows reflect light.

Alsace quarter *D2*

To the N of the esplanade.

On the edge of the esplanade, the Esso building (architects J. and P. Greber and Douglas, 1962) was the first office building to be completed at La Défense. Behind it rises the Septendrion (architect Dufau) whose window panes and aluminium door-frames are bronze coloured.

Place des Corolles *B2*

The square is adorned with a mosaic fresco by Attila, *Le Sculpteur de Nuages,* which adds vivid color to the surroundings. Nearby is Louis Leygue's copper fountain decorated by a sculpture called *Les Corolles du Jour,* from which the square takes its name. Two towers dominate the square: to the N the Europe Tower, which alternates curtain walling with granite panels; and to the E the Aquitaine Tower (architects the Arsene-Henry brothers and B. Schoeller) whose granite cladding repeats the traditional diamond-point motif in reverse. To the S the Terrasse des Reflets, decorated by *The Mechanical Bird*, a sculpture with huge steel wings by Philolaos, gives access to the esplanade.

Place des Reflets *B2*

The square features a sculpture by O. Debré, *La Terre* (The Earth). It is overlooked by the Tower EDF-GDF (architects Gravereaux and Arsac) and the shimmering Aurore Tower (architects Damery, Vetter and Weil) whose windows with projecting sills, rounded at the corners, and smoked glass reflect the green GAN Tower and the rose-colored Manhattan Tower.

Place de l'Iris

One of the most original buildings in the complex is the Manhattan Tower, built in 1985 by M. Herbert and M. Proux. It is one of the first to avoid the monotony of rectilinear constructions with its S-shaped plan and undulating design linking two adjoining structures. Each storey comprises 4000 glass panes that reflect the sky.

The GAN (Groupe des Assurance Nationales) Tower, further to the E, is in the form of a Greek cross, 545 ft./166m high; its curtain wall is made of green-tinted glass enclosed by black aluminium rails which make a delicate pattern on the façade. It is strengthened by a reinforced concrete core. Its architects are J. P. Bisseuil of Paris, and the Americans W. K. Harrison and P. Abramowitz, designers of such famous skyscrapers as the Alcoa Building (1953) in Pittsburgh, and the Phoenix Mutual Insurance Building (1963) in Hartford, Connecticut.

Return to the circular boulevard. From there, take the Ave. Gambetta which leads to Courbevoie.

▷ Works of art at La Défense

The Establissement Public pour l'Aménagement de La Défense (EPAD), which was formed in 1958 to create a commercial district to the W of Paris, quickly adopted a very active cultural policy. With the help of the Ministry of Culture and the societies which had flourished in the 'French Manhattan', it created a real open air museum of contemporary art in the midst of the concrete jungle.

Famous masters of contemporary art are exhibited side by side with less well known artists: A tour of the district will allow you to admire Miró's two gigantic figures; Calder's last work, the monumental red 'stabile'; Mitoraj's *Le Grand Toscan* (The Great Tuscan); Delfino's *Lieu de Corps* (Place of the Body), the white marble *La Dame Lune* by the Argentinian Julio Silva; *Le Somnambule* (The Sommambulist) by De Miller; *Le Danse* by the American Selinger; Guiro's carved wall; *Slat* by Richard Serra, also from the United States, and *The Mechanical Bird* which features a 'kinetic mosaic' by Philolaos. Yaacov Agam's monumental fountain has 66 water jets reaching 49ft./15m high and plays music. The stairway in front of it leads to a gallery which holds art exhibitions (Tues.–Sat. noon–5pm). There you can see Moretti's *Le Monstre* (The Monster), a sculpture with many different textures. The statue by Barrias erected in 1870, in honor of the defense of Paris, and inaugurated in 1883, should also not be missed.

The Denfert-Rochereau district

14th arr./Map ref. 22–D3
Métro: Denfert–Rochereau/Bus: 38, 68
Parking: between the Place Denfert–Rochereau and the Place Saint–Jacques, in the central area.
Taxis: Place Denfert–Rochereau. Tel. 43-54-00-00.

Market: On the open ground between the Rue Brézin, Rue Saillard, Rue Mouton–Duvernet and Rue Boulard (Tues. and Sat. 7.30am– *1.30pm).*

If the Denfert–Rochereau crossroads were not so frequently jammed with traffic they might easily be mistaken for a late–19th c. subprefecture square. The broad, sleepy tree–lined avenues, the many green spaces, the convents, religious establishments, and retirement homes nearby, give the district a provincial atmosphere. Even Bartholdi's impassive Lion, high on its pedestal, seems unable to shake off an air of lethargy.

The Ave. Général-Leclerc, which runs S from the Place Denfert-Rochereau to the remarkable Alésia Church, is one of the capital's busiest and most animated arterial roads. Yet somehow the character of the shops that line it is not quite 'Parisian'. By contrast the charming Rue Daguerre, with its market, provides a centre for the more traditional *'vie de quartier'* which modern shopping centers and complexes have never managed to displace entirely.

Tour of the district

1 hr.

Place Denfert-Rochereau

This is one of the Left Bank's major crossroads. In the middle of the Place Denfert–Rochereau stands the famous Belfort Lion, a small bronze model of the lion at Belfort sculpted by Bartholdi to honor the heroes who defended Paris during the Prussian invasion (1870–71) and their leader, Colonel Denfert–Rochereau. The Place Denfert–Rochereau comprises three squares, each with a monument. In the square to the N a monument by the Morice brothers honors Raspail (1797–1878), the chemist. The politician Ludovic Trarieux (1840–1904) is commemorated by Jean Boucher's monument in the square to the W. Trarieux was one of the few who fought for a review of the Dreyfus case. In the square to the S, stands a monument to Charlet (1792–1845), the painter and draughtsman famous for his military scenes, fashioned by Charpentier. The Gare Denfert–Rochereau (Métro and RER: the Sceaux line) stands on this side, on the corner of the Ave. Renée-Coty and the Boul. Saint-Jacques.

To the SE of the Place Denfert–Rochereau, where the Ave. Général-Leclerc begins, are two villas with sculpted friezes, built by Ledoux in 1784. These are all that remains of the *mur d'octroi* of the Fermiers Généraux (tax collectors). Today these villas house the Inspection Générale des Carrières de Paris et des Services Techniques de la Direction Generale des travaux (General Inspectorate of the Quarries of Paris and of the Technical Services of the General Directorate of Works). The entrance to the Catacombs is in the l.-hand house. An inscription on the building to the W, opposite, recalls that during the 1944 revolt (August 19-25) Colonel Rol-Tanquay (Chief of the French Force of the Interior of the Ile de France) established the command post of the Resistance Movement here.

Avenue Denfert-Rochereau

The Ave. Denfert-Rochereau runs N from the Place Denfert-Rochereau. Originally it was called Rue Inférior, because it lay below the Rue Faubourg-Saint-Jacques to which it runs parallel. In popular parlance this became Rue d'Enfer (Hell Street), whether by phonetic assimilation or because the nearby Château de Vauvert was reputedly haunted, no one can say for certain. In 1879 its name was officially changed to Ave. Denfert-Rochereau in honor of the Colonel of that name who led the defence of Belfort against the Prussians. It is a long, straight, severe street, bordered by high walls behind which religious communities or private estates are sheltered in bucolic gardens.

On the odd numbered side: The unremarkable façade of no. 83 fronts a very pleasant estate *'pour notables de provence'* (for provincial VIPs): it has a central driveway flanked by small mansions and workshops. The Hôtel Fontaine stands at the far end. Built in 1913 by the architect François Le Coeur, its shape and the building materials used (hollow bricks and reinforced concrete) make it one of the first modern buildings of the 20th c. At no. 77, beside the Provincialate (Provincial House) of the Assumptionist Sisters, hidden behind another building is a 'cité d'artistes', which still exists only by sheer force of will and continued donations. These 14 brick studios, almost smothered by the new buildings erected by the Observatory, are the former posthouse stables of the *mur d'octroi*. They are occupied by the sculptors Paul Belmond, Merlet and Longuet, and by the medallion-sculptor Guiraud. The Convent of the Good Shepherd Sisters stands at no. 71; this religious community was founded to help and shelter 'fallen' women. In 1857 it was taken over by the Sisters of St Thomas de Villeneuve, who continued the same work, taking in young girls who were in 'moral danger'. Since 1968 it has housed 'Les Amis de Karen', an organization which offers training for disabled children. There is a water tower in the grounds, first used in 1624, to hold water from Rungis.

On the even-numbered side there is a whole succession of convents, retirement homes, clinics and hospitals. Since 1841, the Visitation Sisters have been at no. 68. This is a contemplative, cloistered order, founded in 1620 by Ste Francis de Sales and Ste Jeanne de Chantal (the chapel is open for Mass Sun. 9.30am and for

Vespers sung in Gregorian chant at 5pm). You may visit the craft shop at no. 68 *bis* which sells items made by the nuns. Within the convent grounds (no. 70), the 18th-c. mansion of the Marquis de Lautrec now serves as a shelter for young women, run by the Association Catholique des Oeuvres de la Protection de la Jeune Filles (Catholic Association for the Protection of Young Girls). At nos. 70 *bis* to 76, what used to be the Novitiate of the Oratory Fathers (founded in 1650) is now the children's hospital of Saint-Vincent-de-Paul. Its chapel, founded in 1655, was consecrated in 1657 to the Holy Trinity and the Child Jesus. The Infant is depicted on the sculpted portal, supported by angels; a Latin inscription from Luke 2:12 (King James' text) is a reminder of the arrival here in 1838 of abandoned children: 'Ye shall find the babe wrapped in swaddling clothes'. At no. 88 is an organization which looks after blind girls: L'Oeuvre des Jeunes Filles Aveugles de Saint-Paul. At one time this building was part of a large estate where Chateaubriand lived with his wife from 1826 to 1836. Mme de Chateaubriand (d.1847) is buried below the chapel's altar. The infirmary that she established in 1819 for sick and elderly priests of the diocese of Paris is at no. 92, called the Infirmerie Marie-Thérèse, in honor of her benefactress, the Duchesse d'Angoulême.

◼ Museum to visit

The Musée Lénine (4 Rue Marie-Rose): the apartment where Lenin lived between 1909 and 1912.

▷ The ghost of Vauvert

The Château Vauvert, built towards the end of the 10th c. for Robert le Pieux, The Pious, stands between the twin promontories of Sainte-Geneviève and Mont Parnasse and is named for the rustic vineyards that originally surrounded it. Soon abandoned, the château became overgrown, a hideout for thieves and vagabonds. The neighbors complained of infernal noises, and little more was needed to convince people that Satan himself had taken up residence there. After all, had it not been the residence of Philippe I, who had been excommunicated for having cast off his wife without due cause? The band of thieves who had in fact taken over the château were careful not to disabuse the locals of these superstitions, but rather to encourage their fear of the 'ghost of Vauvert'. When Philippe Auguste had his famous perimeter wall built around Paris, he carefully excluded the famous château.

The legend was finally killed off when St Louis established a Carthusian foundation here in 1258. The monastery survived in peace and prosperity until 1792. Today, reference to the Château de Vauvert survives in the idiom *'aller au diable Vauvert',* meaning 'to go to the back of beyond.'

Rue Daguerre

The Ave. Général-Leclerc is a busy shopping street which runs S from the Place Denfert-Rochereau, a continuation in effect of the Ave. Denfert-Rochereau. The Rue Daguerre is off to the r. (Calder lived in a small private hôtel here in 1926). The street has a family atmosphere, where everyone knows everyone else – lovingly depicted by Agnès Varda in the film *Daguerreotypes.* It is very much a market street, with a seemingly endless succession of new shops and restaurants.

A l. turn leads into the Rue Boulard: the workshops in the courtyard at nos. 38-38 *bis* are worth a glance.

Halfway down the Rue Daguerre, the Rue Danville leads to the r. The building at no. 7 was constructed in 1906 by Henri Sauvage and Sarrazin.

Take the Rue Sivel, which is opposite.

The town hall of the 14th arrondissement

The Rue Sivel leads to the Place and Square Ferdinand-Brunot, with the town hall, built by Naissant between 1851 and 1858. The registry office where marriages take place is decorated by Maurice Chabas; though based on traditional iconography the work is modern in idiom. The banqueting hall was decorated by R. Poughéon. General Leclerc's division's entry into Paris on August 25, 1944 is commemorated in the town hall by a bas-relief.

In the street which crosses the square there is a monument to Michel Servet, a Spanish doctor and theologian and a disciple of Melanchthon, who was condemned to be burnt at the stake in 1553 by the Grand Council at Geneva, on Calvin's orders. In spring, the games of *boules* (French bowls) have to make way for an antiques market. If you have time, wander about the little streets that lead away from the square, which still retain their provincial charm.

Take the Rue Durou-Choux, and then follow the Ave. du Maine to the S; you will emerge at the Place Victor-Basch, another busy thoroughfare, overlooked by the Church of Saint-Pierre-de-Montrouge, built by Vaudremer between 1864 and 1872. Drawing its inspiration from both Byzantine and Romanesque art, it has been the model for several other late 19th-c. churches.

Les Egouts (The Sewers)

Entrance: l. end of the Pont de l'Alma, corner of the Quai d'Orsay.
Map ref: 14–D1
Métro: Pont de l'Alma – RER: Pont de l'Alma
Bus: 42, 63, 80, 92

Charles V's Provost, Hugues Aubriot, is traditionally credited with opening the first vaulted sewer in Paris, believed to have been below the Rue Montmartre. This waterway, which was for centuries the mainstay of the Right Bank sanitary system, flowed into the Seine slightly to the W of the Place de l'Alma. Over the years, its bed silted up and in 1740 the Ceinture sewer was built to supplement it. In the novel *Les Misérables* this is the huge sewer through which Victor Hugo has Jean Valjean carry Marius to escape from the barricade at the Rue de la Chauverie.

Though the city grew and its population increased, the development of the sewers was relatively rather slow: in 1800 there were only 12.5 miles/20kms of sewers; by 1824 23 miles/37kms; by 1855 there were 103 miles/165kms. None of these sewers was well maintained, and they all discharged into the Seine as it passed through Paris. It was not until the Second Empire that, thanks to the skills of the engineer Belgrand, the system of sewers as they are today was established. Belgrand's key idea was to cut off the meander formed by the Seine as it leaves the city with a huge main sewer that, starting from La Concorde, would discharge the Paris sewage into the river some 12.5 miles/20kms downstream of the village of Asnières. Work began in 1857, and the construction which required digging to great depth over a vast area took four years. By the time Beltrand died in 1878 the network of sewers was almost 375 miles/600kms long. Today the system has a total length of 1280 miles/2050kms, and discharges around 1.7 million cu.yds./1.3million m³ of sewage daily.

The sewage was originally discharged directly into the Seine, but from 1868 it passed through a system of agricultural irrigation as a means of purification. Since 1899 there have been filtration beds at Achères (3236 acres/1310ha), Carrières–sous–Poissy (1623 acres/657ha), and Mery–Pierrelay (4400 acres/1781ha). In all these places, the sewage is used to fertilize agricultural land to a permitted maximum of 21000 cu.yds. per acre/40000m³ per hectare per annum.

Today the volume of sewage is too great for it all to be treated in the filter-beds, which are now supplemented by a filtration plant at Achères (Yvelines) using a far faster biological process (activated sludge). The water is then clean enough to be discharged safely into the Seine.

▷ ## The sewer as seen by Victor Hugo

'The subsoil of Paris, if the eye could penetrate the surface, would present the aspect of a colossal madrepore. There is seen, in the humid haze, the rat, which seems the product of the accouchement of Paris.

'At present the sewer is neat, cold, straight, correct. It almost realizes the ideal of what is understood in England by the word "respectable". It is comely and sober; drawn by the line; we might almost say fresh from the band-box. It is like a contractor become a councillor of state. We almost see clearly in it . . . The sewer has now assumed a certain official aspect. The very police reports of which it is sometimes the object are no longer wanting in respect for it. The words which characterize it in the administrative language are elevated and dignified. What was called a gut is called a gallery; what was called a hole is called a vista. Villon would no longer recognise his old dwelling in case of need . . .'

Victor Hugo, *Les Miserables*, vol 2 (p. 534), translated by Charles E. Wilbur [1968]. Reproduced by kind permission of J.M. Dent and Everyman's Library as publishers.

Visiting the sewers

Mon. and Wed. 2–5pm and the last Sat. in every month except public holidays. Visitors are admitted on a first come, first served basis; no advance booking. After heavy rainfall, the sewers may be closed to visitors. Tel. 43-20-14-40.
(Métro: Ecole –Militaire)

The sewers were first opened for organized tours during the 1867 Universal Exhibition. The main Sébastopol sewer near the Place du

Châtelet was opened first for a tour that was conducted in small wagons; later, boats were used. Since 1972, however, the tours, led by a guide on foot, have been much less picturesque, since the walk is made round a 656 ft./200m circuit clearly defined by lights.

There is an exhibition room with a display of all kinds of documents relating to the Paris sewer network. An audiovisual presentation provides historical and technical information.

The main sewers

Some 900 workers maintain the Paris sewage system, which comprises four principal sewers: the Asnières main sewer (3.75 ml/6km) beginning at La Concorde, where it takes in some sewage from the Left Bank that is piped through a drain running under the Seine; the Marceau main sewer (3.6ml/5.7km) beginning at the Place de l'Alma at the confluence of two drains, one (de l'Alma) with sewage from the Left Bank, the other (Mirabeau) from the 15th arr.; the Clichy main sewer (4.4ml/7km) beginning at the Boul. de Sebastopol, taking in sewage via the Coteaux sewer from the 11th and 12th arr.; and the main sewer du Nord (7.5ml/12km) which begins at the Ave. Gambetta.

The sewer galleries

The sewer galleries enclose the water supply conduits, of which there are two, one serving public and industrial needs, the other domestic. Many also carry telegraph and telephone lines, tubes for the old pneumatic service (*le pneu;* now closed), and pipes of compressed air.

Generally, each sewer follows the line of the street above. Occasionally, where a street is wider than 65.5 ft./20m, there will be a sewer under each pavement. Manholes every 164 ft./50m or so allow access for inspection and maintenance – there are about 26,000 altogether. A plaque on each gallery indicates the name of the street above to which the sewer corresponds.

The Eiffel Tower district***

7th arr./Map ref. 14–C2
Métro: Bir-Hakeim–Grenelle; RER: Champ–de–Mars

Bus: 42, 82
Parking: Place Joffre
Taxis: Quai Branly. Tel: 45-55-85-41

The Eiffel Tower has become such a symbol of Paris that it is difficult to think of one without the other. It overlooks a district which is not at all typical of the rest of the capital. The sumptuous greenery of the Champ-de-Mars, its open spaces, its rectilinear grid of streets and its almost exclusively tourist population give a misleading picture of Paris. Further along, relegated to the other end of the Champ-de-Mars and designed precisely for that site, is the Ecole Militaire, (French Military Academy), forgotten by the casual visitors and overshadowed by the presence of its tall neighbor. This remarkable building gave its name to the district's busiest crossroads nearby.

Beyond the spick-and-span Rue Cler market, around the Church of Saint-Pierre-du-Gros-Caillou are quiet residential streets where life goes at a much slower pace. Some, such as the Ave. Rapp, are worth visiting for the Art Nouveau buildings.

Tour of the district

2 hrs.

The Eiffel Tower***

Champ-de-Mars (daily 10am-11pm; school holidays 9.30am-11pm.) Tel. 45-50-34-56.

Possibly the most famous monument in the world and certainly the most photographed, the Eiffel Tower is always the high point of any tour, with or without a guide. Once the most passionately disputed monument of the capital, the tower now symbolizes Paris in the eyes of the millions of visitors. At night, a new lighting system, installed in 1986, shows off the fantastic metal structure.

History of the tower

The tower was erected between January 28, 1887 and March 31, 1889 by the engineer Gustave Eiffel (1832-1923) as one of the Arts et Manufactures projects for the World Fair (→inset) which was held on the Champ-de-Mars. It was first climbed on June 10, 1889 by Edward VII, then Prince of Wales, and his family. For a long time, the Eiffel Tower was highly criticized for its lack of aesthetic appeal. Huysmans called it a 'hollow candlestick' and Verlaine made detours to avoid seeing it. But, little by little, it became an inseparable part of the Parisian landscape. Eventually, its stubborn modernity won over many artists, as explained in Jean Prévost's book *Eiffel*. Painters such as Le Douanier, Rousseau, Pissarro, Dufy, Desnoyer, Seurat, Utrillo and especially Delaunay, depicted the tower on their canvases. Finally, when it was about to be torn down, it was saved by its potential usefulness as an antennae for French radio and television. This transformation gave the tower a strangely modern, poetic aspect – as Mac-Orlan put it, 'the tower has been accepted into the lyrical world'.

Description

The structure weighs 7700 tons/7000t and comprises 15,000 pieces of metal connected by 2.5 million rivets. The supports for the tower's four metal 'legs' are four masonry blocks 29–46 ft./9–14m deep, with a surface area of 280 sq.ft./26m². The form of the tower was the result of calculation: the engineer did not, in fact, set out to achieve this particular form for aesthetic reasons but the problem was obvious to him: how to make a 986 ft./300m tower stable? This original height was increased to 1.053 ft./320.76m in 1957 by the installation of television aerials. The tower has three platforms which are open to the public: the first at 187 ft./57m; the second at 377 ft./115m; the third at 899 ft./274m with a glass-enclosed lower gallery (orientation panels are above the bays) and, above, an open gallery from which you can see the television aerials and the two lights which seem to be one (→inset). The view* which, on a good day, stretches 42ml/67km beyond Paris, is very clear especially an hour before sunset, but days without mist are rare. Major restoration and modernization have been carried out on the tower over the last few years. A brasserie and a new restaurant have been opened, as well as an audiovisual museum tracing the tower's history. At the foot of the N pillar there is a bust of Eiffel by Bourdelle, installed in 1930.

The Champ-de-Mars*

The old parade ground for the cadets from the Ecole Militaire which could hold 10,000 arrayed for battle, was gradually transformed into gardens between 1890 and 1928 by J. C. Formigé but it is, however, far smaller (52 acres/21ha) since the wide strips along each side were sold as building lots. This district, one of the most luxurious of the Left Bank, was very fashionable between the two World Wars, when Paul Morand and the Guitry family lived there.

The Champ-de-Mars, begun according to Gabriel's plans in 1765, after he had finished the Military Academy, and completed in March 1767, was first used as a racecourse in 1780 (horse racing became popular again during the Restoration). In 1783, the physicist Charles and the Robert brothers launched the first hydrogen-filled balloon here, and in 1874, Blanchard made the first successful attempt with a navigable hot-air balloon. But the Champ-de-Mars was, above all, the setting for revolutionary events: the Festival of the Federation on July 14, 1790 (→ inset), the brutal execution of Bailly, president of the Constituent Assembly in 1793; the 'incorruptible' Robespierre's Festival of the Supreme Being on June 8, 1794, when he decreed a state religion. During the Empire several public ceremonies were held, such as the famous distribution of the Eagles by Napoleon I to his most valiant soldiers. This ceremony has been immortalized on canvas by the painter David. The Champ–de–Mars has also been the setting for most of the world fairs.

From the Champ–de–Mars, at the axis of the Pont d'Iéna, through the trees and beyond the immense arch of the Eiffel Tower, there is a superb view of the Chaillot hill and its palace and greenery. The Champ–de–Mars is cut off on the W by the long Ave. Suffren which marks the border between the district of the Eiffel Tower and its thousands of connections to the Invalides and the district of Javel (far less official and historical in character, and more oriented toward the future) and it is cut off on the E by the Ave. de la Bourdonnais. This section of Paris is full of Art Nouveau buildings. Eclecticism and the use of concrete and corbelled constructions are characteristic of the area, as are sharply delineated surfaces, sculpted reliefs, a frequent use of glass, and the predominantly cubic volumes common both to contemporary architecture and that of the period between the Wars.

Place Joffre

This square separates the Ecole Militaire from the Champ-de-Mars. The bronze equestrian statue of Marshal Joffre by Real del Sarte was erected in 1939.

☐ Ecole Militaire (Military Academy)**

1 Place Joffre (visits by special permission only - contact the Commandant).

This vast and remarkable classical building, around which the district has grown, is one of the great works by Ange-Jacques Gabriel, architect of the Place de la Concorde, begun in 1751. The academy, which had been operating from Vincennes since 1753, took up residence as early as 1756, but it was only from 1768 to 1773 that the buildings facing the Champs–de–Mars were completed. The chapel was finished in 1773. Enlarged during the 19th c. the complex of buildings today covers a surface area of 29 acres/12ha.

In 1751 Pâris-Duverney, financier and supplier to the army, with the support of the king's favorite, Mme de Pompadour, got permission from Louis XV to found and supervise a military academy where 500 impoverished young gentlemen could be trained to serve as officers in the king's armies. Bonaparte was admitted at the age of 15 in 1784 and graduated as a lieutenant in the artillery with the recommendation that he would go far 'in the right circumstances.'

Ten years later Bonaparte, the general, made it his headquarters. In 1787, the Revolution suppressed the institution but the buildings have kept their military traditions, serving as barracks for the Consular, Imperial and Royal Guards. In 1878, Général Lewal used it for the Ecole Supérieure de Guerre which had been created two years earlier. Foch taught general tactics and became Commandant in 1907. In 1944, the Germans, who had taken it over, capitulated on August 25 after a brilliant attack by a division of Leclerc's tank regiment. Today, the Ecole Militaire is the headquarters for further military training schools: Institut des Hautes Etudes de Défense Nationale et d'Economie de Guerre, and its annexes (Ecole d'Etat-Major, for further scientific and technical military education) and the Ecole Supérieure d'Intendance. It was also, until 1966, the college seat for NATO, that is for the officers from nations belonging to NATO.

The exterior

The magnificent NW façade, facing the Champ-de-Mars, consists of a central pavilion embellished with eight Corinthian columns, each two storeys high, a pediment on which two figures hold up the escutcheon of Louis. Pure, refined and classical, the quadrangular dome is supported by beautiful Corinthian pilasters. The entablature is decorated by four figures symbolizing *La Force* (Strength), *La Paix* (Peace), *La France* and *La Victoire;* the last is a likeness of Louis XV dressed in Roman costume and is one of the rare effigies to have escaped destruction during the Revolution. Corner trophies complete this decorative ensemble. The two low-lying wings flanking the main building, with its Ionic columns supporting a sculpted pediment, are the work of Brogniart, a pupil of Gabriel. On the other side, the façade facing the Cour d'honneur, is embellished by a pediment representing France protecting the pupils of the Military Academy and surmounted by a clock flanked by the statues *Temps* (Time) and *Vigilance* by Huez. The Cour d'honneur or main courtyard (Place de Fontenoy), is lined on either side by porticoes with paired Doric columns. Facing you is the colonnaded central building ending in advanced wings. Its façade is decorated with 10 paired columns alternating with windows, Doric at ground level and Ionic at first floor level. In the center is the grand entrance which has four huge columns rising through two storeys up to the pediment under the clock. The quadrangular dome can be seen above it. The mansard roof has dormer windows hiding behind a low stone balustrade running along its length. The sentry boxes are crowned, as they were intended to have been at La Concorde, by statues of groups of children. Louis XV was not at all interested in the academy and gave it no financial help. This fine example of French 18th-c. architecture was built with the proceeds of a lottery and a tax imposed on playing cards.

The interior

The chapel (Masses: Sat. 6pm and Sun. 11am), a masterpiece in the Louis XVI style, was built between the years 1768 and 1773.

The building is surrounded on three sides by monumental Corinthian columns. Above the cornice, on the long sides, small oval windows *(oeil-de-boeuf)* open at the base of a beautiful flattened barrel vault. Facing the altar four Ionic columns support an elegant gallery. In 1773 the chapel was decorated with nine paintings, which depict episodes from the life of Saint Louis (by Vien, Carle Van Loo, Lépicié, Jean II, Restout, Hallé, Durameau, Brenet, Lagrenée the Elder and Beaufort). These were restored to their original places in 1938. The altar was designed by Gabriel and the consoles are the work of Jean Jacques Caffieri. Note the beautiful painting by Doyen on the altar: *La Dernière Communion de Saint Louis* (The Last Communion of St Louis). This chapel, where young Bonaparte was confirmed in 1785 and where Joffre's body lay in state on January 5 and 6, 1931, was re-consecrated in April 1951 for the military personnel of the academy.

The majestic main stairway has a superb wrought-iron banister by the craftsman Fayet, made from designs by Gabriel who was also responsible for the gilded bronze ornaments. Since he had been previously criticized for excessive showiness he had them painted brown, as they remain today. The four niches which overlook the banister once contained statues of Turenne, Condé, Luxembourg and the Maréchal de Saxe: they were hurled to the ground and broken in 1792.

On the first floor, the Salon des Maréchaux boasts delicate wood panelling by Boulanger in the Louis XVI style, a Louis XVI chimney decorated with bronze statues by Jean Jacques Caffieri, and four paintings depicting the *Battle of Flanders* by J.B. Lepaou. This salon was used by Foch for receptions when he was commandant of the Ecole de Guerre before 1914. A room displaying all his souvenirs was set up on November 11, 1960.

The hall of the officers' mess is the old 'chapel of the students' or 'chapel of the infirmary' which Gabriel built between 1754 and 1755. It is a small octagonal building with a flattened cupola, decorated with Ionic columns. The library has been installed in the salons which still preserve the period medallions and woodwork. Leave from the Ecole Militaire, Place Joffre.

The Gros-Caillou district

The name of this district comes from the large rock situated near the intersection of Rue Cler and Rue Saint-Dominique; it marked the boundary of the abbey lands belonging to the Abbaye de Saint-Germaine-des-Prés and the Abbaye de Sainte-Geneviève which were, during the Middle Ages, until the 17th c., the owners of the Plaine de Grenelle. During the 18th c. the rock was destroyed but the name Gros-Caillou remained because of a signpost.

History of the district

As the Hôtel Royal des Invalides and the Ecole Militaire expanded, so the rural inhabitants of the Plaine de Grenelle were replaced by a population of craftsmen and small shopkeepers who relied heavily on the proximity of the Ecole Militaire and the occupants of the Invalides for their livelihood. The village became a market town and, when the Palais-Bourbon was built, the town increased in importance and became the district of Gros-Caillou, crossed by the Rue de l'Université, the Rue Saint-Dominique and the Rue de Grenelle which are, together, infinitely more popular than the sections of these same streets to the E of the Esplanade and the Boul. des Invalides. On the other hand, the Ave. Rapp, Ave. Bosquet and Boul. de Latour-Maubourg have retained their elegance. Although this district has no prestigious monuments, these are many important examples here of Jules Lavirotte's work which has, in a way, become typical of Art Nouveau.

Follow the Ave. de la Motte-Piquet in the direction of Les Invalides.

Rue Cler (to the l.)

The Rue Cler, a busy commercial street, open only to pedestrians up to the Rue de Grenelle, lends charm to the district of Gros-Caillou. No. 33 is characteristic of early 19th-c. Art Nouveau. No. 151 is Jules Lavirotte's first building: the façade which gives onto the street (academic in style), contrasts with the façade over the courtyard. No. 147 is the Lutheran Evangelical Church built by Buhler in 1911 in a Neo-Gothic style.

The Rue Cler comes to an end at the church of Saint-Pierre-du-Gros-Caillou (2 Rue Saint-Dominique), built by Godde; the first stone was laid in 1822 by the Duchesse d'Angoulême. This is a modest basilica formed by four Doric columns surmounted by a pediment.

Rue Saint-Dominique

From Ave. Bosquet to Ave. de la Bourdonnais.

No. 123, beyond Ave. Bosquet, was the old Hôtel de Béhague built in 1866 (old carved wood paneling and a Hispano-Moresque theater); it is now the Romanian Embassy. No. 129 is a curious little place with arches surrounding the Fountain of Mars by Bralle (1806) with reliefs carved by Beauvallet representing Hygieia, goddess of Health, nursing Mars (an allusion to the military hospital of Gros-Caillou); this pump was steam-activated and supplied water to the Ecole Militaire, the district of Gros-Caillou, the Invalides and the Faubourg Saint-Denis.

Remainder of the street → Faubourg Saint-Germain, environs of the Rue de la Grenelle.

Ave. de la Bourdonnais

This wide and very long avenue which runs parallel to the Champ-de-Mars, connects the Place de l'Ecole Militaire to the Quai Branly. Although it is over 200 years old it does not look it. No. 63 is completely covered with sliding glass panels (1962). No. 49 has a memorial plaque to General Castelnau. No. 39 bears an inscription indicating the staff headquarters of the clandestine Resistance Movement whose leaders directed the Parisian uprising of August 1944.

At the Place du Général-Gouraud turn l. into the Ave. E. Pouvillon and then turn r.

Ave. Elisée-Reclus: Lucien and Sacha Guitry lived at no. 18 from 1925 to 1957; a bust of Lucien Guitry has been placed in front of the new building. The house at no. 2 *bis* was built by Deglane.

Return to the Place du Général-Gouraud.

Avenue Rapp

One could say that Jules Lavirotte (→ inset) had command of this street. At the very beginning of the 20th c. he built a house for the ceramicist, Bigot, at no. 29: a concrete structure with a glazed earthenware and brick façade, decorated with animal and floral motifs blending in with feminine forms. This very characteristic Art Nouveau façade won a prize at the Concours des Façades in 1901. At the end of the courtyard at no. 20 is a fountain decorated with a statue of the god Pan. At the far end of the Square Rapp another building by Lavirotte has a watchtower. Next door, no. 4 is a very unusual building decorated with mosaics in which one can distinguish swastikas with the arms bent counter clockwise, the reverse of the Nazi symbol and the Cross of David. This is the headquarters of the Theosophical Society of France. The Ave. Rapp ends at the Place de la Résistance, at the start of the Pont de l'Alma.

The Rue Cognacq-Jay was opened in 1928 on a piece of land belonging to M. Cognacq and his wife (née Jay), founders of the

Samaritaine stores. Nos. 13 and 15 in this short street are occupied by French television.

The Rue Jean-Nicot via the Rue du Colonel-Combes: this street is named after Jean Nicot, the king's ambassador to Lisbon from 1559 to 1561, who first brought tobacco to France. On the corner of the Rue de l'Université is the building by Christian de Portzamparc designed for the Conservatoire du 7th arrondissement (conservatory for the 7th arrondissement).

Further along at no. 12 Rue Surcouf, the office of the SEITA, which houses a fantastic museum (→ Museums) has taken the place of the old Manufacture des Tabacs (Tobacco Manufacturers) destroyed in 1909.

▷ The 'Expositions universelles' (World Fairs)

Most of the international exhibitions (world fairs) have been held on the Champ-de-Mars, which is ideal for this kind of display.

The first, in 1867, dedicated to the 'glory of modern technology', aroused great admiration. The crowds went into raptures and Napoléon III acquired a great deal of prestige. However, the *exposition* had its detractors, in particular, the Goncourt brothers who deplored the fact that the steam engine had replaced paintings as an object of public display! All that remains of this exhibition is the name which was given to the Passage de l'Alma for the occasion, Rue de l'Exposition. The Trocadéro survived for a long time after the 1878 exhibition; it was demolished in 1937. The 1889 exhibition left its mark on the Parisian skyline in the shape of the Eiffel Tower, even though it had been originally slated for demolition. The gallery exhibiting machinery remained open until 1909. Paris owes the Pont Alexandre III, the Grand and the Petit Palais to the 1900 exhibition. The Art Deco style, fashionable at the time, held the place of honor at the 1925 Exhibition of Decorative Arts. Architects such as Ruhlmann, Rateau, Chareau designed a French embassy and a Hôtel du Collectionneur which were housed inside pavilions and made their mark on decorative art. The couturier Poiret's three barges were the biggest attraction. Moored near the entrance, *Amours*, in blue, was the framework for a modern apartment. The second barge, *Orgues,* was white and decorated with 14 hangings painted by Dufy; it housed Poiret's fashion collection. *Delices,* the third, was an epicurean restaurant decorated with huge red flowers. Poiret chose these amusing and somewhat meaningless names as, in the French language, these three words are the only ones of masculine gender in the singular, but feminine in the plural. The impressive building which now houses the Museum of African and Oceanic Arts (→ Museums) was designed by the architects Jaussely and Laprade for the Colonial Exhibition of 1931. The last French world fair took place in 1937, when the Palais de Chaillot and the state and city of Paris Museum of Modern Art were built. It was here that the large fresco by Dufy, *La Fée Electricité* (The Fairy Electricity) was reinstalled. One of his rare decorative works, it is preserved exactly as it was presented in 1937.

> The highest aerial in the world

On November 5, 1898, Eugène Ducretet became the first to establish a radio-electric link in the heart of a city, between the Eiffel Tower and the Panthéon. The tower became the world's highest antenna, but its powerful military transmitter was destroyed in 1940, before the Germans arrived in Paris. Today, the top of the tower carries the television aerials for which the two transmitters are located below ground, near the S column, as is the FM radio transmitter (the whole system was modernized in 1967). There has been a warning light for aircraft on the tower since 1947, but the original single light was replaced in 1952 by a double, synchronized arrangement: these two lights, placed on the N and S corners of the third storey, appear as one to approaching pilots (a flash every 5 seconds, range 112 miles/180km).

> La Fête de la Fédération (Festival of Federation)

July 14, 1790.

This festival commemorating the first anniversary of the storming of the Bastille, was to have taken place on the Champ-de-Mars, which was at the time only a vast plain. Initially, 15,000 people were set to work to level the area but time was short, and it was soon apparent that a larger workforce was needed.

Volunteers came in droves and soon there were 100,000, then 200,000 and finally 250,000 people working on the project - a remarkable mixture of the population toiling away enthusiastically with their spades. On July 14 the work was completed: grandstands were erected, as well as the great Arc de Triomphe, and, most important, the vast Autel de la Patrie (altar of the fatherland) from which Talleyrand, the 'Constitutional Bishop' at the time (he was formerly the Bishop of Autun), said Mass, assisted by 300 priests. Throughout the great day, rain fell intermittently on the crowd of 300,000, and, as Lenotre wrote: 'it seemed to take pleasure in drowning out with torrents of rain, every five minutes, this false Mass held in the open air'.

▣ Museums to visit

Musée de l'Ordre de la Libération (Museum of the Liberation Order) (51 *bis*, Latour-Maubourg): displays relating to the 1940–45 struggles for the liberation of France.

Musée de la Seita (12 Rue Surcouf): the history of tobacco and its uses throughout the world.

▷ Jules Lavirotte

Peculiar? Irritating? Sublime? Baroque? The adjectives that could be used to describe Lavirotte (1864–1928 or 1929) are infinite. The word 'edible', used by Dali to sum up his response to Art Nouveau, would suit Lavirotte perfectly. His first important work, already decidedly Baroque in style, dates from 1899: the mansion at 12 Rue Sédilot whose heavy, almost 'melting' lines, refer to and poke fun at the Louis XV style. In 1900 he committed a second similar offence with the building at 3 Square Rapp, then again in 1901 with 29 Ave. Rapp, his masterpiece which gained him the first of three prizes at the Concours des Façades de la Ville de Paris. Covered in polychrome sandstone by Bigot, this façade mixes a clever cocktail of decorative elements borrowed from all civilizations, with an obviously erotic and deliberately subversive effect.

The Céramic Hôtel Ave. de Wagram (1904), is only a poetic footnote to the building in the Ave. Rapp, and the mansion in the Ave. de Messine is also much more subdued. At the same time that he was at work on these Parisian fantasies, Lavirotte also interested himself in the working-class home (Boul. Lefèbvre, houses in Juvisy). This interest shows the other side of his personality, still very much an enigma and often referred to in a derogatory manner. Most writings falsely cite 1924 as the year of his death.

The Avenue Foch and the Dauphine district*

16 arr./Map ref. 7–A2, B2, B3; 8–C1
Métro: Charles–de–Gaulle–Etoile; RER: Charles de Gaulle-Etoile, Line A.
Bus: 52, 73, 82, 92
Parking: below the avenue between Etoile and Ave. Malakoff
Taxis: 1 Ave. Victor Hugo. Tel. (45-01-85-24) or Métro Porte Dauphine. Tel. 45-53-00-00.

Of all the avenues radiating from the Arc de Triomphe to the Etoile, the most prestigious and magnificent is undoubtedly the Avenue Foch. Reputedly the 'most beautiful avenue in the world', the Ave. Foch can also boast the highest price per square metre in apartments for sale in all of Paris.

The avenue's expansiveness, its beautiful lawns, abundant greenery, and long vista lend it an aristocratic aspect despite the architectural upheavals and land speculation that took place after the last war.

Today the Ave. Foch has lost the fashionable reputation that the splendor of the glittering society of the *Belle Epoque* brought to it and no one goes there any more just to be seen, except at night and for dubious reasons. Equally elegant are the areas around the Ave. Foch as far as the Place Victor Hugo, where equally remarkable pieces of architecture dating from the early 20th c. have been preserved.

Tour of Avenue Foch

30 mins.

Avenue Foch

Laid out in 1854, as the Ave. de l'Impératrice, and also known as the Ave. du Bois-de-Boulogne until 1929, because it is the main road leading to these woods, the Ave. Foch is one of Haussmann's most superb creations. By boldly amplifying the ideas of Hittorff, the architect responsible for the Place de l'Etoile, he laid two lawns, at least twice the size of the parallel side roads, and two roads to serve the houses along the avenue. The avenue is over 393 ft./120m wide. Follow it and you will see opposite the woods (Bois de Boulogne), above Mont Valérien, the slopes of Saint-Cloud, Bellevue and Meudon and the tower blocks at La Défense.

On the r-hand lawn stands a monument to Alphand, the engineer and landscape gardener, who transformed the district and the woods during his role as Directeur des Travaux de Paris (Director of Civil Engineering in Paris). The sculptor Dalou, who was responsible for this statue, placed one of himself to the l. of this group (1893).

The avenue is lined with large residential properties bearing the names of important architects' offices, such as: Dainville, Rives, Walwein, Lefèvre, and others.

The dramatist Henri Bataille lived at no. 14, and died in 1922 at no. 46. No. 19, the old Hôtel Rothschild, was one of the first houses to be built during the Second Empire and the last of its kind to have a private garden; today it houses the Angolan Embassy. No. 28 was for many years the modest workshop of a coal merchant who refused offers of millions of francs to leave. The sumptuous Neo-Renaissance mansion at no. 30, home of the Mexican family Yturbe, saw the foxtrot danced for the first time. At the corner of the Rue Rude, the former home of the Marquis de Breteuil, architect of the Entente Cordiale, is now the Irish Embassy. The magnificent Palais Rose was at no. 50 (→ inset). The building with portholes and studios at no. 53 exemplifies a certain Mannerist tendency of the 1930s. Today the United Arab Emirates are housed at no. 56, which was built by Henri Nénot, the architect of the new Sorbonne. At no. 72 is the entrance to a private drive up to the Villa Saïd: Anatole France lived at no. 5; in 1928 the architect Auguste Perret built the Maison Bresy in the same road. Not far away, in 1918, Debussy died at his home in the Ave. du Bois de Boulogne, now a part of the Ave. Foch. On the opposite side of the avenue at no. 59 are the Ennery and Armenian Museums (→ Museums).

At the angle of the Boul. de l'Amiral-Bruix, the detached house next to the apartment block belonged to Louis Renault, founder of the automobile firm. On this side, the entrance to the subway is protected by a 'butterfly' glass roof, so-called because of its brilliant colors, designed by Hector Guimard; it is composed of panels of enamelled volcanic glass set in a sinuous cast-iron framework: relegated to the outskirts of the town, it bears witness to the total incomprehension of its contemporaries who revolted against these temples of the Apocalypse which were, however, an ambitious attempt to integrate a modern art form into the fabric of the city. Today Guimard's subway entrances are considered to be among his greatest achievements, and are as much a part of Paris as the Eiffel Tower.

The Ave. Foch ends at the Porte Dauphine and the Place du Maréchal-de-Lattre-de-Tassigny. Return to Chaillot either via the Dauphine quarter, or go towards the Etoile by the Ave. Victor-Hugo.

Tour of the Dauphine district

30 mins.

The residential section of this street set within the limits of the Ave. Victor-Hugo, the Boul. Flandrin and the Ave. Bugeaud, consists of mansions in an eclectic architectural style and expensive apartment blocks.

Place du Chancelier-Adenauer

The former Foundation Dosne-Thiers, which lodged and gave grants to students for higher education, has been turned into a residential club without damaging the integrity of the design of its architect, Aldrophe (1890).

Rue de la Faisanderie

The Hôtel Watel-Dehaynin was, until 1975, on the corner of the Ave. Foch. This masterpiece is by the architect Georges Chedanne (1901), who collaborated with the most important artists of the time: Luc-Olivier Merson for the decorative painting, Paul Gasq for the paintwork and Edgar Brandt for the ironwork. A few columns and arches were built at the end of the modern building's courtyard. At no. 49, the Soviet commercial delegation now occupies the former *hôtel* of the Hériot family, owners of the department store Magasins du Louvre, who became famous in the yachting and aviation fields between the two World Wars. This veritable palace was designed by the Danish architect, Tersling (1905); the bas-reliefs are by Ferdinand Faivre.

Rue Emile-Menier

This name is taken from the famous chocolate manufacturer who developed this street. The block at no. 45 was designed by Molinié with sculptures by Garnier, and won the Prix des Façades in 1914; the purity of whole design prefigures the simplification of the modern architecture to come.

Rue de Lota

This street retained a unity of style with its Neo–Gothic, Neo–Flemish and 13th-c. style mansions. The large house at no. 8 was built in 1898 by the architect Richard Bouwens Van der Boijen for his personal use and to house his office on the loggia or gallery level, which is emphasized by a frieze of convex carved ovals or cabochons. Blue and white enamelled bricks cover the façade and follow the curve of the bay windows; inside is an immense painting by Albert Besnard.

Avenue Victor-Hugo

In the past, this beautiful and elegant avenue was called the Ave. Charles-X. Follow it in the direction of the Etoile from the crossroads at the Rue des Belles-Feuilles.

Rue Saint-Didier: no. 60 is the enormous building complex with a shopping gallery on the site of the former Salle de Concerts Humbert-de-Romans (concert hall), designed by Guimard and destroyed as early as 1904.

At the angle with the Rue Mesnil, an open market (Tues. and Thurs.- - Sat. 8am-2pm) adds a little life to the area. No. 8 Rue Mesnil, the Fire Brigade (caserne des pompiers) built in 1935 by Mallet-Stevens, is a rare example of a modern public building from that era.

The 19th-c. Church of Saint-Honoré-d'Eylau still has two interesting paintings: L'Adoration des Bergers* (Adoration of the Shepherds) by Tintoretto and La Nativité de la Vierge (The Birth of the Virgin) by Jean II Restout in 1744. A vast chapel of refuge and parochial center are at no. 66 Ave. Raymond-Poincaré.

In 1942 the Place Victor-Hugo lost the statue sculpted by Falguière and erected in memory of the poet.

Avenue Victor-Hugo, continued

From the Place Victor-Hugo retrace your steps as far as no. 124 where Victor Hugo lived from 1881 till his death (May 22 1885); from the beginning of the century, the building was decorated with a mask of the poet by Faulquereau. No. 111 is an apartment block and shopping gallery with a metal structure attributed to Henri Sauvage and Charles Sarrazin (1906). This belated revival of the Restoration style is an example unique in its time. The buildings at nos. 50 (1902) and 39 (1913) were erected by Charles Plumet (→ inset) and ornamented with sculptures by Lucien Schnegg. They illustrate evolution. No. 50 was Plumet's own residence and office; today it houses the Fondation Olfert Dapper, whose aim is to study and preserve the artistic heritage of Black Africa before colonization. From there cross the Rue Paul-Valéry where, first, Berthe Morisot lived with her husband, Eugène Manet (the painter Edouard's brother) then Paul Valéry, who married Jeannie Gobillard, the artist's niece. He died there on July 20, 1945. Close to the Place Charles-de-Gaulle is the Rue du Dôme where the memory of Charles Baudelaire is kept alive: a plaque at the site of Dr. Duval's clinic, where the poet died on August 31, 1867.

> # The Palais Rose ('Pink Palace')

Undoubtedly this represents the most perfect type of those private mansions which, before the World War I, showed off the opulent life of the wealthy classes.

After his marriage to Anna Gould, a rich American heiress, the Comte de Castellane undertook to build this huge house in keeping with his new fortune, at 50 Ave. du Bois-de-Boulogne (now Ave. Foch). Following the express wishes of his client, the architect Paul-Ernest Sanson took his inspiration from the Grand Trianon at Versailles; his building took its name from the pink pilasters copied from the Trianon. Opened in 1902, it had taken six years of work and four million gold francs to complete. Once finished, the Palais Rose was the scene of the most splendid receptions of the *Belle Epoque*. Its vast main staircase in red and black marble was a masterly adaptation of the famous 'Staircase of the Ambassadors' of the Château of Versailles. The dome was covered with large paintings inspired by Charles Le Brun.

The 'Pink Palace' was occupied during World War II by General Stulpnagel and was used in 1949 for the Soviet delegation at the Conference of Four. After remaining empty for a long time and the successive failure of several propositions for renovation (as an embassy, museum, headquarters, etc.) its ignominious destruction in 1969, to make way for property development, cast no credit on the French government.

> # Charles Plumet

Together with Guimard, Lavirotte and Sauvage, Plumet (1861–1928) was one of the promoters of Parisian Art Nouveau and is the only one to have retained his place in public esteem. His work, with its restrained audacity, is in keeping with the tradition of French art and, as a result, he has at times been described as affected by the critics of today. His first works in the 17th arrondissement (Rue Legendre, Rue de Levis, Rue Léon-Cosnard) in 1883, were neither outstanding nor typical of his style. But two years later his name became known as a result of his work at 67 Rue Raymond-Poincaré.

His first masterpiece (since demolished) at no. 112-114 Rue Malak-off (1898) was a mansion in the Neo-Gothic style. But this, his only building of medieval inspiration, was poorly received at the time. In 1901, after a series of shop decorations which helped his reputation, but which have since disappeared, he completed the building at 50 Ave. Victor-Hugo. This was his most beautiful and characteristic work: here, Plumet showed himself to be the heir to the past and introduced into his aesthetic vocabulary the arched loggia, the traditional curved window and the sculpted décor which were inspired by 18th-c. French art. While creating a few little architectural gems (19 Rue Octave; 17 and 21 Boul. Lannes; 1 Boul. de Montmorency; and finally 39 Ave. Victor-Hugo) he collaborated with Tony Selmersheim to create sets of furniture of such rare elegance that they enabled him to retain the favor of the art critics.

The period after World War I was for him a time of necessary adjustment that, unfortunately, resulted in mediocre works, such as the apartments in the Rue Rafferty. Only the regional towers and the 'Cour des Métiers' erected for the Exposition Internationale des Arts Décoratifs (International Exhibition of Decorative Arts) of 1925 for which he was chief architect still had the necessary qualities to impress the critics favorably.

▣ Museums to visit

Musée d'Ennery (59 Ave. Foch): art from the Far East.
Musée Arménien (59 Ave. Foch): jewelery, *objets d'art* and Arme-nian silverware (14th-19th c.).

Musée de la Contrefaçon (Museum of Forgeries) (16 Rue de la Faisanderie): examples of imitations or copies of objects from Roman times to today.

François-Ier district

8th arr./Map ref. 8-C3, D3
Métro: Alma-Marceau

Bus: 42, 63, 72, 92
Parking: Rue François-Ier Taxis: Place de l'Alma. Tel: 43.59.58.00.

The district of François-Ier was created by Royal decree on July 3 1823 at the same time as the Place François-Ier and the Rue Jean-Goujon, which runs right across the district. Despite the hopes of speculators, the site was developed slowly during the 19th c. (→ inset) and the neighboring streets, almost all of which evoke the era of the 'roi-chevalier', were, for the most part, designed during the Second Empire. Victor Hugo, who lived for some time in the Rue Jean-Goujon, refers in his letters to this deserted town of François Ier where the Neo-Renaissance and Louis-XIII style houses of the 18th c. make up a true anthology of the eclecticism in fashion at the time. This commercial district becomes more lively to the N of the Ave. Montaigne, where shop windows of the great couture houses attract clientele from their palatial homes in the Ave. George V. Once the late-afternoon traffic jams have dissipated at the Carrefour de l'Alma, a subdued atmosphere accompanies the worldly and international crowd of the prestigious Théâtre des Champs-Elysées and the famous '*salle de spectacle*' at the Crazy Horse saloon.

Tour of the district

1½ hrs.

Place de l'Alma

The Place de l'Alma is over 130 years old and an important crossroads for Parisian traffic. In the history of art it is famous as the place where Courbet in 1852, and, 11 years later, Manet, chose to exhibit their work when the official Salon had rejected them.

Avenue Georges V

A few Louis XV mansions remain: at no. 11 and next door, the Embassy for the People's Republic of China; at no. 13, the Spanish Embassy and at no. 15, the old Hôtel de Wagram. The remainder of the avenue has changed considerably since the end of World War II: the American Holy Trinity Church (no. 23) and the restaurant 'Chez Francis' seem to be rare testimonies to an epoch that has ended. Ultramodern buildings have been erected by the resident international companies, banking and industry, some of which are architecturally outstanding: the Heron Building (no. 17), the Banque Française International (no. 30), the Kodak Information Center (no. 38) and the Bank of Brazil.

Rue Marbeuf. This street was once called Ruelle des Gourdes because of the gourds which grew in the neighboring marshes.

The adjacent streets are mainly 18th c., and were named after villages: the Rue Quentin-Bauchart is the extension of the village of Chaillot.

Rue François-Ier

From the Ave. Georges-V to the Ave. Montaigne.

This elegant street, designed by W. Destailleurs, was opened in 1861. Numerous buildings were erected by Lesafouché from 1877. While the Maison Rochas at no. 33 has added a modern façade (1974), the Hôtel d'Ermont, at no. 27, built in 1881 by Chatenay, remains as it was originally.

Avenue Montaigne

In the 17th c. this was known as the Allée des Soupirs (Lane of Sighs), then the Allée des Veuves (Lane of Widows) because, it was said, widows of good breeding, whose mourning forbade them the amusements of the town, could only allow themselves the distraction of strolling down this lane in hopes of a romantic encounter. Marigny turned it into an avenue. Today, the luxurious buildings and the great couturiers have replaced the Bal Mabille (Mabille dance hall), (inset) at nos. 51–53, as well as Dr Ley's clinic, at no. 45, where Gérard de Nerval was once a patient. The former Hôtel Boselli is now the Christian Dior headquarters, while Louis Vuitton, at no. 54, have created their own refined décor with a polychrome façade (architect, Grateau, 1989). The private mansions hiding in their gardens, like the Hôtel Walewski (at no. 6) and the Hôtel Stern are no longer there. Vanished too are Prince Imperial Napoléon's Pompeian villa and the Moorish pavilion built for Ferdinand de Lesseps (at no. 22).

Théâtre des Champs-Elysées**

Ave. Montaigne.

This building, which made its mark on the history of early 20th-c. architecture, and has been completely renovated, is also one of the best concert halls in Paris. The theater, designed by H. Van de Velde, was built by the Perret brothers from 1911 to 1913. Concrete, conventionally used only in utilitarian construction, is used openly here to give a festive appearance. The façade is embellished by remarkable high-reliefs* by Bourdelle: *Apollon et sa Méditation* (Apollo and his Muse), *Les Muses accourant vers lui* (The Muses running to Apollo), *La Musique, La Danse, La Comédie, La Tragédie, La Sculpture* and *L'Architecture*.

There are three theaters built one above the other. The Grand Théâtre (2000 seats) has truly remarkable interior decoration of frescoes by Bourdelle in the atrium and in the passageways leading to the boxes. The ceiling of the auditorium is by Maurice Denis as are the gilded sculptures on the proscenium. La Comédie (655 seats) above the main theater became famous under the direction of Louis Jouvet from 1922 to 1934; note the paintings by Vuillard in the foyer, and the curtain by K.X. Roussel. Le Studio, the avant-garde theater (257 seats), was created in 1923. The Théâtre des Champs-Elysées owes its creation to Gabriel Astruc and Gabriel Thomas. Its early days were dazzlingly brilliant, with the coming of the Ballets Russets and creations like *Jeux*, by Debussy and *Le Sacre du Printemps*, by Stravinksy.

On the Place de la Reine-Astrid, to the E of the Place de l'Alma, is a statue of the Seine by Choin (1964) – a monument testifying to the gratitude of Belgium toward France.

Rue Jean-Goujon

The even numbered side of this street is mostly taken up by the headquarters of the Rhône-Poulenc company and by buildings separated from the street by courtyards and gardens.

The Chapelle Notre-Dame-de-la-Consolation (today the church of the Italian Mission) was built from 1900 to 1901 from the plans of D. Guilbert in a Neo-Baroque style in memory of the tragic fire at the Bazar de la Charité on May 4, 1897. On that day, a film projector started a blaze that left 250 injured and 143 dead, among them the Duchesse d'Alençon. A sort of cloister has been dedicated to the victims of the tragedy. The monument in memory of the Duchesse d'Alençon was sculpted by Hiolin and designed by Guilbert.

The Polish Institute is no. 29. No. 25 comprises several office buildings by Andrault and Parat. The Armenian church is at no. 15. In 1883 Victor Hugo lived at no. 9.

Place François-Ier

Opulent and almost peaceful even though it is situated close to major television and radio stations, this square is surrounded by houses built towards 1865 in the Louis XV style, such as the former Hôtel de Clermont-Tonnerre, at no. 14. In the center of the square is the fountain by Davioud which, like that in the Square Latour-Maubourg, comes from the Place de la Madeleine.

Rue Bayard, which crosses the square, rejoins the Ave. Montaigne to the N: at no. 22 note the façade of the Radio-Luxembourg (RTL) building, decorated by Vasarely (1971).

Rue François-Ier from the Place François-Ier to the Seine: at no. 9, the Hôtel de Vilgruy was built in a Neo-Louis XIII style by Labrouste, who also designed the reading-room and the stack-rooms of the Bibliothèque Nationale (National Library). No. 4 is a Renaissance-style house (architect, Boussard).

One comes out onto the Ave. Franklin-Roosevelt, close to the Embassy of the Federal Republic of Germany (1963).

The Quai de la Conférence (→Quays of the Seine). Return to the Place de l'Alma by following the beautiful walkway created alongside the Seine by Marie de'Medici in 1667 (Champs-Elysées) and, since 1919, named Cours Albert-Ier in the section between the Place du Canada and the Place de l'Alma.

▷ ## The Maison François-Ier

This Renaissance house, whose story begins in the Gâtinais (a marshy area on either side of the Loing river in the *département* of Seine-et-Marne, SE of Paris) played a part in the fashionable life of Paris for a period when, between 1823 to 1956, it became the symbol of the François-Ier district which, at the beginning of the 19th c., was known chiefly for market-gardening. Nevertheless, the residents of the Champs-Elysées were deeply interested in developing this area between the Cours-la-Reine, the Allée d'Antin and the Allée des Veuves (today the Cours Albert-Ier, Ave. Franklin-Roosevelt and Ave. Montaigne). Colonel Brack, who led the enterprise, discovered a Renaissance house at Moret and undertook to move the façade into this future district to 16 Cours Albert-Ier, corner of Rue Bayard. The craze at the time for everything Renaissance was supposed to do the rest. The sculpted reliefs were attributed to Jean Goujon; and the house itself was believed to have been used for the mistresses of François I and of the Duchesse d'Etampes.

The Neo-Renaissance trend did not result in the miracle it was expected to achieve since many streets in the district of François-Ier were not laid out until the Second Empire and were very slowly developed. As for the house, it has now been returned to its original place at Moret where it had been built in 1527 by a certain N. Chabouillé.

▷ ## The Bal Mabille

The popularity of public balls, which had become fashionable in the 18th c., reached an exuberant climax in the mid-19th c. in the pleasure gardens of Paris. The most notorious of these was the Bal Mabille in the Ave. Montaigne: opened by Charles Mabille in 1840, it began as a humble working-class dance hall, but soon became chic, attracting the finest dandies of the day, including Gautier, Eugène Sue, Baudelaire, Nadar and Champfleury. Mabille's sons made it more luxurious with gas lighting and fake palm trees, and an orchestra led first by Polido, then by Olivier Métra. It was frequented by the Jockey Club; the Prince of Wales (later Edward VII) made flying visits just to watch the cancan (and no wonder since, in those days, the dancers wore no bloomers).

All levels of society, foreigners and *gobemouches* (country bumpkins) went there to dance, and to watch the frenzied gyrations of the young men, tall silk hats on the backs of their heads, and the girls, swishing their skirts to show their legs, using the small space left for them by the crowd of onlookers. These dancers came from the lowest stratum of society, but acquired notoriety through their dancing: Céleste Mogador, Môme Fromage (the Cheese Kid), Grille d'Egout (Sewer Grill) and Rigolboche, who became the queen of the cancan. Their wild dancing echoed the wildness of life during the Second Empire, and these public balls saw a great deal of sexual licence, but with the coming of the Third Republic in 1870, everything changed, and the Bal Mabille closed its doors forever in 1875.

The Gare de Lyon-Bercy district

12th arr.
Métro: Gare-de-Lyon
Bus: 20, 29, 57, 61, 63, 65, 87, 91
Parking: SNCF station forecourt and Rue de Châlon
Taxis: in front of the station
Market: Ave. Ledru-Rollin, between Rue de Lyon and Rue de Bercy,
Thurs.–Sat. 7 am–1 pm.

Since the 12th c. the name 'Insula Bercilis' has been used to
designate that rustic area on the Right Bank of the Seine, upstream
from Paris. In the 14th c. it was the domain of the Montmorency
family, but it was in the 17th c. that the first president of the Parisian
Parliament had the château of Bercy built for himself there, whose
famous park was designed by Le Nôtre. The estate was destroyed
by the Revolution and the Commune of Bercy was constituted in
1790.

In order to sell their wine close to the city, but without having to pay
the city toll, the Burgundian and Charolais wine merchants, who
transported their products by river, settled in Bercy, building their
warehouses and cellars on the banks of the Seine. Until 1860 the
many restaurants and cafés, which were set up close by, attracted
crowds of Parisians because the wine, untaxed, was so cheap.
When the Commune of Bercy became part of the city all this came
to an end, and the cellars and shops of the first French wine market
were built. Since the late 1940s this market has declined considerably and the center of activity in Bercy is now around the Gare de
Lyon. Behind the station, the little Chinese restaurants and the
squatters have disappeared from the little island of Châlon, which

has been taken over by demolition teams and construction equipment.

In the coming years this whole sector of the capital will be entirely renovated. The Palais Omnisports de Bercy and the new Ministry of Finance are only two of the most spectacular creations of a vast project which will completely change the district. Behind the Palais Omnisports is a park of about 30 acres/12ha, where the 650 one-hundred-year-old plane trees which still shade the old warehouses will be preserved. The park will also feature playgrounds, terraces and fountains. Meanwhile, alongside the Rue de Bercy and around the Church of Notre-Dame-de-Bercy, a number of residential projects are planned. To aid transport and access to this new district, whose population will be greatly increased, and to relieve the already saturated Pont d'Austerlitz, there are plans to double the width of the Pont de Bercy and to build another bridge further downstream.

Tour of the district

1 hr.

Gare de Lyon

The Gare de Lyon, dominated by its high belfry, was built by Marius Toudoire in 1899 and enlarged in 1927. It replaced the first edifice erected in 1859 by Alexis Cendrier. Situated above the ticket hall, the Galerie des Fresques displays large painted panels evoking the different landscapes passed through on the way from Paris to the Cote d'Azur. On the first floor, the renowned restaurant, Le Train Bleu* (The Blue Train), classed as an historic monument, has preserved intact its extraordinary *fin-de-siècle* décor. Opened in 1901 by Loubet, this restaurant comprises several rooms (*salon doré*, or golden room, *grande salle, salon tunisien, salon algérien*) all decorated appropriately with impressive murals. Forty-five signed paintings by the most famous official artists of the beginning of the century evoke the large towns served by the PLM (Paris-Lyon-Méditérranee). This elaborate décor recalls the days of the *Belle Epoque* and its luxurious trains. Major modernization has recently been carried out on the station to facilitate access for trains from the suburbs and for the TGV (*train à grande vitesse*, or high-speed train). Each year some 76 million travellers pass through the Gare de Lyon and its annex, the Gare de Bercy.

Rue de Bercy

Follow this street in the direction of the Boul. de Bercy to catch a glimpse of the Paris of the 21st c. Since the end of the 1960s the whole district has been completely redeveloped.

The new Ministry of Finance

To the r. of the Rue de Bercy, overlooking the railway lines, the huge glass-and-steel arch (architects, Arretche and Karasinsky) spanning the Quai de la Rapée, was completed in 1986 to house the new Ministry of Finance, formerly in a wing of the Louvre. Major works are under way for the construction of the Ministry of Economy, Finance and Budget. The decision, announced in September 1981, to return this wing on the Rue de Rivoli to the Louvre meant the transfer of the Ministry of Finance to a new building where it would also be possible to group a number of services scattered around Paris. The chosen site, Bercy, was part of a vast plan to shift the center of gravity of Paris towards the E. It meant building 2,850,000 sq. ft./ 265,000m² of offices to house 6500 officials in an area of 8.6 acres/3.5ha. An architectural competition was launched in May 1982, and on December 16 the President of the Republic chose the project submitted by Huidobro and Chemetov.

The new Ministry looks like a viaduct facing the Palais Omnisports of Paris-Bercy. Starting with buildings alongside the railway tracks of the Gare de Lyon with, among other facilities, accommodation for 170 people, a long horizontal platform measuring 1150ft./357m and resting on pillars spans the quays and ends on the banks of the Seine, at a building which accommodates the ministries, thus creating, according to the architects, a monumental gate to East Paris. Behind this platform are buildings seven storeys high built around six square courtyards.

The Palais Omnisports de Paris-Bercy

This sports complex is on the other side of the boulevard and was completed in 1983. It takes up about 20 acres/8ha and can accommodate 17,000 people, with facilities for 22 separate activities. This, the largest *palais* in Paris, is, in fact, a versatile 'geometric' hall because of the flexibility of its design. The center area can be adapted as a skating rink or a concert hall; around this are two tracks built of exotic woods, one for cycling (the Six Day Paris Cycling Race is held here every year), the other for athletics. When not in use they can be covered by movable seating. The *palais* also offers many musical performances including concerts and operas, annually. From the outside the building looks extraordinary, with its grass-covered walls sloping an angle of 45 degrees. It was built on the site of some old warehouses in Grand-Bercy separated from Petit-Bercy by the Rue de Dijon.

The Bercy warehouses

For a long time these enormous warehouses for wine, alcohol, vinegar and oil constituted a veritable city of wine made up of *chais* (wine cellars at ground level), cellars and small houses standing among beautiful trees, a city where all the roads and pathways bore the names of France's best vineyards. The entire district is slated for complete redevelopment.

⚓ The Church of Notre-Dame-de-Bercy

At the end of the Rue de Dijon, standing alone and distant, is the small Church of Notre-Dame-de-Bercy, the oldest church in the 12th arrondissement. It was built in 1825 in the style of a basilica which was popular during the Restoration. It was set on fire during the Commune, flooded in 1910 when the river rose too high, and bombed in 1944. It has recently been completely renovated.

Return to the Gare de Lyon via the Quai de Bercy and the Quai de la Rapée.

Quai de la Rapée

This area will be profoundly affected by the construction work being undertaken to establish a new bridge over the Seine (information office near the Métro); to the l. the metallic viaduct of the subway is visible. Designed at the beginning of the 20th c. this single span of 460ft./140m was much admired, since it was at the time the longest ever built in France. At its foot is the Institute Médico-Légal, built in 1914 to replace the old Morgue (architect, Tournaire) at the S end of the Ile de la Cité. Opposite, on the corner of the Quai de la Rapée and the Ave. Lédru-Rollin, is the former Usine Elévatrice des Eaux de Bercy (pump station, 1887–89) by P. Chabat.

The Hôtel Massilia at no. 13 Boul. Diderot is one of the first examples of the use of a framework in reinforced concrete (architect, M. Oudin, 1911).

The Gare du Nord and Gare de l'Est district

10th arr./Map ref. 6–C3; 12–C1
Métro: Gare-du-Nord
Bus: 26, 30, 42, 43, 46, 47, 48, 49, 54, 58, 65

Parking: Gare-du-Nord

Of the old Parisian districts, the Faubourg Saint-Denis and the Fauborg Saint-Martin are among those which were most radically changed by the urban development of the mid 19th c. Two stations about 110yds./100m apart, and the boulevards serving them, have destroyed the old urban fabric of which only a few traces have survived. On the other hand, the visitor can discover here the very essence of Second Empire Paris, with its arcades, market-places, and broad vistas at the end of which – where once a church would have stood – stands the station, temple of the 19th c.

The whole of imperial policy, interpreted by Baron Haussmann in the terms of urban design, is on display here: a preoccupation with the pragmatic, aesthetic and tactical aspects of city planning. The wide, clean, airy boulevards, bordered with trees, cut the disorderly, turbulent suburbs to the quick, and made possible cavalry charges and the firing of cannon. Concessions were also made to fashion; the little square and the curved ramp in front of the Church of Saint-Vincent-de-Paul, and the transformation of the Classical façade of the Church of Saint-Laurent into a Gothic 'troubadour' pastiche (a so-called Neo-Gothic style of the 19th c.), evidence of a certain bourgeois taste for the theatrical and the picturesque.

Time and usage have somewhat sanctioned these choices, since the liveliest streets in this district, apart from those around the two stations, are still these two traditional old faubourgs.

Tour of the district

45 mins.

Gare du Nord

First there was the Boul. de la Chapelle, point of departure for the N which, under the reign of Louis-Philippe, was transferred to the Place de Roubaix. In 1863, Hittorff (→ inset) built a station so vast that, even now, it can cope with an ever-increasing volume of traffic without needing any drastic changes. Major projects have recently been carried out to improve links with the suburbs. The large innovative glass roofs, with their metal framework, were much admired in their time. The façade of this monumental building is crowned by statues representing those towns of northern France and of Europe accessible by rail from the Gare du Nord.

♣ The Church of Saint-Vincent-de-Paul*

5 Rue de Belzance 7.30am–12 noon; 2pm–7pm. Tel. 48–78–47–47.

At this point, the wanderers will find themselves close to that interesting church which looms from an escarpment above the Place Franz-Liszt.

The exterior

In front of the church an amphitheater with monumental ramps and a central entrance shows the influence of the Piazza di Spagna in Rome. Built in the style of the Latin basilica, as was Notre-Dame-de-Lorette, both these churches are impressive creations of the architecture of the first half of the 19th c. Saint-Vincent-de-Paul was begun in 1824 by Lepère and finished in 1844 by Hittorff. The imposing portico has 12 Ionic pillars. The pediment is decorated by a bas-relief by Leboeuf-Nanteuil representing St Vincent de Paul accompanied by Faith and Charity. Above the pediment the attic storey has statues of the four Evangelists. The two towers, 178ft./54m tall, are decorated with statues of St Peter and St Paul by Ramey; central door with bas-relief of the Apostles.

The interior

The design of the church (262ft/80m long and 121ft/37m wide) is that of a basilica: vestibules, two-storey naves, double side-aisles making five altogether and side chapels. There is neither vaulting nor ceiling – the framework of the roof is visible. But the whole effect is sumptuous because of the perfect unity of the rich decoration and the furnishings.

To the r. in the first chapel: baptismal fonts by Calla. The nave: beneath the tribune, a 56ft./7m long by 10ft./3m high fresco* by Hippolyte Flandrin (– Inset), an immense composition painted on a gold background, dividing the elevation in two. Painted in 1853, it is an important example of the art of the French School. Two long processions of saints, male and female, from the ordinary faithful to the Evangelists and Doctors of the Church, are displayed with all the majesty of Greek processional sculpture on either side of the building. Above the tribunes is a row of columns, and a frieze decorated with medallions. The half dome of the apse is decorated with paintings by Picot: *Christ Enthroned, St Vincent de Paul, The Evangelists*, and *The Apostles* and *Doctors of the Church*. Picot represents the *Seven Sacraments* in the frieze. The stained-glass windows are by Maréchal and Gugnon, and the pulpit was decorated by Duseigneur. The choir stalls were carved by Aimé Millet and by Derre: the wooden sculptures are portraits of all the princes of the House of Orléans who are shown with the attributes of their patron saints; although mutilated in 1848, the statuettes have since been restored. A bronze *Calvary** by Rude (1848–52) stands on the high altar. In the Chapel of the Virgin: a *Christ* on the altar by Carrier-Belleuse.

The visitor interested in Art Nouveau architecture will see, close by, at nos. 14 and 16 Rue d'Abbeville, two remarkable façades decorated with sculptures and painted faience tiles.

Return to the Boul. de Magenta via the Rue des Petits-Hôtels. The 1866 market of Saint-Quentin (85 Boul. Magenta), was part of the Second Empire's spectacular town planning campaign (it has been completely restored).

Rue du Faubourg-Saint-Denis

This very old street, an extension of the Rue Saint-Denis, which connects the palace on the Ile de la Cité to the basilica, was not improved by the renovations entailed in the creation of the Pompidou Center. The Faubourg-Saint-Denis is connected to the Faubourg-Saint-Martin by some rather unappealing little streets. The shops on the Faubourg-Saint-Denis are very varied.

The old Saint-Lazare prison

The telephone exchange and the Square Alban-Satragne have replaced the old Saint-Lazare prison, whose last remaining buildings were razed to the ground in 1935. An old leper-house founded in the Middle Ages by the hospitallers of Saint-Lazare, this building was occupied in 1632 by the Prêtres de la Mission (Priests of the Mission), founded in 1625 by St Vincent de Paul, who died there in 1660. The Saint-Lazare precinct was enormous: in the mid-18th c. it occupied the whole of the area within the limits of the Rue de Paradis, Rue du Faubourg-Poissonière, Rue de Dunkerque and the Rue du Faubourg-Saint-Denis. From the end of the 17th c., the buildings were used as a women's prison during the Terror: the poet André Chénier, Aimée de Coigny, who inspired him to write the elegy *La Jeune Captive* (The Young Girl Prisoner), and the painter Hubert Robert were all held prisoner here.

Only the courtyard and Baltard's chapel remain, after the recent alterations to the old edifice. The architect, G. Lefol, added new 18th-c.-style buildings which conformed to the new use of Saint-Lazare as a health center (police headquarters: Department of Hygiene dispensary entrance, 9 Cour de la Ferme-Saint-Lazare).

At the end of the square, where a monument to St Vincent de Paul stands, the former chapel is now a lecture hall attached to Saint-Vincent-de-Paul, used by the Faculty of Medicine of Paris. The houses beyond (nos. 105–99), which still have some beautiful architectural elements, used to be apartment buildings belonging to the Convent of Saint-Lazare.

Rue de Paradis

This is the kingdom of crystal and porcelain; the main Limoges and Lorraine manufacturers have their sale rooms and exhibition shops here. The Baccarat glassmakers, who have supplied kings, princes, presidents and others for more than 150 years, have installed a beautiful Musée du Cristal (Museum of Crystal, closed weekends), at no. 30 *bis* (→Museums). Next door at nos. 30–32 is the International Tableware Center (trade only) which gathers together, in one place, the most famous names in porcelain-glass-making. At no. 18, an unusual building dating from the end of the 19th c., the former Choisy-Le-Roi (China and Porcelain house), is today the Musée de l'Affiche et de la Publicité (Poster Museum, closed Tues.). The monumental portal, surmounted by columns encasing an enormous oriental vase, gives access to the vaulted hall whose walls are covered in painted ceramic tiles. Note the extraordinary porter's-lodge. Corot had a studio at no. 58 in this street.

Return to the Rue du Faubourg-Saint-Denis via the Rue des Petites-Ecuries, which owes its name to the former little royal stables there. This is also where the well-known jazz club New Morning is (at no. 11).

Rue du Faubourg-Saint-Denis, continued

From the Rue des Petites-Ecuries to Porte Saint-Denis.

France's president from 1895 to 1899, Félix Faure, was born at no. 65; no. 16 is the restaurant Chez Julien, the old *bouillon* (a cheap restaurant where the poor could eat) of the district which has preserved its very characteristic Art Nouveau décor, with glass and enamel panels by Trézel. At no. 12, the Passage du Prado, from which private coaches and public stagecoaches used to depart in the direction of Saint-Denis.

The Rue du Faubourg-Saint-Denis finishes at the Porte Saint-Denis/Grands Boulevards) beyond which the antiquated Rue Saint-Denis, now modernized, rejoins the Place du Chatelet.

Return to no. 54, the Passage Reilhac, where a succession of small courtyards ornamented with fountains and a bronze *torchère* (a kind of outdoor lamp) leads to the Boul. de Strasbourg: this boulevard was opened by Haussmann to relieve the Gare de l'Est and Gare du Nord by connecting them to the center of the city.

Walk up the Boul. de Strasbourg as far as the Rue du Chateau-d'Eau, then turn r. into this street.

Rue du Faubourg-Saint-Martin

This street is an extension, beyond the Porte Saint-Martin, of the old Rue Saint-Martin that, to a great extent, has been rejuvenated because of the Pompidou Center. As in the rest of the district, there is an abundance of wholesale haberdashers and hosiers, as well as numerous little Asian restaurants. At no. 76, on the corner of the Rue du Château-d'Eau, which leads to the Place de la République, is the imposing *mairie* (town hall) of the 10th arrondissement, built between 1892 and 1896 by Rouyer in a Neo-Renaissance style directly inspired by the Hôtel de Ville. Note the interior decoration of the North and South reception rooms (1906–08).

Hôtel Gouthière (6 Rue Pierre-Bullet)

Situated behind the town hall, this charming little mansion was built towards the end of the 18th c. for the engraver, Gouthière. It was remarkably well preserved by its successive occupants who respected the valuable and delicate decoration which the master engraver had so loved. A recent renovation campaign has added nobility to this Neo-Classical home, which looks like a temple with a bas-relief, the *Triumph of Bacchus*, above the façade.

Not far away, at no. 31 Rue du Château d'Eau, is another closed market with an iron structure (1810).

Return to the Rue du Faubourg-Saint-Martin. At the crossroads of the Boul. Magenta, leave the Rue des Vinaigriers which rejoins the Saint-Martin canal and which has several 18th-c. houses.

✝ The Church of Saint-Laurent

Open weekdays 7:30am–7pm, Sun. 1–4pm.Tel: 46-07-24-65.

All that is left of this 12th-c. sanctuary is the belfry. The building here today, consecrated in 1429, was erected on the site of a Merovingian basilica. Work began again during the 15th c. on the nave; the nave and the transept were not vaulted until the 17th c. at the same time as the erection of the façades; finally, in 1712, the Chapelle de la Vierge (Lady Chapel) was built. During the Second Empire, in order to align the church with the Boul. de Strasbourg, Haussmann replaced the Classical W front with a Neo-Gothic façade after having added a bay in the nave. In 1865, the City of Paris ordered several statues for the portal; in 1870 a painting, showing the *Life of St Laurent*, was executed by Balze.

The interior

The nave: a 17th-c. organ case; instrument built by François Ducastel (1682), reconditioned by Cliquot (1766). Side-aisles: stained-glass windows by Pierre Gaudin (1935–39 and 1953–55). Transept: hanging keystones (17th c.), decorated with figures; at the crossing: the Virgin. Sculptures and woodwork from the 18th-c. Chancel: this is the oldest part of the church, which Lepautre refurbished in the Corinthian style in the 17th c. Stained-glass windows by the Polish painter Elesckiewickz (1932). Lady Chapel: built in the 18th c., covered by a small dome decorated with two paintings. Stained-glass windows by Lusson (1874). The little Square Villemin was made in front of the old Villemin military hospital, which is today an architectural school.

Rue des Récollets

There used to be a Couvent (convent) des Récollets (Recollect Friars) here, founded in 1605 through the generosity of the superintendent of finances, Bullion. Beautiful stairways, buildings, a cloister and a chapel restored in 1842 form an 18th-c. ensemble which has fortunately been well preserved.

Gare de l'Est

The Gare de l'Est was enlarged and renovated from 1895 to 1899 and even more drastically from 1924 to 1931. The old façade, on the axis of the boulevard, now forms only the l. wing of the building. On the façade, statues of Strasbourg to the l., and of Verdun (by Varenne; 1930) to the r. On the projecting corner pavilion, to the l., an inscription recalls the old Foire Saint-Laurent (Saint-Laurent Fair). Founded in the 13th c. by Philippe Auguste, this fair was held on the site of the station forecourt (now known as the Cour du 11-Novembre-1918) from 1663 to the end of the 18th c. The land then came under ecclesiastical jurisdiction. This important fair ceased to exist with the increase in similar fairs and fairground amusements.

Just as Montparnasse is the Bretons' territory, so the area around the Gare de l'Est was, traditionally, that of the Alsacians and Lorraines in Paris. The names of the neighboring streets (Rue d'Alsace, Rue de Nancy, Boul. de Strasbourg) and the numerous brassieries (bar-restaurants) are constant reminders of this.

▷ Hittorff

Jacques-Ignace Hittorff (1792–1867), a French architect born in Germany, played an important part in the transformation of Paris in the middle of the 19th c. After training under Percier and Bélanger, he made the traditional Grand Tour of Italy, Germany and England. Later he made his name as an archeologist with his discovery of the polychromy of ancient Greek architecture (1830). Though purists among the older generation of scholars were shocked, subsequent discoveries proved him right. After 1831, Hittorff worked mainly in Paris. He finished the construction of the Church of Saint-Vincent-de-Paul, designed the Place de la Concorde in its present form (1832–40) and the Champs-Elysées (1832–40), where he built two Circuses (Cirque des Champs-Elysées, 1839; Cirque de Napoléon, 1851) with iron and glass domes.

In 1852, he built the Cirque d'Hiver (Winter Circus) where he shouted his interest in new materials, and in 1856, transformed the Place de l'Etoile by erecting the 12 mansions surrounding the Arc de Triomphe. But Hittorff's most significant work is the Gare du Nord, built between 1859 and 1866. The enormous and extremely light glass roofs are still concealed by a monumental façade inspired by Roman baths. Though his role in effecting Baron Haussmann's grand designs went largely unrecognized by Baron Haussmann, Hittorff did, nonetheless, contribute greatly to the transformation of the landscape of Paris, giving it the aspect it retains to this day.

▷ Hippolyte Flandrin

The religious painter par excellence of the 19th c. was Hippolyte Flandrin (1809–64). Born in Lyon, trained at the Ecole des Beaux-Arts, winner of the Grand Prix de Rome in 1832, Flandrin was deeply influenced by Ingres, his teacher at the Villa Medici. Under the supervision of this master, he discovered the grandeur of Raphael; the quality of his compositions, the richness of his drawing and his masterful use of colors, his disdain of fame easily won – all bear the mark of his ardent studies in Rome.

The Saint-Jean Chapel at Saint-Séverin (1839–41), is Flandrin's first monumental work in Paris. The Saint-Germain-des-Prés decorations (1842–46 and 1856–64) and those of Saint-Vincent-de-Paul (1849–53) show his skill in dealing with vast surfaces, and the austere profundity of his inspiration. Outside Paris, Flandrin was responsible for decorating the Church of Saint-Paul at Nîmes (1846–49) and Saint-Martin-d'Ainay at Lyons (1855). He also left a large number of portraits displaying a serene majesty, which show a certain psychological depth.

With his independent and severe personality, Hippolyte Flandrin always remained outside academic quarrels. He was contemptuous of the Purists such as Orsel who, taking the German Nazarenes as an example, made a pretense of reviving the glories of Fra Angelico in the middle of the 19th c. Nor was he affected by Romanticism but remained his whole life a solitary and profoundly classical genius.

▷ Markets

Saint-Quentin Market (covered), 85 *bis*, Boul. Magenta: Mon–Sat. 8am–1pm, 4.30pm; Sun. 8am–1pm.

Porte-Saint-Martin (covered), 31 Rue du Chateau-d'Eau: Mon.– Sat. 8am–1pm, 4–7:30pm; Sun. 8am–1pm

Alibert Market (open air), Rue Claude-Vellefaux: Thurs. and Sun. 7am–1:30pm.

The Gobelins district*

13th arr./Map ref. 23–B3; 24–C3
Métro: Gobelins
Bus: 27, 47, 83, 91
Parking: Rue des Patriarches (5th arr.)
Taxis: 88 Boul. Saint-Marcel. Tel: 43-31-00-00

This district was still, in the mid 15th c., a green and luxuriant valley with the Bièvre meandering between the hills of Butte-aux-Cailles and the Montagne Saint-Geneviève, when the scarlet-dyers from Champagne, Jean and Philibert Gobelin, set up their workshop here, by the stream. Backed by Henri IV and especially by Louis XIV, who reorganized the weavers in 1662, this workshop grew considerably, and from the manufacture of textile dyes the Gobelin brothers expanded their activities and became known for their brilliant tapestries as well. In the 18th c., the production of what had become the Royal manufacture of tapestries and carpets, Les Tapisseries de la Couronne, made the name of the quarter known throughout the whole of Europe.

This was a popular and industrial suburb; many workshops were set up in the 19th c., in particular several tanneries, whose waste products turned the Bièvre into a foul-smelling open-air sewer. The district acquired its present aspect when, in 1910, the Bièvre was covered over and the Avenue des Gobelins and neighboring boulevards were created.

Despite the dense traffic, there remains a certain village charm in the atmosphere at the start of the Ave. des Gobelins and in the little streets around the factory.

Tour of the Gobelins factory**

42 Ave. des Gobelins. Tel: 45-70-12-60. Wed., Thurs. and Fri., 2-4pm. Workshops: guided tours.

Known all over the world for its tapestries for the last three centuries the Gobelins manufactory was attached to the Mobilier National (furniture factory) in 1937. Since 1826, it has also housed the workshops of the Savonnerie who make carpets and, since 1940, the workshops of Beauvais. The weavers follow regulations and traditions dating from the time of Louis XIV, transmitted down the centuries to today.

The history of the factory

The first royal tapestry workshop was at Fontainebleau, but little information about this has survived. At the site where Gobelins stands today, two dyers, Jean and Philibert Gobelin, established themselves in the area around 1440 (it was a Gobelin, the Marquis de Brinvilliers, who married the infamous woman poisoner Marie-Madeleine d'Aubray, who was executed in 1676). In 1601, Henri IV, wishing to create a royal tapestry workshop in Paris, summoned two Flemish tapestry-makers to the old dyeing workshop, Marc de Comans and François de la Planche. In 1662, Louis XIV reorganized the tapestry weavers of Paris with Colbert who centralized the scattered workshops around Paris (in the Rue de la Chaise, at Trinité and the Louvre), and included the Savonnerie carpet manufactory, which moved its looms to the Gobelins in 1826. The collection of manufactures, together with the cabinet-makers, goldsmiths and silversmiths, etc., took the title of royal manufactories of the Meubles de la Couronne (Furnishings of the Crown), confirmed by an edict of 1667. The painter Charles Le Brun (1619-90) was artistic director; Pierre Mignard succeeded him, in 1690. Later, a galaxy of designers, including Van der Meulen, Coypel, Audran and Monnoyer, inaugurated a brilliant period for Gobelins. Though they were not always the directors of the Gobelins, it was artists such as these who inspired the works of art produced there. More recently, Chagall also worked for the Gobelins. Some of the old buildings were set ablaze during the Commune in 1871.

The buildings

The buildings are divided into two separate sections. Facing the avenue, this edifice was built in 1914 by Formigé, crowned by a square cupola with an emblematic light-relief carved by Landowski and, on the first storey, four caryatids by Injalbert. At the back, the old buildings have retained their peaceful and even faintly monastic aspect. Rooms reserved for temporary exhibitions are on the first floor. Louis XIV tapestries hang in the chapel which is no longer in use. There is also a beautiful collection of drawings by Van der Meulen. On display in the Sacristy are models of ornamental pieces and some silver religious vessels which belonged to the former chapel.

The Gobelins workshops

The Gobelins tapestries are woven on looms, many dating from the 19th c. These looms are known as *haute lice* (high warp) looms, which stand upright, and the warp threads are parted manually. This method is considerably slower than the *basse lice* method though specialists agree that is virtually impossible to distinguish on which type of loom a tapestry has been woven. The wefts pass only as far as their color is needed by the pattern, and are then battened firmly down so that the warps are finally completely hidden. The cartoon from which the weavers copy their design stands behind them. Since they work from the back of the tapestry, small mirrors are placed in front so that they can see how the work is progressing by looking through the warps. In the Middle Ages no more than about 20 colours were used, but by the 18th c. in France there were between 400 and 500 tones. Each colored yarn is wound on a separate bobbin, which is passed over and under the warps until the design calls for a different colour. Gobelins, and most European tapestries, were made to be seen from one side only, so the backs are left unfinished with yarn ends hanging loose. A tapestry's fineness is judged by the number of wefts to the centimeter; the coarse Gobelins average eight, but the finest European tapestries average 33. On average, a weaver is able to complete only about 10sq. ft./1m² of tapestry per year.

The mending of old tapestries takes place in workshops specializing in invisible mending, which are found in the Mobilier National.

The Beauvais workshops

Originally the Manufacture Royale established by Colbert in 1664 at Beauvais, these workshops have been set up in the new buildings erected for that purpose in 1940. The weaving technique is different from that used in Gobelins, and is called *basse lice* (woven on a low-warp loom). The loom is placed horizontally in front of the weaver and the warps controlled by harnesses fixed to treadles. The design is reproduced from a cartoon placed underneath the warp; another copy of the cartoon is also hung behind the weaver for reference. François Boucher painted about 45 cartoons for the Beauvais ateliers, including opera scenes and chinoiseries.

The Savonnerie workshops

Established in 1626 in a former soapworks (hence the name) at Chaillot, these workshops invented the 'Savonnerie' technique of rug-weaving. The name now applies to all French hand-knotted carpets, which are made by a method completely different from that used for tapestries. The finished rug has a texture like velvet, the result of using scissors to cut, in a straight line, the rows of knots, which are joined strongly together with hemp thread. In 1826 the manufactury was transferred to Gobelins, where the work continues. Small chair seats and panels, as well as large carpets, are produced.

The Gobelins manufactory also houses the Institut Français de Restauration des Oeuvres d'Art (French Institute for the Restoration of Works of Art).

Tour of the Gobelins district

45 mins.

Avenue des Gobelins

This avenue is the old extension of the Rue Mouffetard, and crosses the whole Gobelins district. At no. 58 the La Fauvette cinema has taken the place of the old Gobelins theater. The sculptor Auguste Rodin, who grew up in the area, decorated the façade which still exists. Take the Rue Abel-Hovelacque, on the r.

Rue des Reculettes, on the r., opens into a district unique in Paris, described by Balzac in *La Femme de Trente Ans* (The Thirty-Year-

Old Woman); again by Victor Hugo in *Les Misérables* and by Huysmans in *La Bièvre*. In 1936 the district was cleaned up and transformed, with the building of the new Mobilier National and the planting of the Gobelins park (1835) in the Square René-Le-Gall.

Follow the Rue Croulebarbe to the r. This was the extension of the old Rue des Gobelins, which ended at what is now known as the Rue Corvisart, which in turn finished at the Croulebarbe gateway of the *enceinte des Fermiers generaux* (tax collectors' boundary wall).

 ## The Gobelins park in the Square René-Le-Gall

Developed by Jean-Charles Moreux, this park stretches along the end of the Rue Croulebarbe, where vegetable gardens were cultivated in earlier times by the workers of the Gobelins, and irrigated by the Bièvre (→inset). In this charming and overgrown rustic garden, a vast playground has been created. Steps, decorated with medallions of pebbles and fossils in the grotesque style of Arcimboldi (1537–93), lead to the paths. The style of the 1930s is evident in the Neo-Classical obelisk, well trimmed hedges and four little summerhouses covered in climbing plants.

On the other side, the new Mobilier National (→inset), transferred from Qual Branly, was designed by A. Perret in 1934; it is characteristic of the architect's style, with its billiard cue-like columns, the open concrete structure and broad façades. The entrance is guarded by two hounds sculpted by Abbal.

Rue Berbier-du-Mets

It Is no longer possible to imagine the old and famous Ruelle des Gobelins as it was in the 17th c. Most of the buildings are modern but the street does run along the façade behind the Gobelins manufactory where you can see some impressive buildings. Above the entrance to the E end of the chapel are two framed inscriptions in marble telling the long history of the Gobelins. The hunting lodge of Jean de Julienne used to be in this area; it may be reconstructed in the Square René-Le-Gall in the near future.

Take the Rue Gustave-Geffroy on the r.

Rue des Gobelins

Until 1636, this rather strange and sombre street, with its old, ruined buildings blackened by time, was called the Rue de Bièvre. Many of its houses seem to have belonged to the Gobelin and Gluck families. The Glucks were another family of dyers who made their fortune when Jean Gluck brought back a new dyeing technique from the Netherlands. His nephew, Jean de Julienne, was known as a collector and art lover. His protégé, Antoine Watteau, was a frequent visitor. At no. 17, at the end of a courtyard, an unusual building with a tower is visible; it is known as the Château de la Reine Blanche (castle of Queen Blanche), built around 1520. It replaced a much older house which was already named after Philippe VI's widow, Blanche de Provence, daughter-in-law of the King of Castille. It is here that historians (for example, Juvénal des Ursins) place the Bal des Ardents of 1393, when Charles VI and four noblemen had their fancy-dress costumes set on fire by a torch carelessly held by the Duc d'Orléans; only the king was saved when his aunt, the Duchesse de Berry, flung the train of her gown around him and smothered the flames. Demolished in 1404, the Château de la Reine Blanche is believed to have been rebuilt for the Gobelin and Cavoye families. Another old house, dating from the end of the 14th or the beginning of the 15th c., still stands.

Boulevard Arago

Follow the street toward the E. From the middle of the 19th c. the Boul. Arago replaced a large part of the old Rue Saint-Hippolyte and the little streets that lead off to the Rue Mouffetard and the Church of Saint-Hippolyte. Today, it is a beautiful main street shaded by a double lane of trees.

Rue Corvisart opens to the l., and passes the former Broca hospital, which was erected on the site of a Franciscan friary, set up here in 1293. Marguerite de Provence, widow of St Louis, enlarged it by adding a house where she eventually died. The Rue des Cordelières, now completely rebuilt, and the Rue Pascal were laid out through the gardens of this friary.

Return to the Boul. Arago.

To the r. is the Rue Broca, formerly the Rue de l'Oursine, from the village of Saint-Médard, which led to the village of Gentilly following the River Bièvre. This street used to serve the large country mansions of the Parisian bourgeoisie. The Hôtel-Dieu des Patriarchs was built by Guillaume de Chanac (where nos. 3–17 stand today, on the other side of the Boul. Arago) and was turned into a Christian Charity hospital – a forerunner of Les Invalides of Louis XIV – to care for wounded veterans. The Rue Broca has retained hardly any reminders of its long history.

▷ The Bièvre

Until it was covered over, in 1910, the Bièvre flowed through this area, past the dyeing workshops and the tanneries which stood on its banks.

The Bièvre (from *bebrá*, beaver), flowed uncovered through Paris for a long time. From its source in Yvelines, in the plains of Trappes, it entered the city near the 'People's Postern', which supplied the Gobelins factories, and crossed the Saint-Martin quarter; today it loses itself in the sewers instead of rejoining the Seine near the Pont d'Austerlitz, as it did before. Though the river itself has now disappeared, its course has left a permanent mark on the topography of Paris in the hollow of the Val de Bièvre which separates the hills of Maison-Blanche and Butte-aux-Cailles (Right Bank) from the heights of Montsouris and the Montagne Sainte-Geneviève (Left Bank).

▷ Mobilier National (National Furniture Storehouse)

The Royal furniture depository at 1 Rue Berbier-du-Mets, created during the reign of Charles X during the second half of the 14th c., was really organized, by Colbert, only in 1663. At that time it comprised all the various pieces of furniture and ornamental objects made for numerous royal residences. The Revolution destroyed or scattered a large part of this heritage, which was partially restored during the Empire. The depository was first installed beside the Louvre, then at the Hôtel de Conti, at the Hôtel d'Evreux and finally at the Hôtel du Garde-Meuble (Furniture Depository) built by Gabriel at the Pl. de la Concorde, now the French Admiralty. Renamed the Mobilier National, the collection finally ended its odyssey in 1936, when it moved to the building which houses it today.

The Mobilier National was created to make, manage, maintain and restore the important heritage of furniture housed in ministries, in museums, in French embassies abroad, and especially in the homes of the heads of state (kings, emperors and presidents), such as Elysée and Rambouillet or in the presidential box at the Longchamp racecourse. The Mobilier National is also responsible for providing the funds to furnish and decorate the apartments used for important visitors to France from abroad.

The Grands Boulevards**

Laid out on the site of Charles V's old ramparts the Grands Boulevards still mark the boundary between the historical center of the city and its suburbs, and the atmosphere differs a great deal on either side of the boundary. Once a carriage-drive and a place for strolling, the Grands Boulevards are now one of the main highways serving the Right Bank, and the traffic is very thick. The boulevards form a great curve which skirts several arrondissements each with its own atmosphere.

The boulevards' exclusive character is preserved by the windows of high-class shops and large travel agencies at the edge of the district around the Madeleine and the Opéra. Elegant cafés abound and at night are filled with the audiences from the Opéra and nearby theaters. The Boulevard des Italiens is lively and popular, especially around the Richelieu-Drouot intersection, but nothing is left of those establishments that gave it a fashionable reputation under the Restoration. The liveliest and most colorful part of the Grands Boulevards stretches from here to the Porte Saint-Martin. The old façades, which are often very handsome, are now hidden behind the signs, bunting and neon lights of fast-food restaurants, ready-to-wear clothes shops, theaters and cinemas, their posters advertising Kung-Fu and American gangster films. At night the Boulevard Montmartre and the Boulevard Poissonière (named after the fishmongers who used it to get to Les Halles) are still very busy, their sidewalks thronged with lottery-ticket sellers, video arcades, street hawkers and shooting galleries. Between the Place de la République and the Bastille the boulevards are less commercial and quieter, except when a demonstration passes by. At the approaches to the impressive rotunda of the Cirque d'Hiver, in the Boul. du Temple and the Boul. des Filles-du-Calvaire, there are many buildings with fine façades dating from the Restoration. Cafés and shops reappear before the Place de la Bastille, along the Boul. Beaumarchais. There you may see, on a street corner, or perhaps set back a little, the silhouette of an old 18th-c. mansion, a sign that you have already entered the Marais.

The history of the Grands Boulevards

The word 'boulevard' (from the Middle Dutch *bolwerc*, from which the English 'bulwark' also derives) gradually lost its first military meaning as it came to evoke the world of the *bon mot*, pure essence of the *boulevardier's* wit. The history of the Grands Boulevards has evolved between these two connotations of the word.

From the Madeleine to the Bastille the route of the Grands Boulevards follows, for part of the way, the line of Charles V's fortified perimeter wall. Built between 1356 and 1360, this wall enclosed the town on the Right Bank from the Tour de Bois (Place du Carrousel) to the Tour Billy (Arsenal) and the Tour Barbeau. The extension of the defensive system soon made it out of date and, moreover, it was breached here and there under the pressure of the population explosion. Gradually, over a couple of centuries, such breaches became officially authorized by the municipality and mills and spinning-factories were put up beside the bastions. However, the building of the Tuileries outside the walls made more drastic measures necessary. On July 12, 1566, the king authorized construction of a new wall. A vast area to the W, later to be called the 'Fossé Jaune', or 'yellow ditch', because of the color of the soil, was enclosed within a line running from Charles V's old ramparts to the Saint-Denis fortifications. Richelieu, who had a personal interest in the project, completed the work in 1647, by which time it too was already out of date. The pointlessness of these fortifications had to be acknowledged, especially since construction was continuing at a great rate outside them. All that could be done was to turn them into a fashionable promenade, and in 1670 this project got under way, beginning on the E side.

By about 1700 the bastions had disappeared one by one. In the E part, the promenade along the Boul. du Temple, with its rows of elms, was attracting crowds: 'People of all classes mixed together, but in an orderly fashion. The carriages . . . sometimes in four lines . . . .' The W., on the other hand, was the sight of large building projects. The boulevard had become the most active district of the capital. The Italian 'bel canto' reigned first at the Théâtre des Italiens (now the Salle Favart), then at the Opéra. The Romantic theater was born at the Porte Saint-Martin, where Hugo and Dumas enjoyed the success denied to them by the Théâtre-Français. A number of discreet little buildings date from the reign of Charles X. Look closely and see how they have kept the Neo-Gothic 19th-c. *fontes troubadour* of their window-ledges and their *portes-cochères*. At the same time the gardens were replaced with cafés and restaurants where the rich and fashionable went to be seen. It was Napoléon III who cut through the heart of this exuberant thoroughfare along the length of which news always spread like wildfire and suppressing forever the 'Boulevard du Crime' (that is, the Boul. du Temple, lined with theaters and mountebanks) to the benefit of the smart, rich Boul. des Italiens and Boul. des Capucines.

Since the 1920s the center of elegance has moved westwards and on to the Left Bank; the brilliance of the boulevards is now nothing but the flashing of neon lights.

Visiting the Grands Boulevards

Departure point: Place de la Madeleine; Map ref. 10–C2, D2; 11–A2, B2; 12–C2, D2
Métro: Madeleine/Bus 24, 42, 52
Parking: Place de la Madeleine.
3 hrs.

The monuments between the Madeleine and Richelieu-Drouot and the cheerful atmosphere that prevails as far as the Porte Saint-Martin will attract those who like walking, and this itinerary has been planned for them.

To get just a general impression of the Grands Boulevards make a trip by car (avoid rush-hour) or by bus 20, starting from the Bastille, for the traffic is one-way E–W between the Richelieu-Drouot intersection and the Place de la République.

Boulevard de la Madeleine

1st and 9th arr.

The boulevard follows the line of the former Rue Basse-du-Rempart, which ran below the ramparts built in the early 17th c. This, which was soon to be turned into a promenade, was bordered by large gardens and private mansions. The Rue Basse-du-Rempart disappeared completely only in the Second Empire, to make way for the wide avenues of today.

Mme Récamier held her salons at no. 32. The basement of no. 15, a large building, was the home of Marie-Alphonsine Plessis, the model for *La Dame aux Camélias*. She was a customer of one of the oldest *magazins de nouveautés* (novelty shops), founded in 1829: the Trois Quartiers. This was rebuilt in the 1930s by Faure-Dujarric. No. 2 is the Hôtel Deshayes and, opposite stands the Hôtel d'Aumont, two mansions built at the end of the 18th c., which have kept intact their elegant round pavilions on the corners of the Rue Caumartin.

Boulevard des Capucines

2nd and 9th arr.

The boulevard is split into two sections by the Place de l'Opéra, which completely changed the face of the area in the Second Empire. The golden age of the boulevard is linked with the creation of the new Opéra and to the setting up around it of the Grand Hôtel, the Grand Café, the Cercle de l'Union and the Jockey Club. In the *Belle Epoque* the sidewalks made a lively picture, with newspaper sellers mingling with audiences from the Théâtre du Vaudeville. On the corner of the Rue des Capucines at no. 43, stood the Hôtel des Affaires Etrangères. On the evening of February 23, 1848, in front of these buildings the shot was fired that unleashed the Revolution. Before the same building, on March 22, 1842, Henri Beyle, the author known by his pen-name Stendhal, an employee of the ministry, was struck down by apoplexy and died, having just emerged from the staff entrance in the Rue des Capucines. No. 35, where the photographer Nadar (→inset) had his studio, is almost unchanged. At no. 28, the Olympia, which replaced the earlier Montagnes-Russes, is the venue for all the great singing stars, while another brilliant star of the music hall, Mistinguette, lived for fifty years at no. 24. No. 27 has the antiquated façade of the luxury Samaritaine, built between 1914 and 1917 by Frantz Jourdain for the

Cognacq-Jays (founders of the Samaritaine shops), who were seeking to enlarge their clientèle; a communicating door linked the shop to the Musée Cognacq-Jay (→Museums), next door at no. 25. The Hôtel Scribe is at no. 14; an inscription records that here, on December 28, 1895 in the Salon Indien of the Grand Café, the Lumière brothers showed their first cinematic projections. Past the Café de la Paix is Garnier's Opéra House** and the Ave. de l'Opéra, which leads to the Palais-Royal. The Opéra Drugstore has replaced, among others, the house at no. 8, where Offenbach died in 1880; only a vestibule with columns in the Napoléon III style remains. At no. 2, on the corner of the Chaussée d'Antin, the Paramount cinema has replaced the Théâtre du Vaudeville, on the former site of the Hôtel de Montmorency, which was built by Ledoux at the end of the 18th c. At nos. 5–7 is a large Palladian building by Lesueur.

Boulevard des Italiens

2nd and 9th arr.

This boulevard takes its name from the old Théâtre des Italiens (1783), later replaced by the Opéra-Comique. In the heyday of the 'Incroyables', the dandies of the Directorate known for their extreme fashions, the boulevard was called 'Petit Coblenz', because the émigrés who took refuge at Coblenz during the Revolution, chose it for their headquarters after their return. At the time of the Revolution, the even-numbered side was called the 'Boulevard de Gand', in memory of Louis XVIII's exile in that town during the Hundred Days; it was the 'in' center of elegance, and gave rise to the term 'gandin', meaning a dandy. The neighborhood remained very fashionable until World War I. The famous restaurants, where the leaders of high society gathered, have all disappeared: Tortoni's confectionery (22 Boul. des Italiens), the Café de Paris (1 Rue du Taitbout), the Café Riche, decorated with mosaics by Forain (16 Boul. des Italiens) and the very fine Passage de l'Opéra, evoked by Aragon in *Le Paysan de Paris*. This transformation of the Boul. des Italiens coincided with the completion of the Boul. Haussmann in 1926, when the district was invaded by bankers and financiers.

The Ford building, designed by Roux-Spitz in 1929, is at no. 36. At no. 31, the Palais Berlitz (architects, Lemaresquier and Laloux) has replaced what was for a long time one of the jewels of the boulevard: the Pavillon du Hanovre at the corner of the Rue de la Michodière and the Rue Louis-le-Grand. It was built at the end of his garden by the Maréchal de Richelieu between 1758 and 1760, to give him a view over the boulevard. Since 1933 it has stood in the Parc des Sceaux, where it was rebuilt stone by stone.

From no. 17 to no. 23, stands the Crédit Lyonnais, founded in 1863. Another large building representative of its time, it belongs to the generation of big banks founded in the Second Empire, whose presence is felt everywhere on the boulevard. The buildings were

1878 by Bouwens van der Boijen, on the site of the
ufflers, then enlarged and finally completed by Narjoux
aloux, the designer of the Gare d'Orsay. Inside, it is decorated
with stonework over a steel framework. Beyond the enormous hall,
the double-spiral staircase is inspired by that at Chambord.

Beyond the Rue des Italiens the newspaper *Le Monde* occupies, like
Le Temps before it, the site of the *hôtel* built in 1719 for the king's
physician, Terray de Rozière.

La Maison Dorée

20 Boul. des Italiens

At the corner of the Rue Lafitte, this restaurant replaced the Café
Hardi, which had been fashionable during the Empire. La Maison
Dorée was built between 1838 and 1839 by Victor Lemaire and
remained for a whole epoch one of the luxurious restaurants where
high society (*le Tout-Paris*) met after the theater. Like David
d'Angers and Alexandre Dumas, the journalist Nestor Roqueplan
was one of the habitués of the restaurant which was close to the
Cité des Italiens, where he had the headquarters of his famous
newspaper, *Le Mousquetaire*. The last Impressionist exhibition in
which Seurat presented *La Grande Jatte*, also took place in the
Maison Dorée. This typical example of the architectural eclecticism
of the period of Louis-Philippe has been converted into an annex of
the Banque Nationale de Paris, which has preserved the Neo-
Renaissance decoration of the façades on the boulevard and the
Rue Lafitte.

On the Rue Taitbout, three new bays have been built, according to
the design of the originals, while a small garden communicates with
the building erected by Dufau in 1974. The composer Grétry lived
from 1795 to 1813 in the 18th-c. mansion at no. 7.

The Opéra-Comique

Via the Rue Marivaux or the Rue Favart

This theatre is still called the Salle Favart, after the celebrated singer
of the 18th c. Oddly, it is separated from the boulevard, to which it
turns its back, by an apartment building. This is the same arrangement as that of the first theater built here in 1783 for the Italian
actors. They refused to have an entrance on to the boulevard for
fear of being mixed up with the mountebanks who worked the
streets.

The present building was inaugurated in 1898. The first theater, built
by the architect J.-F. Heurtier, was destroyed by fire in 1838. A new
building (by Charpentier) was in its turn destroyed by a violent
catastrophe in May 1887, which claimed many victims. There is a

monument to them at the Père-Lachaise cemetery. The present building is the work of Louis Bernier. The main façade, on the Place Boieldieu, is decorated with caryatids, medallions and masks by Peynot, Allar and Michel; there are niches with statues of *Music* and *Poetry* by Peuch and Guilbert; the railings are by Christofle. Beside the main entrance the theater has two side entrances, sheltered by heavy glass porches. Falguière and Mercier collaborated on the sculpted decoration for the interior. Flameng did the mural over the Favart staircase and Luc Olivier Merson that over the Marivaux staircase. The decoration of the foyer, fresh and full of fantasy, very much in the spirit of comic opera, was done by Gervex (*La Foire de Saint-Laurent* (The Fair at Saint-Laurent) and Maignan (*La Dame Blanche* and *Les Noces de Jeannette* ('The Woman in White' and 'Jeannette's Wedding').

The circular ceiling of the auditorium is by Benjamin Constant, the main curtain by Rubé and Masson and the sculpted genii by Marseque. The 18th-c. streets that run alongside the Opéra Comique have retained some of the handsome buildings built in 1780 when the land of the Hôtel de Choiseul was sold: Alexandre Dumas was born on July 27, 1824 at no. 1 Place Boieldieu, and Champollion lived at 4 Rue Favart in 1832.

Before reaching the Richelieu-Drouot intersection, the Boul. des Italiens passes the Passage des Princes (at no. 5 *bis*), which was opened in 1860, and rejoins the Rue de Richelieu (at no. 97). Created by Jules Mirés, it has retained its stained glass and iron arches. Only Sommer has retained its original shop window and its fine display of pipes. The famous Café Cardinal was at no. 1.

The Richelieu-Drouot intersection, busy all year round and at all hours, was bounded to the N and S by gardens in the 18th c. (Crozat and Choiseul). Now the busy Faubourg Montmartre stretches away to the N, with the Drouot showrooms; to the S the Rue de Richelieu rejoins the Bourse.

Boulevard Montmartre

2nd and 9th arr.

From its creation in 1676 until 1860 this mall was very fashionable. At the corner of the Rue de Richelieu a large building stands in place of the mansion built by Brogniart from 1796 to 1808, which housed the famous Café Frascati, destroyed in 1838; the tailor Buisson, made famous by Balzac, lived in the basement. Opposite, on the corner of the Rue Drouot, the Hôtel de Laage was the headquarters of the Jockey Club from 1836 to 1857. At no. 12 is the Passage Jouffroy: the end of the main gallery is decorated with a window and a clock, in which bunches of grapes symbolize the prosperity of commerce; there are toy shops, Asian import shops and bookshops specializing in the theater and cinema. The entrance to the Musée Grévin (→inset) is at no. 10; inaugurated in 1882, it was built on the site of an 'operatic' pub where the baritone Darcier performed his political and folk repertory. As well as its own collections, the Grévin houses the Théâtre Joli, a specimen of pure, turn-of-the-century architecture, with mirrored walls, a stage curtain by Chéret and, above the proscenium arch, a bas-relief by Bourdelle, *Les Nuées* (The Clouds).

The Passage des Panoramas

Opposite, on the odd-numbered side, is the entrance to the Passage des Panoramas, one of the oldest lanes in Paris, which was laid out in 1800 on the site of one of the courtyards of the *hôtel* of the Maréchal de Montmorency, Duc de Luxembourg. The *passage*, built by V. Grisart, owes its name to the two rotundas that flanked its entrance on the boulevard, within which panoramic views (→inset) were shown. The Passage des Panoramas also offered a variety of picturesque shops and restaurants; its popularity was considerable and long-lived, and in the 1820s it was, perhaps, with the Palais-Royal, the most frequented spot in Paris. The Panoramas disappeared in 1831, but such was the reputation of the *passage* that, from 1834, new shopping arcades were added to it: the Galerie Feydeau, the Galerie Montmartre, the Galerie Saint-Marc and the Galerie des Variétés. At no. 47 Passage des Panoramas the decoration inside the shop by the engraver Stern dates from 1840. The *passage* knew even more glorious days in the Second Empire, thanks to the triumph of Offenbach at the Théâtre des Variétés (→below). The stage-door, described by Zola in his novel *Nana* (1879) and opening on to one of the galleries, attracted curious idlers and gentlemen looking for pretty chorus girls.

The Théâtre des Variétés

7 Boul. Montmartre

This theater has never changed either its name or its original façade. It was built in 1807 for Mlle. Montansier, who had just been chased out of the Palais-Royal on the grounds that she was an unworthy neighbor for the Comédie Française. In the 1860s the theater enjoyed the brilliant Offenbach period, when his favourite performer, Hortense Schneider, triumphed in such operettas as *La Belle Hélène, La Grande Duchesse de Gerolstein* and *La Périchole*.

At no. 6 Boul. Montmartre, the atmosphere at the Café de Madrid is not at all what it was in the days when two of its famous patrons, Jules Vallès and Léon Gambetta, escaped from Paris by balloon to avoid the Prussian invasion of 1870.

Boulevard Poissonnière

Most of the old private mansions have retained their 19th-c. wrought ironwork in the upper storeys, but at ground level you are in the realm of plastic and neon and discount shops of all descriptions. The Café Brébant at no. 32 was famous in the Second Empire for its literary dinners: the Dîner des Spartiates, instituted by Goncourt; the Dîner du Boeuf Nature, attended by Zola and other exponents of the naturalist movement. A plaque at no. 27 recalls that Chopin had his first Parisian home (1831-1832) on the boulevard. The Hôtel de Montholon at no. 23 was the scene of a number of *salons*, including that of Mme Edmond Adam, the founder of the *Nouvelle Revue* (1879). The raising of the height of the building and the installation of shops on the ground floor along the boulevard, have destroyed its original majestic proportions. The Théâtre des Nouveautés, built by the architect A. Thiers in 1920, is at no. 20.

The Rex Cinema

1 Boul. Poissonière

Along with the Gaumont-Palace (Quartier Monmartre), which was torn down in 1972, the Rex was Paris's temple of the cinema during the inter-war years. Designed by A. Bluysen and J. Eberson on the model of their '*salles atmosphériques américaines*', this huge concrete cathedral opened its doors for the Christmas vacation of 1932, after only 12 months' construction. The illuminated sign planned for its façade was banned by the police, who considered it a dangerous distraction for drivers.

Inside, a town of Old Spanish inspiration is shown on the walls by special projectors. Although the original services offered – nursery, kennels and hairdressing salon – have disappeared, the main auditorium recovers its former brilliance during the Christmas vacation, when there are aquatic displays.

Boulevard de Bonne-Nouvelle

2nd and 10th arr.

To the S the boulevard runs along the foot of the Butte-aux-Gravois, with its narrow streets that lead up to the Sentier quarter, the center of the ready-to-wear clothing trade.

At no. 38 is the Théâtre du Gymnase; built on the site of the former Bonne-Nouvelle cemetery, it opened in 1820. The names of those undisputed masters of the boulevards, Dumas the Younger, Sardou and especially Scribe (→inset), who put on 150 plays between 1821 and 1830, were constantly on the posters of this family theater. In 1962, the great Marie Bell, an honorary member of the Comédie-

Française, took over the management of the Gymnase and kept it until her death in 1985.

The Porte Saint-Denis

During the demolition of the fortifications surrounding Paris, Louis XIV decided to erect two triumphal gates to mark the entrances to the City: the Porte Saint-Denis and the Porte Saint-Martin, which give access to the streets of the same names, the main N–S thoroughfares of old Paris. These imposing works have a purely decorative and symbolic function; the sculptures decorating them celebrate the king as a warrior and commemorate his victories.

The Porte Saint-Denis was built in 1762 by François Blondel. It is 75ft./23m in both height and width. Against the wishes of the architect and on the orders of the provost, the pedestals of the obelisks were pierced by archways for pedestrians. On the S façade, which faces the boulevard, there is a bas-relief depicting the crossing of the Rhine and allegorical figures of Holland (a grieving woman) and of the Conquered Rhine; on the N façade is *La Prise de Maestricht* (The Taking of Maestricht); all these sculptures were begun by Girardon, finished by Michel Anguier and restored in 1887.

The Rue Saint-Denis, to the S, leads directly to the Halles district; the Rue du Faubourg Saint-Denis, to the N, leads to the Gare de l'Est.

Boulevard Saint-Denis

2nd and 10 arr.

The Passage du Prado at no. 16 is now deserted, but was once the scene of a famous ball; it was laid out in 1785 and later roofed over. At no. 14, the Café de France has taken the place of the Restaurant Maire, a favorite of many café-concert stars in the Second Empire. Crossing the Boul. de Strasbourg, you will see, opposite no. 14, the façade of the Théâtre Antoine. It was at this theater that a revolution in dramatic art was launched at the end of the 19th c. (→inset). To the name of Antoine is joined that of Simone Berriau, in homage to the woman who was its enlightened director for more than 40 years (1943–85). Her productions ranged from boulevard to classical theatre; nor did she neglect the avant-garde, and it was she who discovered Sartre as a dramatic author. No. 9 is a Restoration building of 1828 by Dubois.

The Porte Saint-Martin

This triumphal arch was put up by the city in 1674, designed by Pierre Bullet, a pupil of Blondel; 56ft./17m high and of comparable width, it has a central arcade between two smaller ones. Two bas-reliefs in the Classical manner are sculpted on the central arcade: on the S side, *La Prise de Besançon* (The Taking of Besançon), by Desjardins, and Louis XIV as Hercules trampling underfoot the symbol of the Triple Alliance, by Le Hongre; on the N side, *La Prise de Limbourg* (The Taking of Limbourg), by Legros the Elder and the *Le Défaite des Allemands* (Defeat of the Germans), by Marsy. On the attic storey, to the S, may be seen this inscription, in Latin: 'To Louis the Great, for having twice taken Besançon and the Franche-Comté, and defeated the German, Spanish and Dutch armies: the Provost of Merchants and the councillors of Paris, 1674.'

Boulevard Saint-Martin

3rd and 10th arr.

This boulevard, whose pavements are markedly higher than the street, stretches to the Place de la République. At no. 20, the Théâtre de la Renaissance, built by the architect Lalande on the ruins of the Café Duffieux, opened its doors in 1873. Sarah Bernhardt directed it from 1893 to 1899, performing plays by such writers as Hugo, Sardou and Musset. Firmin Gémier was director for one year, in 1901.

The Théâtre de la Porte Saint-Martin, at no. 16, was built in 75 days by the architect Lenoir, at the command of Marie-Antoinette, who was demanding an immediate replacement for the Opéra, which burned down in 1781. The theater had its days of glory in the 1830s, when actors such as Frédérick-Lemaître, Marie Dorval, Mlle Georges and Bocage performed the great Romantic dramas and melodramas: *La Tour de Nesle, Antony* and *Richard Darlington*, by Dumas, and Hugo's *Marion Delorme*. Sarah Bernhardt directed the theater from 1883 to 1893, performing in such works as *La Dame aux Camélias, Tosca* and J. Barbier's *Jeanne d'Arc* (music by Gounod). In 1897 *Cyrano de Bergerac* had an immense success here but E. Rostand was to disappoint his public greatly in 1910 with *Chantecler*. The theater was completely rebuilt after it was ravaged by fire in 1871 during the battles between the Fédérés (rebels) and the Versaillais (loyalist troops).

At the corner of the Rue de Bondy stood the Théâtre de l'Ambigu, built by Hittorff and Lecointre in 1828; specializing in spectacular melodramas, the theater was tremendously successful with Dumas' *Les Trois Mousequetaires* (The Three Musketeers), *Le Juif Errant* (The Wandering Jew) by Eugène Sue, and *L'Assommoir* by Hugo. In 1965, following management difficulties, the theater was sold and torn down; its place is now taken by the headquarters of a banking company.

In the small square is a bust of composer Johann Strauss (1825–99), composer of *The Blue Danube and Die Fledermaus.*

Place de la République

The vast, long, open space that we now know as the Place de la Republique was developed in stages. To begin with, it was merely the intersection of the Boul. Saint-Martin and the Boul. du Temple with the Rue du Temple and the Rue du Faubourg du Temple; in the 18th c. the present Rue René-Boulanger and the Rue Amelot were added; the inauguration of the fountain (supplied from the Villette basin) built by Girard in 1811, gave the square the name Place du Château d'Eau. Haussmann added the Rue de Turbigo and the Boul. Magenta, and began laying out the Boul. des Amandiers (now the Ave. de la République) and the Boul. du Prince-Eugène (now the Boul. Voltaire) as part of his anti-revolutionary street planning. This led to the razing of the famous 'Boulevard du Crime' and its theaters (→inset). In 1874 Girard's fountain was taken down, transferred to the market at La Villette, and replaced by a similar, but bigger, fountain by Davioud. This in turn was dismantled and removed to the present Place Félix-Eboué; it was replaced in 1883 by the bronze statue *La Republic* by the Morice brothers (with bronze bas-reliefs by Dalou) which gave its final name to the Place de la République. On the NE side, two large buildings guard the entry of the Rue du Faubourg-du-Temple: to the r., the former building of the Magazins Réunis, founded in 1866, in which the exhibitions of the famous Salon des Refusés were held by the Impressionists and other painters rejected by the Academy; to the l., the Vérines barracks (named after Lieutenant-Colonel Vérines, head of a Resistance network, shot at Cologne in 1943), formerly the Prince-Eugène barracks, built in 1854 to house 2000 soldiers on a site partly occupied by the diorama, which was built by Daguerre in 1822. Nearby, in the Rue du Château-d'Eau, the Bourse du Travail was erected by the city in 1890 for the trade unions. Since then it has played a continuous and important part in trade-union affairs.

Boulevard du Temple

3rd and 10th arr.

This boulevard is named after the Order of the Knights Templar, who had at one time acquired nearly a quarter of the land of Paris, before they were suppressed by Philip the Fair; their properties lay to the SW of the modern boulevard (→inset). A plaque at no. 42 recalls that Gustave Flaubert lived there. The Théâtre Déjazet is the only theater of the 'Boulevard du Crime' to have escaped destruction. Built as a ballroom on the site of the tennis court of the Comte d'Artois, brother of Louis XVI, this little theater was originally called the Folies-Mayer. Then, when Hervé, the composer of *Mam'zelle Nitouche* (Mlle. Prude), put on his operettas there, it became the Folies-Concertantes, and in 1859, when Virginie Déjazet took up residence, the Théâtre Déjazet. She put on such plays as *Prés*

Saint-Gervais, *Richelieu* and *Trois Gamins*, light pieces in which she took mostly adolescent rôles though she was past 60, having specialized from the age of five in burlesque parts. Through her own refinement, grace and mischievous wit she created a type of performer, the *déjazets*, and left them her name.

Boulevard des Filles-du-Calvaire

3rd and 11th arr.

The creation of this boulevard was begun in 1670. It owes its name to the convent of the Filles-du-Calvaire, whose gardens it once skirted.

The Cirque d'Hiver

Built at the entry to the boulevard by Hittorff in 1852, the Cirque Napoléon – the original name – gave performances every evening from November 1 to April 30, when the Cirque de l'Impératrice in the Champs Elysées was closed. The *concerts populaires*, founded by Pasdeloup in 1861, took place in the circus on Sundays; they were eclipsed by those of Colonne and Lamoureux, but it is in memory of his generosity that the little square in front of the circus is called the Place Pasdeloup. Above the main door, *L'Amazone* is the work of the sculptor Pradier and *Le Guerrier* (The Warrior) is by Bosio Neveu. Some of the building's polychrome décor has been preserved.

Boulevard Beaumarchais

11th arr.

At no. 40, the café A l'Eléphant got its name from an elephant that escaped from the Cirque d'Hiver in 1912 and took refuge in the café.

The Théâtre Beaumarchais was at no. 25; it was never very successful and was demolished in 1893. From no. 2 to no. 20 stood Beaumarchais' magnificent private mansion, built in 1787 by Le Moine and destroyed in 1826. The winding little streets to the r. lead to the nearby Place des Vosges (→Marais). No. 21 is the back of the Hôtel de Mansart-Sagonne (→Marais, Rue des Tournelles).

> Nadar

Student of medicine, journalist, novelist, serial writer of stories for periodicals, caricaturist and balloonist, Gaspard Félix Tournachon, known as Nadar (1820–1910), made his mark mainly as a photographer. In 1854 he set up his studio at no. 13 Rue Saint-Lazare and began his research on the relatively new wet collodion process. He then made the first aerial photographs, taken from a balloon, which he proposed to use for topographical surveys. When his studio became too small he moved to 35 Boul. des Capucines. In 1861, 25 years after the invention of photography, he filed for a patent on photography by artificial light. To test his invention he then made two documentaries on the sewers and catacombs of Paris. All the most illustrious figures of the time sat in his studio. An incomparable portraitist, Nadar made the best photographic portraits of Victor Hugo, Berlioz, Liszt, Rossini, Baudelaire, Delacroix, George Sand, Wagner, Lamartine and many others. He then abandoned photography and threw himself into aviation; he was obsessed with ballooning and helped to finance the construction of Le Géant, a huge balloon whose first ascent in October 1863 was watched by a quarter of a million people. When Paris was besieged by the Prussians in 1870, he organized regular balloon trips to carry messages over the enemy lines. His experiments exhausted his financial resources and his big studio in the Boul. des Capucines became intolerably expensive, despite the support of Isaac Pereire. Nadar was forced to rent the studio to a group of painters whose first major exhibition there was also their christening: the Impressionists.

▷ The Impressionists on the Grands Boulevards

The taste for modernity attracted Parisians to the Grands Boulevards, rejuvenated by Haussmann, and they were followed by the Impressionist painters.

Some of them – Monet, Renoir, Caillebotte, Pissaro, Degas and Toulouse-Lautrec – immortalized the new capital as Napoléon III had conceived it: a crowd of idlers among green trees; unusual views discovered from roof tops or attic windows; scenes from the theater, the Opéra, and the circus; scenes of the cafés on the Boul. des Italiens where the painters congregated (Café Bade, Café Riche or Chez Tortoni).

Art dealers and galleries had invaded the boulevards and the approaches to big exhibition houses: the Galerie Martinet, where Manet exhibited in 1863; the Maison Goupil; the Galerie Boussod-Valadon, where Vincent Van Gogh's brother worked; the Galerie Berhneim, a favorite with the Impressionists; and last, the gallery of the art dealer P. Durand-Ruel, the Impressionists' strongest supporter, who spread their reputation on the other side of the

Atlantic. Not far away, Samuel Bing's shop displayed the Japanese prints from which they all drew inspiration. It is not surprising that it was in this bohemian district that these avant-garde painters, excluded from the official Salon, mounted their group exhibitions, the first of which was held, ironically, in the studio of the photographer Nadar.

The genre of comic opera

As the name suggests, the origins of comic opera are to be found in a parody of the conventions of Grand Opera; the *opéra-comique* opposes itself to the *opéra-tragique*, as with Opera Buffa and Opera Seria in Italy. The term is found before 1797 referring to plays staged by the former Théâtre des Italiens. From 1713 onwards it was used as the name for certain *spectacles de foire* (at the Saint-Germain, Saint-Laurent and Saint-Ovide fairs). The genre is a cross between the French medieval farces known as *soties*, and the lyrical, comic, or partly-comic plays of Italy. It began mostly in the form of vaudeville, that is, comedies in rhyming couplets, sprinkled with numerous ariettas and parodies of operatic arias. As the famous Monnet, director of the Théâtre des Italiens after 1743, says in his memoirs, the *opéra-comique* was essentially 'the child of French gaiety'.

The passages

What would the Right Bank be without its network of *passages*, those lanes or alleys that serve as shopping galleries, short-cuts and alternative routes for inveterate pedestrians. The passages were, at the beginning of the 19th c., the fruit of an ever-fertile imagination in the service of making a profit, which was so much a part of the development of the boulevards. Of the 140 existing then, only 30 or so survived Haussmann's urban redevelopment. Today they are a sort of refuge for out-of-the-way activities and unusual trades. Some try to survive by erecting dubious neon signs on the boulevard. Others fall into oblivion. A small number, the most beautiful, have been restored and taken over by exclusive shops.

The exploration of these *passages* could make for a pleasant walk through the 1st and 2nd arrondissements.

The Passage des Petits-Pères (1779): 3 Place des Petits-Pères; the Passage du Perron (1784): 95 Galerie de Beaujolais; the Passage Pottier (1787): 23 Rue de Montpensier; the Passage Feydau (1791): 10–12, Rue Saint-Marc; the Passage du Caire (1799): Place du Caire; the Passage des Panoramas (1800): 10 Rue Saint-Marc; the Passage du Grand-Cerf (1824–26): 145 Rue Saint-Denis; the Galerie Vivienne (1824–26): 4 Rue des petits-Champs; the Passage Dauphine (1825):

30 Rue Dauphine (uncovered); the Passage Choiseul (F. Mazois; 1825–27): 40 Rue des Petits-Champs; the Passage Vendôme (1825–27): 3 Place de la République; the Galerie Colbert (1826): 6 Rue des Petits Champs; the Galerie Véro-Dodat (1826): 19 Rue Jean-Jacques-Rousseau; the Passage du Ponceau (1826): 119 Boul. Sébastopol; the Passage Brady (1828): 43 Rue du Faubourg-Saint-Martin and 46 Rue du Faubourg-Saint-Denis, cut in half in 1852 with the opening of the Boul. de Strasbourg; the Passage du Bourg-l'Abbé (1828): 120 Rue Saint-Denis; the Passage Sainte-Avoie (1828): 8 Rue Rambuteau; the Galerie du Prado (1830): 16 Boul. Saint-Denis, on the site of the passage du Bois-de-Boulogne; the Passage des Gravilliers (1834): 10 Rue Chapon; the Passage Sainte-Anne (1834): 59 Rue Sainte-Anne; the Galerie des Variétés (1834): 38 Rue Vivienne; the Galerie Saint-Marc (1834): 6 Rue Saint-Marc; the Passage Puteaux (1839): 31 Rue de l'Arcade; the Passage du Havre (1845–47): 67 Rue Caumartin; the Passage Jouffroy (Destailleur; 1845–47): 12 Boul. Montmartre; the passage Verdeau (1846): 6 Rue de la Grange-Batelière; the Galerie de la Madeleine (1845): 9 Place de la Madeleine; the Passage des Princes (1860): 5 Boul. des Italiens; the Passage Ben–Aïad (1898): 8 Rue Mandar.

▷ The panoramas

This invention, imported in 1796 by the American engineer and inventor Robert Fulton, made it possible to give the viewer the illusion of being in a natural setting.

The spectators, seated at the center of a rotunda on a platform enclosed by a balustrade, were surrounded by a painted 'panoramic view', contrived to give the impression of an endless picture; the edges, as well as the source of light that illuminated the scene, were concealed. Objects were shown according to the rules of one-point perspective, taking the place occupied by the spectator as the central point. These combined effects gave the audience the feeling of being in a balloon over Paris, at Toulon at the moment of its evacuation by the English in 1793, or, still more exotically, in Rome, Naples, Athens or even Jerusalem.

▷ Eugène Scribe

This dramatist (1791–1861) played an important rôle in the history of the theater of the boulevards. He wrote no fewer than 350 works, supplying most of the Parisian theaters with comedies, comic operas, ballets and operas (*Robert le Diable, La Dame Blanche* and *Les Vêpres Siciliennes*, among others).

This abundant output is explained by a well-organized division of labour: one collaborator found the subject, another drafted the plot, a third wrote the dialogue, another set it in rhyming couplets, a fifth made up the jokes, and Scribe then put it all together. In the characters of his theater there is an indifference to ideals and a glorification of materialism meant to appeal to the middle classes of his time.

He amassed a large fortune, which he administered wisely. He died of apoplexy while hard at work on the libretto for *L'Africaine* by the German composer Meyerbeer.

Museums to visit

Musée Grévin (10 Boul. Montmartre): wax models of characters from the history of France, and present-day celebrities.

Musée de l'Opéra de Paris (Place Charles-Garnier): the history of the Paris Opéra and those associated with it.

Antoine and naturalism

A one-time employee of the Paris gas company, André Antoine founded a private theater club, the Théâtre Libre, in 1887, for the production of new naturalistic plays, the principles of which Zola had defined in 1881. It was a revolution without precedent in the French theater. All customs and conventions were overturned. While French actors had traditionally bellowed their lines facing directly out at the audience, Antoine directed actions as if the proscenium were merely a fourth wall of the set: the actors spoke in profile, or even with their backs to the audience; silences, which seemed absolutely interminable at the time, were introduced into the dialogue to express the characters' internal reflexion; striving for effect was suppressed in favor of naturalism and the actors had to 'live' their parts rather than merely perform them. These innovations in acting, directing and playwriting were accompanied by a search for complete authenticity in costumes and décor; Antoine was always prepared to travel anywhere to get it right. Painted canvases and papier-mâché gave way to accessories found outside the theater – not in a set-decorator's shop. People made fun of the water spurting from a little fountain and were shocked to see hunks of real meat on the stage. The Théâtre-Libre d'Antoine, by its decisive break with tradition, marked the advent of 20th-c. theater and with that the invention of a new rôle: the producer.

▷ **Street furniture**

Along with the great Parisian monuments and long rows of buildings, street furniture plays an important part in giving the city its
unique character. The widespread development of pavements
during the Second Empire (415mls/644km between 1859 and 1869)
made the provision of street furnishing not only possible, but
necessary. A vast, systematically coordinated programme brought
to the broad, new avenues their branched lampposts, benches,
newsvendors' kiosks, public lavatories, urinals, billboards and railings for the public squares. This was the work of the Service des
Promenades et Plantations, where Adolphe Alphand commanded a
whole army of engineers and architects (among them Gabriel
Davioud), who devised, designed and organized the distribution of
all these contrivances. The notice-boards that display the regulations governing squares, fountains and kiosks can still be seen in
the Boul. Richard-Lenoir.

The Boul. Saint-Martin still has a few examples of the 8428 benches
designed by Davioud, recognizable by the city emblems they
display and the thick layer of paint covering the original cast iron. A
few of the old-style urinals are still to be found on the Quai
d'Austerlitz and the Quai de la Gare. The Morris pillar, for theatrical
bills, created in 1867 by Gabriel Morris, went on to become a true
symbol of Paris and is now reproduced in modern materials. The
creation of new street furnishings, suspended in 1905, was revived
in the 1970s. The builder Jean-Claude Decaux set up bus shelters,
the automatic public lavatories known as *toilettes sanisettes* and
orientation maps and advertising panels (popularly known as '*lolli-
pops*') – the models for similar innovations since adopted by other
French and foreign cities. The architect Schuss has created two
ingenious new types of kiosk: the green cylindrical style for the
evening newspapers, and the kiosk with a tubular cover which gives
customers shelter from the rain.

▷ **The Boulevard of Crime**

In 1759, this N end of the Boul. du Temple was nothing but a muddy
piece of land surrounded by rows of trees where aristocrats came to
ride in their coaches and to be seen. Later, the *Prévôt des Marchands*
gave permission to entertainers (*amuseurs*) to set up there: the first
theaters were built by Micolet, Audinot and Lazzari. The Constituant
Assembly's decree of 1791 gave more freedom to theaters and brought
about the opening of many new ones, so that in the 19th c. there were,
side by side, Madame Saqui; the Variétés Amusantes; Les
Funambules, where the brilliant mime Dubureau performed (Jean-
Louis Barrault played him in the 1944 film *Les Enfants du Paradis*); the
Folies-Dramatiques, which put on the first performance of *Robert*

Macaire, by Frédérick-Lemaître; the Théâtre Historique, built by Alexandre Dumas; and the Cirque Olympique, specializing in shows with horses, performing animals and battle scenes with several hundred actors. In 1830 the melodrama triumphed and hot tears were shed at the Gaîté! The Emperor inspired many authors, and audiences would shiver with pleasure at the appearance of his famous two-pointed hat. But the decree of 1862, which ordered the destruction of the Boulevard du Crime, put an end to these innocent pleasures. Some theaters were indemnified and set up elsewhere; others disappeared and with them a whole era.

The Grenelle district*

15th arr./Map ref. 13–B2, B3, C3

Just before it leaves Paris the Seine is flanked to the left by a spectacular group of tower blocks. This gigantic ensemble is proof of the architectural optimism and concept of urban renewal that prevailed in the 1960s, when America was often taken as a model. A walk at the foot of these towers on the deserted, windswept pavement, some of it already cracked or broken, brings home both the comparative failure of this enterprise and the potential of this exceptional site on the banks of the river.

At the approaches to the Front de Seine a traditional Parisian quartier contrasts sharply with the glass-and-steel towers: it is an area of bustling activity in the section to the S of the Boul. de Garibaldi, along the Rue Saint-Charles and the Rue Lourmel which becomes much more luxurious nearer the Champ-de-Mars, where many antique dealers have set up elegant shops. Further E, around the Church of Saint-Jean-Baptiste-de-Grenelle, there survives a delightful district whose village character has not changed despite the passing of time. The little Passage des Entrepreneurs, the Place du Commerce with its bandstand and the neighboring narrow streets, with some almost rustic houses, retain the eternal charm of Paris.

The history of the district

The name Grenelle probably derives from *garnella*, which means 'a small rabbit warren'. People came hunting here and cultivated the land which was part of the seignorial domain of Sainte-Geneviève-du-Mont and Saint-German-des-Prés, along with the farm and château of Grenelle. The hamlet of Beaugrenelle came into being with the large building developments of the Restoration. Léonard Violet, a municipal councillor of Vaugirard, wanted to make Grenelle into a new, residential, middle-class district, at the same time planning for an industrial sector between the Rue Saint-Charles and the Seine. Work began in 1824: the engineer-surveyor Herr divided the plan into squares, which were then sub-divided into building plots (this distinguishes Grenelle from Vaugirard, where the village-like streets are not laid out in a grid). The development was completed by the building of a church (1827–28), then a theater (1829), a bridge, a port and a river station.

Grenelle became a commune in 1830, but not for long, for it was annexed with Vaugirard in 1860 to form, with Javel, the 15th arrondissement. The heavy industry along the Seine attracted large numbers of workers to Grenelle, which filled up with cheap housing and was quickly turned into an over-populated slum. Only at the beginning of the 20th c. were numerous apartment buildings for the middle classes built; then, at the end of the 1950s, large clearance schemes removed the factories and replaced them with prestige apartment blocks.

The approaches to the Front de Seine*

Métro: Charles-Michels or Javel
Bus: 42, 70, 62
Parking: Quai André-Citroën between the Pont Mirabeau and the Rue de Javel
Taxis: Place Charles-Michels. Tel. 45–78–20–00. Mirabeau rotary. Tel. 45–77–48–00

1 hr.

Place Charles-Michels

This square, with its plane trees, is still attractive. To the NW stretches the big commercial center of Beaugrenelle, intended to bring together the chief businesses dispersed throughout the 15th arrondissement, which is still organized into separate districts, almost separate villages.

The Beaugrenelle shopping center

This center, the work of P. Gilliéron, located within the triangle formed by the Quai André-Citroën, the Ave. Emile-Zola and the Rue de l'Ingénieur-Keller, has not been as successful as expected. Hardly any access from the street was provided so, to remedy this, an elevated pedestrian walkway was built, running along the Rue

Linois, to encourage the passersby to enter. The luxury boutiques are having to make way for shops more suited to the needs of the locals. It is hoped that when the ZAC Citroën-Cévennes building is finished, more people will use the center.

Rue Beaugrenelle. This small street, to the N of the Pl. Charles-Michels, owes its unity of style to a middle-class housing project by the architect C. A. Lemaire.

The Rue Emeriau rejoins the little Sq. Héricart where, immediately to the r., the Emeriau footbridge gives access to the Parvis du Front de Seine. There is a mosaic mural by Robert Debré (1984).

The Front de Seine

On the site of former chemical factories, this area lies between the embankment, the Rue Emeriau, Rue du Docteur-Finlay, and the Ave. Emile-Zola. Fifty thousand people live here. The operation was launched in the 1960s as part of the renovation of the district. This urban development, intended to be the model for future residential districts in Paris, is the work of the architects R. Lopez, H. Pottier and Proux. It stretches over 62 acres/25ha and already comprises 15 33-storey tower blocks 320ft/98m high, built on 100-ft/30m foundations. Permission to build a sixteenth tower for the ORTF (the French Radio and Television Organization) on the 21,500 sq.ft/1000m provisionally planned was granted in December 1985. The great originality of this scheme lies in its triple level of circulation: road traffic and deliveries at ground-level, a middle level devoted to vehicle parking and a traffic-free upper level for pedestrians with entrances to the buildings and access to the shopping centers, many cultural establishments and schools. The first high-rise block was built at the beginning of the Rue de l'Ingénieur-Keller, to be followed by others named Mars, Mercure, Espace 2000, Avant-Seine, Panorama, Perspective I and II, the Hôtel Nikko, Reflets and the Tour Totem, built by Andrault and Parat and finished in 1978.

After the initial euphoria, this development was seen to suffer from isolation and a lack of communications and commercial links with the traditional old district.

The Rue Robert-de-Flers leads to the Place de Brazzaville, within which is the Square Béla-Bartók (1881-1945), inaugurated in June 1982. It is reached by a stairway at the foot of which stands a statue of the composer, the work of the Hungarian artist Imre Varga, and a gift to Paris from the city of Budapest.

Leaving the square, take the Rue Rouelle, straight ahead; the corner of the street with the Rue Emeriau, occupied by a school, shows a curious contrast with the neighboring contemporary architecture: in 1912 its doors were decorated in colored mosaics by the architect Bouvier. Continue to the Place Saint-Charles, now very disappointing, with nothing of interest to see.

Rue de Lourmel

From the Rue du Théâtre to the Boul. de Grenelle.

No. 42 *bis* (1893) is one of the many works in this district of the architect Th. Judlin: the headquarters of a long-established business. Continue up this busy shopping street towards the N. On the corner of the Rue Fondary (nos. 4 and 6) is the little Church of Notre-Dame-de-Grâce-de-Grenelle, built in 1861 for the religious community of Saint-Vincent-de-Paul. This society, dedicated to caring for the poor, brings together in a shared religious life those consecrated to the work, both ordained and non-ordained.

Higher up, the narrow Rue Fallempin, lined with low houses, has retained its 19th-c. appearance.

Boulevard de Grenelle

Built on the site of the wall of the Fermiers généraux (tax collection), the boulevard marks the frontier between the still working-class part of the 15th arrondissement and the more middle-class 15th as it approaches the 7th.

At no. 87, on the corner of the Rue Dupleix, stands the former Centre Technique de l'Aluminium: now the headquarters of Nouvelles Frontières, the building's smoked glass façade sets off the aluminium alloy bas-reliefs (1947) by T. Riolo and the founder Alexis Rudier. The themes presented are: Lamination, Drawing-out, Water, the Dam, the Camargue, the Power Station, the Curve Hersult 1933, Riveting, Welding. . . . A plaque at no. 8 records the round-up in 1942 of thousands of Parisian Jews in the Vélodróme (cycling arena) who were then deported to concentration camps by the Nazis.

Place Dupleix

This square has an attractive little central garden in which the old bandstand has been preserved. On the l. the Dupleix barracks stand on the site of the former Château de Grenelle, which was converted into a gunpowder factory during the Revolution and entirely destroyed when it blew up soon after. Facing it is the Church of Saint-

Léon built in reinforced concrete faced with brick by Brunet (1927 and 1934).

Now take the Rue du Général-de-Larminat.

The Swiss Village

Closed Tuesday and Wednesday.

Antique lovers make a beeline for this place. Its name dates from the Universal Exhibition of 1900, for which the Swiss government built a faithful reproduction of a village of chalets, with Alpine pastures and mountains. Later a secondhand trade developed there, but it was only in the decade between 1955 and 1965 that the antique dealers took it over. The village was extensively renovated in 1968.

The old village of Grenelle*

Métro: Boucicaut
Bus: 62
Taxis: 45, Ave. Félix-Faure. Tel. 45–58–15–00
Market: Boul. de Grenelle, between Rue Lormel and Rue du Commerce, Wed. and Sun. 7am–1.30pm.
1 hr.

Besides some fine Restoration houses, country houses and workers' dwellings, what is most striking here is the pervasive village atmosphere, despite recent building developments.

Avenue Félix-Faure

This fine avenue is bordered by buildings of the post-Haussmann period. No. 40 is a beautiful natural-stone building with a sculpture illustrating La Fontaine's fable *The Crow and the Fox*, and pretty vine-leaf motifs (architect Audiger, sculptor J. Richard, 1907). Note the friezes at no. 32. No. 31 is a fine building by Clément Feugueur, an architect well represented in the district, and J. Boucher, sculptor (1912); a beautiful wrought-iron gate. No. 21 has pretty balconies. No. 13 has an ochre and white façade with a frieze of flowers in enamelled ceramic (architect, S. Dauger Cornil, 1907).

Place Etienne-Pernet

At the corner of the Rue de l'Eglise is a splendid Art Nouveau building; unfortunately neither its date nor the architect is known.

No. 20 is another building by Clément Feugueur and the sculptor J. Boucher. Follow the wall of the Church of Saint-Jean-Baptiste-de-Grenelle. At nos. 4 and 6 are beautiful village-style houses with tiled roofs, and again at the corner of the Rue Mademoiselle.

♱ The Church of Saint-Jean-Baptiste-de-Grenelle

In 1825, when the new district was inaugurated, the developer-councillor L. Violet insisted on building a church here, because Saint-Lambert was too far away from the new development. This church, named after one of Violet's patron saints, was built by the Compagnie des Entrepreneurs from 1827 to 1828, under the direction of the architect Bontat, but was consecrated only in 1831. The building and the land forming the church square were the gift of the commune. The high altar was made from parts of the altar placed by Louis XIV in Notre-Dame, in fulfilment of his father's vow to dedicate France to the Virgin. The altar was destroyed by Viollet-le-Duc in 1867, but the parish priest obtained its fragments from junk dealers in 1869.

Take the Rue des Entrepreneurs on the l., named in honor of the builders of the hamlet of Beaugrenelle.

Place Violet

The square took its name from the principal director in the Grenelle development. The Château Violet stood on the site of the present fire station. In 1830 Violet, bankrupt for his trouble, was forced to sell it, and it became a boarding school. It was resold to the city in 1860 and became the fire station. Today, the building has been restored; its park was turned into a public square in 1875 and still has a charming bandstand. It was here in 1824 that the festival inaugurating the new district took place, with the *couronnement de la Rosière*, a French village ceremony in which the (supposedly) most virtuous girl of the village is crowned, traditionally with roses. A nearby street is named after this event.

Rue Violet

It was in this street that Violet wanted to build houses for the village notables. In spite of some recent construction the street shows traces of the purpose for which it was first intended (on the l., the Rue Edmond-Roger, laid out in 1927, is entirely occupied by a *UAP* development of middle-class apartment buildings). The street runs along the back of the little Place du Commerce. At no. 69, a house that once belonged to a rich American was used as Grenelle's second town hall from 1842 to 1860; it was a vast Restoration-style house with a small garden in front. Also in the Rue Violet is the 19th-c. Villa Juge with its paved terraces.

Place du Commerce

Known as the Place de la Mairie until 1867, the *place* contains a garden square and a bandstand. To the N, the oblong area formed by the Rue Violet, Rue du Théâtre and Rue du Commerce was owned by the order of the Little Sisters of the Assumption, who played an important social rôle from the moment of their arrival there in 1870, during a period of great poverty, when they nursed the poor in their homes. The small building at no. 9, with an enclosed garden, won the bronze medal in the first competition organized in 1901 by the Comité des Habitations Bon Marché de la Seine (the Committee for Low-cost Housing); the architect was Gonjon.

On the r., the little Passage des Entrepreneurs is no longer used. At no. 3*bis* there is a house in the purest Restoration style with a paved courtyard.

Rue du Commerce

From the Place du Commerce to the Boul. Grenelle

With its row of little shops and 19th-c. façades, this street plunges you back into the atmosphere of the last century. On the r., a former butcher's shop still has its rococo decoration in carved wood and its inscription, '*Boucherie de Premier Ordre*' ('First-class Butcher-shop').

Turn into the Rue du Théâtre. Note the rustic house on the corner, unthreatened for the time being, and enjoy the peaceful charm of the Cité Thure.

Cross the Rue de la Croix-Nivert and explore the Rue Meilhac and the Rue Quinault. The schools here date from the reforms of Jules Ferry. What a contrast to the new nursery school on the corner of the Rue Mademoiselle and the Rue de l'Amiral Roussin. The architect, Klaus Schultze, has created a group of pink and mauve buildings with courtyards like mini-amphitheatres with mosaic surrounds. At no. 23 notice 'The Messenger', a wall painted by Juan-Luis Cousino in 1980.

Go back to the Rue de la Croix-Nivert. The buildings on the odd-numbered side date from the beginning of this century and belong to the insurance company Secours. The Rue Fondary is opposite, with a lovely peasant-style house at no. 89 (now a hotel) with four seated dogs outside (a popular form of ornament). Note the workers' dwellings at 36 Rue de la Croix-Nivert and the tiny Square Garibaldi.

Les Halles district**

1st arr./Map ref. 17–A1, B1
Métro: Châtelet, Les Halles (RER)
Bus 21, 27, 29, 38, 69, 75, 81, 85
Parking: Forum des Halles; Saint Eustache
Taxis: Place du Châtelet. Tel: 42-33-20-99
Market: Rue Montorgueil, daily except Mon. 7am–1pm/4–7pm; Sun. 7:30am–1pm.

The mythical 'hole of Les Halles' has now yielded up its mysteries; the chic young moderns, the truly trendy, have flown elsewhere. Only a few North African tambourine players and a handful of punks hang around the Fontaine des Innocents today. Covered in concrete shopping arcades, cinemas, restaurants and shops of ready-to-wear clothes of run-of-the-mill quality, the *'trou des Halles'*, excavated for the interconnection of the lines of the RER railway system, attracts a young and often suburban public. Around it the *quartier*, one of the oldest in Paris, has not changed much; to the N, the Montorgueil market is still picturesque, to the W, the Rue Saint-Denis is still crowded with a very mixed population as it always has been; to the S, the Rue Saint-Honoré is more middle class. In the evening a typically Parisian public meets in the district's restaurants and many fashionable bars. While there is a degree of typically Parisian snobbery involved in all questions of fashion, it is still here, in the streets rather than in the shop windows, that the style of the day evolves. Not the stiff, conventional style of the *haute couturiers*, but a more spontaneous style, imaginative and eclectic, inimitably Parisian.

History of the Les Halles district

The area was known in the Middle Ages as Les Champeaux (from *campelli*, little fields), a name reflected by the Union des Champeaux, the committee for the defense of the district. In 1183 Philippe Auguste put up two large covered market halls more like sheds to protect the food produce; they were baptised 'Halles' by the Parisians. The king also moved under the same roof the fair which was previously held near the leper colony at Saint-Lazare. This immense market continued to grow over the centuries. In 1851 the architect Victor Baltard built a group of 10 iron pavilions, each one designed for a particular purpose. Napoléon III, who was much impressed by the brand-new Gare de l'Est, had stipulated the use 'of iron, nothing but iron'. He had also said: 'Make me umbrellas'. This produced the strange structure of iron girders and glass roofs so dear to Zola (→inset) which, with the large spaces it contained, its wide, covered streets, its openwork lanterns, windowed bays, spacious basements and distribution of water and light, was copied many times all over France and abroad. The Halles had to be enlarged again in 1936 by the addition of two pavilions to complete the W wing, of which Baltard had been able to complete only four pavilions out of six, which extended their area to more than 10 acres/4ha.

The traffic problems entailed in supplying a wholesale market right in the center of Paris resulted in the decision in 1962 to transfer the Halles to Rungis, where they were installed in 1969. Baltard's pavilions were demolished, except for one, which was re-erected at Nogent-sur-Marne. An immense shopping, cultural and leisure center was erected on the site, completed in 1986: the Carreau des Halles. The vast neighboring sector, between the Rue de Rivoli and the Rue Etienne-Marcel on one side and between the Louvre and Beaubourg on the other, has been rethought: old buildings have been renovated, new ones built, and wherever possible the streets in and out of the district have been taken into underground tunnels, some for traffic alone, others built in conjunction with the RER, Métro and SNCF tunnels. This project has given back to pedestrians over 3 miles/5km of streets.

Tour of the district

2 hrs.

The Carreau des Halles*

The Forum

To the E of the Carreau des Halles (main entrances Rue P.-Lescot and Rue Rambuteau).

Built on the huge RER station of Château-les Halles (→Métro), the Forum was designed by C. Vasconi and Georges Penchreach (1979). It is an underground pedestrian complex on four levels surrounding an open-air patio. The clear glass arcades provide natural light and opens the complex to the surrounding district.

Level 4 is 57ft/17.5m below ground level, and comprises the various entrances to the Forum, together with shops and offices. Near the Porte Lescot it has a gilded bronze bas-relief by P. M. Trémois: 'Light coming from the depths of time'. Level 3, 45ft/13.6m below ground, is the main shopping and entertainment area (two theaters, a music-hall and cinemas). The artist Attila has painted trompe-l'œil porticoes framing Moretti's fresco The Evolution of Man. It communicates with a large sunken patio, the Place Basse, extended by a long gallery. To the N, this gallery gives access to the public services placed beneath the garden, and to the S, to the shopping facilities. On Level 2, 27ft./8.1m below ground, its pillars decorated with a fantastic mosaic of animals by the painter Cueco, a wide balcony beneath the windows overlooks the Place Basse, which has a pink marble sculpture Pygmalion by the Argentine Julio Silva. Level 1, 13ft./4m down, connects with the garden. In addition to shops, it houses the Musée Grévin (waxworks) and the Musée de l'Holographie (→Museums).

The Lescot building

The two main entrances to the Forum are in this L-shaped construction standing on the Rue Pierre-Lescot and the Rue Rambuteau (architect Jean Willerva). It is composed of mushroom-shaped pavilions which make extensive use of reflecting glass. The ground and first floors house the Maison d'Information Culturelle (Cultural Information Center), the Conservatoire of the first four arrondissements of Paris, the Maison des Ateliers Crafts, a municipal children's library, the Maison de la Poésie (Poetry), the Pavillon des Arts, where temporary exhibitions are held, and the Maison du Geste et de l'Image. The upper terrace is an elevated walkway* with views over the Halles gardens, the Forum and the entire district.

The Children's Garden*

Further W, in a hollow beside the Rue Rambuteau between the Forum, the Church of Saint-Eustache and the mall of the main garden, is the imaginative Jardin des Enfants, designed by C. Lalanne. Everything has been scaled down and adapted to children's perceptions of things, their tastes and their dreams. The themes of the garden include: the Tropical Forest, the Soft World (le monde mou) and its 'swimming-pool' of blue balls, the World of Geometry and Sound (le monde géométrique et sonore), the

Volcanic World (*le monde volcanique*), the Great Toboggan of the Island of Mystery, and the Forbidden City and its Labyrinth.

Place Carrée

The sector to the W, between the Bourse du Commerce (the Commodity Exchange) and the Church of Saint-Eustache, comprises an underground area and the garden above it, laid out by Louis Arretche. The whole new development, with the Place Carrée at its center, is strongly linked to the surrounding district, and to the other underground facilities of the Forum: there is direct access to it by RER and the underground road system. The facilities created by Paul Chemetov relate to sports (a swimming-pool giving on to a tropical greenhouse, a gymnasium, a billiard hall) and culture, with an auditorium for 650 spectators, a Maison de la Musique et de la Danse, a photographic gallery and a video library, the aim of which is to provide the capital with a modern system for the gathering of data about its cultural, artistic and urban heritge. The Central Record Lending Library was created by the architects Jean Ravaille and Michael Jeanne. The leisure facilities also include a radio studio, and a shopping center of 130,000 sq. ft/12,000m² with six cinemas.

The Garden of Les Halles

The garden covers 12½ acres/5ha; on the S side, along the Rue Berger, the succession of arcades and porticoes decorated with a sculpture of vegetables and fruits were the creation of François Lalanne. An oblique mall, with three lines of trees and a stream, emphasizes the garden's alignment along the axis of the district's main streets, and lends the eye toward the Church of Saint-Eustache standing at its NW end. The vast round *place* in front of the church (architect, L. Arretche) is laid with paving stones that create a *trompe-l'oeil* labyrinth, and is decorated by a sandstone statue representing *Burgundy*, by Henri de Miller.

Near the Bourse du Commerce, four glass pyramids rise in the heart of the garden to form the large tropical hothouse that graces one side of the swimming-pool, housing a tropical forest, a bamboo forest, a tropical marshland, and a flower garden, with such exotic species as Mexican frangipani and Brazilian jacarandas.

At the NW extremity of the garden, towards the Rue du Louvre is the Centre de la Mer (1988), built with the collaboration of Jacques Cousteau. With nearly 66,000 sq.ft./6000m², it is expected to receive 8000 visitors daily. They will be able to board an underwater exploration vessel, see films and talk with one of the members of the Calypso expeditions.

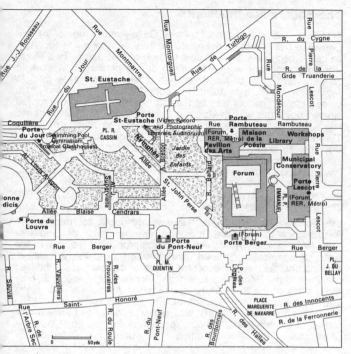

Les Halles

Around the Forum*

The design of the pedestrian area bordering the '*trou des Halles*' is faithful to history. It mixes the sinuosity of the old streets (Rue Saint-Denis, Rue Saint-Honoré) with the straight lines of the 19th-c. and early 20th-c. thoroughfares (Rue Berger, Rue Rambuteau, Rue Pierre-Lescot).

Rue de la Cossonnerie

Leave the Forum by the Porte Lescot, to emerge on the ancient Rue de la Cossonnerie (*c.* 1183), now extensively renovated. At no. 5, there survives a wing of the Cour Batave, a group of buildings dating from 1795, on the *parvis* of the Church of Saint-Sépulcre.

Follow the Rue Pierre-Lescot.

The Square des Innocents

This was the site, probably from Gallo-Roman times, of the Cimetière des Saints-Innocents (Cemetery of the Holy Innocents), so called because it lay beside a church of that name. Two Merovingian sarcophagi were discovered during construction work in January 1973. The cemetery was so close to the Halles that, to separate them, Philippe Auguste, around 1186, built a wall around it. Later a cloister gallery was added, with ribbed vaults and a roofed storey above: this was the famous Saints-Innocents charnel house mentioned by Rabelais, where Villon came to meditate on his *Testament*. The burial places belonged to rich families; the bones from the common graves were stacked in the roofed area. The cemetery was not closed down until 1786, by which time it must have received more than two million dead. The bones still existing at that time were taken to a quarry, renamed the Catacombs. The site of the old cemetery was first turned into a market (1788), then converted to a square (1858).

The Fontaine des Innocents** is a pretty public fountain, and a Renaissance masterpiece. It is the last one in Paris, and was completed in 1549 by architect and sculptor Jean Goujon. In the heart of a typically medieval district, with its crowds, its market, and the charnel house's constant reminder of death, it symbolized the spirit of the Renaissance. Since it was built against a wall, only three sides of the fountain have bas-reliefs (some are now in the Louvre); it stood at the Rue Saint-Denis and the Rue aux Fers (Rue Berger). When the cemetery was closed down, the fountain was moved to the center of the open space thus created. Pajou added a fourth side (1788), which is difficult to distinguish from the others, and which almost reproduces the statue of *La Paix* (Peace) by Goujon on P. Lescot's façade at the Louvre. A new base was substituted in 1865. The W side of the square is occupied by the Berger building, which continues into the Rue Berger (architect, M. Marcot): it houses a Novotel, a block of rented apartments (Orion) and offices. The S side of the square is bordered by a building of 1669 which has one of the longest façades in Paris (394ft./120m.).

Pedestrian gate.

Rue de la Ferronnerie

The street has borne this name since the 13th c.; it was widened after 1669. On May 14, 1610, at about 4:00 in the afternoon, the density of the crowd, the merchants' barrows from the Halles and the narrowness of the street brought traffic almost to a halt, which enabled Ravaillac, who had followed the royal carriage from the Louvre, to get close enough to the king to assassinate him. This occurred between a house with the sign of the Salamander and another with the sign of the '*Coeur couronné percé d'une flèche*' (crowned heart pierced by an arrow: an ill omen?); the latter house is now a restaurant, and has kept the sign. At no. 11, a flagstone marks the spot where Henri IV was assassinated. Ravaillac was executed in the Place de Grève.

Rue Saint-Denis

From the Rue des Lombards to the Rue Etienne-Marcel.

This is one of the oldest streets in Paris parallel to the ancient Roman way, the Rue Saint-Matin. As the fame of the Basilica of Saint-Denis increased, the Rue Saint-Denis grew in importance. The kings of France rode down it in triumph returning from their coronation, the street would then take on a festival air; most elaborate, perhaps, was Louis XI's ceremonial entry, through triumphal arches, clowns, minstrals, and fountains that dispensed free wine, and in which young maidens frolicked. However, kings and queens also made the journey in the other direction, to be buried at Saint-Denis.

Now a pedestrian precinct from the Rue des Lombards to the Rue Etienne-Marcel, the street has seen its population change with the coming of the Forum. While still very busy, the sex shops and *hôtels de passe* (bordellos) confined to the N side of the street are gradually disappearing; they are being replaced by food shops. Some of the houses have triangular pediments and others gabled porches.

Nos. 51, 53 and 57 are 17th- and 18th-c., as is no. 79 (note the wrought-iron). A tall post representing the Virgin's family tree used to stand at the corner of the Rue des Prêcheurs and can now be seen at the Carnavalet Museum. In this section of the Rue Saint-Denis, which was Max Ernst's territory, there are still some handsome houses to be seen, such as nos. 87 and 89.

Cross the Rue de la Grande-Truanderie. It too is changing in character, and has no more of the neighborhood beggars who gave the street its name. It is now a pedestrian precinct and with more elegant fashion boutiques and shops selling unusual articles than disreputable cafés; there are several 16th–17th-c. houses, recently renovated. Since 1919, when a block of buildings separating the two streets was demolished, it has been joined to the Rue de la Petite-Truanderie.

🔱 The Church of Saint-Leu-Saint-Gilles**

Access from Boul. de Sébastopol.

This church, founded in the 12th c., was reconstructed in 1235 and again in 1320, and has been remodelled many times from the 16th to the 19th c. The church (for Saint-Leu read Saint-Lupus) was dedicated to St Gilles, a hermit who lived in Provence.

With no transept, the church is a curious mixture of styles: Gothic in its original structure, Baroque in the chapels and the choir, with 19th-c. additions. The façade and nave are from 1320, the side-aisles from the 16th c. and the choir and chapels from the first half of the 17th. Massillon gave Lenten sermons here in 1611. In 1858 Baltard (→inset) rebuilt the ambulatory to place the apse on the line of the Boul. de Sébastopol, which was laid out in that year. A large square chapel was added to the S. The buttresses are internal, a rare arrangement in Paris. A wide stone staircase leads to the choir, which is much higher than the nave. The church has some important works of art: *St Anne and the Virgin**, a marble group by Jean Bullant (16th c.); three 15th-c. alabaster bas-reliefs from England: *The Last Supper, The Kiss of Judas* and *The Flagellation*. Among the paintings: *Man on his Death-bed* (claimed to be a portrait of St Francis de Sales and wrongly attributed to Philippe de Champaigne); *The Eternal Father* by Jean Jouvenet; *St Jerome at Prayer*, after Georges de la Tour; *The Supper at Emmaus* by Jean II Restout; *The Nativity*, after Simon Vouet. In a chapel to the r. of the choir, the reliquary of St Clotilde in gilded silver; her bones were burnt in 1793 to avoid profanation, and the ashes returned to the church during the Restoration. Under the choir, a crypt from 1780 houses a statue of *Christ Entombed* (18th c.), originally in the former church of Saint-Sépulcre. This is the church of the Chevaliers (Knights) du Saint-Sépulcre, who were ceremonially reinstated there on October 16 1928. Numerous ex-votos.

Take the Rue Pierre-Lescot to the l., where fine Restoration houses are preserved at nos. 17, 28 and 30; no. 28 is decorated in bas-relief.

The Rue Rambuteau

From the Rue Pierre-Lescot to Church of Saint-Eustache.

This street was laid out in the 19th c. and goes by the Lescot building (→ above), then the Children's Garden (above). On its r. is a social welfare building that blends well into its surroundings (architects, Ducharme, Larras and Minost). It runs along the length of Saint-Eustache (→North of Les Halles).

Rue Coquillière

In this street, which affords a wide view of the façade of the Banque de France (→Bourse), François Mansart, around 1630, built a fine mansion at nos. 6–10 for Charles de Laubespine, Marquis de Chateauneuf. The poet Léon-Paul Fargue, 'the wanderer through Paris' as he was called, author of *Le Piéton de Paris*, was born at no.

6 in 1876. The street today is notable for its terraced restaurants, which are particularly attactive in summer.

Rue de Louvre

This street marks the boundary of the Palais-Royal district. Note, at no. 19 (and no. 9 Rue du Coq-Héron) the handsome mansion of Thoinard Vougy, the *fermier-général* (tax collector), possibly built by Boffrand (1730); sculpted door and portal, beautiful interior decoration (guided tours); today it houses the Caisse d'Epargne (Savings Bank). Striking façades at nos. 15 and 16 (the latter is Art Nouveau by F. Jourdain).

The Bourse du Commerce

The Bourse is entered from the Place des Deux-Ecus. It occupies the Halle au Blé (Corn Market) built from 1765 to 1768 on the orders of the *prévôt des marchands*, De Viarmes. It was given an iron cupola in 1811 and remodelled in 1889. On the side of the Rue du Louvre, four columns surmounted by a pediment make a formal-looking façade, while the semicircular NW side on the Rue de Viarmes, is also bordered by similar houses with Doric columns in front of them. Inside is an 18th-c. double staircase with concentric flights in wrought iron. To the E, a column of the former Hôtel de Soissons (→ inset), all that remains of that building.

Rue Saint-Honoré

From the Rue du Louvre to the Rue Sauval.

This is one of Paris' oldest thoroughfares, replacing, since the 13th c., the old Chaussée du Roule which, with the Rue Saint-Denis-Saint-Jacques, formed the famous crossroads of the Gallo-Roman era. It runs westwards as far as the Rue de la Paix (for this section → Tuileries district). To the E beyond the Palais Royal, the Rue Saint-Honoré is livelier and richer in history, with tall façades decorated with garlands, masks and ornamental keystones, and wrought-iron windowsills.

On a window at no. 29, formerly at the sign of the *Montier d'Or*, is a mask of Venus with the symbols of maritime trade; wrought ironwork with the initials R.R.

The fine house at nos. 117–119, which was part of the former Hôtel de Schomberg, was bought in 1616 by the Chancellor d'Aligre, then by the Marquis de Verderonne.

At no. 115 is one of the oldest known pharmacies, established in 1715; it was first the Pharmacie du Mont-Blanc, then passed to a dynasty of pharmacists, the Cadet de Gassicourt family, who supplied ointments and beauty products to Marie-Antoinette and, they say, procured for Count Axel von Fersen the invisible ink he used to write his love letters to the queen. The façade is still very handsome, with its basket-handle windows and its sculpted key-stones.

At no. 108, wrought ironwork. One of the biggest buildings of the steet (18th c.), forms the corner of the Rue Sauval at no. 98. The present no. 96, according to a worn inscription, replaces the house where Molière was born in 1622 and also, it seems, the comedy writer, Regnard, in 1655. This large house once had a decorative corner-post representing an orange tree with seven monkeys, from which it got the name of 'Pavillon des Singes', long since given to the shop of Maître Poquelin, Tapestry Maker to the king and Molière's father. Paris has been generous with the great Molière, allocating him two birthplaces: this one, which according to scholars is the right one, and another not far away, at 31 Rue du Pont-Neuf. The two plaques have different birthdates.

Rue Sauval

Before taking the name of the lawyer-historian of Paris (1623–76) this was called the Rue des Vieilles-Etuves after the public baths, which were closed because of the debauchery that went on there. It has retained most of its 16th- and 17th-c. houses, with their sculpted portals and dark courtyards (see nos. 4, 5 and 6). No. 8 is one of the finest 17th-c. houses in the street.

The Fontaine du Trahoir, in the Rue Saint-Honoré, was formerly called the Croix-du-Trahoir: it was rebuilt in 1776 by Soufflot, with bossages and stalactite work framing a nymph in the style of Jean Goujon, sculpted by Boizot. It replaces the fountain built by François I in the middle of the crossroads formed by the street with the Rue de l'Arbre-Sec, and which had been decorated by Goujon himself. Louis XIII had it moved and placed against a house where the magistrates once took up their positions to witness public executions. Today it is the Maison de l'Andorre.

Rue de l'Arbre-Sec

Walk up this street and back again. The dead tree implied in its name served, in bygone days, as the gallows for the district. The street has changed its name several times and in the 17th c. became fashionably middle class.

At no. 52, Hôtel de Truden (1717–21), where the pediment over the windows carries a *rocaille* ornamental seashell motif, there is also a large decorative balcony.

At no. 48 is the former Hôtel de Saint-Romain, built around 1680. The grouping of nos. 35 and 37 together is unique; at the end of the 16th c. the house was owned by a Marian community. It was restored in the 18th c. and retains from that period some wrought ironwork and arcades. History relates that the young Eugène de Beauharnais hid at no. 39 while waiting for the dark days of the Terror to pass.

Rue Saint-Honoré, continued

Several old houses to see, at nos. 93, 99, 103, 105, 94, 84 and 82, but note particularly the elegance of no. 97, which retains its dormer windows grouped beneath a central pediment with scrolled buttresses; wrought ironwork from the beginning of the 18th c.

Cross the very old Rue Vauvilliers, which must be less sinister than it looks, since Pierre Cardin's boutique is there, as well as a modern furniture shop, a gallery of Far Eastern art and another of curios. No. 9 has a street door framed in ceramic tiles, in the late 19th-c. style.

Rue Saint-Honoré, continued

As far as the Rue du Pont-Neuf

La Renommée des Herbes Cuites, at no. 95, was once the home of the king's surgeon, while at no. 93 Le Bourdon d'Or is now an art gallery: note the Directoire sign. The Passage 91 leads to several courtyards where antique and bric-a-brac shops have been installed. Note the balconies decorated with lyres and garlands and the ornamental brackets of no. 70, the wrought ironwork of nos. 66, 68, 58, 67 and 69 and, above all, the superb balcony* at no. 54 on the corner of the Rue des Prouvaires (meaning 'priests' in Old French), one of the finest balconies to be seen in Paris.

The Rue du Pont-Neuf leads back to the esplanade of Les Halles. No. 31 bears a plaque and a bust of Molière (→ above). Wagner and his wife Minna found their first Parisian lodgings at no. 33 in this street, which at that time was called the Rue de la Tonnellerie.

Continue your walk in the Rue Saint-Honoré, of which most of the low-numbered houses are 17th-c.

North of Les Halles*

At the apse of the Church of Saint-Eustache, where the Rue Montmartre, the Rue Montorgueil, the Rue Turbigo and the Rue Rambuteau converge, the Pointe Saint-Eustache marks the boundary between the esplanade of Les Halles and the densely populated and lively area, developed in the 16th c., when several *hôtels* were built for a firmly established *noblesse de robe* (members of the bourgoisie elevated because of their official functions), and a newly rich middle class.

♱ The Church of Saint-Eustache***

This is a magnificent building, constructed between 1532 and 1637, which shows the persistence of the Gothic style well into the 17th c., not in its decoration, which is Renaissance or even Classical, but in its structure, and its architectural principles, plan, and balanced vaulting.

In the 12th c. a small chapel dedicated to St Agnes was raised here, on the road to Montmartre. It grew (1434) into a church and was rededicated to St Eustace, the Roman general and legendary (and probably apocryphal) hunter. In 1519 planning for the rebuilding of the church began: laying of the foundation stone on August 19, 1532 and commencement of the four chapels on the N side by Pierre le Mercier; S façade (1539–40), nave (1578–1600 and 1618–22) – the old church was probably demolished only as the new building progressed; there was then a noticeable hesitancy about the style of the nave. In 1629, the chapels on the S side transept vaults (1631–34); vaults of the nave (1635–37); finally, on April 26, 1637, consecration. The architects were Charles David and François Petit. Further works on the N portal and on the chapels were carried out, some paid for by Colbert. In the 18th c. the Renaissance W front, which had never been finished, was replaced by a Classical façade with columns, under the direction of, first, Mansart de Jouy (1754), then of Moreau (1772–78), who, in the reconstruction process, did not hesitate to demolish the church's first bay and two accompanying chapels, one of which had been decorated by Mignard. Renamed the Temple de l'Agriculture during the Revolution, it reopened in 1803, was damaged by fire in 1844, and later restored by Baltard.

The exterior

The flying buttresses are traditional Gothic. In the N (giving on to the Impasse Saint-Eustache) and S arms of the transept round-arched doorways are arranged like Gothic portals; their delicate decoration has been restored, but the statuettes in the voussoirs have not been replaced; the N doorway is flanked by twin staircase turrets. Beneath the gable point is the head of a deer with a cross between its antlers, symbolizing the vision that led to Eustache's conversion. The openwork bell tower over the crossing, known as the Plomb de Saint-Eustache, has lost its steeple. In the apse, the chapel dedicated to the Virgin (1630) is larger than the others and protrudes; it is surmounted by a bell-tower rebuilt in 1875. Beside all this, Mansart de Jouy's façade appears alien.

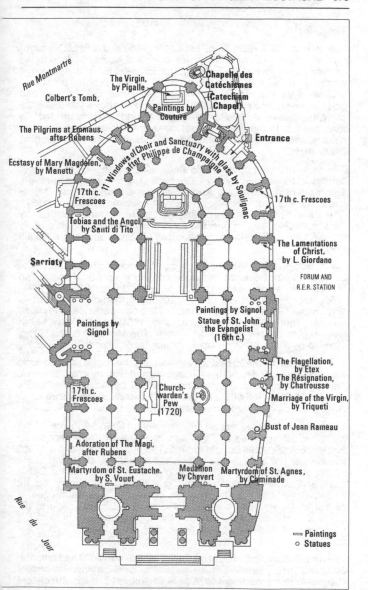

Rue Montmartre

The Virgin, by Pigalle

Colbert's Tomb,

Chapelle des Catéchismes (Catechism Chapel)

Paintings by Couture

The Pilgrims at Emmaus, after Rubens

Entrance

Ecstasy of Mary Magdalen, by Manetti

11 Windows of Choir and Sanctuary with glass by Soulignac after Philippe de Champaigne

17th c. Frescoes

17th c. Frescoes

Tobias and the Angel by Santi di Tito

The Lamentations of Christ, by L. Giordano

Sacristy

FORUM AND R.E.R. STATION

Paintings by Signol

Paintings by Signol
Statue of St. John the Evangelist (16th c.)

The Flagellation, by Etex
The Résignation, by Chatrousse

17th c. Frescoes

Marriage of the Virgin, by Triqueti

Church-warden's Pew (1720)

Bust of Jean Rameau

Adoration of The Magi, after Rubens

Martyrdom of St. Eustache, by S. Vouet

Medallion by Chevert

Martyrdom of St. Agnes, by Caminade

Rue du Jour

— Paintings
○ Statues

Church of Saint-Eustache

The interior

The church (280ft./88m long, 141ft./43m wide and 108ft./33m high) gives an impression of nobility, grandeur and harmony, despite the amputation of part of the nave. Gothic loftiness is combined with a wholly Renaissance decorative style: pilaster columns, super-imposed Classical orders, a triforium with semicircular arches and great arcades, also rounded. The ground plan shows the influence of Notre-Dame: double side-aisles flanking a transept that is spacious inside the building, but does not appear large from the outside, and chapels all contained within its outer wall, surrounding the chancel.

The nave. The 18th-c. organ (85 stops, 7000 pipes), one of the most famous in Paris, built by F. H. Clicquot, is undergoing restoration. The resident organists are André Fleury and Jean Guillou. Organ-chest by Baltard; console remade by Jean Hermann (1967). Churchwardens' pew executed by Lepautre from designs by Carteaux (ca. 1720): during the Revolution it served as an oratory tribune; Cerruti gave the funeral eulogy of Mirabeau here on April 3 1791.

The r. side-aisle (S). Above the door, Martyrdom of St Agnes, after Le Dominiquin. Between this door and the main portal, medallion and epitaph, a fine text by Diderot of General F. de Chevert (1695–1769). 1st bay: the history of the church inscribed on black marble. 2nd chapel (Sainte-Cécile): epitaph of the composer Jean-Philippe Rameau (buried at Saint-Eustache in 1764), and a bust, after Houdon. 3rd chapel (Saints-Innocents): The Marriage of the Virgin, a group by Triqueti. 4th chapel: statues by Etex and Chatrousse.

The transept: In the crossing, the hanging keystone is decorated with two angels carrying the Cross crowned with thorns (30ft./9m). The two arms of the transept have murals by A. Signol: Christ's Passion. At the pier of the S doorway (closed), stone statue of St John (16th c.) and six statues of apostles by Crauk and Husson.

The chancel. Colored marble mosaic paving (1869). High altar of the same period, sculpted by Pyanet in Paris marble from designs by Baltard. Simple stalls bought in 1795. The stained glass of the 11 tall windows of the apse and sanctuary is remarkable, still using in the 16th c. the noble medieval tradition of massive areas of color. Dated 1631 and signed Antoine Soulignac, the cartoons may be by Champaigne, though this remains uncertain. The technique is similar to the stained glass of Saint-Gudule in Brussels: figures (St Eustace in the center surrounded by Apostles and Fathers of the Church) standing out against a background of Classical architecture.

The ambulatory. 2nd chapel on the r. (Sainte-Agnès): The Lamenta-tions of Christ*, painting in the style of Luca Giordano. 3rd chapel (Sainte-Anne): monument to M de la Chambre (d. 1669). 4th chapel

(Sainte-Agnès): 17th-c. frescoes, restored in 1850; reliquary in gilded wood (Louis XIII period) of St Thomas Aquinas. The Louis XVI staircase giving access to the large Chapelle des Catéchismes leaves from the 7th chapel: in the Chapelle des Catéchismes are a *St John the Baptist* by Lemoine and a fragment of an altarpiece (now in the Nantes museum); a naïve sculpture by Raymond, donated to the church, commemorating *The Removal of Les Halles*. Chapel of the Virgin (1630, much restored in 1802): three large murals by Thomas Couture: *Litanies of the Virgin*; above the altar, a beautiful *Virgin**, sculpted by Pigalle for the Invalides chapel. 9th chapel (Saint-Louis-de-Gonzague): Colbert's tomb*, designed by Le Brun, Coysevox carved the statues of Colbert and *Abundance*, and Tuby carved *La Fidélité* (Fidelity). 10th chapel: in the altarpiece, *The Pilgrims at Emmaus**, early Rubens; *Burial of a Martyr*, canvas of the French School (early 17th c.). 11th chapel (Sainte-Madeleine): *The Ecstasy of St Madeleine**, painting by Rutilio Manetti (*ca.* 1627); old frescoes (*Life of St Mary Magdalene*). 12th chapel: dedicated to St Vincent de Paul, who lived in the parish of Saint-Eustache for 10 years (1613–23) while tutoring the Gondi children, Rue Neuve-des-Petits-Champs; 17th-c. frescoes, restored; fine keystone in the vault. 13th chapel; *Tobias and the Angel*, by Santi di Tito (second half of the 16th c.).

The l. side-aisle (N). 2nd chapel (Saint-Joseph): 17th-c. frescoes restored by Basset; inscription to the memory of Anne-Marie Mozart, mother of the great composer, whose requiem was held in the church. *Adoration of the Magi*, after Rubens, in the 3rd chapel. On the tympanum of the door, *Martyrdom of St Eustace* by Simon Vouet. Between this door and the main doorway, medallion of the parish priest Secousse (d. 1771). The superb sacred music attracts many visitors and the Saint-Eustache choir performs remarkably at High Mass each Sunday (11 am).

Rejoin the Rue Coquillière.

Rue Jean-Jacques Rousseau

From the Rue Coquillière to the Rue Etienne-Marcel
For the other section → Bourse district

This street, formerly called Rue Plâtrière, has retained the old buildings on the even-numbered side. Rousseau lived at no. 52, now replaced by a modern building, and the restaurant L'Alsace à Paris stands on the site of his last lodging in Paris. He left it in 1778 for Ermononville near Paris, where he died a few weeks later. One can imagine him painfully climbing the superb staircase of the *hôtel* at no. 68 of Mme Dupin de Chenonceaux, his long-time friend and confidante. This badly deteriorated mansion still retains a fine balcony and a courtyard façade with pilasters and tall windows decorated with mascarons. Note also the innocent-looking lions over the door of no. 56, the door and windows of the Hôtel de Pierre

Sageret (17th c.) at no. 62 and, at no. 64, the handsome façade of a 17th-c. mansion, restored in 1978.

Rue du Jour

This street, which leads back to the façade of Saint-Eustache, was laid over the track that ran alongside Philippe Auguste's perimeter wall; its name comes from the pied-a-terre – 'séjour', as it was then called – of Charles V. Lately, pleasant shops have opened here, but it has kept the unusual and monumental doorway of the Hôtel des Abbés de Royaumont.

At nos. 25–27 the Hôtel de la Porte houses the Musée de l'Avocat (Museum of Law → Museums): note the courtyard pediment, vestibule and fine stairway with stone tracery.

Rue Montorgueil

Extended by the Rue des Petits-Carreaux as far as the Grands Boulevards, this street is invaded daily by market gardeners' stalls. With its delicatessens it retains something of the spirit that once reigned in the district, when the Halles were a gigantic market.

The street, known for a long time as the Rue des Huîtres, retains a few fine houses, like the mansion at no. 15, built in 1729 by the architect Goupy: its handsome façade is listed in the registry of historic monuments. Note the wrought ironwork at nos. 17, 23 and 25; and the enormous gilded snail that is the sign of a renowned restaurant, established in 1832, whose exterior decoration (engraved windows, gilded lettering), and the interior decoration (panelled ceilings) are typical of the 19th c.

Continuation of the street → below.

Rue Mauconseil

The porch of a theater once stood at no. 34, built on land belonging to the Hôtel de Bourgogne. In 1628 it took the name Théâtre de l'Hôtel de Bourgogne, where Gros-Guillaume and Montfleury played, as later did Baron, Armande Béjart, Floridor and the Champmesles. At that time all female rôles were played by men wearing masks. Racine staged *Mithridate, Iphigénie, Andromaque* and *Phèdre* in this theater. Still to be seen, at no. 38, is the Louis XVI bas-relief depicting *Music, Poetry* and *Painting*. The Italians and the famous clown Scaramouche, who could knock a man's hat off his head with a high kick when he was 83, took over the theater. They had to leave in 1697 after an attack on Mme de Maintenon. The Comique Opéra was the last troupe to play here before the theater disappeared.

The Tower of Jean-sans-Peur

20 Rue Etienne Marcel

This square, machiolated tower, all that remains of the former Hôtel de Bourgogne, is also, with the Hôtel de Clisson (→ Marais), the sole surviving remnant of truly feudal architecture in Paris.

After 1408, Jean sans Peur (John The Fearless) fortified the upper storeys to protect himself from the vengeance of the widow of Louis d'Orléans, whom he caused to be assassinated. The house, known as the Hôtel de Bourgogne, which, before Jean sans Peur, had been the home of the Comtes d'Artois, abutted on Philippe Auguste's defensive wall. After the death of Charles the Bold, the grandson of Jean sans Peur, Louis XI, took the *hôtel*, which was becoming a ruin, as Crown property. François I parcelled out the estate as building plots, and the mansion was demolished in 1543.

Today the tower is surrounded by the playground of a municipal school. In the tympanum of one of the external bays two carpenter's planes and a plumbline form the badge (restored) of Jean sans Peur. This badge was opposed to the knotted club of his enemy Louis d'Orléans. Inside, there is still a fine early 15th-c. spiral staircase, the central pillar of which spreads out into the vault in the form of a leafy branch.

Rue Tiquetonne. Most of the houses in this beautiful street (*ca.* 1360) are 17th- and 18th-c. Note in particular the sculpted sign *A l'Arbre de Liège* (no. 10) and nos. 13 and 15; the two storeys on the street and the stairway of no. 13 are listed in the registry of historic monuments.

Rue Dussoubs. This street is laid along the site of an old 13th-c. street and retains several large 17th- and 18th-c. houses.

To the r., the Passage du Grand-Cerf rejoins the Rue Saint-Denis. Previously the courtyard of the Hôtellerie du Grand Cerf, this became the courtyard of the Messageries Royales (royal coach services), and was given a glass roof in 1824.

Rue Greneta

Known in the Middle Ages for a pilgrims' hospice that provided entertainment, notably at the Théâtre Marie-Stuart, the street today has nothing of much interest. However, at the corner with the Rue Dussoubs there is a large, featureless wall which in 1977 was entirely covered by an amusing naïve painting on a sky-blue background.

Rue Saint-Denis

From the Rue Etienne-Marcel to the Grands Boulevards.

This part of the Rue Saint-Denis, running up to the Grands

Boulevards, is known today for its prostitutes, as a red-light district, but long ago kings made their triumphal entries into Paris along this street, which follows an ancient Roman way. Its old houses have not been renovated, as have those near the Forum, and fast-food joints and trendy boutiques have sprung up. At night this street is not very safe. At no. 133, reproductions of old statues, (the originals of which are at Cluny), recall that the Hôpital Saint-Jacques was founded on this spot in 1317 to take in pilgrims.

No. 135 is on the site of the former Porte Saint-Denis, part of Philippe Auguste's fortifications, now called the Porte aux Peintres, from the name of a nearby cul-de-sac. At no. 120, Passage du Bourg l'Abbé was created in 1828.

Léon Blum was born at no. 151 in 1872. At no. 142, a handsome old house with ornamental keystones and mascarons (grotesque heads) dating from the 18th c. and, at the corner of the Rue Greneta Fontaine de la Reine (Queen's Fountain), restored in 1732, but probably dating from the time of Louis XI. Fountains used to run with wine in this street when kings rode down it. There are fine gabled houses at nos. 174 and 176. On the unremarkable façade of no. 170, see the coat of arms and the words *Honni soit qui mal y pense – Dieu est mon roi* ('Evil be to him who thinks evil – God is my king').

Turn l. into the Rue Réaumur and return to the Church of Saint-Eustache by the Rue des Petits-Carreaux: note nos. 45, 40, 37, 19, 9 and, at no. 12, an amusing ceramic sign *Au Planteur*.

Return to the Rue Montorgeuil and note nos. 71, 69, 49–47 and the courtyard of no. 36.

▷ **Zola's Halles**

'. . . and, on the long walks home when all three, Claude, Cadine and Marjolin, circled around the Halles, they caught sight, at the end of each street, of a corner of this iron giant. There were sudden glimpses of unexpected architecture, the same horizon presenting itself in different aspects. Claude most often came back by the Rue Montmartre, after passing the church. In the distance the Halles, seen obliquely, excited him; a big arcade, a high door yawning open: then came the serried pavilions with their two-storeyed roofs, their continuous shutters, their immense awnings: you would have said the profiles of houses and palaces superimposed, a metal Babylon, with the delicacy of an Indian temple, crossed by hanging terraces, aerial corridors, flying bridges flung into space. They always came back there, to that town around which they wandered, without being able to leave it by more than a hundred paces. Above, the shutters are closed, the blinds down. In the covered streets the air sleeps, ash-grey streaked with yellow from the splashes of sunlight falling from the long windows. . . .'

E. Zola: *Le Venture de Paris* (1873)
translated by W. G. Hodgkinson

▷ Victor Baltard and the churches of Paris

Although Baltard (1805–75), son of Louis-Pierre Baltard, and more famous than his father, is remembered chiefly for the old Halles, he also built the Church of Saint-Augustin and for 30 years was principally responsible for the upkeep, restoration and decoration of the churches of Paris. Gifted with an agile, ingenious mind, Baltard never allowed himself to become entangled by taking sides in aesthetic quarrels. Commissioned in 1845 to build Les Halles, he made Napoléon III's idea of the 'umbrellas' his own, and brought to bear on its execution all his skill as a builder, utilizing industrial materials such as iron and glass to simple yet grand effect. Winner of the Grand Prix de Rome for architecture in 1833, Baltard had also studied painting at the Ecole des Beaux Arts. All his life he maintained a preference for colored decorations, which he put to good use in his interior restorations, as at Saint-Germain-des-Prés and Saint-Eustache.

He always involved himself in choosing the painters to work in his churches, and in assigning the locations for their work. He attached great importance to the purely ornamental aspects of a painting, the arabesques or geometric motifs used to frame its different sections; his principal collaborator in this field was Alexandre Denuelle (1818–79).

An audacious builder, a scholarly restorer and a decorator of impeccable taste, Baltard left the mark of his tireless energy and his pragmatic intellect on a great number of Parisian buildings.

▷ The former Hôtel de Nesle and Hôtel de Soissons

On the site of the present Bourse du Commerce there was first an Hôtel de Nesle where Blanche of Castille, Queen of France, lived for 20 years and died on December 1, 1225. Jean de Luxembourg, who was to die at the Battle of Crécy, lived there for 19 years (1327–1346). The *hôtel* later passed to Louis, Duc d'Orléans, who made a magnificent home of it before he was assassinated by his cousin, Jean sans Peur, Duc de Bourgogne. In 1494 Louis II of Orléans, who was not yet King Louis XII, relinquished a part of the *hôtel* to the strange group of women calling themselves the Couvent des Filles Repenties (Convent of Repentant Maidens), who later demonstrated the benefits of true repentance by gaining possession of the whole building. But Marie de'Medici, who had no time for virtue, real or simulated, expelled them and had Bullant build a magnificent mansion for her, the Hôtel de la Reine, which took the name of Soissons when it passed to Charles de Bourbon, Comte de Soissons, in 1606. All that remains of it today is the tall fluted Doric column which may have been used as an observatory by Catherine's astrologer, Rubbieri. The column was saved from destruction by Bachaumont, a noted patron of the arts, who donated it to the city.

▣ Museums to visit

Musée de l'Holographie (Holography Museum) (Forum des Halles, Grand Balcon, Level 1): collection of holograms.

Nouveau Musée Grévin (Forum des Halles, Grand Balcon, Level 1): reconstruction of the *Belle Epoque* waxworks.

Musée de l'Avocat (Lawyers' Museum) (25 Rue du Jour): mementoes, documents and objets d'art relating to famous crimes.

▷ A well-attended church

There are numerous historical figures buried at Saint-Eustache: Colbert, who was a churchwarden as well as a statesman; the poets Voiture and Breserade, Vaugelas, Furetière, La Motte le Vayer, Maréchal de la Feuillade, l'Admiral de Tourville, Chevert, the Garde des Sceaux d'Armenonville, the painter Charles de Lafosse and the composer Rameau. Molière was baptised here as Jean-Baptiste Poquelin in 1622 and Jeanne Poisson, the future Mme de Pompadour, in 1721; Louis XIV came for his first communion in 1649, and in 1662 the composer Lully was married here. La Fontaine had his funeral service in the church. Sophie Volland, Diderot's faithful and beloved friend, was buried here. It was for Jean-Baptiste Poquelin, Tapestry Maker to the King, and not for his son Molière, the great dramatist, that a shortened requiem was held on February 21, 1673. Mirabeau's body was deposited in the church on April 3, 1791, but was removed the same day to the Panthéon.

Saint-Eustache is particularly dear to musicians: besides that of Rameau, the funeral service of Mozart's mother was held here (1778); Berlioz arranged the first performance of his *Te Deum* in the church on April 30, 1855, and Liszt gave his *Grand Mass* here in 1866 and 1886.

▷ The Cour des Miracles

It was Victor Hugo's superb dramatic novel, *The Hunchback of Notre-Dame*, that gave a legendary dimension to the Cour des Miracles, or Court of Miracles.

The most famous legend, for there were many, was that of the cul-de-sac of the Rue Neuve-Saint-Sauveur, now the Rue du Nil, near the Convent of the Filles Dieux and the Rue Montorgueil. Dating from the 13th c., it was made up of a large, muddy courtyard surrounded by tumbledown hovels and reached by a tangle of tortuous alleys. Known also as the 'Piolle Franche', it was a safe haven from the police, who did not often venture there, a refuge for fake blind beggars and false cripples who, on returning within its confines, by a mysterious miracle, threw off their crutches, regained their sight and led their wild 'normal' lives. Towards the middle of the 17th c. this den of thieves extended itself towards the Cul-de-Sac du Petit Jésus, now the Rue des Petits-Carreaux, attracting a growing number of vagrants, who organized themselves into fraternities with an elected 'king'. In 1667, to clean up the district, Nicolas de Reynie, Lieutenant of Police in Paris, decided to get rid of its dubious inhabitants once and for all. The courtyard was surrounded by the police, who let it be known that of the last 12 to come out, six would be hanged and the other six sent to the galleys. All the inhabitants left at top speed, the 'cripples' and 'paralyzed' leading the pack. They were redistributed among the prisons and hospitals of the capital, and the courtyard and its hovels were razed to the ground.

□ The Hôtel de Ville*

4th arr./Map ref. 17–B2
Open Mon., except during official ceremonies. Appointments: Rue Lobau, Porche Rivoli.

The Council Chamber is open to visitors only during public monthly meetings of the Municipal Council. Tel. 42–76–59–37 or 59–28 or 59–34

Métro: Hôtel de Ville, Châtelet
Bus: 38, 58, 47, 67, 70, 72, 74, 96.
Taxis: Rue Lobau
Parking: Rue Lobau

Since 1892, its centenary year, the Hôtel de Ville has recovered a certain *éclat*. Its whitened façades have since then looked down on a large pedestrian precinct, separated from the traffic by fountains on either side, recently created by F. X. Lalanne. The Place is paved in granite with the boat motif of the Watermen's Guild.

This is still the official building of the Municipality of Paris, which itself descends from the Corporation des Marchands de l'Eau (Watermen's Guild), who held a monopoly on river traffic on the Seine, Marne, Oise and Yonne. In the Gallo-Roman period such traffic was in the hands of the Corps des Nautes, whose importance is shown by an inscription dating from the reign of Tiberius.

The first municipal authority was created by St Louis in 1246: the burghers of Paris elected magistrates (*échevins*) to negotiate on their behalf with the central authority; their head was the *Prévôt des Marchands* (Merchant Provost). At that time the seal of the River Traders, with its famous boat, became the seal of the municipality. It was later to form the coat of arms of the city (*Fluctuat nec mergitur*, 'It floats and does not founder'). The municipal ruling body met in an ordinary house near the Abbey of Sainte-Geneviève, which in the 13th c. was known as Parloir aux Bourgeois. The purchase in 1357 by Etienne Marcel, the then Merchant Provost, of an *hôtel* in the Place de Grève (the present Place de l'Hôtel de Ville), called the Maison aux Piliers (Pillared House), became the new meeting place and marked the effective birth of the Hôtel de Ville.

The Place de l'Hôtel de Ville

This square was named the Place de Grève until 1830. It was first enlarged in 1778 and acquired its present dimension under Haussmann. It has recently been made a pedestrian precinct.

From the Gallo-Roman period until the 11th c. there was only a wide beach here among the reeds of the river bank. In 1141 the *Marchands de L'Eau* created a port here to relieve congestion in the Saint-Landry port on the Ile de la Cité. This port and the adjoining square took their name from the foreshore (*grève*) that sloped gently down to the river, between the Pont Notre-Dame and the Pont Marie. A port for coal, wood, corn, wine and hay, the Port de Grève was soon one of the most important in Paris.

In the 13th c. the Place de Grève, wider on the river side than on the land side, was much smaller than the present-day square. When the municipal authority was installed in 1357 in one of the houses at its edge, the Place de Grève became the setting for the great demonstrations in Parisian life: rejoicing, revolts, and even executions were carried out here from 1310 to 1830. It was here that the unemployed used to gather, which gave rise to the expression *être en grève* (to be on strike).

The Hôtel de Ville, continued

History of the building

The southern part of the gabled Gothic building had arcades at ground level, hence its name: Maison aux Piliers. It was rebuilt between 1533 and 1551 by Domineco, known as Il Boccadoro (the Sweet Talker), from Cortone in Italy. The northern part was completed under Henri IV and Louis XIII, between 1608 and 1628. It is thought that Pierre Chambiges was one of the several building contractors.

Under Louis Philippe the building was enlarged and sumptuously decorated (paintings by Ingres and Delacroix), but the Communards burnt it down on May 24, 1871. The present building is a reconstruction (1874–1882) from designs by Théodore Ballu and Edouard Deperthes.

The exterior

The façade, like that of the original, is French Renaissance. Two corner pavilions stand at the end of the two wings, set back 20ft./6m from the main central buildings. The façade has been widened and heightened, the roof-lines raised, the plan of the inner courtyards unified and regularized with spiral staircases at their corners. Innummerable niches, Corinthian columns and plinths have been provided for statues of allegories and 108 eminent men and women: 146 sculptures in all. All the personages depicted are natives of Paris, with one exception: Il Boccadoro. Above the entablature are statues representing 30 towns from all the French provinces. Strasbourg and Metz are still missing. In the center of the main façade is the clock, surmounted by a statue of a young woman seated on a throne, symbolizing 'The City of Paris'. The sculptor was Jean Gauthien. She is flanked by Ernest Miolle's *Education* and *Work*, with *The Seine* and *The Marne* by Ainé Millet on either side.

The interior

Artists well known at the time of the Third Republic shared the huge program of pictorial commissions.

The Salle des Fêtes (Ballroom): its dimensions (164 × 43ft./50m × 43m) make it reminiscent of Galerie des Glaces at Versailles. High arcades support a gallery (now condemned) intended for spectators at balls. Caryatids by Blanchard and Boucher; depictions of the Provinces of France in the spandrels; cottered ceilings by Henry Lévy, G. Fernier, B. Constant and Gervex; 24 crystal chandeliers by Baccarat. The fine simplicity of composition and coloring of the murals *Summer* and *Winter* by Puvis de Chavannes are much admired. He also painted the ceiling of the grand staircase, known as the Escalier du Préfet: Victor Hugo offering his lyre to the City of Paris. The Salon des Arcades (Arcade Room) is formed of triple chambers joined by richly decorated arcades. In the Salon des Sciences: views of Paris, by Lépine; portraits of French scientists. In the Salon des Arts: painting by Léon Glaize; ceiling by Layraud: *Apollo astride Pegasus*. The Salon des Lettres displays portraits of Victor Hugo, Molière, Michelet and Descartes; fireplace decorated by J. C. Thomas; painting by J. Lefèvre. The Galerie Galland, named after the artist, contains paintings illustrating different manual trades. The Salon Lobau: in the antechamber: *Entry of Louis XI into Paris*, by Tattegrain. In the reception room, important paintings of the story of Paris, by J. P. Laurens: *Etienne Marcel saving the life of the Dauphin, Louis VI giving Paris its first Charter, The Great Revolt of the Maillotins, Anne Dubourg and Henri VI, The Arrest of Councillor Broussel, The Reception of Louis XIV at the Hôtel de Ville on 17 July 1789*, and a *Bust of The Republic* by Rodin. In the glass case, signatures of the various heads of state received at the Hôtel de Ville. Central showcase: coat of arms of the City of Paris, with the three decorations awarded to the City of Paris: the Légion d'Honneur, the Croix de Guerre and the Croix de la Libération, bestowed by General de Gaulle on April 2, 1945.

▷ Remains of the former Hôtel de Ville

The fire of 1871 destroyed an important collection of paintings, sculptures, *objets d'art* and documents housed in the Hôtel de Ville.

However, some important pieces were saved and are kept in certain museums. The bronze statue of Louis XIV by Coysevox is in the main hall of the Musée Carnavalet, which also has a bronze of Charlemagne dating from the 10th c., a 16th-c. ceiling-rose, a bronze bas-relief by Lemaire that decorated the tympanum of the main doorway, as well as a coving of this door with the monogram of François I.

Various Paris gardens have received architectural remnants of the building. A few may be seen in the Parc Monceau; the Trocadéro Garden has a pretty Renaissance dormer window frame and, in the Sq. Paul-Langevin, two statues from the façade by Jean Aubry and Pierre de Violle are displayed in their respective niches. Unfortunately they were decapitated during the demonstrations of May 1968.

▷ Tragedies and ceremonies

Riots and festivities succeeded one another in the history of this building.

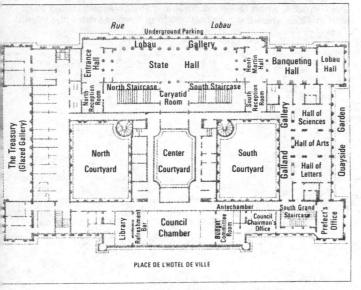

L'Hotel de Ville

First, in 1332, was the revolt of the Maillotins. Etienne Marcel himself was executed for rebelling against royal power in 1357. The 17th c. saw the war of the Fronde. On July 17, 1789 Louis XVI was forced to kiss the tricolor cockade held by Bailly, then mayor of Paris. On July 27, 1794 Robespierre was arrested here and taken to the guillotine the next day. The revolutionary days of 1830 witnessed the stout resistance of the Swiss Royal Guard. It was here in 1848 that Lamartine repulsed the rioters. On October 31, during the siege of Paris, Communard insurgents invaded the Hôtel de Ville where, on March 26, 1871, the Commune was created. On May 24, 1871 the Communards destroyed the building by setting fire to it. In August 1944 the reconstructed building became the headquarters of the uprising of the forces of the Resistance against the German troops of occupation: the Resistance fighters occupied the building and held it against the occupying Germans for five days, until relieved by General Leclerc's division.

Splendid festivities took place at the Hôtel de Ville from the First Empire onwards: in 1810, for the marriage of Napoléon to Marie-Louise; in 1811, for the birth of the King of Rome; in 1814, for the entry into Paris of Louis XVIII; and in 1825 for the coronation of Charles X. In the Second Empire two memorable celebrations were held: in 1854, when Queen Victoria and Prince Albert visited Paris, and in 1856, when the crowned heads of Europe visited the World Fair.

The district of Les Invalides***

7th arr./Map ref. 15–A1, A3
Métro and RER: Invalides
Bus: 28, 49, 63, 69, 83
Parking: Rue de Constantine and Rue Faber
Taxis: opposite 110 Rue de l'Université. Tel. 47–05–03–14
Market: Ave. de Saxe, from Ave. de Ségur to Place Breteuil (Thurs., Sun., 7am–1:30pm).

'Peace lies in the shadow of the sword.' Of all the districts of Paris, this Chinese proverb would apply most aptly to the area between the Hôtel des Invalides and the Ecole Militaire, where the names of the avenues commemorate famous soldiers. It is one of the most airy and tranquil parts of the capital, due to its many green spaces and careful traffic management. Its broad, well-lit, tree-lined streets spread out from the Hôtel des Invalides, a veritable city within the city, still radiant with the austere pomp of the Grand Siècle.

From the era when the nobility began to build their *hôtels* here the district has maintained its residential character. Former convents have been turned into hospitals or places of learning, and few people walk along its sleepy pavements.

Tour of Les Invalides

2 hrs.

The Esplanade des Invalides

The esplanade was laid out in 1704 according to plans by Robert de

Cotte, who turned part of the former Pré-aux-Clercs into a huge square with lawns, surrounded by trees. The statue of a lion brought back from Venice in 1797 by Bonaparte, stood here for nearly 20 years but in 1815 the Austrians reclaimed it and returned it to its column at the entrance to the Piazzetta of Venice. The esplanade, 533yds./487m long and 274yds./250m wide, reveals a superb view* over the quays, the Pont Alexandre-III, and the part of the Ave. Winston-Churchill between the Grand and Petit Palais. The esplanade has recently been redesigned: the streets crossing it enclose large grass spaces and the malls have been replanted with silvery lime trees.

The Rue Fabert runs down the W side of the esplanade, with the Finnish Embassy at no. 2, built in 1965 by J. Goldsberg, and the Austrian Embassy at no. 6. At the NW corner stands the Gare des Invalides, interrupting the view from the esplanade. The building, by Lisch, was erected for the 1900 Exhibition. In 1945 Bigot converted it into the Air France headquarters (booking office and bus station for Orly airport) and it now serves the RER Line C, which runs beneath it. The N façade of Les Invalides is framed by two small squares: the Square d'Ajaccio to the E, with the monument of *Taine et la Défense du Foyer* (Taine and the Defense of the Home), and the Square Santiago-du-Chili to the W.

In the Place Santiago-du-Chili, beside it, statue of Vauban by H. Bouchard (1960).

☐ The Hôtel Royal des Invalides***

Entrance to the main courtyard: Esplanade des Invalides; open daily 10am–7pm. Tel. 45–55–92–30.

The Hôtel and the church together occupy a site of 1,360,000sq.ft./ 126,990m², the N façade is 640ft./195m long. The building houses the Musée de l'Armée, the Musée de l'Histoire de la BDIC, the Musée des Villes-Maquettes (Urban Relief Maps and Plans), and the Musée de l'Ordre de la Libération (→ Museums). It also houses Napoleon's tomb, and so has innumerable links with the history of France and its military annals.

The construction of the *hôtel*, between 1671 and 1676, was the major work of Libéral Bruant, who had already built La Salpêtrière. Bruant's work is austere, but of incomparable majesty. From 1677 onwards Jules Hardouin-Mansart took over the project, as he did for Le Vau at Versailles.

History of the Hôtel des Invalides

The establishment of Les Invalides dates back to Louis XIV. Before him, despite the similar plans of Henri IV and Louis XIII, no special hospital existed for soldiers disabled in the king's service, who, if they were lucky, were taken into monasteries as lay brothers and if not, had to beg. An edict of May 24, 1670 ordered the building of the *hôtel* and another detailed edict of April 1674 founded the institution and detailed its organization. There was soon a large number of inmates, from 5000 to 7000, presided over by a governor. Louis XIV visited the *hôtel* several times, an example followed by visiting sovereigns; the annals mention visits by Peter the Great in 1712 and Gustavus III of Sweden in 1770. The Hôtel des Invalides is the residence of the military governor of Paris, while the *hôtel*'s Commandant Général is responsible for its 32 acres/13ha.

From the beginning of the 20th c. the site has been virtually invaded by numerous army services, and unsightly new buildings have ruined the harmony of its design. André Malraux instigated a restoration program in 1962, and under the direction of J.-P. Paquet, the chief architect of the Department of Historical Monuments, the original character was restored to this admirable group of buildings. Bertrand Mouet and Jean-Claude Rochette are continuing this restoration program. The buildings around de Cotte's pavilion (restored in 1971) have been knocked down so that it can be properly admired, and on the site of a former military cemetery a French-style lawn has been laid, surrounded by dry moats; the stone dressing of Mansart's original moats is still intact.

The exterior

The N. side. The Hôtel des Invalides is separated from the esplanade by dry moats supported by walls to form fortifications in Vauban's style, punctuated here and there by bossages and ending in half-moon formations. Two stone pavilions, set on either side of the entrance gate, display the coat of arms of Louis XIV and are topped by sculpted pomegranates. Inside, a large number of old cannon taken in battle have been placed on the ramparts; their casting is magnificent and most are beautifully decorated. The finest are the 18 cannon of the Batterie Triomphale and, among them, the eight pieces in the series of the Twelve Apostles, cast in 1708 for Frederick I, king of Prussia, brought back from Vienna by Bonaparte. Removed by the Germans in 1940, they were returned in 1946. It was these cannons that, by Imperial decree, saluted the victories of the French armies. Between the rampart of the façade of the buildings is a forecourt with formal French gardens, crossed, in a radial pattern, by five footpaths.

The façade*, restored in 1962, 640ft/195m long, of great purity of line and stylistic simplicity, has four storeys. In the center a magnificent portal projects slightly in a graceful curve; the façade terminates in a pavilion at either end, each adorned with carved stone trophies. On the ground floor, 45 arched doors and windows are surmounted by grotesque mascarons. A cornice runs across the façade at the second storey; above it, the attic storey has dormer windows in the form of trophies. The central pavilion has four paired

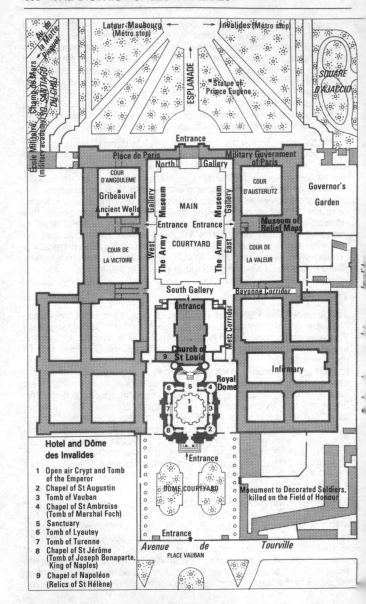

Latour-Maubourg (Métro stop)   Invalides (Métro stop)

SQUARE D'AJACCIO

ESPLANADE

Av. de la Motte Picquet

Champ-de-Mars (military academy) BD. SANTIAGO DU CHILI

École Militaire (military academy)

Statue of Prince Eugene

Entrance

Place de Paris

Military Government of Paris

North   Gallery

COUR D'ANGOULÊME

Gribeauval

Ancient Wells

COUR D'AUSTERLITZ

Governor's Garden

Museum Gallery

MAIN

Museum Gallery

West Gallery

Entrance   Entrance

Main Entrance

COURTYARD

East Gallery

Museum of Relief Maps

The Army

The Army

COUR DE LA VICTOIRE

COUR DE LA VALEUR

South Gallery

Bayonne Corridor

Entrance

Metz Corridor

Church of St Louis

9

6   5   4

7   1   3

8   2

Royal Dome

Infirmary

Hotel and Dôme des Invalides

1 Open air Crypt and Tomb of the Emperor
2 Chapel of St Augustin
3 Tomb of Vauban
4 Chapel of St Ambroise (Tomb of Marshal Foch)
5 Sanctuary
6 Tomb of Lyautey
7 Tomb of Turenne
8 Chapel of St Jérôme (Tomb of Joseph Bonaparte, King of Naples)
9 Chapel of Napoléon (Relics of St Hélène)

Entrance

DÔME COURTYARD

Monument to Decorated Soldiers, killed on the Field of Honour

Entrance

Avenue   de   Tourville
PLACE VAUBAN

Ionic pilasters supporting a flattened arch at the height of the roof, decorated profusely with trophies. The arch frames an equestrian bas-relief of Louis XIV supported by *Prudence* and *Justice*, by Coustou (1735). This bas-relief of Louis XIV in the costume of a Roman general was produced by Cartellier in 1815 after the original was destroyed during the Revolution. Below the pilasters, two colossal statues of *Mars* and *Minerva* frame this magnificent entrance; the originals, by Guillaume I Coustou, were replaced in 1966 by copies. The doors of the three arches of the entrance are in carved wood. The portal is topped by a head of Hercules. The main arch connecting the forecourt to the great courtyard is open to the public; it forms a vestibule supported by four freestanding and 12 engaged Ionic columns.

The main courtyard*, also known as the Cour Royale, is impressive in size (335ft/102m long by 207ft/63m wide), and is used during military parades. Its four sides, each broken by a central pavilion with a triangular pediment, comprise at ground and first floors galleries of wide semicircular arches, forming porticoes. Perhaps this monastic aspect recalls the convents that previously sheltered the disabled soldiers. The dormer windows of the roof again take the form of trophies, all different. Each corner of the courtyard has a square projection surmounted by a group of horses. On the E side, the fifth dormer window (to the r. of the central pavilion) is an architectural pun on the name of the Superintendent of Buildings responsible for the creation of Les Invalides, Louvois: the round window lies between the paws of a wolf – hence *'loup voit'* ('the wolf sees').

In the pediment of the N side an astronomical clock tells the time at the meridian of the *hôtel*, which is marked out by a line of paving stones. The main pavilion on the S side, where two colonnades, one Ionic and one Corinthian, are superimposed, and the arms of France appear in the pediment, is the façade of the Soldiers' Church. In the upper central arch stands the statue of Napoleon as the *Petit Caporal* by Seurre, which from 1833 to 1836 stood on top of the Vendôme Column. The buildings on either side of the courtyard that give on to the E and W galleries house the Musée de l'Armée (→ Museums). In the galleries and courtyard are several very fine old cannons, note especially those in the S gallery. The entrance to the Soldiers' Church is in the center of this gallery.

⚓ The Church of Saint-Louis-des-Invalides (Soldiers' Church)

Open daily 10am–5:45pm in summer; 10am–4:45pm in winter. Mass on Sun.

This church, probably built by Hardouin-Mansart (1679–1708), from designs by Libéral Bruant, has three naves, the two aisles of which are surmounted by galleries. The church is 230ft/754m long and 72ft/23m wide.

The interior*

A balustrade gallery is hung with enemy banners taken in battle. During the night of May 30, 1814 as the Allies entered Paris, Marshal Serurier, Governor of the Invalides, burned over 1400 enemy flags in the courtyard of the Hôtel. Those that remain come from the Senate and the Legislative Corps, who received them as gifts from Napoleon. There are also many flags from foreign campaigns.

The Great Organ (4800 pipes), a magnificent instrument, built by Alexandre Thierry at the end of the 17th c. in a loft designed by Hardouin-Mansart, was completely restored in 1957. The white marble pulpit, with gilded relief, dates from the Restoration. The first performance of Berlioz's *Grande Messe des Morts* (Grand Mass for the Dead) was given here.

In the r. aisle are a chapel and a monument to those generals who fell in battle in World War I. In front of this is a hollow stone from the Sacred Way (Via Sacra) enclosing earth brought from the battlefields of that war. In front of the l. aisle chapel is a similar stone, from the Voie de la Liberté (Road of Liberty) containing earth brought from the N American burial grounds of World War II. Behind the pulpit is an altar dedicated to the memory of those who died during the Indo-Chinese war. The Napoléon Chapel contains three stone slabs from the tomb at St. Helena and the copper sarcophagus and velvet pall used to carry Napoléon's ashes in 1840. There is also a plaster death mask of the Emperor, cast by Antomarchi.

Numerous tombs rest in the vaults: Marshals Jourdan, Moncey, Mouton, Oudinot; Marshal Bessières, the Duc d'Istrie; Marshal Mortier and the victims of the Fieschi assassination attempt on Louis Philippe on July 28, 1835; Marshal Vallée; Admiral Duperré, Marshal Sérurier, Marshal Grouchy, Marshals Bugeaud, Sébastiani, Gérard, Exelmans, Saint-Arnaud, MacMahon, Canrobert, who, in turn, were Chiefs of Staff in World War I. The last to join them, Marshal Franchet d'Esperey (d. 1942), former Commander-in-Chief of the Eastern Army; General Guillaumat (d. 1940) former Commander-in-Chief of the Army of the Rhine, Generals d'Amade (d. 1941) and Gouraud (d. 1946). Marshal Leclerc, liberator of Paris and Strasbourg was also interred here on December 8, 1947; General Giraud in March 1949 and Marshal Juin, victor at Monte Casino, in 1967. The vaults also contain the ashes of Rouget de Lisle, author of *La Marseillaise*, transferred on July 14, 1915 from the cemetery at Choisy-le-Roi; the hearts of Kléber and General Négrier, and also of Mlle de Sombreuil, who threw herself into the midst of the mob during the September riots of 1792 to save her father's life.

The Dôme des Invalides**

Open daily Oct.-Mar 10am-5pm April-Sept. 10am-6pm; June, July, Aug. 10am-7pm.

In the r.-hand corner of the Church of Saint-Louis is the entrance to the corridor of Metz, an extension of the E gallery of the main courtyard. It leads to a small courtyard which gives access to the main courtyard of the Dome. The formal French gardens complement the church's magnificent façade. It was built as a Chapel Royal for the Saint-Louis church.

Begun in 1679 by J. Hardouin-Mansart, but finished only in 1706, it is the most beautiful dome in France and forms a regal crown to Bruand's edifice. It marks the climax of an architectural endeavour which began at the Carmelite church, Saint-Joseph de Carmes, and was developed further at the Sorbonne and Val-de-Grâce. Louis Hautecoeur has shown that Hardouin-Mansart was inspired by designs made by his great-uncle, François Mansart, which had been submitted for the Bourbon chapel at Saint-Denis (1664).

The exterior

The rather sober façade consists of two superimposed orders of Doric and Corinthian columns, surmounted by a triangular pediment. In the niches on either side of the entrance are statues of Charlemagne and St Louis by Coysevox and Coustou. On the upper level are statues, on the l. of *Might* and *Justice*; on the r., of *Temperance* and *Prudence*, also by Coysevox. Above this base the dome rises, resting on a bipartite drum with wide bays and Corinthian columns, flanked by eight projecting arches and an attic storey decorated with a balustrade and pierced with semi-circular windows. The dome is formed of 12 great, gilded sections framing war trophies. It is roofed in lead and surmounted by a pierced lantern and a pinnacle. It was last regilded for the Exposition Universelle (World Fair) in 1937.

The interior*

Its square plan in the form of a Greek cross with a central dome is reminiscent of St Peter's in Rome while the three successive bays of the façade are a further expression of the Baroque style. The proportions, the emphasis on painted decoration, the sculptures and rich mosaic pavements dating from Louis XIV together make this building an architectural masterpiece. A circular glass gallery, designed by Visconti, gives a view of the crypt and Napoleon's tomb.

The tomb of Napoléon* is an imposing monument, designed by Visconti (1843). It has more symbolic value than architectural merit; 13ft/4m long, 6½ft/2m wide and 14ft/4.5m high, the sarcophagus is made from red Finnish porphyry and rests on a base of green Vosges granite. It is surrounded by 12 colossal Neo-Hellenic figures representing Napoléon's victories, among the last works by Pradier.

Decoration of the Dome. On the pendentives, bas-reliefs of the four Evangelists by Charles de Lafosse; on the entablature below the windows, sculptured medallions of the most important French kings; above the windows, panels of the Apostles painted by Jouvenet. In the center of the Dome, a painting of St Louis delivering up his sword to Christ. Inspired by the plans for the Bourbon funeral chapel, this dome was the first to have a central opening, allowing a view through to a secondary dome.

R. side Saint-Augustine Chapel: tomb of Joseph Bonaparte, Napoléon's elder brother and King of Naples (d. 1844). Six paintings and cupola by Louis de Boullongne. Central bay: a cenotaph commemorating Vauban (1807) containing the Marshal's heart; *Science* and *War*, by Etex. Overdoors; bas-reliefs showing St Louis directing the construction of the Quinz-Vingts and the *Taking of Damietta*. Chapel of Saint-Ambrose: the tomb of Marshal Foch (d. 1929), an imposing monument in bronze by Landowski (1937). The sarcophagus contains the mortal remains of the Marshal, the plinth has a group of eight helmeted soldiers carrying his funerary statue on a shield of laurel leaves.

Chancel. High altar in marble with an interesting baldachin dating from the time of Louis Philippe: above and behind, the *Assumption* and in the vault, the *Holy Trinity*, painted by N. Coypel. Behind the High Altar a glass door gives a view of the interior of the Church of Saint-Louis. On either side of the High Altar stairs lead to the entrance of the crypt housing Napoléon's tomb. At either side of the entrance mausoleums contain the remains of Marshals Bertrand and Duroc, who followed Napoléon to St. Helena.

The Crypt. The bronze crypt door is flanked by two colossal statues of *Civil* and *Military Might* by Duret. The inscription on the impost may be translated as: 'I desire that my body be laid to rest on the banks of the Seine, among the French people whom I have so loved.' This was the Emperor's last wish. The Emperor's tomb is by Jouffroy. The gallery surrounding the sarcophagus is decorated with ten bas-reliefs after Simart, illustrating the greatest achievements of Napoléon. In the crypt where, beneath a simple slab, lies 'l'Aiglon' (Napoléon II) is a statue of Napoléon in coronation robes in white gilded marble by Simart.

L. side. Chapel of Saint-Grégoire: tomb of Marshal Lyantery (d. 1934) whose ashes were brought back from Rabat on May 10, 1961 and placed here on March 22, 1963: the bronze sarcophagus is by the master iron-worker R. Subes. It stands on two marble pedestals. (A. Laprade, architect; 1962). Six paintings by Gabriel Doyen, a pupil of Carle Van Loo. In a niche an urn contains the heart of La Tour d'Auvergne (d. 1800) who is buried in the Panthéon.

Central bay: the tomb of Turenne*, designed by Le Brun, made by Tuby, shows *Wisdom with the Crown of Thorns* and *St Louis Curing the Sick*; this tomb was transferred here from Saint-Denis on Napoléon's orders. Chapel of Saint-Jérôme: the tomb of Jérôme, youngest brother of Napoleon and king of Westphalia (statue by Guillaume). The ashes of Napoléon ('l'Aiglon' as he was called after Rostand had made him the eponymous hero of his drama) were brought from Vienna and placed in the chapel by the Germans in 1940. On December 18, 1969 they were put in the crypt.

Hôpital des Invalides

The Hospital and Rest Home of Les Invalides stand on either side of the domed façade. The dispensary of the Institution Royale is still within the hospital. Attractive woodwork in the Capuchin style is complemented by antique pharmaceutical jars; they frame Parmentier's famous works. During Louis XVI's reign Parmentier assumed the position of apothecary, and his laboratory can be found here. The Hospital itself is one of the most advanced in Paris, specializing in the care of wounded veterans.

General de Gaulle donated a pool for physiotherapy.

Tour of the district

Place Vauban

The court of the Dome opens onto the semicircular Place Vauban adorned with monuments to Marshal Fayolle (1852–1928) and Marshal Gallieni (1849–1916), both by Jean Boucher.

The Ave. de Tourville: no. 4, designed in 1891 by the architect Dutarque and decorated by the sculptor Laurier and the statue, (sculptor Fossé), is an excellent example of Second Empire eclecticism with its exotic flavor of Moorish arches on the first-floor strengthened by many-colored stained-glass windows.

Boulevard des Invalides

To the Church of Saint-François-Xavier

This impressive boulevard was created between 1704 and 1761. It runs beside the gardens of the Hôtel Biron, now the Rodin Museum (→ Museums) and the Lycée Victor-Duruy which, at no. 33, occupies part of the site of the old Couvent des Dames du Sacré-Coeur de Jésus. At no. 35, the Roussel Laboratories replaced the Hôtel Vertillac-Rohan some 30 years ago. From this pavement, looking through the railings, the beautiful façades of two grand houses are visible, the Hôtel de Bourbon-Condé and the Hôtel

Montesquiou-Fezensac (see nos. 12 and 20 Rue Monsieur) and, on the corner of the Rue Oudinot, the Brongniart town house (see no. 22 Rue Oudinot).

⚱ The Church of Saint-François-Xavier

12 Place du Président Mithouard; open daily Tel: 47–88–32–12.

A good example of late 19th-c. architecture, the church was begun in 1861 by Adrien Lusson and completed in 1874 by Joseph Uchard. The design of the façade is Italian Renaissance in inspiration.

The interior. In the 2nd chapel on the r. is a beautiful *Last Supper* painted by Henri Lerolle (1894). The cupola over the crossing is decorated with the *Four Prophets* by Elie Delaunay (1876) and the *Twelve Apostles* by Alexandre Denuelle. At the base of the arch of the choir *Angels* by Alexandre Falquière. The vestry, where weddings are solemnized, contains Tintoretto's *Last Supper.* Inquiries can be made at the sacristy to the l. of the choir. In the 2nd chapel on the r. of the retrochoir (behind the high altar) the *Crucifixion of St Peter* by Luca Giordano (mid-17th c.). In the Mass Sacristy *The Holy Family* by Lubin Baugin.

Boulevard des Invalides, continued

In front of the Church of Saint-François-Xavier stands a monument to François Coppée with a medallion by Saupique (1959). At the E end of the church in the Place Denys-Cochin is a new statue of General Mangin (1866–1925) by Raymond Martin (1954) replacing that of Réal del Sarte, melted down during the German occupation. At no. 52 pause to admire the superb garden façade of the Hôtel Masserano with its fluted pilasters. Its entrance is in no. 9 Rue Masseran. Brongniart built the house in 1787 for the Prince de Masserano, Spanish Ambassador to France in 1805, later Grand Master of Ceremonies to Joseph Bonaparte. The house contains a superb salon decorated with Louis XV woodwork brought from the mansion of Baron de Gargan (22 Place Vendome). It was described in the novel *La bal du comte d'Orgel* (1924) by Raymond Radiguet.

At no. 5 Rue Duroc the Valentin Haüy Association for the Blind is a society for mutual assistance where unsighted people can work. A shop inside the building sells their handiwork (brushes, basketwork, knitwear and other goods).

▣ The Valentin-Haüy Museum is in the same building (→Museums) with a library concerning the History of the Blind (open Thurs. 2pm–5pm).

Institut National des Jeunes Aveugles (National Institute for Blind Children)

56 Boul. des Invalides

This Institute was founded in 1793 by Valetin Haüy, the first inventor of raised characters which allowed the blind to read. Louis Braille (1809–52), inventor of the system of reading which bears his name, died in this building.

The mansion was built by Philippon in the 19th c. and is decorated with a carved pediment by Jouffroy. The chapel contains important paintings by Henri Lehman (visits by request). A statue of Valentin Haüy stands in the middle of the courtyard. The collection of the Musée Historique Louis Braille (tel. 45–67–35–08.) traces the education of young visually handicapped people since the 18th c.

Opposite, at 84–88 Rue de Sèvres, stood the famous Couvent des Oiseaux, '*Collège des filles gracieuses de l'artistocratie*' ('A school for the charming daughters of the aristocracy', as Jules Vallès called it). On its site and cutting across two blind alleys are the Ave. Daniel Lesueur and the Ave. Constant-Coquelin. Follow the Rue de Sevres W.

Hôpital Necker – Hôpital des Enfants-Malades (Hospital for Sick Children)

At nos. 149–151 the Necker-Enfants Malades complex is one of the biggest hospitals in Paris (907 beds), famed chiefly for its care of patients with kidney diseases. It is also an important teaching and University center (CHU). The two hospitals are side by side, but under the same management since 1921 (entrance at no. 149). A hospital was founded here in 1724 in the buildings of an old educational institution, La Maison Royale de l'Enfant Jésus. An inscription can still be read on the façade: 'Hôpital des Enfants Malades' (Hospital for Sick Children); 200 beds were made available for children under 15 years of age, and in 1808 an innovative move was made in separating the acutely and chronically sick from those with contagious diseases. The Necker Hospital at no. 151 stands on the site of the former Benedictine nunnery of Notre-Dame-de-Liesse. The community was suppressed, and Necker, with the support of the curate of Saint-Sulpice, founded in 1779 a Hospice for the parishioners of both Saint-Sulpice and Gros Caillou. There were to be 120 beds, with no more than one patient per bed, and it was this hospice which became in 1802 the Necker Hospital, directed for a time by Mme Necker. Laennec taught here from 1816 to 1823 during which time he discovered auscultation (examination by sound). A plaque with his bust commemorating his invention of the stethoscope is visible from the street.

Rue Maurice-de-la-Sizeranne opens onto the front of the two

hospitals. At no. 8, note a charming little country pleasure house whose entrance used to be at 90 Rue de Sèvres. The façade and pediment of this 18th-c. mansion can be admired through the railings. During the 19th c. it housed the novices of the Sisters of Saint-André. Today it is the Sainte-Jeanne-Elizabeth school. Return to the Rue de Sèvres.

Ave. de Saxe on the r. recalls the name of the famous Marshal, illegitimate son of the king of Poland, who led the armies of Louis XV to victory at Fontenoy. Foch lived at no. 52 in 1918.

Place de Breteuil

This square opens onto a splendid view along the avenue of the same name. Lined with trees, lawns and flower-beds, it was cut through the axis of the Dôme des Invalides in 1680. In the center of the square, Pasteur's monument was the last important work by Falguière, erected in 1904 by national subscription, on the site of ancient artesian wells. Around the pedestal unrolls a massive sculpture of figures modelled in the round: 'Workers of the Fields enjoy in peace those benefits obtained for them by the great wisdom of Pasteur which protects them from death.'

Continue along the Ave. de Saxe to where it joins the Ave. de Ségur, where André Masson lived, and where you will see the monumental building of the Ministry of Post and Telecommunications (1935–38).

Place de Fontenoy

This beautiful semicircular *place* with trees planted in alternate rows, is in front of the majestic courtyard of the Ecole Militaire (Tour Eiffel district). A pyramid with curving sides stands in the center, a memorial to officers and other ranks who died in the defense of their country. On its NE side the square is bordered by the Ministry of Public Health and Social Security (L. Aublat, 1930) and the Ministry of Transport and the Merchant Service (interesting building by Ventre, 1932). The Unesco building is to the SW.

☐ UNESCO*

7 Place de Fontenoy (closed Sat. and Sun, open Mon to Fri. 9am-noon and 2–5pm). Tel. 45–68–03–59.

Headquarters of the United Nations' Educational, Scientific and Cultural Organization, the UNESCO building occupies 7 acres/3ha contained between the Place de Fontenoy and the Ave. de Saxe, the Ave. de Ségur, Ave. de Suffren and Ave. Lowendal. Built between

1955 and 1958 by the architects Breuer (USA), Nervi (Italy) and Zehrfuss (France), this vast complex of four buildings was conceived as an international attempt at capturing the artistic and architectural mood of the mid-20th c. It was inaugurated on November 3, 1958.

UNESCO's aim is to 'contribute to the maintenance of peace and security by encouraging, through education, science and culture, cooperation between nations to ensure universal respect for justice, law, and the fundamental rights and liberties of all, without distinctions of race, sex, language or creed, rights which the Charter of the United Nations recognizes for all people'. These fundamental goals are declared in the Act of Constitution, negotiated in London in 1945 by the representatives of 44 nations, convened at the initiative of the United Kingdom and France. The Organization was officially created a year later, in Paris, when 20 countries ratified the Constitutional Act. In November 1958 at the opening of the new session, the number of member-states rose to 87, and today stands at 161.

The Buildings

The architects' use of the most advanced techniques has produced a balanced project which blends admirably with its site. The exceptional handling of the precast concrete gives it the quality of a more noble medium. The main building houses the Secretariat*; seven storeys high (92ft/28.5m) and Y-shaped supported on piles. Its three façades are slightly concave, 407ft/124m, 446ft/136m, and 486ft/148m long. This arrangement has allowed the completion of the semicircle behind the Ecole Militaire on the Place de Fontenoy planned by Gabriel. On this N façade, travertine (a type of marble) facings surround the windows, and on the two other sides a complicated network of vertical and horizontal anti-glare laminations, and grey glass sun-filters have been used. The three sides together have a total of 1068 windows and 87,300 sq.ft/8109m² of glazed surfaces. In the center of the Ségur façade the fire escape rises in an airy spiral, its 151 steps encircling the central water pipe. The entire Secretariat rests on 72 massive concrete pillars, with an immense ground-floor hall set between them, paved with Norwegian quartzite. The decoration on this storey was carried out by three painters: Afro (Italy), Apper (Netherlands), and Matta (Chile) and the French photographer Brassaï, whose gigantic photographic enlargement decorates the restaurant.

A lobby links the Hall with the building containing the conference rooms (35,300 sq.ft/3282m²) which is set into the angle formed by the Ave. de Segur and the Ave. de Suffren. This building, trapezoidal in form, is only 46ft/14m high. It is one of the purest expressions of the use of concrete in building. Its framework is that of a double portico in the shape of an M; its 229ft/70m central projection rests on six columns. Its walls are of fluted concrete and the accordion-pleated roof is ribbed in copper. It houses the Plenary Sessions Chamber (1000 seats), the Great Commission Chamber which is decorated with a large fresco by the Mexican Tamayo: *Prometheus presenting Man with Fire*, and there are six committee rooms. The Hall is decorated with a vast composition (262 sq.ft/80m²) by Pablo Picasso. Painted on wood, it symbolizes the victory of the forces of Light and Peace over those of Death and Evil. Fourteen member countries are in charge of the management, decoration and furnishing of the headquarters building, which makes it a truly international museum of the modern decorative arts.

The third, small, cubic building to the E, in the angle formed by the Ave. de Saxe and Ave. de Segur is four storeys high and is reserved for permanent delegations and non-governmental organizations (NGOs). On one of its outside walls at ground-level, a mosaic by Bazaine overlooks a charming Japanese garden, designed by Isamu Noguchi, which borders the Ave. de Ségur. It contains 88tons/80tonnes of rocks, a stream, and an ornamental lake with a bridge. On one large stone with a splashing fountain, the Japanese character for 'peace' has been engraved.

On the W, bordered by the Ave. de Suffren and Ave. de Lowendal, a wide piazza opens out, whose most striking feature is the great entrance to the secretariat annex sheltered by a porch roof, whose form resembles a nun's coif. The piazza is adorned with a giant black steel mobile (32ft/10m) high by Calder, and a monumental *Reclining Figure* by the English sculptor Henry Moore in travertine marble. The two walls set at right-angles and at the end, towards the waiting hall, are covered by two large compositions by Miró, executed on ceramic by Artigas, *Sun* and *Moon* (Winner of the Guggenheim Award, 1958).

In 1963, faced with an increase in the number of member countries and an extension of the organization's activities (2000 people work in Paris alone), the construction of two floors underground was undertaken, supplied with natural light from six low level patios, (architect, Bernard Zehrfuss). Inaugurated in November 1965, it was decorated by the landscape artist Burke Marx (Brazil). In the patio in front of the Executive Council Chamber is the model of the admirable monument to Sibelius, by Eila Hiltunen, which is in Helsinki. The model was given by the Finnish government in 1967. In the hall which links the two buildings is a bronze high-relief by Jean Arp, and tapestries by Lurçat and Le Corbusier.

On the 99,200 sq.ft/9,220m² of land donated by the French government, other buildings include no. 1 Rue Miollis (15 arrondissement), used as an annex. Designed by B. Zehrfuss, these buildings are constructed on a concrete sub-foundation with steel structure and white-paneled cladding.

> Napoléon's Ashes returned to France

'I desire that my body be laid to rest on the banks of the Seine, among the French people whom I have so loved.' This was Napoléon's last wish as written in his will, and to fulfil it, Louis-Philippe decided to return Napoléon's ashes to Paris. After seven years of negotiation with England, the king of France was authorized to send his son, the Prince de Joinville, to St Helena to bring back the Emperor's body. The funeral took place on December 15, 1840, in a flurry of snow which ceased only when the funeral cortège reached the Invalides. 'Suddenly the cannons fired, simultaneously from three different points on the horizon making a superbly powerful triangle of sound. Drums beat distantly in the fields. The Emperor's funeral carriage appeared. The sun, veiled until that moment, re-appeared at the same time. The effect was stupendous.' (Victor Hugo)

Museums to visit

Army Museum (Hôtel des Invalides): Military history, weapons and historic objects.

Museum of Relief Maps and Plans (Hôtel des Invalides): Collections of models of strongholds and ports, and plans of the fortifications by Vauban, from the 17th c. until modern times.

Museum of the History of the B.D.I.C. (Hôtel des Invalides): Artistic and historic documents from the 20th c.

Museum of the Order of Liberation (51 *bis* Boul. de Latour-Maubourg): Documents, uniforms and objects concerning the Resistance, Free France and the deportation.

Rodin Museum (5 Rue Duroc).

Louis Braille Historic Museum (56 Boul. des Invalides): Apparatus and documents concerning the history of the visually handicapped.

> Aptly named streets

Many of the streets around the Invalides near the Military Academy were named after the most famous military leaders of the Monarchy.

From the region of Louis XIV, Duquesne (1610–88), who fought with distinction against the Dutch in the Mediterranean; Vice-Admiral d'Estrées (1624–1707), who took Cayenne from them; Marshal Vauban (1633–1707), who surrounded the kingdom with fortifications; Admiral de Tourville (1642–1701); and Marshal Villars (1653–

1734), who won the decisive victory of Denain in 1712 during the Wars of the Spanish Succession, are all commemorated.

From the reign of Louis XV, both Lieutenant-General Chevert (1695–1769) and Marshal de Saxe, who demonstrated their strategic skills during the War of the Austrian Succession, are commemorated; as are La Bourdonnais (1699–1753), Governor of the Iles de France and Bourbon; Marshal de Lowendal (1700–1755), who distinguished himself at the Battle of Fontenoy in 1745; and Vice-Admiral de Suffren (1729–1788), who fought against the English in the United States and India.

From the region of Louis XVI, Lieutenant-General La Motte-Picquet (1720–91), who fought brilliantly during the American War of Independence.

The Italie district

13th arr./Map ref. 24–C3
Métro: Italie.
Bus: 27, 47, 57, 67, 83
Parking: Ave. d'Italie
Taxis: corner of Ave. d'Italie. Tel: 45–86–00–44.

An aerial view of Paris would show that only two districts are distinguished by their skyscrapers: the areas round the Place d'Italie and the Front de Seine (15th arr.). In the latter case, tower blocks have risen between the Seine and the old factories along the Quai Citroën; in the former district they have pushed into the heart of an old *quartier*, giving rise to strong contrasts.

A contrast, for example, between the past and the present at Butte-aux-Cailles to the W, with its rustic, evocative street names – Rue des Peupliers (poplars), Rue du Champ-de-l'Alouette (field of larks) and so on – evidence that before becoming a great metropolis Paris was a collection of villages. To the E, on the other hand, large groups of tower blocks have completely altered the urban fabric of 19th-c. Paris. A contrast also in the pace of life – Butte-aux-Cailles seems drowsy and provincial compared to the frantic activity of the Ave. d'Italie, Ave. de Choisy and Ave. d'Ivry. The Place d'Italie, dominated by the hulk of the Galaxie shopping center, is in-between, a sort of urban no-man's land which illustrates the area's diversity: middle-aged housewives, shopping baskets in hand, jostle happily with the young inhabitants of the tower blocks, 'Walkmans' hanging from their shoulders.

Tour of the district

30 mins.

Place d'Italie

This large circular *place* lies at the northernmost point of what could be called the promontory that stretches between the Seine and the Bièvre, marking the boundary of the heights of the Butte-aux-Cailles and Maison Blanche. The hub of seven important thoroughfares, the *place* has a charming little garden at its center with an ornamental pond and a monument commemorating Marshal Juin's Tunisian and Italian campaigns in 1942 and 1944.

On the N side of the *place* stands the Mairie (town hall) of the 13th arrondissement, built by Bonnet (1867–77); the Registry Office for marriages was decorated by R. Boulanger. The Place d'Italie was developed on the site of an ancient crossing of Roman roads leading to Italy. Until 1672, travellers to the S of France crossed this square and took the Ave. d'Italie, then called the Chemin de Turin. The crossroads increased in importance after the building of the *enceinte* of the Fermiers Généraux (tax collectors') wall; the lines of the walls are traced by the Boul. de l'Hôpital and the Boul. Auguste-Blanqui. The city gate at the Barrière d'Italie, built by Nicolas Ledoux in the late 18th c., was demolished in 1877.

The entire sector S of the Place d'Italie was subjected to major redevelopment in the 1970s. Over an area of 264 acres/107ha on either side of the Ave. d'Italie, 13,000 new apartments were built to house 45,000 people. Six schools, four *crèches* (for infants under two years old) and day-nurseries, three youth clubs, three health clinics and an arts center complete the development, plus over 20 acres/8ha of new green space and playing fields. To provide a better transport service for the area, the population of which has doubled, it is planned to introduce a fast lane in the center of the Ave. d'Italie, which has been widened to 180ft/55m.

At the SW corner, take the Rue Bobillot leading to the Place Paul-Verlaine.

Place Paul-Verlaine

This is the heart of the Butte-aux-Cailles quartier, which looks like the picturesque Paris before modernization. The square has a little garden with a bust of Sergeant Bobillot, killed in Indo-China in 1885. Beyond the garden is the Butte-aux-Cailles (public swimming-pool). Built in 1924 by L. Bonnier, with a variety of unmatching dyes, it is served with running water by an artesian well 1918ft/584.5m deep, providing daily over 6,000 litres/130,000 gallons of water rich in iron at 52°F/28°C. Take the Rue Vandrezanne on the l. and turn r. down the little Passage Vandrezanne: at a glance you have a striking overall picture of the district's past and present. Behind the small, low old-fashioned houses lost in the profuse vegetation of their gardens can be seen the tall, many-windowed silhouettes of neighboring skyscrapers. Follow the Rue Moulin-des-Prés, and at no. 68 look into the Square des Peupliers, which shelters many little houses in an almost rural quiet.

Turn r. down the Rue des Peupliers as far as the Place de l'Abbé Henocque, a little square, charmingly provincial with the Red Cross Hospital (Hôpital des Peupliers).

At the end of the Rue Charles-Fournier stands the Church of Sainte-Anne-de-la-Maison-Blanche, built between 1894 and 1921 in the Neo-Roman style. Inside, stained glass and mosaics were designed by Mauméjean in 1938.

From the Place de l'Abbé Henocque, take the Rue Henri-Pape on the r., passing through a neighborhood of small private houses dating from the turn of the century. Often identical, with small front gardens, these little houses could almost be mistaken for a pleasant English suburb.

Return to the Place Paul-Verlaine via the Rue Moulin-des-Prés, continue past the intersection and return to the Place d'Italie via the Rue Simonet, and turn r. down the Rue des Cinq-Diamants. Here the narrow streets lined with old workshops afford a glimpse of the working life of the district, and still retain an old-world charm.

Boulevard Auguste-Blanqui

From (Métro) Galacière to the Place d'Italie.

This extension of the Boul. Saint-Jacques leads from the Place Denfert-Rochereau to the Place d'Italie. On the corner of the Rue Abel-Hovelacque stands the Ecole Robert-Estienne, a technical training college for printing and publishing. On the Boulevard at no. 25, the leading French socialist Auguste Blanqui died in 1881. At no. 50 is the Sainte-Rosalie chapel: no. 96 is the Orthodox Church of France.

Avenue de Choisy

S of the Place d'Italie, on the other side of the Ave. d'Italie, the ongoing renovation on the district has progressed much further. On the l. going down the avenue is the Square de Choisy, with the Eastman Foundation (Dental Institute) on one side. A sculpture by the American Richard Serra was installed here in October 1985; it consists of two gigantic curved steel blades. At no. 81 the Lycée Gabriel-Fauré is decorated with a mosaic by Rohner. The Church of Saint-Hippolyte at no. 27 was built between 1909 and 1924 by the architect Astruc. The entire sector between the Ave. de Choisy and the Ave. d'Ivry is occupied by apartment blocks recently put up. A substantial segment of Paris's Asian population lives here (→ inset).

Rue de Tolbiac

Go past the Lycée Claude-Monet on the l. Beside it rises the buildings of the University campus Paris I, their glass cells stacked around a central axis. A little further on, at nos. 7, 9 and 15 Rue des Hautes Formes, those interested in contemporary architecture can see the group *Les Hautes-Formes* (Tall Forms), considered to be one of the four most important post-war designs by the architect C. de Portzamparc, and which provides housing for 210 people. It is full of light and tranquillity, making brilliant use of a small and unpromising site.

> Chinatown in Paris

The city authorities' allocation of housing to refugees from SE Asia determined the future of this area in the 1970s. Since the previous inhabitants had been rehoused elsewhere, and the apartment blocks between the Place d'Italie and the Porte de Choisy were almost empty, this is where refugees from Vietnam, Cambodia, Laos, Thailand and even the People's Republic of China settled temporarily. Once the process had begun, the new refugees who arrived in ever-increasing numbers were drawn toward the area, where they settled in as well as they could, in turn bringing over relatives and friends. Today, between the Ave. de Choisy and the Ave. d'Ivry, more than half the inhabitants come originally from South-East Asia. These refugees represent an arbitrary convergence of ten nationalities and as many different cultures, which nevertheless have been able to organize themselves, recreating a parallel and independent society in which they can eat, shop, and find entertainment, all within the community. On Sundays, when Asians from all over Paris come here to shop, the area really seems like another country, the signs in ideograms, the shop windows offering everything from embroidered dressing-gowns to spring rolls.

> Street markets

On the Ave. d'Italie, even-numbered side, from no. 186 to the Rue Bourgon: 7am–1:30pm.

Boul. Auguste-Blanqui, odd-numbered side, between the Place d'Italie and the Rue Barrault: Tue., Fri., Sun., 7am–1:30pm.

On the (odd nos). of the Rue Bobillot, between the Place de Rungis and Rue de la Colonie: Tue., Fri., 7am–1:30pm.

Place Jeanne-d'Arc: Thur., Sun., 7am–1:30pm.

Jardin des Plantes** (Botanical Gardens) district

5th arrondissement/Map ref. 24–C2, D2
Métro and RER: Gare d'Austerlitz, Jussieu, Monge
Bus: 25, 57, 61, 65, 89, 91
Parking: Underground, 4 Rue du Marché-des-Patriarches
Street market: Place Monge, Wed., Fri., Sun., 7am–1:30pm

Away from the impeccable flower-beds along the central paths, the Jardin des Plantes has an air of centuries-old neglect, which nevertheless lends it a delightful charm all year round. Although right in the center of Paris, it takes on a slightly provincial character when, on fine Sundays, families come out to walk round the menagerie, the aviaries or the greenhouses.

The neighboring district also has a rustic atmosphere with its narrow, secluded little streets and hidden squares, such as the one in which the remains of the 2nd-c. Roman amphitheatre (Arènes de Lutèce) lie. Watching over the neighborhood is the minaret of the Paris Mosque – an unexpected touch of the exotic. The liveliest part of the district lies round the utilitarian block forming the Jussieu campus (natural sciences) of Paris University. Almost a town unto itself, Jussieu welcomes every day over 10,000 students and researchers who come here to work, invading the cafés, restaurants and bookshops of the neighboring streets.

Museums to visit

Muséum d'Histoire Naturelle (Natural history), 57 Rue Cuvier: anatomy, paleontology, geology and botany.

Collection des Minéraux de Jussieu (4, Place Jussieu, Block 25): mineralogical collection of the Sorbonne.

Musée de la Sculpture en plein air (Quai Saint-Bernard): post-war outdoor sculpture.

History of the district

The history of the district around the Jardin des Plantes is inseparable from that of the two major institutions to have occupied a large part of the area (one of which still does): the Abbaye de Saint-Victor and the Jardin du Roi (→ Jardin des Plantes, below).

The borough of Saint-Victor was formed around the abbey, which was bounded by the Seine and the present-day Rue Linne, Rue Cuvier and Rue des Bernardins. The borough was cut in two by Philippe Auguste's perimeter wall (Rue des Fossés-Saint-Bernard), the eastern part remaining outside along with the abbey, itself surrounded by walls. Beyond that stretched cultivated fields, vineyards and marshy wasteland, bordering the Seine: an area of small-holdings and enclosed plots reflected in the street names (Clos du Chardonnet, Clos des Arènes, Clos Patouillet). With the exception of the nearer foothills of the Montagne Sainte-Geneviève, the region was still sparsely settled in the 17th and 18th centuries. The extensive King's Garden (Jardin du Roi until 1793), the abbey garden and those of other religious houses gave it a rural character, except at its southern fringe (around the present-day Rue Monge). As the Faubourg Saint-Victor, the village came within the 18th-c. Paris boundary, which assigned precise limits to the city.

The area was increasingly built up in the 19th c; the population grew considerably, leading to the construction of new residential neighborhoods, on the little island next to the huge Halle aux Vins (bonded warehouse now transferred to Bercy) and to a concentration of people in the parts already developed. In the early 19th c., a very unwholesome neighborhood developed here, which was cleared during the construction of the Rue Monge (1859) at the same time as the buildings along the river boldly took on a new look à la Haussmann. The district gradually assumed the character recognizable today: a residential area in central Paris, well-to-do but not overly luxurious, with the whole range of 19th-c. and early 20th-c. architecture and little pockets of older (17th and 18th-c.) or more recent (late 20th-c.) buildings, all of which can be seen on a walking tour.

Tour of the Jardin des Plantes (Botanical Gardens)

Main entrance: Place Valhubert; access also from the Rue Buffon, the Rue Geoffroy-Saint-Hilaire, and the Rue Cuvier. Open daily, 7:15

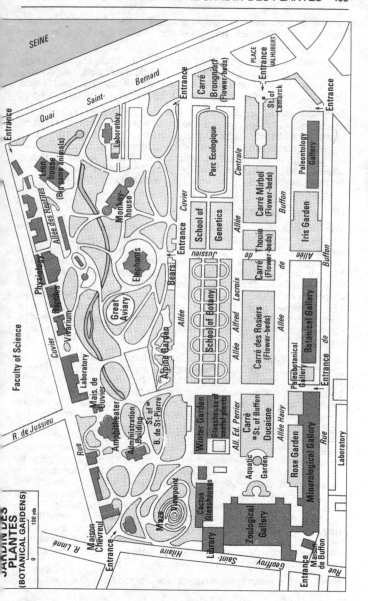

SEINE

Quai   Saint-   Bernard

Entrance

Entrance

PLACE
VALHUBERT

Entrance

Entrance

Faculty of Science

Laboratory

Lion
house
(Big game animals)

Allée des Reptiles

Physiology

Monkey
house

Cuvier

School of
Genetics

Parc Ecologique

Carré
Brongniart
(Flower-beds)

St. of
Lamarck

Paleontology
Gallery

Cuvier

Entrance

Reptiles

Vivarium

Great
Aviary

Elephants

Bears

Jussieu

Allée

Centrale

Carré Mirbel
(Flower-beds)

Iris Garden

R. de Jussieu

Laboratory

Mais. de Cuvier

Alpine Garden

School of Botany

Allée   Alfred   Lacroix

Allée   de   Buffon

Carré
Thouin
(Flower-beds)

Carré
(Flower-beds)

Botanical Gallery

Amphitheater

Administration
Building

St. of
St-Pierre

B. de St-Pierre

Winter Garden

Glasshouse of
useful plants

Carré des Rosiers
(Flower-beds)

Allée   de

Paleobotanical
Gallery

Allée   de   Buffon

Rue

All. Ed. Perrier

Carré
St. of Buffon
Ducaisne

Allée Hauy

Entrance

Maison
Chevreul

Cactus
Glasshouses

Aquatic
Garden

Rose Garden

Laboratory

R. Linné

Maze

Viewpoint

Library

Zoological
Gallery

Mineralogical Gallery

Rue

Entrance

Saint-   Hilaire

Geoffroy

Maison
de Buffon

Entrance

Rue

JARDIN DES
PLANTES
(BOTANICAL GARDENS)

0   100 yds

or 8am until sunset. Admission is free, but separate entry charges apply for the galleries, Winter Garden, Alpine Garden, menagerie and vivarium.

A detailed tour of the Natural History Museum, including a thorough look at the Museum galleries and zoological gardens, takes half a day, and is worth a special visit. However, without too much haste, you can have a general overview of the gardens in about an hour.

Originally the King's Garden, and the oldest garden in Paris, the Jardin des Plantes was officially designated as the National Museum of Natural History by the Convention on June 10, 1793. It covers 70 acres/28ha. Features of the garden are its beautiful views, its labyrinthine paths and its remarkable Alpine Garden. Including scientists and gardeners, 1,500 people help to make this one of the foremost institutions in the world for the study of plant life.

History of the Garden

The idea of a botanical garden first emerged following the extensive studies of 16th-c. botanists. After the creation of the garden at Montpellier, Henri IV and Sully conceived a plan to establish a similar garden in Paris. The plan was carried out in 1626 under Louis XIII, by Jean Hérouard and Guy de La Brosse, physicians to the king; La Brosse was the first Superintendent of the Jardin Royal des Plantes Médicinales (Royal 'physic garden') as it was then known. The definitive organization of the garden's administration took place in 1635. Thanks to support by Gaston d'Orléans, and later by Colbert, chairs in Botany, Chemistry and Natural History were created.

Under the dynamic leadership first of Louis XIV's doctor Fagon, then of Tournefort, who travelled the world in search of plants, botanical science made great strides. But it was Buffon, in the course of his long career as curator (1739–88) who fulfilled the founders' plans, developed and coordinated the various departments and enlarged the whole establishment. The Jardin du Roi thus played an important role in the 18th c. when the sciences, particularly natural history, became so prominent. Buffon was assisted by the famous Louis Daubenton, *'garde et démonstrateur du cabinet du roi '* (keeper and lecturer to the King's cabinet) and by the Jussieus' nephew, Antoine-Laurent. He was succeeded by Bernardin de Saint-Pierre. It was the latter who reorganized the Natural History Museum, broadening its scope to include minerals, fossils and animal skeletons. He was also responsible for re-stocking the menagerie with some animals surviving from the old Royal Menagerie at Versailles, at the end of the 18th c., but chiefly with animals confiscated from travelling circuses. Condorcet later instituted botanical gardens in all the main provincial cities, as part of the national effort at public education.

Nearly all the great French naturalists worked here: Daubenton, A.-

L. de Jussieu, Fourcroy, Brongniart, Portal, Geoffroy Saint-Hilaire, Lamarck and Thouin, were among those elected to the 12 professorial chairs created by the Convention. Other well-known names are Haüy, Vauquelin, Lacépède, Cuvier, Chevreul, Milne-Edwards, Quatrefages, the Becquerels, Gaudry, Edouard Perrier, M. Boule and A. Lacroix. At present there are 25 professorial chairs.

The Botanical Garden

Enter from the Place Valhubert, and the monument to Lamarck (1744–1829) by Fagel (1908) is straight ahead, opposite the entrance. Botanist, then Professor of Zoology, Lamarck claimed that animal species derived from one another through an evolutionary process caused by environmental pressures (the theory of spontaneous generation). Criticized by Cuvier, his theories on evolution were not pursued in his lifetime but were taken up by Darwin in 1869. Beyond the monument extends a vast area of cultivated ground divided by long paths: the Allée Centrale slightly to r. of the entrance, Allée Cuvier on the r. and Allée Buffon on the l. The whole forms the Botanical Gardens including the Botanical School, at the end of which can be seen greenhouses and the building housing the Zoological Gallery.

Gardens to the r. (between the Allée Centrale and the Allée Cuvier)

The Carré Brongniart, at the beginning of the path, is dominated by the statue of a hunter of bear-cubs by Frémiet; here are trees and shrubs with unusual growth patterns. Next comes the Parc Ecologique (Ecological Garden), established in 1938, which is interesting for its reproduction of specific eco-systems, from the sandy soils of the Ile-de-France to Mediterranean woodlands. This is one of the oldest urban centers for research in plant ecology. On a lawn stands a Velani oak from Asia Minor, whose edible acorns taste like chestnuts. Some Judas trees, planted by Buffon around 1785, border the Allée Cuvier; their unusual flowers bloom in May. Beyond the Ecological Garden stretch the beds known as the School of Genetics and School of Botany, systematic collections of plants comprising some 2600 hardy medicinal or edible species (extensively renovated in 1954). Here you can see the first Corsican pine, planted in 1768 from seeds brought back by Turpot. At the edge of the Allée Cuvier is a Canadian sugar maple which has beautiful red foliage in autumn. On the other side of the path, the Alpine Garden* presents plants in their natural surroundings. By clever use of orientation, shade and soil type, the gardeners manage to grow a few metres apart 2000 plants and shrubs from Corsica, the Caucasus, Morocco, the Alps, the Himalayas and elsewhere. To the r., near the Alpine Rock and Cuvier's house, is a living fossil: the great Metasequoia. These primitive conifers were only known in fossilized form until the discovery in 1940 of examples growing in Eastern China.

Gardens to the l. (between the Allée Central and the Allée Buffon)

Return towards the statue of Lamarck to take the Allée Buffon on the l. On your r. the beds are filled with ornamental plants. Edged by two remarkable rows of plane trees pruned in the French manner, the six plots forming the garden flower in successive stages from April to November. There are 150 varieties of dahlia, 60 varieties of canna, and quantities of other species, all labelled.

The Museum Galleries

To visit the collections → Museum of Natural History

On the l. the Paleontology Gallery, a beautiful brick building whose façade was decorated by the ornamental sculptor Allar. In front of it stands a striking reproduction of a stegosaurus. The building is ornamented with interesting bas-reliefs. Garden side: *Le dressage des chevaux* (breaking-in of horses) by Marqueste; *Crocodiles attacking Nubians* by Barrias. Rue Buffon side: *The Bear Hunter* by Frémiet; *The Eagles' Attack* by Coutan. On the side of the Allée de Jussieu lies the iris garden where from mid-May to the end of June 400 varieties of iris are in bloom. Next is the Galerie Botanique (Botany Gallery) at the far end of which is the broad trunk of the ancient *Robinia* (false acacia), the first ever planted in Europe, by the scholar Robin in 1601, and the oldest tree in Paris. He planted another in the Square Saint-Julien-le-Pauvre. Nearby stands the 'Plaisanterie' table in conchitric (shelly) limestone weighing 2.2 tons/2t. discovered at a depth of 6½ft/2m in the forest of Chantilly. It is named after the mare who provided the horsepower necessary to dig it up.

Next come the Mineralogical Gallery with minerals and precious stones, built in 1833, with an ancient *sophora japonica* or Pagoda Tree, brought to France in 1747 by Bernard de Jussieu, growing in front of it. The 440 ancient varieties of rose tended here are the ancestors of the 90 modern varieties displayed in the central flower-beds. Some of the root stocks conserved here, with those at the Bagatelle (Bois de Boulogne) provide samples for research into new varieties. Bordering this rose garden are 260 old varieties of iris.

La Maison de Buffon (Buffon's House)

At the end of the Mineralogical Gallery pass under an arch to reach the extreme SW part of the Institute. To the l. of a small courtyard stands this attractive dwelling. Buffon bought it in 1772, stayed there whenever he was in Paris, and finally died there in 1788. Today it houses the nature conservation service and the museum bookshop. This is one of the ways into the Gardens, at the corner of the Rue Buffon and Rue Geoffroy-Saint-Hilaire (→ below).

The Zoological Galleries

All along one side of the gardens stretch the Zoological Galleries built by the architect André. Except for the exhibition rooms along the front, they have been closed since 1965. However, in the basement the ultramodern equipment installed in 1985 houses about 2,000,000 specimens of creatures preserved in alcohol, stuffed or dried. Some are now extinct. It represents a zoological collection of inestimable value.

The Zoological Gallery (1877) is ornamented by portraits of the early professors in the Institute, and in the center, L'Histoire Naturelle by E. Guillaume. Above the massive doors the coat of arms of the museum represents the animal, vegetable and mineral kingdoms around a hive, symbol of Freemasonry - very active in scientific circles in the 18th c. The interior was lit by a huge stained-glass window; the need for repairs, (now in progress) recently led to the gallery's closure. At the foot of the r.-hand staircase, Buffon's brain is preserved inside a pillar.

Museum Central Library*

Open daily except Sun., Mon. and public holidays 9:30am–5:30pm. Tel. 47–04–53–94.

The Museum Central Library is a modern building extending from the N side of the Zoological Gallery on the site of the old Cabinet Royal d'Histoire Naturelle. It was opened in June 1963 and houses some 750,000 printed books, 4000 geographical and geological maps, 4000 prints and photographs, and 3000 manuscripts, the most valuable of which are by Plumier, Tournefort, Buffon, Lamarck, members of the de Jussieu family, Cuvier, and others.

The Early Book Division* contains illustrated botanical and zoological works, as well as the personal libraries of Cuvier, Chevreul (chemistry and alchemy) and Prince Charles-Lucien Bonaparte (ornithology and ichthyology).

Its most valuable items are the Royal Manuscripts** on vellum (inset), a collection of 6000 paintings of plants and animals begun in 1630 by Nicolas Robert for Gaston d'Orléans and continued to the present by such artists as Aubriet, Van Spaendonck, Huet and Redouté. Two walls of the entrance hall are decorated with Raoul Dufy's frescoes, The Naturalists and The Explorers. At the junction of several alleys in front of the Zoological Gallery are a lily pond and the statue of Buffon by Carlus (1908).

The Greenhouses

Winter Garden open daily except Tue. 1:30pm–5pm. Sun. 10:30am–5pm.

The l. of the two square greenhouses (1830) is devoted to Australian plants, that on the r. to plants from Mexico. These greenhouses were erected during the reign of Louis-Philippe by Rohault de Fleury, one of the first architects to experiment with iron as a building material. Behind them is the Winter Garden (1938), a large greenhouse over 180ft/55m long, 73ft/20m wide and 52ft/16m high, reserved for tropical plants. Removal of certain plants to the annex of the Jardin des Plantes at Chèvreloup justifies the forthcoming demolition of the small greenhouses standing alongside.

Le Labyrinthe (The Maze)

The Maze, dating from 1640, is laid out on two hillocks overlooking the NW part of the gardens. It is one of the most delightful parts of the garden, planted with aromatic herbs with highly evocative scents. It was here that Chateaubriand used to meet Hortense Allait, and here that the curator Buffon welcomed Marie-Antoinette and, later, where Mme Roland was received by her friend, the naturalist Bosc.

On the slopes of the huge maze stands the famous cedar of Lebanon*, the first to be planted in France, by Bernard de Jussieu in 1734, to whom it was given by Kew Gardens, as well as other rare trees, dating from the 18th c., among them two maples from Crete planted by Tournefort in 1702. Near the top of the hill and not far from the cedar, is the grave of Daubenton (1716–1800), marked by a column. Like Buffon a native of Montbard (Côte d'Or), Daubenton assisted him during the garden's greatest period, and became curator of the Cabinet Royal du Jardin des Plantes.

On the summit stands the little Pavillon de Bronze*, a gazebo erected by Verniquet, with its skeleton sphere of hoops and its sundial with the inscription *Horas non numero nisi serenas* (I mark only the cloudless hours). Known as 'Buffon's Arbour' (*gloriette de Buffon*) it is the oldest metal structure in the world (1786). Together with the greenhouses and galleries it shows the degree of innovation in some of the architecture in the Jardin des Plantes. The original iron framework was cast in Buffon's own foundries in Montbard. Between 1983 and 1984 it was restored to its original appearance, with the exception of the solar gong. This used to ring each day at noon when a magnifying glass concentrated the rays of the sun to burn through a thread (replaced daily) from which a weight hung.

The way to Cuvier's house

The NW entrance to the garden lies at the corner of the Rue Geoffroy-Saint-Hilaire and the Rue Cuvier. Just to the r. of the entrance as you enter stands H. Jacquemart's Lion Fountain (1857) on the site of what was once a reservoir fed by the Bièvre, while just to the l. is the house in which A.-L. de Jussieu and Chevreul once lived.

From this point, continue to walk parallel with the Rue Cuvier to reach, on the l., an old house completely covered with ivy near the Sequoia, beneath which is the N entrance to the Museum (57 Rue Cuvier) opening onto the forecourt. On the r. stands L. Faguel's statue of Eugène Chevreul, director of the Museum, famed for his work in colour theory, and the analysis of fatty acids; he isolated stearic, oleic and palmitic acids, important in the manufacture of soap and candles. To the r. of the statue grows a monkey-puzzle. Opposite is the elegant Hôtel de Magny*, erected by Bullet around 1650 and purchased by Buffon in 1787; Lacépède, Daubenton and Fourcroy all stayed here at various times. Today it houses the administrative staff of the Museum. Although defaced during the 19th c., the *hôtel* still retains a fine pediment*.

A little beyond is the large amphitheater begun by Verquinet, but of which the structure and exterior are essentially the work of Legrand and Molinos (1794). It is due for restoration. The Ecole Normale held classes here in 1795. Gay-Lussac, Chevreul and Gabriel Bertrand all worked in the adjacent chemical laboratory (1832–50, 1830–89 and 1890–1900 respectively).

On the l. of the lecture theater stands Baron Cuvier's house, in which that great scholar died in 1832. Regarded as the founder of comparative anatomy and paleontology, he studied the anatomy of living species as well as of fossils and identified and named the pterodactyl. Above the bust of Cuvier on the façade an inscription reads: 'In the Museum's applied physics laboratory, Henri Becquerel discovered radioactivity on March 1, 1896'. The Friends of the Museum have their offices on the ground floor.

Cuvier's house leads from the old Comparative Anatomy Gallery (by F. Dutert), behind which modern laboratories on the Rue Cuvier were completed in 1942. Against the wall of the building, on the garden side, may be seen a cross-section from the trunk of a sequoia tree* some 2000 years old, presented by Californian veterans of World War I in 1927. Chess players provide this corner of the gardens with an almost provincial atmosphere, accentuated by the somewhat dilapidated buildings.

Nearby is another entrance to the zoo, which forms a separate section.

From Cuvier's house, keeping the zoo wall on your l., walk between the seal pool (on the l.) in front of which stands J. Félon's fine bonze group *Women Riding on a Dolphin* (1863), and Louis Holweck's monument (1907) to Bernardin de Saint-Pierre (1737–1814), its pedestal ornamented with the figures of Paul and Virginie from his novel of that name. A romantic novelist and disciple of J.-J. Rousseau, he is less well known as the scientist and curator of the gardens who founded the menagerie in 1793.

The Menagerie

Open daily 9am–5pm (winter); 9am–8pm (summer)

While there are three entrances inside the gardens, there is only one from the outside, on the corner of the Rue Cuvier and the Quai Saint-Bernard.

The animals are housed in a very different fashion from those in the Vincennes Menagerie which also comes under the management of the Museum. Here the emphasis is upon study, and most of the specimens may be approached more closely. This is the place for small mammals and for one of the best collections of birds, reptiles and insects. The old gardens, too, with their fine trees and flowers, provide a delightful setting.

If you come in through the SW entrance near Cuvier's house and the laboratories, you will see on your immediate l. the vivarium created in 1928, very attractively arranged. Small mammals and insects are shown in well-lit, glass-fronted cages against accurate reconstructions of their natural habitats. This is a live exhibition, the make-up of which is frequently changed.

Proceed along the walk parallel with the Rue Cuvier; on the l. is the reptile house (1874). In the first section there are crocodiles, alligators and tortoises, and caged snakes (python and boa), iguanas and monitor lizards. The second room contains poisonous snakes, small lizards, turtles and amphibians. Further on are the aviaries with birds of prey and, towards the Quai Saint-Bernard, a small building on the l. housing monkeys, lemurs, parrots and rare birds.

In the NE corner of the garden a fine lion house was erected in 1937 (architect, Berger), decorated with bas-reliefs by Hilbert. In front stands Jouve's sculpture, *Lion Killing a Goat*. Siberian tigers, Chinese panthers, caracals and other large cats may be seen both from inside and outside the building, due to interconnected cages.

Cross the little river running the length of the zoo and walk back toward the SW to see the main attractions on the way: the large monkey house, erected in 1927, the rotunda (1802), the recently installed bear-pits, the large aviary for waterfowl (1888) and the wild goats and sheep.

The Museum has its annexes on the far side of the Rue Buffon and is responsible for running the zoological park in the Bois de Vincennes (Bois de Vincennes) as well as the Musée de l'Homme (→ Museums). It also arranges interesting temporary exhibitions, especially a *Salon du champignon* (mushroom exhibition), held every autumn.

The Museum also owns the arboretum at Chèvreloup, with its important collection of coniferous trees (30 Route de Versailles, 78150 Rocquencourt; tel. 39-55-53-80).

Tour of the district

2 hrs.

Leave the Jardin des Plantes via the SE exit (Buffon's house), to emerge at the corner of the Rue Buffon and the Rue Geoffroy-Saint-Hilaire.

Rue Buffon: the Museum bookshop stands on the corner of this rather narrow, uninteresting street; on the odd-numbered side are several old houses in which employees of the gardens once lived, as well as the Museum's annexes, while much further down, at no. 15 *bis*, there is a large public library. If you are prepared to walk that far you will pass nos. 27–29, a badly restored house once belonging to Buffon.

The Rue Geoffroy-Saint-Hilaire was once a main thoroughfare in the Faubourg Saint-Victor. Like the Rue Lacépède, for a short time it was called the Rue Coupeau, from the great heap of rubbish and rubble which went to form the *butte* known as Coupeau or Copeau, on which the maze in the Jardin des Plantes was laid out. The street used to cross the Bièvre, which ran approximately between where nos. 31 and 29 now stand and where there was a watermill.

For the rest of the street → Districts: Saint-Marcel.

The Centre Universitaire de Censier

If you are interested in university architecture of the 1960s, go down the Rue Censier as far as the Centre Universitaire de Censier (Paris-III, New Sorbonne: literature, languages, sociology and an annex of Paris-VII). When the refectory on the corner of the Rue Geoffroy-Saint-Hilaire was erected by Pottier and Tessier in 1965, it was judged a highly successful piece of architecture. The lecture halls (entrance on the Rue de Santeuil) were built between 1964 and 1966 (architect, Carlu). The whole block has been blighted by their unimaginative, utilitarian style. Urban renewal has obliterated all trace of the Hôpital de la Miséricorde or Hôpital des Cent-Filles, founded in the 17th c. to take in orphaned girls.

The entire block replaced the old leather market built between 1865 and 1868, which itself replaced the original market on the Right Bank. Part of the building burned down in 1906 and was reconstructed to house the district's trade in skins, which goes back over the centuries to the tanners and leather-dressers along the Bièvre. No. 8 is a typical 1930s apartment building. The Rue du Gril leads to the main gate of the Paris Mosque. You will already have noticed its domes – it is the main reason for using this particular exit from the Jardin des Plantes. As you pass the Rue Georges-Desplas, note on your l. a group of buildings in brick with painted tiles, erected as part of the second stage of the cheap housing scheme (HBM) of the 1920s and 1930s.

The Paris Mosque and the Institut Musulman**

1 Place du Puits-de-l'Ermite. daily except Fri. and Muslim religious festivals, 10am–noon/2pm–5.30pm.

The Institut Musulman comprises three distinct sections: a religious section, including the Mosque; an educational section, in which Arabic and Islamic culture is taught; and a commercial section. The group of buildings was erected between 1922 and 1926 under the supervision of the architects Heubès, Fournez and Mantout in the Hispano-Moorish style, in which North African influences predominate.

To the r. of the religious section is the entrance to the garden and the (modern) ritual ablution rooms in the basement. There is the Grand Patio (Main Patio) inspired by the Alhambra, with its woodwork in cedar and eucalyptus and a fountain in the center. Mosaic freizes round the walls bear quotations in Kufic script from the Koran. Note the traceried capitals of the arches. The Prayer Room* has rugs hanging on the walls, cedar paneling and a line of vigil lights in which electricity has replaced oil. The floor is covered by a selection of very beautiful carpets woven in different parts of the Muslim world from the 17th c. to the present day. At the far end is the mihrab, or niche, which marks the direction in which Mecca lies. The domes were decorated by teams from North Africa, which tried to outdo one another in ingenuity: each is unique.

Return to the entrance and you will see the minaret, standing nearly 100ft/33m high, to which the public is not admitted.

From the main forecourt, with its garden, fountains and gallery supported by pink marble columns, note the magnificent eucalyptus, nutwood and *bois de corail* door with its stucco frame.

Opposite is the lecture room, with a carved and painted wood ceiling. There is a fine library (closed to visitors) which contains several valuable editions of the Koran, as well as many commentaries upon it, and books in both Arabic and French which form the basis of Islamic culture.

Behind this group of buildings (entrance at nos. 29 and 31 Rue Geoffroy-Saint-Hilaire) are Turkish baths, with a dressing-room, restroom and three steamrooms, open on different days for men and women; a Moorish cafe; an Arabic restaurant in which alcohol is barred but where you can eat genuine couscous and drink mint tea; and shops selling items of Muslim art. When you leave the Mosque, it is pleasant to linger by the willow and the fountain in the Place du Puits-de-l'Ermite and notice how the disparate styles of the houses and the different cultures of those living round it still blend into one harmonious whole. The Rue Quatrefages runs from the NE corner of the square. Although nothing remains to prove it, this street was created in the 16th c. and, in the 17th c., ran alongside one of the largest hospitals of the era. Take the Rue du Puits-de-l'Ermite (named after the 16th-c. tanner, Adam L'Hermite) running from the S end of the square up to the Rue Monge. On the corner are some fine wrought-iron railings in front of what was once a café and wine-merchant's.

Place Monge

Turn r. down the Rue de la Clef – once the Chemin du Pont-aux-Biches which crossed the Bièvre a little lower down – then turn l. down the Rue Dolomieu to reach the Place Monge. Surrounded by austere apartment blocks dating from the days of Baron Haussmann, the square comes to life on market-days (Wed., Fri., and Sun. mornings). It was built in 1859 when the Rue Monge took over from the Rue Mouffetard as the highroad to Italy, within a grid system for the Left Bank which included the Boul. Saint-Germain, the Boul. Saint-Marcel, the Rue Gay-Lussac and the Rue Claude-Bernard. The S side of the square is blocked off by one of the barracks for the Garde Republicaine erected in 1840 by Rohault de Fleury and the elder Hermant, who designed the façade, inspired by Florentine originals.

Rue Lacépède

Continue for a short way down the Rue Monge before turning r. into the Rue Lacépède. The 19th-c. buildings which line it give no indication that the street was already in existence in the 14th c. No. 7 is an attractive small Louis XV town house built for Dr Pourfour du Petit. The façade is decorated with garlands and it has an arch with corbels above the main doorway. Behind the house lies the garden which once had an underground passage to the Sainte-Pélagie prison nearby, between the Rue de la Clef, the Rue Larrey and the

Rue Quatrefages. This was the scene of the famous escape of 28 prisoners in 1834.

The Cuvier Fountain*

Before proceeding to the Roman arena walk down the Rue Lacépède as far as its junction with the Rue Geoffroy-Saint-Hilaire, the Rue Linné and the Rue Cuvier, to look at the superb fountain, a memorial to Cuvier, which abuts the house on the corner of the Rue Cuvier. It was erected in 1840 by Vigouroux to replace the one designed by Bernini in the 17th c., which stood beside the old Tour Alexandre, the prison of the Abbaye de Saint-Victor. Feuchères carved the female figure symbolizing *Natural History*, surrounded by different species of animals, including a crocodile with its head turned in an anatomically impossible position. Nos. 47 and 67 Rue Cuvier are mentioned in the description of the surrounding wall of the Jardin des Plantes.

Walk back up the Rue Lacépède and turn r. down the Rue de Navarre, which takes its name from the old Collège de Navarre nearby, while on its N side was the Convent of the Congregation of Notre-Dame where, in 1765, young Manon Philipon (the future Mme Roland) was a pupil.

The Roman Arena of Lutetia**

Entrances in the Rue de Navarre and at 49 Rue Monge.

Entrance to the Roman arena of Lutetia is via the square leading off the Rue Navarre. 'Theater' would be a better word than 'arena', since the tiers of seats are broken on the E side by a proscenium and the whole was used both for theatrical performances and for the usual spectacle of the Roman amphitheater, perhaps both for reasons of economy and because they could be exhibited simultaneously. The arena appears to have been built towards the end of the 1st c. AD, outside the city limits, on the E slope of the Montagne Sainte-Geneviève, overlooking the Bièvre, with the Seine in the background. The Barbarian invasions in the second half of the 3rd c. mark the beginning of its destruction. Dressed stone was removed to provide the foundations of the walls of the Ile de la Cité. At the beginning of the 4th c. burials took place within the ruins of the arena, which thus became a small pagan cemetery. The site was gradually lost to view, long buried, especially by the earth thrown up to form ramparts, when, in the 14th c., the moat was dug round Philippe Auguste's city walls. Until the middle of the 19th c. the precise location of the arena was unknown, although its memory lingered on in ancient documents and place names; the site was long known as the Clos des Arènes. These remains came to light in 1869, after the construction of the Rue Monge and the allocation of sites alongside it to developers. The preservation and restoration of this monument of the Roman occupation was not achieved without a struggle. The Compagnie Générale des Omnibus were the arena's landlords, and it was not until 1883 and with the support of Victor Hugo and Victor Duruy, that the second stage of excavation could be undertaken. Further remains were uncovered between 1915 and 1918 and the final work of restoration began (→ inset).

The W tiers of the amphitheater today lie buried below the buildings in the Rue Monge and, although the remainder has perhaps paradoxically been over-restored, it still requires great imagination to picture the arena as it was. It is now a public garden: the *pétanque* players have staked their claim; local children use it as their sports field, and during the summer various outdoor events take place. Behind the stage, fragments of Gallo-Roman buildings have been reassembled from the remains of the medieval city wall in which they were reused. The bust which you can see is that of Dr. Capitan, who supported the restoration of the arena and the laying-out of the public gardens in the square which bears his name.

Leave by the Square Capitan to find yourself in the Rue des Arènes. No. 5 is an amusing Gothic Revival house in which the writer Jean Paulhan lived from 1940. Walk down to the Rue Linné, and turn l. It was once part of the Rue Saint-Victor, which ran from the Abbey walls right out into the country. No. 25 was the entrance to the former 19th-c. Saint-Victor reservoir which supplied a section of the Left Bank with water from the Ourcq, taken from the Bassin de la Villette in very wide bore pipes across the Seine. Nos. 41–45 are old 17th and 18th c. houses. You now reach the Place Jussieu, the tables outside the cafés crowded with students from the nearby Faculty of Sciences. On the E side of the square are some interesting Neo-Renaissance houses erected by Giraud around 1840. The Rue Jussieu running from the W side of the square was also the former Chemin due Faubourg Saint-Victor. During the 18th c. it was the site of the annual Saint-Clair Fair, held every July. No. 25 has a 19th c. street sign marking the site of the old wine shop, Le Buisson Ardent (The Burning Bush).

The Jussieu Faculty of Sciences

The campus of the Universities of Paris-VI (Université Pierre et Marie Curie) and of Paris-VII (natural sciences) stands on the original site of the old Abbaye Saint-Victor, renewing the tradition of the medieval university (→ inset). But it should be remembered that between times this was the location of the wine market and the slang name for the present university buildings is the 'Halle aux Vins'. This long relapse from learning started in the 17th c. when a warehouse for wine already stood on the corner of the Quai Saint-Bernard. In 1812 this was replaced by a larger market, itself further enlarged in 1868 to comprise a group of warehouses divided by roads running at right angles, each bearing the name of a famous vintage. The Bercy warehouses on the far side of the Seine took most of the trade, leading to a commercial decline and the gradual acquisition of the market's 351/2acres/14ha by the Faculty of Sciences to meet their ever-increasing need to expand. Between 1958 and 1961, out of sight of the square, two long, massive and gloomy buildings were erected, one fronting the Quai, the other on the Rue Cuvier (architects, Seassel Casasan and Coulon). When the entire site became free in 1965, the architect Albert was entrusted with the master plan. He followed the rules of an aesthetic of deliberate austerity which, in the opinion of some, was too severe. The result was steel and glass buildings in a checkerboard pattern, standing on piles, each surrounding a central court to be decorated by contemporary artists. Some of these commissions were completed – for example Arp's work in Court 26–15; Vasarely in Courts 23–12, although it is necessary to be several floors up to appreciate his pattern of aluminium strips; Stahly's in Court 22–33; the base of the pool in Court 32–43 by A. Beaudin, with the designs for the marble flooring by J. Largrange and the two gables flanking the entrance by L. Gischia. The Zamansky Tower named after the then Rector of the University overlooks the entire complex. Erected in 1970 and modified according to Albert's original plan, it was left incomplete at the architect's death in 1968, and today has a derelict air, emphasized by the deliberate harshness of the architecture. Not until 1986 was a plan put into effect to complete the original work: wall paintings commissioned from artists of differing styles (Quai Saint-Bernard) and new sculpture (Rue Cuvier entrance by P. Manoli: Court 46–55 by A. Steiner). The building of the Institut du Monde Arabe and the layout of its surroundings are sure to improve the way in which the Faculty of Sciences fits into its urban environment. The Department of Mineralogy has some fine collections displayed in the Musée des Minéraux (→ Museums).

Rue des Boulangers

Behind the square take the odd little Rue des Boulangers, with its steep incline and bulging house-fronts, which indicate that the street was here long before its modern neighbors.

It existed already in the 14th c. with its sharp right-angle bends, and derives its name from the bakers who worked here in the 16th c. Nearly all the houses are 17th- or 18th-c., while the lower walls and foundations of those at the end of the street are older still: 15th- and 16th-c. Note especially the arch over the side door of no. 5 (17th-c.); the rounded attic windows of nos. 7–13 (18th-c.); the lower wall of no. 16 (17th-c.); and the arched doorway of no. 22 (17th-c.). No. 30 is a large 17th-c. house of which only the cornice is visible from the street (the block on the far side of the forecourt once overlooked a large garden). No. 34 has a fine doorway with wooden tympanum, wrought iron fanlight, carved mascaron forming the keystone and curving cornice (early 18th-c.). Nos. 19–31 opposite stand on the site of the outbuildings of the English Sisters' convent where George Sand once stayed.

Rue de Cardinal-Lemoine

Between the Rue Monge and the Rue des Ecoles.

Turn r. down the Rue du Cardinal-Lemoine (for the upper part of the street → Districts: Rue Mouffetard). No. 49 is the beautiful Hôtel Le Brun* built in 1700 by Boffrand (inset) for a nephew of the famous painter. Watteau spent the last years of his short life here between 1718 and 1721, and Buffon lived here in 1766. The Hôtel Le Brun is the finest in the district. The mezzanine floor comprises seven bays and the first floor is paneled. The semicircular arched gateway is decorated with a carving of Bacchus wreathed in vines. The mansion is built according to Vitruvius' Golden Section. Three projecting bays of the façade are crowned by a triangular pediment. The projection onto the forecourt carries the arms of Le Brun surmounted by a count's coronet. Today the Hôtel Le Brun houses the national headquarters of the HLM and is not enhanced by the two modern buildings on either side. For the remainder of the Rue du Cardinal-Lemoine → Latin Quarter.

Slightly to the r. the Rue des Fossés-Saint-Bernard follows the line of the old city moat which, at that time, was interrupted by the Porte Saint-Victor (the gate stood at the corner of the Rue des Ecoles) and the small La Tournelle fort on the banks of the Seine. (In the 17th c. this was replaced by the Porte Saint-Bernard, a decorative triumphal arch.) The street leads to the Institut du Monde Arabe.

The Institut du Monde Arabe (IMA)

23 Quai Saint-Bernard, main entrance across the square in the Rue des Fossés-Saint Bernard. Open daily except Mon. 1pm–8pm; groups and school parties at special times. Tel. 46–34–25–25.

Ideas for the IMA had been discussed since 1974, but took official shape only in 1980 when France and 19 Arab states signed a document approving the statutes of an institution, of recognized public value, to foster in France a knowledge of Islamic and Arabic civilization, and encourage cultural exchanges between the Arab and the Western worlds. The founding member-states were Algeria, Bahrain, France, Iraq, Djibouti, Jordan, Kuwait, Lebanon, Mauritania, Morocco, Oman, Qatar, Saudi Arabia, Somalia, the Sudan, Syria, Tunisia, the United Arab Emirates, the Arab Republic of Yemen and the Yemen People's Democratic Republic. In 1984 they were joined by Libya. Other states are welcome to join. The costs of construction, equipment and administration are shared equally between France and the Arab partners and governed by agreements between the financial parties involved. The first site earmarked on the Boul. de Grenelle had to be abandoned after protests by adjoining property owners, and the Quai Saint-Bernard location was chosen in 1981. At the same time a limited competition was organized within the framework of major State building projects; the winning design came from Jean Nouvel and the Architect Studio.

The exterior

The modernity of the building is not obtrusive: its lovely curving W façade is broken by the *Tour des Livres* (Book Tower), its existence glimpsed through the glass. The lynchpin of the whole building stands out like the prow of some enormous ship where the Boul. Saint-Germain runs down to meet the Seine. It balances the E front of Notre-Dame, since the architects' intentions have been to integrate modern methods and materials (steel and glass) into the old city, and the site itself, while linking it with the Arab tradition. The N façade, which curves along the line of the Boul. Saint-Germain, attempts to bridge the gap between the latter's mid–19th-c. façade and the group of modern buildings that make up the Faculty of Sciences, and uses stone as the buildings opposite do, while the entrance on this side echoes in its proportions the Porte Saint-Bernard, demolished in the 19th c. On the S façade modern technology follows a North African tradition, for thousands of photoelectric cells automatically filter the sunlight passing through the glass bays of the library. The white marble in the patio and its position in the middle of the building also echo the Arab tradition.

The interior

The IMA provides over 318½sq.ft/26,900m² of floor space allocated to the museum and its annexes (→ Museums), the media archive, a 360-seat auditorium in the basement and a restaurant on the top floor with a magnificent view of Paris.

The media archive has four departments: the newsroom (Basement no. 2) with the latest information on the Arab world and periodicals in French and Arabic. Here exhibitions on specific topics are mounted and debates are held. The audiovisual area (Basement no. 1) contains six sets of individual audiovisual equipment, photographs, documentary films, a music archive of video discs and videotapes and a wide screen television showing extracts from Arab programmes. The Library (Reading Rooms on the 1st, 3rd and 5th floors) builds up collections of publications in the Arab world in Arabic and in other languages – effectively French and English.

Admission is free, but a fee is levied on loans from specific parts of the collections. The documentation center on the 7th floor can accommodate 24 readers and has files of press-clippings on specific subjects.

▷ The Greenhouses: structural masterpieces of metal architecture

Adolphe Thiers, Minister of the Interior, intended the Museum's glasshouses to be worthy of the Jardin des Plantes. The Museum's architect, Charles Rohault de Fleury, satisfied this ambition in 1833 by designing 'the earliest structure comprising an exterior surface of glass on an iron framework'.

Before studying architecture, Rohault de Fleury had been a pupil of the Ecole Polytechnique, and as a result of this dual training, had a first-rate knowledge of the properties of iron. Although seldom used as a building material at the time, iron had the advantage of strength and therefore could span a greater distance with few supports, and these supports themselves could be extremely slender. Taking advantage, too, of the superiority of French glaziers, the architect used panes 8in/20cm by 12in/30cm to provide the maximum sunlight to the interior. The greenhouses were designed as two pavilions at either end of a walk, and received the gardeners' seal of approval. Steam-heated by the most up-to-date boilers, they must have seemed the height of luxury to the general public especially given the inordinate price of glass panes. In 1871 they suffered from shelling during the siege of Paris and the architects who subsequently tried to enlarge them were less skilful; the gardeners complained above all that the overtly opaque structure provided insufficient sunlight.

▷ Manuscripts on vellum

The unique smoothness and whiteness of vellum, a superfine parchment made from stillborn calf- or goatskin, has for centuries enabled miniaturists to use it for finely detailed pictures. This is particularly advantageous for natural history plates, which demand accuracy in coloring and in the texture of fur, feathers and the leaves and petals of plants. The collection of manuscripts on vellum in the museum stems from Gaston d'Orléans, brother of Louis XIII. He was an obsessive collector and showed a keen interest in natural history. The earliest paintings of flowers and birds were made from live specimens in the Château de Blois, which he owned. At his death, five great folio volumes were bequeathed to Louis XIV's library. Louis added to the collection and Nicolas Robert, who had previously worked for Gaston d'Orléans, was appointed 'King's Miniature Painter in Ordinary'; the royal Jardin des Plantes and menagerie at Versailles supplied him with models. His work was continued by Jean Joubert, Magdeleine Basseporte and Gerard Van Spaendonck. After the French Revolution the tradition was revived by Pierre-Joseph Redouté, Adèle Riché, Nicolas Huet, Léon de Wailly and many others whose signatures may be found on plates regularly added to the collection until 1905 and which amount to some 6000 paintings in all.

▷ The trees of Paris

As well as those in the Bois de Vicennes and Bois du Boulogne, there are more than 157,000 trees in Paris. Planes and chestnuts predominate in the streets, interspersed with strains deriving from the ancient forests of Europe and species from the five continents. The most remarkable are:–oldest tree: *Robinia pseudoacacia* (Locust tree) in the Square Viviani, planted by Robin in 1601; thickest tree (23ft 10in/7.05m circumference): an Oriental plane in the Parc Monceau; tallest tree (138ft/42m): a hybrid plane in the Ave. Foch; most twisted branches: the dwarf beech (Fau de Vergy) in the Square des Arènes-de-Lutèce; oddest shape: the Weeping Atlas Cedar, Square Debussy; most deeply fissured bark: the Amur Cork tree (*Phillodendron*); Square du Collège de France; most spiny tree: the Honey locust (*Gleditsia triacanthos*) in the Champ-de-Mars, which owes its name to the soft pulp in the hanging red-brown seed pods; most inaccessible tree: the Monkey puzzle in Ave. Foch, so named from the sharp-edged leaves surrounding its branches; tree with the most curious flowers: Dove tree or Handkerchief tree, whose flowers have two large white bracts in May–June: Jardin du Trocadéro.

▷ The famous Jussieu family

Antoine de Jussieu (1686–1758), physician and professor at the Jardin du Roi; his brothers Bernard (1699–1777) and Joseph (1704–79), botanists; their nephew Antoine Laurent (1748–1836), botanist and Director of the Museum; his son Adrien (1797–1853), botanist when the garden was at its greatest.

▷ Georges-Louis Leclerc, Comte de Buffon

Born at Montbard (Côte d'Or) in 1707, Buffon was the son of a councillor of the Burgundian Parlement. Fascinated by nature, he studied every possible aspect of it both in France and abroad and, at the age of 26, succeeded Jussieu at the Académie des Sciences. In 1739 he was appointed Curator of the King's Garden. He held the post for 50 years, reorganizing the garden, doubling its surface area and enriching the natural history collections. He surrounded himself with able collaborators such as Daubenton, Thouin, Lamarck and Antoine-Laurent de Jussieu, nephew of the famous brothers. Buffon was the father of 'transformism' (the theory of evolution) a theory based on the notion of the evolution of species under the influences of domestication and the natural environment. He set out to demonstrate his thinking in his *Histoire Naturelle*, followed by *Epoques de la nature* (published 1749–89), enormous undertakings of 44 volumes, that occupied him for nearly 40 years and gained him his election to the Académie Française in 1752. The company of this extraordinary man was sought by the great and powerful: Catherine II, Tsarina of Russia; Prince Henry of Prussia; Joseph II, Emperor of Germany. His prestige was so great that a statue was erected to him during his lifetime. But it was in his native town, where he felt most at ease, that he wrote most of his work. He installed a forge there, which he operated himself, and in which he made the wrought iron that the architect Verniquet used to build the gazebo (his *Pavillon*) of the Jardin des Plantes' labyrinth. He died in his house in the Gardens at Paris in 1788.

▷ Sainte-Pélagie

The Sainte-Pélagie prison was originally a convent founded in 1665 by Mme de Miramion in the grounds of the Hôpital de la Pitié, to which convicted prostitutes were sent and where other women who had dishonoured their families or scandalized the public came 'voluntarily' to repent. The two classes of inmates sat on different sides of the chapel which they shared. The entire complex was turned into a political prison during the French Revolution; among those incarcerated there were the future empress Josephine, Mme du Barry, the painter Hubert Robert, and Mme Roland, who made the most of her imprisonment by writing her memoirs. Successive régimes made equally full use of it during the 19th c. and among its famous detainees were Béranger, Paul-Louis Courier, Lamennais, Blanqui, Proudhon, Jules Vallès, H. Rochefort and Gustave Courbet. Despite the erection of the Pavillon des Princes for special prisoners, conditions in the prison grew steadily worse, and the decrepit, cramped, unhealthy state of the prison led to its being demolished in 1899.

▷ The Arena in Roman times

The type of amphitheater which could be used both as an arena and as a theater was peculiar to Gaul. The arena of Lutetia was the largest – roughly 430ft/130m by 330ft/100m – and the most typical. Through J. Formigé's restorations and P. M. Duval's more recent studies, we have a good idea of what this building in local sandstone must have looked like, although none of the 35 tiers of seats which it is presumed to have contained has been discovered. The arena could hold over 15,000 spectators and its façade was recessed with 41 bays, each divided by a half-column, sunk into the wall, similar to the arenas at Nîmes and Arles, although one storey lower than these. Two broad entrances sloped down to the *cavea*, the interior of the arena, an irregular oval roughly 170ft/52m by 150ft/46m, encircled by a podium wall topped by a parapet. Into this wall five large recesses were sunk, the three closest to the main entrances possibly being the *carcares*, or cages for the wild beasts. The tiers are broken by a big stage, about 135ft/41m long, in which nine niches were cut, both to enhance the acoustics and as a decorative feature, many fragments of which have been unearthed.

▷ The Abbey of Saint-Victor

The famous Abbaye Saint-Victor has completely disappeared, although recently its ground plan has been used in a design by Jacques Lagrange for the open space between Towers 46 and 56 of the Jussieu Faculty of Sciences, erected between 1960 and 1970 on the site of the old wine warehouses. Originally this was a Merovingian burial ground, which gained notoriety when a female hermit, Basilla, built her cell there. In 1108 Guillaume de Champeaux gave up his position at the cathedral school of Notre-Dame to set up a retreat on the banks of the Bièvre with a few followers, as recorded by Robert de Thorigny. In 1113 Louis VI founded the Royal Abbey of Canons Regular of the Lateran, which during the 12th c. was to know a period of brilliance with Hugues, Adam, Achard and Richard of Saint-Victor. It was rebuilt in the 16th c., but engravings by Marot (17th c.) show that it retained its Norman belfry. During the 17th c. the abbey gained fresh fame from men such as Santeuil and Jean de Thoulouse, but it was soon destroyed during the French Revolution. The recumbent statue of Guillaume de Chanac from the infirmary chapel now lies in the Louvre. A few arches, remains of the abbey outbuildings, can still be seen in a house on the corner of the Rue Linné and the Rue Cuvier. A substantial part of the abbey's library was transferred to the Bibliothèque Nationale.

▷ Germain Boffrand

Gabriel-Germain Boffrand (b. Nancy, 1667–1754) was the greatest French Rococo architect of the 18th c. as well as an interior decorator, government official, financier, man of letters and engineer. He began as a sculptor in Paris under Girardon, then studied architecture with J. Hardouin-Mansart, with whom he later collaborated. In 1709 he became a member of the Académie and, in 1711, was *Premier Architecte* to the Duc de Lorraine for whom he built the Château of Lunéville (1702–06) and its chapel (1720–23). Very little of his work in Lorraine survives. He had great influence outside

France, following Mansart as architect to Leopold of Bavaria, and later worked for the Elector of Mainz for whom he built La Favorite near Mainz. His ideal was elegant informality allied to a sophisticated simplicity, as in the brilliant Château de Saint-Ouen. His finest interior is probably that of the Hôtel de Soubise with its oval drawing-room, the acme of the Louis XV style, now the Archives Nationales (→ Districts: Le Marais). He was not only employed extensively by the nobility in Paris, but was also architect of the Hôpital Général and became Inspector General of Highways and Bridges in 1732. Most of his Parisian buildings have disappeared including his orphanage, the Hôpital des Enfants-Trouvès on the Ile de la Cité, but among the survivors are the Hôtel Le Brun which made his reputation, and the Hôtel Seignelay (1713), the Hôtel de Torcy (1714) and the Hôtel Amelot (→ Districts: Faubourg Saint-Germain). He was also responsible for the enlargement, restoration and interior decoration of such extant buildings as the Petit-Luxembourg, the façade of the Arsenal fronting the Boul. Morland, the Blessed Sacrament chapel in the Church of Saint-Merri, and an extension to the Hôpital de la Salpétrière. He was the technician who sank the celebrated well at Bicêtre and the inventor of a new type of pump. He made a fortune by the speculative building of large *hôtels* (and lost most of it in the Mississippi Bubble of 1720).

In 1745 he published *Livre d'Architecture contenant les principes généraux de cet art* (*The Book of Architecture Containing the General Principles of this Art*).

The Javel district

15th arr./Map ref. 19–A1
Métro: Charles-Michels or Javel
Bus: 42, 62, 70
Parking: Quai André-Citroën between the Pont Mirabeau and the Rue de Javel
Taxis: Place Charles-Michels. Tel: 45–78–20–00.
Market: Rue Saint-Charles, Tues, Friday, 7.30am–1pm

Javel, on the outskirts of Paris, is typical of the working city of the inter-war years. It was for a long time the least popular part of the 15th arrondissement, but the apartment blocks being erected on the site of the former Citroën car plant bear witness to the fact that as far as architecture and town-planning are concerned, the district is now one of the pace-setters for the French capital.

History of the district

In the 17th and 18th c. Javel was an uninhabited area of fields and meadows, as it was subject to frequent flooding. However, lying on the banks of the Seine, slightly off from the center of Paris, it was a suitable site for the chemical works which, encouraged by the Comte d'Artois, was set up in 1777 to produce the famous disinfectant *Eau de Javel*. From then on this isolated district was divided between factories and market-gardens.

Even after it became part of the 15th arrondissement in 1859, very little urban development went on. Only a population of day-laborers and wretchedly paid workmen lived there, among the encampments of the rag-and-bone merchants. The major industrial turning-point came in 1915 with the establishment of Andre Citroën's car plant to create a bleak landscape of quaysides, warehouses, sheds and blank brick walls. When the car plant closed in 1976, and with it a number of other factories, Javel was left crippled, but on the threshold of major changes.

Today the district is making good all those years of neglect and finding its landscape and population radically altered by the major development plans now being put into effect. So hurry if you want to see the last traces of a poverty-stricken, industrial area of Paris, the last cramped 19th-c. houses in cul-de-sacs and narrow alleys where the grass pushes up between the paving stones.

Tour of the district

1 hr.

Rue Saint-Charles

From the Place Charles-Michels to the Rue de Javel.

The street was laid down after 1868. It is a tree-lined and full of shops, while its 4- or 5-storey apartment blocks, typical of the unpretentious side of the 19th-c. development, lend it the charm of the French provinces.

One may wonder whether the Impasse Saint-Charles will continue to look like a village street when all the construction works which shake it today are completed. Where it cuts through the Rue de Javel there is a fine 1904 apartment block with a sculptured façade.

Rue de La Convention

From the Rue des Bergers to the Rue de Lourmel.

The street was laid down from 1888 to 1890 and runs between

comfortable apartment blocks typical of the feverish property speculation of post-Haussmann Paris in the early years of the 20th c. when building land became a rare commodity.

On the r., at the corner of the Rue des Bergers, is the sculptured façade of no. 32, an apartment block with a most attractive façade with wrought-iron balconies and ornamental brickwork, erected by Clément Feuguer. He designed a number of similar buildings in the 15th arrondissement, including, in 1907, the nearby 64 Rue de Cévennes, an apartment block with a frieze of turquoise blue glazed bricks. No. 78 is the Hôpital Boucicaut, founded with money left to the Assistance Publique by the widow of Aristide Boucicaut. Designed by the architect Legros, father and son, it was formally opened by President Félix Faure on December 1, 1897. Originally 15 beds were reserved for members of the staff of the Bon Marché stores, founded by Boucicaut.

Avenue Félix-Faure

From the Rue de la Convention to the Boul. Victor.

Notice the 19th-c. countrified house standing on the corner of the Rue Maridor. Walk on towards the Balard Métro station to come into the contemporary 15th arrondissement. Opposite no. 126 is the entrance to the Square Jean-Cocteau within the ZAC Saint-Charles initiated in 1982 (ZAC = *Zone d'aménagement concerté*, or planned redevelopment area). Its architecture is typical of the 1980s and was the idea of a Parisian town-planning studio.

Le Verseau, an apartment block at nos. 20–24 Rue Modigliani, provides a striking display of coloured tiles. A fountain sculpted by Y. Chevallier stands at the junction of the Rue Modigliani, the Rue Saint-Charles and the Rue Balard. Well-to-do apartment blocks in brick and masonry seem almost out of date in this floodtide of contemporary building.

Walk as far as the Boul. Victor. If you appreciate 1930s architecture note the luxury apartment block at no. 3, built in the 'transatlantic-liner' style in 1934 by P. Patout, while no. 8, the Ministère de la Marine, is by A. Perret (1932).

Rue Saint-Charles, continued

From the Rue Lablanc to the Rue Cauchy and the Parc André-Citroën.

In the sector between this street, the Rue Balard and the Rue Leblanc, the demolition men have cleared what has become the last and largest piece of building land in Paris, the Citroën car plant, a site of some 86½ acres/35ha beside the Seine. The huge development plan is as far-reaching as the site at its disposal. Round the

Rue Balard will be erected shops, offices, a hospital and a vast housing estate for which 2500 housing units have already been built. There are plans for a 35-acre/14ha park (see below). Since traffic along the Quai André-Citroën uses an underpass, the redevelopment includes a wide riverside promenade which will give access to pedestrians to the banks of the Seine. Work began in 1983 and is to be completed in 1990–93.

Parc Citroën-Cevennes

The park will cover some 32 acres between the Seine, the Rue Leblanc, the Rue Balard and the Rue Cauchy.

The project combines the two winners of a planning competition held in 1986 by the City authorities. Its creators are the architects Patrick Berger, Jean-François Jodry and Jean-Paul Viguier and the landscape gardeners Gilles Clément and Alain Provost.

The new district has been planned around this park on the banks of the Seine. Work has already begun and the project should be completed around 1993.

Walk back up the Rue Saint-Charles and pass the tiny Grenelle cemetery in which is buried the family of Violet who built the hamlet of Beaugrenelle in 1824. Violet, himself, however, rests in the Père-Lachaise cemetery. No. 197 is an early 20th-c. gritstone suburban house in complete contrast with its ultra-modern surroundings.

In the Rue Cauchy, which once led to one of the three encampments of the rag-and-bone men, the few shanties still standing are doomed to speedy destruction.

Turn r. down the Rue Gutenberg and the Rue Emmanuel-Chauvière. Suddenly you have left Paris for a country town, with its low houses, grass sprouting between the uneven paving-stones, the bench beneath the tree.

In the Rue Sébastien-Mercier, on the corner of the Rue Léontine, note the stone-faced red brick apartment house with bow windows, by the architect Charles Chevillard.

At the Rond-point du Pont Mirabeau stands a huge block of apartments, typical of the 1930s, faced with yellow tiles. The Gare de Javel was built for the Alma Station during the 1889 Exhibition, and was moved here in about 1895.

Rue de la Convention, continued

From the Pont Mirabeau to the Rue Gutenberg.

Nos. 9, 17–21, and 25 are good, solid middle-class buildings. On the corner of the Rue Saint-Christophe stands the Church of Saint-Christophe-de-Javel, built of reinforced concrete from 1926 to 1934 by the architect Charles H. Besnard (1881–1946), who invented a system of prefabricated building in 1916. The figure of St Christopher, carved in high-relief on the façade, is by P. Vigoureux; inside there are frescoes by J. Martin-Ferrières (1933).

The Imprimerie Nationale (National Printing Press)

27–35 Rue de la Convention (guided tours Oct. 1 – June, 30, except during school holidays, on written application to the Director). For security reasons children aged 14 and under are not admitted. (Groups are restricted to 20).

In 1640 Louis XIII founded the Imprimerie Royale and housed it in the Louvre. The matrices and punches for the fount of Greek types known as the *grecs du roi* cut by Garamond during the reign of François I, as well as the punches for Arabic, Turkish and Persian founts assembled by Savary de Brèves, were deposited here in 1603. The Imprimerie itself also commissioned several founts of type which are milestones in the development of typography and bear witness to the creative and stimulating part which it played. They include such faces as the Grandjean *romain du roy* for the age of Louis XIV, Luce in the reign of Louis XV, the millimetric Didot of the First Empire, the Marcellin-Legrand of the reign of Charles X and, closer to our own time, the Gauthier of *ca.* 1950.

It has been known as the Imprimerie Nationale since September 1870, but before that had been called 'Nationale', 'Impériale' or 'Royale' according to the régime of the time. The Convention moved the press to the Hôtel de Penthièvre and then Napoléon moved it once again in 1809 to the Hôtel de Rohan in the Rue Vieille-du-Temple. Finally, in 1925, it was housed on a site in the Rue de la Convention in buildings especially designed for it. During the French Revolution the Imprimerie was made publisher of the Bulletin des Lois and in 1823 it became responsible for all government printing. Since 1910 it has been a department of the French Treasury. A decree of December 4, 1961 redefined its privileged position as a government printing office and its public obligations. The Imprimerie is entrusted with the task of printing all government and official documents such as year-books, tax-reforms, Treasury debentures and bonds, identity-cards, official forms, examination papers, and so on. To do this, it was enlarged in 1974 by the addition of more presses in Douai.

In addition to being the government printing office, the Imprimerie has to preserve the traditional art of printing. It owns 224,000 woodcut letters and 92,000 steel punches of which it has exclusive use. It is a living museum of printing technology. Finally, it is an active publishing house issuing nine series of prestigious publications produced by traditional methods. Furthermore the Imprimerie owns a copy of every piece of print from its presses since its foundation. In 1986 joint action by the Treasury and the Ministry of Education made it into a national studio of typographic design, run by the Ecole Nationale Supérieure des Arts Décoratifs, which aims to exploit new areas of typographic design and to train specialists in the latest printing technologies. During the tour you can inspect the main engraving studio and see mechanized typesetting and printing by hot metal and off-set.

Back in the Rue Gutenberg, walk down to the Place Alphonse-Hubert where a group of low-income housing owned by the city of Paris is undergoing renovation.

☐ The Louvre Palace***

1st arr./Map ref. 16–D1; 17–A1
Métro: Louvre, Palais-Royal
Bus: 21, 24, 27, 69, 72, 74, 81, 85, 95
Parking: Place du Louvre
Taxis: Place André-Malraux, Palais-Royal Métro station. Tel: 42-60-61-40

The largest building in Paris, this is one of the finest palaces in the world. To the E, the Cour Carrée is surrounded by the buildings of the Old Louvre, while to the W those of the New Louvre frame the Square du Carrousel, two long galleries linking them to the Pavillon de Flore and the Pavillon de Marsan, between which, until it was burned down in 1871, stood the Tuileries Palace.

For three hundred years the kings of France and two emperors tried to link up the two palaces; when that was finally achieved during the Second Empire it lasted for only a few years. The current program of major building works, which has simplified museum visits by providing a single main entrance under the famous glass pyramid, therefore follows a long tradition. Like its predecessors, the 20th c. will have made its contribution to the palace whose history has always been entwined with that of France.

The history of the Louvre

(See also pages 1284–87)

The Middle Ages

Immediately before setting out on the Crusades, Philippe Auguste determined to fortify the new districts of Paris on the Seine's right bank. Therefore, from 1190 to 1202, he had a wall built down to the river, close to the Church of Saint-Germain-l'Auxerrois, strengthened at that point by a fortress. The site was already known as the Louvre. The precise derivation of the word is unknown. It may indicate that a lepers' hospital once stood here, or a kennel for wolfhounds (*lupara*) or a blockhouse (*lower* in Frankish). Philippe Auguste's fortress — its outer walls were discovered to the SW of the Cour Carrée during archeological excavations in 1863 — was built more or less four-square. Towers stood at the corners of the outer walls and in the middle of the N and W sides. Gates were set in the center of the E and S sides, and buildings erected against the W and S walls. A vaulted room, with pillars crowned by polygonal abacuses and foliated capitals, was discovered in 1866 under the Salle des Caryatides. In the middle of the courtyard stood a massive keep which was at one and the same time a prison, a treasure house, an arsenal and a symbol of royal power. It was here that Ferrand, Count of Flanders, was incarcerated after the Battle of Bouvines. A fort defended the Louvre on the riverside. The foundations of the medieval Louvre, the moats and the base of the keep, are now on view to the public.

The fortress attracted the people and soon a new district sprang up between the Louvre and the tile-works to the W of it. When Etienne Marcel rebelled against the Dauphin Charles in 1358, he built a new wall along the banks of the Seine which turned in at right-angles across what is now the Square du Carrousel. On his return to Paris, Charles had the wall finished (1383). The Louvre was no longer just a fortress: it was soon to become a royal residence. Charles V added extra storeys, had windows pierced in the walls and decorated the building with statues. He built wings to the E and N and commissioned Raymond du Temple (*ca.* 1365) to provide a grand staircase — the *grand-vis*. He set up his library in a tower in the NW courtyard, filled the Louvre with works of art and had a garden laid out to the N with porticoes and wooden summerhouses.

Then came the civil wars and the English invasion, during which the Duke of Bedford removed the royal library. In the 15th c. the kings of France abandoned the Louvre to take up residence on the banks of the Loire.

François I and Henri II: Pierre Lescot's Louvre

In 1527 François I notified the magistrates of Paris of his intention to reoccupy the Louvre. He began by demolishing the old keep, blocking the S entrance and turning the riverside advanced defenses into a tilt-yard for tournaments. Outbuildings were erected to the W of the Louvre. When the king received the Emperor Charles

V in 1533 he had the Louvre redecorated in the latest fashion. Compared to his fine residences in the Valois and Touraine, François I found the Louvre gloomy and uncomfortable, and instigated a program of suitable embellishments, entrusted to Pierre Lescot on August 2, 1546. The latter planned on the former W wing, an *hôtel* with a central staircase, porticoes on the N and S wings with the main entrance in the E, but the buildings were barely begun when François I died in 1547.

On July 10, 1549 Henri II instructed Lescot to alter his plans to what became *Le Grand Dessein* (the Grand Design). While François I had envisaged building his palace on the same area as that covered by Charles V's, Henri II determined to increase the size of the Cour Carrée fourfold, which meant that Lescot had to move his staircase to an extension built N of the W wing. At the same time he planned to erect identical blocks on all four sides of the courtyard. Only the W wing and part of the adjoining S wing were finished at this time and decorated by Jean Goujon who, in 1550, completed the decoration of the Salle des Caryatides. Above was the guard room (now the Salle La Caze) and the king's antechamber (now the Salle Henri II). The king's private apartments were situated in the SW pavilion (now part of the Salle des Sept-Cheminées or Room of the Seven Chimneys or Fireplaces). The S wing was completed and decorated between 1561 and 1564.

Catherine de' Medici and Henri IV: the Galerie du Bord de l'Eau and the Galerie d'Apollon

After Henri I received a fatal blow in the eye during a tourney and died in the Hôtel des Tournelles (1559), Catherine de' Medici no longer wished to live there and, in 1563, had Philibert Delorme draw up plans for the Tuileries 550 yards/500m away on the clayfields where tiles were manufactured (*tuiles*: tiles, hence the name). She did not want to live in the Louvre palace but planned a covered way between it and the Tuileries: the Galerie du Bord de l'Eau, along the banks of the Seine. Building began at the E end but in 1572 an astrologer persuaded the queen that she would die on the site and all work stopped. The Wars of Religion had also halted construction several times. The Louvre itself now played a tragic role in the history of France. While it has never been proved that, encouraged by his mother Catherine de' Medici, Charles IX actually fired on the Huguenots from the palace windows during the St Bartholomew's Eve Massacres, the Louvre was tainted by the rumor. Later the palace suffered from the rivalry between Henri III and his heir and brother, the Duc d'Alençon. Henri III was so frightened by the barricades erected in front of the Louvre that he fled Paris. In 1591, during the Wars of the League, the Duc de Mayenne hanged four members of the Council of Sixteen (districts of Paris) found guilty of the murder of Président Brisson, from the beams of the Salle des

Gardes (now the Salle des Caryatides)– the ceiling was not vaulted until the reign of Louis XIII.

In 1594, when the first of the Bourbon kings, Henri IV, was finally able to enter Paris, having abjured his religion and become a Catholic ('Paris is worth a Mass' he cynically remarked), he immediately resumed work on the Louvre. In 1604 the Petite Galerie (the Galerie d'Apollon of Catherine de' Medici) was completed, and its sumptuous first floor became the Galerie des Rois. Henri added another storey to the Long Gallery connecting the Tuileries to the Louvre, and built the Flore wing. Between 1595 and 1597 the Grande Galerie was erected, perhaps to the plans of Métezeau and Jacques II Androuet Du Cerceau, and the whole was completed in 1608. The king had dreamed of realizing Henri II's *Grand Dessein* but was carried back to the Louvre on May 14, 1960, dying from Ravaillac's knife thrust.

The 17th century and the reign of Louis XIV

During the regency of Marie de' Medici the only apartments to be decorated were those belonging to the Queen Mother herself on the ground floor of the Cour Carrée. Construction of the Louvre started again in 1624. Jacques Le Mercier, who followed Pierre Lescot's original plan, erected the Pavillon de l'Horloge on the line of the Pavillon des Tuileries and the N portion of Lescot's wing. In 1641 Poussin was commissioned to decorate the Grande Galerie, but soon returned to Rome (1642). Once again this Grand Design was halted by another royal minority and by the Civil War of the Fronde. On October 21, 1652 Louis XIV re-entered the capital and summoned the Parliament of Paris there. The Court was established in the Louvre. The king's mother, Anne of Austria, instructed Le Mercier to arrange her winter apartments in those which had belonged to Marie de' Medici. Known, too, as the Appartement des Bains, they amazed the Queen Mother's contemporaries. In 1654, opposite the Collége des Quatre-Nations, which he had just built, Le Vau took over the work of Lescot and Le Mercier and divided the ground floor of the Petite Galerie into the summer apartments of Anne of Austria. Romanelli painted the ceilings and the sculptor Michel Anguier modelled the stucco which still survives. At the same time Le Vau widened the corridor between the Pavillon du Roi and the Petite Galerie to take in the Cabinet du Roi. He fitted out Mazarin's apartments on the second floor of the Pavillon du Roi and in Lescot's wing, the chapel on the first floor of the Pavillon de l'Horloge, and the apartments of the young queen Maria Theresa (now the Galerie Charles X) above the Queen Mother's winter apartments. These were the rooms where Pierre Beauchamp's ballets were danced to poems by Benserade, in which Louis XIV himself performed, where he fell in love first with Marie Mancini and then Louise de La Valliére and where he received foreign ambassadors. On October 24, 1658, on a stage erected in the Salle des Caryatides, Molière performed for the first time before the Court.

After the Peace of the Pyrenées in 1659, Mazarin devoted considerable funds to work on the Louvre. Le Vau extended the S wing and resumed work on the N wing for which Le Mercier had laid only the foundations. However, on February 6, 1661 the Galerie des Rois was seriously damaged by fire. Le Vau now doubled the size of the gallery to enlarge the Queen Mother's apartments and create ground-floor rooms to house the king's collection of antiquities with, on the first floor, a library and small rooms, known as the *cabinets du roi*, for pictures. Le Brun and a team of painters and sculptors decorated the Galerie d'Apollon (Gallery of Apollo) from 1661 to 1680.

In 1664 Colbert, having been appointed Superintendent of Buildings, asked the most distinguished architects in France and Italy for plans to complete the palace. He even summoned the great Bernini from Rome, but his designs proved quite impractical both for the French climate and the French way of life. A committee made up of Le Vau, Lebrun and Claude Perrault, physician and architect and brother of Colbert's head clerk, but better known as the brother of Charles, author of the world-famous fairy tales, produced plans for the S and E façades. Colbert vacillated and war slowed down the pace of building which came to a halt when, between 1678 and 1680, the king removed his Court and administration to Versailles. The Louvre was handed over to the Academies and left to artists, including Coypel and Boucher, and these privileged people throughout the 18th. c. treated it as if it were a conquered country, yet it had always been the intention of Henri IV, generous and broad-minded as he was, that the Louvre should be the palace of kings and artists (→ inset).

From Louis XV to the Bourbon Restoration

In the mid-18th c., during the reign of Louis XV, the Marquis de Marigny (Minister to the King), entertained the idea of regaining possession of the Louvre to house the Grand Conseil and the Royal Library. Gabriel and Soufflot restored the colonnade and cleared the shanties lived in by jugglers and entertainers which had been built against the walls, disfiguring the Cour Carrée, but financial difficulties prevented completion of the scheme.

The Marquis de Marigny had also dreamed of turning the Grande Galerie into a museum, a scheme taken up during the reign of Louis XVI and realized under the Republic and the Empire. To display the works of art belonging to the nation and those ceded to France under peace treaties, Raymond created the Musée Napoléon in the Queen Mother's former apartments. Percier and Fontaine now drew up plans and, in 1806, began the long N gallery between the Pavillon

Marsan and the Pavillon de Rohan, finishing it in 1816. The artists and the Institut were driven from the Louvre. The Cour Carrée was completed at last. The French style of Lescot's roof was preserved on the W, while on the other three sides a second floor was added following the plans drawn up during the reign of Louis XIV. The colonnade was enhanced.

During the reigns of Louis XVIII and Charles X the Cour Carrée sculptures were set in place. Charles X commissioned Fontaine to turn Maria Theresa's apartments into the Musée Charles X for the recently acquired Greek and Egyptian antiquities. The Pavillon du Roi, previously enlarged by Perrault, became one huge room, known as the Salle des Sept-Cheminées (Room of the Seven Chimneys).

Napoléon III and the Louvre

During the Second Republic Duban restored the Salon Carré and the Galerie d'Apollon and Napoléon III finished the building of the Louvre. Between 1852 and 1857, first Visconti, then Lefuel, completed the N and S sides of the square known as the Cour Napoléon-III. The buildings on the S side were devoted to the arts; those on the N housed the officers of the Imperial Household and of the Telegraph Service. From 1863 to 1868 Lefuel altered the W end of the Grande Galerie du Bord de l'Eau, built the pavilion which would become the Salle des Etats and provided a number of small gateways to ease the flow of traffic.

The Communards burned down part of the buildings on the Rue de Rivoli but they were immediately restored by Lefuel and assigned to the Treasury. The Louvre Museum took over the whole of the Cour Carrée and the S part of the New Louvre with the exception of the Pavillon de Flore and the bays adjoining the Grande Galerie — these became the Ministry for the Colonies and subsequently an extension of the Treasury. These buildings, vital for the museum's expansion, were extensively restored in the 1960s and are now part of the museum.

The Grand Louvre

In the autumn of 1981 it was decided to hand back to the Louvre Museum the wing at that time occupied by the Treasury between the Cour Napoléon and the Rue de Rivoli, since the museum was desperately short of space for workshops and facilities for visitors. These comprised only 5% of the surface area of the museum, while in most of the world's great museums space is almost equally divided between services and exhibition areas. The space made available by the departure of the Treasury was not enough to solve the problem. In July 1983 the Chinese-born American architect Ieoh Ming Pei was asked to draw up a remedial plan. His solution was to create new space in the basement of the Cour Napoléon, which would also allow the museum to be transformed from a corridor 2600ft/800m long into a compact grouping round a central point. A huge glass pyramid now gives light to the main entrance (underground reception area) from which there are three entrances to the palace, the whole of which will be used to house the museum's collections. The Departments of Oriental, Egyptian, Greek and Roman Antiquities are being expanded. The sculpture, which is at present displayed in the Aile de Flore, will be divided between the N and S wings of the Cour Napoléon. The large pieces of statuary outside the building will be removed to Les Cours de Finances and placed behind glass so that they can be seen from the Passage Richelieu. The Department of Painting will expand on to the second floor of the Aile des Finances and of the Cour Carrée to take advantage of overhead light. The entrance lobby in the Cour Napoléon has been given the infrastructure needed to provide an information service for visitors, a meeting point for group tours, as well as temporary exhibition rooms, a lecture theater and a restaurant. To the W a shopping arcade leads to the parking lot beneath the Place du Carrousel.

A pyramid was chosen because, being so close to the Seine, it was impossible to excavate below about 26ft/8m, providing insufficient height for so vast a floor area. The glass pyramid therefore provides light and space to an area that could otherwise seem oppressively confined. Furthermore, the visitor is immediately aware of the position of the main entrance. These twin demands led to the architect's choice of a pyramid. Surrounded by seven black granite fountains and three smaller pyramids which provide natural light for the underground corridors leading off towards the Louvre's pavilions, this glass pyramid, a simple architectural structure in an airy, uncluttered, transparent, geometrical shape, 'set in the midst of fountains which give it life and movement as they mingle their reflections with those of sky and clouds', reconciles past and the present without detracting from its setting. (See p. 445)

A tour of the exterior

¾hr.

To simplify its description, the present-day Louvre may be divided into three main parts: the Old Louvre around the Cour Carrée, the Petite Galerie and the Grande Galerie du Bord de l'Eau; Napoléon III's New Louvre standing on either side of the Square du Carrousel; and, finally, the Galerie Nord, running from the Pavillon de Rohan and the two former pavilions of the Tuileries Palace.

The Old Louvre

The Colonnade**

The main façade of the palace is the E front, nearly 575 feet/175m long, overlooking the Place du Louvre. Just who was responsible for designing the celebrated colonnade is still not settled and continues the quarrel which set Boileau against the Perrault brothers in the 18th c. Le Vau's first scheme, which included a central pavilion and a domed pavilion at either end, was begun in 1661 but abandoned in 1664. In October 1665 fresh foundations were dug in accordance with Bernini's plans, but the Italian architect's scheme was quickly shelved. In 1668 Louis XIV approved Le Vau's second plans. However, the decision taken in 1668 to double the length of the S wing along the Seine meant that the colonnade had to be lengthened at either end. This explains why this façade is out of proportion in relation to the N façade along the Rue de Rivoli. Since Le Vau was kept busy at Versailles at that time, it would seem that the combined influence of his collaborator and son-in-law François d'Orbay, and of Claude Perrault proved decisive. The latter had advocated removal of the pavilions from the plan to give the colonnade the greatest possible depth and to ensure the harmony of its horizontal planes. Perrault wanted statues along the balustrade and had substituted niches for the windows of the earlier plan, which were restored during the First Empire. Work on the colonnade was interrupted in 1678. Between 1756 and 1757 the façade had to be restored. The pediment is by Lemot who, in 1808, carved *Minerva surrounded by the Muses* and *Victory crowning the bust of Napoleón I* (replaced by that of Louis XIV under the Bourbon Restoration).

The square in front of the colonnade was cleared in the middle of the 18th c. Finally, on the urging of André Malraux, the dry moats included in the original plans but never completed in the 17 c., were dug between 1964 and 1967 along the foot of the colonnade to reveal the monumental stylobate and restore to it its true proportions. These dry moats, 82ft./25m wide and nearly 25ft./7.50m deep, turn in at r. angles at each end so as to keep the corner pavilions free. The counterscarp is crowned with a stone balustrade. In the middle of the façade a semi-circular projection and a fixed stone bridge some 16.5ft./5m long and over 26ft./8m wide leads to the main entrance to the palace. This bridge was built to 17th-c. designs, using the stones from the stylobate of Le Vau's original façade, begun in 1661 and abandoned in 1664.

The Cour Carrée***

By crossing the bridge and going through the main entrance you reach the heart of the Old Louvre (369ft./112.50m long).

The W wing is the oldest and falls into three sections. The S section** (to the l. of the Pavillon de l'Horloge) was the work of Pierre Lescot, Jean Goujon and their assistants during the reigns of François I and Henri II. It is one of the masterpieces of French Renaissance architecture. Above a ground floor with Corinthian pillars and wide semicircular arches rises the main storey, of Composite order, above it an attic storey supporting a steeply pitched and heavily leaded roof. The façade is divided by three projections with curved pediments. Above the gate the *oeils-de-boeuf* (small oval windows) are framed by allegorical figures by Jean Goujon and surmounted by a black marble slab bearing a commemorative inscription (before 1550). The decoration of the three pediments is magnificent. The first, on the l. contains the figures of Ceres, Neptune, Plenty, Pan and a faun below the motto of Henri II, 'Donec totum impleat orbem'. The second, in the middle, symbolizes War, with Mars, Bellona, two Victories and a group of captives, while the third, on the r., is devoted to Science accompanied by Archimedes, Euclid and the Geniuses. The Pavillon de l'Horloge (also known as the Pavillon de Sully) was erected by Le Mercier in 1624; the caryatids were carved by Guérin, Buyster and Poissant from models by Sarrazin. The S section (to the r. of the Pavillon de l'Horloge) is the work of Le Mercier (1624) but was decorated only after 1820, except for the *oeil-de-boeuf* window sculpted by Van Obstal in the 18th c.

The S wing was begun at its W end (to the r.) by Lescot who built the first *travée* and built as far as the central pavilion during the reigns of Charles IX and Henri III (note the monograms R and H between the columns), but this further end was not decorated until the reign of Henri IV. The central pavilion and the E section are by Le Vau.

The N wing was started by Le Mercier and continued after 1660 by Le Vau. Since he was also responsible for the central pavilion, the E wing and half of the S wing, he erected single-handedly the greater part of the Cour Carrée from 1660 to 1664. However, he kept to Lescot's overall plan.

The pediments of the three pavilions belong to different dates. On the E pediment in 1758 Guillaume Coustou carved *Geniuses supporting the Royal Arms* which were replaced by a cockerel entwined by a snake during the Revolution. On the N pediment in 1811 Claude Ramey depicted the *Genius of France* in the guise of Napoleon summoning Minerva, Mercury and the gods of Peace and Law-making to replace Mars and the trappings of war superseded by Victory. In the same year J.-P. Sueur carved *Minerva accompanied by the Arts and Sciences* for the S pediment.

Every year, from the end of June to the end of August, the Cour Carrée provides the setting for the Louvre Festival.

The outer façade (N of the square), on the Rue de Rivoli is very severe. It was started from the W (Pavillon de Beauvais) by Le Mercier, and finished by Le Vau and Claude Perrault.

The S façades (overlooking the Seine)

The S façades of the Old Louvre comprise the external façade of the S wing of the Cour Carrée, the Petite Galerie and the Grande Galerie.

The S façade of the square was erected by Perrault in front of the façade built by Le Vau from 1660 to 1663. Its overall arrangement is that of the colonnade, but without the upper gallery, so that the double columns are replaced by simple Corinthian pilasters framing the windows. The Infante's gardens were here. At the far W end of this façade stands the former Pavillon du Roi, linked with the Petite Galerie by a kind of galleried bridge, enlarged to its present size by Le Vau in 1665.

The Petite Galerie, running S at a r. angle, was begun by Catherine de' Medici in 1566 and continued by Henri IV from 1594 to 1608. Barthélemy Prieur's sculptures date from the reign of Henri IV. After the fire of 1661, Le Vau altered the first floor façade containing the Gallerie d'Apollon. In 1849 Duban restored it to its original condition, as depicted in an engraving by Marot.

The Grande Galerie

The Grande Galerie may be divided into a number of sections. There is the Pavillon du Salon Carré, built by Henri IV, who had the ground floor furnished as the Salle des Ambassadeurs covered with marble. The height of the pavilion was raised by Le Vau to accommodate the Salon Carré. The Pavillon du Salon Carré was the setting for the annual exhibition of paintings presented to the king and this event soon took the name of 'Salon'. The E section of the gallery was erected between 1594 and 1608, probably by Métezau, and comprises a ground floor with vermiculated bosses between Tuscan pilasters, a mezzanine floor and a floor with wide windows and niches in between. The decorative sculptures were continued in 1850. The Porte Barbet-de-Jouy stands in the center. The gallery's ground and mezzanine floors were occupied from 1608 to 1806 by artists, who lived there with royal permission. Next comes a pavilion which is the twin of the Pavillon du Salon Carré and is currently occupied by the French museums' directorate. The Pavillon Lesdiguières, built during the reign of Henri IV, stands at the point where Charles V's original wall turned at r. angles to the N. Near the pavilion once stood the Tour de Bois from the reign of Charles V, and the Porte Neuve, opened in the reign of François I and demolished in that of Louis XIV. The Carrousel gateways were built by Lefuel in the mid-19th c. On the pediment stands *The Genius of the Arts*, a bronze haut-relief on a gold ground, by Mercié.

It replaced the equestrian statue of Napoléon III by Barye, who is responsible for the two side figures. The Pavillon La Trémoille is similar to the Pavillon Lesdiguières and is the work of Lefuel. The W section of the Grande Galerie was erected from 1594 to 1608 and is the undoubted work of Jacques II Androuet Du Cerceau. This gallery was decorated on a grand scale which Percier and Fontaine copied from the other side of the Square du Carrousel, from the S side of the N Gallery. These decorations were stripped off by Lefuel in 1863 to be replaced by others matching the W section of the Grande Galerie. In the center, the Porte des Lions, called after Barye's sculptured group, stands symmetrically with the Porte Barbet-de-Jouy.

To the W the Grande Galerie ends in the Pavillon de Flore, which was part of the Tuileries Palace. If you go through the ticket offices opposite the Pont du Carrousel, on the l. you can see the large pavilion which Lefuel erected between 1863 and 1868 against the N façade of the Grande Galerie to house a new Salle des Etats and the Emperor's stables.

The New Louvre

Lefuel erected the buildings of the new Louvre between 1852 and 1857 to the plans of Visconti as an extension of the old Louvre in a W direction on either side of the Cour Napoléon and the Square du Carrousel.

To the E they link up with Lescot's and Le Mercier's W wing of the Cour Carrée, the gound floor of which has been restyled, as indeed has that of the Pavillon de Sully in the center, to match the new façades.

The W façade of the old Louvre is joined to the buildings of the new by two similar small constructions, the stylobate of which was also restyled appropriately by Lefuel: on the r. is the N façade of Anne of Austria's apartments (1652); on the l. a symmetrical replica by Percier and Fontaine.

The Pyramid (La pyramide)

The center of the Cour Napoléon is occupied by the glass pyramid built by I. M. Pei in 1988 for the entrance to the museum. With a height of 69ft/21m, and 98ft/30m square at its base, it is constructed in Saint-Gobain transparent low-reflection glass on an aluminium frame supported by a stainless steel substructure. The framework appears simple but is in fact extremely complex and carries within it a system to control condensation in this giant green-house. The base of the pyramid, and the small pyramids and triangular

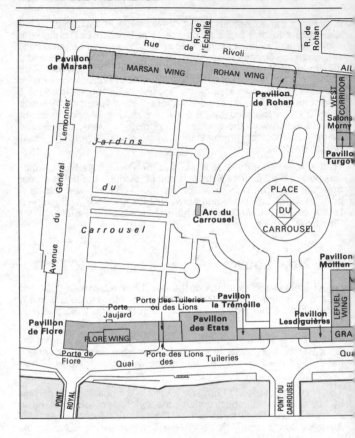

fountains that surround it, are in black Brittany granite, echoing the color of the roofs of the old palace. The paving of the courtyard, in Fontainebleau stone, is based on a 19th-c. project, hitherto unrealized. In front of the pyramid, off-center in relation to the courtyard, but directly in line with the view of the Tuileries gardens, the Place de la Concorde and the Champs-Elysées, is a lead cast of the equestrian statue of Louis XIV, sculpted by Bernini at the end of the 17th c. The marble original is in the Petites Ecuries at the Château de Versailles.

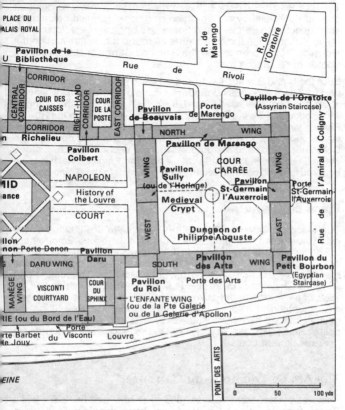

The Louvre

Pavilions and façades of the Cour Napoléon

Looking from E to W, these comprise: on the S wing, the Pavillon Daru; the Pavillon Denon, topped by a pediment by Simard (notable for having the only sculpture of Napoléon III in Paris; two groups by Barye), which is the main entrance to the Museum; and the Pavillon Mollien in the corner. On the N wing are the Pavillon Colbert, the Pavillon Richelieu (two groups by Barye) and the Pavillon Turgot in the corner.

The façades are set back between these pavilions and bordered at ground floor level by a Corinthian portico with fluted columns in accordance with Percier's and Fontaine's original plans (later taken up by Visconti). On the entablature all round the square and on the recessed façade overlooking the Place du Carrousel, Lefuel set the statues of 86 famous men.

Both the N and S wings incorporated three inner courts within their design. The S wing has no modern façade over the riverside since it abuts the Grande Galerie on this side. On the other hand the N wing, occupied by the Treasury since 1871, presents to the Rue de Rivoli a façade split in the middle by the Pavillon de la Bibliothèque which once housed the Louvre Library. It was burned down by the Commune (1871) and restored. Its interior decoration makes it one of the finest existing examples of the Second Empire style. It is to be restored and will be included in any future visit to the Grand Louvre.

Place du Carrousel

The Place du Carrousel lies within the Louvre itself, between the two wings of the new palace, and during the Second Empire bore the name of Napoléon III. In the 13th c. it was the site of the Hospice des Quinze-Vingts, founded by St. Louis for the blind, and of the mansions of the rich such as those of Mme de Rambouillet and Mme de Chevreuse, of streets like the Rue Saint-Nicaise and, in 1662, of the tournament (*carrousel*) that gave it its name. Napoleon I and Napoléon III cleared it of houses. During the Revolution the guillotine stood here from August 22, 1792 until May 10, 1793, only being removed on January 21, 1793 to the Place de la Concorde for the execution of Louis XVI.

The Arc de Triomphe du Carrousel*

This was erected from 1806 to 1808 by Percier and Fontaine, while Denon executed the sculptures to celebrate Napoleon I's victories in 1805. It is one of the most typical examples of the First Empire style. The arch was designed as a triumphal entry to the Tuileries Palace.

Modelled on the arch of the Roman emperor Septimius Severus (and nearly 48ft./14.60m high, 64ft./19.50m wide and 29ft./8.75m deep), the arch is flanked by eight rose marble Corinthian columns with, on the top, statue of soldiers of the Grande Armée in their different uniforms, their realistic representation making them particularly interesting. The ensemble was to have been completed by Lemot's group of bronze statues of the Emperor in a chariot drawn by the famous antique Horses of St Mark, looted from Venice, led by Victory and Peace. However, the chariot remained empty as Napoleon refused to have his statue set in it – the statues itself may be seen at Malmaison – and in 1815 the horses were returned to Venice. They were replaced by copies, and in the chariot Bosio placed an allegorical bronze statue celebrating the Bourbon Restoration. The four sides are decorated with six marble bas-reliefs: *The Capitulation of Ulm, The Battle of Austerlitz, The Meeting of Napoleon and Alexander at Tilsit, The Entry into Munich, The Entry into Vienna* and *The Peace of Pressburg.* The vista** from the arch across the Tuileries Gardens, up the Ave. des Champs-Elysées to the Arc de Triomphe de l'Etoile on the skyline, is one of the grandest and most impressive to be found in Paris.

Galerie Nord (The North Gallery)

The North Gallery stretches between the Rue de Rivoli and the Carrousel gardens, parallel with the S Grande Galerie, and once linked the Louvre with the Tuileries Palace. Nowadays it comprises three parts:

The Pavillon de Rohan stands at the junction of the gallery with the buildings of the new Louvre and was erected by Percier and Fontaine in 1816 and subsequently restored. The façade overlooking the Rue de Rivoli is ornamented with eight statues: from l. to r., Hoche, Kléber, Desaix and Marceau (→below), and Masséna, Lannes, Soult and Ney (→above). The E portion of the gallery was built by the same architects in 1806. They copied the original arrangement of the W section of the Grande Galerie (overlooking the river), later to be altered by Lefuel in a totally different style. It has Colossal columns supporting alternately curved and triangular pediments. Lastly there comes the W section of the gallery, burned down in 1871, but restored by Lefuel and enlarged on the garden side from 1875 to 1878. The architect here copied the N façade of the Grande Galerie, which he himself had erected between the Salle des Etats and the Pavillon de Flore under Napoléon III, in a style taken from the Tuileries Palace.

The old Tuileries Palace

All that remains of this old palace, burned down by the Communards, are the Pavillon de Marsan (N) and the Pavillon de Flore (S).

History of the palace

This palace stood on a site known as the Sablonnière, occupied from the 12th c. by tile-kilns. François I had acquired for his mother, Louise de Savoie, a small country house standing in the Clos des Tuileries. After Henri II had been carried mortally wounded from the jousts in the Faubourg Saint-Antoine to die in the Hôtel des Tournelles, Catherine de' Medici refused to live there any longer and purchased the Clos Le Gendre and the Clos des Cloches on either side of the house which had belonged to Louise de Savoie. In 1564 she instructed Philibert Delorme to build her a palace; he drew up vast plans of which only a small part was actually realized; a central pavilion attached to two main buildings with projecting porticoes along the garden front. When Delorme died in 1570, Jean Bullant took over, erecting a pavilion to the S, but in 1572 Catherine de' Medici called a halt to the building operations, allegedly because she was upset by the prophecy of her death there by an astrologer. She ordered Bullant to erect the Hôtel de Soissons, of which only the astronomical pillar near the Bourse de Commerce remains. Henri IV had the palace extended. Jacques II Androuet Du Cerceau linked Bullant's pavilion with the corner Pavillon de Flore (1608).

Gaston d'Orléans and his daughter, La Grande Mademoiselle, lived in the Tuileries until 1652. Louis XIV handed over the palace to his younger brother, the Duc d'Anjou. In 1659 Le Vau created pavilions to the N matching those to the S to house the Salle des Machines. The Apollo Gallery was restored and two storeys completed. In 1664, in collaboration with François d'Orbay, he completely refurbished the interior of the palace to allow Louis XIV to reside there during the work on the Louvre.

Louis XV spent his minority in the palace. The Salle des Machines was adapted for the opera house when the auditorium in the Palais-Royal was burned down. Louis XVI took up residence in the Tuileries after October 6, 1789, but on June 20, 1791 the royal family had to flee. They were arrested and returned. On June 20, 1792 a Paris mob broke into the palace and forced the king to put on a red Cap of Liberty. On August 10, an armed mob attacked the Tuileries; the king ordered his Swiss Guards not to fire; two of them were massacred and the king deposed. On May 10, 1793 the Convention started its sessions in the Tuileries in a hall put up on the site of the theater. On November 4, 1796 the Conseil des Anciens took its place until driven out by the coup d'état of 18 Brumaire. It was in the Salle Verte, on the ground floor of the Pavillon de Flore, that the Committee of Public Safety sat in permanent session.

Bonaparte took possession of the Tuileries on February 1, 1800 and until 1870 the palace was the seat of the government. Percier and Fontaine once again remodelled the interior, altering the staircase, the reception rooms and the state apartments and installing a chapel in what had been the pavilion of the Salle des Machines. On July 29, 1830 and February 24, 1848 the palace was once again seized by the people of Paris and sacked. From 1849 it housed an annual exhibition of paintings. The Empress Eugénie commissioned a suite of apartments from Lefuel. It was through the Grande Galerie du Bord de l'Eau that she escaped to Belgium on September 4, 1870 when the Tuileries was occupied by the Gardes Nationales.

In May 1871 the palace was set on fire by the Communards, but the main building was saved. After the Franco-Prussian War both Lefuel and Viollet-le-Duc suggested restoring the Tuileries, the bulk of the building being virtually unharmed, but the newly established Third Republic voted for demolition. In 1884 the royal palace was razed and in 1889 a garden was laid out on the site.

Meanwhile, items salvaged from the palace had been dispersed all over France, to many European countries and even as far afield as America. Thus stones from the pavilion standing on the Place du Carrousel were used by Conte Pozzo di Borgo to construct his palazzo at La Punta, near Ajaccio in 1886. Even in Paris some pieces have been preserved in the Tuileries gardens (near the Jeu de Paume), in the gardens of the Palais de Chaillot, at the Ecole des Ponts et Chaussées, at the Ecole des Beaux-Arts and at the Ecole Spéciale de l'Architecture.

The pavilions

The Pavillon de Marsan at the end of the N Gallery was rebuilt by Lefuel. Its upper floors house the Musée des Arts de la Mode, while the ground floor and the W end of the gallery are occupied by the Musée des Arts Décoratifs (→Museums). The Pavillon de Flore is on the other side of the gardens. It, too, was once part of the Tuileries Palace. During the Second Empire it was altered by Lefuel and is decorated, on the Seine side, by Carpeau's famous group, *The Triumph of Flora**; the pediment is by the same celebrated sculptor. This façade overlooks the Pont Royal.

Tour of the interior

1 hr
For opening times →Museums

The buildings around the Cour Carrée and all the S part of the palace, including the S half of the new Louvre, are occupied by the Louvre Museum (→Museums). A tour of the interior of the palace is usually combined with that of the museum. However, if you pay the museum's admission fee, you can, after viewing the outside of the Louvre, see the best-preserved portions of the interior quite quickly. The conversion of a palace into a museum meant substantial alterations, so that the only rooms to retain their original decoration are some of the royal apartments and the adjoining rooms, all lying in the oldest part of the palace, namely Lescot's wing and, especially, in the Petite Galerie. The recent enlargement of the museum has uncovered the foundations of the old medieval Louvre, reached through the new reception hall, itself an interesting example of contemporary architecture.

The tour starts on the ground floor of Lescot's wing, in the Salle des Caryatides (→Louvre Museum, map of Department of Greek and Roman Antiquities).

The Hall Napoléon*

The major event of the opening of the pyramid and the new reception hall in 1989 has deflected the attention of some from the primary rôle of the Louvre as a museum. It is true that this great luminous hall, like a contemporary cathedral, is itself a monument. The great simplicity of construction of this volume, over 164ft/50m square, conceals much refinement, especially in the choice of materials. The Burgundy stone of its walls harmonizes with the colors of the façades of the palace seen through the transparency of the pyramid. The coffers of the ceilings of the three main entrance-ways to the museum's departments were cast in moulds of Oregon pine, the textured pattern of the concrete following that of the grain of the wood. This concrete itself was the subject of careful study, both for its color and its composition, in which there is a quantity of silicates that reflect light and give a slight sparkling effect. In the midst of this Pharaonic décor the free-standing metallic staircase, the hydraulic piston of the lift and the elegant glass-sided escalator bring a note of technological modernity.

The medieval Louvre*

Leave the reception hall following the 'Louvre médiéval' arrows: direction Sully. At the end of the corridor you come to the Salle Le Vau, into which have been moved the remains of the abutments of the bridge that Louis XIV's famous architect built in front of the Pavillon Sully, then surrounded by moats.

Next you will enter the Crypte Sully and see, on the r., the remains of the fortress built by Philippe-Auguste from 1190 to 1202. The floor has a colored drawing showing the site of the Tour de la Librarie which occupied the N-W corner of the castle. Then you come to the moats which surrounded the medieval defensive wall; the tour continues along the foot of this. The whole of Philippe-Auguste's fortress was destroyed from the 16th c. onwards, but only to ground level. Below there survived the fortress's founda-tions, notably those of the towers and the curtain wall which was protected by the moats that had been filled in. The removal of 565,000 cu ft/16,000m³ of earth which led to a few archeological finds, and the covering of the moats with a concrete slab, now allow the visitor to inspect the only remains of Parisian military architecture of the end of the 12th c.

To the r. of the entrance is the base of the Tour du Milieu, then standing isolated in the middle of the moat, the pile of the bridge that led from the castle to the king's garden. The Tour de la Taillerie then marked the N-E corner of the enciente. Further on you will pass the substructure of the eastern gate which was flanked by two towers. The pile of the drawbridge still exists in front of the defensive wall. You will then leave the outer moats to cross over the foundations to come to the moat that surrounds the enormous circular keep. The tour of department devoted to the medieval Louvre ends with a visit to the Salle Saint-Louis. Originally a low room, built with the rest of the fortress around 1200, it was given a new roof with rib-vaulting in about 1230–1240, the time at which the carved capitals and polygonal abacuses were added. The vaulting of the room disappeared with the construction above it of the Salle des Caryatides in the middle of the 16th c.

Leave the archeological crypts following the direction Sully. On the ground floor on the r., at the top of the staircase, is the entrance to the Salle des Caryatides.

The Salle des Caryatides**

This room is earlier than the apartments of Catherine de' Medici and takes its name from the splendid caryatids which Jean Goujon created in 1550 as supports for the gallery, above which the large bronze bas-relief is a copy of Benvenuto Cellini's *Nymph of Fontainebleau*. All the other decorations, as well as the monumental Renaissance-style chimney-piece, were produced under the supervision of Percier and Fontaine, except for the two allegorical statues incorporated into the latter, which are by Jean Goujon.

From June 10 to June 20, 1610 a wax effigy of the murdered Henri IV was displayed in the Salle des Caryatides, and from June 21 to 29 his coffin lay there in state. In this room Molière staged his earliest plays, here the Institute held its public meetings between 1796 and 1806 and here, on April 10, 1957, the President of the French Republic gave a banquet for Queen Elizabeth II and Prince Philip.

The summer apartments of Anne of Austria**

At the end opposite the gallery by the Corridor de Pan and the Archaic Greek Room (with Prud'hon's ceiling painting of *Thetis invoking Jupiter*) you will reach, on the r., the summer apartments of Anne of Austria, created in 1654 on the ground floor of the Petite Galerie. Starting with the Rotonde de Mars, decorated with stucco figures by Michel Anguier, they comprise a suite of five rooms, their ceiling also decorated in stucco (that in the Salle des Antonins is by Girardon) and by mythological paintings by Romanelli (note, particularly, the fine ceiling in the Salle des Saisons). The Salle des Antonins was divided in two: one half being Anne of Austria's bedchamber, the other the study in which she conferred with her ministers. From the Rontonde de Mars take the Escalier Daru down to the Cour du Sphinx with its fine E façade by Le Vau (1659–61).

The Escalier Daru leads to the Galerie d'Apollon on the first floor of the Petite Galerie.

The Galerie d'Apollon***

→ *Louvre Museum, map of 1st floor of Objets d'Art*

Its proportions (201ft./61.39m long, 31ft./9.46m wide and 36ft./11m high) make this one of the finest galleries in the world. It was built in the reign of Henri IV and, after a fire, restored under the supervision of Le Brun in the time of Louis XIV. In the 19th c. it was completed in something resembling the Louis XIV style.

Above the entrance is *The Earth Awakens*, a painting by J. Guichard after Le Brun. In the centre of the vault is Delacroix's large-scale composition, *Apollo vanquishing the Phythian Serpent*, the only 19th-c. original among all the paintings here. The other four large cartouches (ornamental panels) in the form of a scroll depict *Night* or *Diana*, *Evening* or *Morpheus* by Le Brun; *Castor* or *The Morning Star*, by Renou, and *Dawn* by Le Brun, retouched by Charles Muller. On the sides of the vault are *Winter* by Lagrenée le Jeune, *Spring* by Gallet, *Summer* by Durameau and *Autumn* by Taraval. Above the window which looks out onto the Seine is Le Brun's *The Triumph of Neptune and Amphitrite, or The Awakening of the Waters* restored by Popleton. On the walls hang 19th-c. Gobelins tapestry portraits of 18 of the chief artists who worked in the Louvre. Cross the Rotonde d'Apollon with its ceiling painting, *The Fall of Icarus*, by Merry-Joseph Blondel (1891), and enter the Salle des Bijoux. The ceiling of the Salle de Bijoux is painted by Jean-Baptiste Mauzaisse: *Time showing the Ruin he inflicts and the Masterpieces he leaves behind for Discovery* (1822). The room itself was once the Cabinet du Roi and gives access to what was the Pavillon du Roi in the SW corner of the Cour Carrée on the first floor of which were the king's apartments and the Salle des Gardes.

Beyond the Salle des Bijoux lies the Salle des Sept-Cheminées. On the coving of its ceiling are winged figures by Joseph Duret (1851). The Salle Henri-II (to the l.) was the antechamber of the king's apartments. The splendid gilded ceiling by Francesco da Carpy (1557) was completed during the reign of Louis XIV. Since 1953 a breath of life and fresh air has been brought to this Renaissance setting by *The Birds*, three compositions by the contemporary painter Georges Braque. The Salle Henri-II gives access to the Salle La Caze (or Bronze Antiques room). At the far end may be seen the Escalier Henri-II, one of the first great straight staircases in France, constructed between 1550 and 1555 by Pierre Lescot. Its decorations were carved by Jean Goujon and his students. Return to the Salle des Sept-Cheminées and turn l. towards the Department of Egyptian Antiquities. The succession of rooms along the S side of the Cour Carrée makes up the Galerie Charles X.

The Galerie Charles X

This gallery replaces the apartments furnished by Le Vau in the 17th c. for the young Queen Maria Theresa, wife of Louis XIV. Subsequently, after the Bourbon Restoration, the rooms were redecorated (1826–27) to house the collections of Egyptian art. Beyond the Salle des Sept-Cheminées, the Salle Clarac, its ceiling painted with a copy of Ingres' *The Apotheosis of Homer*, acts as an antechamber to the Galerie Charles-X which overlooks the Cour Carrée and the Galerie Campana running along the riverside.

The description of the ceiling paintings follows in room order. In the Galerie Charles-X they are: Room H (250) *Vesuvius receiving from Jupiter the Fire which is to destroy Herculaneum and Pompeii, while Minerva pleads for the Cities* by François Heim; Room G (248) *The Nymphs of Parthenope led by Minerva to the Banks of the Seine* by Charles Meynier; Room F (246) *Cybele protecting Herculaneum and Pompeii against Versuvius* by François-Edouard Picot; Room E (244) known as the Salle des Colonnes, *The Law protecting the Arts* by Antoine-Jean Gros; Room D (242) *Study and Genius unveiling Egypt and Greece* by François-Edouard Picot; Room C (240) *Julius II ordering Bramante, Michelangelo and Raphael to build St Peter's* by Horace Vernet; Room A (236) *The Genius of France inspiring the Arts and Protecting Mankind* by Antoine-Jean Gros.

The Galerie Campana

This gallery was decorated at the same period to receive the prestigious collection of Greek art which has given it its name. Ceiling paintings comprise: Room A (253): *Poussin presented to Louis XIII by Cardinal Richelieu* by Jean Alaux; Room B (251): *Henri IV shows clemency after the Victory of Ivry* (1833) by Charles Steuben; Room C (249): *Puget presents the Milo of Crotona to Louis XIV in the gardens of Versailles* by Eugène Devéria; Room D (247): *François I receiving the paintings brought from Italy by Primaticcio* by Evariste Fragonard; Room E (245): *The Rebirth of the Arts in France* by François Joseph Heim; Room F (243): *Bayard arraying François I in Knight's Armour* by Evariste Fragonard; Room G (241): *Charlemagne receiving Alcuin who Presents his Manuscripts* by Jean Victor Schnetz; Room H (239): *Louis XII proclaimed 'Father of his People' before the States General of 1506* by Martin Drolling; Room I (237): *Bonaparte Ordering the Expedition to Egypt* by Léon Cogniet.

The Galerie Campana and the Galerie Charles-X meet in the hall of the Escalier Percier. During the Bourbon Restoration substantial construction works were carried out in this part of the Louvre, in the S wing of the Cour Carrée and in the Colonnade. At both ends of the latter the architects Percier and Fontaine erected two monumental staircases, the Escalier du Nord and the Escalier du Midi. Turn l. from the staircase landing into the Colonnade to reach the Salles de la Colonnade.

The Salles de la Colonnade

The ceiling and the old pieces of paneling in the antechamber come from the Council Chamber in the Pavillon de la Reine at Vincennes (1654–1658).

The alcove room is decorated with paneling from the King's Bedchamber in the Louvre, remodelled by Le Vau in 1654. The ceiling is from Louis XIV's bedchamber. The *Slaves* and *Trophies* on the springs of the arches are the work of Girardon and Regnauldin, the *Famed* are by Laurent Magnier and Legendre. In the alcove into which Henri IV was carried after Ravaillac's assassination attack stand four Genii supporting a canopy by Gilles Guérin. The mid-17th-c. bed comes from the Château d'Effiat. The tapestry, *The Legate received in Audience*, is part of the series of the *History of the King* after Le Brun (Gobelins, 1667–1672).

Most of the paneling in the Chambre de Parade dates from the reign of Henri II and comes from the former Pavillon du Roi. The fine wood ceiling was carved by Francesco da Carpi in 1558 to Pierre Lescot's designs and was brought here during the Bourbon Restoration. It was the ceiling of Henri II's *chambre de parade*. The doors are attributed either to Jean Goujon or to Maître Ponce. They were completed and the pediments added by Utinot and Laurent Magnier (ca. 1660). Wall tapestries show the *Story of Deborah* by Pietro da Cortona and Romanelli (mid-17th c.) and *The Sacrifice at Lystra* from the series of the *Acts of the Apostles* after Raphael (Mortlake Workshop, England; 1630–1635).

▷ Living at the Louvre

There is a side to the Louvre which is easy to forget — that for centuries it was a home to artists. Henri IV was the first to reserve the ground floor of his recently erected Galerie du Bord de l'Eau as a home for the artists who worked for the Crown. To be assigned quarters in the Louvre in some sense set the seal of official approval on the artist's work, but it also had solid material advantages since the Crown bore the costs of furnishing and upkeep; such rooms were much sought after.

Their earliest occupants included the painters Jacob Bunel and Marin Bourgeois, the sculptors Pierre de Francheville and Guillaume Dupré and the tapestry-weavers Maurice Dubois, Girard Laurent and Pierre Dupont, inventor of the Savonnerie technique. Under Louis XIII there were the painters Simon Vouet, Daniel Dumoustier and Tortebat, the sculptor Louis Lerambert and the engraver Michel Lasne. In Louis XIV's reign there were the painters

Charles Errard, Jacques Stella, the Coypels and Blin de Fontenay, the engravers Claude Mellan and Sylvestre, the sculptors Le Hongre, Coysevox and Girardon, the cabinet-makers A. C. Boulle and Oppenordt, and a host of printers, goldsmiths and tapestry weavers. During the 18th c. the painters Boucher, Desportes, Chardin, Restout, Greuze and Fragonard were lucky enough to be assigned lodgings in the Louvre, as were the sculptors Le Moyne and Pigalle and several goldsmiths and tapestry weavers. The Swedish painter Alexander Roslin also enjoyed this privilege. The painter J.-L. David had several studios there, the architect Gabriel made his home in the Orangerie, while Guillaume Coustou took up residence in a tiny lodging in the Cour Carrée. When Napoleon took possession of the Louvre in 1806 he turned the artists out, and they moved into unused portions of the Sorbonne, leaving behind a dilapidated palace. They had even knocked holes in the walls for stove pipes, and squatters had defaced the buildings. The Louvre was also the home of the Academie Royal de Peinture et de Sculpture and certain rooms were set aside for academicians' reception-pieces and works presented to the Académie by other artists.

Excavations in the Cour Napoléon

Within the overall plan of the Grand Louvre, alterations to the cellars of the Museum enabled a large-scale 'rescue dig' to be undertaken in the Cour Napoléon and the Carrousel garden between March 1984 and March 1986. These uncovered the foundations of the building which lay between the Louvre and Charles V's city walls of which the ground-plan was known from 17th-c. maps. The district had its hour of glory in the 17th. c. before it became the slum described in Balzac's *La Cousine Bette* and its destruction when the Louvre was joined to the Tuileries in the 19th c. Excavations have also shown that this was an area of farmland long before it became built-up in the 13th c. Countless items, such as jewelry, knives, clay pipes and pottery, reveal what a busy craftsmen's district this once was. In the Cour du Carrousel 12 tile-kilns were unearthed to provide rich additional evidence of artisanal activity from the 15th to the 17th c. Over 5000 plaster moulds, terracotta mouldings, and painted figurines have also been discovered, which Bernard Palissy used in the building of the Grotto of the Tuileries Palace.

The Luxembourg Palace and Gardens**

6th arr./Map ref. 16–D3
RER: Luxembourg

Bus: 21, 27, 38, 58, 82, 83, 84, 88, 89
Parking: Rue Soufflot
Taxis: Place Edmond-Rostand. Tel: 46-33-00-00.

Since 1958 this former royal palace with its echoes of Florence has been the home of the French Senate. It is surrounded by one of the largest gardens in the French capital (nearly 62 acres/25ha). The Luxembourg Gardens combine the classical parterre with its straight paths, with the less formal English-style garden with winding tree-shaded alleys. This two-fold aspect, and the fact that the gardens are in the heart of Paris, attract a large and varied crowd of visitors; schoolchildren, students and artists mingle with the solid middle classes and monks and nuns from nearby religious houses.

History of the Luxembourg Palace

Its name, Lucotitius, hence the diminutive 'Luco' given to it by its regulars, must have been applied by its Roman rulers to this faubourg of Lutetia. It was the site of a Roman encampment. The ruined castle of Vauvert which stood here in the 10th c. (→Denfert-Rochereau) was demolished by the Carthusian monks of the Order of St Bruno when St Louis gave them the site in 1275 to build their monastery and grow the fruit and vegetables on which they lived. The history of the palace and its gardens starts with Marie de' Medici, homesick for her native Florence, who in 1612 purchased the Hôtel de Luxembourg, next door to the house in which her fellow citizens, the Gondi, lived. The Queen loved this faubourg — so peaceful and more healthy than the Louvre — and she acquired various plots of adjacent land as far as the boundaries of the Charterhouse to the S. She did not pull down the Hôtel de Luxembourg (it became the Petit Luxembourg) but in 1615 her architect Salomon de Brosse began to build a palace to remind her of the Pitti Palace of her childhood with its Italianate stone bosses, Tuscan capitals and ringed columns. The cupola, the fourth in Paris to be gilded, was meant to proclaim the grandeur of the Queen Regent. In 1622 she commissioned Rubens to paint the famous series of pictures now hanging in the Louvre; around 1625 she settled into the Grand Luxembourg. She was not happy there for long; setting herself at the head of the ultra-Catholic party in opposition to Richelieu, she was exiled to Cologne and died there, penniless in 1642.

The palace became the Palais d'Orléans, when Marie's second son, Gaston d'Orléans, inherited it on the death of Louis XIII in 1642. Its next owners were, successively, Catherine-Marie, Duchesse de Montpensier, sister of the Guises and heroine of the Fronde (1672); Louis XIV (1694), who made Mme de Maintenon governess here to the illegitimate children he had had by Mme de Montespan; then the Orléans family. Finally in 1778 Louis XVI gave the Luxembourg to his younger brother, the future Louis XVIII, Comte de Provence. He sold about 25 acres/10ha of land where the Rue Guynemer is now, and lived in the Petit Luxembourg until he fled the French Revolution on June 20, 1791.

During the Revolution the gardens were enlarged when the Carthusians' property was confiscated, stretching for nearly a mile/1400m as far as the Palais de l'Observatoire, running from N to S as Marie de'Medici had originally planned. First, the palace was turned into a small-arms factory and then, under the innocuous name of Maison Nationale de Sûreté, into the prison in which were confined Camille Descoulins, Fabre d'Églantine, Danton and Joséphine de Beauharnais, the future empress. After the 9th Thermidor, David was imprisoned in the Luxembourg where he made the first sketches for his painting: *The Rape of the Sabines* as well as the only landscape he ever painted – the view from his window (→ Louvre Museum).

In 1794 the Directory moved the seat of government to the Luxembourg and it was here that, on December 10, 1797, General Bonaparte presented the Treaty of Campo Formio. Following the 18th Brumaire, the 'Palais Directorial' became the 'Palais du Consulat' until 1800. Under the First Empire it was the 'Palais du Sénate' and subsequently the 'Palais de la Pairie'. Chalgrin drastically altered the interior to meet its purpose. Out of Marie de' Medici's private apartments he created the ushers' chamber and the courtiers' chamber. In 1815 Marshal Ney was imprisoned and tried in the Luxembourg, then executed by firing squad on the other side of the gardens towards the Ave. de l'Observatoire. Under Louis-Philippe, Charles X's ministers were put on trial in the Luxembourg in 1830, as was Louis-Napoléon Bonaparte after his landing at Boulogne in 1840. The palace was considerably enlarged from 1836 to 1841 by A. de Gisors, who erected a new façade overlooking the garden (sculptures by Pradier), copying exactly its predecessor, with two pavilions at the corners. During the Second Empire a throne room was built jutting into the courtyard and it was then that the gardens took their final shape. They were cut back on the Rue de Vaugirard side, and the building of the Rue Auguste-Comte caused the loss of the nursery and botanic gardens. The remaining gardens were laid out with parterres in the French style and framed by landscaped gardens along the Rues Guynemer and Auguste-Comte. These contrasting styles were a great success, as was the restoration of the Queen Mother's small parterre in front of the Petit Luxembourg.

From 1940 to 1944 the Luxembourg was the headquarters of Marshal Sperrle, Commander-in-Chief of the Luftwaffe on the Western Front. The Gemans altered the interior of the palace drastically and built heavily protected air–raid shelters under the gardens. Fortunately they had no time to use them, for the whole position was taken on August 26, 1944 by a few tanks from the Leclerc Division.

Tour of the Luxembourg

2 hrs.

Palace**

Entrance, 15 Rue de Vaugirard; guided tours: Tel. 42–34–20–60

The ground floor is closed to visitors: on the first floor the sculpture gallery, lecture and committee rooms and the Salon Victor Hugo are profusely adorned with statues and paintings which are obviously official commissions. The library: in the central dome and in a semicircle above the window respectively are two magnificent paintings** by Delacroix executed in 1847 (→ inset), *Dante and Virgil walking in Limbo* and *Alexander placing Homer's poems in Darius' Golden Casket*. The ceiling of the Galerie des Jordaens (an extension of the library) is decorated with 12 paintings of the signs of the zodiac by Jordaens, purchased in 1802 at the time of Chalgrin's interior alterations. This gallery was, in fact, the first public picture gallery (1750). The luxurious gilt Cabinet Doré had been Marie de' Medici's audience chamber: on the ceiling allegorical figures painted by Decaisne. Period paneling from the queen's apartments in the Louvre frames panel paintings by Theodor Van Tulden. The Bureau des Tabacs: Marie de' Medici's former bed-chamber: on the ceiling is Jadin's *Aurora rising from her Couch*. The main staircase is hung with Gobelins tapestries and occupies the site of the Galerie des Rubens. The 24 paintings, executed from 1621 to 1625 by Rubens, which once hung there, are now in the Louvre; they illustrate the life of Marie de'Medici and her political activities. The incidents were selected by Richelieu, concerned for his own future, and to cement the reconciliation between the Queen Mother and her son, Louis XIII. At the head of the public staircase, paintings by Lucien Simon and Maurice Denis (1928) have 'Peace' as their theme. The chapel is from Louis–Philippe's era. On the second floor, in the W wing, above the door leading to muniment rooms (closed to the public), a plaque (1935) commemorates Marshal Ney.

The Petit Luxembourg

Entrance, 15 Rue de Vaugirard (visits only by permission of the President of the French Senate).

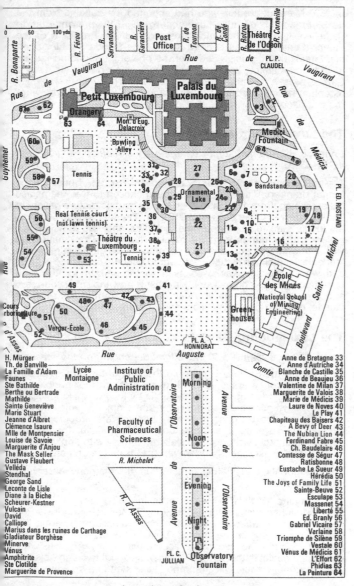

Luxembourg Gardens

In 1627 Marie de'Medici, who had acquired the building from the duke, François de Pinay-Luxembourg in 1612, presented it to Richelieu. It is now the official residence of the President of the French Senate. On the r. hand side of the façade a tablet commemorates the physicist, Sadi Carnot, one of the founding-fathers of thermodynamics, who was born here when his father, Lazare Carnot, was a member of the Directory. The interior includes reception rooms decorated by Boffrand (1711); the state drawing-room is decorated by Louis de Boullongne.

■ The Luxembourg Museum

Entrance, 19 Rue de Vaugirard; temporary exhibitions all year. Tel: 42-34-25-95.

The old Luxembourg Museum was, from 1886 to 1937, housed in the former orangery. The location had been chosen to free the palace gallery which, from 1750, had been the first public picture gallery in Paris, known in those days as the 'Salon'. The Marquis de Marigny, the king's Minister, had been the instigator and had enriched the gallery with paintings from the royal collections. The remains are visible of what was once the convent of the Filles du Calvaire, whom Marie de' Medici had settled next door to her own residence in 1622, and whose cloister was used as a winter garden for the Petit Luxembourg. Their chapel stood in what is now the small courtyard and through the railings you can see its delightful Renaissance façade, restored by A. de Gisors and re-erected there.

▲▲ The Luxembourg Gardens *(See map on p. 461)*

Open 7.30 or 8.15am – 5.00 or 9.30pm, depending on the season.

Only during the Second Empire did the idea of the public garden, now taken for granted, prevail over that of the prince's or nobleman's garden opened to the public by its owner's kindness or whim. The vulgar herd was not given untrammelled enjoyment of the Luxembourg Gardens until they became the property of the Comte de Provence (the future Louis XVIII). Then, for a small admission charge, visitors could slake their thirst with drinks, coffee or milk, and satisfy their hunger with fruit from the orchard.

The memorials and statues erected in the gardens deserve a moment's pause.

The Fontaine Médicis** (Medici fountain, 1624), not far from the Saint-Michel corner, between the Boul. Saint-Michel and the Rue de Médicis, is crowned by a pediment bearing the queen's arms. It is probably by Salomon de Brosse, built in the style of the Italian grotto, although the decorative sculptures are by Auguste Ottin (1866) and depict in the centre Polyphemus about to crush Acis and Galatea under a rock, with Pan and Diana standing on either side.

Alexandre de Gisors, architect of the French Senate, in 1864 set up immediately behind it the First-Empire Fontaine du Regard*, removed from the crossroads in the Rue Saint-Placide. Its twin pilasters and pediment frame the bas-relief of *Leda and the Swan* by Achille Valois on the Rue de Médicis side. The two water nymphs that recline above the pediment were carved by Jean-Baptiste Klagmann (1864). Beyond, and towards the Place Paul-Claudel, a monument by Watkin erected in 1956 in honor of the students killed in the wartime Resistance movement stands beside busts of Murger by Théophile Bouillon (1895) and of Théodore de Banville by Jules Roulleau (1892).

Next, walk towards the main entrance on the Boul. Saint-Michel, to the l. of which you will first see Auguste Rodin's medallion portrait of *Stendhal*, then *George Sand* by François Sicard (1905) and an outstanding piece of Romantic sculpture, *Vedela, druidess of the Bructeri*, by Hippolyte Maindron (1844). On the other side of the central alley Eugène Lequesne's *Dancing Fawn* compliments Denys Puech's memorial to Leconte de Lisle (1898).

As you approach the large fountain, do not miss Zacharie Astruc's *Mask Seller* (1883), its plinth adorned with the masks of Corot, Dumas, Berlioz, Carpeaux, Fauré, Delacroix, Balzac and Barbey d'Aurevilly. The statues of the Queens of France and other famous women on the terrace were erected by Louis-Philippe. To the l. and r. of the large fountain stand two 16th.-c. marble statues in the Antique style – a *Nymph* and *David slaying Goliath*.

On the Rue Auguste-Comte side, two groups of animal sculptures, *The Nubian Lion* by Auguste Cain (1870) and *A Bevy of Deer* by Le Duc (1886), stand next to *Ferdinand Fabre* by Laurent Marqueste (1880) and *Baudelaire* by Fix-Masseau. Henri Gauquié's memorial to Watteau (1896) comprises a pewter bust of the painter and *Youth*, a marble statue in the 18th-c. 'gallant' style. The group, *The Joys of Family Life*, is by Horace Daillion (1889).

Now walk towards the Rue Guynemer. The beehives, rose garden and orchard towards the Rue d'Assas and the Rue Guynemer are a small reminder of the horticultural traditions of the Carthusians and their nursery garden, which were on the site of the present Rue Auguste-Comte, before Baron Haussmann got to work. On the lawns pay particular attention to Raoul Verlet's and Paul Gasq's memorial to Massenet, depicted with his heroine, Manon, and to a much reduced copy of New York's Statue of Liberty, presented to the City of Paris by Bartholdi and restored to mark the bicentennial of the USA. Under the arbors may be found the Luxembourg puppet theater. It dates from 1931, but its predecessors go back to 1881. Nearby is the riding school designed by Charles Garnier, architect of the Paris Opéra.

On the other side of the alley leading to the entrance on the Rue Guynemer, do not miss Dalou's *Triumph of Silenus* and the bust of

Verlaine by Rodo de Niederhausen. Beside the Rue de Vaugirard (to the r. of the entrance on that street) is a little-known work by Antoine Bourdelle, a bust of Beethoven. Beside it stand *L'Effort* by Pierre Roche (1907) and Emile Chatrousse's *The Spring* and *The Brook* (1869). Dalou's statue of Delacroix* is by the private gardens of the French Senate.

▷ **Delacroix's official commissions**

Eugène Delacroix (1798–1863), the leading painter of the French Romantic school, took on many commissions for public buildings in Paris. His first commission in 1826 from the Conseil d'Etat had for its subject the Emperor Justinian I preparing his *Corpus juris civilis*. Unfortunately it perished in the fire of 1871. However, his first important work was the decoration of the king's drawing-room in the Chambre des Deputés (1834), a notable painting in grisaille. The choice of this particular painter for so important a public building had been dictated by Thiers' wish to ingratiate himself with Talleyrand, Delacroix's putative father. Despite criticisms, Thiers went on to entrust him with the decoration of the library, which he completed in 1846. Simultaneously, Delacroix had been commissioned in 1840 to decorate the library of the French Senate. This immense volume of decorative painting was triumphantly crowned by his work in the Chapelle des Saints-Anges (Chapel of the Holy Angels) in the Church of Saint-Sulpice. To be closer to the task which so absorbed him, the painter moved (1857) to the Place Fürstenberg, where he died six years later, exhausted by his superhuman endeavours to complete the chapel. This, the painter's last studio, has now been converted into a Delacroix museum.

▷ **Famous walkers in the 'Luco'**

These gardens have always been famous not only for their peaceful atmosphere but for their freshness and charm, which provided all the reasons Diderot and Rousseau needed for strolling there, the latter trying, as he walked, to sharpen his dulled memory on Virgil's *Eclogues*. Watteau sought inspiration here when his friend Audran was park-keeper. The latter was something more than this, being himself an enlightened artist, whose work was later to be found at the Gobelins tapestry works, and he admitted Watteau to what was still a private garden. The Luxembourg was well used by residents in the district and much loved by such writers as Baudelaire, Lamartine, de Musset, Verlaine, Hugo, George Sand, Balzac, André Gide (who lived close by), Hemingway, Brasillach, Sartre and many more. Being on the edge of the Latin Quarter and the largest green open space there, it is also the students' garden where they rub shoulders with those in search of peace and quiet, and children with their own amusements – Punch and Judy, model yachts, the riding school, sweet stalls and ponies.

The Madeleine district***

8th arr./Map, ref. 10–C2
Métro: Madeleine
Bus: 94, 84, 52, 42, 24
Parking: Place de la Madeleine, odd-numbered side
Taxis: 8 Boul. Malesherbes. Tel: 47–42–54–73.

The Place de la Madeleine appears quite different according to whether it is viewed from in front or from behind the huge peripheral rectangle of the church. The impressive vista of the Rue Royale, the Place de la Concorde and the Palais Bourbon can seem overwhelming. A passerby, standing dwarfed at the foot of the Hollywood-like staircase that leads to the entrance of the church, must be intimidated by so much grandeur. But a picturesque flower market, numerous cafés and elegant boutiques bring humanity to the other sides of the square.

Behind the church, illegally parked cars betray the proximity of the Maison Fauchon (the temple of gourmandise for Parisians, perhaps even for all French people). At the approach of Christmas and the New Year, these refined boutiques are beseiged by clients who, forgetting their good manners, elbow their way in to order their *foie gras* or their large boxes of *marrons glacés*. The adjacent streets (scene of some of the most important building developments during the Restoration), are now calm. Nearby, the little Square Louis-XV, with its melancholy chapel, seems unaware of the passerby on the boulevard.

Tour of the district

45 mins.

⚱ The Church of Sainte-Marie-Madeleine*

Open weekdays 7:30am–1pm, Sun. 8am–1pm, 4–7pm. Tel: 42–65–52–17.

The Madeleine is one of the most famous buildings in Paris. Its history is as long and stormy as that of the Panthéon, with which it is practically contemporary. But the Madeleine is different from the Panthéon in that it is still today the parish church of a particularly well-to-do and elegant district. The remarkable sumptuousness of the Madeleine and its unusual character – an ancient Greek temple set in the heart of Paris – explains the attraction which it exerts on the imagination.

History of the church

In the 13th c. the Church of Sainte-Marie-Madeleine was built at the beginning of the present Boul. Malesherbes in the suburb of La Ville-Evêque. In the 19th c. the development of the district required a larger church. The plan for a new building, to be located at the end of the Rue Royal and complete the large group in the Place Louis-XV, took shape in 1757. The first stone was laid in 1764. Constant d'Ivry had designed a church on a Latin cross plan, crowned with a dome. After his death in 1777, the designs were radically changed by his successor, Guillaume Couture. The Latin cross became a Greek cross, accentuating the resemblance to the Church of Sainte-Geneviève (Panthéon) by Soufflot, built in the same period. The Revolution halted construction. The unfinished building was suggested for various purposes: Assemblée Nationale, Bourse, Bibliothèque Nationale. Napoléon eventually decided to turn it into a Temple de la Gloire (temple to the glory of the Great Army) and entrusted the completion of the work to Barthélemy Vignon, so again the existing structure was razed. The contemporary face of the Madeleine is Vignon's work, although the Restoration again changed. Vignon died (1828) and the work was completed by Jean-Jacques Huvé. In 1837 the building was nearly chosen as Paris's first railway terminal, but consecration took place in 1845. The decorations, remarkably homogeneous, date from the years 1830 to 1840. The State bore all the costs but the church was ceded to the City of Paris in 1842.

The exterior

From outside the Madeleine looks like a Greek temple. The church is completely encircled by 52 Corinthian columns, and is of impressive dimensions: 355ft/108m long, 141ft/43m wide and 60ft/20m tall. A 13½ft/4m pedestal and a broad perron add further dignity to the building. The church has a single nave with three bays, each covered by a dome, and a semi-circular choir covered by a half-domed vault. The bronze doors are adorned with bas-reliefs of the *Ten Commandments* by Henri de Triqueti. The huge main pediment which represents the *Last Judgement* is by Philippe-Henri Lemaire. In the niches in the walls under the portico, are 32 statues of male and female saints by important sculptors of the time, including Leboeuf-Nanteuil, Duret, Feuchères, Bosio, Dantan, Duseigneur, Ramey, Maindron, Caillouette, Jouffroy and Raggi.

The interior

The organ is a superb instrument by Cavaillé-Coll (1846, restored in 1927). In the vestibule to the r., *Le Mariage de la Vierge* (The Marriage of the Virgin), a group by James Pradier; holy water stoups by Antonin Moine. 1st bay: on the pendentives of the dome, statues of four Apostles by Jean-Pierre Roman and François Rude. In the lunette to the r.: *Conversion of Mary Magdalene* by Victor Schnetz. Below, statue of St Amelia by Théophile Bra. 2nd bay: *Apôtres* (Apostles) by Denys Foyatier. Lunette to the r., *La Madeleine au pied de la croix* by François Bouchot. Statue of *Christ the Savior* by Francisque Duret. 3rd bay: *Apôtres* (Apostles) by Pradier. Lunette to the r., *La Madeleine en prière* by Abel de Pujol. Statue of St Clothilde by Antoine Barye.

The half-dome (58ft/18m in diameter) is adorned with Jules Ziegler's painting of the *History of Christianity*. The figures of heroes gathered round Christ and Mary Magdalene go from Constantine to Napoleon, Joan of Arc, Dante and Raphael. The mosaic below, after a cartoon by Joseph Lameire, is the only important addition made to the original decoration: *Le Christ et les propagateurs de la foi en Gaule* (Christ and the missionaries of the Faith in Gaul, 1893). The high altar, with the carved group above, *Le Ravissement de Ste Madeleine* (Mary Magdalene ascending to Heaven) and the two angels that flank it, are the work of Charles Marochetti.

Returning down the nave: 3rd bay: Lunette to the l, *Morte de Ste Marie Madeleine* (Death of St Mary Magdalene) by Emile Signol. Sculpture of St Augustin, by Antoine Etex. Second bay: (Lunette), *Ste Marie Madeleine au sepulcre* (St. Mary Magdalene at the Sepulchre) by Leon Cogniet. *La Vierge et l'Enfant Jesus* (The Virgin and the Infant Jesus) by Charles-Emile Seurre. First bay: Lunette: *Le Repas chez Simon* (Supper at the house of Simon the leper) by Auguste Couder. *St Vincent de Paul* by Bernard Raggi. In the vestibule to the l., *Le Baptême du Christ*** (Baptism of Christ) is one of Rude's masterpieces.

Place de la Madeleine

Designed at the same time as the church, the square occupies the site of the dependencies of the Prieuré de la Ville-Evêque , the fief of the Bishop of Paris since the 6th c.

W side: the Galerie de la Madeleine, built in 1840, is one of the typically Parisian *passages* of the Right Bank. Beside it, forming a corner with the Boul. Malesherbes, is a large building (no. 9) built under Louis-Philippe by Charpentier, with sculptures by Klagmann (landmarked), where Marcel Proust passed his childhood. On the ground floor, the chic and famous Lucas-Carton* restaurant (book at least a week ahead) has kept its marquetry decorations (1903) attributed to L. Majorelle. No. 7 is where Jules Simon, the academician, historian and minister, lived. On the ground floor is the famous goldsmith Odiot.

S side: the view of the Rue Royal, hidden by the façade of the Palais-Bourbon (Assemblée Nationale), opens up.

E side: near the church a little flower market (daily exc. Mon. 8am–7:30pm), established since 1832, gives a little color to the square. An American clothing store is installed at no. 2 in the building which was formerly famous for the Café Durand frequented by Zola among others. The Boul. de la Madeleine leads towards the Opéra and the Place Vendôme nearby. At the corner where the boulevard meets the Place de la Madeleine, the department store Aux Trois Quartiers, founded in 1829 and reconstructed in a restrained style by Faure-Dujarric in 1932, provides a calm atmosphere in which to shop.

N side: gourmet food reigns. At no. 26, the Fauchon shops offer nearly 20,000 products from all over the world, with a dazzling window display. No. 21 is the Epicerie Hédiard, 130 years old and the grocery *par excellence*. Further on is the large Confiserie Tanrade with hand-made chocolates (18, Rue Vignon). Wines not to be found anywhere else can be bought in the cellars of Au Verger de la Madeleine at 4 Boul. Malesherbes. The Théâtre de la Madeleine (19 Rue de Surène), inaugurated in 1924, was, from 1930 to 1942, Sacha Guitry's principal theater where, with Yvonne Printemps and Pierre Fresnay, he staged his plays and reviews. Today this theater houses the Valère-Desailly Company.

Rue Tronchet

This street, which was laid out in 1842 on the site of the priory of the Benedictines of La Ville-l'Evêque, is named after the lawyer, François Tronchet (1725–1806), defender of Louis XVI. Its continuation as far as the Boul. Haussmann dates from 1862.

The buildings in this street show the commercial trend of their owners who built them to earn money from their capital. They built shops along the road, while they lodged in the rear of the buildings looking out on to courtyards. Chopin lived at no. 5 from 1839 to 1842. Alfred de Musset had a pied-à-terre at no. 9, and Lamennais who quarrelled with the clergy, was to have lived at no. 13 but died excommunicate before he could move in. The Galerie Palacio de la Madeleine is on the site of the old market.

At no. 7, is the Hôtel de Pourtales, built in 1836 by Duban, who had already built the Ecole des Beaux-Arts.

The enthusiasm that James-Alexandre Pourtalès-Gorgier (1776–1885) felt for all aspects of the arts led him to commission Duban to design a Renaissance-style mansion to house his Etruscan glass, picture and antique collections. Along the arcaded courtyard on the r. the gallery contained priceless paintings including works by the Carrache brothers, Guido Reni, Holbein, Murillo, David and the famous *Corps de Garde* by Le Nain, now in the Louvre. The auction sale which dispersed the collection in 1863 lasted several days. Acquired in 1917 by an insurance company — which made some discreet alterations — the mansion is not usually open to visitors.

The Rue de Castellane, on the site of the large Hôtel de Soyecourt where the Maréchal de Soubise died, is outstanding for the harmony of its Restoration buildings.

Rue Greffulhe: no. 7 has a plaque and a medallion recalling that the composer, Reynaldo Hahn (1874–1947), friend of Proust, died here.

Rue des Mathurins

This district is dedicated to fashion, and in the 19th c., was very literary. The Rue des Mathurins has kept some of this nostalgic cultured atmosphere from the time when Marie d'Agoult held her salon at no. 10 and Sophie Gay entertained at no. 40 in the house where Germaine de Staël died. In the Théâtre des Mathurins, constructed in 1906 by Lucien-German Guitry, father of Sacha, a medallion commemorates Georges (d. 1939) and Ludmilla Pitoëff (d. 1953), two artistes who, between 1927 and World War II, were responsible for the memorable evenings for which the place was renowned.

⚱ The Chapelle Expiatoire

Entrance: 29 Rue Pasquier; open daily April–September 10am–5.45pm, rest of year 10–4. Tel: 42–65–35–80.

This is the chapel built by Fontaine for Louis XVIII from 1815 to 1826, in memory of Louis XVI and Marie-Antoinette. It was built in the Square Louis-XVI, itself established on the site of the old Cimetière de la Madeleine de la Ville-Evêque. It is there that the people who died in the fireworks of 1770 and nearly 3000 victims of the Revolution were interred. These included the 600 Swiss guards killed in the Tuileries on the evening of August 10, 1792, Louis XVI, Marie-Antoinette, Philippe-Egalité, Charlotte Corday, Mme Roland, Custine, Mme du Barry, Camile and Lucile Desmoulins,

Malesherbes, Danton, Hébert, Fabre d'Eglantine, Barnave, Bailly, Lavoisier, Brissot, Vergnaud and Chaumette.

Immediately after their execution, the bodies of the King and Queen were entombed here. The altar to the crypt is in the exact place where their remains were found on May 18, 1814 and where they stayed until their transfer to Saint-Denis, January 1815.

The cloister 'formé d'un enchaînement de tombeaux' ('formed by a chain of tombs'), as Chateaubriand wrote in his Mémoires d'outre-tombe, looks strange today. The little square offers a melancholy peace in the middle of the hurly-burly of the boulevard. At the extreme end of the row, to the r., is a monument to Charlotte Corday, who assassinated Marat in his bath on July 13, 1793, and opposite, to the l., one of Philippe-Egalité, Duc d'Orléans and father of Louis Philippe.

There are two marble groups in the chapel, given by the Duchess of Angoulême, daughter of Louis XVI. To the r., Louis XVI by Bosio, supported by an angel to whom the artist has given the likeness of the Abbé Edgeworth, the king's confessor (on the pedestal is engraved the testament of December 25, 1792). To the l., Cortot's Marie-Antoinette agenouillée aux pieds de la Religion (Marie-Antoinette kneeling at the feet of Religion) shown in the likeness of Mme Elisabeth. (On the pedestal is the letter that the Queen addressed to Mme Elisabeth on October 16 1793.) Above the portal, La Translation à Saint-Denis, bas-relief by Gérard. Steps lead down to the crypt, which is very austere.

The tour can be finished by rejoining the Boul. Malesherbes, which leads to another great 19th-c. church, Saint-Augustin (→Saint-Lazare).

At the corner of the Rue des Mathurins and the Boul. Malesherbes, at no. 32, an elegant iron and glass rotunda can be seen; it is practically unique in Paris (1903).

▷ The Kiosque-Theater of the Madeleine

Like London and New York, Paris has a theater ticket kiosk which is opposite 15 Place de la Madeleine.

All the unsold seats for the current day are put on sale at half price from 12:30 onwards. Almost all the private theaters, some subsidised theaters, the Lucernaire, the Théâtre de Chaillot, the Maison des Arts de Créteil, the Théâtre de Boulogne Billancourt, the Théâtre Gérard Philipe, the Théâtre de la Ville, the TMP Châtelet, music halls (Alcazar, Olympia) as well as opera and ballet (Opéra, Orchestre de Paris, the Salle Gaveau and others) are obliged to provide the Kiosque-Théâtre with a minimum of four seats for each of their performances. The Kiosque-Théâtre is open

Tues-Fri, 12:30-8.00pm, Sat. 12:30pm for matinees; 2-8pm for evenings; Sun. 12:30-4:30pm.

The Marais***

Traditionally, the area known as the Marais (the marsh) – once an uninhabitable swamp – is the part of Paris bounded to the S by the Seine, to the E and N by the Boul. Beaumarchais and the Boul. du Temple, and to the W by the Rue Beaubourg and the Rue Turbigo. Although this elegant district remains the heart of historic and tourist Paris *par excellence*, visitors may still be surprised at the liveliness, even the hustle and bustle of the area. The population which lives and works here has always been extremely varied, and this diversity is reflected in the dwellings. Mansions are juxtaposed with modest houses and boutiques, unusual in Paris.

Today a largely immigrant population supports itself with craft and cottage industries. Many Asian merchants specialize in fancy leather goods and exotic jewelry, while the clothing workshops, once centered arond the Carreau du Temple, are the fiefdom of the Yugoslavs, and the ready-to-wear boutiques are often owned by repatriated French-Algerians.

The S part of the district and the area around the Place des Vosges are distinctly more residential, with luxury shops (antiques, art galleries), fashionable couturiers and elegant restaurants. Many people from the worlds, of the theater and the arts live here. The construction of the new districts of Les Halles and Beaubourg nearby has sparked new interest in the Marais which, up until the present, has not been of interest to property developers. It is likely that the renovation of the E districts of Paris (Bastille and its surroundings) will have a similar impact. However, it is feared that the large amount of luxury building and renovation might accelerate the migration of the working class to the suburbs – which has already begun – and that the Marais might be left with a population of the rich, and administrative buildings. The area stands to lose a great deal of its charm and gaiety, its picturesqueness and cheerful character, and to become a moribund 'museum' district.

There are three planned walks to help the visitor discover the Marais: the Place des Vosges area, the Saint-Paul quarter, and the Temple and Rue des Archives district. Avoid the Marais on the weekend, when many of its old mansions, which are occupied by businesses, are closed, while others, which have become private residences, are equipped with numerical coding systems to forbid access. Do not be discouraged by closed doors, but try to see courtyards and hidden staircases. Sometimes a polite smile at the caretaker is sufficient. A tip may be even more effective.

History of the Marais

Though there is evidence of a basilica on the site of the Church of Saint-Gervais since the late 4th c., the ancient parish of Saint-Paul had its origins in a small 7th-c. chapel. It was only during the 12th c. that this district, devoted to grazing land and market-gardening, really began to be occupied. The Ordre Militaire du Temple (Knights Templar) established its authority to the N and outside the walls of the town in a vast and arrogantly fortified enclave, surrounded with cultivated land. It was here that small merchants and craftsmen grew rich by evading official taxes and dues. At the beginning of the 13th c. many religious congregations followed the example of the Templars (Priory of Sainte-Catherine du Val-des-Ecoliers, Convent of the Blancs-Manteaux, Convent of Saint Croix-de-la-Bretonnerie, Convent of the Carmes-Billettes) while in the mid-13th c. Charles d'Anjou, king of Naples and Sicily and brother of St Louis, installed his residence on the site of no. 7 on the present-day Rue de Sévigné; the Rue de Roi-de-Sicile recalls his stay in Paris. In the 14th c. Charles V fled from the Palais de la Cité to the Hôtel Saint-Pol, the royal residence, situated between the Seine and the Rue Saint-Antoine. Of this collection of modest buildings interspersed with gardens and orchards, abandoned and divided up from the 15th c. onwards, only the place-names still evoke memories: Rue des Lions (menagerie), Beautreillis (vine), Rue de la Cerisaie (cherry orchard), Rue des Jardins-Saint-Paul. It was Charles V who closed the E extremity of the district: building the Bastille. Following the king's example, both laity and clergy built sumptuous dwellings (the Hôtel Clisson, Hôtel du Prevot Hugues Aubriot, and a little later the Hôtel des Archevêques de Sens). After the cramped and badly ventilated Hôtel Saint-Pol, Charles VI preferred the Hôtel des Tournelles, which was much more open, situated N of the Rue Saint-Antoine. It was here, in 1559, that Henri II lost his life in a tournament. His queen, Catherine de'Medici, loathing the hôtel, had the Tournelles torn down. The Marais, though abandoned by the Court, did not decline completely. The Hôtel Carnavalet and the Hôtel Angoulême were there to witness the splendors of the Renaissance and the triumph of the Italianizing style.

At the dawn of the Grand Siècle, the enlightened king, Henry IV, the first French king with an interest in urban designs, gave the Marais a new lease on life. The Place Royal project of 1605 was his own conception, and gave birth to the present-day Place des Vosges. The golden age of the Marais had begun. Both the *noblesse d'épée* (the old aristocracy) and the *noblesse de robe* (the newly elevated nobles drawn from the ranks of bourgeoisie), parvenu financiers, bourgeois merchants – everyone wanted to have a mansion here. The great architects, painters, sculptors worked here: Androuet de Cerceau, Le Muet, Le Vau, the Mansarts; Vouet, Le Brun, Mignard, Coysevox, to name only the most well known. It was a triumph for the worlds of letters and the arts: Mlle de Scudery, Mme de Sévigné, Scarron and his wife François d'Aubigné, the future Mme de Maintenon, held their salons here. Music was brilliantly represented with Marc-Antoine Charpentier in the Jesuit church, and the Couperins at Saint-Bervais. The Comédiens du Marais (future Comédiens Français) were Installed in the Rue Ville-du-Temple in 1634.

The early 18th c. was even more marked for its superb buildings – the Hôtel de Rohan, Hôtel de Soubise, the Hôtel d'Albret – though decline had already set in. The Palais-Royal came back into fashion during the Regency, while the old Marais district, with its narrow streets and relatively tiny courtyards, suddenly appeared less comfortable. More sweeping vistas and larger tracts of land were sought after, as fashionable districts of Saint-Germain and Saint-Honoré came into their own. The Marais still offers some brilliant examples of Louis XVI architecture, with the Hôtel d'Hallwyll and the Hôtel de Sandreville bearing witness to the Neo-Classical style characteristic of the end of the century.

The events of the Revolution dealt a fatal blow to the Marais. The mansions were abandoned by their emigré owners; the beautiful apartments were divided up, pillaged and sacked, while a new population of artisans and small shopkeepers moved in. In the 19th c. this slow degradation continued with the development of cottage industries. The courtyards of the old mansions were cluttered with workshops, lean-to sheds and warehouses. Even more damaging, perhaps, was the administrative vandalism which lasted for a century and a half, and caused the irreparable destruction of the Hôtel du Grand Prieur, the Hôtel Effiat and many others. The courageous and enlightened restoration policies of the Commission du Vieux Paris since 1898 have gone some way to repairing the damage.

Today the Marais is the subject of emotional debate. Malraux's bill of 1962 allowed the Conseil Municipal to initiate a plan to renovate the Marais, supported by various cultural associations. But despite much admirable restoration, the battle for the rehabilitation of the Marais is not yet won.

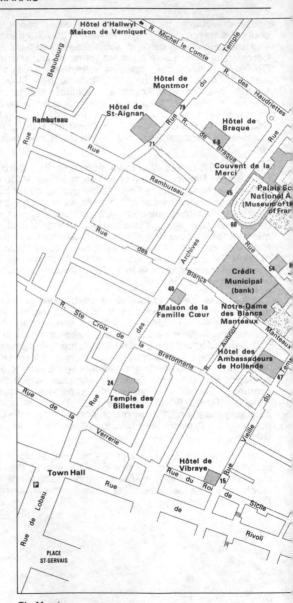

The Marais

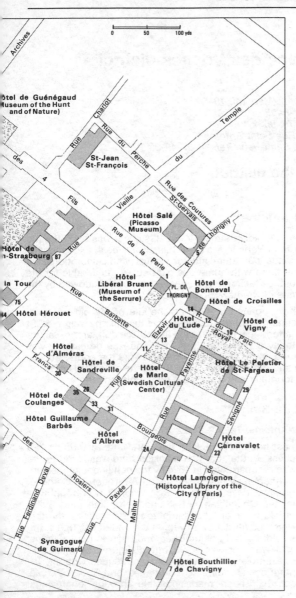

The Place des Vosges district***

3rd and 4th arr./Map. ref. 18–D2
Métro: Saint-Paul
Bus: 29, 69, 79, 96
Parking: 16 Rue Saint-Antoine
Taxis: Métro Saint-Paul. Tel: 48–87–49–39.

Tour of the district

1½ hrs.

Rue Saint-Antoine**

This is one of the oldest streets in Paris, since it was once the old Roman road from Paris to Melun. It has always been exceptionally wide, which made it a natural site for festivals and celebrations. On the N side it is lined with numerous old houses remarkable for the narrowness of their façades. The street is now overshadowed by the enormous mass of the new Opera House.

The Rue Caron, opened in 1783 on the site of the old priory of Sainte-Catherine-du-Val-des-Ecoliers, created in the reign of St Louis, leads, after a few paces, to the little Place du Marché-Sainte-Catherine*, today a pedestrian precinct. The Rue de Jarente was laid down at the same time as the square: note the courtyard, the paved porch and the staircase of no. 8, and the courtyards of no. 4. A Louis XVI fountain is at 2 Impasse de la Poissonnerie.

The Hotel de Sully***

62 Rue Saint-Antoine. Tel: 42–74–22–22

One of the most beautiful hôtels in the Marais, its restoration is a complete success. In the 16th c. a mansion here was razed to the ground, but was reconstructed in 1624 by the rich financier Mesme-Gallet. The architect may have been Jean I Androuet Du Cerceau. The *hôtel*'s greatest days began in 1634 when it was bought by Henri IV's minister, Maximilien de Béthune (better known as Sully) who spent his fortune on the sumptuous decorations for this mansion, in which he hardly ever lived. At the end of the 18th c. the mansion was sold, partially demolished and used to house shops; and after World War II it was constantly disfigured by makeshift buildings. An exemplary reconstruction by Jacques Dupont, In-specteur Général des Monuments Historiques, and Robert Vassas, chief architect, has been made possible through engravings, architectural drawings and archival research. Today the Hôtel de Sully is the head office of the Caisse Nationale des Monuments Historiques et des Sites, or CNMHS (National Historical Monuments and Sites Commission), which holds temporary exhibitions there.

The exterior (free entrance into the courtyard 10am–6pm). An intrusive building, added in the 19th c. between the lovely entrance pavilions with rounded pediments, has been demolished. The exceptional beauty of the stone of this *hôtel* has retained a Renaissance aspect with lavish ornamentation and the placement of its staircase. On its courtyard and garden façades the figures in bas-relief represent the *Elements* and the *Seasons*. Voltaire was beaten up under the portal by servants of a nobleman whom he had ridiculed – which made him a lifelong enemy of the nobility.

The interior (for visits: contact CNMHS, tel: 48–87–24–14 or 42–74–22–22) is remarkable for its staircase with an ornamental ceiling, its painted ceilings and the wainscotting with painted and gilded pilasters in Sully's apartments. Between 1634 and 1641, Sully built an orangery known as the 'Petit-Hôtel de Sully' at the end of his garden. This opened on to 7 Place Royale. It was detached from the mansion in the middle of the 19th c. but has now been rejoined. The cellars have been restored (open 10am–7pm). A door at the bottom of the garden gives access to the Place des Vosges or take the Rue de Birague, which was built in 1605 to give access from the Rue Saint-Antoine to the Place des Vosges.

Place des Vosges**

This was the first square in Paris, created by Henri IV, who took up a project of Catherine de' Medici, intended to replace the Hôtel des Tournelles. Access from the Rue Saint-Antoine is by the Rue de Birague, passing through the 'Pavillon du Roi'.

History of the square

Following a fatal lance thrust in the eye by his Scottish captain, Henri II was carried to the Hôtel des Tournelles where he finally died after six days on his deathbed. Poor Montgomery was executed, although it was an accident. Queen Catherine conceived a loathing for the enormous palace, built in 1388 for Pierre d'Orgemont, and which at the beginning of the 15th c. occupied all the space bounded by the Rue Saint-Antoine, the Rue des Tournelles, the Rue de Turenne and the Rue Saint-Gilles. Jean, Duc de Berry, had lived here as had the Duc d'Orléans, the mad king Charles VI, the Duke of Bedford, Regent of France after the death of his brother Henry V, and Louis XI; Louis XII died here. The sovereigns did not abandon it even when the Louvre returned to favor. In 1559, the marriage of Elizabeth of France to Philip II of Spain, the occasion on which the tragic tournament was held, was celebrated with great pomp in the presence of Queen Catherine and the king's mistress, Diane de Poitiers. With the king dead, Charles IX allowed Catherine to have the palace destroyed. An impressive horse fair took its place. Here, too, the famous duel between Henri III's favorites (three of the four were killed) and the Duc de Guise's men, was fought. At first Henri IV had no fixed ideas about the land. He built a silk factory (1604), then decided to border this with a public square whose three other sides would consist of housing for the workers. This project was not realized and the factory was demolished in 1607, and in 1609 buildings identical to those on the other three sides were erected in its place. The people's square became aristocratic; Henri IV wished it to be reserved for commerce, festivities and courtly activities. The architects' names are not known; they may have been Louis Métezeau and Jacques II Androuet Du Cerceau. In 1605 letters patent stipulated the indivisibility of both the plots of land and the buildings and a unity of building materials and design. Each building was to be two storeys high above arcades which formed galleries. The Place Royale, as it then was, was inaugurated on April 5, 6 and 7, two years after the death of its creator, on the occasion of the double marriage ceremony of Louis XIII and the Spanish infanta Anne of Austria, both aged 10, and of Madame, the king's sister, with the prince of Spain, which took place there. The great period of the Place Royale was, it would seem, the Louis XIII era; a play by Corneille was entitled *La Place Royale* (1634). But Louis XIV liked the Place Royal no more than he liked the Louvre, and the nobility had deserted it. However, until the 19th c. the *noblesse de robe* (nobles elevated from the bourgeoisie, by virtue of their functions) and the high financiers had remained faithful. With the coming of the Revolution, the Place Royale lost its statue of Louis XIII and became the Place de l'Indivisibilité at the same time as it was adapted to serve as a site for military fairs. And on September 23, 1800 it was renamed Place des Vosges in honor of the Vosges department, which had been the first to pay its taxes. After having been sorely neglected, the Place des Vosges has regained its elegance, and is trendy and a trifle snobbish.

Tour of the square

The Place des Vosges is a large rectangle surrounded by 36 *pavillons* or houses, with two taller buildings at either end, facing each other, the King's Pavilion and the Queen's Pavilion. The houses have a unity of design and are all built of red brick or plastered with rough cast to imitate brick, with white stone facings on the cornices, entablatures and window-frames. The king's instructions were meticulously followed by Sully: the height of the houses had to be roughly equal to their width, and the height of the blue slate roofs half that of the façades. Two storeys high, they are supported on arches which form galleries. The king was mainly preoccupied with the façades, which explains the variety of the

Place des Vosges

courtyards. Differences in the bull's eye (*oeil-de-boeuf*) windows are obvious; and balconies have been added to certain buildings. Malraux's 1965 restoration project was slow and not always completely accurate.

The equestrian statue of Louis XIII, in the middle of the square, is by Cortot and Dupaty. A sculpture of small distinction, it replaces the statue which was placed there in 1639 and destroyed during the Revolution. The Place des Vosges has regained its theatrical character and, in addition, several high-class shops: antique dealers, book shops, art galleries. In summer, musicians and itinerant artists liven up the arcades, and the cafés spread their tables further into the square.

A tour of the square should start from the l. of the Pavillon du Roi, that is with the uneven numbers. The Pavillon du Roi, at no. 1, is taller than the adjoining houses and, on the Rue de Birague side, has a profusion of decorative motifs (antique trophies symbolizing the Arts and Arms entwined with an H). On the square side, the head of Henri IV is carved on a medallion. At no. 1 *bis* is the Hôtel de Coulanges, built in 1606. Marie de Rabutin-Chantal, the future Mme de Sévigné, was born here on February 5, 1626. No. 7 is the Petit-Sully, originally meant as a hothouse for lemon trees, and the Orangery of the Hôtel de Sully (→above). At no. 9 is the Hôtel de Chaulnes, where the great 19th-c. tragedienne Rachel (d. 1858) lived a year before her death. To the r. in a vast courtyard surrounded by low old parish buildings, is an imposing mansion with a triangular pediment (J. Hardouin-Mansart, mid 17th c.). It still has its stone staircase, painted beams and Louis XVI décor. It has been occupied by the Académie d'Architecture since 1967. The Hôtel de Loménie de Brienne at no. 11 is where the courtesan Marion Delorme lived and received flocks of rich admirers (1639–48). Boussuet, the preacher and writer lodged at no. 17 (1682–84). A mansion at no. 21, the former home of Cardinal Richelieu, was bought in 1659 by his great-nephew. In front of the cardinal's house on the day his edict against duelling was proclaimed, François de Montmorency and Des Chapelles fought against Beuvron and Bussy. Alphonse Daudet also had an apartment here. The Hôtel de Bassompierre is at no. 23. Its remarkable staircase has balustrades adorned with large sculpted vases. No. 25 has a charming courtyard and steps with a wrought-iron handrail. No. 28 is the Pavillon de la Reine (the largest) and the Hôtel d'Espinoy. The *pavillon*, which has kept its original wainscotting in two rooms both registered as national historic places, is situated at one end of the Rue de Béarn and faces the Pavillon du Roi. No. 24 was the mansion of Louis Barbier de la Rivière, Bishop of Langres. This house, confiscated in 1793, was the town hall of the old 8th arrondissement until 1860. Today it is a synagogue. Part of its decoration and two of its painted ceilings by Le Vau and Le Brun have been removed to the Musée Carnavalet. Philippe, Marquis de Dangeau, owned the Hôtel de Dangeau at no.12, decorated by Le Sueur and Le Brun; it has belonged to the Ville de Paris since 1869. At no. 10 is the hôtel of Claude de Chastillon who, in 1605, was Henri IV's topographer and who undoubtedly played a great part in the city-planning projects. He is responsible for practically all the reproductions of maps and famous monuments of Paris of his time. Théophile Gautier and Alphonse Daudet lived for a time at no. 8. No. 6, where Victor Hugo lived from 1832 to 1848, was bought by the city of Paris in 1873 to house the Musée Victor Hugo (→Museums). Turn back to rejoin, on the r., the Rue du Pas-de-la-Mule, which is very uneven because the Boul. Beaumarchais, which it rejoins, was built over the old rampart.

Rue des Tournelles

The slope of this street has made certain modifications necessary in the architecture of several of its buildings. Note the courtyards of nos. 28, 56 and 60. To the r., no. 28 is the Hôtel Mansart de Sagonne* , built between 1674 and 1685 by Jules Hardouin-Mansart, grand-nephew of François Mansart, the Superintendent of Royal Buildings and renowned architect of the chapel of the Invalides, the chapel stables and the Orangerie and Trianon at Versailles, the Place Vendôme and the Place des Victoires.

The mansion is isolated from the street by outbuildings. Mansart had it decorated by Le Brun and Mignard, the greatest painters of his time: two of the original painted ceilings were discovered in 1939. The garden side can be seen from no. 23 Boul. Beaumarchais. Further along at no. 50 there is an imposing façade, recently restored, and a Louis XIII staircase with oak tracery. Take the Rue Verlomme to rejoin the Rue de Béarn.

Rue de Béarn: To the l., the N side of the Pavillon de la Reine can be seen. Follow the street to the r. An immense police barracks replaces the convent of the Minims (17th c.), the cloister of which survived until 1912. Cross the Rue des Minimes: at no. 12 the 17th-c. façade and the wrought-iron staircase are all that remain of the convent.

Rue Saint-Gilles

The immense Hôtel de Venise extends from no. 8 to no. 16. It was the site of a sort of industrial city; at no. 12 a large 17th-c. carriage archway and a *porte cochère* remain; to the r., at no. 10, there is a wrought-iron staircase. At no. 22 there is a *hôtel* erroneously known as Delisle-Mansart: this folly, with its multi-faceted design and a rotunda overlooking the garden, in fact dates back to the mid-18th c.

Rue de Turenne

The Hôtel de Montresor * is at no. 52–54. A municipal school since 1905, the façade of these magnificent twin mansions has recently been restored along with the superb Louis XIII staircase. At no. 59, on the corner of the Rue Villehardouin, there is beautiful niche with a statue of the Virgin. No. 66 still shows traces of the Hôtel de Turenne built for the famous marshal's father.

Rue Villehardouin*

For a short while in 1637 this street was named Rue des Douze-Portes (twelve doors) because of the twelve similar houses built here. Though extra storeys have been added to some, others are well preserved, no. 24 in particular. Some have kept their *porte-cochères* or staircases (see nos. 20 and 17).

The Hôtel known as 'du Grand Veneur' . . . .

60 Rue de Turenne

This building, with a boar's head on the façade, was begun in 1637, and underwent numerous modifications at the end of the century when it was bought by the chancellor Boucherat, who considerably enlarged it, adding the huge arched portal. Although the Marquis d'Ecquevilly, who was the owner in 1773, never held the title of Grand Veneur (Master of the Royal Hunt), he had the mansion decorated on both the street and courtyard sides with bas-reliefs relating to hunting, and reconstructed the r. wing and the magnificent staircase with finely carved banisters. The mansion was spoiled in the 19th c., first by a religious community and then by a business concern. But the mansion, which, together with its neighbor the Hôtel de Hesse (no. 26) is currently being extensively restored, should regain some of its former splendor. Opposite, at no. 67, two bulls' heads supporting the balcony are a reminder of the impressive butcher's shop which occupied the premises at the beginning of the 19th c.

⚱ The Church of Saint-Denis-du-Saint-Sacrement*

68 bis Rue de Turenne (9am–12pm/4:30–7pm. Tel: 42–72–28–96)

The church was built by Godde between 1826 and 1835 on the site of the Benedictine Convent of the Adoration Perpétuelle du Saint-Sacrement, established about 1684 by the Duchesse d'Aiguillon. It is one of numerous restoration churches. Its Neo-Classical façade with a peristyle of Ionic columns is surmounted by a pediment sculpted by Feuchères (1884): *La Foi, L'Espérance et la Charité* (Faith, Hope and Charity).

The interior

The organ was built by the Maison Daublaine-Callinet under the artistic direction of Félix Danjou (1839). The r. side aisle: the chapel of Sainte-Geneviève on the other side of the façade: *La Déposition du Croix* (Deposition) by Delacroix, (1844), lit from the foot of the altar; marble statue of St Geneviève by Perraud (1868). Chapelle de la Vierge (to the r. of the choir): *Notre-Dame-du-Bon-Secours* by Joseph-Désiré Court (1844); *La Vierge et L'Enfant Jésus* (Virgin and Child), marble by Debay (1861). The choir: the half-dome is decorated by Abel de Pujol (commissioned in 1861), in the upper part *Le Père Eternel* (Eternal Father); *Christ et la Vierge entoures d'Anges* (Christ and the Virgin Surrounded by Angels); below, *St Denis prechant dans les Gaul* (St Denis Preaching in Gaul), frieze in grisaille. The r. side aisle: Chapelle Saint-Denis to the l. of the choir: *Les Disciples d'Emmaus* by Picot (1840); marble statue of St Denis by Jules Thomas (1867). Chapel St-Jean-Baptiste on the other side of the façade: marble statue of the patron saint by Crauk (1863).

Rue Saint-Claude: at no. 1, the Hôtel Cagliostro (1719) whose façades were decorated with plaster work during the reign of Louis XVI.

Rue des Arquebusiers: nos. 8, 10, 11 and 13 are 18th-c. houses. At the back of no. 11 the Galerie-Orangerie, built for Claude de Guénégaud (17th c.), is visible. The Rue Saint-Antoine can be rejoined via the Rue de Turenne to reach one of the other two walks in the Marais.

▷ A respect for heritage

A look at the history of the Marais shows that the respect for
national heritage which inspired today's conservation plans is an
entirely new sentiment. A veneration for the past certainly did not
concern François I or Charles IX when they demolished the Hôtel
Saint-Pol and the Hôtel des Tournelles. This was also true of the
17th- and 18th-c. architects who often made way for their own
buildings by pulling down the mansions so admired today, and of
Louis XVI who had the convent de Saint-Catherine-du-Val-des-
Ecoliers razed to the ground. Neither the Revolution nor
Haussmann's 'Century of progress' had any respect for the city's
heritage: the Church of Saint-Paul disappeared in 1799, the Couvent
des Minimes, the Couvent des Célestins and the Couvent de l'Ave-
Maria fell one by one during the 19th c., as well as many of the
mansions. The 20th c. carried on with this devastation: in the name
of public health whole blocks were crossed off the map, such as the
area round the Hôtel de Sens. In 1927 Cognacq-Jay, a great art
lover, had the Hôtel de la Vieuville destroyed to make way for the
warehouses for his department stores. Later, another *hôtel* in the
Marais, spared on this occasion, received the collection which bears
his name. This posthumous redemption is indeed a sign of the
times.

▷ The *hôtel* between courtyard and garden

One of the particular charms of the Marais is its ability to surprise.
The splendor of its historic mansions is often hidden, because even
if the edges of places used for festivities apartments were turned to
face outward like real theater boxes (Place des Vosges, Hôtel de
Beauvais), the accent was generally on the building at the end of the
courtyard. This layout, rigorously planned around a central
courtyard, often with a garden, is characteristic of these mansions.
Some, such as the Hôtel de Châlon-Luxembourg, have only two
parallel buildings; but where the size of the land permitted, they
were joined by a wing, as with the Hotel de Saint-Aignan, or even
better by two, as with the Hôtel de Mayenne and the Hôtel de Sully,
the concern for symmetry being essential. For a regular plan it was
necessary to resort to illusion, arcades and blind windows (Hôtel de
Saint-Aignan), painted vistas like the Hôtel d'Aumont or the Hôtel
de Fieubet. The mansions attract the attention of passersby by their
portals, sometimes veritable triumphal arches attached to streetside
constructions which are often little more than enclosing walls.

▷ Henri IV, urban designer

When he entered Paris in 1594, Henri IV declared his intention of
living there and making his city '*un monde entier et un miracle du*

monde' (a whole world and a miracle of the world). He concentrated his earliest efforts on the Louvre (the Petite and Grande Galleries, and the Tuileries), ordered work to recommence on the Pont-Neuf, initiated the Place Dauphine project and lengthened the route to the Left Bank with the Rue Dauphine. Taking up an idea of Catherine de'Medici, he designed the Place Royal (now the Place des Vosges) and had work started on it with the least possible delay. His death interrupted the great Place de France project Temple (→quarter). Henry IV was also concerned with the upkeep of the streets, the collection of garbage and the public water service (restoration of the fountains, installation of the first pump, La Samaritaine). Putting into practice the lessons of an Italian model, he was the instigator of a movement which, after him, could serve as an example for all France: he can be justly considered the first urban planner not only for Paris, but for the whole country.

The Saint-Paul district**

4th arr./Map ref. 18–C2
Métro: Hotel-de-Ville
Bus: 38, 47, 58, 67, 69, 70, 72, 74, 75, 76, 96
Parking and taxis: Rue Lobau

Tour of the district

3 hrs.

Place Saint-Gervais

The square, which is dominated by the church of the same name, extends between two large annexes of the Hôtel de Ville and the former barracks, all built by Haussmann. In 1912 an elm was planted in the center of the square to revive the tradition of Saint-Gervais, according to which judges administered justice under an elm. The elm motif is also be be found on the surrounding buildings (→below) and on a sign in the Musée Carnavalet.

☦ The Church of Saint-Gervais-Saint-Protais**

Open daily except Mon. 6:30am–8pm. Tel: 42-72-64-99.

This is the church of one of the oldest parishes on the Right Bank. It is a surprise to find a magnificent Gothic church behind a Classical façade.

The history of the building

The origins of Saint-Gervais-Saint-Protais go back to the 6th c. Apparently, one church on this site was rebuilt in the 13th c. The present church, begun in 1494, was not completed until the 17th c., as shown by the numerous dates carved on the keys of the vaults and on the stained-glass windows. The Chapelle de la Vierge (Chapel of Our Lady), choir and transept date from the 16th c. The nave was built between 1600 and 1620 and on July 24, 1616 Louis XIII laid the first stone of the façade. In the 17th c. Marie de Rabutin-Chantal was married to the Marquis de Sévigné here. Many famous people are buried here, notably Scarron (first husband of Mme de Maintenon) (d. 1660), the Flemish painter Philippe de Champaigne (d. 1674), Chancellor Le Tellier (d. 1685) and Chancellor Boucherat (d. 1669). In 1793 the church was converted into the Temple of Youth, after its numerous tombs had been desecrated and its statues destroyed. Between 1840 and 1870 the City of Paris commissioned many decorations for the chapel in the side aisles, notably from Caminade, Alexandre Hesse, Glaize, Jobbé-Duval and others. Statues were commissioned for the façade and the stained-glass windows were restored by Gsell and Prosper Lafaye. On Good Friday, 1918 a German shell caused part of the vault to collapse, killing more than 100 people. For some years, the church has been served by the Fraternité Monastique de Jérusalem (→inset).

The exterior

The façade, dating from 1621, was for a long time thought to be by Salomon de Brosse, but today it is attributed to Clément II Métezeau. This was the first example in Paris of the superposition of the three Classical orders: Doric on the ground floor, Ionic on the first floor, Corinthian on top. The statues were remade in the 19th c.: *Moïse écrivant le Pentateuque* (Moses writing the Pentateuch), by Dantan, and *St Gervais* by Jouffroy (1849).

The interior

The nave. The 18th-c. organ case is partially reconstructed with some elements of the old 17th-c. case. The organ originally belonged to the famous dynasty of French musicians, the Couperin family; François Couperin composed his two masses here in 1685. The most recent restorations date from 1874, when the mechanics were entirely restored to their original condition. On either side of the 19th-c. pulpit are *The Four Evangelists* in bronze, by Leboeuf-Nanteuil and Laitié (1825). Note the 17th-c. churchwardens/ pew,

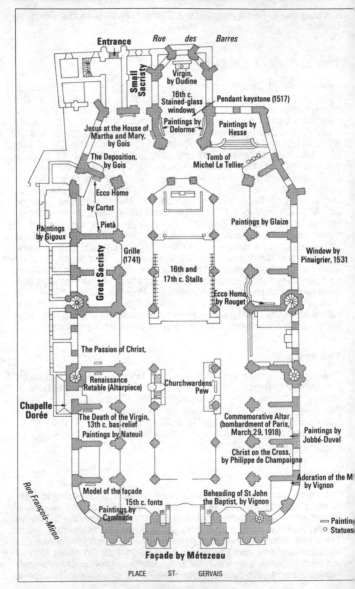

Entrance

Rue des Barres

Virgin, by Oudine

Small Sacristy

16th c. Stained-glass windows

Pendant keystone (1517)

Paintings by Delorme

Paintings by Hesse

Jesus at the House of Martha and Mary, by Gois

Tomb of Michel Le Tellier

The Deposition, by Gois

Ecco Homo by Cortot

Pietà

Paintings by Gigoux

Paintings by Glaize

Great Sacristy

Grille (1741)

Window by Pinaigrier, 1531

16th and 17th c. Stalls

Ecco Homo by Rouget

The Passion of Christ,

Renaissance Retable (Altarpiece)

Churchwardens' Pew

Chapelle Dorée

The Death of the Virgin, 13th c. bas-relief

Paintings by Nateuil

Commemorative Altar (bombardment of Paris, March 29, 1918)

Paintings by Jobbé-Duval

Christ on the Cross, by Philippe de Champaigne

Adoration of the M by Vignon

Model of the façade

Rue François-Miron

15th c. fonts

Paintings by Caminade

Beheading of St John the Baptist, by Vignon

— Painting
○ Statues

Façade by Métezeau

PLACE   ST-   GERVAIS

Saint-Gervais-Saint-Protais

the central section by Jacob Desmalter was unfortunately removed in 1877 to a side-chapel on the r.

The r. side-aisle. Above the entrance to the r., *Décollation de St Jean Baptiste* (Beheading of John the Baptist) by Claude Vignon, 17th c. 1st chapel: *L'Adoration des Mages** (Adoration of the Magi), also by Claude Vignon. 2nd chapel: *Le Christ en Croix* (Christ on the Cross) attributed to Philippe de Champaigne; above, *Retour de Tobie* (The Return of Tobias), cartoon for a tapestry attributed to Sébastien Bourdon; *Grégoire le Grand et Vital intercédant auprès de la Vierge pour les âmes du Purgatoire* (St Gregory the Great and St Vitalis interceding with the Virgin for the Souls in Purgatory), picture by Sebastiano Ricci, 18th c. 3rd chapel: murals by Jobbé-Duval (1869); altar commemorating the bombing of March 29, 1918. 4th chapel: *St Catherine*, marble statue by Cortot; seven small panels representing scenes from the *Life of Christ* (17th c.). R. transept: large retable with altar cloth dating from the 17th c. illustrating Pentecost; opposite, *St Ambrose and the Emperor Theodosius* by Couder (1827).

The chancel has a double row of stalls (family subjects) which date partly from the reign of Henri II and partly from the 17th c. Principal altar ornaments: 18th-c. bronze-gilt cross and candelabra by Soufflot, from the old Abbaye de Sainte-Geneviève. To the r. and the l. of the high altar there are wooden statues of St Gervais and St Protais, the church's patron saints, by Michel Bourdin (17th c.) At the entrance to the chancel, against the NW pillar of the transept, a 14th-c. Virgin and Child in stone.

The ambulatory. 1st chapel: 16th-c. stained-glass window depicting *Le martyre des St Gervais et Protais*; *Ecce Homo* by Rouget (1835). 2nd chapel: large stained-glass window of 1531, *Jugement de Salomon*, attributed to Pinaigrier (restored in the 19th c.) 3rd chapel: on the retable of the altar: *St-Geneviève rendant la vue a sa mère* (St Genevieve restoring her mother's sight) by Boulanger (1841); murals by Glaize (1863) depicting the life of St Geneviève. 4th chapel: tomb of Michel Le Tellier, Grand Chancellor under Louis XIV by Mazeline and Hurtrelle (statue of the Chancellor and two allegorical figures; this monument is incomplete; – part of it is in the Louvre). Three praying statues (the Duc and Duchesse de Tresmes and the Duc de Gesvres) from the old Célestins' church, were placed in this chapel in 1977. The murals by Alexandre Hesse (1863) recall the lives of St Gervais and St Protais. 5th chapel: Chapelle de la Vierge: At the junction of the double arch an open-work stone crown (1517) by the Jacquet brothers, 8ft/2.5m in diameter, hangs from the vault. Three windows showing the Life of the Virgin, are attributed to Pinaigrier, restored in 1846 by Gsell; murals by Delorme (1842); statue of the Virgin by Oudiné (1844). 6th chapel: *Descente de la Croix* (The Deposition), group sculpted by Gois (19th c.) 7th chapel: plaster *Pietà and Ecce Homo* by J.-P. Cortot (19th c.); the chapel communicates with the Chapelle Saint-Joseph, constructed in 1697 by the Chancellor Louis Boucherat (Louis XV confessional) and is decorated with murals by Gigoux (1863). 8th and 9th chapels: the large sacristy in the N choir aisle has a fine iron grille by Vallet (1741), decorated with 18th-c. wainscotting.

The sacristy is below the tower; *Christ en Croix* sculpted by Préault (1840). To the l., in the wall of the tower, is the church consecration stone (1420).

The l. transept: scenes from the *Passion*, painting on wood attributed to H. Aldegraever (16th c.).

The l. side-aisle. 1st chapel: 17th-c. retable with 19th-c. plaster statues; at the end, the old wooden choir screen with openwork design from the Chapel Dorée (for visits, apply at the sacristy) was built out of alignment in 1628 by Antoine Coussault, Counsellor of State. Its 17th-c. decoration, a series of small pictures of Flemish inspiration representing the *Life and Passion of Christ*, have been preserved. 2nd chapel: an altar frontal consisting of a medieval bas-relief depicting *The Death of the Virgin*; medallion by Charles Bordes (1863–1909), choir master of the Chapelle de Saint-Gervais and founder of the Schola Cantorum; paintings by Auguste Hesse and Nanteuil recall the *Life of St Laurent* (1860–73). 3rd chapel (baptismal fonts): 15th-c. baptismal fonts; 17th-c. statue in wood of John the Baptist; wooden model of the portal by Métezeau; two 17th-c. window fragments, *Baptism of Christ* after Raphael, *Christ and St Nicholas*.

Rue François-Miron

The stepped street which flanks the N side of the church is part of the old Rue Saint-Antoine, and one of the most impressive in the district. It took its name from a 17th-c. merchant provost.

A fine group of 18th-c. houses has been restored (1957), as have the houses of the adjacent block, by the architect Laprade. These houses, from nos. 2 to 24, are the old Pourtour Saint-Gervais* (the Saint-Gervais boundary) going back to no. 17 Rue des Barres. These houses, built in 1732 as church workshops on the site of 15th-c. buildings, all bear on their first floor balconies the symbolic elm in wrought-iron, work of the master ironsmith J.-B Bouillot. A sensitive piece of restoration (1945–49) refurbished the original arcades and the old road signs. At no. 2 is the entrance to the old cemetery. Nos. 2–4 were the house of the Couperin family, the famous dynasty of organists (at Saint-Gervais) and composers. François, known as Couperin le Grand, was born in 1668 in the old 15th-c. dwelling which stood on the same site. Ledru-Rollin was born at no. 10 in 1807. The Discothèque de France, founded in 1960, was installed at no. 12 in 1967. At no. 14 is an attractive balcony with a particularly detailed elm motif. The building departs from the most common design in the area with a *piano nobile* (main floor with reception rooms) taller, than usual. It was built in 1727 by J. A. Gabriel and magnificently restored in 1965. Opposite, in the Place Baudoyer, is the town hall of the 4th arrondissement. It houses a public library and organizes exhibitions.

Rue des Barres

From no. 15 the old Saint-Gervais charnel-house can be seen through a gate. No 12 is a double-gabled house* which formed part of the Hôtel de l'Abbaye de Maubuisson. Restoration work has uncovered the original half-timbering and the foundation of a turret which no longer exists, and refurbished the corbelling. It is occupied by the Accueil des Jeunes en France, an organization that provides various services to young tourists. A wide opening at the corner of the Rue des Barres and the Rue de l'Hôtel-de-Ville now gives a fine view* from the *quai* onto the apse and the S façade of the church, partly uncovered in 1946. The Rue de l'Hotel-de-Ville. To the r. a fragment of the old Hôtel-d'O (17th c.) has been mounted on the modern buildings of the Compagnons du Devoir du Tour de France (the committee that organizes the famous bicycle race). The gate at no. 62, decorated with pigeons, came from an old inn, L'Auberge du Pigeon-Blanc.

Rue du Pont-Louis-Philippe

At no. 6, the exterior and interior decoration of a former dairy has been preserved. In the courtyard of no. 22 *bis* is a Renaissance-style house* with a brick façade and curious stone pilasters. It overlooks the entrance to another house with Corinthian pilasters of carved wood and a staircase with a balustrade which is said to have been made for Marie Touchet, favorite of Charles IX (visit by request). At no. 13 on the corner of the Rue Cloche-Perce, there is a gabled half-timbered house dating from the late Middle Ages. No. 42 is the Hôtel de la Barre de Carron, built in 1742 by P. de Vigny with a Louis XV façade adorned with wrought ironwork. At nos. 44-46 is a late 16th-c. – early 17th-c. building, the former house of the Abbey of Ourscamps. It now belongs to the Association du Paris Historique (68 Rue Francois-Miron), which is restoring it and has uncovered some Gothic cellars. No. 48 is a Directoire house. The wine merchant's gates date from this time. At the corner of the Rue Tiron, a bakery has retained its old shop front.

Rue Geoffroy-l'Asnier

Walk up this street and back again. At no. 26 the Hôtel de Châlons-Luxembourg*, built shortly after 1625 by G. Perrochel, has a magnificent doorway. He carved the interlaced P and B (for his wife,

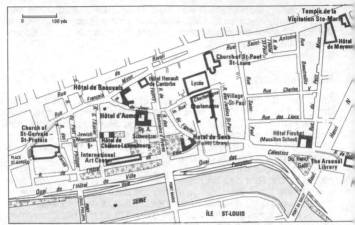

The Saint-Paul district

F. Buisson) on the dormer pediments. A certain Béon de Lux-embourg bought it in 1658, and from 1659 her name was added to that of Châlon as shown on the portal. There is a pretty Louis XIII pavilion in the courtyard. Gabriele D'Annunzio, the Italian poet, stayed here in 1915. Today it houses the Institut d'Histoire de Paris. The sumptuous portal* is one of the rare examples of Baroque in the Marais. The carriage entrance, with magnificent carved doors, is framed by Ionic columns supporting a large arcade. The tympanum is ornamented with a broad shell motif and a lion's head. The mansion is a fine example of the Henri-IV – Louis- XIII style, built of brick with stone quoins and set between courtyard and garden. At no. 22, a 17th-c. building has a carved door and a staircase with balustrade. At the end of the courtyard is a Louis XIII *hôtel*. Also note the staircases at no. 20.

At the corner of the Rue Geoffroy-l'Asnier and the Rue du Grenier-sur-l'Eau is the Memorial to an Unknown Jewish Martyr inaugurated on October 30, 1956 (architects: G. Goldberg, A. Persitz and L. Arretche). Below the courtyard in the crypt is the tomb of the unknown martyr. Behind it, no. 17 is clad in marble: its four floors house the archives of the Centre de Documentation Juif de Paris (Jewish Study Center) and a library (open daily except Sat. and Sun. morning, 10am–12pm and 2pm–5pm). To the side, towards the Seine, are buildings reserved for the enlargement of the Cité des Art (→below). During construction in 1985 a Gothic cellar was discovered.

☐ Hôtel de Beauvais**

68 Rue François Miron

This mansion, an architectural *tour de force* by Antoine Lepautre, was built in 1657 on the site of two dwellings belonging to the Abbaye de Chaalis of which Gothic cellars are still visible (to visit, apply to the Association du Paris Historique, 68 Rue François-Miron). The mansion was built for Pierre Beauvais with money he received in exchange for looking the other way while the 14-year-old Louis XIV was being taught the facts of life by Beauvais' 40-year-old wife, Catherine-Henriette Bellier, lady-in-waiting to Louis' mother Anne of Austria, and known as 'Cateau-la-Borgnese' (because she had only one eye). It was from the *hôtel's* balcony that Anne of Austria, Princess Henrietta of England, Cardinal Mazarin, Turenne and their followers watched the young Louis XIV and Marie-Thérèse enter Paris on August 26, 1660. After the death of the owners this great house passed through many hands, including those of the Bavarian ambassador, who lodged there for five months in 1763, during which time his guests included the seven-year-old Wolfgang Amadeus Mozart, his father Leopold, and his sister: a plaque commemorates their visit. Queen Christina of Sweden stayed here later. In the 18th c. the façade was mutilated, and a new row of windows was put in on the first floor. The portal, which is set back, has a half-dome supporting the balcony. It has been surrounded by shops ever since it was built.

When the architect Lepautre constructed this mansion for the Beauvais, it was considered the most sumptuous in Paris. Its highly original plan was imposed by its irregularly shaped plot. The inner courtyard, a semi-oval surrounded by Ionic pilasters, is unusual. The five doors decorated with grotesque masks are from the old stables. At the end, on the l., is a very beautiful staircase with wrought-iron handrail. The other side of the façade is decorated with Ionic and Corinthian pilasters. On the ground floor the circular vestibule with eight Doric columns is decorated with rams' heads (*têtes de bélier*), which recall the name of the first owner, Catherine Bellier. The main staircase, with Corinthian columns and stone banisters, and the hall, decorated with bas-reliefs, reveal the grandiose ambitions of its creators. Unfortunately none of the original interior decoration remains. The *hôtel* is now empty but in 1990 it will be restored, together with the neighboring Hôtel du Président Hénault (no. 82). On leaving, note the coal merchant's shop. The Hôtel Hénault de Cantorbe, also called the Hôtel du Président Hénault, at no. 82 Rue François-Miron, was built during the early 18th c. on the site of the Hôtel Du Guesclin. Note the balcony with ornamental brackets. In the courtyard to the r., there is a broad flight of stairs with wrought-iron handrail.

Rue de Fourcy

The pavement was recently enlarged by an arcaded passage. A gate will give access to pedestrian walkways which will provide links between the Rue François-Miron, Rue de Fourcy and Rue de Jouy. The restoration of the block should be finished in 1990. Opposite, the 17th-c. mansion at no. 6 has been restored and turned into a youth center (MIJE).

Rue de Jouy. An old knife-grinder's sign has been remounted on a modern building which forms the corner. The restoration of the even-numbered side, by the OPHLM of the City of Paris, has now been completed. In practice it concerned only the façades. Note the façade and Louis XV portal of no. 12.

The Hôtel d'Aumont*

7 Rue de Jouy

The mansion, which houses the Tribunal Administratif de la Seine, was built in 1648 for Michel-Antoine Scarron, uncle of the poet Paul Scarron, by Le Vau. In 1656, Antoine d'Aumont commissioned François Mansart to alter the garden façade and parts of the house. The interior decoration by Le Brun and Simon Vouet still exists. Condemned in the 18th c., mutilated in the 19th c., the mansion was bought by the City of Paris in 1932. It was restored, enlarged and partly reconstructed only in 1960. No more sumptuous mansion exists which so satisfactorily combines two different architectural styles. Of the rich interior decoration (visits by request) two ceilings with painted beams survive. One ceiling has arches carved by Le Brun. In the courtyard concerts and plays are sometimes given during the Festival of the Marais. Mansart's façade on to the garden can be seen through the gates of the big garden, unfortunately closed to the public since 1985.

The Rue Charlemagne, which existed from the 14th c. onwards under the name of Rue des Prêtres-Saint-Paul, took the name of the neighboring school in 1844. At no. 25 the Louis XVI façade has been reconstructed.

The Rue du Figuier, which is flanked by new buildings, recalls in its narrowness, its medieval past.

To the r., between two recently restored 17th-c. buildings (nos. 18 and 20), is another medieval street, the former Rue Percée, whose name is still carved there. Today it is the Rue du Prévôt, so named in 1877 in honor of Hugues Aubriot who lived there in the 14th c. in a luxurious *hôtel* which extended to where the Church of Saint-Paul stands today. Note the door at no. 8.

Rue Saint-Antoine**

→*Place des Vosges district*

This street is a continuation of the Rue de Rivoli, which it does not resemble at all. Running parallel to the Seine, it was the old Roman road to the E. It still retains a number of tall, narrow 17th-c. and 18th-c. dwellings. Although they lack the prestige of the large *hôtels* of the Marais, they constitute in themselves a homogenous ensemble and are not without charm. This portion of the street is very lively, partly due to the stalls of the street vendors. The Hôtel Séguier, at no. 133, dates from the early 17th c. It has a beautiful ornate balcony decorated with chimerae, dating from 1728, and a Louis XIII staircase. A Wallace fountain stands opposite no. 121. The Ionic pillars and the staircase at no. 111 are worth seeing. The Lycée Charlemagne (no. 101) is in the former Maison Professe des Jesuites, and the school library occupies the apartment of Père Lachaise. In the passage the cupola of the main staircase can be seen; it was painted in the 17th c. by Gherardini.

It is to be hoped that the current restoration of the school will enable visitors to see the frescoes long hidden under a false ceiling in the old library.

⚓ The Church of Saint-Paul-Saint-Louis**

99 Rue Saint-Antoine (open 8am–7:30pm). Tel: 42–72–30–32.

History of the building

This is one of the rare buildings in Paris that can be called 'Jesuit'. The foundation of the 'Grands-Jésuites' or Church of Saint-Paul-Saint-Louis in the Rue Saint-Antoine dates back to 1580. Only later, from 1627 to 1641, the Jesuits, with strong support from Louis XIII, built a church worthy of their powerful position. Three architects, members of the Society, were responsible for the construction of the church. The Baroque portal is by Father Martellange; the overall design is by Father Derrand and Father Turmel. The work was carried on by Father Martellange until 1629. In that year Father Derrand replaced him: it fell to him to finish the upper parts of the church, raising the dome, the largest in Paris at that time, and the chief innovation of the Jesuit style) and constructing the façade. The church was finished in 1641 and Richelieu celebrated the first Mass there on May 9. The rather ornate interior and the furnishings were completed by Father Turmel in 1647. The church was known for the richness of its furnishings and works of art. These are now dispersed, among other places, to the Louvre and Chantilly. The high altar, now vanished, was particularly sumptuous. In its center four pictures alternated, according to the liturgical calendar. One, *La Présentation au Temple*, by Simon Vouet, is in the Louvre. Until 1762, the year when the Jesuits were again expelled from the kingdom, the church enjoyed a truly golden age. The Saint-Louis pulpit became famous for its great preachers, such as Bossuet, Fléchier and above all Bourdaloue, of whom Mme de Sévigné was a great devotee ('he preached like an angel', she said). On the Maître de Chapelle's lectern there are also some famous names, including those of Marc-Antoine Charpentier and J.-P. Rameau. The church contained the magnificent mausoleum of Henri II de Bourbon (today in Chantilly). The hearts of Louis XIII and Louis XIV and of other great princes were kept here for many years. During the Revolution the church served as a repository for books from the numerous monasteries in the district, and in 1792 was robbed of its works of art, and the Culte de Raison was celebrated there briefly around 1793. In 1802 the old Jesuit church was appropriated as a parish church, dedicated under the double name of Saint-Paul-Saint-Louis, the Church of Saint-Paul-des-Champs having been demolished in 1797. Baltard undertook its restoration under the Second Empire, which involves mainly the renovation of the façade and the alteration of the choir. The church was pillaged twice during the 19th c., in 1831 and 1871.

The exterior

The façade, built by Father Derrant, has three storeys (two Corinthian and one Composite). Its decoration recalls the Flemish Baroque style. The statues having disappeared in the Revolution, in 1860 the City of Paris commissioned the three to be seen today: *St Louis* by Lequesne, *St Anne* by Etex and *St Catherine* by Préault. The clock comes from the former Church of Saint-Paul-des-Champs. The apse is visible from the Rue des Jardins-Saint-Paul, and from Philippe Auguste's old ramparts.

The interior

The nave. The plan, directly inspired by the Gesù church in Rome, has neither aisles nor ambulatory. The side chapels, covered with small domes, are intercommunicating and have aisles. The large arcades are surmounted by galleries. The entablature frieze is decorated with foliage, heads of cherubim and monograms of Christ and the Virgin. Either side of the entrance: shell-shaped holy water stoups donated by Victor Hugo, who lived in the Place des Vosges.

The transept. Over the crossing of the transept is a dome, 180ft./ 55m high, whose pendentives (curved triangular sections formed by the intersection of two arches) are adorned with large medallions depicting the Evangelists. This was the first dome of such a size built in Paris and was the forerunner of the domes of the Sorbonne, the Val-de-Grâce and the Invalides. The paintings between the windows were executed in 1873 by P.-J. Blanc and represent Robert the Pious, Clovis, Charlemagne and St Louis.

The r. transept. This Chapelle de la Vierge (Chapel of Our Lady) was first dedicated to St Francis-Xavier. On each side of the altar two 18th-c. plaster statues: l., *La Religion instruisant un Américain* (Religion instructing an American Indian) by Adam; r., *L'Ange de la Réligion foudroyant l'Idolatorie* (The Angel of Religion Striking Idolatry with Lightning) by Vinache. On the wall to the l.: *Louis XIII offre le Modèle de l'Eglise St Louis* (Louis XIII offering a model of the Church to St Louis) from Simon Vouet's studio; on the wall to the r.: *La Mort de St Louis* (Death of St Louis) by Jacques de Letin; these canvases are part of a series of four, commissioned in the mid 17th c. to decorate the transept; the fourth has unfortunately disappeared.

The l. transept. In this chapel stood the monument containing the heart of Henri II de Bourbon, Prince de Condé (today in Chantilly). On the l. wall: *St Louis recevant la Couronne d'Epines des Mains du Christ* (St. Louis receiving the Crown of Thorns from the Hands of Christ) from the studio of Simon Vouet; this work belongs to the same group as that in the r. transept. On the r. wall: *Le Christ au Jardin des Oliviers** (Christ in the Garden of Olives) by Delacroix, a painting commissioned by the City of Paris and exhibited at the Salon in 1827.

The chancel. Set into the modern altar is a 17th c. gilt bronze bas-relief depicting *Les Pèlerins d'Emmaüs* (The Pilgrims at Emmaus) by François Anguier. It comes from the high altar of the Church of Val-de-Grâce. On the apse wall *The Four Evangelists* painted by Decaisne (1840–43). The two side chapels, enclosed by 17th-c. wrought-iron gates, are decorated with beautiful Louis XIII paneling. It is in these chapels that the monuments destroyed in the Revolution containing the hearts of Louis XIII and Louis XIV were kept; Louis XIII's monument and the medallions sculpted by Sarrazin are preserved in the Louvre. It was originally intended for the Chapelle des Valois at Saint-Denis.

Leave by the picturesque Passage Saint-Paul. Opposite, on the corner of the Rue Saint-Paul and Rue Neuve-Saint-Pierre is a section of wall from the N tower of the old 13th-c. Church of Saint-Paul which was destroyed in 1799.

A little further on, to the r., the Rue de l'Hôtel-Saint-Paul, which took its name from Charles V's residence.

Rue Beautreillis

Walk up this street and back again. It was laid down in the 16th c. across the gardens and vineyards of the Hôtel Royal Saint-Pol which extended as far as here. Some beautiful houses have been preserved. Baudelaire lived with Jeanne Duval (1858–59) in the Grand Hôtel de Charny at no. 22, built in 1676. The portal is decorated with mascarons and brackets, sculpted doors and, under the vault, doors surrounded with paneling in the purest Louis XIII style. Note the unusual passage at the Petit Hôtel de Charny (no. 16), the wrought ironwork at no. 11, the late 16th-c. houses and courtyards at nos. 7 and 9. No. 10, the Hôtel des Princes de Monaco, is one of the finest 16th-c. houses in Paris.

Before rejoining the Rue Saint-Antoine note on the left the ancient wine-merchant's.

The Hôtel de Mayenne, also called the Hotel d'Ormesson

21 Rue Saint-Antoine. (open during the school term).

The mansion was built in 1613 for Henri de Mayenne from plans by Jean or Jacques II Androuet Du Cereau, and was one of the first examples of a mansion built between courtyard and garden. It was considerably modified in 1709 by Boffrand, who, in order to install a mezzanine floor, replaced the tall windows of the ground floor with arcades. The window's four curved pediments can still be seen. After 1870 the two corner pavilions were linked by an attic storey. The original structure can be envisaged by comparing it with the Hôtel de Sully (→ Place des Vosges district). In a courtyard, to the r., is a corbelled turret and, to the l., a gallery and a graceful staircase at the end of the courtyard. The mansion has been occupied since 1870 by the Brothers of the Ecoles Chrétiennes previously installed in the Rue Francs-Bourgeois, whose name the school has kept.

♱ The Temple de la Visitation Sainte-Marie*

History of the building

This circular church was built between 1632 and 1634 on the site of the Hôtel d'Etampes as a chapel for the Convent of the Visitation-Sainte-Marie. It was François Mansart's first major work. The Minister of Finances Fouquet, and Jeanne de Chantal, later canonized, the first Mother Superior of the order, which was founded in 1610 by Francis de Sales, were buried here. Vincent de Paul was chaplain of the convent. Closed in 1793 and made into a repository for confiscated books, the church became Protestant in 1802. It was badly damaged in 1871 and had to undergo a complete restoration. Remains of the convent can be seen at no. 19. It is still a Protestant church.

The interior

This is a fine circular building, decorated with Classical garlands, draperies and Corinthian pilasters. Between the W aisle and the S part of the nave, a small crypt contains a number of desecrated sarcophagi, still containing bones, some of which might well be those of Fouquet or St Jeanne de Chantal. In a church out-building to the E of the choir, fragments of a 17th-c. ceiling with frescoes were found in 1948.

Return as far as the Rue du Petit-Musc, a corruption of the phrase '*La pute y muse*' ('the whore loiters here'). This street was in the past frequented by sailors from the port of Saint-Paul. There are some old houses, including nos. 33 and 27.

Rue Charles-V (to the r.)

This fine, calm and dignified street was cut through the former Hôtel Saint-Pol in the 16th c. (→inset). It was formerly called the Rue Neuve-Saint-Paul. It has retained some beautiful 17th-c. portals (particularly at no. 15), some fine wrought ironwork (note the Regency balcony at no. 2) and staircases (at nos. 15 and 21). The Hôtel de Brinvilliers (or d'Aubray) at no. 12 was built around 1620 for Balthazar Gobelin, whose son Antoine, the Marquis de Brinvilliers, was married to Maire-Madeleine d'Aubray, the notorious poisoner who was beheaded in the Place de Grève in 1676, and then burnt, 'so that', in the words of Mme de Sévigné, 'we are all breathing her now'. The mansion has an impressive portal and a large courtyard lengthened by a garden. The l. wing retains a fine staircase and a carved ceiling. The r. wing ends in a half tower with a conical roof.

Rue Saint-Paul: At no. 28 note the wine merchant's gate. No 8 is an 18th -c. building; in the courtyard, both wings have large staircases with wrought-iron banisters.

Rue des Lions

This street was laid out in the 16th c. near the Hôtel Saint-Pol menagerie. There is a 16th-c. corbelled turret at the corner of the Rue Saint-Paul. The Hôtel Louis XIII is at no. 12. The little 17th-c. mansion at no. 11 was the home of the Marquise de Sévigné from 1644 to 1650; note the portal with studded panels. A passage in a modern building at no. 10 leads to a 1642 mansion with a courtyard and two staircases. One of them, at the end of the courtyard to the r., has interlacing motifs and carved panels, as well as a stone urn, which are particularly worth seeing. Note the courtyards at nos. 9 and 7 and the portal at no. 5. The house known as the Hôtel des Parlementaires de la Fronde (18th c.) at no. 3 has an attractive staircase to the l. and in the courtyard, to the r., a Louis XV fountain which was restored in 1970. The garden façade of no. 1, the Hotel de Fieubet, is by Jules Hardouin-Mansart (→ below).

The Quai des Célestins

The *quai* bears the name of a huge Carmelite convent, later a Celestine monastery, which was in an area today covered by the Place de la Bastille and extending as far as the Seine.

The Hôtel de Fieubet*, on the corner of Quai des Célestins and the Rue du Petit-Musc, is imposing. Gaspard Fieubet, chancellor to Anne of Austria, had it built by Jules Hardouin-Mansart in place of an early 17th-c. mansion, of which some elements still remain. The interior was decorated by Le Brun and his pupils. The original gardens were splendid with fountains and a vista painted on a party-wall. It was altered completely but not improved by the Comte de Lavalette in 1858, with the addition of a belvedere, bell-tower dome, caryatids and swags. In 1877 the Fathers of the Oratory put up a building along the wing which faced out onto the Rue du Petit-Musc. Note the façade on to the garden and the turret on the corner. It still contains the Massillon school, and the first sphinxes seen in Paris still guard the door. The Hotel Nicolai (17th c.) at no. 4 was possibly built by François Mansart. It retains its proportions and very fine wrought-iron banisters. The sculptor Barye died there in 1875. At the corner of the *quai* and the Rue Saint-Paul is the Hôtel de la Vieuville. Built in the 16th c., it was destroyed in 1927 and replaced by the enormous warehouses of the Samaritaine, now converted into apartments.

Take the Rue de l'Ave-Maria, named after a convent which disappeared in the 19th c.

The Rue des Jardins-Saint-Paul (to the r.) provides a fine view of the E end of the Church of Saint-Paul-Saint-Louis. The demolition of the houses on the W side, alongside the little Charlemagne school, has freed part of the perimeter wall of Philippe Auguste (→inset) of which Rabelais, who died in this street in 1553, said '*une vache avec un pet en abatroit plus de six brasses*' ('a cow could knock down six arm spans of it with one fart').

The Saint-Paul village

The area bounded by the Rue de Jardins-Saint-Paul, Rue Saint-Paul, Rue Charlemagne and Rue de l'Ave-Maria, known as the Saint-Paul village, is a good example of the preservation of an area which had been condemned. Many of the old houses have been restored. There remain some 17th-c. staircases and medieval cellars, such as that at no. 14 Rue des Jardins-Saint-Paul. At street level the antique shops, second-hand shops, arts and craft workshops are spread around a pleasant pedestrian precinct. A large second-hand fair, during which the whole village is transformed into a souk, takes place four times a year.

The Rue des Jardins-Saint-Paul runs into the Rue Charlemagne. At no. 8 there is a fountain from 1846. Two 17th-c. buildings, nos. 4 and 6, have recently been restored.

The Rue Eginhard to the l.: (on the l.), a 17th-c. outdoor well has been restored; the small Lycée Charlemagne school is at no. 13 on the site of the convent of the nuns of Ave-Maria.

Rue du Fauconnier (l. of the Rue Charlemagne): no. 11 is a large 17th-c. mansion occupied by a youth center, the MIJE, and the only old building in this medieval street.

The Hôtel de Sens

1 Rue du Figuier. Tel: 42-78-17-34

With the Hôtel de Cluny and the Jacques Coeur house, this fine mansion is one of the rare examples of medieval Parisian civil architecture. It now houses the Forney library, devoted to the fine arts.

This *hôtel* is the third Hôtel de Sens and it is to Tristan de Salazar, bishop of Sens, that this fortified mansion is owed, built between 1474–75 and 1519. Until 1623, the bishopric of Paris was suffragan to the metropolitan see Sens. Thus the *hôtel* was occupied by the Bourbons and the Guises and by Monseigneur de Pellevé, who turned it into a stronghold of La Ligue (the confederation of Catholics against the Calvinists). While Henri IV was entering Paris, monseigneur died of apoplexy and outrage in this house. Henri IV, finding it unoccupied, lodged his ex-wife, the extravagant Marguerite of Valois (la Reine Margot), there in 1599. She made this citadel of faith a place of romance and sometimes tragedy before she left it for the Pré-aux-Clercs. The bishops of Sens remained the owners of the mansion after the creation of the bishopric of Paris, when they began to rent it out. Art students, laundry maids, jam makers and stage-coach offices lodged in turn within these walls. The City bought it in 1916 when it was in a state of near ruin. The restoration, a bold project begun in 1936, lasted until 1962. The Hôtel de Sens has been largely reconstructed, but rather poorly. It is better to ignore the reconstructed architectural details and allow the overall aesthetic charm of the *hôtel* to take effect. Its corner turrets, a large and a small door each with a basket-handle arch, its square tower cut by a machiolated balcony, which encloses a spiral staircase, are all contrary to the spirit which prevails in other great residences of the Marais.

The Forney Library (open from Tue.–Fri. 1:30pm–8pm; Sat. 10am–8:30pm), founded in 1886 with a legacy from the Parisian industrialist, Forney, was transferred during 1961 to 1962 from no. 12 Rue Tiron. The library, which is devoted to decorative arts, techniques, and arts and crafts, offers rich and varied resources to lovers of art and architecture and has kept to its original aim of providing an information center on Parisian artisans. It puts at the public's disposal 150,000 books, 2000 periodicals, 24,000 exhibition and museum catalogs, 250,000 prints, 45,000 slides, a collection of wallpapers, designs for furniture and metalwork and samples of materials from various factories in France, England and Holland and a collection of 3,000 old and 10,000 modern posters. The library organizes exhibitions of arts and crafts, the decorative arts and of its own collections.

The Rue de l'Hôtel-de-Ville runs along the quays. In front of the W façade of the mansion is a fine example of a French-style garden.

La Cité Internationale des Arts

Opposite the garden façade of Le Vau's Hôtel d'Aumont, the N and S sides of the Rue de l'Hôtel-de-Ville have been demolished to make way, on the N side, for the large parallelepipedal building (architects, Tournon and Cacoub) which is the Cité Internationale des Arts, inaugurated in 1965. Subsidized in part by the City of Paris, this Cité provides facilities for both French and foreign art students. With some old buildings a little further down the street and the new buildings in the Rue Geoffroy-l'Asnier, it consists of 230 studios. It contains a restaurant, a library, conference rooms and halls for theatrical performances, concerts and exhibitions.

The monastic brotherhoods of Jerusalem

'Ce que les premiers moines allaient chercher au désert, tu le trouveras aujourd'hui dans la ville' (What the first monks sought in the desert you will find today in the city), proclaims the *Book of Life* of the monastic brotherhoods of Jerusalem, who have brought new life to the old parish church of Saint-Gervais since November 1, 1975. It is this philosophy that inspires the monks and nuns to create in Paris—under the double sign of Babel and Jerusalem— an oasis of peace, prayer and silence in which to live by the values of the monastic tradition. In the midst of the bustling city, beneath the Gothic vaults of this church facing toward Jerusalem, Gregorian chant and the strains of the Orthodox liturgy conjure up Byzantium, rising like incense below the gilded icons (Mon– Sat, at 7am, 12:30 and 6pm; Sun at 11am).

▷ The Middle Ages recalled at Saint-Gervais in the Saint-Paul district

The Marais knew its first golden age under the medieval monks and kings. In the Saint-Paul district, apart from a fragments of Philippe Auguste's wall and a section of the wall of the former Church of Saint-Paul in the street of the same name, only the street names recall this lost splendor. The Rue Beautreillis, Rue de la Cerisaie and Rue des Lions recall the Hôtel Royal Saint-Pol, while the Quai des Célestins and the Rue de l'Ave-Maria evoke the vanished monasteries. There are more tangible remains on the Saint-Gervais side: houses in the Rue des Barres and the Rue François-Miron and Gothic cellars at nos. 44–46 and 68 Rue François-Miron; a saddler's shop in Rue Geoffroy-l'Asnïer, and above all the Church of Saint-Gervais and the Hôtel de Sens, all proclaim the enduring presence of the late Middle Ages. But it is, perhaps, in the Rue François-Miron and Rue Saint-Antoine and in the winding streets (Rue des Barres, Rue du Figuier, Rue Charlemagne, Rue du Prévôt and Rue Eginhard) that the Gothic spirit and its lack of symmetry can best be seen, recalling an era before rectilinear squares and long vistas became all-important.

The Festival of the Marais and the Association du Paris Historique

In 1962 the first festival of the Marais took place, and its success continues to grow with every passing year. Based on the aims of its founder, Michel Raude, and the preservation committee set up by the inhabitants, it was designed to draw public attention to the plight of a district whose rich heritage seemed destined to disappear. It is true that the district has been partly 'saved', and the renewed attention it attracts early each summer, thanks to the shows and concerts organized by the festival in many of the churches, *hôtels*, cellars, courtyards and so on, is no doubt responsible.

The Association pour la Sauvegarde et la Mise en Valeur du Paris Historique (Association for the Preservation and Development of Historic Paris), formed after the passing of the Malraux Law on the protection of heritage, with which the festival is closely linked, has played and continues to play an important rôle in organizing group visits, providing various publications, carrying out historical research, building an imposing collection of photographs and taking charge of restoration projects.

The Association's information center is at 68 Rue François-Miron (open Mon–Sat 2–6pm; closed Aug–Sept; tel: 48.87.74.31).

The *hôtels* of the Marais open to the public

The inner courtyards and apartments of certain private mansions now housing museums or libraries are open to the public.

Hôtel de Guénéguaud (→Musée de la Chasse et de la Nature)
Hôtel de Rohan-Strasbourg (temporary exhibitions)
Hôtel Salé (→Musée Picasso)

Hôtel Libéral-Bruant (→ Musée de la Serrure)
Hôtel Lamoignon (Bibliothèque Historique de la Ville de Paris)
Hôtel de Marle (→ Musée Tessin)
Hôtels Carnavalet and le Peletier-de-Saint-Fargeau (→Musée Historique de la Ville de Paris)

Hôtel de Sully (temporary exhibitions)
Hôtel de Sens (Bibliothèque Forney)

▷ The Hôtel Saint-Pol

Charles V, while he was still only Duke of Normandy, had acquired a huge house in this district of orchards, kitchen gardens and vineyards. Over the years he became proprietor of various other houses between the quay and the Rue Saint-Antoine. This ill-matched assortment of buildings linked by courtyards, arcades and alleys, which covered an area twice the size of the medieval Louvre, was known as the Hôtel Saint-Pol. Charles VI (le Bien-Aimé) was born here on December 8, 1368. Charles V died here in 1380. Following the death of Charles VI, who ended his days here in madness, and the departure of the King of England's Regent, the Duke of Bedford, the kings abandoned the Hôtel Saint-Pol for Les Tournelles, and the mansion, filled with gloomy memories, was gradually demolished. Its memory lingers on only in the names of the district's streets.

▷ Philippe Auguste's Wall

In 1190 when Philippe Auguste was leaving for the Crusades, he ordered the construction of a wall with strong towers and fortified gates around the northern part of Paris as far as the Seine. The wall went N from the Seine at the Louvre as far as what is now the Rue Etienne-Marcel, returning towards the Rue Rambuteau and Rue des Francs-Bourgeois. It then made a right angle at the point on the Rue Sévigné where the fire station now stands, to rejoin the Seine again in the middle of the Quai des Célestins. The Left Bank perimeter was not built until 15 or 20 years later. It left the Seine opposite the Louvre, went around what is now the Panthéon and rejoined the river at the end of the Boul. Saint-Germain. It had six gates on each bank. Apart from a fragment on the Rue des Jardins-Saint-Paul, there are still some remains visible here and there on both banks of the Seine (for example, the Rue Clovis on the Left Bank).

▷ Bourdaloue at the church of Saint-Paul–Saint-Louis

The church of Saint-Paul–Saint-Louis was too small to hold the crowds that came to hear the sermons of Bourdaloue, a Jesuit father who made his first appearance in a Parisian pulpit in 1669. Though he was in Fénelon's opinion 'A great man, but no orator,' he filled his audience with boundless admiration. The letters of Mme de Sévigné bear witness to the strong impression he made. His style was professional: his explanations were methodical, with multiple points of reference; he detailed each step in his chain of reasoning, and summarized his ideas so they would be easy for listeners to follow. Addressed to a public enamored of reason and clarity, his method could not fail to gain their admiration. His moral rigor, not to say harshness, inspired Mme. de Sévigné to remark, 'He knocks like a deaf man' – and such austerity was thought appropriate in a Jesuit.

Bourdalue preached for forty-two years; eight days before his death, in 1704, he was still in the pulpit.

The Temple and Archives**

District: 3rd and 4th arr./Map ref. 18–B2, C1
Métro: Hôtel-de-Ville, Rambuteau, Temple
Bus: 38, 47, 58, 67, 69, 70, 72, 74, 75, 76, 96
Parking and taxis: Rue Lobau

Tour of the district

3 hrs.

The Rue du Temple

From the Place de l'Hôtel-de-Ville to the Rue Saint-Merri.

The road begins at the corner of the Bazaar of the Hôtel-de-Ville, whose basement is known to all handymen. It is one of the old Paris streets, dating from early 14th c. It has kept its original name, taken from the Commanderie du Temple (→inset).

It is an unusual street, with its clearly defined wholesale and semi-wholesale shops (leather goods, ornate jewelry and Parisian goods, but also goldsmiths, gilders and silver merchants) and vestiges of an elegant past. The Rue de Temple still has some very beautiful 17th-c. mansions, many of them unfortunately not yet restored.

In this busy, popular and cluttered street, the eye is continually drawn to windows adorned with sculpted masks or keystones and to wrought-iron balconies (nos. 10, 12, 18: wrought ironwork staircase). Balzac lived at no. 122, and nos. 101–103 were the Hôtel Montmorency, home of Fouquet. No. 20, today a cinema, was a salt-tax office. No. 22 is an 18th-c. mansion with mansard roof, door and staircase. On the corner of the Rue Saint-Croix-de-la-Bretonnerie, no. 24 has a square turret dating from 1610.

Rue Saint-Merri

Very near the squalid dead-end alley known as Cul-de-Sac-du-Beouf, note the beautiful Hôtel Le Rebours, altered around 1685 for the nobleman of the same name, President of the Grand Council. You should see the courtyard even though it is cluttered with outbuildings, the vestibule and staircase, and the mascarons. The street side has a triangular pediment with a bull's-eye window (*oeil-de-boeuf*) set into it; wrought ironwork. No. 9, opposite the Hôtel Potier de Blanc-Mesnil (1630), has a pretty pediment with a shell motif and a monogram over the door, the letters P, B and M interlaced.

Rue du Temple, continued

From the Rue Saint-Merri to the Rue des Haudriettes

At the corner of no. 25 is a bas-relief (cherubs) listed in the registery of historic monuments. The old Auberge de l'Aigle d'Or at no. 21 was a stagecoach terminus in the 19th c.: Louis XII staircase in the corridor; fine courtyard with registered façades (windows with corbelled pediments, dormer windows, bull's-eyes windows, wrought ironwork); beautiful staircase at the end to the l.; today a café-théâtre, a dance and music school and a resturant give the place an air of privilege, but the buildings themselves are very dilapidated. No. 45 has a beautiful 18th-c. façade and staircase. At no. 57, at the end of the courtyard, is the *hôtel* (1665) of Maximilien Titon, an arms dealer; its pediment is attractive but dilapidated. The Passage Sainte-Avoye (1828) opens up at no. 62 on the site of the Hôtel Neuf-de-Montmorency. Nos. 62 and 72 are old houses. Above the door of no. 72 an engraved plaque indicates the Hôtel de Savoye.

The Hôtel de Saint-Aignan**

71 Rue du Temple

This extraordinary mansion, in its sumptuous and dilapidated elegance, looks like a romantic theater set. It was built between 1640 and 1650 by P. Le Muet for one of the finest intellects of the day: Claude de Mesmes, Comte d'Avaux, member of the Great Council, Maître des Requêtes (rapporteur of the Council of State), Surintendant des Finances (financial secretary), and one of the three plenipotentiaries at the Congress of Munster for the signing of the Treaty of Westphalia (1648). After being owned by, among others, Louis de Rochechouart, Duc de Mortemart, the mansion was split up and rented as apartments and studios. During the last few years restoration has been taking place slowly so as not to disrupt the offices where part of the Archives de Paris is installed. The mansion has recently been assigned to the Musée d'Art Juif (Museum of Jewish Art).

Beyond the monumental but sober portal, the *hôtel* was built between the courtyard and the garden. Corinthian pilasters frame each bay of the façade, while the ground floor arcades support an entablature of tall windows. Note that the l. side of the courtyard, painted with *trompe-l'oeil*, in which the desire for realism has gone so far as to paint inside shutters behind the glass of the false windows. This décor was designed to hide an unattractive vestigial section of Philippe Auguste's wall.

Rue de Braque

Walk up this street, and back again. It is named after an old family which once owned the land here (14th c.). At nos. 4–6 is the Hôtel Lelièvre*, built in 1673 for the nobleman of La Grange. It was divided up between his children and redecorated. There are superb *rocaille* portals and balconies and a magnificent staircase at no. 4. There is still a ceiling painted by Le Brun in a former drawing-room. There are remains of former habitations in the courtyard of no 5. No. 3 has a gate adorned with pine cones, a traditional decorative motif on the gates of taverns. No. 7 is the little Hôtel des Mesmes, which formerly backed on to the Grand Hôtel de Mesmes, also known as the Hôtel Neuf-de-Montmorency (→inset). Verennes, minister for Foreign Affairs of Louis XIV, lived there; a recent renovation has completely changed its original character. No. 8 has a magnificent door. The Rue de Braque allows the best view of the turreted Gothic gateway of the former (Hôtel de Clisson → Hôtel de Soubise).

The Hôtel de Montmor**

79 Rue du Temple

This mansion, luxurious in its time, was built in 1623 for Jean Habert, Seigneur of Montmor. (Champaigne painted a masterly group portrait of Habert de Montmor's children, now in the Musée de Rheims). His son, Henri-Louis de Montmor, a man of great literary and scientific culture, sheltered the empiricist philosopher Gassendi, from 1653 until Gassendi's death in 1655. This friend of Mme de Sévigné created his own private academy of sciences in his *hôtel*, which was the seed of the Académie des Sciences (1667).

Descartes, Chapelain, Guy Patin, Huygens and Personne de Roberval were all habitués of this house where Molière came to read his *Tartuffe* in private when it was banned. Colbert bought the rich library with its manuscripts, now in the Bibliothèque Nationale.

The monumental carriage entrance opens on to a paved courtyard. The main building is at the back, with a wing at either end, turning towards the interior in an elegant curve. The arcaded ground floor supports a first floor with a flat string-course, which is curved on the second floor; fine wrought ironwork. Note the staircase with its wrought-iron balustrade.

Rue Michel-le-Comte

This was once a fashionable street inhabited by bankers and stockbrokers. Its name has its origins in the popular Parisian saying: '*Ça fait la Rue Michel*' ('Here's the Rue Michel. Here's the bill.'). It has several early 17th-c. houses. At no. 16, the Hôtel Le Tellier, behind an insignificant façade, lies a lovely little courtyard in a mixture of 15th- and 17th-c. styles. In the 15th c. this was the Auberge de l'Ours et du Lion. In the 17th c. it became the residence of the administrator Le Tellier. Lenoir de Mezières, Payeur des Rentes (a financial official), has his mansion at no. 19. There is a beautiful door but regrettably tall outbuildings in the courtyard. No. 21 is the mansion that belonged to Louis XVI's architect, Verniquet (→ inset). The main 17th-c. building overlooks a courtyard and, on the other side, to the gardens of the Hôtel de Saint Aignan (→ above). No. 29 has fine wrought-ironwork and no. 30 is an attractive little building dating from 1666.

The Hôtel d'Hallwyll**

28 Rue Michel-le-Comte

This beautiful mansion was remodelled in 1765 by Ledoux. The director-general of French finance, Necker, lived here from 1757 to 1766 and his daughter, the future Mme de Staël, was born here. It is the former Hôtel de Bouligneux, rented in part to the Thélusson bank (Necker and Thélusson, both members of the Swiss Guards, were associates). Its owner, Franz-Joseph d'Hallwyl, who was a colonel in the Swiss Guards, had it altered by Ledoux; it was one of the architect's first important works in Paris, but already the heavy columns around the door and the way the dividing walls on the inner side of the street elevation were set in, show his typical style. (→ inset). The second courtyard, too narrow to make a garden, was bordered by two colonades. The impression of space was given by a *trompe-l'oeil* painting on a blank wall on the other side of the Rue de Montmorency. The restoration of the Hotel d'Hallwyll has been under discussion for years. It is astonishing that the authorities have only just started work to save this important building, the only extant mansion by Ledoux in Paris.

Return by the Rue du Temple.

Rue des Haudriettes

This 13th-c. street takes its name from an old order of nuns. No. 16 is a gabled house. No. 12 is an attractive little stone house with 17th-c. dormer windows. At nos. 4–6 is the Renaissance Hôtel de Bondeville, with registered façades overlooking a courtyard, a pretty door which has a triangular pediment and keystone carved with the head of an old man wearing a crown of oak leaves.

At the corner of the Rue des Archives is the Haudriettes fountain, which was designed in 1765 by Moreau, to replace the Fontaine du Chaume which stood at the corner of the Rue des Francs-Bourgeois (the men who pay no tax–the inmates of the almshouses, c.1334) before it was removed to make way for the Hôtel de Soubise. Note the attractive relief of a nymph by Mignot.

Visitors short of time should take the Rue des Haudriettes to rejoin the itinerary starting from the Hôtel de Guénégaud (→below). The tour of the N of the district follows for those with more time.

Rue du Temple, continued

From the Rue des Haudriettes to the Square du Temple.

Here is a delightful ensemble of 17th-c. houses. At no. 84 mascarons, remodeled façade. At no. 85: façade on to the street, passage way, courtyard with mansard roofs worthy of restoration. No. 80, gabled house, was La Croix Blanche tavern during Louis XV's reign. At nos. 101–103: beautiful 18th-c. façade of the Hôtel de Montmorency, entrance at 5 Rue de Montmorency (→Beaubourg). At no. 131, façade with dormer windows. In the 18th c. no. 153 was a hiring office for *Les Vinaigrettes*, two-wheeled sedans and single-seater hand-drawn carriages.

The Square du Temple

Even if nothing of the past remains here, this square is still historically evocative. Charming and parochial, the Square du Temple, with its rock-work, ornamental ponds, its monument to the memory of the singer and writer of popular songs, Béranger (d. 1857), has replaced the old domaine of the Knights Templar, which used at one time to extend over a large section of Paris. Its center used to be the fortified enclosure, an area now bounded by the Rue du Temple, Rue de Bretagne, Rue de Picardie and Rue Béranger.

The famous tower or keep of the Knights Templar, dating from 1265 to 1270, stood on the corner of the Rue Eugène-Spuller and Rue Perrée. To the l. it encroached slightly on to the pavement and square, and to the r. it lay along the N wing of the town hall of the 3rd arrondissement.

The church (c. 1140) was built on a circular plan like the Temple in London, which can still be seen today. In the early 13th c. choir and porch were added. The enclosure comprised a complete community of noble families and artisans who, not belonging to the corporations, were exempt from taxes – a refuge for bankrupts who found protection, and criminals. A palace for the Grand Prior of the Order of St John was built there in 1667 by the Prior Jacques de Souvré according to plans by P. Delisle-Mansart (on the W part of today's square at the entrance to the Rue du Temple). It resembled the Hôtel Soubise. It was here that Philippe de Vendôme led his sybaritic life. The courteous Prince de Conti was Grand Prior when the young Mozart played in the great hall, as shown in the painting by Ollivier now in the Louvre: *Le Thé à l'anglaise chez le Prince de Conti* (Afternoon tea at the Prince de Conti's). The prince also received the lionized J.-J. Rousseau (1765). In fact all Parisian high society (*le tout* Paris) came to visit the philosopher. The events of the Revolution and the incarceration of the royal family in August 1792, made the Tour du Temple notorious. Successive governments tried to wipe out these memories by altering the place. The tower was demolished in 1808 and the land divided up. In 1814 a convent of the order of the Assumption replaced the Grand Prior's palace. This became a barracks in 1848 and was torn down in 1853 to make way for the square. The sole survivor of the royal family, Mme Royale, then the Duchesse d'Angoulême, came here on a pilgrimage on her return to France before her death in 1851. She planted a weeping willow which died a few years later.

╪ The Church of Sainte-Elisabeth*

195 Rue du Temple

The foundation stone of this Franciscan church was laid by Marie de'Medici in 1628. It was completed in 1645 but underwent many 19th-c. modifications with the construction of the Rue Turbigo. The architect Godde lengthened the nave and built the chancel to form a semicircle with the ambulatory. In 1938, Sainte-Elisabeth became the church of the Order of St John of Jerusalem (Knights of Malta), whose coat of arms is above the high altar.

The interior

The nave. Only the first four bays date from the 17th-c. Entablature adorned with religious emblems and Instruments of the Passion; 19th-c. organ case and pulpit. The organ (1853) was built by Suret.

The l. side-aisle: Chapelle des Catéchismes has four large canvases commissioned by the City of Paris between 1848 and 1872. The Chapelle Sainte-Élisabeth: above the altar, *Ste Elizabeth de Hongrie déposant sa Couronne aux Pieds de l'Image du Christ* (St Elizabeth of Hungary laying her Crown at the Feet of Christ's Image) by Blondel (1824). The choir is decorated with a painting by Jean Alaux (c. 1840): *Glorification de St Elisabeth de Hongrie.* In 1844, the ambulatory was decorated with murals by Bézard, Boh, Jourdy and Roger; it also has 100 16th-c. carved wooden panels from the choir stalls of the Abbey of Saint-Vaast at Arras, acquired in 1845 by the parish curate, illustrating scenes from the Old and New Testaments.

Take the Rue Dupetit-Thouars which owes its name to a ship's captain who died heroically at the Battle of Abokir. At Rue Dupetit-Thouars and the Rue Gabriel-Vicaire, on the wall of a nursery school, is a plan of the Temple carved in stone.

The Carreau du Temple

Open Tue–Sat 9am–12:30pm; Sun 9am–1pm

The Carreau du Temple has been a famous clothes market since the end of the 18th c.

Originally, inside the grounds of the Temple, was a rotunda built in 1781 by Pierre de Montreuil. This oval building, surrounded by a colonnade, served as a ground-level covered gallery. The rotunda sheltered wanted debtors and bankrupts. The building, which was preserved during the Revolution, became the home of secondhand clothing merchants. It was subsequently completed as a market in 1809 by the addition by Molinos of four wooden pavilions toward the street on the ruins in the old Temple area. These pavilions received picturesque, evocative names according to their speciality: the Palais-Royal (lace and silks); the Flore pavilion (bedding, linen, cottons); Le Pou Volant (secondhand clothes) and finally La Forêt Noire (leather goods and old shoes) – the last two had a sinister reputation. In 1863 the unhealthy pavilions were destroyed (note vestiges of the stone frames of the side-entrance) to make way for cast iron and glass buildings, part of which can still be seen today. They are not the work of Baltard, as has often been claimed, but of Legrand and Mérindol. The first Paris Fair was held there in 1904. But the new Marché aux Puces at Clignancourt offered too much competition and the Carreau closed down; after 1904 four of the six pavilions were demolished.

In 1973 the authorities condemned the two remaining pavilions but the inhabitants of the district, the 360 market traders, protested successfully. Today, the newly renovated Carreau animates the district. At 7:30am, an old bell signals the start of business, stall-holders come and go with large baskets of merchandise, cajoling the passing customers. From leather jacket to shoes, Parisians buy their bargain wardrobe at Carreau du Temple.

Proceed along the Rue Dupuis.

Rue Béranger

This street was formerly the Rue de Vendôme, opened in 1696 by Philippe de Vendôme, Grand Prior of the Temple, and lined with sumptuous mansions. The Hôtel de Mascrani at no. 2 was constructed about 1696 on land acquired by the Temple. Partly demolished in 1903, it has been scandalously altered during renovations. The Hôtel Peyrenc de Moras* at no. 3 and the Hôtel de La Haye* at nos. 5 and 5 *bis* were built in the early 18th c. and joined together a little later by Bergeret de Frouville, the king's financial adviser. The Hôtel de La Haye was the last residence of the popular songwriter, Béranger (→inset). The City of Paris bought the two mansions in 1881 and 1889. At present they are occupied by a school association. Note the decoration of the portals and doors, decorative ironwork and carved keystones. A smile at the concierge of no. 5 should suffice to obtain entry to the courtyard. If not, offer a *pourboire* (tip). The actor, Frédérick Lemaître, who was the glory of the theater of the Boulevard du Crime, lived at no. 10. At no. 16, the Passage Vendôme (1827) has an equally attractive façade in Restoration style. It was built on the site des Convent of the Filles du Saint-Sauveur.

Rue Charlot

As far as the Rue de Bretagne.

Claude Charlot arrived in Paris in great poverty, the son of a peasant from Languedoc. Yet within a few years this remarkable man has amassed a huge fortune through speculation to become one of the most powerful financiers in the capital. He was in a way the creator of the district, since after the death of Henri IV and the abandonment of the Place de France project (→inset), he was quick to divide up the vast terrains acquired by the Temple, building streets, many mansions and apartment blocks.

In the triangle formed by the Rue Charlot and Rue de Turenne note the fountain built by Jean Beausire in 1699 for Chancellor Boucherat. Many houses in the street have retained beautiful features, wrought-ironwork in particular. No. 58, the Hôtel de Chamillart (early 17th c.), was occupied in 1699 by Michel de Chamillart, Louis XIV's minister, and has a beautiful door, and a courtyard with a balustrade testifying to a glorious past. It deserves restoration. No. 56 belonged to the printer Sebastien de Cramoisy (1611) and to the Duc de Brisac, Governor of Paris. The painter Troyon died at no. 57, the *hotel* of the Marquis de Boulainvilliers. Note the door and the strange little pilasters at ground floor level around the courtyard. No. 44, at the corner of the Rue de Bretagne, is a fine gabled house which for a long time bore the sign of *Les Trois Mousquetaires* (The Three Musketeers). At no. 38, passage with beams, picturesque courtyard. At no. 33, a 17th-c. staircase. At no. 28, the Hôtel de Bérancourt 1680: door, mascarons, mansard roof, very pretty courtyard. At no. 26, dormer window with pulley. At no. 17, at the corner of the Rue Pastourelle, another fine gabled house.

Walk along the Rue de Poitou which has kept many of its modest old dwellings. Continue as far as the Rue de Saintonge.

Rue de Saintonge

The street was opened in 1626 by C. Charlot. It is quite spoiled now, especially in the N part. At no. 64, nothing remains to recall the house – certainly the post office that replaces it does not – in which Robespierre lived from October 1789 to July 1791, nor the house at no. 13 where Pascal lived with his family between 1648 and 1651. However, there are still some interesting features in the street. No. 4: carved swags above the windows; no. 8: austere Louis-XIII façade, but two staircases, and in the courtyard a registered frieze* of birds pecking fruit; no. 12: 'Rue de Touraine' carved on an old road sign; no. 15: shop decorated with small oil paintings under glass; no. 20: beautiful façade with pediment.

Rue de Bretagne

This section of the city was also opened up by Charlot in 1626. The odd-numbered houses are mostly old. A little to the E, on the corner of the Rue Vieille-du-Temple, at no. 1, is a superb house*, an apartment block built in 1777 for Pierre Guérard by the architect Jean-Louis Blève. It is a very good example of Louis-XVI architecture (rare in this district), with its windows framed by stone balustrades surmounted by pediments, and its decorations of swags. The bas-reliefs of *Les Cinq Sens* (The Five Senses) by Hollande are not carved but cast, as was the custom at the time. Go along the Rue de Bretagne to the W. At no. 41 is the Enfants-Rouges market created by letters patent in 1616 on land belonging to Charlot. It is probably the oldest market in Paris still functioning (→inset).

Rue des Archives

As far as the Rue Pastourelle.

This street links the Temple district to the Place de l'Hôtel-de-Ville. At no. 90 there are remains of the Chapelle de l'Hôpital des Enfants-Rouge. The children at this orphanage wore red uniforms as a sign that they lived on public charity. The ophanage, which was founded by François I and his sister Marguerite d'Angoulême, was pulled down in 1772. At no. 81, on the corner of Rue Portefoin (beautiful façades) is a Louis XIII house with Louis XV staircase and vestibule. Valentine Conrart, first permanent secretary of the Académie Française, lived here from 1672 to 1675. At no. 79, Louis XIII mansion, with mansard roofs and triangular pediments. No. 78 is the Hôtel de Tallard*, also known as Amelot de Chaillou, which was reconstructed in 1660 by Bullet for Jacques Amelot de Chaillou, Maître des Requetes (rapporteur of the Council of State). It owes its present name to the Comte de Tallard who owned it from 1722. The façade on to the courtyard is at right angles to an arcaded ground floor and first floor with tall windows. The staircase by Le Muet is considered to be one of the most beautiful in Paris. The mansion has just been restored.

Rue de Beauce is reached by the Rue Pastourelle (many fine 17th-c. houses) where part of a façade with beautiful medallions overlooks a garden.

Rue des Archives, continued

As far as the Rue des Quatre-Fils.

No. 76 is the fine Hôtel Le Pelletier de Souzy (1642) which belonged to Etienne-Jacques Turgot, grandfather of the minister, until 1710. No. 72, the 17th-c. Hôtel de Villefix has a registered door, triangular pediment, mascarons and swags of fruits and flowers in the sculpted decoration. The mansion at no. 70 was built for the financier Michel Simon in 1610; door and the back of the façade registered as historic monuments; staircase at the end of the courtyard to the l.; dormer window with pulley. At no. 62, the Hôtel de Montgelas, rebuilt in the early 18th.: door, mascarons.

The Hôtel de Guénégaud**

60 Rue des Archives

This magnificent mansion was built by François Mansart for Henri de Guénégaud des Brosses, Tresorier de l'Epargne (treasurer of savings). It was very dilapidated when it was acquired in 1961 by the City, who rented it to M and Mme Sommer; they had it restored (architect, A. Sallex, 1964–66) to contain the Musée de la Chasse et de la Nature (→ Museums). The restored French garden in front of the beautiful back elevation is visible from the Rue des Quatre-Fils.

Rue des Quatre-Fils

The street got its name from a 14th-c. sign *Aux Quatre fils Aymon* (the Four Sons of Aymon). Bordered on the numbered side by the bland façade of the depôt of the Archives, the street borders the gardens of the Hôtel de Guénégaud. No. 22 is the Hôtel du Président d'Arçonville. De Sèze, Louis XVI's lawyer, lived at no. 20, which he bought in 1793: wrought ironwork, staircase, mascarons, mansard roofs; on the façade some 18th-c. elements have been replaced; the portal is as beautiful as that of no. 16.

The S part of the Rue Charlot (→above) is reached by the Ruelle Sourdis, opened in 1626, between nos. 3 and 5. It has remained very picturesque and typical of the little old streets of Paris, with their central gutters, boundary stones and corbels.

Rue Charlot, continued

As far as the Rue du Perche.

At no. 7 a beautiful courtyard is unfortunately spoiled by outbuildings. No. 8 is the *hôtel* of the chief treasurer and paymaster of Turmenyes. It belonged to Debeleyme, Prefect of Police, who introduced the omnibus and public gas lighting. At no. 12, the Hôtel de Brossier (17th c.): fine carved door and elegant dormer windows.

⚲ The Church of Saint-Jean-Saint-François

13 Rue du Perche

The church, originally a simple chapel built by the Capuchins, on the site of a tennis-court, was completed in 1715 and established in the parish in 1791 as a second succursal chapel of Saint-Merri under the name of Saint-François d'Assise. Closed in 1793, it was reopened in 1803 with the priests in charge of the chapel coming from Saint-Jean-en-Grève (the reason for the double dedication). The present choir was built in 1828 by Godde, as was the Chapelle des Catéchismes and the presbytery. Baltard added the porch in 1855. The church is today the seat of the Apostolic Exarchate of Armenia.

The interior

The nave: organ commissioned in 1833 by Dominique and Aristide Cavaillé-Coll, and renovated several times; organ case by the master sculptor Lienard. César Franck was organist from 1851 to 1858. The wide rectangular bays contain eight large paintings, six commissioned during the Restoration from Degeorge, Ary Scheffer, Lordon, Trézel, Franque and Gaillot. The chancel: at the entrance, on the l., *St François d'Assise recevant les stigmates** (St Francis of Assisi receiving the Stigmata), marble sculpture by Germain Pilon, c. 1580; on the r., St Denis, marble sculpture by the brothers Gaspard and Balthazar Marsy (17th c.). On the chancel walls, 17th-c. canvases, four showing the *Life of St Francis* by Frère Luc. The paneling is from Billettes. Reliquary containing the veil and bones of St Isabelle, sister of St Louis.

Rue Vieille-du-Temple

From the Rue de Belley to the Rue des Coutures-Saint-Gervais.

This was an old route leading to the Commandery of the Temple (→ above). This ordinary street was once elegant, and many beautiful façades alternate with small shops.

Walk a short distance to the Rue de Belley to see nos. 102–104, 106 and 110. These three *hôtels* were built on land from the former Hôtel d'Epernon. The Hôtel de Ferrary (17th c.) at nos. 102–104 is an annex of the Lycée Victor-Hugo. Unfortunately it is closed to visitors but the courtyard can be seen. At no. 106 the Hôtel Megret de Sérilly (early 17th c.) takes its name from the Trésorier Général des Guerres who owned it from 1776 until the Revolution. Fine façade over the street with a triangular pediment decorated with two carved lions; the elegant courtyard deserves restoration. It has a brick facing, apparently false, as with many of the façades of *hôtels* in the Place des Vosges. No. 110, the Hôtel d'Hozier (17th c), belonged from 1735 to 1798 to the famous family of genealogists: magnificent door decorated with emblems of War; regrettably high outbuildings; beautiful staircase at the end of the courtyard on the l.; in the tablet above the door is written '126', the former royal number, which the house had when the district was inhabited by the nobility.

Return to the corner of the Rue Vieille-du-Temple and Rue des Coutures-Saint-Gervais to see the beautiful garden façade of the Hôtel Salé (→below). Part of the gardens on the Rue Vieille-du-Temple side was the site of the former Marais tennis court which, from 1620 to 1673, became the theater of the Comédiens du Marais. The first performance of *Le Cid* was given here.

The Rue des Coutures-Saint-Gervais was cut in 1620 on land belonging to the Hôpital Saint-Gervais. All the houses on the even side are more or less from this period and give a good idea of an early 17th-c. middle-class home.

Rue de Thorigny

This street has preserved many 16th-c. houses which have recently been restored at great cost. President de Brosse lived at no. 4 which was built in 1660 by Jacques Brunand. Balzac lodged at no. 9 and Mme de Sévingé was a tenant at no. 8. But the street is well known because of the Hôtel Salé.

⌐ The Hôtel Salé***

5 Rue de Thorigny

This beautiful mansion was restored in 1985 in order to contain the Musée Picasso (→ Museums). The Hôtel Aubert-de-Fontenay or de Juigné, known as the Hôtel Salé, was built from 1656 to 1660 for a gentleman from Tours, Pierre Aubert de Fontenay. A financier who married money, he was a salt tax collector, hence the name Hôtel Salé (Salted) – although the hôtel was at first called the Hôtel de Juigné. Aubert had the mansion for only a year. Compromised in the Fouquet case, he could not honor his debts and his goods were confiscated. The mansion, let by Aubert's debtors, was occupied successively by the Venetian ambassador, the Maréchal de Villeroy, then acquired in 1728 by Nicolas Le Camus, President of the Cour des Aides (customs dues paid by rich and poor), who had the interior refurbished. The mansion was impounded during the Revolution as belonging to an *emigré*, and resold. It was occupied by the Ecole Centrale des Arts et Manufactures (Central School of Arts and Crafts) from 1829 to 1824, then by a wrought-iron craftsman who carefully preserved the interior decoration. Finally, the Ecole des Métiers d'Art took it over and damaged it considerably.

The mansion, constructed according to a plan which was an innovation for the period, was designed by Jean Boullier de Bourges, a little-known architect whose other buildings have disappeared. The double depth of the main building allows a magnificent staircase** , an architectural tour de force, to be given a central place without breaking up the row of rooms overlooking the garden. The domestic parts, the kitchen and stables, have been lengthened and relegated to the back yard with an exit on to the Rue des Coutures-Saint-Gervias. The façade overlooking the beautiful semicircular courtyard is more successful than that on to the garden, which is more austere. The dogs, represented in the abundant carved decoration, are part of the Aubert coat of arms. The mansion has been superbly restored and the museum arranged with respect to the dimensions of the rooms by the architect R. Simounet. Unfortunately the paneling of the large room, dating from the time of President Le Camus, has been covered over.

Place de Thorigny. This is the centre of an area chosen for a pilot renovation operation now constituting a composite ensemble; unfortunately, the restoration obscures the fact that this is the very heart of a district dear to the actresses Madeleine and Armande-Grésinde-Claire-Elizabeth Béjart, and consequently familiar to Molière, who married the latter.

Rue de la Perle

This street takes its name from a sign on a tennis court situated on the even-numbered side of the street. The odd-numbered side has numerous buildings by Libéral Bruant, in particular the mansion* at no. 1, Hôtel Libéral-Bruant, which the architect of the Invalides built for himself (1685) in an elegant Italianate style very different from the Invalides. The house is of modest dimensions but distinguished by a pediment covering the entire façade; its tympanum is pierced by an oculus (circular opening) at the apex and decorated with two cupids and horns of plenty. The stairway, decorated with *trompe-l'oeil* paintings, has survived. From 1771 to 1788 the buildings were rented to the engineer Perronet who set up the first Ecole des Ponts et Chaussées (School for Bridge-building and Highways). After various setbacks in the 19th c., the *hôtel* was bought back from the City of Paris by the Société Bricard, which restored it to house the Musée de la Serrure (→ Museums).

Rue Vieille-du-Temple, continued

Further on, the Rue de la Perle goes past the front of the Hôtel de Rohan-Strasbourg (→below) and on the even-numbered side the outbuildings of the old Hôtel Barbette. This mansion, which was on the site of the Rue Barbette, was built in the 14th c. and sold to Isabeau of Bavaria (1401) who lived there. Later it passed to Diane de Poitiers and was sold by her daughters and the land divided up into lots. The *hôtel* has a badly damaged door and two medallions.

The Rue Barbette was flanked with beautiful mansions of which few are left.

☐ The Hôtel de Rohan-Strasbourg**

87 Rue Vieille-du-Temple (group visits, for exhibitions and conferences by permission).

This mansion is a complement to the Hôtel de Soubise (→below). It, too, was built by Delamair and at the same period. It has been given over to part of the Archives Nationales since 1927. The former outbuildings and stables now house the Minutier Central de Paris where solicitors' files of the Seine district are stored, and are at the public's disposal. A law of March 14, 1928 allows solicitors to deposit archives over 125 years old there. One of the annexes, the Hôtel de Boisgelin, is also used by the National Archives; it contains newly created services (microfilms, economic and private archives) and has the most modern equipment.

It was Armand de Rohan-Soubise, a cardinal and Bishop of Strasbourg, who had this house built on land that his parents, the Soubises, had granted him. It was separate from the neighboring mansion, the Soubise Palace, but communicated with it by the shared garden. The *hôtels* bear no resemblance to each other but both are superb. The mansion remained in the hands of the Rohans, four of whom were cardinals, until the Revolution, after which, in 1808 it became the Imprimerie Imperiale (Royal Press) until 1925.

The exterior

The main courtyard is reached through the gate in the Rue Vieille-du-Temple, open only during certain exhibitions. The high, severe E elevation of the mansion dominates the end of the courtyard. A passage to the r. leads to a second courtyard: over the door of the former stables, which contain 52 stalls, is the famous high-relief by Robert Le Lorrain: the *Chevaux d'Apollon* (Horses of Apollo**), one of the most beautiful 18th-c. French sculptures, showing the quivering horses at a drinking-trough. The main façade, with its fine attic storey, faces W onto the garden, which is shared by both mansions.

The interior

On the first floor is the famous Cabinet des Singes*, the small 'Monkey Room', with panels painted in a highly imaginative style by Huet between 1749 and 1752, which have remained intact. Cardinal Edmond de Rohan said his Mass in the corner of this room, hidden by a missing panel showing the *Jeu de la Main chaude* (a card game), and was arrested here during the 'Necklace affair', a plot to defame Marie-Antoinette. The large music room still has its four overdoors by J.-B.-M. Pierre. Another room is charmingly decorated with Aesop's *Fables* on green and gold paneling from the Hôtel Soubise. A Gobelins tapestry hangs in the antechamber and the former dining room is decorated with Beauvais tapestries from Boucher's *Suite Chinoiserie**. On the main staircase, which dates from the Louis-Philippe period, there are two tapestries showing the story of Achilles, woven for the first Cardinal de Rohan (one is a gift from the Librairie Hachette).

Rue Vieille-du-Temple, continued

As far as the Rue des Francs-Bourgeois. (See also below.)

No. 75 is the beautiful Hôtel de La Tour du Pin: courtyard with pilasters, carved keystones, wrought ironwork. Regrettably, the house has been heightened. No. 54 is the Hôtel Hérouët, built about 1510 for J. Hérouët, Louis XII's treasurer; despite bomb damage in 1944, the pretty turret survives. It has been very badly restored. Today the *hôtel* is an art gallery.

Rue des Francs-Bourgeois

From the Rue Vieille-du-Temple to the Rue des Archives.

No. 53 has the remains of the monastery of the Blancs-Manteaux, an order of mendicant monks, and the flat apse of this old religious community's church (→below). At nos. 55–57 are the 19th-c. buildings of the Crédit Municipal (→inset); at no. 57 a tower from Philippe Auguste's wall and part of the rebuilt façade of the Hôtel de Noiron (difficult to see).

The Quadrilatère Archives

The other side of the Rue des Francs-Bourgeois forms the S side of what is known as the Quadrilatère Archives, an annex of the Archives Nationales. The Archives Nationales shop sells an excellent brochure, modestly priced, containing the history and description of the various buildings contained within the Quadrilatère Archives.

No. 54 is the Hôtel de Jaucourt or Le Camus: the latter name is more appropriate, since Jean Le Camus, Lieutenant Civil (a civic official), was the principal owner who actually lived in the mansion (1684–1710). Its small dormer windows with pediments are 16th c., but the buildings facing onto the street and the entrance date from 1687, with great modifications from 1772 to 1792. The hôtel, which was acquired by the Archives Nationales in 1982, has been restored. The Hôtel de Fontenay is at no. 56; it was part of the Bérulle estate which extended to the next plot of land (no. 58), split up among the family in 1611. Various owners acquired the property until it was assigned in 1720 to François-Victor Le Tonnelier de Breteuil, Marquis de Fontenay-Tresigny, Parliamentary Councillor and then Secretary of State for War. It was he who had the charming main building between the courtyard and garden built by the architect Vinage in 1733. In 1751 the house was sold to Gilbert Claustrier who destroyed the old façade over the street, and the existing façade built by Mansart de Sagonne (1752). Restored in 1961, the hôtel contains the Direction des Archives de France. The Hôtel de Breteuil is at no. 58. This is the other part of the Bérulle house, where the future cardinal passed his childhood. In 1630 the Le Tonnelier de Breteuil family occupied it, despite many vicissitudes, until 1787. The decoration of the door probably dates from 1738. The mansion was acquired by the Archives Nationales in 1862, and used for a while as the Ecole des Chartes. At no. 58 bis is the Hôtel d'Assy, which was rebuilt by Le Muet in 1642 for its new owner, Denis Marin de la Châtaigneraie, was bought in 1706 by Chaillon de Jonville, Receveur Général des Finances (General Collector of Taxes) for Caen. He enlarged the house with wings facing onto the courtyard. There was more construction work from 1731 until 1733: a new wing enclosed the courtyard and the interior was redecorated. The very beautiful paneled salon is attributed to Oppenordt. The mansion is occupied by conservation offices and the private apartment of the Director General of the Archives Nationales.

The Hotel de Soubise, formerly the Hôtel de Clisson, then the Hôtel de Guise***

60 Rue des Francs-Bourgeois, on the corner of the Rue des Archives.

The portal of the Hôtel de Clisson (58 Rue des Archives) is all that remains of the manorhouse which Olivier de Clisson, Constable of France and a former companion in arms of Du Guesclin, built (c., 1371–80). The beautiful gateway, with its Gothic arch and corbelled turrets, used to be at the corner of an alley-way, no longer extant. The two medallions over the double arcade were not put up until the 19th c. The painted arms over the door are those of the Guises. The building lies along the Rue de Chaume (des Archives), not perpendicularly like the Hôtel Soubise. What remained was destroyed in the second half of the 19th century to make way for the present large warehouses of the Archives Nationales.

It was exactly here that the Constable was attacked (June 13, 1392) by the murderers of Pierre de Craon. He survived. The Dukes of Clarence and Bedford lived here during the English occupation. This very medieval mansion passed from hand to hand through the Albrets and the Penthièvres to Philibert Babou de la Bourdaisière, François I's Financial Secretary. In 1553 it became the Hôtel de Guise when it was bought by Anna d'Este, wife of François de Lorraine, Duc de Guise and head of La Ligue (to defend the Catholics against the Calvinists). It was within these walls that the St Bartholomew's Day massacre (1572) was planned. The descendants of Balafré lived in fine style in this vast house where the arts and letters were honoured and where Corneille, Malherbe and Quinault were entertained by Henri II de Lorraine, grandson of François. It was here, too, that the Duc de Guise's equerry, Gaignières, a remarkable man, assembled a fabulous collection of architectural drawings and plans and projects for tombs. The Guises, who lived here for 36 years (1553–1688) in the old Hôtel de Clisson, carried out some important building projects. The painter and sculptor Primaticcio and Niccolò Dell'Abbate were put in charge of the decoration and transformed the Clisson chapel, remains of which can still be seen.

The two daughters of the Princess Palatine, Duchess of Hanover and the Princesse de Condé, sold the house to François de Rohan, Prince de Soubise, who charged the then unknown Delamair with the reconstruction of the old house (1705–09) and Boffrand with the decoration. When the Hôtel de Soubise, by order of Napoleon (March 6, 1808), became State property in order to contain the Archives Nationales, annexes were constructed bordering the Rue des Quatre-Fils and the Rue des Archives.

The portal onto the Rue des Francs-Bourgeois (*L'Histoire* after Eugène Delacroix in the tympanum) gives access to the semicircular main courtyard (*Cour d'honneur*) of exceptionally pleasing dimensions. It is surrounded by beautiful porticoes of 56 paired columns which form a covered walk. At the end a harmonious façade consists of a ground floor where the paired columns reappear between the windows, and only one upper storey: in the center two superimposed orders are crowned by a triangular pediment, with two reclining figures representing *Prudence* and *Wisdom*; four groups of children symbolizing the *Spirits of the Arts* surmount the balustrade at the base of the French-style roof. Between the windows on the first floor the figures of the *Four Seasons* by Robert Le Lorrain have been replaced by copies. The Prince (ground floor) and Princess (first floor) de Soubise's apartments, which still have their magnificent 18th-c. Roccoco decoration, contain the Historical Museum of France (→museums), which celebrated its centenary in 1967. The history of France is told with original documents from the time of the Merovingians to the present day.

The transfer of The Archives Nationales (→ inset) will permit the extension of the museum.

Rue des Archives

From the Rue des Francs-Bourgeois to the Rue des Blancs-Manteaux.

At nos. 45–47 was the Couvent des Pères de la Merci, a religious community established here in 1613 by Marie de' Medici. The fathers devoted themselves to ransoming the captives of the Barbary pirates, even going so far as to offer themselves as hostage in exchange. The building was reconstructed by Godeau (1721–27). Closed in 1790, the convent was sold as national property in 1789. Registered door, sundials, staircase. The new demolished church stood on the corner of the Rue de Braque.

Rue des Blancs-Manteaux

This road has numerous old façades (wrought ironwork), and a visit to the Church of Notre-Dame-des-Blancs-Manteaux (the only remains of the monastery), which occupies the Square Charles-V-Langlois, is worthwhile.

Beyond the Rue du Temple it becomes the Rue Simon-le-Franc which dates from the 13th c. Some old houses are still there. Today it opens up a view over the Beaubourg Center.

☖ The Church of Notre-Dame-des-Blancs-Manteaux

12 Rue des Blancs-Manteaux (open Tues–Sun. from 10am–noon and 4–7pm). Tel: 42-72-09-37.

This church was so named because of the white cloaks worn by the impoverished mendicant friars of the Augustinian order. They were known as the Serfs of the Virgin; they founded the monastery in 1258. When the order was suppressed in 1695 its possessions went to the Benedictines of St William, the Guillemites, then in the 17th c. to the Benedictines of the congregation of Saint-Maur. The monastery became a center of learning, as respected as that of Saint-Germain-des-Prés. The church was rebuilt from 1685 to 1690 by Dom Antoine de Machy. The monastery was closed during the Revolution. In 1802 it became the parish church. A Catechism chapel was built in 1844 on the r. side of the church, then Baltard added a bay to the nave and applied the 18th-c. facade of the Church of Saint-Elio when it was removed from the Cité by Haussmann) to the S. elevation (Rue des Blancs-Manteaux*). Other interesting items: stalls, paneling, pulpit organ case, were acquired in the 19th c. Concerts of organ music are held in the church.

The interior

The nave. The church, without a transept, faces N. The large arcades with semicircular arches support an entablature with small bas-reliefs of, to the l., the Old Testament and to the r. the New Testament. Over the arcades are medallions carved with the busts of Saints and Apostles. The organ case, built in 1864, is attributed to the architect Varcollier who reused the paneling – notably the large fluted columns with Ionic capitals – from the former Abbey of Saint-Victor for the gallery. The instrument, which suffered severe bomb damage in August 1944, has been completely restored. The magnificent pulpit, which was acquired in 1864, dates from 1749 and is of Flemish origin. The canopy is surmounted by statues of St Michael and the four Evangelists. The parapet and staircase are decorated with marquetry panels inlaid with pewter and ivory representing the Parables and scenes from the New Testament.

The r. side aisle. Above the door: *L'Adoration des Bergers* (Adoration of the Shepherds) by J.-M. Bralle, commissioned in 1821. Chapelle des Catéchismes dedicated to St Geneviève. Around the high altar, three pictures commissioned under the July Monarchy, showing the life of St Geneviève. On the r-hand wall: *Jésus donne les Clefs à Saint Pierre* (Jesus giving the Keys to St Peter) by Norblin (1864), *Jésus au milieu des Docteurs* (Jesus surrounded by the Doctors) by Jollivet (1865) and *Le Christ au milieu des Enfants* (Christ surrounded by Children) by C.-H. Michel. On the wall facing the high altar: collection of 17th-c. paintings with, above, *La Mort de St Anne* (Death of St Anne) by Joachim Sandrart (17th c.). Returning by the r. side aisle, *La Multiplication des Pains* (The Multiplication of Loaves and Fishes) by Claude II Audran (1683).

The choir: the balustrades (early 18th c.), come from the former Château de Bercy. The woodwork on the posts also comes from Saint-Victor, like the organ. The stalls are 17th-c.

The l. side-aisle contains several pictures commissioned during the July Monarchy and under the Second Empire.

Opposite the church, the pretty Rue Aurbiot takes its name from Prevost Hugues Aurbiot, who appears to have been the first prisoner of the Bastille after he had finished building it. The street, now renovated, is bordered with 17th- and 18th-c. houses.

The Rue des Guillemites is a little less well preserved. Return by the Rue des Archives.

The Rue des Archives, continued

As far as the Rue Sainte-Croix-de-la-Bretonnerie.

The restoration of a building at no. 40 in 1971 revealed a beautiful house* which probably belonged to Jacques Coeur's son, Geoffrey, who may have had it built. What is certain is that it once belonged to Marie Coeur, daughter of Geoffroy, who died there in 1557. With its mullioned windows and decorative red brick masonry, this seems to be one of the first buildings in Paris to mix stone and brick. Beautiful Regency style doorway.

The Rue Sainte-Croix-de-la-Bretonnerie

Cross this street, which takes its name from the Priory of Sainte-Croix-de-la-Bretonnerie, which once stood at the corner of the Rue des Archives, but of which nothing remains, not even the church attributed to Pierre de Montreuil. The street has retained several beautiful inner courtyards and many attractive façades at nos. 2–10, 3, 13, 16 (where the astronomer François de Lalande once lived), 17, 18, and others.

☥ The Temple and the Cloître des Billettes

22 Rue des Archives

The evangelical church of the Billettes, constructed in 1756 by the Carmelites, stood on the site of a chapel and a monastery of the brothers of the Charité-Notre-Dame (known as the Billettes) who succeeded the Carmelites in 1633. The monastery was occupied from 1290; according to the chronicles of St Denis, it was in a house on this site that a money lender is said to have cut up a host (communion wafer) with a knife; the host began to bleed and the man threw it into a pan of boiling water which immediately turned red, hence the street's original name: Rue òu-Dieu-fut-bouilli (the Street where God was boiled). The man was burnt at the stake and soon after a church was built on the site in the late 16th c., with the triple dedication to the Holy Trinity, the Virgin and All Saints. In 1663 it was taken over by the Carmelites of the Observance des Rennes, called the Carmes-Billettes, who rebuilt the church from 1755 to 1758. It became a Lutheran church in 1812. Concerts are given here regularly.

The circular choir is linked to a nave of four bays flanked by side-aisles with two tiers of galleries, punctuated with Ionic pilasters. Of the old monastery there remains a pretty cloister*, completed in 1427, with four galleries of 14 tierce-point (triangularly arched) arcades with Flamboyant vaults. It is the only medieval cloister remaining in Paris. Since its restoration, it has been the venue for exhibitions, making it accessible to visitors.

Rue de la Verrerie. In the 12th c. there was a glassworks in this street. Later, the Confrérie des Peintres sur Verre et Emailleurs (Brotherhood of Glass Painters and Enamellers) took up residence here. Most of the houses on the even-numbered side are old.

Turn left into the Rue du Roi-de-Sicile, named after Charles d'Anjou, brother of Saint Louis, King of Naples and of Sicily, whose residence was to the extreme E. Nearly all the S side was destroyed to make way for the Rue de Rivoli. A few attractive houses remain.

Cross the Rue Bourg-Tibourg, which is named after the locality which was brought within the limits of Paris by the construction of Philippe Auguste's perimeter wall. Most of the buildings date from the 17th and 18th c., and while not luxurious, have much charm.

Rue Vieille-du-Temple, continued

From the Rue du Roi-de-Sicile to the Impasse du Trésor.

The Hôtel de Vibraye (1650) is at no. 15: door with triangular pediment, keystone carved with acanthus leaves, mascarons in the courtyard. At no. 17: door, wrought ironwork, mansard roofs. At no. 20: Impasse d'Argenson with, at the end, the remains of the mansion of the famous police lieutenant who was Louis XV's Minister of War. An old carved sign for the Cul-de-sac d'Argenson. Note the decoration on the façade of no. 21.

The Impasse du Trésor

This street was built on the site of the Hôtel du Maréchal d'Effiat, father of Cinq-Mars, Louis XIII's favourite who was executed for conspiring against Richelieu. It is closed off by a 19th-c. fountain, which is not in use. It is unfortunate that one of the most beautiful mansions of the Marais was sacrificed to make way for a useless cul-de-sac. No. 24 is an unusual mansion which, in 1792, was the property of the architect Varin. It is not known whether he designed it: façade, passage with a coffered vault, massive pillars, registered doors, courtyard. No. 33 is an attractive corner house: old street sign. At no. 36, which was reconstructed in 1660: registered door, wrought ironwork, courtyard. At no. 44: portal, doors, registered staircase in poor state of repair. No. 43 was where the Passage des Singes once started, a picturesque succession of courtyards leading to the Rue des Guillemites. It was demolished by a disastrous development which also left only a façade at no. 45.

Rue des Rosiers

Turn r. into this former *chemin de ronde*, the Philippe Auguste perimeter wall, which in the W section still follows its sinuous medieval route. This is the center of the Jewish district (→inset). Numerous old houses: at no. 32: courtyard; no. 23: door; nos. 20, 28: staircase; no. 16: remains in the courtyard. Nearby is the Rue des Ecouffes, the origin of whose name remains obscure. Philippe de Champaigne died at no. 2 (inscription). Many beautiful 17th- and 18th-c. houses: no. 25: door, attractive building overlooking a courtyard, staircase; nos. 23, 21, 13, 10, 5: door and courtyard; and no. 2: gabled house, old gate, shop decorated with oil paintings under glass.

Go l. into the Rue du Roi-de-Sicile. It owes its name to Charles d'Anjou, brother of St Louis, king of Naples and Sicily, who had his residence at the E end. Practically all the S side was demolished during the construction of the Rue de Rivoli. Some attractive façades on the even-numbered side.

Take the Rue Ferdinand-Duval (13th c.) on the l., which was called Rue des Juifs until 1900. At no. 20 there is an interesting courtyard (possibly early 17th c.) with pilasters, Corinthian capitals, mansard roofs and alternating triangular and curved pediments; fine door. Much wrought ironwork (nos. 16, 18). No. 1: door.

Take the Rue des Rosiers again to rejoin the Rue Vieille-du-Temple.

☐ The Hôtel des Ambassadeurs de Hollande**

47 Rue Vieille-du-Temple

This superb mansion proclaims the power of its various owners. Today it belongs to the Paul-Louis Weiler Foundation and is in the course of being restored.

In the 15th c. the Hôtel de Rieux, built near the Barbette postern for the companions of Du Guesclin, stood on this site. It was near this house that Louis d'Orléans, brother of Charles VI, was assassinated at the instigation of Jean sans Peur (→below) while leaving the Hôtel Barbette. The mansion passed from hand to hand. In 1655 it was acquired by the Amelot de Chaillou family, the Viscounts de Bisseuil, who embarked on its reconstruction, following plans by P. Cottard. Pierre-Antoine Caron de Beaumarchais lived here (1776–87) and wrote his *Marriage of Figaro*. Ever short of money but never of ideas, he founded an enterprise, which, under a commercial disguise was designed to provide arms to the American insurgents against the English. He also turned the house into a shelter for impoverished nursing mothers. It has never been very clear why the mansion was called Hôtel des Ambassadeurs de Hollande. Some historians have explained it with reference to some sort of sign; others have suggested the name recalls the chaplains of the chapel of the Dutch Embassy who occupied it, one of whom is said to have baptized the infant Germaine Necker (the future Mme de Staël) here.

The mansion, which must have been sumptuous, was one of the most beautiful in the Marais, but it has been badly damaged over the centuries. However, the imposing portal with the bas-relief of Romulus and Remus (1660) was restored in 1970 and substantial work was carried out in 1977 in the first courtyard, which has preserved four big sundials and carved windows. The second courtyard, which is even larger, has Corinthian pilasters and porticoes with garlands. The so-called Italian Room is covered by a domed ceiling painted by L. de Boullongne. The mansion had, like the Hôtel Lambert, a magnificent gallery which has been reconstructed with a ceiling painted by Michel Corneille.

Opposite, at no. 48 Rue Vieille-du-Temple, the Laboratoire d'Hygiène of the City of Paris occupies the former Blancs-Manteaux market, which was built from 1811 to 1819 on the site of the Saint-Gervais hospital (Rue des Hospitalières-Saint-Gervais). There are two fountains with Assyrian bulls' heads in bronze appliqué attached to the outside of the building that was the market butcher's shop.

Rue des Francs-Bourgeois

From the Rue Vieille-du-Temple to the Rue Elzévir (for the last part of this street →above).

This is the richest and most handsome section of this street. At no. 38, the Allée des Arbalétriers is a good example of a medieval street, with its large cobblestones, boundary stones and corbelled houses. It continued to the S as far as Philippe Auguste's perimeter wall, serving as a practice field for crossbow men, and led to a second entrance at the Hôtel Barbette. It was very likely here that Louis d'Orléans, leaving after a visit to Isabeau of Bavaria, was assassinated on the orders of his cousin Jean sans Peur. At nos. 34–36 is the Hôtel Poussepin, built in 1603 for Jean Alméras on the site of the old Maison d'Aumône, created to house 48 poor people who were also to be free from taxation, hence the name Francs-Bourgeois: attractive courtyard, 17th-c. painted ceilings. Today it is the Centre Culturel Suisse which puts on some interesting events (concerts, exhibitions, plays). No. 30 is the Hôtel d'Améras, built about

1611 for Pierre d'Améras, councillor and financial secretary to the king. It is a fine example of Henri IV architecture, whose monumental portal recalls certain works by Salomon de Brosse; 18th-c doors. No. 35 is the Hôtel de Coulanges. Modified on numerous occasions, the mansion bears the name of the famous family that owned it during much of the 17th c. The portal dates from 1707. In the courtyard, the r. wing and the central part of the building probably date from the early 17th c. The l. wing was rebuilt in 1660. A circular pavilion built in 1770 looks onto the garden. This is today the Maison de l'Europe, a center for cultural meetings and exchanges. At no. 26 is the Hôtel de Sandreville which in the 16th c. was called the Hôtel Morrier, but was split in two after a family division in 1604. The façade on to the street was extended by two storeys and redecorated in the Louis XVI style, rare in the Marais. Its owner at the time was Louis-Charles Le Mairat, President of the Chambre des Comptes (Chamber of Commerce). The *hôtel*'s garden used to extend as far as the Rue Barbette. It is to be hoped that the restoration currently in progress will pay scrupulous attention to the original appearance of one of the oldest mansions in the Marais. At no. 33, behind a bleak 19th-c. façade, the remains of the Hôtel de Guillaume-Barbes, which was named after the treasurer of the French and Swiss Guards who had taken part in the development of the Ile Saint-Louis. The mansion, built in the 17th c., had its front part cut off by an 1868 decree regulating the alignment of the street.

Rue Elzévir

Enter this small street, which takes its name from a Dutch family of printers, and offers an attractive view of the gardens of the Hôtel de Marie (→below).

At no 4 is the Hôtel de Savourney (c. 1586), the main part of which, between the courtyard and garden, has been restored. Part of it can be seen from 3 Rue Payenne to where the gardens once extended. The wings and the building onto the street are later additions. No. 8 is the Hôtel de Donon, built about 1575 for Médéric de Donon, Controller of the King's Buildings. It is a building of exceptional interest, thought to be the work of Philibert Delorme. The garden extended as far as the Rue Payenne. The front building on the street is 18th c. The City of Paris acquired the mansion in 1975, but neglected it, and its present state is causing concern. It has now been assigned to the Musée Cognacq-Jay, which will install its collections in the house after restoration. At no. 14 the name of Mme de Sévigné crops up once again and, at no. 16, that of Ninon de Lenclos, the celebrated courtesan.

Rue des Francs-Bourgeois, continued

As far as the Rue Pavée

At nos. 32 and 29 *bis* is the Hôtel d'Albret**, built on the land belonging to the Anne, Duc de Montmorency, gentleman-in-waiting to the king. Following exchanges and inheritances, the mansion passed, not to Jeanne d'Albret, as is generally supposed, but to Madeleine de Guénégaud, wife of César d'Albret. The building, assigned to the Direction des Affaires Culturelles de Paris, is undergoing restoration.

It is a very beautiful house, though of a composite style: the building at the end of the courtyard is 16th c., modified in the 17th and 18th c; the r. wing was built in the 17th c. A passage for carriages leads to the inner courtyard of the *hôtel* (no. 29 *bis*). It is possible that a part of the building was by François Mansart. The main building onto the street, recommenced in 1740 with designs by the architect Vautrain, boasts superb Rocaille decoration.

☐ The Hôtel Lamoignon**

Entrance at 24 Rue Pavée

This is one of the largest houses in the Marais and one of the most interesting, partly because of its date of construction (1584). The central part of the building was constructed on the site of the old Hôtel de Beauvais (mid 16th c.) by Diane de France, Duchesse d'Angoulême, legitimized daughter of Henri II and a young Piedmontese, Filippa Duco. She chose as her heir Charles de Valois, her nephew, and the bastard son of Charles IX and Marie Touchet. It was he who had the wings built (1624). That on the r. was built in 1834 as an enlargement of La Force prison.

The main façade on to the courtyard, with its Corinthian pilasters, is one of the oldest examples in Paris of a Colossal order (columns rising from the ground through several storeys up to the cornice). The architect may have been Jean-Baptiste Androuet Du Cerceau. Observe the rounded pediments, the decoration of dogs' heads, bows, arrows and quivers (which recall Diane's passion for hunting), the letter D and crescents.

From 1658 to 1677 the mansion was rented to Guillaume de Lamoignon, the first president of the Parliament of Paris, then in 1688 bought by his son, Chrestien François de Lamoignon, who laid out a magnificent garden and built the grand entrance (1718). This bears the initials L and M for Lamoignon de Malesherbes. The decoration on the tympanum includes two cupids, one holding a mirror and the other a serpent, symbolizing Truth and Prudence, M de Lamoignon's outstanding virtues. At the corner of the Rue Pavée and Rue des Francs-Bourgeois is a pretty square turret supported on squinches. On its base are the letters S C, for St Catherine, to show in whose territory the mansion stood. The façade on to the garden can be seen from the Rue des Francs-Bourgeois. The mansion was restored (1949–60) and a new building added (1966) to contain the Bibliothèque Historique de la Ville de Paris (open daily except Thurs., bank holidays, 9:30am–6pm) which left the Hôtel Le Peletier for the Musée Carnavalet. The large room on the ground floor, today a lecture hall (90 seats), has kept its beautiful ceiling, with 16th-c. painted beams and joists. The shops, which have 12ml./20km of metal shelving, occupy seven floors, two of which are in the basement under the main courtyard.

The Rue Pavée

Until 1848, no. 22 extended toward the S as far as the Prison de la Petite Force (1784), of which a wall with vermiculated (decorated with uneven shallow channels, like worn tracks) bosses still stands. The prison, which was linked to the Grande Force, was used for female prisioners. Those who were faithful to Marie-Antoinette and shared her early days of captivity at the Temple were detained there, including the Princesse de Lamballe, Mme de Tourzel and her daughter. At no. 13 is part of the Hôtel d'Herbouville (1770), the old mansion of the dukes of Lorraine, which was rebuilt in 1643 and split in two after 1681. At no. 11 the Hôtel des Marets has a Louis XIII door, and no. 13, the Hôtel d'Herbouville, has an 18th-c. entrance. These two mansions, which are occupied by the highways department of the City of Paris, are in a pitiful state. No. 12 is the Petit Hôtel de Brienne, built in 1632, which belonged to the Loménie de Brienne family from 1969 to 1784 when it was bought by Tronchet, one of Louis XVI's legal advisers, who died there in 1806: pretty courtyard, staircase. No. 10 is a synagogue by Guimard (1913), with an interesting four-storey façade with bay windows.

The Rue Malher, which branches off on the l. from the Rue Pavée, is on the site of the former Rue des Ballets and La Grande Force prison. The latter was a political prison from 1782, where 75 Girondins were held, and which gave onto the Rue du Roi-de-Sicile where, before the prison gate, 171 prisoners, including the Princesse de Lamballe, were massacred, beheaded and dismembered by the mob (September 2–7, 1792).

Rue Payenne

Return to the Rue des Francs-Bourgeois to reach this street, which was finished in 1545, and retains much of its charm. Its even-numbered side is occupied by the Musée Carnavalet (conservation offices) and by the attractive little Square Georges-Caïn, which has a small lapidary collection belonging to the City of Paris. The square is bounded in the N by the elegant *orangerie* (allegory of *Truth* in the pediment) of the Hôtel Le Peletier de Saint-Fargeau (→ below), and to the E by the mansion itself. The rear façade is also worth seeing: the carved decoration on the tympanum of the pediment is the figure of an old man with wings looking at an hourglass. No. 5 is the house that François Mansart built for himself, where he lived until his death in 1666 with his nephews Pierre Delisle-Mansart and Jules Hardouin-Mansart, both architects. The house was altered completely when it was converted into a 'temple of the religion of Humanity' by the positivist church of Brazil in 1903. The temple was dedicated to the memory of Clotilde de Vaux, a friend of Auguste Comte; on the façade is written *'L'amour pour principe, l'ordre pour base, le progrès pour but'* (Love as the principle, order as the foundations, progress as the goal), which recalls the Brazilian national motto, 'Order and Progress'.

The Hôtel de Marle*, or du Polastron-Polignac

11 Rue Payenne

This mansion, built in the late 16th c., was acquired in 1572 by the councillor Hector de Marle, who lived there for over 30 years. In 1609 it was sold to Charles Duret de Chevry, who had also lived in the adjoining mansion, the Hôtel du Lude, as well as at 8 Rue du Parc-Royal. In the 18th c. the mansion, designed by Philibert Delorme, belonged to Yolande de Polastron, wife of Armand de Polignac and a favourite of Marie-Antoinette's. The center building, with its two wings projecting on the garden side visible from the Rue Payenne, seems to date from Hector de Marle's period. A careful restoration has preserved the beautiful roof, attributed to Philibert Delorme. The two courtyard wings may be of a later date, possibly 1640. The mansion has retained several of its ceilings with painted beams (16th and 17th c.) and a staircase with banisters dating from the second half of the 18th c. Acquired and restored in 1967 by the Swedish Government, it now houses the Swedish Cultural Center (open daily except Sun. 2pm–6pm) which offers frequent exhibitions, Swedish cinema, theater, conferences, and language and literature courses. On the first floor is the Musée Tessin (→ Museums).

The Hôtel du Lude*, or de Châtillon

13 Rue Payenne

Dating from the Louis XIII period, this hotel also belonged to Duret de Chevry, and was rented for most of the 17th and 18th c., among others, to the Duchesse du Lude and the widowed Duchesse de Châtillon. Françoise d'Aubigné, the future Mme de Maintenon, lived here. The courtyard, which is covered with Virginia creeper, has much charm, but the building has, regrettably, had extra storeys added. Remarkable staircase, beautiful portal with a sculpted cartouche.

No. 15 Rue Payenne is a Louis XIII house.

Rue du Parc-Royal

The odd-numbred side of this street is bordered by the Square Léopold-Achille, while the other side is lined with a series of *hôtels*, mostly from the Louis XIII period (the Place des Vosges is not far away), which have deteriorated with age. The Hôtel de Bonneval at no. 14 was probably rebuilt c. 1786 in its present Neo-Classical style (façade and l. wing) by its owner at the end of the 18th c., M de Bonneval. The main part of the building was rebuilt in 1975: unusual stepped pediment. A magnificent hall with a painted cupola and a beautiful staircase can be seen in the l. wing. No. 12 is the Hôtel de Croisilles, built from 1619 onwards for Nicolas de Croisilles, Councillor of State and steward of Mgr le Duc d'Angoulême; it was enlarged in 1691 following the acquisition of two building plots and the street. In 1898 it became the Cercle Amicitia, a centre for impoverished young Christian girls. The street side façades are 19th-c. Assigned to the Ministry of Culture to house the library and archive of France's historic buildings commission (the Bibliotheque des Monuments Historiques) it is in the course of restoration. At no. 10, the Hôtel de Vigny (visits on request; tel: 42–71–22–02) was built about 1618 and enlarged in 1628, probably by Louis Le Vau (staircase, wings projecting in to the garden). It takes its name from the widow of the State Auditor Jacques Olivier de Vigny, its owner in the 18th c. In 1960 it was bought by the Ministry of Education, which intended to demolish it. But restoration work carried out by a team of generous amateurs brought to light ceilings with painted beams, which ensured its conservation. Since then another magnificent painted and stuccoed ceiling has been discovered on the first floor; the work of Nicolas Loir and Jacques Gervaise (1669–70). The mansion, which is a registered historic monument, has been assigned to the Centre National de Documentation du Patrimoine (National Documentation Center) (→inset). No. 8 is the Hôtel Duret de Chevry. King's Councillor, Intendant of Finance and President of the Chamber of Commerce, the rich and powerful Charles Durey de Chevry was a favorite of Sully. His mansion was built from 1618 to 1619. All that remains are the two wings onto the courtyard. The main part of the building (which has been extensively restored) between the courtyard and the garden is now a 19th-c. pastiche. At no. 4 is the Hôtel de Canillac. Since the beginning of the 17th c. it has been altered many times, sometimes drastically (the main building has had extra storeys added, and a passage cut through it), but it has retained one of the most beautiful staircases* in Paris, both in its structure and decoration, exemplary of early 17th-c. style.

Rue de Sévigné

This was formerly the Rue de la Culture-Sainte-Catherine, created in 1544 on land belonging to the priory of Sainte-Catherine-du-Val-des-Ecoliers (→Place des Vosges district). At no. 52 are the remains of the Hôtel de Flesselles (1680) whose remarkable painted ceiling is in the Musée des Arts Décoratifs. It belonged to the last of the Provost Marshals, who was torn to pieces by the mob on July 14, 1789. No. 48, the Hôtel de Jonquières, is a dilapidated Louis XIII house; the bas-relief by Fortin (1810) of *La Charité* comes from the old Popincourt fountain in the Rue de la Folie-Méricourt.

The Hôtel Le Peletier de Saint-Fargeau

29 Rue de Sévigné

This mansion was built from 1686 to 1689 by P. Bullet for the financial administrator, Le Peletier des Forts. In the 18th c., a descendant of this family, Le Peletier de Saint-Fargeau, became a member of the Convention. Having voted for the death of Louis XVI, he was stabbed on the eve of the execution in the gardens of the Palais-Royal by the King's ex-bodyguard, Pâris.

Above the door (on the impost) the monogram MLP can be seen. This mansion, designed in a very austere style, is arranged around a rectangular courtyard visible from inside the museum bordered by two-storey buildings above an arcaded ground floor. The windows are surrounded by a simple frieze. The beautiful orangerie, visible from the Square Georges-Caïn, is also the work of P. Bullet. In contrast, the buildings that border the Square Leopold-Achille are 19th- and 20th-c. The buildings suffered considerably from being used for a time as a school. They were bought by the City in 1897 to house the Bibliotheque Historique, which was transferred to the Hôtel Lamoignon in 1968. Recently work has been carried out to convert the *hôtel* into an annex of the Musée Carnavalet (→ Museums), for the collections concerning the history of Paris from its origins to the 18th c.

The Hôtel Carnavalet***

23 Rue de Sévigné

The mansion, forever linked to the memory of Mme de Sévigné, and today the historical museum of the City of Paris, is a superb example of civil architecture of the Renaissance and the 17th c.

History of the building

Curiously, the mansion bears the name of a lady to whom it owes practically nothing, which hardly does justice to the two owners chiefly responsible for its appearance. Nicolas Dupuis built the *hôtel* between 1548 and 1560 for Jacques de Ligneris, President of the Parlement of Paris. In 1578 it was acquired by Françoise de Kernevenoy, widow of the Breton king of Kernevency, whose name was gradually corrupted to Carnavalet. The financier Claude

Boislève bought the mansion in 1654 and in 1660 gave the famous architect François Mansart the task of enlarging and modernizing it. The mansion was then rented to Marie de Rabutin-Chantal, Marquise de Sévigné, who lived there from 1677 until her death in 1696. The illustrious letter writer loved her mansion dearly, calling it her 'Carnavalette', receiving there many of the greatest men of letters of the day. The City of Paris bought it in 1866 to have its historical collections. The architect Parmentier restored the oldest part of this building to their original state, and the museum opened its doors in 1880. The museum continued to expand and more space was needed for the increasing number of collections. Buildings were added with three courtyards, whose classically designed flowerbeds contribute to the charm of the Carnavalet.

Tour of the exterior

The museum is a combination of two *hôtels*, that built by Pierre Lescot in 1544 in the Renaissance style, and the other by François Mansart in the middle of the 17th c. The portal with its Renaissance bossages, guarded by Goujon's lions, framed by Mansart's elegant architecture, is first to greet the visitor. The bas-reliefs are mid-16th c. but the tympanum is somewhat later. Jean Goujon also carved the keystone with a statue of Plenty; its supporting globe was changed to a carnival mask, a punning reference to the name 'Carnavalet'. Above the door of the *hôtel* at first-floor level are two large carved figures of *La Force* (strength) and *La Vigilance* by Gerard van Obstal (17th c.). The main building is Gothic in style, contrasting with the 17th-c. wings. The l. has cherubs holding torches, and the statues of the Four Seasons, probably executed in the workshop of Goujon. In the center of the courtyard stands the bronze statue of Louix XIV*** in the garb of a Roman general with his 17th-c. perruque, by Coysevox (1689), brought here from the Hôtel de Ville. Two of the mansion's three garden courts can be seen through the doorway over the Rue des Francs-Bourgeois, framed in its Nazarene arch, although it is not possible to reach the gardens without walking through the museum. The l. wing consists of a 16th-c. loggia to which Mansart added another storey. The r. wing, also by Mansart, mirrors the one opposite, with four divinities carved in bas-relief by van Obstal.

Rue de Sévigné, continued

As far as the Rue Saint-Antoine

At no. 13 is a former annex of the Hôtel Bouthiller de Chavigny: gate with registered doors. No. 11, the Théâtre du Marais, constructed by Beaumarchais with bricks from the demolition of the

Bastille, was inaugurated on September 1, 1791. Napoléon I's decree governing Parisian theaters (1807) closed it along with many others. The hall, which was destroyed in 1812, was replaced by baths, which existed until the 1960s. The street façade with its pilasters and wrought ironwork, has been preserved. At nos. 7-9 is the Hôtel Bouthiller de Chavigny. Around 1265 the Hôtel de Charles d'Anjou, the residence of the brother of St Louis, stood on this site. The old mansion was rebuilt in the Renaissance, then bought by Claude Bouthillier de Chavigny, Secretary of State under Louis XIII; he had it enlarged by François Mansart (wing onto the courtyard). From 1698 to 1713 the *hôtel* was inhabited by the Duc de La Force and known by his name. Sold again, it was divided in two. The W part became the sinister Prison de La Force (→above). The E part was acquired by the Intendant of Finance, Jacques Poulletier, who had it altered by the architects Bullet and Jacques Gabriel. From 1801 to 1813 it was the headquarters of the Administration des Pompes Funèbres (a service that oversaw burials and funerary monuments), and today it is a fire station. The facade is austere but there are some fine features in the courtyard. The barracks can only be entered during the July 14 ball. The Raspail clinic was at no. 5 (1840-48).

> The Order of the Knights Templar

The capture of Jerusalem in 1099 necessitated maintaining a permanent army in Palestine. Military personnel and communities of soldier-monks were needed to defend the sacred places and the pilgrims. The Order of the Temple, a name recalling the Temple of Solomon in Jerusalem, created by Hugues de Pays in 1119, expanded rapidly, attracting France's greatest nobles. Its 9,000 *commanderies*, spread throughout Europe and the Near East, assured it an important political and economic role. It was the Templars who created the first international bank as it were, instituting early forms of the letter of exchange and the cheque drawn against a deposit. The Temple, which was installed near Saint-Gervais in the early 12th c., moved in the middle of the century to the district which still bears its name. The Templars, who at this time were guardians of the royal treasury, gradually became administrators of the royal finances and later the king's principal creditors. It is well known how Philippe IV (le Bel), burdened with financial difficulties at the end of his reign, and angry at the power and influence in Europe of the Knights Templar, whose wealth he doubtless wished to appropriate, relentlessly and brutally destroyed the Order. This dramatic episode ended in 1314 with the burning at the stake of two Temple dignitaries, Jacques de Molay and Geoffroy de Charnay. Pope Clement V, who was devoted to the King of France (to whom he owed his election) had in 1312, at the conclusion of a shameful trial, ordered the supression of the Order. The Temple property passed to the Hospitalers of St John of Malta.

▷ **The Verniquet plan**

The historian Edmé Verniquet (1727–1804) is first and foremost the creator of a masterly plan of Paris. The plan, commissioned by Louis XVI in 1783, was completed in 1792. Composed of 72 26×17¼ in./44×66cm engraved sheets, it was the first map worked out by trigonometry and therefore scientifically accurate.

It served as a reference throughout the 19th c., notably for the first cadastral survey of Paris (1808) which was used to plan street widening and the expropriation of property that it entailed. It is especially valuable in that it gives us a true and precise picture of how Paris was before the wholesale destruction of convents, mansions and churches, brought about first by the Revolution and then by the 19th-c. city administration. The bronze engraving plates, hidden by Verniquet's daughter Madeleine following a dispute over money, have not been found to this day.

▷ **Claude-Nicolas Ledoux**

This Parisian architect (1736–1806), taught mainly by Blondel, soon quarreled with his master, who had little time for his aesthetic biases. Under the influence of Palladio, he favored a monumental use of the Classical orders, rather than superimposition of the orders and he was inspired by the cyclopean fantasies of Piranesi. In addition, his architectural conceptions drew strength from the Rousseauist vision of a new society. While in the provinces his genius can be judged from his surviving buildings; in Paris his engravings, meticulously executed by his office, show his prodigious feeling for setting, together with his evident attention to simplicity and efficiency. Finally, contemporary opinion, equally divided between indignation and admiration, is an indication of how revolutionary his architecture appeared, with its constant use of columns and unusual proportions. These mansions, built from 1765 to 1795, were all situated in the Chaussée-d'Antin and the new Poissonnière districts. The principal ones were: the Hôtel d'Hallwyll (1766); the Hôtel d'Uzes (1768), violently criticized by Blondel; the house (1770) for Mlle Guimard (a dancer who was the mistress of the Prince de Soubise), which included a private theater and a winter garden; a curious group of buildings designed for the West Indian nabob Hosten (1792; since demolished), a complex that included not only the owner's house, but 15 identical houses to be rented out; the Pavillon de Louvenciennes, a landmark of French Neo-Classical architecture, begun in 1771 for Mme du Barry; and finally, above all, the Hôtel Thélusson (1778). This mansion, which was built for the widow of the Swiss banker, was a popular place for strolling, and something of a curiosity on account of the enormous triumphal arch which served as its entrance; its English-style landscaped garden, with a grotto hollowed out under a central rotunda; the underground passages for carriages, with a roundabout; and finally the ingenuity and sumptuousness of its interior decoration.

▷ The royal family in the Temple

The royal family (Louis XVI, Marie-Antoinette, the king's sister Mme Elisabeth, the Dauphin's sister Mme Royale and the seven-year-old Dauphin) were imprisoned by order of the Revolutionary Commune on the evening of August 13, 1792, first in the little tower adjoining the dungeon of the Temple Prison, then in the Temple itself. The king left it on January 21, 1793 to go to the guillotine. Mme Royal was the last prisoner and was not freed until after the 9th Thermidor (November) reaction in 1795. As for Louis XVII, the only fact on which historians agree is that the body of the dead child found in the Temple on June 8, 1795 was not his. Although the number of pretended dauphins now totals 43, his disappearance will doubtless always remain an enigma. (→The Sainte-Marguerite cemetery).

▣ Museums to visit

Musée Carnavalet (23 Rue de Sévigné): history of Paris and *objets d'art* from the 16th to the 19th c.

Institut Tessin (11 Rue Payenne): Swedish artists (17th to 19th c.). Maison de Victor Hugo (6 Place des Vosges): mementoes and drawings of Victor Hugo displayed in his former mansion.

Musée Picasso Hôtel Salé, (5 Rue de Thoringy): Picasso bequest. Musée de l'Histoire de France Hôtel de Rohan, 60 Rue des Francs-Bourgeois: documents on the history of France from its origins to the Revolution.

Musée Kwok-On (41 Rue des Francs-Bourgeois): Asian theater and music; costumes, masks, puppets, musical instruments (Noh, Kabuki, etc.).

Musée de la Serrure (1 Rue de la Perle): collection of door furniture including locks, keys, handles and wrought ironwork.

Musée de la Chasse et de la Nature (60 Rue des Archives): hunting objects, arms, collections of animal paintings.

▷ Pierre Jean de Béranger

'*La tyrannie ne pourra jamais s'asseoir définitivement dans un pays où l'on chante*' ('Tyranny can never take root permanently in a country that sings'). These words of Béranger (1780–1857), *chansonnier* and polemicist, sum up the views of this independent and courageous man, so unjustly forgotten today. As a child he knew the elation of storming the Bastille, but also the horrors of the subsequent massacres. A confirmed liberal, he was always distrustful of the excesses of popular revolutions. Having had little education, he became an assistant in the office of his father, a banker of little talent. He was already interested in nothing but poetry and, in 1804, reduced to near povery, he sent his verses to Lucien Bonaparte, who took him under his wing. Assured of a modest income, he devoted himself to writing songs (such as *Le Vieux Sergent, Le Dieu des bonnes gens*), which were immediately popular. Having seen in Bonaparte the guarantor of liberal ideas, he did not cease to lampoon the authoritarianism of Napoléon. However, after the Bourbon restoration, he felt compelled to glorify the dethroned Emperor, a stand which brought him to trial, with a first detention of three months (1822), followed by a prison conviction of three months and a 10,000 franc fine (1829). The popularity of the poet can be gauged by the fact that the fine was paid by public subscription. He was seen as an inspirer for the revolutionary days of 1830. The abolition of monarchy by divine right filled him with joy. After 1833, he ceased to publish his writings. He was elected deputy in 1848, but promptly resigned. An enemy of any constraint of liberty, of power and pomp, he wished to exert political influence by virtue of his songs alone.

▷ The Place de France project

Visitors to this district will be amazed to discover how many streets bear the names of French provinces: Poitou, Saintonge, Bretagne, Normandie and so on. It is a reminder of Henry IV's scheme which, in addition to the Place Dauphine and Place Royale (now Place des Vosges), proposed the creation of a Place de France. The decision by the Grand Prior of the Temple to divide up the *marais* (marsh) outside the Temple's enclosure resolved the king to acquire the land in 1608. The plan for the *place* is known from a drawing by the engineer Claude Chastillon. It was to back onto the rampart and was to be semicircular, reached on the suburban side by a monumental gate and a bridge spanning the moat, and on the town side by eight radiating streets, bearing the names of the French provinces and bordered by identical houses, built in a mixture of stone and brick, as was common at the time. Where the streets emerged into the square there were to be seven symmetrical pavilions, with a covered gallery at ground level, corner turrets with windows all round on the first floor, and the whole roofed over with tiles. The assassination of the king in 1610 put an end to this grandiose scheme.

▷ Markets

Marché des Enfants-Rouges (39 Rue de Bretagne): Mon.–Sat. 8am–1pm and 4–7:30pm; Sun. 8am–1pm.

Marché du Temple (Rue Perrée): Tues.–Sat. 9am–noon, Sat. and Sun 9am–1pm; shops open until 7pm.

> The Crédit Municipal, the former State pawnshop

As early as the 14th c. Italy had establishments that issued loans against a security, designed to help people who were momentarily short of cash. The first in France, was at Avignon (1577). The Paris pawnshop was created by letters patent in 1777 and installed in a number of adjoining houses, acquired in 1777, 1779 and 1789, in the Rue des Blancs-Manteaux. The Lieutenant-General of the Police and the General Hospital shared the administration. The benefits that accrued were handed over to the General Hospital on the principle that money that came from the poor should return to the poor. The pawnshop which from the time of the Empire fell under the authority of the Ministry of the Interior, was prodigiously successful during the whole of the 19th c. Picturesque expressions such as *aller chez ma tante* (going to my aunt's house) and *au clou* (to put one's modest treasures in hock) hid a cruel privation. The establishment, which fell into disuse at the beginning of the 20th c., got a new lease of life in 1985. With newly renovated offices and up-to-date technological equipment, the Crédit, as well as providing traditional loans against a security, now offers full banking services. There is also a special office where expert advice can be obtained on selling by auction. Some clients even use the Crédit Municipal as a furniture store. But whether you leave your iron or your grandmother's diamond ring there, you are always assured of a warm welcome.

> The Centre National d'Accueil et de Recherches des Archives Nationales (CARAN), (National Archives Research Center)

Since 1908, with successive acquisitions (the Hôtels de Soubise, de Rohan, d'Assy, de Breteuil, de Fontenay and de Jaucourt) of buildings erected in the 19th c., the State has established the National Archives firmly in the quarter that now bears its name. However, given a rate of increase in the number of visitors during the last 20 years of over 250% (with 15,000 readers in 1986) and, at present, five reading rooms offering a total of only 170 seats, it is obvious that extra accommodation is essential. In an open competition in 1983, Stanislas Fiszer's design was accepted. Work began on the new building in March 1986 and the building was opened in March 1988. Despite protests in certain quarters, the new Archives have proved to be one of the true successes of contemporary architecture. The varied design of the street facade takes the neighboring buildings into account: the Hôtel Boisgelin to the east and large, windowless warehouses to the west. The bronze bas-relief by Yvan Themier depicts the heroes of a 12th century epic poem, *Les Quatre Fils Aymon*. The garden façade is entirely of glass on a framework of slender pillars, giving an impression of lightness. The large number of materials employed (stone, concrete, plaster, steel, wood) may not suit all tastes, but the quality of the finish is remarkable. Beyond the handsome and spacious entrance hall lie a large reading room (350 seats), a catalogue room, a room where microfilms can be read and areas for specialist research: sigillography, onomastics, Parisian topography. The furniture has been specially designed. Though the centre will be further improved when the computer systems are fully operating, it already represents an outstanding resource for researchers. It contains reading rooms equipped with modern technology computers, microfilm reading equipment, special research services, which should facilitate both the work of researchers and the librarians (access underground between the reading rooms and the depots ensures the safety of documents). There will be a reception and information bureau and a cafeteria. Finally, the completion of the project for CARAN will allow access to the gardens of the archives by readers and visitors. The model, which was on display in 1984, aroused public indignation because of its modernity, which was felt to be inappropriate to the area, though it is worth remembering that the Marais was created during a period extending from the 12th c. to the present day. Its various styles and periods have, with the passage of time, blended harmoniously. Only the future can tell if CARAN's contribution to the 20th c. will be a success.

▷ The Jewish quarter

Visitors are assured of a complete change of scene when they explore the Rue des Rosiers and the adjacent streets. This district, dating from the 13th c., is one of the oldest Jewish areas of Paris. It is only by chance that it remains an isolated enclave today. The new Jewish settlements began in 1809, and grew after 1880 and in the early 20th c. with the arrival of refugees from Central Europe (mostly from Poland, but also from Russian and the Slavic provinces of Austria). The character of this largely Ashkenazi community has changed recently, with the arrival of Sephardic Jews, 'repatriated' immigrants from North Africa. The district is picturesque, with kosher food shops, restaurants offering traditional Jewish cuisine as well as succulent Central European specialties (the best-known is the famous Goldenberg's) side by side with shops selling religious objects, or record shops where Enrico Macias is the uncontested star. Signs written in Hebrew, old people hailing each other and conversing in Yiddish (some have never even left the quarter) and a few remaining Orthodox Jews in their long black coats all contribute to the personality of the district. Visitors should try *falafel*, a delicious Middle Eastern sandwich made with fried chickpea croquettes, or buy some smoked salmon (from shops whose names are well known to Parisian high society) and perhaps end their walk with a visit to the *hammam*, or public baths (4 Rue des Rosiers; open Wed. and Fri. for women, Thurs, and Sat. for men). Avoid visiting on Saturday, the Sabbath, when all the shops are closed.

The Bibliothèque Historique de la Ville de Paris (Historical Library of Paris)

In 1752 the tenant of the Hôtel Lamoignon was Antoine Moriau, Procurator to the king. This enlightened bibliophile amassed a considerable library, which he bequeathed to the City on his death (1759). The first library of the City of Paris, inaugurated in 1762, was open to the public two afternoons a week and was situated in the same place to which the collection was to return two centuries later. Having occupied the Hôtel Carnavalet, then the Hôtel Le Peletier de Saint-Fargeau, the Bibliothèque Historique de la Ville de Paris has been housed in the Hotel Lamoignon since 1969. It comprises more than 800,000 volumes and 20,000 manuscripts relating to the history of Paris and the Revolution. It possesses an imposing collection of original documents, including letters of Boileau and Voltaire, Mme d'Epinay's memoirs, Fouquier-Tinville's letters, the papers of Camille and Lucille Desmoulins, Flaubert's notebooks, and the letters, manuscripts and papers from George Sand's family. The topographical section has a unique collection of maps of Paris from the 16th c.

The library also houses the Service des Travaux Historiques de la Ville de Paris, which is responsible for the publication of the principal texts of the municipal history of Paris. It also organizes documentary exhibitions and has a constantly updated section on current affairs, where documents of all kinds relating to contemporary Parisian life are on display (posters, tracts, handbills, invoices, etc.).

The Centre National de Documentation du Patrimoine (National Heritage Documentation Center)

On December 19, 1984, the Ministry of Culture inaugurated the Centre National de Documentation du Patrimoine in the Hôtel de Vigny. In 1964, on the initiative of André Malraux, a general inventory of France's monuments and artistic treasures was made.

This enormous census covered both public and private monuments and works of art. In 20 years more than 80,000 files have been compiled (covering about 200 districts, and about 1.2 million photographs, 4,000 maps and 20,000 tables). The results of this project have been widely distributed in the numerous and highly specialized publications concerning the inventory and by exhibitions all over France. Eventually it became apparent that such a mass of documents could not be operationally effective without computerization. The center now makes available to researchers the following services: a specialized library, the consultation of files on microfiche, data sources available by request from specialist-operated computer terminals. This exceptional research facility will be complete when the Bibliothèque des Archives des Monuments Historique is installed in the neighboring Hôtel de Croisilles.

The Boulevards des Maréchaux

Tour of Paris, departure point: Porte de Saint-Cloud
Métro: Porte de Saint-Cloud
Bus: 22, 62, 72, PC. Catch the bus for Petite Ceinture Intérieure (PC Int) on the Boul. Murat near the church.
Parking: Porte de Saint-Cloud, Ave. de la Porte-de-Saint-Cloud
Taxis: Porte de Saint-Cloud. Tel. 46–51–60–40.

Unlike other touring itineraries, the route along the *boulevards extérieurs* is not determined by the history of a district or a monument, but simply by a street system that provided motorists with the only means of skirting Paris before the *boulevard périphérique* (outer ring-road) was built (→inset). Driving along the Boulevards des Maréchaux gives a rapid, if superficial, impression of Paris, although as a tour it is amazing for the abrupt contrasts that history, architecture and the inhabitants themselves provide. It is very different from touring the city center, where one district tends to merge imperceptibly into another.

The buses on the Petite Ceinture (*la PC*) route link the outer districts, making possible a complete circuit of the city, which is best thought of as a complement to other tours. This route takes travellers from one particular destination to another through districts which sometimes contain little of interest. An integral part of the city, the Boulevards des Maréchaux, unlike the *boulevard périphérique*, are not the exclusive preserve of the motorist, and you can stop whenever you wish. The boulevards give glimpses of the little-known aspects of Paris – the vast expanse of the railroad tracks, or the busy ports of the Seine. If the city is the stage, then these are the wings.

History of the Boulevards des Maréchaux

These boulevards encircling Paris follow the line of the fortifications built at the instigation of the historian and statesman, Adolphe Thiers, from 1841 to 1844. Some 24miles/39km long, these defenses were pierced by 52 entrances corresponding to the present-day 'gates' of Paris. From 1860 onwards the Rue Militaire, the sentry walk which ran round inside the fortifications, was transformed into boulevards, which were then named after the Marshals of the First Empire. Beyond, an area some 650ft./200m wide, in which building was prohibited, separated Paris from its suburbs. This area became known as *la zone* in Parisian slang. Although it should have provided the French capital with a green-belt, the frequent granting of special dispensations has meant that 'the zone' has been almost completely built over.

Gardens and playing fields still bear witness to the original ban on construction. The fortifications themselves were demolished from 1920 to 1929, and it was at this time that the Boulevards des Maréchaux took on their present appearance. Most of the buildings lining them were erected at the turn of the century or between the two World Wars. More recently, urban renewal in such districts as the 13th and 20th arrondissements has produced new apartment buildings giving the boulevards a more modern look.

Northern Circuit

From the Porte de Saint-Cloud to the Porte Dorée.
2 hrs.

Porte de Saint-Cloud

The Porte de Saint-Cloud, like so many of the other 'gates' of Paris, has a bus station for suburban service, and is enlivened by large *cafés-brasseries*, and, except for a few hours during the night, it is the scene of ceaseless activity. It is a major road junction, the start of the roads to Sèvres and Saint-Cloud which cross Boulogne-Billancourt.

Two monumental fountains in the square are floodlit after dark. They were designed by the architects Pommier and Billards; Paul Landowski's sculptures depict Paris, the Seine and its tributaries.

To the S in the Ave. Georges-Lafont, stand the gates of the sports arena, the Stade Pierre-de-Courbetin, named after the baron (1864–

1938) who revived the Olympic Games. This covered stadium was erected from 1936 to 1938 by the architects Crevel, Carré and Schlienger, for indoor sports of all kinds – gymnastics, boxing, fencing, shooting, and so on, but above all for tennis. On the N side of the square, well clear of other buildings, stands the Church of Sainte-Jeanne-Chantal, which was begun in 1936 by the architect Barbier, and completed after World War II. The square bell-tower on one side is a separate building. Inside, the church contains a monumental copper cross by the sculptor Jean Touret (1971), who is also responsible for the high altar, a copper cube embossed with the stylized figures of the twelve apostles, and for the wooden statue of the *Risen Christ* (1970). The stained-glass windows are by Le Chevalier (1954).

Boulevard Murat

The bus route runs toward the Porte d'Auteuil across the 16th arrondissement. This is one of the most luxurious districts in Paris, dotted with substantial and imposing apartment houses erected from 1930 to 1950. No. 95 was designed by the architect Paul Guadet for himself in 1906, and constructed in concrete by the imaginative Perret brothers. The tiles decorating the façade are the work of Bigot (→Montparnasse). The Parc des Princes, on the l., a sports stadium holding 50,000 spectators, was designed by the architect Taillibert and opened in 1972. Its facilities for competitors, spectators and press, radio and television commentators alike, allow it to be used for international events (→Calendar of Events). Opposite the Parc des Princes is the Lycée Claude-Bernard (architect, Umbdenstock, 1935).

The Ave. du Parc-des-Princes, parallel to the Boul. Murat, is a continuation of the Ave. du Général-Sarrail. It passes the Stade Jean-Bouin (renovated in 1967) on the l. and, at the Porte Molitor on the r., the Lycée La Fontaine (architect, Héraud 1938), and on the l. a memorial to the athlete and journalist Frantz Reichel (1871–1932) by the sculptor A. Maspoli. At the far end of the Ave. de la Porte Molitor, the Piscine Molitor (public swimming-pool) can be glimpsed.

Between the Lycée La Fontaine and the Porte d'Auteuil stretches a wide expanse of playing fields. Beyond and to the W of the Municipal Flower Gardens (→Bois de Boulogne), on the l. is the Stade Roland-Garros (entrance on Ave. Gordon-Bennet), the site of major tennis tournaments (→Calendar of Events). It always attracts vast crowds for the French Open and the elimination round of the Davis Cup and similar competitions.

Porte d'Auteuil

At the top of the Rue d'Auteuil, a wall painted with an advertisement extolling the products of a biscuit manufacturer, evidence of the return to Paris of this means of advertising. Standing on the corner of the Ave. du Maréchal-Lyautey is a fountain with a sculpted group depicting four young women (Raoul Lamourdedieu, 1926).

Boulevard Suchet

The boulevard stretches from the Porte d'Auteuil to the Porte de la Muette and is lined with elegant apartment buildings built from 1925 to 1920. A more pleasant route, by car, would skirt the Bois de Boulogne by the avenues named after the marshals of World War I, Lyautey, Franchet d'Esperey, Maunoury and Fayolle. Between the Ave. du Maréchal-Lyautey, alongside the Auteuil Racecourse and the Boul. Suchet, a whole series of luxurious apartment buildings has been erected, separated by small private gardens (the Squares Malherbe, Racan, d'Urfé, Alfred-Capus, de Padirac, des Aliscamps and de Rocamadour). Farther off, between the Ave. Franchet-d'Esperey and the Boul. Suchet, is a series of small squares surrounded by wealthy private houses, among them the Square Tolstoï with Gurdjan's marble memorial to Tolstoy (1935) and Jean Cassou's *Mother and Child* sculpture (1934), and the Square Henry-Balaille with Marguerite de Bayser-Gratry's bronze gazelle (1930).

You reach the Porte de Passy. At the corner of the Ave. Raphaël and the Boul. Suchet is a white marble allegorical group by Georges Bareau.

Porte de la Muette

Place de Colombie

The Place de la Colombie stands at one of the main entrances to the Bois de Boulogne. On the S side it is dominated by beautiful apartment buildings (architect, J. Walter, 1931) and decorated on the N side by the memorial to Peter I of Serbia and Alexander I of Yugoslavia by Real del Sarte (1936): the green bronze group on a rose granite pedestal shows Alexander I on horseback between his father, King Peter, and Maréchal Franchet d'Esperey. The Organization for Economic Cooperation and Development (O.C.D.E.), at the SE corner of the Place de Colombie (Rue André-Pascal), occupies the last surviving section of the old Parc de la Muette, which surrounds the modern château built by Baron Henri de Rothschild. The O.C.D.E. has owned both park and house since 1948 and they have become international territory. The house contains 18th-c. Gobelins tapestries and modern Lurçat tapestries of the Four Seasons (1940).

Boulevard Lannes

This boulevard links the Porte de la Muette with the Porte Dauphine and runs parallel to the Ave. Louis-Barthou and the Ave. du

Maréchal-Fayolle along the edge of the Bois de Boulogne. Between the latter and the Boul. Lannes, the Sq. Claude Debussy is the setting for a memorial to the composer (1862–1981) in the shape of a portico overlooking a pool of water (by the Martel brothers, 1932). The imposing building at 40 Boul. Lannes has been the Soviet Embassy since 1978. No. 32 is a swimming-pool (Piscine Henri-de-Montherlant). Paul Claudel died at no. 11 in 1955, and Edith Piaf lived at no. 67 until her death in 1963.

The Centre Universitaire Dauphine-Paris IX

From 1955 to 1959, on a vast site of nearly 4 acres/16,000m² between the Boul. Lannes and the Boul. Fayolle, the architect Jacques Carlu erected NATO Headquarters. In 1966 when France withdrew, the organization was transferred to Belgium and the huge six-storey building, shaped like the letter A, was taken over by the French Ministry of Education. Since then it has housed the Centre Universitaire Dauphine, with a capacity of 8000 students, who take courses in applied economics, administration and business management.

Porte Dauphine

This gate, at the W end of the Ave. Foch, named in honor of Marie-Antoinette, is at the main entrance of the Bois de Boulogne. Several memorials stand in the Place du Maréchal-de-Lattre-de-Tassigny, into which the Ave. Foch runs, including one erected in 1956 by the architect André Hardy to the champion racing driver J. P. Wimille, with a bronze bust by Buisseret. In the center of the square stands Kaeppelin's huge monument (1981) to Maréchal de Lattre de Tassigny (1889–1952), while on the corner of the Ave. Foch there is a bronze bust of the liberator of Paraguay in 1811, Pedro Juan Caballero. A traffic underpass gives easier access to the Boul. de l'Amiral-Bruix.

To go from the Porte Dauphine to the Porte Maillot, take the Boul. de l'Amiral-Bruix alongside the Stade Jean-Pierre-Wimille. On the l., at the far end of the stadium, lies the Sq. Anna-de-Noailles.

Porte Maillot

This is a highly important junction in the W of the French capital, between the Ave. de la Grande-Armée and the Ave. Charles-de-Gaulle, in Neuilly, at the NE entrance to the Bois de Boulogne. This new district is entirely commercial between the Etoile and Neuilly, crossed daily by hundreds of motorists. The square is made more lively still by its numerous restaurants. A development plan for the area has recently been published. An underpass between the Boul.

Pershing and the Boul. de l'Amiral-Bruix speeds the flow of traffic along the outer boulevards.

Originally, the Porte Maillot (formerly Mahiaulx or Mahiau) was separate from the Porte de Neuilly, although they were neighbors. From it ran the Route de La Révolte, the present-day Boul. Gouvion-Saint-Cyr; in 1715 the pediment had to be removed to allow Louis XIV's hearse to pass on its way from Versailles to Saint-Denis. Nowadays custom has substituted the name Porte Maillot for Porte de Neuilly.

Near the Boul. de l'Amiral-Bruix stands the great memorial to General Koenig and the Resistance. On the corner of the Ave. de la Grande-Armée and the Ave. Malakoff the architect Dufau has erected a fine building faced with blue glass.

The whole of the N side of the square is filled by the Centre International de Paris and the Palais des Congrès. This vast building, erected by the architects Guillaume Gillet, Serge Maloletenkov and Henri Guiboud, which replaces the old Luna-Park so dear to an earlier generation of Parisians, comprises a horizontal trapezoidal structure dominated by a tall tower which seems to be translucent. It contains 19 conference rooms, three exhibition halls, the Hotel Concorde-Lafayette (superb panoramic restaurant) and a lecture-theater with sophisticated audiovisual equipment; every seat is wired for six-language simultaneous translation. The Palais des Congrès is directly linked with the *boulevard périphérique* and with the highways to Roissy–Charles-de-Gaulle and Orly airports.

Boulevard Pershing

This boulevard runs from the NW corner of the square, at the end of the tunnel which carries traffic along the outer boulevards, and merges with the Boul. Gouvion-Saint-Cyr.

The Chapelle Notre-Dame-de-la-Compassion, a private chapel belonging to the Comte de Paris, once stood at 25 Boul. Pershing. It was taken down stone by stone and rebuilt in its original form at the corner of the Place de la Porte des Ternes and the Boul. Aurelle-de-Paladines, on the site of the old Ballon des Ternes (a bronze by Bartholdi was melted for scrap in 1942). The chapel is a mausoleum in the form of a Latin Cross, erected in 1843 on the site of the house in which Louis-Philippe's son, Ferdinand, Duc d'Orléans, died following a carriage accident on July 13, 1842. Its reconstruction allowed the incorporation of a basement meeting hall.

Inside on the r. stands the Duke's cenotaph (he is buried at Dreux) carved by Triqueti from Ary Scheffer's designs, showing the Duke in the uniform of a general officer stretched out on a mattress. An angel kneels in prayer, one of the last works of Princess Marie d'Orléans, and a bas-relief shows France holding a funeral urn and a lowered flag. The stained glass was made at Sèvres from Ingres' designs (original cartoons in the Louvre); behind the high altar is Triqueti's *Descent from the Cross* after Ary Scheffer's designs.

Boulevard Gouvion-Saint-Cyr

The whole of the outer district to the l. was built from 1920 to 1938 on the site of the old fortifications. Note Perruch's buildings with their strong vertical lines at nos. 3 and 5 Rue Dobropol, on the l. of the boulevard, and at no. 42 Boul. Gouvion-Saint-Cyr. In the Place Jules-Renard stands the new headquarters of the Paris fire department. On the Boul. Gouvion-Saint-Cyr is one of the entrances to the Porte de Champerret underpass.

Porte de Champerret

This important junction at the end of the Ave. de Villiers is the center of a district built during the 1930s.

To the W in the Square de l'Amérique-Latine stands the statue of the Venezuelan general, Francisco de Miranda (1750–1816) after Lorenzo Gonzales, with the busts of seven South American writers set on either side. To the N, at the corner of the Ave. Stéphane-Mallarmé and the Boul. de la Comme, stands the Church of Sainte-Odile, built of reinforced concrete with red brick facing (1938–1946). The church by architect Barge, with its three flattened domes and rocket-like bell-tower over 230ft/72m high, is decorated with stained-glass windows by F. Decorchemont depicting St Odile and the saints of France, with capitals carved by Anne-Marie Roux.

Boulevard Berthier

In the 19th c. artists and actors showed a particular liking for the 17th arrondissement, and many had private mansions built here. Some of them still stand on the boulevard between the Porte de Champerret and the Porte de Clichy. The painter Pierre Carrier-Belleuse had his studio at no. 31; at no. 23 *bis* the music-hall artiste Yvette Guilbert (1898–1944) had a Neo-Gothic mansion built by A. Selonier in 1900. On the even-numbered side of the boulevard, between nos. 134 and 142, note the Habitations à Bon Marché, or HBM (low-cost housing), erected in 1933 by the architects Bassompierre, Rutte and Sirvin. At no. 72 are the warehouses where scenery for the Opéra Comique is stored (built in 1895), and at no. 36 those of the Paris Opéra.

In the Ave. de la Porte-d'Asnières stands a series of split-level apartment buildings with multicolored façades erected from 1950 to 1960.

Beyond the Porte d'Asnières (traffic underpass) the street passes beneath the railway tracks from the Gare Saint-Lazare. The Porte d'Asnières is the gateway to one of the most heavily populated districts of N Paris, in which noteworthy architecture is rare.

The Porte de Clichy is one of the N exits from Paris, rebuilt and enlarged in 1936 with the underpass between the Boul. Berthier and the Boul. Bessières. On the l. stands the Lycée Honoré-de-Balzac.

The Parisian cemetery of Les Batignolles

8 Rue Saint-Just

There are entrances to this cemetery in the Ave. de la Porte-de-Clichy and the Ave. du Cimetière on the r. Here lie buried Paul Verlaine (d. 1896); set and costume designer of the Ballets Russes; Léon Bakst (d. 1924); the famous barrister Henri Robert (d. 1936); the great Russian bass Feodor Chaliapin (d. 1938); the composer Alfred Bruneu (d. 1934); Gaston Calmette, publisher of the newspaper *Le Figaro*, murdered by Mme Caillaux in 1914; the poets Léon Dierx (d. 1912) and André Breton, master of surrealism (d. 1966); the writer Blaise Cendrars (d. 1961); the pioneer flyer Lucien Bossoutrot (d. 1958); show business personalities such as Charpin (d. 1944), star of Marcel Pagnol's stage and screen dramas, and the nightclub singer René Dorin (d. 1969); and the hero of the French Resistance, Georges Médéric, who poisoned himself after his arrest in 1943.

Boulevard Bessières

This boulevard links the Porte de Clichy with the Porte de Saint-Ouen, by an underpass between the Boul. Bessières and the Boul. Ney. A recently built apartment building stands at nos. 31–35. Faced with ceramic tiles, it is unusual in design, an arch across the end of the Rue du Général-Henrys. No. 17, an apartment building by Feine (1911), is typical of working-class housing of the early 20th c.

Boul. Ney: the Hôpital Bichat is at no. 17, rebuilt in 1928 and now considerably enlarged by a tall, airy addition, a marked contrast to the older buildings.

The Boul. Ney continues past the Porte de Montmartre.

Porte de Clignancourt

An underpass in line with the Boul. Ney links Paris with Saint-Ouen. This is the location of the Saint-Ouen Flea Market (Sat., Sun., Mon.), the largest and most highly regarded in the French capital (→Flea Markets). It is crowded and bustling, with the racks of the clothing merchants, many of them selling leather goods, almost blocking the pavements.

Follow the Boul. Ney and pass the Collège Maurice-Utrillo at no. 100 on the l.

Then go under the Pont des Poissonniers (rebuilt in 1958) and under the railway tracks from the Gare du Nord.

The district between the Porte des Poissonniers and the Porte de la Villette is less thickly populated and full of vast warehouse complexes used mainly by haulage contractors.

Porte de la Chapelle

This is the main N exit from Paris, at the end of the Rue de la Chapelle, and the start of the Autoroute du Nord (northern highway). Although a few apartment buildings have recently been erected, this is a somewhat depressing district and becomes more so on either side of the next boulevard – a world of warehouses, railway sidings and factory buildings. At the junction, on the r., stands the contemporary postal and telecommunications building.

Boulevard Macdonald

This interminable boulevard is the continuation of the Boul. Ney beyond the Porte d'Aubervilliers. On the r. is La Villette (amusement park), with its Géode, a sphere covered with mirrors, and the red airplane on top of a concrete pillar marking the site of the concert hall known as Le Zénith. On the l. is the Hôpital Claude-Bernard (infectious diseases) rebuilt from 1904 to 1930. Beyond the bridge over the Canal Saint-Denis, a long underpass enables drivers to avoid traffic jams at the Porte de la Villette.

The Porte de la Villette (bus: PC, 130, 149, 150, 152) lies to the NE of Paris at the end of the Rue de Flandre and the beginning of the Route du Bourget.

Beyond the bridge over the Canal de l'Ourcq, from which the Grands Moulins (mills) of Pantin may be seen on the l., the Boul. Sérurier, the continuation of the Boul. Macdonald, overlooks the wide, flat, open country of Pantin on the l. and runs alongside the *boulevard périphérique*. Silos and other industrial buildings catch the eye.

The Ave. Jean-Jaurès, which runs parallel to the Canal de l'Ourcq, still contains some of the best restaurants for meat dishes in Paris, a reminder that this is where the municipal slaughterhouses once stood.

Porte de Pantin

Bus: PC, 75, 151

On the corner of the Ave. Jean-Jaurès stands the Sainte-Claire chapel, built of reinforced concrete, a nave over 65ft/20m wide and chancel roofed by a half-dome (architect, Le Donné, 1958). The high altar has mosaics by Irène Zack. On the other side of the *boulevard pérphérique* is a large sports complex (architect, Jean Peccoux, 1971). It contains a stand for 3000 spectators and a building whose important feature is its upstairs indoor arena over 275ft/84m by 170ft/52m. The technique used for the roofing is especially interesting: it consists of laminated wooden beams supporting a ceiling of wooden strips laid crosswise, glued and stapled to the beams.

The Boul. Sérurier runs between the Porte de Pantin and the Porte des Lilas, climbing the slopes of Belleville. It is more interesting than the Boul. d'Indochine running along the E slope of the ridge. The landscape changes; the working-class atmosphere is stronger and the streets are redolent of the old days of the Commune. It is still hard-working Paris, and full of life, but no longer looks the same.

Beyond the Porte Brunet (Bus: PC, 75) the boulevard continues to climb towards the steeply sloping Butte du Chapeau-Rouge on which the beautiful square of the same name was laid out in 1939 (fountains, large shaded areas) from which there is an extensive view of the Pré-Saint-Gervias.

Porte du Pré-Saint-Gervais

Bus: PC

The Church of Sainte-Marie-Médiatrice was built in fulfilment of a vow made by Cardinal Suchard in 1944 for the preservation of Paris and consecrated on December 8, 1954 by Cardinal Feltin. The church stands on a rise with a wide square in front of it. Its framework is of reinforced concrete filled in with quarry stones from Saint-Maximin. The lofty façade is flanked on the r. by a votive tower topped by a eternal flame. On the l., separate from the church, stands the 190-ft/158m bell-tower; to the r. is a domed baptistry. The nave is covered by a very low brick vault. The stained-glass windows are by the master craftsman, Loire. The crypt is dedicated to those who died during the Liberation; the cement pillars bear incised decoration by R. Courtin.

The church is at present in the middle of a vast building-site intended for a children's and a maternity hospital, the Hôpital d'Enfants and the Maternité Robert-Debré (architect, Pierre Riboulet).

Between the Church of Sainte-Marie-Mediatrice and the Porte des

Lilas one of the largest reservoirs in the world was constructed from 1961 to 1963 from pre-stressed concrete and then turfed over.

The Porte des Lilas at the end of the Rue de Belleville still evokes something of the old Paris remembered from popular songs. To the S, between the Ave. Gambetta and the Boul. Mortier, the Square du Docteur-Variot lies in front of the Stade Nautique des Tourelles, one of the largest swimming-pools in Paris (architect, Bévière, 1924). On the l. side of the Boul. Mortier, the Caserne Mortier at no. 148 stands immediately opposite more barracks, the Caserne des Tournelles, built in 1881. The Boul. Mortier runs S past the Porte de Ménilmontant (Place de l'Adjutant-Vincenot).

Note the little brick and stone houses in the Rue du Capitaine-Tarron (on the r. just before the Porte de Bagnolet).

Porte de Bagnolet

Lying to the E of Paris, this 'gate' is overlooked to the NE by the stepped terraces of the Square Séverine. It is also one of the largest crossroads in Europe, with nearly 1½ miles/2300m of overpasses in an intricate circle. It serves as the starting point of the Paris–Strasbourg highway and is one of the access points to another, the Autoroute du Nord. It is more than a crossroads, since the Bagnolet road is designed to syphon off traffic flowing between the *boulevard périphérique* and the communes of Bagnolet, Montreuil and Romainville, and in itself it provides a highway–Métro link comprising a bus station for ten different routes, a Métro station (Galliéni-Parc de Bagnolet) and a parking lot for over 2000 vehicles. The district has been altered beyond recognition by demolition and reconstruction. A typical example is the neighborhood around the Rue Vitruve.

The Boul. Davout links the Porte de Bagnolet with the Porte de Vincennes. In recent years many HLM apartment blocks have been built along it. Designed in the spirit of what is often called the post modernist aesthetic, they are evidence of a desire to make these districts look more attractive.

Beyond the Porte de Montreuil on the l. is a secondhand market (Sat., Sun., Mon.) – really just another flea market. Along the boulevard at the corner of the Rue de La Volga a new square has been laid out, the Jardins Charonne.

The Porte de Vincennes is the main exit from Paris to the E. From it the Cours de Vincennes, which starts from the Place de La Nation, continues as the main road to Vincennes and Nogent.

The Boul. Soult links the Porte de Vincennes with the Porte de Charenton to the S. No. 38 is the Lycée Paul-Valéry (architects, Dhuit and Donelle, 1958–60). Behind it is a huge sports stadium.

Porte Dorée or Porte de Picpus

This 'gate' stands at the end of the Ave. Dausmenil and provides the main access to the Bois de Vincennes. To the E it opens on to the broad Place Edouard-Renard, with floodlit fountains, ornamental pools and, at the far end, a large bronze gilt statue by Drivier (1935) of *La France Colonisatrice*, emblematic of the colonialist ideology of that period. Behind it to the l. is the Musée des Arts Africains et Océaniens (→Museums). Immediately opposite a memorial was unveiled in 1949 to General Marchand (1863–1934) who led the famous Congo-Nile Expedition of 1898 (sculptor, Baudry, 1949).

The Southern Circuit

From the Porte Dorée to the Porte de Saint-Cloud.

2 hrs.

Boulevard Poniatowski

Follow this boulevard SE from the Porte Dorée as it runs alongside a number of playing-fields at the edge of the Bois de Vincennes, among them the Stade Léo-Lagrange. Also on the l. lies the Plateau de Reuilly on which, every spring, the Foire du Trône, or Ginger-bread Fair, is held (→Nation District).

The Boul. Poniatowski passes the Porte de Charenton, goes under the railway bridge from the Gare de Lyon and drops down to the Quai de Bercy (→Quays) where there is a large train station and some warehouses. A spectacular piece of redevelopment is under way that will alter the entire district, with modern housing, and a new Ministry of Finance (→Gare de Lyon) and a park. On the l., on the corner of the Quai de Bercy, is a bastion, the last survivor of Thiers' fortifications.

Bear r. to cross the Seine by the Pont National (→ Bridges), which is the longest in Paris; it was built in 1852 and gives a fine view over the city and the riverside. The Bercy and Tolbiac docks display all the signs of a healthy commercial activity; there is a station built of concrete and the tall building of the Ciments Français company, erected by the Arsène-Henry brothers in 1968.

Boulevard Masséna

Go straight along this boulevard, which passes over the railway lines from the Gare d'Austerlitz and, on a new overpass some 357 yds/326m long, over the hollow in which the Porte de Vitry lies. At the Porte de Vitry (Bus: PC, 27) stands a fire station designed on contemporary lines (architect, Willerval, 1969). No. 24 *bis* Boul.

Masséna is the Villa Planeix. It comprises three studios and was erected in 1927 by Le Corbusier. Designed with simple lines, these apartments are early examples of the use of the mezzanine, one of the innovative features of the architect's buildings.

Porte de Choisy

This 'gate' stands at the end of the Ave. de Choisy. In recent years the whole district, bristling with office buildings, has undergone considerable changes. It is now the Chinatown of Paris (→Place d'Italie). Asian immigrants have settled here in large numbers; along the streets and between the buildings Vietnamese restaurants display their exotic signs one after another, while shops cater for the inhabitants as if they had never left home.

Porte d'Italie

This is the main exit from Paris to the SE at the end of the Ave. d'Italie and the beginning of the Route Nationale N7. The square is surrounded by large apartment buildings and skyscrapers, each named after an Italian town, and is flanked by two other squares, named after the aviators Hélène Boucher and Robert Bajac. An underpass in line with the *boulevard périphérique* allows drivers to avoid crossing the square. To the W, in the Square Rosny-Aîné, stands a bust of that writer.

Boulevard Kellermann

This boulevard links the Porte d'Italie with the Porte de Gentilly. On the l. there is a pleasant walk down a grassy alley. Here is the connecting road leading to the Autoroute du Sud. Immediately beyond it stands the Monument des Mères Françaises (monument to French mothers) unveiled in 1938, the work of the official sculptor at the time, Henri Bouchard. Between the boulevard and the *boulevard périphérique* lies an oasis of greenery, the Parc Kellermann and the Gentilly Cemetery. The boulevard goes over an embankment across the valley of the Bièvre, where playing fields and recreation areas have been laid out in the river banks. Here the boulevard passes over the Poterne des Peupliers. Between the boulevard and the Rue de Tobliac, the Peupliers district has preserved its charm amid the skyscrapers. The wooden seats and people chatting to one another from their doorsteps might make you think you were in some overgrown village. On the r., beyond the Poterne des Peupliers, is the Garde Républicaine. In front of no. 91 is a sculpture by Di Teana. Further along the boulevard on the l. is the huge university stadium, the Stade Sébastien-Charléty. The entrance to no. 83 is flanked by two groups in stone of young athletes, by L. Gilbert.

The boulevard continues past the Porte de Gentilly bus: (PC, 21).

Boulevard Jourdan

This boulevard passes between the Parc de Montsouris on the r. and the Cité Universitaire Montsouris on the l. Opposite the Fondation des Etats-Unis a statue of the philosopher Thomas Paine was unveiled in 1948. Paine (1737–1809) took part in both the American and the French Revolutions; his bronze gilt statue is by Gutzon Borglum (1934). A little beyond on the far side of the Cité Universitaire station (RER: ligne de Sceaux) stands the equestrian statue of General San Martin (1778–1850) erected in 1960, a copy of the one in Buenos Aires. Pass the Parc de Montsouris and note the Bardo, a replica of the Bey of Tunis's palace left from the 1867 World Fair. Further along stands the Hôpital Universitaire (architect, U. Cassan). On the corner of the Boul. Jourdan and the Rue Tombe-Issoire are the buildings of the Ecole Normale Supérieure des Jeunes Filles (architect, Drevel, 1950), formerly located at Sèvres. The school hall is decorated with paintings by Yves Alix and Pierre Guastala.

Porte d'Orléans

This, the main S exit from Paris, lies at the end of the Ave. du Général-Leclerc and is the beginning of the access road leading to the motorway, the Autoroute du Sud. This was the 'gate' through which Leclerc's division entered Paris on August 24 and 25, 1944 and it was here that the memorial to Marshal Leclerc stands, an impressive stainless steel sunburst, over 72ft/22m high, by Raymond Subes; at its foot is the bronze gilt statue of the marshal by sculptor R. Martin. On the N side of the square in front of the memorial, the Kufra Oath and the main events in the marshal's life are inscribed in gold letters on a steel screen in the shape of flames. On either side of the Porte d'Orléans are squares, gardens and a stadium. Typical of Paris municipal housing policy before World War II are the brick apartment buildings around the Porte d'Orléans: no. 117 Boul. Jourdan and 138 Boul. Brune (architects, D. and L. Brandon, 1926); 189 Boul. Brune (architects, C. Genêtre and L. Mounie 1936).

Boulevard Brune

This boulevard runs from the Porte d'Orléans to the Porte de Vanves. On the r.-hand side it is bordered by apartment buildings erected at the beginning of the 20th c. The Symbolist poet Jean

Moréas (1856–1910) lived in the modern building at no. 210 in 1904. The boulevard continues past the Porte de Châtillon. At no. 26 stand the red brick buildings of the Institut de Puériculture of the Faculty of Medicine, a Franco-American foundation (Duval, Gonse, Bresse and Houdon, architects, 1933). No. 123 is the mail-sorting office of the Paris-Brune district (architect, Tourry, 1961).

Between the Porte de Châtillon and the Porte de Vanves, parallel to the Boul. Brune, runs Ave. Maurice-d'Ocagne. On its l. side stands the municipal stadium, the Stade Jules-Noël, with Saupique's stone statue of an athlete hurling the discus outside the entrance; and, further on, a school complex.

Cross the Ave. Georges-Lafenestre (Porte Didot), where there is a flea market (Sat., Sun.).

Beyond, the Ave. Marc-Sangnier runs alongside a sports complex (on the l.) with a swimming-pool and the Lycée François-Villon, as the boulevard approaches the Porte de Vanves.

Boulevard Lefebvre

Beyond the Porte de Vanves this boulevard goes under the railway tracks from Montparnasse. It crosses the Porte Brancion,the starting point of the Route de Clamart, and the Porte de Plaisance, between which, on the l., lies the Square du Docteur-Calmette, planted with poplars. No. 52 houses the laboratories of the Ecole des Ponts et Chaussées (1938).

The reinforced concrete and red brick church of Saint-Antoine-de-Padoue, built by Azéma from 1934 to 1936, stands at no. 52. Its elegant bell-tower, nearly 160 ft/46m high, is surrounded by statues of St Francis of Assisi, St Louis, St Clare and St Elizabeth of Hungary by Delamarre and Vezien. Inside are Stations of the Cross and statues by Delamarre; Jean Bernard's fresco of the *Crucifixion* with St Francis of Assisi and St Anthony at the foot of the cross; the Beatitudes depicted in oculi. Beyond the church the Boul. Lefebvre runs alongside the Parc des Expositons.

Porte de Versailles

This important crossroads at the end of the Rue de Vaugirard is the beginning of one of the main roads to Sèvres through Issy-les-Moulineaux. The square is framed by porticoes which are the entrances to the Parc des Expositions, a vast enclosure for trade and corporate exhibitions, stage shows and political rallies (→Calendar of Events); at the entrance at the E end stands the Palais des Congrès and at the W end, an enormous exhibition center covering nearly 2½ acres/10,000m², erected from 1956 to 1957. These old buildings proved inadequate, and in 1970 a new building was put up beside the *boulevard périphérique* covering over 22 acres/90,000m², comprising three floors for exhibitions, rooftop rooms and many other amenities.

In 1960 the architect Pierre Dufau built a Palais des Sports in the W part of the exhibition ground. It was designed to replace the old Vélodrome d'Hiver, with seating for 6000 spectators under a dome nearly 200ft/60m in diameter made of aluminium lozenges resting on concrete porticoes, a new system derived from the latest construction methods of the aerospace industry. Constant improvement and enlargement have made this one of the main venues for concerts and dance spectacles in Paris. An overpass, some 950 yds/870m long, carries the *boulevard périphérique* over the exhibition ground.

Boulevard Victor

This boulevard stretches from the Porte de Versailles to the Seine. On either side of the Porte de Sèvres on the N edge of the Issy airfield, the French Air Ministry has erected what amounts to a small town, and there are substantial offshoots of the French Admiralty here as well. The building at no. 30 Boul. Victor was formerly the Ecole Nationale Supérieure de l'Aéronautique (architect, L. Tissier; sculptor, H. Bouchard, 1932) since transferred to Toulouse; no. 28 was built by L. Tissier in 1936 as the Musée de l'Air, now moved to Meudon. Outside no. 26 stands the sculptor Louis Leygue's memorial to the legendary air ace Guynemer (d. 1917). Beyond and in succession stand, at no. 26 Boul. Victor, the French Air Ministry, a huge T-shaped building faced with brick, the flatness of its long white horizontal surface relieved by engaged pillars; the memorial to Jean Moulin (1899–1944), leader and hero of the French Résistance; at no. 24 the external services of the French Air Ministry and the Officers' mess of the 117th Bataillon de l'Air; at no. 2 the barracks of the Issy Base, the Caserne Guynemer. To the N an underpass below the loop railway links the Boul. Victor to the Place Balard, at the end of the Ave. Félix-Faure. To the S the Ave. de la Porte-de-Sèvres gives access to the Paris Heliport at Issy-les-Moulineaux; at the entrance stands a monument commemorating the first flight of 1km over a closed circuit in 1908, with a medallion showing Gabriel Voisin and Henry Farman by Paul Landowski (1929). The last military installations were removed from this vast open space of 100 acres/41ha once construction of a semicircular, 19-storey skyscraper had been completed on the N edge of the *boulevard périphérique*. On the far side of the boulevard, immediately opposite this building, 320ft/100m from the heliport, now stands a new Sofitel, distinguishable by its external elevator shafts. Last, a number of sports fields are to be laid out in the grassed-over center section of the old airfield. Toward the W end of the Boul. Victor are the two headquarters buildings of the EDF

(Electricité de France) company. One is faced with sheets of glass mounted in aluminum frames, the other with stamped metal panels with inset windows, while nearer the boulevard itself stands the white buildings of the SNECMA (National Society for the Study of Construction of Aero-engines). Beyond the crossing with the Ave. de la Porte-de-Sèvres, on the l.-hand side, at no. 8 Boul. Victor, is an impressive grey concrete building erected in 1930 by A. and G. Perret for the French Admiralty to house a test tank and the offices of the naval architecture department. Opposite, at nos. 3 and 5, the apartment buildings erected by P. Patout between 1929 and 1934, on a long, narrow plot, is shaped like a transatlantic liner.

In recent years the W end of the Boul. Victor has been completely reconstructed so as to rise gently on an embankment and pass over the Invalides-Versailles railway line and the l. bank of the Seine. To the r. there is a panoramic view of the French capital, punctuated by the skyscrapers of the Front du Seine, and the Eiffel Tower. In the foreground, the site of the former Citroën car factory is currently being redeveloped (new housing and a park).

The new connecting road now crosses the Seine by the Pont du Garigliano (→Bridges), passes over the r. bank, then tunnels under the Ave. de Versailles to rejoin the Boul. Exelmans, which has been cleared of the old railway bridge that carried the loop railway and has been reconstructed as an express highway. Accordingly the PC now heads back along the Ave. de Versailles for the Porte de Saint-Cloud. However, you may take the Boul. Exelmans and go straight through to the Porte d'Auteuil. No. 39 Boul. Exelmans is a townhouse erected in 1895 by the architect Guimard on the site of the studio of the sculptor J. B. Carpeaux (1827–75).

▷ ## The Boulevard Périphérique (the outer ring-road)

Designed for fast-flowing traffic, this urban expressway encircles the Boulevard des Maréchaux and is built over what was once the fortified zone. Nearly 22 ml/35km long, its construction began in 1957 and was completed in 1973. There are no traffic lights, and a speed limit of 50 m.p.h./80 k.p.h. is enforced. Although it avoids the 70 junctions with the Boulevards des Maréchaux, the *boulevard périphérique* nevertheless has 35 interchange points including such major ones as at the Porte de la Chapelle, Bagnolet and Bercy. Its creation involved setting up 83 civil engineering projects of varying degrees of complexity. It also provides access roads to the highways linking Paris with the rest of France, and from it there is a panoramic view over Paris and the suburbs. During rush hours it no longer fulfils its purpose, since traffic is brought to a virtual standstill by enormous jams.

The local radio station FIP (France-Inter Paris: 90.35MHz) regularly reports traffic conditions on the *boulevard périphérique*. Otherwise telephone 42–76–52–52 for road closures.

> Outer Paris markets

Opening times: 7am–1:30pm
14th arr.: Boul. Brune (Thurs., Sun.)
15th arr.: Boul. Lefebvre (Wed., Sat.)
16th arr.: Boul. de l'Amiral-Bruix (Wed., Sat.); Ave. de Versailles (Tues., Thurs., Sun.); Porte Molitor (Tues., Fri.)

17th arr.: Boul. Berthier (Wed., Sat.)
18th arr.: Boul Ney, nos. 4–30 (Wed., Sat.); near the Rue Jean-Varenne (Thurs., Sun.)

19th arr.: Ave. de la Porte-Brunet (Wed., Sun.)
20th arr.: Boul. Mortier (Thurs., Sun.), Boul. Davout (Tues., Fri.)

Note also the flea markets on Sat., Sun., Mon.

> The 'Gates' of Paris

Many of the 'gates' of Paris advertise their presence to the stroller by the large brick apartment buildings near them. These buildings, known as Immeubles à Loyer Normal (ILN), or Rent-Controlled Apartments, were erected by the Paris municipal housing department from 1923 onward. The buildings around the Porte d'Orléans are the best examples of this architecture and attain a certain dignity with their bow-windows, gables and façades crowned by the glass roofs of artists' studios.

> First flights over Paris

The airfield at Issy succeeded the lawns of Bagatelle as the testing ground for early aircraft, Archdeacon being the first to test his machines here in 1905.

From 1907 onward the aircraft constructors Blériot (the first to fly across the English Channel in 1909) and Voisin regularly made test flights from here.

Some notable dates in the history of the airfield: January 13, 1908: first flight of 1km over a closed circuit (Henry Farman in a Voisin biplane); August 7, 1908: start of the Circuit de l'Est, the first major air race in stages from town to town (won by Leblanc in a Blériot); May 21, 1911: start of the Paris–Madrid Air Race in which Jules Védrines was the only pilot to finish, and in which Bertaux, the French Minister of War, was killed by an aircraft as it took off.

The Métro

Telephone inquiries regarding services throughout the Paris Region, Information Center: Tel. 43–46–14–14.

1st train: 5:30am; last train 12:30am; interval between trains: 1 min. 35 sec. – 8 min., depending upon the time of day.

RATP (Régie Autonome des Transports Parisiens), the independent State-run Paris transportation company, controls the Métro as well as the buses. More than ever before, the subway system Métro has become the most efficient, swiftest and least tiring means of getting around in Paris. Clearly and logically marked, even foreigners find it easy to use. Every station and every station platform displays a map of the network of 13 different lines serving 363 stations on nearly 120mls/192km of track.

The history of the Métro

Work on the Métropolitain (to give it its full name) began at the end of 1898 and the first line, nearly 6¼m/10km long, from the Porte Maillot to the Porte de Vincennes, was opened unofficially on July 19, 1900. This new means of transport, which was both cheap and swift, became so popular that in its first six months of operation it carried more than 15 million passengers.

Thereafter the network was rapidly developed, as the record of its track mileage shows – 8.07mls/13km (end of 1900); 19.88mls/32km (1905); 43.5ml/70km (1910); 49ml/44km (1935); 98.18mls/158km (1920); 67.11ms/108km (1925); 72.7mls/117km (1930); 89.49mls/144km (1935); 98.18mls/158km (1940) and 102.53mls/165km (1945). After World War II, in 1952, Line no. 13 was extended from the Porte de Saint-Ouen to the Pleyel road-junction, but for the next 18 years there was no expansion of the network. The name of the civil engineer Fulgence Bienvenüe (1852–1936), Inspecteur Général des Ponts et Chaussées, will always be linked with this gigantic undertaking.

Expanding the network: the RER

At first the underground system had been confined to the capital, but from 1934 onwards plans were made to extend it to the inner suburbs. In 1938 came the Gare du Luxembourg–Massy-Palaiseau and the Robinson branch of the Sceaux Line. Then, on August 1,

1964, the Massy-Palaiseau–Saint-Rémy-les-Chevreuse line run by French National Railway (SNCF) was handed over to the RATP as inheritors of the network run by the old Paris Metropolitan Railway Company. The Sceaux line became the first link in the RER, the Réseau Express Régional or Regional Express Network, created to address new needs arising from the economic growth of the Paris region. This network was built between 1969 and 1981, to provide a unified system linking the various lines: in the E, Boissy-Saint-Léger and Marne-la-Vallée; in the W, Saint-Germain-en-Laye, Saint-Quentin-en-Yvelines, Versailles; in the S, Sceaux, Saint-Rémy-les-Chevreuse, Versailles; and in the N, Roissy, Mitry-Claye. In the center of Paris the Châtelet–Les Halles Station functions as a railway turntable.

Development plans for the future

For some years the Métro network has been under intense renovation. At the same time as the stations have been rebuilt (→below), passenger capacity has been increased by lengthening station platforms to allow the use of longer trains. This has already brought about a marked improvement in the carrying capacity of the network as a whole. To speed the modernization of the rolling-stock, new trains of standard type have been introduced on Line 3, Pont de Levallois–Gallieni. These trains are better lit, less noisy and more comfortable. At the same time more escalators have been installed and access-ways at interchange stations improved. All these measures are aimed at improving the efficiency and comfort of a means of transport used by 4 million passengers a day (something of the order of 2 million individuals, each on average making two journeys a day).

Engineers of the RATP have introduced many new features: automation of the trains, centralized traffic control, time-limits set for stops at certain stations, mechanized ticket machines. Automation is completed by a system of centralized control and automatic regulation for the running of trains. In a central control-room, a number on a control panel shows precisely where every train in the network is at any given moment, while the official in charge can keep both train and station staff informed at all times by high-frequency telephone, and control all points and signals in the network.

The overground Métro

To look down on Paris from a Métro railway bridge is to gain a fascinating view of many different buildings and districts. Just under 6 miles/9.5km of the system runs above ground, but it is easy to enjoy, since it is confined to three lines: Line 5 (Porte d'Italie–Porte de Pantin), Line 2 (Porte Dauphine – Nation) and Line 6 (Nation-Etoile via Denfert-Rochereau).

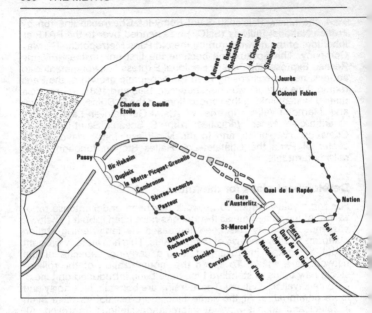

Elevated Métro Lines

Although F. Bienvenüe was responsible for building the Métro, the design and decoration of the bridges (1902–06) were entrusted to J.-C. Formigé. Despite the tendency of the period toward overly lavish ornamentation (→Champs-Elysées, Grand and Petit Palais) the architect did not hide the metal structure.

Place d'Italie-Porte Pantin (Line 5)

Between the Saint-Marcel and Quai de la Rapée stations the Métro crosses a bridge with a remarkable view* over the Salpêtrière (→Saint-Marcel). The line then runs through the Gare d'Austerlitz before crossing the Seine on the Pont d'Austerlitz (→Paris, Bridges), with a very fine view** of the Ile de la Cité and the E end of Notre Dame. The line then dives underground just by the Morgue (municipal mortuary).

The Circle Line (Lines 2 and 6)

This line, which encircles Paris, is in fact made up of two lines linking Nation and Etoile via Barbès-Rochechouart and Denfert-Rochereau respectively. Constructed at the beginning of the 20th c, it quickly replaced the inner circle railway line. Because it followed the line of the outer boulevards, which replaced the Fermiers-Généraux (perimeter wall), a number of bridges could be built. These bridges are confined to the poorer districts, however, and the Métro plunges underground whenever it approaches a wealthier area.

On the Nation–Etoile Line via Denfert, the Métro emerges in the 12th arrondissement between the Bel-Air and Dausmenil stations and then again at Bercy, where there is a view of the new Palais Omnisports* with its grassed walls and the large buildings on the river's edge for the future Ministry of Finance* (→Gare de Lyon). The Métro crosses the Seine on the Pont de Bercy near the river port of Plaisance and then goes underground again at the Nationale station. The line resurfaces in the 13th arrondissement between Corvisart and Saint-Jacques where modern skyscrapers contrast starkly with the remaining older buildings. Between Pasteur and Passy, the elevated line marks the frontier between the fashionable 7th arrondissement and the more working-class 15th arrondissement. From it the leafy carpet of treetops along the Ave. de Breteuil* with the Dome of the Invalides*** at the end, can be seen. The line crosses the Seine over the fine Pont de Bir-Hakeim**. On the r. the Trocadéro Gardens* (→Chaillot) face the Eiffel Tower; on the l. the round bulk of the Maison de Radio France (→Auteuil) complements the slender shapes of the towers of the Front de Seine (→Grenelle). The white bulk of the Sacré-Coeur** (→Montmartre) stands out in the distance.

The Etoile–Nation Line via Barbès runs above ground only between the Anvers and Colonel-Fabien stations. It runs alongside the picturesque Magasins Tati and their crowded approaches, past the walls of the Hôpital Lariboisière and then clatters over the sidings of the Gare de l'Est and the Gare du Nord. Near Stalingrad the line bustles irreverently up to Ledoux's Rotonde** (→La Villette), leaves the canal-basin of La Villette on the l. and the Canal Saint-Martin on the r., before running the length of a series of apartment buildings.

The Métro stations

In recent years the stations have been given a facelift, in the form of new, brightly colored tiles, and have been enlivened by the addition of boutiques offering a variety of goods and services – from Asian imports, to groceries, key-cutting, and bars. Special attention has been paid to certain stations, either because of their name or their location. Below is a list of outstanding Paris Métro stations.

Abesses: a rare example of the Art-Nouveau openwork metal arches which H. Guimard had built between 1900 and 1913 at the entrances to the Métro. The most ornate have been scrapped, but 90 of Guimard's 141 unroofed Métro entrances survive.

Auber : temporary exhibitions and concerts held during the Spring under the context of the Week of Music in the Métro.

Bastille (Line 5): remains of the State prison destroyed during the French Revolution.

Barbès-Rochechouart : reminds the traveller of the French Resistance, whose members hid in and travelled through the tunnels of the Paris Métro.

Champs-Elysées: permanent exhibition in connection with the Palais de la Découverte.

La Chapelle–Gare du Nord (RER): fresco by Nicolas Stravolpoulos.

Châtelet–Les Halles: bas-relief by Tremois and sculpture by Signori.

Croix-Rouge (closed to the public): *trompe-l'oeil* painting of the seaside.

Défense: fountains and monumental stained glass.

Saint-Lazare: is quite simply the busiest Métro station in Paris.

Hôtel-de-Ville: decorated in the colors of the City of Paris, it tells the story of the Place de Grève and the town hall.

Jussieu: decorative theme evoking the Muséum National d'Histoire Naturelle.

Liège: 6576 ceramic tiles depict the province of Liège.

*Louvre**: contains copies of several masterpieces in the museum. It was the first station to be refurbished (1967).

Montparnasse-Bienvenüe: the building of the Métro is the theme for its decoration.

Miromesnil stages temporary exhibitions.

Pelleport: the station entrance, designed by Plumet in concrete and sandstone, is typical of the 1930s.

Porte Dauphine →Abesses.

Porte des Lilas →Pelleport.

République: the passageways between platforms are decorated by the students of the Ecole des Beaux-Arts.

Réaumur-Sébastopol: the history of the newspaper industry.

Saint-Augustin: temporary exhibitions.

Saint-Denis Basilique: the decorative theme is the basilica of the kings of France.

Saint-Germain-des-Prés: permanent exhibition relating to the abbey, the district and the history of printing.

Saint-Fargeau →Pelleport.

Varenne: exhibition of copies of Rodin's works.

Victor-Hugo: evokes the writer's life and works.

> The last twenty-five years of the Métro

Some important dates

August 1966: Line 4 completely re-equipped with rolling stock with pneumatic tyres.

July 25, 1968: Moving escalators put into service at the Montparnasse-Bienvenüe station.

February 1972: First operational use of automatic ticket-gates.

February 1975: The line between Saint-Lazare-Champs-Elysées-Clemenceau opened.

May 1976: This line extended to Saint-Denis-Porte de Paris and Saint-Denis-Basilique.

November 1976: This line further extended to Invalides and Châtillon-Montrouge.

October 1977: The new Les Halles station opened as an interchange station with the Châtelet-Les Halles railway station.

December 1981: The RATP network connected with the SNCF rail network on the RER's Line B.

Main stages in setting up the RER network

December 1969: Nation–Boissy-Saint-Léger.
February 1970: Charles-de-Gaulle-Etoile–La Défense.
November 1971: Auber–Charles-de-Gaulle-Etoile.
October 1972: La Défense–Saint-Germain-en-Laye.
December 1977: Marne-la-Vallée branch line (Fontenay–Noisy-le-Grand–Mont-d'Est).

December 1977: Luxembourg–Châtelet-Les Halles.
December 1977: Completion of the Marne-la-Vallée branch line with the Noisy-le-Grand–Mont-d'Est-Torcy section running through the communes of Noisy-le-Grand, Champs-sur.Marne, Noisiel, Lognes, Torcy and Bussy-Saint-Martin.

December 1981: Châtelet-Les Halles–Gare du Nord.
1988: Saint-Michel station opened.

> Tickets

To save time at the ticket office, buy a booklet of ten first or second class tickets, rather than a single ticket, which will always cost more. Once you pass the barrier your ticket will be valid no matter how long your journey and how many times you change lines en route. The only exceptions to this are stations beyond Charenton-Ecoles on Line 8, the stations between Carrefour Pleyel and Saint-Denis on

Line 13 and all RER lines beyond the city limits of Paris. Remember, too, that a Métro ticket may be used on buses.

All Métro stations also supply weekly, monthly or annual season tickets (the Orange Card), valid for unlimited travel on the Métro and the buses. Tourists, however, are better advised to use the special tourist tickets offered by the RATP which give complete freedom of the network (first-class on Métro, RER and buses) for one, four, or seven consecutive days.

▷ Archeology and the Métro

The only historic remains which can actually be seen in the subway system are those of the prison-fortress at the Bastille station.

Nonetheless, while the different tunnels were being pierced, the foundations of the gateway of the Porte du Temple were found, while remains of Charles V's city wall were discovered at the end of the 19th c. at Strasbourg-Saint-Denis, the Place de la République and the Boul. Beaumarchais. At Jussieu on Line 10, were found the remains of a Gallo-Roman abbey and a Merovingian cemetery.

While constructing Line 7 in front of the colonnade of the Louvre, tunnellers unearthed the foundations of the Hôtel de Bourbon, almost completely demolished in 1527.

The Parc Monceau* district

8th arr./Map ref. 3–A3
Métro: Monceau
Bus: 30, 84, 94
Taxis: 1 Ave. de Villiers. Tel. 46–22–00–00
Markets: daily except Sun. and Mon. mornings, in the pedestrian precinct of the Rue de Villiers.

The old village of Monceau – or Mousseaux, or even Mouceaux, as it was known two centuries ago – existed as early as the reign of Charles the Bald (840–77). It was a fine, old village with windmills, set deep amid the meadows, woodlands and vineyards, whose main square was the present-day Place de Lévis, living quietly through good years and bad. However, on January 1, 1860, the outlying communes, Mousseaux among them, were absorbed into the capital. At the same time Baron Haussmann began the most drastic program of urban redevelopment that Paris had ever known. The wasteland on either side of the Fermiers-Généraux (perimeter wall) was split up into lots by the property developers of the day, and on the gently rolling plain – which must have been rather dreary except in summertime – they built what was to become one of the most elegant *quartiers* of Paris, ringing the park with ostentatious mansions.

The original architecture has survived to the present virtually intact, and the many mock Renaissance manor-houses and sham 18th-c. mansions still display the taste of the bankers and captains of industry for whom they were built. Nor do the rather starchy bourgeoisie who live in the district seem to have changed much. In the shady old-fashioned paths of the Parc Monceau, well-brought-up little girls are still to be seen taking their baby brothers out in their prams, Rolls-Royces of baby-carriage design, under the solemn gaze of their governesses. To this sense of stepping backward in time is added a touch of exoticism by the presence of the remarkable Russian church in the Rue Daru, erected in the same period.

Tour of the district

1 hr.

◢ The Parc Monceau*

The park forms one of those green oases which are to be found here and there in Paris.

History of the park

The land was once part of the seigneury of Clichy, and at one time belonged to Grimod de La Reynière, who sold it to the Orléans family. The Duc de Chartres, the future Philippe Egalité d'Orléans, had the trees planted and gave the painter-writer Carmontelle the task of designing a magnificent garden, which became known as 'Folie de Chartres' (→inset). Carmontelle was both a draughtsman and a theater designer, and he created a 'garden of illusions' full of picturesque details. In 1783, the Scottish landscape-gardener, Thomas Blaikie (1750–1838) laid it out in the English style. On October 22, 1797 Garnerin (1796–1823) made the first recorded descent by parachute from a height of 1000 ft/310m into the park. Napoleon gave it to the second arch-chancellor of the Empire, Cambacérès, but when the Bourbons were restored to the French throne, it was returned briefly to the Orléans. In 1852 it was acquired by the State and considerably reduced when the financier. Pereire sold half the land as building plots for luxurious *hôtels*. In 1861 the engineer, Alphand, turned the park into public gardens, making

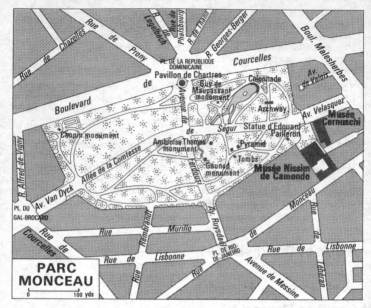

Parc Monceau

fresh use of existing ruins and adding new buildings, such as the arcade of the Hôtel de Ville, later destroyed during the uprising of the Commune.

A tour of the park

The round Pavillon de Chartres stands at the N entrance by the Boul. de Courcelles. This is an 18th-c. tollhouse built by Ledoux as part of the Fermiers-Généraux wall, now a warden's lodge. This Barrière de Chartres, or Rotonde du Parc Monceau as it is also known, is essentially a watch-tower within the Duc d'Orléans park. Of modest proportions and surrounded by a 16-column peristyle, the ground and first floors were used by the officials who levied the tolls, while the Duc d'Orléans kept a room opening onto the circular terrace. The whole building was restored in 1986.

The Naumachia, at the NE corner, is a huge oval pool partly surrounded by a Corinthian colonnade which, according to a dubious tradition, was brought by Catherine de'Medici from the basilica of Saint-Denis where it was the projected mausoleum for Henri II and herself. It was never finished and was pulled down in

1719. When they come to restore the colonnade, the parks depart
ment of the City of Paris is determined to resolve the mystery of i
origin. Beside it stands a Renaissance arcade, brought from the old
Hôtel de Ville. The river and its bridges, the monuments to Gounod
by Antonin Mercier (1897), to Chopin by Jacques Froment-Meurice
(1906), to Ambroise Paré by Alexandre Falguière 1902 and to Guy
de Maupassant by Raoul Verlet (1897), monuments once thought
ridiculous but today seen as moving tributes, the tombs of unknown
origin brought here at the creation of the garden, as well as the
memory of Marcel Proust (→inset), who knew these shaded walks
well – all these are indissociable from the Parc Monceau.
Carmontelle's last work for the park, the pyramid, is the setting of a
short story by André Pieyre de Mandiargues. Near the Musée
Cernuschi (→Museums) stands a Japanese funerary lamp
presented to the City of Paris by the Governor of Tokyo in 1986 to
commemorate the celebrations of the Year of Japan.

Hôtels round the Parc Monceau

During the Second Empire these mansions were built on land which
had originally belonged to the park, and as a group they are unique
in Paris. They stand on either side of the W, S and E entrances to the
Parc Monceau.

To the W, on the Ave. Van-Dyck, famous for its literary associations,
stands a mansion that Philippe Hériat took as the setting for the
'Boussardels, stockbrokers, bankers, property developers and
relatives of Baron Haussmann'. In reality, this luxurious dwelling,
decorated by Dalou, was erected by H. Parent for Emile Menier,
founder of the dynasty of chocolate manufacturers.

Follow the Rue de Courcelles on the l. as far as the junction with the
Rue de Monceau to pass no. 45, where Marcel Proust's parents lived
from 1900 on.

Walk as far as the Boul. Haussmann and back: no. 158 was another
luxurious mansion by Parent, built between 1860 and 1875, which
now houses the Musée Jacquemart-André (→Museums).

Take the Rue Rembrandt: on the corner is a famous and unusual red
building, shaped like a pagoda. It is C. T. Loo's specialist shop for
Asian art. Several apartment buildings in this street show a nostalgia
for the Renaissance while others are resolutely modern in style (see
no. 7).

Take the Rue Murillo on the r. In the courtyard of no. 9 may be seen
the carved medallions brought here after the Tuileries Palace was
burned down.

The street runs into the Ave. Ruysdaël between the S entrance to
the Parc Monceau and the Place Rio-de-Janiero, where Marshal de
Lattre had his last home in Paris (no. 4).

Follow the Rue Monceau towards the Boul. Malesherbes. No. 63 is the Musée Nissim-de-Camondo (→Museums); like the Musée Jacquemart-André, it is the former home of those who donated main collections. This beautiful house, remodelled between 1910 and 1914 by Sergent, is reminiscent of the Trianon.

Go l. along the Boul. Malesherbes as far as the Ave. Vélasquez, which leads to the E entrance to the Parc Monceau with, on either side, a late 19th-c. mansion: no. 5, which belonged to the art collector and banker, Chauchart, and no. 7, are owned by another banker, Cernuschi, which is now the Musée Cernuschi (→Museums).

The Rue de Miromesnil, lying further to the S, contains a number of antique shops. Both Axel von Fersen (Marie-Antoinette's lover) and Chateaubriand lived at different times in no. 31. At the turn of the century the Comtesse de Baulincourt held a literary salon at no. 12, to which both the Goncourt brothers and Marcel Proust often came. At no. 104 they would also have met the widow of Georges Bizet, Geneviève Halévy, daughter of his old composition teacher, and future wife of the barrister Emile Straus, an illegitimate son of one of the barons Rothschild.

N of the Parc Monceau

Stretching as far as the Boul. Pereire lies a whole district which, since it was first created, has been the domain not only of well-to-do members of the financial and industrial worlds, but of literary and theatrical luminaries as well. As there are no sites of historic or artistic importance, this tour simply takes in places associated with famous people, and important museums and monuments.

The Boul. de Courcelles: the most interesting part follows the line of the Fermiers-Généraux (perimeter wall). Gaston Arman de Caillavet and Robert de Flers, who collaborated on so many successful light comedies for the Paris stage, lived at nos. 40 and 70 respectively.

The very long Rue de Courcelles is the former high street of the hamlet of Courcelles. Today it is a busy shopping street between the Boul. de Courcelles and the Place du Maréchal-Juin. Saint Saëns lived at no. 83 *bis*, and the writer Henri Barbusse died at no 105.

Rue Cardinet: in 1901, at the time of his first marriage to Lilly Texier, Claude Debussy lived at no. 58, where he wrote his opera *Pelléas et Mélisande*; it was in Messager's home, almost next-door, that he gave a recital of the piano version to the director and singers of the Opéra-Comique.

The Ave. de Wagram: this broad thoroughfare, long known as the Boul. de l'Etoile, is full of cafés and brasseries, but the further it gets from the Place de l'Etoile, the more middle-class it becomes. Its appearance also changes as the late 19th-c. apartment buildings give way to contemporary buildings. The Symbolist painter Odilon Redon lived at no. 129.

Ave de Villiers: Alexandre Dumas the younger lived at no. 98; Puvis de Chavannes died at no. 89; and the Musée Henner (→Museums) is housed at no.43.

Place du Général-Catroux

Once known as the Place Malesherbes, this square is close to the Parc Monceau and its rotunda. It is interesting for its statues and the Neo-Gothic architecture of the private houses around it. In the gardens in the middle of the square are memorials to both the Dumas. That to the father, Alexandre, is by Gustave Doré; at the feet of the author of *The Three Musketeers* is the heroic figure of d'Artagnan. The son's memorial by the sculptor Saint-Marceaux is more recent (1906). Another figure from the turn of the century is Sarah Bernhardt, and her statue by François Sicard shows her in the role of Phèdre. Around the square at no. 1 is the mansion erected by the architect Victor-Jules Février for the banker Gaillard and inspired by the Louis XII wing of the Château de Blois. It now houses a branch of the Banque de France. Nos. 2, 10, and 16 are also worth more than a passing glance. The composer Gounod lived at no. 20.

The neighboring streets, too, contain architectural pastiches typical of the eclectic taste of the *fin de siècle*.

Thus at no. 42 Rue Fortuny stands one of the strangest mansions in the whole of the Plaine Monceau, built in 1879 by Boland for the master glass artist, Ponsin. Although it has recently been restored and the façade remodelled, the two huge draped figures sculpted in the style of Jean Goujon, the medallion of Bernard Palissy and the rich decoration of masks and satyrs, have been retained. Note, too, nos. 8 and 9, the former in Norman style.

On the corner of the Rue de Prony stands a very beautiful Art Nouveau apartment building.

The auditorium of the Ecole Normale de Musique at no. 78 Rue Cardinet has a façade by A. Perret, strongly inspired by Classical antiquity (1929).

Visit the nearby Batignolles district.

▷ The Folie de Chartres, or Parc Monceau

The pavilion or rotunda at the entrance was originally a toll house. It is high, surrounded by pilasters and built entirely of yellow marble from Siena and red marble from Languedoc. Yet if the Duc de Chartres looked out from it now he would not recognize his park, reduced to a third of its original size. The naumachia is still there, but the winding paths, typical of Chinese gardens, are no more. With them have gone the follies, the covered galleries plunging through a forest of exotic shrubs and trees; the greenhouses; and the Chinese pagoda mirrors painted with arabesques, one of which could swing open to reveal a garden laid out in an underground gallery, its walls covered with *trompe-l'oeil* paintings. The duke would be unable to find his grotto designed in the English fashion popular at the time with the waterfall close by, the cavern in which he held his supper parties, his Roman temple or his Dutch windmill.

Louis Carrogis, master of this duke's entertainments, explained that 'it was in no way an English garden that they wished to create at Monceau, rather they wanted to bring together a single garden all ages and all lands. It was fantasy, pure and simple.'

▷ In the footsteps of Marcel Proust (1871–1922)

The private literary world of Marcel Proust is closely tied to Haussmann's districts in the western part of Paris. All the rituals vital to his existence took place in the narrow square formed by the Madeleine, the Saint-Augustine *quartier*, the Champs-Elysées and the Parc Monceau.

Although born in Auteuil during the Commune, he soon returned to his family's apartment at 9 Boul. Malesherbes. He received his schooling at the Lycée Condorcet and his adolescence was spent among friends, books and long walks on the bridle paths along the Ave. Gabriel where he met his first love. In about 1900 the Proust family moved to 45 Rue de Courcelles near the Parc Monceau where Proust loved to commune with himself in the cool shade of the trees. It was an age, too, of ostentation, when society dined out, especially at the Ritz, or practised conversation at nearby salons such as those of Madeleine Lemaire, of the Comtesse de Baulincourt or the widow of the composer Strauss. Here Proust met Robert de Montesquiou, Anatole France and the Comtesse Greffulhe, people whom he was later to combine with other models to create the characters of Charlus, Bergotte and the Princesse de Guermantes. After his mother's death he moved in 1906 to 102 Boul. Haussmann, where he lived the life of a recluse and, working from his bed, began to write *A la Recherche du temps perdu* (*Remembrance of Times Past*). After World War I, stricken by attacks of asthma, Proust shut himself away at 44 Rue Hamelin Chaillot in an apartment 'as uncomfortable as it was expensive' and there, in a cork-lined room, far from the neighborhoods he loved, he finished his great work. He died there on November 18, 1922.

▣ Museums to visit

Musée Jacquemart-André (158 Boul. Haussmann): works of art from the Renaissance to the 18th c. (open Wed.-Sun. 1:30–5pm).

Musée Nissim-de-Camondo (63 Rue de Monceau): 18th-c. furniture and *objets d'art* (open Wed.-Sun. 10am–noon and 2–5pm).

Musée Cernuschi (7 Ave. Vélasquez): ancient and modern Chinese art; arched bronzes, etc. (open 10am–5:40pm except Mon.)

Musée Henner (43 Ave. de Villiers): works by this late 19th-c. painter.

▷ Russia comes to Paris

Five minutes from the Etoile and the Parc Monceau, between the Rue de Courcelles and the Faubourg Saint-Honoré, the Rue Daru gives you the opportunity of taking a stroll to discover what present-day Russians would consider the most traditional aspect of their country.

No. 12 is the Russian Orthodox Church of Saint-Alexander-Nevsky, consecrated in 1861 and built in the Neo-Byzantine style by architects of St. Petersburg's Academy of Fine Arts. It is as famous for the singing of its services in Russian (every Sun.: 10am–12:30pm) as for its unusual architecture and interior decoration (paintings, icons). The Byzantine elements are found in the Greek cross ground plan, the tympanum covered with mosaics on a gold ground and the frescoed cupolas; in Russia the five gilded 'onion' domes symbolize lighted candles whose flames (the spires) soar to Heaven.

Outside the church are two grocers with tearooms and restaurants attached, the Daru and A la Ville de Petrograd, offering a wide range of Russian delicacies. Close by, at 12 Rue Pierre-le-Grand, the Russian bookshop (open daily except Mon., 10am–1pm and 3–7pm) also sells Russian crafts, records, samovars, dolls, etc.

Butte Montmartre***

18th arr./Map ref. 4–C1, C2, D2
Métro: Blanche
Bus: 30, 54, 68

Parking: 4 Rue Coustou; 11 Rue Forest; 9 Rue Caulaincourt; Place d'Anvers
Taxis: Place Blanche. Tel: 42-57-00-00. 4 Rue du Mont-Cenis. Tel: 42-59-00-00
Markets: Rue Lepic and Rue des Abbesses, daily except Mon.

A visit to Montmartre can be a bewildering experience – you miss so much of it if you are in a hurry. The district is best known for its brash, aggressive side; this is the tourists' Montmartre at the top of the *butte* (the hill), centered upon the Sacré-Coeur and the Place du Tertre. The tourist trade has ruined the streets of the old village and turned it into a stereotype that unadventurous crowds come to photograph. If you are prepared to wander off the beaten track, you will find the real village still exists, only it has moved elsewhere.

The working-class village of Montmartre, round the Rue Lepic and the Rue des Abbesses, still preserves the almost vanished atmosphere of pre-war Paris. It remains working-class, full of activity in the mornings, when it echoes with the shouts from the stall-holders of the Rue Lepic; there is a substantial population of retired people and students; and the district still remains very much alive. Further off, on the N side of the hill, you may find that spaciousness and quiet which have become such rare commodities in Paris, which explains why the houses and gardens in the Ave. Junot are now so much sought after.

The tour outlined below is for the idle, inquisitive stroller, who will be led through places of interest for their simple charm alone – for Montmartre's architecture is more modest than in many other parts of Paris. The highlights of a walk through the district may well be an arbour, a balcony, a statue – charming details that do not figure in the text. Note that this tour, though no longer than many other, is tiring, because the streets are steep, and there are many steps to climb.

The history of the Butte Montmartre

Although the hilltop has always been consecrated to the gods, it seems that Montmartre was dedicated not to Mars, but to Mercury: it was the Mons Mercurii, rather than the Mons Martis, as the modern name would lead one to expect. It was Hilduin, Abbot of Saint-Denis, who, in the 9th c., gave it the name Mons Martyrium (the martyrs' mount). According to legend (→inset), St Denis and his companions Rusticus and Eleutherius are supposed to have suffered martyrdom near what is now 9 Rue Yvonne-Le-Tac, where, much later, Ignatius of Loyola and his six followers founded the Society of Jesus (Jesuits).

Slightly before A.D. 1000 the Capetian kings gave the land to the Montmorency family. It later passed to the monks of Saint-Martin-des-Champs and, in 1133, Louis VI, le Gros (the Fat), and his wife Adelaïde of Savoy, founded the Benedictine abbey of Montmartre on the land. The Dames de Montmartre occupied the abbey until the Revolution.

From earliest times Montmartre was a battlefield, for the hamlet, known far and wide for its windmills (there were over 30 in the reign of Louis XIV, but only two remain) and for its vineyards, was a natural strategic stronghold. From these heights in 1590 Henri IV bombarded Paris, much as he would have preferred to conquer it without the use of arms. Though Napoléon planned to erect a Temple of Peace on these heights, the Russians occupied them in 1814 and the British in 1815. In 1860 the Commune of Montmartre was, like so many outlying communes, absorbed into Paris, but in 1870 it became the birthplace of the revolutionary Commune. At the end of the 19th c. Montmartre attracted many painters, and gained its place in the history of art.

Tour of Montmartre

2 hrs.

The Rue Caulaincourt passes over the Montmartre Cemetery on a viaduct, then climbs to the Place Constantin-Pecqueur, making it one of the best ways up the hill by car.

On reaching the Place Constantin-Pecqueur, cars then turn r. into the Ave. Junot, or carry straight on up the gentler gradient of the Rue Lamarck.

Place Blanche

This is where the tour will start, if you are on foot, close to the Moulin-Rouge, where Toulouse-Lautrec came each evening to sketch the habitués and the performers. All that remains of the windmill are the great sails revolving above the square. The building is now a cinema and cabaret which remains faithful to the French cancan, to La Goulue (the Glutton) and to Valentin le Desossé.

Rue Lepic

Until 1864 this street was called the Rue de l'Empereur, named after the general who defended the hill in 1814. It begins as a busy shopping route, with market stalls and shopkeepers displaying their goods in the street. Note the ceramic tiles of the Lux Bar on the corner of the Rue Coustou. Turn r. down the Rue Constance to reach the Impasse Marie-Blanche. No. 7 is a Neo-Gothic house built with material salvaged from the Hôtel de l'Escalopier, which was pulled down in 1882.

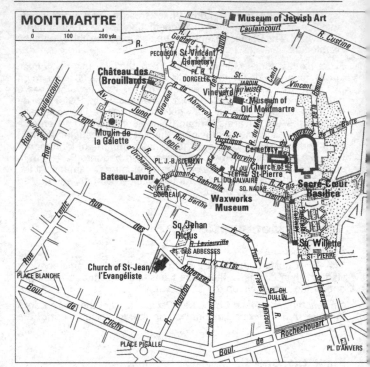

Butte Montmartre

Rue Lepic, continued

Walk back to the Rue Lepic, which takes on a far more residential character as it swings in a wide curve to turn more gently round the hillside. The poet Jehan Rictus lived at no. 50 from 1918 to 1933. Albert Guillaumin once lived on the first floor of no. 54, while the Van Gogh brothers shared an apartment on the third. On the r., the Rue de l'Armée-de-l'Orient is bordered by painters' studios built in the 1930s. Back in the Rue Lepic, no. 64 is a beautiful early 19th-c. apartment building ornamented with statues. Beyond it, at no. 65, a short flight of steps leads to a terrace which leads down to the Ave. Junot.

The Moulin de la Galette (no. 77) and the Moulin du Radet (on the corner of the Rue Lepic and the Rue Girardon) are the sole survivors of the 30 windmills on the hill, so celebrated in paintings, drawings and songs. The Moulin de la Galette, also known as the Moulin Blute-Fin, was built in 1622. At the beginning of the 19th c. the mill was owned by the Debray family and it is said that in 1814 four Debray brothers were killed defending their property against the Prussians. Later, a son of this family converted the mill into a dance hall. From the 1860s on it became a haunt of artists such as Toulouse-Lautrec, Van Gogh, Willette, Emile Bernard, Utrillo and Renoir, whose painting of it, now in the Musée d'Orsay, made the Moulin de la Galette famous. Below the mill, residential buildings have been erected, preserving the style of the period.

The Mire du Nord, hemmed in by these new buildings (apply to the caretaker, 1 Ave. Junot), is a small stone pyramid erected by Cassini in 1736 to provide a trigonometrical point with which to determine the meridian of Paris.

To the r. in the Rue Tholozé at no. 28 is Studio 28, the first Cinéma d'Art et d'Essai (Art and Experimental Cinema) to be opened in Paris in 1928. Louis Buñuel's *L'Age d'Or* was shown for the first time here in 1930.

Avenue Junot*

Via the Rue Girardon on the l.

This broad and peaceful thoroughfare runs past the many painters' studios and family houses and was opened in 1910, having been built over some wasteland of ill repute known as Le Maquis. No. 13 was Pulbot's house (→inset), decorated with mosaics which he designed. No. 15 was the Romanian poet Tristan Tzara's house, built for him in 1926 by the Austrian architect A. Loos; it is the only example of this Viennese architect's work to be found in Paris. At no. 23 the flight of steps to the Rue Lepic and the houses surrounding it, stand on the site of the Moulin-Neuf. No. 25, the Villa Léandre, built in 1926 in the English style, occupies the site of the Moulin des Prés.

Turn r. down the Rue Simon-Dereure, noting the 1930s bas-relief depicting a sculptor above the doorway of no. 27, then climb the flight of steps leading to the Allée des Brouillards.

The Château des Brouillards is a fine white house erected at the end of the 18th c. for Legrand-Ducampjean. It, and the Folie Sandrin, are the only two architectural 'follies' in Montmartre. The family of musicians, the Casadesus, once lived in the Château des Brouillards and, in 1895, Renoir had his studio in a pavilion nearby.

The flight of steps at the end of the Rue Girardon leads to the Place Constantin-Pecqueur where you will find P. Vannier's memorial to the painter Steinlen (1859–1923), unveiled in 1936.

Take the Rue Lucien-Gaulard which leaves the square at no. 10 and leads to the Saint-Vincent cemetery.

The Saint-Vincent Cemetery

This, the second cemetery in the former Commune of Montmartre, was opened on January 5, 1831, eight years after Le Calvaire Cemetery was closed. Originally the entrance was in the Rue Saint-Vincent, hence its name, and among those buried here are the novelist and founder of the Club des Hydropathes, Emile Godeau (d. 1906); the actor Harry Baur (d. 1943); the composers Honneger (d. 1955); and Inghelbrecht (d. 1965); the artists Steinlen (d. 1923); E. Boudin (d. 1898); Chéret (d. 1932) and Utrillo (d. 1955), who is buried with his wife Lucie Valore (d. 1965); the sculptor Carrier-Belleuse (d. 1887); the engraver J. J. Daragnès (d. 1950) and last, the novelists Marcel Aymé (d. 1967) and Roland Dorgelès (d. 1973).

Return to the Place Constantin-Pecqueur and follow the Rue Caulaincourt as far as the Rue des Saules.

Rue des Saules

In the 17th c. this street was known as the Rue de la Saulsaie from the willows (*saules*) which grew there. Today it contains a number of buildings dating from 1900 to 1925. The Musée d'Art Juif (→Museums) is in the N section at no. 42.

The Lapin Agile (no. 4) preserves the memory of all who made Montmartre so famous just before World War I. Once known as the Cabaret des Assassins, it acquired its name from the signboard painted by the humorist André Gill, depicting a rabbit (*lapin*) escaping from a stock-pot. Gill's Rabbit (Le Lapin à Gill) soon became Le Lapin Agile (the 'Agile Rabbit'). Aristide Bruant bought the cabaret in 1902 and made Frédé manager. The latter soon made it the haunt of all Montmartre's writers up to 1941.

Cross the Rue Saint-Vincent, so often celebrated in the songs of Aristide Bruant (he lived at no. 30). Toulouse-Lautrec immortalized the singer in a poster, depicting him in profile with his black cape and red scarf. Pass the vine planted in 1933 to preserve the memory of the vineyards of Montmartre. Festivities are held each year at the time of the grape harvest. There are public gardens at no. 17.

To the l. the Rue de l'Abreuvoir runs down to the Rue Girardon; the odd-numbered side of the street is bordered by the gardens of the former Folie Sandrin. The street was often painted by Utrillo and it was the painting of no. 2 (*La Petite Maison Rose*) which established his fame.

Rue Cortot

On the r. of the Rue des Saules.

No. 12 houses the Musée de Montmartre (→Museums) and is the oldest mansion on the hill. It formed part of the estate purchased in 1680 by Rosimond (Claude la Roze), an actor in Molière's company, and a scholar and dramatist (d. 1686). From 1875 onwards it was the home of a number of famous artists, and legend has it that it was in the garden of this house that Renoir painted *The Swing*. It was here that the painter Emile Bernard entertained Van Gogh and Gauguin. Camoin, Othon Friesz, Raoul Dufy, Suzanne Valadon, Utrillo and Poulbot had studios here. The writers Léon Bloy and Reverdy also lived here for a time, as did André Antoine, founder of the Théâtre-Libre.

Rue du Mont-Cenis

The water tower that supplies the district stands at the junction with the Rue Cortot; completed in 1927, it has a capacity of 18,700gal./700m³. The Rue du Mont-Cenis follows the path taken by the martyred St Denis (→inset); it linked the abbeys of Saint-Denis and Montmartre and was used as a processional route until 1784. It is now the preserve of restaurants and souvenir shops.

Rue du Chevalier-de-la-Barre

The first part of the street is purposely designed to attract tourists, but it houses the only Carmelite convent in Paris (no. 34) as well as a Benedictine monastery. It was here that the Generals Lecomte and Thomas were murdered by the Fédérés (soldiers of the Commune), so beginning the uprising which developed into the Commune.

⚲ The Sacré-Coeur Basilica*

Open daily 6am–11pm; the Dome, 10am–5pm, 9am–6pm in summer (admission free); the Crypt, 2pm–5pm except Sat., daily 9am–6pm in summer.

This overwhelming building, which crowns the hill, is hardly one of the most successful religious edifices erected in Paris during the 19th c. In 1674 public devotions to the Sacred Heart were first instituted in the great Abbey church of Montmartre by the abbess Françoise de Lorraine, soon after the first revelations made at Paray-le-Monial to the Blessed Marguerite-Marie Alacoque on December 27, 1673. During the Franco-Prussian War of 1870 Alexandre Legentil and Rohault de Fleury made a vow to erect a basilica dedicated to the Sacred Heart on the hill. In 1873 the

National Assembly authorized its construction, which was financed by private subscription. Work began in 1876, with plans by Abadie, under the supervision first of Daumet, next of Laisne and Rauline, then of Rauline alone and, from 1904 onward, of Lucien Magne, who was responsible in particular for the bell-tower (1905–10). The basilica was consecrated on October 16 1919. During the night of April 21–22, 1944, during an air attack on the Gare de la Chapelle, incendiary bombs landed on the forecourt of the basilica, shattering most of the stained glass.

Overall the building is inspired by the Church of Saint-Front in Périgueux. The ground was unstable, which required the sinking of 38 shafts to a depth of nearly 125ft/38m, filled with rubble and linked by arches to provide the foundations. Outside the basilica two equestrian statues by H. Lefebvre depict St Louis and St Joan of Arc, the latter being one of five statues of that saint to be found in Paris. Inside, the chancel vault is decorated by a vast mosaic by Luc-Olivier Merson. The crypt runs under the side-aisles, transepts and choir. In its center is a mortuary chapel with statues of Cardinal Guibert by Noël and of Cardinal Richard by Lefebvre on either side of the entrance. On the altar is a *Pietà* by Courtan.

The Dome: to find the guard who conducts tours go up to the first terrace or platform overlooking the Church of Saint-Pierre. From the second, or Stained-glass Gallery, there is a view of the whole interior of the basilica. Above is the external gallery, called the Gallery of the Columns, after the 80 columns with different capitals that it comprises, from which there is a view* of the area for a radius of over 30 ml./50km. To the N lie the Gare du Nord, Saint-Vincent-de-Paul, the Buttes-Chaumont with the relay tower of the television center, the bell-towers of Belleville, and the Père Lachaise Cemetery; then, further to the r., the town hall of the 10th arrondissement, the July Column, the dome of the Salpêtrière, the Hôtel de Ville, Notre-Dame, the Tour Saint-Jacques, the Panthéon, the domes of the Sorbonne, the Val-de-Grâce, the Observatoire and Saint-Germain-l'Auxerrois. Lastly, there are the Tour Montparnasse, the Louvre, the Opéra, Sainte-Clotilde, the Vendôme Column, the Invalides, the Eiffel Tower, the Front de Seine buildings, the Palais de Chaillot, the Arc de Triomphe and the skyscrapers of La Défense.

The bell-tower holds one of the heaviest bells in the world. Called La Savoyarde and cast by the Paccard Brothers of Annecy in 1895, its timbre is remarkable. It was the gift of the four dioceses of the Savoie. The bell itself weighs 18.5 tons/8835kg, the clapper another 1904lb./850kg.

The Montmartre reservoirs lying alongside the Rue Azaïs were built from 1887 to 1889 by Bechmann and Journet from plans by Diet. In the Neo-Byzantine style of the Sacré-Coeur, they hold 2.67 million gal./11,000m³.

Nearby, in the Rue du Cardinal Dubois, is the Montmartre cable railway (→inset) which runs alongside the Square Willette.

Square Nadar and Square Willette

These two squares lie below the vast forecourt of the basilica. On the r. in the little Square Nadar stands the plinth of the now vanished statue of the Chevalier de la Barre. Erected in the heyday of anti-clericalism, immediately opposite the basilica porch, it was subsequently removed to a less provocative location. The Square Willette, laid out as a series of terraces on the S side of the hill, with shrubberies, lawns, flowerbeds and trees, drops in a series of slopes and steps down to the Place Saint-Pierre.

Place Saint-Pierre

The Halle Saint-Pierre, a building devoted to the sale of textile fabrics, was originally erected in 1868 to house a covered market. Its architect is unknown, but from the style he appears to have been a follower of Victor Baltard (1805–74). Today, with several other markets, it has been restored to bear witness to the 19th-c. fashion for cast-iron structures. The Halle Saint-Pierre has recently been subdivided to house a gymnasium (the Gymnase Ronsard) as well as the Musée d'Art Naïf and the Musée en Herbe (→Museums). Inside, the glazing and the iron framework are displayed to their best advantage.

The large fountain in the square is decorated with three groups of sea gods, carved in stone by Paul Gasq (1932). As you walk down, on the l., near the Rue Foyatier, there is a small fountain carved by Emile Derré in 1906, depicting a young woman surrounded by children.

Take the cable railway, which will bring you back to the Rue Cardinal-Dubois. In this street, on the corner of the Rue Foyatier, stands one of the original pavilions from the Exposition Universelle of 1900; it now houses the Imprimerie Lacourière et Frélaut. Picasso, Miró, Chagall and many others came to work in this famous engraving studio. Take the Rue Saint-Eleuthère which runs alongside public gardens with a small open-air theater (Arènes de Montmartre).

The Church of Saint-Pierre-de-Montmartre*

This church is one of the oldest in Paris and represents the faith that has endured since the dawn of Christianity.

The building appears to have been erected on the site of a very early shrine to St Denis, which in turn replaced a Gallo-Roman temple. The monks of the rich Abbey of Saint-Martin-des-Champs founded a house on the site of the Oratoire Saint-Denis, destroyed in 944. Around 1133 they were replaced by the Benedictines, for whom Louis VI le Gros (the Fat) and his consort, Adelaide of Savoy, founded the royal Abbey of Montmartre, in which Queen Adelaide later died (1154). The church was consecrated on Easter Monday 1147 by Pope Eugenius III, with St Bernard and Peter the Venerable as his deacons, in the presence of Adelaide's son Louis VII and his court. The four marble Roman columns on either side of the choir on the inside of the façade of the church came from the original Gallo-Roman temple. Thomas à Becket and Ignatius of Loyola worshipped here. After the Revolution in 1794 when it became the Temple of Reason, the church was deconsecrated, fell into disrepair and was abandoned in 1871. It was restored by the architect Sauvageot and reconsecrated in 1908.

The uninspired W front dates from the 18th c., the two apsidal chapels, the transept and the bay adjoining the nave, from about 1147; the oldest ogival arch (also 1147) in Paris, roughly hewn, can be seen above the choir. With Saint-Martin-des-Champs and Saint-Germain-des-Prés, the church is among the oldest in Paris. The pentagonal apse, with six ogival branches, replaced the original half-dome of the apse toward the end of the 12th c. The nave vaulting was reconstructed in the 15th c. The side-aisles are not vaulted. The tombstones of the abbesses include that of the foundress, Adelaide of Savoy, in the l. side-aisle and that of the last abbess but one, Catherine de la Rochefoucauld (d. 1760) in the N apse. The last abbess, Louise-Marie de Montmorency-Laval, was guillotined in 1794 and is buried at Picpus. In the 19th c. the organ made famous by Antoine Boesset (1586–1643), Louis XIII's Super-intendant of Music, was replaced by the one from Saint-Pierre-des-Arcis (1770). In 1954 the church was given a complete set of modern stained-glass windows designed by the master glazier Max Ingrand, donated by Demarest.

Standing on the church's *parvis* is a great cross, all that remains of the Chapelle-Saint-Denis cemetery, brought when the cemetery was closed in 1878. To the l. (N) lies the cemetery of Le Calvaire, also known as the Saint-Pierre cemetery (open November 1 and 2). It goes back to Merovingian times, and among those buried there are the navigator Bougainville (only his heart is interred here), Desportes (first mayor of Montmartre), and members of the families of Fézensac, Fitz-James, and of course, the brothers Debray, Montmartre millers, their tomb crowned by a miniature windmill. To the r. (S) lies the Jardin du Calvaire (Calvary Garden; closed to the public), on the site of the old Benedictine abbey; the figure of Christ on the Cross is said to have come from Mont-Valérien.

Rue Saint-Rustique

This quiet little street is one of the few on the hill to have remained unchanged. Where it meets the Rue des Saules, a plaque on a restaurant wall, 'A La Bonne Franquette', recalls that, as Aux Billards de Bois at the turn of the century, this was the meeting place of painters such as Diaz de la Peña, Pissarro, Sisley, Cézanne, Toulouse-Lautrec, Renoir and Monet, and of the writer Emile Zola. Here, in this garden, Van Gogh painted *La Guinguette* (*Garden of an Inn*, 1886), now in the Musée d'Orsay.

Place du Tertre

Overrun by cafés and restaurants, the square is the tourist center of Montmartre. Thick with easels and instant portrait sketchers, it has become the market for so-called 'Montmartre paintings'. It is easy to overlook the square itself, surrounded by pretty, low houses, where the abbey's gallows and stocks once stood. No. 3, which is now Pulbot House, became Montmartre's first town hall in 1790; no. 6 is the restaurant, La Mère Catherine, founded in 1793; while no. 21 is the Syndicat d'Initiative (tourist bureau) du Vieux Montmartre.

The Place du Calvaire is the smallest square in Paris. It lies away from the crowd and provides a splendid view* of the capital.

In the nearby Rue Poulbot is the Musée de Cire Historial de Montmartre (→Museums).

Rue Norvins

Between the Place du Tertre and the Place Jean-Baptiste-Clément.

This street comprises the old Rue des Moulins and Rue Trainée (*trainée* is the old word for a terrace of houses) and was the village high street in the 11th c. Here restaurants, art galleries and souvenir shops all rub shoulders. No. 22 is the Folie Sandrin (1774) which between 1820 and 1847 became Dr Blanche's private clinic, where the poet Gérard de Nerval was a patient in 1841. Although it has been heavily restored, the building preserves the general arrangement of its original façade. At no. 22 *bis* the land and buildings belong to the City of Paris, which has made them an artists' colony. The land beside the Rue de l'Abreuvoir remains undeveloped, and is the last example of Montmartre's 19th-c. wasteland.

On the l. lies the Place Jean-Baptiste-Clément (1836–1903), named after the composer of the song *Au Temps des Cerises*; he was also mayor of the Montmartre Commune in 1871. A former water-tower, built in 1835, stands here. Its external octagonal shape and Renaissance-style fountain have been preserved.

A flight of steps leads to the steeply sloping Rue Ravignan, which widens to form the little Place Emile-Goudeau. The Rue d'Orchamp* on the r., where painters' studios stand next to family houses, is one of the most peaceful on the hill. At 13 Place Emile-Goudeau is the Bateau-Lavoir (→inset), burned down in 1970 and rebuilt in 1978 as a modern artists' colony.

Few except local residents use the Rue Barielle or the Rue Berthe, which link the Rue Ravignan with the Square Willette, and so they keep their peaceful charm – surprising, given that they are so close to the Place du Tertre. Rather romantic houses, with oculi (round windows) surrounded by garlands or putti and now restored, stand next to pleasant shops. Picasso's first Paris lodgings were at 49 Rue Gabrielle. The Rue Ravignan runs into the Rue des Abbesses (market) not far from the Place des Abbesses.

Place des Abbesses

This square is also sloping and is flanked to the N by the Square Jehan-Rictus, laid out on the site of Montmartre's former town hall, later that of the 18th arrondissement, where Clemenceau, then a young lawyer, was mayor. Verlaine was married here on August 11, 1870.

The awning over the entrance to the Place-des-Abbesses Métro station is one of the last two survivors of the glass roofing that Hector Guimard created for the entrances to the Métro stations in Paris (the other is at the Porte-Dauphine station). Apart from their utilitarian function, these glass and iron structures were conceived with the intention of preserving the character of Paris as a city of the arts.

♪ The Church of Saint-Jean-l'Evangeliste was designed by A. de Baudot (1894–1904). He was a pupil of Labrouste and a disciple and collaborator of Viollet-le-Duc. The interlocking arches of the façade are reminiscent of Islamic architecture. This was the first religious building to be built of reinforced concrete; its cabochons and rose facing has given it the nickname St-Jean en Brique (the Brick St John). The sculptures (two angels, St John, and the holy-water stoups) are by Arthur Guéniot. Inside, the walls and pillars are decorated with stylized flowers motifs, typical of the art of 1900.

To the r. of the church a flight of steps leads to the Rue André-Antoine. Even before he founded the Théâtre-Libre, Antoine made his debut at no. 37, in a tiny auditorium in 1887. The painter Seurat died at no. 39.

Rue Yvonne-Le-Tac

No. 9 is the former convent of the Auxiliatrices de la Rédemption. Their chapel (1887) was built on the site of another, founded in the Middle Ages where the Sanctum Martyrium, or Martyr's Chapel, had stood on the spot traditionally identified with the beheading of St Denis. It was in this chapel that Ignatius of Loyola, founder of the Society of Jesus, on August 15, 1534 formally pronounced his first Jesuit vows with his six companions. The shrine became derelict and was restored by the Abbess Marie de Beauvilliers. During the rebuilding the presumed place of St Denis's martyrdom was discovered. The chapel and its abbey enjoyed a period of prosperity. Razed to the ground during the Revolution, the chapel was not rebuilt until 1887.

By taking the Rue Yvonne-le-Tac and the Rue des Trois-Frères, you can reach the quiet Pl. Charles-Dullin.

The Théâtre de l'Atelier

Place Charles-Dullin

Charles Dullin (1885–1949) set up his Théâtre de l'Atelier in the old Théâtre de Montmartre. An extremely versatile actor, whose most famous rôles included Jonson's Volpone and Molière's Harpagon, he led the French theatrical revival of the 1920s. Later as a producer, he was the teacher of a new generation of actors and producers such as J.-L. Barrault and J. Vilar.

Place Pigalle

Via the Rue d'Orsel on the l. and the Rue Houdon.

The Place Pigalle is built on the site of the old Montmartre tollgate and in the 19th c. was the center of the artists' and writers' colony. Isabey, Puvis de Chavannes and Boldini had a studio at no. 11. No. 9 was La Nouvelle Athènes (→inset). Today the square is full of strip clubs.

The brasserie café-bar La Pigalle, at no. 23 Boul. de Clichy, is an interesting example of the decorative style of Parisian cafés in the 1950s. The décor by M. Gridaine (1955), has been preserved in its entirety and is now registered with the Inventaire des Monuments Historiques (Historic Monuments Commission).

Boulevard Rochechouart

This street is named after Marguerite de Rochechouart, Abbess of Montmartre from 1717 to 1727. There is no need to walk down it to conjure up that famous but now vanished cabaret, 'Le Chat Noir'. Opened in 1881 at no. 84, by Robert Salis, it had a signboard painted by Willette. Writers, poets and music-hall singers congregated there to perform. All that remains of it are the ticket booth, lobby and stairway, typical of the monumental Bauhaus style, now part of the La Cigale cinema. There are few other vestiges of the boulevard from the turn of the century, but note the façade of the Trianon cinema (no. 80), once a light opera theater, and the bas-relief over the entrance to a former dance hall, the Elysée-Montmartre cinema (no. 72), which retains its original elegant *Belle Epoque* façade beneath the cinema posters. Gustave Charpentier, who wrote the opera *Louise*, lived at no. 66, Renoir at no. 57 and Caillebotte at no. 29.

Boulevard de Clichy

Walk down this boulevard where numerous artists' studios still exist on the N side (9th arr.) to remind you that during the *Belle Epoque* this was one of the temples of painting. Degas lived and died 1917 at no. 6, and Picasso lived at no. 11 and no. 13. Van Gogh, Toulouse-Lautrec, Seurat, Bonnard and Van Dongen all had their studios and apartments here and bought their paints and canvases from local shopkeepers. There was also a series of famous cabarets; the Théâtre de Dix-Heures (no. 36) has replaced La Lune Rousse, and the Théâtre des Deux Anes (no. 10) what used to be the Cabaret des Truands.

The Rue Rachel on the r. leads to the Montmartre cemetery, but the great tragedienne herself is buried in the Père Lachaise cemetery.

On the corner of the boulevard and the Rue Caulaincourt, a hotel stands on the site of the old Gaumont-Palace (→inset).

Place de Clichy

Unlike the Place Pigalle, the Place de Clichy is not completely taken over by tour buses. The brasseries, cinemas and shellfish stalls all round it give the square the lively atmosphere of a working-class district. Built on the site of the old Clichy tollgate, it was in 1814 the scene of hard fighting between the National Guard, led by Marshal Moncey, and the Cossacks attempting to seize Paris. In the middle of the square stands a monument by Doublemard, erected in 1869 in memory of Marshal Moncey and the battles of 1814.

The North, or Montmartre cemetery

Entrance: 20 Rue Rachel. Tel. 43–87–64–24.

This cemetery is nearly as extensive and famous as the Père Lachaise cemetery. It was opened in 1798, closed, and reopened in 1831.

Tour of the cemetery

Immediately before you as you enter is the *grande allée* leading to the Carrefour de la Croix from which can be seen, immediately on the l., the tomb of Cavaignac. The 1st section starts immediately to the r. of the entrance and continues along the Ave. des Polonais at the top of the steps.

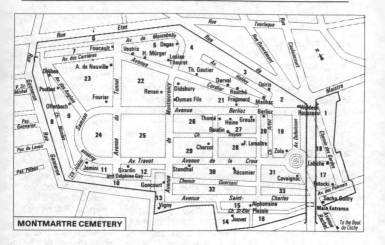

1st section

Immediately to the r. of the entrance is the simple grave (rough stone rising from the grass) of the great actor Lucien Guitry (d. 1925) and of his son, the playwright and actor Sacha Guitry (d. 1957); Jean Béraud (d. 1935), painter of Parisian life.

2nd section

Francisque Sarcey, the theater critic (d. 1899); Waldeck-Rousseau, one of the Président du Conseil under the Third Republic (d. 1904); Admiral Porlier (d. 1890), with L. Morice's statue, *La Pleureuse* (*The Weeping Woman*).

3rd section

The Pam family grave, with a caryatid by Bartholomé; Halévy, composer of *La Juive* (d. 1862), marble statue by Duret; the three Johannot brothers, engravers and Romantic book-illustrators; Théophile Gautier (d. 1872), with Cyprian Godebski's statue, *La Poésie*; Osiris, with Mercié's bronze copy of Michelangelo's *Moses*.

4th section

Marshal Lannes, Duc de Montebello (d. 1809), of wounds received at the Battle of Essling; only his heart is buried here – his body lies in the Panthéon; the painter Edgar Degas (1834–1917), bronze medallion by Chauvenet (1961); Countess Marie Potocka, Princess Soltikoff, a small, richly decorated Russian chapel; the architect Ignace Hittorff (d. 1867); Victor Brauner*, the painter (d. 1966), whose tomb is decorated with one of his works.

5th section

Miecislas Kamienski, a Polish volunteer with the French Army, killed at Magenta in 1859, a bronze statue of him dying by Franceschi; the painter Paul Delaroche (d. 1856), a memorial designed by Duban; Horace Vernet, painter (d. 1863); composer Adolphe Adam (d. 1856); Gaetano Vestris, whose dancing was 'un chef d'oeuvre de noblese et de grâce', in the 18th c. (d. 1808); Henri Murger (d. 1861), author of *La Vie de Bohème*, whose tomb, erected by public subscription, is crowned by Millet's statue, *La Jeunesse Youth*; the painter Henner (d. 1905); Antoine Sax, inventor of the saxophone (d. 1894).

6th section

Jacques Charon (d. 1975), in his time the doyen of the Comédie-Française.

9th section

Léo Delibes, composer of the opera *Lakmé* (d. 1891), medallion by Chaplain; Jacques Offenbach, famous composer of operettas (d. 1880), with a bronze bust by Franceschi; the engraver Pierre Thomire (d. 1843), with his self-portrait in bronze, a statue exhibited in the Salon of 1810; Fernand Piestre, the painter known as Cormon (d. 1924); Francisque Poulbot (d. 1946), famed for his sketches of the slum children of Montmartre.

12th section

Delphine Gay (d. 1855), writer and first wife of Emile de Girardin, and Emile de Girardin (d. 1881); the composer Victorin de Joncières (d. 1903), with a bust by Marqueste.

13th section

The writers Edmond and Jules de Goncourt (d. 1896 and 1870); the tomb of the Félix-Hinoult family, in the Egyptian style; Alfred de Vigny (d. 1863).

14th section

The painter Jules Lefebvre (d. 1912), with his bust and marble bas-relief, *La Verité* (Truth), by Ernest Dubois; Narcisso Diaz de la Peña, painter (d. 1876); the actor and film star, Louis Jouvet (d. 1951).

15th section

Alphonsine Plessis, known as Marguerite Gautier, Alexander Dumas the Younger's 'Dame aux Camélias' (d. 1847).

17th section

The celebrated pamphleteer Henri Rochefort (d. 1913); Eugène Labiche, writer of comedies (d. 1888); the writer Maxime Du Camp (d. 1894).

18th section

Ponson du Terrail (d. 1871) creator of the blood-and-thunder character, Rocambole; the journalist Castagnary (d. 1888), bust by Rodin; the sculptor Gérôme (d. 1904); the Wallet family tomb in which lies Théophile Delcassé (d. 1923), architect of the Entente Cordiale between France and Great Britain.

19th section

The diplomat and historian, the Comte de Ségur (d. 1830); Napolean I's secretary, Claude Meneval (d. 1850); the Seveste family vault, built like a Doric temple.

20th section

The famous chef Antoine Carême (d. 1833); the public executioners, the Sansons; since 1971 Hector Berlioz (1803–69), one of the greatest French Romantic composers, has been buried in this section beneath a black marble monument; Emile Zola (d. 1902),

whose tomb is by the architect Frantz Jourdain, the bronze bust by
Solari (1860).

21st section

Joseph-Louis Duc, who restored the Palais de Justice (d. 1879); the
Neo-Classical tomb of the Daru family (1829); the composer Francis
Thomé (d. 1909), memorial by Landowski and Nénot; the novelist
and dramatist Alexandre Dumas the Younger (d. 1895), with reclin-
ing statue by Saint-Marceaux; the painters Jean-Honorè Fragonard
(d. 1806), Alexandre Fragonard (d. 1850) and Carle Vernet (d. 1836);
Dr Péan (d. 1898); the politician Jules Simon (d. 1896); the dramatist
Henri Meilhac (d. 1897), monument by Bartholomé; the painter
Gustave Guillaumet (d. 1887), medallion by E. Barrias; the film
director François Truffaut (d. 1984).

22nd section

The philologist and philosopher Ernest Renan, one of the greatest
French 19th-c. writers (d. 1892); Renan's uncle, the painter Ary
Scheffer (d. 1858); the actor Samson (d. 1871), bronze bust by
Crauk; Marie Taglioni, the greatest ballet dancer of her day (d.
1884); the great ballet dancer Vaslav Nijinsky (d. 1950); the
Duchesse d'Abrantès (d. 1838), with a medallion.

23rd section

The utopian socialist philosopher Charles Fourier (d. 1837); the
politician Henri Brisson (d. 1912); the military painter A. de Neuville
(d. 1895).

24th section

The music-hall singer Gustave Nadaud (d. 1893).

25th section

Léon Fournier (d. 1953), the dramatist and music-hall singer known
as Xanrof, composer of *Le Fiacre*, and his wife, the singer Marguerite Carrère (d. 1952); the writer Jérôme Tharaud (d. 1953); the writer
and university teacher Jacques Decourdemanche, known as
Jacques Decour, shot by firing squad in 1942.

26th section

The poet Marceline Desbordes-Valmore (d. 1859), with an epitaph erected in 1930; Victor Massé, composer of *Les Noces de Jeanette* (d. 1881).

27th section

Baudin, killed at the barricades (1851) while serving as Representative of the People; the pharmacist Pelouze (d. 1867); Troyon, the painter (d. 1865); the painter Freuze (d. 1805), his tomb adorned by a statue, *Jeune Fille à la Cruche Cassée* (Young Girl with a Broken Jug); André Jolivet the composer (d. 1974); the famous German poet Heinrich Heine, who died in exile, in 1856.

28th section

The composer of *Mignon*, Ambroise Thomas (d. 1896); the poet Méry d. 1866, with L. Durand's bronze statue, *La Poésie* (Poetry); the famous actor Frédérick Lemaître (d. 1876), with a bronze bust by Granet; the publicist Auguste Nefftzer (d. 1876), founder of the newspaper *Le Temps*, with a statue by Bartholdi; Edmond Audran (d. 1901), composer of *La Mascotte*; the singer Pauline Viardot (d. 1910); the animal sculptors Auguste Cain (d. 1894) and Mene.

29th section

The magistrate and journalist Gustave Chaudey, executed during the Commune, with Renaudot's bronze portrait medallion; Dr Charcot (d. 1893) and his son, Dr Jean Charcot (d. 1936), the polar explorer who drowned when his ship, the *Pourquoi Pas?* went down off the coast of Iceland; the lawyer Janson de Sailly (d. 1829); the railway engineer Eugène Flachat (d. 1873); the conductor Charles Lamoureux (d. 1890); a tall obelisk surmounted by a cross, erected in memory of the Duchesse de Montmorency-Luxembourg (d. 1829); Jacques Charon, the actor (d. 1975).

30th section

Henri Beyle, the novelist Stendhal (d. 1842), his tomb bears the epitaph 'To live, To Love, To be Milanese' (medallions after David d'Angers); Récamier (d. 1849), friend of Chateaubriand and one of the most famous beauties of the 19th-c.; her intimate friend, the writer Balanche (d. 1847); A.-M. Ampère (d. 1836), discoverer of electro-magnetism; the dramatist Georges Feydeau (d. 1921); the dancer Thérèse Aubry (d. 1829), who performed as the Goddess of Reason in 1793.

31st section

Emma Livry, the ballerina from the Opéra, who died from injuries she suffered in a fire at the age of 17, in 1863; the Marquis de Coëtlogon's pyramid; the Cavaignac family vault containing the remains of Jean-Baptiste Cavaignac, Deputy in the Convention (d. in Brussels in 1823) and of his sons Godefroy Cavaignac (d. 1845) and Eugène Cavaignac (d. 1857), head of the government that quelled the Revolution of 1848, with a bronze statue* by Rude of Godefroy Cavaignac.

32nd section

The French Romantic painter Théodor Chassériau (d. 1856).

33rd section

The novelist and poet Louise Colet (d. 1870), friend of Flaubert.

▷ The legend of St Denis

This legend, which was very popular during the Middle Ages, told how St Denis, who first brought the Gospel to Paris in the 3rd c., was arrested in the Faubourg Saint-Jacques with his two companions, the deacon Eleutherius and the priest Rusticus; they were condemned to death when they refused to abjure their faith. Imprisoned and tortured in the Cité, they were led toward the top of the Butte Montmartre to be executed in front of the Temple of Mercury. However, before they had climbed halfway up the hill Denis was beheaded. He then picked up his blood-covered head, washed it in a spring (Rue Girardon) and carried it N, to die on the spot where St Geneviève later built one oratory which ultimately became the basilica of Saint-Denis.

▷ Francisque Poulbot

This draughtsman, poster designer and illustrator (1879–1946) settled in Montmartre and gained fame by creating the archetypal Montmartre dead-end kid, a latter-day version of Victor Hugo's Gavroche, as poor, rebellious and mischievous as he, and deeply sensitive. His creation became so popular that at one stage the deprived children of Paris were known as 'little Poulbots'. Copies and reproductions of this artist's paintings and watercolors are to be found all over Montmartre.

Sunset over the Adriatic

Everybody on the Butte was convulsed with laughter by this practical joke, except for the one person it was intended to take in – Apollinaire. Roland Dorgelès, the novelist, detested 'modern' painting and 'Picasso's gang', the painters of the Bateau-Lavoir. One day he thought of tying a paint-brush to the tail of Lolo, the donkey belonging to the guitarist and landlord of the Lapin Agile, Frédé (his niece married Mac Orlan). Under the watchful eye of a bailiff, Lolo conscientiously completed her task and the result, a painting entitled *Sunset over the Adriatic* by Boromali, was officially exhibited at the Salon des Indépendants du Cours-la-Reine, where it had a resounding success. Critics were divided in another Battle of the Ancients and Moderns. However, Apollinaire, whom Dorgelès wanted to convince of the worthlessness of the Bateau-Lavoir painters, was the only one not to be taken in. The painting was soon sold for 400 francs and the proceeds given to the artists' orphanage.

Suzanne Valadon and Maurice Utrillo

Both Suzanne Valadon and her son Maurice Utrillo have helped to immortalize the Montmartre of painters and Bohemians. Suzanne Valadon (1865–1938) whose beauty made her the queen of Montmartre, was the daughter of a local laundress, and first worked as a circus acrobat before becoming the model for Renoir, Puvis de Chavannes, Toulouse-Lautrec and Degas, the last named encouraging her to take up painting on her own account. She specialized in vigorous nudes and naïve still-lifes; her use of impasto gave a freshness to her work. Her son, Maurice Utrillo (1883–1955), was a true child of Montmartre. Early in life he became an alcoholic and in 1902 it was his mother who made him take up painting as a form of therapy. Self-taught, he had only the painter Quizet and his mother to advise him. Keeping himself aloof from the artistic world, he let first his mother, and then his wife, Lucie Valore, guide his career. Collectors and dealers soon discovered his painting and its success surrounded Utrillo with investors and speculators. Throughout his career he painted views of the suburbs of Paris sometimes from postcards, a few churches, but especially Montmartre. Utrillo's best works belong to his 'White' period (1909–15), so-called because of the predominance of white, producing subtle milky tones. The strength and simplicity of his art, the original way in which he looked at the city, a touch of poetry, all the elements that gave his earlier paintings their quality of melancholy harmony, are missing from his later work in brighter colors. His work was unequal but his street scenes have a beauty of composition that has rarely been equalled.

▷ Public Transport in Montmartre

A bus service, the Montmartrois, with vehicles specially built to negotiate the narrow streets of the Butte, runs from the Place Pigalle to the 18th arrondissement town hall, via the Place du Tertre.

The cable railway (on which Métro tickets are valid) swiftly takes you up to the foot of the basilica of the Sacré-Coeur. It leaves from the end of the Rue Foyatier, skirting the Square Willette.

▷ The Bateau-Lavoir

This temple of art and poetry was so named by Max Jacob after the laundry boats once moored on the Seine. Its strange shape was the result of being built on uneven ground, so that it had one floor on the Rue Ravignan, and three on the Rue Garreau. Also known as *La Maison du Trappeur* (the Trapper's House) this dirty, comfortless shack was home from 1890 to 1920 to many artists and writers, who had to take it in turn to sleep on the bed. Picasso and Fernand Ollivier, Juan Gris, Van Dongen, Herbin, Marcoussis, Braque, Gargallo, Manolo, A. Salmon, Francis Carco, Mac Orlan, Reverdy, Apollinaire and many others all lived and worked in the Bateau-Lavoir during an important moment, not only in their own lives, but also in the history of art. It was here that, between 1906 and 1907, Picasso painted *Les Demoiselles d'Avignon*, regarded as the source picture of Cubism. And it was here, in 1908, that he gave the legendary banquet for Henri 'Le Douanier' Rousseau.

▷ Café life of the Impressionists

Between 1866 and 1874 painters whom a critic christened 'Impressionists', but who were really still only the 'Batignolles Group', fell into the habit of meeting on Thursday evenings in the Café Guerbois (now 9 Ave. de Clichy). This was the setting of Manet's painting – now in the Philadelphia Museum of Art – *Le Bar Bock*. Painters, critics and collectors would leave their nearby studios and gather in the café to argue about art, united in their desire to fight the art of the establishment. They included Manet, Monet, Renoir, Sisley, Cézanne, Pissarro, Degas, Bazille as well as Duranty and Nadar. Manet, older than the others, took the intellectual lead. Although its individual members argued among themselves, the group gained strength and cohesion. After 1876 the Impressionists abandoned the Café Guerbois, which had become too crowded, and met at the Café de la Nouvelle Athènes (9 Place

Pigalle). Two tables were permanently reserved for Manet, Degas and their friends, Renoir, Pissarro and Raffaelli who regularly met there until 1885, with the writers Duranty and Villiers de l'Isle-Adam. Degas used the café as the setting for his painting *L'Absinthe* (The Absinthe Drinker), now in the Musée d'Orsay.

The Gaumont-Palace

Often likened to the prow of a ship cutting the waves at the corner of the Rue Caulaincourt and the Boul. de Clichy, the Gaumont-Palace was demolished in 1973 and replaced by a hotel. In 1908 the Hippodrome in the Place de Clichy had been turned into a cinema (the Hippo-Palace). In 1911 this was purchased by Léon Gaumont, who turned it into the film mecca of Paris. Henri Belloc rebuilt the old cinema in 1931, and G. Peynet modernized it in 1954. The vast auditorium with 5000 seats, the luxurious materials used (pink granite for the façade, black marble in the foyer), the technical improvements aimed at providing perfect acoustics, and the gigantic screen (over 7200 sq. ft./670m^2 in area), all made this *the* cinema for major premieres and official gala performances. It then fell victim to the reorganization of the film industry, which saw the large cinema swept away by the smaller and more economical auditorium. The Gaumont-Palace belonged to an age in which the cinema offered total entertainment. In addition to the film itself, there were variety acts during the intermission, the whole setting to enjoy, and the cinema organs to provide the music. These organs are the sole survivors of the cinema and are preserved in all their old glory in the Baltard Pavillion in Nogent-sur-Marne.

Museums to visit

Musée de Montmartre (12 Rue Cortot): posters, drawings and documents relating to the history of Montmartre.

Musée du Cire (Place du Calvaire): tells the story of Montmartre through the medium of its waxwork figures.

Musée d'Art Juif (42 Rue des Saules): Jewish religious and plastic art from the 14th to the 20th c.

Halle Saint-Pierre (2 Rue Ronsard): Musée d'Art Naïf Max-Fourny and Musée en Herbe

The Faubourg Montmartre and the Faubourg Poissonnière

9th arr./Map ref. 11–A2, B1, B2
Métro: Richelieu-Drouot
Bus: 20, 39, 48, 67, 74
Parking: Parc Chauchat-Drouot
Taxis: Richelieu-Drouot Métro station. Tel: 42–46–00–00

Spectacular changes occurred in the districts beyond the Grands Boulevards during the 18th c. when large numbers of private mansions were built. During the 19th c. trade and industry gained the upper hand, as witnessed by the covered passageways in the approaches to the boulevards, and by the factories in the Faubourg Poissonnière. Today, because the narrow streets are so often jammed with traffic, and there is a cruel lack of fresh air and green spaces, this is one of the most undeservedly little known districts of Paris.

Here and there, however, it is more authentically Parisian in character than many other parts of the city more frequented by tourists. The neighborhood around the new public auction house, the Nouveau Drouot, with its antique shops and passages, the area around the Folies Bergère with its synagogues, furriers and Asian restaurants, partake completely of the atmosphere of Paris. The district, the shrine of Parisian Neo-Classicism, has not been turned into an open-air museum like other historic areas of the capital. Here the craftsmen of the leather and jewellry trades and the shopkeepers who live in the Faubourg Poissonnière continue to earn their daily bread and give life to the district.

Tour of the district

1 hr.

The 9th arr. Town Hall*

6 Rue Drouot

This is one of the oldest town halls in Paris. It was erected from 1748 to 1752 as the Hôtel d'Augny by Charles-Etienne Briseux, author of several treatises on architecture, and later purchased by the municipal authorities in 1849. Access to the Salle des Mariages on the first floor where weddings take place is by a registered staircase: the room has retained its Empire decoration.

The Hôtel Drouot (Nouveau Drouot)

9 Rue Drouot (Mon.-Sat. 11am-6pm; closed Sun. and July 25 to Sept 15 except for special sales. Tel: 42-46-17-11).

Since 1851 the main public auction-rooms have been located where the La Grange-Gatelière farmhouse once stood. The new buildings, with 16 rooms, which were opened on May 13, 1980 (architect J. J. Ferniet), preserve some of the original cast ironwork, but with their small, round windows and arcades they have been criticized for combining too many different styles. The cramped facilities have not prevented many important auctions from taking place, despite the dominance of the art market by British houses such as Christie's and Sotheby's. A number of antique and stamp dealers have set up in the immediate vicinity of the Nouveau Drouot in the Rue Chauchat.

Rue Drouot (end)

The Protestant Church (no. 16) was originally a warehouse erected in 1827 and adapted in 1843 by the architect Fau, who added a porch and a small bell-tower. The interior is still imposing. An apartment building by Viollet-le-Duc survives at no. 23.

Rue de la Grange-Batelière

The name of this street goes back to the 13th c. and derives from the battlemented farmhouse (*grange bataillée*) belonging to the canons of Saint-Opportune, which stood on the site of the present-day auction rooms. The Hôtel de Novilos at no. 10 (imposing Louis XVI façade decorated with swags) was once the meeting place for a literary circle comprising Arago, E. de Girardin, Hugo, Roqueplan, A. de Musset and Sainte-Beuve. At no. 9 is the exit of the Passage Jouffroy, built in 1846. Now given over to toyshops and second-hand bookshops, it provides access to the Hôtel Chopin and is the location of the Musée Grévin's exit (→Museums). The arcade is part of the boulevards, unlike the Passage Verdeau (entrance at 6 Rue de la Grange-Batelière), which is more hidden.

Rue du Faubourg-Montmartre

The numerous Neo-Classical buildings in this street are the scene of a nightlife that blends popular entertainment with exoticism and snobbery. This may best be seen in the juxtaposition of the Chartier restaurant at no. 7 with that temple of Parisian nightlife, the Palace, at no. 8. Access to the Cité Bergère, an alley created in 1825 in which a large number of *hôtels* are located, is at no. 6. Heinrich Heine lived at no. 3 and Chopin at no. 4. *L'Equipe*, a sports newspaper, has its offices at no. 10. Further along, where the Rue Cadet branches off, is the local outdoor market. On the corner of the Rue de Provence is one of the finest surviving 19th-c. grocer's and confectioner's shops, its interior and fittings preserved intact.

Rue Richer

This is one of the late–18th c. streets that converge upon the Folies-Bergère at no. 32. This intricate network of streets poses problems for tour buses. The Folies-Bergère puts on one of the most traditional shows in Paris. It was opened in 1869, but the present interior and façade are Art Déco.

Rue de Trévise

This street, with its uniform range of 1840s and 1850s buildings, is the Armenian quarter of Paris. At no. 32 the façade over the garden of the Hôtel de Bony is visible, a Neo-Palladian work by Joly, built during the Bourbon Restoration. The interior* of this *hôtel* has been preserved, but the building has long been due for demolition and only recently appears to have been saved. Its outbuildings have survived, as has the carriageway leading to the Rue Bleue (no. 13).

Not far away, beside the Poissonnière Métro station, the Square Montholon is an oasis of greenery in this heavily built-up area. It has cast-iron railings from the Second Empire and two venerable Oriental plane trees standing nearly 100ft./30m high.

Rue Bleue

Charles Henri Sanson, Louis XVI's executioner, was born in a house on the site of no. 14. At no. 5 is the Cité Trévise, carved out in 1840 and distinguished from a mere passageway by the square decorated with a fountain at its center. The fountain's statues are copies, after Germain Pilon, of the Virtues (order of angels) on the funeral monument for the heart of Henri II in the Louvre. At 25 Rue Bleue, the Leclaire company was formed in 1911, selling zinc oxide to replace the white lead used in the building trade which caused serious illness and even death, among the construction workers.

Rue du Conservatoire

In the 18th c. the Hôtel des Menus-Plaisirs, the mansion in which the Court festivities and the grand entertainments of the kings of France were held, stood on the land between the Rue du Conservatoire and the Rue du Faubourg-Poissonnière. François Bélanger (1745–1818) was in charge of it, which explains his involvement in a number of developments in the district (→inset). The Church of

Saint-Eugène-Sainte-Cécile* (1854–55, even-numbered side of the street and 6 Rue Cécile) was built by Louis-Auguste Boileau, one of the first to use iron construction in church architecture. Although built with structural iron, the church's outward form is a polychrome Neo-Gothic, which makes it an experimental work of the first importance in the history of architecture. The Conservatoire** was established at no. 2 during the Revolution and some sections of the building dating from the First Empire remain unaltered, notably the columned vestibule, the staircase and the Salle Pompéïenne (1811), renowned for its splendid acoustics, by Delannoy, the architect responsible for the Galerie Vivienne. The Conservatoire de Musique moved to the Rue de Madrid before World War I and the buildings now house the Conservatoire National Supérieur d'Art Dramatique.

Rue du Faubourg-Poissonnière

From Bonne-Nouvelle to the Rue des Petites-Ecuries.

The street offers such an array of buildings and town houses that it would bear comparison with the Marais or the Faubourg Saint-Germain had it not been deserted by the nobility and rich bourgeoisie during the reign of Louis-Philippe. No. 9 has a Neo-Classical façade by Trouard (1758); no. 13, on the corner of the Rue Bergère, is an apartment building by Bélanger (c. 1780); nos. 15 and 17 together form an interesting telephone exchange building (1912) with a canopy and mosaics by a forerunner of modern architecture, F. Lecoeur. Bélanger decorated and lived in no. 19 from 1797. The entrance is on the street. Across the courtyard you can see a small town house erected by Hittorff from 1819 to 1921. The largest mansion in the district is the Hôtel de Chéret (no. 30) erected by Lenoir le Romain in 1773. Its courtyard remains virtually unaltered and the porte-cochère has a vaulted ceiling painted with *trompe-l'oeil* coffering.

The Rue Gabriel-Laumain is a typical passageway cut from 1820 to 1824. It leads in the heart of the block to a turning circle for coaches and gives access to the small town house at no. 6*bis*.

Rue des Petites-Ecuries

The Hôtel Botterel-Quintin at no. 44 was erected by Pérard de Montreuil and Duboisterf (1785, and from 1790) and still has its beautiful façade with a porch with a column on either side, its Pompeian-style staircase and its richly decorated dining-room.

Rue du Faubourg-Poissonnière, continued

From the Rue des Petites – Ecuries to the Rue Lafayette.

The Hôtel Cardon (no. 50) was erected by Goupy in 1773. Corot died at no. 56 in 1875. Nos. 58 and 60, the Hôtel Titon* and the Hôtel Goix*, were built by Jean-Charles Dalafosse from 1776 to 1783. The courtyard of no. 58, with its urns, pediments and banisters, demonstrates the refined taste of this expert decorator. The oval drawing-room at no. 60 has been preserved. No. 65 may have been erected by Durand in 1788. The restaurant at no. 80 has retained a gate dating from 1800 which once served to advertise a wine-merchant's shop. The district was known as La Nouvelle-France and barracks of that name were installed at no. 82 in 1780, and rebuilt in 1931.

Take the Rue des Messageries, once a *passage* with stables and a provincial atmosphere. The round *place* at the junction with the Rue d'Hauteville, created in 1772, was also used as a turning place by coaches (→ Rue Gabriel-Laumain).

The rear of the Hôtel Titon overlooks the far end of the Cité Paradis.

Rue d'Hauteville

No. 58, the Hôtel de Bourrienne** (open Wed., Sat. and Sun. 2–4pm; about 45 min.), is one of the few Parisian Empire buildings to have survived in its entirety. The winter garden, dining-room, drawing-room, bathroom, and other rooms, were decorated by Lecomte in a style close to that of Percier and Fontaine. The building can really be compared only with the Hôtel de Beauharnais. There are the remains of other town houses at nos. 53 and 26.

▣ Museum to visit

Musée de la Franc-Maçonnerie (16 Rue Cadet): history of Free-masonry.

▷ Memories of the Second Empire

Napoléon III was born on April 20, 1808 at 17 Rue Laffitte, where his mother, Hortense de Beauharnais, wife of Louis Bonaparte, King of Holland, presided over a brilliant salon. And it was only a short distance away from this spot that Napoléon III nearly met his death on January 14, 1858 when, on his way to the Opéra, which from 1821 to 1873 stood at 6 Rue Le Peletier, he and the Empress Eugénie escaped an assassination attempt by Orsini in which nearly 150 people were injured by a bomb.

These two street are also full of memories of the great painters of that era. Monet was born at 19 Rue Laffitte on November 14, 1840, and Ambroise Vollard, the dealer who so staunchly supported the avant-garde painters of the 1900s, had his gallery in the same street. Le Divan, the café patronized by Balzac, Henry Monnier, Gavarni,

Théophile Gautier, Gérard de Nerval and Baudelaire was at 3 Rue Le Peletier. Until 1873 Degas regularly visited the Opéra at no. 6 to paint the ballet dancers. The Rue Le Peletier was also the scene of two sensational Impressionist exhibitions (the second and third).

Parisian Neo-Classicism

The very definition of Neo-Classicism (ca. 1750–1830) raises certain problems. It is often considered to be a style as distinct as Renaissance, Baroque or Rococo although within its design it contains the seeds of eclecticism. Certainly references to Classical Antiquity play a dominant role, but more important still, Neo-Classicism is remarkable for its internationalism (it is the pre-eminent style from Rio to St Petersburg), for the primacy it accords to theory (it is a highly intellectual movement), and finally, for its rationalism, which makes it appear as the first 'modern' movement.

Within this broad framework there exists, perhaps, a specifically Parisian type of Neo-Classical architecture. From the time of the Revolution Paris was not merely the political center of Europe, but also its intellectual center, which explains, why the most outstanding examples of Neo-Classical architecture were built there (the Ecole de Chirurgie, the Panthéon, the Odéon, the Rue de Rivoli) and why its most influential theoreticians, such as Jacques François Blondel, Ledoux and Durand, published their books in Paris. There is a characteristic touch of severity in Parisian Neo-Classicism; it avoids the use of polychrome, so admired in Central Europe, and uses forms simplified to the utmost degree. The high cost of land certainly compelled architects to limit the scale of their buildings and reduce their ornamentation. It is important to realize that a substantial number of Parisian buildings date from this period, especially so in the 9th arrondissement.

Bélanger and Paris

François-Joseph Bélanger (1744–1818) was both a fine architect and an extremely shrewd businessman. He is most generally known as the architect of the exquisite Bagatelle in the Bois de Boulogne, which he built in 64 days for the king's brother, the Comte d'Artois, to win a bet with Marie-Antoinette, and for the Folie Saint-James at Neuilly, for the completion of whose rockery he commandeered every farmer's cart in Fontainebleau.

Traces of his work in Paris are less spectacular. Like his colleague Brongniart, he speculated in such districts as the Faubourg Poissonnière, then undergoing wholesale development. When the Lycée Condorcet in the Chaussée d'Antin was divided up, Bélanger invented the back staircase. In the Saint-Georges *quartier* at 13–15 *bis* Rue Saint-Georges, is the unified façade which he gave to three town houses. After the Revolution, he designed the remarkable iron and glass dome for what was then the Halle au Blé or corn exchange (1808–13) in Paris, which is now the Bourse de Commerce, as well as the original layout of the Bains Vigier, which still exist near the Place de la Concorde.

The Montparnasse Cemetery*

14th arr./Map ref. 4–C1, C2
Métro: Edgar-Quinet, Raspail
Bus 58, 68

The Montparnasse, or Southern, Cemetery is divided by the Rue Emile-Richard into a large and a small section. It covers nearly 45 acres/18ha of what was once land belonging to three farms. All that remains of these is an old mill-tower, dating from the 14th or 15th c., which stands in the W corner of the cemetery.

History of the cemetery

In 1654 the religious Order of St John of God (Saint-Jean-de-Dieu) opened their private burial ground on this piece of land. In 1785 they also began to inter those who had died in La Charité hospital, run by the brothers in the Rue des Saints-Pères. It was a national conse-quence that the Prefect of Paris, Frochot, should choose this spot as one of the three extramural Parisian cemeteries. Land was pur-chased at various times until it amounted to some 25 acres/10ha and the first burial took place on July 25, 1824. In the beginning this cemetery was assigned to the inhabitants of the arrondissements on the Left Bank and to the bodies of executed criminals who, until 1883, were buried in a special trench. The cemetery was doubled in area in 1847, and split in two in 1891 when the Rue Emile-Richard was built.

The site is flat and the graves are set out in a rectilinear pattern. This is the smallest of the Paris cemeteries and, although less pictur-esque than Père-Lachaise, it contains nevertheless the graves of many famous painters, writers and publishers. The funerary monu-ments are much the same as in other cemeteries. Since 1874, the cemetery has been devoted exclusively to concessions in perpetuity.

Tour of the cemetery

Main entrance: Boul. Edgar-Quinet
7:30am–6pm Mar. 15–Nov. 5; 8am–5:30pm, Nov. 6–Mar. 14; open Sat.
at 8:30am, Sun. and public holidays at 9am.

Suggested routes through the cemetery

Use the main entrance on the Boul. Edgar-Quinet. On the r., near the gate, lies the grave of Jean-Paul Sartre (d. 1980) and of Simone de Beauvoir (d. 1986). Proceed as far as the outer wall, then turn l. into the Ave. de l'Ouest. In the 5th section, on the l., the painter Soutine (d. 1943) is buried, while a little further on, on the same side in the 6th section, the poet Charles Baudelaire (d. 1867) lies in the Aupick family vault. Still to the l., the sculptor Henri Laurens (d. 1954) lies buried in the 7th section. As you proceed you will see on your r., in succession, the graves of the publisher Louis Hachette (d. 1864), the Surrealist poet Robert Desnos (d. 1945), the Romanian poet Tristan Tzara (d. 1963), founder of Dadaism and, last, the monument of the sculptor Antoine Bourdelle (d. 1929).

To Charles Baudelaire's cenotaph

Having reached Antoine Bourdelle's grave turn l. into the Allée Dalou. In the 9th section on the r. stands the tower of La Charité mill. At the Ave. Principale, on the l., you will see the grave of the sculptor Dalou (d. 1902). Cross the avenue and take the Chemin Raffet opposite. In the 11th section on the l. the artist Raffet (d. 1860) and the philosopher Edgar Quinet (d. 1865) are buried. Continue to the Ave. de l'Est and turn l. A little further on, on the l. in the 11th section, stands the grave of Le Verrier (d. 1877), the astronomer who discovered the planet Neptune and established the French meteorological service. Next turn r. into the Ave. Transversale. Against the outer wall stands Charles Baudelaire's cenotaph, carved by J. de Charmoy (1902).

To Brancusi's *Le Baiser* (The Kiss)

Walk back along the Ave. Transversale as far as the roundabout. Then turn r. down the Ave. Principale and r. again into the Ave. du Nord. There, turn r. into the 13th section for the graves of the actress Jean Seberg (d. 1979) and the composer Saint-Saëns (d. 1921). The sculptor Constantin Brancusi (d. 1957) is buried in the 18th section, opposite. Continue along this avenue, cross the Rue Emile-Richard and enter the small cemetery. Turn l. at the gate. In a corner, by the outer wall, is a tomb decorated with a Cubist sculpture by Brancusi, called *Le Baiser* (*The Kiss*).

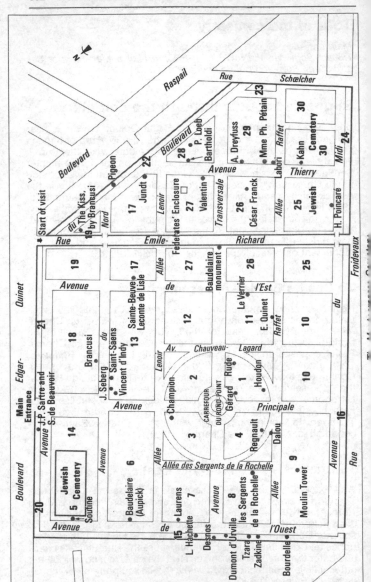

The Montparnasse Cemetery

To the Grave of Henri Poincaré

Proceed down the Ave. du Boulevard alongside the wall. To the r. note the fine *fin de siècle* tomb in which Charles Pigeon is buried, with life-size recumbent statues of him and his wife beneath a side canopy. Turn r. into the Ave. Thierry. In the 28th section, to the l., the graves of the sculptor Bartholdi (d. 1904) and of Colonel Alfred Dreyfus (d. 1935) whose famous court-martial so bitterly divided France between 1894 and 1906. Continue to the Ave. du Midi running along the outer wall and turn r. in the 25th section and you will find the grave of the mathematician Henri Poincaré (d. 1912).

Leave the cemetery, emerging into the Rue Emile-Richard on the corner of the Rue Froidevaux.

Tour of the cemetery by section

The list below comprises the names of the more famous people buried in the cemetery together with tombs of architectural interest.

1st section

The sculptor Houdon (d. 1828); Chauveau-Lagarde (d. 1841), the lawyer who defended Marie-Antoinette before the Convention; the botanists Antoine-Laurent de Jussieu (d. 1836) and Adrien de Jussieu (d. 1853); the painter Baron Gérard (d. 1837), with a medallion by Dantan and bronze bas reliefs of two of his paintings, *Belisarius* and *Christ*; the geologist Elie de Beaumont (d. 1844); F. Rude (d. 1855), with Cadet's bust of the sculptor and a sketch for the Arc de Triomphe, *Le Départ*; Vaneau, a student of the Ecole Polytechnique, killed in Paris during the revolution of 1830.

2nd section

The poet Hégésippe Moreau (d. 1938), bust by Mme Coutanson; the archeologist Lenoir (d. 1865); the artist Léon Willette (d. 1926); the Abbé Grégoire (d. 1831), a member of the Convention; and the writer J.-K. Huysmans (d. 1907).

3rd section

The scholar and philologist Littré (d. 1884), compiler of the famous dictionary of the French language; the jurist Ortolan (d. 1873), bronze bust and bas-relief by Schoenewerk; the sculptor Ramey (d. 1838); P. Véron (d. 1900), bronze bust by Gauthenin; the bookseller and publisher Honoré Champion (d. 1909), monument by Bartholomé; the engraver Bertrand Andrieu (d. 1822).

4th section

The physician Orfila (d. 1853), marble pyramid and medallion; the writer and philosopher, Father Gratry (d. 1872); the painter Henri Regnault, killed in action at Buzenval in 1871; the sculpter Dalou (d. 1902); the geographer Malte-Brun (d. 1826); Pégoud, the first aviator to loop the loop, shot down in 1915; the famous Romanian pianist Clara Haskil (d. 1960).

In the middle of these first four sections, in the Allée Principale, stands Daillion's *Le Souvenir* (Memory), a monumental bronze angel on a stone plinth.

5th section

The lawyer and politician Crémieux (d. 1880); and the painter Soutine (d. 1943).

6th section

The sculptor Esparcieux (d. 1840), bust by David d'Angers; Marie Dorval (d. 1849); actress and friend of de Vigny, the geographer and publicist Adolphe Joanne (d. 1881), founder of the *Guides Joanne*, now the *Guides Bleus*; his son and succesor Paul Joanne (d. 1922); the physicist and astronomer Biot (d. 1862); the painter Eugène Carrière (d. 1906); the counsellor of state Charles Robert, bust by Dalou; General Aupick, his wife and his stepson, Charles Baudelaire (d. 1867): also 27th section; and the aviator Maryse Bastie (d. 1957), whose grave has a huge carved block of stone beside the Ave. Principale.

7th section

The sculptor Antoine Etex (d. 1888), marble self-portrait bust; the publisher and writer Jules Hetzel (d. 1886); the archeologist Quatremère de Quincy (d. 1849); the surgeon Dr Velpeu (d. 1867); the sculptor Henri Laurenc (d. 1954), his own statue, *La Douleur* (Sorrow); the Russian painter Pougny (d. 1961).

8th section

The economist Adolphe Blanqui (d. 1854); the tragic actor Mounet-Sully (d. 1916) and his brother, Paul Mounet (d. 1847); General Mangi's family vault; Tristan Tzara (d. 1963), the founder of Dadaism.

9th section

The old tower of the La Charité mill, 14th or 15th c.; the writer Jules Sandeau (d. 1883); the composer Emmanuel Chabrier (d. 1894), bust by Constantin Meunier; Louis Binger (d. 1936), explorer of the Ivory Coast; the poets Vincent Muselli (d. 1956) and Maurice du Plessys (d. 1924); the professor of medicine Charles Richet (d. 1935).

10th section

The Romantic writer Aloysius Bertrand (d. 1841); Lachaud (d. 1882), one of the greatest French lawyers of the 19th c.; General Comte Lepic (d. 1827); the zoologist Milne-Edwards (d. 1885); Dr Brown-Séquard (d. 1894); the politician Etienne Arago (d. 1892); the painter Fantin-Latour (d. 1904); the composer Samuel Rousseau (d. 1904); the lawyer de Moro-Giafferi (d. 1956); Louis Loucheur (d. 1931), Minister of Labor, who brought in the act which bears his name and provided for cheap rental housing; Emile Faguet (d. 1916), professor and critic.

11th section

The writer and philosopher Edgar Guinet (d. 1865); the artist Raffet (d. 1860); Le Verrier (d. 1877), the astronomer who discovered the planet Neptune; the caricaturist Cham, pseudonym of the Comte de Nóe (d. 1879); the architect of the Paris Opéra, Charles Garnier (d. 1898); the memorial to the aviator François Coli (d. 1927) who vanished in an attempt to fly the S Atlantic with Charles Nungesser.

12th section

The sculptor Diébolt (d. 1851); the publisher Plon (d. 1895); the painter Bouguereau (d. 1906); the tragic actor de Max (d. 1925); the etcher and engraver Auguste Lepère (d. 1918).

13th section

The poet Théodore de Banville (d. 1891); near the junction of the Ave. du Nord and the Ave. Principale, not far from one another, the two great composers Saint-Saëns (d. 1921) and Vincent d'Indy (d. 1931); the singer Sylvia Lopez (d. 1959); the diplomat Paul Cambon (d. 1924); the composer and organist Louis Vierne (d. 1937); the surgeon Lisfranc (d. 1847), high-reliefs by Elschoecht; the actress Jean Seberg (d. 1979).

14th section

Pierre Larousse (d. 1875), publisher and compiler of the famous encyclopedic dictionary, the *Grand Dictionnaire Universel*, fine bronze bust by Perraud; the Catholic pamphleteer and publicist Louis Veuillot (d. 1883); the historian Henri Martin (d. 1883); Sister Rosalie (d. 1856); the writer Feuillet de Conches (d. 1887); Emile Deschanel (d. 1903), writer and father of Paul Deschanel; Paul Deschanel (d. 1922), President of the French Republic; and the mathematician Emile Picard (d. 1941).

15th section

General Hulin (d. 1841), marble bust by David d'Angers; red pyramid with bust by Dantan the Elder erected by the Société de Géographie to the memory of the unfortunate explorer Dumont d'Urville who, after having twice circumnavigated the globe, was killed in a railway accident at Saint-Germain-en-Laye on May 8 1842, together with his wife and young son; General Charles Duvivier (d. 1852); the anthropologist P. Broca (d. 1880); the sculptor Antoine Bourdelle (d. 1929); the poet Robert Desnos, who died in the Theresienstadt concentration camp just after its liberation, 1945; the bookseller and publisher Louis Hachette (d. 1864); the politician Pierre Laval (d. 1945).

16th section

The chemist J.-B. Dumas (d. 1890); the painter Girodet (d. 1824); the sculptor Bonnassieux (d. 1892).

17th section (large cemetery)

The critic Sainte-Beuve (d. 1869), bust by J. de Charmoy.

17th section (small cemetery)

The painter Gustave Jundt (d. 1884), bronze statue, *L'Enfance* (Childhood), and bust by Bartholdi; the monument to the poet Leconte de Lisle (d. 1894), which stood, with his bust by Moulin, under an acacia tree, was moved to the island of Réunion in 1977; the painter and poet Jules Breton (d. 1898), bust by Houssin; the musicologist Bourgault-Ducoudray (d. 1910); the geographer Emile Levasseur (d. 1911); the artists Achille and Eugène Devèria (d. 1857 and 1865 respectively).

18th section

Aristide Boucicaut (d. 1879) and his wife (d. 1887), founders of the Bon Marché department stores; Comte de Gaspari (d. 1879), fine marble memorial with bronze bust; Dr Récamier (d. 1852); de Cardaillac (d. 1890), medallion by Crauk; the poet Léon-Paul Fargue (d. 1947); the Romanian sculptor Brancusi (d. 1957), his sculpture, *Le Baiser* (The Kiss) stands in the small cemetery.

19th section (large cemetery)

The historians Augustin and Amédée Thierry (d. 1856 and 1873 respectively).

19th section (small cemetery)

The critic Ferdinand Brunetière (d. 1906), bust by Allouard; *Le Baiser* (The Kiss), Cubist sculpture by Constantin Brancusi (→18th section).

20th section

H. Ruhmkorff (d. 1877), inventor of the induction coil which bears his name; Bullier (d. 1869), with marble medallion bust by Desprez; and the writers and philosophers Jean-Paul Sartre (d. 1980) and Simone de Beauvoir (d. 1986).

22nd section (small cemetery)

The sculptor and poet Zacharie Astruc (d. 1907), with bust and bas-relief by R. Sudre; the writer Catulle Mendès (d. 1909); the director of sophisticated film comedies Becker (d. 1960); the politician Paul Reynaud (d. 1966); the monumental tomb of Charles Pigeon on which the sculptor shows the industrialist awake in bed, realizing the need to invent the bedside lamp.

24th section (small cemetery)

The Hollywood film star Maria Montez (d. 1951); the actor Georges Berr (d. 1941).

25th section (large cemetery)

Conté (d. 1805), inventor of the pencil.

25th section (small cemetery)

The mathematician Henri Poincaré (d. 1912).

26th section (small cemetery)

The composer César Franck (d. 1890), medallion by Rodin; memorial to the dead of the Franco-Prussian War of 1870-71; the novelist Guy de Maupassant (d. 1893); the painter Octave Tassaert (d. 1874); the novelist Paul Bourget (d. 1935); the novelist Paul Féval (d. 1887); and the poet and novelist Pierre Louÿs (d. 1925).

27th section (large cemetery)

Although J. de Charmoy's memorial (1902) to Charles Baudelaire (d. 1867) stands here, the author of *Les Fleurs du Mal* is actually buried with his mother and stepfather in the Aupick family vault (6th section); the politician Boulay de la Meurthe (d. 1840), bust by David d'Angers; the novelist Victor Cherbuliez (d. 1899); the painter Othon Friesz (d. 1949); Wattiez (d. 1911), monument by Carrier-Belleuse.

27th section (small cemetery)

Common grave of the victims of the Commune June 21-23, 1871; the novelist Edouard Estaunié (d. 1942); the actor Max Dearly (d. 1943); the poet Laurent Tailhade (d. 1919); the composer Maurice Emmanuel (d. 1938).

28th section (small cemetery)

Colonel Herbinger (d. 1886), bronze bust by Etex; Bartholdi (d. 1904), sculptor of the Lion of Belfort and the Statue of Liberty, with obelisk and bronze by himself; Colonel Alfred Dreyfus (d. 1935), victim of the celebrated 'Affaire' that divided France into two camps between 1894 and 1906; the auto manufacturer André Citroën (d. 1935); the sculptor Jean Arp's relief on the tomb of Pierre Loeb (d. 1965); the Herbette sepulchre statue and bas-relief by Roty.

29th section (small cemetery)

The poet Charles Cros (d. 1888), one of the inventors of the phonograph and of color photography; the philospher Caro (d. 1887), caricatured in *Le Monde où l'on s'ennuie*; the mathematician Joseph Bertrand (d. 1900); the famous assize-lawyer F. Labori (d.

1917); the wife of Marshal Pétain (d. 1962) and her son, the director P. de Hérain.

30th section (small cemetery)

The Jewish Cemetery: the poet Gustave Kahn (d. 1936).

> Epitaphs

Long epitaphs, often dedicated to wives or children, are typical of the first half of the 19th c. They could be bought from the monument masons, who maintained collections of them, and did not hesitate to sell the same epitaph several times over. In general they address the passerby, recalling the most important moments in the life of the departed. Some would not be out of place in a biographical dictionary.

> Graves and family vaults

Single burials were customary from 1804 to 1830, and these were generally made directly in the ground. When several members of the same family were buried, each was given a separate grave and the whole plot was railed off. After 1830 the family vault became the fashion, a solid structure with room for a number of coffins. Title to the burial plot was handed down to the descendants of the original purchaser. However, there was no need for occupants of the vault to be members of the same family. When colleagues are interred in the same tomb the inscription *Deux amis* ('Two Friends') takes the place of the traditional 'Such-and-such Family' or 'Family Vault'. Since the collapse of the 88th section of the Père-Lachaise Cemetery in 1874, the four major Parisian cemeteries have ruled that all burial plots should be sold in perpetuity and that the tombs should be built of durable materials.

The Montparnasse district*

6th, 14th and 15th arr./Map ref. 4–C1, C2
Métro: Montparnasse
Bus: 28, 48, 58, 82, 89, 91, 92, 94, 95, 96
Parking: under the station, 48–50 Ave. du Maine and under the shopping center, Rue de l'Arrivée and Rue du Départ.

Taxis: 73 Boul. du Montparnasse. Tel. 42–22–13–13

This district of Paris has been home to so many artists for so long, that it has certainly earned the right to the name of the Greek mountain dedicated in Antiquity to Apollo, god of beauty, music and poetry. The area around the Gare Montparnasse has obviously changed greatly since the 1920s, when it was the haunt of Picasso, Max Jacob and Modigliani. Nonetheless, there are still plenty of artists' studios in the little streets round the station and the peaceful Montparnasse Cemetery, like that in which the sculptor Antoine Bourdelle once lived. Moreover, because the railway line from Brittany terminates at the Montparnasse station, this is the district of Paris long favored by Bretons, who have established their book-shops, their various societies and their *crêperies* here.

Into a world practically unchanged in the past 75 years sprang the contemporary architecture of the Centre Maine-Montparnasse, its tower exemplifying the concepts behind urban-planning of the early 1970s, when the American way of life was still taken as a model. At the foot of the Tour Montparnasse, the Boul. du Montparnasse has changed far less. It is very much alive and the many cinemas, cafés and fashionable brasseries around the Carrefour Raspail stay open until the early hours.

Tour of the Maine-Montparnasse development

A vast development scheme, which Raoul Dautry first put forward in 1934, was finally adopted in 1958 and eventually begun in 1961. It began with the demolition of the Boul. Edgar-Quinet and the Ave. du Maine, thus freeing a huge area between the Rue du Départ and the Rue de l'Arrivée. The aim was to give the Left Bank the center that it had always lacked and to provide a counterpart in S Paris to La Défense, the new district to the W.

The old Gare Montparnasse had been opened in 1852, but practically all that remained from that period was the façade, the rest having been altered several times. This façade was on the Place du 18-Juin-1940, then called the Place de Rennes, opposite the Rue de Rennes, when an appalling railway accident occurred in 1898. A Granville-Paris express train ran out of control right through the front of the station, leaving the engine hanging in space over a newspaper kiosk. It was in this former station that Marshal Leclerc set up his headquarters during the Liberation of Paris and here that the German General von Choltitz signed the surrender of the garrison of 'Gross Paris' at 5pm on August 25, 1944. The station was subsequently used only for suburban service, since two new stations had been built behind it for the main railway lines: the Gare Maine-Arrivée (1929) and the Gare Maine-Départ (1936). Both these stations were swept away by the Maine-Montparnasse development.

The plans for this development involved an area of nearly 20 acres/ 8ha, and construction of the entire complex including and enclosing the new station was completed in 1974. From the architectural point of view, the design, which entailed the reconstruction of an entire district, is characterized above all by vertical use of space. The area, over 984ft./300m long and 328ft/100m wide, between the new station and the Place du 18-Juin-1940, is filled successively by a huge open square surrounded by flower-beds, a tower and a shopping center. Lopez, Beaudoin, Arretche, de Hoym and Dubuisson were the architects responsible for the development.

A new section was opened in 1987.

The Tour Montparnasse*

Open daily Apr.-Sept.; 9:30am-11:30pm, 10am-10pm, Oct.-Mar.; closed 6pm Tues. and Thurs. except during July and Aug., public and school holidays.

An oval cylinder standing over 688ft/209m high in line with the Rue de Rennes, this steel and smoked glass tower comprises 58 floors, mostly offices, and accommodates over 7000 people daily. The tallest building of its kind in Europe, it dominates an area 12mls/ 20km diameter and is thus a landmark visible anywhere in Paris. Its foundations go down 230 ft/70m to support 120,000 tons of masonry. The view from the open-air terrace on top is of course exceptional and slightly different from that from the top of the Eiffel Tower, since it includes the Left Bank and the mansions and their gardens in the Faubourg Saint-Germain. On the 56th floor there is a bar with a panoramic view, and exhibition halls. In the shopping center at the foot of the tower, with branches of the Galeries Lafayette, Habitat, and others, there are also several restaurants, a swimming-pool, squash courts, a fencing school and, overlooking the Place du 18-Juin-1940, the offices of the Centre International du Textile. There are underground parking lots. The tower is separated from the station by a terrace paved with pink Sardinian granite; the Ave. du Maine passes underneath.

The Gare Montparnasse

The station, a U-shaped terminal, serves part of the W suburbs of Paris, Brittany, Mayenne and Basse-Normandie. The vast concourse that connects with the Métro is decorated with large compositions by Vasarely. Between the station parking lot and the taxi stand there is even a chapel dedicated to St Bernard, completed in 1969. Its style is restrained; the lectern was carved from a railroad tie sleeper, and only a simple plaque draws attention to its existence.

The Vaugirard Building, a glass, steel and concrete tower, comprising 17 floors and 5 basement levels, is an L-shaped structure over 720ft/250m long and over 820ft/60m high, one wing running parallel with the Boul. Pasteur. In the angle of the two wings, the huge Sq. Max-Hymans covers a three-level underground parking lot. Most of these buildings are occupied by the offices of Air France and a bank, the Caisse Nationale de Crédit Agricole.

The Plaisance Building comprises apartments built by the architect Dubuisson and a major postal station designed by the architect Arretche.

Between the ends of these gigantic buildings the railway tracks are spanned by a bridge, the Pont des Cinq-Martyrs-du-Lycée-Buffon, along the axis of the Boul. Pasteur.

Tour of the Montparnasse district

1 hr.

Boulevard de Vaugirard

This street runs along the NW side of the Gare Montparnasse. At no. 18 the central accounting office of the French telephone company is housed in a building erected in 1935 by Debat and Ponsan that combines functionalism with the classicism of its two lower floors. The Musée de la Poste (→Museums) is located at no. 34, in the Maison de la Poste et de la Philatélie, to which it was transferred around 1975 from its original home opened in 1946 in the 18th-c. Hôtel de Choiseul-Praslin in the Rue Saint-Romain. The architect André Chatelin created the building, which is ornamented with moulded concrete prisms. At the end of the boulevard, on the l., can be seen the bronzed glass windows of the Crédit Agricole offices (architect, R. Genin, 1975).

Go through the Galerie Vaugirard, a shopping arcade recently opened next door to the Musée de la Poste, to reach the Rue Falguière. The Paris Art Centre (36 Rue Falguière) uses renovated former artists' studios to house exhibitions of modern art.

Turn r. into the Rue Antoine-Bourdelle to visit the Musée Bourdelle (→Museums). After leaving the museum cross in front of the station and beyond it take the Ave. du Maine underpass below the Maine-Montparnasse development.

Avenue du Maine

This is one of the district's main thoroughfares. On the r., cross the Rue du Commandant-Mouchotte, named after the officer commanding the Alsace Group, killed in an air battle in August 1943. From it you can see the tall outlines of the Hôtel Méridien some 360 ft/110m high (architect, Pierre Dufour, 1975), and a vast complex of offices, housing, nightclubs, a theater and a skating-rink, shopping arcades, cafés and banks. It was in this street that R. Bofill built two housing projects in the Neo-Classical style, (1984–86): (→Plaisance district).

Rue de la Gaîté

The Rue de la Gaîté runs off on the l. of the Ave. du Maine and was a street of surburban cafés in the days when wine was cheaper beyond the tollhouses that surrounded Paris. Undismayed by the opening of the cemetery close by, it continues to be a center of popular entertainment. Today sex shops stand next door to theaters, of which the best known are Bobino, the old-fashioned music hall, the Gaîté Montparnasse, which first opened its doors in 1868, and above all the Théâtre-Montparnasse at no. 31. From 1930 to 1942 its director was Gaston Baty, and here he staged *The Threepenny Opera, Macbeth, Les Caprices de Marianne*, and other productions that emphasized the stagecraft of his actors, as well as music and lighting. During the 1950s Marguerite Jamois was director, and under her régime the Montparnasse became Jean Anouilh's favorite theater, where *The Lark, Poor Bitos* and *Becket* were first produced. The theater has recently been refurbished, and now includes an old café while preserving its 1886 décor.

Boulevard de Montparnasse

This district really comes to life in the evenings. So many attractions are packed together between the place du 18-Juin-1940 and the Carrefour Raspail: there are cafés, *cafés-théâtres* (do not miss Le Lucernaire, 53 Rue Notré-Dame-des-Champs), nightclubs (Rue Bréa, Rue Vavin, Rue Delambre as well as on the boulevard itself), many cinemas and large brasseries. At the Carrefour Vavin, where the Boul. Montparnasse intersects the Boul. Raspail, stand the four best-known (→inset): Le Dôme, La Rotonde, Le Select and La Coupole, of which only the last two have preserved their original décor. Since 1939, at the edge of the intersection, Rodin's long and often bitterly criticized statue of Balzac* has stood on an island in the Raspail.

The Rue de la Grande-Chaumière begins at the Carrefour Vavin. Its name comes from the famous pleasure-gardens that stood on the site from 1780 to 1855, where such dances as the polka, the cancan and the cachucha were launched. No. 14 is the Académie de la Grande-Chaumière, an academy of painting and sculpture opened in 1904. When Gauguin returned from Tahiti in 1893, he rented an apartment at no. 8.

Boulevard Raspail

Between the Carrefour Vavin and the Rue Campagne-Première.

Walk back up the boulevard toward the Place Denfert-Rochereau. No 216 is a fine apartment building in imitation of artists' studios, erected by Bruno Elkouken in 1934 around a cinema, the Studio Raspail, at a time when films were gaining acceptance as the seventh art.

Rue Campagne-Première

This street was given its strange name by the man who built it, General Taponnier, who christened it in memory of his first campaign at Wissembourg in 1793. Between the wars many artists lived here, including Modigliani, Pompon, Othon Friesz, Miró, Picasso, Max Ernst, Giacometti and Kandinsky. No. 31, a large block of studios*, erected by A. Arfvidson in 1911, marks the turning point between the decorative architecture of the *fin de siècle* and the modern architecture that emphasized masses and volumes. Its façade is decorated with glazed sandstone by Bigot. The father of modern photography, Eugène Atget, had his studio at no. 17 from 1898 to 1927.

Boulevard Raspail, continued

Between the Rue Campagne-Première and the Place Denfert-Rochereau.

Since 1907 the Ecole Spéciale de l'Architecture (founded in 1865) has been located at no. 254. The columns in the courtyard come from the Tuileries Palace. In the Rue Schoelcher there are some fine studios: no. 5 (architect, Follot, 1911) and no. 11 *bis* (architect, Gauthier, 1927) overlooking the Montparnasse Cemetery. The very active American Center for Students and Artists (no. 261) was built around 1920 on part of the gardens of the Infirmerie Marie-Thérèse (Ave. Denfert-Rochereau) which has a cedar supposed to have been planted by Chateaubriand.

Retrace your steps to visit the Montparnasse Cemetery (→inset).

▣ Museums to visit

Musée Bourdelle (16 Rue Antoine-Bourdelle): Antoine Bourdelle's sculptures displayed in his old studio.

Musée de la Poste (34 Boul. de Vaugirard): history of writing, letters and everything relating to postal services.

▷ Artists' studios

The essential requirements of an artist's studio are high ceilings and wide doorways through which the finished works may be taken, and large facing windows, preferably north, so that the quality of the light does not vary. In Paris the studios of several sculptors have been preserved, including those of Bourdelle, Zadkine and Bouchard, while Brancusi's has been moved in its entirety from the Impasse Ronsin to Beaubourg (→Museums, Bouchard, Bourdelle, Zadkine, and Brancusi's studio under the Pompidou Center). You may also visit the comfortable homes in which painters such as Delacroix, Henner and Gustave Moreau had their studios (→Museums, Delacroix, Henner, G. Moreau). However, most of the studios are fragile buildings that proliferated on the outskirts of the city, in Montmartre and to the S of Paris in the 14th and 15th arrondissements. Between the wars they became very fashionable with the discerning middle classes. Although these studios have often been swept away in favor of more profitable forms of housing, Paris has retained several groups of fine multi-storey studios, such as 31 Rue Campagne-Première or 216 Boul. Raspail. Others are grouped in quiet lanes such as the Villa Seurat (→Parc Montsouris district).

▷ The great Brasseries at the Carrefour Vavin

Montparnasse soon succeeded Montmartre as the melting pot of modern art, and there is a touch of nostalgia in recalling today those who used to haunt the four large brasseries at the Carrefour Vavin. Artists from all over the world – Brancusi, Chagall, Foujita, Friesz, Kisling, Matisse, Max Jacob, Picasso, Pascin, Modigliani (whose death, followed by the suicide of his pregnant mistress, Jeanne Hébuterne, caused much sadness in the district) – and the models, such as Alice Prin (nicknamed Kiki), who sat for them, collectors and dealers, could all be found in the years before World War I and in the 1920s at Le Dôme or La Rotonde. Here many must have encountered Lenin and Trotsky, unaware of their historic significance. La Coupole, opened on December 20, 1927, took the lead. Its decoration was put in the hands of 30 painters; and it survives to this day, having seen a long succession of artistic personalities. After

Hemingway, Dali, Giacometti, Sartre, Simone de Beauvoir and many others, the likes of the rock singer Sapho, Régine, Gonzague Saint Bris and the actress Jane Birkin continue to make this great café an exclusive rendezvous.

The Parc Montsouris district*

14th arr.
RER: Cité-Universitaire
Bus: 21, 67, PC
Parking, Porte d'Orléans
Taxis: 1 Place du 25-Aout-1944. Tel.45-40-52-05

The busy, and already almost suburban, neighborhood around the Rue de la Tombe-Issoire had a genuine working-class atmosphere which attracted literary and artistic bohemia between the wars. Despite a number of major construction developments that have, since the 1950s, changed both the appearance and the atmosphere of this corner of Paris, in many parts it still has an almost rural charm.

It is enough to stroll down the narrow streets round the 100-year-old Montsouris reservoirs or, better still, into the little culs-de-sac round the park, to see how true this is.

The park adds greatly to the attraction of the district. It has been landscaped on uneven ground with wide, gently rolling expanses of lawn and, although most Parisians seem unaware of it, it is one of the largest open spaces in the capital. First thing in the morning students from the nearby Cité Universitaire use it for jogging.

The Cité Universitaire itself is a veritable city within a City. International in outlook, its student residence welcome students from all over the world who come to study at the University of Paris. A microcosm of the world, the 'Cité-U' has also served as a laboratory for modern architecture and in this respect the Foundation Suisse (Swiss House), designed by Le Corbusier, and Claude Parent's Foundation Avicenne are outstanding.

Tour of the district

2 hrs.

The Parc Montsouris*

The park was laid out from 1875 and 1878 and, with its hollows and hillocks, it is charming and very peaceful during the week, popular with students from the neighboring Cité Universitaire, children and the artists who live around the park in the little houses that line the picturesque culs-de-sac.

Alphand intended it as the counterpart of the Parc des Buttes-Chaumont to the N. The problem was to accommodate the ground, broken by quarries, and the two sets of railway tracks that crossed it. Thus the park is effectively split in two, but the division has been cunningly concealed. The park has plenty of broad lawns, clumps of trees, a grotto and a waterfall.

The Bardo*

W part of the Park

This building is the Tunisian pavilion built for the 1867 Exposition Universelle (World Fair) on the Champ-de-Mars, a reproduction of the palace of the Bey (ruler) of Tunis. The municipal authorities subsequently purchased it from Baron de Lesseps on condition that he have it re-erected in the Parc Montsouris. That task was entrusted to Davioud, the architect who frequently cooperated with the engineer Alphand and the landscape gardener Barrillet-Deschamps in designing open spaces of Paris. He re-erected the fragile wooden structure on a masonry base at the highest point in the park. The French meteorological service took over the building and in 1869 it became a meterological observatory. There the scientists worked until they were driven out in 1974 when the decaying buildings threatened to fall down around them. Shards of stained glass and a frail structure of beams were all that remained of the original Moorish splendor.

Restoration of the building was determined by an agreement signed between the Parisian municipal authorities and the Tunisian Minister of Culture. Under it the Tunisian Government took over the building on a renewable 99-year lease at the nominal rent of 100 francs per year and on the condition of fully restoring the building before turning it into a Tunisian cultural center. Renovation began in 1986, some structural elements being dismantled and rebuilt in Tunisia. The Bardo became a registered monument only in 1985.

To the r. is a modern meteorological tower, but behind it stands a four-sided marker, about 13ft/4m high, with an opening in its upper section. This is the Observatory's old surveying marker, set up in 1806 (Napoleon's name has been removed).

Beside the RER line, near the iron bridge over the tracks, stands a pyramid erected in memory of the members of the Flatters Expedition, who were sent out to survey the trans-Saharan railway line and were murdered by the Touaregs in 1881.

The Lake

E part of the Park

The lake is fed from the S by a waterfall above which is a terrace with benches. Not far off is the Pavillon du Lac. There is a tragic story connected with the lake's inaugural celebration: on the day Napoléon III was to perform the official ceremony, the lake suddenly dried up, and the engineer responsible for the project killed himself in despair. Nearby is a beautiful fountain decorated with a group by the sculptor Baucour, *Le Premier Frisson* (The First Tremor).

Northwest of the Park

This quiet and airy district saw, between the wars, the construction of a number of attractive apartment buildings and artists' studios.

Rue Deutsch-de-la-Meurthe

From this street run several other quiet little streets. The Rue Braque (formerly the Rue du Douanier) is where Georges Braque had his studio, at no. 6, built by A. Perret in 1927. Note, too, no. 8, a house by Zielinsky (1932), and no. 5, a studio by R. Fischer (1929). The Rue Nansouty leads to no. 14, the Villa Guggenbuhl, with its stark lines, designed by A. Lurçat in 1927. No. 2 Square du Monsouris is the Maison Gaut (architect Perret, 1923) while no. 17 is a 1930s-style house.

Avenue Rielle

No. 53 is the celebrated house and studio built by Le Corbusier for his friend Amédée Ozenfant in 1923. Only the saw-toothed factory-style roof has been changed and flattened to make a terrace. Both nos. 55 and 57 are houses designed by J. Dechelette in 1925. A little further on (50 Ave. René-Coty) is the strange studio on stilts erected by J.-J. Lemordant in 1929, standing snugly against the side of the Vanne Montsouris reservoir.

Rue Saint-Yves

This old cobbled street runs along the side of the Monsouris reservoir, built in 1874 to take water from the rivers Vanne, Loing and Lunain. The iron shelter overlooking it (11 Rue du Tombe-Issoire) dates from 1900. No. 11 is the Cité du Souvenir, founded by the Abbé Keller to provide 300 dwellings for parents with large families.

Nos. 3, 5 and 7 Rue Gauguet (to the l.) are large studios with living accommodations designed in the international style (architect Zielinsky, 1930). Nicolas de Staël once lived in no. 7.

Rue de la Tombe-Issoire

This street is the old Orléans road and its name is an odd relic of the chivalrous epics. In the *chanson de geste* of Guillaume d'Orange, the hero of that name came here and killed the giant, Isoré, king of the Saracens. Isoré's tomb gave the street its name, Tombe-Issoire. The street was much livelier between the wars than it is today, when there were cafés frequented by writers, and artists' studios close by; now the area has been almost completely rebuilt.

The Villa Seurat stands in a private cul-de-sac leading off the Rue Tombe-Issoire. It was erected in 1925 and is a model of consistency of style. Almost all its studio-houses are the work of André Lurçat, although no. 7 *bis* is by August Perret. Lurçat, Henry Miller, Anaïs Nin, Chana Orloff, Gromaire, Soutine and Salvador Dali all lived in the Villa Seurat during the interwar years.

The Rue Marie-Rose joins the street almost directly opposite the Villa Seurat. A plaque on no. 4 commemorates this as one of the houses in Paris where Lenin stayed from 1909 to 1912. Accordingly, all Soviet statesmen coming to France pay it an official visit. No. 7, opposite, is the entrance to the red brick chapel of the monastery of the Franciscan missionaries (architects, Gélis and Hulo, 1936).

Southeast of the Park

No. 3 Rue de la Cité-Universitaire is an apartment building built around 1930 by Roux-Spitz; the aviator Mermoz lived here before his disappearance in the S Atlantic in 1936.

The Paris University Residential Campus, Boul. Jourdan

The first student residence for the University of Paris was built here in 1922, when Paul Appell was its Rector. Today, university accommodation stretches for over a kilometer along the Boul. Jourdan on either side of the Porte d'Arceuil and covers nearly 100 acres/40ha of the land cleared when the fortifications were demolished. Its creators were motivated by the desire to promote international

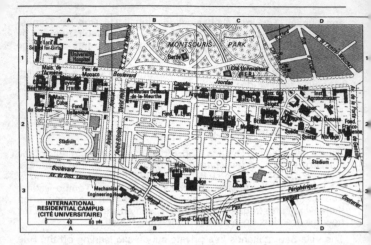

understanding and to improve the living conditions of the university students. It now comprises 37 student residences housing 6000 young people of both sexes, nearly two-thirds of whom are non-French, drawn from 120 different countries. It is truly an international university campus, unequalled anywhere else in the world. It has enabled the University of Paris to revive a tradition dating back to the 12th-c., and to give a worthy reception to its foreign students.

The Cité-Universitaire is served by its own Métro station (RER, Sceaux Line) which brings the campus within minutes of the Latin Quarter. Its creation was the concept of a group of prominent people, including a generous benefactor, Emile Deutsch de la Meurthe, the Minister of Education, André Honnorat, and the Rector of the University of Paris, Paul Appell. As a legal entity, the Cité is a State-approved foundation, formed as an association in accordance with the Law of 1901, with a board and a managing director. Between 1925 and 1960, 35 student residences were built, each financed by a different country or group of individuals. Since these projects were all begun at different dates and commissioned by people with widely differing tastes, the Cité comprises an equally wide variety of architectural styles, but each building shares the common aim of providing its residents with comfortable, human-scale accommodation. In each student residences, 60 of the students come from the country that financed the building's construction, the remainder from other countries.

In addition to these student residences, the Cité Universitaire, thanks to the generosity of John D. Rockefeller Jr., provides a central building open to all students, the Maison Internationale (architect, Fr Larsen), built in 1935 in the Louis XIII style. The building houses such facilities for on-campus residents as a library, a restaurant, common rooms, a swimming-pool, etc., as well as a theater open to the public, with three auditoriums (La Reserre, the Grand Théâtre and La Galerie). The Foundation Deutsch-de-la-Meurthe (37 Boul. Jourdan), the first building to be erected (1921), and the nucleus of the campus, was designed by Lucien Bechmann in a style reminiscent of that of traditional British colleges. From 1927 to 1960, the Foundation was to be joined by 35 other buildings set in a pleasant open space, provided with plenty of sports facilities, including running tracks and tennis courts. These student residences are meticulously designed and generally include in both external and internal detail something evocative of the country that funded their construction.

The Student Residences

Maison des Etudiants Canadiens (architect, Thomas Vannier): 31 Boul. Jourdan.

Fondation Belge Biermans-Lapôtre (architect, T. Gueritte): 9A Boul. Jourdan.

Maison des Etudiants Argentins (architect, M. Betourné): 27A Boul. Jourdan.

Fondation de l'Institut Agronomique (architect M. Patouillard): 7B Boul. Jourdan.

Maison du Japon* (architect, P. Sardou): 7C Boul. Jourdan.

Maison des Etudiants de l'Asie du Sud-Est (architects, Martin and Vieu): 59B Boul. Jourdan.

Fondation des Etats-Unis (architect, Leprince-Ringuet): 15 Boul. Jourdan.

Maison des Etudiants Arméniens (architect, Léon Nafilyan): 57 Boul. Jourdan.

Maison des Etudiants Suédois (architect, M. Persson): 7F Boul. Jourdan.

Maison des Etudiants Danois (architect, M. Gottlob): 7H Boul. Jourdan.

Fondation Hellénique (architect, M. Zanos): 47B Boul. Jourdan.

Fondation Rosa-Abreu-de-Grancher (architect, P. Laprade): 59A Boul. Jourdan.

Maison des Provinces de France (architect, A. Gueritte): 55B Boul. Jourdan.

Maison Franco-Brésilienne* (architects, Le Corbusier practice and Lucio Costa, 1959): 71 Boul. Jourdan.

Maison de l'Inde (architect, M. Leclaire): 7B Boul. Jourdan.

Maison du Liban (architects, Vernon and Philippe): 9E Boul. Jourdan.

Fondation Suisse* (architect, Le Corbusier, 1932): 7K Boul. Jourdan.

Collège d'Espagne (architect, P. Irisarri): 7E Boul. Jourdan (closed since 1968).

Collège Néerlandais* (architect, M. Dudok, 1927): 61 Boul. Jordan.

Collège Franco-Britannique (architects, Martin and Vieu): 9B Boul. Jourdan.

Maison de Monaco (architect, J. Médecin): 47A Boul. Jourdan.

Fondation Victor-Lyon (architect, L. Bechmann): 29 Boul. Jourdan.

Maison des Elèves-Ingénieurs des Arts et Métiers (architect, U. Cassan): Rue Pierre-Masse.

Résidence Lucien-Paye (architects, Laprade, Vernon and Philippe): 7N Boul. Jourdan.

Maison de la Tunisie (architect, Sebag): 45A Boul. Jourdan.

Maison du Mexique (architect, Medellin): 9C Boul. Jourdan.

Maison du Maroc (architects, Laprade, Vernon and Philippe): 1 Boul. Jourdan.

Maison de Norvège (architect, Philippot): 7N Boul. Jourdan.

Maison des Industries Agricoles et Alimentaire (architects, Thieulin and Vigan): 5 Boul. Jourdan.

Maison Heinrich-Heine (architect, Maître): 27C Boul. Jourdan.

Maison du Cambodge (architect, Audoul, 1957): 27B Boul. Jourdan (closed).

Maison d'Italie (architect, Klien, 1959): 7A Boul. Jourdan.

Résidence André-de-Gouveia (architect, M. Crépet): 7P Boul. Jourdan

Foundation Avicenne* (architects, C. Parent and M. Fourough, 1966–68; sculptor, André Bloc): 27D Boul. Jourdan

Pavillon André-Honnorat: 21 Boul. Jourdan (reserved for female students).

From the architectural viewpoint pride of place is often given to Le Corbusier's Fondation Suisse and Dudok's Collège Néerlandais, while the more recent Foundation Avicenne is held up as an example of the best French architecture of the 1960s.

✠ The Church of the Sacré-Coeur

In the Commune of Gentilly.

Endowed by the Lebaudy family and built in 1936 by the architect Paquet as the chapel for the Cité Universitaire, the church has been cut off from the campus by the construction of a highway, which can be crossed by a footbridge.

The clock tower is supported by four angels sculpted by Saupique, who was also responsible for the façade. The interior contains a set of the *Stations of the Cross* painted by A. Zarraga and the stained glass is by Gruber. The church has now been allocated to the Portuguese community of the diocese of Paris.

▷ The Revival of Religious Art

Around 1920, Maurice Denis, in collaboration with Georges Desvallières, founded the Ateliers d'Art Sacré. These studios were located in the Place Fürstenberg and were intended to provide an artistic education and training, especially for painters, and more particularly in ecclesiastical art. Young artists were instructed in the techniques of mural and easel painting, sculpture, gold- and silver-smithing, stained glass and embroidery. The one thing lacking was a school of architecture. Among the many artists who used these studios were Albert Dubos, Pierre Couturier, Henri de Maistre, and Pauline Peugniez. Unfortunately the public response was distinctly tepid.

A few years later a church-building program, the Chantiers du Cardinal, breathed fresh life into this area. In 1932 Cardinal Verdier decided to build churches in the newly built up districts of Paris and its suburbs. His appeal was so successful, that new building expanded at a rate that exceeded any program ever devised by a metropolitan for his diocese. These new churches included, in Paris itself, Saint-Antoine-de-Padoue; the church in the Cité Universitaire in which Gruber set the earliest abstract stained-glass windows, and the church of the Saint-Esprit. The latter was designed by the architect Tournon and decorated by artists of the Ecole des Beaux-Arts and the Ateliers d'Art Sacré. The murals by Maurice Denis, Henri de Maistre and Pauline Peugniez, and the *Stations of the Cross* by Desvallières are fine examples of religious art of the period.

The Rue Mouffetard district**

5th arr./Map ref. 23–B2; 24–C2
Métro: Censier-Dubenton
Bus: 27, 47, 21, 83
Parking: Metro 4 Rue de Marché-des-Patriarches
Taxis: Place Monge. Tel. 45–87–15–95.
Place des Gobelins. Tel. 43–31–00–00.

The Place de la Contrescarpe opens out from the orderly, quiet surroundings of the Rue Descartes or the Rue de l'Estrapade into a different world. Steep, narrow, busy streets make the La Mouffe district seem like a little village in the middle of Paris. The intelligently restored old houses that line these little streets add to the unusual charm of the place. The combination of so many attractions has inevitably drawn lovers of the picturesque in droves, and it is hard to find an empty table on a summer evening on the terraces of the Greek restaurants that line the Rue Mouffetard. Of course there is something slightly bogus about the gaudy colors of the market stalls; not all the bare beams inside the houses are genuine and even the down-and-outs in the Place de la Contrescarpe seem like actors hired to give a touch of local color. However, despite the dubious authenticity, in the shadow of the Tour Clovis and the Panthéon a few winding streets and charming little squares still keep intact the true character of the Left Bank.

History of the district

The Bourg Saint-Médard, with its neighbor, Saint-Marcel, is one of the oldest within the confines of the capital. Documentary evidence for its existence goes back only to the 12th c., but it must have been there much earlier. In the days when Paris was 'in the country' this was an area of stone quarries, arable land, meadows, and vineyards, where a number of the rich and powerful had built their country residences in the 13th and 14th c. Among these huge feudal estates were the Séjour d'Orléans, which the Queen, Isabeau of Bavaria, gave to her brother-in-law Louis, Duc d'Orléans in 1402, the mansion belonging to Charles V's architect, Raymond du Temple, and the Maison des Patriarches. Lying within ½m./1km of Philippe Auguste's Wall, the medieval town came into the hand of the all-powerful Abbey of Sainte-Geneviève, and eventually the houses along the Rue Mouffetard joined up with those of the Bourg de Sainte-Geneviève within the city walls. From the 15th c. onward the large estates were broken up and parcels of land purchased for the most part by shopkeepers and craftsmen. Inns and shops, craft workshops and butchers' stalls crept into the district, giving it its busy working-class atmosphere. During the 17th and 18th c. what had been a country town now became part of the big city, absorbed by the suburbs to the S of Paris, under the name of the Faubourg Saint-Marcel. It was included within the city limits set by Louis XV in 1724 to stop the uncontrolled outward spread of Paris. During the 19th c. the district became even more working class, and even impoverished. Some of its small bars, the Quatre Sergents de la Rochelle, for example, or the Vieux-Chêne, became famous meeting places or rallying points for workers during the revolutions of the 19th c. Until a fairly recent date many of the unpretentious 16th-, 17th-and 18th-c. suburban houses, built of rubble stone, covered with roughcast plaster and half-timbered, had acquired a distinctly unhealthy look.

During the 1960s and 1970s urban renewal overtook this district, which, miraculously, had been spared by Baron Haussmann. Property developers were quick to recognize the attractiveness of the old-world village atmosphere of the district. All renovations are strictly controlled and must conform to the overall character of the area. Although this is now a district inhabited by the well-to-do, and the craftsmen have disappeared, the little food shops permanently occupy the whole lower end of the street, for they are its principal and officially recognized attraction.

Tour of the district

1½ hrs.

The Church of Saint-Médard**

141 Rue Mouffetard (8:30am–12:30pm/3pm–7:30pm, closed Mon.; Tel. 43-36-14-92)

This shrine stands at the point where the old Roman road to Lyon crossed the Bièvre, and its origins go back beyond the 9th c. The Flamboyant Gothic façade and nave of the present building were probably rebuilt during the latter half of the 15th c. The choir and chapels were added from 1560 to 1586 and there were further additions in the 17th c. The church belonged to the Abbey of Sainte-Geneviève, which administered it until the Revolution. During the persecution of the Jansenists, members of the sect found refuge in the parish of Saint-Médard and several, including Pierre Nicole (d. 1695), are buried in the church. In 1784 the architect Petit-Radet, in line with the then fashionable classical revival, transformed the chancel pillars into fluted Doric columns, as was done at Saint-Germain-l'Auxerrois and at Saint-Nicolas-des-Champs. In addition he built the large Chapelle de la Vierge at the E end of the church. In 1864 the houses that hemmed in the church were demolished, and the present square lies over part of the old cemetery. Its patron,

St Médard, advisor to the Merovingian kings of the 6th c., gave wreaths of roses to young girls known for their virtue.

The interior

Nave: organ case by Germain Pilon (1645); above it Christ descends from Heaven between two angels. The pulpit is dated 1718 and on its base are the names of the churchwardens who underwrote it.

R. side-aisle and its chapels: 1st chapel contains fragments of 16th-c. stained glass depicting Christ's descent into Limbo; above the altar is a 16th-c. triptych with a *Pietà*. 2nd chapel: on the l., *Pietà* by Gullemot (1819); on the r. a copy by Bona (1783) of Restout's *The Paralytic Healed at the Pool of Bethesda*.

Chancel: finished in the 17th c., it is wider and higher than the nave and its pillars were fluted and given Doric entablatures by Petit-Radet in 1784. Circuit of the chancel and its chapels starting from the r.: 1st chapel: *St Joseph walking with the Christ Child* by Zurbarán (17th c.); 2nd chapel, *Christ Entombed* after Philippe de Champaigne; 3rd chapel on the l., *The Annunciation with Six Prophets* (17th c.) and r., *St Cecilia* (17th c.); 5th chapel, the Chapelle de la Vierge (Chapel of Our Lady), by Petit-Radet 1784: on the r., *St Médard Crowning the first Rosière* (virtuous girl crowned with roses) by L. Dupre (1837) and, on the l., *The Marriage of the Virgin* by Caminade (1824); 6th chapel, *St Geneviève Reading while Tending her Sheep*, attributed to Charles Eisen (mid-18th c.); 7th chapel, *Religion* by Challe (18th c.).

L. side-aisle and its chapels: 1st chapel, *Christ Driving the Money-changers from the Temple*, painted by Natoire in Rome in 1728; vaulted roof decorated with heavily restored murals; 2nd chapel: *The Baptism of Christ* after Magnard above the altar; on the altar, a 17th-c. painted terracotta statue of St Denis.

Rue Mouffetard**

From the Church of Saint-Médard to the Rue Daubenton.

This is one of the oldest streets in Paris and was once a major thoroughfare. Originally a Gaulish track, it then became part of the great Roman road between Lutetia (Paris) and Rome via Sens and Lyon. This crossed the Bièvre over a bridge that originally ran from 4 Rue de Bazeilles to what is now the Place d'Italie. During the 17th and 18th c. it was known as the Grande-Rue-du-Faubourg-Saint-Marcel, which it crossed until the Ave. des Gobelins was built from 1868 to 1869 and cut it short. The part that remains and climbs the S slope of the Montagne Sainte-Geneviève has kept the original medieval layout of the plot of land and, although the houses on it have been altered over the years, they stand on the same foundations and have much of the overall appearance which they had then. Some small shops have very old painted signs. All the houses at the end of the street are old (nos. 135–117: no. 126, a house with a large dormer window is late 16th-c.) although they have sometimes been altered to suit the taste of the 17th and 18th c. No. 135 has a restored Louis XIII façade, and the houses opposite have mansard roofs; no. 134 is amusingly painted, and on the façade of no. 122 a very fine carved well is the street sign for *A la Bonne Eau*, altered to *A La Bonne Source* (at the sign of the clear spring).

In the Rue Daubenton (formerly Rue des Boulliers), just beyond the side entrance to Saint-Médardt no. 41, the remains of two bricked-up arched gateways can be traced, one of which led to the cemetery.

Place des Patriarches

In the square, a group of contemporary buildings with a classical flavor fills part of the site of the huge 14th-c. feudal mansion, the Maison du Partriarche (later, des Patriarches). In its list of owners in 1396 is the name of a high church dignitary, the Archbishop of Rheims and Patriarch of Alexandria. The mansion and its land gave way in 1830 to a covered market, then to a bathhouse that has become a municipal gymnasium.

Rue de l'Arbalète

On the l. of the Rue Mouffetard.

It is a surprise to be greeted by the exotic aromas and merchandise of the Village Africain. There are amusing bunches of grapes in stucco decorating the wall of the bar at the street corner which led to the now vanished 17th- and 18th-c. convents of the Sisters of Divine Providence and the Sisters of Silence. Nos. 9–21 are built on the site of the Apothecaries' Garden, the forerunner of the Jardin des Plantes, where medicinal plants and herbs were grown in the 16th c. Michelet lived in this street, and Seurat had a studio here. In 1840 Rodin was born at no. 3.

Rue Mouffetard, continued

From the Rue de l'Arbalète to the Rue du Pot-de-Fer.

Continue up the Rue Mouffetard passing a succession of houses whose structures are very old, though some were renovated or had storeys added in the 17th and 18th c. (nos. 114–112, 106–102, 94–82, for example), alternating with later buildings (nos. 100–96). The gateway of no. 81 is surmounted by a triangular pediment (doubtless the remains of a 17th-c. chapel); it leads into courtyard with a tall gabled house. Nos. 74–76 are the municipal library specializing in detective fiction. At no. 73 a modern alley leads through to the Rue Gracieuse and houses the 5th arrondissement cultural center. The entrance to the vast d'Albiac estate is believed to have stood in this vicinity in the 15th c. No. 69 is the Maison du Vieux-Chêne, a revolutionary club in 1848 and subsequently a dance hall. The oak tree in relief on its street sign is one of the few carved wood examples still left in Paris (another is at the Arbre à Liege, Rue Tiquetonne). No. 61 is the barracks of the Garde Républicaine, built in 1840 on the site of the Convent of the Sisters of Mercy founded in the 17th c. Opposite, on the corner of the Rue-de-Fer is the 'Iron Pot' fountain, one of the 14 fountains that Marie de'Medici had built on the Left Bank in 1624, fed by an aqueduct that replaced the Gallo-Roman Arceuil aqueduct, and was intended to bring water to the Luxembourg Palace. It was rebuilt in 1671 to a design by Le Vau.

Rue du Pot-de-Fer*

On the r.

Once a cart track through the vineyards, this is an attractive little street, with restaurants spilling their tables out onto the pavements. No. 1 is a gabled house; no. 7 has a pretty 18th-c. doorway.

Rue Mouffetard, continued

From the Rue du Pot-de-Fer to the Place de la Contrescarpe.

Return along the Rue Mouffetard and pass no. 53, remembering the fantastic treasure discovered here in 1938 when the old house was demolished. It consisted of 3350 *louis d'or* ($4.25/£2.5 million today). This was divided between the traceable descendants of the original owner of the hoard, Louis Nivelle, a lawyer in the 18th-c. Paris Parlement; the Paris municipal authorities who owned the site on which the gold was found; and the workmen who found it. No. 36 was once part of the barracks of the Gardes Françaises (→Rue Tournefort, nos. 7–11). At the Place de la Contrescarpe there is another painted street sign, Au Nègre Joyeux, at no. 11.

Place de la Contrescarpe*

The *place* takes its name from the backfilling from the moat dug outside Philippe Auguste's wall, altered under Charles V, which follows the Rue de l'Estrapade, Rue Blainville and Rue du Cardinal-Lemoine. The square was laid out in 1852, formed by the demolition of some old houses. It is far removed from the crossroads that once stood outside the city walls. It has always been, and remains, a place for meetings and festivities. The shady trees and the old façades seem to retain a charm born of all these festivities. No. 1 has a tablet commemorating the old 'Cabaret de la Pomme-de-Pin' (Pinecone Cabaret), which actually stood opposite, immortalized by Rabelais, where members of the original Pléiade met in the 16th c., among them, Ronsard, Baïf and du Bellay. Not far away on the r. at

50 Rue Lacépéde stands a contemporary building housing a child care center and public showers, built in a style blending traditional and modern elements.

Rue Rollin

Before proceeding down the Rue du Cardinal-Lemoine to the N, turn off to the r. into the provincial, literary world of the Rue Rollin, the end of which, cut off by the creation of the Rue Monge, seems to be suspended in space. The street is lined with old houses, mostly restored, some with very fine doorways. No. 2 vies with 67 Rue du Cardinal-Lemoine for the honor of being the house in which Pascal died: Bernardin de Saint-Pierre lived at no. 4, where he wrote *Paul et Virginie*. Emile Zola lived here in 1860, the philosopher Descartes always stayed at no. 14 when he came to Paris.

Rue du Cardinal-Lemoine

Originally known as the Rue des Fossés-Saint-Victor, this street, in the Middle Ages, as the name implies, was the track that followed the moat below the city walls down to the Seine and became a street only in 1684 when the moat was filled.

The old paved alleyway of no. 75 leads to a pretty Directoire house* with its two main sections facing one another across a square of grass. This stands on the site of the house that belonged to the congregation of the Pères de la Doctrine (Fathers of the Christian Doctrine), founded in the 17th c. No. 71 is the house to which the writer Valéry Larbaud moved in 1920. No. 65 is the former Collège des Ecossais (Scottish College); this district was full of colleges and foundations that housed students during the Middle Ages. Some were established by foreign benefactors for their compatriots, like the Scottish College, founded in 1326 by David, Bishop of Moray, in the heart of the University quarter and later moved here in the 17th c. The present building, erected from 1662 to 1667, had to be shored up a year later when the level of the street was lowered to a gentle downward slope. A new gateway was built below the original entrance, which was then turned into a window, hence the unusual arrangement of an entrance right in the middle of this severe classical façade. It has always belonged to English Catholics; the current tenants are Dominican nuns, who continue the educational tradition with a students' hostel for girls and a primary school. Through the entrance you can glimpse a beautiful staircase with oak banisters, but the five-bay chapel which contains a huge 17th-c. altarpiece is closed to the general public (visits available by arrangement through the Caisse Nationale des Monuments Historiques).

For remainder of the Rue du Cardinal-Lemoine →Jardin des Plantes district.

Rue Clovis

Turn l. into the Rue Clovis to find yourself in the part built in 1809 on the site of the chapel of the Collège de Boncourt. The coat of arms set on the façade of no. 1 – a lion passant* gardant (with head facing the viewer, body in profile, with one foreleg raised) on a shield surrounded by Scottish thistles – reminds us that his land was given by the City of Paris to the Scottish College. The ivy-covered wall at no. 3 is a surviving section of Philippe-Auguste's city wall*. Enter the courtyard of no. 7 to see a substantial portion of it, interesting not for its beauty, but because it reminds us that the city once ended here.

For the N and W continuation of the Rue Clovis → the district of Montagne Sainte-Geneviève.

In the Rue Descartes on the l. you are once more standing on part of the great Roman road which linked Lutetia (Paris) with Rome. Early in the 20th c. sarcophagi from the Merovingian cemetery of Saint-Peter-Saint-Paul were unearthed at no. 31. No. 36 is the Lycée Henri-IV, while no. 45 is a gabled house.

Passing the Rue Thouin, note that in the 17th c. there was a tennis court where nos. 2–6 now stand, while no. 10 *bis* is the Armenian church, opposite a small contemporary building at no. 7. Return briefly to the Rue Mouffetard where there is another street sign from a butcher's shop at no. 6, a bas-relief of a bull (18th c.), probably one of a pair of which the other has been lost.

Turn r. into the Rue Blainville. Formerly a cart-track running around the outside of the moat, it now climbs towards an intersection where a shady garden has recently been laid out. There are old houses on either side of the street. No. 5 has fine wrought ironwork.

Rue de l'Estrapade

This street is a continuation of the Rue Blainville. During the 17th c., as in the Rue Thouin running alongside the old city walls, you would have found two tennis courts, Monplaisir, on the site of nos. 3–7, and Le Grand Braque, a little further on. In 1749 Diderot was arrested at no. 3 and imprisoned in the keep of Vincennes castle for the undisguised atheism of his *Lettre sur les Aveugles*. Nos. 5–7 is a fine 18th-c. mansion. No 9 is an old house with a tiled roof that still has the amusing cut-out metal sign (*ca.*1914) of the coffee-roaster who occupied the building at the beginning of the century. No. 11 is the 18th-c. house in which the pamphleteer Paul Louis Courier (1772–1825) lived.

For the remainder of the Rue de l'Estrapade and the Place de L'Estrapade → the Montagne Sainte-Geneviève district.

Take the Rue Laromiguière (on the l.), on the even-numbered side of the street to see a group of old houses that have been carefully restored; the range of color in their plasterwork makes a pretty effect. Once known as the Rue des Poules, in the 17th c. it led to the cemetery (on the site of no. 11, and of no. 8 Rue Amyot) granted to the Protestants under the Edict of Nantes (1598) and deconsecrated when the Edict was revoked in 1685.

Rue Amyot (once called Rue du Puits-qui-Parle, or Talking Well Street, after a well with a famous echo). At no. 11 there is a delightful old pavilion in a garden, but unfortunately it can hardly be seen from outside. Turn back towards the Rue Tournefort and get a clear view of the rear of the turreted house that stands on the street corner and also of no. 15.

Rue Tournefort

Turn sharp l. down the Rue Tournefort to pass the site of what was once the barracks of the Gardes Françaises (nos. 7 and 11, running right back to the Rue Mouffetard). This was built in 1775 to end the system of billeting soldiers with the inhabitants. Opposite there used to stand yet another tennis court, La Mort-qui-Trompe. In 1978 the whole district became the object of a vast restoration project. Nos. 16 and 18 formed part of what was once the Community of Saint-Aure (18th c.) which then occupied the entire block as far as the Rue Lhomond. It began life as a sort of reformatory and then became a boarding-school for girls of poor families; the future Comtesse du Barry, Jeanne Bécu, was among its pupils. The buildings have now been converted to luxury apartments, but the garden side of the house, unfortunately inaccessible to the public, preserved its fine Baroque façade. The chapel attached to the school as well as the massive Church of Christ-Roi erected by Astruc from 1935 to 1940 have both disappeared. On the fine building at the corner of this street and the Rue du Pot-de-Fer, the curved cornerstone is incised on both sides with their former names. Rue du Pot-de-Fer is the same, but the Rue Tournefort was originally called Rue Neuve-Sainte-Geneviève, and there it is, carved, but with the word 'Sainte' scratched out during the Revolution. Balzac locates the Pension Vauquier in his novel Le Père Goriot (1819) a little further down the street. No. 25 has a plaque indicating that Mérimée lived there in 1820.

Place Lucien-Herr

This square forms the frontier between the popular tourist-area of the Rue Mouffetard and the intellectual and residential district of Val-de-Grâce. With your back to the Rue Jean-Calvin (fortunately its construction was halted before it cut right through the Rue Mouffetard) you will see an interesting contemporary fountain (Bernadette Gourner, 1982) below the unusual and picturesque projecting front of a small terraced restaurant.

Follow the Rue Lhomond (→Val-de-Grâce district) for a minute and turn l. down the ancient Passage des Postes* to come out again in the Rue Mouffetard opposite the Passage des Patriarches.

▷ The Miracles of St Médard

For more than five years a strange phenomenon was observed around the tomb of the deacon François Pâris in the little parish cemetery of Saint-Médard. Pâris, a fervent Jansenist who had lived an exemplary life devoted to asceticism and charity, died in 1727, and was venerated by the local inhabitants as a saint. At a time when the Jansenists were being persecuted, his grave became a shrine for oppressed Jansenists and the focus for a cult that quickly assumed bizarre forms. There were miraculous cures, real or imaginary, arousing intense excitement, which soon gave way to a variety of trances, visions and convulsive fits. The peaceful little graveyard became the scene of masochistic frenzy and mass hysteria. More and more people became infected by this madness until the authorities felt compelled to put a stop to it. Veneration of Deacon Pâris was forbidden and the cemetery was closed one day in 1732. The following day this anonymous and ironic epigram was pinned to the gates: 'In the King's name, God is forbidden to perform miracles in this place'. This was not enough to put a stop to the ecstasies of these Jansenists fanatics or *convulsionnaires* – they simply went underground and continued to haunt the district until 1762.

▷ What's in a name?

The name, Rue Mouffetard, is very familiar to Parisians, but few know its derivation, for which two very different etymologies have been claimed. The most generally accepted and amusing claims that 'Mouffetard' is derived from the word *mofette* related to the French name for the skunk, *la mouffette*, supposedly used to describe the sickening stench emanating from the River Bièvre, polluted as it was by butchers and skinners. These tradesmen had established themselves in the Saint-Médard district round the Pont-aux-Tripes in the early 14th c., and were soon followed by tanners and dyers who used the river water to wash out the guts of the slaughtered animals. The second, more scholarly derivation, which would appear more likely since it is supported by old documents, attributes the name to the linguistic corruption over the centuries of the name of the hill which the street climbed over or skirted in the 13th c., from the Latin *Mons Cetardus*, through Mont Cétard, Montfétard, Moufftard, to Mouffetard.

▷ Old Paris street signs

Until street numbers appeared in 1805, the only way of indicating or finding a house was by means of a sign. Although they must have existed well before 1200, this is the first date for which there is concrete evidence for their use in Paris. Rare in the 13th c., they became more widespread in the 14th and especially the 15th c., and thereafter came into general use, not only for business premises, but also for private houses. They were of many different sizes and materials – carved wood, stone bas-reliefs, wrought metalwork, terracotta – but always brightly painted and in countless shapes. In addition to the traditional representation of the tools of a particular trade or goods sold by the individual vendor, religious imagery was also common, such as the Three Wise Men, or a patron saint often displayed as a statue within an arched recess. There were also many animal or vegetable subjects such as The Crown and Lion or The Golden Apples; the stars provided such themes as The Golden Crescent; from myth and fable would come, for example, The Siren, while other signs might be based on puns and riddles. Shop signs were often hung on an iron pole suspended from a bracket, but as commercial competition grew fiercer the signs grew larger and heavier, noisier in the wind and a source of peril to the passerby, until in 1761 they were banned by Sartines, the chief of police. Thereafter there was a rash of signboards painted and nailed to the walls of houses and shops, one of the most famous of them being the shop sign that Watteau painted for Gersaint: *L'enseigne de Gersaint* (1720, Berlin, Charlottenburg), an illustration of the quarrel between the ancients and the moderns.

Nowadays houses use a different language to identity themselves, but some of the old signs are still to be seen and the Musée Carnavalet has preserved plenty of fine examples.

> The Hôtel des Patriarches and the Saint-Médard riot

The 16th-c. owner of the Hôtel des Patriarches was a Calvinist sympathizer who rented one wing of the mansion to followers of the reformed religion to use as a place of worship. It was one of the two Protestant churches within the suburbs of Paris to whose existence the Queen, Catherine de'Medici, turned a blind eye. It was here that the first blood of the Wars of Religion was shed in Paris, when Protestants who had gathered to hear a sermon clashed with Catholics who were ringing the bells for vespers at the nearby Church of Saint-Médard. Thus December 27, 1561 became known as the day of the Saint-Médard riot. Mutual provocation, intolerance and fanaticism inevitably caused collision between two communities separated only by the width of a street and a garden. The clash was violent, with dead on both sides, and when the Protestants sacked the Catholic church, the Catholics retaliated the following day by burning down the Protestant chapel. A few months later the Massacre of Vassy took place and brought to an end the policy of religious toleration attempted by Catherine de'Medici. The terrible Wars of Religion were unleashed.

▷ Avoiding the crowds

The two busiest times and places: the market place during the day, and the restaurants in the evenings.

Market: at the end of the Rue Mouffetard and the immediate vicinity. During market hours (Tues.–Sat. 9am–1pm, 4pm–7:30pm; Sun. 9am–1pm) the area becomes a semi-pedestrian precinct from which cars are banned.

Restaurants: a number of Greek restaurants are concentrated at the top of the Rue Mouffetard and around the Place de la Contrescarpe; they become very crowded and lively on summer evenings.

For guided tours consult the program of the Caisse Nationale des Monuments Historiques, 62 Rue Saint-Antoine, tel. 42-78-73-81. Concerts are held in the Church of Saint-Médard, especially during the autumn festivals of the 5th arrondissement.

Best advice: of course you should visit on a market day to enjoy the merchants' beautiful displays, but avoid the late-morning crush on Sat. and Sun.

La Nation district

12th arr.
Métro and RER: Nation
Bus: 56, 86
Parking: 75 Boul. de Picpus; Cours de Vincennes between the B. de
Charonne and the Rue des Pyrénées
Taxis: 1 Ave. du Trône. Tel. 43–73–29–58

The Cours de Vincennes probably has more statues and monuments than any other great street on the E side of Paris. The long perspective framed by Ledoux' two columns supporting statues of St Louis and Philippe Auguste offers a panorama of Paris with the symbolic profile of the Eiffel Tower rising in the background. The Place de la Nation itself is an important traffic circle, spacious but rather bland, from which the main thoroughfares to the E of the capital radiate. Dwarfed by the size of the square, Dalou's colossal symbolic bronze group *The Triumph of the Republic* seems unable either to fill the space assigned to it or to overawe the acrimonious post-mortems on their shots conducted behind it by the *boules* players.

During the Revolution the square was far less pleasant. No fewer than 1306 victims of the Terror were guillotined here and their memory still lingers close by in the pastoral atmosphere of the Picpus cemetery, a private burial ground for emigrés. Although there are no outstanding monuments in the vicinity of the Place de la Nation, there are still many interesting examples of 19th- and 20th-c. architecture, such as the notable Church of the Saint-Esprit.

Tour of the eastern section

From the Place de la Nation to the Porte de Vincennes.
45 mins.

Place de la Nation

This traffic circle over 900 ft/250m in diameter, forms a triumphal entrance to Paris. It was once known as the Place du Trône, named after the dais or 'throne' that was put up for the triumphal entry into Paris of Louis XIV and his bride the Infanta Maria Theresa on August 25 and 26, 1660. From 1793 to 1880 it was known as the Place du Trône-Renversé (Overturned Throne Square) and the guillotine was erected here when the inhabitants of the Rue Saint-Honoré grew tired of the sight of the passing tumbrils. (From 25 Prairial [June 13] – 9 Thermidor [July 27] in Year II of the Republic [1794], 1306 victims, and probably more, including André Chénier, were guillotined.) The square took its present name on July 14, 1880.

It is embellished by Dalou's monumental bronze group, *The Triumph of the Republic**. This important sculpture was designed for the Place de la République, but the judging panel turned it down and it had to wait 20 years before it found its final, but illegal, resting place in 1899 in the Place de la Nation. To the E, and framing the Ave. du Trône, stand the two pavilions, each surmounted by a Doric column (100 ft/30.50m high) which were built as tollgates by Ledoux in 1788 as part of the Fermiers-Généraux' city wall, and the sole surviving remains of the Barrière de Vincennes. During the reign of Louis-Philippe the columns were crowned by statues of Philippe Auguste and St Louis by Etex and Dumont.

The Cours de Vincennes

The spacious Cours de Vincennes is the main thoroughfare of a district that was developed from 1930 to 1960. It provides a pleasant stroll for lovers of 19th- and 20th-c. architecture and is particularly busy on market days.

To the l. at the entrance to the Rue des Pyrénées, the Church of Saint-Gabriel built by Murcier in 1937 and decorated with paintings by A. H. Lemaître (1942). The Lycée Hélène Boucher (architect, L. Sallex, 1938) is named after the heroic woman pilot 'killed on the field of honor in the sky' in 1934: its entrance hall is decorated with paintings by Sigrist. No. 89 is the Lycée Maurice-Ravel, while nos. 84 and 86, opposite, house the Ateliers Bricard (architect, Alexandre Borgeaud, 1902–04). On the same level with no. 101 stands the railway bridge erected in 1888 as part of the Petite Ceinture (inner circle) to link all the other lines together.

The Cours de Vincennes now reaches the Porte de Vincennes. The Rue Marsoulan on the l.-hand side of the Cours de Vincennes leads to the Square Courteline where a bust of Georges Courteline by Benneteau (1935), is a reminder that the novelist and playwright lived in the vicinity from 1907 to 1923 at 43 Ave. Saint-Mandé (commemorative plaque). Follow the Ave. de Saint-Mandé to the W. The Ave. du Bel-Air on the r. leads back to the Place de la Nation.

Tour of the southern section

From the Place de la Nation to the Avenue Daumesnil.
1 hr.

Go along Boul. Voltaire. The Rue des Immeubles-Industriels (first l.) built by Emile Leménil (1872-73) provides a Parisian example of workers' housing conceived according to the principles of the phalanstery of Charles Fourier (1772-1837). Turn r. into the Rue du Faubourg-Saint-Antoine and take the first street on your l.

Rue de Picpus

The original name may have been Rue Pique-Puce (Fleabite Street), but the derivation is uncertain. Like many Paris streets today, it has two faces: the modest houses, craftsmen's workshops, convents, impoverished old people's homes and orphanages cannot hide the major upheavals that have changed the district. In the 16th c. it was a road through the fields of Picpus; later it led to the religious houses established in these rustic surroundings; now it runs beneath massive skyscrapers. At the end of the Rue Picpus, on the l. note the buildings of the Institution Eugénie Napoléon with its entrance at 254 Rue du Faubourg-Saint-Antoine. Hittorff built it in 1857 for the educational establishment founded by the Empress Eugénie. Ninon de l'Enclos owned a country house where no. 12 now stands. At the junction with the Rue Fabre-d'Eglantine a tall circular building houses the headquarters of the French forestry commission, the Office National des Forêts, with the Centre Technique du Bois behind it.

The Picpus Cemetery*

Open daily except Mon. 2-6 pm (Oct. 15-Apr. 16, 2-4 pm).
Tel. 43-44-18-54.

Open the tall gate of no. 35, and step straight into the 18th c., for this was once the Community of the Canonesses of St Augustine, and now shelters the 'graveyard of the nobility' situated at the end of a roughly paved courtyard. Installed at Picpus in 1647 by Cardinal de Retz and President Tubeuf, the convent was suppressed and appropriated by the State in 1790. In 1805 it was revived by the

Sisters of the Perpetual Adoration of the Sacred Heart. They are still there and their convent includes an old people's home. The Chapel of the Adoration on the r. contains a much-venerated dark wood statue of Our Lady of Peace, originally from the Capuchin convent in Rue Saint-Honoré. It stands over the altar behind which there is a list of the names of the 1298 (actually 1306) people guillotined at the Barrière du Trône. Enter the gardens with their sycamores and ash trees, vegetable and flowerbeds and fruit trees, their paths where you will pass silent nuns dressed all in white with their lace wimples, and Paris seems a million miles away. At the end to the l. (NE corner), you can see the lintel over what was the hole in the wall through which the tumbrils came; nearby are traces of the third common grave, dug, but never used, and the site of the grotto in which the bodies of the guillotined were stripped.

The cemetery contains the tombs of the victims' families: La Fayette, Montalembert, Chateaubriand, Crillon, Gontaut-Biron, Quélen, Choiseul, La Rochefoucauld, Montmorency, Rohan, Noailles, Tuscher de la Pagerie, Salignac-Fénelon, and others, as well as the grave of the historian Théodore Gosselin, who wrote under the name of Georges Lenotre (d. 1934), with a memorial by P. Sardou. In a peaceful grassy corner at the far end stands the tomb of the Salm-Kyrbourg family, whose descendant, the Prince de Salm, originally bought the plot where the noble victims' bodies had been thrown. It was here in 1929 that two common graves were discovered containing the remains of the victims of the guillotine, among them André Chénier and the 16 Carmelite nuns from Compiègne, martyred on July 17, 1794.

When you come out into the Rue Picpus, where Mlle Clairon, the famous 18th-c. tragedienne, had her country house (at no. 82), you will see an old people's home, an orphanage and, on the corner of the Rue Senterre, the Hôpital Rothschild. Cross the Boul. de Reuilly and continue along the Rue Picpus. Take the Rue Sidi-Brahim (1st r.), which comes out into the Ave. Daumesnil opposite the Church of the Saint-Esprit.

✝ The Church of the Saint-Esprit

Open daily 8 am–noon and 3–7.30 pm. Tel. 43–07–52–84.

Erected from 1928 to 1935, this church is a veritable manifesto in stone of inter-war religious art. The architect Tournon used reinforced concrete with an external brick facing; the plan is based closely on that of Santa Sophia at Constantinople (Istanbul). Religious architecture has here returned to its Byzantine roots, yet to this archaic design, the architect adapted the most up-to-date techniques of his day.

The exterior is faced with cut Burgundy bricks, except for the domes on which the concrete is left bare. The buttresses are crowned with pinnacles. The 12 months of the year are carved in bas-relief by L. Gibert, Guignier and Muzinger.

An imposing flight of steps leads to the circular narthex, surrounded by seven blind arches decorated with the Unterstellers' monochrome frescoes of the *Creation*. The narthex gives on to the crypt and baptistery.

The crypt (wrought iron gate by Raymond Subes) is over 108 ft/33 m wide and nearly 89 ft/27 m long, with room for 1500 worshippers. Two of the four pillars supporting the dome divide it into three naves. Despite the statues of Our Lady of Peace and St Joseph, and Sarrabezolles' carved decorations, the overall impression is austere. Marcel Imbs designed the stained glass which was executed by Douzier.

The interior of the church itself is imposing. The decorations (walls and pillars) evoke the Church Militant, those of the dome the Church Triumphant. The concrete is covered with Venetian enamel mosaics designed by Marcel Imbs and executed by Gaudin. The pillars bear the emblems of the religious orders. On the surrounding walls compositions tell the story of the spreading of the Gospel throughout the world. Nearly 30 artists were assembled to create these murals. The most outstanding part is the apse, with Maurice Denis's *Pentecost* (1934) showing the descent of the Holy Ghost upon the apostles reunited around Our Lady in the Upper Room; then St Paul with the Fathers of the Greek Church with the Church of Santa Sophia in Constantinople, and the Fathers of the Holy Roman Church, with the basilica of St Peter at Rome; on the lower half of the walls are the *Seven Sacraments*. To follow this evangelical epic on the outer walls, start at the Martyrs' Chapel (l. of the apse), proceed as far as the Confessors' Chapel and come back up the r. side-aisle via the Virgin's Chapel and the Chapel of Labour. On the lower halves of the walls of these side-aisles are Stations of the Cross by Georges Desvallières. The stained glass in the upper lights is very clear and becomes more opaque lower down. It is by Barillet and Hébert-Stevens in the 1st chapel. The chancel is completely faced in multi-colored marble and surrounded by gilded rails designed by Chéret. There is a marble ciborium (vessel for the consecrated host) over the high altar which is decorated with Dunand's gilded reredos depicting the *Vision of the Lamb* from the book of Revelation.

Place Félix-Eboué*

via the Ave. Daumesnil

In the center of the Place stands Davioud's fountain, originally set in 1862, in the Place du Château-d'Eau, or what is now the Place de la République. It was replaced there by the statue of the Republic, and set up here. Proceed along the Ave. Daumesnil to reach the town hall of the 12th arrondissement built from 1874 to 1877 by Hénard. Inside, the ground staircase is decorated with paintings by E. Thirion that have as their theme the trades and industries of the 12th arrondissement.

Rue de Reuilly

This street begins in the Place Félix-Eboué (named after a governor of Chad, a Gaullist) and walking along it you pass no. 77, the Convent of La Providence-Sainte-Marie. The heart of St Catherine Labouré, a Sister of Charity canonized in 1947, who spent 46 years here (1830–76), is preserved in the chapel. Opposite, the new Church of Saint-Eloi has been erected in the heart of a block of houses under restoration. This brick and iron structure is dominated by a beacon nearly 120 ft/35m tall (architect, Marc Leboucher 1966–67). No. 57, the Ecole Boulle 1895, a trade school for the furniture industry, lies at the end of a blind alley (architect, Mussigmann, 1889–92). No. 36 is the old Church of Saint-Eloi (1856), partly rebuilt in 1880. The barracks at no. 20. are on the site of the Royal mirror factory, founded in 1634 and moved to Saint-Gobain in 1840. No. 9 is the site of Citizen Santerre's brewery; he lived from 1752 to 1809 and, in 1793, was General of the Parisian Garden Nationale and governor of the Temple prison during the imprisonment of the French Royal Family.

▷ **The Gingerbread Fair**

The Place de la Nation was the site of a gingerbread fair, also known as the Foire du Trône, which was first held over a thousand years ago. In 957 the neighborhood was afflicted by a terrible famine, and the monks of the Abbey of Saint-Antoine gave the starving villagers of Pique-Puce little piglet-shaped cakes of rye flour, aniseed and honey (piglet-shaped for St. Antony's emblem), in honor of their patron, St Antony the Hermit, who was fed on milk and honey in the desert of the Thebaid in the 3rd c. Until the 17th c. the Abbey of Saint-Antoine-des-Champs retained the privilege of selling these little cakes during Easter Week. However, it was not until 1719 that a regular annual fair came into being, held in the abbey enclosure. In addition to the usual itinerant merchants, the fair attracted increasing numbers of mountebanks. During the 19th c. the Gingerbread Fair took over the Place du Trône, later to be known as the Place de la Nation. It then expanded considerably, filling the neighboring streets for several weeks. By 1880 the number of stall-holders had risen to 2424. Since 1965 the Foire du Trône has settled at the entrance to the Bois de Vincennes, on an open site of nearly 25 acres/10 ha, the Pelouse de Reuilly. It is the largest fair of its kind in France, and during April and May each year it attracts more than 5 million visitors.

Markets

Cours de Vincennes, between the Boul. de Picpus and Boul. Arnold-Netter: Wed. and Sat., 7.30 am–1.30 pm.

Boul. Rue de Reuilly, between the Rue de Charenton and the Place Félix-Eboué: Tues. and Fri., 7.30 am–11.30 pm.

Boul. Poniatowski (odd numbered side): between the Ave. Daumesnil and the Rue de Picpus, Thurs. and Sun., 7 a.m.–11.30 pm.

Museum to visit

Musée des Arts Africains et Océaniens (293 Ave. Daumesnil): works of art, artifacts and figurative art from Africa and the Pacific.

Notre-Dame***

1st arr./Map ref. 17–B2, B–3
Métro: Cité
Bus: 21, 47, 85, 96

The cathedral of cathedrals, 'the parish church of French history', stands tall on the SE tip of the Ile de la Cité.

The history of Notre-Dame

In 1160 Maurice de Sully, Bishop of Paris, undertook to erect a single great and imposing building to replace the churches of Notre-Dame and Saint-Etienne. Work began in 1163 during the reign of Louis VII, and continued until 1334.

The first stage (1163–82) saw the completion of the choir except for the roof, its double side-aisles and galleries, and the E wall of the transept. Sculptors started work on the doorways in the façade, and the high altar was consecrated on May 19, 1196. The second stage (1180–1200) saw the erection of the W wall and the W piers of the transept, the last three double bays of the nave (with the bays of the two side-aisles) the sanctuary, ambulatory and the galleries. In the third stage (1190–1220) the two rectangular towers were begun and the linking bay of the nave; the W. front was erected up to the level of the rose window, which was added from 1220 to 1225, and the foundations for the first double bay of the nave were laid; the nave itself was built (with the neighboring bays of the side-aisles and the galleries) from 1210 to 1220. The fourth and last stage saw the S tower (1225–40) and the N tower and the lofty gallery between the two, completed (1235–50).

Masterbuilders of genius

Nobody knows the names of the earliest architects who built the cathedral under Maurice de Sully and Eudes de Sully, bishop from 1197 to 1208 (no relation to the former). During the 13th and early 14th c. the church was added to and slightly modified. Already the roofing had been replaced; from 1225 to 1235 the upper portions were altered to increase the national light of the clerestory by enlarging the windows and lowering the level of the rose windows. Finally, as the pious donations increased, more chapels were needed (the church was first conceived with no chapels). The arms of the transept had to be lengthened (N *ca*. 1250; S in 1258). The master mason Jean de Chelles had begun the façade of the N transept in 1250. He was succeeded around 1265 by the great builder Pierre de Montreuil (d. 1267) who began the façade of the S transept in 1258 before completing the arms of the transept, the chapels and the Red Door, and began replacing the flying buttresses of the chancel. Pierre de Chelles built the rood screen from 1300 to 1318 and in 1296 began the chapels at the E end, which Jean Ravy was to continue as master of works from 1318 to 1344. Jean Ravy completed the chapels radiating out to the N and raised the bold flying buttresses of the apse with their 50-ft./15m. span. These are the same buttresses which are so breathtaking today. His nephew, Jean le Bouteiller, took over from him until 1363 when Raymond du Temple, his deputy since 1359, became solely responsible for directing construction.

The desecration of a masterpiece

For three centuries despite changes in taste, this Gothic masterpiece was left untouched. Adversity struck at the end of the 17th c. when Louis XIII had Robert de Cotte demolish the rood screen, the choir stalls, the bas-reliefs of the choir-screen, the high altar and many tombs, to fulfil a vow he had made that entailed the redecoration of the chancel. During the 18th c. the canons replaced the stained glass with clear glass and whitewashed the walls. In 1771 Soufflot demolished the pier and part of the tympanum of the central Porte de Jugement, thus ruining it, simply to allow the processional dais to pass through.

There remained only the Revolution, when the Kings of Judah on the W facade, which the mob believed were statues of the kings of France, were destroyed in 1793 and replaced by copies in the 19th c. They were to turn up again, very mutilated, and fragments are now in the Musée de Cluny (→Museums). All the great statues above the doorways were prised out, too, except the Virgin and Child (Notre Dame de Paris) above the cloister door (Porte du Cloître); the cathedral itself was looted and the Goddess of Reason in the person of Mlle Maillard, enthroned on the high altar.

A poet and an architect

All that remained of the masterpiece was its skeleton, and in places that was crumbling. Victor Hugo's novel of 1831, *Notre Dame de Paris* (*The Hunchback of Notre-Dame*), his personal expression of the Gothic Revival, started a movement which culminated, in 1844, in the decree by which Louis-Philippe ordered the restoration of the cathedral. The task was entrusted to Lassus and, after his death in 1857, to Viollet-le-Duc (d. 1878), on whom the major burden of the restoration fell. He accomplished it by a remarkable combination of knowledge, skill and daring (→inset) for which he is still criticized.

Today the cathedral is again being restored. The nave is being completely cleaned, the chapels will be properly lit, and the paintings are gradually being restored.

The influence of Notre-Dame

It is hard to exaggerate the importance of Notre-Dame in architectural terms. It was the first Gothic church to surpass Cluny. The cathedral is the last of the great galleried churches springing from Saint-Denis and the Anglo-Norman cathedrals of Noyon, Senlis and above all of Laon, and the first to use flying buttresses. In Notre-Dame this tradition flowers with a unique breadth and perfection, which overshadows all other religious architecture of the Ile de France by its harmony and its balance of strength and finesse. The art of Jean de Chelles and Pierre de Montreuil, whose influence spread to the Neckar and beyond, to Uppsala in Sweden (where the cathedral was built by Estienne de Bonneuil, a journeyman stone-mason, who left his work at Notre-Dame for that purpose) shows the classically harmonious Gothic art at its best. The influence on music exercised by the cathedral towards the end of the 12th and during the 13th c. is a point generally overlooked. The School of Notre-Dame-de-Paris, with its masters, Léonin (or Leoninus, composer of *organa*) and Pérotin (or Perotimus Magnus, writer of liturgical works), both of whom worked at Notre-Dame, led the polyphonic movement and took it to heights previously undreamed of.

Tour of the exterior

The layout of Notre-Dame is utterly simple, grand and harmonious and has been described by Marcel Aubert as 'a long nave leading to the choir, enclosed by double side-aisles, divided almost halfway along its length by a wide transept barely projecting beyond the outer walls, the whole held in place and supported by buttresses'.

Numerically its dimensions express perfect harmony. Notre-Dame is just over 343ft/35m from floor to the vaults; the same in width; the towers are 226ft./69m high; the surface area is 59,200sq.ft./5500m² over all and 976 sq.yds/816m² between the fulcra of the building. Viollet-le-Duc calculated that the cathedral could hold about 9000 people, including 1500 in the galleries.

The W façade

Overlooking the parvis.

It is tempting to believe that the church must have been conceived all at once and by one architect, so perfect is its uniformity and grandeur. It is dominated by two great rectangular towers just over 226ft/69m high, on three levels harmoniously proportioned and clearly distinguished one from another.

The portals

In the center is the Portail du Jugement (Portal of the Last Judgement), nearly 23ft/7m high. The original dates from around 1220, but most of the portal was restored in the 19th c. On a trumeau (pillar) supporting the middle of the tympanum is a huge statue of Christ teaching (1885). The six archivolts (above the tympanum) show the Heavenly Court. In the tympanum (ruined by Sufflot when he breached it) is the Last Judgement. Viollet-le-Duc restored the two lower lintels; below is the Resurrection, and above the Weighing of the Souls (by St Michael); the elite are led to heaven by angels and the damned to hell by demons. The Wise and Foolish Virgins (respectively opening and closing the doors to Paradise), carved in exquisite detail on the piers on the outer sides of the double doors, are modern. In the embrasures on either side of the piers the Apostles, by Viollet-le-Duc, stand above medallions in bas-relief, showing the Virtues (upper row) and the Vices (lower row).

The Porte de la Vierge or Portal of the Virgin (on the l. facing the cathedral), is some years older than the Last Judgement Door (c. 1210) and its composition is remarkable. On the trumeau stands a statue of the Virgin and Child trampling the Serpent underfoot (modern). The lower part of the beautiful tympanum shows, below, the Ark of the Covenant, three kings and three prophets; above, the Dormition of the Virgin with Christ and the Apostles and, at the apex, the Coronation of the Virgin (early 13th c.) showing Christ handing a sceptre to His Mother. On the arch above the tympanum, are figures of prophets, kings, patriarchs and angels framed by delicate foliage, fruit and flowers. Small bas-reliefs on the side walls and plans of the arches show the monthly labors of both rich and poor (and give real insight into life at that time) and the signs of the zodiac. Viollet-le-Duc added the statues in the embrasures showing St Denis with two angels, St John and St Stephen (St Etienne).

The sculptures of the Portal of St Anne were mainly carved from 1160 to 1170 for a narrower doorway. They are the oldest statues in the cathedral. They fill the two upper levels of the tympanum. At the apex is a seated Virgin in Majesty with the Christ Child on her lap and two angels with a king, supposedly Louis VII, and a bishop meant to be Maurice de Sully; behind them the figure of the famous scribe Barbedor. On the trumeau a long, slender statue of St Marcel or Marcellus shows him killing the dragon by thrusting his crozier down its throat (copy of the 12th-c. original kept in a chapel in the N tower). On the double lintel are scenes from the Life of St Anne (lower lintel) and the Virgin (central). The four archivolts framing the tympanum show a heavenly court of angels and kings; the statues on the embrasures at the sides of the portal were recarved in the 19th c.

The wrought-iron hinges, especially those of the Portal of St Anne, are the original medieval masterpieces (restored). In the four niches in the buttresses between the doorways are modern statues of St Stephen, the Church, the Synagogue (with a blindfold) and St Denis. A similar niche cut at right angles in the r.-hand buttress, holds a modern statue of St Marcel trampling the dragon underfoot.

The galleries

The Gallery of the Kings of Israel and Judea runs across the façade above the portal. On it stand statues of the 28 monarchs whom St Matthew lists as Jesus Christ's ancestors. The originals, believed to be kings of France, were destroyed in 1793 by the Commune and these have been recut according to Viollet-le-Duc's sketches, but the heads of the former were recently rediscovered among 360 sculptured fragments unearthed in 1975 (→Musée de Cluny). Above the Gallery of the Kings is a balustrade known as the Gallery of Our Lady adorned with modern statues of the Virgin between two angels. Behind them is the rose window*, 31½ft/9.6m in diameter, the largest built at that period (1220–25). Flanked by double windows surmounted by relief, arches with statues of Adam (r.) and Eve (l.), it is exquisite.

A superb row of openwork arches links the two towers. The spires designed for them were never built and, finally, were deemed unnecessary. At the corners of the buttresses are colossal statues of gargoyles, night birds and devils partly concealed by the balustrade running above the arches. All were designed by Viollet-le-Duc and one of them, the Stryge gargoyle of Notre-Dame, has been popularized by Méryon's famous print.

The towers

10am-5pm

The S tower houses the famous great bell Emmanuel, weighing 12.79 tons/13t. The clapper weighs just over 1090lb./500kg and since 1953 has been operated electrically. When it was recast in 1686 women threw their jewelry into the heated bronze, and this is said to account for its pure tone. The N tower has a staircase with 387 steps. Halfway up is the cathedral shop, in which are displayed several paintings by Guido Reni (*ca*. 1636), Ludovico Carracci (17th c.), Carle Van Loo (1743) and Etienne Jeaurat (18th c.), as well as original stone carvings from the cathedral, in particular the statue of St Marcel (or Marcellus) from the pier of the Portal of St Anne and 12 mutilated figures some of which may come from St Stephen's Portal. The towers are 226ft./69m high. From the S tower platform there is a magnificent view of the spire, the flying buttresses and Paris in general.

The N and S façades and the apse

These comprise three distinct, recessed and superposed levels. The boldness of Jean Ravy's elegant flying buttresses of the apse, with their span of 50ft/15m, is still much admired.

The S door or St Stephen's Portal

A Latin inscription at the base of this magnificent portal shows that it was begun in 1257 by Jean de Chelles and finished by Pierre de Montreuil. Geoffroy-Dechaume's statue of St Stephen stands on the pier; the tympanum, comprising three tiers, is carved with the life and death (by stoning) of the saint, with, on either side, under the six modern statues of the Apostles, light bas-reliefs of student and university life (13th c.). A splendid rose window and a pierced gable with a statue of St Marcel are over the door.

The N or Cloister Portal

This was built at about the same time as the S Portal (1250) by Jean de Chelles. On the trumeau of the portal there is a fine original statue of Our Lady, holding the Christ Child, standing in an attitude of easy elegance – the Gothic slouch – the only full-length medieval statue for the doors of the cathedral (early 13th c.). The tympanum has scenes from the childhood of Christ, the life of the Virgin and the legend of Theophilus, the deacon who sold his soul to the Devil and was saved by the Virgin.

The Red Door

Beyond the N door

This little door, the work of Pierre de Montreuil, was used only by members of the cathedral chapter. On the tympanum is the crowning of the Virgin between St Louis and Margaret of Provence (*ca.* 1260). On the archivolts scenes from the life of St Marcel. To the l. of the Red Door, bas-reliefs inlaid into the chancel chapels' foundations, show seven scenes, the Death, Burial, Resurrection, Assumption and Coronation of the Virgin, the Last Judgement with the Virgin interceding with her Son, and the Legend of Theophilus (early 14th c.). The spire above the transept crossing stands over 147ft/45m above roof level and over 295ft/90m above the ground. It was reconstructed from 1859 to 1860 by Viollet-le-Duc, who copied the original (1220–30) which had been destroyed during the Revolution. It is built of 500 tons of oak, covered with 250 tons of lead and weighs just over 738 tons/750t. Copper figures of the Evangelists and Apostles stand at its base; one of them is a self-portrait of the architect.

Tour of the interior

8am–6.30pm daily (in summer), chancel open Sun. 11am–3.00pm (in winter). Tours conducted Mon.–Fri. at noon; meet below the organ loft. Tel. 43–54–22–53. Concerts every Sun. 5.45pm (admission free).

The interior comprises a sort of pre-nave of two bays lying below and between the towers, a central nave and four aisles for the three portals (something quite unprecedented); the side-aisles are flanked externally on either side by seven chapels which continue round the apse, making 27 chapels in all. The elevation is on three levels, and the galleries can hold 1500 people. The vaulting, supported by 75 piers, is sexpartite, one bay of quadripartite vaulting being divided transversely into two parts so that each bay has six compartments. These are characteristic of Notre-Dame. The first nine bays (13th c.) are similar, while the tenth is a reconstruction by Viollet-le-Duc in the 12th-c. style of architecture. It is on four levels.

The three great rose-windows*

These are the only windows to have preserved any of their 13th-c. stained glass. The rose-window of the nave in the W facade was almost completely refurbished by Viollet-le-Duc, but still has fragments of the original 13th-c. glass. It depicts the Labors of the Months, the signs of the Zodiac, the Seven Virtues and the Seven Deadly Sins, the Prophets and, in the center, the Virgin. The N rose

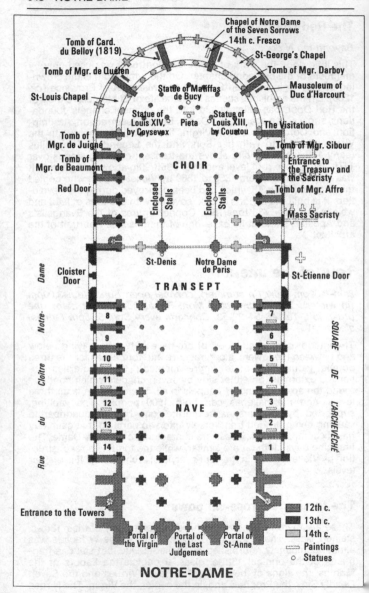

Chapel of Notre Dame
of the Seven Sorrows
14th c. Fresco

Tomb of Card.
du Belloy (1819)

St-George's Chapel

Tomb of Mgr. de Quélen

Tomb of Mgr. Darboy

Statue of Matiffas
de Bucy

Mausoleum of
Duc d'Harcourt

St-Louis Chapel

Statue of
Louis XIV,
by Coysevox

Pieta

Statue of
Louis XIII,
by Coustou

The Visitation

Tomb of
Mgr. de Juigné

Tomb of Mgr. Sibour

Entrance to
the Treasury and
the Sacristy

Tomb of
Mgr. de Beaumont

CHOIR

Red Door

Enclosed
Stalls

Enclosed
Stalls

Tomb of Mgr. Affre

Mass Sacristy

St-Denis

Notre Dame
de Paris

Cloister
Door

St-Étienne Door

TRANSEPT

8

7

9

6

10

5

11

4

12

3

NAVE

13

2

14

1

Entrance to the Towers

Portal of
the Virgin

Portal of
the Last
Judgement

Portal of
St-Anne

12th c.
13th c.
14th c.
Paintings
Statues

Dame
Notre-
Cloître
du
Rue

SQUARE DE L'ARCHEVÊCHÉ

NOTRE-DAME

window is virtually intact and depicts the Virgin surrounded by high priests, judges, kings and prophets from the Old Testament. The S rose window (thoroughly restored in 1737) depicts the Wise and Foolish Virgins, male and female saints, the Twelve Apostles and Christ in the center.

The Nave

Cliquot's organs (1730) were restored by Cavaille-Coll in 1868 (6000 pipes, 110 stops, five manuals). A new console with electrical controls was installed in 1962, making the organ in Notre-Dame the largest in France (with 113 stops today). The windows in the nave and the rose windows in the gallery were given a complete set of modern, abstract stained glass to replace the gloomy grisaille 19th-c. glass. In 1962 Jacques Le Chevalier installed these new windows and, using medieval manufacturing processes, created a symphony of color of which the predominant strains are pure blue and red.

The side-chapels of the S side-aisles (r.)

The side-chapels are hung with the large religious paintings known as 'Mays' because every May 1 the Goldsmiths' Guild offered one to the Cathedral.

1st Chapel: the original chapel of the Goldsmiths' Guild (→inset) and assigned to them again in 1964; rail by Subes; copper gilt repoussé altar and crucifix by Philippe Kaeppelin; on the wall *The Stoning of St Stephen*, 'May' offering for 1651, by Charles Le Brun. 2nd Chapel: *The Martyrdom of St Andrew*, 'May' for 1647, by Charles Le Brun; in its original place over the altar, *The Martyrdom of St Bartholomew* by Lubin Baugin (17th c.). 3rd Chapel: *The Crucifixion of St Peter*, 'May' for 1643, by Sébastien Bourdon. 4th Chapel: *St Peter Preaching in Jerusalem*, 'May' for 1642, by Charles Poerson. 5th Chapel: *Cornelius the Centurion at the Feet of St Peter*, 'May' for 1639, by Aubin Vouet; 16th-c. woodwork inserted in 1865. 6th Chapel: *The Conversion of St Paul*, 'May' for 1637, by Laurent de La Hyre; above the altar, *The Nativity* by Le Nain (17th c.); stained-glass window by Didron depicting the Tree of Jesse (1864). 7th Chapel: *St Peter Healing the Sick with his Shadow*, 'May' for 1635, by Laurent de La Hyre.

The S arm of the transept

Thanks to the strength imparted by the flying buttresses, the rose windows (→above) are very large, measuring nearly 43ft/13m across.

Here hangs *The Fountain of Wisdom*, painted by A. Nicolas in 1648.

Against the SE pillar of the transept, to the r. of the chancel, stands the famous 14th-c. statue of the Virgin from the chapel of Saint-Aignan, known as Our Lady of Paris (Notre Dame de Paris), a usurped title since the only statue which deserves it is that of the Virgin on the Cloister Portal (→above). Next to it an inscription commemorates the fact that the process for the rehabilitation of Joan of Arc was begun in Notre-Dame. On the paving opposite the first pillar separating the two side-aisles of the ambulatory, an inscription commermorates the conversion of the 20th-c. poet Paul Claudel on December 25, 1886.

The chancel

The chancel is enclosed by a small section of railing. It was completely redecorated in fulfilment of Louis XIII's vow, by Robert de Cotte in the reign of Louis XIV, from 1708 to 1725.

It contains fine early 18th-c. paneling* comprising 52 high and 26 low stalls (from an original total of 114) by Louis Marteau and Jean Noël, from designs by J. Dugoulon and R. Charpentier. The high backs of the stalls are carved in bas-relief and divided by trumeaux decorated with foliated scrolls and carvings of the Instruments of Christ's Passion. At either end there is an archepiscopal stall surmounted by a baldachin with groups of angels carved by J. Dugoulon from designs by Vassé. The bas-relief on the r.-hand stall shows *the Martyrdom of St Denis*, that on the l. the *Miraculous Cure of King Childebert* by St Germanus (Bishop of Paris). The other carvings include some scenes from the Life of Christ and of Our Lady and allegorical figures.

Behind the high altar stands the *Pietà* by Nicolas Coustou (1723) between statues of Louis XIII by Guillaume Coustou (r.) and Louis XIV (l.), a fine piece by Coysevox, both dating from 1715, and six angels carrying the Instruments of the Passion.

The ambulatory

In the first three bays are the remains of the old choir wall* which formerly enclosed the choir. On the outer sides are 14th-c. bas-reliefs begun by Jean Ravy and finished in 1351 by his nephew, Jean Le Bouteiller, later restored and repainted by Viollet-le-Duc. The oldest (N side): 14 scenes relating to the Birth and Life of Christ before His Passion; the nine subjects on the S side show Christ appearing to his disciples after his Resurrection.

In the ambulatory itself (starting from the r.) there are: a memorial tablet commemorating the cathedral's eighth centenary; the tomb of Monsignor Affre; the tomb of Monsignor Sibour, and against the choir wall the tomb of Cardinal Dubois (d. 1929) by H. Bouchard.

The Chapel of Saint-Guillaume: *The Visitation by* Jean Jouvenet (1716); monument to Jean Juvénal des Ursins and to his wife, Michelle de Vitry (15th c.); mausoleum of Lieutenant-General Henri-Claude d'Harcourt (d. 1711) by Pigalle. The Chapel of Saint-Georges (from 1379 until the Revolution known as the chapel of the Cordwainers Guild): the tomb of Monsignor Darboy by Bonnassieux; a statue of St George; opposite, against the choir rail, a memorial to Cardinal Verdier (d. 1940). The Chapelle Notre-Dame-des-Sept-Douleurs (Chapel of Our Lady of the Seven Sorrows); the kneeling statues of Albert de Gondi, Duc de Retz, Marshal of France (1522–1602), and of Pierre, Cardinal de Gondi, Bishop of Paris (1532–1616) and, on the r.-hand side, a 14th-c. fresco (restored) depicting the *Virgin and saints with the soul of Bishop Matiffas de Bucy* (d. 1304) whose remains were translated to a place behind the high altar. The Chapel of Saint-Marcel: the tombs of Cardinal de Belloy (d. 1818) by Deseine, of Monsignor de Quélen (d. 1839) by Geoffroy-Dechaume and, opposite against the choir rail, the memorial to Cardinal Suchard (d. 1949). The Chapel of Saint-Louis: the tomb of Monsignor de Juigné (d. 1809), after Viollet-le-Duc. In the chapel just before the Red Door are monuments to Monsignor de Beaumont d. 1781 and Marshal de Guébriant (d. 1643), and the kneeling statue of Cardinal Morlot (d. 1862).

In the N crossing of the transept, a bare patch on the wall shows where the 'May' offering for 1649, *St Paul Preaching to the Ephesians*, by Eustache Le Sueur, has been removed to the Louvre. Nicolas Coustou's statue of St Denis stands against the NE pillar of the transept.

The side-chapels of the N side-aisles (l.)

8th Chapel: the tomb of Canon Etienne Yver (d. 1468) on which his naked body is seen being eaten by worms, while his soul kneels begging Christ for mercy. 9th Chapel: *The Jewish Exorcists, the Sons of Scaeva, beaten by the Devil* by Matthieu Elyas, 'May' for 1702, and, above the altar, *The Martyrdom of St Catherine* by J. -M. Vien (1752). 10th Chapel (dedicated to Our Lady of Guadaloupe, Mexico): *Agabus Foretells to St Paul his Sufferings in Jerusalem*, by Louis Chéron, 'May' for 1687. 11th Chapel: *St Andrew Shivers with Joy at the Sight of what he is to Suffer*, by Gabriel Blanchard le Neveu, 'May' for 1670; monument to Cardinal Amette by Hippolyte Lefebvre (1923). 12th Chapel: *The Flagellation of St Paul and St Silas* by Louis Testelin, 'May' for 1655. 13th Chapel: *St Paul Blinds the False Prophet Barjesus* by Nicolas Loir, 'May' for 1650, and, above the altar, *Our Lady of Mercy* by Lubin Baugin (17th c.). 14th Chapel: baptismal fonts carved by Bachelet from Viollet-le-Duc's designs; *The Descent of the Holy Ghost* by Jacques Blanchard, 'May' for 1634, and, opposite, *The Adoration of the Shepherds* by

Jérôme Franck (1585). Below the N tower there is a statue of Our Lady Protectress (*Notre-Dame de Bonne-Garde*) by Vassé, 1722.

The Chapter sacristy and the Treasury

Entrance on the r.-hand side of the ambulatory; Mon.-Sat. 10am–6pm, Sun. 2pm–6pm.

The items displayed in the Treasury were rearranged in 1963 for the cathedral's eighth centenary. Valuable 19th-c. manuscripts and printed books are exhibited in the corridors as well as a selection of vestments, among them those given by Napoléon III in 1856 for the christening of the Prince Imperial. There are also souvenirs of the three Archbishops of Paris who were murdered – Monsignor Affre, Monsignor Sibour and Monsignor Darboy – as well as of Viollet-le-Duc and his restoration work (1844–64) and of Paul Claudel (1868–1955) and his conversion on December 25, 1886; 19th- and 20th-c. gold and silver work is assembled in the main room. At the entrance stands a Madonna and Child by Odiot, presented by Charles X in 1826. Among the many chalices, ciboria, reliquaries, altar-cruets, ewers, sets of altar plate and processional crosses, the following are especially noteworthy: reliquary for the Holy Crown of Thorns made by C. Cahier in 1804; the custodial by L. Legay (1814); the set of altar plate by C. Cahier presented by the king's brother Monsieur (later Charles X) in 1823; the amethyst-studded chalice given in 1823 by the Knights of the Holy Sepulchre; several items presented by Napoléon III or designed during his reign by Viollet-le-Duc and executed by the goldsmiths Maison Poussielgue-Rusand, and in particular another reliquary for the Holy Crown of Thorns dated 1862 and a set of altar plate decorated with filigree and enamel work and presented to Canon Deplace in 1867. Also of interest are the Popes' mementoes; the ciborium of Leo XIII (1887); the chalice and ciborium of John XXIII (1961 and 1963), and of the Archbishops. Among other gifts are the Goldsmiths' Monstrance by Chéret (1949) and two terracottas by J. -B. Carpeaux, a Crucifixion and a Deposition.

The most important item is a fragment of the True Cross, kept inside the Palatine Cross* made for it by Famechon, displayed, together with one of the nails from the Cross, since 1828. The cross is so named because it belonged to Anne de Gonzago of Cleves, Princess Palatine, active in the Fronde (d. 1684). With this fragment is a gold plate with an inscription in Greek showing that it belonged to the Byzantine emperor Manuel Comnenus (d. 1180). Relics of St Louis are displayed in the same case (his tunic, his scourge, a fragment of his jawbone and a rib). Other relics, in particular the Crown of Thorns which St Louis acquired from Baldwin II, King of Jerusalem, are only displayed during Lent and Holy Week.

On the walls of the Chapterhouse hangs a collection of 258 cameos portraying all the popes from St Peter to Pius IX. A piece of furniture designed by Viollet-le-Duc and painted by Perrodin houses all items dating from before the French Revolution, including ivory crucifixes, amphora, chalices, shrine reliquaries, and altar-cruets, most notable being an ebony and copper cross on which hangs the ivory figure of Christ, attributed to Girardon.

> Viollet-le-Duc

Reactions to Eugène-Emmanuel Viollet-le-Duc (1814–1879) are deeply divided. Though he came from a rich cultured and enlightened family, he always opposed the 'establishment'. He was at one and the same time architect, archeologist, restorer, decorator, artist, writer and theoretician. After helping to build barricades in the uprisings of 1830 and refusing to go to the Ecole des Beaux Arts, he met Professor Mérimée (author of *Carmen*), Inspector in the newly founded Commission for Historic Monuments, and this decided his future. Inspired by Victor Hugo and Arcisse de Caumont, he rediscovered and restored the Middle Ages to a place of honor, saving Vézèlay (his first job, in 1840), rebuilding Pierrefonds and restoring Eu, Notre-Dame in Paris, Sens, Saint-Sernin in Toulouse, the cathedral of Clermont-Ferrand and the city of Carcassonne. He has been severely criticized by those who judge his restorations to be based upon Romantic concepts of the Medieval rather than the real thing, and yet in most instances they are discreetly done, historically respectful and, in any case, archeologically sound, because he always undertook the most detailed research before beginning any work. The decision taken at Notre-Dame is typical of the dilemmas which confronted Viollet-le-Duc. He had to decide between reconstructuring a 12th-c. nave or restoring a 13th-c. one. In the end he decided to contrast the two styles by leaving in the transept crossing a specimen of 12th-c. architecture, despite the fact that although the two styles certainly existed, they did not exist simultaneously.

Viollet-le-Duc's contribution as a restorer should not blind us to the fact that he was an original architect as well (apartment buildings in the 9th arrondissement of Paris, the Church of Saint-Denis, country-houses) and designer (religious furnishings, stained glass, furniture at Pierrefonds, the Emperor's suite, interior decoration).

> Memorable events

There is space here to list only a few important dates.
1229: On Maundy Thursday, Raymond VII, Count of Toulouse, came to do penance. 1239: St Louis, barefoot, carried the Crown of Thorns into the cathedral and soon afterwards his coffin was brought here from Tunis. 1302: Philippe IV le Bel (the Fair) opened

the first Estates-General. 1430: Henry VI of England, aged 10, crowned King of France. 1437: Charles VII celebrated the recapture of Paris with a *Te Deum*. 1558: Mary Stuart married François II. 1590: the leaders of the Holy League swore never to recognize the Huguenot Henry of Navarre as king: he had already, in 1572, been married to Marguerite de Valois (La Reine Margot) in a most peculiar ceremony, with the bride standing inside, and the groom outside the church. 1594: on March 24 Henri IV offered thanks for the recapture of Paris. 1625: Charles I of England married Henrietta Maria by proxy. 1660: *Te Deum* offered for the marriage of Louis XIV. The Duc de Luxembourg was nicknamed *le tapissier de Notre-Dame* for the numerous captured enemy flags, which he hung on the cathedral walls. 1668: Turenne publicly abjured Protestantism. 1687: Bossuet delivered the funeral oration for Condé on March 10. In the 18th century, despite Versailles, Notre-Dame still held its own, and it was here that the Queens of France, Marie Leszczynska and Marie-Antoinette, came to pray after the births of their children. During the Revolution Mlle Mailland, a singer and prostitute, was crowned Goddess of Reason. Many treasures were destroyed. 1804: Napoleon I and Josephine were crowned by Pius VII on December 2: a year later the standards captured at Austerlitz provided new wall-hangings. 1811: baptism of the King of Rome.

After the restoration of the cathedral, it was once again the setting for Imperial ceremonial for the marriage of Napoléon III and Eugénie de Mantijo on January 30, 1853, and for the baptism of the Prince Imperial in 1856. Since 1918 the old church seems more than ever to have regained its status with the State funerals of Maurice Barrès (1923), Marshal Foch (1929), Marshal Joffre (1931), Raymond Poincaré (1934), General Leclerc (1947) Marshal de Lattre de Tassigny (January 1952), Paul Claudel (February 1955), Marshal Juin (February 1967), but above all with the thanksgiving for the Liberation of Paris on August 26, 1944 and the Victory *Te Deum* on May 9, 1945. On November 12, 1970, in the presence of many foreign heads of state, the official memorial service took place following the death of General de Gaulle.

▷ The Goldsmiths' 'Mays'

Until the Revolution Parisian goldsmiths occupied a special place in Notre-Dame, where they had their own chapel. In 1349 they founded the Fraternity of St Anne and St Marcell which undertook each May Day to present a green May tree to the Virgin. By the end of the century a portable altar made of green branches replaced the tree.

From 1630 to 1707 the tradition developed new forms, as the goldsmiths presented each year a painting to be hung in the blind arcades of the nave and chancel. These offerings came to be known as 'Mays', after the original trees. These 76 paintings were all commissioned from artists of renown and measured 11ft/3.50m high by 8½ft/2.75m wide. Their subject-matter was usually a scene from the Acts of the Apostles. They were dispersed during the Revolution and many of them were lost. However, the Louvre, some provincial museums and a few churches (Saint-Thomas-d'Aquin in Paris, for example) have saved some of them. Happily, the most substantial collection of these paintings, seven in all, hangs in the side-chapels of Notre-Dame. This tradition was renewed in 1949.

▷ Organ recitals

Several churches in Paris deserve a visit either because of the quality of their organs or because of the talents of their organists. The best time is generally during Mass on Sunday mornings, especially High Mass, but many organists give recitals on Sunday afternoons.

Notre-Dame (daily 5.45 pm; admission free); and the churches of Saint-Roch, Saint-Germain-des-Prés, Saint-Eustache, Saint-Séverin, Trinité, La Madeleine, Saint-Louis-des-Invalides, Saint-Germain-l'Auxerrois, Saint-Louis-en-l'Isle, Saint-François-Xavier, Saint-Merri.

▷ Louis XIII's vow

Louis XIII had vowed to consecrate his kingdom to the Virgin if a son were born to him. After 23 years of marriage, his wish was fulfilled by the birth of the Dauphin Louis, later Louis XIV, in 1638. However, the king died before he could realize his vow to erect a new high altar in Notre-Dame and place in the chancel a sculptured *Pietà*. Sixty years later Louis XIV fulfilled his father's promises.

The alterations accomplished by Robert de Cotte utterly transformed the Gothic chancel, and its pointed arches were completely hidden behind semicircular marble arcading. On either side of the high altar bronze angels were set beside the statues: one of Louis XIV by Coysevox and the other of Louis XIII by Guillaume Coustou, while the heartrending *Pietà* by N. Coustou was placed behind it. The stalls erected by Dugoulon and Charpentier were surmounted in the ambulatory by eight paintings designed to complete the whole, of which only one, *The Visitation* by Jean Jouvenet, is preserved today in the Chapel of Saint-Guillaume. The stone chancel screen was cut back so that, of the 14th-c. bas-reliefs, only scenes from the *Life of Christ and His Apparitions*, were left.

Notre-Dame-des-Champs district

6th arr.
Métro: Vavin, Notre-Dame-des-Champs. RER: Port-Royal
Bus: 38, 82, 83, 91
Parking: Boul du Montparnasse (corner of the Rue de Chevreuse).
Taxis: Place du 18 June 1940. Tel: 42–22–13–13.

From the Ecole des Mines, past the Stanislas College and the
Faculty of Pharmacy, to the Catholic Institute, there is a veritable
belt of secondary and higher educational buildings that surround
the S part of the Jardin du Luxembourg. Near Montparnasse, the
first indication of which is the Closerie des Lilas, is the Notre-Dame-
des-Champs *quartier*, not so long ago inhabited by the art students
who attended the academies in the Rue de la Grande-Chaumière or
Rue du Montparnasse and were sometimes entertained by Gertrude
Stein at her home in the Rue de Fleurus.

Today the population in these quiet streets is less bohemian, and
painting is only discussed at the Institute of Art beside the Square
d'Observatoire. From Montparnasse to the Vavin intersection, the
busy shopping streets are lined with elegant boutiques, frequented
by the pupils and students of the neighboring schools. Further E, at
the magnificent Observatoire fountain near the Jardin du Luxembourg, the wide, open streets are more residential.

Tour of the district

45 mins.

Place Camille-Jullian

The Centre Universitaire Jean-Sarrain (Rector of the University of
Paris from 1947 to 1961) on the square, has a concrete structure
with a curtain wall façade (architect, André Lacoste, 1960). In 1838
open-air dancing in a garden, the summer Prado, took place on this
site. In 1847 it was replaced by the Closerie des Lilas, which became
the Bal Bullier, closed a few years before World War II.

The Avenue de l'Observatoire

From the Place Camille Jullian to the Luxembourg.

This wide and shady avenue offers a fine view of the Jardin du
Luxembourg and its palace above which rises the white mass of the
Sacré-Coeur. In front of no. 20 is one of Rude's great works, the

statue of Maréchal Ney (shot on December 7, 1815 outside no. 43). The Closerie des Lilas café, behind (on the corner of the avenue and the Boul. Montparnasse), is one of the most famous in Paris. In the 1920s it was first a literary café favored by the Symbolist poets, Baudelaire, Verlaine and Charles Cros; later it was the haunt of the writers of the *Nouvelle Revue Française*: Gide, Jarry and Charles-Louis Phillippe; and finally of the next generation: Carco, Apollinaire, Paul Fort and Charles Vildrac.

The Institut d'Art et d'Archeologie (entrance at 3 Rue Michelet) is one of the many institutes that border the W side of the avenue. This large red brick building, decorated with bas-reliefs representing famous works, was constructed by Paul Bigot in 1927, and is a rare example in Paris of historicist architecture, as opposed to that of the modern movement. It houses the Bibliothèque Jacques-Doucet, and the University of Paris holds its history of art and architecture courses there. The Library was founded in 1909 by the couturier and collector, Jacques-Doucet (1853–1929), who bequeathed it to the University of Paris in 1918. It comprises about 300,000 volumes on art of all periods and from all centuries, 300 manuscripts, 2000 files of manuscript documents, a series of 3000 old anthologies on decoration, architecture, festivals and costumes, a collection of old and modern French and foreign prints, and a photographic library with over 200,000 photographs. Jacques Doucet also gathered a very variable collection of literature, which is kept at the Bibliothèque Saint-Genèvieve (→ Quai de Latin).

No. 4 is the Faculty of Pharmacy, built from 1876 to 1885 by Charles Laisne (in the vestibule, frescoes by Albert Besnard). His botanical garden gradually diminished as the faculty increased. At no. 2 the Institut International d'Administration Publique occupies the Moorish-style buildings designed by Ad Yvon for the Ecole Coloniale.

For the S end of the avenue →Faubourg Saint-Jacques.

♣♣ The gardens of the Observatoire

The central part of this wide Ave. de l'Observatoire, between the Place Camille-Jullian and the Rue Auguste-Comte, comprises a beautiful series of flower-beds shaded by chestnut trees and decorated with statues. *Le Fontaine de l'Observatoire* (observatory fountain) created by Davioud in 1875, is adorned with Carpeau's famous group of the four quarters of the globe: *Les Quatre Parties du monde* (Oceania, the fifth, omitted in the interest of visual balance). The bronze horses are by Fremet.

The gardens of the Observatoire, which were designed by Chalgrin during the First Empire, replaced the Carthusians' cloister. These monks, part of the Order of St Bruno created in 1086 near Saint-Pierre-des-Chartreux in the Dauphiné, were installed here in 1257 by St Louis. It was a verdant area, covered with vineyards and woods, hence the name 'Vauvert'. Later it got such a bad reputation that the expression 'Au diable Vauvert' was coined. When the Carthusians arrived they enlarged and improved the domain, which was open to the public, except for the nuns' quarters. The entrance was at 64 Boul. Saint-Michel. Until 1960, inside the cloister was a chapel built by Eudes de Montreuil in 1325, which was decorated three centuries later by Coypel, Champagne, Boullongne, Jouvencet and Charles de Lafosse. After the expulsion of the Carthusians in 1790, part of the gardens were linked to the Jardin du Luxembourg.

The Rue Michelet separates the two gardens. At no. 9 the Institut d'Etudes Slaves (Slavic Studies), in the house of the historian E. Denis (1849–1921), contains souvenirs of Leo Tolstoy, bequeathed by one of his granddaughters. The Rue Auguste-Comte, at the end of the gardens, is for the most part bordered by the Lycée Montaigne (architect, Charles Le Coeur, 1886–90).

Rue d'Assas

As far as the Rue Vavin.

This street was created in 1728. At no. 100 *bis*, at the end of the cul-de-sac, is the Musée Zadkine, in the sculptor's old studio. No. 93 is the Faculté de Droit et de Sciences Economiques, built by Lenormand and Carpentier from 1959 to 1964, and later enlarged on the Rue-Notre-Dame-des-Champs side by buildings designed by Lods, Dupont and Beauclaire. Bartholdi, sculptor of the Statue of Liberty in New York, died at no. 82. Jules Michelet, the historian, lived at no. 76 from 1869 to 1874. The Swedish dramatist, writer and painter, August Strindberg (1849–1912), stayed at the Orfila pension at no. 62 from 1895 to 1896, as shown by a tablet.

Rue Vavin

Walk up this street and down again to see the building** designed by Sauvage in 1912 (→ inset); it is covered in white ceramic tiles and has stepped terraces. Not far off, on the other side of the Boul. Raspail, the beautiful glass façade of an office building can be seen. It was built in 1980 (architect, M. Berbert). The Rue Vavin has some nightclubs and numerous shops that stock artists' materials. The painter Othon Friesz (1879–1949) died at no. 73. Fernand Léger lived at no. 86 in 1913. At nos. 107–109 is the Ecole Alsacienne, founded in 1876 by the families who had to leave Alsace in 1871. Many well-known personalities were educated there, including André Gide.

The Rue Vavin rejoins the Boul. du Montparnasse at La Coupole restaurant and the Select brasserie (→ Montparnasse district).

The Rue Guynemer goes along the Jardins du Luxembourg and

rejoins the Rue de Vangirard near the Allée du Seminaire. At No. 14 are the first Parisian apartment buildings to have concrete frameworks hidden by polished stone façades. They were built by Roux Spitz in 1928.

The Rue de Fleurus is a beautiful street which opens up a vista of the Jardin du Luxembourg. It is linked to the history of Cubism, since it was at no. 27 that Gertrude Stein received Picasso, Juan Gris and many others. The Rue Madame in the 16th c. was called Rue du Gindre (as can be seen from the old plaque affixed to no. 23). No. 65 is an 18th-c. mansion built by Chalgrin for Anne de Caumont La Force. The painter Hippolyte Flandrin lived at no. 54.

Rue Cassette

This street is one of the oldest in the district, with many registered 18th-c. houses. Rainer Maria Rilke was living at no. 29 when World War I broke out, and his belongings were sequestered. Montalembert lived at no. 18 in a beautiful mansion that belonged to Le Brun. Alfred de Musset's family had an apartment at no. 27. Jarry, creator of *Ubu Roi*, had an apartment at no. 20. The attractive Louis XVI cul-de-lampe (ornamental lamp support) with a Virgin, is all that remains of the large Jesuit noviciate in the Rue du Pot-de-Fer (corner of the Rue Honoré-Chevalier).

Rue de Vaugirard

From the Rue Cassette to the Rue d'Assas.

The Carmelite seminary at no. 70 is now attached to the Catholic Institute.

The Couvent des Carmes Déchaussés (Barefoot Carmelites) was built in 1611 by Nicolas Vivien. It became a prison in 1790 and in September 1792 was the scene of a massacre when some 120 priests were murdered and most of their bodies thrown down a well that lay between 4 Rue d'Assas and 102 Rue de Rennes

More than 700 people including Joséphine de Beauharnais passed through the Carmelite prison. In 1797 after peace was restored, the convent was bought by Mlle de Soyécourt and, following that, acquired by the archbishopric, which founded several scholastic establishments here. Lacordaire, having restablished the Order of St Dominic, installed the Dominicans here until 1867. He himself lived in a cell which is now the chapel of the rector of the Catholic Institute. Mementoes of the ardent preacher have been preserved.

The Church of Saint-Joseph-des-Carmes (open daily ex. Mon., Sun. and public holidays, 2.30pm–3.30pm) was built between 1613 and 1620, as the chapel of the Carmelite convent. Its Italian dome was the second to be built in Paris after the small domed hexagon of

Marguerite de Valois' chapel, incorporated in the Ecole des Beaux-Arts. The dome is a simple shell of wood and plaster that aims to imitate the much earlier stone domes of Italy. But the building is interesting mostly for its relics of the Revolution. It is now the chapel of the Catholic Institute.

Inside, the dome is decorated with frescoes: *Elie enlevé au ciel* (Elijah taken up to Heaven) by Bartholet Flémalle, a 17th-c painter from Liège; the Carmelites considered the prophet Elijah as their founder. On the high altar, *La Preséntation au Temple* (Presentation in the Temple) by Quentin Varin (1624); alabaster bas-relief *La Cene* (The Last Supper); funerary monument containing the heart of Mgr Affre.

In the transept, *Virgin and Child*, marble group by Raggi after Bernini; *Christ glorieux, entre Ste Thérèse et St Jean de la Croix* (Christ in Glory between St Teresa and St John of the Cross) painting by Michel Corneille (1642–1708).

The Chapelle du Sacré-Coeur and the Chapelle de Saint-Elie, are splendidly decorated with paintings framed with sculptured angels attributed to Simon Vouet. To the r. of the choir is an elegant little chapel, its decoration, contemporary with the building, is Flemish, mostly by Van Thulder. The church dates from a time (between the Fontainebleau school and Vouet's return to Italy) when, because of the lack of well-known French painters, Flemish artists were called upon.

The crypt contains the remains of 120 massacred priests in two ossuaries; the tomb of Frédéric Ozanan, the Catholic writer, who set up the St Vincent de Paul meetings (1813–53), and the tomb of Cardinal Baudrillart (1859–1942), former rector of the Catholic Institute.

For the section of the street alongside the Jardin du Luxembourg →Saint-Sulpice district and the Luxembourg.

The Catholic Institute

Corner of the Rue Vaugirard and the Rue d'Assas.

This is the most respected teaching establishment in France. Founded in 1875, it was largely rebuilt in 1930. Edouard Branly taught physics here until the end of his career and is remembered by a plaque and a small memorial museum (→ Museums). Another small museum, Bible et Terre Sainte (Bible and Holy Land), contains objects found during excavations in the Holy Land.

The courtyard of the Catholic Institute communicates with the garden where the beautiful building of the Carmelite seminary, a prison during the Revolution, can be seen. There is also a simple stoop bearing the inscription: *Hic ceciderunt* (Here they fell), which marks one of the places where the massacre of September 1792 took place. Rue d'Assas (→above): no. 28 is the site of the house where the physician Foucault died. It was here in 1851 that he made the first experiments on the rotation of the earth.

Boulevard Raspail

This boulevard was built in several stages from 1866 to 1901. It has always been an elegant upper middle-class street. Among the houses that had to be demolished for its construction was one in the Rue Notre-Dame-des-Champs where the young Victor Hugo and his family lived from 1827 to 1830.

The Alliance Française (whose headquarters in 1911 were at no. 101) which was founded in 1884, is 'a national association for the propagation of the French language in the colonies and abroad'. It has a well-known active theater.

Rue Notre-Dame-des-Champs

Between the Rue de Vaugirard and the Rue du Montparnasse.

This small section of the street has more character. There are some beautiful portals, witness to mansions which were formerly of some splendor (nos. 17, 19 18).

The Collège Stanislas (main entrance at 28 Rue du Montparnasse) at no. 22 has kept the magnificent though dilapidated portal of the 18th-c. Hôtel de Mally. The college was founded in 1804. Edmond Rostand, Georges Guynemer, the generals Henri Gouraud, Charles de Gaulle and the commander of *L'Herminier* studied here. The old college was entirely reconstructed in 1967 to now plans that allowed the enlargement of the gardens The classrooms, study rooms and recreation terraces were regrouped in a seven-storey concrete and glass building constructed on a star-shaped plan (architects, Barge and Sire).

Rue du Montparnasse

The Church of Notre-Dame-des-Champs (corner of the Boul. du Montparnasse) is a Roman pastiche (1867–76) built by Girain. Its particularly light interior is adorned with a series of paintings by Aubert. Sainte-Beuve lived at no. 11 around 1850, but died at 11 Rue du Montparnasse in 1869. Edgar Quinet lived at no. 32 from 1840 to 1851, and Augustin Thierry died there in 1856. Rejoin the Boul. du Montparnasse and follow it in the direction of the Place du 18-Juin-1940.

Rue de Rennes

This and the Boul. Raspail are the only relatively modern main thoroughfares in the district. Following the construction of the Gare Montparnasse in 1840, the street was cut and lined with beautiful five-storey buildings from 1854 to 1867. It was planned to go as far as the Seine and rejoin the Rue du Louvre at a bridge near the Mint, but in fact it finished in front of the Church of Saint-Germain-des-Prés. On the r. at no. 40 is an Art-Nouveau building* constructed around 1902 by Paul Auscher for the great Félix Potin shops.

▣ Museums to visit

Musée Zadkine (100 *bis* Rue d'Assas): sculptures by Ossip Zadkine displayed in his studio.

Musée Branly (21 Rue d'Assas): Edouard Branly's apartments.

▷ Henri Sauvage and 26 Rue Vavin

Henri Sauvage (1873–1932) was first heard of as a member of the Nancy School using a version of Art Nouveau in the construction of the Villa Majorelle (1898). Then, turning his attention towards functional public housing, he founded the Société des Logements Hygiéniques à Bon Marché with Frantz Jourdain in 1903. The famous 'terraced' sports center in the Rue Vavin was commissioned by a cooperative association. Here Henri Sauvage created a truly avant-garde building, abandoning the sinuous Art-Nouveau plant motifs for a simplicity of volume and a restraint of decoration which were not widely adopted until after World War I. The system of terraced construction, which 'gave the street more light', as well as letting air and sun into the dwellings, was used again and developed by Henri Sauvage in another building in the Rue des Amiraux (→ La Chapelle, Clignancourt district). This modernity which was freely expressed in the two buildings, was not to be found in the neighboring building (dating from 1925) at 137 Boul. Raspail. The architect, anxious to conform to the surroundings of a Haussmannian street, designed an utterly ordinary building.

L'Odéon district*

6th arr./Map ref. 16–D3, 17–A3
Métro: Luxembourg. RER, Odeón
Bus: 21, 27, 38, 81, 84, 87
Parking: Place Saint-Sulpice
Taxi: Carrefour de l'Odeón, 91 Boul. Saint-Germain. Tel: 43–26–00–00.

Towards the end of the *Ancien Régime*, around 1779, the whole sector around the new Odeón theater was divided into lots. The historically aristocratic Rue de Tournon and Rue de Condé, as well as the old Palais du Luxembourg nearby, attracted a rich and fashionable clientele. Today, the five streets that converge before the theater's monumental façade, retain their air of distinction, their elegant boutiques, old bookshops, and young fashion houses. Further down, in the Rue Monsieur-le-Prince and Rue d l'Ecole-de-Médecine, there are many remarkable buildings, such as the admirable refectory of the Cordeliers Convent, which has been recently restored. During the day these main streets are frequented by students who come to shop in the numerous scientific and university bookshops. Further down still, at the Carrefour de l'Odéon, the dense, jostling mass of people from the Boulevard Saint-Germain crowds up against the Statue of Danton. Opposite this statue are the courtyards of the Commerce-Saint-André where Marat printed his revolutionary newspaper and where Dr Guillotin used sheep in experiments with his dreadful machine. The *quartier's* many cinemas and cafés are lively well into the night.

Tour of the district

45 mins.

The Odéon theater**

The old Théâtre-Français is a beautiful Neo-Classical building. It is one of the rare Paris theaters, like the Opéra and the Marigny Theater which is detached. It is surrounded by arcades and, until 1818, had two arches spanning the Rue Corneille and Rue Rotrou, which sheltered spectators from the rain as they descended from their carriages.

The Théâtre-Français was built between 1779 and 1782 by Peyre and de Wailly in the gardens of the former Hôtel de Condé, which had been bought by the king and offered to the city as a site for a theater. It was intended to house the Comédie Française, which, for several years, had been installed in the Tuileries Palace theater. In 1797, with a new company, the theater took the name Odéon. The company was not successful. In 1807 the building burnt down and a similar one was reconstructed by Chalgrin that same year. Beaumarchais's *Marriage of Figaro*, which was created and performed in the new theater in 1784, was highly successful. The Odéon, which was linked on many occasions with the Comédie-Française, passed to the Jean-Louis Barrault Company in 1959, who remained there until 1968. In May of that year, during the student riots, the theater was occupied for a month and badly damaged. The Odéon frequently receives famous foreign companies. In the interior, the auditorium has a ceiling by André Masson (1965).

In the foyer, which was renovated in 1875, there is a bust of Antoine (1858-1943), the actor, producer, and then director of the Odéon from 1906 on. Eight large portraits of famous 19th-c. actors in memorable rôles from the repertory form part of the mural decoration: E. Geoffroy (Carolus-Duran), L. A. Delaunay, F. Berton, H. Lafontaine, J. P. F. Provost, J. I. Samson, Bocage, P. F. Beauvallet.

Place de l'Odéon

This is a quiet and attractive semicircular square into which runs the fan of roads made at the same time as the theater was constructed in the gardens of the former Condé. An architectural plan was drawn up for the Place and for the Rue de l'Odéon. It was at no. 2, in a third-floor apartment that he shared with Lucile, that Camille Desmoulins was arrested in 1794 (the inscription at no. 1 is innaccurate). At no. 1 is the Franco-American Center, which after the Benjamin Franklin bookshop replaced the old and venerable Café Voltaire. For over 150 years the café was the literary haunt of the Encyclopedists, the Romantics and the Symbolists. Between the wars it was a meeting-place for writers and, in particular, for the 'lost generation' of Americans: Scott Fitzgerald, who lived in the neighborhood in the Rue de Vaugirard, T. S. Eliot, Ezra Pound, Hart Crane, Hemingway, Kay Boyle, Sinclair Lewis, Gertrude Stein and all the others who, like them, came and went between the Voltaire and the bookshops of Adrienne Monnier and Sylvia Beach.

Rue de l'Odéon

Lying opposite the theater, this is the most important street that enters the Place de l'Odéon. It was the first in Paris to have sidewalks with curbside gutters. As in the past, it is still bordered by attractive shops. There are many interesting houses (nos. 9, 10, 11, 12, 14, 16), which date mainly from the 18th c., as do the two mansions on the street where it meets the Carrefour de l'Odéon. No. 7 was Adrienne Monnier's bookshop, *Les Amis des Livres*, which was for many years the meeting-place for Gide, Martin du Gard and Valéry, while Americans from the Voltaire met opposite at no. 12, Librarie Shakespeare, which was Sylvia Beach's bookshop. In 1922 the first edition of Joyce's *Ulysses* was published here; the author and publisher were prosecuted in the United States for obscenity. The Rue de l'Odéon meets the Carrefour de l'Odéon near the Place Henri-Mondor which, until the 18th c., was called the Carrefour du Riche-Laboureur.

At the passageway, glance at the wrought ironwork of the old houses on the Rue des Quatre-Vents. It dates from the early 15th c. and gets its name from a sign showing cupids blowing at the four points of the compass.

Boulevard Saint-Germain

From the Place Henri-Mondor to the Boul. Saint-Michel.

This section was once called the Rue des Boucheries because of the 22 butchers' stalls that stood here during the Revolution. The street is lined on both sides with publishing houses, and with the medical publishers near the Faculty of Medicine. To the W it goes towards Saint-Germain-des-Prés; to the E it rejoins Boul. Saint-Michel, passing in front of the Librarie Hachette (no. 79), founded in 1826 by Louis Hachette, who preferred the bookshop to higher education. The boulevard crosses the Rue Hautefeuille at this point and on the wall of the bookshop itself is a plaque recalling the site of the Hôtel d'Aligre where Charles Baudelaire was born in 1821.

Rue de l'Ecole-de-Médecine

This street, formerly the Rue des Cordeliers, existed in 1300. All the land between nos. 25 and 21 was occupied by the Franciscan convent of the Frères-Mineurs (or Cordeliers, a name derived from the cord they wore round their habits) which was founded in 1230. In the Middle Ages it was a center of learning comparable to those of the Dominicans. The convent, which had received its lands from St Louis, extended as far as the present Lycée Saint-Louis. It was suppressed during the Revolution and requisitioned by Camille Desmoulins for the Cordeliers' club (1791).

Approximately at the site of the triangle at the corner of the Rue Antoine-Dubois is the house in which Marat was living when Charlotte Corday stabbed him in his bath on July 13, 1793. Of the huge conventual buildings, which were reconstructed by Anne of Brittany in the Flamboyant Gothic style in the late 15th c., only the refectory remains (15 Rue de l'Ecole-de-Médecine). This well-proportioned refectory is one of the rare vestiges of medieval monastic architecture still in existence in Paris.

Marat's body was laid out here before burial in the garden of the Cordeliers.

The Ecole pratique de médecine (University of Paris-VI-Pierre-et-Marie-Curie) was built between 1877 and 1900 on the site of the Cloître des Cordeliers. It has a large annex at no. 45 Rue des Saints-Pères (built from 1937 to 1953) for the first years. The Musée Duputren is housed here (→ Museums).

The old Faculté de Médécine

12 Rue de l'Ecole-de-Medecine

This comprises a vast group of buildings between the Boul. Saint-Germain and the Rue Hautefeuille, partly occupying the site of the Collège Royal de Bourgogne, founded in 1331, and of the Chapelle des Prémontrés. Although for two centuries the Faculté de Médecine never had any premises of its own it still held a significant position in the University. From 1281 it became a separate body, with its own statutes, confirmed by Philippe de Valois in 1331. In 1267 it elected its first dean, whose 235 successors followed each other uninterruptedly until the Revolution. Under the *Ancien Régime*, doctors and surgeons formed two absolutely distinct and rival corporate bodies. From 1472, the former established their school in the Rue de la Bucherie while the latter, from the 13th c., held their meetings near the Cordeliers' convent. It was for the Academy of Surgeons that the old part of the present-day building was constructed. And it was there that the two rival corporate bodies were united by the Convention Nationale in the Ecole de Santé (School of Health) on December 4, 1794. With the re-establishment of the University under the Empire, the school was given the name of the Faculté de Médecine. These vast buildings now house the administrative headquarters of the Université René-Descartes-Paris-V, as well as the library, the museum and archives of the Faculty of Medicine. Louis XV entrusted the plans of the Académie de Chirurgie (Academy of Surgeons) to the architect Gondouin who only completed part of the grandiose scheme, (1769-86), which was continued on the same scale by Ginan from

1878 to 1900. This last phase of construction did away with Courbet's studio in the W. The old part, which marked a return to the Classical Antique style of the 18th c., has four rows of columns forming an Ionic colonnade (Rue de l'Ecole-de-Médecine) which precedes a large, well-proportioned courtyard, also surrounded by an Ionic colonnade, while the large lecture room opens up under a Corinthian peristyle. A statue of Bichat, the 18th-c. anatomist, stands in the center of the courtyard.

The library (open to doctors and medical students; for visits, see the concierge; closed in Aug.) contains several hundred thousand works, 100 early printed books, 1100 manuscripts, of which two are from the 15th c., the letter of the doctor and writer Guy Patin (1601–72) and the 24 volumes of *Commentaires*, which are the day-to-day history of the Faculté de Médecine from 1395 to 1786 written in Latin; old book bindings. The Musée d'Histoire de la Médecine (→ Museums) is on the second floor.

On the corner of the Rue Hautefeuille and Rue Pierre Sarazin, the old mansion, which retains its attractive octagonal turret, was completely restored in 1977.

At 5 Rue de l'Ecole-de-Médecine, the Institute of Modern Languages of the Faculty of Letters occupies the old premises of the 'long-gowned' Brotherhood of Surgeons, who performed every kind of anatomical operation until the 17th c. 'Short-gowned' surgeons (usually only barbers) could only act as midwives or undertake bleeding. St Louis founded the Brotherhood, dedicated to the healing saints, Cosmas and Damien, in the 13th c. The lecture room, built in 1691, is covered by a dome with tall windows and crowned with small turrets with round windows called *lanternes*. It was the Ecole des Arts Décoratifs until 1933. Sarah Bernhardt was born in this house on October 25, 1844, as recorded by an inscription. To complete this walk, take the steps from the Rue Antoine-Dubois to rejoin the Rue Monsieur-le-Prince, perhaps by Rue Dupuytren. This was built in the 17th c. over the Cordeliers cemetery and it was where Armande Béjart lived after the death of her husband Molière.

Rue Monsieur-le-Prince

Before acquiring this princely title, the street, which takes its name from the Prince de Condé, was simply called Rue des Fossés, and ran along Philippe Auguste's wall, which moreover forms the base of the foundations of a few houses (nos. 41 to 47). Beautiful houses, whose imposing character is still clearly evident, can be seen all along the street (note particularly the balconies, wrought ironwork, carved brackets, and mascarons). No. 4, the Hôtel de Bacq (1740), has a lovely portal which can be seen from the Rue Dupuytren. No. 10 houses the International Association in the Auguste Comte

■ house, which is the reference center and museum of Auguste Comte (1798–1857), founder of positivism. The apartment where he lived until his death in 1857 can be viewed by appointment. Cadoudal (head of the Vendée, in opposition to the Republic) must have been arrested just opposite. Saint-Saëns lived at no. 14 from 1877 to 1889; Yves Brayer has his studio at no. 22, which belonged to La Gandara before him, who died in 1917. Pretty courtyard.

The Rue Racine was cut across the Clos des Cordeliers. George Sand, who was a typical Left Bank habituée, lived at no. 3.

The top end of the Rue Monsieur-le-Prince was called the Rue des Francs-Bourgeois-Saint-Michel in the 17th-c. The English poet Longfellow (1807–82) lived at no. 49. The imposing Lycée Saint-Louis occupies the sites of the Cordeliers' garden, the Collège d'Harcourt (founded 1280) and the Collège de Justice (created in 1354 by Jean de Justice). Blaise Pascal lived in no. 54, which still exists, from 1654 until he left to die in 1662 at the house of his sister, Gilberte. He was living here during the great spiritual experience, the famous 'night of fire' on November 23, 1654, and wrote *Les Pensées* and some of the *Provinciales*. Very beautiful houses at nos. 58, 60, 63, 65. The street goes as far as Boul. Saint-Michel. Take the Rue de Vaugirard (→Saint-Sulpice district) to reach the Rue de Condé.

Rue de Condé

This street is named after Henri II de Bourbon, Prince de Condé, but during the Revolution was called Rue de l'Egalité. A calm and somewhat austere street, it has a number of old houses. Nos. 1 to 5 have registered façades. At no. 8 Maurice Sand had an apartment that George Sand, his mother, shared for a while. Notice the brackets and wrought ironwork at no. 10. The Hôtel d'Henri II de Condé (on the site of nos. 9–25) belonged to the Condé until 1764 when he moved to the Palais-Bourbon. The Marquis de Sade was born in this *hôtel* (1740) when his mother was lady-in-waiting to the princesses. In 1773 Louis XV bought the land and gardens. For some time Pascal and his family lived at no. 20. Before her marriage to Camille Desmoulins (guillotined because he was suspected of moderation during the Terror, 1749), Lucile Duplessis lived at no. 22. After her outraged letter to Robespierre she was guillotined in her turn (1794). Note the wrought ironwork at no. 24, the Hôtel Gramont-Caderousse, and the stairs, courtyard and sculptures. The 18th-c. mansion at no. 25 was rented by Beaumarchais when he was writing *The Barber of Seville*. It is here that Alfred Valette and his wife, the novelist Rachilde, founded *Le Mercure de France* in 1903. It is now the headquarters of the *Revue des Temps Modernes*. At no. 28 is the old Hôtel du Président Le Rebours.

Rue de Tournon

This street was created in 1540. The land belonged to the abbey of Saint-Germain, and it took the name of the cardinal of Tournon, who was then abbot. It is a street full of fine architecture with elegant up-market ready-to-wear clothes shops and old bookshops. At no. 16 is the finest bookshop in Paris. A series of large private *hôtels* line the even-numbered side of the street and apartment houses, largely old, line the odd-numbered side. At no. 14 is the 17th-c. Petit Hôtel d'Entragues, and at no. 12, the Grand Hôtel d'Entragues, reconstructed by Neveu in Louis XVI's reign. Elizabeth, Comtesse d'Houdetot, indifferent to Rousseau's ardour, died here in 1813 and, after her, the dowager Duchesse d'Orléans, widow of Philippe Egalité. Note the ironwork and sculpted keystones on the registered façades on the road and courtyard. No. 27 was the house of the Chevalier d'Airain (Jacques Casanova de Seingalt), which was built on a site which François I offered to Clément Marot, his valet, and a great poet. In 1792 an unusual man lived and died at no. 19. He was John Paul Jones, who after having been the first admiral of the American navy, became rear-admiral of Catherine II the Great of Russia's fleet.

The actor Gérard Philipe (1922–59) died at no. 17; crowds packed the street to mourn, some even trying to climb up to the balcony of the room where he was laid out, wearing the costume of 'Le Cid', his greatest rôle. Josef Roth, the Austrian novelist and critic, came here after being driven from Vienna, and lived at no. 18 from 1937 to 1939. The Hôtel du Maréchal d'Ancre (later known as the Grand Hôtel de Nivernais) at no. 10, passed to the Duc de Luynes after the Italian soldier of fortune, Concino, confidant of Marie de' Medici and made marshal by her, was killed in 1617. Louis XIII (Marie's son) often stayed here and was in the *hôtel* on November 11, 1630, '*la journée des Dupes*'. When the power struggle between the Queen Mother and Cardinal Richelieu reached its climax, the Queen extracted a promise from her son to get rid of the cardinal, but he reneged, on what history called 'the day of the dupes', and as a result his mother was exiled and spent the remaining 12 years of her life in Cologne in miserable poverty.

Théroigne de Méricourt opened a club at no. 8, which was frequented by Danton, Desmoulins and Fabre d'Eglantine. G. Pierné had an apartment there from 1990 to 1937. No. 6 is the beautiful Hôtel de Brancas which, during the Regency, was reconstructed by Pierre Bullet, the designer of the Château de Champs-sur-Marne and the Crédit Foncier, Place Vendôme. On the pediment of the portal are allegorical statues of Justice and Prudence. The mansion was occupied by the Academie d'Equitation de La Martinère, which in 1764 became the property of the Duc de Brancas who gave it his name. Today it is the Institute Français d'Architecture, created in 1981 for the promotion of architecture. There is a beautiful staircase in the main building. In the courtyard is a library that specializes in

20th-c. architecture and urban planning. Temporary 20th-c. architectural exhibitions are held in the stables (entrance between no. 6 and no. 8) and the orangerie at the end of the garden. Gambetta lived on the top floor of no. 7, the Hôtel du Sénat, and A. Daudet also stayed there. The journalist, Hébert (Père Duchesne) lived at no. 5 in 1793. He had a mistress, Mlle Lenormand, who was a famous clairvoyant, consulted by Revolutionary leaders. At no. 4 is the Hôtel Jean de Palaiseau* which was refurbished in the 18th c. for the Montmorency family. Notice the peristyle in the courtyard, the front-staircase with columns and the staircase with wrought-iron bannisters. The façade and one of the rooms are registered. Lamartine, Ledru-Rollin and Renan all lived in this beautiful house. At no. 2 is the 18th-c. Hôtel de Châtillon* where the daughter of Boucher, the painter, died, and Balzac lived from 1827 to 1830. Later the poet, V. de Laprade and Musset lived there and finally, from 1874 to 1881, this literary house was inhabited by André Gide.

▣ Museums to visit

Musée d'Histoire de la Médecine (12 Rue de l'Ecole-de-Médecine): history of the teaching of medicine and surgery.

Musée Dupuytren (15 Rue de l'Ecole-de-Médecine): collection of anatomical specimens.

L'Opéra district**

9th and 2nd arr./Map ref. 10–C2
Métro: Opéra
Bus: 20, 21, 22, 27, 29, 42, 52, 53, 66, 68, 95
Parking: Rue de la Chausée-d'Antin
Taxis: Place de l'Opéra. Tel: 47–42–75–75.

Like the Place des Vosges and the Place Vendôme, the Avenue and the Place de l'Opéra form a cohesive, uniform group of buildings designed as a setting for the new theater built under the Second Empire. Here Haussmannian urban planning can be seen, with its distinctive appearance of wide vistas and monumental façades, whose whiteness contrasts vividly with the polychrome of the Opéra.

This Garnier 'palace', which is considered to be the finest architectural example of the Napoléon III style, now dominates one of the busiest intersections in the capital. It is surrounded by international banks, foreign tourist offices, and travel agencies. The district is very lively during the day, but calmer in the evening when the offices close. Later, after the Opéra and neighboring theaters have emptied, the cafés along the Boulevard des Capucines, such as the Café de la Paix (the most famous) are full of people.

Tour of the district

45 mins.

The Opéra**

Place de l'Opéra is open daily (except May 1 and July 14 and days with matinee performances), 11am–4.30pm. Performances daily except Tues. and Wed. Ballets: reservations 14 days in advance. Best seats: dress circle, 1st and 2nd floor boxes, 4th floor front row seats.

The Opéra, or the Académie Nationale de Musique et de Danse, is a sumptuous building by the architect Charles Garnier (1825–98). After the assassination attempt on the Emperor on January 14, 1858 by Orsini near the Peletier room, it was decided to build a new opera in a safe, open area. Charles Garnier won the architectural competition in 1861, though his design did not win the support of Napoléon III and Eugénie. The Empress is said to have attacked the architect asking, 'What is this style? It isn't a style; it's not Greek, nor is it Louis XVI'. 'No, Madame,' Garnier is supposed to have replied. 'These styles have had their day. This is the Napoléon III style, and you complain?' Upon which the Emperor murmured, 'Don't worry, she knows nothing at all.' In fact the building became the archetype of the Napoléon III style – eclectic, Baroque and excessive. The first stone was laid on July 21, 1862, after vast foundations had been laid below ground. However, the Prussian war and the Commune held up construction until 1875, when the Opéra was finally inaugurated, with great ceremony by MacMahon, President of the Third Republic.

Although the surface area of the theater is one of the largest in the world, there are only 2131 seats; much of the space is taken up by rehearsal rooms, foyers, the library, the museum, and, areas devoted to public circulation. In fact it was in these spaces (vestibules, staircases, landings, etc.) that the magnificent rituals of fashionable bourgeois society accompanying every performance took place. The Opéra, designed in the most brilliant period of the Second Empire, was, thanks to the new director Louis Véron, able to accommodate scenery was on a scale lavish enough to please even Meyerbeer. The upkeep of such an establishment is extremely hard to sustain, despite State subsidy. But the Opéra still remains one of the most illustrious opera houses in the world.

The exterior

Because of its broad, flat dome, the Opéra has a stocky silhouette which, however, disappears as you approach, and its polychrome decoration and spatial variety come into focus. On the main façade, emphasis has been placed on the first floor, which consists of a large open gallery or loggia above the arcaded entrance hall. The loggia is accentuated by Corinthian columns with monolithic shafts of Ravière stone. Between them, above the tall windows, small circular *oeil-de-boeuf* windows shelter busts of famous composers and librettists. Other composers are portrayed in medaillons carved in bas-relief on the spandrels between the arcades leading to the foyer from the square. Antique bronze gilt masks by Klagmann are set closely together along the top of the façade with, at either end, immense bronze winged allegorical figures of *Music* and *Poetry* by Gurnery. While the dome corresponds to the cupola above the amphitheater, a triangular pediment corresponds to the front of the stage, which is one of the largest in Europe. At the apex of this low-pitched gable, almost hidden behind the dome, is a statue of *Apollo of the Golden Lyre* (by Millet) with winged horses (Pégases) by Lequesne at each end. Garnier used 73 sculptors for the Opéra décor. On the *avant-corps* (projecting ends) at each side of the steps leading up to the building are four huge allegorical sculpted groups: *Music* (Guillaume), *Lyric Poetry* (Jouffroy), *Lyric Drama* or *Opera* (Perraud) and *Dance* (Carpeaux). When this last work was unveiled it was considered indecent. During the night of August 27 1869 the sculpture was defaced with a bottleful of ink. An attempt was even made to remove it from view. In 1965 Carpeaux' work of art was placed in the Louvre (it is now in the Musée d'Orsay); replaced by a replica by Paul Belmondo, in the Opéra forecourt. On the side façades, which are more austere, are the semicircular pavilions. The one to the E (Rue Auber) has a separate entrance courtyard and a double access ramp, designed so that the Emperor could be driven to the level of the dress circle. After Orsini's assassination attempt, this found favor with the Emperor. Today it is the entrance to the library and museum. The pavilion on the W side is for season-ticket holders. The building is surrounded by a balustrade, and further on by branched street lamps or bronze flares, designed by Chabaud, and by marble columns with lanterns.

The interior

1st vestibule: statues of Lully, Rameau, Gluck and Handel by Schoenewerk, Allasseur, Cavelier and Salmson respectively. 2nd vestibule: box office open 11am–6.30pm. Season-ticket holders enter a huge circular vestibule where, in the center of the vaulted ceiling, in a pseudo-Arabic inscription, Charles Garnier has signed and dated his work; then, through a gallery, the Grand Staircase can be reached (ornamental basin with the bronze *Pythoness* by Marcello).

Only the Grand Staircase shows a certain bravura. The imprint of different historical styles and the polychromy of its balustrade of onyx and verde and rosso antico (red and green marble) combine to make it a powerfully original work. The white marble staircase (nearly 33ft/10m wide) curves up to divide at the entrance to the amphitheater and the stalls at a central landing which is guarded by Thomas' monumental caryatids. The candelabra set at intervals along the balustrade are by Carrier-Belleuse. Two perpendicular flights lead to the Avant-Foyer which leads to the Grand Foyer. On every floor arcades of huge marble columns allow opera-goers to take part in the social parade where they can see and, more importantly, be seen (on Friday evenings everyone wears evening dress). Allegorical ceiling paintings by Pils add to the overall polychromy.

The Grand Foyer is approached through the Avant-Foyer, whose domed ceiling is covered with mosaics by Salviati, after Curzon. It is one of the most beautiful parts of the Opéra, 177ft/54m long, 46ft/13m wide and 39½ft/18m high. At the central entrance are two mirrors by Saint-Gobain; at the sides, paired columns; at either end, chimneypieces adorned with caryatids, behind which are the octagonal salons (W salon, décor painted by Burrias; E salon by Delaunay). The Grand Foyer is decorated with allegorical paintings by Paul Baudry. Bouchard's monument to the composer Camille Saint-Saëns (1835–1921) was inaugurated in March 1938. The glass doors link the foyer with the Loggia, which overlooks the Ave. and Place de l'Opéra. By the middle door, is a bust of Garnier by Carpeaux.

The red and gold Auditorium* today appears a little outmoded but very characteristic of the period, with five tiers of quite uncomfortable boxes. Eight large columns, of highly polished scagliola (marble), support the dome from which hangs a large chandelier weighing 6½tons/6t. The old ceiling by Lenepveu has been hidden since 1964 by a new ceiling by Chagall, inspired by nine famous operas and ballets (Mozart's *The Magic Flute*, Wagner's *Tristan and Isolde*, Berlioz's *Romeo and Juliet*, Debussy's *Pelleas and Melisande*, Ravel's *Daphnis and Chloë*, Stravinsky's *The Firebird*, Tchaikovsky's *Swan Lake*, Adam's *Giselle* and Mussorgsky's *Boris Godunov*).

The stage, which is 170ft/52m wide, 196ft/60m high and 121ft/37m deep, can hold up to 450 performers and accommodate a formidable amount of stage machinery. It is linked to the Foyer de Danse, which boosts a mirror 22ft/7m by 32ft/10m is decorated with paintings by Boulanger. The latter is the scene of many of Degas's ballerina paintings.

Place de l'Opéra

The square, which interrupts the vista of the Ave. de l'Opéra, is dominated by the Opéra house itself, and is one of the great street intersections of Paris, scarcely able to cope with its border of traffic. Indeed, its Second Empire designs overlie a much older urban fabric, and cut in two the Boul. des Capucines, beloved by 19th-c. Parisians. The façades of the buildings surrounding the square have Corinthian pilasters rising two storeys to conform to a design made compulsory by a decree of 1860.

The Grand Hôtel was built during the Second Empire in a quarter undergoing complete reconstruction to provide 700 bedrooms and 70 salons for the important visitors expected in Paris for the International Exhibition of 1867. This imposing building was constructed by the architect Armand on the site of what had been a kitchen garden in Louis XV's reign. To conform with regulations currently in force in that area (whose notable buildings include the Hôtel Scribe, and the Jockey Club), the 39ft/120m-long façade had to have a Colossal order of Corinthian pilasters, while the main entrance on the Boul. des Capucines was surmounted by columns and atlantes (male figures) supporting the entablature. The hotel, which was originally equipped with the latest in modern comforts, underwent unnecessary refurbishments in 1956 and 1976 which left scarcely anything of the original décor. However, the large dining room was preserved. This semicircular room, which is on three levels, has a luxurious décor of moulded plaster ornaments by the gifted sculptor Millet. The Café de la Paix forms a part of the Grand Hôtel. Its décor, by Garnier, has been restored. Somewhat old-fashioned, but sumptuous, it remains a meeting-place popular with after-theater diners and tourists from all over the world.

Four wide main streets fan out from the Place de l'Opéra: Boul. des Capucines, Rue de la Paix, Ave. de l'Opéra and the Rue du 14-Septembre.

Avenue de l'Opéra

S of the square

With its beautiful shops, this is one of the main tourist attractions of Paris. Crowds of German, English, American and Japanese visitors stream along this world famous avenue. The characters on the shop signs indicate a considerable amount of Japanese trade. The avenue was planned in 1853 and constructed from 1854 to 1876. Had there been no change of régime it would still be the Avenue Napoléon. First the site (the Butte Saint-Roche), had to be levelled,

but one of the mills, the Radet, was removed to Montmartre. The
98ft/30m wide avenue, which was designed to link the Louvre with
the new Opéra, is pure Haussmann in concept, with its well-built
five-storey buildings whose solidity is emphasized by the iron
balconies. The layout of the earlier quarter, with 17th- and 18th-c.
houses, can be found in the adjacent streets. No. 29 is the National
Center for the Visual Arts, with a *trompe-l'oeil* entrance.

Rue de la Chaussee-d'Antin

To the E of the Place de l'Opéra on the l. in Boul. des Capucines and
the Boul. Haussmann. This whole district was completely
transformed in the first half of the 18th c. by Pardaillan Goudrin,
Duc d'Antin. Among the famous who lived in this fashionable street
was Rossini, who lived at no. 2 from 1857 until 1868. The portal is
decorated with gorgons' heads.

The cutting of the Rue Meyerbeer entailed the destruction of many
famous houses, including: no. 5, originally built by Brongniart, in
which the Marquis d'Epinay died, one of the Grimm brothers lived,
and Mozart passed five months in 1778 after his mother died.
Chaplin lived here from 1863 to 1936. Germaine Necker de Staël was
brought up in a sumptuous mansion at no. 7 (now demolished)
where her mother received Gibbon, Buffon, Saint-Lambert and
Marmontel. In 1798 it was bought by the banker Jules Récamier,
whose wife held the most distinguished salon of the Directoire here.
The Temple of Terpsichore at no. 9 was nothing more than the
Hotel de la Guimard (Fragonard decorated this beautiful mansion,
built by Ledoux in 1773, for the Prince de Soubise's mistress).

No. 10 was the birthplace of the writer Fernand Gregh (1873–1960).
It dates from the Restoration and has kept its beautiful colonnade.
The Revolution suddenly rose up from the past in April 1977 when
workmen at no. 20 discovered the 21 heads of the Kings of Judah,
which had adorned the façade of Notre-Dame. They were saved by
the Royalist Lakanal, a scholar and brother of one of the members
of the Convention (→ Musée de Cluny). The hotel was part of three
buildings which Lakanal had constructed. Moreau also lived there.

For the rest of the Rue de la Chaussée-d'Antin, → the Saint-Lazare
district. The Boul. Haussmann, which runs along the N of the Place,
is flanked by two of the largest shops in Paris, Galeries Lafayette
and Printemps Saint-Lazare, with their magnificent main halls.

Rue Edouard-VII

*To the E of the square, end street to the r. in the Boul. des
Capucines.*

This, like the Boul. Haussmann, is one of the rare main

throughfares in the district to have been constructed in the 20th c. The project was launched in 1911. The architect Nénot opted for a right-angled layout whose two sides join at an irregular octagonal *place* with arcades; in its center is the equestrian statue of Edward VII by Landowski. The Société Generale took over the whole site except the theater in the Place Edouard-VII. Since 1984 it has been called the Edouard VII – Sacha Guitry theater, in honor of the actor-playwright who created *Désiré* there in 1927. The square is linked to the Square de l'Opéra-Louis-Jouvet, where the Anthénée theater is situated. On the eve of World War II and in the early war years, Louis Jouvet, the Anthénée's director since 1934, brought such brilliance to the theater, that those who saw *La Guerre de Troie n'aura pas lieu* or any of Giraudoux's other plays will never forget the experience. Jouvet, like his master Molière, died on stage, on August 16, 1951.

▷ The birth of the opera

Opera developed in France under the influence of Italian lyric works, reinforced by *pastorales* (early opera-ballets) and Court ballets. The official founders of French opera were the Abbé Pierre Perrin and Robert Cambert (murdered by his valet while working in London in 1627). Louis XIV gave them the monopoly for performance of opera in the French language in 1669. But when Perrin, the victim of unscrupulous entrepreneurs, was languishing in prison for debt, Lully bought the licence from him, and it is Lully who always gets the credit for being the 'Father of French opera'. The Royal Academy of Music was opened on the site of the present 42 Rue Mazarine and 43 Rue de Seine, occupying several halls, the last and most renowned being those in the Rue de Richelieu (now the Square Luvois), that in the Rue Peletier, which burned down in 1873, and the hall in the former Théâtre des Italiens.

The Académie Nationale de Musique et de Danse is controlled by a director nominated by the government.

▷ Traces of the first gas and electric lighting

Although Lebon invented gas lighting in 1791, it was not until 1829 that public street lighting was first used in Paris. The first attempt at urban electric lighting took place in 1878 during the International Exhibition, when the Ave. de l'Opéra was lit at 32 points. These beautiful lamps can still be seen. Paris has preserved numerous examples of these early lighting devices: the beautiful lamps and rostral columns (decorated with ships' prows) in the Place de la Concorde, installed by the architect Hittorff in 1840; the group of sculpted candelabra on the Pont Alexander III; the bronze torches by Félix Chabaut around the Palais Garnier; the candelabra in the

Place de l'Hôtel-de-Ville; and the lamps in the Place de la République, where gas lighting devices from 1860 can still be seen.

A more recent curiosity is a lamp run on a solar powered system in the Place de l'Alma.

The Palais de Justice**

4 Boul. du Palais, 1st arr./Map ref. 17–A2, B2
Métro: Cité
Bus: 21, 38, 81, 85, 96
Parking: Rue de Harlay
Taxis: Place du Châtelet.Tel: 42–33–20–99. 29 Quai Saint-Michel.
Tel: 43–29–63–66.

The great mass of the Palais de Justice, which fills nearly all the W part of the Cité, is one of the most evocative of buildings, with its old towers lining the quays and a history going back over sixteen centuries. Inside it is full of the bustle of palais life, but visitors must above all see the Sainte-Chapelle, a miracle of Gothic splendor recalling the revolutionary history of the Conciergerie.

The history of the Palais de Justice

In the words of the Palace's historian, H. Stein, it is probable that there has always been a Cité building that was first only a fortress, then the home of the Kings of France, the scene of royal courts, and finally the center of all the capital's judiciary services. The palace of the Roman governors and emperors, including Julian the Apostate, must have been situated here in the Cité's fortified area. The Merovingian kings, and later the Capetians, succeeded them. Louis VI le Gros (the Fat) and Louis VII le Jeune (the Young) died here. Philippe Auguste was born and lived here in the palace, and here Joinville wrote his life of St. Louis. The building, which was enlarged during the reigns of Philippe le Bel (the Fair) and Enguerrand de Marigny, had from the early 15th c. on, the appearance of the castle reproduced in the famous miniature from the Duc de Berry's *Les Très riches Heures* (Book of Hours). In the late 14th c., the king began to spend less time in the palace and more in the Hôtel Saint-Pol and the Louvre, which was to become the royal residence. The departure of the Dauphin, the future Charles V, was caused by the tragic events of February 22 1357, when he saw his palace invaded and his advisers slain in front of him by Etienne Marcel and his followers. The palace then became the seat of the Parliament.

The devastating fires of 1618 and 1776 led to modifications and enlargements. Salomon de Brosse, architect of the Palais du Luxembourg and Saint-Gervais, was commissioned to repair the ravages of the first fire and, over a century and a half later, Desmaisons and Antoine (1783–86) built the entrance and the monumental façade on to the Cour du Mai. The plans for extensions were continued in 1825 and completed during the Second Empire by the architect Joseph-Louis Duc and his colleagues, and by Daumet after 1879. From 1911 to 1914, Albert Tournaire built the wing over the Quai des Orfèvres, at the corner of the Boulevard du Palais.

Formerly the palace was more disorganized and more picturesque. Galleries, haberdashery shops and bookshops enlivened it. Their memory lingers on in the Corneille's Galerie du Palais, or in Boilescu's Le Lutrin. Mention should also be made of the engravings by Abraham Boss, Moreau or Lancelot. The shops were damaged by the fire of 1776. The last one disappeared in 1840.

Tour of the Palais de Justice

Tel: 43–29–12–55

The exterior

The Tour de l'Horloge (clock-tower)

This square tower (154ft/47m high), which stands on the corner of the quay and the Boul. du Palais, dates from the reign of Jean le Bon (14th c.). It had the first public clock in Paris, commissioned by Charles V from Henri de Vic in 1371. It was renovated during Henri III's reign and decorated with sculptures by G. Pilon (figures of, to the r., *Justice*, and to the l., *Law*), which were restored in 1685 and again in 1851 by Toussaint. Frequently overhauled since then, the clock now no longer works.

The N façade

This façade is on the Quai de l'Horloge side, and the waters of the Seine washed against it until 1611, when the level of the quay was raised. Beyond the Tour de l'Horloge, the façade has three round towers topped with turreted roofs. They are, respectively: the Tour César (Caesar's Tower), which adjoins Philippe le Bel's apartments; the Tour d'Argent (Silver Tower), where the crown jewels were stored (both towers were built about 1300), and the Tour Bonbec. This tower, built in 1250 and renovated after a fire in 1935, was isolated in the past. From the 15th to the 16th c. it served as a torture chamber (→inset).

The towers and the lower parts of the building between the Tour de l'Horloge and the twin towers, are the remains of the royal palace of the Capetians, dating from the early 14th c. The dry moat that runs along the façade between the Tour de l'Horloge and the Tour Bonbec indicates the original ground level. The upper parts of the building, and the façade between the Tour d'Argent and the Tour Bonbec, were reconstructed in the 19th c. by the architect Joseph-Louis Duc (1802–79), who is responsible for three-quarters of the whole building. Finally, the whole of the block to the W of the Tour Bonbec, which is used by the Cour de Cassation (Supreme Court of Appeal), was built by Duc in the Corinthian style; it has a central pavilion with a pediment, decorated with caryatids. Before returning to the Boul. du Palais and the main façade, you can visit the Conciergerie (→inset), the oldest prison in Paris, with its entrance between twin towers. The E façade of the palace is on the Boul. du Palais. Leave the Tour de l'Horloge, to see first the Civil Court, built in 1853, then the façade of the huge lobby called the Salle des Pas-Perdus, which is pierced by wide bays.

The Cour du Mai

The palace's main entrance, in the center, leads to this impressive looking courtyard, the work of the architects Desmaison and Antoine (1783–86). Its name is due to an old custom whereby the Clerks of the Court (an important corporation) planted a tree here on the first day of May each year. On the boulevard side it has magnificent railings from 1787, restored in 1877. In front of the main façade at the far end of the forecourt is a broad staircase in the Louis XVI style. The height of its projecting Doric avant-corps is increased by four allegorical statues on the balustrade above the columns. *Abundance* and *Strength*, by Pierre Berruer, and *Prudence* and *Justice*, by Frédéric Lecomte. This avant-corps has a quandrangular dome, decorated at its base by two genii (winged figures) supporting an escutcheon with the royal arms, by Pajou. On either side of the iron railings on the boulevard, two Classical pavilions stand at the ends of the galleries that enclose the two sides of the courtyard: the r. pavilion has a fine Louis XVI staircase leading directly to the Galerie Marchande and the Salle des Pas-Perdus (this is the most-used entrance to the palace); the pavilion on the l. has two vaulted passages that link the Cour du Mai with the courtyard of the Sainte-Chapelle. To the l. of the entrance to the Saint-Chapelle is a Henri IV façade.

The Police Correctionelle

Leaving the palace by the Cour du Mai, to the r., the building of the Police Correctionelle (the petty crimes court) stands on the boulevard; its façade is copied from galleries of the Cour du Mai. Beneath this building is a vaulted passage (usually closed) giving access to the Sainte-Chapelle courtyard. On the l. of this passage, on the boulevard, a plaque put up on January 31 1967 marks the site of the former Saint-Michel chapel, where Philippe Auguste was baptized in 1165 and where, in 1210, he installed the headquarters of the Brotherhood of the Pilgrims of the Mont-Saint-Michel; in 1470 Louis XI transferred the headquarters of the Order of Saint-Michel there (this is the origin of the name of Boul. Saint-Michel).

The interior

Mon.-Fri., 9am-6pm

Inside the palace, the most-visited parts are the Salle des Pas-Perdus and the Chambre Dorée.

The vestibule (Galerie Marchande)

Opposite the central entrance is a staircase decorated with a 18th-c.-style statue of Law. This leads to the chambers of the Court of Appeal and to the lawyers' robing room. To the r., the gallery leads to the Salle des Pas-Perdus.

The Salle des Pas-Perdus

This magnificent hall is the true center of the palace, and from midday onwards is full of activity. It comprises two enormous naves, separated by a row of semicircular arches. A plaque commemorates the re-establishment of the Bar in France, and a monument to the memory of Berryer, the 19th-c. lawyer and adversary of the Second Empire, designed by Lebas, has a figure resting its foot on a tortoise, an ironic symbol of the slowness of justice.

The Salle des Pas-Perdus replaced the Grande Salle, one of the most famous halls in the France's history, decorated in the past with royal statues. At the end of the hall was the black marble table, of which a fragment is now in the *musée lapidaire* in the Salle des Gens d'Armes, that was used for the signing of treaties and official contracts, ceremonies accompanied by memorable banquets. The entire hall was the center for State ceremonies. Burnt down in 1618, the Grande Salle was rebuilt by Salomon de Brosse in 1622. Burned again during the Commune (1871), it was once more rebuilt by Duc and Daumet, in the same style.

At the r.-hand end, opposite the War Memorial, a majestic double staircase leads to the chambers of the Civil Court and to the office of the Clerk of the Court. Beneath the staircase, a passage gives on to a pretty vestibule, where there are various courtrooms, the library, and the President's office. This part of the palace dates from 1853.

The Chambre Dorée

Several chambers of the Civil Tribunal open off the Salle des Pas-Perdus, among them the First Civil Court, formerly the Grand-Chambre, or Chambre Dorée, with its ceiling of flattened rib vaults and pendentives. This is a remnant of the old palace and has played a major role in its history. Originally it was probably the bedchamber of St Louis, and it was later part of the premises of the Paris Parliament. Here, from April 6, 1793, the Revolutionary tribunal sat, and condemned many famous figures, among them Marie-Antoinette. Restored in 1856, burned by the Communards in 1871, the Grand-Chambre was reestablished in the original Louis XII style of 1502 by Duc and Daumet.

The Galerie des Prisonniers and the Galerie Lamoignon

These form a single long gallery with flattened vaulting; part of it is new. It has three fine pediments, probably from the end of the 18th c.; their decorations recall earlier jurisdictions. To the l., this gallery leads to the Galerie Duc, which contains the entrance to the lawyers' robing room, and to the r. leads to the Galerie Saint-Louis, rebuilt by J. -L. Duc in 1866. At the end of the Galerie Saint-Louis, the Galerie des Bustes (busts of jurists and magistrates) leads (to the l.) to the Supreme Court of Appeal, or Cour de Cassation* (to visit, consult a guard here if no public hearing is taking place). The chambers and offices of the Cour de Cassation offer an interesting and intact example of Second Empire interior decoration.

At the end of the Galerie Lamoignon is the Harlay Vestibule, again the work of J. -L. Duc. Note, at the r.-hand or N end, the statues of St Louis and Philippe Auguste. Between them a door opens into the Civil Chamber of the Cour de Cassation (above); this is the entrance to public hearings.

⌐ The Conciergerie**

1 Quai de l'Horloge (open daily, 10am-7pm Apr.-Sept. 30 10am-5pm Oct 1-Mar. 31). Tel. 43-54-30-06.

The Conciergerie is an important remnant of the palace of the Capetians, occupying the lower floor of the N wing of the palace. The accused wait here to go before the Cour d'Assizes or the Cour des Appels Correctionels (or Court of Petty Appeal) – whose sentences are not necessarily petty, and can range from five days to five years. The Conciergerie, Paris's first prison, looms large in the history of the Revolution. The present entrance dates from 1864; it gives onto a small courtyard with, on the r., the doorway to the Salles des Gardes.

The Salle des Gardes

This fine, well-restored building of the first quarter of the 14th c. measures 75ft/22.8m by 39ft/11.8m, with a vault of 23ft/6.9m high. Three massive columns divide it into two naves, each of four rib-vaulted bays. To the r., on the window side, are two small outside staircases. The one on the r. leads to the Tour de César (not open to the public), where Ravaillac (Henri IV's assassin) and Lacenaire were imprisoned on the ground floor, as were, on the first floor, Prince Pierre Bonaparte (in 1870) and Prince Jérôme Bonaparte (in 1883). The l. staircase leads to the Tour d'Argent (Silver Tower), where Damiens was imprisoned, before being executed by quartering (pulled apart by four horses) for striking Louis XV with a penknife. The young Duc d'Orléans was imprisoned on the first floor in 1890. To the r., down a few steps, a door gives on to Marie-Antoinette's staircase. At the end of the hall, another door leads to the Salle des Gens d'Armes.

The Salle des Gens d'Armes* (Hall of the men-at-Arms)

Sometimes wrongly called the Salle Saint-Louis (this great hall is in fact owed to his grandson, Philippe le Bel), it is a magnificent architectural composition (1301–15), which archeologists compare only to the Mont Saint-Michel monastery and the Palais des Papes (Papal Palace) in Avignon. Including the Rue de Paris (→ below), the hall measures 227ft/69.3m by 90ft/27.4m, with a height to the top of the vaults of 28ft/8.55m. Three rows of columns and pillars (69 in all), differing in form, divide it into four naves, one of which has 13 bays, the others nine, all with rib vaulting. Two chimney-pieces stand against the N wall and two more against the S. This is the lower storey of the old Grand-salle (Salle des Pas-Perdus), which was reached by a spiral staircase that still exists. Burned in 1618, the

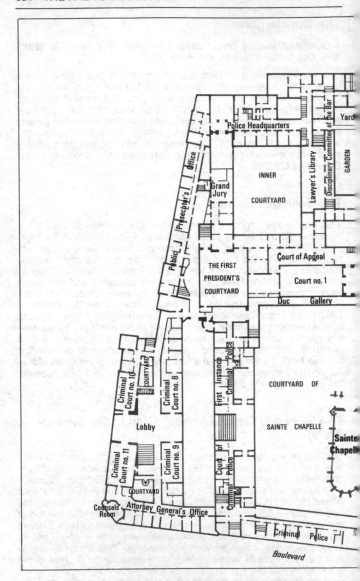

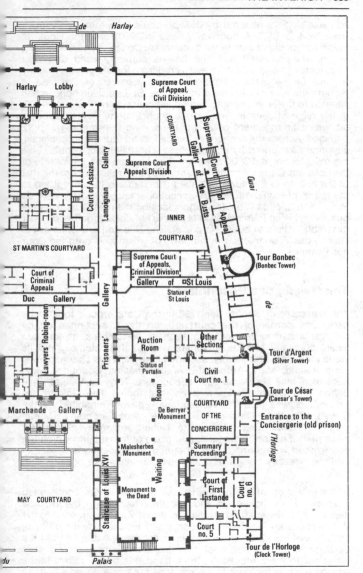

Palais de Justice

hall was skilfully restored by Joseph-Louis Duc, then by Daumet, from 1868 to 1880. A doorway (made in 1966) onto the Boul. de Palais allows direct access via a staircase. Concerts and exhibitions are now organized here. The hall is currently used to house fragments of stone sculpture recovered from the old palace, notably a piece of the black marble table and a carved capital said to recount the love of Abelard and Héloïse. St. Louis' kitchens, a hall situated to the N, is wrongly named, since it was built around 1350, in the reign of Jean le Bon. It is a square room, vaulted above a staggered arrangement of 21 columns, nine freestanding and 12 engaged. Across the corners of the hall stand four great fireplaces, supported by curious flying buttresses. These fireplaces could serve the royal family and 3000 retainers. The four bays on the W side of the Salle des Gens d'Armes, separated by iron railings from the rest of the hall, form the corridor called Rue de Paris because it led to the rooms of the Revolutionary executioner known as 'Monsieur de Paris'. Here the '*pailleux*' (prisoners lacking the means to bribe the guards and keep themselves '*à la pistole*') huddled together on their miserable pallets of straw (*la paille*). The Rue de Paris ends at the Galerie des Prisonniers, the windows of which look onto the Cour des Femmes.

The Galerie des Prisonniers

The massacre of September 1792 in the Conciergerie took place here. One corner of the courtyard, on the l., sectioned off by railings, was reserved for men. With its portcullises, its fountain where so many famous prisoners washed their clothes, and its stone table, the melancholy, secluded courtyard has changed little. Mme Roland, Marie-Antoinette, André Chénier, Cadoudal, Mme Récamier, Mlle de Sombreuil, Labédoyère, Ney, La Valette, Proudhon and Orsini all knew it as it is today. The Galerie des Prisonniers was also the Revolutionary prison, inhabited by the Queen, Danton, Desmoulins, Hoche, the Girondins, Marat, Couthom, Saint-Juste, Chaumette, Hébert and many others. But more than a prison, it was a sordid place of transit, into which the condemned were herded and where, in an atmosphere of weirdly artificial vivacity, anguish mingled with elegance, gaiety and intrigue.

In the l. section of the gallery is a small room where condemned prisoners were locked up and had their hair shorn before their departure for the scaffold. At the end, a gate was the entrance to the Conciergerie during the Revolution, preceded them by the office of the Clerk of the Court (now a refreshment room; entrance from the Cour du Mai). It was through this gate that the condemned were taken out to the tumbrils. On the r.-hand side of the gallery at the end, on the l., is the door (the same door, but since moved a little) of Marie-Antoinette's cell (→ inset); the room is unrecognizable, having been converted into an expiatory chapel in 1816. Adjoining it is Robespierre's cell (to which, wounded, he was brought in the evening of 9 Thermidor), which leads to the Salle des Girondins.

The Salle des Girondins

An oratory dedicated to the Virgin by Louis VII, this former Conciergerie chapel, again a chapel during the Restoration, has retained, with its altar, its original appearance; the upper storey was taken off in 1869, by order of the Empress, so that the prisoners might hear Mass. This is where the Girondins spent their last night. Opposite the entrance, in a glass case, a collection of souvenirs of the period includes a crucifix found in Marie-Antoinette's cell and a facsimile of a note written by the Queen with a pin; articles of linen and other objects (the armchair is from the Tuileries); the lock of Robespierre's cell and a blade of the guillotine used during the Terror; a medallion of Mme Elisabeth, the King's sister. Three other glass cases contain the orders for commital to prison of famous people (including Hugo and Clemenceau), and engravings of scenes of the Revolution (the originals are at the Bibliothèque Nationale).

The Sainte-Chapelle***

4 Boul. du Palais. Tel. 43-54-30-09 (open 9.30am-6pm, Apr. 1-Sept. 30; 10am-4pm Oct. 1-Mar. 31; guided tours by the CNMHS.

This royal shrine, unfortunately enclosed in an inadequate space, is the oldest part of the Palais de Justice complex, coming before the buildings of the Conciergerie. St Louis built this monumental reliquary for the fragments of the True Cross and, especially, the Crown of Thorns, which he had bought at vast expense from Baudouin II, Emperor of Constantinople. The architect was perhaps Pierre de Montreuil; the plans date from 1241. Begun in January 1246, the church was consecrated on April 25 1248. It was burnt down in 1630 and only slowly rebuilt. In about 1790 its demolition was considered, but in the 19th c., interest in the Middle Ages revived greatly, and the building was restored toward the end of Louis-Philippe's reign by Duban, Lassus, Viollet-le-Duc and Boeswillwald. The paintings and stained glass are currently being restored.

The exterior

The building is admirable for its elegance and lightness: the windows are so large in relation to the slender stone framework that it seems to remain standing only by a miracle of equilibrium. In appearance it is extremely high (139ft/42.5m) for its length (118ft/

36m) and breadth (56ft/17m); this is because it comprises two superimposed chapels. The very low ground-floor chapel was for the servants, the upper for the royal family and courtiers. Only the S side is exposed to view, the N side being obscured by the building of the later wing of the Cour du Mai. The tall windows are surmounted by delicately carved gables and a graceful balustrade. Beneath the 4th window on the r., in the upper storey, a narrow passage gave access from the oratory chapel called the Oratoire de Saint-Louis: monarchs were able to attend services here, hidden from public view.

The main portal on the W façade is composed of two superimposed porches. Over the upper porch, the great rose window with Flamboyant tracery, rebuilt in the reign of Charles VIII, is surmounted by a balustrade carved with fleurs-de-lis; two angels on the ledge crown the monogram of King Charles. A 19th-c. statue of the Virgin decorates the pier of the door of the lower chapel. On the tympanum is a bas-relief: *Le Couronnement de la Vierge* (The Crowning of the Virgin), also 19th-c.

The interior

The height of the vaulting in the lower chapel is 22ft/6.6m. Its square vaults are supported on 14 single-shafted columns. Some tombstones, mostly of the 14th and 15th c., are set in the floor, and that of Jacques Boileau can still be seen. The poet, his brother, was at first buried in the Saint-Chapelle, but during the Revolution his remains were transferred to Saint-Germain-des-Prés. An internal staircase leads from the lower to the upper chapel.

The upper chapel: this royal chapel marks the culmination of all the research of the Gothic period into vaulting and lighting. The thrust of the vaults is carried outside by prominent buttresses, leaving the walls free of interior support structures, then to frame delicate stained-glass windows.

The windows: each of the 15 windows (50ft/15.4m × 14ft/4.25m) is a dazzling jewel case. They have been skilfully restored by Lusson, following the designs by Steinhell, and under the direction of F. de Guilhermy. It is hard to tell the old parts from the new; out of 1134 scenes, 720 are thought to date back to the 13th c. The three central windows of the apse are devoted to the New Testament (from l. to r.: St John the Evangelist, Jesus and St John the Baptist, the first on the r. of the nave to the history of the relics. St Louis, his brother Robert, and a queen (probably Blanche de Castille), are frequently depicted in scenes of the translation of the Crown of Thorns and the fragments of the True Cross. All the other windows relate to scenes from the Old Testament, including the great rose window, which shows the Apocalypse.

The remaining architecture (67ft/20.5m under the vault) disappears beneath the 19th-c. gilding and polychrome decoration reconstructed from 13th-c. fragments. A blind arcade runs beneath the windows, with quatrefoils framing scenes of the martyrs. On ornamental supports (*culs-de-lampe*) set against the pillars, statues of the Apostles carry consecration crosses (marking the consecration of the church). The third, fourth and fifth statues on the l. are 14th c. Four have been remodelled after the originals when they still existed, but were broken in several places; two that were missing have been remade. Two niches, below the windows of the fourth bay on either side of the chapel, were seats of honor reserved for the King, the Queen and other members of the royal family. In the second bay, on the l., is the doorway to the external gallery that communicated with the chapel. Behind the altar, above the center of a lovely blind arcade with an opening in it, is a wooden arched baldachin, a 19th-c. replica of the one destroyed in the Revolution, beneath which the relics (now at Notre-Dame) were displayed. Two wooden staircases lead up to the platform. From the porch of the upper chapel a door communicates directly with the Galerie Marchande in the Palais de Justice. In the Sainte-Chapelle courtyard, on the r. on leaving the chapel, note the tall 16th-c. building, the façade of which is decorated with fleurs-de-lis; its dormer windows were altered in the 19th c. This was the Sainte-Chapelle foundry, and is all that is left of the canons' living quarters.

The torture tower

The Tour Bonbec (Bon-Bec: babbler) was so named because it was here that even the most recalcitrant prisoners became eloquent.

Several degrees of 'questions' were inflicted on the accused according to the importance of their alleged crime, the purpose of the operation being to make them admit their misdeeds and denounce their accomplices. For the water torture or 'question' they were forced to drink from a hollow ox horn a quantity of water determined by the gravity of the offence: for an ordinary question, four pints, for an extraordinary one, eight. A question 'boot' (*les brodequins*), was applied only to those accused of serious crimes because it maimed, crushing the legs and feet between two planks, gradually squeezed together by wooden wedges struck with a mallet. Ravaillac underwent this torture after the assassination of Henri IV on May 4 1610. The *pelote* entailed tying up the prisoner and then steadily tightening the bonds until they bit their way into the flesh.

Under Louis-Philippe, work on the Conciergerie led to the discovery, on the ground floor of the Tour Bonbec, of earlier instruments of torture. Below ground, two *oubliettes*, in the form of wells furnished with iron spikes, made traps that opened under the feet of the unfortunate condemned who were impaled on the spikes and died a slow death. Thereafter the river waters carried the corpses away.

▷ A concierge at the Conciergerie

The concierge (caretaker) was originally a powerful lord who had the right to administer '*basse*' and '*moyenne*' justice (low justice dealt with property, contracts and fines; middle justice came somewhere between this and 'high' justice, which dealt with the most serious crimes, punishable by death, mutilation or corporal punishment). The concierge collected rent from the many shops on the ground floor of the palace. These included: goldsmiths, engravers, booksellers, hairdressers and wine merchants. In 1596 there were 224 merchants, according to an Italian traveller. At this time even a blacksmith had set up his anvil in the Salle des Gens d'Armes. Moreover, when the buildings were converted into a prison, the concierge also collected rent for the dungeons and payment for the rental of cell furniture.

▷ An unsuccessful escape plot

Marie-Antoinette was first imprisoned in 1743 between the corridor that led to the visiting room and the Cour des Femmes. In mid-September, despite strict surveillance, an officer named de Rougeville, known to the Queen, was able to enter her cell in disguise. He dropped a carnation near the hem of her dress. The flower was said to have contained a tiny piece of paper with plans for her escape. A woman named Harel, who had replaced the Queen's former attendant, removed for having mended the Queen's mourning dress, noticed this incident and reported it to Fouquier-Tanville. From that time on the Queen had no privacy, and was watched by guards; even when using the toilet. The gendarmes were replaced by Lebeau, head of La Force prison; and Mme Richard, the concierge of the Palace (who had been kind to the Queen), her husband and her son, were all imprisoned. The Queen was transferred on September, 11 1793, further away from the entrance, to a cell which later became an expiatory chapel. Here she stayed for another 35 days until October 16 (old style). Defended by Chauveau-Lagarde, she heard her death sentence pronounced at 4.30am after an examination lasting three whole days. At 12.15 the Queen's head fell beneath the blade of the guillotine, which was operated by Henri Sanson.

The Palais-Royal district**

1st and 2nd arr./Map ref. 10–D3
Métro: Palais-Royal
Bus: 21, 27, 39, 48, 67, 69, 72, 74, 81, 85, 95
Parking: Rue des Pyramides
Taxis: at Métro Palais-Royal. Tel: 42–60–61–40.

From whichever direction you approach the Palais-Royal, you will be surprised by the contrast between the noisy activity of the adjacent districts – the Opéra, Les Halles and the southern border formed by the Rue de Rivoli – and the calm of this harmonious complex of buildings.

However, its special atmosphere does not mean that the district is static or boring. From the Palais-Cardinal, through the turbulence of the Revolution until today, the Palais-Royal has been, from time to time, the arena of lively argument, the most recent concerning the erection of Buren's columns in the main courtyard. Also, the fashionable dress shops, bridgeheads of the nearby Place des Victoires, are found more and more among the medal-makers in the Galleries.

Around this enclosed space, 'this little town within a large town, a little town guarded by its cats', according to Cocteau, streets, through which a constantly changing public strolls, form the frontiers. Here are magistrates of the Conseil d'Etat and officials of the Ministry of Finance on the Place Colette, researchers and scholars in the Rue de Richelieu on their way to the Bibliothèque Nationale, and elegant women from the Place des Victoires passing stockbrokers from the nearby Bank of France. They all have one thing in common: they have fallen under the spell of this unique place.

History of the district

The establishment of the Court at the Louvre in the 16th c. led to the construction of many large private houses in new, rather bucolic districts for which the 17th c. was the golden age. At this period, the old perimeter wall of Charles V was pushed back toward the N, highlighting the major axes of the district established around the Palais-Cardinal. Along a modern network of streets rose the classical mansions of the nobility, admired by everyone, even the Italian architect and sculptor Bernini, who was hard to please. Originally Richelieu's creation, the district was completed under Cardinal Mazarin and Louis XIV.

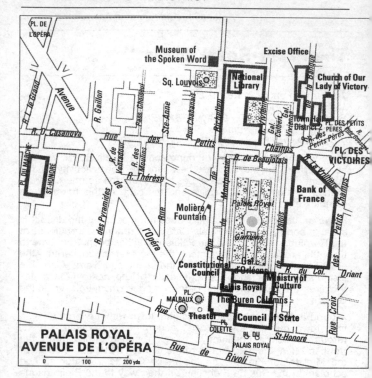

**PALAIS ROYAL
AVENUE DE L'OPÉRA**

0   100   200 yds

☐ **Tour of the Palais-Royal**

The Palais-Royal has two main parts: the palace itself, occupied today by the Conseil d'Etat, may only be visited under certain conditions; and the galleries surrounding the gardens on three sides. These annexes of the palace house the constitutional Council and the Ministry of Culture. The Comédie Française is attached to these buildings.

From the Palais-Cardinal to the Palais-Royal

The Palais-Cardinal was the luxurious dwelling built by Armand Jean du Plessis, Duc de Richelieu (the future Cardinal). As his favor and fortune grew he bought land and houses near the Charles V rampart. In 1629 he chose as his architect Jacques Le Mercier, famous creator of the Clock Pavilion at the Louvre who would later build the Sorbonne, which would house the Cardinal's tomb. The garden was entrusted to Desgots, the king's gardener, who made it the largest then in Paris, with an ornamental pool fed by the pump of the Samaritaines. The sumptuous life of 'the Sphinx of the Red Robe' as the 19th-c. historian, Jules Michelet, called him, was expressed in his art collections, his library and his great theater in the Italian style.

The Cardinal died there in 1642, having wisely made a gift of his home to the king in 1633: the Palais-Cardinal then became the Palais-Royal. Anne of Austria stayed there as Regent with her son, the future Louis XIV, still a child; but following the troubles of the Fronde uprising, the Queen left the Palais-Royal and escaped to Saint-Germain-en-Laye. The palace was then occupied by her sister-in-law, Henrietta Maria, who took refuge in France after the execution of her husband, Charles I of England. The palace was refurbished for the marriage of her daughter, Henrietta of England, to Monsieur, brother of Louis XIV, soon to become the Duc d'Orléans.

The Orléans domain

Louis XIV, who had resided at Versailles since 1682, was no longer interested in the Palais-Royal and gave it in 1692 to his brother, Monsieur, and to his male heirs, who kept it until 1848.

Four princes of this house inherited the palace during the 18th c. and embellished it, giving it the appearance it has today. The moment Monsieur became the owner he made important alterations that his son, the Regent, Philippe d'Orléans, was obliged to complete. The most brilliant period of the Palais-Royal lasted until his death in 1723. Loving the arts and sciences, he made his home the center of a new creative spirit and of pleasure. The Palais-Royal suppers given to his intimate friends date from this time. He had the second-floor apartments renovated by Oppenordt and a picture gallery decorated by Coypel. The Regent's collection of paintings was one of the largest after that of the king.

After the fire at the palace opera house in 1763, his grandson, Louis-Philippe, had the oval grand staircase and the octagonal pavilion on the Rue de Valois rebuilt by Constant d'Ivry. Moreau Desproux constructed the façades on the Cour de l'Horloge while Constant d'Ivry rebuilt the present central building on the main courtyard, which was completed by Louis and Fontaine in the next century. Louis-Philippe d'Orléans, the future Philippe Egalité, was the last owner of the Palais-Royal before the Revolution. Of a lively and enterprising mind, an enthusiast for anything new and a wild spendthrift, he sank himself in debt. In an attempt to solve this situation, he undertook a large construction project. The Duke became a promoter and, reducing the area of the garden by a third, built around it a large group of dwellings, the ground floors of which were to be occupied by galleries and shops.

Victor Louis, the architect of the Théâtre de Bordeaux, enclosed the garden with colonnades and, from 1781 to 1784, built 60 uniformly designed buildings for rent, each corresponding to three arcades of galleries comprising a ground floor with a mezzanine, a floor with symbolically decorated windows, then at the top, an attic storey with a balustrade. The three streets behind these houses were named after the Duke's three sons, Valois, Montpensier and Beaujolais. On the side separating the main courtyard from the garden, the Duke built huge temporary galleries in wood and glass bordered by shops rent commercially and known as 'The Tartars' Camp'. Although householders were deprived of their view over the garden, the development was a success, the shops rapidly found takers and the Palais-Royal became the most popular spot in Paris for shoppers, strollers, and pleasure-seekers. After the second fire at the palace opera-house, the Duc d'Orléans asked Victor Louis to build the auditorium of the Théâtre-Français and the theater of the Palais-Royal.

The throbbing heart of the Revolution

From the time of the Regency the Palais-Royal, with its gambling clubs and pleasure houses, was a place noted for its social freedom, especially as the police had no right to enter the princely domain. At the dawn of the Revolution, debating societies proliferated there. On 12 July 1789 Camille Desmoulins, standing on a table outside the famous Café de Foy, called the crowd to arms and, with the leaves of a chestnut tree in the garden, made the first cockades that Parisians wore as a sign of hope. Philippe Egalité's Palais-Royal became the Palais Egalité, and its garden became the garden of the Revolution. It remained one of the centers of revolutionary harvest until 1794. It was in a restaurant in the Galerie Montpensier that Le Peletier de Saint Fargeau, a member of the National Convention, was killed by a former royal guard on January 20, 1793, the night before the execution of Louis XVI.

From a place of fashion to a deserted garden

During the Consulate and the Empire, the popularity of the fashionable Palais-Royal only increased. Fifteen restaurants, 29 cafés, 17 billiard rooms, 24 jewellers, plus bookshops, clockmakers, wigmakers and shoeshiners – not to mention the infamous trade plied by the young ladies of the Palais-Royal, which attracted an international clientèle – kept the place humming. In 1814, drawn there by the ambiguous reputation of the place, Allied soldiers were given a warm welcome in the cafés and by the *belles* of the Palais-Royal. The return of the Orléans family put an end to this life of pleasure.

Louis-Philippe, then Duc d'Orléans, took possession of his ancestors' palace and set about clearing it up, giving Fontaine the task of restoring it in 1815. In 1825 the architect replaced the notorious wooden galleries, now completely dilapidated, with the well-proportioned Orléans Gallery, a vast portico with two colonnades, matching the classic style of the quadrilateral conceived by Victor Louis. The Valois wing was entirely restored and the Montpensier wing was built. Before taking up residence at the Tuileries, the Duc d'Orléans, who had become king under the name Louis-Philippe I, lived for two years at the Palais-Royal. The garden lost its prostitutes and its gambling dens following the Duke's strict prohibitions, which marked the beginning of the Palais-Royal's decline.

In 1854 the property of the Orléans family was confiscated by Napoléon III and the Palais-Royal was given to King Jérôme, Bonaparte of Westphalia, and then to his son, Prince Jérôme-Napoléon Bonaparte. At the time of the Commune, part of the palace was set on fire, but was later restored to house the Conseil d'Etat and the present Ministry of Culture. Inhabited by artists and writers – among them Colette and Jean Cocteau – the palace has become like Sleeping Beauty's, and maintains gentle drowsiness. It took the controversy over Daniel Buren's columns to make the Palais-Royal once again a place for promenading and heated discussion.

The main courtyard

From the Place Colette, a passage between the palace and the Théâtre-Français gives access to the main courtyards, which are separated from the garden by the Orléans Gallery, a vast portico with a double colonnade built by Fontaine. In 1985 and 1986 the main courtyard was rearranged for use as a parking lot, arousing some lively arguments regarding the installation of Daniel Buren's columns on this historic site. In the gallery, two existing ornamental fountains have been decorated with mobile steel spheres by the sculptor Pol Bury (1985).

The Galerie de Valois

In the main courtyard, the r. wing of the Palais-Royal displays on its lower section the last traces of the Palais Cardinal built by Le Mercier: a decoration of anchors and ships' prows in honor of Richelieu, Grand Admiral and Superintendant of Shipping. This wing is occupied by the Ministry of Culture. The numerous arcades of the Valois Gallery house administrative offices. It was in the cellar of the Café Février at no. 113 that the royal guard, Pâris, killed the member of the National Convention, Le Peletier de Saint-Fargeau, the night before the execution of Louis XVI. At no. 153 is Guillaumont, heraldic engraver, the oldest establishment of the Palais-Royal along with the Grand Véfour. Founded in 1761 on the Place du Palais-Royal and, in 1784, installed in the Montpensier Gallery, it has moved in recent years to the Valois Gallery. No. 156 is the site of the Café Valois which, with the Café des Milles Colonnes and the Café du Grand Véfour, was frequented by former emigrés and their bodyguards. Further up was the Restaurant Brauvilliers, the most famous restaurant in Paris during the Revolution. No. 177 was the shop of the cutler, Badin, where Charlotte Corday bought the knife with which she stabbed Marat on July 13, 1793.

The gardens of the Palais-Royal*

A sculpted group in bronze by Gérard Garouste (1986) and another by Anne and Patrick Poirier representing the *Birth of Pegasus* has here installed here.

Rue de Valois. Enter this street by a passage from the Galeries des Prouse. No. 3 is the Pavilion du Palais-Royal, built by Constant d'Ivry and Moreau (1766) facing the Place de Valois. The Place de Valois is the former Cours des Offices or Cours des Fountaines government offices. The Offices built by Cartaud in 1750 still exist for the most part. The Passage de la Verité runs between the Rue des Bons-Enfants and the Place de Valois. Return to the Rue de Valois. At nos. 6–8, the Hôtel Mélusine, built around 1550, has a balcony (built in 1636) supported by brackets with lions' heads. In 1638 Richelieu presided here over the first sessions of the French Academy. At no. 8 above the door, a bull indicates the 19th-c. restaurant which bore the sign of the 'Boeuf à la Mode'. At no. 11 is an inscription to the memory of the magician, Robert Houdin, who owned the Théâtre des Soirées Fantastiques (1845).

The Galerie de Beaujolais

This gallery borders the N side of the garden and owes its fame to the oldest establishment of the Palais-Royal: the Grand Véfour, nos. 79–82. Founded in 1781 when Philippe Egalité had just finished his galleries, it was first called the Café de Chartres, then the restaurant of Véfour the Elder, known as the Grand Véfour. The Prince Murat, Count Rostopchine, the Duc de Berry, the Prince de Joinville, the Duc d'Aumale, Lamartine and Sainte-Beuve, Thiers and MacMahon frequently visited the Grand Véfour. Above the café, on the first floor, was the apartment of Montansier (→below). Nos. 83–86 was the site of the restaurant Le Véry, where the artist Fragonard died from apoplexy while eating a sorbet during the summer of 1806; no. 88 was the Restaurant des Trois-Frèbes-Provençaux. Nos. 89–92 and 103 were the Café Caveau and Café du Lemblin, well-known meeting places for the high-class prostitutes or 'nymphs' of the Palais-Royal in the 9th c. Rue de Beaujolais. The writer Colette lived at no. 9 from 1927 to 1929 and from 1938 until her death (August 3, 1954); she is commemorated by a plaque on the street, a medallion in the gallery and a letter C marking her window on the garden side.

The theater of the Palais-Royal

This theater, on the corner of the Rue de Montpensier, was created by Victor Louis and has been altered many times. Opened in 1784, it only took off in 1790 under the direction of Mlle Montansier. It has often changed its name (Théâtre du Péristyle Egalité, Théâtre de la Montagne, etc.) because its director, who was very involved in politics, knew how to adapt herself to events. Having known the *Ancien Regime* and survived the Revolution, it continued its activities under the Empire, installed on the boulevards. The golden age of the Théâtre de Palais-Royal began in 1840 when nearly all the plays of Eugène Labiche were performed there.

The Galerie de Montpensier

This borders the garden on the W side. Nothing remains to recall the cafés of the Revolution and the Directoire (at nos. 7–12) or the Café Foy where Camille Desmoulins harangued the crowd. An important part of the gallery and the W wing of the palace, known as Montpensier, is occupied by the Conseil Constitutionel. This wing formed part of the buildings erected from 1817 to 1830 by the architect Fontaine on Louis-Philippe's orders. The interior decoration owes much to Prince Jérôme-Napoléon Bonaparte and his wife, Marie-Clothilde of Savoy, in particular an oratory, planned by Viollet-le-Duc, which still exists. The prince received all the liberals of his time there: Sainté-Beuve, Taine, Flaubert, Renan, Emile de Girardin, Paul de Musset. The Rue de Montpensier communicates by several passages with the Rue de Richelieu. Cocteau, Colette's neighbor, spent the latter part of his life at no. 36. Notice the fire escape from the Théâtre du Palais-Royal added in 1880 by the architect Paul Sédille.

Tour of the district

45 mins.

The Théâtre-Français

Complete visit the third Sun. of the month. Apply to the Caisse Nationale des Monuments Historiques (tel. 48–87–24–12). Group visits by requests on Sun. mornings.

The theater is situated on the corner of the Place André-Malraux and the Place Colette. During performances the auditorium, the foyer and the gallery containing busts of famous French theater people may be seen.

The building, abutting onto the Complex of the Palais-Royal, was created between 1786 and 1790 by Victor Louis for the Théâtre des Variétés Amusantes. It has been rebuilt and restored several times, especially after the fire of 1900, which cost the life of a young actress when it destroyed the stage and auditorium. The most recent restorations were made from 1973 to 1974 to remedy its dilapidation. The Comédie-Française was created in 1680 by Louis XIV. He ordered the companies of the actors of the Théâtre du Marais, the troupe formed at Molière's death, and the actors at the Hôtel de Bourgogne to unite. By royal decree of 21st October, the existence of the actors of the Comédie-Française was legalized. The Revolution divided the company; the monarchists escaped the guillotine by a miracle, but they were all reconciled by 1799 when they were installed in the theater built by Victor Louis. In 1812 Napoléon signed the Decree of Moscow, which made the theater directly dependent on the State and regulated its administrative organization. The statute of April, 27 1850 ordered the appointment of an administrator by the State. The last important reforms were made in 1975 under the administration of Pierre Dux; they concern the social and financial organization of the Comédie-Française. On the outside in the Rue de Richelieu, medallions representing Corneille, Molière, Racine and Hugo adorn the portico; there is a medallion of the actor, Mounet-Sully, in Rue Montpensier.

The interior

In the vestibule the public may admire Houdon's *Seated Voltaire**, presented by Voltaire's niece to the actors of the Comédie-Française, as well as Molière's armchair, used in his portrayal of *Le Malade Imaginaire*. The Galerie des Bustes is adorned with works by the greatest sculptors of the 18th and 19th c., among which the marble bust of *Piron* should be noted; its sculptor, Caffieri, gave it in exchange for a ticket for life to the Théâtre-Français. Also of note are *Dufresny* by Pajou, *Victor Hugo* by Dalou and *Duman the Younger* by Carpeaux. The ceiling of the auditorium is decorated with a huge composition by Albert Besnard (1913): near the stage stand *Molière, Racine, Corneille* and *Victor Hugo*. The Comédie-Française owns many other works of art which are dispersed throughout the theatre: *Statue of Talma* (d. 1826) by David d'Angers; statues by Duret of *Tragedy* (Phèdre, played by Rachel, d. 1858) and of *Comedy* (Célimène, a character in *La Misanthrope*, portrayed by Mlle Mars, d. 1847); a portrait of *Talma* by Delacroix; and works by Lemoine, Caffieri, Van Loo, Mignard, Coypel, Largillière, and Nattier.

Place du Palais-Royal

First you notice the Palais-Royal's Cour de l'Horloge (Courtyard of the Clock), designed by the architect Moreau-Desproux in 1763. The main façade is crowned by an attic storey (decorated by Augustin Papou) with a pediment showing the arms of the Orléans which has now been replaced by a clock. On the corner of the Rue Saint-Honoré and the Rue de Valois, an inscription on the façade of the Palais-Royal is a reminder that it was here that the theater of the Petit-Cardinal was opened in 1641, and that it was occupied by Molière's company from 1661 to 1673. On this stage Molière, playing Argan in *Le Malade Imaginaire*, was struck by a fatal illness on February 17, 1673. The Petit-Cardinal was replaced by the Académie Royale de Musique, with Lully, the so-called creator of French Opera, at its head. In 1780, the amphitheatre of the palace was destroyed to make way for a new auditorium constructed to the W of the palace by Victor Louis (→Théâtre-Français).

Le Louvre des antiquaires (antique-dealers)

Louvre: main entrance at 2 Place du Palais-Royal (open 11am, except Mon. 11am–7pm, tel: 42–97–27–00).

This occupies what were once the Grands Magasins du Louvre founded by Alfred Chauchard and built by Percier and Fontaine. Three levels of luxurious galleries are devoted to more than 200 shops where you can browse around or use your knowledge to discover some rare, unusual or precious object.

Rue de Richelieu from the Place du Palais-Royal to the Rue des Petit-Champs

Go along this street, which begins at the Place André-Malraux, to reach the Bibliothèque Nationale. Opened by Richelieu in 1634, it was laid out in a N–S direction which was a novelty for Paris. Later it was called the Rue de Richielieu. It was at no. 1, that the fire at the gunsmiths', Fauré-Lepage, founded in 1716 and still existing today, set in motion the revolution of 1830. No. 21 is the Hôtel Dodun built by Bullet in the Regency style between 1726–28. A magnificent staircase, partly damaged, remains. At no. 23, the painter, Mignard, died in the 17th-c. mansion. At no. 37, the Molière fountain by Visconti (1844) was raised by national subscription. The seated statue of Molière is by G. Seurre; the standing figures of Serious Comedy and Light Comedy are by Pradier. This fountain conforms to the old type of Parisian fountain, built on a street corner against the houses. Molière died on the site of the present no. 14 on February 17, 1673 at ten o'clock at night, following the fourth performance of *Le Malade Imaginaire*. The present house dates from 1765. At no. 39, in a house dating from 1670, Diderot died (1784) 12 days after moving into the apartment given to him by Catherine the Great of Russia. The future Marquise de Pompadour lived at no. 50. At no. 66 Brillat-Savarin died in 1826. Celebrated for his *Physiology of Taste*, he made a true art of gastronomy. No. 69 is on the site of the house where Stendhal wrote *Le Rouge et le Noir* (*The Red and the Black*).

For the rest of the →Rue de Richelieu, Bibliothèque Nationale district.

▷ The Associate Actors

The statute of the actors of the Comédie-Française is unique. The Society of the Actors of France is made up of the *pensionnaires*, artists under a renewable yearly contract, and the *sociétaires* (members), chosen from among the *pensionnaires*, who are associates linked to their theater by a contract which may last from 10 to 30 years; the status of every member is reviewed every five years. The actors collect an annual basic allowance (the *feux*) awarded for each performance in which they take part. At the end of every run, 75% of the profits are shared among the members proportionate to the number of shares or fractions of shares – counted in twelfths – that the actors hold in the Society. (The remainder of the profits are distributed, 15% to the personnel in a profit-sharing arrangement and 10% to reserve funds.) Proposals for nomination to the Sociétariat, the allotment of the twelfths and the termination of contracts are discussed at the meeting of the administrative committee each December. The committee is composed of seven *sociétaires* and the Administrator.

The Panthéon**

5th arr./Map ref. 23–B1
Métro, RER: Gare du Luxembourg.
Bus: 84, 89. Parking: Rue Soufflot
Taxis: Place Edmond-Rostand. Tel: 46-33-00-00

The Panthéon is one of the best-known monuments of the capital. This magnificent achievement which, despite its cruciform ground plan, is not a church, remains slightly isolated in the largest deserted square. It has a long and complicated history.

The history of the Panthéon

Louis XV once vowed, while gravely ill, that if he survived he would build a church: the result was Sainte-Geneviève, built to replace the Abbaye Sainte-Geneviève. The greatest French Neo-Classical architect, Soufflot, drew up his first plans in 1757, and Louis XV, accompanied by the Dauphin, laid the first stone during a grand ceremony in 1764. Unusually for that period, the architect was a great admirer of the Gothic, and hoped here to recapture its élan, but at the same time his monument, one of the first examples of Neo-Classicism, demonstrates an uncompromising admiration of Greek and Roman antiquity. The higher the building rose, the more its daring style made it vulnerable; it cracked, and it was said that Soufflot died of grief. The work was, however, continued by his disciple Rondelet, but at the cost of modifications which made the building's style heavier.

In 1791, with the church barely finished, the Constituent Assembly commissioned the archeologist Antoine Quatremère de Quincy to transform the church into a temple intended to receive the remains of the great men of the era of French liberty – the Panthéon. Mirabeau was the first of this long series of heroes, followed by Voltaire, Le Peletier de Saint-Fargeau, Joseph Bara, Rousseau and Marat.

But as times changed, some of the great men became less great: Mirabeau and Marat had to go. In 1806 the Panthéon, returned to religion again, became the Church of Sainte-Geneviève, then once more the Panthéon from 1831 to 1852, and then again the Church of Sainte-Geneviève. In 1871 Millière, a member of the Commune, was executed by firing-squad on the steps. When Victor Hugo was buried there in 1885, the imposing monument once more became the resting-place for great men and one woman, Mme Berthelot. Since 1918 official ceremonies have increased: the transfer of Gambetta's heart and of the ashes of Jean Jaurés; the State funerals of Paul Painlevé, Raymond Poincaré, Jean Perrin, Paul Langevin, Victor Schoelcher and Félix Eboné. The most recent ceremony, and one of the most moving, was the 1964 transfer of the ashes of Jean Moulin (d. 1913), founder of the Resistance movement, who died under torture by the Nazis.

Tour of the Panthéon

Place du Panthéon/temporary entrance E side. The nave is closed for restoration/Visits to the crypt, the scale model and the galleries of the Dome. Open daily 10am–12.30pm/2pm–5pm. Tel. 43–54–34–51. 1hr.

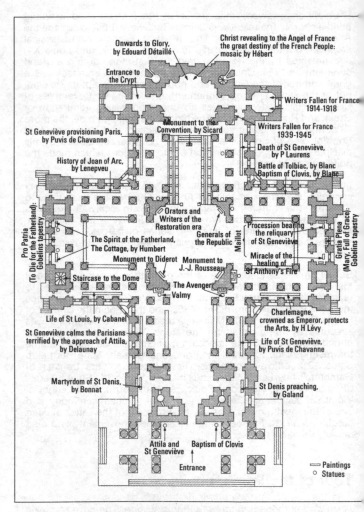

Onwards to Glory, by Edouard Détaillé

Christ revealing to the Angel of France the great destiny of the French People: mosaic by Hébert

Entrance to the Crypt

Writers Fallen for France 1914-1918

St Geneviève provisioning Paris, by Puvis de Chavanne

Monument to the Convention, by Sicard

Writers Fallen for France 1939-1945

Death of St Geneviève, by P Laurens

History of Joan of Arc, by Lenepveu

Battle of Tolbiac, by Blanc
Baptism of Clovis, by Blanc

Pro Patria (To Die for the Fatherland): Gobelins tapestry

Orators and Writers of the Restoration era

Generals of the Republic

Procession bearing the reliquary of St Geneviève

Gratia Plena (Mary, Full of Grace): Gobelins tapestry

The Spirit of the Fatherland, The Cottage, by Humbert

Monument to Diderot

Monument to J.-J. Rousseau

Miracle of the healing of St Anthony's Fire

Maillot

Staircase to the Dome

The Avenger
Valmy

Life of St Louis, by Cabanel

Charlemagne, crowned as Emperor, protects the Arts, by H Lévy

St Geneviève calms the Parisians terrified by the approach of Attila, by Delaunay

Life of St Geneviève, by Puvis de Chavanne

Martyrdom of St Denis, by Bonnat

St Denis preaching, by Galand

Attila and St Geneviève

Baptism of Clovis

Entrance

Paintings
Statues

The Panthéon

The exterior

The Panthéon is built on the plan of a Greek cross, with the central transcept surmounted by the famous dome. Wide steps lead up to a Corinthian peristyle, whose 22 columns freely imitate the Pantheon in Rome. David d'Angers sculpted the bas-relief of the pedestal *La Patria* between *Liberty* and *History*, distributing crowns of laurels to the great men. Beneath the peristyle are three doors decorated with garlands and bas-reliefs; on either side of the central door, marble groups: *the Baptism of Clovis, Attila and St Geneviève*. Dimensions of the building: length 361ft/110m; width 269ft/82m; height from the top of the lantern of the dome 272ft/83m.

The interior

Each nave is bordered by side-aisles demarcated by a colossal set of 100 Corinthian columns; three peristyles support an entablature decorated with friezes of swags and garlands. By sealing up the windows (the outlines can still be seen from the outside), the Revolution provided the artists of the next century with huge inner walls, which they brought to life, creating one of the greatest decorative ensembles of the era. Originally, the Panthéon had been entirely conceived as the tomb for St Geneviève, which occupied the center, beneath the dome. Today, the center is empty and the naves are full of monuments.

R. aisle: scenes from *The life of St-Geneviève* (first part) by Puvis de Chavannes, works by Galand and Lévy; Gobelins tapestry.

The choir, r. side: *Death of St Geneviève and her funeral celebrations* by J. P. Laurens. At the end are plaques with the names of writers who died for France during the two World Wars. At the back of the choir is a colossal group of statues: *The Convention*, by Sicard. In the apse, *Vers la Gloire* (Onwards to Glory), a painting by Edmund Détaillé; above the vault, *Christ revealing to the Angel of France the Great Destiny of the French People*, a mosaic from the cartoons of Hébert (characteristic of late 19th-c. official art). In the l.-hand corner at the end, the entrance to the crypt (→below). L. side: *St Geneviève watching over Paris* and *St Geneviève provisioning Paris*, this is by Puvis de Chavannes; the most famous decorative piece in the building. Against the pillar: *Mirabeau*, by Injalbert.

The Dôme**

In the center, the dome is supported by four pillars by Rondelet, which link four great arches. The dome consists of three cupolas: the first, open in the center, allows the second to be seen; it is decorated by a Gros fresco representing *The Glorification of St Geneviève* and showing France's most famous kings, Louis XVI and

Louis XVIII. To see it distinctly and in its entirety go up to the gallery of the first cupola. On the pendentives are various allegories relating to the First Empire: *Glory, Death, Mother Country*, and *Justice*, by Gérard. Against the first pillar of the dome, on the r., is the cenotaph of Jean-Jacques Rousseau. From l. to r. are pictures of *Music, Truth, Philosophy, Nature* and *Glory*, by Bartholomé. Against the second pillar, to the r., is a monument to the generals of the Revolution, by Gasq. Against the second pillar, to the l., is a monument to the orators and publicists of the Restoration, by Marqueste. Against the first pillar, to the l., stands a statue of Diderot, by Terroir. It was under the dome that Foucault publicly experimented with the pendulum to demonstrate the earth's rotation in 1851.

L. transept: compositions by Cabanet and Lenenpveu; Gobelins tapestry (*Pro Patria*); *To Unknown Artists*, sculpture by Landowski, to the r. L. side-aisle: compositions by Delaunay and Bonnat.

The crypt (take the stairs in the l. corner at the end of the building): It is divided into several galleries by Doric columns. Before the entrance door, above an inscription to the memory of the generals of 1870 to 1871, is a niche where, on November 11 1920, the second anniversary of the Armistice, Gambetta's heart was brought from the house of Jardies to be housed in the Panthéon. This ceremony was accompanied by the transfer of the remains of the Unknown Soldier to the Arc de Triomphe. To the r., the tomb of Jean-Jacques Rousseau: a hand holding a torch rises from the tomb, symbolizing the influence of his work after his death. Next door, to the l., the tomb of Voltaire and, in front of it, his statue attributed to Houdon; to the l., beyond that of Voltaire, the tomb of Soufflot from 1829. Between the four central pillars, there is a remarkable echoing effect. The Galerie des Couronnes contains the tombs of Lannes; Lazare Carnot and his grandson Sadi Carnot, President of the Republic, assassinated in Lyons in 1894; Marceau; T. C. de la Tour d'Auvergne, killed at Oberhausen in 1800 (his heart is in the Invalides); Baudin; Victor Hugo; Emile Zola; Berthelot and Mme Berthelot in the same tomb; Paul Langevin (d. 1948); Paul Painlevé (d. 1933); Jean Perrin (d. 1948); Jean Jaurès (d. 1924); Victor Schoelcher; and Félix Eboné (d. 1949). Louis Braille (d. 1952) and Jean Moulin (d. 1964) have also received the honors of the Panthéon. Four vaults hold the remains of the great digitaries of the First Empire (1806), 40 in all, making a total number of people interred in the Panthéon. Inscriptions have also been put up to the memory of Georges Guynemer, Antoine de Saint-Exupéry and Bergson. The tour of the galleries of the dome gives a wonderful panoramic view** of Paris.

> Puvis de Chavannes

In the vast spaces of the Panthéon, Pierre Puvis de Chavannes (1824–98) was able to express his art freely, emerging as the foremost French fresco painter of the 19th c., working in the manner of the Italian Quattrocento, with simplified forms and flat areas of color. This artist, who in the eyes of his contemporaries was a revolutionary, and was for long refused entrance to the Salon, is thought today to have been ahead of his time, and timeless. He was neither an Impressionist nor an academician, and hardly a Symbolist. To the intimacy of easel painting he preferred mural art which, according to J. Foucart (in a catalogue of work, *Puvis de Chavannes*, 1976), seemed like 'the slow and majestic progression of a film in slow motion'. It is an art, at once intellectual and decorative, sensitive and elegant. From 1893 to 1895 he decorated the Boston Library.

> Neo-Classical architecture in Paris

The artistic return to antiquity, viewed in a more strictly archeological manner following excavations at Paestum, Pompeii and Herculaneum, and the return to a more severe geometric style in reaction to the delicacy and profusion of the Rococo, became apparent at the start of Louis XV's reign.

The king himself and the Marquise de Pompadour favored it. It was an architecture of idea produced by theorists and architects who had been to Rome. The Panthéon, by Soufflot, is the first building of this type. It was part of a general plan, of which only one other building, the Faculty of Law, was completed. Of the numerous projects of the time, few were completed, in general, only isolated buildings have survived.

The following is a short list of architects who built Neo-Classical works in Paris. Among the earliest were Peyre and de Wailly, creators of the Odéon, (1767–1782); E. L. Boullée, very original, only one example of whose work remains, the Hôtel Alexandre, 16 Rue de la Ville-L'Evêque (1763); then Antoine, creator of La Monnaie (the Mint) in 1767 and the Hospice de La Rochefoucauld, Ave. du Général-Leclerc. Chalgrin constructed many buildings and monuments, including the Arc de Triomphe at the Etoile, Saint-Philippe-du-Roule (1772–84), and the Seminary of the Saint-Esprit, 30 Rue Lhomond (1769). Belanger, builder of many Paris *hôtels*, is responsible for the Bagatelle in the Bois de Boulogne, and the *folie* Saint-James at Neuilly. One of the most famous and most original personalities was C. N. Ledroux. Only a few of his buildings survive: the Pavillons de Barrières (1785), the Cours de Vincennes, the Place Denfert-Rochereau and the rotundas of La Villette and the Parc

Monceau; mention should also be made of the Hôtel d'Hallwyl, 28 Rue Michel-le-Comte. A. T. Brongniart is in some respects close to this style. If the present Bourse now owes little to him, his elegant *hôtels*, the Lycée Condorcet at 8 Rue du Havre (1779) and the entrance to the Père-Lachaise cemetery, are remarkable. C. Percier and P. F. L. Fontaine, architects of Napiolia, were the creators of the Arc de Triomphe du Carrousel; Fontaine later produced the expiatory chapel (1851–26).

Other Parisian Neo-Classical works: Hôtel de Gallifet, 50 Rue de Varenne, by Legrand; the Hôtel de Salm (1782), Rue de Lille, by Rousseau; the Ecole de Médecine in the street of the same name, by J. Gondoin; the Madeleine by Constant-d'Ivry, Couture, Vignon, then Huvé, and, following the same course, the façade of the Chambre des Députés by Poyet (1808). Also churches, such as Notre-Dame-de-Lorette (1823–36) by L. H. Lebas, or Notre-Dame-de-Bonne-Nouvelle by Godde, and entire streets, such as the Rue Monsieur, Rue du Faubourg-Poissonnière, Rue de la-Tour-des-Dames and Rue des Colonnes.

The Passy-La Muette district

16th arr./Map ref. 13–A2, B2
Métro: Passy RER, Line C, Metro Boulainvillers
Bus: 72
Parking: Ave. du Président-Kennedy
Taxis: Place du Docteur-Hayem. Tel: 42-24-99-99.

People no longer come to take the waters at Passy and no one now cultivates the vine here, but certain streets climbing its hillsides have retained a little of their country character. Others, more luxurious, between the Métro's admirable viaduct and the Trocadéro Gardens, owe their picturesqueness to the steepness of the terrain and the variety of their architecture. At the top of the hill, the Place de Passy seems still to be the heart of an old village, even if those who frequent it today are elegant and sophisticated. To the W the La Muette intersection gives onto the Ranelagh's lawns, where the local children, kilted or velvet-trousered, come to take the air.

Hardly anything remains of the large parks like La Muette and Beauséjour where the king and a few aristocrats had summer places and hunting lodges, but the district is still very quiet and the proximity of the Ranelagh and the Bois de Boulogne adds greatly to its attractiveness.

History of the district

The name of Passy still evokes the little village of the past that was the scene of many of the *Ancien Régime's* festivities. It was originally a hamlet founded by the woodcutters of Nigeon, mentioned for the first time in a charter of May 1250. Its fame began in the 15th c. with the discovery of sulphated and ferruginous waters; these springs bubbled to the surface in the former Parc Delessert (→inset). With the aid of financiers, Passy reached its pinnacle of fame in the 18th c. The Château de Boulainvilliers, which had been bought and rebuilt in the 17th c. by the financier Claude Chahu, had existed at Passy since the 15th c. In 1722 the powerful banker Samuel Bernard bought it for his mistress, Mme de Fontaine. One of his sons later rented the château to the tax farmer general Le Riche de la Pouplinère, for whom it provided the setting for magnificent entertainments. There was much dancing then: one of the first collections of engravings of the quadrille is called *Spirées de Passy*. There too, between the Rue Beethoven and the Rue de l'Alboni, Jean-Jacques Rousseau stayed with his friend Mussard in 1752, and wrote *Le Devin du Village*. Passy was elevated to the status of the commune in 1790, and then annexed to Paris in 1860 by the Second Empire. The place was already favored by artists and writers: Rossini, who had a chalet there (as well as a mansion in the Chaussée d'Antin), died there in 1868, as did Lamartine in 1869.

Tour of the district

2 hrs.

Rue d'Ankara

In the shadow of the immense Maison de la Radio (→Auteuil), on the edge of the Ave. du Président-Kennedy and facing the Font de Seine, there is a small district which is still countrified, a little provincial with its centuries-old boundary stones and bumpy streets. At no. 17, a fine classical *hôtel* with a garden, the residence of the Turkish ambassador. Adjoining, the Chancellory (H. Beauclair, architect; 1976) is a curved building clad in suspended glass panels, without vertical supports.

This property, known as the Domaine de Lamballe, had first belonged, in the 17th c., to Claude Chahu, Passy's *seigneur*. It was later bought by the Duc de Lauzun, who eventually married Louis XIV's cousin, La Grande Moiselle. The widow of the Prince de Lamballe, Marie-Thérèse de Savoie-Carignan, acquired it from the Duc de Luynes in 1783. After her death, her nephew and heir, C. - E. de Savoie-Carignan, rented it to a private tenant who created a pleasure garden here. Following that, the physician Esprit Blanche bought it and converted it into his famous sanatorium: Gérard de Nerval came here twice (1853–54) and Gounod in 1857; Maupassant died here in 1893. The land was sold off, and between 1925 and 1930, over it were laid the Rue du Général-Mangin and the Ave. de Lamballe.

Rue Berton

Formerly Rue du Roc, this is unquestionably one of the most charming streets in Paris. While the part lying near the Rue Raynouard is modern in appearance, the beginning of the street is like a country lane, squeezed between old ivy-covered walls. At no. 24, a rustic doorway leads to the courtyard of Balzac's house entrance: 47 Rue Raynouard, now the Musée Balzac. On the r. of the doorway is a boundary-stone from 1731, which marked the limits of the *Seigneuries* of Passy and Auteuil. At the corner of the Rue Berton and Rue Raynouard, workers building terraces have uncovered a coffin of a type never used after the 14th c., proving that the district was inhabited earlier than that.

Rue Raynouard

This fine middle-class street, formerly Rue des Francs-Bourgeois, bears the name of the historian of the Knights Templar, who died at no. 34. The architect Robert de Cotte and the Abbé Prévost, author of the novel *Manon Lescaut*, lived on this street. On the l., at nos. 52–68, is the site of a pavilion that was part of the Hôtel de Valentinois, which in the 19th c. belonged to a rich textile industrialist, David Singer. A medallion and inscription on the chamfered face of the corner recalls that Benjamin Franklin lived in the pavilion from 1777 to 1786, and erected France's first lightning conductor on it. Opposite, at no. 69, is the site of a terrace of the park of Château de Passy; note the balusters, the bull's-eye (*oeil-de-boeuf*) window, and the lion's head. No. 54 is by Auguste Perret. Toward the Place de Costa-Rica, at nos. 51–53, a modern building, also by Perret, replaces the house of the celebrated archeologist-architect Quatremère de Quincy. At nos. 49–47 there used to be a large property belonging to Jean de Julienne; after a century it was divided up and one part of it, no. 47, became the Maison-Musée Balzac. Gérard de Nerval spoke of this house. It still has great charm and is, amid the modern buildings, a reminder of the old Passy. Rousseau wrote *Le Devin du Village* in the house that stood on the site of no. 21; the Duc de Lauzun and Mme du Barry had properties, now vanished, in the part of the street between the Rue de l'Annonciation and the Place de Costa-Rica. Follow the Rue de l'Alboni and turn r. down the Sq. de l'Alboni to come to the Rue des Eaux. At the end of the street at 5 Square Charles-Dickens, cut into the side of the hill, are the vast medieval cellars of the Musée du Vin (→ Museums). The museum was opened in 1983 by the Confrèrerie des Echansons de France. The cellars are those of the former Minim monastery Friars, which stood on the site until the Revolution; they comprise more than 1000m of well-arranged galleries, in which exhibitions and wine tastings are organized.

Ave. Frémiet: this is the outcome of an operation by a single speculator, who hired the architect Vêque to design all the buildings; these are notable for their abundant carvings. Return to the Place de Costa-Rica.

Rue Franklin

This street bears the name of Benjamin Franklin, whose bust stands in the little garden that overlooks the Place du Trocadéro, at the corner of the street. At no. 8, the Maison de Georges Clemenceau is now a museum devoted to the memory of that statesman. No. 13 is considered the oldest building in Passy, and at no. 25 is the first Parisian building* (erected in 1903) of reinforced concrete and glass bricks, by the Perret brothers (→inset).

Rue Scheffer

To the l. of the Rue Franklin.

At no. 39, an elegant Art Nouveau building by the architect Louis Herscher (1911). At no. 40, the poet Comtesse Anna de Noailles lived and, in 1933, died.

Rue Le Tasse

To the r. of Rue Franklin.

This street alongside the Trocadéro Gardens. Begun in 1904, it was a luxury development that brought together a number of high quality architectural creations: at the end of the avenue, overlooking the Seine, is the former hôtel of the Chilian Errazu family, designed in the style of an 18th-c. pavilion by Walter Destailleur; no. 7 is a 1907 building by Louis Sorel, a model of modern construction in its time, with the use of corbelling and simplicity of decoration. The other buildings and *hôtels* are the work of René Sergent, who had his office in the attic storey of no. 3. No. 5 is occupied by the Moroccan Embassy. Return again to the Place de Costa-Rica.

Rue de Passy

This is the former main street of the village of Passy. It is a busy shopping street where small boutiques and large stores rub shoulders, while the most refined luxury articles sell next door to mass-produced goods and ready-to-wear clothes; the multi-storey Franck et Fils has all the temptations that fashion has to offer. General Moreau lived at no. 7 in 1797, and Prud'hon died at no. 12.

Rue Claude-Chahu

To the r. of Rue de Passy.

At no. 9 is an extraordinary apartment building in the modern style, erected in 1903 by the architect Charles Klein; this is his only known work. The building has a concrete frame with a façade dressed in mauve and green sandstone; the principal decorative element is a thistle motif by the ceramicist Emile Müller.

Place de Passy

A very attractive place in summer, when the restaurant's tables spread far out into the street, leading the district a holiday air; in winter it is rather more like the square of a small town. The Pâtisserie Coquelin is a veritable shrine for gourmands.

Rue de l'Annonciation

At first sight a little dull, this street is nevertheless interesting for its mixture of the working and middle classes. At no. 10, the Church of Notre-Dame-de-Grâce-de-Passy was built in the middle of the 19th c. (altered several times) on the site of a chapel erected in 1666 by the financier Claude Chahu, seigneur of Passy. It has a painting by Luca Giordano: *The Crowning with Thorns*.

Passy's first cemetery, at the corner of the Rue de l'Annonciation and Rue Lekain, has long since been removed, though the private tomb of the influential Delessert family survived for many years before it was removed. Follow the Rue Lekain, then its extension, the Rue Alfred Alfred-Bruneau.

Rue des Vignes

This street's name evokes the vineyard through which it ran at the time of the *Ancien Regime*. At no. 5, in the 18th c., stood the Théâtre de la Popelinière, built by the farmer general of that name in the gardens of his Château de Boulainvilliers, and where Rameau gave concerts. The automobile builder Louis Mors had the present concert hall built in 1890; Wagner's *Das Rheingold* was performed there for the first time in France in 1900. The hall has been enlarged, but has retained its remarkable decoration of Neo-Renaissance paneling and woodwork; a registered historical monument, the hall today houses the Ranelagh experimental cinema. The composer Gabriel Fauré (1845–1924) died at no. 32.

At no. 52, lies the Station Boulainvilliers, on the Auteuil-Invalides line; the architect Barret designed this station in brick and stone with sandstone decorative motifs. Glass-tiled footbridges and glass-roofed stairways lead to platforms set below ground level to keep them smoke-free. This line, called the Petite Ceinture, was reopened in 1988. Turn r. into the Rue de Boulainvillers, which runs across the gardens created by Le Nôtre for the former Château de Passy. Luxury apartment buildings and a few boutiques set the tone of the street. Pierre Louÿs (1870–1925) lived in the street and Fernand Gregh died there in 1960. René Boyslesve used it as the setting for his *Leçon d'Amour dans un Parc* and *Souvenirs d'un Jardin Détruit.*

The former Domaine Royale de La Muette

The Chaussée de La Muette begins at the Carrefour de La Muette. The Château de La Muette stood to the r. of it.

The Domaine de La Muette may have taken its name from a kennel, or perhaps from the *mues* (shed antlers) of the deer kept there. The original hunting lodge was converted into a château by Philibert Delorne in the 16th c., following which it was inherited by *La reine Margot,* the cast-off wife of Henri III. It was embellished by Louis XIV's Regent, whose daughter, the Duchesse de Berry, used it for the amorous assignments for which she was notorious. Louix XV lived there until he attained his majority; he restored it completely for Mme de Pompadour and, on her death in 1764, rebuilt it. Louis XVI, while still Dauphin, lived in it and received Marie-Antoinette there on her arrival at the French Court; it was there also that he issued the Edict of La Muette, by which he renounced the right of *joyeux avenement* (accession tax). In 1783 the first hot-air balloon ascent was made there by Pilâtre de Rozier and the Marquis d'Arlandes. On July 14 1790, for the Fête de la Fédération, the Commune of Paris gave a banquet there for 5000 deputies from the army corps and the communes of France. The château and the park, which had been declared State property, were bought in 1820 by Sébastien Erard, the well-known piano maker, who years before had made his debut as a pianist before Marie-Antoinette in this very place. La Muetté remained in the Erard family until 1920. The last to inherit it, the Comte de Franqueville, had always fought for its conservation, but after his death the property fell into ruin and was broken up. The last stones of the château disappeared in 1926, but a large part of the park remains, bordered by the Boul. Suchet, the Allée Pilâtre-de-Rozier and the Rue de Franqueville, surrounding the modern château erected by Baron H. de Rothschild (now the property of the O.E.C.D.), opposite the Place de Colombie. Close to the Passy station, the grounds of Villa Beauséjour lead on to the

Boul. Beauséjour. The name is that of a large park where Mme Récamier, Chateaubriand, the Princesse de Talleyrand and the Princesse de Lieven had their country houses. The villa contains some fanciful Russian *izbas* (log huts), mementoes of the World Fair of 1867. Return to the Chaussée de La Muette to cross the Ranelagh Gardens.

The Ranelagh Gardens

These gardens, covering 123½ acres/50 ha, in the past formed the setting for the public ball, which had a charge for admission, 'in imitation of Lord Ranelagh's in London'. The ball was then all the rage, for Marie-Antoinette herself did not disdain to come to dance at it. Today the Ranelagh is one of the most popular gardens with children, who come for its merry-go-rounds, donkey rides and Punch-and-Judy shows. There are a few descriptive sculptures. In the center is the La Fontaine monument, stripped in 1942 of its statue (by Dumilatre, 1891); its replacement, by Correia, was erected in 1983. To the l. runs the Ave. Ingres, where Rossini died (at no. 5) in 1868; to the r. is the Ave. Prud'hon. The Musée Marmottan (→Museums) is in the Rue Louis-Boilly (via Ave. du Ranelagh). The buildings at nos. 5, 7 and 9, by Charles Labro (1912), are representative of the sobering of architectural style just before World War I. Follow the Boul. Suchet as far as the Place de Colombie.

Avenue Henri-Martin

The avenue is shaded by the expensive buildings that line it. The central reservation has, unfortunately, been made into a parking lot. At the corner of the Rue de Franqueville is a large residential development in the Classical style of the interwar years, the work of the architect Roux-Spitz, who set up his office here; at the time (1931) it was one of the earliest co-ownership operations. At the corner of the Ave. Victor-Hugo, stands a statue, by Rodin, of the poet surrounded by the Muses; the present bronze was cast only in 1964, from the original plaster mould. The chalet where Alphonse de Lamartine died stood between nos. 113 and 107. At no. 71 is the *mairie* (town hall) of the 16th arr., built by Godebouf from 1868 to 1874. The banqueting hall was decorated by Chauvin and the semicircular hall by E. Lévy (1887).

Avenue Georges-Mandel

This former section of the Ave. Henri-Martin was renamed in 1945. At no. 42 *bis* stood the mansion of the Duc de Gramont, a member of the Académie des Sciences. His wife was the daughter of the famous Comtesse Greffulhe, who was the inspiration for Marcel Proust's Duchesse de Guermantes, and the most beautiful woman in Paris. Built by the architect Adda in 1910, it was destroyed in 1963. At no. 43, the mansion designed by Henri Grandpierre in 1904 houses the Foundation Singer-Polignac. The Institut de France organizes concerts in the round concert hall in the Rue Cortambert, with its decorative painted frieze by Jose-Maria Sert, representing Apollo on his chariot.

Rue de la Pompe

Retrace your steps as far as this very long street that links the district of La Muette to the Ave. Foch. The Lycée Janson-de-Sailly (no. 106), was built by Laisné from 1881 to 1883. At no. 89 an inscription recalls that from October 1940 to June 1942 Pierre Brossolette and his wife kept the bookshop here that became the meeting place for many Resistance fighters. At no. 51 is a Spanish church, decorated with 16 scenes from the *Life of the Virgin* (Lucien Jonas, 1944). The Rue de la Tour takes you back to the Place de Costa-Rica. With the Rue de Passy, it is one of the two old village streets; at no. 66 you can see a remnant of its ancient buildings in a tower, now much restored.

▷ The Waters of Passy

The health-giving reputation of the waters of Passy emerged in the 15th c., at the time when the village was raised to the status of a *seigneurie*. However, it was only in the middle of the 17th c. that the Faculty of Medicine began to take an interest in their curative properties. These mineral waters became truly established in the 18th c. with the discovery of new springs that began to attract high society and to bring about the expansion of the village. In the 19th c. all the properties where the springs were sited (20 acres/8 ha) were bought by Benjamin Delessert, philanthropist and founder of the Caisse d'Epargne. Remaining open to those wishing to take the cure, the property, arranged in terraces on the hillsides, was then embellished by a Swiss chalet, adding a picturesque note. On part of the estate Delessert built a sugar refinery and a spinning-mill; in 1824 these were linked to his home by the first suspension bridge built in France. The Parc des Eaux de Passy was broken up in 1930, leading to the laying out of the Ave. Marcel-Proust, Ave. René-Boylesve and the Ave. du Parc-de-Passy, while the lower part of the Rue Berton was widened and became Rue d'Ankara; buildings rose along the quay, one of which contains an early civil defense shelter. On the heights of Passy, from no. 17 to no. 27 Rue de Raynouard, large residential developments by the architects Julien et Duhayon (1931) and Nafilyan (1933) came to dominate the Seine with the mass of their structures. After the war, temporary administrative buildings were put up on what remained of the park; there

there they remain, in spite of the green-space classification that forbids building on the land.

▷ The Perret brothers, 25 *bis* Rue Franklin

Neither Auguste (1874–1954) nor Gustave Perret (1876–1952) was an architect; both were builders. That did not matter. An architectural diploma was not yet required of builders, and when they built 25 *bis* Rue Franklin it was not their first architectural venture: they had already, in 1899, put up the Casino in Saint-Malo and, in 1902, the building at 119 Ave. de Wagram.

The Perret family owned the plot at 25 *bis*. The building was to provide both their office (on the ground floor) and their home (on the top floor). Building for oneself often leads to acts of daring that working for others would not permit: this edifice may truly be considered the first French building of the 20th c. (it was erected in 1903), by virtue of the simplicity, even austerity, of its lines and volumes. The 'apostle of concrete', Auguste Perret, here demonstrated for the first time the aptness of the epithet he was given later, even if he hid his audacity beneath a polychrome sandstone facing by Bigot, a concession to the taste of the period. It would not be the case two years later: concrete appeared naked on the façade of the garage (now sadly demolished) in the Rue de Ponthieu, consecrating the birth of contemporary French architecture. The Perret family lived in the Rue Franklin until 1929, the year in which 51 Rue Raynouard was built; by then famous and solicited from all sides, their office had become too small to deal with the ever increasing volume of public commissions.

▣ Museums to visit

Musée Marmottan (2 Rue Louis-Boilly): Napoleonic art and Impressionist paintings.

Musée des Lunettes et Lorgnettes (2 Ave. Mozart): collection of eyeglasses and binoculars from the 16th to the 20th c.

Musée Balzac (47 Rue Raynouard): rooms occupied by Balzac from 1840 to 1847.

Musée du Vin (2 Rue des Eaux): objects and documents illustrating viniculture. Musée Clemenceau (6 Rue Franklin): mementoes of statesman Georges Clemenceau.

The Père-Lachaise Cemetery**

20th arr.
Métro: Père-Lachaise
Bus: 61, 69
Parking: 146 Rue de Charonne
Taxis: 65 Boul. de Ménilmontant. Tel: 48–05–92–12

The Père-Lachaise Cemetery stands on a hill where the boundaries meet of what were once the three villages (which now comprise the 20th arrondissement): Belleville, Ménilmontant and Charonne.

It covers an area of just over 116 acres/47ha and is the largest and most frequently visited of the Paris cemeteries. In summer it becomes a vast and picturesque garden, with its mass of greenery, romantic walks and statues. People visit it not simply to commune with the spirits of the great and famous who lie buried here, but also to view an important aspect of 19th-c. sculpture. Among the most famous sculptors and architects whose work is represented are Rude, Chapu, David d'Angers, Barrias, Garnier, Guimard, Visconti, and many others.

Walking through the cemetery, you will come to appreciate the extraordinary variety of the funerary monuements, ranging from a simple headstone to the most sumptuous mausoleum; lovers of 19th-c. architecture will find here a compact collection of all the styles of monument masonry in fashion during the period.

Remember, however, that the oldest parts of the cemetery are those near the main entrance. They cover an area of uneven ground and are divided by many winding paths. This portion of the cemetery has been registered as an historic monument since 1962. The more recent sections are on the high ground near the Avenue Gambetta and are laid out in rectangular blocks with paths running at right angles between them, as if drawn with a ruler.

History of the cemetery

In the 12th c. the land was known as the Champ de l'Evêque (The Bishop's Field) because it was jointly owned by the Bishop of Paris, who had his wine press here. In 1430, a wealthy merchant built his country house here, the Folie Regnault. House and land passed through the hands of different owners until 1626, when the hill was purchased by the Jesuits as a place of retreat and was named Mont-Louis, in honor of St. Louis. In 1665 and 1709 it became famous as a favorite haunt of Louis XIV's confessor, Father François de La Chaize. The estate decayed after 1763, when the Jesuits were expelled. In 1803 it was sold to Frochot, the Prefect of Paris, who converted it into a cemetery. Officially opened on May 21 1804, the Mont-Louis estate became the E cemetery, one of three outside the limits of the old city walls.

The first burial there was that of an auctioneer's clerk. The architect Brongniard was commissioned to lay out the original 42 acres/17ha. He aimed to create a new type of cemetery with the graves placed in a garden setting. To popularize this new burial ground, the city authorities ordered the remains of some of the famous to be transferred to it – for example, the remains of Héloïse and Abelard in 1817.

The result was a positive infatuation with the cemetery, which was several times enlarged and became one of the most famous spots in Paris. In it are buried a host of celebrated people from the past and present.

Tour of the cemetery

Main entrance: Boul. de Ménilmontant. Open weekdays Mon. Mar.16–Nov. 5, 7.30am–6pm; Nov. 6–Mar. 15 8am–5.30pm; on Sat. opens at 8.30am; Sun. and public holidays 9am. The tour lasts 2 hrs.

How to find some famous graves

Go through the main entrance on the Boul. de Ménilmontant and along the Ave. Principal, turning r. into the Ave. du Puits, which leads to the Ave. Casimir-Périer running the length of the 7th section. At the corner, on the r., a path leads to the tomb of Héloïse and Abelard.

The tomb of Héloïse and Abelard*

The mausoleum is enclosed by wrought iron railings. Two recumbent stone figures lie beneath an arched canopy which came from the Abbey of Paracelet. The tomb contains the remains of Héloïse (d. 1164) and of Abelard (d. 1142), rescued in 1800 by the archeologist Alexandre Lenoir. The City of Paris erected the mausoleum in 1817.

Leave the 7th section and follow the Ave. Casimir-Périer on the r. as far as the intersection, in the center of which stands the statue of Casimir Périer (d. 1832), Président of the Council under Louis-Philippe. The sculpture and the three reliefs are by Cortot. Turn r. at this junction to enter the 16th section. Behind the chapel erected here on the corner, lies the grave of the rock singer Jim Morrison (d. 1971).

Jim Morrison's grave

The interesting thing about this simple grave is the hooligan cult that has grown up around it. Nearby graves have been desecrated by all kinds of graffiti scratched or sprayed on them. Hastily drawn arrows on the walls of nearby sculptures point to the location of the grave. The cemetery administrators regularly clean up the graffiti, but they are constantly renewed by fans of this singer, who died of an accidental overdose in Paris. This rather special form of devotion has been practised for the last 15 years.

To the grave of Champollion the Younger

Walk back towards the junction of the Ave. Casimir-Périer. If you go round to the l. you will pass in succession the graves of the mathematician Gaspard Monge (d. 1818) and of the chemist and revolutionary Raspail (d. 1878) whose tomb by Etex is in the form of the prison cell which was condemned after the revolution of 1848. Proceed to and along the Ave. des Acacias: on your l. stands the obelisk which marks the grave of the Egyptologist Champollion the Younger (d. 1832). Follow the Ave. des Acacias. A little further on to your r. is the grave of the mathematician Michel Chasles (d. 1881).

Princess Elizabeth Deminoff's mausoleum

A little further to the r. stands the base of the mausoleum of Princess Elizabeth Deminoff (d. 1818), whose son married Princesse Math-ilde, a cousin of Napoléon III. The monumental tomb, designed by Quaglia, is three storeys high and has a marble canopy. Go up the steps alongside the mausoleum and proceed down the Chemin du Dragon; on the r. is the grave of General Foy* (d. 1825) with statue and bas-reliefs by David d'Angers. Further along this path, on the l., the poet Anna de Noailles (d. 1933) is buried in a Byzantine-style chapel. Follow the Chemin du Dragon to the Chemin Masséna.

Napoleon's Marshals

On the l. is the vault of Marshal Ney, executed by firing squad in 1815; close by, on the r., David d'Angers' equestrian group decorates the grave of General Gobert (d. 1808). Beyond, on the l. are the graves of Marshal Masséna (d. 1817; bust by Bosio), and of Marshal Lefèvre (d. 1820). Continue past the intersection of the Chemin du Dragon to the tomb of Murat (d. 1815). Go back down the Chemin Jordan: three rows away on the r. lies David d'Angers' simple grave (d. 1856).

The sarcophagi of Molière and La Fontaine

Walk along the Chemin Molière where it forks off from the Chemin Jordan, leading to the sarcophagi of Molière (d. 1673) and of La Fontaine (d. 1695), on the r. of the path. Their bodies were brought here in 1817, but it is doubtful whether the remains really are those of the two great writers.

Sarah Bernhardt's grave

Continue down the Chemin Molière to the Chemin Laplace: turn r. down it to reach the Ave. Transversale no. 1. At the meeting of the ways, take the Chemin Perignon. In line with this path stands a chapel, a few yards behind which lies the grave of the great tragedienne Sarah Bernhardt (d. 1923).

Simone Signoret's grave

Go back and take the Chemin du Quinconce; turn r. into the 44th section as far as the Ave. Transversale no. 2. Walk past the Columbarium on your r., then take the little cul-de-sac which divides the 44th from the 91st section. The film star Simone Signoret (d. 1985) is buried to the r. of this path. Walk back to the Ave. Transversale no. 2 and bear r. In the 92nd section, between two chapels, lies the journalist Victor Noir, murdered in 1870 by Prince Pierre Bonaparte. Dalou's bronze was paid for by public subscription. Follow this path to the end and turn l. into the Ave. Circulaire. Level with the Ave. Transversale no. 3 stands the memorial to the victims of the Mauthausen concentration camp. Turn down here on your r., in the third row, is the grave of the singer Edith Piaf (d. 1963). Walk back to the Ave. Circulaire and continue l.

The Mur des Fédérés (Federalists' Wall)

Opposite the memorial to the victims of Ravensbruck concentration camp stands the Mur des Fédérés, before which the last 4 Communards were shot, on May 28, 1871. On the r., near the wall, is their communal grave. They were buried where they fell, after fierce fighting among the graves. There are few Communard tombs in Paris, one being that of Jean Baptiste Clément (d. 1903), composer of *Le Temps des Cerises*.

To Oscar Wilde's grave

Proceed along the Ave. Circulaire; on the l. in the 97th section are the graves of members of the Central Committee of the French

Communist Party – Jacques Duclos (d. 1975), Maurice Thorez (d. 1964) and Paul Vaillant-Couturier (d. 1937) – as well as that of the Surrealist poet Paul Eluard (d. 1952). Beyond stand various memorials to the concentration camp victims. Proceeding, turn l. into the Ave. Carette. The chemist Chaptal (d. 1832) is buried on the r. Beyond is the grave of the conductor Edouard Collone (d. 1910), founder of the Concerts Colonne, and finally Epstein's *Sphynx*, marking the grave of Oscar Wilde (d. 1900). Follow the Ave. Carette, then turn r. into the Ave. Transversale no. 3, which comes out into the Ave. des Combattants Etrangers Morts pour la France (Ave. of the Foreigners who fell fighting for France) in which are various memorials, including those to the Garibaldians of the Argonne, the Belgian troops killed in World War I, and the Greek volunteers.

The Columbarium

On the l. stands the main entrance to the Columbarium, in which the ashes of those who have chosen to be cremated are placed. Within, at the end of the great hypostyle hall, stands a sculpted stone group by Paul Landowski depicting *Le Rectour de l'homme ansein de la Nature* (Man's Return to the Bosom of Nature). The crematorium is in the center of the building. It was begun in 1886, designed by Formigé, and came into operation on April 27, 1889. After cremation, the ashes are enclosed in urns and placed in identical niches; they include the composer Paul Dukas, the film director Max Ophuls, the humorist Pierre Dac and the dancer Isadora Duncan, among many other famous names.

Allan Kardec's grave

Further on, beyond the junction with the Ave. Transversale no. 2, lies the founder of the spiritualist movement, Allan Kardec (d. 1869), buried on the l. His tomb is built like a dolmen, with a bust by Capellaro. The tomb has become a place of worship and is visited regularly by groups of spiritualists.

To Balzac's grave

Continue into the Ave. Transversale no. 1, and bear l. toward the mausoleum of Félix de Beaujour (d. 1836), President of the Council during the Consulate. It is a colossal obelisk over 52ft/16m high. Go back and take the Chemin Delavigne: on the r. lie the graves of Balzac (d. 1850) with his bust by David d'Angers, and of his wife, Mme Hanska.

To Gérard de Nerval's grave

Proceed along the Chemin Delavigne to the intersection, then turn l. up the Ave. Delacroix where, on the l., is the sarcophagus, made of volcanic rock from the quarries of Volvic in the Puy-du-Dôme, of the painter Eugène Delacroix (d. 1864). Slightly beyond, to the r., lies the grave of the poet and novelist Gérard de Nerval (d. 1855).

To Géricault's grave

Retrace your steps and walk down the Chemin de Mont-Louis. Beside the Ave. de la Chapelle stands the grave of the publisher Del Duca, decorated with Messina's *Descent from the Cross* in bronze. Now go to the promenade in front of the chapel overlooking Paris. To its r. stands the monumental tomb of President Thiers (d. 1877). Follow the Ave. de la Chapelle into the 12th section, where, on the r., lies the grave of the painter Géricault (d. 1824), with Etex's copy in relief of his famous painting *Le Radeau de la Médusa* (The Raft of the 'Medusa').

To Chopin's grave

Beyond Géricault's grave take the path r. which runs down into the 11th section. Again turn r. into the Chemin Denon; on the r. lies the grave of Frédéric Chopin (d. 1849), with the composer's profile portrait and a statue of the Muse Erato by Clésinger. Not far away, the composer Cherubini (d. 1842) lies buried.

To the graves of Alfred de Musset and Colette

Go back and turn l. down the Chemin du Coq, which becomes the Chemin du Père Eternel. On the l., note the grave of the tragedienne Mlle Georges (d. 1867) and further on, where the S Ave. Laterale forks off, Dubois' fine statue; *Femme agenouillée* (Kneeling Woman). Take the S Ave. Laterale on the r., and you will see on the l. Bartholomé's *Monument aux Morts** (Monument to the Dead). Walk back down the Ave. Principale: on the r., in the 4th section, Alfred de Musset (d. 1857) and the novelist Colette (d. 1954) lie buried.

Tour of the cemetery by section

Below are listed the names of the most notable people buried in the cemetery as well as tombs of special architectural interest.

1st section

Clothilde de Vaux (d. 1846), who inspired the philosopher Auguste Comte; the philanthropist Edmé Champion (d. 1852) and the chemist Paul Champion (d. 1884); Gustave Froment (d. 1865), who invented the gyroscope and built the electric telegraph.

2nd section

Jean Faure (d. 1889), father of President Félix Faure, and the engraver Pierre Tardieu (d. 1842). Beside the wall stands the Art Nouveau Family tomb of E. Caillat.

3rd section

The aviation and automotive pioneer Ernest Archdeacon (d. 1950); the alienist Jacques Moreau de Tours (d. 1884); Jean Schnetz (d. 1870), painter and Director of the School of Rome; and the novelist Jules Romains (d. 1972).

4th section

The La Rochefoucauld family tomb; the scholar François Arago (d. 1853) with a bust by David d'Angers; Auber (d. 1871), composer of over 50 operas, most notably *La Muette de Portici*, with bust by Dantan; the philosopher, politician and writer Victor Cousin (d. 1867); Ledru-Rollin (d. 1875); the painter Thomas Couture (d. 1879) with a bronze bust and winged figure by Barnas; President Félix Faure (d. 1899); the sculptor Falguière (d. 1900); Marqueste's statue. *Inspiration*; Sergeant Hoff, hero of the Franco-Prussian War (d. 1902); statue by Bartholdi; the famous singer Adelina Patti (d. 1919); the architect Visconti (d. 1854), who designed Napoléon's tomb and the Louvre; the archeologist Beulé (d. 1874); the sculptor Dantan (d. 1842); Achille Fould (d. 1869), Napoléon III's Finance Minister; cenotaph of the composer Rossini (d. 1868), whose body was buried in Florence in 1887; Louis Poinsot (d. 1859), mathematician; the poet Alfred de Musset (d. 1857), buried under a willow tree as he requested; Arsène Houssaye (d. 1896), writer; Baron Haussmann (d. 1890), architect and urban designer; the Generals Lecomte and Clément Thomas, shot by the Communards in 1871: Cugnot's statue *La Patrie* (The Motherland); Lebas (d. 1873), the engineer, who brought to France the obelisk from Luxor and erected it in the Place de la Concorde; Lenoir and Vavin (d. 1892), with a statue titled *La Pleureuse* (The Weeping Woman); the painter Paul Baudry (d. 1887), with bronze by Mercié; the novelist Colette (d. 1954); the sculptor Bartholomé (d. 1928), close to his masterpiece *Monument aux Morts* (Monument to the Dead) stand-

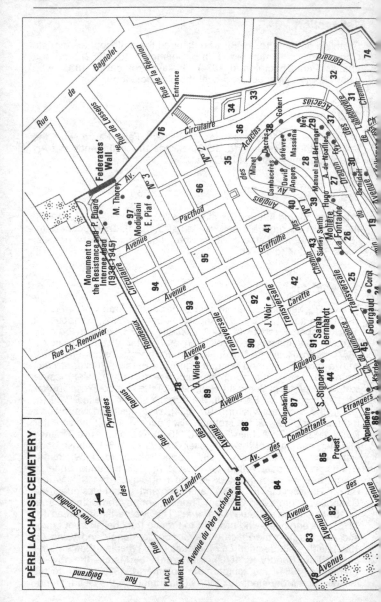

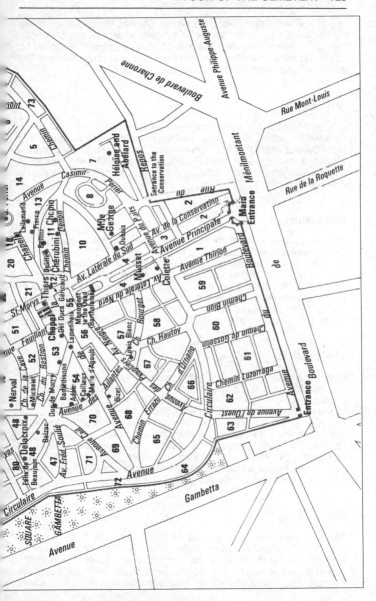

ing in the Ave. Principale; the jeweller Charles Christofle (d. 1868); Jules Claretie (d. 1913), writer and Administrator of the Comédie-Française; the composers Gustave (d. 1926) and Henri Goublier (d. 1951); Pierre Jansen (d. 1907), astronomer and physicist, and the astronomer Joseph Lefrancois de Lalande (d. 1807).

5th section

Marshal Maison (d. 1840), commander of the French expedition. Charles-François Lebrun, Duc de Plaisance (d. 1824), politican and third Consul after the 18 Brumaire coup d'etat, covered by a granite temple; the composer Francis Poulenc (d. 1963); the journalist Claude Terrien (d. 1966), who wrote under the name of Claude de Fréminville.

6th section

The monument erected by the City to the members of the Parisian Garde National who fell in the fighting of June 1832; Cyrano de Bergerac (1619–55) the writer whom Edmond Rostand made the hero of his play of that name; Napoléon III's surgeon Nélaton (d. 1873); the de Lesseps family tomb, housing the remains of Ferdinand de Lesseps, builder of the Suez Canal; the watchmaker Casimir Becquerel (d. 1860); the writer Lucien Prévost-Paradol (d. 1870), and the painter Antoine Vollon (d. 1900).

7th section

The Jewish cemetery. Here lies the tragedienne Rachel (d. 1858); the strange mausoleum of Jacques Roblès (d. 1893), with Précault's *Silence* in semi–high relief; the mausoleum of Héloïse and Abélard, to which their remains were transferred in 1817; Pierre Decourcelle (d. 1926), popular novelist; family tomb of the printers, Firmin-Didot; the watchmaker Lepaute (d. 1789), the dramatist William Busnach (d. 1907); Lucien Fugère (d. 1935); the composer Françoise Hoffmann (d. 1928); the painter François Picot (d. 1868); the Rothschild family tomb; the painter Pissarro (d. 1903), and Pierre Lazareff, journalist for *France-Soir*.

8th section

The anatomist Pierre Béclard (d. 1827) and his son Jules (d. 1887), with Bra's bronze bust of the latter, who was Permanent Secretary of the Academy of Medicine; the famous actress Mlle Mars (d. 1847); cenotaph of the family of Joseph Lesurques (d. 1797), implicated in the celebrated case of the Lyons Mail; the famous anatomist Xavier

Bichat (d. 1802), aged 33; the naturalist Cuvier (d. 1894); the chemist Dulong (d. 1838), medallion by David d'Angers; the sculptor Cavelier (d. 1894); Marie-Joseph de Chenier (d. 1811), poet, politician, and brother of the poet André Chénier; the actress Yvonne de Bray (d. 1954); Napoleon's historian, Frédéric Masson (d. 1923), Louis Bertin (d. 1841), publicist and founder of the *Journal des Débats*; Emilie Couverchel (d. 1866), who is supposed to have lived for 147 years.

9th section

Paul de Saint-Victor (d. 1881), critic and historian, bronze bust by Guillaume; Berthelier (d. 1881), painter, bronze bust by Rougelet; Royer-Collard (d. 1846), philosopher and politician; Mlle George (d. 1867), the famous tragedienne, and successively, the mistress of Napoléon, Talleyrand, and Metternich; André de Fouquières (d. 1959); red marble temple of the Worms de Romilly family erected in 1867; General Henri Choury de la Vigerie (d. 1893), and the sculptor Paul Dubois (d. 1905).

10th section

The tomb of the bronze-founder and gilder Ravrio (d. 1814), designed by himself; Denon (d. 1825), archaeologist, a member of Napoleon's expedition to Egypt, and curator of the Louvre with a bust by Cartellier; Gohier (d. 1830), president of the Directory, with a medallion by David d'Angers; Delambre (d. 1822), astronomer responsible for defining and measuring the meter; George Sand's son-in-law, the sculptor Clésinger (d. 1883); the painter Guillaume Dubufe (d. 1909), with a monument by Bartholomé and Formigé; the composer Gustave Charpentier (d. 1956); Aimée de Coigny (d. 1820), the 'Young Captive' of André Chénier's famous poem; the writer Rémy de Gourmont (d. 1915); Jacques Tenon (d. 1816), surgeon; the famous physicist Edouard Branly (d. 1940); Pierre Agier (d. 1823), president of the Revolutionary Tribunal; the German astronomer Johann Burckardt (d. 1825); Henri Franquetot, Duc de Coigny and Marshal of France (d. 1821); the chemist Antoine Labarraque (d. 1850); the historian and orientalist Silvestre de Sacy (d. 1838); and Miguel Asturias (d. 1974), writer.

11th section

Jean-Louis Barthou, Minister for Foreign Affairs, assassinated in Marseilles in 1934 by Yugoslav terrorists; the musician and instrument maker Erard (d. 1831); the well-known watchmaker Bregeut (d. 1823); the composers Boïeldieu (d. 1834), Grétry (d. 1813), Bellini (d. 1835), Cherubini (d. 1842) and Wilhem (d. 1842), with a medallion of the latter by David d'Angers; the singer Tamberlick (d. 1889) with a memorial by Godebski; the poet Jacques Delille (d. 1813); Lesueur (d. 1837), composer and Berlioz' teacher; the Chevalier de Boufflers (d. 1815), poet and soldier; Bernardin de Saint-Pierre (d. 1814), writer; Laharpe (d. 1803), critic; the physicist and pioneer balloonist Charles (d. 1823), whose young wife was the 'Elvire' of Lamartine's *Meditations*; Louise Dugazon (d. 1821), actress; the politician Regnault de Saint-Jean-d'Angely (d. 1819); the painter De Nittis (d. 1884); the Carnot family tomb; the poet Parny (d. 1814); Habeneck (d. 1849), conductor of the Paris Conservatoire orchestra; the composer Frédéric Chopin (d. 1849); Jean Neveu and his sister, the famous violinist Ginette Neveu 1919–49, killed together in an aircrash; Lakanal (d. 1845), a member of the Convention; Guy Target (d. 1807), the lawyer who defended Cardinal de Rohan in Marie-Antoinette's Diamond Necklace affair; Guillaume Bervic (d. 1822), engraver; Adélaïde Dufresnoy (d. 1825), novelist; the composer and piano-manufacturer Pierre Gaveau (d. 1825); Charles Messier (d. 1817), astronomer; Maria Milanolho (d. 1848), violinist; the architect of the Bourse. Brogniart (d. 1813) who was responsible for the lay-out of the original cemetery.

12th section

Talma (d. 1826), the first actor to perform in period costume; the painter Géricault (d. 1824); Riesener (d. 1828), Delacroix' uncle; the sculptor Jean Carnès (d. 1894), with bronze self-portrait bust; the playwright Ernest Capendu (d. 1868); the composer Isouard (d. 1818), whose real name was Nicolò.

13th section

Mme Lavoisier (d. 1836), wife of the famous chemist who was guillotined in 1794; the composers Méhul (d. 1817), Hérold (d. 1833), Gossec and (d. 1829). Ignace Pleyel (d. 1836) and Gabriel Pierné (d. 1938); the balloonist Mme Blanchard (d. 1819); the Duverger de Hauranne family vault; Rudolphe Kreuzer (d. 1831), the violinist and composer; the composers Montan (d. 1844): his real name was Henri Berton, Henry Février (d. 1957), Honoré Langle (d. 1807) and Ferdinand Paër (d. 1839); the student Lallemand, the first political victim to be buried in the cemetery, killed in an uprising in 1820.

14th section

The Moreau-Vauthier family vault, statue by Moreau-Vauthier; Admiral Pothuau (d. 1882); the Marquis de Lauriston (d. 1828), diplomat and Marshal of France; the physicist Augustin Fresnel (d. 1827), famous for his research into the nature of light; a tablet at the foot of a tree marks the grave of Tallien (d. 1820), who was instrumental in the overthrow of Robespierre; Auguste Cahours (d. 1891), chemist; Pierre Réal (d. 1834), Fouché's assistant.

15th section

Amusat (d. 1856), surgeon, with bronze medallion by Bogino; Léon Cognier, painter with a fine stone medallion; the author Melchior de Vogué (d. 1910); the Belgian writer Georges Rodenbach (d. 1898).

16th section

Jim Morrison (d. 1971), whose real name was James Douglas, lead singer of the California rock group, The Doors, whose grave has become the focus of a unique cult; General de Labédoyère (d. 1815), executed by firing squad after the Bourbon Restoration for greeting Napoléon at Greenable on his return from Elba; Sophie Germain (d. 1831), the mathematician; celebrated artist and stage designer Christian Bérard (d. 1949).

17th section

Marshal Victor, Duc de Bellune (d. 1841); Desiré Dalloz (d. 1869), jurisconsult and his brother Armand (d. 1867), authors of standard legal treatises; Michel Chasles (d. 1881), mathematician; the philosopher Pierre Laffite (d. 1903) disciple of Comte; Auguste Comte (d. 1847), founder of the positivist school of philosophy; Panckoucke (d. 1798), the publisher; Admiral Abel Aubert du Petit-Thouars (d. 1864).

18th section

Gaspard Monge (d. 1818), the mathematician and one of the founders of the Ecole Polytechnique; the playwright Robert de Fleurs (d. 1927), Professor Hachette (d. 1834), of the Ecole Polytechnique; Dr Gall (d. 1818), one of the first to study phrenology; Raspail (d. 1878), chemist; the physicist Joseph Fourier (d. 1830) commemorated by a bronze bust; the famous Egyptologist Champollion (d. 1832), with an obelisk bearing a medallion; Marshal Kellermann, Duc de Valmy (d. 1820), whose heart is buried on the battlefield of Valmy; Jacques Laffite (d. 1844), financier; Francis Salabert (d. 1946), music publisher; and the specialist in mental illness, Philippe Pinel (d. 1826).

19th section

The memorial chapel of Princess Deminoff (d. 1818); Hahnemann (d. 1843), founder of homeopathy; Duret (d. 1865), sculptor; Delsart (d. 1900), singer; Denis Poisson (d. 1840), mathematician; the Garnier-Pagès family tomb; and the naturalist Geoffroy Saint-Hilaire (d. 1844), with a medallion by David d'Angers.

20th section

The actresses Raucourt (d. 1815), Clairon (d. 1803) and Contat (d. 1813); Claude Bernard (d. 1878), the famous physiologist; the painter Isabey (d. 1855); the Abbé André Morellet (d. 1819), writer and philosopher; Napoleon's financier, Gabriel Ouvrard (d. 1826); General Auguste Rochechouart (d. 1858); Jacques Pajou (d. 1828), painter.

21st section

Dr Hyacinthe Vincent (d. 1950), discoverer of anti-typhoid vaccine and measures to prevent gangrene; General Ernest Courtot de Cissey (d. 1882), Minister of War.

22nd section

Désaugiers the songwriter (d. 1827), Gustave Doré (d. 1883), the book-illustrator; the actress Mme Crosnier (d. 1907) with a portrait bust; and the painter Joseph Vien (d. 1848).

23rd section

The painter Ingres (d. 1867), with a bust by Bonnassiex and marble tomb by Baltard; General Baron Gourgaud (d. 1852), who accompanied Napoleon into exile on St Helena; the painters Boilly (d. 1845) and Dubufe (d. 1864); monument in memory of the great botanist Michel Adamson; the famous genius of Art Nouveau jewellery and glass, René Lalique (d. 1945); the painter Jean Raffaeli (d. 1924).

24th section

Daubigny (d. 1878), painter; the Comtesse de Genlis (d. 1830), bluestocking and writer, governess of the children of Philippe Egalité and inspector of primary education under Napoléon; the Marquis de Perignon (d. 1818), Marshal of France; Pradier (d. 1852), sculptor, with bust carved by his pupils, and graceful bas-reliefs on his tomb; Honoré Daumier (d. 1879), painter and caricaturist; Camille Corot (d. 1875), painter; Hyacinth Loyson (d. 1913), founder in 1879 of the breakaway Gallican Church, with a monument by H. Andersen and H. Hébrard; Jacques Cellerier (d. 1814), architect, who made the famous elephant erected in the Place de la Bastille, described by Victor Hugo in *Les Misérables*; Henri Fouques-Duparc (d. 1933), pianist and composer; and General Andoche Junot, Duc d'Abrantès (d. 1813).

25th section

Admirals Hamelin (d. 1864) and Roussin (d. 1854), the latter the pioneer of French transatlantic steamships; the Gémond family tomb 1842, a massive pyramid; Baron Gros (d. 1835), painter; the chapel of General d'Aboville (d. 1891), framed by two cannon; the tombs of La Fontaine (d. 1695) and of Molière (d. 1673) erected in 1817 (whether their occupants really are the writers is doubtful); and the playwright d'Ennery (d. 1898).

26th section

The chemist Gay-Lussac (d. 1850); Léon Faucher (d. 1854), publicist; Paul Meurice (d. 1905), playwright and friend of Victor Hugo; Alphonse Daudet (d. 1897), novelist; Marchand (d. 1876), personal valet to Napoleon in exile on St Helena; Augustin Legendre (d. 1874).

27th section

Admiral Bruat (d. 1855), with tomb carved by Maindron; the lawyer Paillet (d. 1855), with marble bas-relief by Doublemard; Couder (d. 1873), painter; the Duc de Gaete (d. 1844), statesman and financier; Victor Hugo's father, General Hugo (d. 1828); Charles Dupaty (d. 1825), sculptor; Gaston (d. 1899) and Albert (d. 1906) Tissandier, pioneers of the dirigible balloon with electric motor.

28th section

Boissy d'Anglas (d. 1826), President of the Convention; Marshal Lefebvre (d. 1820), and his wife, known as Mme Sans-Gêne (Mrs Inconsiderate); Marshals Masséna (d. 1817) and Reille (d. 1860), with a tomb by Jacques and Bosio; the writer Beaumarchais (d. 1799); the economist Saint-Simon (d. 1825), who founded his own school of social science; Brillat-Savarin (d. 1826), author of the gourmet classic *Physiologie du Goût* (*The Physiology of Taste*); Barras (d. 1829), the conspirator of 9 Thermidor and a member of the Directory; General Haxo (d. 1824), painter; Daunou (d. 1840), politician, scholar and historian, with a medallion by David d'Angers; the Lameth brothers, all three cavalry colonels (d. 1829, 1832, 1853); Judith Frère, the songwriter, Bèranger's 'Lisette'; General Foy* (d. 1835), David d'Angers' statue and bas-reliefs make this one of the finest tombs in the cemetery; Prince Georges Bibescu (d. 1887) and Anna de Noailles (d. 1933), poetess; the politican Jacques-Antoine Manuel (d. 1827) and the songwriter Béranger (d. 1857), reunited in the same grave, with medallions (Manuel's by David d'Angers); Napoléon's architects (d. 1897); the large chapel of the philanthropist Sir Richard Wallace (d. 1890), who bequeathed the Wallace Collection in London; Benjamin Antier (d. 1970), playwright.

29th section

Marshal Ney (d. 1815); Merlin de Thionville (d. 1833), member of the Convention; the inventor of the telegraph Claude Chappe (d. 1805); the scholar Dacier (d. 1833); Paul Lelong (d. 1846), architect; Dulong, the deputy killed in a duel by Marshal Bugeaud in 1834; Benjamin Constant (d. 1830), politician and author of *Adolphe*; the German poet Boerne (d. 1837), medallion and bas-relief by David d'Angers; Garnier-Pagès (d. 1841), politician; the poets Jean de Tinan (d. 1898) and Vielé-Griffin (d. 1937); Henri Lavedan (d. 1940), writer; the painter Constance Mayer de la Martinière, who committed suicide in 1821 for love of the painter Paul Prud'hon, who lies buried in the neighboring 30th section.

30th section

Dr Serres (d. 1868), member of the Academy of Sciences, with a fine marble medallion; Lanjuinais (d. 1827), member of the Convention; the painter Pierre Prud'hon (d. 1823); the Marquis de Caulaincourt (d. 1827), diplomat, named Duc de Vincenze by Napoléon; Sieyès (d. 1836), one of Napoleon's fellow Consuls; Comte Roy (d. 1847), financier and statesman; Martin du Nord (d. 1847), politician.

31st section

The Doric temple to the Duc de Bassano politician, (d. 1839); Talleyrand-Périgord (d. 1883); beautiful chapel of Panhard-Dufour (d. 1897); Joseph Barbet de Jouy (d. 1896), writer.

32nd section

The painter Hersent (d. 1860), medallion and bas-reliefs by Lanno; General Mounier (d. 1860); the Belgian painter Alfred Stevens (d.

1906); the composer Bazin (d. 1878), marble bust by Doublemard; Jean Huvé (d. 1852), architect of the Madeleine; Félix Ravisson archeologist (d. 1900).

33rd section

Gustave Roger (d. 1879), tenor at the Paris Opéra.

34th section

Maurice Duplay, cabinet-maker and friend of Robespierre; Eléonore Duplay (d. 1832), Robespierre's fiancée; Jean d'Arcet (d. 1844), chemist.

35th section

Granite pyramid crowned with trophies to the Inspector General of Engineering, Dabadie (d. 1820); Clara Peabody (d. 1882), large memorial, with bronze high-reliefs ; Lieutenant-General Belliard (d. 1832), a peer of France; the Montmorency family tomb 1830; the playwright Scribe (d. 1861); Tony Noël (d. 1909), sculptor, bust by P. Gasq; the music-hall artiste Theresa (d. 1913), whose real name was Emma Valladon; Camille Flers (d. 1868), landscape painter; Savary, Duc de Rovigo (d. 1833), Napoléon's Minister of Police from 1810 to 1814.

36th section

The Schichler family tomb, 1867, Admiral Bruix (d. 1805); Georges Pouchet (d. 1894), professor at the Muséum, medallion by Vasselot; Edmond About (d. 1879), writer, bronze statue by Crauk; Léon Say (d. 1896), politician and economist; photographer Félix Nadar (d. 1910), the Protestant preacher Athanase Coquerel (d. 1868); Seguin (d. 1875), railway engineer.

37th section

Marshal Gouvion-Saint-Cyr (d. 1830), marble statue by David d'Angers; Marshal Macdonald, Duc de Tarente (d. 1840); General Gobert (d. 1808), magnificent equestrian statue and bas-reliefs by David d'Angers; Baron Larrey (d. 1842), surgeon-in-chief of the Grande Armée, pyramid shaped tomb; the Frochot family chapel, with hauts-reliefs by Raggi.

38th section

Guillaume Dupuytren (d. 1835), who revived clinical surgery, founded the Anatomical Society and operated on Charles X for cataract.

39th section

Marshal Suchet, Duc d'Albuféra (d. 1826), bas-reliefs by David d'Angers; Charles X's minister, Jean-Baptiste de Martignac (d. 1832); Jean-Baptiste Say (d. 1832), economist and industrialist; Raoul Duval (d. 1887); Admiral Duc Ducrès (d. 1820), huge tomb with beautiful bas-reliefs; Edmond de Bourke, a Danish citizen, (d. 1821), marble bas-reliefs; Marshal Beurnonville (d. 1821); Cambacérès (d. 1824), Bonaparte's fellow consul, the sculptor David d'Angers (d. 1856), in a plain grave with no ornamentations; the Boode family tomb in the style of a Greco-Roman temple; Camille Jordan (d. 1821), politician and publicist, marble statue; Brion (d. 1863), sculptor; Parmentier (d. 1813), agriculturist who introduced large-scale potato growing to France; Prosper Enfant (d. 1864), known as 'Le Père Enfantin', one of the founders of Saint-Simonianism, large bust by Aimé Millet; Baron Oberkampf (d. 1837), industrialist; Laréveillière-Lépaux (d. 1824), member of the Directory; Latreille (d. 1833), naturalist; Charles Cade de Gassicourt (d. 1831), Napoléon's chief pharmacist; family vault of Marshal Murat; and Marshal Sérurier (d. 1819), Governor of the Invalides.

40th section

Jean Vaillier (d. 1883), archeologist, large statue- *Le Bon Pasteur* (The Good Shepherd); Jean Perrégaux (d. 1808), financier and creator of the Banque de France; Armand Trousseau (d. 1867), doctor; and Admiral Laurent Turgeut (d. 1839), First Lord of the Admiralty.

41st section

E. Du Sommerard (d. 1885), founder of the Musée de Cluny; Alphonse Daudet's grandson Philippe, whose murder in 1923 roused suspicions of government complicity; Alphonse Herman (d. 1896), composer; the painters Luc (d. 1902) and Olivier Merson (d. 1820); Adam Prazmonksy (d. 1885), astronomer; the Comte de Volney (d. 1820), philosopher and writer.

42nd section

André Devambez (d. 1944), painter; François Richard-Lenoir (d. 1839), well-known industrialist; and Marie Vuillame (d. 1933), singer.

43rd section

Picard (d. 1828), playwright and member of the Académie Française; the British Admiral Sir Sidney Smith (d. 1840); Jules Cousin (d. 1899), founder of the Musée Carnavalet; General Louis Letort, killed at the Battle of Ligny in 1815.

44th section

The tomb of Hyppolyte-Léon Rivai, better known as Allan Kardec (d. 1869), founder of the spiritualist movement, is a granite dolmen on which stands a bronze bust by Capellaro. It is always covered with flowers and is the object of an organized cult. General Michel Ordener (d. 1862), who distinguished himself at Waterloo; J. -J. Veyrassat (d. 1893), animal painter; the great tragedienne Sarah Bernhardt (d. 1923); the poet Sully-Prudhomme (d. 1907); Georges Goyau (d. 1939), historian; Charles Durier (d. 1899), founder of the French Alpine Club; Jeanne Ludwig (d. 1898), actress; General Marbot (d. 1854), whose memoirs chiefly concern Napoleon and who was model for Conan Doyle's character Brigadier Gerard; Simone Signoret (d. 1985), actress.

45th section

Bosio (d. 1845), sculptor, whose statue of Louis XIV stands in the Place des Victoires, and who also decorated the Vendôme Column and the Chapel of Atonement; the Aguado family tomb, decorated with statues (Beneficence and the Arts), and bas-reliefs; Jean Beaudelocque (d. 1810), doctor; Marie de Senonnes (d. 1828), subject of a famous portrait by Ingres.

46th section

Claude Vignon (d. 1888), sculptress, with bronze self-portrait bust she designed for her own grave; Auguste Vitu (d. 1891), journalist, bust by Guilbert; Félix Pyat (d. 1889), revolutionary; Vice-Admiral Lalande (d. 1844).

47th section

General de Wimpfen (d. 1884), bronze bust; Eude (d. 1889), sculptor, medallion by Pacou; Henri Mazel (d. 1947), writer; Princess Dolgorouka, with white marble statue.

48th section

The gigantic monument for the ex-consul Félix de Beaujour; family tomb of Mme Diaz-Sentos, Duchesse de Duras (d. 1827); Frédéric Soulié (d. 1847), with bronze medallion by Clésinger; Lachambeaudie (d. 1872), writer of fables, bronze bust by Taluet; Emile Souvestre (d. 1854), novelist and playwright; Honoré de Balzac (d. 1850), bronze bust by David d'Angers; Jean Pacini (d. 1866), composer.

49th section

Charles Delescluze (d. 1871), journalist, and a leader of the Commune; Charles Nodier (d. 1844), writer, and one of the early French Romantics; Casimir Delavigne (d. 1843), poet and dramatist; the great Romantic painter Eugène Delacroix (d. 1864), in a tomb copied from that of Scipio; Barye (d. 1875), sculptor, bronze bust; Crozatier (d. 1855), sculptor and caster, bas-reliefs by Bosio; Gérard de Nerval (d. 1855), poet and novelist; Frédéric Bérat (d. 1855), composer of *Ma Normandie*; Pierre Chanlaire (d. 1817), geographer.

50th section

General Uhrich (d. 1886), who defended Strasbourg during the Franco-Prussian War; Claude Choiseul (d. 1711), Marshal of France.

51st section

 A terrace with a magnificent view* over Paris. In the centre on the site of the Jesuits' house stands the cemetery chapel, 1834; Paul de Musset (d. 1880), brother of Alfred and writer; Charles Steuben (d. 1856), painter; Pierre Tirard (d. 1893), politician; Saint-Marceaux' statue *Devoir* (Duty).

52nd section

Michelet (d. 1874), who in the 19th c. aroused new interest in the study of history, with high-relief by A. Mercié; Buloz (d. 1877), founder of the *Revue des Deux Mondes*. The Rond-Point Michelet, close to Michelet's grave with Dupré's *Monument des travailleurs municipaux* (Memorial to the Municipal Workers) 1899; Maurice Merleau-Ponty (d. 1961), philosopher.

53rd section

Henry Becque (d. 1899), dramatist; Barbedienne (d. 1892), metal-caster, bust by Chapu, tomb by Boucher; Heibuth (d. 1889), painter; Cartelier (d. 1831), sculptor, medallion bust by Rude, bas-relief by Seurre; De Sèze (d. 1828), with a lawyer Louis XVI pyramid; Gaston Boissier (d. 1908), Roman historian; Cino Del Duca, publisher, with Messina's fine bronze *Descent from the Cross*; Félicité de Lamennais (d. 1854), the famous philosopher, buried in a communal grave by his own wish, between the 53rd and 54th sections.

54th section

The de Morny Chapel, designed by Viollet-le-Duc; Théodore Barrière (d. 1877), playwright, with marble bust; the lavish marble and bronze tomb of Dr. Ricord (d. 1889); the Countesse d'Agoult (d. 1876), pen name Daniel Stern – Liszt's mistress and mother of Cosima Wagner; sculptures by Chapu; Robichon's *Memorial to the Defenders of Belfort*; Guillaume Dode de la Brunerie (d. 1851), Marshal of France; Paul Le Brasseur (d. 1896), actor.

55th section

Great mausoleum of Adolphe Thiers (d. 1877), with Chapu's sculptures; Rebert (d. 1880), Baron Taylor (d. 1879), the patron of literature; Cornélie Falcon (d. 1897), singer; Guérinot (d. 1891), architect, with Barrias' statue *La Pleureuse* (The Weeping Woman).

56th section

General Neigre (d. 1817), his grave surrounded by stone cannons and cannon-balls; containing the heart of the great Neo-Classical painter Jacques Louis David (d. 1825), whose body is buried in the principal cemetery in Brussels; General de Chassloup-Laubat (d. 1833); Raymond Radiguet (d. 1923), author of *Le Diable au Corps* (*The Devil in the Flesh*); Emile Cheve-Paris (d. 1864) musical theorist.

57th section

Hippolyte Flandrin (d. 1864), painter, marble bust by Oudine; Emmanuel Grouchy (d. 1847), Marshal of France; Count Pozzo di Borgo (d. 1842), Corsican opponent of Napoleon, who served the Russian Czars as ambassador in Paris and London; Louis Funck-Bretano (d. 1946), historian; Jean Vanni-Marcoux (d. 1962), singer.

59th section

Marshal Augereau (d. 1816); Debureau (d. 1846), the famous mime; Eugène Burnouf (d. 1852), orientalist; General Arthur Morin (d. 1860), mathematician; Pierre Brasseur (d. 1972), film actor.

60th section

Dr G. Piogey (d. 1894), bronze bust by Barbedienne; the de Broglie family vault; Julien Dupré (d. 1910), landscape and animal painter; Valentin Haüy (d. 1822), founder of the Institut des Jeunes Aveugles (School for Blind Children) and inventor of a system of printing characters in relief for their use.

63rd section

Alfred Chauchard (d. 1909), multi-millionaire founder of the old Magasin du Louvre.

64th section

Georges Méliès (d. 1938), cinema pioneer, bust by Carvinnani 1954; Robert Kemp (d. 1959), critic; monuments erected to the Gardes Nationaux killed at Buzenval, January 19 1871, and to the soldiers who fell in the Franco-Prussian War 1870–71.

65th section

Mame Carvalho (d. 1895), singer, memorial by A. Mercié; Spuller (d. 1896), politician; Spuller (d. 1896), politician; Etienne Melingue (d. 1875), Etienne Pihan (d. 1878), orientalist; Marie Royer (d. 1873), actress.

66th section

Jules Vallès (d. 1885), publicist and revolutionary, bust by Carlier; Pierre Flourens (d. 1867), physiologist; Alphand (d. 1891), stone pyramid and bronze bust by Courtan; Anatole de la Forge (d. 1891), politician, bronze by Barrias; Charles Floquet (d. 1896), politician, monument by Dalou and Formigé; the painters Georges Seurat (d. 1891) and Edouard Detaille (d. 1912); Alexandre Walewski (d. 1868), Napoléon I's son by Marie Walewska.

67th section

Louis Blanc (d. 1882), French socialist; the composers Edouard Lalo (d. 1892) and Ernest Chausson (d. 1889); Claude Guillaume (d. 1905), sculptor; Emile Meunier (d. 1881), chocolate manufacturer; Philippe d'Ornano (d. 1863), Marshal of France, and his wife, Marie Walewska (d. 1817), Napoleon's Polish mistress.

68th section

Bizet (d. 1875), the famous composer of *Carmen*, bronze bust; Georges Enesco (d. 1955), Romanian violinist and composer; Joseph-Robert Fleury (d. 1890), painter; Félix Potin (d. 1896), made famous by the chain of shops bearing his name.

69th section

René Mouchotte (d. 1943), pilot hero of World War II; Georges Hainl (d. 1873), cellist and composer; Jean Cail (d. 1871), industrialist.

70th section

Frédéric Dorian (d. 1873), politician, bronze bust by Aimé Millet; Aimée Desclée (d. 1874), actress, bust; Gaëtan Leymarie (d. 1901), Kardec's disciple.

71st section

Crocé-Spinelli and Sivel, balloonists killed when their balloon Zénith crashed in 1875, bronze recumbent statues by Dumilâtre; Bernard Desly (d. 1855), writer; André Murat, journalist, founder of *L'Ouvrier*.

72nd section

Jean Reynaud (d. 1863), bronze bust by David d'Angers and marble statue, *Immortality*, by Chapu.

73rd section

Jean Peltier (d. 1845), physicist and discoverer of the Peltier Effect; Gaston Plante (d. 1889), inventor of the accumulator storage battery.

74th section

Rosa Bonheur (d. 1875), painter, in the Micas family tomb.

75th section

Benoît Malon (d. 1893), deputy, monument with medallion by Bartholomé; Alexandre Massol (d. 1875), philosopher.

76th section

The bodies of several members of the Paris Commune lie buried here, including Jean-Baptist Clément (d. 1903), poet and song-writer, composer of *Le temps des Cerises* (Cherry Time); Edmé Chabert (d. 1890), founder of the Workers' Party; Karl Marx's son-in-law, the writer Paul Lafargue, who committed suicide with his wife in 1911; Valerien Wrobleski (d. 1908), a general under the Commune; Paul Brousse (d. 1912), social theorist.

79th section

Villiers de l'Isle-Adam (d. 1889), a leading Symbolist poet.

80th section

Jules Berry (d. 1951), actor.

81st section

The actress Déjazet (d. 1875); Henri Moissan (d. 1907), Nobel Prize for chemistry, 1906; Xavier Ruel (d. 1900), founder of the Bazar de l'Hôtel de Ville.

82nd section

Ernest Guiraud (d. 1892), composer; Alfred Picard (d. 1913), scholar; marble Byzantine chapel for Yakoulef (d. 1882), with an unusual sculpture of a man and a woman kneeling facing one another, clasped in each other's arms; Fulgence Bienvenüe (d. 1936), who planned the Paris Métro system.

84th section

Louis Verneuil (d. 1952), playwright; three war memorials with statue to the Czechs, the Belgians and the Italians.

85th section

Marcel Proust (d. 1922); novelist; Paul Souday (d. 1884), critic, bronze bust by L. Cladel; the composers Louis Lacombe (d. 1929) and Reynaldo Hahn (d. 1947), friend of Proust; Trujillo (d. 1961), Dominician president; Virginie Oldoni, Comtesse Verasis de Castiglione (d. 1899), Napoléon III's mistress; the Muslim cemetery.

86th section

Guillaume Apollinaire (d. 1918), World War I poet; Henri de Regnier (d. 1936), poet and novelist, a founder of the Symbolist Movement; the Abbé Rousselot (d. 1924), founder of experimental phonetics, bust; Jean Pezon (d. 1897), a animal-trainer, with a statue of him riding his lion, the celebrated Brutus; the Montfort-Revillon family chapel.

87th section

Monument and Colombarium in which are preserved the ashes of the composer Paul Dukas (d. 1935); Jules Guesde (d. 1922), founder of the Workers' Party; Camille Pelletan (d. 1913), Minister of the Navy; Paul Rivet (d. 1958), founder of the Musée de l'Homme; the dancers Isadora Duncan (d. 1927) and Loie Fuller (d. 1928); the singer-composers Fragson (d. 1913) and Montéhus (d. 1952); Max Ophuls (d. 1957), film-director; Harry Pilcer (d. 1961), dancer and actor; Stan Golestan (d. 1956), Hungarian musician; Henri Torrès (d. 1966), famous lawyer.

88th section

Bernard Grasset (d. 1955), publisher; Léon Juhaux (d. 1954), trade unionist; Marie Laurencin (d. 1956), painter; memorial slab to the Compagnons de la Libération.

89th section

The Labaudy family tomb; Chaptal (d. 1832), chemist and Member of the Institute; Alice Ozy (d. 1893), actress, friend of the painter Chasseriau and known as 'the modern Aspasia'; *Madonna and Child* marble group by Gustave Doré; René Piault (d. 1903), bronze bust by Rodin; Oscar Wilde (d. 1900), with Epstein's strange *Sphynx*; Edouard Colonne (d. 1910), conductor who founded the Concerts Colonne, bust by Sorensen Ringi; the poets Jean Moréas (d. 1910) and Edmond Haraucourt (d. 1941); the writers Georges Courteline (d. 1929); Henri Duvernois (d. 1937) and Franc-Nohain (d. 1935); General Ferrié (d. 1932); Marie Delna (d. 1933), singer; Charles Lecoq (d. 1918), composer; Edouard Pailleron (d. 1899), playwright; Alphonse Bertillon (d. 1914), criminologist; Albert Carré (d. 1938), director of the Paris Opéra; Alex Fischer (d. 1934), writer; René Mesmin (d. 1931), aviator, killed in a crash in Russia; Ernest Pacra (d. 1925), founder of the concerts which bear his name.

90th section

Romain Coolus (d. 1952), playwright; Romain Coolus (d. 1952), playwright; Stephen Heller (d. 1888), virtuoso musician; Marcel Vertez (d. 1961), painter; Emile Waldteufel (d. 1915), composer.

91st section

Blanqui (d. 1881), revolutionary, recumbent bronze statue by Dalou; Théry (d. 1909), racing driver, memorial by Marc Robert; Albert Schlumberger (d. 1897), chemist.

92nd section

Victor Noir (d. 1879), journalist murdered by Prince Pierre Bonaparte, recumbent bronze statue by Dalou; victims of the fire in the Bazar de la Charité (1897), Formigé's monument; J. Cornély (d. 1907), journalist, memorial by Moreau-Vauthier; P. Marinowitch (d. 1919), pilot.

93rd section

Planquette (d. 1903), composer of *Les Cloches de Corneville*; Alfred Capus (d. 1922) and Miguel Zamacois (d. 1955), playwrights; Ziem (d. 1911), painter, memorial by Victor Ségoffin; Félix Galipaux (d. 1932), actor; the famous clown George Footit (d. 1921); Pierre Levegh, racing-driver, who was killed when his car exploded among the spectators at the Le Mans 24-Hour Race in 1955, causing many casualties.

94th section

Philippe Gaubert (d. 1941), composer and conductor; Alain (d. 1951); real name Emile Chartier, philosopher; Gramme (d. 1901), inventor of the dynamo; Yvette Guilbert (d. 1944), actress and singer; Gertrude Stein (d. 1946), painter and writer; Alexandre Stavisky (d. 1934), financier, center of notorious scandal; Fernand Foureau (d. 1914), explorer; Emile Dupont (d. 1945), founder of the Cafés Dupont.

95th section

Elémir Bourges (d. 1925), writer and Member of the Académie Goncourt; André Gill (d. 1887), artist, bronze bust by Laure Coutan; Joffrin (d. 1890), politician, monument by Suchetet; Boussingault (d. 1887), chemist and agronomist; Félia Litvin (d. 1936), singer; Adeline Dudlay (d. 1934), actress; Eugène Pottier (d. 1887); Onésime Reclus (d. 1916), geographer.

96th section

Eugène Delaplanche (d. 1891), sculptor, with bronze bust by A. Levasseur; memorial to the victims of the fire in the Opéra-Comique 1887; René Doumic (d. 1937), critic, director of the *Revue des Deux Mondes*; Modigliani (d. 1920), painter; Camille Erlanger (d. 1919), composer; Jean Grandrey-Rety (d. 1962), music-critic.

97th section

The Mur des Fédérés, the wall against which the 147 surviving defenders of the Commune were executed by firing-squad, and buried where they fell; Barbusse (d. 1935), author of the outspoken novel of World War I, *Le Feu*; the poets, Paul Eluard (d. 1952) and Jean-Richard Bloch (d. 1947); Jean Guignebert (d. 1958); the Communist deputies and party leaders Marcel Cachin (d. 1958), Maurice Thorez (d. 1964), Paul Vaillant-Couturier (d. 1937), Pierre

Sémard (d. 1942) and Raymond Losserand (d. 1942); General Malleret-Joinville (d. 1960); Edith Piaf (d. 1963), the great singer; memorials to the French men and women who were deported and died in the concentration camps of Auschwitz, Buchenwald-Dora, Mauthausen, Neuengamme, Ravensbruck and Mont Valérien; the grave of those killed with the Brigade Fabien; monuments to those who died in the Polish town of Wolomin, and to those who were killed in the Métro disaster at Charonne on February 8, 1962.

▷ Mausoleums

The Père-Lachaise Cemetery contains a considerable number of tombs of such unusual size that they are generally called mausoleums, an illusion to the vast funerary buildings of Classical Antiquity and specifically to the tomb of King Mausolus. The vault is below ground, beneath a memorial on which its occupant's portrait and the outstanding incidents in his or her life are often depicted. These tombs are generally created for famous or powerful people, and many have been paid for by public subscription. Frequently other members of the family are discreetly laid to rest in the same vault. The mausoleums were public tributes to the memory of distinguished soldiers, statesmen or artists; by the end of the 19th c., they tended to be less frequently erected, as space in the cemetery grew more scarce.

Among these tombs of various types, mention should be made of Félix de Beaujour's monumental obelisk (48th section), put up by the architect Cendrier; the Neo-Grecian memorial to Princess Deminoff, 19th section, built of white marble and designed by Quaglia; the recumbent statues of Héloïse and Abelard (7th section), and the many memorials to Napoleon's Marshals (28th, 29th and 38th sections).

▷ Funerary architecture

The development of funerary architecture in the cemeteries of Paris falls neatly into three periods.

Most of the memorials from 1794 to 1830 are standing or flat tombstones. Their shapes were inspired by the architecture of Classical Antiquity, very fashionable during the Neo-Classical period: stelae, pyramids, obelisks, columns, imitation sarcophagi, and so on. Their decoration, too, looked back to antique motifs: urns, amphoras, winged hourglasses, crowns of laurel etc. Deaths heads and bats, statues of weeping women or of genii (winged youths) also can be found, as well as roses and hearts and epitaphs that borrowed the up-to-minute vocabulary of the French Romantic movement.

After 1830, chapels became increasingly frequent. These were small buildings designed for devotions, with altar and prie-dieu, laid out in straight rows, which altered the original lines of the garden. From the mid 19th c. on, they became common features of all cemeteries.

Since the beginning of the 20th c., such large buildings have become less common. The most usual type today is the flat slab gravestone with a headstone. They are becoming more simple in design, and the same models are repeated *ad infinitum*. Traditional materials, such as white marble or Volvic (volcanic) work, have been replaced by pink, grey, or blue granite.

> ## The Garden of Rest and the battlefield

Twice in the history of Paris, the Père-Lachaise Cemetery has been turned into a battlefield.

On March 30 1814, students of the Ecole Polytechnique and of the Ecole des Maison Alfort fortified the cemetery in an attempt to repulse the Russian attack.

In May 1871 the Versailles Government's troops finally crushed the Commune when they launched their attack on the Fédérés. A bloody battle ensured among the graves and the last 147 Communards were shot by firing-squad against the wall (Mur des Fédérés) on May 28; 11,018 bodies were buried where they fell, in a communal grave.

The Plaisance district

14 arr.
Métro: Gaîté/Bus: 28, 58.
Parking 48/50 Ave. du Maine.
Taxis: Place du 18-Juin-1940. Tel: 42–22–13–13.

The name 'Plaisance' evokes an image of pleasure and diversion. And indeed, at the end of the 18th c., this was first an area of open fields where cabarets and small theaters had just begun to appear. But the Industrial Revolution and the 1841 construction of the western wharf on the site of the future Gare de Montparnasse attracted a population of migrant workers from the western provinces, and by the time this agreeable district was incorporated into Paris on January 1, 1860, it was becoming one of the worst examples of proletarian poverty.

Although whole blocks had been declared unfit for human habitation from the beginning of the 20th century, it was not until after World War II that plans were finally drawn up for slum clearance. The most ambitious of these was begun in 1966 and involved the development of some 62 acres/25ha, on which 4,400 decayed dwellings were to be replaced by 5,700 new housing units in the Vandamme-Plaisance areas. The most recent and most spectacular project affects the Guilleminot area and involves some 27 acres/11ha bounded by the Avenue du Maine, Rue Vercingétorix, Rue de Gergovie and Rue Raymond-Losserand. Since 1974, the aim has been to build 4,040 housing units, and the project has in part been entrusted to an architect of international repute, Ricardo Bofill.

The plan for an urban expressway, called the Radiale Vercingétorix, which was to link the Porte de Vanves with the Maine-Montparnasse business complex, was dropped in 1977 in favor of public gardens between the Rue Vercingétorix and the railway tracks.

Tour of the district

45 mins.

As you exit from the Gaîeté Métro station, take the Rue Vercingétorix, with its recently built 17-storey buildings on the l., and the 330ft/100m-high Hôtel Paris-Montparnasse (formerly the Sheraton) on the r. (The hotel was built in 1975.)

Ricardo Bofill's housing complexes and public squares*

You will soon reach the Place de Catalogne. This vast circular *place* some 100 yds/100m in diameter, provides one of the few examples of the *place publique* created in the 20th-c. It is flanked by one of two tiered blocks designed for the area by the Catalan architect Ricardo Bofill. To lend dignity and spaciousness to everyday life, the architect conceived a complex in the Neo-Classical style with pediments, pilasters, columns and entablatures. Note the fountain (sculptor Shamai Haber), an immense disk composed of 300,000 blocks of Brittany granite. It is particularly effective at night with the floodlights playing on the water. The originality of the building lies in the use of precast concrete components both in the structure itself – uprights, cross pieces and slabs – and in the external decoration. This grand setting provides 574 housing units of which 425 are for low-income families. Continue under the main archway and through the building to reach the two inner squares.

The Place de l'Amphitheatre. Access to this semicircular, turf-banked open space is on the r. The architect's plans have been fulfilled down to the smallest detail: the balconies, balustrades, fountain basins and even the paving stones at the S. end are of precast concrete. At night, the projecting elements of the façade are set off, to great effect, by the play of light and shadows produced by the floodlights set between the huge pilasters. From here there is an interesting view of the public gardens under construction and of a second amphitheater with terraced grass banks.

The Place des Colonnes. Access is on the l. hand side of the central passageway. This second great open space is an ellipse flanked by a complex of buildings with glistening façades completely glassed in. The existence of transparent columns is hinted at by the concrete plinths and capitals at their extremities. Accessible from the rest of the district and with its wide expanse of lawn, this *place* affords a huge open public space.

ⳇ The Church of Notre-Dame-du-Travail*

35 Rue Guilleminot (open daily 8am–8pm; tel: 43-20-09-51)

The Church of Notre-Dame-du-Travail, erected by Jules Astruc between 1898 to 1902, is an unusual example of the adaptation of building in metal to ecclesiastical architecture. When it was first built, it stood on the line of the Rue Vercingétorix, but today it lies within the heart of a new, grassy pedestrian precinct and the buildings that concealed its N façade have been demolished.

The apostle of the poor, Abbé Soulange-Bodin (1861–1925), was the guiding force behind the idea of building a church dedicated to work, and he intended it to be a 'universal sanctuary' for workers and a place for 'the reconciliation of Capital with Labor'. The Abbé Soulange-Bodin helped various cooperative organizations for the needy; the mutual aid association, the workers' club, and the consumers' cooperative.

The exterior

Since the church was built with the strictest possible budget, its working-class parishioners raising part of the funds themselves, it displays an odd mixture of materials: cut stone for the main façade, milled rubblestone in the wall foundations, lower-quality stone for the side façades, bricks for the upper levels and specifically some 133 tons/135f of riveted steel and iron for the structural framework. One windowless wall has been decorated by Geneviève and Henri Taillefert, using a traditional method incorporating a whitewash undercoat; an impressive fresco, depicting the interior, which draws the visitor to this unusual church. The façade is broken by the arch of the main doorway, its interior surface decorated by little columns. In the central gable-end is a blind circular recess. In Astuc's original plans, this was to have a stained-glass window. Similarly, the façade should have been flanked by two imposing bell-towers. However, poverty ruled the day, and neither the bell-towers nor the window were installed. The tympanum of the façade has a neo-Byzantine false mosaic which is actually a painting under glass. On this façade hangs the Sevastopol Bell, a trophy from the Crimean War (1854), donated to the parish of Plaisance by Napoléon III in 1861.

The interior

The metal structure frames a wide nave, flanked by side aisles opening onto chapels with galleries above. The whole decorative scheme is Art Nouveau, splendidly restored by Geneviève and Henri Taillefert, with painted foliage on the walls around the sober colors of the stained-glass windows. The semicircular apse houses a plaster statue, by Camille Lefebvre, of the *Madonna and Child* (1897). The base, decorated with themes from the 'world of work', recalls the days of the Guilds. The two apsidal chapels with half domes are located on either side of the apse; the one on the r. dedicated to the Sacred Heart, and that on the l. to St Peter. After restoration, the original circular paintings will be reinstalled in the different chapels. Among them, Jean Huberti's delightfully naïve paintings are noteworthy, depicting the patron saints of different trades: St. Joseph, patron of carpenters, dressed as a workman (1900); St. Luke, patron of artists; St. Elegius, patron of metalworkers, etc.

Leave the church and walk back to the cul-de-sacs off the Rue Didot, via the Rue de l'Ouest and Rue de Gergovie, if you want to see the vast change which has come over the district. The modern buildings are left behind as you enter streets with buildings that go back to the early 20th c., their courtyards often with artists' studios or craftsmen's workshops (examples of the former at 99 Rue de Gergovie). Turn r. at the corner of the Rue d'Alésia into the Rue Didot. As you pass the end of the Rue Jacquier, notice the towers of nos. 5 and 7, once the Crèche Fortado-Heine, erected by Paul Blondel in 1884, and now a social security office. Former country bridlepaths lead off the Rue Didot: Villa Duthy, Villa Deshayes and the Villa Jamot. The last is the most unusual, as you will discover by going through the entrance hall of the apartment building at no. 105. After going round a gigantic fig-tree, you enter a rural Paris in which six villas stand peacefully in their little gardens.

▷ Markets

On the space between the Ave. Villemain and the Rue d'Alésia; Tues. and Fri. 7am–1.30pm. Between nos. 33–73 and Boul. Brune: Thurs. and Sun. 7am–1.30pm.

The Ponts de Paris (The bridges of Paris)***

The Seine enters Paris a little before the Pont National, about 300 mls/500km from its native Burgundy, where its source lies in the forest of Chanceau in the Côte-d'Or, at an altitude of 1500ft/470m. The section passing through Paris is 8m/13km long; and except for rare periods, the height above sea level is virtually constant, varying around 86½/26.39m. As the Seine enters Paris, it has already left the country and the woods long behind, and as it passes under the Pont National it has already grown familiar with the urban landscape, the busy harbor and H/M, silos and factories.

The river is inseparable from the history of the capital. There were, nevertheless, many centuries when the Lutetians, and later the Parisians, appeared to have little regard for the river, treating it as though it were invisible. They asked nothing of it apart from protection and subsistence: the river brought grain, wood and stones for building. But, it brought danger, too: it was by the Seine that the Barbarians and the Norsemen invaded. With Henry IV things changed: the King forbade houses on the Pont-Neuf, and, after him, city planners, were instrumental in making the inhabitants of the capital take an interest in the river which linked them to the world. Today, the 32 bridges that cross the Seine allow easy communication between the two banks, and since the establishment of the quays, the river has become an integral part of the town's landscape.

The history of the bridges of Paris

The Seine, the first main route through Paris, was originally crossable by ferryboat only. Until the 16th c., two bridges are known to have existed: the Grand Pont to the N of the Ile de la Cité, on the main arm of the river but its exact position has not been determined, and the Petit-Pont, to the S on the smaller arm, last repaired in 1852. At the end of the Middle Ages, in order to link the opposite banks of the Ile de la Cité, the 'cradle' of Paris, more bridges were built: to the S the Petit Pont and the Pont Notre-Dame, and to the N the Pont au Change and the Pont Saint-Michel. Constructed in wood, these bridges were battered by boulders and ice, destroyed by fires or the impact of boats, or cut in two when invasion threatened, but always untiringly rebuilt. Lined with houses and small shops on both sides, they were centers of commerce and places for strolling.

It was not until the 18th c. that the method of construction evolved to the point where the bridge became a really important factor in the city, from a utilitarian as well as an architectural viewpoint. Seven bridges were built in this era, and three reconstructed. Three of these can still be admired: the Pont-Neuf, the Pont Marie, and the Pont Royal.

In the 18th c. few projects were undertaken, but Louis XVI's orders to demolish the houses that congested the bridges, and certainly the creation of the Ponts et Chaussées (Bridge and Roads Corporation) by Colbert in 1716, had a considerable influence on construction in the 19th c., when more than 21 bridges were built, and numerous reconstructions carried out. One reason for this was technological progress: the use of iron under the Empire, suspension bridges during the Restoration, and later the advent of steel. Under Haussmann's influence, there were not merely new bridges, but a complete restructuring of the crossings of the Seine, finally aligning them with the new major routes of the capital, and attempts at solving the traffic problems.

In the 20th c., these problems are still not resolved, despite the construction of bridges on the Boul. Périphérique to the W and E of Paris. It is likely that at the end of the 20th c. there will be a highway to the E of Paris near the Pont d'Austerlitz.

The principal bridges of Paris

The Pont Alexander-III

7th, 8th arr. Map ref. 9–A3, 15–A1

This bridge, with its exuberant architecture, is very representative of the decorative art of the Third Republic. It is named after Czar Alexander III, father of Nicholas II, who laid the foundation stone in October 1896, a time when France and Russia enjoyed good diplomatic relationships. The bridge was completed in only two years (1898–1900), and inaugurated at the World Fair in 1900. Its design was subject to very strict controls to prevent it from blocking the view of the Invalides or the Champs-Élysées; it had also to be supported by as few arches as possible in order to ease the irregular flow of water at this spot, because of the river's curve and the bridge's proximity to the Pont des Invalides.

The structure, entirely of metal, was the work of the engineers Résal and d'Alby, and constituted a technical feat. The steel arch (118ft/ 107.5m) crosses the Seine in a single span, brought as low as possible, producing a great thrust of pressure on the abutment-piers, the ornamentation of which acts as a counterweight. The decoration. on the R. Bank on the top of the r. column *La*

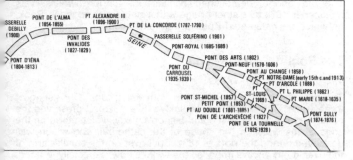

The principal bridges of Paris

Renommeé des Sciences (The Fame of Science) by E. Frémiet; at the base, *La France Contemporaine* (Contemporary France) by G. Michael. The l. column, *La Renommée des Arts* (The Fame of Arts) by Frémiet; at the base, *La France de Charlemagne* by A. Lenoir. The stone lions are by Gardet. On the L. Bank, the l. column *La Renommée du Commerce* by P. Granet; at the base, *La France Renaissante* (France Reborn) by J. Coutan. L. column: *La Renommée de l'Industrie* by C. Steiner; at its base *La France de Louis XIV* by L. Marqueste; lions by Dalon. The entire bridge is decorated with motifs recalling the marine flora and fauna by A. Poulin. The keystones are decorated with two compositions in hammered copper: upriver, the Nymphs of the Seine carrying the coat of arms of Paris; downriver, the Nymphs of the Neva carrying the arms of Russia, by G. Récipon. On the parapet at the base of the columns: four groups of water sprites with fishes and seashells. Four large bronze branched lamps complete the decoration of the bridge, surrounded by cupids and sea monsters by H. Gauquic.

The Pont de l'Alma

7th, 16th arr. Map ref. 14–C1

The original bridge dating from 1855 has completely disappeared. It commemorated the Franco-British victory over the Russians at Alma in the Crimea in 1854. Against the central piers are statues representing soldiers of the four armies that took part in this battle: a grenadier and a Zouave by G. Diebolt, and a chasseur and artilleryman by Arnaud. The Zouave was soon adopted by the Parisians as a popular gauge in estimating the height of the Seine in flood.

The old bridge, demolished because of its narrowness, was replaced in 1974 by a steel bridge with a single pier, to the R. Bank, on which the celebrated Zouave was reinstalled.

The Pont del'Archevêché

4th, 6th arr. Map ref. 17–B3

The best view** of Notre-Dame is from this bridge. Consisting of three arches, it was built very quickly (1826–1828). It preserved the name Archevêché, after the archbishop's place, which stood on the edge of the water in the shade of the cathedral, and which was destroyed during the riots of 1831. Built over on the smaller arm of the river, it has always impeded the water's flow, especially in flood, because of its two piers, the straight arches, and its lack of headroom under the central arch.

The Pont d'Arcole

4th arr. Map ref. 17–B2

The project to link the Place de Grève to the future Place du Parvis-de-Notre-Dame goes back to 1756. But it was only in 1828 that the footbridge to Grève was built, a pedestrian suspension toll bridge. In 1830 a young insurgent was killed while waving the tricolor as he was going to the Hôtel de Ville. Dying, he cried: 'Remember that my name is d'Arcole'. This was the name that was given, in 1898, to the footbridge, replaced in 1954 by an iron bridge.

The Pont des Arts*

1st, 6th arr. Map ref. 17–A2

The construction of the Pont des Arts is due to Bonaparte, who was First Consul at the time. It marked the first use of cast iron in the 19th c. This bridge, built between 1802 and 1804, was the third of its kind, the first two being in England. It takes its name from the Palais des Arts, as the Louvre was known under the First Empire, when it was linked to the Collège des Quatre-Nations (today the Institut). It was a pedestrian toll bridge built above the level of quays, and it was a veritable hanging garden, with shrubs, flowers and branches for pedestrians to enjoy. Part of it was rebuilt under the Second Empire, but its original structure was too light and the nine arches hindered navigation. Damaged several times by barges, it was finally closed to the public in 1970 for reasons of safety. Between 1982 and 1984, it was rebuilt in a style similar to the original.

Now reopened, the new footbridge differs from the old: it is made of steel rather than cast iron, and has only five arches. Decorated with shrubs and benches which tend to recreate an illusion of the original garden, it offers an interesting view of the Louvre, the Institut and the tip of the Île de la Cité.

The Pont d'Austerlitz

5th, 12th arr.

Since the 18th c., various projects have been proposed for the construction of a bridge to link the Jardin des Plantes to the R. Bank. In 1802, construction of a cast iron bridge began, the second one of its kind in Paris after the Pont des Arts footbridge. Opened to traffic in 1807, it commemorated the victory of the Napoleonic troops over the Austrians and the Russians in 1805. In 1854 it was replaced by a stone bridge with wide pavements, which were further widened in 1884.

The Austerlitz Viaduct*

12th, 13th arr.

This metal bridge was built between 1903 and 1904 by J. C. Formigé exclusively for the Métro. With its 459ft/140m arch, it holds the record as the longest span in Paris. This technical feat (L. Biette, engineer) was called for because of the proximity of the Pont d'Austerlitz; an increase of piers in the river would have hindered barge traffic. J. C. Formigé, architect of Métropolitan superstructures, carried out the decoration of the bridge.

The Pont de Bercy

12th, 13th arr.

This bridge, inaugurated by Louis-Philippe in 1832, and modified at different times, took on its present appearance in 1904 when it was raised to accommodate the Métro. The road would no longer take traffic, after the new Minister of Finance installed the Quai de la Rapée. A second road, on the upriver side, will be completed in 1991.

The Pont de Bir-Hakeim**

15th and 16th arr. Map ref. 13–B1

The former Passy viaduct became the Bir-Hakeim Bridge in 1949. It commemorates the battles in which the Free French army resisted Rommel's armoured divisions in the Libyan Desert, during May 1942.

It was one of the viaducts developed at the beginning of the 20th c. to provide an above line for the Métro, and replaced a footbridge built for the Exposition Universelle (World Fair) of 1878. The collaboration of L. Biette (engineer) and J. C. Formigé (architect for the Métropolitan Railway Board) produced one of the great successes of steel architecture. This double bridge, 778ft/237m, serves at the same time, for the Métro, cars and pedestrians, and combine functionalism with eclecticism. The piers are decorated with monumental cast iron groups, and the masonry with four bas-reliefs: upriver, *The Seine* and *Work* by J. Coutan; downriver, *Electricity* and *Commerce* by A. Injalbert. The bridge rests on the Allée des Cygnes (Quays) where there is a statue of *France Reborn* (Wederlinck, 1930), presented by the Danish community in Paris.

The Pont du Carrousel

1st, 6th and 7th arr. Map ref. 16–D3

Originally called the Pont du Louvre, it later took the name of a neighboring street, Rue Saint-Pères (a distortion of Saint-Pierre). It owes its present name to a fête held by Louis XIV in 1662, on a large piece of land facing the Louvre, in which a tournament with five troops of 10 well-drilled horses was the main attraction.

Built in 1834 and inaugurated by Louis-Philippe, its construction, by the engineer Polonceau, entailed numerous technical innovations, such as building all three arches at the same time, and distributing the stress in a new way.

Being too narrow for traffic, the bridge was rebuilt in 1939, a little farther downriver, crossing the Seine from the Quai Voltaire to the Louvre. At either end are four seated statues, retained from the first bridge, by L. Petitot (1846); on the R. Bank, *Industry* and *Wealth*; on the L. Bank, the *Seine* and the *City of Paris*. It is lit at each end by two monumental branched lamps designed by the cast-iron sculptor R. Subes. They have an unusual telescopic design: 39ft/12m by day, 72ft/22m at night; this enables them to light up the whole bridge, despite its size.

The Pont au Change

1st, 5th arr. Map ref. 17–B2

Rebuilt many times, this bridge was first constructed in the 9th c. by Charles the Bold, out of wood. It was known as the King's Bridge, from which Parisian birdwatchers would release thousands of birds to greet the arrival of the Sovereign. In 1141, Louis VII Le Jeune (the Young) issued a decree forcing the goldsmiths, and especially the moneychangers, to rebuild it. It got its present name at this time. It was an elegant place, with a flower and bird market, and it was the royal route for processions to Notre-Dame. Vulnerable to fire and frequently damaged by floods, the bridge was rebuilt in stone in the 17th c., designed by J. Androuet Du Cerceau. It was lined with houses, as was the custom, and was widened into a V-shape on the

R. Bank, with two separate accesses from the square, where there was a sculpted group by F. Guillain (now in the Louvre) representing Louis XIII, Anne of Austria and the young Louis XIV.

The existing bridge dates from 1860, the era of Haussmann's great projects. It was built in line with the new arterial road, Boul. du Palais, itself in line with the new Place du Châtelet.

The Pont de la Concorde

7th, 8th arr. Map ref. 9–B3

Until the beginning of the 18th c., the river could only be crossed by ferry at this point. The bridge, planned in 1725, was not built until 1788, and finished in 1791. The upper part was constructed with stones from the Bastille so that Parisians could tread on that symbol of royal despotism. Like the square from which it extends, the bridge's name often changed depending on political events; the Louis XVI bridge, the Revolution, the Concorde, again Louis XVI, and finally Pont de la Concorde, which has been its name since 1830. Its architect, Perronet, was the first director of the Ecole des Ponts et Chaussées (School of Bridges and Roads), created by Colbert. Napoleon put up statues of eight generals who had died in battle. These were replaced during the Restoration by 12 monumental white marble statues of four great ministers (Colbert, Richelieu, Suger and Sully), four soldiers (Bayard, Condé, Du Guesclin, Turenne) and four naval officers (Duguay-Trouin, Duquesne, Suffren and Tourville). They were too heavy for the bridge, and were removed to Versailles. The bridge, widened in 1931, returned to its original appearance. Overloaded with traffic, it nevertheless offers two magnificent views*: one of the Place de la Concorde*, the other of the Palais Bourbon.

The Passerelle Debilly footbridge*

7th, 16th arr. Map ref. 14–C1

This was built for the World Fair of 1900, to allow visitors to reach the numerous 'palaces' on both banks easily, without having to leave the enclosure of the Fair. It is an iron footbridge by Résal, architect of the Pont Alexandre-III. Like the neighboring Quai Debilly, (since baptized the Ave. de New York), its name commemorates one of Napoleon's generals killed at Iéna. The footbridge has recently been completely renovated.

The Pont au Double

4th, 5th arr. Map ref. 17–B2

In 1626, the overcrowded conditions of the Hôtel Dieu hospital were so bad that it became imperative to enlarge it by joining the old buildings of the Ile with those on the R. Bank. The work, conceived by the architect Gamard, was completed in 1631. The bridge, which had two arches, went from the corner of the archbishop's garden to the Rue de la Bûcherie. It took three sick wards, leaving a third of its width open to the public. The hospital decided that to finance the building of the bridge, the patients would have to pay a fee twice (when leaving as well as when entering); hence the origin of its name.

The bridge collapsed several times. It was always rebuilt, as were the three sick wards which partly covered it, despite the disapproval of the riverside residents, who disliked this proximity to disease. The hospital dumped its garbage straight into the river, without any concern for hygiene. The wards stayed until 1835. The present bridge dates from 1882: in cast iron, with one arch, it was built in line with the Rue d'Arcole. Excavations made during its reconstruction brought to light a hoard of treasure: Celtic weapons, Roman statues, Merovingian jewelry, seals from the Middle Ages and swords from the Renaissance.

The Pont du Garigliano

15th, 16th arr.

This name recalls a battle at Monte Cassino in Italy in May 1944. The bridge has taken the place of the former Viaduc d'Auteuil, erected in 1865. Built in stone on two levels, the upper part is the track for the *Petite Ceinture* railway, and the lower level is for pedestrians and for cars, which were few at a time when Auteuil was still only a village.

This viaduct was also called the Pont du Point-du-Jour (Bridge of Daybreak), the name of a place nearby where duels, traditionally held at dawn, were regularly fought. After the alterations to the Boulevards des Maréchaux in 1920, the viaduct became unsuitable for traffic and too low for navigation. In 1966 it was replaced with the present concrete bridge.

The Pont Gentry

Lying upstream from the Pont d'Austerlitz and provisionally called Pont Gentry, this bridge is the work of the architect L. Arretche and will link the Lyon and Austerlitz railway stations. The work will be completed in 1992.

The Pont de Grenelle

15th, 16th arr. Map ref. 13–A3

The first Pont de Grenelle was built in 1825, at the same time as the port and the station of the same name. On its completion in 1827, it was found to lie outside the perimeter of Paris, since the village of Grenelle had not yet been annexed. Its wooden arches were replaced in 1875 with an iron framework. Totally rebuilt in 1968, this bridge rests on the W extremity of the Allée des Cygnes, where there is a reduced bronze replica of New York's Statue of Liberty by Bartholdi, presented by the United States to France, and erected for the World Fair of 1889. Standing 30ft/9m high, she looked toward the E so that she would not turn her back on the Elysée. When the Ile de Cygnes was recognized for the 1937 World Fair, the statue was turned round to face the American continent.

The Pont d'Iéna

7th, 16th arr. Map ref. 13–B1

This bridge is positioned to have a double view of the Palais de Chaillot and its fountains on the R. Bank, and the Eiffel Tower and the École Militaire on the L. Bank. The bridge celebrates the victory of Napoleon's army over Prussia at Iéna in 1806; the construction of this bridge was ordered that same year. Work began in 1809 but was not finished until 1813. In 1815 the Prussian general Blücher wanted it destroyed; only Louis XVIII's persistence saved it; it then took the name of the Pont de l'Ecole Militaire until 1830. It was very busy during the World Fairs of 1889 (inauguration of the Eiffel Tower), 1900 and 1937, which were held between the Trocadéro and the Champ-de-Mars. At the time of the construction of the new Palais de Chaillot, replacing the earlier Palais de Trocadio, for the Fair of 1937, it was widened.

At first the pylons were decorated with Napoleonic eagles, replaced by S under Louis XVIII. These were succeeded in 1852 by eagles sculpted by Barye. Four equestrian groups (1848–53) were placed at the entrances to the bridge: R. Bank, an Arab by Feuchère and a Greek by F. Préault; L. Bank, a Gaul by A. Préault and a Roman by L. Dumas.

The Pont des Invalides

7th, 8th arr. Map ref. 9–A3

In 1827 this was a suspension bridge, as were many others in Paris at the beginning of the 19th c. Being unstable, it was entirely rebuilt in 1879 following severe deterioration due to the breaking up of the ice after the freeze. Enlarged in 1956, this bridge is not, as its name suggests, aligned with Les Invalides (→Pont-Alexander-III). The central pier is adorned with sculptures: upriver, *La Victoire Terrestre* (Terrestrial Victory) by V. Vilain, and downriver *La Victorie Maritime* (Maritime Victory) by G. Diebolt. The other four piers are decorated with trophies of war sculpted by H. Daillon.

The Pont Louis-Philippe

4th arr. Map ref. 18–C2

One of the first suspension bridges, taking its name from Louis-Philippe, who inaugurated it in the presence of Thiers, July 1833, for the anniversary of the 1830 Revolution. Because of this it was for some time called the Pont de la Réforme. It was a direct link between the Right Bank and the Quai des Fleurs, on the Ile de la Cité, resting on the small square at the end of the Ile St-Louis. Burnt down in 1848, it was rebuilt in 1862, slightly upriver.

The Pont Marie**

4th arr. Map ref. 18–C2

This bridge, one of the oldest in Paris, linked the R. Bank to the Ile Saint-Louis. It bears the name of the property developer Christophe Marie, who built it with his own money in return for a territorial concession on the Ile Saint-Louis in 1614. A humpback bridge, it has five arches; the timberwork of the piers is original.

In 1658, following the thaw, two of its arches collapsed, carrying with them 22 of the houses that stood there. This part was rebuilt, but the houses were not replaced; the other buildings disappeared in 1788. Since then, this 18th-c. bridge has been only slightly modified, once, in 1950.

A freshwater fish market nearby sold directly to the boats moored to the bank. A chain was hung across the river between the Barbeau Tower and the Loriaux Tower in Charles V's perimeter wall, to impede the passage of boats during invasions by the Norsemen.

The Pont Mirabeau

15th, 16th arr.

Made famous by Apollinaire's poem, this bridge was built of iron at the end of the 19th c. (1890–96), by Résal, engineer of the Pont Alexander-III and the Debilly footbridge. Decorated with coats of arms and bronze statues of four sea gods by A. Inhalbert, it was not repaired and reinforced until 1957.

The Pont National

12th, 13th arr.

This is the second bridge upriver from Paris, after the bridge of the Périphérique E, and one of the first constructed (in 1853) by Haussmann along the axis of the Boulevards des Maréchaux. It allowed the passage, simultaneously, of the *Petite Ceinture* railway and the Boulevards. Enlarged several times, it is also one of the longest bridges in Paris.

The Pont-Neuf***

1st, 6th arr. Map ref. 17–A2

This is the most famous, most popular and also the oldest bridge of Paris, despite its name. Immortalized by Victor Hugo, it has been painted, engraved or drawn in every era, from Leclerc and Callot to Pissarro and Derain. Built to allow a king to pass more easily from one bank to the other, and to ease the relations between the Louvre and the Abbey of Saint-Germain-des-Prés, Henry III placed the first stone on May 31, 1578. Work continued, sometimes with long interruptions, over 29 years. It was Henry IV who inaugurated and baptized it in 1607, with the name that it still has today.

Conceived by five architects including Andronet du Cerceau and des Isles, it really consists of two halves, not quite in line: one has five grounded arches and the other has seven, linked by an artificial terreplein. The result is the joining of two small islands: the Ile aux Juifs and the Ile du Patriarche or de la Gourdaine. From the time it was opened the Pont-Neuf was extremely popular. For its time, its dimensions were remarkable: 912ft/278m long and nearly 92ft/28m wide, it is still one of the largest bridges in Paris. The half circles on top of each pier are decorated with comic reliefs of the shops and charlatans on the bridge: tooth pullers and other comic characters such as Pantaloon. The first stone bridge without houses, it was a popular place for walking, because its footpaths were separated from the traffic, protecting pedestrians from the mud and galloping horsemen. It became the site for a permanent fair, and its popularity increased when a pump, for supplying the Louvre with water from the river, was installed under one of the arches. Because it was decorated with a sculpture of the Samaritan woman giving Christ water to drink, it became known as La Samaritaine, a name later taken by a department store. Although repaired several times, the Pont-Neuf has hardly been altered since it was built; the wooden posts forming the base of the piers date from the 16th c. The 19th-c. branched lamps are by Baltard. The rounded arches were once carved along the top with 385 grotesque masks, some of which are preserved in the Cluny and Carnavalet museums.

At the very tip of the island is the Square du Vert-Galant, named affectionately after the womanizing Henri IV. It is the departure point for the Pont-Neuf launches, dominated by the equestrian statue of Henri IV, although this is a copy of the original (→ inset).

The Pont Notre-Dame

4th arr. Map ref. 17–B2

The first bridge on this spot for which there is historical evidence was a wooden footbridge, called the planches Milbray (half an arm-span), on which stood numerous mills. Destroyed in 1406 by a flood, several wooden bridges succeeded it between 1413 and 1499, but all collapsed. The construction of a stone bridge, around 1500, is attributed to Fra Giacondo of Verona. It was surmounted by 68 identical houses in brick and stone, numbered in gold, this was the first attempt to number houses in Paris. Due to the elegance of these houses, the bridge remained for a long time the most fashionable in Paris, always lively, since it was on the royal route for solemn processions and triumphant entries into Paris. The houses were demolished in 1787 by order of Louis XVI. Contrary to popular opinion of the time, it had been established from 1769 that the buildings standing on the bridges weakened rather than reinforced the structure. The so-called Notre-Dame water pump which stood there from 1676 to 1853, was installed on the parapet upriver from the bridge. The bridge was put out of service while work was underway to lower the levels of the neighboring banks. In 1912, the three median arches were replaced by a single iron arch, and the parapet was decorated with acanthus leaves.

*The Notre-Dame is one of the few in Paris to have retained its original name.

The Petit-Pont

1st, 5th arr. Map ref. 17–B2

As its name indicates, this bridge has for nearly 2,000 years been the shortest in Paris (131ft/40m). It was one of the few ways by which the inhabitants of the Ile could get to the S bank of the river. In Roman times, it linked the Cité to a new district, known from the 13th c. on as the Latin Quarter. Destroyed and rebuilt several times during the invasions of the Norsemen, the bridge was rebuilt in stone in 1186 by Maurice de Sully, Bishop of Paris. It was defended at the S end by the Petit Châtelet, which disappeared in 1782.

If the chroniclers are to be believed, traffic on the Petit-Pont has always been heavy, because it was one of the few routes across the river. Like the others, it was a toll bridge, except for the travelling acrobats (*saltimbanques*), who were only expected to act the fool to get across; they paid with '*monnaie de singe*', empty promises – the expression has persisted. The present bridge has only one arch, for ease of navigation, and dates from 1852.

The Pont Royal**

1st, 7th arr. Map ref. 16–C1

Built from 1685 to 1689 by Father Romain and J. Gabriel, from plans by J. Hardouin-Mansart, this bridge was entirely financed by Louis XIV, for which reason it was called the Pont Royal (Royal Bridge).

The only bridge downriver until the construction of the Pont de la Concorde, it gave access to the Left Bank, thereby facilitating installation of the nobility in the suburb of Saint-Germain. It was on this bridge, then called the Pont National from 1792 to 1804, that Bonaparte placed cannons to defend the Tuileries, where the Convention and the Committee of Public Safety sat.

Like the Pont-Neuf and the Pont Marie, it is registered as a historic monument, and underwent only slight alterations in 1850. On the last pillar on either bank you can still see the hydrographic scale showing historical low-and-high-water level marks.

The Pont Saint-Louis

4th arr. Map ref. 17–B2

This bridge links the Ile Saint-Louis to the Ile de la Cité. It dates from 1614 as a wooden footbridge built, by Christophe Marie (see Pont Marie), close to the Port Saint-Landry, one of the chief centers for the victualling of the capital. Various wooden bridges succeeded it until 1842, when a suspension bridge was built, replaced by an iron footbridge in 1861. It consisted of one single arch, which was knocked down by the impact of a barge in 1939. A temporary footbridge was installed in 1941, and an iron pedestrian bridge has linked the two islands since 1969.

The Pont Saint-Michel

4th, 5th arr. Map ref. 17–A2

This bridge is named after the Palace chapel (since demolished), dedicated to the Archangel Michael, where Philippe Auguste was baptized in 1165. It offers beautiful views of Notre-Dame, upriver. In 1378 the *Prévot des Marchands* Aubriot ordered the building of a stone bridge at this spot; executed by the cheap labor of the convicts of the Petit Châtelet, it took nearly 10 years to build. It was first called the Neuf-Pont, or the Petit Pont-Neuf. Like those on Pont au Change, the shops on the Pont Saint-Michel belonged to specialized tradesmen: secondhand goods dealers, dyers, tapestry-weavers, perfumers and booksellers. Their dwellings were demolished between 1786 and 1807. The bridge was rebuilt in 1857 to head into the Boul. Sébastopol. For the foundations, a system new to Paris was used: that of foundation cylinders, or caissons. The imperial N, for Napoléon III, is owed to Haussmann.

The Solférino Footbridge

1st, 7th arr.

A cast iron bridge was built here in 1859 to make the Tuileries gardens accessible to the residents of the Faubourg Saint-Germain.

It became dilapidated and was replaced in 1960 by a temporary footbridge for pedestrians only. It takes its name from the battle in which Napoléon III beat the Austrians in 1859, during the Italian Campaign.

The Pont Sully

4th arr. Map ref. 18–C3

This bridge, named in honor of Maximilien de Béthune, Duc de Sully, a minister of Henry IV, replaced two footbridges built in 1838, and dates from 1876. It is unusual in that it is composed of two separate metal bridges, resting on the tip of the Ile Saint-Louis. Like the little Square Barge which is to be found on the upriver end of the isle, the bridge crosses part of the French-style gardens of the former Hôtel de Bretonvilliers, from which there is one of the most typically Parisian views over the quays of the Ile Saint-Louis and the E end of Notre-Dame.

The Pont de Tolbiac

12th, 13th arr.

The name of the this bridge recalls the victory of Clovis over the Alemanni at Tolbiarum in 496. Built in brick from 1879 to 1882, it has five arches. The only notable incident in its history occurred when an English plane crashed into it during World War I. It lies near the Port de la Gare, where there is a concrete mixing plant, which receives barges laden with sand and gravel.

The Pont de la Tournelle

4th, 5th arr. Map ref. 18–C3

This bridge takes its name from one of the square turrets of Philippe Auguste's Wall (late 12th c). Originally a wooden bridge linking the Ile Saint-Louis to the R. Bank from the widest side of the river, it was frequently washed away by floods and always rebuilt. It was finally constructed in stone in 1656 by Christophe Marie, when the islet was being developed by him into building plots. In 1851 it was enlarged and rebuilt in alignment with the Pont Marie; it was last altered in 1929. Since 1928 a tower in dressed stone has stood on one of its piers, with a statue of St Geneviève by Landowski. The tower commemorates the deposition here of the reliquary of Paris's patron saint in 885 (→Church of Saint-Etienne-du-Mont).

▷ # Les Bateaux-Mouches

From the 17th c. through the first years of the 20th c., the Seine was much more lively than it is today. In 1665, Colbert granted letters patent to the boatmen who transported Parisians by water, and by the 18th c. there was a regular boat service between the Pont Royal, Saint-Cloud and Sèvres. Apart from the licensed boats, there were numerous craft that carried local people from one bank to the other; and naturally, the river dwellers and rich families had their own private boats.

In the middle of the 19th c., two boat companies were authorized to set up in Paris for the World's Fair of 1867, and found instant success. Their boats were built in the Mouche à Lyon district; the name 'Bateaux-Mouches' stuck. From 1888 to 1934, after which they ceased operation, these water 'carriages' transported up to 25 million Parisians every year. The development of many types of public transport in the center of Paris (omnibuses, tramways, buses and the Métros) at the end of the 19th c. entailed the decline of the river service. Today the Bateaux-Mouches and the launches that cross the Seine are only used by tourists.

> # Floods

Paris has endured numerous floods. The first to be recorded occurred in 585. Since then there have been many, of varying suddenness and severity. In 1685, the level of the Seine reached a height, never since exceeded, of 29½ft/9m. There were neither quays nor parapets to contain the water, and the bridges hindered their dispersal. Each flood brought with it the collapse of several bridges and destroyed the houses built on them.

The 19th c. accomplished a great deal in stabilizing the banks (→History of the Quays). In 1867 the first dam was built down-stream, at Suresnes, in order to maintain a constant water level. In 1885 the first network of river-level monitoring points was set up. From the beginning of the 20th c., seven anti-flood stations were brought into service, which, from December to April, pumped up water and returned it further downriver.

After the celebrated flood of 1910, during which the water level reached 28ft 3in/8.62m, and almost covered the head of the Zouave at the Pont de l'Alma, Paris equipped itself with anti-flood parapets on top of the embankments, which controlled the approaches to the river and could be quickly closed in case of floods. At the time of the reconstruction of certain bridges, particular care was taken with the positioning of the arches. But Paris still had major floods of the river banks, in 1955 and as recently as 1982 (28ft 2in/6.15m).

The Service de la Navigation de la Seine built three barrage-reservoirs upriver: one on the Seine itself (1966), the other two on its tributaries, the Yonne (1950) and the Marne (1974), which could contain up to 30m³. A fourth barrage on the Aube, containing 175m³, was completed in 1989. Their role is not only to reduce the level of the water in Paris, but also to restore the level at times of low water. In the 1980s, the Service de la Navigation, Quai Saint-Bernard, modernized its flood warning center by linking its 80 monitoring points to the *télématique*, a computerized visual system.

▷ **Boat trips**

Sailing between the Pont d'Iéna and the Pont d'Austerlitz, the Bateaux-Mouches offer an unusual way to visit the most beautiful places and monuments in the capital. Several companies offer cruises with commentary in several languages.

The Bateaux-Mouches, Port de l'Alma, Right Bank, open daily, 10am–noon, 1–7pm, and 8–11pm, tel: 42–25–96–10; trips last 1¼ hr., lunch and dinner by reservation, tel: 42–25–96–10; supper-concerts June–Oct., leaving at 3.45pm. Itinerary: Pont Sully–Pont Mirabeau.

The Bateau Parisiens – Vedettes Tour-Eiffel, Pont de la Bourdonnais (Left-Bank opposite Ave. de la Bourdonnais) and Quai Montebello (Left Bank by Notre-Dame), daily 10am–6pm Mar.-Nov., 10am–11pm. Departures in season: every 20 mins., tel: 45–51–33–08.; trips last 1 hr. Lunch and dinner by reservation, tel: 47–05–09–85.

Itinerary: Pont Bir-Hakeim–Pont Sully

The Vedettes du Pont-Neuf, Square du Vert-Galant du Ile de la Cité, daily, Oct 15–Mar 31, 10am–noon, 2pm–5pm; Apr. 1–Oct. 15, 10am–noon, 1.30–6pm, 9–11.30pm; departures every 30 mins. Tel: 46–33–98–38; trips last 1 hr.

Itinerary: Pont d'Iéna-Pont Sully

The Vedettes de Paris – Ile-de-France, Port Suffren (Left Bank), daily, Oct 1–Apr. 15, 9am–5pm; Apr. 16–Sept. 30, 9am–11pm; departures every 30 mins. Tel: 47–05–71–29; trips last 1 hr.

Itinerary:Pont de Bir-Hakeim – Pont d'Austerlitz

Paris-Canal, daily Apr. 1–Nov. 15, 9.30am–2.30pm, departs from Quai Anatole-France (Left Bank near the Deligny swimming-pool), arrives Parc de la Villette (Café de l'Horloge, 212 Ave. Jean-Jaurès); 2.30pm–5pm in the opposite direction. Tel: 48–74–75–30. Trips last half a day.

▷ The ever-lively Pont-Neuf

The Pont-Neuf, from the time it was built, aroused great enthusiasm because of its architectural innovations (its width, prospect of the river). It was here also that the most famous of all the water pumps stood (La Samaritaine). It rapidly became the site of a permanent and crowded fair and the theater for millions of picturesque scenes: the mountebank Tabarin's stage; flower sellers, peddlers, secondhand booksellers and tooth pullers. Its name figures in the history of the theater as the place where farce originated. The popular tunes used in comic-opera were even called the '*pont-neufs*'.

It is still a special meeting place: each June, from 1978 until 1983, a festival was held recreating the atmosphere of the bridge and the Place Dauphine between the 16th to the 18th c. (various entertainments, fireworks, refreshment stalls). It had to be stopped, because it became too popular! It was also this bridge that was transformed, from September 23 to October 6, 1985, by the artist Christo, who wrapped it in fabric, leaving only the road surface uncovered. On such occasions it finds again the *joie de vivre* of days gone by.

▷ The horse in quest of a rider

A bronze horse was given to Marie de'Medici by her father, Cosimo II, Grand Duke of Tuscany, intended to bear a statue of Fernando of Tuscany. But the statue was shipwrecked with the boat that was carrying it, and finally took its place in the Square du Vert-Galent only in 1614. In 1634 the horse acquired a statue of Henry IV by Giambologna and Tacca which was melted down during the Revolution in 1792, and so it found itself again without a rider. The bronze slaves adorning the pedestal were saved and are now in the Louvre. In 1818 Lemot erected the present statue, and it is said that the caster, an ardent Bonapartist, benefited from the occasion by hiding inside the statue a copy of Voltaire's *La Henriade* (on the League and Henri IV) with other writings, as well as a small statuette of the Emperor.

▷ The pumps

In the maintenance of the water supply, a constant concern of Parisians, the Seine plays an important part. The water from the river, although polluted, has throughout history been drawn by pumps. The first and most famous is La Samaritaine. A royal edifice dating from 1688, it was placed against the second arch of the Pont-Neuf, on the Right Bank, downriver. It is surmounted by a bell-tower containing an astronomical clock. On its side, a bas-relief in gilded bronze shows the Samaritan giving Christ water to drink at Jacob's well. The pump was destroyed in 1813. Another pump, known as Notre-Dame, blocked up two of the five arches of the bridge of the same name from 1676 to 1853 which made navigation extremely perilous at this spot. Finally, a third, at the Pont de la Tournelle, served the districts further afield. All three were phased out in the 19th c. canalization of spring water which rendered the pumps on the Seine increasingly useless.

Les Puces* (Flea markets)

There are three flea markets in Paris, all taking place at the entrances to the city. The largest is at Saint-Ouen but the others, at Montreuil and Vanves, should not be passed up.

On a Saturday morning, when commerce and its offices sleep, Paris's flea markets wake up for three days. At seven in the morning everyone gets busy, and while trousers are hung on rails at the Marché Malik and tinkling chandeliers are lit at the Biron, tramps, following the traditions of the '*biffins*' (rag-pickers) of the 19th c., spread out a few sorry bits and pieces on a blanket. These markets make up an exceptional social and ethnic microcosom which, by virtue not only of the days on which they take place (Sat., Sun., and Mon.; trading is not allowed on other days) but also by the colorful and cosmopolitan crowds, and the diversity of the goods offered for sale, occupies a unique place in the world. Not just markets for antiques, but also for new and second-hand goods, they are like gigantic supermarkets which draw customers from every class and all walks of life. These are places where both the essential and the frivolous can be acquired; anything goes – from the purchase of a bath to a Louis XV commode, from a kitchen cupboard to a rare book.

Surrealists, intellectuals and artists have all contributed to the fame of 'Les Puces'. André Breton was a frequent visitor, 'in search of those things to be found nowhere else, old-fashioned, in pieces, unusable, almost incomprehensible, in the end, perverse . . .' (Nadja). Fashions were launched here; it was from Saint-Ouen that the revival of Second Empire style began, and that '30s furniture was rediscovered.

At the end of every week, about 150,000 to 300,000 people (gawkers, buyers, tourists or Parisians), will pass by, and 1,300 merchants will set up their stalls here. In the antique trade, flea markets play the part of wholesalers. Many antique dealers from Paris and the provinces come here to stock up, attracted by constantly changing merchandise which has been scrounged and restored during the week. Starting at dawn on Saturday mornings, they scour the markets feverishly.

Since their founding a hundred years ago, the flea markets have evolved from hawkers trading just within the law to an established trading center which, to judge from the amount of foreign currency that it attracts, has some real economic importance.

The history of Les Puces

In 1841 Adolphe Thiers, President of the Council, decided to surround Paris with a fortified wall, the '*fortifs*', which were completed in 1844. On the Paris side the wall was bordered by an interior Boul. Périphérique which, in 1864, was turned into a series of outer *boulevards extérieurs* named after field marshals of the Empire. On the suburban side a *non aedificandi* (no building area) was laid out, 820ft/250m wide. Used for military maneuvers and for strolling, the '*zone*', as it was nicknamed, became a place where, from 1860 onwards, the poorer population, such as tramps and rag-pickers, found shelter.

In the 1880s, there were an estimated 30,000 of these rag-pickers (or '*biffins*'), whose history has been bound up since the Middle Ages with that of all the *Cours des Miracles* (places that the police could not enter), which abounded all over Paris. At a time when social disparity and differences in wealth were much more marked than now, the gathering of refuse discarded by the rich could support an entire colony. In the middle of the 19th c., rags, metals and food were systematically collected to be resold. Established in the '*zone*' (and, in particular, around the commune of Saint-Ouen), the rag-and-bone collectors sold the fruits of their harvest. This is how the custom of going to Saint-Ouen to buy second-hand goods came about.

In 1920, when the demolition of the '*fortifs*' began, the first organized market was set up. Still faltering at the beginning of the century, the antique trade became institutionalized, particularly with the development of the flea market of Saint-Ouen. The rag-pickers didn't disappear; despite being chased away regularly, they always managed to find a corner at the edge of the markets. Once a menace, now part of tradition, they continue to hover about the flea market. The markets will continue to change; current planning foresees their transformation in a way which, while securing for them some measure of respectability, many detract from their unique character.

The Saint-Ouen marché aux puces**

Saint-Ouen
Open Sat, Sun, Mon.
Métro: Porte de Clignancourt
Bus: 56, 85, PC.
Parking: Ave. de la Porte-de-Clignancourt; Saint-Ouen: Rue Marie-Curie. Marché Serpette
Taxis: Porte de Clignancourt. Tel. 42–58–00–00

Motorists should take care to park their cars in authorized places, since the '*contredanses*' (parking tickets) flourish at Saint-Ouen, and the visit should be made on foot.

Access: Take the Ave. de la Porte-de-Clignancourt. After the Porte de Clignancourt, cross a market selling new clothing: the Marché de Paris. Cross the bridge over the ring road; the Ave. Michelet leads into the Commune of Saint-Ouen. This avenue is lined with street-hawkers' displays and stalls, ironmongers, second-hand clothes merchants, bric-a-brac sellers etc. Rue des Rosiers, which is the main artery of the flea markets, opens up on the l. of the Ave. Michelet.

The Marché Vernaison

99 Rue de Rosiers. Tel: 40–10–27–76

This was the first organized market. In 1920, Romain Vernaison, its founder, bought a plot of land of 222 acres/90ha, on which he built booths for hire. There are now more than 300 stalls.

Since its inception, the Vernaison market has suffered from the presence of dealers in 'stylish' new furniture, but these are disappearing. In its winding alleyways there are many finds to be made: second-hand dealers with luster drops for chandeliers or glass pearls for sale; sellers of country furniture, ornaments or pictures; popular art. Some more specialized stalls offer old photographs, prints, posters, postcards, old gramophones and records. Besides the traditional fortune-tellers, the Vernaison market shelters another institution: the restaurant Chez Louisette, where an accordionist always plays along with some passing Edith Piaf. By preserving the atmosphere and appearance of the old flea markets, the Vernaison market will always be a delight to visit. The adjoining Marché Antica was opened recently. A small open market, its few stalls offer ordinary merchandise comparable to that found in antique shops in Paris or the provinces.

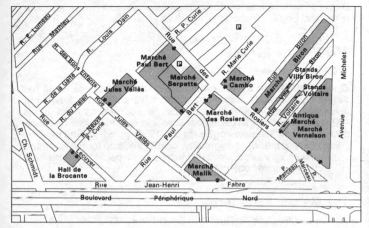

Marché aux Puces (Flea Market) of Saint-Ouen

The Marché Biron

85 Rue des Rosiers, 118 Ave. Michelet. Tel. 40–11–59–69

Sheltering over 200 stalls, it was built in 1925 on some marshland at the instigation of the rag-pickers, who wanted to stay at Saint-Ouen. It has two parallel alleys, one covered, one open, distinguished by the type of goods for sale in each.

The open alley is lined by large, glassed-in stands where the style of Napoléon III reigns supreme: gilded furniture, tinkling chandeliers and bronzes, and late 19th-c. paintings. A few dealers provide an exception: a bookseller, a specialist in African art and North African jewelry, a dealer in picture frames or a seller of etchings. A dealer in antique glass will try to help you find pieces to replace those missing from your set. The covered alley is principally reserved for country furniture, as well as old drawings, nautical paraphernalia and seashells, or musical instruments.

The Marché Cambo

75 Rue des Rosiers.

Set up in 1970, it consists of about 30 stalls, divided between two levels. Its has two unique specialities: late 19th-c. paintings from the

Barbizon school, lesser-known Impressionists and post-Impressionists, and English mahogany furniture.

The Marché Serpette

110 Rue des Rosiers. Tel. 42–59–54–14

Opened in 1977 in an old garage, this is the prototype of all the modern flea markets. It is more comfortable and covered over, but less true to the ideals of the picturesque older flea markets. It has 120 stalls. It is this market that started the cult for 1930s furniture, and which saw the new vogue for the 1950s pieces. Some dealers, seeking a reputation for originality, cultivate a taste for the eccentric – unusual or very large pieces of furniture, or paintings of off-beat subjects or peculiar objects.

The Marché Paul-Bert

96 Rue des Rosiers; 18 Rue Paul Bert. Tel. 40–12–14–86

This is one of those places where haggling over prices is still a pleasure. Its beginnings are linked with the Occupation. The municipality at that time insisted that the places in the market be reserved for people whose property had been taken by the Nazis. Today, its 225 stands, spread over seven alleys, offer a varied merchandise. Everything imaginable is for sale: furniture, fabrics, crockery, old prints and drawings, paintings from all periods. Time and curiosity are needed to visit this market, where the disorder of the stalls will entrance the amateur bargain-hunter. The café Bert, at the corner of the market entrance on the Rue Paul-Bert, is one of the traditional meeting places at the flea markets.

The Marché des Rosiers

3 Rue Paul Bert

This is principally given over to objects from the *Belle Epoque* and Art Déco, and particularly to costume jewellery.

The Rue Paul Bert is lined with second-hand and antique shops all the way to the Rue Jules-Vallès. Take the Rue Jules-Vallès on the r., where one of the largest scrap metal merchants in France salvages all manner of things.

The Marché Jules Vallès

7 Rue Jules-Vallès. Tel: 40–11–54–41

This market was founded in 1938 by a Venetian, Amadeo Cesana, who bought an area of waste land of about 1794 sq. yd./1500m². Its two parallel alleys of stalls are the domain of the second-hand trade in all its guises. Some stalls are more specialized: old toys, articles from the turn of the century, weapons, prints, exhibition catalogues, art books, postcards. Its location, slightly away from the center, should not discourage the visitor – regular visitors know that it can sometimes reward them with a lucky find. In the Rue Lécuyer, parallel to the Rue Jules-Vallès, there are warehouses piled with things of all kinds.

The Marché Malik

53 Rue Jules-Vallès; 59 Rue Jean-Henri-Fabre. Tel: 40–11–93–84

Recently converted and roofed over, this market was organized in 1920 by a Yugslavian 'prince', Malik Hajrullac, on an area of ⅛ acre/3000ml. With more than 100 stalls, the market specializes in both new and second-hand clothing and accessories: spectacles, buttons, paste jewelry called *'strass'* after its inventor; trinkets lie next to jeans, 1950s dresses and leather jackets. On Sundays the Malik market is the busiest of all.

The Rue Jean-Henri-Fabre and the neighboring streets are filled with clothing merchants. Domestic appliances, televisions, radios, stock from bankrupt businesses and goods seized by Customs are sold from large warehouses. Ends of lines in furniture and bedding are also sold off here at very low prices.

The Marché aux puces de la porte de Vanves* (flea market)

14th arr.
Open Sat., Sun.
Métro: Porte-de-Vanves.
Bus: 48, 58, PC.
Taxis: Porte de Vanves. Tel: 45–39–87–33

The Porte de Vanves, also known as the La Porte Didot flea market, was set up in the 1920s. Lying away from overcrowded street, with a tranquil atmosphere suggesting the slight superiority of more carefully chosen goods, it has had growing success.

Entrance: at the Place de la Porte-de-Vanves, take the Ave. Marc-Sangnier. The market is situated between the Ave. Marc-Sangnier, Ave. Georges-Lafenestre and the Boul Périphérique. Unlike the Marché de Saint-Ouen, there are no fixed stands: the dealers just spread their wares out on the pavements, which explains why not much furniture is sold here. The local people stay on good terms with the dealers, who will usually barter, looking for second-hand items: paintings, prints, old linen, jewelry.

The Marché aux puces de la Porte de Montreuil (flea market)

20th arr.
Open: Sat., Sun., Mon.
Métro: Porte-de-Montreuil
Bus: PC.
Taxis: Porte de Montreuil Tel: 43–70–00–00

Since the 17th c., rag-pickers have always been forced out of the center of Paris. Some migrated eastward, and the market at Montreuil is linked to this movement. The flea market at Montreuil is paradise for those who love haggling, and for those who live in hopes of fereting out a rare treasure. Second-hand clothing takes up the greater part and there is a constant throng of people around the piles of '*fripes*' (old clothes). On Sundays, the second-hand dealers are joined by those selling 'new' clothes and hardware. Entrance: between the Boul. Périphérique and the town of Montreuil, the market is divided into several zones. On some Sundays, when the police are feeling lenient, unfettered piles of merchandise spill out over the pavements. The second-hand dealers are further away, along the Boul. Périphérique. Their goods, which are sometimes displayed on the ground, are very varied. Salvaged goods, a few bits of furniture, and curios or paintings, frequently form unusual compositions which are interesting to look at in their own right.

▷ **Practical advice**

The markets are open on Saturdays, Sundays and Mondays. Saturday is the quietest day and all the stalls are open. On Sundays, it is better to go toward the end of the morning, before the afternoon crowds. On Mondays, all the 'new' shops are open, but many of the stalls are shut. There are removal firms that specialize in carrying away every kind of merchandise imaginable. Art Transit (Marché Biron Stall 63. Tel: 42–52–24–97). Camard (Marché Paul-Bert, Alleyway 1. Tel: 40–12–84–45).

The Quays of the Seine***

Of all the thoroughfares in Paris, the oldest and most majestic is, without any doubt, the wide natural channel through which the Seine flows. Facing the Seine in a majestic procession, Paris's great monuments seem to escort the river through the city. The quays, in fact, offer the most remarkable views of the capital.

The quays, gradually recovering land from the parking lots, warehouses and sand quarries, offer exceptional walks in all seasons and at all times of day. Early on a summer morning, when the sun is rising over the Seine, or in the evening, when it is setting once again, the view from the quays is profoundly moving. And yet, of the 19mls/30km of river banks, only a third is reserved for pedestrians.

Among many others, the following walk suggests an itinerary into the heart of Paris. For the visitor passing through, it is an introductory route that will give an overall impression of the city; it may also provide the image of Paris that will linger longest in the memory.

The history of the quays

The physiognomy of the banks of the Seine has changed considerably over the centuries. The Seine was 1½ ml./3km wide 200,000 years ago, and, at the end of the last glaciation, it branched in two, to the N and to the S. The N branch, which used to flow in a wide arc as far as the mills of Belleville, Montmartre and Passy, gradually disappeared. The present River Seine originates from the second branch.

Toward the 4th c., the Seine, then some 131 ft./40m wider than today, flowed freely; the Ile de la Cité, formerly Lutetia, was much narrower. Gradually the embankments, then the quays, which were successively built on over the years, encroached on the river itself. There were no quays, as the word is understood today, until the 14th c. The river banks were still natural verges, often with towpaths, sometimes interrupted by small groups of houses built on solid piles and a multitude of ports with a variety of activities. The first quay, the Grands-Augustins, was built of stone by Philippe le Bel (the Fair) in 1313. By the end of the 14th c., the R. Bank had been furnished with several unconnected quays running alongside important buildings, such as the Louvre, the Hôtel de Ville, and the Célestins convent. François I was responsible for linking the quays already in existence around 1530, during the construction of the Nouveau Louvre. In 1604, under Henri IV, the Quai des Ormes, now the Quai des Célestins, was extended toward La Grève; at the same time, the construction of new bridges entailed raising and paving the neighboring quays. In 1610, the Quai de Chaillot (now the Quai de New-York) was also lengthened. Under Louis XIII, the little isle de Notre-Dame and the isle aux Vaches were joined together to form the Ile Saint-Louis, the development of which, including construction of the quays, was entrusted to Christophe Marie as part of a deal with the Crown.

Even though the first quay was built on the L. Bank, the R. Bank was the beneficiary, in the 17th c., of the longest continuous succession of quays, built between the Arsenal and the Jardin des Tuileries. As a result, the view over the river was opened up and protection against flooding was improved.

There was a marked step forward in urban planning during the reign of Louis XV. The King, wanting a large river bordered by quays and ports, commissioned plans for development from P. L. Moreau. Houses built either on the bridges or on the quays overhanging the river were demolished by a decree of 1769. Moreau was also responsible for designing the Quai Saint-Bernard, the Quai des Ursins (today the Quai aux Fleurs), the Quai Bignon (today the Quai Saint-Michel), the Quai de la Pelleterie (today the Quai de la Corse) and others, plans of which were realized much later. Under Louis XVI, an edict confirming the decree of Louis XV resulted in the demolition of most of the houses on the bridges as well as the houses on the Quai de Gesvre.

Napoléon was responsible for the construction of the quays planned during Louis XV's reign. Wishing to return to inland water transport the importance it had lost during the Revolution, he had the river banks raised and the Quai du Louvre reconstructed. He also ordered the rebuilding and completion of many other quays: the Quais de Montebello, des Grands-Augustins, de la Conférence and de Billy, d'Orsay and des Invalides. In addition, the towpaths were improved, a path for carts was created, and the area allocated to merchandise in the ports was increased. To ease navigation, the Emperor also cleared the river of its clutter of water mills and wash-houses. The profession of *maître de pont* (bridge master), which had been abolished during the Revolution, was re-established, and the port police instituted. Projects begun under the Empire were completed during the Restoration. The banks upstream were developed and, between 1833 and 1837, alterations were carried out on the Quai de la Grève (now the Quai de l'Hôtel-de-Ville) and the Quai de la Mégisserie.

The Seine, however, continued to be frequently impassable due to flooding and remained dangerous because of its strong current. In 1839 it was decided to transform the banks completely; but the work, begun in 1846, was not completed until 1855. The river, once dredged and enclosed between two stone ramparts, became calmer, protecting Paris from the frequent and often unexpected floods. The banks and the level of the ports as far as the Place de la Concorde were raised. During the Second Empire, the mobile dam at La Monnaie was built on the smaller arm of the river with plans by the engineer Poirée. Strangely enough, Haussmann as Prefect of the Seine, made few alterations to the quays; he only widened the Quai Conti and planted trees on the banks of the Seine, to make it a pleasant place for strolling.

The port, which had hitherto been too important to sacrifice even one square meter of space, lost its previous economic importance with the coming of the railway. The waterways were then essentially devoted to the transport of heavy goods. Further dredging and other modifications continued from 1870 to 1900.

The first half of the 20th c. was a black period for the quays of Paris: indiscriminate construction, poor maintenance of the supporting walls of the raised quays, the use of the quays as parking lots (near the Pont-Neuf, the Pont Royal and the Ile de la Cité) and a lot for impounded cars (at the Port de la Tournelle) gave the quays a dirty, run-down air. Quays were converted to main roads to help cope with the enormous increase in traffic within Paris. From 1961 to 1967, a freeway was built on the R. Bank from one end of the city to the other; in 1976, another was built on the L. Bank, but shorter than the first, due to numerous protests.

The interest displayed by Parisians toward their quays made the authorities take note of the importance and potential beauty of the area. As a first step, they turned the Port de la Tournelle and several parking lots over for redevelopment as gardens and parks, with trees and foot paths. An example of this is the site between the Pont de Sully and the Pont des Arts.

Strolling along the quays

Today it is possible, especially in the center of Paris, to find very pleasant areas to stroll. Start in the Tino-Rossi gardens, which have an open-air sculpture museum, go along the banks of the Quai Saint-Bernard, then continue along the quay and cross to the middle of the Pont Sully, staying on the Ile Saint-Louis; take the Quai d'Anjou, then the Quai de Bourbon, as far as the tip of the island, and finally cross the Passerelle Saint-Louis footbridge. Once on the Ile de la Cité, walk along the Quai aux Fleurs and part of the Quai de la Corse, cross the Seine again on the Pont au Change, and turn l. at the Quai de la Mégisserie as far as the Pont-Neuf. Cross this bridge to get to the L. Bank; take the Quai des Grands-Augustins, and then the Quai Saint-Michel, Quai de Montebello and Quai de la Tournelle.

The quays within the city are listed alphabetically. The description of each quay and the nearby buildings goes from upstream to downstream.

The Quai Anatole-France

7th arr. Map ref. 16-B1, C1

Bounded by the Pont Royal and the Pont de la Concorde, this quay used to be the eastern section of the Quai d'Orsay before 1947, when it took the name of the French novelist who lived close by at 15 Quai Malaquais, from 1844 to 1853. At the time, his father had a bookshop at no. 9 Quai Voltaire. The construction of the quay, in freestone, was begun in 1708 by C. Boucher d'Orsay, *Prévôt des Marchands,* but completed only under the Second Empire, between 1802 and 1815, when it was given the name Quai Bonaparte.

The Caisse des Dépôts et Consignations, rebuilt after the Commune fire in 1871, occupies the site of several mansions, the most important of which was by Robert de Cotte (1727), chief architect to the King. All that remains is a registered pediment, dismantled and rebuilt stone by stone, of Minerva looking at an architect's plan. The Gare d'Orsay, built in 1897 for the World Fair of 1900 by the Orléans Railway Company (architect, V. Laloux), is an interesting example of interior architecture in iron. This station has just been restored to house the Musée d'Orsay, and was devoted to art from 1848 to 1914. Between the Rue de Bellechasse and the Rue de Solférino is the Hôtel de Salm-Kyrburg, built between 1782 and 1790 by P. Rousseau. Once bordered by a terraced garden, the hôtel was acquired in 1804 by the Grande Chancellerie de la Légion d'Honneur, and today houses the palace and museum of the Légion d'Honneur (→Museums). Beyond the Rue de Solférino, you can see the modern CNRS building, the gardens of the Hôtel de Beauharnais (1714), today the GFR Embassy, and the neighboring mansion, the Hôtel de Seigneley, with its 18th-c. decoration. Below is the Deligny swimming-pool, opened in 1785.

The Quai André-Citroën***

15th arr. (towpath). Map ref. 13–A3

Originally, this quay was an old towpath along the river bank. It begins near the Pont de Grenelle; it is the last Parisian quay on the R. Bank before the suburbs. It bordered the old borough of Javel, whose windmill gave the quay its first name. In 1777, several industrialists were authorized to set up factories for the manufacture of potassium hypochlorite, now known as *eau de javel* (bleach). In 1958 this quay was named after the car manufacturer who established his factories here in the 1920s. They have now been demolished and replaced by a large 6–acre/15ha park and a complex comprising a hospital and residential, office and commercial buildings. The quay has been cleared of its port installations to make way for the park.

The Quai d'Anjou***

4th arr. Map ref. 18–C3

This quay begins at the upstream tip of the Ile Saint-Louis and ends at the Rue des Deux-Ponts. Built during the belated development of the island, from 1630 to 1647, it displays an architectural uniformity which makes it one of the most beautiful quays of the capital. Note also two remarkable mansions: the Hôtel Lambert, architect, Le Vau, (1640), and the Hôtel de Lauzun (1656) (→Ile Saint-Louis).

The Quai de l'Archevêché**

4th arr. Map ref. 17–B3

In the 13th c., this part of the Ile de la Cité was a small island known as 'la Motte aux Papelards'. At that time, it was surrounded by a construction which is today the base of the supporting wall of the quay. The quay took the name of the former archbishop's palace built in 1697, pillaged and set on fire in 1831 (during the anti-legitimists' uprising). The area is taken up almost entirely by the Square–Jean XXIII (the former Square de l'Archevêché), which lies beside the apse and S wall of the cathedral, which was built at the heart of a network of back streets which disappeared when the quay was reconstructed during the Second Empire. This calm, remote isle of greenery, less visited than the parvis, invites strolling. At the tip of the island another garden has housed the Crypte du Mémoriale de la Déportation (crypt in memory of those deported by the Nazis) since 1961 (→Ile de la Cité).

The Quai d'Austerlitz

13th arr. Map ref. 24–D2

This quay was built at the beginning of the 18th c.; then it was called the Quai de l'Hôpital because it lay near the gardens of the Hôpital de la Pitié–Salpêtrière. It extends from the Pont de Bercy to the Pont d'Austerlitz.

The station barrier which constituted part of the Fermiers-Généraux perimeter wall used to face the Pont de Bercy. It was here, upstream from the viaduct to the Métro, that a new bridge was planned to link the Gare d'Austerlitz to the Gare de Lyon, once the new Ministry of Finances had been built on the R. Bank. The Entrepôts Généraux (general warehouse) and the customs buildings standing on the banks hide the river from view. No. 55 used to be the Garde Nationale prison, nicknamed '*Hôtel des haricots*' (bean mansion) in irreverent homage to the officers' mess. It was destroyed in 1805, while work on the Gare d'Austerlitz was nearing completion. Enlarged and rebuilt in 1867 by the architect Renault, the station opens on to the Place Valhubert, where you will find the entrance to the Jardin des Plantes.

The Quai de Bercy

12th arr.

This quay was built at the end of the 17th c. and lies between the Pont National and the Pont de Bercy. Until the end of the 19th c. the land of the Bercy family stretched away on either side of the Pont de Tolbiac. Upstream loomed the Château de Bercy, built from 1658 to 1714. Its park, designed by Le Nôtre, was gradually divided into plots after 1804, and finally destroyed to make way for the wine merchants' warehouses, some of which still line the quay. As the shipping and receiving area for wine, it became the most important wine market in Europe. But new storage techniques caused its gradual decline. In 1978, the City of Paris bought the site, which is now scheduled for development. This project will include, most notably, a green area surrounding part of the old wine stove houses, now registered as historic monuments, a viti-vinicultural center, and a shopping precinct devoted to wine and fine foods. The park suffered other incursions during the 19th c. First, the fortification of the city cut it in two. Of these fortifications, one redoubt remains further upstream, near the Boulevard Périphérique. From 1847 to 1852 the installation of the railway completely destroyed vast green areas, and the château was razed a few years later, in 1861.

Upstream from the Pont de Bercy looms the Palais Omnisports de Bercy, a sort of temple with turfed sloping walls, including both a sports complex and concert halls. The ceaseless flow of traffic arriving from the R. Bank freeway makes the quay particularly noisy, and not really suitable for strolling.

The Quai de Béthune**

4th arr. Map ref. 18–C3

Situated on the Ile Saint-Louis, this quay begins at the Pont Sully and ends at the Pont de la Tournelle; unlike the other quays, this one does not have low banks. In 1806 it was named after Maximilien de Béthune, Duc de Sully, Henri VI's chief minister. However, the superb wrought-iron balconies that decorate the façades of this quay have earned it another name, Quai des Balcons (→ Ile Saint-Louis).

The Quai de Bourbon**

4th arr. Map ref. 18 C2

Starting at the Pont Marie on the Ile Saint-Louis, this quay runs alongside the downstream tip of the island to end at the footbridge that links the Ile Saint-Louis to the Ile de la Cité. Built in 1614, it owes its name to the royal house of Bourbon.

At no. 1, the Cabaret du Franc Pinot, dating from the 17th c., was restored in 1977. Until the 19th c. this was one of the docks for the passenger barges that carried travellers from Melun. Also moored here were special boats with tanks for live freshwater fish. Of the beautiful mansions on the quay (→ Ile Saint-Louis), do not miss the Hôtel Charron at no. 15 and the Hôtel de Jassaud at no. 19.

The Quai Branly

7th and 15th arr. Map ref. 13–B2, 14–C1

This quay, situated between the Pont de l'Alma and the Pont de Bir-Hakeim, was built in 1808 and was part of the Quai d'Orsay until 1941. It then took the name of the French physician, Edouard Branly (1844-1940). Its high banks, bordered with greenery, offer a pleasant place for a stroll, but its low banks are cluttered with harbour installations and silos.

At no. 11, the old stables built in 1864 for Napoléon III, now converted into apartments, are decorated with a sculpted pediment of an eagle. The tall silhouette of the Eiffel Tower, symbol of Paris since the World Fair of 1889, dominates this quay.

The Quai des Célestins**

4th arr. Map ref. 18–C2, C3

Situated on the R. Bank between the Pont Sully and the Pont Marie, this quay was built at the end of the 14th c. under Charles V. Lined with elm trees at that time, it was called the Quai des Ourmetiaux; in 1868, it was renamed after the huge Célestin convent. This convent replaced the Carmelite convent, which had been established on the L. Bank of the Bièvre. It was built on land stretching from the present Place de la Bastille to the Seine, where the barracks of the Garde Républicaine now stand. For centuries the convent and its church were the honored burial places of princes and nobles, until they were razed during the Revolution.

To the E, the houses are separated from the river by the triangular Square Henri-Galli, which enclosed within its SE corner the subfoundation of one of the eight towers of the Bastille (known as La Liberté, 1370) rebuilt with blocks of stone discovered during the construction of the Métro in 1899. Behind the square, the Bibliothèque de l'Arsenal is visible.

On the corner of the quay and the Rue du Petit-Musc is the Hôtel Fieubet (17th c., altered in the 19th c.), which houses the Ecole Massillon (→ Marais, district Saint-Paul). The Hôtel Nikolai, no. 4, was once part of an older mansion. The sculptor Barye died there in 1875. The 16th-c. Hôtel de la Vieuville, formerly adjacent, was unfortunately destroyed in 1927 and replaced by the warehouses of the Samaritaine department stores. These were converted into apartments from 1979 to 1980. The Barbeau Tower, which stood level with no. 32, marked the E end of Philippe Auguste's perimeter wall; the remnants, as well as the E end of the Church of Saint-Paul, can be seen by taking the Jardins-Saint-Paul (→ Marais, Saint-Paul district). Thanks to a clear space on the same level as Rue du Fauconnier, one of the oldest buildings in Paris is visible: the Hôtel des Archevêques de Sens (→ Marais, Saint-Paul district), with its Gothic portal framed by two turrets like watch towers with pepperpot roofs. Today it houses the Bibliothèque Forney, dedicated to books on arts and crafts. It is open to the public and exhibitions are frequently held there.

The Quai de la Conférence

8th arr. Map ref. 9–A3

This quay links the Place de la Concorde to the Place de l'Alma. Its name commemorates the conference held in Surêsnes when Henri IV formally renounced Protestantism, cynically remarking 'Paris is worth a Mass', and the surrender of Paris in 1593. This quay merges with the part of the route to Versailles that was transformed in 1616 by Marie de' Medici into an elm-lined carriageway, the Cours-La-Reine, whose W section was renamed Cours Albert Ier in 1919. The Maréchal de Bassompierre completed the development by building a quay and raising the river banks. The quay was raised during the 18th c. Until 1775 it was very fashionable.

Close to the Place de la Concorde, on a monumental plinth, stands a bronze statue of Albert I, King of the Belgians, by A. Martial (1938). The impressive outlines of the Grand and Petit Palais (→Champs-

Elysées), built for the World Fair of 1900, dominate the quay. The enormous glass roof of the Grand Palais, illuminated by the setting sun, is best viewed from the Pont Alexandre-III (also built for the 1900 Exhibition). On either side of this bridge stand equestrian statues of Simon Bolivar by E. Frémiet and the Marquis de Lafayette by Bartholdi, presented by the students of the Ecoles des Etats-Unis (American States Schools). At 34 Cours Albert-Ier is the Brazilian Embassy. Do not miss, at no. 40, the Art-Nouveau house of the master glass artist René Lalique, with its elaborate front door. On the corner of the Ave. Montaigne and the Cours, a sculpted stone group by Rudder (1923), illustrates the *Reconnaissance de la Belgique à la France* (the gratitude of the Belgians to the French) and, in the center of the Place de l'Alma, a bronze statue by G. Choain symbolizes the Seine (1962). Near the Pont de l'Alma a column decorated with bas-reliefs is surmounted by a statue of the Polish poet and patriot Adam Mickiewicz, sculpted by Bourdelle in 1929.

The Quai de Conti**

6th arr. Map ref. 17–A2

This quay, which was built from 1651 to 1760, stretches from the Pont-Neuf to the Passerelle des Arts and is overlooked by two impressive buildings: the Monnaie (Mint) and the Institut de France. After several name changes, the quay was finally given the name Conti, after the family of princes whose residence used to be where the Hôtel de la Monnaie stands today.

No. 1 is at the Curie intersection named after the scientist Pierre Curie, husband of Marie, who was run over by a horse-drawn carriage and killed here in 1906. It is a big brick building by architect J. Marrast, dating from the early 19th c. Originally it was to have stood in line with the Pont-Neuf between the Rue Dauphine on the l. and on the r. an extension of the Rue de Rennes, which was planned on the site of the Rue de Nevers. Under the arch is an inscription dated 1655 taken from C. Le Petit's *Paris Ridicule* relating to the Pont-Neuf. In its upper section, a sculpted group by C. Sarrabezolles represents *La Gloire de Paris* (Glory of Paris). Between the Rue Guénégaud and the Impasse Conti stands the Hôtel des Monnaies (the Mint). This sober edifice, by the then unknown J. D. Antoine, was the forerunner of a new architectural style on a grand scale, which reached its peak under Louis XVI (Saint-Germain-des-Prés; for visits to the Musée de la Monnaie →Museums. No. 13, the small Hôtel Guénégaud, set slightly back, was built by F. Mansart (1659) and lived in until the end of the 18th c. by a Corsican family with whom Bonaparte had lodged in 1792. Today it is an art gallery. No. 15 was built during the reign of Louis XIV. In front of the Passerelle des Arts, the buildings of the Institut de France form a harmonious group dominated by the famous dome. Louis Le Vau was responsible for the design of the Collège des Quatre-Nations College of Four Nations, founded by Mazarin for the provinces of Alsace, Artois, Piedmont and Roussillon, under his ministry, and which is now the headquarters annex for the five Académies de l'Institut, the most famous of which is the Académie Française. Its library, the Bibliothèque Mazarine, is housed in the Tour de Nesle. With the Cardinal's legacy as the core of its collection, this library houses some exceptional works, mostly relating to historical and religious subjects (→Saint-Germain-des-Prés).

The Quai de la Corse

4th arr. Map ref. 17-B2

Situated on the Ile de la Cité between the Pont d'Arcole and the Pont au Change, this old section of the Quai aux Fleurs dates from 1769 and was renamed the Quai de la Corse in 1929. It has no private dwellings, but is lined with the buildings of the maternity department of the Hôtel-Dieu (→Ile de la Cité), the Marché aux Fleurs flower market: Open daily except Sat. 8am-7:30pm, and the Tribunal de Commerce built under Napoléon III in 1865 by A. N. Bailly (→Ile de la Cité).

The Allée des Cygnes (Swans' Walk)

15th arr.

This isle seems to be moored between the Pont de Grenelle and the Pont de Bir-Hakeim. The *allée* as it appears today was created in 1825 by the developers of the Port de Grenelle to serve as a jetty for the port. There had been a charnel-house on the site for horses in the 18th c. The *allée* took the name of the islet that formerly lay upstream, close to the L. Bank, between the Pont des Invalides and the Pont d'Iéna, which was joined to the river bank in 1820 at the old site between the Quai Branly and the Rue de l'Université. It was on this islet that Louis XIV, by a decree of 1676, had put swans brought from Denmark and Sweden. Before this, during the 16th c., it was called the Ile Maquerelle, a corruption of *mâle querelle* (literally, 'male quarrel'), because of its frequent use by duellists.

The 'Swans' Walk' offers a very pleasant stroll at the level of the water between two rows of fragrant trees - poplar, lime, maple and chestnut trees. It is also the home port for the pleasure cruise boats (bateaux-mouches). At its W end, like the figurehead on a prow of a ship, stands the original small-scale model of New York's Statue of Liberty by Bartholdi, presented to the city by the American colony in France. It was installed for the 1889 World Fair and has been restored in time for its centenary. At its E end is the stern figurehead, *La France Renaissante* (France Reborn) by Wederkinch, presented by the Danish colony in Paris.

The Quai aux Fleurs*

4th arr. Map ref. 17–B2

Situated on the Ile de la Cité, this quay begins at the pedestrian Pont Saint–Louis, which joins the island to the Ile Saint–Louis, and ends at the Pont d'Arcole. One large section of this quay, formerly known as the Quai de la Pelleterie between the Pont d'Arcole and the Pont au Change, was renamed Quai de la Corse in 1929. Built towards the end of the 18th c. and raised in 1804, it is situated beside the Port Saint–Landry, the first and oldest port of the Cité until the construction of that at Place de Grève.

At nos. 9 and 11, two 19th-c. semi-detached houses with an inscription, above which are two sculpted heads representing the ill-starred lovers Héloïse and Abelard (→Ile de la Cité). They are a reminder that the home of Heloïse's uncle Canon Fulbert stood nearby. From here, the absence of houses on the quay gives a view of a medieval house in the Rue des Ursins. Opposite no. 21 is the Rue de la Colombe, its name unchanged since 1223. Further along the street, a slanting section of paving stones indicates the former site of the island's perimeter wall.

The Quai de la Gare

13th arr.

Originally a 17th–century towpath, this quay begins at the level of the Pont National and ends at the Pont de Bercy. It owes its name, not to the proximity of the Gare d'Austerlitz, but to an old project, begun in the 18th c., for building a dock for storing grains and flour to alleviate Paris's river traffic and to build up a reserve stock for the months when the river would freeze over or for times of lower water. The Parlement of 1765, however, asked that the project be postponed, since it was judged to be too costly.

On the banks further upstream are the Grands Moulins de Paris and the concrete–manufacturing factories of the Bétons de Paris company. Not far away is the compressed air factory, built in 1890, which distributes throughout Paris compressed air for a multitude of uses: the operation of a variety of machines, elevators, automatic clocks, etc.

The Quai de Gesvres

4th arr. Map ref. 17–A2

This short quay with a long history lies between the Pont d'Arcole and the Place de Châtelet. The first quay built here, the Quai Pelletier, stretched upstream from the Place de Grève, now the Place de l'Hôtel-de-Ville, to the Rue Saint-Martin. Its construction, which began in 1675 to facilitate travel between the Louvre and the Faubourg Saint-Antoine, entailed the displacement of the small tanneries on the bank and to the E and the disappearance of the sloping land known as the Tuerie (killing place) where butchers came to slaughter their animals. This first section was originally known as the Quai Neuf, then became the Quai de la Tannerie and finally took the name of the *Prévôt des Marchands* who had built it. It was widened in 1830. The second section of the present Quai de Gesvres, built after the 1641 fire at the Pont au Change, was situated between the Rue Saint-Martin and the Place du Châtelet. Louis XIII authorized the Marquis de Gesvres to build a quay at his own expense on the same level as the neighboring bridges, the Pont au Change and the Pont Nôtre-Dame. It was supported by arcades that formed a vaulted gallery encroaching on the river and sheltering, in its crannies, both shops and vagabonds. In 1860, at the time of the reconstruction of the two neighboring bridges, the gallery was separated from the river by a wall and converted into a tunnel; it was used in 1913 for the Métro's no. 7 line (Ivry-Villejuif). The construction dating from the time of Louis XIII is still visible in the Métro, at the Châtelet station: its walls have now been covered in mosaics and a small basement window and one of the old sheltering arches are still visible.

The two quays were joined together in 1868 under the name of the Quai de Gesvres. It is now occupied by various official buildings: the Assistance Publique, the headquarters of the companies of urban transport under the Préfecture de Police, as well as the Théâtre de la Ville (→Châtelet), built by Davioud at the same time as the Théâtre Musical de Paris, which stands opposite.

The Quai des Grands-Augustins**

6th arr. Map ref. 17-A2

Situated between the Pont Saint-Michel and the Pont-Neuf, this is the oldest quay in Paris. It was built in 1313 under Philippe le Bel (the Fair) and widened in 1809. Originally called the Quai Pont-Neuf, in 1670 it was renamed after the Grands-Augustins, one of the largest monasteries in France, established by St. Louis in the 13th c. The monastery's grounds once extended from the Rue de Nevers to the W to the Rue Christine in the S, the Rue des Grands-Augustins to the E, and the Rue Dauphine to the N. In 1293, monks from the eremitical order of Saint-Augustin settled in this area. A papal reform in 1588 divided them into the Grands and Petits Augustins, and the Déchaussés (Discalced) or shoeless monks. Only the Grands Augustins remained at the old monastery, whose huge house and Flamboyant Gothic church were destroyed during the Revolution in 1797.

This quay is bordered by a beautiful row of tall houses (16th–19th c.). Near where no. 33 stands today, from the late 17th c. to the 19th c., there was a chicken, butter and egg market, known as the Marché de la Vallée. No. 35, on the corner of the Rue Séguier, is a two-storey mansion with high windows decorated with bas-reliefs. It belonged to the Montholon family in the 16th c. and later to the printer Firmin Didot, during the 18th c. On the corner, No. 51 is the famous Lapérouse restaurant, which has stood there since the end of the 18th c.

The Quai de Grenelle

15th arr. Map ref. 13–A3, 13–B2

Between the Pont de Bir-Hakeim and the Pont de Grenelle, this quay is separated from the Seine by the Invalides–Versailles railway. Above the railway line is a walkway. An important section of this quay runs along the Front de Seine (→ Grenelle), a district which has been completely renovated since 1961 by the City of Paris. The Port de Grenelle and the Allée des Cygnes, which form a protective dyke, date from 1825.

The Quai Henri-IV

4th arr. Map ref. 18–D3

This quay starts at the level of the Arsenal basin and ends at the Boul. Henri-IV, which becomes the Pont Sully. Henri IV who often passed this way left it his name. Where the bridge spans the Arsenal basin, Pont Morland, is the Tour de Billy, built into Charles V's perimeter wall. The basin itself was dug on the site of the wall's old moat. The royal arsenal, created in 1563 by Henri II, stretched from the Bastille to the Boul. Morland. The land beyond formed the Ile Louviers, which served as a depot for firewood from the nearby Port des Célestins. The small arm of the Seine, which was filled in 1843, allowed the construction of a rapidly developing port for floating timber.

No. 30 is the Archives de Paris, formerly the archives of the Seine, which houses the certificates of births, deaths and marriages from 1860 on, Paris building permits dating from 1880, and collections on the history of Parisian public buildings, private properties and topography. There is also a map library. Documents are available for public viewing.

No. 38 is a mansion decorated with sculptures. The quay is not suitable for strolling because of heavy traffic. At this level, the freeway, after passing over the upper section of the quay, runs down again towards the river bank by the Pont Henri-IV.

The Quai de l'Horloge***

1st arr. Map ref. 17–A2

This quay on the Ile de la Cité starts at the Pont au Change and ends at the Pont-Neuf. Begun in 1580, it was raised in 1611. It runs alongside the Palais de Justice, the former palace of the kings of France, the construction of which dates back to the 11th c. and which Philippe le Bel (the Fair) enlarged in the 12th c. All that remains of the old Capetian palace, which was completely transformed in the 19th c., are the four towers and the lower parts of the building beside the quay. The dry moat which runs parallel to the façade shows the original level of the ground before the quay underwent many alterations; all the façades of the palace were restored under Louis-Philippe, and again after 1872. First named the Quai des Morfondus (the fed up) – an allusion to the hours of waiting endured by litigants – then the Quai des Lunettes (spectacles) – because of the numerous opticians doing business there, the quay was finally named after the tower further upstream, the Tour de l'Horloge (Clock Tower).

The Quai de l'Hôtel-de-Ville

4th arr. Map ref. 18–C2

This quay starts at the Pont Marie and ends at the Pont d'Arcole. Until 1830 it was called the Quai de Grève because of the adjacent port. It was twice raised, from 1673 to 1675 and from 1740 to 1798; it was altered one last time between 1835 and 1837.

In the Rue de Jony, the Hôtel d'Aumont stands at no. 7, built by Le Vau in 1648 and completed by Mansart in 1656, with decoration by Le Brun and a formal French garden (→ Marais Saint-Paul district). Further on is the Cité Internationale Arts (International City of Arts; architects, Tournon and Cacoub, 1965) which houses the arts foundation formed by the Finnish painter Eero Snellman. French and foreign artists can live here for a year. Further along stands the gloomy barracks known as the Annexe Lobau, built in 1854, which now houses the services of the Mairie de Paris (town hall). Continue along the quay and you will reach the Hôtel de Ville. From the quay, overlooking the private gardens of the mayor of Paris, you can see the equestrian statue of Etienne Marcel begun by J. Idrac and completed by L. Marqueste in 1888. Marcel, a rich draper and a merchant provost, defied royal authority during the 14th c. He died at the hands of the mob in 1358. You will come to the Place de l'Hôtel-de-Ville, recently refurbished. In the Middle Ages it was called the Place de Grève (foreshore: Hôtel de Ville) and is important in the history of Paris as a gathering place for the unemployed, which gave rise to the expression *'faire la grève'* (to go on strike).

The Quai Kennedy

16th arr. Map ref. 13–A2, B2

The former Quai de Passy begins at the Rue Beethoven, close to the Trocadéro gardens, and ends opposite the Pont de Grenelle, opposite the Maison de Radio-France (→Auteuil). For a long time it was a towpath, bordered by the Barrière des Bonshommes. This barrier, built by Nicholas Ledoux, was part of the Fermiers Généraux perimeter wall and marked the city's W border. On the site of the country houses of the village of Passy now stand tall apartment buildings.

The house at no. 18 Rue des Eaux is a reminder of the ferruginous waters which made the city famous as a spa as early as 1650. No. 42 has sculpted pillars and an ornate door. Access to the river has now been blocked by the freeway on the R. Bank.

The Quai du Louvre**

1st arr. Map ref. 17–A1

A first quay built during the 14th c. was rebuilt by François I at the time of the construction of the Nouveau Louvre. It underwent further alterations at the beginning of the 18th c. and during the construction of the Passerelle des Arts in 1810. During the Second Empire it was extended to its present length, stretching from the Pont-Neuf to the Pont du Carrousel by joining it with the Quai de l'Ecole and the Quai de Bourbon.

Opposite the Pont-Neuf stands the department store La Samaritaine (→Châtelet) with its beautiful Art Deco façade (architects Jourdain and Sauvage), dating from 1928. The houses between the store and the Louvre have preserved their original appearance; the building at the end is by the architect Hittorff.

Behind these buildings, but partly visible from the quay, are the Church of Saint-Germain-l'Auxerrois (→Châtelet) with its Romanesque belfry (architect Ballu, 1861) and Perrault's superb colonnade which marks the entrance to the Palais du Louvre. Follow the façade by Le Vau, then the first section of the Galerie du Bord de l'Eau, built for Henri IV. The entrances, built in the 19th c. by Lefuel, are decorated with sculptures representing, at the base of the arcades, to the r., *La Marine Marchande* (the Merchant Marine), to the l., *La Marine de Guerre* (the Navy) by E. Jouffroy and, on the pediment, *Le Génie des Arts* (The Genius of the Arts), a high-relief in beaten copper by A. Mercié. On either side of this the two figures representing rivers are by Barye.

From the 13th to the 19th c. the river banks sheltered the busy Port Saint-Nicolas, which provided the capital with food imported from the provinces and from Holland. In 1942 the port was replaced by a pleasure garden.

The Quai Malaquais*

6th arr. Map ref. 16–D2

This quay was built in 1552 as protection against flooding and stretched from the Rue de Seine to the Rue du Bac. It was called Mal-Acquet, a name taken from the neighboring port to which access was difficult. From 1641 to 1662 it was named Reine-Marguerite after the Queen, whose domain stretched alongside the Seine to the Rue de Bellechasse in the W.

At no. 3, the Louis XIII Hôtel Dorat has a wrought-iron balcony; it was the home of the Maréchal de Saxe from 1744 to his death in 1750. The statue of Voltaire by Caillé is in the small square to the l. At no. 5 the Hôtel de Chateauneuf, built in 1625, displays its five semicircular arcades, their tall, elaborately designed windows adorned with delicate balconies and medallions on the imposts. In 1791 Marie-Antoinette unsuccessfully planned her escape from this house. The Hôtel de Garsalan at no. 7, built for J. de Garsalan, advisor and *maître ordinaire* of the Treasury in 1622, underwent several alterations, as did the Hôtel de Chateauneuf. The Champion bookshop, on the ground floor, is over a century old. The Hôtel de Transylvanie at no. 9, built from 1622 to 1628, owes its name to F. Rackoczy, prince of Transylvania. Exiled from his country, he took refuge in France and set up the Académie de Jeu, which plays an important role in the novel *Manon Lescaut* by the Abbé Prévost. This mansion has preserved its Directoire décor on the first floor, and its 17th-c. ceilings with painted beams. At no. 13, the Salle Melpomène, a building of Classical inspiration, was designed by the architect Duban in 1845 for the Ecole des Beaux-Arts (School of Fine Arts). At the same time the school annexed no. 15, where Anatole France lived from 1844 to 1853, after moving from no. 19. At no. 17 the Hôtel de la Bazinière, also known as the Hôtel de Chimay, was built in 1640 by F. Mansart and decorated by Le Brun for Bertrand de la Bazinière. It was altered during the 18th c. for Marie-Anne Mancini, Duchesse de Bouillon. La Fontaine and Henriette de France, daughter of Charles I of England, often stayed here as guests of the duchess. Anatole France was born at no. 19 on April 16 1844, and George Sand wrote *Lélia* and lived here from 1832 until 1836.

The Quai du Marché Neuf

4th arr. Map ref. 17–B2

The construction of this quay, situated on the Ile de la Cité, was begun under the Empire but not completed until 1860; it stretches from the Petit Pont to the Boul. du Palais and runs along the side of the Préfecture de Police (Police Headquarters), which takes up almost the entire quayside. The quay got its name from the fish and vegetable market which was held here from 1568. It has a very narrow bank. The house where Théophile Renaudot founded France's first newspaper, *La Gazette de France*, in 1631, was at no. 8 (since demolished).

The Quai de la Mégisserie*

1st arr. Map ref. 17–A2, B2

This quay lies between the Pont au Change and the Pont-Neuf; its first building dates from 1369. At that time, it was named Quai de la Saunerie because it was near a salt storehouse. With the quays on the Ile de la Cité, it is among the oldest in Paris, after the Quai des Grands-Augustins. It was rebuilt under François I from 1530 to 1539 and owes its present name *mégisserie* (tanning) to the tanners who cured their leathers here for five centuries until they were pushed out toward the banks of the Bièvre, on the l. bank. The riverbed here was very deep, forming a kind of gorge where the current was particularly strong. Moreover, the two bridges (Pont Notre-Dame and Pont au Change) stood very close to one another, were cluttered with buildings, and had been built in such a way that their arches were not aligned, making navigation difficult for the river pilots. The zigzagging that passing beneath these bridges required caused so many accidents that the place was nicknamed the Vallée de la Misère (Valley of Woe).

The quay begins at the former Théâtre du Châtelet, known today as the Théâtre Musical de Paris, built by Davioud. It ends at the Rue du Pont-Neuf, created in 1866, on the corner of which the shop La Belle Jardinière, built in 1867, used to stand. This quay is known for its corn chandlers, fowlers and its animal sellers.

The Quai de Montebello*

5th arr. Map ref. 17–A3

This quay begins slightly downstream from the Pont de L'Archevê-ché and ends at the Petit Pont. It commemorates Maréchal Lannes, Duc de Montebello, killed at Essling, Austria in 1809. The quay was not built until 1811 to 1813. It runs parallel to the ancient students' district of the Middle Ages where lectures, known as *'collèges'*, were held in the open air. Behind the small Square René-Viviani is one of the oldest churches of Paris, the Church of Saint-Julien-le-Pauvre (→Latin Quarter, Maubert-Saint-Séverin) consecrated to the Greek Catholic rite since 1889, but used as a university church from the 13th to the 16th c.

The small churchyard shelters a venerable tree, now propped up on all sides, and reputed to be one of the two oldest in Paris: a robinia, or false acacia, said to have been planted in the 17th c. Set a little further back, at no. 39 Rue de la Bûcherie, is one of the smallest houses in Paris, which has a lean-to roof with one slope only. Until 1782 the Petit Châtelet, the fortress which governed L. Bank access to the Ile de la Cité, stood at the start of the Rue de Petit-Pont. Not far from there was the Port aux Bûches, where the firewood and logs floated down the river were stored before the Port de Bercy was established.

The Quai de New-York

16th arr. Map ref. 13–B2

Also known as the Ave. de New-York, this quay begins at the Pont de l'Alma and ends at the Pont de Bir-Hakeim. It has changed names several times over the centuries. Known until 1610 as the Quai de Chaillot, it was really no more than a reinforced supporting wall. While it was called the Quai de Billy in 1807 it gave its name to the nearby footbridge, the Passerelle Debilly, and it then became the Quai de Tokyo in 1918. It was not until 1945 that it was given its present name.

The quay is dominated by the Palais de Tokyo, built in 1937 by Dondel, Aubert, Viard and Dastugue (→Chaillot). It stands on the site of the Savonnerie carpet factory founded by Louis XIII on the site of a soap factory. The Savonnerie was reorganized by Colbert in 1663 and amalgamated with the tapestry works at Gobelins in 1826. The former National Museum of Modern Art, which is now at the Pompidou Center, was originally installed in the l. wing of the palace. To the r. you can visit the Musée d'Art Moderne de la Ville de Paris (Museum of Modern Art of the City of Paris); (→Museums) An abundance of sculpted decorations covers the façades and the terraces on the side of the quay. On the wings, to the l., Triton, three nymphs, centaur and Eros by M. Gaumont; to the r., Actaeon, *La Chasse* (The Hunt) and Hercules by L. Baudry. The basin at the base of the fountain is supported by bronze sea horses by F. Févola; around the fountain are four recumbent nymphs by L. Dejean, L. Drivier and, (the two center nymphs), A. Guénot, together with two full-length statues: *Une Femme Maure* (Moorish woman) by A. Quiquaud and *Une Jeune Vendangeuse* (Young woman harvesting grapes) by P. Vigouroux. One either side of the great stairway at the back: to the r., *La Légende de la Mer* (Legend of the Sea), to the r., *La Légende de la Terre* (Legend of the Land) by A. Janniot (1930).

Further downstream, the quay is overlooked by the Trocadéro gardens, the stage for numerous fêtes and often lit up at night. The gardens were designed as they are today during the construction of the new Palais de Chaillot by the architects Carlu, Boileau and Azéma for the 1937 Art and Technology Exhibition (→Chaillot). On either side of the ornamental lake are sculptures: above, to the l., *L'homme* (Man) by P. Traverse; to the r., *La Femme* (Woman) by D. Baqué; in front of them, two fountains in gilded bronze: on the l., a bull's head with a deer by P. Jouve; to the r., two horses' heads and a dog by G. Guyot. Below, two massive stone statues: to the l., *La Joie de Vivre* (the Joy of Living) by L. Drivier; to the r., *La Jeunesse* (Youth) by P. Poisson.

The Quai des Orfèvres*

1st arr. Map ref. 17–A2

This quay stretches from the Pont Saint-Michel to the Pont-Neuf on the Ile de la Cité. Around 1600 a first quay was built during the construction of the Pont-Neuf and the Place Dauphine. Rebuilt in the 18th c., it owes its name to the numerous goldsmiths (*orfèvres*) who worked in the area. It runs alongside theTribunal Correctionel (court of summary jurisdiction) built from 1907 to 1914 by A. Tournaire and decorated with four female statues in the turn-of-the-century style: *La Verité* (Truth) by A. Lombard, *Le Droit* (Law) by A. Allar, (*L'Eloquence*) by R. Verlet and *La Clémence* (Clemency) by J. Coutan. The sundial is decorated with a bas-relief by A. Injalbert representing *Time and Justice*.

The Quai d'Orléans*

4th arr. Map ref. 15–A1, B1

On the Ile Saint-Louis, this quay begins at the Pont de la Tournelle and ends at the Rue Jean-du-Bellay, near the Passerelle Saint-Louis. It was built from 1630 to 1647 and dedicated to Gaston d'Orléans, Louis XIII's brother. No. 6 houses the library of the Polish historical and literary society and also the Polish Musée Adam-Mickiewicz (→Museums).

Apart from nos. 18 (17th c.) and 20 (18th c.) the remaining houses on this quay date from the 19th c. (→Ile Saint-Louis).

The Quai d'Orsay**

7th arr. Map ref. 9–A3, B3

Not long ago this was the longest quay in Paris, known as the Quai de la Grenouillère. It has since lost both its ends (today the Quai Anatole-France and the Quai Branly) and now stretches only between the Pont de la Concorde to the E and the Pont de l'Alma to the W. The reconstruction of the quay and the alteration of the banks of the Seine began in 1703 and ended in 1813 when the Ile des Cygnes was joined to the L. Bank. C. Boucher d'Orsay, who carried out the works, gave the quay his name.

Upstream, the façade of the Assemblée Nationale, called the Palais-Bourbon (→Faubourg Saint-Germain) has been built askew in relation to the alignment of the quay (architect Poyet, 1806) in order to make it parallel to the façade of the Church of La Madeleine at the end of the Rue Royale, on the opposite bank. To the r., the Hôtel de Lassay (→Faubourg Saint-Germain) built by Aubert in 1724, has been the residence of the President of the Assemblée since 1843.

Downstream, at no. 37, the Neo-Classical Palais des Affaires Etrangères (Foreign Office) built by J. Lacornée at the beginning of the Second Empire, has Doric columns on the ground floor and Ionic columns on the first floor. In front of the building stands a monument in bronze to Aristide Briand by P. Landowski 1937. Further along, the esplanade in front of the Invalides is the best place to view the façade of the Hôtel des Invalides built by Libéral Bruant (d.1697) for Louis XIV. The *hôtel* comprises a home for disabled soldiers, a military hospital, the Musée de l'Armée (→Museums) and Napoleon's tomb (→Invalides). To the Soldiers Church (Eglise des Soldats) completed in 1676, J. Hardouin Mansart added the famous dôme of the Invalides, completed in 1706. The esplanade was altered from 1979 to 1980 according to designs conceived by Robert de Cotte in 1750.

The buildings beyond the esplanade are an architectural medley. No. 59 is the South African Embassy (architects Lambert, Thierrat, Garet, 1974); the American Church is a Neo-Gothic reconstruction (architect, Caroll Greenough, 1927-31). From nos. 67 to 91 is a new district created since 1930 on the site of the old Magic-City amusement park, which shows some characteristic examples of modern architecture. Edouard Bourdet (1887-1945), the playwright, died at no. 71. Jean Giraudoux (1882-1944) died at no. 89, in the building designed by Roux-Spitz (1931).

The Quai de la Rapée

12th arr.

This quay was only a path going from the Pont de Bercy to the Boul. de la Bastille, opposite the Arsenal basin. It owes its name to the 18th-c. Hôtel de la Rapée, an aristocratic country residence, now gone, which belonged to General Commissioner de la Rapée at the Ministry of War under Louis XV.

Upstream is the Barrière de la Rapée from the former tollhouse, which levied dues on all goods entering Paris by way of the river. Downstream, at no. 48, lost among the modern buildings, a factory in brick, which looks like a fortified castle, houses the RATP (Parisian transport headquarters). The clock of the Gare de Lyon, built from 1899 to 1900 by Marius Toudoire, can be seen from the quay. The neighboring district has been almost completely rebuilt in the 20th c. There are plans for a new bridge opposite the Passage

Genty and the Rue Van-Gogh, to improve the flow of traffic, which will increase when the new Ministry of Finance is installed at no. 16 on the quay (→Gare de Lyon). The only building between the river bank and the street, under the Métro bridge, is the Institut Médico-Legal at no. 12 (no admittance: →inset) built in 1923. The Port de la Rapée has set up its huge warehouses of stone, wood, plaster and building materials of all kinds, on the banks on the site of the former Port Mazas or Port au Plâtre (plaster), which existed as early as the 16th c.

The Quai Saint-Bernard

5th arr. Map ref. 18-C3

Situated between the Pont d'Austerlitz and the Pont de Sully, the name of this quay comes, no doubt, from the name of one of the gates in Philippe Auguste's perimeter wall, rebuilt on a monumental scale under Louis XIV; the Saint-Denis and Saint-Martin gates, to the N of Paris still exist; the Saint-Bernard gate was destroyed in 1787.

The quay runs alongside the Pierre and Marie Curie University buildings and continues past the gates of the zoo at the Jardin des Plantes. From the 16th to the 18th c. it was a popular place for swimming. Downstream, the Port Saint-Bernard, which faced the wine market built by Louis XIV, served as a dock for the wine-laden boats waiting to be inspected. Napoleon had wanted to assemble all the wine merchants there and had built a wine market (the Halle aux Vins) expressly for that purpose in 1814. This market at Jussieu had exceptionally fine arched cellars, but the competition of the railways brought about its decline under the Second Empire. The market was destroyed in 1960 when building began on the Faculté des Sciences (University of Science) which borders the quay. At the beginning of the Pont Sully, the Institute of the Arab World (architects J. Nouvel, P. Soria and G. Lezenes, 1987), has a façade with a motif, inspired by traditional Muslim art, which changes according to the light, with the help of a photo electric cell inside the window (→Jardin des Plantes district). The banks of the Port Saint-Bernard have been transformed into a promenade with lawns, terraces and playing-fields. They were rechristened the Jardins Tino-Rossi in 1985. The City of Paris installed an open-air museum of contemporary sculpture (→Museums) modelled on the Hakone Museum near Tokyo. Works of 29 artists have been either donated or lent to this museum. Among the artists represented are César, Zadkine, Stahly, Ipoustéguy and Rougemont.

The Quai Saint-Michel*

5th arr. Map ref. 17-B2

The site of this short quay between the Pont Saint-Michel and the

Petit Pont was the subject of many projects before it was built from 1812 to 1816. Earlier the space had been taken up by houses overhanging the low bank and separated by narrow, perpendicular alleys, two of which have survived: Rue du Chat-qui-pêche (the fishing cat), the narrowest street in Paris (8 ft./2.5m), and the Rue Xavier Privas. Today the river bank, along the smaller arm of the Seine, is very narrow at water level and the quay overhangs the slope itself.

At the end of the Place Saint-Michel, the fountain attached to the gabled wall of the first building was created by Davioud from 1856 to 1860 and restored in 1980. The central niche houses a bronze group: *St Michel Terrassant le Démon* (St Michael Slaying the Demon) by F. Duret. (→Latin Quarter).

The Quai de la Tournelle***

5th arr. Map ref. 17–B3, 18–C3

Situated between the Pont Sully and the Pont de l'Archevêché, this quay has a splendid view of the back of Notre-Dame. It was created in 1554 as the Quai des Bernadins and, in 1750, took the name Quai de la Tournelle from an old square tower which had been part of Philippe Auguste's perimeter wall in the Middle Ages, and was linked to the Loriaux tower on the Ile Saint-Louis by a chain forming a barrier across the Seine to prevent attacks. The Port de la Tournelle specialized in the hay trade from the 16th c., then in wood and coal. After the police automobile pound was moved in 1976, the banks were landscaped and the quay was restored.

At no. 15 is the famous restaurant, La Tour d'Argent (the Silver Tower); closed Mon. opened in 1582 during the reign of Henri III, whose successor Henri IV is said to have been introduced to the use of the fork here. A small museum, the Musée de la Table (→Museums) was installed on the ground floor in 1958. No. 27 has a 17th-century façade (architect, Ledu). This was the point of departure for the passenger barge travelling to Fontainebleau when the court resided there. No. 37 is a 17th-c. mansion (the upper section has been altered). No. 47 is called the Hôtel de Miramion because it was used, from the 17th c. to the Revolution, by the order of the Filles de Sainte-Geneviève Miramiones, founded by Mme de Miramion. In 1810 the house became La Pharmacie, the central pharmacy for all Parisian hospitals, and was later converted, in 1934, into the Musée de l'Assistance Publique (the national welfare system: →Museums). The neighboring mansion at no. 57, was built in 1637 for F. de Nesmond, private secretary to the Prince de Condé. The Nesmond family was the first to engrave their name on the door of their house. Such an action caused a scandal. But the inscription remained. During the Revolution, it was changed to *'Hôtel cy-devant Nesmond'* (residence of the late Nesmond) which can still be read on the portal. The mansion was completely restored and converted into apartments from 1978 to 1979. No. 61, an 18th-century mansion, has recently been restored. The Rue de Bièvre is named after the river (Gobelins district) which now flows underground and this street marks the end of the quay.

The Quai des Tuileries**

1st arr. Map ref. 10–C3

This quay starts downstream from the Louvre *guichets* in front of the Pont du Carrousel and ends at the Pont de la Concorde. Its name comes from the old Palais des Tuileries nearby. Until 1731 a narrow path separated the dry moats of the Tuileries from the Seine. This path was widened after the demolition of the Porte de la Conférence (→Tuileries) and was converted into a quay in 1806 on Napoleon's orders, then bordered with plane trees during the Second Empire.

The quay runs parallel to the second section of the Grande Galerie du Louvre, from the entrance gates at the Carrousel to the Pavillon de Flore, which was built in the reign of Henri IV and entirely rebuilt in 1863 by Lefuel. The richness of the sculpted decoration and, in the center of façade, the door flanked by Barye's two bronze lions have always been much admired. The façade on the Seine side of the Pavillon de Flore, also rebuilt by Lefuel, is decorated with two works by Jean–Baptiste Carpeaux: above, the semicircular pediment, *France carrying light throughout the world and protecting Agriculture and Science* and, below, a charming group: *Le Triomphe de Flore* (The Triumph of Flora), half-size plaster models, at the Musée d'Orsay. Downstream, the Jardin des Tuileries is partially hidden from view. It was entirely rearranged by A. Le Nôtre on Colbert's orders; the gates and the balustrade on the quay side were restored in 1980. The quay then opens up onto the Place de la Concorde. This vast square was laid out from 1757 to 1763 by Gabriel, but was not given its final appearance until 1830 when Hittorff took over the project.

The Quai Voltaire

6th and 7th arr. Map ref. 16–C1, C2

This quay, which was known first as Quai Malaquais, then as Quai des Théatins, took the name Quai Voltaire in 1791. It stretches from the Rue des Saints–Pères to the Rue du Bac. Some of the most important Parisian antique dealers have their shops here.

At no. 1, the Hôtel de Tessé was built toward the end of the 18th c. by the architect Le Tellier. No. 9 was the home of the Comte Charles–Gustave Tessin, Swedish Ambassador Extraordinary, an important patron of the arts and collector to whom the National Museum of Stockholm owes a large part of its collection of French paintings. Vivant Denon, a director of the Louvre, also lived here. Ingres died at no. 11. Delacroix lived and had his studio at no. 13 before Corot moved in; in 1789 it was the headquarters of the Moniteur Universel. Nos. 15 to 25 housed the former convent of the Théatins, of which only the S portal remains, in the Rue de Lille. No. 17, where Ingres had a studio, was also the entrance to the convent. No. 19 used to be a 17th-c. inn. Baudelaire stayed here from July 1856 to December 1858; Wagner wrote *Die Meistersänger* (Dec. 1861 to February 1, 1862), Sibelius and Oscar Wilde also lived here; in the small drawing-room on the r. are souvenirs of Baudelaire. Montherlant took his own life in 1972 at no. 25, in an apartment overlooking the quays. Musset lived in a house that belonged to the Théatins. No. 27 is the Hôtel de la Villette where Voltaire's turbulent life came to an end. He was living with his niece, Mme Denis, at the home of the Marquis de Villette, where he entertained Condorcet, Camille Desmoulins, the Lameth brothers and Franklin; however, when he was dying, he was moved to the wash-house at the end of the garden, despite opposition from Dr Tronchin and the Marquise de Villette; his highly dramatized funeral seemed more like a macabre play. At no. 29, the Hôtel de Mailly–Nesle dates from the 17th c. Marie, Comtesse d'Agoult, writing under the pen-name Daniel Stern, lived here in 1830, and the philosopher and economist Victor Considérant, in 1848. Today it is the headquarters of the Documentation Françaises.

The Georges-Pompidou freeway

This freeway on the R. Bank is the W–E thoroughfare that allows travellers to cross Paris quickly from the Pont du Point–du–Jour to the bridge resting on the Quai d'Ivry without traffic lights or intersections. At either end it joins the Boulevard Périphérique. The total one–way length of the freeway is 8 mls/13km in two lanes; it consists of 3 mls./5km of quays, 3 mls./5km of river bank and 2 mls./3km of tunnel; it allows the motorist to avoid 22 traffic circles. The traffic flow on the R. Bank, which was once 75,000 cars per day, has doubled.

As early as 1961 a first section of road, measuring 2625 ft/800m on the river banks, was put into service between the Ave. de Lamballe and the Rue Beethoven; moreover, the 138 ft./142m tunnel from the Place de l'Alma, dates from 1956. But the remainder of the work was realized in the space of four years, from the beginning of 1964 to the end of 1967. To ease traffic in the rapidly changing E districts of Paris, the freeway will be widened from three to five lanes at the Pont d'Austerlitz, and the intersections with the Quai Henri IV, the Pont Morland and the Boul. Bourdon will be rearranged. Driving along the freeway when the sun is setting affords a most beautiful view of the Left Bank, the bridges and the islands.

▷ The Baths

It was a long time before the Parisians had running water in their homes. However, the first cold-water baths were installed on ships along the Seine as early as 1688. They took their water from the Seine, filtering it through sand.

In 1761, the first hot-water bathing establishment was opened near the Pont de la Tournelle by M. Poitevin. These ships proliferated, offering more and more individual bath-tubs. A glance over the Seine would reveal the entire fleet of Paris baths: Le Bain de la Samaritaine, Le Bain Royal, Le Bain des Fleurs and, for the ladies, Le Bain Henri-IV. In most of these *'Bain à quat' sous'*, so-called because of their low entrance fee, the user could also enjoy bread rolls, sausages, brandy and soup. These baths looked like a floating city on the Seine. Pools for collective bathing did not yet exist.

In 1765 M. Déligny opened an establishment especially for swimmers and created the world's first swimming school, near the Pont de la Concorde, where the pool named after him stands today. A second swimming-pool was opened on the Quai de Béthune at the tip of the Ile Saint-Louis by Petit. These two floating establishments had two revolutionary advantages: they were open to the air and their sloping deep ends made diving possible. There were also changing rooms and a rest area in the stern. The river itself offered no competition since the police had outlawed swimming in the river in 1800 – not because it was dangerous, but because it was indecent.

Establishments offering private bath tubs continued to do business alongside those with communal bathing. In 1823 the Vigier baths had more than 200 bath-tubs in a two-storey building. The water supply still came from the river. At the beginning of the 20th c. there were some 20 or so 'floating baths': the last, the Royale, was closed in 1976 and then sunk. Of the first two swimming-pools, only the Deligny pool remains (→Quai Anatole-France). After numerous refurbishments, it is still very popular, more because of its sunny location than for the pool itself.

▷ The second-hand booksellers: a Parisian way of life

The origin of the word *bouquiniste* (second-hand bookseller) is uncertain: it could derive from the English *book,* or from the German (*Buch*); or perhaps from the smell of goat (*bouc*), from the goatskin used for bookbinding at the time.

Having set up their stalls a short time after the completion of the Pont-Neuf, the second-hand booksellers were periodically driven away by royal decrees. It was only in 1891 that they were authorized to keep their stalls, which had to be of a standard size and color, on the parapet instead of having to take them away each evening. Nowadays the City of Paris regulates the second-hand booksellers who are closely identified with Paris, 'the only town with its library out doors', as Hanotaux used to say. Whereas a number of kiosks are open throughout the winter especially on Sundays, the majority wait for good weather and then stay open all week. Real finds are, however, becoming less frequent and book lovers only rarely get their hands on a much-coveted book.

▷ What to look for in the second-hand book stalls

Left Bank
The Quai de la Tournelle: paperbacks published between 1900 and 1950; science fiction, crime novels; books and magazines for the cinema lover.

The Quai de Montebello: the sea, history, war; old engravings, maps of the world, postcards, old school textbooks, literature, old books, paperbacks from between the wars, engravings, minor manuscripts from the 16th c., antiphonaries.

The Quai Saint-Michel: unusual books, books on crafts, colored engravings, old prints.

The Quai des Grands-Augustins: records (rock, the '60s, jazz), old geographical maps (16th-19th c.), rare maps; *Pléiade editions*, comic strips, works by Daumier, old newspapers, old postcards; history and politics, French and foreign paperbacks; old and modern books: politics, history and romantic literature.

Right Bank
The Quai de la Mégisserie: old photographs, old pens; stamps; pre-war novels, paperbacks, engravings of hunting scenes; literature, philosophy, sociology, English books, French comic strips, American comic books.

The Quai de Gesvres: history, art; cinema, comic strips.

▷ The Paris Port Authority

The Port Autonome de Paris (PAP; Paris Port Authority) was created by the State in 1970 as a result of the administrative division of the region of Paris in order to manage and develop the 300 ports established over the 312 mls./500km of navigable waterways throughout the Ile de France. It is the most important river port in France, second in Europe, and it continues to deal with 15% of the traffic within the City of Paris (discounting the transport of metals). This method of transport is economical, reliable, regular and can take care of the heaviest goods. The PAP's aim is to aid businesses in finding the best solution for transporting their goods. The PAP also regulates the use of the space along the river banks, such as mooring places for residential and leisure barges, and is responsible for rent collection. Its administrative offices are at 2 Quai de la Grenelle.

> ## 'Avaleurs de Nef' (Ship gobblers)

From the 14th to 18th c., a group of more or less stable corporations organized the landing stewards, grain carriers, timber loaders and river pilots, each group had its own duties and privileges. As early as the 14th c. crossing Paris on the Seine had become increasingly difficult, giving rise to the organization of a body of pilots specializing in this work, overseen by the *Prévôt des Marchands* (provost marshal).

They were called *'avaleurs de nef'* (ship gobblers), and were responsible for directing boats through the arches of the bridges, amid the middle of the strong currents. The boats were incapable of navigating the river without these pilots, who took charge of them, one at a time, in order of arrival. On arriving at the port, the landing stewards would take over and secure them to their moorings; the *'planchéeurs'* (plank layers) would then link them to the river bank with a footbridge, after which porters, unloaders and rollers would take charge of the merchandise, once the measurers and tellers had checked the products and the officers of the Hanse had levied taxes on the goods.

Under the *Ancien Régime* the activities of these *'avaleurs'* were made official; they were given the name of *maîtres de pont* (bridge masters) during the 18th c., then *chefs de pont* (bridge foremen) in the 19th c., until they were disbanded in 1854.

> # The Morgue

Set up in 1923 on the Quai de la Rapée in buildings erected in 1914 by the architect Tournaire, the Institut Médico-Légal, which has replaced the old Morgue, is still commonly known by that name. In the past it was open to the public on Sundays and was even a place for family outings. People came to see the corpses that had been found on the roads and the drowned bodies fished from the Seine. A small opening allowed visitors to view the corpses in order to identify them. And this is, indeed, the first meaning of the word: *morguer* means to look, to observe. In fact, before the 17th c. the morgue was a detention center where the accused awaiting trial were incarcerated and searched: at the time it was situated on the ground floor of the Grand Châtelet. The prisoners were closely watched by their *morgués* (guards) not only for supervision, but also in order to commit to memory their faces and any distinctive features. This highly supervised cell was moved to the W side of the building in the 17th c., and the premises were then used to display corpses for identification. The Institut Médico-Légal is now closed to the public.

▷ Fishing in Paris

Contrary to appearances and despite its murky look, the waters of the Seine in Paris are increasingly safe for fish, and the river is home to bream, tench, carp, pike and trout.

Until World War II urban fishing had been an important activity, which declined because of the increasing pollution of the water. Under pressure from fishing societies, the City of Paris made an enormous effort to clean up the water and to restock the river with fish and aquatic plants. Tests are carried out on the water eight times a year; the environment is becoming purer.

The City of Paris has launched operation *Seine propre 1984– 1994* to control the waste matter put in the Seine.

The Union of Parisian Fishermen, which manages all the fishing agreements for the Seine in Paris, has a membership of approximately 3500.

The Latin Quarter**

Since the Middle Ages, with the opening of the first colleges, then of the Sorbonne, this area has been frequented mainly by students. Because learning was exclusively the province of the church it was all in Latin, which the students also spoke among themselves; Rabelais gave the quarter the name it bears to this day.

The scholarly tradition still endures. The greatest *lycées,* numerous schools and scholarly institutes, and the most prestigious Parisian universities have their seats around their illustrious doyen, the Sorbonne.

But the district has changed a lot. Pedestrian precincts filled with Asian restaurants and knickknack shops and hidden streets whose picturesque qualities have been wisely left unspoiled by discreetly luxurious development projects, make us forget that these alleyways around Saint-Séverin and on the slope of the Montaigne Sainte-Geneviève as far as the Place Maubert, were once the haunts of rowdy students and petty crooks. The romantic fiction of the half-starved student toiling by candlelight in a gloomy garret crumbles before the Greek restaurants and opulent shop fronts. Even the Boul'Mich' is not what it was: its cobblestones have disappeared and the cafés full of artists and politicians have given way to fast-food restaurants and enticing ready-to-wear boutiques. Nevertheless the Latin Quarter still has a unique character, inimitably Parisian, thanks to its perpetual activity, day and night, and thanks to the large number of students from all over the world, who come together as at an obligatory crossroads between the library, a café, a lecture hall or film society meeting.

The following tour of the Latin Quarter is divided into three walks, centered around the Saint-Sevérin district, the Montagne Sainte-Geneviève, and the Boulevard Saint-Michel.

Saint-Séverin district*

5th arr./Map ref. 17–A2, A3, B2, B3, 23–A1, B–1
Métro: Saint-Michel
Bus: 24, 47, 63, 86, 87
Taxis: Place Saint-Michel. Tel. 43-29-63-66.
Parking: Place du Parvis-Notre-Dame.

The district around Saint-Séverin is one of the oldest in Paris. Created in the 13th c., its winding medieval alleyways were laid across cultivated fields, after their first proprietors (Mauvoisin, by the Seine; Garlande, further to the S). Development started in 1202, on the fief of Garlande, which belonged to the Abbey of Sainte-Geneviève. Clusters of houses sprang up (Rue Galande, Rue du Fouarre, Rue des Trois Portes and Rue de la Bûcherie). When the University was set up on the Left Bank (1215), numerous residential colleges were built to attract students from the provinces; those for students from Narbonne and Bayeux were in the Rue de la Harpe. The college of Picardy was the last to be opened and was still active under Louis XV.

The network of streets created during the Middle Ages is punctuated by clearings made in the course of the urban development of the second half of the 19th c.: Rue des Ecoles (1854), Rue Lagrange (1887), Rue Dante (1896), Rue Saint-Jacques, Rue Boutebrie as well as the Place Maubert have been widened. The Saint-Séverin quarter has seen great social changes in its time. The commercial and upper middle classes lived here until the 18th c., but the population was much less affluent in the 19th c. – Huysmans in *La Bièvre et Saint-Séverin* (1898) evokes a life of disreputable cabarets and vendors of cooked mussels. The district was so filthy and unhealthy that it came close to being destroyed.

Thanks to restoration it has now taken out a new lease of life, combining its picturesque and commercial aspects. Architectural

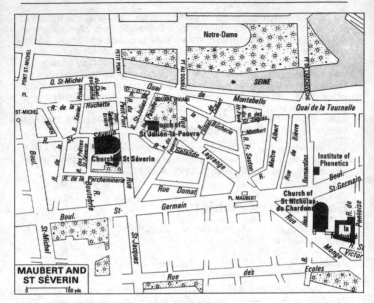

The Saint-Severin district

enthusiasts should make this tour in the morning, since in the evening the streets are too busy.

Tour of the district

1½ hrs.

✝ The Church of Saint-Séverin**

1 Rue des Prêtres–Saint–Séverin
Open Tues. – Sat. 11am–1pm, Sun. 9am–1pm, 3–8pm; closed Mon.
Tel. 43-25-96-63.

The Church of Saint-Séverin, one of the most beautiful in Paris, is especially interesting for its Flamboyant Gothic architecture. It inspired Robert Delaunay to paint a series of famous canvases.

History of the church

Around 1650 in the fields bordering the Seine, an oratory was built to the memory of a hermit called Severius; nothing is known of him except that Clodoald, the future St Cloud, son of Clovis, was his follower. Burnt down by the invading Norsemen, the oratory was replaced by a chapel in the 11th c. Toward the end of the 12th c. the priest Foulque of Neuilly preached the Fourth Crusade from here.

The construction of the present building was begun in the first half of the 13th c., continuing until the 15th c. in the Flamboyant Gothic style of which the church is a perfect example. At the beginning of the 16th c. chapels were opened off the side-aisles and in the broad double ambulatory, the church's most remarkable feature. Like many Parisian churches Saint-Séverin was unfortunately altered in the 17th c. according to current fashion. The choir lost its Gothic characteristics and was redecorated by J. B. Tuby from designs by Le Brun (1682–83). All this was paid for at vast expense by Mlle de Montpensier, 'la Grande Mademoiselle', eccentric daughter of Gaston d'Orléans who, having quarrelled with her own parish church, Saint-Sulpice, adopted Saint-Séverin. It was during this time that the 15th-c. rood screen disappeared. Closed in 1793 and used as a gunpowder and saltpeter warehouse, and then a granary, the church was not reconsecrated until 1803. In 1837 the portal from the church of Saint-Pierre-aux-Boeufs in the Ile-de-la-Cité was transferred to Saint-Séverin's façade, when that church was demolished to make way for the Rue d'Arcole. From 1840 to 1870 several artists were brought in to decorate the side chapels: Paul and H. Flandrin, Signol, Schnetz, Gérome, Biennoury, and others.

The exterior

The portal of the W front or main façade (Rue des Prêtes-Saint-Séverin), dating from the mid-13th c. (see above), is surmounted by a tympanum with Ramus' *Virgin and Child Between Two Angels* 1839; the door panels with Peter and Paul are 17th c. On the NW corner of the main façade is a 13th c. square tower two storeys high with large Gothic bays, framed by slender columns; its pinnacled turret and balustrade are 15th c. On the N side is a door which, until 1839, was the main entrance; the tympanum has a bas-relief by Maillot: *St Martin of Tours Giving half his Cloak to a Beggar* (1853). A niche in the corner beside it holds a statue of St-Séverin by Thomas (1847) on a Flamboyant dais.

By walking round the church via Rue Saint-Sévern and Rue Saint-Jacques you can see the Flamboyant arcades above the chapels decorated with gargoyles shaped like birds and animals. On the S side of the church (Rue de la Parcheminerie) are the rib-vaulted galleries of the charnel houses of Saint-Séverin (15th c.).

In 1428 the *Oeuvre Saint-Séverin,* the church's charitable foundation belonging to (Abbots des Eschallis) bought the *hôtel* to create a cemetery on the site. Three galleries were built: the W gallery where the bones were interred, was not finished until 1608. This type of cemetery (another is at Saints-Innocents) is very old and probably derived from the Roman atrium, as the word *aître* indicates (*Aître Saint-Maclou,* for example, the Saint-Maclou cemetery in Rouen). The faithful also called them *paradisius,* from which the word *parvis* (the square) in front of a church, comes. Part of these galleries was demolished in the 19th c. The gables date from restorations carried out around 1920.

The interior

The nave. The organ case* was built by the cabinet maker Dupré with carvings by Fichon (1745); the organ loft is closed off by an elegant wrought-iron rail. The instrument, which goes back to the 18th c. and still has its original stops, was greatly admired by Fauré and Saint-Saëns, both of whom played on it. In 1962 it was completely restored, and again, partially, in 1982.

The first three bays are 13th-c. and the next five 15th c.; the difference in style is very noticeable. The adaptation of the later construction to the earlier can be seen in the way in which the ribs of the double arches fall back on the 13th c. columns. The rose window in the W façade has the most beautiful stained glass in the church; it shows The Tree of Jesse (early 16th c.), but is unfortunately hidden by the organ. The windows in the first three bays have late 14th-c. stained glass, restored in the 19th c. They are from Saint-Germain-des-Prés and depict large figures of the apostles. The windows of the following bays and those in the apse have stained glass from the second half of the 15th c.

The r. side-aisle and its chapels. The side chapels are covered with murals commissioned by the City of Paris in the 19th c. 1st chapel: *The Baptism of Christ* and *The Preaching of John the Baptist* by P. Flandrin (1843). 2nd chapel: *The Life of St. Anne* by Heim (1849). 3rd chapel: *The Marriage of the Virgin* and *Flight into Egypt* by Signol (1845). 4th chapel: *The Life of St Andrew* by Schnetz (1849); a door leads to the charnel house. 5th chapel: *St Paul and St Peter* by Biennourt (1850), 6th chapel: *St Mary Magdalene* by Murat (1844). The stained glass of the triforium is by Emile Hirsch (1876).

The chancel. The chancel has no transept; it was modernized in the 17th c. by Le Brun. The pointed Gothic arches were changed into rounded arcades. Only three of these have retained their marble cladding, by Tuby (17th c.).

The double ambulatory and chapels. The chapels of the side-aisles were decorated with murals in the 19th c. 7th chapel: paintings by H. Flandrin (1840). 8th chapel: *Life of St Geneviève* by Alexandre

Hesse (1850). 11th chapel: *Adam and Eve Chased from Paradise* by Mottez (1865). 12th chapel: *The Communion of St Jerome*, and *Les Pestifières de Marseille* (The Plague-stricken from Marseilles) by Gérôme (1850). 10th chapel: *The Virgin and the Infant Jesus* by Bridan (18th c.), a door leads into the chapel built by J. Hardouin-Mansart (1673). The double ambulatory is a rare feature in Parisian churches, most of which follow the influence of Notre-Dame. Built from 1489 to 1494, it is a Flamboyant Gothic masterpiece. Eight slender columns surround the central pillar. The complex ribs separate into abundant sheaves like a mass of vegetation (they have been compared to a grove of palm trees) gives a striking impression of lightness and dynamism. In the chapels of the apse stained glass by Jean Bazaine (1966) depicts the Seven Sacraments.

Against the wall of the tower above the holy water stoup is an inscription to the memory of Bertrand Ogeron, governor of Haiti from 1664 to 1675, who died in the parish in 1676. To the l. of the entrance: *St Luke writing the Gospels*, 17th-c. painting from the French school. The 16th c. chapels extend for two bays; the 19th c. murals have almost completely disappeared. 2nd chapel: red marble high altar (17th c.) probably executed when the pillars were clad in marble. Above the sacristy door is a picture of *St Paul* by Claude Vignon (17th c.) In the sacristy: *The Crucifixion***, painting on wood by Peter Bruegel the Younger.

Rue des Prêtres-Saint-Séverin

This medieval street was enlarged by royal edict in 1837. The l. side is taken up by the church and its Neo-Gothic presbytery (alterations from 1913 to 1922). A children's library is on the r. side of the street. During construction work in 1973 Merovingian sarcophogi were discovered.

Rue de la Parcheminerie

In the Middle Ages this street was full of life, thronged with professional letter writers, booksellers, copyists, parchment sellers (hence its name). This street of intellectuals was then called the Rue des Ecrivains (Writers' Street). No. 29 is a Louis XV house built for Claude Dubuisson, Comptroller of the Mint (note the windows, keystones, friezes, balconies, and inner staircase). Also note no. 28, an old house with, on the ground floor, inventory tablets from two medieval shops. In 1906 the street lost many old houses when the Rue Saint-Jacques was widened.

The Square André-Lefevre, which was created in 1923, is on the S side of the Saint-Séverin charnel house. Two beautiful catalpa trees frame a bust of Emile Verhaeren (1855-1916), a French-speaking Flemish poet (bronze by C. Scrouvens).

Rue Boutebrie. This 13th-c. street (its name is a corruption of Erembourg de Brie) still has some of the oldest houses in the *quartier* on the even-numbered side. No. 6 is a beautiful gabled house (16th c.) No. 8 has four storeys and a staircase inside (hard to see) from the late 16th c., decorated with large plant motifs. On the N side is a Louis XIII house at no. 10. The famous manuscript illuminator Honoré lived in the street at the end of the 13th c.

Take Boul. Saint-Germain, which, in this section, has absorbed the old Rue du Foin, before turning r. into the Rue de la Harpe.

Rue de la Harpe

Known first as the Via Inferior because it ran parallel to Rue Saint-Jacques, this ancient street was for centuries frequented by students, because the thermal baths (*les thermes*) and the colleges of the Montagne Saint-Geneviève stood there; the street joined Rue Monsieur-le-Prince. Its S end was absorbed in 1855 during the expansion of the Boul. Saint-Michel. The street takes its name from a sign depicting King David. For a long time now, the section between the Rue Saint-Séverin and Rue la Huchette has been known as the Petite-Bouclerie.

Today it is a pedestrian precinct teeming with life; in 1948 it already had the cabaret, La Rose Rouge, which soon moved to Saint-Germain-des-Prés. The odd-numbered side of the street is lined with fine 17th-c. mansions (nos. 23, 27, 29, 51, 53). No. 47 is a beautiful 18th-c. house. No. 45 is a large mansion from the mid-18th c. (wrought-ironwork and mascarons on the street side and on the courtyard). No. 35 was built in the Louis XV period (arcades with mascarons and a tympanum at mezzanine level lavishly sculpted in wood). Mme Roland, the revolutionary whose house was the chief *salon* of the Girondists, was arrested in this street on June 2, 1793. Between the Rue Saint-Séverin and Rue de la Huchette are old houses at nos. 15, 5, 12, 10, and 8.

Rue Saint-Séverin

This part of the street, between the Rue de la Harpe and the Boul. Saint-Michel, dates from 1855 and the creation of the Boul. Saint-Germain. In the 1960s, the little district of Saint-Séverin became the model for the renovation of the old quarter of the city, which had previously involved the almost total destruction of a given area. This 'islet' of city blocks following a 13th-c. plan stretched from the Seine to the Boul. Saint-Germain, and from Rue de Poissy to the Boul. Saint-Michel. The architects Albert Laprade and Claude Charpentier wanted 'to make perceptible a type of architecture without which the quality of life would be unthinkable'.

COLOR SECTION

Arc de Triomphe *(Photo: G.A.D.)*

The Grande Arche, La Défense *(Photo: V.C.L.)*

MAPS OF PARIS

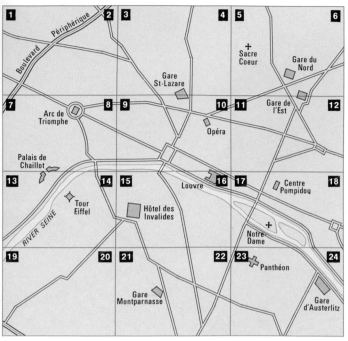

0   100   200   300   400   500 yards

5 miles = 1 inch

▬▬	Principal Road	✈	Airport terminal
▬▬	Principal shopping street	*Palais de l'Elysée*	Building of interest
┼┼┼	No entry street	*Ministère du Travail*	Public building
▬▬	Pedestrian street	✛	Religious building
GARE DE L'EST	Main line railway station		Park or garden
BALARD ○	Underground station	MATHURINS ✴	Theatre
OPERA ●	Underground interchange	COURREGES	Shopping store
PORT ROYAL ○	R.E.R. station	BRITISH AIRWAYS ▲	Useful address
JAVEL ◗	R.E.R. and Underground interchange	TOURISME SNCF ☆	Information bureau

© GEORGE PHILIP LTD. 1989

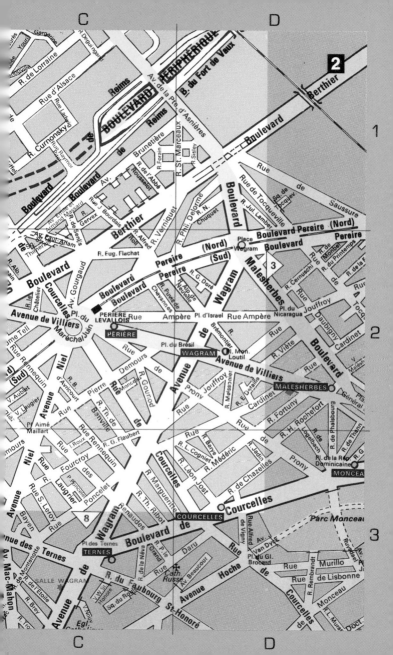

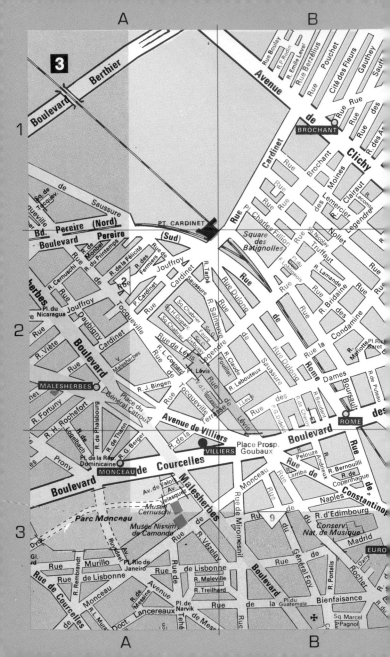

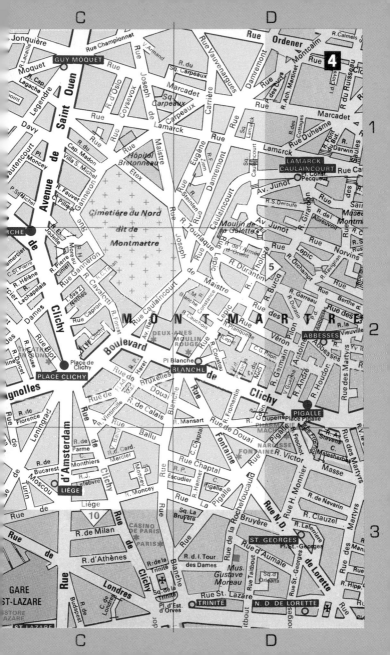

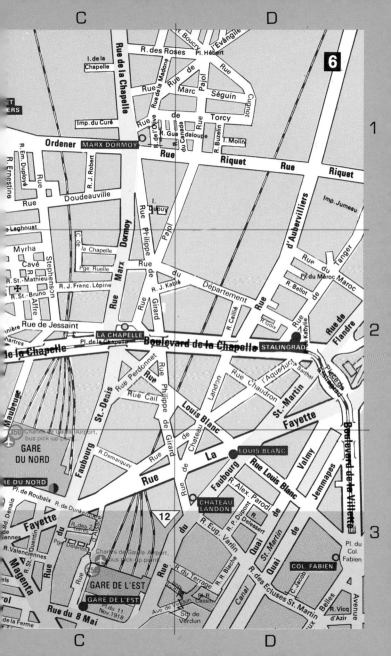

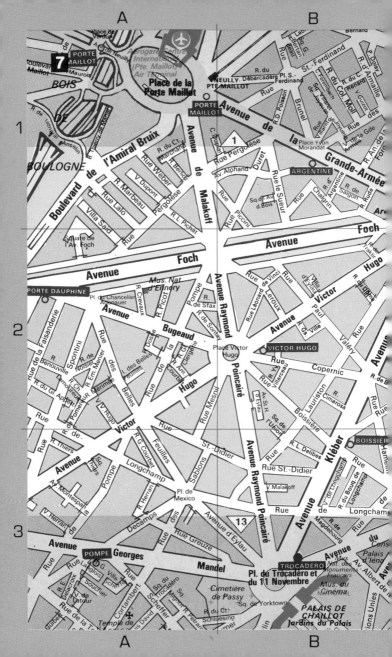

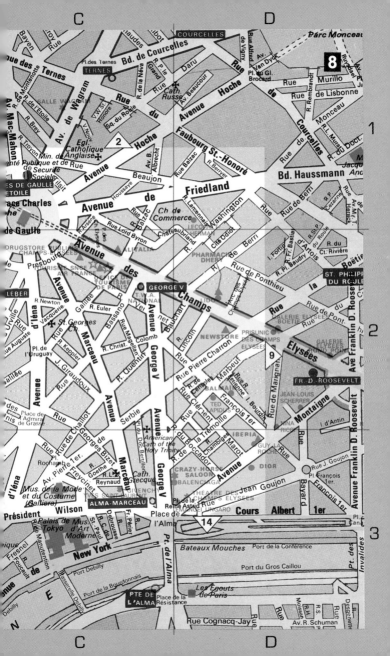

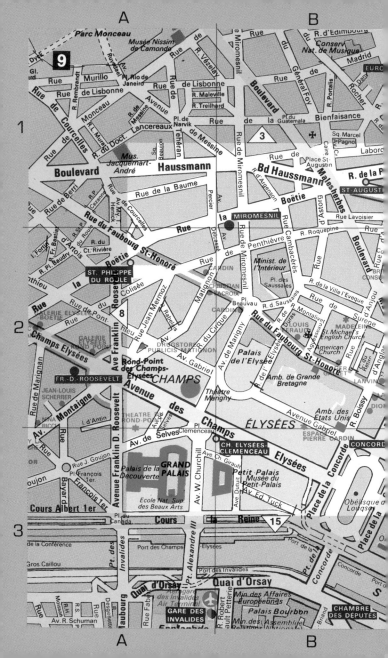

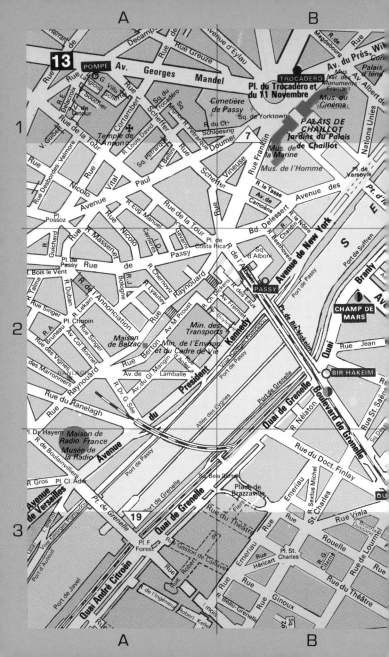

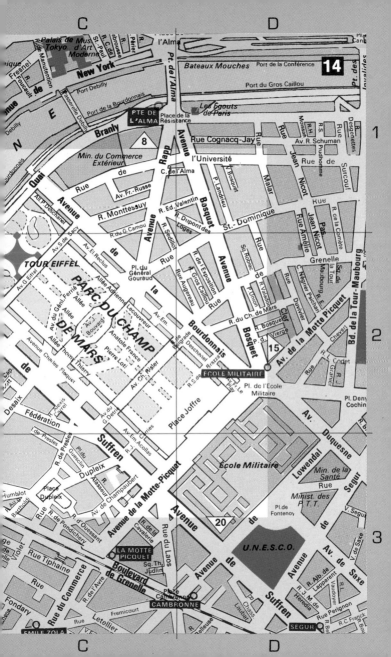

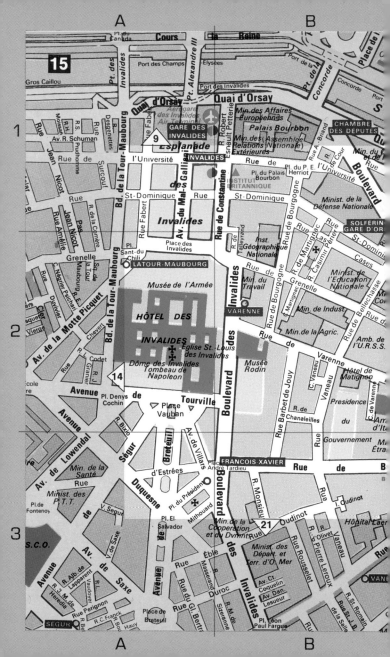

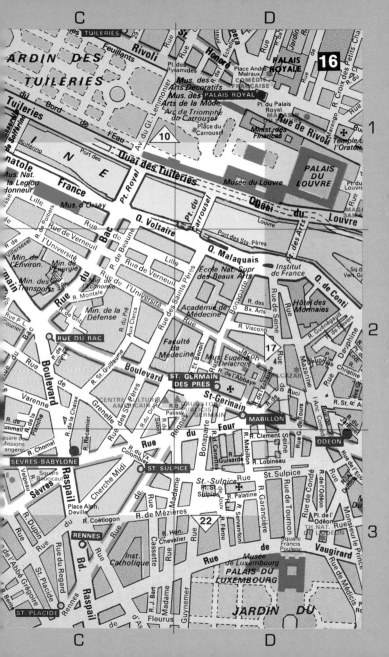

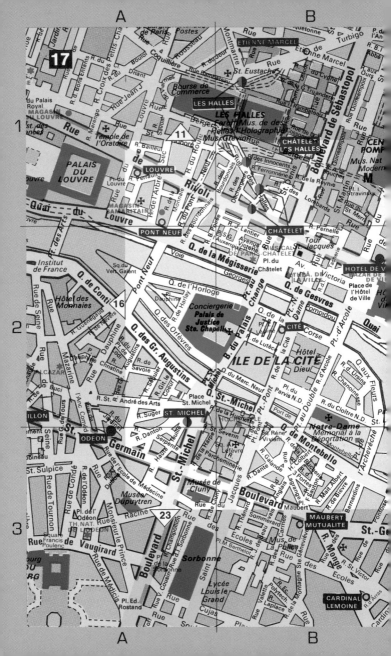

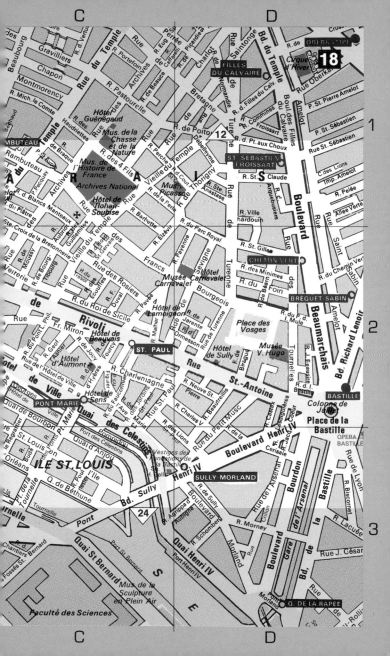

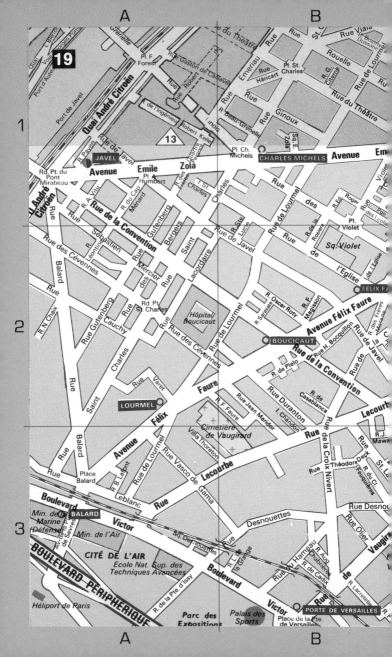

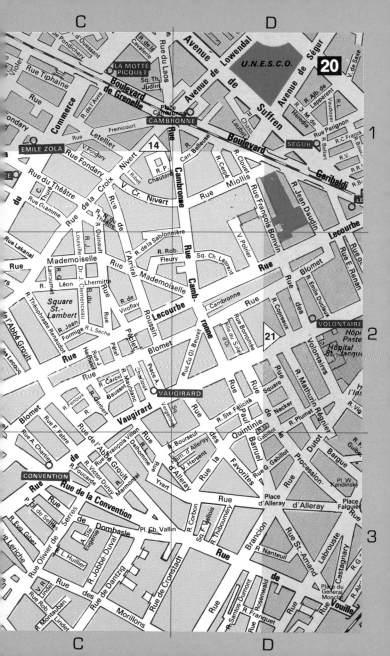

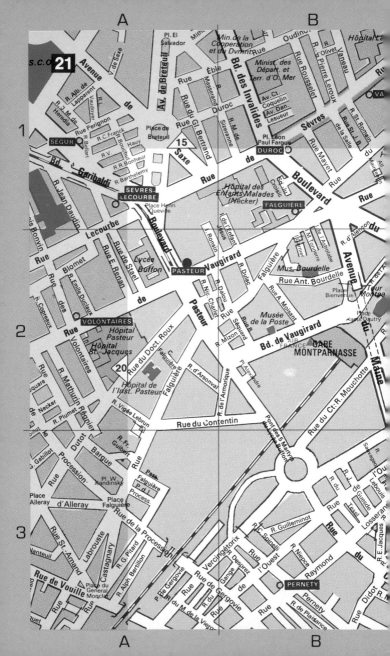

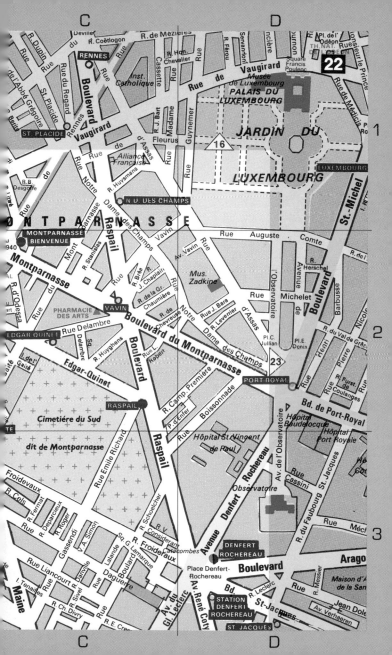

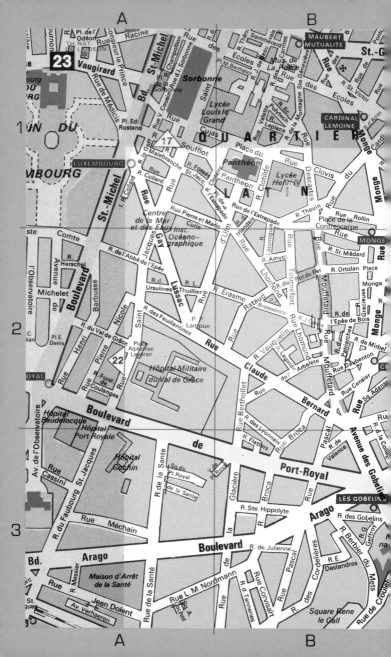

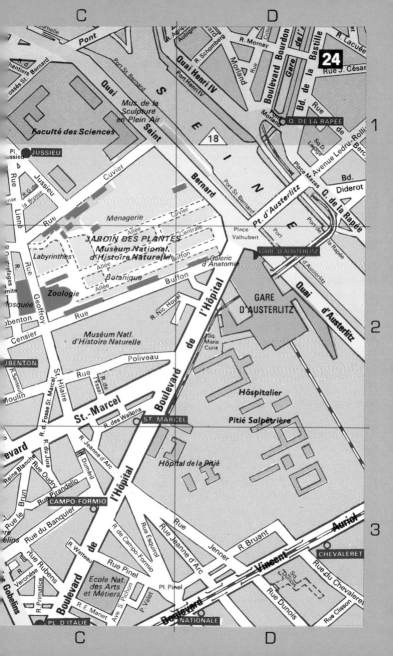

The Eiffel Tower from the Place de la Concorde *(Photo: D. Wimsett)*

Forum des Halles *(Photo: A. Rye)*

The Louvre

The Pyramid *(Photo: V.C.L.)*

The interior of the Pyramid
(Photo: B. Bansse)

Overleaf
Pompidou Centre
(Photo: J. C. Davies)

No. 34 is a beautiful *hôtel* dating from the mid 18th c. (wrought iron, dormer windows on the street, mascarons and two iron staircases in the courtyard). In this street, be sure constantly to look up at the balconies, wrought ironwork and fanlights of these houses (nos. 20, 16, 14, 12, 8, 4 from the 17th and 18th c.). No. 14 is from the Louis XIV period, recently restored. At no. 13, above a cinema, note the carved stone sign: *Au Cygne de la Croix* (the Swan of the Cross). The narrowest house in Paris is no. 12, which was the home of the Abbé Prévost, author of *Manon Lescaut*. Level with no. 4 *bis* is the cul-de-sac Salembrière (private, and closed by an iron gate), from the first half of the 13th c. Its name comes from the Salimbene family, undoubtedly of Italian origin, who owned the mansion.

Reach the Rue Xavier-Privas, to the r. of Rue Saint-Séverin, by retracing your steps. Built in 1219, this was for a long time the chief street of the leather-trade. In 1929 it was named after the poet-singer Xavier Privas. Nearly all the houses date from 17th or 18th c. The three 18th-c. mascarons at no. 20 are from the original façade. The 17th-c. house at no. 5 has a wooden sign carved in high relief showing a cockerel in the moulding.

Rue de la Huchette

This street is nearly 800 years old and has kept the same name since the 13th c. It was known above all for its diamond cutters, and for the *rôtisseurs* who sold roasted meat. The shop sign of La Huchette (a small flat-topped chest) is probably the origin of the name. The street crosses the Clos de Laas. In the 13th and 14th c. the Parisian residence of the abbots of Pontigny was on the N side. After the Liberation it gained a certain notoriety when Americans, following in the footsteps of Hemingway and Henry Miller, came to the charming Hôtel de Mont-Blanc. This mansion was also a haven of peace for Pablo Neruda when he was the Chilean ambassador to Paris.

Today a pedestrian zone, half-Greek half-Asiatic, it has preserved some beautiful 18th-c. wrought ironwork from the time when it was the preserve of foreign ambassadors. Make a detour to the r. to appreciate the street in its entirety. No. 23 is the Théâtre de la Huchette, opened in 1948. In 1957 it put on two plays by Ionesco, *La cantatrice chauve* (The Bald Primadonna) and *Le Leçon* (The Lesson), both of which are still playing the longest record in French contemporary theater. The Louis XIV façade of no. 14 has been whitewashed; it has a black marble *Y* which was the sign of a haberdasher-hosier. Nos. 17 and 15 are mid-8th c. The 17th-c. staircase has been preserved inside no. 11, which used to be the Restaurant Bouillon, described by Huysman as 'the Café Anglais of down-and-outs and the destitute'. Between the two World Wars it was replaced by a famous black *bal-musette* (popular dance-hall with accordion music). No. 10, where Bonaparte lived, was built in the mid 18th c. At no. 4 a stone sign *A la Hure d'Or* (The Golden Boar's Head) can still be made out, on a tablet fixed to the façade of the 18th-c. building.

Rue du Chat–qui–pêche (the Fishing Cat) has not changed since its creation at the end of the 18th c. It is still as narrow, approximately 8ft/2.5m, as dark and as dirty. Though not picturesque, it still attracts tourists. For some time parking has been forbidden on both sides of the street.

Place du Petit–Pont. The Petit Châtelet, a fortress protecting the Left Bank from incursions, was rebuilt in stone by Charles V in the 14th c. Charles VI housed the Provost of Paris there. Having been used for a long time as a prison, the Petit Châtelet was pulled down in 1782, to make way for modifications to the Hôtel–Dieu and the development of the Place du Petit–Pont.

Rue du Petit-Pont

This street was created in the 12th c. at the end of the bridge of the same name. Several of the houses show signs of its refurbishment in the 18th and 19th c.; note the windows and wrought ironwork at nos. 5, 7, 9 and 15. Nos. 9 and 11 have been recently restored. The street was widened in 1907, and only the houses on the odd numbered side are original. For a short stretch the Rue du Petit-Pont is the first section of the Rue Saint–Jacques.

In the Rue Saint–Jacques, there is a beautiful 18th-c. house (no. 21) at the end of the courtyard. For the continuation of Rue Saint–Jacques, →the Montagne Saint–Genevieve.

Rue Galande

This ancient street takes its name from the fief of Garlande. Formerly it was the Lyons–Paris Roman way which led towards the Gobelias and Italie districts. In the 17th c., it was widened and became chic, with opulent houses where the nobility and gentry lived. But in the following century it went downhill and was known for its infamous taverns.

At the corner of the Rue Saint–Julien–le–Pauvre and Rue Galande (56 Rue Galande), the sign of the *Trois Mailletz* (Three Mallets) hangs above the door of a nightclub appropriately recalling the house in the name of Maillet, known to have stood here in 1465.

No. 52, the Caveau des Oubliettes nightclub, is a 17th-c. house built on medieval foundations; it has a winding staircase well worth seeing. On the Saint–Julien–le–Pauvre side, the medieval appearance was added in the 19th c. – fake half-timbering and little false windows with ogive arches. The cellars are the home of the old

■ French *chanson*. They also contain a small museum of instruments of torture (open to patrons only, from 9pm to 2am) with a *grand guignol* atmosphere.

The boutique Le Chat Huant is at no. 50, in a medieval house restored in the 17th c.; it still has a beautiful triple-coved winding staircase (admission by advance request). Behind the façade of nos. 59–61, dating from 1910, is a fine stairwell with wooden banisters, possibly 17th c. (access limited to inhabitants of the building). No. 65 has the restored façade of a former noble residence; it was the *hôtel* of the Châtillon family in the 16th c.; of Lamoignin, the first president of the French Parlement, in the 17th c. and of Lesseville in the 18th c.

No. 46 is the Auberge des Deux Signes (Inn of the Two Signs) which has some precious archeological features: the great Gothic windows with pointed arches of the W gable from the chapel of Saint-Blaise, and a beautiful old well and a spiral staircase from the Priory of Saint-Julien leads down to vaulted cellars. The Saint-Blaise chapel was the refectory of Saint-Julien-le-Pauvre when the church was a priory affiliated with Longpont. In 1476 the stonemasons and carpenters established their confraternity there. It was partially rebuilt in 1684; destroyed except for the façade in 1770.

On the façade of no. 42, now a cinema, a bas-relief shows St Julian the Hospitaller in his boat. Old houses at nos. 31 and 29 are probably 16th c. No. 31 still has its projecting gables and sculpted pike (this fish was a popular image).

Rue des Anglais already existed in the reign of Philippe Auguste, and owes its name to the English students who lodged here in the Middle Ages; late in the medieval period, the abbots of Pontigny had their residence on the E side. The street has been greatly altered by the creation of the Boul. Saint-Germain.

Rue Domat

This is the former Rue de Plâtre. Its old houses on the odd-numbered side were demolished in 1860. An alley at no. 12a (no longer passable) still retains vestiges of the Collège de Cornouailles founded in 1317 for Breton students and was rebuilt in the 18th c. La Cornouaille, the oldest and most traditional part of Brittany, is also the French name for Cornwall; the Bretons are ethnically closest to the Welsh and the extinct Cornish tribes. To the S the street was the boundary of the Jewish cemetery of the Rue Galande, the existence of which is verified by a 13th-c. charter (the Jews were expelled in 1394).

Turn r. into Rue Dante (completed 1901).

Rue du Fouarre

One of the most famous streets of medieval Paris, created at the end of the 12th c. and the first street that really belonged to the University which has completely disappeared, this was originally called Rue des Escholiers (the old word for scholars). However, the people called it Rue Trou-Punais (Filthy Hole) - which requires no explanation. The name *Fouarre* comes from *feure*, an archaic word for straw, which refers to the straw on which the students from the local colleges sat during lectures. Tradition has it that Dante was one of them, perhaps in 1304.

At no. 8 note the wrought ironwork and mascarons from the beginning of the 18th c. (the shell of the building is older). Rue du Fouarre, which originally began at the Quai de Montebello, has been considerably shortened, and only a few old houses remain on the even-numbered side, including no. 8, and only one house (modern), on the odd-numbered side. The College of the Nation of Picardy, which still existed under Louis XV, also stood on that side at the corner of Rue Galande. Rue de Fouarre runs into Rue Lagrange.

The Square René-Viviani

This square, named after the President of the Council at the start of World War I and the result of enlarging an earlier small churchyard belonging to Saint-Julien-le-Pauvre, is surrounded by lime trees and lilacs. It owes its existence to the demolition of an annex of the Hôtel-Dieu hospital built in the 17th c. and destroyed in 1909. The false acacia or robinia planted by the botanist Robin in 1601 is the doyen of Parisian trees; it has to be supported by a prop. A stone sarcophagus, possibly from an archeological dig in the neighborhood, was placed at the side of the Rue Saint-Julien-le-Pauvre. Other stone fragments came from the restorations of Notre-Dame. There is a remarkable view of the cathedral from here.

⚓ The Church of Saint-Julien-le-Pauvre**

Rue Saint-Julien-le-Pauvre
9am - 1pm, 2:30 - 6:30pm.

This ancient sanctuary, built on the pilgrims' route to the sanctuary of St James of Compostela, in Santiago de Compostela, has become one of the capital's most venerated churches. From earliest times there was an oratory on this site dedicated to St Julian the Hospitaller (also known as the Poor), but perhaps also to the 3rd-c. martyr, St Julien de Brioude. The oratory quickly became a church, to which was added a hospice for pilgrims and penniless travellers. The church and the hospice were ravaged several times by the

Norsemen during the 9th c. Around 1165 to 1170, the monks of the Abbey of Longpont, daughter-house of Cluny, rebuilt the sanctuary as a priory. In the time of Petrarch, Maître Albert and Villon, the University held its official meetings in the priory. The church was ransacked by anti-establishment students in 1524, and university meetings were barred. In 1563 it became the chapel of the Hôtel-Dieu hospital, but by the 17th c. it had become so damaged that it was partly demolished. It was rebuilt shortly afterward and acquired its present façade. During the Revolution it was used to store animal fodder. Since 1889 the Church of Saint-Julien-le-Pauvre has belonged to the Greek Orthodox Church with the liturgy of St John Chrysostom.

Outwardly the church looks like a country church, without flying buttresses and Gothic in style but still showing Romanesque influence. Huge buttresses support the small projecting side-chapels that surround the apse, and modillians (small brackets similar to the original ones) now support the roof.

Inside, the church consists of a nave with four bays but no transept, and two side-aisles. It was covered over in the 17th c. with heavy semicircular vaulting; the vaulting of the S aisle was restored, but that of the N aisle, which is one bay longer than the S aisle, is intact. The whole of the chancel is like a small-scale Notre-Dame. Its two bays are covered with sexpartite vaulting. The piers have admirable capitals (acanthus, harpies). The apse has notable cross vaults and is enclosed and flanked by two projecting side-chapels from the earlier church. It is built in three sections, each pierced with windows and with two superimposed bays of unequal length. In the S side-aisle, tombstone inscriptions from the 15th c. (in the chapel a marble Virgin, modern); at the high altar a medieval bas-relief. In the N side-aisle, a fine 17th-c. cast-iron lectern; a 16th-c. *Crucifixion* in low-relief. The iconostasis depicts a *deesis* (image of supplication) by an artist from Damascus. Several types of *deesis* exist, but Christ is always to be found in the center of the composition with (on either side and in attitudes of supplication) the Virgin and St John the Baptist, or St Peter and St Paul, or even the archangels Gabriel and Michael. Near the portal* is an old well formerly inside the church and, in front of the entrance to the Caveau des Oubliettes, a large paving stone from the Roman road from Paris to Orléans, found in 1927 opposite the Collège de France in the Rue Saint-Jacques.

Rue Saint-Julien-le-Pauvre

Established in the 13th c., this narrow street was enlarged by the extension of the Square Viviani. The houses on the even-numbered side are old and beautiful. At no. 16 is a 17th-c. arcade; at no. 14, the mansion of Isaac de Laffemas, who was governor of the Petit Châtelet; this *hôtel* has a magnificent portal* from the end of the

17th c. - try to see the façade on the courtyard, the pediments and overhanging dormer windows. Nos. 10, 6 and 4 are houses built in the 17th and 18th c. on medieval foundations. All these houses were constructed above three levels of cellars belonging to the Petit Châtelet.

Rue de la Bûcherie

Up to the Rue de Hôtel-Colbert.

Established in 1202 near the Port aux Bûches (known since the 16th c. as the Quai de la Rapée), this was the wood merchants' street. It is cut off today by the Square René-Viviani and lined with houses that saw the Petit Châtelet razed to the ground in 1782.

The bookshop Shakespeare and Co. at no. 37 is a meeting place for intellectuals and poets from all over the world. George Whitman, the owner, is the grandson of the American poet Walt Whitman. He nearly always has the book you want.

The first Faculty of Medicine (1472-1775) of which a late 15th-c. building survives (corner of Rue de l'Hôtel-Colbert). The rotunda, an old amphitheater* (to visit, enquire at the Paris *Mairie*) was built in 1744 by Barbier de Blinière and is attached to the NE corner of the Gothic hall, without closing off any of its entrances, except at the base of the E side. The Danish anatomist J. B. Winslow (b. at Odense, 1669) gave his inaugural lecture here. Inside, the frieze of the circular entablature, supported by eight Doric columns, is decorated with cocks, storks and pelicans, traditional medical emblems. Restoration became necessary in 1903. Today the building is an administrative office for professional training for the City of Paris.

Rue de l'Hôtel-Colbert, mentioned in 13th-c. records, was called until 1829 Rue des Rats, perhaps through corruption of the name of the Hôtel d'Arras which may have stood here. There are several fine 17th-c. *hôtels* including nos. 12 and 14, the latter with a pair of bricked-up dormer windows.

A little further up on the l. is the beginning of the Rue de Trois-Portes which existed as early as the 13th c.; the three doors are thought originally to have been gates preventing access to the street, in order to protect its inhabitants from the rogues and students of the Rue du Fouarre.

Return to the Rue de la Bûcherie; the façade of no. 11 is decorated with garlands, surmounted by a pediment. Note the pediments and wrought ironwork of nos. 9 and 7, built in the 17th and 18th c. respectively. No. 9 has an old well in the courtyard.

Rue Frédéric-Sauton. Before 1806 this was the Rue du Pavé of the Place Maubert. It was renamed Frédéric-Sauton in 1912, after a former municipal councillor of the district. The street has a series of old houses; most of their cellars communicate with those of the Rue Maître–Albert.

The Impasse Maubert

The College of Constantinople, the first of the Parisian colleges, was situated here, built in 1206 by the Patriarch of Constantinople, at the time of an attempted reunification of the Greek and Latin churches. Long the haunt of petty thieves and tramps, this area is now inhabited by students, the middle class and aristocrats, a fact that is not always apparent at first sight. At no. 4 Godin de Sainte-Croix had his 'poisoning laboratory'. One of his most faithful clients was the notorious Marquise de Brinvilliers (*ca.* 1630–76), who murdered her father and two brothers in order to secure the family fortune for herself and her adulterous lover, causing a scandal that ignited the infamous Poison Affair; she was finally beheaded and burnt.

Place Maubert. The Rue Frédéric-Sauton ends in this square, whose colorful market obliterates its sinister history (→Montagne Sainte-Geneviève).

Rue Maître-Albert

For a long time this street was known as Rue Perdue (Lost Street). The Collège Saint-Michel had an entrance on the odd-numbered side; in the 19th c. the street was renamed, after the famous Dominican scholar Albert the Great, who taught in the Place Maubert in the 13th c. Once a haunt of beggars, the street has since 1975 become decidedly gentrified - galleries, artists' studios, craft shops and the renovation of old comfortable homes have transformed the whole area. The 17th-c. *hôtel* at no. 7 is the finest house in the street. Zamor, the black servant boy who betrayed Mme du Barry, died at no. 13. No. 14 is another fine 17th-c. mansion. All these houses and those in the neighboring streets are linked by subterranean passages.

Before reaching the quays, cross the Rue des Grands-Degrés, where Voltaire was a lawyer's clerk.

Follow the Quai de la Tournelle to the r.

Rue de Bièvre

This street dates from 1250. It took its name from the branch of the river that enters the Seine nearby (→Gobelins). Once idyllic, it became a haunt of tramps, drunks and rag-and-bone men and remained so until 1950. Today it has recovered a certain dignity, since politicians moved in to find peace and quiet. The houses have been meticulously restored and a garden laid out. No. 12 is an old outbuilding of the Collège de Chanac, founded in 1348, originally dedicated to St Michael (note the statuette of the archangel slaying the dragon above the entrance door).

▷ Commissions from the City of Paris in the 19th c.

The Revolution had emptied the churches. When the freedom to worship was returned under the Consulate, celebrations resumed in buildings stripped of all finery. From the start of the Restoration until the first few years of the Third Republic, successive régimes endeavored to return to the churches some of their former splendor. Many paintings and sculptures were put back in place. On the initiative of the Comte de Chabrol, Prefect of the Seine from 1814 to 1830, who enjoyed the total confidence of Louis XVIII and Charles X, the City of Paris began to commission works annually to redecorate the churches.

The first commissions were huge canvases, such as those that still adorn the nave of Saint–Jean–Saint–François (→Marais, Archives). After 1820, the municipality commissioned more and more murals. Eclectic in its choice, the Service des Beaux–Arts de la Ville favored no particular movements. The heirs of Davidist Classicism (Drolling, Granger) were invited to work in the churches as well as the archaizing mystics (Orsel, Périn, the disciples of Ingres Flandrin, Signol) and certain Romantics (Delacroix, Chassériau, Achille Devéria). An equal number of commissions went to a variety of sculptors, from the austere Ottin to the fiery Préault.

The 19th c. saw a great flowering of religious art, following the long period of contempt, during which all manifestations of the art were dismissed under the general epithet of *sulpicien*. Today, the great variety produced by this movement is there to be rediscovered, thanks in large part to the many commissions granted by the City of Paris.

▣ Museums to visit

Musée de l'Assistance Publique (Museum of Public Assistance, 7 Quai de la Tournelle): the history of Parisian hospitals.

Musée de la Table. Restaurant de la Tour d'Argent, 15 Quai de la Tournelle: Table settings and gastronomy.

▷ Not to be missed

The Hôtel de Cluny and the thermal baths.
The Sorbonne.

The Panthéon, Place Soufflot and Rue Soufflot.
The rood screen at Saint-Etienne-du-Mont.
The Henri IV Lycée.
The Churches of Saint-Séverin and Saint-Julien-le-Pauvre.

▷ ## The old houses of Paris

The Saint-Séverin district, which still has several 16th-c. houses, is
one of the oldest of the capital. It is difficult to date with any
certainty houses built in a similar fashion in the course of several
centuries. In the 3rd arrondissement, the house at 3 Rue Volta was
reputed to date from the 14th c.; a recent study showed it to have
been built from 1644 to 1654 – proof of the durability of construction
in wood.

By a statute of August 18, 1667, the Treasurers of France made the
owners coat the surfaces of buildings with wooden walls with
plaster, to protect against fire. 'In the future we charge the proprietors to cover the wooden surfaces with lathe, nails, and plaster,
inside as well as outside, in such a way that they are in a state to be
able to resist fire. . . .'

It is not known how effective the regulation was, but it is sometimes
possible to recognize a timber-framed house beneath the plaster of
its façade. The house at 6 Rue Boutebrie, which can be compared to
31 Rue Galande, illustrates how a projecting gable can be buried in
plaster. Furthermore, in the 17th and 18th c. old houses were often
modernized, which entailed piercing additional windows, building
additional storeys or altering the decoration of the façades by
adding string courses or wrought-iron brackets.

The Montagne Sainte-Geneviève**

5th arr./Map ref. 17-A2, A3, B2, B3
Métro: Saint-Michel, Maubert-Mutalité
Bus: 21, 27, 63, 85, 86, 87
Parking: Opposite 37 Boul. Saint-Germain
Taxis: Place Saint-Michel. Tel. 43-29-63-66
Market: Place Maubert, Tues., Thurs., Sat. 7am – 1:30pm

The Montagne Sainte-Geneviève was originally the town founded
by the Romans, to counterbalance the Gallic town on the Ile de la
Cité. In the Middle Ages the area reverted to a country village except
for a number of churches (the biggest was the Abbaye Saint-
Geneviève founded in the Merovingian period), which no doubt

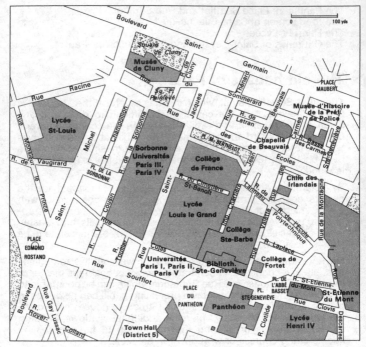

Sainte-Geneviève District

became the focal points for urban development from the 12th and 13th c. onward. Later, the district was organized around the colleges, forming a dense network of courtyards, backyards, chapels and so on.

The only major development in the 18th c. was the construction of the Panthéon and its surrounding buildings; the area had until then been occupied by gardens and vineyards belonging to the abbey. The Rue Soufflot, begun in the 18th c. but only finished in the 19th, completed, with the Rue des Ecoles, the street system organized around the two main N–S axes: the Rue Saint-Jacques and the Rue de la Harpe. Both streets were widened, the Rue de la Harpe becoming the Boulevard Saint-Michel, and losing most of its past in the process.

Tour of the district

3 hrs.

This walk begins in Gallo-Roman Paris, at the Cluny Roman baths, and climbs towards the Panthéon through the University district, ending at the approaches to the Church of Saint-Nicolas-du-Chardonnet.

The whole district, clinging to the sides of the Montagne Sainte-Geneviève, is crisscrossed with steeply climbing streets and lanes, their walls sometimes covered in Virginia creeper or ivy, their houses built tall, with courtyards front and back. You will find yourself continually retracing your steps, pushing through a doorway to take just a few paces down an alley, and it is not easy to recommend one particular itinerary.

The Cluny Baths**

Entrance: 6 Place Paul-Painlevé; visits to the interior every Wed. 3pm.

In the garden of the Hôtel de Cluny, at the corner of the Boul. Saint-Germain and Boul. Saint-Michel, you can see some beautifully preserved remains. Contrary to a well-established tradition, this was not the palace of Julian the Apostate, but a Gallo-Roman bathhouse in Lutetia, built at the end of the 2nd or the beginning of the 3rd c. by the powerful corporation of Parisii boatmen, the Nautes. These were the buildings of the Thermes du Nord of the Gallo-Roman city, which was organized along two parallel thoroughfares (present-day Rue Saint-Jacques and the Route de Chartres, now the Boul. Saint-Michel). At least three large rooms can still be made out: the frigidarium, at the back, is the only one to have retained its ribbed vault (late 2nd c. - early 3rd c.), resting on eight ornamental brackets representing the prows of armed ships and, until 1820, supporting the hanging gardens of the Abbots of Cluny. To the W is the tepidarium, its walls lined with baths in niches, now undergoing restoration, and before which the two hypocausts (the underground furnaces) for heating the water are still visible; the caldarium, in the SW corner, has collapsed.

Rue de Cluny

The street was laid out on the site of a hospice and a chapel of Saint-Mathurin, which had been built in the 12th c. on a part of the baths' gardens bordering the main Roman road. In addition to part of an arcade visible at no. 7, other arcades can be seen in the neighboring Chinese restaurant, as well as at 20 and 22 Rue Du Sommerand. It was here in 1407 that the Provost of Paris, having wrongly condemned two students to be hanged at Montfaucon, was

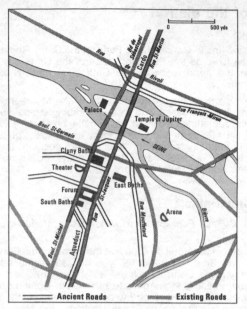

Gallo-Roman Paris

forced to take them down from the gibbet himself and kiss them on the lips. The students were then buried with great ceremony in the Saint-Mathurin chapel.

☐ The Hôtel de Cluny**

Entrance: 6 Place Paul-Painlevé

Adjoining the baths, the Hôtel de Cluny is without doubt the most beautiful example of civic architecture in Paris. After the devastations of the 9th to 12th c., the land here was built over; then the whole area was bought up in 1330 by Pierre de Châlus, the twenty-first Abbot of Cluny. He rebuilt the first *hôtel* as a town house for abbots visiting Paris from the monastery in Burgundy. The *hôtel* that survives today was built between 1485 and 1498 by Jacques d'Amboise, brother of the Cardinal-Minister, it was completed only in Charles VIII's reign. The buildings were pillaged during the Revolution, and in 1807 were occupied by a printer, some coopers and washerwomen. Now restored, the *hôtel* houses rich collections of medieval sculpture and *objets d'art* (→Musée de Cluny). Mary Tudor, daughter of Henry VII and widow of Louis XII, known as La Reine Blanche because white was the royal color of mourning, lived at the *hôtel* in 1515. At various times in the 17th c. the Cardinal of Lorraine, Marie Angélique Arnaud, Mazarin and the other papal nuncios all lived here.

The N façade, on the Boul. Saint-Germain side, is the simplest in style. It overlooks a small garden, which offers a view of the corbelled apse of the chapel projecting forward at the first-floor level. Two doorways to now vanished buildings may be seen: the entrance to the Collège de Bayeux (14th c.) and the doorway to the Church of Saint-Benoît-le-Bétourné (16th c.). Beneath the chapel is a pretty portico, the central pillar of which has a capital with a crowned *K* (the monogram of Charles VIII) and an escutcheon with the coat of arms of Jacques d'Amboise.

The inner courtyard is open to the public. The flattened arch of the doorway is surmounted by the Amboise coat of arms. The main building, opposite, has a projecting pentagonal tower containing a staircase (on its base are depicted the attributes of St. James, an allusion to the name of the founder, Jacques d'Amboise). This building and the two wings that between them enclose three sides of the courtyard are decorated with Gothic mullioned windows, a balustrade around the edge of the roof, and magnificent emblazoned dormer windows. The W wing is pierced by four large Gothic arches, surmounted by sculpted gables, forming a porch. A passage in the E wing to the r. leads to the garden.

The Square Paul-Painlevé separates the Hôtel de Cluny from the Sorbonne. There are statues of Puvis de Chavanne, Montaigne by Landowski and *La Louve Romaine* (the Roman She-wolf), given to Paris by Rome in 1962 on the occasion of the twinning of the two cities.

Rue de la Sorbonne

Cross this street without entering it. In the 5th c. at the corner with the Rue des Ecoles, stood the Saint-Benoît monastery, where François de Montcorbier, better known by the name of François Villon (→inset), grew up; it was there that he killed the priest, Sermoise, in a brawl, and from then on led an unsettled, violent life. The Rue de la Sorbonne was first called Rue Coupe-Gueule, then Rue des Deux-Portes, because it was closed off by gates at either end for reasons of security. Note the Librairie des Cahiers, where Péguy printed the *Cahiers de la Quinzaine*.

Take the Rue Champollion, which dates from the 18th c., noting the interesting staircase it still retains at no. 5. Racine and Marmontel are thought to have lived in the street, known today for its cinemas showing experimental and art films.

You come out into the Place de la Sorbonne, laid out in 1634 on the sites of the Collège des Dix-Huit and the Collège de Calvi. It is bordered by cafés and bookshops, leads to the Boul. Saint-Michel, and is dominated by the dome of the Chapelle de la Sorbonne (→Sorbonne).

Walk back up the Rue Victor-Cousin, which dates from the 13th c., then take the Rue Cujas to the l., also laid out in the 13th c., when it was named the Rue Saint-Etienne-des-Grès. At that time it was longer, since it gave access to the Abbaye Sainte-Geneviève.

Cross the Rue Toulier, where the poet Rainer Maria Rilke had his first Parisian lodgings in a squalid hotel, to arrive at the Rue Saint-Jacques.

Rue Saint-Jacques

For the very beginning of this street, refer to the Saint-Séverin district.

This was probably Paris's first street. Originally a Gallic track, then a Roman way (Via Superior), it ran parallel to the system of conduits bringing water to the baths. This great, historic Roman road, 'the link in the chain forever connecting Paris to life in the world outside', as the French historian Jullian said, also appeared on Peutinger's famous map of the roads of the Roman Empire, and pieces of paving have been discovered as solid as that of modern roads. It was 30ft/9m wide, ran around Philippe Auguste's perimeter wall and, especially in this part (Val-de-Grâce), was bordered by numerous large monasteries.

The Lycée Louis-le-Grand, facing the back of the Sorbonne, was rebuilt by Lecoeur at the end of the 19th c., and all that remains of the original building of 1628 are the two wings to the r. and l. of the central courtyard. It was founded for the Jesuits under the name of Collège de Clermont, thanks to a legacy from Guillaume Duprat, Bishop of Clermont; they later renamed it 'Louis-XIV'. The students were so numerous that the Collège Louis-le-Grand had to be enlarged in 1641 by the addition of the Collège de Noirmoutiers and, in 1683, by the Collège du Plessis. Molière, Crébillon, Dupuytren, Le Brun, Robespierre, Hugo, Littré, Delacroix and Baudelaire were among its better-known pupils. Lower down, at 67 Rue Saint-Jacques, there is a pretty Louis XV house. For the continuation of Rue Saint-Jacques, →Val-de-Grâce district.

Rue Soufflot, upper part

This street, which climbs toward the Panthéon, was begun in 1760 and completed a century later; today it is full of legal publishers.

Nothing in Paris better reveals the important Roman site of the beginning of the capital's history. The Roman forum on the summit of the Montagne Sainte-Geneviève stood between the roads to Orléans and Chartres; it was rebuilt in the 3rd c. and fortified in the 4th. There were also a temple and a civil basilica on the site. On these Gallo-Roman foundations a chapel and a hospice were built for pilgrims travelling to the shrine of St James of Compostela; both were later given over to the Dominicans who, as they were also called Jacobins gave their name to the old highway that became the Rue Saint-Jacques.

The 'Universal Teacher', St Albert the Great, taught here, as did his pupil, St Thomas Aquinas. The Parloir aux Bourgeois stood on the site of the present 20 Rue Soufflot until 1357, when it was transferred to the Grève; the original building was demolished only in 1861. The Faculty of Law, at the corner of the Rue Soufflot and Rue Saint-Jacques, occupies the site of Paris's first church, Saint-Etienne-des-Grès, founded by St Denis and demolished in 1792. For the lower part of the Rue Soufflot →Boulevard Saint-Michel.

Place du Panthéon

Dominated by the famous Sainte-Geneviève church, now the Panthéon, the square is bordered toward the Rue Soufflot by the curving façades of two Classical buildings. The *mairie* (town hall) of the 5th arr., in the S corner of the square, which matches the Faculty of Law, was built by Hittorff from 1844 to 1846. The Faculty of Law building, begun by Soufflot in 1771 and completed in 1822, has been altered and enlarged several times, especially after 1960 (buildings of the Rue Cujas). It stands on the site of the Collège de Lisieux, built in the 14th c. and transferred to the vicinity of the Abbaye Sainte-Geneviève in the following century. The entrance of a new library, built in 1958 in the Rue Cujas, has the original door of the Collège de Barbes. A large annex has been erected in the Rue d'Assas.

The Sainte-Geneviève library**

10 Place du Panthéon (open daily except Sun., 10am-8pm; stockrooms open 10am-noon, 2pm-6pm except Tues. am and Sun.); Bibliothèque Jacques Doucet (open Mon., Tues., Fri., 2pm-6pm).

This library, which borders the N side of the square, is the only monastic library in Paris to have survived the Revolution and its collections are among the largest in the capital. It was created in 1624 to receive the treasures accumulated in the Abbaye Sainte-Geneviève (now the Lycée Henri-IV). It stands on the site of the Collège de Montaigu, which was renowned for its teaching, but also for the poor treatment of its students, among whom were Ignatius de Loyola, Rabelais, Erasmus and Calvin; it was also called the Hôtel des Haricots (beans), a dry reference to the staple diet. The architect built a vast edifice of severe lines (1844-50), with vaults carried above a steel framework; this method had previously been used only at the Monnaie (Mint) in Nantes, at the Ecole des Beaux-Arts in Paris and, still earlier, by Bellanger for the cupola of the Halle au Blé (now the Bourse de Commerce).

Ground floor

The vestibule: large model of the corvette *L'Aurore* (1768), planisphere and terrestial globe by Coronelli (1693). Reading Room of the *Réserve:* pastel portraits of the Kings of France from Louis IX to Louis XIV (17th c.); marble busts of Charles Maurice Le Tellier, Archbishop of Rheims and Michel Le Tellier, Chancellor of France, by Coysevox; of César Le Tellier, Marquis de Courtanvaux, by Bridan; plaster busts of Rotrou, Boileau, Corneille, Quinault and Piron, by J. J. Caffieri; of Pascal, Achille de Harlay, Descartes, Le Nain, Cassini and others. Stockroom: plaster busts of Rameau and Pingré by J. J. Caffieri of Le Brun; by Coysevox, of Maurice of Saxony by Lemoine; portrait of a black nun, known as *La Religieuse de Moret,* said to be the natural daughter of Marie-Thérèse, wife of Louis XIV; ethnographic objects, mostly American, called *sauvageries,* collected in the 17th c.

The Jacques-Doucet literary library, bequeathed to the University in 1929, has been housed in the stockroom of the Bibliothèque Sainte-Geneviève since 1932. It has about 25,000 volumes, by authors of the 19th and 20th c. Its richest heritage lies in manuscripts of Baudelaire, Verlaine, Rimbaud, Mallarmé, Tristan Tzara, Breton and Malraux, among others. The Director's office (visits arranged on written request): exceptional astronomical clock** (16th c.) by Oronce Fine. A large chest with a marquetry top depicting the coat of arms of Louise-Adelaïde d'Orléans, Abbess of Chelles (1739); magnificent table in sculpted oak (18th c.); marble bust of the Grand Arnault, by Coysevox; plaster busts of Buffon by Houdon, of the Cardinal de la Rochefoucauld by De Buyster, of the Grand Condé by Debrais and others.

Principal treasures of the *Réserve:* a series of bindings of the 17th-19th c. for famous booklovers (or with coats of arms). Among the most precious illuminated manuscripts must be mentioned a Carolingian volume of the gospels from the 9th c.; an English Bible copied in the 12th c. by Manerius; the *Chronicles of St Denis* (end of the 13th c.); the psalter of Margaret of Burgundy (13th c.); an edition of Livy from Charles V's library (14th c.); the *De proprietatibus rerum* by Barthélemy l'Anglais (15th c. translation) and, above all, *The City of God* by St. Augustine, from the school of Jean Fouquet (second half of the 15th c.). Around 1600 incunabula (books printed before 1501) and illustrated 16th-c. volumes. An important series of editions of *The Imitation of Jesus Christ* (Delauny collection).

The staircase is decorated with a bust by Daumas of Ulrich Gering, who set up the first printing-press in Paris in 1470; bust of Labrouste, architect of the library (by E. Guillaume) and of Cardinal de la Rochefoucauld (1558-1645) by Barthélemy.

First floor

The great Reading Room** with 750 seats uses cast- and wrought-iron structure to create a vast open space. Dating from a few years before the Bibliothèque Nationale 1844-58, the Bibliothèque Sainte-Geneviève 1844-50 saw one of the first applications of the rationalist thought maintained by Labrouste against the theoreticians of the Académie des Beaux-Arts. Between the two entrance doors is a Gobelins tapestry, after Balze, depicting *L'Etude surprise par la Nuit* (Study Surprised by Night). The library has about 2 million volumes, of which nearly 4000 are manuscripts, and about 40,000 engravings, of which 10,000 are portraits. Among the main collections are the unique theological collection of Catholic and Protestant works; a collection of works on Spain, Portugal and South America, and collections of scientific and literary periodicals. There are busts of Mansart and Robert de Cotte by Coysevox, of Ingres (bronze) and Carpeaux (granite) by Bourdelle.

✝ The Church of Saint-Etienne-du-Mont***

Place Sainte-Geneviève. 7.30am-noon, 3pm-7pm. Tel. 43-54-11-79.

While far from being among the oldest, this is certainly one of the most remarkable of Parisian monuments. Not only does it house the reliquary of St Geneviève, the object of many pilgrimages, it also contains the remains of Racine and Pascal. Architecturally, it is much more 'the fruit of the dreams of those who built it', in a century of uncertain values, than the expression of some overall guiding thought. Saint-Etienne-du-Mont is very much the church of its time, combining the old forms, the fashion of the period, Italian influences and a fundamentally Gothic structure. The complexity of its interior is an exceptional example of stylistic transition.

History of the building

The massive increase in the number of parishioners in this college district, mainly students and their teachers, necessitated the construction in 1492, of a much larger church. In the 13th c. it was decided to build beside the abbey church of Sainte-Geneviève, a church dedicated to St. Etienne. Work continued throughout the

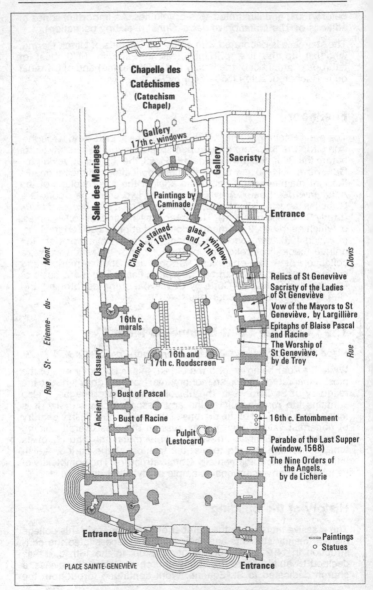

Chapelle des Catéchismes (Catechism Chapel)

Gallery 17th c. windows

Sacristy

Gallery

Salle des Mariages

Paintings by Caminade

Entrance

Chancel stained-glass windows of 16th and 17th c.

Relics of St Geneviève

Sacristy of the Ladies of St Geneviève

Vow of the Mayors to St Geneviève, by Largillière

16th c. murals

Epitaphs of Blaise Pascal and Racine

The Worship of St Geneviève, by de Troy

Ossuary

16th and 17th c. Roodscreen

Ancient

Bust of Pascal

Bust of Racine

16th c. Entombment

Pulpit (Lestocard)

Parable of the Last Supper (window, 1568)

The Nine Orders of the Angels, by de Licherie

Rue St- Etienne- du- Mont

Rue Clovis

Entrance

Entrance

Entrance

PLACE SAINTE-GENEVIÈVE

=== Paintings
○ Statues

The Church of Saint-Etienne-du-Mont

16th c.; the choir, its ambulatory, the rood loft and the belfry tower were completed in the middle of the century, the nave and transept in about 1585. The first stone of the façade was laid in 1610 by Marguerite de Valois (la Reine Margot) first wife of Henri IV, and the church was consecrated on February 15 1626. The rood screen narrowly escaped destruction in the 18th c., and is the only one in existence in Paris, saved because of its wide arch. During the Revolution Saint-Etienne-du-Mont became the Temple of Filial Piety and as such served the theophilanthropic movement until 1803; at this time the church was stripped of its works of art. In the years 1802 to 1807 the S wall was exposed by the demolition of the abbey church of Sainte-Geneviève. In 1861 deterioration of the façade made complete restoration necessary, which was carried out by Baltard and finished in 1868.

The exterior

The façade, built between 1610 and 1622, mixes Classical forms with Gothic tradition. The central part is composed of three super-imposed pediments, the upward sweep of the belfry accentuating their form and the differences in style and decoration. Above the main entrance door is *The Martyrdom of St Etienne* (St Stephen) by G. J. Thomas; in the pediment of the portal, the *Resurrection,* by De Bay. These works were modified by Baltard. On the N side (Place de l'Abbé Basset) a small portal in the Doric order built in 1632. The S wall (Rue Clovis) was exposed by the demolition of the abbey church at the beginning of the 19th c.

The interior

The church, designed asymmetrically with side-aisles almost as high as the nave, is reminiscent of the German Gothic *hallen sirche.* Their vaults fall back onto thick cylindrical pillars, joined together by a gallery running all round the church.

The nave. The organ loft* built by the master joiner Jean Buron (17th c.) is exceptional in the harmony of its volumes and the richness of its ornamentation, dominated by a depiction of the *Risen Christ Surrounded by Angels*; this is the oldest wholly-preserved organ loft in Paris. Organ recitals are given regularly. The pulpit (1651) is the work of the master joiner Germain Pilon, carved by Claude Lestocard from designs by Laurent de la Hyre; it is supported by a figure of Samson and decorated with statues of the Virtues. The stained-glass windows*, mid-16th-late 17th c. To the l. facing the choir, The Descent from the Cross, after Raphael; The Resurrection; The Coronation of the Virgin. To the r., The Ascension; The Incredulity of St. Thomas; The Pilgrims at Emmaüs; The Holy Women at the Sepulchre.

The r.-hand side-aisle and its chapels. 3rd chapel: inscriptions to the memory of famous people buried in the suppressed churches and monasteries of the parish; in 1794 and 1795 the remains of Mirabeau and Marat were translated from the Panthéon to the little cemetery beyond the E and of the church. 4th chapel: *The Nine Orders of Angels* (archangels, angels, seraphim, cherubim, etc.), by Louis de Licherie 1679. Between the 6th and 7th chapels, marble plaque to the memory of the saints and blessed of the order of preaching friars called Jacobins; below, a plan of the former monastery that stood in the Rue Saint-Jacques. 7th chapel: the altarpiece, depicting *St Charles Borromeo*, was given in fulfilment of a vow made by Quentin Varin; *Manna in the Desert*, executed by the pupils of Philippe de Champaigne.

The choir. The rood loft**, built at the same time as the choir *ca.* 1530, probably by Antoine Beaucorps, from designs by Philibert Delorme, is composed of an arch, 29½ft/9m across, allowing the congregation a clear view of the ceremonies performed in the chancel, which is why it was left in place. Access to the rood loft is by two elegant open spiral staircases. The architecture is pure Gothic but there is nothing medieval about the decoration, and the whole seems inspired by the Renaissance. The Classical twin side doors (1600–05) are thought to be by Pierre Biard, one of the sculptors of the Grande Galerie in the Louvre. The stained-glass windows of the apse, from the mid 16th c., depict the Apparitions of Christ after his Resurrection.

The ambulatory and its chapels commencing to the r. of the choir. On either side of the 1st chapel, epitaphs of Racine written by Boileau and Pascal, both buried in the church; above the entrance to this chapel, ex-voto to St Geneviève by De Troy 1726. Between the 1st and 2nd chapels, on either side of a small door, two plaques recount the history of the abbey church of Sainte-Geneviève, which adjoined Saint-Etienne; above this door, another ex-voto to St Geneviève, by Largillière 1696. 2nd chapel Sainte-Geneviève: 19th-c. reliquary in gilded copper containing a fragment from the saint's original grave, rediscovered in 1802. In 1793 her remains were exhumed and burnt in the Place de Grève. Her life is also evoked in the stained-glass windows of the chapel. A window of 1882 shows the façades of Saint-Etienne and Sainte-Geneviève before the demolition of the latter at the beginning of the 19th c. Between the chapel of Sainte-Geneviève and the Chapelle de la Vierge, a door gives onto the sacristy, the Chapelle des Catéchismes and the cloisters known as the Charniers (Charnel House Cloister). The Chapelle des Catéchismes, built by Baltard, contains paintings by Giacometti and Timbal (1864) and four statues by Chapu and Allasseur. In the Charnel House Cloister, built from 1605 onwards around the apse, 12 beautiful stained-glass windows of the early 17th c.; their color and vitality make them closer to the art of the painter than to that of the stained-glass artist; note particularly The Miracle of the Rue des Billettes (1st window), The Mystic Vessel or

Our Lady (2nd window), Manna (9th window) and The Mystic Wine Press or The Grapes of Wrath (10th window). The Chapel of the Virgin is to the r. Returning into the church: four paintings by Caminade 1830–37. 6th chapel: *The Virgin, John the Baptist and St Gerard Sagredo*, by Girolamo di Santa Croce. 7th chapel: medallion of Frédéric Ozanam by A. Cario (1914), recalling his founding of the Society of St. Vincent de Paul in May 1833 in the parish of Saint-Etienne-du-Mont. 8th chapel: murals from the end of the 16th c. Chapels of the l. side-aisle: 4th chapel: bust of Racine. 5th chapel: bust of Pascal.

] Lycée Henri-IV

Entrance, 23 Rue Clovis: visits by prior request to Mme la Proviseur the headmistress. Tel. 46-34-02-20.

This is one of the great Parisian lycées. It occupies the former building of the Abbey of Saint-Geneviève.

History of the building

This, in the Roman period, was the rich district and the 'sacred hill of pagan Lutetia' (Jullian). After defeating the Visigoths near Poitiers, Clovis built a rich basilica dedicated to saints Peter and Paul on the summit, on the site of a pagan temple. He and his wife Clotilde were buried there. The first church was erected between 506 and 520; it was decorated with mosaics. In the 6th c. the remains of Paris's patron saint, St Geneviève, were transferred there and the basilica was eventually dedicated to her; it stood on the site of the present-day Rue Clovis and was destroyed by the Norsemen in 857. Another church was built there in the 12th c. This survived until the Revolution, when it was replaced by the Panthéon, originally intended to be the Church of Sainte-Geneviève. The abbey was occupied by canons regular, and had to be reformed several times when conduct fell below the required standards. The abbey gradually extended its influence in this rural, vine-growing area rivalling the Abbey of Saint-Germain-des-Prés, acquiring complete legal jurisdiction, even for capital crimes; the Chancellor of the University was also placed under its control. Sainte-Geneviève was for the E part of the Left Bank what Saint-Germain was for the W: the center of urban expansion. Just as there was the Bourg Saint-Germain, so there was the Bourg Sainte-Geneviève. The son of the Regent, known to his entourage as Louis le Pieux (the Pious), was a frequent guest at the abbey, which owes its library to him. With only his books, his medals and a handful of friends, Louis d'Orléans ended his days in the house at the corner of the Rue Clovis and Rue Descartes, now the presbytery of Saint-Etienne-du-Mont.

Tour of the building

The tower rising within the perimeter wall of the lycée, wrongly named the Tour de Clovis, with a Romanesque base and Gothic upper storeys, is a relic from the basilica; it was used by the physicists Ampère, Arago and Dulong for their experiments. Of the medieval monastery buildings, there survive the kitchens (12th c.) and, beneath them, two Gothic cellars built one above the other, each with two bays partly 12th c.; the former refectory (13th c.), with ribbed vaults and over 98ft/30m in length, now the lycée's chapel and visible from the Rue Clotilde. Of the buildings from *ca.* 1675, there survive a fine staircase, the former chapel of the Abbot, now the Salle des Actes, and, most importantly, the galleries of the library, now converted into a foyer. These galleries, in the form of a huge cross, are lit by a central cupola decorated with a large painting by Restout: *The Triumph of St Augustine* (1730). Finally, the medal room of the *Génovéfains*, the canons of Sainte-Geneviève of 1753, with its harmonious Louis XV decoration. The cloister (1746) is bordered by barrel-vaulted arcades. The second courtyard dates from the 17th c.

Rue Valette

Laid out in the 11th c., this street was called Rue des Sept-Voies until the 18th c. At no. 6 the Bibliothèque Nordique (open Mon.-Fri. 2-6pm), rebuilt in 1961, houses the Finnish-Scandinavian collection of the Bibliothèque Sainte-Geneviève: 145,000 volumes, among which are some rare, old editions. The library contains a copy of everything written in French on the Nordic countries and receives the main daily newspapers from them. At no. 4 is the entrance to the Collège Sainte-Barbe, with its curious brick and stone façade. Founded in 1450 by Geoffrey Normand, it is the oldest of the private colleges, and the only one to survive from the Middle Ages. Among its pupils are Ignatins de Loyola, Montgolfier, E. Scribe, the mathematician Bertrand, Meissonnier, Labrouste, G. Eiffel, who built the refectory vault, L. Blériot, J. Jaurès and Charles Péguy. The basic design is by E. Lheureux 1881. Go to no. 21 to see the courtyard and Gothic cellars of the Collège Fortat, created in 1937 for students from Aurillac; Calvin lodged here from 1531 to 1532 and the so-called Tour de Calvin (Calvin's tower), 15th c., where he lived during his student days at the Collège de Montaigu, became, curiously, a center for the Catholic League in 1576. No. 7 dates from 1673, no. 9 from the beginning of the 17th c.

Rue Laplace to the r. of Rue Valette

This street once contained several colleges including La Merci and Les Ecossais at no. 10. The entrance to the Collège de Grassins

(1659) can still be seen at no. 12. Nos. 10 and 18 are 16th-c. houses. At no. 9, a large workers' apartment building of 1910 (architect G. Vaudrier). Almost all the houses are old; some have been restored, but those that have not still have medieval cellars. Jehan de Meung or Jean de Meun, 1240–1305, author of the second part of *Le Roman de la Rose,* lived in this street.

The former Ecole Polytechnique

The entrance to what used to be the Ecole Polytechnique is in a small, antiquated square, decorated with a semicircular fountain. The school was founded on March 11 1794 by the Convention and, through the dominant influence of the mathematician Monge, was originally called the Ecole Centrale de Travaux Publics (Central School of Public Works) intended to replace all the specialist engineering schools. It assumed its permanent name and character in 1795 and was reorganized in 1852. First installed (1794) in the Palais–Bourbon, the Polytechnic was transferred here in 1805, then to Massy–Palaiseau in 1977. It occupied the sites of two earlier colleges: the famous Collège de Navarre at 5 Rue Descartes, founded in 1304, among whose pupils were Gerson, Henri IV, Richelieu and Bossuet; and the Collège de Boncourt (14th c.) at no. 21, joined in 1638 to the Collège de Navarre, which was also joined to the Collège de Tournai on the Rue Clovis side.

The enclosed gardens are open to the public. The entrance through the portal built by Renié in 1838, leads into the Cour de Navarre. Three contemporary bronze sculptures have recently been erected: in the square ornamental pool, *La Spirale,* by Meret Oppenheim; set around the pool, a column by Côrne Mosta–heint and three figures by Giuseppe Penone. To the I., the buildings erected in the 19th c. on the site of the magnificent library of the Collège de Navarre are now occupied by the Centre d'Etudes et de Systèmes de Technologies Avancées (Center for Advanced Technological Studies and Systems) and sports facilities. Opposite is the Bâtiment Joffre, formerly the Bâtiment des Bacheliers de Navarre, built by J. J. Gabriel in 1738. Behind, a passage gives access to the annex of the Collège de France, to the Bibliothèque Byzantine and the Bibliothèque d'Histoire des Textes Grecs. To the r., on the Boncourt site, the Ministry of Research occupies the former residence of the Governor–General of the school.

Take a look into the Rue de l'Ecole–Polytechnique, laid out on the site of the Collège de Grassins and which, like the Rue Laplace, leads into the Rue Valette.

Rue de la Montagne-Sainte-Geneviève

This is one of the oldest streets in Paris. Laid out in the 12th c. under the name Rue des Boucheries, it surrounds itself with the mystery of its front and back courtyards, dark corners and passages plunging off to who knows where.

Returning toward the Place Sainte-Geneviève, you can admire, at no. 47, a handsome 17th-c. building, the former Collège de Huban, known as the Collège de l'Ave Maria; at no. 51, a 16th-c. building that was formerly a cabaret. Go back down the street: at no. 40, a very old cabaret, with a sign depicting St Geneviève and, in the Revolution, changed 'to the late St Geneviève, rendezvous of the Sans-Culottes'. In the courtyard of no. 34 are traces *ca.* 1740 of the Collège des Trente-Trois, the 33 years of Christ's life, founded by Claude Bernard. The site of the ancient Collège de Dacia, which from 1275 to 1430 was for Danish students, was at the corner of the Rue Bassé-des-Carmes. Between the Rue des Ecoles and the Place Maubert, the street occupies the site of two other colleges, the Collège de Laon and the Collège de la Marche.

Follow the Rue de l'Ecole to the l.

Rue des Carmes

This street was laid out on the Clos Bruneau, whose vineyards were famous, and whose name is still recalled by an unevenly paved cul-de-sac. A little lower, at no. 1 *bis*, is the Musée Historique de la Préfecture de Police (→Museums). The Collège des Lombards was at nos. 15 and 17; founded in 1334, it was ceded in 1677 to Irish priests in exile; the small chapel, rebuilt in 1738 by Boscry, has a handsome façade with an elliptical porch, surmounted by a damaged pediment that recalls certain works by Bernini. Since 1925 the chapel has been given over to the Syrian Melchite rite of St Ephrem.

At the corner of the Rue des Carmes and Rue de l'Ecole is the Impasse des Boeufs, which formerly gave on to the back of the Collège des Lombards and the Collège des Trente-Trois.

Rue de Lanneau

This street, another of the oldest in Paris, was laid out in 1185. It was first called Rue du Mont-Saint-Hilaire, then Rue Saint-Hilaire, after the parish church of Saint-Hilaire-du-Mont, which stood at the corner of the Rue des Sept-Voies. This, in the Middle Ages, was a noisy, lively street and, in the 16th and 17th c., printers and bookbinders lived in and around it including the Gourmonts, the Estiennes, the bookbinder Clovis Eve. Most of the houses are from that period. In recent years craft shops and pleasant little restaurants have been set up here – the Rue de Lanneau is becoming gentrified. The Maison du Puits-Certain at no. 11, has been an inn since 1627.

Cross the Rue d'Ecosse to the l., formerly Rue du Chaudron, from which a passage once led to the Saint-Hilaire church. The Collège de Toul used to stand on the l. and a part of the Collège de Coqueret on the r.

Impasse Chartière

to the l. of the Rue de Lanneau

This street has existed since 1860 but, cut off by the building of the Collège Sainte-Barbe, is today only a cul-de-sac.

In the 16th c. it had a printing-press, two bookshops, two bookbinding workshops and five colleges, including the famous Collège de Coqueret. It might almost be said that this college, founded in 1439 and dissolved in 1568, was the cradle of the French language. It had as pupils Ronsard, Baïf and Joachim du Bellay who, in 1549, with Jodelle, Rémi Belleau, Pontus de Tyard and the Hellenist Dorat, founded the first French Pléiade (named after a group of poets in Ptolemaic Egypt), while Du Bellay was writing his *Défense et Illustration de la Langue Française*. The college stood on the l., on the site of the present-day outbuildings of the Collège Sainte-Barbe, whose curious metal structure is worthy of note.

Return to the Rue de Lanneau, which ends at the E side of the Collège de France.

The Thermes de l'Est

These Roman baths (2nd-3rd c.) stood at the intersection of present-day Rue de Lanneau with the Rue Jean-de-Beauvais, the Impasse Chartière and the Place Berthelot, and comprised many rooms. The caldarium and frigidarium were rectangular, the tepidarium circular; the other rooms were built inside one another like Chinese boxes. These baths were partially uncovered during construction of the extension to the Collège de France.

The Collège de France*

11 Place Marcelin-Berthelot (interior open only to those attending lectures).

The college was founded in 1530 by François I, in response to the entreaties of France's greatest humanist, Guillaume Budé. In the 17th c. it became the Collège Royal de France; with the coming of the Revolution the adjective was dropped. Originally it taught Latin, Greek and Hebrew, unsupervised by the theologians, since the college was independent of the University. Ever since, it has remained the model of the unbiased institution, where knowledge is cultivated for its own sake. Lectures are open to the public and free of charge. The teachers are appointed by the government irrespective of creed. Among others, Claude Lévi-Strauss, A. Leroi-Gourhan, Georges Duby, Y. Bonnefoy, E. Le Roy-Ladurie, Pierre Boulez and André Chastel all teach at the Collège de France. The old college, built slowly from 1610 to 1778, when it was completed by Chalgrin, has its entrance, with a concierge, on the Place Marcelin-Berthelot; the inscription *Docet omnia* (All are taught here) sums up the universality of its teaching. In the courtyard is a marble statue of Champollion by Bartholdi (1875). In the W courtyard, decorated with an elegant portico by Letarouilly (1830-1840), which can be seen through the gate in the Rue Saint-Jacques, is a marble statue of Guillaume Budé (1468-1540) by Max Bourgeois and busts of Vatable, Turnèbe, Gassendi, Fine, Ramus and Danès. Vestibule of the r. wing: busts of scholars. Teachers' common room: two paintings by Lethière and Thévenin: *François I Signing the Act of Establishment of the Collège de France, Henri IV Endowing the College Chairs;* old portraits of Guillaume Budé, Danès and others. Room no. 3 *bis*: *The Death of Delille*, canvas by Camus (Abbott Delille died in this room). Room no. 4, called the Salle des Langues (Language Room), where Champollion, Silvestre de Sacy, Burnouf and Renan all taught: busts of Burnouf by Eugène Guillaume and Renan by Falquière. Room no. 8, the room of the Bergson lectures. Room no. 9: medallions of Michelet, Quinet and Mickiewicz, who all taught here. The little laboratory where Magendie, Laënnec, Flourens and the great physiologist Claude Bernard worked (the last from 1847 to 1878), see inscription outside, overlooks the Rue Saint-Jacques. On the first floor, reliquary of Claude Bernard, with mementoes, manuscript of the *Introduction à l'Etude de la Médecine Expérimentale* (Introduction to the Study of Experimental Medicine), and so on, in Bernard's office. In the courtyard, the Fontaine du Collège de France (1812).

Since 1930 the old college has been modernized and extended. The old building was returned to the faculty of the arts, while large, modern buildings for the sciences, designed by the specialist architects A. and J. Guilbert, were erected to the E, at the side of the Impasse Chartière. A new building, which is 98ft/30m high, with basements 49ft/15m deep, houses physics and chemistry laboratories, with all the latest equipment; the laboratory of Frédéric Joliot (d.1958) where he set up his cyclotron, is in the lower basement. The corner building houses the general services and the physics and chemistry lecture rooms (176 and 108 seats respectively). The entrance hall is decorated with two large paintings by Pierre Bompard: *Air and Water* and *Earth and Fire*, and with a bronze sculpture by Poisson. Another building, between the old college and the Rue Saint-Jacques, is devoted to biology.

In the square of the Place Marcelin-Berthelot are bronze statues of Dante by Aube, and of Ronsard; on the staircase, a statue of Claude Bernard by Guillaume, who died at 40 Rue des Ecoles (plaque).

Behind the College de France the Rue du Cimètiere Saint-Benoît is a reminder of the Church of Saint-Benoît, which was named, not for that patriarch of Norcia, but from the Old French expression *Benoiste Trinité* (Blessed Trinity). Originally the altar was at the W end, but during a 16th-c. renovation it was moved to the E and the church was renamed Bétourné, it was destroyed in 1854.

Rue Jean-de-Beauvais

Created in the 14th c., this was for a long time the printers' street. François I visited Robert Estienne, who lived at no. 17. The house thought to have been the birthplace of Alfred de Musset (1810) disappeared with the construction, in 1934, of the huge concrete Ecole Speciale des Travaux Publics, du Batiment et de l'Industrie (High School of Public Works, Construction and Industry). The street crosses the Rue des Ecoles, beyond which the chapel of the Collège de Dormans-Beauvais, founded in 1370, still stands (open only for services; see note affixed to the door). This chapel was built in 1375 by Robert de Temple, architect to Charles V, and its Gothic spire is the only one of this period surviving in Paris. The nave has five bays and the apse is pentagonal. The tracery of the high windows comprises three trefoil compartments while a sculpted cornice supports a pointed barrel vault, created by Jacques de Chartres. Since 1885 the chapel of Dormans-Beauvais, much changed, has been devoted to the Romanian Orthodox church. The streets run on to the Boul. Saint-Germain near the Place Maubert.

Place Maubert

Much more middle-class today than it has ever been since it was created slightly N of where it now is, the Place Maubert has borne, since 1202, the corruption of the name of the famous Dominican friar, Maître (Albert Albert the Great), second abbot of Saint-Geneviève.

In the Middle Ages it was a path between the traditional old school in the cloister of Notre-Dame and the newly-born colleges of the Montagne Sainte-Geneviève. After the departure of the students to the slopes of Sainte-Geneviève, the place embarked upon the most sinister and tragic period in its history, as a place of execution: people were tortured, hanged, broken on the wheel, pilloried and burnt as heretics here, including the unfortunate printer and philosopher Etienne Dolet, burnt alive in 1546. His statue, in belated homage, by the sculptor Ernest Guilbert, disappeared during the German occupation. So many Huguenots were burnt here that it became a place of pilgrimage for followers of the Reformation. Barricades were raised here too, and for centuries, until quite recently, this 'Maubert cesspit', as Erasmus called it, retained its evil reputation.

♦ The Church of Saint-Nicolas-du-Chardonnet*

30 Rue Saint-Victor (8am-7pm).

Follow the Rue Monge, from which you will see this church, especially interesting for its historical mementoes and for the tombs of Le Brun and his mother.

History of the church

The history of the shrine goes back to the 13th c. when it was erected in a field of thistles (*chardons*), but the foundation stone of the present church was laid in 1656. The lower part of the bell-tower is all that remains of the former church, and even that dates from its later period of construction (see inscription on the outer wall dated 1625). Charles Le Brun, who was a parishioner of Saint-Nicolas, is believed to have designed the side façade with its beautiful carved door, on the Rue des Bernadins. When the church was consecrated in 1667, the vault and the first two bays of the nave had not been built, and it was finally completed, still without its façade, thanks to lotteries organized in 1716 and 1763. The cutting of the Boul. Saint-Germain necessitated alteration to the apsidal chapel, carried out by Baltard. Finally, in 1934, the architect Claude Halley erected the present façade on the Rue Monge in the Neo-Classical style.

Since 1977 the church has been used by members of the Catholic traditionalist movement, presided over until his death in 1984 by Mgr Ducand-Bourget. Masses are celebrated in Latin, according to the rite of St Pius V.

The interior

The nave. The organ loft came from the old Church of Saints-Innocents, upon its closure in 1787; the case is by the joiner Oger, the instrument itself by François Thierry. On the inside of the W wall to the l., *The Presentation in the Temple,* a painting of the 18th c. French school. The r.-hand side aisle and its chapels. In the first bay of the aisle: *The Martyrdom of John the Baptist* by Charles Le Brun. 1st chapel: *The Baptism of Christ* by Corot and *Jesus Healing the Blind Man of Jericho* by Desgoffe. 3rd chapel entrance to the Chapelle des Catéchismes: *Death of St Francis de Sales* and *Martyrdom of St Cyricus and St Julitta* by Durameau (18th-c.). The r. transept, Chapelle de la Communion: above the altar *Pilgrims at Emmaus** by Brother André (early 18th c.), elsewhere, *Melchizedek's Sacrifice* and *Manna* by N. Coypel the Younger (1713).

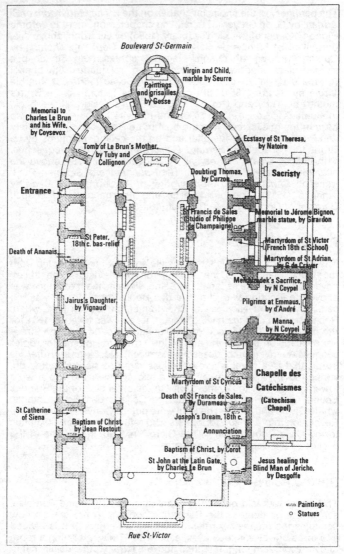

Boulevard St-Germain

Virgin and Child, marble by Seurre

Paintings and grisailles by Gesse

Memorial to Charles Le Brun and his Wife, by Coysevox

Tomb of Le Brun's Mother, by Tuby and Collignon

Ecstasy of St Theresa, by Natoire

Entrance

Doubting Thomas, by Curzon

Sacristy

St Francis de Sales (Studio of Philippe de Champaigne)

St Peter, 18th c. bas-relief

Memorial to Jérome Bignon, marble statue, by Girardon

Death of Ananais

Martyrdom of St Victor (French 18th c. School)

Martyrdom of St Adrian, by G de Crayer

Jairus's Daughter, by Vignaud

Melchizadek's Sacrifice, by N Coypel

Pilgrims at Emmaus, by d'André

Manna, by N Coypel

Martyrdom of St Cyricus

Chapelle des Catéchismes

(Catechism Chapel)

Death of St Francis de Sales, by Durameau

Joseph's Dream, 18th c.

Annunciation

St Catherine of Siena

Baptism of Christ, by Jean Restout

Baptism of Christ, by Corot

St John at the Latin Gate, by Charles Le Brun

Jesus healing the Blind Man of Jericho, by Desgoffe

⊏⊐ Paintings
○ Statues

Rue St-Victor

St Nicolas-du-Chardonnet Church

The periphery of the choir. 1st chapel: on the r. *The Martyrdom of St Adrian*, by G. de Crayer (17th c.). 2nd chapel: monument to Jérome Bignon, Keeper of the King's Library (1656) by Girardon; above this, portrait of St Francis de Sales. 3rd chapel: *Doubting Thomas* by Curzon (19th c.) 4th chapel: Regency confessional. 5th chapel: stained-glass window with relics, 18th-c. reliquaries. 6th chapel (Chapelle de la Vierge): decoration by Gosse (1857–63), marble *Virgin* by Seurre (1861). 8th chapel: to the l., tomb of Le Brun's mother by Tuby and Collignon to Le Brun's design; at the back, monument to Le Brun* (d.1690) and his wife by Coysevox; at the base of the obelisk carrying the bust of Le Brun, two figures: Piety and Penitence; above the altar and on the ceiling, paintings by Le Brun. 10th chapel: *St Bernard Celebrating Mass* by Sacquespée. 11th chapel: *Death of Ananias* by Sacquespée (1678); above the altar 18th-c. bas-relief in wood: *The Repentance of St Peter*. The l. transept: *Christ Raising the Daughter of Jairus from the Dead* by Vignaud (1819). The l. side-aisle and its chapels: 2nd chapel: *Baptism of Christ* by Jean Restout (18th c.).

Rue Saint-Victor

The present route of this street recalls an older street that led from the Place Maubert to the Abbaye de Saint-Victor. The abbey covered a large area as far as the Seine, since its main entrance was above the junction with the Rue des Boulangers. No. 42 was the seminary of Saint-Nicolas-du-Chardonnet, founded in 1612, where Renan studied. Things have changed: its site was taken in 1931 for the building of the Maison de la Mutualité. No. 14 is a fine three-storey mansion built at the end of the 17th c. for the master roofer Jacques Auvray (porch, bossages, cornices). No. 8 was an *Hôtel à la corde,* that is, a hotel where penniless vagrants slept standing up, supported by a rope under their arms; at dawn the ropes were lowered, and they fell to the floor. On the other side of the Rue des Ecoles, in the Rue d'Arras, was the Collège des Bons-Enfants, where Calvin and Vincent de Paul were pupils. Converted during the Revolution into a prison for priests who refused to swear allegiance to the Civic Constitution of the Clergy in 1790, it was one of the scenes of the September massacres.

Rue de Poissy

This street was laid out at the same time as the Rue de Pontoise, across the gardens of the Bernadine convent. A fire station now occupies the monastery refectory* at no. 24 (→inset). It is divided into three ogival-vaulted naves, each with 17 bays, forming a room of over 230ft/70m long. It stands above a large Gothic cellar that in 1709 was filled in by the Bernadines themselves up to the sub-structure of the vaults, after flood waters from the Seine had made the cellar unusable. A study center for Paris and the Ile de France occupies part of the first floor.

Follow the Boul. Saint-Germain to the l. towards the Place Maubert.

Rue des Bernadins to the r.

This street formerly ran alongside the wall of the Bernadine Convent. At no. 19 stood the Hôtel de Torpane, a remarkable civil building of the late Middle Ages, constructed in 1566 by Jacques Lefèvre, adviser to Charlex IX. It was demolished in 1830. The botanist Jussieu lived at no. 11. Note the old houses at nos. 16, 12, 8 and 6. The street ends where the Pont de l'Archêveché meets the Quai de la Tournelle.

> François Villon

> *Human brothers who after us will live,*
> *Let not your hearts to us be hardened,*
> *For if to us your pity you will give,*
> *By God's mercy yourselves will be pardoned.*

So begins the *Ballade des Pendus,* the epitaph that Villon himself wrote while waiting to be hanged for a crime which, for once, he had not committed. François de Montcorbier (1431-63?), known as Villon after the chaplain of Saint-Benoît le Bétourné who was his tutor, is the first great French lyric poet. Holder of a Master of Arts degree from the Sorbonne (1542), he shared the tumultuous life of the scholars of the Latin Quarter immortalized by Rabelais in *Panurge.* Association with the crooks and the *cabarets* (taverns) of the Rue Saint-Jacques led him first to theft, then to murder. Pardoned, he did not mend his ways and led a vagrant existence punctuated by brief spells in prison. After 1463 he wrote no more and disappeared, leaving to posterity several collections of poetry, including *Le Lais* or *Petit Testament* and *Le Grand Testament.* Villon revived the personal and realistic tradition of the 13th c., which had been abandoned in favor of courtly and allegorical themes. A direct reflection of his life, Villon's rhythmic poetry, often written in slang, dwells often on death. His own impending death and that of others inspired him to write moving, macabre verses, evoking the pitiless fate that strikes rich and poor without distinction.

> The long history of the Université

For three centuries the Sorbonne has been the temple of culture and learning. Before it, however, and independently, the Université existed for centuries. It was originally established in the school of the cloister of Notre-Dame, but in 1108 Guillaume de Champeaux, who taught there, crossed the bridge to continue his teaching at the Abbaye Saint-Victor.

From that moment on the Université took up residence on the Left Bank. In 1118 Peter Abelard, who is widely believed to be the real founder of the Université, was forced to leave the cloister because of the hostility of the canons who were scandalized by his non-conformism. He was followed by 3000 students who sat in the fields between the Rue Guerlande or Garlande and the Rue du Fouarre, while he championed the conceptualist position in the *querelle des universaux* (debate on university propositions).

These small, isolated centers of learning joined together to acquire greater autonomy from royal and religious authority, and from 1209 to 1210 joined together in one association. This was the Universitas, to which Philippe Auguste accorded the privilege of being under ecclesiastical jurisdiction; a few years later, in 1231, the Université was placed under pontifical authority; in 1252 it received its own seal.

Licensed teachers brought their pupils together at a street corner, in front of a window or at a street intersection. Only in the 13th c. did students' inns begin to multiply under the name of *collèges.* Eventually there were four *nations,* comprising several colleges, and grouping students together by their places of origin, a tradition that still lives on in Nordic countries, the *nation* of France was at 8 Rue du Fouarre. There was the Collège d'Harcourt (seat of the *nation* of Normandy), the Collège de Coqueret, and the Collèges de Calvi, des Ecossais for Scottish students, de Dacia for Scandinavian students, the *Nation Anglaise* which, during the Hundred Years War, became German, the Collège des Irlandais, and many more. The Université originally had three faculties: Theology, Canon Law and the Arts (something that resembled the French *baccalauréat); the* Faculty of Medicine dates from 1331. Throughout the Middle Ages the Université de Paris shone brilliantly, eclipsing Bologna, its senior, and Oxford, its junior. Scholars travelled great distances to hear St Bonaventura, Albert the Great, Thomas Aquinas and, later, Malebranche and Massillon. In 1793 the Convention dissolved all the universities and Latin, which had been the language of the University of Paris, was no longer the official tongue. The Université was re-established under imperial patronage by Napoléon in 1806, and in 1821 it was centralized at the Sorbonne.

▷ # Who was St Geneviève?

St Geneviève, who lived from about 420 to 500, was not a simple shepherdess, as she is often presented, but a rich Gallo-Roman landowner. Her life is well known from accounts written down shortly after her death.

She was born at Nanterre, to which people still make a pilgrimage.

Her parents, Sévère and Géronte, may have had property there. When she was a little girl, Geneviève Genovafa met the bishop St Germanus of Auxerre, who was on his way to Britain, and told him she wished to devote her whole life to God. The bishop encouraged her and when she was 15 presented her with the veil of a dedicated virgin. Even at this early age she performed a miracle, curing her mother's blindness with water from the well at Nanterre.

Later she came to Paris, where she spent most of her life, and was renowned for her virtue, generosity and courage, but also for her criticism of the morality of others. In 451 her response to the invasion of the Huns earned her widespread esteem: she refused to panic and flee like many others, but simply prayed with a few women friends that Paris should be spared. Their prayers were answered, and Attila went elsewhere. Later, when the town was suffering shortages from the exactions of the Franks in the surrounding countryside, she organized an expedition to find wheat in the region of Troyes. She then grew wheat herself and made bread which she distributed to the poor.

Her many miracles made St Geneviève into a popular figure: several times a candle extinguished by rain or wind relit itself in her hands (in the Middle Ages she was often represented holding a candle relit by an angel); she cured many sick people; she turned away rain and calmed a storm. Consequently people began to worship her and, even after her death, saw her miraculous powers at work when, during an epidemic of ergot poisoning caused by a fungal infection in rye, her relics were paraded through the streets in a public procession and the epidemic ceased, an event celebrated annually in Paris. Her relics were also carried through the city at times of natural catastrophes or to repel invasions; it is the latter aspect of her cult that has given her a national, even patriotic value, and she remains in every way the patron saint of Paris.

▷ **Procession of the relics of St Geneviève**

From the Middle Ages to the 18th c. Parisian life was rich in processions. Every year great ceremonies were held on August 15, Corpus Christi and Rogation Days. But other occasions (famine, epidemics, the King's ill-health) impelled Parisians to invoke their patroness, St Geneviève. Her relics were then publicly venerated with special processions: five in the 13th c., an equal number in the 14th c., 11 in the 15th, 44 in the 16th, seven in the 17th and three in the 18th. The ceremony was very grand. Besides the regular and secular clergy, representatives from every public organization participated. The reliquary of the patron saint of Paris left the Abbey of Sainte-Geneviève where it was kept until the Revolution, when the remains were burnt and the ashes scattered and the procession set off for Notre-Dame. All along the route houses were decorated and the ground strewn with flowers and foliage. Other reliquaries were exposed to public worship and associated with the procession, such as that of St Marcel. The two ex-votos by Largillière and J. F. de Troy, large canvases commissioned by the municipal magistrates and kept at Saint-Etienne-du-Mont, bear witness to these exceptional days.

▣ Museum to visit

Musée d'Histoire de la Préfecture de Police (1 bis Rue des Carmes), accounts of famous trials and history of the police from its beginnings, including criminals' weapons and royal warrants. Open Mon.-Thurs. 9am-5pm, Fri. 9am-4:45. Tel. 43-29-21-57. Ext. 336.

▷ The former Collège des Bernadins

The Bernadine monastery shows how important university studies had become for Cistercians during the 13th c. In 1246 Etienne de Lexington, Abbot of Clairvaux, set up a college in the Clos de Chardonnet, inside Philippe Auguste's perimeter wall, that became the college for the entire order. The monastery buildings and the church were rebuilt from 1338 onward, only the refectory being retained from the 13th c. The most spectacular part of the church was a double spiral staircase set into the S part of the apse that allowed the monks to come down from their dormitory via the sacristy, for the evening services.

In the Revolution the church was desecrated, then destroyed. The refectory became a fire station due to vacate the premises in 1988. In 1886 in the course of clearing out a wood yard, and in 1978 during excavations for an underground parking lot, sculpted elements of the 14th-c. church were uncovered.

The Boulevard Saint-Michel*

6th and 5th arr./Map ref. 17-A2, A3
Métro: Saint-Michel, Odéon
Buses: 21, 24, 27, 38, 81, 85, 96
Parking: Rue de Harley (1st arr).
Taxis: Place Saint-Michel. Tel. 43-29-63-66.

A walk along the Boulevard Saint-Michel offers an occasion for nostalgia but almost nothing to sustain it: no trace remains of the great events that have taken place here. Ideas flourished, and the convulsions of the Revolution that shook all Paris spread from here, but lovers of art and architecture will find absolutely nothing worth a second glance – only the layout of the street itself, popularly known as the 'Boul. Mich', has never been altered. Although its history is shorter than that of the Rue Saint-Jacques, because it was not created until 1869, under the Second Empire, the Boulevard Saint-Michel soon established itself as the heart of the Left Bank. It also goes back to a Roman road that ran parallel to the Rue Saint-Jacques and led to Chartres, but which lost its importance during the Middle Ages because it ended without a bridge across the Seine. The street survived nonetheless, with the name Rue de la Harpe, continuing as far as the gate in Philippe Auguste's perimeter wall, called the Porte Saint-Michel. Beyond the wall, the street became the Rue de l'Enfer. Finally, the S section of the Boulevard Saint-Michel has been laid out over the more recent Rue de l'Est.

The literary cafés, which have existed along the boulevard almost since its beginning, are chiefly responsible for its fame. Their greatest hour of glory was under the Third Republic, when the small literary groups to which they gave shelter made and unmade the world daily. Wine and witticisms were dispensed in equal amounts; a cynical poet once asked for 'gall in a long glass'. The boulevard was the birthplace of Symbolism, and Verlaine frequented almost all its establishments.

Visit to the boulevard

45 mins.

Place Saint-Michel

In the Middle Ages this square was known as the Place du Pont-Saint-Michel, and lay near the Macon watering trough and several alleys that were prostitutes' territory. It was named in honor of Michelle de France, daughter of Charles VI.

It is a busy intersection where Davioud's fountain (1860), ornamented with a statue of St Michael killing the dragon (bronze by Duret). After serving as a swimming-pool during the crazy parties that used to end the students' year-end Four Arts Ball, the site seems to have become the rallying place for the young from all quarters of the globe. The Place has often witnessed revolutionary unrest. Under the Second Empire, the Café de la Renaissance (no. 4) was a Republican meeting place, and it became the center of the Commune in 1871. Literary gatherings took place at no. 1 in the café first called L'Avenir, then the Caveau du Soleil d'Or – a sordid tavern where the Hydropathes (→below), Laurent Tailhade, Maurice Boukay and, of course, Verlaine, gathered round its old piano –

before it became the Café du Départ around 1900. Later, in August 1944, the tanks of the Liberation rolled down the boulevard while students were fighting the Nazis on the Place; the many who died are commemorated by marble plaques. But nothing remains to recall the turbulence of the student revolt of May 1968, except the frequent presence of the police.

Boulevard Saint-Michel

N section as far as the Pl. Edmond-Rostand.

The liveliest part of the boulevard stretches from the Place Saint-Michel up to the Place Edmond-Rostand. Always thronged by a hurrying, colorful crowd, this area competes with the Grands Boulevards as one of the few places where you can buy on the street newspapers, scarves, souvenirs, theater guides, and so on until late at night. Logically enough, shops keeping conventional hours include some good bookshops (Gibert, Hachette, PUF), but they are being replaced more and more by fast food restaurants. The Café de Cluny at no. 20 is one of the few famous cafés to have survived under its original name. It had a brilliant clientele, more political than literary, which in the 19th c. included lawyers, exiled Turks, Romanians and Irish Feiners; booklovers also came here to discuss the history of Paris. The poet Ponchon, and later André Thérive (1923) would stay here until the small hours.

On the opposite side, the Boul. Saint-Michel runs beside a garden in which the Roman ruins of the thermal baths of Cluny lie (→Montagne Saint-Geneviève), admirably preserved and dominated by the mansion of the former abbots of Cluny. A little higher up on the l. the Rue des Ecoles begins. On the corners two famous establishments once stood: The Café Soufflot, now the Select-Latin, opened under the Second Empire. While the students of the Ecole Polytechnique played billiards upstairs, the atmosphere on the ground floor was more serious around 1869; the café was the center for the Young Turks, led by Kemal Bey (later Ataturk) and Tahsin. Opposite, La Vachette (no. 27) was from 1865 to 1911, the rendezvous for a group of poets led by Jean Moréas, noted for his exchanges with Isidore, the waiter. The latter prided himself on his poetry. One day he chanted: 'For Master Moréas, I bring a *café tasse!* ' Some of the most famous men of the day came here: Verlaine, L. Tailhade, Huysmans, Maurras, Mallarmé, Héredia, F. Coppée, R. Loüys and P. Bourget. Further up, at no. 35, La Source, Verlaine's favorite café, has been replaced by a fast-food restaurant. At the back of the room there used to be a famous spring (*une source*), beneath a round ceiling, which is still there. At nos. 29 to 33 walk past the site of the colleges of Seez, Narbonne and Bayeux whose 14th-c. portal has been removed to the Musée de Cluny. Further on, at no. 40, the Collège d'Harcourt, seat of the Nation of Normandy, was founded in 1280 and established on this site in 1311.

It became the Lycée Saint-Louis, and its façade on the boulevard was built by Bailly in 1861. Racine, Boileau, Diderot, Talleyrand, the Abbé Prévost and Gounod were pupils there. A Roman theater, built under the Antonine emperors and capable of holding between 4000 and 5000 people, was found on this site.

Place de la Sorbonne*

This opens up opposite the Lycée Saint-Louis, and is dominated by the chapel of the Sorbonne (La Sorbonne). A monument to the 19th-c. philosopher Auguste Comte by Injalbert (1903) stands in the center. On the corner at 47 Boul. Saint-Michel, the Café d'Harcourt echoed, from 1880 to 1939, to the tumult of students, while the Café de la Rive Gauche on the corner of the Rue Cujas became famous as the birthplace of the bizarre Society of Hydropaths founded on October 11, 1878, by Emile Goudeau. Among this happy crowd of versifiers and singers were poets (J. Richepin, M. Rollinat, J. Moréas, H. de Régnier, E. Haraucourt) and politicians, particularly Barrès, and the singers from the Chat Noir cabaret.

Rue Soufflot – lower section

For a long time this street was flanked by two famous cafés: to the l., at no. 63, was the Taverne du Panthéon, known between the two World Wars as the Capoulade; writers from the *Mercure de France* met there, but it was above all, a place to talk politics. Opposite, at the Café Mahieu, the publisher Bernard Grasset held court. The MacDonald's that now replaces it, has kept the old tables and chairs. At no. 69 is the Café Rouge, famous for its concerts (note the monogram C.R.). Finally, at no. 73, the Café François I (decorated with palms, stalactites and weapons) was home to the first Symbolists, Verlaine, Jules Laforgue and others. For the upper part of Rue Soufflot →Montagne Sainte-Geneviève.

Place Edmond-Rostand

From this *place* onwards, the Boul. Saint-Michel changes character and becomes quieter, almost suburban. It recalls the atmosphere that prevailed until 1687 when the Porte Saint-Michel, which was on this level, was demolished. It separated the city surrounded by walls to the N from the suburbs in the S. A pretty fountain was erected on the *place*, but it was destroyed in the 19th c. when the *place* was incorporated into the boulevard that took its name.

Boulevard Saint-Michel

S section as far as the Boul. de Port-Royal.

Jules Vallès lived and died at no. 77, César Franck at no. 95. No. 93 is the original American Foundation for Students, created in 1919. On the r., in front of the Luxembourg Gardens there was a row of private residences of which only one remains, the Hôtel de Vendôme, built in 1707 by Courtonne; it became the Ecole des Mines (no. 60*bis*). Only the garden façade retains its original appearance; the boulevard façade dates from 1855 onwards. The Ecole des Mines was founded in 1783; it houses an interesting museum of mineralogy (→Museums). Further down still, a rustic atmosphere predominated for a long time, preserved by the *guinguettes* (cafés with dancing in the open-air). The Café du Chalet where the painters Ranvier and L. Français met is on the r. The Bal Bullier, now the Rue Georges Bernanos, with its curious, brightly colored papier-mâché arcades, was well known to the students. It has been replaced by a university sports center. Finally, on the r., is the Closerie des Lilas (→Notre Dame-des-Champs) in front of which rises the unusual station of the Réseau Express Régional, the former Sceaux line, built in 1894 and restored in 1986.

▣ Museums to visit

Musée de Cluny (6 Place Paul-Painlevé): medieval art.
Musée de Minéralogie (60 Boul. Saint Michel): a collection of French minerals, meteorites.

▷ Memorable days in student life

The most impressive ceremony is the *rentrée,* at least during the first year. The students, often accompanied by their families, go to enroll in their faculties (*la fac*), and this may take place in June, at the end of the summer or even as late as the beginning of the semester in October. There are stacks of forms to fill out, the difficult choice of major and minor subjects, the schedules, the panic at the book lists handed out by the professors. . . . Then the year rolls by more or less peacefully until the time comes for cramming, when the much dreaded examinations approach, to take place in May and June. While the libraries are stormed by some students the more relaxed study in the cafés. For the studious tourist, the most interesting ceremony occurs when theses are defended, generally around Easter. This glorious crowning of scholastic endeavor is the only ceremony that has retained some solemnity. It takes place before a restricted audience, mostly composed of friends and guests, although the curious may be admitted if they can find a seat. The courteous debate on learned subjects is not necessarily arduous and the criticism, subtle or scathing, of the President of the Jury is applauded as much as the defense of the doctoral candidate. Apart from their course work, students used to amuse themselves by organizing mock protests against particular professors. And the *bal des Quartre-z-arts* (the Four Arts Ball) should not be forgotten; it ended the year in a joyous tumult, with the students running noisily through the streets in disguise, all night long, often capping the festivities with a bath in a fountain, dressed or undressed.

The Réaumur district

2nd, 3rd arr./Map ref. 11–A2, B2, B3; 12–C3
Métro: Bourse
Buses: 20, 29, 39, 67, 74, 85
Parking: Place de la Bourse
Taxis: 64 Rue de Bretagne (Square du Temple). Tel. 42-78-00-00.

The Rue Réaumur, with its fantastic and monumental façades, preserves something of the pomp that banks and newspaper companies liked to display in their architecture during the triumphant era of capitalism at the turn of the century. Today, the flashy shop windows and neon lights of the ready-to-wear clothing manufacturers compete with one another in a luminous and colorful show of market place aggression. In the street, choked by delivery vans, newspaper vendors and the men unloading bales of material or clothing rush around in feverish activity.

After the Boulevard de Sébastopol and the watch tower of the Félix-Potin building, the Rue Réamur is much quieter; it passes between the Church of Saint-Nicolas-des-Champs and the former Abbey of Saint-Martin-des-Champs, which houses the Musée des Techniques (Museum of Technology). Isolated in a little square, the old abbey has kept its rustic character, despite the proximity of the noisy Arts-et-Métiers intersection. At this spot in the Rue Réaumur the store windows are peopled surrealistically with naked mannequins.

To see this street at work and to appreciate its architecture, walk through it on a weekday since the buildings are often closed during the weekend.

Tour of the Rue Réamur

Departure point: Place de la Bourse/45 mins.

Like the Rue des Immeubles-Industriels opened in the Nation *quartier* in 1873, the Rue Réamur is an example of a street designed exclusively for industrial and commercial buildings. It was built close to the heart of the Parisian business world between 1897 and 1905. During this time some 20 buildings were put up to accommodate offices, ready-to-wear clothing manufacturers, print shops and allied industries. The extraordinary originality of the architecture springs both from its astonishing stylistic unity and from the great diversity of its façades. In fact, the construction of Rue Réamur was marked by the new regulation of 1902 which favored variety in the treatment of façades and roofing effects, permitted rounded corners and encouraged gigantic bow windows that interrupted the regularity of the balconies systematically aligned on the second and fifth floors, common practice since 1859. At the same time, to encourage architectural invention, the Municipality set up a contest, the Concours de Façades (→inset).

These buildings, while preserving a bourgeois, even luxurious appearance, are perfectly adapted to their objective: to offer floors free of interior walls, allowing for vast open spaces, chiefly for garment manufacture and printing. Many buildings make use of metal, either exclusively (no. 124), or combined with stone (nos. 69, 82-98, 91, 97, 118, 126 and 130).

Rue Réamur

From Place de la Bourse to Rue Montmartre.

No. 132, the corner building, constructed by Jacques Hermant in 1901, is a good example of the ostentatious architecture typical of the great banks. Guiral de Montarnal's building of 1898 (no. 130) is worth a visit for its entry hall and staircase. The visitor is surprised by the monumental staircase, which has two flights built slightly at an angle to the street axis. Everything is admirably preserved: the original flight of stairs in copper, the decoration (plane tree foliage) and stained glass. You must go to the mezzanine floor to discover a staircase built in a delightful elliptical curve, and to use the elevator by Roux-Combaluzier of the same period.

Rue Montmartre

From Rue Réamur to Rue de Cléry.

Not far from where the Rue de Réamur crosses at no. 95, is one of Paris's first apartment buildings, with a façade entirely of glass, except for the balustrades of glazed brick. It was built in 1898 by the architect S. Périssé.

Rue Réaumur, continued

From Rue Montmartre to Rue Saint-Denis.

The building at no. 124, generally attributed to Georges Chédanne, dates from 1903. The entirely metal framework and the inner courtyard ensure the maximum amount of light. Built to house a printing press, this edifice in riveted steel shows great originality. The bow windows suspended from the fourth floor allow a white mosaic to be seen. The fifth floor has apartments and is differentiated from the rest of the building by a brick facing. No. 118, constructed by Guiral de Montarnal, is one of the most beautiful and elegant buildings in the street; it dates from 1900. An award winner in the Concours de Façades, it presents beneath a flattened arch an immense expanse of window on three levels stretching across the entire width of the building. Graceful scrollwork in metal and stone enhance this bay, also framed in stone. The building by Walawein (no. 116, 1897) also won a prize in the Concours de Façades in spite of its sober decoration, due to its not being completed as planned and the façade which is remarkable only for its considerable expanse of glass. At no. 100, the large façade put up in 1924 sheltered the *'Intransigeant'* newspaper, and later *France-Soir*: the rotary press in the basement printed this paper until 1980. The two pediments above the wings are decorated with bas-reliefs by Navarre and represent *Typographers* (on the r.) and *Journalists* (on the l.) Do not hesitate to enter the main vestibule, which has a grand staircase, an elegant grey stained-glass window characteristic of the 1920s, and a floor decorated with the name of *Intransigeant*. The décor typifies the opulence of the Parisian press of the time. In a corner to the l. a plaque indicates the site of the former Cour des Miracles, a neighborhood haunted by beggars and vagabonds in the Middle Ages, and described by Hugo in *The Hunchback of Notre-Dame*. The building constructed by Jolivard and Devillard at no. 97 has two projecting side wings. Below that on the r. the opening of the Sentier Métro is oddly tucked away.

Rue Saint-Denis

Between Rue Réaumur and Rue Turbigo.

Continue along to no. 155 to see the store called *La Soie,* built in 1898 by Henri Rouville. The depth of the building is over 180ft/55m. As in most stores selling textiles, its long corridor is lit by a skylight.

Rue Réaumur, continued

From Rue-Saint-Denis to the Boul. de Sébastopol.

Between no. 82 and 98 stretches the Réaumur department store which Constant Bernard built in 1897. The part situated in the angle of Rue Réaumur and Rue Dessoubs was put up in 1926. The building at no. 69 constructed by Ernest Pergod in 1898, was designed as a graphics studio. The third floor skylight gives maximum light. The façade clearly separates the stonework from the metalwork. Two medallions placed on either side of the central bay represents *Industrial Art* on the r. and *Commercial Art* on the l. Almost effaced above the doors is the inscription *Industries et Beaux-Arts*.

There is a highly original building at nos. 61–63. Built by Sirgery and Jouannin around 1900 on a very small piece of land only 6½ft/2m long, it has an impressive, eclectic façade and is occupied by a clothing factory. It is a good idea to enter through the Romano-Byzantine doors and climb the stairs to the third floor, where you can appreciate the almost laughable dimensions of the building. At no. 51, near the exit of the Réaumur Métro, the massive Félix Potin rotunda, built in 1910 by Charles Le Maresquier, is decorated in exuberant colors with bees symbolizing high finance and abundance. A vast dome surmounted by a bell-tower crowns the whole. These domes, visible all along the Rue Réaumur, are a characteristic of the bourgeois buildings of the 1900s and are nicknamed *poivrières* (pepperpots). Beyond the Boul. de Sébastopol and the Arts-et-Métiers intersection, no. 39 (architect G. Salard) is ornamented with two astonishing grotesque caryatids (1901) by Pierre Roche, the Symbolist sculptor.

Tour of the Réaumur district

45 mins.

Boul. de Sébastopol

Between Rue Réaumur and Square Chautemps.

Created between 1855 and 1858 by Baron Haussmann to serve as a strategic route in the event of riots, frequent in this well-populated district, this street offers a broad view from the Place du Châtelet to the Gare de l'Est. After it crosses the Rue Réaumur, the Boul. de Sébastopol runs along one side of the Square Emile-Chautemps with the Conservatoire des Arts et Métiers on the E and the Théâtre de la Gaité Lyrique on the S. This theater was originally a showcase for the King's favorite dancers, later became the Théâtre de la Gaité Lyrique and then, in 1907, the Opéra Municipal de la Gaité. Parisians enjoyed many fine performances here until World War II. Between 1974 and 1979 Sylvia Montfort created and developed here Paris's first *centre d'action culturelle*.

Today, only the theatre's facade and the foyer have been conserved: the rest of the theatre has been completely rebuilt. Its floors now include boutiques as well as activities for children. Open during the week, 1–8pm; Wed. 9am–8pm; Sat. Sun. and school holidays, 9am–10pm.

The Conservatoire des Arts et Métiers

292 Rue Saint-Martin. Tel. 42-71-24-14. Church and museum open Tues.-Sat. 1–5:30pm; Sun. 10am–5:15pm/Refectory, now the Library, Mon.-Fri. 2–8:30pm; Sat. 1–7pm; Sun. 9am–12 noon.

This institution of industrial engineering, occupying the former Abbey of Saint-Martin-des-Champs, houses the Musée National des Techniques, the science museum of Paris, (→see Museums). Apart from the admirable church and refectory, the former buildings of the abbey were rebuilt in the 18th c. by Antoine, restored and enlarged from 1845 to 1897 under the direction of Léon Vaudoyer, then restored by Henri Denoux on the eve of World War I. The former abbey of Saint-Martin-des-Champs was in all probability built over the site of the basilica of Saint-Martin, which had replaced the primitive oratory erected there by an inhabitant grateful for the miracles the saint had performed in Paris. The Abbey lay on the pilgrimage route to Santiago de Compostela and at the crossroads of the main commercial routes between the basilicas of the kingdom. In 1061 Henri I elevated the Church of Saint-Martin-des-Champs to the status of an abbey; destroyed by the Norsemen, the church was solemnly dedicated in 1067. After Philip I presented it to the Abbey of Cluny (1078) it became a center of learning on the R. Bank to be compared with that of Saint-Germain-des-Prés on the L. Bank. The extant church and refectory give an idea of its former splendor. A papal bull mentions, in 1096, 33 churches dependent on the abbey of Saint-Martin. The buildings, which had been occupied during the Revolution by the Société des Jeunes Français, an educational institution, then by a small arms factory, were rebuilt in 1798 as the Conservatoire des Arts et Métiers by the decree of 19 Vendémiaire, Year III (October 10, 1794) at the suggestion of the Abbé Grégoire.

The main courtyard contains a modern second portal ornamented with busts of Coulomb and Chaptal. To the l., statues of Nicolas Leblanc (1742-1806) by Hiolle and of Denis Papin (1647-1714) by Aimé Millet. The monks' refectory is situated to the r. of the courtyard. This fine hall, built before 1250, is one of the masterpieces of Pierre de Montreuil, great architect of the Sainte-Chapelle and one of the masters of Notre-Dame. Today it holds the library. Inside, a magnificent hall with a surprising boldness and lightness (140ft/42.8m long, 38ft/11.7m wide), divided into two aisles whose double ogive vault rests on seven central columns as well as on the slender engaged columns set against the side walls. The 16 keystones of the bays are ornamented with foliage and fruit. Most of the light comes from twin bay windows surmounted by a rose window. Outside, projecting from the N wall, is the admirable stone reader's pulpit, with its steps out into the thickness of the wall.

♣ The Church of Saint-Martin-des-Champs

The church is situated to the S of the refectory on the other side of the former cloister bordering the Rue Réaumur. The church belongs to two distinctly different periods. The nave, with no side-aisles, lit by beautiful Gothic windows covered by a wooden vault, dates from the end of the 13th c. The vault and the walls are decorated with recent paintings. The tower, projecting on the S side, was built at the beginning of the 12th c. on the S arm of the transept of the church of 1067. The façade over the courtyard is visible through the railings of the Rue Saint-Martin: the portal is a fantastically conceived reconstruction of 1885, and the turret on the r. is quite recent. From the Rue Réaumur, you can easily see the S side of the nave built at the end of the 13th c., the Romanesque tower and, particularly, the beautiful 12th c. chancel (1130-40), with its double ambulatory flanked by seven chapels whose exterior walls are also Romanesque. This multi-foiled chevet was situated on the edge of the Saint-Martin courtyard which linked Saint-Martin to Saint-Nicolas. The choir (1130-40) is probably the first Parisian edifice in which the ogive vault appeared; it also shows tentative efforts which are of great interest in the history of the origins of the Gothic style. The sanctuary is surrounded by a double ambulatory flanked by a large, trefoil absidal chapel and by six small, rounded chapels. Many elements are still purely Romanesque, notably the capitals; the greater part of the bays of the ambulatory have only groin vaulting and the chapel windows have rounded arches. To sustain the thrust of the ogive vaults of the chancel, the architect built small buttress walls on the transverse ribs of the ambulatory; they are the oldest in France and the forerunner of the 13th-c. flying buttress.

Take the Rue du Vertbois which runs along to the N of the Conservatoire buildings. At the corner of the Rue Saint-Martin, the Fontaine du Vertbois (1712) has been built onto a tower of the fortified perimeter wall; the tower and the fountain were heavily restored in the 19th c.

To the r. begins the Rue Vaucanson where, at the end of the 19th c., the Central School of Arts and Crafts was situated on the site of the Saint-Martin market.

Continue down the Rue du Vertbois as far as the Rue Volta, which you take to the r. Recent discoveries show that the half-timbered house at no. 3 is not the oldest house in Paris as was popularly supposed until 1978, but a very successful 17th-c. imitation. Its structure, however, is characteristic of medieval houses.

Rue Turbigo

From Rue Volta to Rue Saint-Martin.

Created in 1854, this street is named for the battle that saw a French victory over the Austrians on June 2, 1859. In 1867 in this street Ernest Cognacq opened his first store, called Au Petit Bénéfice. Future founder of the Samaritaine department stores, he bequeathed his collections to the City of Paris (→Musée Cognacq-Jay). Important archeological explorations have revealed, from nos. 40–48 Rue Turbigo, a number of substructures of the former buildings of the Rue Au-Maire. In the same neighborhood, the graves of the Saint-Martin cemetery have been recovered, filled with human bones.

Take the Rue Saint-Martin on the r.

⚱ The Church of Saint-Nicolas-des-Champs*

254 Rue Saint-Martin. Tel. 42-72-92-54. Open Mon.–Sat. 9am-7pm; Sun. noon-4pm.

This huge church was originally only a simple chapel, erected in the parish in 1184. It was rebuilt at the end of the 12th c., then again in the 15th c.; the façade, the bell-tower and the first seven bays are from this period. During the second half of the 16th c., the nave was lengthened by four bays and the side-aisles with their chapels were built, as well as the fine S portal. The expansion was finally completed in 1615. Around 1745, following the fashion for the return to the antique, the columns of the choir were fluted and topped with Ionic pilasters, and the stained-glass windows were replaced with clear glass. Closed in 1793, the church became the Temple of Hymen and of Fidelity. It was reconsecrated in 1802 and restored in 1823 and in 1843; the portal of the W façade was then embellished with new statues. Finally, in 1854, the construction of the Rue Turbigo opened up the S and E façades.

The exterior

The N façade dates from the 15th c.; the portal is framed by a Flamboyant Gothic arch; the statues are by Desprez 1843. S face: 16th-c. portal*, masterpiece of Renaissance religious architecture, inspired by a design by Philibert Delorme for a door of the Hôtel des Tournelles; the panels are sculpted with female torsoes, angels, animals and foliated scrolls.

The interior

In the nave, the organ-case, the oldest parts of which go back to

1610, was altered in 1632 and enlarged in 1773. The organ loft is of this period. The case is richly decorated: the central turret is surmounted by a statue of St Nicholas between two musician angels. The instrument, although remodeled in 1930, is not in good repair.

R side-aisle, 2nd chapel: to the r. *Virgin and Saints* by Aspertini (16th c.); to the l. the *Consecration of St Augustine* by Hilaire Olivet (18th c.); 4th chapel: to the l. *Souls in Purgatory* after Sebastiano Ricci; 7th chapel: to the l. St Geneviève by E. Jeaurat (18th c.); to the r. *St Geneviève as a Child, blessed by St Germain* by Joseph-Nicolas Jouy (1845).

The chancel contains a monumental twin-sided marble high altar of the 17th c. In the center, two works by Simon Vouet (1629); below, *The Apostles at the tomb of the Virgin*; above, *The Assumption*, retable on the high-altar; elsewhere, *St Nicholas and John the Baptist* by J. B. Robin (1775), four stucco angels complete the decoration. Paschal Easter candlestick in copper-gilt, 9ft/2.75m high.

Periphery of chancel beginning r., 1st chapel; *Baptism of Christ* by Gaudenzio Ferrari (16th c.); 2nd chapel: *The Circumcision* by Finsonius (*c.* 1615); 4th chapel: r. *Virgin of the de Vic Family*, called the *Virgin of Victory of François II Pourbus* (*c.* 1610); in the vault, murals by Georges Lallemant (16th c.); 5th chapel: to the r. *The Ascension* by C. Vignon (1650); the remainder, 17th-c. murals. 6th chapel: St *Vincent de Paul Ransoming the Galley-Slaves* by Léon Bonnat (1865); murals (17th c.). 9th chapel axial: to the l., *Adoration of the Shepherds* by Noël-Nicolas Coypel (18th c.); to the r., *The Rest on the flight into Egypt* by Caminade (1817); marble Virgin by Delaistre (1817). Opposite, on the back of the high altar, *St Charles Borromeo giving Holy Communion to Plague Victims in Milan*, and *The Eternal Father* by Godefroy (18th c.). 11th chapel: (17th c.). murals in the vault. 12th chapel: to the l. *St Nicholas in the Tempest* by J. B. Pierre (1747), canvas in grisaille; in the vault, murals by Georges Lallemant (16th c.) 15th chapel: to the r., *St Vincent de Paul giving alms to a Beggar* by Brisset (1858). On the back wall, a *Calvary* painted on wood (16th c.), between two paintings after Rubens, *The Ascent to Calvary* and *The Deposition*; above, plaque commemorating the call of Louise de Marillac to found the order of the Filles de la Charité (Daughters of Charity). The chapel is paved with black marble tombstones with the names of the great families buried in the church. 16th chapel: to the l., *St Bruno (founder of the Carthusians) refusing the gifts of Count Roger* by J. P. Laurens (1874). L. side-aisle: 1st chapel (Chapelle des Catéchismes), generally locked: *Jesus Blessing the Little Children* by Noël Hallé (1775), canvas from the former Collège des Grassins; the artist had painted the same subject for Saint-Sulpice. 8th chapel: *St Louis Distributing Alms*, attributed to Stella (17th c.)

▷ # The Concours de Façades of the City of Paris

The construction of Rue Réaumur, opened with great solemnity in 1897, was the origin of the Concours de Façades, a competition organized by the City of Paris between 1898 and 1936. At first it was concerned only with the Rue Réaumur, but it was soon evident that it had to be extended to all Paris, with the aim of stimulating originality and variety in the decoration of Parisian buildings. The model was Brussels, which had invented a similar competition a short time before. The six buildings annually awarded a prize brought fiscal and financial advantages to their owner and architects.

Guimard was one of the laureates of 1898; the adjudication always took place the following year with Castel Béranger, Rue La Fontaine, as the proud inscription on the façade bears witness. Buildings of no great merit generally received awards, but some interesting works among them were given prizes: Lavirotte, 29 Ave. Rapp, 34 Ave. de Wagram and 23 Ave. de Messine; Arfvidson, 31 Ave. Campagne-Première; Herscher, 39 Rue Scheffer. After World War I, this competition continued until 1936, twinned with another for shop windows. But even though Roux-Spitz (14 Rue Guynemer) or Guimard (18 Rue Henri-Heine) were among the prizewinners, the competition had lost its importance. Modernism won fewer prizes there, putting an end to a laudable idea whose passing nonetheless was unregretted.

The Saint-André-des-Arts district**

6th arr./Map ref. 17–A2
Métro: Saint–Michel, Odéon
Bus: 21, 24, 27, 38, 63, 81, 85, 86, 87, 96
Parking: 27 Rue Mazarine
Taxis: Carrefour de l'Odéon. Tel. 43-26-00-00.

This small *quartier* between the Boul. Saint–Germain and the Seine quays retains all the atmosphere of 17th-c. Paris. Though it still bears traces of its chaotic medieval layout, the strict planning of the *Grand Siècle* (17th c.) is visible throughout. Alleyways such as the narrow Rue de l'Hirondelle and the winding Rue Hautefeuille are a legacy of the Middle Ages. On the other hand, the Rue Dauphine with its continuation over the Pont–Neuf represents the first deliberate act of urban planning, recognizing the natural course of the Seine as the main artery of the Paris landscape. Its old façades and large mansions, which have a more rural charm than those of the Saint–Germain district, have always attracted artists and writers.

Today, while the outskirts of the district are noisily enlivened by the picturesque market on the Carrefour de Buci and by the café terraces of the Boul. Saint–Germain and the Place Saint–André-des–Arts, the interior streets are quieter. At night a few bars and excellent film clubs impart a discreet atmosphere to the district.

Tour of the district

1 hr.

Place Saint-André-des-Arts

This district was laid out on the site of the College of Autun and the Church of Saint-André-des-Arts, neither of which is still there. This church, built in 1210, housed the tombs of Ambroise Paré and Christophe de Thou, now in the Louvre. Voltaire was baptized here. The raised terraces of the cafés give this lopsided square a summer atmosphere. In 1818 Gounod was born at the former no. 11 on the corner of the Rue Danton.

Notice opposite, at 1 Rue Danton, the forerunner of all the reinforced concrete buildings constructed by Hennebique and Arnaud from 1898 to 1900.

Rue Saint-André-des-Arts

Formerly this street bore the name Grande Rue Saint-Germain and was the continuation of the Rue de la Huchette, which led to the village of Saint-German-des-Prés across the Clos de Laas. Beyond the perimeter wall it was known as the Sente du Pilori (Pillory Path). It is an interesting street whose superb balconies, carved keystones and wrought ironwork can be admired despite its extreme liveliness in the evenings. In the 18th c. nos. 23 and 25 were built by J. R. Cochois on the old foundations of the Hôtel de la Verrière (17th c.). At no. 27, is the Maison des Trois Chapelets (House of the Three Rosaries), built in 1640 for the historian A. Duchesne, and rebuilt in 1748 by Dairler; three large arcades can still be seen. The Baroque balcony and mascarons of women's heads date from the 18th c. No. 30, once the Hôtel Montholon (18th c.) where Billaud-Varenne, who lived on the site of the Lycée Fénélon, was married, is now a cinema. There are beautiful houses at nos. 31, 33 (Louis XV), 35 and 37 (Louis XIII). Look into the courtyards at no. 41: 18th-c. Flamboyant Gothic corbels and former outbuildings of the Hôtel de Château-vieux on the Rue de l'Eperon. At no. 45 is the Lycée Fénélon, the first of its kind for girls, opened in 1883. Inside an 18th-c. staircase and drawing-room have survived. At no. 52 the beautiful Hôtel Du Tillet de la Bussière* (1750) still has its semicircular roofed bays, balconies supported by corbels decorated with rams' heads, wrought ironwork and an elegant courtyard. At the corner of the mansion you can see that the word 'saint' of Saint-André was scratched out during the Revolution. The Hôtel de La Vieuville is at no. 47 and at no. 49 the Hôtel de Châteauvieux, rebuilt in 1728, replaced the Hôtel de Navarre, which was inhabited by Louis XII and at that time occupied all the land as far as the Rue de l'Eperon. The mansions at nos. 51 and 53 date from the 17th-18th c. (courtyards). At no. 58 the 18th c. mansion has been disfigured. The portal at no. 60 is of a fine Renaissance design. The other parts of the buildings are of a later date.

On the l. before the Carrefour de Buci is an entrance to the courtyard of the Commerce-Saint-André (→below) and just by it is the Bar Mazet, haunt of the international hippie fraternity. The Porte de Buci which closed the Rue Saint-André-des-Arts, was situated just about here. In 1418 the Burgundians entered by it to massacre the Armagnacs, who were then the masters of Paris. The gate was demolished in 1672.

The Rue Mazet gives access to the Rue Dauphine, which was once the counterscarp of Philippe Auguste's wall. It has lost a lot of its former charm. No. 6 was the Magny restaurant, frequented by Flaubert, George Sand, Sainte-Beuve, Renan, Pauline Viardot, Turgenev, *et al.*

At the corner of the Rue Mazet and Rue Saint-André-des-Arts stands a small statue of St Andrew.

Rue Dauphine

Built in 1607 as a continuation of the Pont-Neuf, this street was, for a long time, one of the most chic streets in Paris and de Sartines, Lieutenant de Police, chose to install the first street lamps here. The houses are built over very beautiful Gothic cellars (no. 34). No. 61 was built in 1769. On the site of nos. 44-46 stood the Porte Dauphine, completely destroyed in 1672. The plaque, which was put up in 1673, is the oldest in Paris. Nos. 41, 37, 35, 33 and 30 date from the 17th c. Sartre and the existentialists crowded into no. 33, the cabaret Le Tabou, for lively jazz sessions when Saint-Germain-des-Prés had become the center for the new intelligentsia. The Passage Dauphine, leading to the Rue Mazarine, is at no. 30. The underground parking lot here, contains remains of Philippe Auguste's Wall. No. 31 is a beautiful mansion* with magnificent 18th-c. wrought ironwork. At the end of the courtyard is the Café Belge, which was frequented in the 19th c. by bohemians and *grisettes*, young, working-class women, some of whom were part-time prostitutes, who came to see Henri Murger. The fashion for eating onion soup in the small hours started here. At no. 16 around 1660 the Hôtel de la Curée was replaced by the Hôtel de Moüy.

Rue de Nesle

Originally called Rue d'Anjou-Dauphine, this street was built on the site of the gardens of the Hôtel de Nesle. Raoul de Nesle was Constable of France in the 14th c. Most of the houses on the even-numbered side date from 1607 to 1620. No. 13 was rumored to have been an underground passage leading to the Tour de Nesle on the bank of the Seine.

The street ends at the Impasse de Nevers, which has hardly

changed since the Middle Ages. Most of the buildings date from the 15th c. Rejoin the Rue Dauphine.

Rue Christine to the l., built in 1607, is named after Christine of France, daughter of Henri IV and Marie de' Medici. Almost all the houses date from this time. No. 1 at the corner of the Rue des Grands-Augustins is magnificent.

Rue des Grands-Augustins

This street is named after the convent which extended from the quay to the Rue Christine. It is a street with literary associations, and there are still some beautiful old houses (nos. 28, 26, 24, 21, 19, 17, 16 and so on, mostly 18th c.).

Follow this street in the direction of the Rue Saint-André-des-Arts, then go down again towards the quay. La Bruyère lived at no. 25 from 1676 to 1691, then Augustin Thierry had an apartment there from 1820 to 1830; Heinrich Heine stayed there in 1841. No. 23 was the Hôtel des Charités-Saint-Denis (17th c.) Emile Littré was born at no. 21 in 1808 and the mathematician Laplace lived at no. 12 in 1802. At nos. 5 and 7 the Hôtel d'Hercule (15th c.), was demolished in 1675 and divided up among the numerous younger branches of the House of Savoy. No. 7 has a beautiful 17th-c. courtyard and no. 5 was the Hôtel de Savoie-Carignan. At no. 1 on the corner of the Rue du Pont-de-Lodi, the Restaurant Lapérouse dates from the 18th c. and has preserved its original beams. In the courtyard of no. 3 which formed part of the Hôtel de Savoie-Nemours (1628) are remains of the refectory of the convent of the Grands-Augustins, over which this street was built in 1802.

Rue de Savoie

Returning along Rue des Grands-Augustins, on the l.

This street was laid out over the grounds of the Hôtel de Savoie-Nemours. Most of the houses are 18th c. There was once a mansion at no. 29. Sophie Germain (1776–1831), mathematician and philosopher, died at no. 13. Nos. 10 and 6 have interesting courtyards. Blaise Cendrars, the writer, lived at no. 4. Picasso had a studio in this street.

Rue Séguier

In 1179 this street replaced a path which crossed the Clos de Laas. From the 16th c. until 1864 it was called Rue Pavée-d'Andouilles or Rue Pavé-Saint-André-des-Arts. Begin the tour from the quay.

No. 2 was the Didot printing house (18th c.). No. 6 was part of the

Hôtel de Nemours, then the Hôtel de Montholon, where Giraudoux lived. The Belgian poet Henri Michaux lived at no. 8. No. 3 dates from the 18th c. On nos. 9, 11 and 13 stood the house of the *Cordonniers*, so-called for the cords around their waists, brothers of the order of Saint-Crépin (*ca.* 1645). At no. 16 is the Hôtel de Moussy, with a beautiful Louis-XV door and courtyard. Elegant houses with wrought ironwork are at nos. 10, 12, 16 and 17. No. 18 was the Hôtel de Nevers, afterwards the Hôtel d'Aguesseau and then the Hôtel de la Roche-Aymon. Albert Camus lived here. The courtyard is magnificent.

Rue Gît-le-Coeur

To the l. of Rue Saint-André-des-Arts.

The street, which took its name in the 13th c. from Gilles-le-Queu or Guy-le-Queux (the cook), has also been called Guy-le-Preux. No. 12 is a large 18th-c. mansion. There are 17th-c. houses at nos. 10 and 11. Nos. 5, 7, 9 were the *hôtel* of Pierre Séguier, Marquis d'O; it became the Hôtel de Luynes, owned by Racine's uncle. Note the 17th-c. building in the courtyard of no. 5. No. 4 has a 17th-c. door and a courtyard altered in the 18th c.

The street communicates with the Place Saint-Michel (→ Latin Quarter, Boul. Saint-Michel) via the old Rue de l'Hirondelle.

Rue de l'Hirondelle: nos. 23, 25 and 27 (18th c.) formerly belonged to the college of Autun. At nos. 22 and 20 an 18th-c. house has kept the sign of the Salamander emblem of François I which marked the *hôtel* of Anne de Pisseleu, Duchesse d'Etampes and mistress of the King.

From the Place Saint-Michel recross the Place Saint-André-des-Arts.

Rue Hautefeuille

In the Middle Ages, before it was shortened, this ancient street led to the Château Hautefeuille outside the ramparts, sheltered by large trees. Many beautiful early 17th-c. houses (nos. 1*bis*, 8 and 10 and doubtless, from the reign of Louis XV, nos. 4 and 7). No. 3, the Hôtel Le Clerc de Lesseville, was built in 1683. At no. 5, on the corner of the Impasse Hautefeuille, is the former *hôtel* of the abbots of Fécamp, where Diane de Poitiers may have stayed or at least visited the Cardinal of Lorraine, whose residence it was. Later, the notorious poisoner, the Marquise de Brinvilliers, plotted there with her lover, who lodged at the *hôtel*. The turret dates from the 16th c. In the courtyard of no. 5, note the wooden sign, 'La Serpente', taken from the street of the same name.

Rue Serpente on the r. Only these few old 18th-c. houses recall the old path which, around 1179, snaked across the fields. At no. 15 an inscription indicates that here stood the Collège de Suesse or Collège d'Uppsala, founded in 1291 for 12 Finno-Swedish students from the University of Paris.

The Rue de l'Eperon is very tranquil. No. 12 is from the 17th c. and no. 10 from the time of Louis XVI. The poet Théodore de Banville died here.

A little further on to the r. is the Rue Suger which seems somewhat neglected, although it has several interesting houses. No. 16 is a beautiful 17th-18th c. mansion. No. 12 was Nicolas Cottignon's *hôtel* (1625), which was later modified. No. 11 dates from the 17th c. Joris-Karl Huysmans, author of *A rebours,* was born at no. 9; finally, no. 5 is part of the former college of Boissy, from the 18th c.

Rejoin the Rue de l'Eperon, to the l., and turn r. into the small Rue du Jardinet, where Saint-Saëns was born in 1835. In this street there used to be an entrance to the Lycée Fénélon.

The Cour de Rohan**

Access from the Rue du Jardinet until 8pm; after 8pm access from the Boul. Saint-Germain.

This courtyard belonged to the mansion that the archbishops of Rouen used as a pied-à-terre, which explains its name. It consists of three charming small courtyards of a somewhat old-fashioned character. The first, to the E, has a well with a decayed coping. The second is the most unusual with its *pas-de-mule* (three-legged wrought-iron mounting block) and beautiful 1636 *hôtel.* The yard to the W has a fragment of Philippe Auguste's Wall, forming a terrace. From there the Cour or Passage du Commerce-Saint-André, which was built in 1776 above the dry moats surrounding the wall, is reached. Most of the houses date from the same year. The critic and writer Sainte-Beuve lived at no. 2 from 1831 to 1841. No. 4 has the basement of one of Philippe Auguste's towers. In 1793 the Marzt printing house was at no. 8, where the future Marshal Brune was head of the composing room. In a neighboring shop, Girondin Brissot's widow set up a reading room with the books of her guillotined husband. At no. 9 Dr. Guillotin is supposed to have tried out – probably on sheep – his 'philanthropic decapitation machine'; in fact he only suggested the idea, and it was a Dr Louis from the College of Surgeons who had one built.

Rue de l'Ancienne-Comédie

A passage links this street directly to the Passage du Commerce-Saint-André. Formerly the Rue des Fossés-Saint-Germain, the street got its present name when the Comédie-Française left it; the company had had its *hôtel* here at no. 14 in the *Jeu de Paume* (old tennis court) of the Etoile. It was formed in 1680 by the merging of the Hôtel de Bourgogne and the Guénégaud companies, the latter having been set up by Armand Béjart, Molière and La Grange. It remained here from 1689 to 1770. After its departure, David, Horace Vernet and Gros had a studio here. On the façade is a haut-relief representing *Minerve* by Le Hongre.

At no. 13 the Restaurant Le Procope succeeded the famous Café Procope. Founded in 1675 in the Rue de Tournon by a Sicilian, Francesco Procopio dei Coltelli, it was one of the most popular cafés in Paris. When the Comédie-Française settled down opposite in 1689, it became a rendezvous for actors. Many generations of writers and politicians met here. After Voltaire and the Encyclopedists came those who made the Revolution: Danton, Desmoulins, Marat, Robespierre; after them, the Romantics: Musset, George Sand and the bohemians of the time, and finally Gambetta and his journalist friends. Towards the end of the century it regained its literary character with Verlaine, Paul Arène, Charles Cros and Oscar Wilde. Its décor dates only from 1893.

Rue de l'Ancienne-Comédie leads into the Boul. Saint-Germain.

Place Henri-Mondor

The boulevard, which is very much wider at this point, becomes the Place Henri-Mondor. Nothing in the area resembles the maze of winding streets where those involved in the French Revolution lived. Marat and Legendre lived in the Rue des Cordeliers (now Rue Ecole-de-Médecine) and Fabre d'Eglantine in the Rue de l'Ancienne-Comédie. The Simon family, Louis XVI's jailers, lived at no. 87, and Danton had a huge apartment where he was arrested in 1794, in the very spot where his statue stands today.

> The Wallace Fountains

Public hygiene was a major preoccupation during the Second Empire and the Third Republic, which is why the period saw a proliferation of water supply points and the installation of many drinking fountains and fire hydrants. The English philanthropist Sir Richard Wallace donated 66 drinking-fountains to Paris.

The first of the popular Wallace fountains was installed in 1871 on the Boul. de la Villette. While the name of the generous donor is remembered, the sculptor, Charles Lebourg, is less well known. The model has a bronze base ornamented with dolphins, while four caryatids support an elegant dome patterned with scales and topped by more dolphins. Despite the destruction or sale of some, numerous examples can still be seen on a walk round Paris (e.g. Boul. Richard-Lenoir).

The Wallace donation included two other less well-known models: the Wallace wall fountain (one survives in the Rue Buffon) and the small-scale Wallace fountain, the traditional drinking fountain of the squares, with the tap in the center of a sunflower.

Among the strangest of the many Paris fountains was the hot water fountain built around 1890. On inserting a coin, the Parisian wishing to take a bath or wash a vehicle could obtain eight litres of hot water. The last fountain of this type, worked by gas, exploded in the Place Saint-André-des-Arts in 1893.

▷ 'Tabou'

The story of the Tabou, first and last of the 'cellars' of the great Saint-Germain-des-Prés era, sums up the story of them all. Immediately after World War II at the Club Saint-Germain, or the Vieux-Colombier or La Rose Rouge, the same strange ambience of what rapidly became known as 'existentialism' could be found. It was evoked in the works of Sartre, who is credited with the philosophy. Social life was awakening once again in a moment of utopian brotherhood after the lean years of the war. Devotees clustered around the new intellectuals. Little sleep (so they say) and a uniform of trousers and black sweater was the particular fashion that characterized the young Parisian existentialist. Le Tabou opened in 1947. It engaged Boris Vian and his two brothers as the jazz band. Juliette Greco, Anne-Marie Cazalis, Raymond Queneau and Léo Malet came as both clients and performers, and after them, Roger Pierre, Jean-Marc Thibault, Jean Poiret, Mouloudji and Fernand Raynaud. The jazz club became well known through the elections of Miss Fantasy, especially during the 'Nuit de la Luxure'. Since then, its success has been continuous. Today it has a largely black clientele.

▷ Not to be missed

Rue Saint-André-des-Arts and its 18th-c. mansions: nos. 33, 41, 47, 49, 52.

The Cour de Rohan.

The Hotel de Fécamp, Rue Hautefeuille.

▷ The craft of making books

The craft of bookmaking dates from the Middle Ages when Paris was an important center for the production of manuscripts. There was a street, Rue des Ecrivains, devoted to it and a guild at the Church of Saint-Jacques-de-la-Boucherie. These 'writers' were mainly just copyists, but they also did the illuminations. One of their specialities was 'books of hours'.

After Gutenberg invented movable type, it was introduced to Paris by the Germans: In 1470 Gering, Friburger and Crantz were summoned by the rector of the Sorbonne and installed in their first workshop. In 1473 they moved to the Rue Saint-Jacques to the Soleil d'Or, which became the center of some of finest work produced. Henceforth, the Rue Saint-Jacques became the center of the Parisian book trade, with its innumerable printers and booksellers, which at first were not separated: Jean Petit, Josse Bade, Kerver, then in the 17th c., Cramoisy, the Mariettes, all around where the Sorbonne is today. The street, quiet today, then buzzed with intense activity. Other streets were also connected with the printing trade: the Mont Saint-Hilaire (Rue de Lanneau) and the Rue Jean-de-Beauvais with the Estiennes and the Ballards, music printers.

Later the bookshops moved to the Palais de Justice, where prints were largely sold. The publishers produced less material and had less contact with the public. They nonetheless remained on the Left Bank, especially on the Boul. Saint-Germain and the neighboring streets where the main offices of Hachette, Presses Universitaires de France, Magnard and many others are located. The bookbinders remained for a long time in the Saint-André-des-Arts district where they found both their clients and their materials (skins, gold leaf, etc.).

Today printers are usually to be found in the provinces or abroad, and bookbinders in the suburbs, while bookshops are everywhere. Only the antiquarian bookshops remain traditionally concentrated in the 6th arrondissement: Argences (38 Rue Saint-Sulpice), Brieux (48 Rue Jacob), Clavreuil (37 Rue Saint-André-des-Arts), Dasté (16 Rue de Tournon), Galantais (27 Rue de Seine), Jammes (3 Rue Gozlin), Kieffer (46 Rue Saint-André-des-Arts), Laget (75 Rue de Rennes), Saffroy (4 Rue Clément).

The Faubourg Saint-Antoine*

11th and 12th arr. Map ref. 18–D2, D3
Métro: Bastille
Bus: 20, 29, 65, 69, 76, 86, 91
Parking: Place de la Bastille, between the Boul. Bourdon and the Boul. de la Bastille

Taxis: 2 Rue Faidherbe. Tel. 43-72-00-00.

To find the true character of this district you must go beyond the flashy shop windows of the Faubourg Saint-Antoine, where Moorish figures serve as lamps and porcelain tigers crouch beside cheap gilt furniture like a stage-set for some regatta. At the heart of this inner suburb lies one of the last authentic areas of Paris, with its market, bars, saucy down-and-outs and genuine craftsmen whose amazing skills are well recognized in the name 'Rue de la Main-D'Or' (Golden Hand). It is at the ends of courtyards and in back alleys that, in the same way and with the same tools, the traditions of three centuries of fine quality furniture-making are still carried on.

Yet this lively and colorful district has not stood still. The Auvergnats who came to take over the wood and coal trade at the beginning of the 20th century were followed by the African immigrants from both North and Subsaharan Africa, and Southeast Asians. This extraordinary mixture of cultures and races has made this historic district completely unique in Paris. Recently the fashion industry has taken over the area. Numerous young artists and fashion designers have opened workshops or boutiques here and the Rue de Lappe and the Rue de Charonne are being invaded by contemporary art galleries. The imminent opening of the Nouvel Opera of the Place de la Bastille will doubtless intensify this phenomenon.

The history of the Faubourg

The Faubourg Saint-Antoine developed around the fortified royal abbey of Saint-Antoine-des-Champs, founded in 1198. By freeing the craftsmen who worked around the abbey from the restrictive supervision of the guilds, Louis XI firmly established the furniture industry in the Saint-Antoine district. Boulle, Riesner, Cressent, Leleu and Jacob were among the most celebrated of the cabinet-makers. It was through them that the district's fame extended far beyond the kingdom's borders in the 17th and 18th c. At this time some cabinet-makers' workshops employed over 100 workers, whose wretched conditions were at the root of serious social unrest. The local people were naturally at the center of the insurrections during the time of the Revolution. Later, they threw up barricades during the revolutionary days of 1830 and 1848, and during the Paris Commune.

Tour of the district

1 hr.

Rue de la Roquette

This street to the NE of the Place de la Bastille owes its name to the Petite Roche, Rochette or Roquette, which was the country house of the Valois. In 1636 the estate passed to the hospitallers of the Roquette, whose convent was founded there three years later by the Duchesse de Mercoeur. This busy shopping street has been somewhat changed by the appearance of some bars and fashion boutiques.

Verlaine lived at no. 17 and Michelet at no. 41. A little further on at no. 51 *bis* is the Church of Notre–Dame–de–l'Esperance with its polygonal steeple, built in 1930 by the architect Barbier. At no. 84 there is a monument to the East European Jews who died for France during World War I. Much further on, at no. 148, is the site of the Grande–Roquette prison, demolished in 1899. On the corner of the Rue de la Croix–Faubin can be seen the five flagstones on which stood the guillotine that was in use here for many years. The second prison, known as the Petite–Roquette, was situated at no. 143 until quite recently. Today the playgrounds and lively atmosphere have completely changed the street, which is considerably more animated than it used to be.

Rue de Lappe

Follow this street to the r. The Rue de Lappe, which is mentioned as early as the 17th c., had its heyday in the 19th c. It was here that dance halls and *bals-musettes* (dance halls with accordion music) proliferated, frequented by people from all social classes. Until the 1930s it was fashionable to go slumming in the Rue de Lappe to mix with *les apaches*, the local toughs and their girls. The apache dance was rather risqué but not really violent, to judge from contemporary photographs, but it did have a lot of twirling lifts. The American G. W. Smith introduced the *apache* dance to America and thrilled audiences with the sight of girls in slit skirts and berets being spun around acrobatically by their cloth-capped partners. Today the street is calmer. The Balajo and the Boule Rouge are still there but the boutiques and trendy art galleries have changed the atmosphere. Asian restaurants have not completely eclipsed the traditional Auvergnat shops, with their copper counters and clogs hanging alongside the drying sausages.

Rue de Charonne

Go along this street to the l., following the route of the old way to the village of Charonne. Note the large glass roof at no. 22, which covers the two buildings joined to form the V-shaped inner courtyard (*ca.* 1896). Note the façade of the Café Vrai Saumur on the corner of the Ave. Ledru-Rollin. Built in 1902, it has the sinuous curves of Art Nouveau architecture and has recently been cleverly restored.

No. 53, hidden by a modern building, is the Hôtel de Mortagne*, built by Delisle-Mansart in 1660. Enter the Passage Dallery on the l. to see both sides of the building. In 1746 Vaucanson assembled a collection of machines here, which was to become the nucleus of the Conservatoire des Arts et Métiers collection. Louis XVI, who was extremely interested in the machines, bought the mansion and turned it into the Royal Collection of Machinery *(le Cabinet de mécanique du roi)*. The mansion was divided up in the 19th c.

A little further down at no. 94 is the Salvation Army hostel, also called the Palais de la Femme, a large building characteristic of the 1920s architects Labussière and Longerey. No. 98 is the site of the Filles-de-la-Croix convent where Cyrano de Bergerac is said to have found refuge and to have been buried. But after the expulsion of the nuns, the tomb of this man who apparently bore little resemblance to Edmond Rostand's hero could not be found.

Take the Rue Saint-Bernard to the r., which leads to the Church of Saint-Marguerite at no. 36.

✝ The Church of Sainte-Marguerite

Open Mon.-Sat. 8am-noon, 3-7pm; Sun. 8am-noon. Tel. 43-71-34-24.

Originally this church was a chapel built by Antoine Fayet, curate of Saint-Paul, at his own expense to serve as a chapel of ease for his church. It was enlarged in 1669 and again in the 18th c. In 1760 Victor Louis, who designed the Grand Théâtre of Bordeaux, donated the sketches for the Ames du Purgatoire (Souls in Purgatory chapel).

The interior

In the nave, which has basket-handle arching (there is a pulpit, 1704) decorated with four bas-reliefs: *Sermon on the Mount* and *Preaching of John the Baptist, St Peter* and *St Paul*. In the r. transept: Chapel of the Virgin; in the l. wall successively: *The Foundling Institution* by Louis Galloche (1732), *Anne of Austria and S Vincent de Paul, St Vincent de Paul Teaching the Poor* by Frère André (18th c.). The paintings by Galloche and Frère André form part of a series of 11 pictures depicting scenes from the life of St Vincent de Paul, commissioned by the priests of Saint-Lazare, for their monastery in the Faubourg Saint-Denis. Around the chancel on the wall to the l. of the sacristy door: *The Visitation* by Suvée

(Salon painting of 1781). Behind the high altar, white marble *Pietà* carved for the tomb of Catherine Duchemin (d.1698), wife of Girardon. This work by two of his pupils, E. Nourisson and Robert Le Lorrain, to his own designs, was originally placed in the Church of Saint-Landry in the Cité. Going back to the l. of the chancel to the Chapel le des Ames du Purgatoire (Souls in Purgatory) chapel built by Victor Louis (1760). *Trompe-l'oeil* décor by Paolo-Antonio Brunetti. Under the archway at the end: *Souls in Purgatory* by Briard. In the transept to the l., Chapelle de Sainte-Marguerite: to the r. of the altar, *St Ambrose Presenting a Letter to God from Theodosius* by Lagrenée (1764); on the r. wall, in the center: *St Margaret Driven out by her Father* by Vafflard (1817) and a marble statue of St Margaret by Leboeuf-Nanteuil (1827), to the l., *S Francis de Sales Installing St Vincent de Paul as Chaplain of the Dames de la Visitation* by Jean Restout (1732); to the r., *St Vincent de Paul Commanding the Priests of his Congregation to Care for the Soldiers* by J. B. Féret (1731). These two pictures are part of the same series as those in the Chapel of the Virgin.

The Cemetery

Visits by arrangement.

In a small cemetery (not open) surrounding the church is the tomb of the cabinet-maker Georges II Jacob (d.1803). It was also here that the body of Louis XVII is said to have been buried in 1795. From 1637 to 1804 the cemetery was the burial ground for the Temple district; the charnelhouse was on the site where the Chapelle des Catéchismes stands today. A child was buried there on June 10, 1795. The exhumations between 1846 and 1894 gave disturbing results. Some bones of a child were uncovered as well as some bones of a young man, 15 to 18 years old. Lenotre suggests that the young king's coffin, brought from the Temple, was perhaps buried more deeply. The hypothesis of the substitution of a child for the true Louis XVII has its supporters, since it has been established that the child who died at the Temple was not the son of Louis XVI. However, some still believe that the little king died at the Temple and was buried in the Church of Saint-Marguerite. It remains one of the mysteries of Paris. The grave is just on the l. by the Ames du Purgatoire chapel. Its small stone cross is inscribed: 'L. . . XVII 1785–1795' and underneath '*Attendite et videte si est dolor sicut dolor meus*'. (Listen and behold: If there is sorrow it is my sorrow). Further on are some graves from the old cemetery. In the center is a crib built in 1904; there is a calvary dated 1717.

Rue Saint-Bernard runs into the Rue du Faubourg-Saint-Antoine, after crossing the Square Raoul-Nordling, which is named in memory of the Swedish consul who persuaded the German general commanding Paris not to order its destruction.

Place du Docteur-Beclère

It is here that the Fontaine de Montreuil was built in the 18th c. to mark the beginning of the street of the same name. At the corner of the Rue Montreuil and Rue du Faubourg–Saint–Antoine is the site of the former Folie Titon, where the first hot–air balloons were made in 1783, by the Montgolfier brothers; they were helped financially by Réveillon, who popularized wallpaper. It was here that the first bloody riots of 27 and 28 April 1798 took place. They were directed against the Réveillon workshops and their owner had to flee. Heavily suppressed by the Swiss and the French guards, this popular uprising was a forerunner of the Revolution.

The Saint-Antoine hospital

Opposite the fountain is the entrance to the hospital, which occupies a large part of the former Royal Abbey of Saint–Antoine–des–Champs. This famous nunnery, which was founded in 1198 by Foulques, curate of Neuilly, formed a community outside the town, and gave its name to the whole district. The abbesses were usually princesses of the blood royal. The buildings which still exist today are those which were reconstructed around 1770 by the architect Lenoir, known as Le Romain. Mme Geoffrin, famous for her wit, was at the abbey in 1771. Her visit has been commemorated in the delightful paintings by Hubert Robert.

The former buildings consist of a beautiful façade, two storeys high, surmounted by a triangular pediment. It dates from 1767. André Wogenscky built the first health clinic of the University of Paris (CHU), for 850 students, as part of the building's expansion from 1964 to 1965. The architect, a former colleague of Le Corbusier, understood how to temper the severity of the building, which has a concrete frame and a façade of glass and steel, by the use of light and shade on the outside of the building. A balanced harmony of colors enhances the interior, with black, white, grey, orange–red and dark blue. There is also a mobile by Marta Pan, a mural by James Guitet and a window by James Koenig. Robert Wogenscky decorated the recreation room, which opens onto a garden terrace.

Those interested in modern architecture should visit the remarkable kitchen building of the Saint–Antoine hospital at 30 Rue de Citeaux (architect Ciriani, 1985).

Rue du Faubourg-Saint-Antoine

From Place du Docteur Beclère to Rue d'Aligre.

Follow this street toward the Place de la Bastille. No. 151 is an 18th-c. house, in front of which was the barricade where the Deputy Baudin was 'killed for 25 francs' on December 3, 1851. This sum was the daily salary of a deputy, while workers were considered well paid if they got five francs. The story may not be true, but it clearly shows the relationship between the proletariat of the district and the parliamentary victims of the coup.

Follow the Rue d'Aligre to the r. as far as the Place d'Aligre, which should be seen in the morning when its colorful and lively market is open (→inset).

Opposite the pleasant Square Trousseau, which has retained its bandstand, is a group of stone and brick buildings constructed in 1905 for the Rothschild Foundation. The complex, which was created 'for the improvement of material living conditions for the workers', is characteristic of public housing projects constructed early in the century by philanthropic foundations. Above the main entrance, which is in the Rue de Prague, is an edifying bas-relief, paying tribute to *Work and the Family*.

Rue du Faubourg-Saint-Antoine, continued

From Rue d'Aligre to the Quinze-Vingts Hospital.

The Rue du Faubourg-Saint-Antoine, as far as the Bastille, still has some of its former character, with its elegant curved balconies, wrought ironwork and windows, while behind its façades stretches a complicated network of passages and courtyards. The kingdom of the wood craftsmen, although declining, can still be seen operating here. In its way the Faubourg Saint-Antoine is a noble *quartier*: skills pass from one generation to the next; there are carpenters, cabinetmakers, carvers, bronze and marquetry workers and gilders. It is a street known for its fine workmanship. Over the centuries furniture famed throughout Europe has been made here. To the tradition of woodwork must be added that of insurrection, since the district has always been quick to rebel against power. Although this is now a thing of the past, the political and trade union demonstrations that go from the Bastille to the Nation along the Faubourg-Saint-Antoine are a tribute to the street's traditions. At the beginning of the Rue de Charonne, note the large Trogneux fountain, built in 1710.

At no. 50, on the l., go down the Passage de la Boule Blanche (closed at night) as far as the entrance to the Quinze-Vingts Hospital.

The Quinze-Vingts Hospital

28 Rue de Charenton

In 1260 St Louis founded this hospital for 300 blind people. Originally situated in what is now the Place du Palais-Royal, since 1790 the hospital has occupied the former barracks of the Black

Musketeers (so called because of the color of their horses). They form an imposing group of buildings constructed between 1699 to 1701 to plans by Robert de Cotte.

Rue du Faubourg-Saint-Antoine, continued

From the Quinze–Vingts Hospital to the Bastille.

No. 46 is a furniture shop constructed by Robert Le Sage and Charles Miltgen in 1907. At no. 25 are the Le Bihan shops, formerly the Wimphen shops, built from 1893 to 1894 by Charles de Montalto.

▷ # Entertainment

The district, which is traditionally a shopping area, is particularly lively in the Rue du Faubourg–Saint–Antoine between the intersection at Ledru–Rollin and at Faidherbe–Chalingy.

Markets

The Aligre market, Place d'Aligre. Secondhand bric-a-brac and clothing: daily 7:30am–7:30pm.

Rue d'Aligre, fruit and vegetables: Tues.–Sun. 7:30am–12:30pm.

Covered market between Rue D'Aligre and Rue de Cotte: Tues.–Sun. 8am–1pm, 3:30–7:30pm, Sun. 8am–1pm.

Theaters

The Bastille Theater (76 Rue de la Roquette), the Espace Kiron (10 Rue de la Vacquerie) and the Théâtre des Athévains (46 Rue Richard–Lenoir), present mime, dance and avant-garde theater.

Contemporary art

A dozen or more art galleries have just opened up in the area. One of the most important, the Lavignes–Bastille gallery (27 Rue de Charonne; tel. 47-00-88-18) now puts on exhibitions three times a year.

Note also: the Claire Burrus gallery (30–32 Rue de Lappe, 75011; tel. 43-55-36-90); J. and J. Donguy (57 Rue de la Roquette, 75011; tel. 47-00-10-94); the Gutharc Ballin gallery (47 Rue de Lappe, 75011; tel. 47-00-32-10); Antoine Candau (17 Rue Keller, 75011; tel. 43-38-75-51).

L'Espace Bastille, 5 Rue de la Roquette, is a center for various cultural events: exhibitions, festivals and salons.

Over the last few years, artists in the neighborhood have held open days for the public in their studios during the July Bastille celebrations and the related International Contemporary Art Fair held in October and November.

The Faubourg Saint-Germain**

The atmosphere of this sprawling district varies widely from one neighborhood to another. To the E in the Rue de Sèvres and Rue des Saints-Pères, you can peer into the elegant shop windows of the top fashion designers and fashionable interior decorators. This is the busiest and most commercial part of the district. Between the Boulevard Saint-Germain and the Seine and around the Musée d'Orsay, quiet and unobtrusive streets shelter art galleries and antique shops that attract a distinguished clientèle of collectors and connoisseurs.

However, the heart of the Faubourg, lying to the W between the Rue de Babylone and the Seine, stretches as far as the Boulevard des Invalides. This is the powerhouse of French political life and the place where ties with foreign states are made, for most of the foreign embassies and French government ministries now occupy what were once the mansions of the nobility. The Chamber of Deputies, as well as a republican administration, seems quite at home in aristocratic quarters. Most of the austere façades of these houses have a history and often conceal an imposing forecourt or a secret garden. As you walk down the quiet streets past these noble mansions, you can only marvel at the good taste and inborn refinement of the society that built them, and which once set the tone not merely for the whole of France, but for all Europe as well. The size of the district suggests four separate itineraries: focused on the Rue des Saints-Pères, the Rue de Grenelle, the Sèvres-Babylone *quartier,* and the Palais-Bourbon.

History of the district

In the 8th c. the abbey founded by King Childebert two centuries earlier as the Abbey of the Sainte-Croix-Saint-Vincent, to enshrine a fragment of the True Cross and St Vincent's tunic, received the body of St Germain, Bishop of Paris. Thereafter it became known as the Abbey of Saint-Germain-des-Prés (St-Germain-in-the-Fields), evidence that it then stood out in the country. The Abbey demesne more or less covered what is now the Faubourg, being bounded on the N by the Seine, on the E by the Rue des Saints-Pères, on the S by the Rue de Sèvres and on the W by the Boulevard des Invalides. In essence it comprised arable land, vineyards and meadows, with a stretch of woodland, where the Invalides now stands, kept as a hunting park.

The district began to be developed and became more thickly populated in the reign of Henri IV. Convents and the houses of religious orders were the first to appear: Augustinians of the Saint-Sépulcre (Holy Sepulchre), Carmelites, Cordeliers, Dames de la Providence, Bernardines, Theatins and Jacobins. In 1564 the erection of the Château des Tuileries made it necessary to establish a ferry on the site of the present Pont-Royal 'to carry stone back and forth' from the quarries of Notre-Dame-des-Champs, and thus to create the major N-S axis, the Rue du Bac (or Bacq) (Ferry Street). This was the first link between the King's city and the abbots' country estate. What were once modestly known as 'the little cowpath' (Rue de Grenelle) leading to the village of Grenelle and 'Warren Street' (Rue de Garenne) by the early 18th c. had become the Rue de Grenelle and the Rue de Varenne, fine streets lined by elegant mansions with forecourts and gardens.

From the very beginning of construction, the location of the Faubourg Saint-Germain, on the direct route to Versailles and close to the Louvre and the Tuileries, gave it a markedly aristocratic character. It reached the peak of its fortunes during the minority of Louis XV, when the young king made his home in Paris. Here was a site – similar to the Place des Vosges and the Place de l'Etoile – in which the ingenuity of architects and the skill of decorators could have full play, and in the first half of the 18th c. they covered it with a harmonious complex of *hôtels,* without benefit of any formal urban planning at all.

That this new district was exclusively residential was in itself something new. Unlike the Marais, where palaces and mansions were engulfed by shops and traders' stalls, commerce, the theater and places of entertainment were effectively confined to the Rue du Bac and Rue de Bellechasse. Simultaneously a new *art de vivre* was born, and architecture strove to reflect the latest needs of a worldly, cultivated aristocracy. Palaces and mansions were built to be unobtrusive and comfortable, yet luxurious, and set within spacious and elegant gardens. These gracious houses stood side by side and belonged to the greatest names in France: the Duchesse de Bourbon, the Princesse de Bourbon-Condé, Louis XIV's grand-daughters Mlle de Sens and Mlle de Charolais, the Duchesse de Maine, the Duc de Castries, and the Comte de Matignon.

The French Revolution emptied the faubourg. The aristocracy either emigrated or went to the guillotine. Its mansions were sold by auction and their contents sometimes incorporated into the national depositions. During the First Empire these town houses were not disdained by some of the more notable members of the new ruling class. Napoléon's mother, Madame Mère, his brother Lucien, Cambacérès, Talleyrand, Kellermann, Davout, Corvisart and Chaptal all took up residence next door to the old aristocratic families, some of whom had returned to live in their favorite district. But it was after the Bourbon Restoration that the faubourg slowly regained its aristocratic cachet, when the nobility returned as a group entirely separate from the rest of society, in a district with an atmosphere all its own. It was then that the gulf widened between the Left and Right Banks. The Faubourg Saint-Honoré which, during the 18th c., had rivaled the Faubourg Saint-Germain in its high-born residents and the beauty of their homes, no longer had the same prestige. If Stendhal, Balzac, Flaubert, and Proust as well, are to be believed, the inhabitants of the two banks of the Seine were utterly at odds over all aspects of life: the fervor of their faith, the strictness of their morals, their lust for money, their taste for adventure, the cut of their clothes, their speech and manners, even their carriages, were different. At the close of the 19th c. the building of the Boulevard Saint-Germain not only altered the appearance of the district but transformed its attitudes of mind, as it drove its residents to new quarters in the districts created by the expansion of the capital. Civil servants drove out the lingering shades of Mme du Deffand, a princess of Monaco, a Duc de Chaulnes, a Comte Loménie de Brienne and a Marquis du Châtelet.

Now ministers and ambassadors, generals and diplomats have taken possession of the reception rooms with their Rococo paneling, dining-rooms with their mahogany sideboards and boudoirs hung with silk from Lyons.

The Rue des Saints-Pères district*

7th arr./Map ref. 16-C2,D2
Métro: Saint-Germain-des-Prés, Rue du Bac
Bus: 24, 27, 39, 48, 63, 95
Parking: Boul. Saint-Germain opposite Le Drugstore; Square Boucicaut
Taxis: Rue du Bac Métro station. Tel. 42-22-49-64.

This walk will tempt those who like beautiful things, taking you past some of the most famous antique dealers in Paris. Avoid Sunday and Monday, when art galleries and antique shops are closed.

Tour of the district

2 hrs.

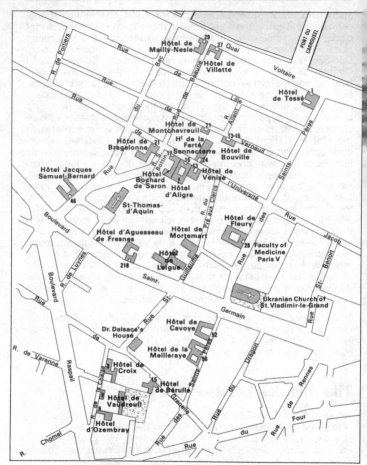

The Rue des Saints-Pères district

Rue des Saints-Pères

As far as the Rue de Lille.

The name of this street is a corruption of Saint–Pierre, to whom was originally dedicated what is now the chapel of St Vladimir the Great

(→below). No. 2 was once the Hôtel Tessé*, by Pierre–Noël Rousset and its beautiful Louis XVI façade stretches into the Rue de Lille (no. 2) and beyond to 1 Quai Voltaire. The author Visconti lived here in 1797 and after him Pradier who sculpted two of the Muses on the Molière fountain, and Barbet de Jouy. The side-wall of no. 6, the Hôtel Pidoux (→below), is ornamented by a balcony supported by four lions' heads, typical of the French Regency.

Rue de Lille

As far as Rue du Bac.

This street follows the line of one of the paths in La Reine Margot's garden and, until the time of the Convention, was named Rue Bourbon, after the Duc de Verneuil, a natural son of Henri IV and abbot of Saint-Germain-des-Prés. Its present name is a tribute to the heroic defense of Lille in 1792.

Proceed along this street as far as the Rue du Bac and then retrace your steps.

No. 1 is the Hôtel Pidoux*, built in 1640. The fine entry, with a grotesque head carved on the façade, and the Rococo balcony show how sumptuous the mansion was. Under Louis XVI it housed the Comtesse d'Artois' stables. Opposite, the Ecole des Langues Orientales (School of Oriental Languages) occupies a mansion built on the site of the gardens of the Hôtel Tessé and remodelled in the 19th c. by Faure–Dujarric. Nos 11, 13, 14, 15 and 16 are all beautiful 18th-c. mansions. Pay special attention to the wrought ironwork at no. 9 and to the sundial at no. 14. The entrance to the Théatin Church of Sainte-Anne-la-Royale still stands at no. 26, crowned by an angel which must have been carved by a leading Parisian sculptor of the day. The rest of the church, begun in 1666 and finished by Desmaisons in 1746, was demolished in 1800. Continuing along the Rue de Lille you will come to the headquarters of the Federation of French Baptist Churches at no. 48. The building was erected in 1873 and baptisms by total immersion still take place there, although strictly confined to adults.

An alternative way back to the Rue des Saints-Pères is via the Rue de Verneuil. (→The Palais-Bourbon District).

Rue des Saint-Pères, continued

From Rue de Lille to the Boul. Saint-Germain
From the beginning of this street →above.

The composer Charles Marie Widor lived at no. 7, formerly the Hôtel de Falcony, erected in 1647 but entirely rebuilt during the 18th c. In 1908 the historian Michelet lived at no. 10. Other buildings, without such claims to fame, deserve a glance for their courtyards or balconies. Juliette Bernard, the future Mme Récamier, lived at no. 13, the 18th-c. Hôtel de Bernage. No. 28, the Hôtel de Fleury, built by Antoine in 1773, has a fine classical façade, pure Louis XVI, overlooking the forecourt and a magnificent staircase (registered). Since 1985 it has housed the Ecole des Ponts et Chaussées (School of Civil Engineering); in the forecourt stands an obelisk, in memory of former pupils killed in action. There is fine Empire furniture in a first-floor reception room. No. 30, which is now the home of the Maison Debauve et Gallais, a very old firm of manufacturers of 'fine and hygienic chocolates', was erected on the site of the old Protestant cemetery. Among the bodies exhumed were those of the Androuet du Cerceau and the Gobelins families, Salomon de Brosse and Conrart. Protestant burials used to take place after dark, without any ritual. Columns from the cemetery of Saint-Benoît-le-Bétourné are in the forecourt. (→Latin Quarter: the Montagne Sainte-Geneviève). Nos. 34–42 inclusive are a group of old houses with their original staircases, wrought ironwork and carvings.

The Faculty of Medicine

The entire odd-numbered side of the Rue des Saints-Pères from the Rue Jacob to the chapel of St Vladimir the Great is occupied by the huge, imposing bulk of the Faculty of Medicine, built from 1937 to 1953 by the architects Madeline and Walter. The façade is ornamented with 45 medallions depicting the history of medicine from its legendary beginnings. The main entrance has a door with heavy bronze panels decorated with bas-reliefs by Landowski.

The building houses 7 lecture halls seating 3000, 21 seminar rooms, 12 dissection rooms, 147 laboratories, and a 300-seat restaurant, and stands on the site of the old La Charité hospital, which was established here in 1608, replacing an earlier hospital founded in 1602 by Marie de' Médici on the Quai Malaquais. It had to remove here when Marguerite de Valois chose the original site for her own residence.

☥ The Chapel of Saint-Pierre

Corner of Rue des Saints-Pères and the Boul. Saint-Germain.

The little Square Tarass-Chevtchenko (with a memorial to this writer) separates this chapel from the Boul. Saint-Germain. Founded in the 6th c., it was completely rebuilt in the 18th c. and set aside for the La Charité hospital. It retains the fine Neo-Classical façade designed by Clavareau during the Revolution, which bears the fasces of the Roman lictors. At this time it became the School of Clinical Medicine in which Corvisart and Laennec taught, and from 1850 to 1900 it was home to the Faculty of Medicine.

In 1942 the building was consecrated to the Ukrainian Uniat faith as the chapel of Saint-Vladimir-le-Grand. It has a fine iconostasis. Like the Greek Uniat (or Greek Catholic) Church, the Ukrainian Uniats have their own ecclesiastical hierarchy adhering to an Orthodox rite and discipline, but submitting to papal authority. The head of the church in France, the Exarch, is a suffragan (diocesan bishop) subordinate to the Roman Catholic cardinal of Paris, who functions as the metropolitan (provincial archbishop) for the Uniat church. The Ukrainian Uniat Church has some thirty or forty thousand members in the Paris region, and in Sochaux-Montbéliard, Lille, Amiens, Rheims, Lyons and Montargis.

Rue de l'Université

Between Rue des Saints-Pères and Rue du Bac.

Famous for its interior decorators and antique dealers, the aristocratic Rue de l'Université has hardly changed in the last century. Once it was a country lane, called the Chemin des Treilles and later the Chemin de la Petite Seine, which wound its way across the Pré-aux-Clercs.

Professor Debré lived at no. 5 from 1926 until his death in 1978. At nos. 7–9 Le Vau built one of the first *hôtels* in the faubourg for President Tambonneau, and in 1793 Chappe installed his signaling system called *telegraphe par signaux* there, which was used a year later to announce the retaking of Condé-sur-l'Escaut. The house was destroyed at the start of the 19th c. to make way for the Rue du Pré-aux-Clercs, whose name evokes the time when scholars left the University to follow Abélard and sit in the fields to listen to his teaching (→inset). No. 16 was the home of Berthie Albrecht, a founder member of the Resistance group, Combat, who was executed in Fresnes prison in 1943. Chaveau-Lagarde, the lawyer who defended Marie-Antoinette and Charlotte Corday, lived at no. 18, behind which there are an interesting courtyard and pavilion.

The Ecole Nationale d'Administration

13 Rue de l'Université

This fine 18th-c. mansion* has undergone considerable alteration. It is said to have been the Embassy of the Venetian Republic, and for many years it housed the hydrographic service of the Marine Ministry. It is now the home of the Ecole Nationale d'Administration, which is not a branch of the University of Paris, but controlled by the Prime Minister's office. A highly functional modern building for the students has been erected opposite the garden front (G. Gilbert, architect: 1978). The original Ecole d'Administration was founded by Jean Reynaud and Hippolyte Carnot during the Second Republic in 1848, but lasted only a few months. The present institution only dates from 1945 and is designed to train candidates for the higher branches of the civil service. Students are recruited by competitive examination from university graduates, graduates of the Institut des Sciences Politiques or civil servants of at least four years' standing. They are allocated to four different sections – general, economic and financial, welfare, and foreign affairs.

Rue de l'Université, continued

For over a century the Hôtel d'Aligre* (also known as the Hôtel de Beauharnais) at no. 15 has been the home of the *Revue des Deux Mondes* (founded 1829). The mansion was erected in the latter part of the 17th c. and was first owned by the Aligre family and later by a Beauharnais. Another owner was the 1913 Nobel laureate, Charles Richet. No. 17, the Hôtel Bochart de Saron, was built in 1639 for François Lhuillier, father of the poet Chapelle. It has had strong literary connections ever since; Tallemant des Réaux lived there from 1646 to 1655 and it now houses the Gallimard publishing house. The garden façade has a central projecting avant-corps with beveled corners. The mansions at nos. 19 and 21 date from 1639, and are now an annex of the Treasury and Economics Ministry. No. 24, the Hôtel de Sennecterre, built by Gobert, has a fine staircase and is now an annex of the Ministry of Industry.

For the remainder of Rue de l'Université →the Palais-Bourbon District.

Pass the end of the Rue de Beaune in which Mme. du Deffand (no. 3) and Chateaubriand (no. 5) once lived.

The *Nouvelle Revue Française* is published from 5 Rue Sébastien-Bottin on the l.

Rue du Bac

From the Seine to the Boul. Saint-Germain.

The street takes its name from the ferry (*bac*) that carried stone for the Château des Tuileries across the Seine when Catherine de' Médici started building. The carts came in from the country along a grassy track that ran from the present Rue de Sèvres to the point at which the Pont-Royal now stands. It became a paved street in 1642.

On the r., in the section leading down to the Seine, Chateaubriand is supposed to have lived from 1815 to 1818 on the site of nos. 31–27. No. 21, the Hôtel du Président Hénault, is one of the few old mansions to survive on the odd-numbered side of the street; 18th-c. houses include nos. 12 and 24.

In the section between the Rue de l'Université and the Boul. Saint-Germain: Fouché lived at no. 28, while in 1932 André and Clara Malraux had an apartment at no. 44, a mansion built in 1696. Next door, no. 46, is the splendid *hôtel* which Jacques-Samuel Bernard built for himself on inheriting a fortune from his father, a wealthy banker, in 1740. He loved luxury and died, a ruined man, in this house with its vast frontage of 131ft/40m on the Rue du Bac and nearly 196ft/60m on what was then the Rue Saint-Dominique (now the Boul. Saint-Germain). Chaptal and Barras lived there. The corbeled arch of the doorway is topped by a mascaron, and the carved initials 'S.B.' The woodwork from the drawing-room with overdoors by Carl Van Loo was removed and reinstalled in the Hôtel de Rothschild in the Faubourg Saint-Honoré; it is now in the Jerusalem Museum. There are two magnificent staircases.

The odd-numbered side of this section of the street was pulled down when the Boul. Saint-Germain and the Rue de Gribeauval were built. Further down the latter stands the Church of Saint-Thomas-d'Aquin.

For the remainder of the Rue du Bac →Sèvres-Babylone district.

♀ The Church of Saint-Thomas-d'Aquin*

Place Saint-Thomas-d'Aquin (closed noon - 2 pm). Tel. 42-22-59-74.

The Dominicans opened their novice house in the Faubourg Saint-Germain in 1631. When the friars decided to rebuild it completely from 1682 to 1688, in the Jesuit style, Pierre Bullet was commissioned to design the church, although his plans were not followed through and the nave lacks two of the bays shown in the original drawings. The friars' chancel, behind the high altar, was built in 1722 and the façade from 1765 to 1769. The novice house has survived, but is now used as offices by the central supply department of the French Army. The simple façade is broken by two fine doors designed by François-Charles Butteux (1769).

The interior: chapel on r., *Death of Saphira* by François Picot (1819) and *Assumption* by Salvator Rosa (*ca.* 1660); 2nd chapel: *The Virgin Appearing to St Jerome* by Giovanni Francesco Barbieri called Guercino (1650) and *St Germanus of Auxerre Presenting St Geneviève with a Medal* by Louis Lagrenée (1771). R. arm of the transept: both arms and the flattened dome of the crossing were decorated by Joseph Blondel (1830-50). Transept r. arm: above the altar, *St Vincent de Paul* by Jean-Baptiste Stouf (late 18th c.). At the far end of the r. hand side-aisle a passage leading to the sacristy contains fine mid-18th c. paneling and a painting by the Dominican Frère André, *St Dominic Expounding his Rule* (1738).

Chancel: the ceiling of the Chapel of Our Lady is painted with *The Transfiguration* by François Lemoyne (1724); above the altar, *The Transfiguration* by Jean Restout (c. 1760), between *Carrying the Ark of the Covenant* and *Aaron Blessing the People* by Blondel (1841).

Transept l. arm: above the altar, *Madonna and Child* by Gilles

Guérin (early 17th c.); 1st chapel: *St Peter Curing the Cripple* by Léon Pallière (1819).

Boulevard Saint-Germain

Between Rue du Bac and Rue des Saints-Pères.

This is not the most interesting part of the boulevard, but it is wide and very pleasant in the spring when the horse-chestnut trees are in bloom. Guillaume Apollinaire lived at no. 202 from 1913 until his death on November 9, 1918. There are a number of specialist antique shops, including one for Empire furniture, another for antique clocks, watches and walking-sticks and the Galerie Nikolenko, of which the stock-in-trade is Russian icons.

The Rue de Luynes was begun in 1901 on the site of the Hôtel de Luynes, one of the greatest mansions in the Faubourg, built by Le Muet in 1661 for Marie de Rohan-Montbazon, Duchesse de Chevreuse. In the 18th c. Brunetti decorated the staircase; his frescoes have been reinstalled in the Carnavalet Museum, while the Louis XVI paneling from the Grand Salon has been taken to the Louvre.

Rue Saint-Guillaume

From the Boul. Saint-Germain to the Rue du Pré-aux-Clercs.

This is the oldest portion of the street. No. 16, the Hôtel de Créqui, was built by Le Muet from 1660 to 1664 and enlarged a century later (see the 18th-c. retaining wall in the second court). The mansion is full of literary history: it was here that Lamartine began his *Jocelyn,* Renan lived here in 1877, and at the beginning of the 20th c. Proust, Colette, Saint-Exupéry, Ravel and Reynaldo Hahn all frequented the Saussine family's brilliant literary and musical salon. No. 14 is a *hôtel* erected for the Mortemart family at the end of the 17th c. It retains its original entrance (registered), the original courtyard staircase with a beautiful handrail and vestibule. No. 11 is an early 18th-c. mansion.

Rue des Saints-Pères

From the Boul. Saint-Germain to the Rue de Sèvres.

When the Boul. Saint-Germain was built it swept away the house in which the world-famous *memoirist,* Louis de Rouvroy, Duc de Saint-Simon, was born. Note the pediment, the masks over each window and the folding doors of no. 50. Opposite is no. 52, the Hôtel de Cavoye, purchased by one of Louis XIV's gambling companions, Louis d'Oger de Cavoye. It preserves its magnificent entrance; both its façades and a salon which was originally in another house, are registered. Salomon de Brosse lived in the mansion which stood on the site of no. 54, the present Bibliothèque et Musée de l'Histoire du Protestantisme Français (→Museums), built by L. A. Boileau in 1873. No. 56 is the hôtel erected by Gittard for Marie de Cosse who had married Charles, Duc de la Meilleraye, Marshal of France and a hero of the Thirty Years War. Note the entrance, forecourt and staircase. Having housed for many years the Ecole Nationale d'Administration, now at 13 Rue de l'Université, it now belongs to the Institut d'Etudes Politiques (Institute of Political Studies). Other old and interesting houses include nos. 58 and 60 (note the dormer windows with pulleys). Chateaubriand lived at no. 63 from 1811 to 1814. No. 76, the Catholic bookshop, is a very ordinary building, but is the first example of the use of concrete roughcast on iron (architect, E. Dupuis, 1878).

Rue de Sèvres

From Rue des Saints-Pères to the Sèvres-Babylone intersection.

Walk as far as the Sèvres-Babylone intersection and back again. This E end of the street has greatly altered in character since the 1960s. Nowadays it is very busy and youthful, like the nearby Rue du Four and Rue du Dragon. This is one of the centers of the rag trade; here are all the boutiques that *make* Paris fashion. They have replaced the Premonstrant convent, suppressed in 1789; no. 11 is built where its gateway stood. It was at no. 11 too, that J. K. Huysmans lived from 1872 to 1898 in the courtyard where previously the painter Martin Drolling (1786-1851) had a studio. No. 21 stands on the site of the house in which Drolling died.

Rue Récamier

This street was built across the grounds of the Abbaye-aux-Bois (→inset), a Bernardine convent. This little street has always been quiet and is now a pedestrian precinct, with attractive shrubberies. The convent buildings have been replaced by the Théâtre Récamier (architect, C. Blondel, 1908), and the Ligue de l'Enseignement et de l'Education Permanente founded by Jean Macé at no. 3. At the end of the street there is a pleasant little terraced public garden enclosed by the backs of the fine mansions in Rue de la Chaise and Rue de Grenelle as well as by elegant modern buildings.

From the Rue de la Chaise (→below) the only surviving fragment of the convent may be seen: its staircase has been reinstalled at the Château de Breteuil (→).

Rue de Grenelle

To Rue Saint-Guillaume

The name of this street comes from the word *garanella,* a corrupt diminutive of the medieval Latin *warrena,* a rabbit warren or fish pond; the Rue de Varenne has the same derivation. Long ago it was only a track, the little Chemin aux Vaches (cowpath) which led from the Abbey of Saint-Germain-des-Prés into the countryside. Like the Rue de Varenne, this is the wealthiest and most ambassadorial street in the Faubourg. It is also a publishers' street. At no. 15, the Hôtel de Bérulle, erected by Pierre-Claude Convers in 1776, has a curved façade on the street to facilitate the coming and going of carriages. During the 1920s it housed the offices of Recherches Surréalistes. No. 14 is another 18th-c. building, with a very modern garage next door.

No. 20 is a small 17th-c. town house that belonged to Mme de Beauvais, nicknamed Catheau la Borgnesse (One-eyed Kate), for whom a magnificent house was built in the Rue François-Miron, and who was also given an extensive property at no. 79 Rue de Grenelle, where she taught the young Louis XIV the art of love. Many houses have retained their lofty windows and 18th-c. balconies: note nos. 22, 24, 26 and 28.

Rue Saint-Guillaume, continued

Walk up and down this 16th-c. street, which will be forever associated with the Ecole Libre des Sciences Politiques and the Institut d'Etudes Politiques de Paris, academic centers that have trained generations of higher civil servants for more than a century. On the even-numbered side of the street, between the Rue de Grenelle and the Boul. Saint-Germain, are the Fondation des Sciences Politiques, the Institut des Hautes Etudes de l'Amérique Latine and the Centre Français du Droit Comparé (Center for Comparative Legal Studies). Wagner's brother-in-law, Emile Olivier, lived at no. 31. In the forecourt of this house stands a structure that marks an epoch in French architecture, Dr Dalsace's house* (visits permitted), created by the furniture designer P. Chareau in 1931. This house was the first in France to use glass bricks from the Saint-Gobain factory. Their use, together with an original handling of interior spaces, makes this building a daring and innovative experiment.

The Institut d'Etudes Politiques is now at no. 27, the former Hôtel de Mesmes owned by the Duc de Mortemart. In 1945 it took over from the Ecole Libre des Sciences Politiques, founded by Emile Boutmy after the Franco-Prussian War (1870-71) to give the elitist education appropriate for those destined for the higher echelons of public and private administration. Its students follow a three-year course in one of the four departments - general administration, economics, international relations (for entrants to the diplomatic and consular services) and public service (for candidates for the Ecole Nationale d'Administration exams). A garden separates the Institut des Sciences Politiques from its annex in the Rue des Saints-Pères.

Rue de la Chaise

This little street opens opposite the Rue Guillaume. It is very attractive, with beautiful mansions dating from the second half of the 18th c. No. 1 is the Hôtel de Brosse (1760) and no. 3 was built in 1640 for the Comte des Vertus and from 1785 to 1810 belonged to the Béthune-Pologne family. Most of the houses on the even-numbered side of the street are old: note the windows, mascarons and carved masks.

The Hôtel de Vaudreuil, also known as the Hôtel de Borghèse, occupies nos. 5–7. Its entrance, between two pavilions crowned by a triangular pediment, shows how magnificent this mansion must have been when it was built in 1763. It was owned by the Comte de Vaudreuil, friend of the Comte d'Artois and of Marie-Antoinette. It became the Ministry of Foreign Affairs and then, in 1803, was purchased by Elisa Bonaparte, who gave it to François Borghèse, brother-in-law of Pauline Bonaparte-Borghèse. With the fall of Napoléon the mansion passed to the Crussol d'Uzès family, and then to the Dominicans. For 60 years it was a private nursing home and was only saved from demolition in 1960 thanks to a forceful campaign for its conservation. In 1973 the building erected along one side of the courtyard was regarded as a controversial attempt by the architects J. J. Fernier and A. Biro to integrate contemporary architecture into a classical setting.

Another fine entrance at no. 9 leads into the former Hôtel d'Ozembray, now an annex of the department of the Fondation des Sciences Politiques.

Rue de Grenelle. Walk back down this street to look at nos. 31, 33, 35, 37, 34, 36 and 38 – all beautiful 18th-c. houses.

Boulevard Raspail

Between the Bac and the Sèvres–Babylone intersections.

This section is the most recently built (1904–07) of this fine thoroughfare begun in 1866. Nos. 28–30 are carefully finished buildings of the 1930s by P. Abraham. No. 36 is the hôtel in which Marc Sangnier (b.1873) lived and died in 1950. He founded Le Sillon and the Auberges de Jeunesse (Youth Hostels) and was one of the most outstanding members of the Catholic social movements of the first half of the century. There are some antiques and furniture shops, overshadowed by the department store Le Bon Marché (→the Sèvres–Babylone district, the Cherche-Midi, Notre-Dame-des-Champs and Montparnasse districts) for a description of this boulevard.

▷ Not to be missed

Concentrating on a few places of outstanding historic interest will allow you to make a quick visit to the Faubourg Saint-Germain.

Rue de Varenne, bordered by the finest mansions in the faubourg: the Hôtel de Boisgelin, the Hôtel de Galliffet, the Hôtel Matignon and the Hôtel Biron, whose large garden and rooms now house works by the sculptor Rodin (→Museums). The rare occasions on which visitors are allowed inside the vast Palais-Bourbon and its neighbor, the Hôtel de Lassay beside the Quai d'Orsay, provide an opportunity to appreciate Delacroix's decorative paintings.

The Rue de Lille leads to the Hôtel de Beauharnais (Empire décor), the Hôtel de Salm-Kyrkburg, now the Musée de l'Ordre de la Légion d'Honneur (→Museums), and the Musée d'Orsay, the old railway station recently converted into a museum to house the French national collection of 19th-c. art (→Museums).

▷ The Pré aux Clercs

Since the Middle Ages this famous *clos* (enclosed field) has been one of the liveliest places in Paris. Enclosed by the lands of the Abbey of Saint-Germain-des-Prés, the *pré* stretched along the Seine from the present-day Rue Bonaparte and the Champ-de-Mars to where the Rue de l'Université and Rue de Lille now run. Students acquired the habit of coming to the *pré* for relaxation, and the monks resented the constant intrusion of these youthful members of the university. This led to constant confrontation and occasional bloodshed. The authority of the Pope himself was invoked to settle these disputes and, in 1215, an agreement was reached between the abbey and the university, under which the close was divided into two distinct parts. Despite this, the rector of the university came each year at Easter to lay claim to his lands.

In the 17th c. the *pré* was a frequent setting for duels, as well as for hunting. 'La Reine Margot' bought part of it, which she laid out as a park. All this was changed after her death in 1615, when the ground was divided into lots for development.

▣ Museums to visit

Musée d'Orsay (formerly Gare d'Orsay): 19th-c. art.

Musée de la Légion d'Honneur et des Ordres de la Chevalerie (2

Rue de Bellechasse): history of the orders of chivalry from their foundation; collection of insignia, arms and historic souvenirs.

Musée Rodin (Hôtel de Biron, 77 Rue de Varenne): sculptures by Auguste Rodin.

Musée Valentin-Haüy (5 Rue Duroc): exhibition of objects and techniques developed for teaching the blind.

Musée du Protestantisme Français (54 Rue des Saints-Pères): documents illustrating the history of French Protestantism.

Musée Orfila (45 Rue des Saints-Pères): anatomy and anthropology.

Musée Dina-Vierny (59 Rue de Grenelle): painting and sculpture of the first half of the 20th c.

> Some antiques shops (Left Bank)

In the area between the Quai Voltaire, the Rue des Saints-Pères, Rue de l'Université and Rue du Bac are the leading Parisian antique dealers. Here are some of them:

Objets d'art from the Haute Epoque
Brimo de Laroussilhe: 7 Quai Voltaire
Gabrielle Laroche: 12 Rue de Beaune
Furniture and objets d'art (17th and 18th c.)
Galerie Perrin: 3 Quai Voltaire
Galerie Camoin: 9 Quai Voltaire
Marc Revillon d'Apreval: 23 Quai Voltaire
Pascal Sarfati: 5 Rue de Beaune
Galerie Delvaille: 15 Rue de Beaune
Paintings and drawings
Michel Segoura: 11 Quai Voltaire
Galerie de Jonckheere: 21 Quai Voltaire
Galerie Leegenhoek: 23 Quai Voltaire
Galerie Bailly: 25 Quai Voltaire
Textiles and tapestries
Galerie Chevalier: 15 Quai Voltaire
Asian and Near Eastern Art
Galerie Samarcande: 13 Rue des Saints-Pères
La Chine des Ts-ing (Qing): 14 Rue de l'Université
Myrna Myers: 11 Rue de Beaune
Porcelain
Vandermeersch: 27 Quai Voltaire
Antique clocks and watches
Jean-Pierre Rochefort: 14 Rue des Saints-Pères
Antiquarian books
Christian Galantaris: 15 Rue des Saints-Pères
Nautical antiques
La Rose des Vents: 25 Rue de Beaune

Curios

Le Cabinet de Curiosité: 23 Rue de Beaune

In May, all the antiques shops stay open until 10pm during the five days of the 'Objet Extraordinaire' festival, when they present to passersby a remarkable collection of rare and beautiful objects.

▷ The Abbaye-aux-Bois

As early as the 16th c., nuns of the Annonciades de Bourges (Order of the Annunciation), founded in Bourges around 1500 by St Jeanne de France, daughter of Louis XI, and wife of Louis XII, had established a convent on the site of what is now the Rue Récamier. In the mid–17th c. they were succeeded by the Bernardines, an order stemming from the Cistercians. Their abbesses were drawn exclusively from the noblest families in the kingdom and all the nuns had to be of noble birth. The convent was suppressed in 1790 and became a prison during the Terror, but when peace was restored, one wing was converted into a retreat. In middle age and with her fortune gone, Mme Récamier came here. From 1819 to 1949 she lived in the Abbaye–aux–Bois and made it famous: her salon, the most influential of the time, drew all the leading figures of the day, politicians, writers and painters, attracted by her beauty, charm and friendship. Chateaubriand, who lived in the Rue du Bac, visited his old friend every day to read aloud passages from his *Mémoires d'Outre-Tombe.*

The Rue de Grenelle district**

7th arr./Map ref. 15–B2, 16–C2, D2
Métro: Rue du Bac
Bus: 63, 64, 69, 83, 84
Parking: Square Boucicaut
Taxis: Bac Métro station. Tel. 42-22-49-64.- Chambre-des-Députés Métro station. Tel. 47-05-03-14.

This austere and peaceful quarter contains the highest proportion of *hôtels* erected in the 18th c. by famous architects. Today ambassadors and ministers have taken the place of princes of the blood.

It is advisable to visit the Rue Grenelle, Rue Varenne and Rue Saint-Dominique during the week when the carriage entrances of the *hôtels* are open and the fine façades of the mansions are visible. Few of the buildings are open to visitors, but enquiries may be addressed to the Caisse Nationale des Monuments Historiques et des Sites (62 Rue Saint-Antoine; Tel. 42-74-22-22) or to the private cultural societies, which list their forthcoming programs of visits in the newspapers.

Tour of the district

2 hrs.

Rue de Varenne

Between Rue du Bac and the Boul. des Invalides.

The rabbit-warren over which this street was built in 1605 has long since vanished, and it was not until the 18th c. that most of the beautiful houses that line it were built. For the past two centuries the Rue de Varenne has been one of the most sought-after addresses in Paris and its prestige has rubbed off on the streets nearby. The section between the Rue du Bac and Rue de la Chaise, distinguished though it is, has no buildings of outstanding interest, and is not discussed below.

In 1849 the actress Marie Dorval, mistress of the poet Alfred de Vigny, died at no. 38. Nos. 48, 43 and 41 are 18th-c. houses. Antoine erected no. 45, the Hôtel de Narbonne-Sérant, also called the Hôtel de Janvry, in 1785: above the four Ionic columns of the entrance is a notable entablature. No. 47 houses the Italian Embassy in the former Hôtel de Boisgelin**, also known as the Hôtel de La Rochefoucauld-Doudeauville, built around 1787 by the architect Cartaud; some of its paneling comes from the Château de Bercy.

The Hôtel de Galliffet**

50 Rue de Varenne

Built from 1775 to 1796 by Legrande, this *hôtel* now houses the Italian Cultural Attaché's offices. During the Directory it was the Ministry of Foreign Affairs, where Talleyrand entertained Josephine and Bonaparte and where Mme de Staël met the future Emperor for the first time.

The façade overlooking the courtyard displays eight Ionic columns and an entablature with medallions (decorative brackets). On the garden façade, six half-engaged columns support a balcony with copies of the statues of the nymphs on the Fontaine des Innocents. There is a similar arrangement of columns within, on the staircase, the semicircular vestibule, and the state drawing-room*, which together make up one of the finest Louis XVI interiors in Paris.

From no. 51 Cité Vaneau, looking r. the W side of the Italian Embassy and a number of luxurious 19th-c. mansions can be seen.

Before reaching the Hôtel Matignon, note the beautiful portal at no. 56 Rue de Varenne, the Hôtel de Gouffier de Thoix (1719).

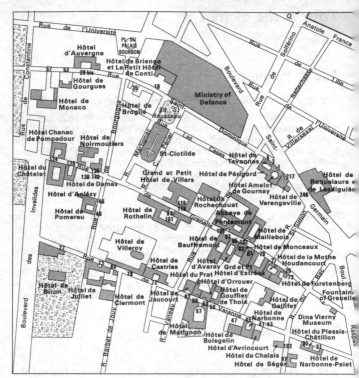

The Rue de Grenelle district

The Hôtel de Matignon**

57 Rue de Varenne

This is one of the most beautiful of all the mansions in the Faubourg. Since 1958 it has been the official residence of the French prime minister.

Jean Courtonne began this building in 1721 for the fourth son of the Maréchal de Luxembourg and it was still uncompleted when it was sold to Jacques Goyon de Matignon, Comte de Thorigny. When the eldest daughter of the Prince of Monaco became Comtesse de Matignon, she had the mansion finished and decorated. After the Revolution the *hôtel* had many different owners, notably Talleyrand, who gave sumptuous receptions here. In 1815 Louis XVIII exchanged the Hôtel de Matignon for the Elysée Palace, owned by the Duchesse de Bourbon. It was next bequeathed to Louis-Philippe's sister who lived there until 1847, when it passed to the Duc de Montpensier. The Duc de Galliera, its next owner, made it available to the Comte de Paris, who used its state rooms on May 15 1886 for a lavish wedding reception for his daughter Marie-Amélie and Manuel of Braganza, heir apparent to the crown of Portugal. The result of this *fête* was the passing of a law exiling both Royalist and Bonapartist pretenders. The mansion later became the Austro-Hungarian Embassy (1888-1914) and since 1935, has been the residence of the Président du Conseil. In January 1959, under the Fifth Republic, the Hôtel de Matignon was made the official home of the prime minister, as the head of government is now known.

The noble Ionic *porte-cochère* opens on to a broad semicircular main courtyard and the two façades each have projecting avant-corps center sections with beveled corners. Inside, the mansion has preserved part of its extravagant Rocemille decoration with a ground-floor *salon* with 18th c. white-and-gold carvings, as well as the rooms that Duban redecorated for the Duc de Galliera in the 19th c. On the first floor there are panels painted with pastoral scenes by Fragonard. The garden is the largest private garden in Paris and stretches as far as the Rue de Babylone (→below), where there stands a charming little Louis XV pavilion.

Rue de Varenne, continued

No. 58, the Hôtel de Fouquières, constructed in 1736, serves as an annex to the Hôtel de Matignon. No. 60, the Hôtel du Prat built in 1720 by Leroux, which belonged both to the Montmorency and the Béthune families, has façades registered as historic monuments over the courtyard and garden (pediment), wrought ironwork and ornamental panels framed by swags. The Hôtel de Seisac at no. 69 is also known as the Hôtel de Clermont. Built by Leblond (1711-14) it was modernized under Louis XVI for Pierre-Gaspard-Marie Grimond d'Orsay. It, too, is an annex of the Hôtel de Matignon. From the street the two courtyards are visible. At no. 72, the Grand Hôtel de Castries (see inscription over the gateway) built around 1700, the reactionary Marquis de Castries and the radical Charles Comte de Lameth fought a duel in 1790, and a riot broke out and the mansion was sacked. It became the Ministry of War from 1790 to 1804 and now houses the prime minister's parliamentary delegate. The Petit Hôtel de Castries (erected 1770) now demolished, stood on the site of today's no. 74; it was the birthplace of the diplomat and archeologist, the Comte de Vogüe. The site has been absorbed by the Ministry of Agriculture.

No. 73, the Hôtel de Broglie*, was built in 1735 for the Comte de Longonay; the façade and other portions of the building were altered in 1785 by J. B. Leboursier. In 1752 the mansion belonged to the Comte Victor-François de Broglie. It was confiscated during the Revolution and became the prize in a lottery. In 1826 it was owned by Marechal Lannes' widow, the Duchesse de Montebello, who was responsible for some of the decoration. The Russian princes Gortchakov used it as their pied-à-terre in Paris and then, during World War I it became the headquarters of the American Expeditionary Force. No. 75, the Hôtel de Châtillon, serves as its annex. One would never think that behind Emmanuel Brune's somewhat heavy façade at no. 78 is a mansion built in 1724 by Debias-Aubry, decorated by Leroux. Marechal de Villeroy owned it in the mid-18th c., and after him the Comte de Tessé. The forecourt and garden façades, with their central avant-corps and triangular pediments, are registered monuments. Today the building is the Ministry of Agriculture.

On the corner of the Rue de Varenne and the Boul. des Invalides stands no. 77, the magnificent Hôtel de Biron**, now the Musée Rodin (→Museums) built by Aubert and Galonee in 1728. Recent developments enable the whole complex, including gardens only slightly smaller than those of the Hôtel Matignon, to be seen from the street. The mansion belonged to Peyrenc de Moras, who made his fortune from John Law's fraudulent Mississippi Scheme; later it was rented to Louise de Bourbon, widow of the Duc de Maine. Passing into the ownership of the Gontaut-Biron family, it was sold in 1824 to the Dames du Sacré-Coeur (Sisters of the Sacred Heart) and remained their property until 1904. Rodin moved there in 1907. The original paneling from the two side pavilions has been replaced in the *hôtel,* having been removed by the aristocratic nuns as too ostentatious. A glassed window in the garden wall enables Rodin's *The Burghers of Calais** to be seen from the street.

Proceed to the Boul. des Invalides.

Rue de Grenelle

From the Boul. des Invalides to Rue de Bourgogne.
For the beginning of the street. → *The Rue des Saints-Pères district.*

This street is as prestigious as the Rue de Varenne. No. 142, the Hôtel de Chanac-Pompadour, by Delamair (1704) is famous for its Rococo boudoir. In 1782 Brogniart installed a bathroom in the basement. The building is now the Swiss Embassy.

No. 127 is the Hôtel du Châtelet, a fine example of Louis XV architecture by Cherpitel (1770). This sumptuous dwelling enjoyed a succession of official tenants: Napoléon's Superintendent of the Imperial Household, then his royal successor in 1814. Subsequently it was the Turkish Embassy and the Archbishop of Paris's palace; it is now the Ministry of Labor. The part of the façade projecting on to the forecourt (the *avant-corps*) is ornamented by a Colossal order of four Corinthian columns. The garden façade is less severe; its *avant-corps* has beveled corners and the windows are decorated with swags. Within, there is an elegant pilastered octagonal drawing-room and a Louis XVI dining-room decorated with wall fountains.

Nos. 138-140, the Hôtel Noirmoutier, was built in 1724 by Courtonne for the Duc de Noirmoutier. Mlle de Sens, great-granddaughter of Louis I de Bourbon, Prince de Condé, commissioned Lassurance to redecorate the house and lived here until 1765. Marshal Foch lived in 138 for 10 years until his death in 1929, when the mansion became the official residence of the prefect of the region. No. 140 became the Institut Géographique, and no. 134 is a typical Art Nouveau Mansion by Lavirotte.

Rue de Bourgogne

Walk along this street and back again. It was built in 1907 and named after Louis XIV's grandson, although it remains solidly middle class, not to say archepiscopal. It is the main shopping street for this part of the Faubourg and renowned for its *pâtisseries*. It contains two late 18th-c. mansions at no. 46, the Hôtel d'Anlezy, and no. 48, the Hôtel Choiseul-Praslin, now known as the Hôtel de Pomereu. The first archbishop had his palace at no. 50. Modern apartment buildings now stand in what was once the garden of a Salesian convent.

Rue de Grenelle, continued

From the Rue de Bourgogne to Rue de Bellechasse.

No. 122 was the entrance to a Carmelite convent which was suppressed in 1790 and over which were built the Rue Casimir-Pèruer, Rue Champagny, Rue Martignac, Rue Las-Cases, the Square Samuel-Rousseau and the Church of Sainte-Clothilde. A tablet on the wall of no. 123 reminds us that the Resistance hero Pierre Brossolette lived here (1932–44). No. 118, the Petit Hôtel de Villars (1714) still retains its original paneling; Delacroix had a studio here from 1823 to 1827. The building is now a private school, the Cours Paul-Claudel.

No. 116, the Grand Hôtel de Villars, dates from the mid 17th c. It was completely altered and rebuilt for Marshal de Villars in 1709; in 1772 it was owned by the Duc de Brissac who went to the guillotine in 1792. In 1795 it housed the Ministry of the Interior; it was as head of this department that Lucien Bonaparte moved in. After being the Turkish Embassy for a time, the *hôtel* has been the town hall of the 7th arrondissement since 1862. Boffrand built the original portal on the l.; it was remodelled in 1830 by Visconti for the Forbin–Janson family.

Go through the side door of no. 115, the Hôtel de Sommery, to see a tablet to the actress Adrienne Lecouvreur (1692–1730). The tablet, engraved by her lover and sole heir d'Argental, was rescued from the attics of the mansion. On the wall of no. 103 is a tablet whose inscription translates as: 'From this building the first regular French television programs were transmitted in November 1935.' No. 110, the Hotel de Courteilles, also called de Rochechouart, built by Cherpitel in 1778, has a façade with 10 fluted Corinthian pilasters two storeys high. It contains an exquisite octagonal pilastered Louis XVI salon. Since 1829 it has been the Ministry of Education. The lettering on the balconies of no. 101, the Hôtel Rothelin–Charolais, tells you that it was built by Pierre Cailleteau, called Lassurance, in 1704 for the Marquis de Rothelin. It was acquired in 1736 by the celebrated Louise–Anne de Bourbon, Princesse de Charolais; in 1825 it became the Ministry of the Interior. When, in 1860, it housed the Austrian Embassy the fame of the salon over which Pauline de Metternich presided brought the mansion back into the fashionable world. It now houses the Ministry of Industrial Redeployment.

Rue de Bellechasse

From the Rue de Grenelle to the Boul. Saint–Germain.

This street was built in 1805 on the site of the convent of the Dames de Bellechasse. This abbey of the Bernardines of Pentémont, an offshoot of the Cistercians, was founded in 1671 in the Rue de Grenelle and was an aristocratic school for girls (Jefferson's daughter was a pupil during his embassy) and a retirement home for noble widows and elderly spinsters. The surviving abbey buildings on the Rue de Bellechasse (nos. 37–39) now house the offices of the Secretary of State for Veterans' Affairs.

♣ Rue de Grenelle, continued

From the Rue de Bellechasse to the Rue du Bac.

No. 106 is a Protestant church, the Temple de Pentémont, formerly the abbey church of the Bernardines of Pentémont. It was built by Contant d'Ivry from 1747 to 1756 and comprises a rotunda with two transepts and a deep chancel. The transepts are lined with striking Ionic pilasters. The fine façade is an early example of the Louis XVI style. No. 104, formerly an annex of the Abbaye de Pentémont or Panthémont, as it was also called, is now used by the Ministry of Defense. The beautiful early 18th c. Hôtel de Maillebois* (no. 102) is by Deslisle–Mansart. The Duc de Saint–Simon lived here from 1750, writing his *Mémoires*, until his death in 1755. The *hôtel* was completely altered by Antoine in 1783. Mme de Staël presided over a famous salon here, which was especially influential in November 1800 at the time of the coup-d'état of the 18 Brumaire. Robert Browning and his wife Elizabeth Barrett later rented the mansion.

☐ No. 87, the Hôtel de Bauffremont*, built from 1721 to 1736 by Pierre Boscry, has known such various owners as the Comte d'Orouer, Pâris de Marmontel, the Comtesse de Boisgelin, the Archbishop of Bourges and the Princesse de Bauffremont, daughter of the Duc de Montmorency, and on two occasions has served as the Austrian Embassy. This superb building has kept its triangular pediment above the avant-corps in the façade overlooking the forecourt and the curved façade over the garden with a rounded avant-corps (both are registered). The richly furnished salons were paneled in white and gold by the famous decorator Nicolas Pineau (1733).

No. 85, the Hôtel d'Avaray*, is the residence of the Dutch Ambassador (the Chancery is at 8 Rue Eblé). The mansion was built by Leroux in 1718 and for two centuries belonged to the Bésiade d'Avaray family. It is a unique example of continuity of ownership in the Faubourg Saint-Germain. The Dutch government purchased the building in 1920 and restored it with as much good taste as luxury. Today over the gateway you may read the device of the House of Orange, 'Je maintiendrai' (I will maintain).

No. 83, the Hôtel Bonneval or de Monceaux, was erected in 1672 and during the early years of the Empire was owned by Maret, Duc de Bassano. No. 86, the Petit Hôtel d'Estrées, built for the Duchesse d'Estrées in 1709, was at one time occupied by the Comte Daru, Intendant of Napoleon's armies and a relative of the novelist Stendhal, whom he employed in his department.

No. 79, the Grand Hôtel d'Estrées, was erected by Robert de Cotte in 1713 for the Duchesse d'Estrées. It also belonged to a daughter of the Regent, the Duc d'Orléans, and then passed through the hands of many different owners until the end of the 19th c., when it became the Russian Embassy at which Nicholas II and the Czarina stayed during their state visit to Paris in 1896. It is still the Russian Embassy, or rather the private residence of the Ambassador of the USSR, since the chancery and reception rooms were transferred to the Boul. Lannes in 1978. Painted pale pink and white in the Scandinavian tradition, its façade was extensively altered during the 19th c. The house contains a very fine staircase.

The austere *hôtel* at no. 77 was built for the Comtesse de Lamothe-Houdancourt in 1708 by Delisle-Mansart, architect of the Hôtel de Fürstenberg no. 75 erected about 1703. In 1675 he also erected the mansion at no. 86, which retains some of its original décor inside. No. 73, the former Hôtel de Galliffet, now houses the Italian Cultural Institute. Legrand started building it in 1775 and it has now absorbed the Hôtel Talon. The doors of nos. 67–69 and the Louis-Philippe wrought ironwork are worth seeing.

Just before reaching the Boul. Raspail, you pass, opposite nos. 59–57, the lovely Fontaine des Quatre-Saisons*, also known as the Fontaine Bouchardon or the Fontaine de Grenelle. It was built in 1739 to supply the district with water. It is decorated with large allegorical statues of the City of Paris with the Seine and the Marne at its feet, and delightful bas-reliefs of the seasons. Water flows from the four mascarons on the base. Commissioned by Turgot, this early example (1739–46) of Neo-Classicism which became all-pervasive a few years later, was admired by everybody except Voltaire: 'A great deal of stonework for a very little water', he commented.

Alfred de Musset spent most of his life (1824–40) as a writer at no. 59, leaving it in 1839 to travel to Venice with George Sand. The Musée Dina Vierny (→Museums) is to be opened in a mansion behind the fountain, with sculptures by Maillol donated by the Catalan sculptor's former model.

Proceed to the intersection of the Rue du Bac and the Boul. Saint-Germain.

The Boul. Saint-Germain

From Rue du Bac to Rue Saint-Dominique.

No. 246, the Hôtel de Roquelaure, begun by Lassurance in 1722, was completed 10 years later by Leroux for the Maréchal de Roquelaure. Today it houses the Ministry of Transport, but during the 18th and 19th c. it was owned by Président Molé, the statesman Cambacérès, and Louis-Philippe's mother, the Duchesse d'Orléans. Two fine salons with Rocaille paneling, one designed by Nicolas Pineau with overdoors painted by Natoire, are among the most admired in the Faubourg. No. 248, the Hôtel des Lesdiguières, built in 1740, has a fine garden façade and is an annex of the Ministry of Transport.

Rue Saint-Dominique

Between the Boul. Saint-Germain and the Church of Sainte-Cloth-ilde.

This street, built in the 18th c., owes its name to the Dominicans, who occupied the former Jacobin convent. The Church of Saint-Thomas-d'Aquin now stands on the site of the convent beside the path which led from the meadows of Grenelle to the Rue des Saints-Pères. When Baron Haussmann built the Boul. Saint-Germain in 1866, his plans involved the destruction of numerous mansions and the disappearance of part of the Rue Saint-Dominique, so that what was originally no. 67 is now no. 1.

No. 1, the Hôtel Amelot de Gournay (also known as the Hôtel de Tingry-Mortemart), was built by Boffrand in 1712 around a fine oval courtyard, the concave façade broken by a Colossal order of pilasters. The stables could hold 21 horses. The garden communicates with the garden of the Hôtel de Varangeville at no. 217 Boul. Saint-Germain. This is now the Maison de l'Amérique Latine and has a first-class restaurant. Mme Swetchine, who played an important role in the 19th-c. religious life, lived from 1818 to 1857 at no. 5, formerly the 17th-c. Hôtel de Tavannes. In 1883 Gustave Doré died at no. 7, where he had lived with his mother. Look at the great arched portal decorated with scallop-shells and ornamental brackets. Cross the Rue de Bellechasse and at no. 27 you can see the artist's studio, its façade decorated with casts of the Parthenon sculptures and Gustave Doré's initials.

Nos. 8, 10 and 12 Rue Saint-Dominique are Saint-annexes or offices of the Ministry of Defence housed in the former Convent of the Daughters of St Joseph (1641). After being supplanted in royal favor by Mme de Maintenon in 1674, Mme de Montespan retired to this convent for orphaned girls. Mme du Deffand (1697–1780) held her salon here in 1755, 'hung with gold-flecked watered silk with flame colored bows'. She lived here for 23 years presiding over a salon to which came the leading intellectuals of the day. She tried to rival the literary salon of her niece, Julie de Lespinasse, who lived at no. 6, where she died on May 22, 1776, with her faithful lover d'Alembert at her side.

Nos. 14–16 are mansions built by Debias-Aubry in 1724 and 1728, now occupied by the Ministry of Defense. The smaller of the two, no. 14, built for Président Duret, is known as the Hôtel de Brienne; the larger belonged to Françoise de Mailly. Both were bought by Louise-Elizabeth de Bourbon, dowager Princesse de Conti, who lived in them until 1776. Subsequent owners were the Duc de Richelieu, Charles de Loménie de Brienne, Minister of Finance to Louis XVI, Lucien Bonaparte in 1802 and finally, in 1804, Napoléon's mother, Laetitia Bonaparte, 'Madame Mère'. The Ministry has preserved the original decoration in a number of rooms, notably the Empire salon, Laetitia Bonaparte's small boudoir and the blue drawing-room with Louis XV paneling. In 1944–45, General de Gaulle set up the Provisional Government here.

In the Square Samuel-Rousseau, opposite the Church of Sainte-Clothilde, stand Lenoir's statue of César Franck, who was organist at the church, and *L'Education Maternelle* by Delaplanche.

⚓ The Church of Sainte-Clothilde

23 bis Rue Las-Cases (8am–1pm, 5–7pm. Tel. 47-05-22-46).
This parish church of the Faubourg Saint-Germain was erected between 1846 and 1856 and designed by Christian Gau. After his death in 1853, Théodore Ballu took charge of construction. By adopting a Neo-Gothic style for this new church, the first of its kind to be built in Paris, Gau shows how interest in the Middle Ages was growing during the Bourbon Restoration and under the July Monarchy. Inspired by 14th-c. architecture, the ground plan of the church is that of the Latin cross. Among the carvings decorating the façade,

the fine statues by Geoffroy-Dechaume (*ca.* 1855) of St Clothilde and of Clovis, stand out on either side of the main doorway.

The interior

The nave: The stained-glass windows in the side-aisles were executed by the firm of Lusson from Paul Jourdy's cartoons (r.-hand side) and Auguste Gallimard (l. side). *The Stations of the Cross* are the work of Francisque Duret (seven stations in the r. side-aisle and transept) and of James Pradier (the remainder in the l. side-aisle and transept). Jules Lenepveu's paintings, *The Conversion of St Valeria* and *The Martyrdom of St Clothilde and St Valeria,* hang in the r. arm of the transept. The chancel is divided from the ambulatory by a screen on the back of which are four reliefs by Eugène Guillaume. Ambulatory: 1st chapel, *St Remigius* by Alexandre Pils and Isidore Laemlein; 2nd chapel, *St Joseph* by Louis Bézard; 3rd chapel, *Chapel of Our Lady* by Leneupveu; 4th chapel, *Holy Cross* by Pierre Brisset; 5th chapel, *St Louis* by William Bouguereau. L. arm of the transept: Desiré Laugée's paintings: *The Baptism of Clovis* and *St Clothilde Distributing Alms.*

Rue Las-Cases, built on the site of the convent of the Dames de Bellechasse, is named after the author of the *Mémorial de Sainte-Héléne.* No. 13, a 19th-c. mansion, is the Australian Embassy. No. 29 is the Catechism Chapel of the basilica of Sainte-Clothilde, built by Destailleur in 1887 and decorated with sculptures by d'Astanière and bas-reliefs after Fra Angelico. It is open for Mass only (Sat. 5pm; Sun. 10am).

Rue Saint-Dominique, continued

From the Church of Sainte-Clothilde to the esplanade of the Invalides.

No. 35, the Hôtel de Broglie*, built in 1724 for Charles-Guillaume de Broglie, was purchased by Napoléon's physician, Baron Corvisart. In 1818 the mansion was sold to the Comte d'Haussonville, who enlarged it. Ingres' portrait, which immortalized the beauty of the Comtesse d'Haussonville, is now one of the treasures of the Frick Collection in New York. The mansion has kept its fine carved doorway, the garden façade visible from the Rue Las-Cases and late 19th-c. paneling, and is now the offices of the Secretary of State for Communications.

Beyond the Rue de Bourgogne, the group of mansions on the odd-numbered side of the street houses the headquarters of the Crédit Nationale; their gardens may be seen from the vestibule of no. 18 Rue de Bourgogne. No. 41 Rue Saint-Dominique is the Hôtel de la Vallière, which belonged to the Talleyrand-Périgord family at the beginning of the 19th c. No. 43 is the Hôtel de Ravanne; nos. 45–47 were once the Hôtel de Seignelay, home of the inventor of gas-lighting, Leblond. In 1829 it was replaced by a Louis XVI mansion which Froëlicher built for the Duc de Montmorency. Between 1839 and 1840 Bailly was summoned by the Prince de Luxembourg to erect the *hôtel* at nos. 49–51.

On the even-numbered side of the street, no. 28, the Hôtel de la Tour d'Auvergne, also called de Caraman, was built for Camus Destouches around 1710. The Comte de Caraman received Marie-Antoinette here, on July 22, 1774, when she came in search of ideas for her garden at the Petit Trianon. 'The Queen remained for two hours, walking, eating ices and talking with Mme de Caraman who had come from Roissy', he recounts in *Les Bonheurs et les Dangers du Comte de Caraman ou la vie d'un gentilhomme au XVIIIe s.* (The Good Fortune and Perils of the Comte de Caraman, or The Life of an 18th-c. Gentleman). The architect Lefranc enlarged the *hôtel* and added an extra storey from 1934 to 1935, and it is now the Maison de la Chimie (Chemistry), with reception, lecture and seminar-rooms.

The Hotel Kinsky at no. 53, was designed by Nicolas Ledoux in 1770 for Président de Gourgues. It was decorated by Princess Kinsky, granddaughter of the Palatine of Hungary, Count Pálffy, and the *soirées* given by this great patron of music were famous. One may still admire the Louis XV state salon as well as the ceiling painted by Julien de Toulon in 1779. It is the headquarters of the Directorate of Music and Theater, a department of the Ministry of Culture. No. 55, the small Hôtel de Monaco (damaged), houses the Directorate of Professional Training.

The Hôtel de Monaco, also known as the Hôtel de Sagan, is at nos. 57–59. It was originally a mansion built by Brongniart from 1774 to 1777 for the estranged wife of Honoré Grimaldi, Prince de Monaco; her lover, the Prince de Condé, lived in the Palais-Bourbon. In 1838 its new owner, the English banker Williams Hope, commissioned Fédel to build him a mansion more in keeping with 19th-c. taste. It was here that the Princesse de Sagan gave the Bal des Animaux which Proust evokes in *Le Côté de Guermantes* (The Guermantes Way). Since 1936 the building has housed the Polish embassy, with the Chancery entrance on the Rue de Talleyrand.

This walk ends on the esplanade of the Invalides, with its fine view of Hardouin-Mansart's dome.

For the remainder of the street →the Eiffel Tower district.

 ## Street numbering

The naming of streets in Paris was, for a long time, a matter of simple tradition, formal identification dating only from 1729. The names of streets were then carved on a tablet or cartouche set into the façades of their first and last houses. However, the work of numbering begun at the same time had to be abandoned, most of the nobility refusing to allow the disfigurement of their *portes-cochères*. Complete and systematic numbering came only in 1806, with streets generally classified according to direction, into those parallel to the Seine numbered in black and those perpendicular to it numbered in red. Numbering in parallel streets followed the direction of the current of the Seine, and in perpendicular streets proceeded outward away from the Seine. In both cases even numbers were on the r., odd numbers on the l. This arrangement is still in use today, although after 1826 the system of the metal signs with white letters or numbers on a blue background was substituted for the old sculpted signs, examples of which can still be seen on certain old buildings.

The Sèvres-Babylone district

7th arr./Map ref. 15–B3, C3

Métro: Sèvres-Babylone
Bus: 83, 68, 39
Parking: Boucicaut
Taxis: 1 Place Alphonse-Deville (Hotel Lutetia). Tel. 45-48-84-75.

This walk starts in the bustling commercial center around the Bon Marché department store, leads through the ancient quarter of hospices and 19th-c. writers' homes and finishes in the religious fiefs of the Sisters of St Vincent-de-Paul and foreign missions.

Tour of the district

1½ hr.

Rue de Sèvres

For the beginning of the street →The Rue des Saint-Pères district.

This is one of the streets in the center of Paris that has changed most since the end of World War II. Formerly, it played a more serious role, with convents and hospitals. Today the hospitals have been enlarged but most of the convents have been replaced by modern buildings and innumerable fashion boutiques. It was this very old street, known as the Chemin de la Maladrerie, that led to Sèvres in the 13th and 14th c.

At no. 33, between two boutiques and set back, a modern door opens into the Neo-Gothic Church of Saint-Ignace. This church is linked to the Jesuit community of Paris and to the Centre des

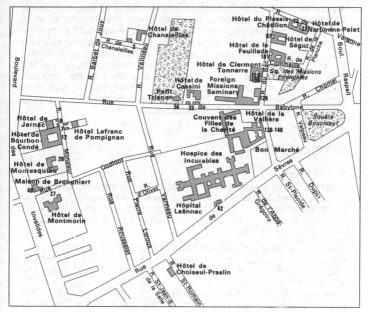

Sèvres-Babylone district

Etudes et Recherches (35 Rue de Sèvres), whose members are mainly students and teachers of theology, philosophy and the humanities. Le Corbusier had his studio and apartment at no. 35.

The Square Boucicaut

This square is built over the old leper house of the Saint-Germain-des-Prés abbey. Inaugurated in June 1873, the square is named after the founder of the Bon Marché department stores. An imposing white marble monument, by the sculptor Moreau-Vauthier, dating from 1914, pays hommage to the philanthropic works of the Baron Hirsch and Mme Boucicaut. It was presented by the financier Osiris, the benefactor of the Pasteur Institute, who himself is represented behind the monument.

The shops of Bon Marché

These are the oldest *magazins de nouveauté* (novelty shops), described by Zola in *Au bonheur des Dames*. Originally, Bon

Marché was a little shop that a store manager of the Petit-Saint-Thomas, Aristide Boucicaut, acquired under the Second Empire, and greatly enlarged after 1870. The main store was built in 1870 by Louis-Charles Boileau, and the metallic framework was by Gustave Eiffel. Although the interior is heavily modified, the huge windows and the pretty wrought-iron balustrades still remain around the first floor. The new store dates from 1923, the work of the younger Boileau, who also designed the Hôtel Lutetia. During the *Belle Epoque*, the annual sale of lace and household linen was considered to be a great event in the district.

Laënnec Hospital

42 Rue de Sèvres

Since 1878 this hospital has replaced the old Hospice des Incurables, founded by Cardinal François de la Rochefoucault, abbot of Sainte-Geneviève in 1635. The building was built in 1643 for the incurably ill, who would not be accepted by the general hospitals of Paris and the province.

The chapel, built by Gamard, has maintained its old façade and entrance, with beautiful folding doors, topped with a triangular pediment surmounted by the traditional medieval small rose. The whole edifice is dominated by a well-designed skylight. At the transept crossing is a short wooden spire, one of the only two authentic ones in Paris (the other is in the chapel of the Collège de Beauvais).

Laënnec never worked in this hospital, although it was named in memory of him as the inventor of the stethoscope. A project to turn the hospital into a convalescent home proposes the restoration of all the old buildings. The modern buildings all along the Rue Vaneau would be demolished to allow a clear view of the entire hospital.

Rue de Sèvres, continued

No. 95 is the Congrégation de la Mission, founded by St Vincent de Paul whose remains lie in the chapel in a silver shrine. The Chapel of the Lazarites, as it is called, dates from the Restoration.

Near the Vaneau Métro stop is the Egyptian fountain, or the Fontaine du Fellah, built by Bralle and Beauvallet, one of those built in 1810 in Paris, when the waters of the Ourcq were brought to the capital: this is testimony to the passion for all things Egyptian inspired by the Egyptian campaign. On the corner of the Rue Saint-Romain, and slightly set back, is the Grand Hôtel Choiseul-Praslin, built in 1729 by Sulpice Gaubier; it was enlarged and embellished in the second half of the century by the Duc de Praslin, ambassador and minister (while he was the Admiralty Minister he organized and provided for the circumnavigation of the world by Bougainville). For a long time the *hôtel* housed the Postal Museum; it has beautiful paneling. Nos. 84–86 are the site of the famous and aristocratic Convent des Oiseaux. At no. 137, behind the façade, are pretty 19th-c. houses.

Rue Rousselet

Léon Bloy lived at no. 22, Barbey d'Aurevilly at no. 25 and, in 1906, Paul Léautaud. As Edmond de Goncourt wrote: 'A remarkable street and an unusual district, this corner of Paris, where Barbey d'Aurevilly lodges. This Rue Rousselet, with the Rue de Sèvres lost in the distance, is like the suburb of a small town where the nearby military college gives the neighborhood a soldierly air.'

Rue Oudinot

This is the former Rue Plumet, the setting for the meeting of Cosette and Marius in *Les Miserables*. General Hugo, father of the poet, lived there. François Coppée lived at no. 12. No. 19 was the nursing home of the Brothers of Saint-Jean-de-Dieu, where Villiers de l'Isle-Adam (died 1889), as well as Marechal Joffre (1931) and Paul Bourget (1935). No. 20 was the birthplace of Pierre de Coubertin, who re-established the Olympic Games; he lived there from 1863 to 1909. No. 27 is the Hôtel de Rambouillet de la Sablière (early 18th c.), which later belonged to Montmorin, Louis XVI's last Minister of Foreign Affairs, and father of Pauline de Beaumont, friend of Chateaubriand; it is now occupied by the Ministry of Overseas Territories. At no. 22 is a mansion built by Brongniart (1785) for himself, where the façade overlooks 49 Boul. des Invalides; the Lupée family acquired it in 1881, and placed the head of a wolf, their family crest, above the door.

Rue Monsieur

Retrace your steps to find this street, opened in 1779, in order to allow Monsieur, the King's brother and Count of Provence, access to his stables (now destroyed). Several fine houses remain. No. 20 is the Hôtel de Montesquiou-Fezensac, built by Brongniart in 1781; the outer façade is accentuated by a cornice topped by an attic storey with a pediment; the garden is a registered monument, as are the façades on this side, where the attic storey is surmounted by triangular pediments; today it is the Ministère de la Coopération. At no. 15 is a Jesuit community; Teilhard de Chardin stayed here when he was in France. No. 12 is another house (visits by request; tel. 47-83-42-49), built by Brongniart in 1786, for Louise-Adèlaide de

Bourbon-Condé. The façades on the courtyard have lost the reliefs by Clodion, now in the Metropolitan Museum in New York. The garden can be seen from the Boul. des Invalides. Inside the house is a beautiful oval salon and a dining-room decorated with huge landscapes by Watteau de Lille. At no. 8 is Jarnac's house, built by Legrand in 1783: the family of Rohan-Chabon lived here, the then Minister Villèle and Dupuytren and the Duchess de Valençay. Several rooms have retained their decoration from the end of the 18th c. Paul Bourget lived at no. 7 from 1880 to 1935, in a town house that, in 1786, belonged to Lefranc de Pompignan, where the sumptuous decorations proclaim the beginning of Romanticism.

Rue de Babylone

To the Rue Barbet-de-Jouy.

This street with its exotic name replaces the rustic lane that meandered into the fields of Grenelle. It has kept the name of Bernard, bishop *in partibus* of Babylon, who founded at no. 22, the Seminary for Foreign Missions (→below). Turn l. to see La Pagode, a cinema known to all film enthusiasts, at 57 *bis*: it is a Chinese-style pavilion, with a façade decorated in faience. It was built in 1895 by Alexandre Marcel and, from 1905 on was used as a reception hall for the Chinese Legation, installed at no. 57. The street runs along the barracks of the French guards, taken by storm in 1830 by insurgents led by Vaneau, a graduate of the Polytechnique.

Rue Barbet-de-Jouy

This street, developed in 1838, is named after the curator of the Louvre who, in 1871, saved the museum from fire. It has been altered a great deal over the past few years.

At nos. 33–39, the two old houses of Luppé and Montebello (1860) have been joined and are occupied by the offices of the prefecture of the region. Opposite, at no. 40, a curious building, heavily decorated, typical of the Napoléon III style. No. 32, the Hôtel de Rambuteau, is the Archbishop of Paris's Palace, the archbishopric having been transferred to the Rue-de-la-Ville-l'Éveque. No. 25 is the Tunisian Embassy, and no. 27 the Swedish Embassy, the latter built on the site of an old house where the painter Kissling lived. At no. 20 is the religious association, the Maison d'Ananie. No. 16 was the *hôtel* built by Rateau for Jeanne Lanvin; all the decorations were donated to the Musée des Arts Décoratifs. (→Museums).

Cut through the Rue de Chanaleilles to rejoin the Rue Vaneau.

Rue Vaneau

Most of the old houses have now gone, but this street remains a haven of peace between the aristocratic Rue de Varenne and the bustling commercialism of the Rue des Sèvres. André Gide lived here from 1926, and died at no. 9*bis*. Nos. 15 and 16 are annexes of the Hôtel Matignon. No. 20 is the Syrian Embassy.

On the corner of the Rue des Chanaeilles the fine Hôtel de Chanaeilles, built in 1770, is still at no. 24. The banker Ouvrard offered the *hôtel* to Mme Tallien, before she became the Princesse de Chimay. Nicknamed Notre Dame de Thermidor, together with Vigée-Lebrun and Josephine de Beauharnais, she launched the fashion of the Merveilleuses, wearing transparent Grecian gowns. The façades of the *hôtel*, the roofs (apart from the new wing), the paneling and stucco are all registered. The pilot and author Antoine de Saint-Exupéry lived in this mansion in 1931. Stavros Niarchos, who acquired the *hôtel* in 1951, had the building remodeled on the side of the Rue de Chanaleilles, to install some splendid lacquered paneling from the Place Vendôme.

The historian Georges Lenotre lived for 56 years (1876–1932) at 40 Rue Vaneau. Renan, the writer, lived at no. 29 from 1864 to 1877.

Rue de Babylone, continued

From Rue Vaneau to Rue de Bac.

A public garden was opened on the site of the old kitchen gardens of the Sisters of Saint-Vincent-de-Paul, where the convent opened on to 136 Rue du Bac (→below). Opposite are the gates, unfortunately closed, of the Hôtel Matignon's garden. No. 32, in the old Hôtel de Cassini built in 1764 by Belisard, is the Secrétariat d'Etat à la Function Publique; one of the salons is decorated with paneling from the former Hôtel de Créqui in the Rue d'Anjou.

Rue du Bac

Between Rue de Babylone and Rue de Varenne.

For the start of the street, see the Rue des Saints-Peres district. At nos. 134 and 136 is the Convent of the Sisters of Saint-Vincent-de-Paul where the remains of St Louise de Marillac, founder of the Filles de la Charité, were placed. No. 140 is the chapel of La Médaille Miraculeuse (daily 7:30am–1pm, 2:30pm–7pm) where, on July 18, 1830, the Virgin appeared to Sister Catherine Labouré, a nun from the Charité de Saint-Vincent-de-Paul; she was beatified, then canonized by Pious XII. Her reliquary rests below the altar of the Virgin. This is an important place for religious believers, visited by Roman Catholics the world over. Pope John Paul II came here on May 31, 1980.

No. 128 is the Seminary of the Foreign Missions founded in 1663. A very beautiful garden. The chapel, built in 1691 by Lebas-Dubuisson, presents an elegant Classical façade, consisting of two storeys of Ionic and Corinthian pilasters, surmounted with a pediment. It became a parish church between the Revolution and 1870, and here Chateaubriand's funeral took place in the presence of an enormous crowd.

At nos. 118–120, Hôtel de Claremont-Tonnerre; it consists of twin *hôtels*, built at the end of Louis XIV's reign, and joined together later; the *portes-cochères* have two medallions by Toro representing the Four Continents. Chateaubriand lived at no. 120 from 1838 until his death in 1848; every day he visited Mme Récamier at the Abbaye-aux-Bois (→inset).

Opposite the *hôtel* in the Square des Missions Etrangères, created by the City of Paris in 1945, is Gambier's bust of Chateaubriand. The mathematician Laplace (1749–1827) died in the house at no. 108. At no. 102, the Hôtel de Sainte-Aldegonde (some features are registered); note the porch, the staircase and the snake emblem of the Colberts; the Princesse de Chalais, granddaughter of the minister, lived in the house. No. 105 is the Hôtel de la Feuillade, built towards the end of Louis XIV's reign. In 1825 Princess Galitzine was the owner of the *hôtel* at no. 99, dating from the end of the 17th c. The inn of the Two Angels, which occupied the site of no. 98 was, at the time of Tournebut and Cadoudal, a nest of conspirators. No. 97 is the Hôtel de Ségur, built about 1720: note the balconies, the mascarons and the registered portal; in a corner of the courtyard is a large circular sculpted gallery. At the intersection of the Rue du Bac and Rue de la Varenne, at no. 85, note the unusual façade with a pediment, heavily restored and a little too white, which is all that remains of the early Couvent des Récollets which, for two centuries, occupied the length of the odd-numbered side of this section of the Rue du Bac. As far as the Boul. Saint-Germain the houses in this section, mainly commercial, are old.

The Palais-Bourbon district***

7th arr./Map ref. 15–B1
Métro: Chambres-des-Députés, Invalides
Bus: 83, 63
Parking: beneath the Esplanade des Invalides, entrance Rue de Constantine, Rue Faubert.
Taxis: 110 Rue de l'Université. Tel. 47-05-03-14.

This walk takes you around the two great *hôtels*, the Palais-Bourbon and the Hotel de Lassay. This *quartier* figures prominently in the history of French parliamentary politics, and it is easy to

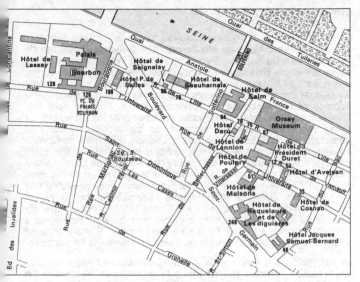

The Palais-Bourbon district

imagine how glamorous life was in the 18th c., at the time of its first owner, the Duchesse de Bourbon.

Stroll toward the imposing Gare d'Orsay, a fine example of the grandeur of Paris in 1900, and now the new museum of the 20th c.

Tour of the district

2 hrs.

☐ The Palais-Bourbon**

Visits allowed only between sessions.
To attend a sitting of the National Assembly, send your request in writing to the Quaestor, or see the visiting times in the CNMHS: Tel. 42-74-22-22 and those of private cultural organizations.

In line with the Pont de la Concorde and the Palais-Bourbon, where the National Assembly sits, is the Church of la Madeleine at the end of the perspective beyond the Rue Royale and the Place de la Concorde.

History of the building

The palace was built on land acquired by the legitimized daughter of Louis XIV and Mme de Montespan, the Dowager Duchesse de Bourbon (Mlle de Nantes). Begun by Giardini in 1722, continued by Lassurance, the palace and terraced gardens sloping down to the Seine were finally completed by Aubert and Gabriel in 1728. Louis XV bought the property 28 years later to make it part of the general scheme of the Place de la Concorde, but in 1784 he sold this 'dwelling of agreeable proportions, built not only for show, but for living comfortably and for oneself', as the architect Patte had described it in 1760 to the duchess' grandson, the Prince de Condé. He enlarged and embellished it, adding two wings to the main courtyard. Finally the Hotel de Lassay (the Marquis de Lassay was a close friend of the duchess) was added; it was known as the Petit Bourbon. The Revolution broke out before work was completed and the palace was confiscated to become a chamber for the Council of the Five Hundred (*Conseil des Cinq-Cents,* 1795). It was completely remodeled and where the salons of the main building had been, a council chamber was built by Gisors and Lecomte. It was then used to store archives and the Hôtel de Lassay became the Polytechnic.

In 1807 under the Empire, Napoléon commissioned Poyet to build the N façade. Overlooking the Place de la Concorde, it balances the Neo-Classical façade of the Madeleine, characteristic of the period 1803–07. Under the Restoration the *hôtel* was returned to the Prince de Condé, but his son soon rented it to the State, which later bought it from the Duc d'Aumales. In 1827 it was taken over by the Legislative Assembly. Gisors' and Lecomte's conference hall, dilapidated beyond repair, was demolished in 1830, to be replaced by the present salon, the work of the palace architect Jules de Joly (1828–32). Three other salons, the corridors and the library were added at the same time. At the end of the large courtyard opposite the Concorde bridge a raised main courtyard was constructed, reached by two broad steps, allowing direct access to the central hall (Casimir-Perier) by a Neo-Classical portico and a ceremonial bronze door. Since these alterations were completed in 1932, the palace has not undergone any substantial changes. Part of the r. wing was badly damaged in an explosion on the night of March 23 to 24, 1961. Restored and refurbished in 1962, the building was enlarged in 1972. Seat of the legislative body, then of the Chamber of Deputies (the last session of which was held on May 16, 1940), the Palais-Bourbon was, during the German occupation, the administrative headquarters of Grand Paris. The Germans were driven out on August 25, 1944 by a detachment of the Leclerc division after a bloody battle in which the building was damaged and 30,000 books in the library destroyed. The National Constituent Assembly, elected on October 21, 1945, held its first session at the Palais-Bourbon on November 6. The Constitution of the Fourth Republic (1946) replaced the Chamber of Deputies with the National

Assembly, a designation which was retained by the constitution of 1958.

The exterior

The main entrance opens to the S on to the Place du Palais-Bourbon. The wings of the main courtyard and the buildings on this side date from the second half of the 18th c. Walk round the palace to the E, following the Rue Aristide-Briand.

Poyet's façade. This First Empire Neo-Classical façade, overlooking the Pont de la Concorde, is simply a decorative veneer with no logical relationship to the building. The haut-relief on the pediment by J. P. Cortot (1842) represents France surrounded by Freedom and Order, with the spirits of Commerce, Agriculture, Peace, War and Eloquence. On the wings, set back, are two allegorical bas-reliefs: to the r., *Prometheus giving life to the Arts*, by Rude (1835); to the l., *Public Education* by Pradier (1839). On the steps two statues: to the r., Themis by Houdon, to the l., Minerva by Roland. At the base of the steps four politicians: Sully by Beauvallet, L'Hospital by L. Deseine, d'Aguesseau by J. Foucou, and Colbert by J. Dumont.

The interior

In the center, the Council Chamber (1828–32) occupies the site of the Duchesse de Bourbon's salons: a semicircle decorated with 20 marble Ionic columns with gilded bronze capitals; sunken panels and arabesques in the vault are by Adam and Gosse. On either side of the bureau used by the president (formerly used by the Council of the Five Hundred) are statues of the *Liberty of Public Order* by Pradier; above the columns in the attic storey, Reason, Justice, Prudence and Eloquence by Desprez, Dumont, Allier and Foyatier; between the pedestals of the columns, bas-reliefs by Roman: *France Giving Laurel Wreaths to the Arts and Industry*; above, Gobelins tapestries: *The School of Athens*, after Raphael; on the gallery, a fine bas-relief, *The Fame of History* (1798), framing two eagles changing into a cockerel on the fall of the Empire; this gallery, as well as the president's chair, in mahogany and gilt bronze, dates from the Council of Five Hundred. The Council chamber is surrounded by two large rooms: to the W, the Salle des Pas-Perdus to which journalists and authorized personnel have access; to the E, the conference hall, strictly reserved for deputies.

The Salle des Pas-Perdus or Salon de la Paix is the lobby: ceiling painted by Vernet, with allegories of *Peace* (to the r., Sea Gods fleeing before steamships; to the l., *Scientific Progress and the Genie of Steam on land*; below, peers and magistrates, the university and the diplomatic corps). The Council Chamber: in the vault, historic scenes painted by Heim; behind Raggi's statue of Henry IV, flags captured as war trophies from the Spanish Campaigns during the First Empire; paintings by Vinchon (*Reunion of the States*), Ary Scheffer (*Burghers of Calais*) and Vincent (*The Arrest of President Molé*); a fine green marble fireplace surmounted with a bust of the Republic and the Crown.

The vestibule or Salle des Distributions: statues of Cicero and Demosthenes.

The Library: reserved exclusively for members of the Assembly, under exceptional circumstances consultants are admitted with special permission. Situated to the E, near the Council Chamber, it forms a gallery with rounded ends covered over with half-domes, and divided into five vaulted bays, each with a dome supported by pendentives. These 20 pendentives (four to each dome) and the two end half-domes are decorated with famous paintings** by Eugène Delacroix, one of the most important works of the Romantic master and a masterpiece of the 19th c. Delacroix fulfilled his 'need to excel', as he wrote in a letter.

The decorations, commissioned by Montalivet in 1838, which necessitated many plans, sketches, cartoons and modifications; the work took nine years; from 1845, the painter was at the same time decorating the Peers Chamber in the Palais du Luxembourg. The gallery was poorly lit and Delacroix, while painting the subjects of the half-domes directly on to the wall, suffered severely from the heat. The pendentives were painted on canvas in the studio, then mounted, and finally retouched *in situ* by the artist. These magnificent paintings trace the history of civilization with the two semicircles forming sources of light, symbolizing the beginning and the end. To the S, *Orpheus Bringing Civilization to the Savage Greeks*; to the N, *Attila Trampling Underfoot Italy and the Arts*. The five domes each contain four subjects relating to a central theme: 1st dome (S), the Sciences: *Hippocrates Refusing Gifts from the King of Persia, Archimedes Killed by a Soldier, Aristotle Describing the Animals Sent by Alexander, Death of Pliny the Elder*. 2nd dome, Philosophy: *the Chaldean Shepherds, who Invented Astronomy, Socrates and his Daemon, Herodotus Questioning the Magians on their Traditions; Death of Seneca*. 3rd dome, Legislation: *Lycurgus Consulting the Pythian Oracle, Numa and the Nymph Egeria, Demosthenes Haranguing the Waves, Cicero Accusing Verres*. 4th dome, Theology: *The Creation of Eve*, the *Babylonian Captivity*; the *Death of John the Baptist*; the *Coin of the Tribute*. 5th dome (N), Poetry: the *Education of Achilles, Alexander and the poems of Homer, Hesiod and his Muse, Ovid among the Barbarians*.

The gallery, lit by 10 semicircular bays, is broken along its length by two monumental white marble fireplaces, with four sides. At either end are busts of Voltaire and Diderot by Houdon, each standing on a piece of furniture in the so-called Egyptian style.

The collections: the Library, which dates from the Convention, contains more than 350,000 volumes. The old collection begins with a small number of incunabula, of which the oldest is a Catholicon of 1460; note also a superb copy of the Mainz Bible (1462). An important collection of works of all kinds (notably the humanities, jurisprudence and history) from the 16th and 18th c., of which many are richly bound in leather, some with coats of arms. The modern collection, from the 19th c. onward, is constantly updated. The manuscript collection consists of over 1500 volumes; the oldest is a Bible from the 10th c. The most remarkable are the original manuscript of the trial of Joan of Arc, illuminated medieval manuscripts, 20 autograph manuscripts by J. J. Rousseau (*Confessions, Emile, La Nouvelle Héloïse, Lettres,* the score of *Le Devin du Village,* etc.), an important collection of extracts from the registers of the Parlement of Paris, administrative manuscripts on the history of the provinces, some curious oriental manuscripts and, especially, an Aztec divinatory codex.

In a room adjoining the library the small museum of the history of the Palace and its Assemblies has been set up. There is a fine marble bust of a member of the Convention, J. A. Crueze-Latouche, then a senator, who became President of the Council of the Five Hundred; a collection of medals, letters and insignia of the deputies dating from the Constituent Assembly of 1789; engravings and various mementoes.

Between the debating chamber and the main courtyard are three rooms reserved for discussions and correspondence of the deputies: these rooms and the Conference Hall are known as the 'corridors' of the Assembly. The ceiling of Abel de Pujol's salon is decorated with grisailles (historical subjects) by Abel de Pujol. In the center, the Casimir-Perier room or vestibule, the bronze door of which opens on to the main courtyard, is decorated with bas-reliefs and statues: Mirabeau and Bailly, by Jaley; Casimir-Perier, by Duret; General Foy, by Desprez. At the end, a bronze bas-relief by Dalou: *The Sitting of the National Assembly on June 23, 1789.* The Delacroix or King's Room (the niche where the throne of Louis-Philippe was placed can still be seen) has more decoration* by Delacroix, commissioned by Thiers in 1833, and restored in 1929. Symbolizing the sources and manifestations of the strength of the State, Delacroix painted on the frieze, scenes relating to Justice, Agriculture, Industry and War, which he also represented on the ceiling accompanied by their emblems. In this room, without any obvious interior architecture or any normal light, Delacroix had wanted to give an impression of monumentality rather than decoration, hence the large grisaille figures representing rivers and seas: six rivers of France, the Ocean and the Mediterranean.

The Palais-Bourbon is linked to the Hôtel de la Présidence or Hôtel de Lassay by the large and magnificent Galerie des Fêtes, which dates from 1848: it is balanced by the Galerie des Tapisseries, the former picture gallery of the Duc de Morny, president of the Legislative Body of the Second Empire.

☐ The Hôtel de Lassay**

Entrance 128 Rue de l'Université (same visiting conditions as for the Palais-Bourbon).

On the Quai d'Orsay next to the Palais-Bourbon, the Hôtel de Lassay, built by Aubert between 1722 and 1724, is today the residence of the President of the National Assembly. The façade overlooking the Seine consists of wide semicircular arched bays beneath a balustrade carrying statues. It became the Petit Bourbon when the Prince de Condé annexed it to his palace (1768). It was reserved for the President of the Chamber from 1823, when the Duc d'Aumale sold it to the State. Under the Second Empire, it was the residence of the ostentatious Duc de Morny. He kept a suite of five elegant rooms, arranged and decorated in the delicate style of the 18th c. with beautiful Louis XV woodwork.

Follow the Quay d'Orsay (→Quays) and rejoin the Rue de l'Université, either via the Rue de Constantine, or go back by the Rue Aristide-Briand.

The Ministry of Foreign Affairs

130 Rue de l'Université; 37 Quai d'Orsay.

Built between 1845 and 1853 by Lacornée, this is the headquarters of the French Diplomatic Service: the Quai d'Orsay. Many sovereigns and heads of State have been received here since 1900. This was the scene of a violent fight on August 25 1944: a large part of the Chancellery buildings had to be rebuilt. On the quay, a monument to Aristide Briand (d.1932) by Landowski and Bouchard.

Virtually opposite the residence of the President of the Chamber, at 101 Rue de l'Université, is a modern building, erected in 1975 for the services of the Palais-Bourbon and the Ministry of Foreign Affairs. Each deputy has his own office. The Place du Palais-Bourbon forms a fine architectural ensemble with its sober, elegant Louis XVI *hôtels*. It was designed for the Prince de Condé. In the center, an allegorical statue of *The Law* by Feuchères (1855); President Paul Reynaud lived at no. 5 from 1936 until his death in 1966.

Take the Rue Aristide-Briand.

Rue de Lille

As far as the Boul. Saint-Germain.

For the beginning of the street, → Rue des Saints-Pères district.

Since January 1957, no. 121, the former Hôtel Turgot* (18th c.), the façade of which is visible from the Rue de l'Université, has housed the Dutch Institute. It contains an important art library and the famous collection of Dutch and German paintings amassed by Fritz Lugt (1884–1970). The concerts, conferences and exhibitions that take place throughout the year are an important part of the cultural life of Paris. Glance down the passage in the courtyard of no. 119.

Cross the Rue de Courty where, in 1959, the historian-sociologist André Siegfried died, and where Marcel Achard lived (1899–1974). The street is two centuries old.

The large property at 288 Boul. Saint-Germain, on the corner of the quay, has been occupied by the European Parliament since 1980. The odd-numbered side of the boulevard is mainly occupied by buildings erected by Bouchot to enlarge the Ministry of Defence. The headquarters of the Chiefs of Staff of land armies are here.

Rue de Lille, continued

As far as the Rue de Solférino.

The construction of the Boul. Saint-Germain caused the loss of two or three 18th-c. mansions in the street. Mlle Clairon, the famous actress, died in 1803 on the site of the present no. 105. No. 93 is an early 19th-c. mansion. At no. 80, the *hôtel* built by Boffrand in 1714 was sold to the Marquis de Seignelay; in 1839 it was bought by a great-nephew of the financier John Law, the Maréchal de Lauriston. The first-floor salon overlooking the garden is a Rococo masterpiece. In the garden – which is laid out in terraces, as are all the gardens of the *hôtels* along the quay – in the middle of the lawn is a small marble plaque bearing the name 'Coco'; it was here that Mme de Tourzel buried Marie-Antoinette's little dog. Now the home of the Ministère du Commerce et de l'Artisanat (Commerce and Crafts), the two façades and two salons are registered historic monuments.

The Hotel de Beauharnais**

78 Rue de Lille.

One of the most beautiful mansions of the suburb, this is the residence of the German Ambassador.

In the 18th c. the *hôtel* was sold by Boffrand to Jean-Baptiste Colbert, nephew of the great statesman, then passed to the Duc de Neufville-Villeroy. Prince Eugène de Beauharnais, son of Joséphine, acquired it in 1803, and had it converted by the architect Bataille, spending on it the then enormous sum of 1.5 million francs. His sister, Queen Hortense, lived there. Through Eugène de Beauharnais, who, in 1822, married off his eldest daughter to Oscar

I of Sweden, son of Bernadette and Desirée Clary, and through her and her brothers and sisters who ruled in Portugal and in the German principalities, the blood of the Beauharnais runs in the veins of all the ruling families of Europe. In 1814 Frederick William III, King of Prussia, installed his legation there and acquired the *hôtel* in 1817 for 250,000 francs. It remained the legation of Prussia until it became the German Embassy in 1871. It was taken back by the French state in 1945, and returned to West Germany in 1961.

The unusual Neo-Egyptian peristyle (1807) erected on the courtyard façade is totally characteristic of the fashion popular since the Egyptian Expedition. The harmonious, sober façade overlooking the gardens is visible from the Quay Anatole-France, between nos. 13 and 23.

The magnificent interior décor and the furnishings have been preserved, making an outstanding Empire collection. On the first floor the most remarkable room is the Salon Vert, decorated with two huge fantastic landscapes painted by Hubert Robert, and a superb fireplace in antique green marble with a gilt bronze mantlepiece. The grand apartments on the second floor consist of the Salon du Trône, the Salon Rose, with a mosaic chimneypiece, and the magnificent Salon des Saisons, in the Pompeian style, the figures of the seasons, which gave the room its name, are by Boisfremont. On the same floor, Queen Hortense's apartment, consisting of the bedroom, a music room, a 'Turkish' boudoir and a 'Pompeian' bathroom, bear witness to the refinement and sophistication of the era. The *hôtel* is everything Eugène de Beauharnais could have wished for. Bismarck stayed here for a few weeks in 1862 as minister of the Prussian Legation.

Cross the Rue de Solférino. This large and airy main street gives a fine perspective over the greenery of the Tuileries and beyond the Seine, and runs along the side wall of the Grande Chancellerie of the Legion of Honor (→below). Jules Romains lived at no. 6 from 1947 to 1972. The headquarters of the Socialist Party is at the corner of the Rue de l'Université at no. 30, in the former Hôtel de Broglie.

Hôtel de Salm-Kyrkburg**

64 Rue de Lille.

Built by Pierre Rousseau from 1782 to 1787, since 1804 this has been the headquarters of the Grande Chancellerie of the Order of the Legion of Honor. Burnt down during the Commune, it was perfectly restored in every detail. As in the Hôtel du Châtelet, note the even more varying styles of the façades overlooking the courtyard and the garden: on one side Roman severity with the triumphal entrance arch, the pavilions on the street decorated with *Fame* by Moitte, the Sacrifices in the Antique style by Boquet and Roland, and the colonnades in the courtyard; on the other side, the charm of the

18th c. in the semicircular pavilion crowned with statues by Moitte. In San Francisco, the Palace of the Legion of Honor, which dominates Golden Gate Park, is the replica of this *hôtel* in Paris and another palace (twice as large) at Rochefort-en-Yvelines.

For the Musée de l'Ordre de la Légion d'Honneur et des Ordres de Chevalerie (→Museums).

Rue de Lille, continued

From Rue de Bellechasse to Rue du Bac.

On the even-numbered side of the street the Rue de Lille is mainly taken up by the Gare d'Orsay and offices of the Caisse des Depôts et Consignations which have absorbed the Hôtel de Choiseul-Praslin. But on the opposite side, at no. 67, is President Duret's *hôtel,* burnt down under the Commune, rebuilt by Marcou, today it is the headquarters of the Caisse des Dépôts et Consignations, a public office that handles, among other matters, court-ordered deposits of money. It was built in 1706 for the Marquis de Dangeau, known for his diary of life at the Court of Louis XIV.

The former Gare d'Orsay*

This stands on the site of the Palais d'Orsay (1838) built for the Minister of Foreign Affairs. Burnt down by the Commune, the land was bought back by the Orléans Railway Company (note the initials P. O., for Paris-Orléans, on the façade), which commissioned Laloux to build a station. This task began on July 14, 1900, but was almost abandoned by 1939 as the platforms were not long enough for the electric trains. The building escaped demolition and since December 1986 has been the museum of the 19th c. (→Museums). A tribute to this era, it seemed as if the Academy was attempting to take over new construction techniques.

On the long façade by the *quai* are statues of Bordeaux, Toulouse and Nantes by Hugues, Marquestre and Injalbert.

Rue de Bellechasse between the Seine and the Boul. Saint-Germain. In this section, the street is far less commercial and ministerial than S of the Boul. Saint-Germain. There are several 18th-c. mansions at nos. 5, 11, 11 *bis,* 13 and 15 where Bernardin de Saint-Pierre, author of *Paul et Virginie,* lived from 1801 to his death in 1814.

Rue de l'Université, continued

Between the Boul. Saint-Germain and Rue du Bac.

For the beginning of the street, see the Rue des Saints-Pères district. Lamartine lived at no. 82 from 1833 to 1853. At no. 80 the

Hôtel de Nointel has two connected courtyards with arcades and pediments. The mansion at no. 78, built in 1687, has been recently restored.

No. 51 is the magnificent Hôtel Pozzo di Borgo** (so-called since 1817), also called de Soyécourt. It was built from 1707 to 1708 by Lassurance. Beyond the great portal flanked by two Doric columns, the main building comprises a projecting section or avant-corps decorated with two orders of pilasters supporting a triangular pediment. This superb residence, parts of it registered monuments, has retained a certain number of its original decorative features, most notably a salon by Leroux, with rocaille woodwork.

Venture into the Rue de Poitiers, opened in 1680 on the lands of Marguerite of Valois. Note the Hôtel de Poulpry (1703): from 1707 to 1708 Watteau decorated the salons with grotesques that are among his first works.

Rue de Verneuil

Opened in 1640 in the large Pré aux Clercs, it has maintained a lot of its old look. The charming Hôtel d'Avejan at no. 53 stretches all the way to the Rue de l'Université (nos. 60–64). It was built in 1725 for the Marquis d'Avejan, a King's Musketeer, and bought for 50 francs by M. J. J. Hartman with the winning ticket no. 4858 of the lottery of Biens Nationaux in 1795. The *hôtel* was restored by D. Canal. Today it houses the Centre National des Lettres and the Maison des Ecrivains (tel. 45-49-30-85). This center aims to support publication, stimulate literary creativity, facilitate the translation of foreign works and encourage the public to read. No. 47 is the Hôtel de Saint-Thierry (18th c.). It was in the inn on the corner of the Rue du Bac that, in 1796, the famous crime of the Courrier de Lyon was planned. No. 21 is the Hôtel du Montchevreuil (1785). Nos. 13, 15 and 17 date from the 18th c; note the pediments and decorations on the façades.

The Saint-Germain-des-Prés district**

6th arr./Map ref. 16–2C, 2D
Métro: Saint-Germain-des-Prés, Mabillon
Bus: 39, 48, 63, 70, 86, 87, 95, 96
Parking: Boul. Saint-Germain opposite Le Drugstore.
Taxis: Saint-Germain-de-Prés Métro station. Tel. 42-22-00-00.
Mabillon Métro station. Tel. 43-29-00-00.

Markets: Rue de Buci, Rue Lobineau, Rue Clément and Rue Mabillon, Mon.–Sat. 8am–1pm, 4pm–7pm; Sun. 8am–1pm.

Like the Eiffel Tower or Montmartre, Saint-Germain-des-Prés is one of those legendary places that symbolize Paris in tourists' imaginations. Since the end of World War II, despite changing fashions, this area has remained chic. Nightspots in cellars, and *drugstore cafés* may have had their day, but artists, writers, politicians, actors and journalists still meet at Le Flore, Les Deux Magots or the Brasserie Lipp, which have become fixtures in the cultural life of Paris.

The network of streets and small squares behind the church has preserved many 17th-c. buildings. This is one of the most sought-after addresses in Paris; though the *quartier* lies in the heart of the capital it still retains something of the atmosphere of a village, typified by the Rue de Buci market.

The banks of the Seine opposite the Palais du Louvre, and close to the Pont Neuf built by Henri IV, were once extremely fashionable. It was here that the former Collège des Quatre-Nations was erected (the building now houses the Institut).

The curved wings of its façade and the oval dome are imbued with the Baroque spirit of French architecture at the start of Louis XIV's reign. Its neighbor, the Hôtel des Monnaies (the Mint), was built a century later and bears the marks of a Neo-Classicism dawning. For generations the nearby streets were the home of painters and writers; now they house a multitude of antiquarian booksellers' and antique dealers' shops and art galleries.

S of the Boul. Saint-Germain, the Rue du Four (the square in which the Saint-Germain market was once held) and the surrounding streets are more commercial, with ready-to-wear boutiques, couturiers and fashionable shoe shops.

History of the district

The district of Saint-Germain-des-Prés (Saint-Germain-in-the-Fields) was originally the domain of the Benedictine abbey of the same name, one of the most famous in the whole of France. The abbey owned an enormous agricultural estate stretching as far E as the present Petit-Pont, covering what are now the 6th and 7th arrondissements, as well as numerous other pieces of land all around Paris. The abbey's possessions were thus an essential nucleus of the city's growth.

The small town that grew up around the abbey in the 9th c. had by the 13th c. become a built-up area bounded by the Rue du Vieux-Colombier and the Rue des Saints-Pères. During its heyday in the beginning of the 14th c. luxurious mansions were built, one of the largest of which was the Hôtel de Nesle, standing more or less on the site now occupied by the Hôtel des Monnaies (the Mint).

Standing outside Philippe-Auguste's Wall, and therefore slightly remote from life inside the capital, the little town of Saint-Germain tried to be self-sufficient. Known in the Middle Ages as 'the town of Saint-Germain', the abbey was a virtual monastic city, enjoying complete autonomy, with its own courts of law, and independent of the diocese of Paris, since its abbot was answerable to the Pope alone. Walled and moated, it contained a public bakery and its own prison. The little town had its own annual fair, which brought economic, artistic and intellectual expansion in its wake. It also had its own hospital, run by the order of the Frères-de-la-Charité, on the corner of the Rue Jacob and the Rue des Saints-Pères. When Mazarin founded the Collège des Quatre-Nations on the Quai Malaquais, he established a haven of learning, and many theaters opened in the faubourg.

Throughout the 17th c. the walls around the abbey were gradually torn down. Houses for lay people were erected around and outside the cloisters and new streets built, including the Rue Sainte-Marthe across what is now the *parvis* in front of the church and the Rue Childebert, swept away by the Boul. Saint-Germain. The Revolution helped the district to expand by destroying some of the abbey buildings (the Chapel of our Lady, for example), and by cutting new roads across the heart of the old monastic estate. The main cloister was torn down to build the Rue de l'Abbaye. Later the Saint-Germain *quartier* was to be radically altered by Baron Haussmann's plans which destroyed many small streets, old mansions and private houses when the two main thoroughfares, the Boul. Saint-Germain and the Rue de Rennes, were built.

Although much has been destroyed over the centuries, the buildings erected in its place have continued to make the district a cultural and intellectual center. The Ecole des Beaux-Arts was built on the site of the convent of the Petits-Augustins, the new School of Medicine replaced the La Charité hospital, while the boulevards have carried on the traditions of the Saint-Germain fair with their big cafés and basement nightclubs. Finally a whole host of art galleries, bookshops and publishing houses have chosen the side streets as their home.

The tour of the district is arranged in three stages: the Church of Saint-Germain-des-Prés, the area to the N of the Boul. Saint-Germain and the area to the S.

Tour of the district

♣ The Church of Saint-Germain-des-Prés**

History of the church: This is the oldest of Paris's great churches, built at the beginning of the city's history, on a spot previously dedicated to pagan gods. In 52 BC, Camulogenus, chief of the

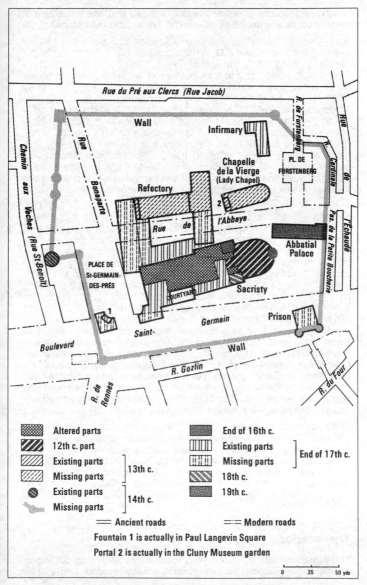

Abbey of Saint-Germain-des-Prés

Aulerci, set up camp here to resist Caesar's lieutenant, Labienus, encamped near where Saint-Germain-l'Auxerrois now stands.

Saint-Germain-des-Prés has been Christian soil since the Merovingian period. In about 543, on the advice of St Germanus, future Bishop of Paris (555), the son of Clovis, Childebert, returned from Spain, built a basilica and a monastery in the fields (prés) to house St Vincent's tunic and fragments of the True Cross. The abbey became the Saint-Denis of the Merovingian kings, of Queen Fredegonda and of St Germanus himself (d.576), who was buried in the St Symphorien Chapel. Recent excavations in this chapel have revealed the foundations of the Merovingian basilica (closed to the public). From the 8th c. on the abbey was governed as a city into itself, while the monks adopted the Benedictine rule. The monks played a dominant role in Parisian intellectual life until the Revolution, vastly extending the scope of their scholarship and laying the foundations of modern archeology and paleography.

The abbey church had been sacked by the Norsemen in 845, 857, 861 and 900, and fallen into ruin during the 10th c. The reconstruction, which began around 1000 and took over a century to complete, employed the innovations of Romanesque architecture. The nave (late 11th c.) was flanked by three towers, two on either side of the E end (torn down in the 19th c., only their bases remain) and the massive belltower above the narthex which for nearly a thousand years has been part of the Paris skyline, one of the oldest surviving belfries in France. The nave was completed in 1050, but vaulted only in the 17th c. A new chancel with arcaded galleries was built around 1163 on the pattern of those at Senlis, Saint-Denis and Noyon. For the first time in France a solution was found to the problem of ambulatory vaulting. It appears that the great Pierre de Montreuil, who worked on the transept of Notre-Dame and perhaps the Sainte-Chapelle, enlarged the church in 1245 by building the Chapel of Our Lady and the cloister (remains of the latter are to be seen in the little garden on the N side). Because of its copper-sheathed roof the church was known as Saint-Germain-le-Doré (the Gilded). The S and W doorways were added in the 17th c.

The abbey was suppressed in 1790, its famous library destroyed by fire in 1794, and the statues on the W door vandalized. All that remains today is part of the abbatial palace and the church itself, from which, however, the royal tombs have disappeared. Godde restored the building from 1821 to 1823, demolishing the three upper storeys of the towers at the E end, and V. Baltard commissioned H. Flandrin to decorate the chancel (1842–48) and the nave (1856–63).

The interior

The nave: murals* by Hippolyte Flandrin (painted 1856–63). Each arcade is surmounted by two paintings, one representing a New

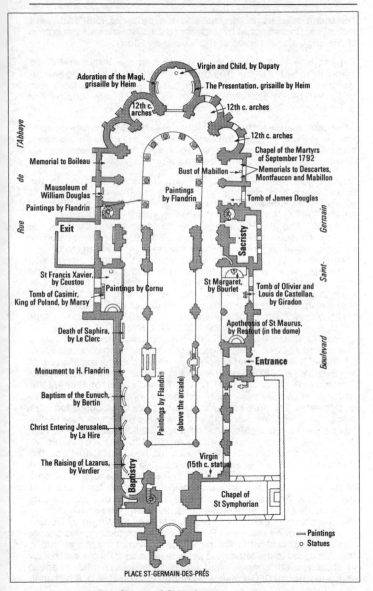

The Church of Saint-Germain-des-Prés

Testament mystery or dogma and the other its Old Testament archetype. Carved pulpit by Jacquot (1829). The capitals are copies of the originals preserved in the Musée de Cluny.

R.-hand side-aisle: 15th-c. marble statue of the Virgin and Child originally in Notre-Dame. The doorway in the 4th bay (Porte Sainte-Marguerite) dates from 1646. The chapel in the S transept was dedicated by St Francis de Sales in 1619; in the dome, *The Apotheosis of St Maurus* by Restout (1756).

S transept: marble statue of St Margaret (1705) by Jacques Bourlet, a monk in the abbey, and the tomb of Olivier and Louis de Castellan, killed in the King's service in 1644 and 1669 respectively, by Girardon, with statues of Faith and Piety.

The chancel has four bays. The small marble columns in the triforium are from the original 6th-c. Merovingian basilica of St Vincent; their capitals and bases are 12th c.; murals by H. Flandrin (1846): *Christ's Entry into Jerusalem* (l.) and *Christ Carrying the Cross* (r.). The ambulatory has five radiating chapels with ogival vaulting, consecrated in 1163. From 1957 to 1958 they were carefully cleaned, revealing their magnificent white stonework. In the course of restoration, behind a rough wall in the two S apsidal chapels and in the NE chapel, some beautiful blind arcading supported on little columns was uncovered. Despite their late date (*ca.* 1157) some of the capitals on these columns preserved the figurative tradition of Romanesque decoration; wrought-iron grilles by R. Subes. In the first bay polychrome stone bas-relief by Charlier in memory of Mgr de Montmorency-Laval (1623–1728), first Bishop of Quebec. 1st chapel (St Teresa and the Child Jesus): mausoleum of Lord James Douglas (d.1645), a Scottish gentleman in the service of Louis XIII, by Michel II Bourdin. 2nd chapel (since 1936 the Blessed Martyrs of the September 1792 Massacres and in particular the Blessed Dom Chevreux, Superior General of the Benedictines of Saint-Maur, martyred in Les Carmes prison): below the window, the tombstones of Descartes (the philosopher's remains have been deposited here since 1819, with the exception of his head which is now in the Musée de l'Homme), Montfaucon and Mabillon; bust of Mabillon. 3rd chapel: 12th-c. blind arcading revealed in 1958; two attractive 18th-c. white marble medallions with the heads of Christ and the Virgin carved in profile set in the reredos. 4th chapel: 12th-c. blind arcading also opened up in 1958. Windows composed of fragments of 13th-c. stained glass depicting the Annunciation, the Marriage of the Virgin, St Anne and St Joachim, and the Works of Mercy. Chapel of Our Lady at the E end: rebuilt in 1819, altering the architecture of the church; murals by Heim; marble statue of the Virgin by Dupaty (early 19th c.). As always in Romanesque architecture, this chapel was once identical with the others. The growth of the Marian cult in the 13th c., led to the attempt to provide her a second place of honor in churches. 6th chapel: blind arcading as in the other chapels; statue in wood of St Germanus by Muriel Pulitzer (1961). 8th chapel:

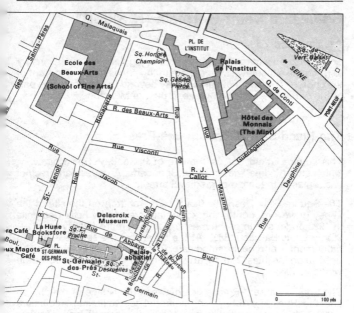

North of Saint-Germain Boulevard

the poet and critic Nicolas Boileau's tombstone from the Sainte-Chapelle; *St Peter Preaching the Gospel* by Jeaurat (1763). 9th chapel: tomb of William Douglas (d.1611) a Scottish nobleman at the court of Henri IV, attributed to Michel Bourdin; mural showing St Cornutus (2nd half of 19th c.).

N. transept: against the gable end, the tomb of John Casimir, King of Poland (d.1672). He abdicated in 1668 and became Abbot of Saint-Germain-des-Prés in 1669. His body was taken back to Poland, only his heart is buried in Saint-Germain; statue of the kneeling figure of the king by the Marsy brothers; statue of St Francis Xavier by Guillaume Coustou (1772). L.-hand side-aisle: memorial to H. Flandrin designed by Baltard with marble bust by Oudiné (1865); The *Death of Saphira* by S. Lerclerc and *St Philip Baptizing the Eunuch* by Bertin, two May Day offerings made to the church in 1718. *Christ Entering Jerusalem* by La Hire and *The Raising of Lazarus* (1677) by Verdier.

Boulevard Saint-Germain (N Side)**

2 hrs. [→ *map, page 919*]

Sometimes on summer evenings actors, jugglers and musicians try to re-create a medieval atmosphere in the *parvis* (square) in front of the church. The wall that curves away beyond the presbytery is part of the old abbey with, in a niche, a bust of Mabillon.

The Place Saint-Germain-des-Prés

This square is laid out on the site of the abbey's main gateway, which stood in line with the Rue Bonaparte. A pedestrian precinct has replaced the maze of medieval streets.

The Square Félix-Desruelle lies S of the church on the site of the abbey graveyard, containing a fountain erected by Félix Desruelle in 1923 and a statue of the master potter Bernard Palissy (*c.* 1510–90) by Louis Barrias (1883). At the far end of the square there is a monumental portico in stoneware from Sèvres with Art-Nouveau decoration by Jules Coutan, artistic director of the Sèvres porcelain works in 1900.

The Square Laurent-Prache lies between the N side of the church and the Rue de l'Abbaye. A memorial to Guillaume Apollinaire (1880–1918) was unveiled in June 1959, with a female face in bronze by Picasso, who presented it to the city in memory of his friend.

Rue de l'Abbaye

This street was built in 1800 over the remains of the monastic buildings.

The abbatial palace takes up nos. 1–5 on the odd-numbered side of the street. It was constructed in 1586 for the head of the Holy League, Cardinal de Bourbon, Charles, the then Abbot of Saint-Germain-des-Prés, who became King of France in 1589. Apart from the Hôtel Scipion, the abbey is the oldest stone and brick edifice in Paris. With its twin-casement windows with alternate triangular and round pediments, it seems ahead of its time, anticipating Louis XIII architecture. This substantial building, in which Pradier once had his studio, underwent major restoration in 1977–8 (architect, Yves Boiret); and small outbuildings were removed which since the 19th c. had disfigured its ground floor. The house of the architect Louis Baltard, in which his son Victor was born, is now visible. The whole group of buildings currently houses local and parochial services. The gardens adjoin the church gardens toward the boulevard.

Rue de Fürstenberg*

Named after the late 17th-c. Cardinal Egon von Fürstenberg, this street is built over what was once the forecourt of the abbey. The Abbot's palace had its main entrance where the Rue de Fürstenberg meets the Rue du Colombier (today Rue Jacob), where one of the pillars of the abbey gatehouse still stands. On the site of the abbey outbuildings, at no. 6, the painter Eugène Delacroix had an apartment and a studio from 1858 to 1863 when he was working on the frescoes at Saint-Sulpice and painting *La Descente au Tombeau* (The Entombment of Christ) and *La Montée au Calvaire* (The Way to Calvary). It is now the Musée Delacroix (→Museums). Manet and Bazille also had lodgings in this street.

The Rue Cardinale, built in 1700, winds along between old houses. It, too, keeps the name of Cardinal von Fürstenberg alive. The Passage de la Petite-Boucherie leads off it and back to the boulevard.

At the end of the 17th c. the Passage de la Petite-Boucherie was built on abbey lands. Its oldest houses are early 18th c., the most remarkable being the house on the corner of the Rue de l'Echaudé which, like that further on at the corner of the Rue de Seine, is shaped like the triangular cake called an *echaudé,* a speciality of the district that gave its name to the street.

The Rue de Bourbon-le-Château was built c. 1610 and is lined with curio shops and art galleries. Note the ironwork at no. 1 and the *maison-puits* at no. 2; this is a circular yard surrounded by high walls, with Restoration ironwork; note the banisters and the glass canopy above the stairwell.

Rue de Buci*

For centuries this was an important Left Bank thoroughfare. Its colorful market brings it to bustling life every day. The Chouan leader and Royalist conspirator Cadoudal held secret meetings with his accomplices at no. 40. No. 30 is a Louis XV mansion. In 1728 the dramatist Boizard de Pointeau installed the Opéra-Comique at no. 12 and had a star carved on the façade in memory of the Etoile (Star) tennis court in the Rue de l'Ancienne-Comédie which had sheltered the Comédie-Française in 1668 (→inset). Favart had his first play performed on this stage in the Rue de Buci in 1734. Apollinaire used to meet his friends at no. 10. The butcher's shop at no. 4 has replaced the Café Landelle where the first Masonic Lodge was founded in Paris in 1732. In the following year a new set of customers appeared when poets, singers and painters, led by Crébillon, Helvétius and Rameau, met to dine and discuss literature.

The Rue Grégoire-de-Tours is as busy today as it was in the 16th c., with its Breton crêperies, Asian shops, jewelers and art galleries. Nos. 11, 12, 13 and 15 are Louis XIII houses.

There is a fine Louis XVI apartment building at the Carrefour de Buci. On the site of this intersection the first recruiting booth in Paris was opened in 1792 to enlist volunteers for the defence of France. In the same year and on the same spot priests who had refused the oath to the Constitution were killed, the first victims of the September Massacres. In the Revolution of 1848 barricades were erected here.

Rue Mazarine

This street of art galleries and antiquarian booksellers, known at various times as Rue des Buttes, Rue des Fossés and Rue des Fossés-Nesle, today takes its name from the cardinal. Most of its houses are old and often pierced by passageways leading to courts and backyards. No. 42, La Bouteille tennis court, was leased on October 8, 1670 to the poet and abbot Pierre Perrin, to whom Louis XIV had given the monopoly for performance of opera in the French language. For this purpose he was to set up academies of music so that opera could be staged there. This must therefore be accounted the cradle of the Paris Opéra. In 1672 Lully took advantage of Perrin who had been put in debtors' prison by unscrupulous entrepreneurs and moved the Opéra to the Rue de Vaugirard. No. 30 is the former Hôtel des Pompes (→inset). The poet Robert Desnos lived at no. 19 from 1934 until his arrest by the Gestapo in 1944. Nos. 17–5 are old houses built on land that once belonged to the Collège des Quatre-Nations. Champollion deciphered Egyptian hieroglyphics at no. 28 where Horace Vernet later had his studio. Molière established the Illustre Théâtre (→inset) at no. 12.

Take the Rue Guénégaud at the corner of no. 15.

Rue Guénégaud

Built over what were the gardens of the Hôtel de Nevers, part of one side of the street is lined by the side wall of the Hôtel des Monnaies (Mint: below) and by some prominent art galleries. In the courtyard of no. 29, in the bookshop of the publishers Editions du Seuil stands a tower disappearing through the ceiling, the remains of Philippe-Auguste's wall. All along the street there are fine wrought-iron balconies. Nicolas de Blegny lived at no. 12; in 1692 he published the *Livre Commode des Adresses*. The Jansenist lawyer and friend of Buffon, Armand Camus, who played an influential rôle in the National Assembly lived at no. 7. Sent to arrest General Dumouriez, he was captured and handed over to the Austrians and, in 1795, was one of the five hostages exchanged for Louis XVI's daughter, still held prisoner in the Temple. No. 2 is the shop where the Mint (Hôtel des Monnaies) sells reproductions of ancient medals, contemporary strikes and limited editions of important medallions (open Mon.-Fri. 9am-5pm; Sat. 9-11:45am).

☐ The Hôtel de la Monnaie (Mint)**

11 Quai Conti (open Mon.-Sat. except public holidays 11am-5pm. Tel. 43-29-12-48).

More colloquially known as *la Monnaie,* this splendid and virtually unaltered 18th-c. building was erected from 1771 to 1777 by J. D. Antoine, who used the uneven ground to great advantage. This is the first large-scale example of Louis XVI architecture, typified by its emphasis on the harmonious balance of volumes. It was Antoine's first important work, and he lived in the *hôtel* until his death.

The exterior

The façade (126yds/117m long) has an avant-corps projecting from a central block of five arcades flanked by six Ionic columns, the attic storey crowned by six allegorical statues of Prudence, Might, Justice, Trade, Peace and Plenty. The work of J. P. Pigalle, Mouchy and Lecomte, they were strengthened and restored in 1884. The monumental gateway bearing Louis XV's monogram has a bronze tympanum on which the supporters of the fleur-de-lis escutcheon are Mercury and Ceres. The four medallions bearing the monogram of the Republic are later additions. The façade projecting onto the Rue Guénégaud is decorated with statues of the four elements by Duprez and J. J. Caffieri. A semicircular court is near the back of the building, ornamented with busts of Henri II, Louis XIII, Louis XIV and Louis XV. The central pavilion is ornamented with Doric columns and the attic storey is surmounted by the seated statues of Loyalty and Plenty.

The interior

The beautiful coffered entrance leads into the luxurious interior of the Mint which may be seen during visits to the Musée de la Monnaie (→Museums). During special exhibitions you can see the grand hall of the Mint, a vast basilical chamber in which, under the glazed dome, Mouchy's stucco statue once gazed down at the coin presses.

The Workshops (guided tours Mon. and Wed. 2:15pm; closed July and Aug.): Installed by Charlemagne in his palace in 805, the Mint moved successively to the Marais, the Saint-Jacques-de-la-Boucherie *quartier* and finally, in the 14th c., to the present Rue de la Monnaie. Henri II established another Mint on the Ile de la Cité devoted to striking medals, which was moved to the Louvre in Louis XIII's reign. In those days forgers received short shrift; they were thrown alive into cauldrons of boiling water and then hanged. Louis XV established the Mint on its present site. The Abbé Terray, Contrôleur Général des Finances, laid the foundation stone on April 30, 1771. At the beginning of the 19th c. the minting of medals was transferred to the Mint and in 1878 both functions were placed under a single directorate.

Since 1973 all coins have been minted at the coin factory in Pessac in the Gironde. Only two active workshops remain at the Quai Conti, the precious metal mint (closed to visitors) and the medal mint in which the old coin presses are kept. You cannot see the preliminary operations or what happens after the medals are struck, but you can watch the manufacture of the matrices and the process of striking medals.

The Quai Conti: between the Mint and the Institut, at no. 13, stands the little Hôtel de Guénégaud built by Mansart in 1659 and owned at the end of the 18th c. by the Permon family, relatives of the future Duchesse d'Abrantès, who was frequently visited by the young Bonaparte in 1792. The surgeon Larrey lived here from 1805 to 1832; the house is now the Galérie Katia Granoff. No. 15 was built during the reign of Louis XIV.

☐ The Palais de l'Institut de France***

23 Quai Conti (parties may visit the courtyards and the Salle de La Coupole Sat. and Sun. 3–4pm upon written application to the Secretary of the Institut).

This palace, surmounted by its famous cupola, forms a splendid and harmonious group of buildings opposite the Pont des Arts. Louis Le Vau drew up the plans aligning the palace with the Cour Carrée of the Louvre on the other side of the Seine and Lambert and d'Orbay supervised the actual building from 1663 to 1691. The rounded wings end in two large square pavilions, with a Jesuit-style chapel in the center. The palace regained its past glories after restoration and repointing of the stonework (1961–62 and 1974). It hosts sessions of the five national academies of which the most famous is the Académie Française and houses the venerable Mazarine Library.

History of the building

In his will Cardinal Mazarin left 2 million livres in cash and another 45,000 worth of land to found a college for 60 gentlemen from the four provinces ceded to France under the Treaty of Münster: Artois, Alsace, Roussillon and Piedmont (Pignerolo). Hence the Collège

Mazarin was often called the Còllege des Quatre-Nations. During the Revolution part of the Collège Mazarin was turned into a temporary prison in which David, Dr Guillotin and Mme de Tourzel were held. Next it housed the three central Parisian schools. The Institut, formed by the Law of October 25, 1795 (3 Brumaire, Year IV) under the terms of the Constitution of the Year III and temporarily housed in the Louvre, was given in 1805 tenancy of the former Collège Mazarin. The architect Antoine Vaudoyer, who was commissioned to restore the building, built the arcades, the domain of the print sellers, which were demolished in 1875.

The Mazarine Library

Open Mon.-Fri. 10am–6pm; closed August 1–15.

The library is housed in the E pavilion of the palace built, as a tablet records, on the site of the Hamelin Tower (part of Philippe-Auguste's 13th-c. city wall), better known as the Tour de Nesle because it controlled the approaches to the vast grounds of the mansion of that name. The Tour de Nesle was demolished in 1665.

Cardinal Mazarin's private library was assembled by the learned Gabriel Naudé, and became the first public library in France when, from 1643 onward, Mazarin opened it to scholars one day a week. Scattered during the troubles of the Fronde (the civil war between the nobles) and later reassembled, the books were bequeathed by the Cardinal to the Collège des Quatre-Nations founded under the terms of his will. In 1689 it was opened twice a week and from 1789 onward, every day. During the Revolution it was considerably enriched by libraries confiscated from religious houses and émigré noblemen. From 1923 to 1945 it was controlled by the Bibliothèque Nationale, but is now administered by the Institut. The building itself was restored recently (1970–71).

The library contains 450,000 printed books, 4600 manuscripts, 2100 incunabulae (books printed before 1501 and 6000), *mazarinades* (17th-c. political pamphlets), a collection of outstanding quality, mostly of historical interest. Access is by an elegant staircase installed by Vaudoyer in 1824, a minor masterpiece of Restoration architecture. All in all the library has a distinctly 17th-c. air. The columns with their Corinthian capitals come from the original library, as does the paneling in the Reading Room with Mazarin's devices. Many antiquities are on display, some from the Cardinal's own collections, *objets d'art* and chandeliers by Boulle and Caffieri.

The Palace courtyards

Behind the Mazarine Library there is a second rectangular courtyard, with the entrance to the Institut on the l. From here you can see members of the Académie Française arriving every

Thursday to work on the French dictionary. Finally, beyond this, is the charming little courtyard which was once the kitchen yard of the college, with a gateway onto the Rue Mazarine (no. 3). An old well decorated with wrought iron stands in front of an ivy-clad wall. The building on the far side houses the Bureau des Longitudes.

The Institut de France (visitors should return to the 2nd courtyard, with the entrance to the administrative offices and the meeting rooms).

Five academies comprise the Institut de France. The most famous of these is the Académie Française, founded by Richelieu in 1635, restricted to 40 members and specifically entrusted with the compilation of a dictionary of the French language. The Académie des Inscriptions et Belles-Lettres was founded by Colbert in 1664 and publishes reports and collections of historical documents (open meeting Fri. at 3:30pm). The Académie des Sciences was founded by Colbert in 1666 and publishes weekly reports (open meeting Mon. at 3 pm). The Académie des Beaux-Arts was established in 1816 as the successor body to the 4th Class of the Institut as constituted in 1803. The Académie des Sciences Morales et Politiques was founded in 1832 as the successor to the 5th Class of the Institut suppressed in 1803; it publishes its transactions (open meeting Mon. at 2:45pm).

Each of the academies meets formally and separately once a year under the cupola, and jointly there in plenary session each October 25, the anniversary of the foundation of the Institut. Newly elected members are admitted to their respective academies under the cupola. Members of the public may attend with tickets obtainable from the Secretary's office (23 Quai Conti).

Every year the Institut awards many prizes and is also a patron of literature, science and the arts. It has been bequeathed over 900 legacies since 1810, and in Paris owns the Musée Marmortan, the Musée Jacquemart-André and the Bibliothèque Thiers.

The interior

Regular meeting room of the three Academies of Sciences, Beaux-Arts, and Inscriptions et Belles-Lettres: statues of Racine by Boizot, of Puget by Desprez, of Molière by Duret, of La Fontaine by Seurre the Elder, of Corneille by Laitié and of Poussin by Julien; busts of Gross by Dantan, of Cuvier by Pradier, of Bonaparte by Guillaume, etc. Regular meeting room of the Académie Française and of the Académie des Sciences Morales et Politiques, as well; it lies beyond the first room; at the far end hang portraits of Cardinal Richelieu, the full length being a copy of the painting by Philippe de Champaigne, that of the cardinal on his death-bed an original work by the artist. The fine carved wooden door was for many years in the French National Records Office and only returned in 1931. During the First

Empire, what had been the chapel of the Collège des Quatre-Nations was restructured to become the formal meeting room in which new members were admitted to the Académie Française, where the Institut held its annual plenary meeting and where the five academies each held their annual meetings. The architect Vaudoyer radically changed its character by installing galleries and tiers of seats in the side chapels and entrance and, in particular, by hiding the upper portions of Le Vau's cupola behind the false front of a flattened dome. This was removed in the restoration completed in 1962. Le Vau's dome was revealed once more and its skylight replaced. The drum is decorated with a verse from Ezekiel and medallions of the Twelve Apostles by Desjardins, two of which were recut by Paul Belmondo. The floor level was lowered to accommodate the tiers of seats without upsetting the architectural balance.

Mazarin's tomb, designed by J. Hardouin-Mansart and executed in 1689 by Coysevox, Le Hongre and Tuby, has been returned to its original place in the vestibule after a stay of over a century in the Louvre.

Rue de Seine

From the River Seine to the Rue des Beaux-Arts.

This section of the street from the river to the Boul. Saint-Germain dates back to 1250, although the first building along it did not appear until about 1535; and it was extended to the Rue de Tournon at the time of the Consulate.

The earliest houses were built on the site of the outbuildings of Marguerite of Valois' (La Reine Margot) palace. Nos. 2 and 4 were the now demolished mansion belonging to Victor Riqucti-Mirabeau. Today it is the Square Honoré-Champion, a patch of grass with Léon Drivier's statue of Voltaire, unveiled in 1960. No. 6 was built in 1625, perhaps by Pierre Le Muet for Jacques de Garsanlan, Treasurer to the Duc d'Orléans. It still has its fine façade. At no. 10, in a considerably altered 17th-c. mansion, the *Journal des Débats* was founded, and David had his studio and Rosa Bonheur her drawing school here.

Rue des Beaux-Arts

This street was built in 1825 on the site of the Hôtel de la Rochefoucauld, whose gardens and buildings ran as far as the Rue Bonaparte and the Rue Visconti (no. 14). From the start the street was the haunt of painters and writers. Gérard de Nerval lived at no. 5 and when in 1831 Lacordaire opened the first free school at no. 3 *bis*, without permission from the university authorities, the police moved in and forced him to close. Fantin-Latour had his studio at no. 8, while Corot had his at no. 10, the house in which both

Merimée and Ampère also lived. A carved medallion commemorates the death of Oscar Wilde at no. 13 in 1900. No. 11, the Galerie de la Maison des Beaux-Arts, regularly gives students of the school (→below) the opportunity to exhibit their work.

The Rue des Beaux-Arts ends opposite the main entrance to the Ecole des Beaux-Arts.

☐ The Ecole des Beaux-Arts*

14 Rue Bonaparte (groups only, admitted with prior written permission. Tel. 42-60-34-57).

The school is housed in the remains of the 17th-c. convent of the Petits-Augustins, the 18th-c. Hôtel de Chimay and accommodation built for the purpose in the 19th c. Originally the land was part of the E end of the Pré-aux-Clercs which 'La Reine Margot', Henri IV's discarded first wife, bought for the site of her palatial mansion. Its entrance stood on the Rue de Seine and its gardens ran down to and along the riverside. The Queen had the chapel of Les Louanges built and then, after her death, the Augustinian fathers moved in. They were expelled during the Revolution, and what had been their convent became in 1795 the Musée des Monuments Français (→inset) and then, in 1816, the Ecole des Beaux-Arts. F. Debret was commissioned to erect new buildings designed to house the studios. From 1820 onwards he was responsible for the building on the S side of the gardens known as Les Loges and began the l. wing of the Palais des Etudes (Study Center). The building was completed by F. Duban, who replaced Debret in 1832.

Tour of the Ecole des Beaux-Arts

The forecourt: in the center stands a Corinthian column. The bronze statue of Plenty by G. Pilon which used to surmount it is now in the church. On the l. early 16th-c. statues from the former mansion known as the Hôtel de la Trémoille; above, Balze's painting on faience, after Raphael, *God the Father Blessing the World.* Most of the sculptures which stood in the forecourt have been returned to the places from which they were taken, including the famous façade from the Château de Gaillon (→ Eure).

The Conventual Church of the Petits-Augustins (open for special exhibitions): erected 1617 to 1619. The projecting central avant-corps of the main façade of the 16th-c. Château d'Anet has been built on to the gabled façade of the church. The former is one of Philibert Delorme's masterpieces and the first example in France of the superimposition of the three Classical orders. It has been restored as a museum of Renaissance art. In the vestibule there is paneling from the Château d'Anet and at the far end mouldings of the copy made by Sigalon of Michelangelo's *Last Judgement*. The chapel known as Les Louanges (open for special exhibitions) adjoins the church and flanks Rue Bonaparte. Its six-cell, ribbed dome is the oldest in Paris (1608). It, too, is now a museum, devoted to the work of Michelangelo.

The Palais des Etudes (Study Center) which fronts the far side of the main courtyard was erected from 1858 to 1862 by F. Duban. Known as Les Loges, the building to the S is by F. Duret (1820–32). The garden, to the N contains bas-reliefs (J. Goujon's studio) from the attic storey of the Cour Carré of the Louvre as well as a row of arcades from the lower storey of the 16th-c. Hôtel de Torpane which stood in the Rue des Bernardins. The beautiful façade of the 17th- and 18th-c. Hôtel de la Bazinière, also known as the Hôtel de Chimay, purchased for the Ecole des Beaux-Arts in 1884, overlooks one side of the gardens. The Cour du Mûrier (Mulberry Tree Court), named after the tree which A. Lenoir planted here, is the former Augustinian cloister converted to a Pompeian atrium by F. Duban in 1836.

Walk down the Rue Bonaparte towards the Seine to see the school buildings along the Quai Malaquais. No. 13 is in the Classical idiom erected by Duban, housing the main exhibition hall for students' work (open for special exhibitions).

The school's library in the E wing of the Palais d'Etudes produces a remarkable overall effect with its coffered ceiling, doors taken from the Château d'Anet and furnishings designed by Duban. The pictures displayed above the bookcases come from what was the Académie Royale de Peinture et de Sculpture. The library was opened in 1864 and contains over 120,000 old books on art and architecture, 100,000 prints, 20,000 photographs, 12,000 old master drawings, 700 incunabulae printed before 1501, 25,000 architectural drawings, as well as paintings, miniatures and manuscripts. The whole of the library was restored in 1975. The school also has an information and documentation center and a newspaper room for students.

Rue Bonaparte

From the Seine to the Rue Visconti.

There are still a few fine mansions with original sculpted doorways, wrought ironwork and elegant, well-proportioned forecourts. Nowadays art galleries have proliferated. Nos. 5, 7 and 9 are 18th-c. mansions. Marshal Lyautey lived in no. 5 from 1911 to 1934. The Marquis de Persan, Chief Marshal of the Household of the Comte d'Artois in 1789, had his town house at nos. 7 and 9. Monge lived there in 1803 and Manet was born there in 1833. No. 6 was built for Louis Le Barbier in 1631 and heavily restored in the 18th c. Derain had his studio opposite no. 14, the main entrance to the Ecole des

Beaux-Arts, while Lachaud, the lawyer in the notorious Lafarge case, had an apartment at no. 11. No. 16 is the Académie de Medecine, housed in a building erected by Ronchet in the early 20th c., with a fine library. Nos. 20, 22 and 28 are Louis XIII mansions. Paul Delaroche lived at no. 20 from 1832 to 1854. The abbey gardens stretched as far as nos. 27 and 28.

Rue Visconti

This is one of the oldest streets in the district, built in 1540 across the small Pré-aux-Clercs. It was not named after the architect Joachim Visconti until the 19th c. It would be tempting to say that it is still the hidden backwater which it was at the close of the 16th c. when it afforded a refuge to Protestants, among them Bernard Palissy. So many Huguenots lodged here that Agrippa d'Aubigné called it 'Little Geneva'. Its inhabitants escaped the Massacre of St Bartholomew's Day.

The longest of all the narrow streets of Paris, it was this street that the artist Christo chose for his *Iron Curtain* on June 27, 1962 to coincide with his exhibition at the Galerie Drouin. The *Iron Curtain* was simply a pile of metal drums across the street.

Nearly all the houses are 17th c., with their original great carved portals, wrought-iron banisters and charming forecourts. Nos. 24, 22 and 20 stand on the site of the huge mansion which, in 1559, belonged to Nicolas Vauquelin and subsequently to Nicolas Fontaine, who had close connections with Port-Royal. Racine died here in 1699. Walk back to no. 22 to admire the fine staircase with its wrought-iron banisters. The executive committee of the Décades de Pontigny held their meetings at no. 23, with Paul Desjardins and André Gide in the chair. No. 21 is the Hôtel de Ranes (*ca.* 1660) while at no. 17, on June 4, 1827, Balzac opened a printing press, which failed to make his fortune and later became the Deberny type foundry. Adrienne Lecouvreur lived at no. 16, where she entertained Maurice de Saxe and Voltaire, and Fontenelle died there on March 20, 1730. It has a 17th c. staircase with wrought-iron banisters behind a portico with pediment.

Rue de Seine, continued

From the Rue Visconti to the Rue Jacques-Callot.

For the beginning of this street, → above.

George Sand, who shocked the district by wearing men's clothes, lived at no. 31, a building at present occupied by the Akademia Raymond Duncan, founded by Isadora's brother. No. 26 is the site of Le Petit Maure, the tavern in which the poet Saint-Amand (1594–1661) died. This large house has preserved its wrought ironwork, fine windows and 17th-c. inn sign.

On the l.-hand side is the Rue Jacques-Callot. Although most of its houses are old, this is a new street. Note the picturesque Café de la Palette. The large block of studios of the Ecole des Beaux-Arts was designed by Roger Expert in the 1930s.

Rue de Seine to Rue Jacob

Note the portal of no. 36 and the strange sign, an inverted dove against the sun, at no. 38. Baudelaire lived at no. 35 from 1854 to 1855. No. 41 is a *hôtel* which still retains its two original dormer windows on the top floor with their pulleys for hoisting goods or furniture. No. 42, the Maison d'Angleterre on the corner of the Rue de Seine and the Rue de l'Echaudé, is another house built in the shape of the triangular cake known as an *echaudé*, one of the specialties of the district. No. 57 is a beautiful Louis XV mansion. Mickiewicz wrote *Pan Tadeusz* in 1834 at no. 64 (→ Musée A. Mickiewicz). The whole street is now given over to art galleries, bookshops or publishers' offices.

Rue Jacob

Since 1836 it has taken its name from the altar which Marguerite of Valois ('La Reine Margot'), set up when she regained her freedom and dedicated to the Patriarch Jacob in the garden of her mansion in the Rue de Seine. For many years there was a restaurant, A l'Autel de Jacob (Jacob's Altar), and there is now a well-known cabaret, L'Echelle de Jacob (Jacob's Ladder).

The street still retains a few old houses, but the most interesting surviving features are indoors and in the courtyards and you will often have to push open doors to see ironwork and carvings (note nos. 3, 9, 11, 13, 15, 22, 26 and 28). No. 7 is a mansion built about 1640, in which Racine lived after he left Port-Royal in the same year. Maurice de Saxe is said to have lived at no. 12; go inside to see the pretty courtyard and garden and the fine staircase with 17th-c. wrought-iron banisters. Jean-Casimir, King of Poland, is believed to have lived in no. 11, after being dethroned in 1668 and before becoming Abbot of Saint-Germain-des-Prés. It has a magnificent 17th-c. staircase with a stone baluster. Wagner had an apartment from mid-October 1841 to April 7, 1842 on the far side of the courtyard of no. 14. No. 18 was erected about 1925 by Gabriel Veissiere for the publishing house Gautier Languereau, on the site of the offices of the Hetzel firm, publishers of Jules Verne's novels. Proudhon wrote his two *Memoires sur la Propriété* (1839 and 1841) at no. 19. In 1824 Delacroix had a studio at no. 20 where he painted *The Massacre at Chios* (→Musée Delacroix), but at the beginning of the 20th c. Nathalie Clifford Barney, whom Remy de Gourmont nicknamed the Amazon, gathered a fashionable literary circle here.

In the garden (closed to the public) stands a charming little Empire temple with Doric columns, a Temple of Friendship according to the inscription, 'To Friendship', which it bears. No. 22, known as 'Adrienne Lecouvreur's House', has a charming façade overlooking the garden. Ingres lived at no. 27; Colette and her first husband Willy at no. 28 in 1895, and Auguste Comte at no. 36.

Rue Saint-Benoît

Built in 1680 over the moat surrounding the abbey, it was only given its present name in the 18th c. The bistros at the top of the street were among the most popular during the 1950s. The second basement nightclub (*cave*) to be opened in Paris after Le Tabou in the Rue Dauphine, was here, and it regularly attracted such artistes as Juliette Gréco and Boris Vian. Sainte Beuve lived at no. 5 and Léo Larguier died here. In 1845 the painter Boilly, who sketched many scenes of Parisian life, died at no. 6. No. 11 is a restaurant opened in 1900, L'Assiette au Beurre, with an Art-Nouveau façade: inside there are several bronze figurines of the same period. Buloz set up the offices of the *Revue des Deux-Mondes* at no. 20.

Boulevard Saint-Germain (S Side)*

1 hr.

The Boul. Saint-Germain between the Rue des Saints-Pérés and the Carrefour Mabillon.

Starting from the Quai de la Tournelle in 1855, Baron Haussmann built this boulevard to run to the Quai Anatole-France. The section between the Rue Saint-Benoît and the Mabillon intersection was the last to be built (*ca.* 1878), sweeping away the Rue Taranne and the Rue Sainte-Marguerite.

On the corner of the boulevard and the Rue des Saints-Pères the old street name of Rue Taranne can still be seen. Nos. 175–155 Boul. Saint-Germain are houses surviving from this street, and they show how rich and elegant it was. Jean Gautherin's statue of Diderot (1885), which now faces no. 145, stood until 1947 outside no. 169 (that is, 2 Rue Taranne), on the site of the house in which the author of *Jacques le Fataliste* slaved away for years trying to forget his marital and financial difficulties. This stretch of the boulevard retains some splendid 18th-c. mansions with their original wrought ironwork, carved keystones and balconies supported by corbels.

You are now in the heart of the Saint-Germain-des-Prés of the 1950s; the Deux Magots (there is a Deux-Magots literary prize) and the Café de Flore haunted by the shades of Malraux, Camus, the Préverts, the Allégrets and Pierre Mac Orlan, and with its memories of Jean-Paul Sartre, Simone de Beauvoir, Mouloudji and Juliette

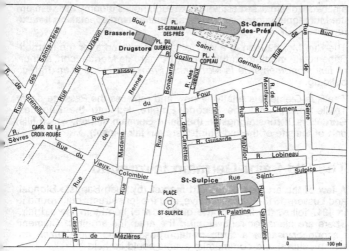

South of Saint-Germain Boulevard

Gréco. Le Flore has been a literary café for the best part of the century – Maurras and his companions of *l'Action Française* used to meet here around 1900 and Apollinaire was a regular customer. On the other side of the boulevard, the Brasserie Lipp, once the haunt of writers and politicians such as Valéry, Herriot, Léon Blum, Giraudoux, Saint-Exupéry and Max Jacob, is now more popular with journalists and the film world. Le Drugstore, nearby, opened in 1965 and decorated by Slavik, is no longer fashionable.

Beyond, in the Rue Gozlin, the bar Le Village is another of the centers of *'germanopratine'* life in the district.

At the intersection of the boulevard and the Rue de Rennes stands a fountain, nicknamed Embacle ('Logjam'), the work of the sculptor Charles Daudelin, presented to the municipal authorities by the Québec Government. The far end of the Rue de Rennes is closed by the dominant outline of the Tour Montparnasse. The street itself was built by Baron Haussmann and finished in 1878. It is now, particularly in its nearer section, given over to the luxury trades.

The abbey prison, scene of massacres in 1789, used to stand near the Carrefour Mabillon. Opposite, the Café Rhumerie Martiniquaise and the Café Mabillon are always crowded.

S of the boulevard and W of the Rue de Seine you are once more in a network of small streets which, though not as gloomy as those on the Montagne Sainte-Geneviève, are just as tangled, making it hard to plan a walk.

The Rue Montfaucon is a very old street, named after the learned Benedictine monk from the abbey, Bernard de Montfaucon, author of *Les Monuments de la Monarchie Française*. No. 3 is an 18th-c. building.

The Rue Clément is relatively new and replaces the Passage de la Treille which, until the Second Empire, led into the Rue des Cordeliers. It runs alongside the Saint-Germain market, which fills part of the site of the old Saint-Germain fair (–inset).

▷ The Old Saint-Germain fairground

A few of the arcades of the old market (by Jean Baptiste Blondel and Lusson; 1813–18) still survive, and the four streets built round it in 1817 follow the lines of the outer row of booths in the old fair. There are plans for redeveloping the area: the architect Clément Cacoub envisages a large multipurpose public open space on which cultural and commercial events could be held.

The Rue Mabillon is built over the Passage de la Foire Saint-Germain, taking its name from the father of the science of paleography, a monk in the abbey of Saint-Germain, Jean Mabillon (1632–1707). Gangways leading up from nos. 8 and 10 show that the ground level has been raised; the other side at a lower level is that of the old Saint-Germain fairground. Roland Dorgelès, the writer, spent the last years of his life at no. 2.

The Rue Guisarde was built in the 17th c. on the site of the meeting-place of the Holy League, the Hôtel de Guise. There are several old houses, the street was somewhat dowdy, but it has now caught up with Saint-Germain-des-Prés.

Rue Princesse: the princess after whom the street is named may have been Mlle de Montpensier, who assembled the followers of the Holy League around her in the now vanished Hôtel de Roussilion. During the Revolution the street was known as the Rue de la Justice, but for us it remains very much Chardin's street. The painter was born in a house which stood on the corner of the Rue du Four; he lived at no. 2 with his first wife and at no. 13 with his second. The private Club Le Castel is located here. The street was opened in 1630. The houses on the even-numbered side are 17th c., as are nos. 15 and 17.

Rue des Canettes

Its present name goes back to 1636, but the street was there in the 13th c., when it was the Rue Saint-Sulpice. Its façades, with their escutcheons, mascarons and swags are worth seeing. The sculptor Jean-Jacques Caffieri (1725–92) spent his whole life at no. 20: go inside to see the pretty courtyard and half-timbered façade. Nos. 16 and 18 are 18th-c. houses: No. 18 has a bas-relief depicting ducklings on a pond, from which the street gets its name. No. 17 was the home of the husband of the notorious Comtesse de Lamothe, of the Diamond Necklace Affair. In 1887 the long-forgotten poet Gabriel-Tristan Franconi was born at no. 13. In 1918 he died defending 'his house, his street and the Place Saint-Sulpice' against the enemy. Nowadays a multitude of small restaurants have opened in the street.

On the other side of the Rue du Four lies the 15th-c. Rue des Ciseaux. Today this little street is one mass of clubs and restaurants.

Rue du Four

In the Middle Ages a footpath followed the line of the Rue Saint-André-des-Arts and the Rue de Buci beyond Philippe Auguste's city wall and along what is now the Rue du Cherche-Midi. Rue du Four takes its name from the public bakery owned by the abbey, in which citizens of the township of Saint-Germain had to bake their bread. The opening of the boulevard and the Rue de Rennes has completely altered the character of the street, and with few exceptions most of the buildings date from the 19th c. No. 33 retains its 17th-c. gateway, well and staircase. A plaque on the wall of No. 48 commemorates the place where Jean Moulin held the first meeting of the Conseil National de la Résistance. During the 1950s the Rue du Four was one of the centers of existentialism. Now commerce has largely superseded philosophy.

Rue Bonaparte (between the Boul. Saint-Germain and the Place Saint-Sulpice): this section of the street is dominated by the luxury ready-to-wear trade with several top couturiers, and antique shops.

You now come to the square in front of the Church of Saint-Sulpice.

Rue du Vieux-Colombier

This street takes its name from the abbey dovecote. It dates from the 13th c. and has a long intellectual tradition.

Molière, Racine, Chapelle and La Fontaine used to meet in Boileau's lodgings in this street around 1661 to 1665. Mme Récamier, too, lived here. No. 1, the 18th-c. Hôtel de Louvencourt, has its very fine original façade. The fire station (no. 11) occupies the site of the convent of the Sisters of Mercy (Filles de Notre-Dame de la Hiséricorde) which was suppressed during the Revolution, while in the old church hall (no. 21) Jacques Copeau in an effort to 'bring back true beauty and poetry to the theatre' (1913), founded the Théâtre du Vieux-Colombier which, after its hour of literary glory, finally closed its doors in 1971.

Rue du Dragon

Although it was called the Rue du Sepulchre from the 14th c. until 1791, the inhabitants preferred the name 'Dragon', which decorated the monumental gateway of the Cour du Dragon. A copy of this dragon is displayed above the corner balcony of no. 44. Although the group of 18th-c. buildings that gave the street its name disappeared in 1957, some of the 17th- and 18th-c. houses and mansions are almost intact, such as nos. 2, 6, 10, 27 and 33. During the 17th and 18th-c. a colony of Flemish painters lived at no. 37, once the Hôtel de la Chasse (plaque). Victor Hugo composed his *Odes et Ballades* at no. 30 in 1821 and, on October 12, 1822, he married Adèle Foucher in the church of Saint-Sulpice with Alfred de Vigny as witness. No. 31 is the Académie Jullian, founded in 1860. Jacques Copeau lived at no. 19, while, on the far side of the forecourt of no. 10, stands the small 18th-c. town house in which the writer and Nobel prizewinner, Roger Martin du Gard (1881–1958) lived. No. 7 is the site of an entrance to the Cour du Dragon which communicated with 50 Rue de Rennes. Here, during the 17th and 18th c., young gentlemen were instructed in horsemanship, fencing and dancing at the Académie Royale. No. 5 is the American Cultural Center.

The Rue Bernard-Palissy, turning off on the r., was once the little Rue Taranne. With its old houses it does not seem much changed since the 18th c.

▷ Not to be missed

The Church of Saint-Germain-des-Prés (11th and 12th c.): murals by Hippolyte Flandrin (19th c.) Rue de Fürstenberg: a secluded street with the Musée Delacroix (the artist's former studio). Rue de Buci with its colorful market. The Hôtel de la Monnaie (Mint) and its museum. The palace of the Institut de France with its beautiful façade over the Seine. Rue Mazarine, Rue Jacques-Callot, Rue des Beaux-Arts and Rue de Seine, for their art galleries.

▷ Remains of the Abbey

Square Laurent-Prache: bays from the Chapel of Our Lady built by Pierre de Montreuil in the 13th c. and demolished in 1802. 16 Rue de l'Abbaye: in the stairwell there is the gable end (with window embrasure) of the monks' refectory by Pierre de Montreuil dating from 1239 to 1244. 4 Rue de Fürstenberg: set into the outer wall of the building a pillar surmounted by a firepot motif, marking the entrance to the abbey. 18 Rue de l'Echaudé: remains of a pillar from the abbey's N gateway. 20 Rue de l'Echaudé: remains of a pillar from the abbey's S gateway. 19 Rue Jacob: remains of the infirmary in the foundations of the building.

▷ A new use for the royal tennis courts (Les Jeux de Paume)

In 16th-c. Paris there were hundreds of indoor courts for 'real' (i.e. royal) or 'court' tennis as opposed to lawn tennis, not yet invented. More than any other, this was the 'noble game' played by royalty and the nobility; 'real' means 'royal'. There was a guild for the Maîtres Paumiers et Raquettiers with a three-year apprenticeship for the master's certificate.

Two players, using the palm of the hand either bare or gauntleted, and later a racket, hit a ball to each other across a net. The game was played in a huge rectangular room known as a *jeu de paume,* specially built for the purpose, with wooden pillars supporting a gallery for spectators. The rules of the game were complicated: the ball had to bounce off the wall when serving; a point was scored when the player hit it into the gallery; the onlookers were protected by a net. The walls were as much a part of the game as the ground.

In the early years of the 17th c. the game went out of fashion, and by 1760 only 13 courts were left in Paris. Troupes of actors took over the disused courts; Molière's Illustre Théâtre opened in Les Mestayers court (12–14 Rue Mazarine); the Opéra-Comique in La Diligence court (12 Rue de Buci) and the 'Grand' Opéra in La Bouteille court (42 Rue Mazarine).

▷ The first Parisian fire brigade

Until the end of the 18th c. there was no public service for the specific task of fighting the fires which took such a dreadful toll in towns mainly constructed of wood. When disaster struck, clergy, master masons, carpenters, thatchers and tilers were called out as well as the *quarteniers,* men picked in each district of Paris for such emergencies. Public pumps seem to have appeared only in 1669. François Dumouriez du Périer, Molière's manservant and an actor with the Comédie-Française, discovered fire pumps when he was traveling in Holland. In 1705 he left the stage to exploit the royal monopoly that he had been granted to manufacture these wonderful machines. The pumps were then allocated to different Parisian districts and firemen and firemen's assistants entrusted with the task of operating them under the supervision of the lieutenant-general of police or the merchant provost. Dumouriez du Périer's own home (30 Rue Mazarine) became the general headquarters of the fire-pump service, and so the first Parisian fire brigade was formed.

▷ Saint-Germain-des-Prés: art galleries

During the 1920s the first art galleries opened in Saint-Germain-des-Prés. For 50 years this was the only place in Paris where contemporary or avant-garde painting was on view. Today some of the galleries have grown old with the artists whose work they show and are part of art history, while others, opened more recently, exhibit the work of young and relatively unknown painters. There are just too many galleries to say that there is a general trend; all, however, are devoted to contemporary art, even though some take a more historical approach by exhibiting 20th-c. masters as well. Every two months a leaflet listing current exhibitions is published, available in all galleries.

Fabien Boulakia: 20 Rue Bonaparte, 75006, tel. 43-26-56-79; Isy Brachot: 35 Rue Guénégaud, 75006, tel. 43-54-22-40; Galerie Breteau: 70 Rue Bonaparte, 75006, tel. 43-26-40-96; Jeanne Bucher: 53 Rue de Seine, 75006, tel. 43-26-22-32; Claude Bernard: 5, 7, 9 Rue des Beaux-Arts, 75006, tel. 43-26-97-07; Galerie Clivages: 46 Rue de l'Université, 75007, tel. 42-96-69-57; Denise René: 196 Boul. Saint-Germain, 75007, tel. 52-22-77-57; Lucien Durand: 19 Rue Mazarine, 75006, tel. 43-26-25-35; Erval: 16 Rue de Seine, 75006, tel. 43-54-73-29; Georges Fall: 57 Quai des Grands-Augustins, 75006, tel. 46-33-52-45; Liliane François: 15 Rue de Seine, 75006, tel. 43-26-94-32; Galerie Jacob: 28 Rue Jacob, 75006, tel. 46-33-90-66; Bernard Jordan: 54 Rue de Verneuil, 75007, tel. 42-96-37-47; Samy Kinge: 54 Rue de Verneuil, 75007, tel. 42-61-19-07; Krief-Raymond: 50 Rue Mazarine, 75006, tel. 43-29-32-37; Lara Vincy: 47 Rue de Seine, 75006, tel. 43-26-72-51; Adrien Maeght: 46 Rue du Bac, 75007, tel. 42-22-12-59; Albert Loeb: 12 Rue des Beaux-Arts, 75006, tel. 46-33-06-37; Galerie Montenay-Delsol: 31 Rue Mazarine, 75006, tel. 43-54-85-30; Galerie de Paris: 6 Rue du Pont-de-Lodi, 75006, tel. 43-25-42-63; La Pochade: 11 Rue Guénégaud, 75006, tel. 43-54-89-03; Nathalie Seroussi: 34 Rue de Seine, 75006, tel. 46-34-05-84; Darthea Speyer: 6 Rue Jacques-Callot, 75006, tel. 43-54-78-41; Stadler: 51 Rue de Seine, 75006, tel. 43-26-91-10; Trigano: 4bis Rue des Beaux-Arts, 75006, tel. 46-34-15-01; Dina Vierny: 36 Rue Jacob, 75006, tel. 42-60-23-18.

▷ Alexandre Lenoir and the Musée des Monuments Français

After the nationalization of church property in 1790, the convent of the Petits-Augustins was chosen as a State depository. The archeologist Alexandre Lenoir (1762–1839), appointed curator, decided to turn it into a museum and collected all the items he thought worthy of preservation from the churches and convents of Paris. Among those objects saved from destruction were the magnificent royal tombs erected in the Church of Saint-Denis. After all the works of art had been restored, the Musée des Monuments Français opened in October 1795. Lenoir was a born educator and arranged the museum in such a way that visitors could follow the progress of French sculpture from the 12th c. to the height of its achievement in the 17th c. Each century was appropriately lit – semi-darkness for the Middle Ages and full light for the 17th c., for example. Lenoir also published a catalogue for visitors.

The Museum was closed when the Bourbons were restored and most of the exhibits were returned to their places of origin, Versailles or the Louvre. Others remained in the gardens or the courtyards which Duban had remodeled. Artists of the Romantic Movement were constant visitors and so the Musée des Monuments Français helped to encourage that re-evaluation of medieval art that took place in the first half of the 19th c.

▷ The Saint-Germain fair

In 1482 the market held in the township of Saint-Germain was turned, with the consent of Louis XI, into an annual fair for the benefit of the abbey, where business, gambling, public entertainment and pleasure were given free rein. It was very important to the Paris economy and attracted a mixed crowd – by day commoners strolled around, while the nobility and gentry flaunted themselves until late at night. Henri III and later Henri IV, with their respective Queens, were regular visitors. All tastes were catered for: there were taverns for those who loved good drink and tobacco; travelling showmen performed for the idle crowd; and strolling players staged dramas or operas. The fair was always the scene of brawls and minor riots. Nor was the king himself spared, for 'in 1579 the king [Henri III] was insulted by a gang of youths'. In 1762 most of the building erected for the stallholders was destroyed by fire. This was the beginning of the end, which came in 1790 with the Revolution. The site itself was finally reorganized as the local market in 1818. In 1900 part of the land was used to build examination halls for the university, with covered premises for stallholders at ground level. A cultural center has been suggested for the remaining land.

▷ From coffeehouse to café

Whether they are in a hurry or have time on their hands, Parisians never miss the opportunity of stopping at one of the 12,000 cafés set at strategic intervals around the capital. The café first began to make itself an integral part of the landscape over three hundred years ago. Coffeehouses were first seen in the Levant and in 1643 a Levantine opened the ancestor of the modern café in the covered way which led under the Petit Châtelet from the Rue Saint-Jacques to the Petit Pont, a coffeehouse which served the passerby with a decoction of coffee called *cahouet.* The proprietor achieved only limited success. In 1692 an Armenian called Paskal was the next to open a coffeehouse, and when this failed he took his business to London and made a fortune. The idea took root, however, and soon in Paris there were not only plenty of stalls selling spirits, liqueurs, fortified wines, and coffee, but also Turkish coffee vendors, trays hanging round their necks, pouring coffee for the passersby. The first coffeehouse to be furnished with any degree of luxury was opened by Francesco Procopio from Palermo in 1702. Under the French form of his name – Procope – his café still stands in the Rue de l'Ancienne-Comédie, then the Rue des Fossés-Saint-Germain. In their early years coffeehouses had a very bad name. Open until the early hours, they sheltered all the riffraff of the night. Subjected to strict legal control, their tone gradually improved. In 1723 there were some 300 coffeehouses in Paris; by the end of the 18th c., nearly 800. They were cheerful places, favoring talk and the exchange of ideas; places, too, where newspapers could be read, and rallying points in time of revolution.

Not, however, until the 19th c. did the coffeehouse become the large café known today, where people go to see and to be seen. The most chic cafés moved successively from the Palais-Royal to the Grands-Boulevards, the Champs-Elysées, Montparnasse and finally Saint-Germain-des-Prés. The Café de Flore and the Deux Magots were open to the boulevard; the close confines of the old-style tavern vanished, and chairs and tables spilled onto the terrace. Here anyone could relax and watch the world go by in the street. The Brasserie Lipp, with its tiled interior by Léon Fargue (*ca.* 1880), shows the deliberate attempt to give public rooms the décor of the drawing-rooms to which high society had long been confined. A century later found Le Drugstore, a café fitting into the heart of a shopping arcade.

The Faubourg Saint-Honoré**

8th arr. Map ref. 8–C2, D2; 9–A2, B2
Métro: Georges V
Bus: 22, 31, 43, 52, 73, 83
Parking 101 Ave. des Champs-Elysées

Taxis: I Ave. de Freidland. Tel: 45–61–00–00.

The Rue du Faubourg-Saint-Honoré runs through the 8th arrondissement, one of the most elegant districts in the capital. Near the Place de l'Etoile the street is mainly residential; the Salle Pleyel, an imposing concert hall, and the Fondation Nationale des Arts Plastiques are its only cultural institutions. From the intersection at Saint-Philippe-du-Roule to the Palais de l'Elysée many art galleries and antique shops entice elegant tourists from the Champs-Elysées and numerous business people who work nearby in imposing corporate headquarters.

As for the impressive Rue Royale, the opposite sides of the Rue du Faubourg-Saint-Honoré vary greatly in character. The odd-numbered side is lined with the porchways of former 18th-c. mansions that now house foreign legations. The Hôtel d'Evreux (or Palais de l'Elysée), the most sumptuous, is the official residence of the French president. Across the street the most prestigious *maisons de couture* are grouped around luxury boutiques specializing in clothing and interior decoration. On one pavement bored guards stand sentry, while on the other the wealthy windowshop.

History of the Faubourg

Forming the backbone of this district, the Rue du Faubourg-Saint-Honoré is the former Chaussée du Roule, which once meandered through the countryside to the hamlet of Le Roule. Only in 1722 did the hamlet become a suburb of Paris. Between the Avenue Hoche, which it crosses before reaching the Place des Ternes and the Church of Saint-Philippe-du-Roule, the twisting Rue du Faubourg-Saint-Honoré is the old village high street of Le Roule.

In the 18th c. the royal nursery that stocked the Luxembourg and Tuileries gardens with trees and plants stretched for 10.5ha/26 acres, a long fertile ribbon between the Champs-Elysées and the Rue du Roule, from the great sewer near the Tuileries gardens as far as the Rue de Chaillot (Rue de Berri). After 1719 a new nursery was planted on the other side of the Rue du Roule. This enlarged area became the profitable preserve of the Comte d'Artois, brother of Louis XVI. The former, assisted by the architect Bélanger, embarked on ambitious plans to develop this almost virgin territory. A model town named Nouvelle Amérique was to be built around a Place Franklin, intersected by the Rue Washington and Rue Lafayette, names famous since the American War of Independence. Plans for a Nouvelle Ville des Adelphes and then a Nouvelle Londres soon followed.

In the end only the stables of the Comte d'Artois saw the light of day, with their monumental entrance overlooking the Rue du Faubourg-Saint-Honoré. These Neo-Classical buildings designed to house about a hundred horses were destroyed during the Second

Empire. All around mansions and *folies* or pleasure houses sprang up during the 18th c. (Hôtel d'Evreux, Hôtel de Charost, Hôtel d'Argenson, Folie Marigny, Hôtel de Duras). Higher up in the Faubourg the Beaujon charter house (inset) opened its boundaries to include the Ruggieri brothers' amusement park and a roller coaster known as the Montagnes Françaises (from Montagnes Russes, meaning Russian Mountains, the usual French term for a roller coaster or switchback railway), and the new Quartier Beaujon came into being, attracting a galaxy of 19th-c. artists and writers.

Tour of the Faubourg

2 hrs.

Rue Balzac

At the intersection of this street and the Ave. de Friedland in the Place G.-Guillaumin is a statue of Balzac by Alexandre Falguière. The monument was erected in 1902 to the memory of the writer who lived nearby (22 Rue Balzac) and is essentially a watered-down version of Rodin's Balzac. The latter statue was refused for this site, despite Zola's support, and found a home, in the Boul. Raspail, only in 1939.

Work began on the nearby Hôtel Potocki (27 Ave. de Friedland) in 1858, under Jules Reboul. Part of the luxurious décor has been preserved. In 1923 the *hôtel* became the headquarters of the Chamber of Commerce and Industry of the city of Paris. Viart and Dastugue converted it, constructing new buildings with gardens; Ruhlman was responsible for the decoration. The ballroom has not been altered.

At 22 Rue Balzac a plaque commemorates Honoré de Balzac, who died on August 15, 1850 in a mansion that stood on this site until its demolition in 1882. With it disappeared the last traces of the Folie Beaujon (→inset) and of Balzac's residence here (→inset). A few stones of the Chapel of Saint-Nicholas, built by Beaujon, escaped destruction and were placed in the gardens of the Baronne Salomon de Rothschild.

Rue Berryer

At the end of this street is the *hôtel* of the Baronne Salomon de Rothschild. The gardens were extended into the grounds of Balzac's house. Here one can see the replaced stones from the Chapel of Saint-Nicholas and the Pavillon Balzac, a small rotunda with a room in the Moorish style. The Hôtel Rothschild, begun in 1872 by Léon Ohnet, was completed in 1878 by Justin Ponsard. The baroness bequeathed her mansion to the State while her collections enriched those already housed in the Musée des Arts Décoratifs and in other national museums. After accommodating the Bibliothèque Doucet and the Maison des Artistes in 1976 the building became the headquarters of the Fondation Nationale des Arts Graphiques et Plastiques.

Rue du Faubourg-Saint-Honoré

From the Ave. Hoche to the Rue de Berri.

At no. 208 the former Hospice Beaujon, founded in 1784 by the financier Beaujon for the education of the poor children of the *quartier*, is a splendid edifice constructed by Girardin. Since 1936 the buildings have been used as the police training academy. The austere partitioned façade and the monumental entrance are all that survive of the Beaujon estate. Beyond the intersection with the Boul. Haussmann and the Ave. de Friedland the buildings are not as old. On the site of no 170 stood the house where Mme de Genlis, governess of Philippe Egalité's children, died, and at no. 166, Mme de Maintenon's country house.

Cross the Rue de Berri. In this street dating from 1778, Princess Mathilde, daughter of Jérôme Bonaparte, occupied an apartment at no. 20 after the war of 1871, until her death in 1904. Her salon was frequented by all the great political, literary and artistic figures of the turn of the century. At no. 6 Rue d'Artois, which crosses the Rue de Berri, Alfred de Vigny died aged 66.

♁ The Church of Saint-Philippe-du-Roule*

154 Rue du Faubourg-Saint-Honoré (Open daily. Tel: 43-59-24-56).

Built from 1774 to 1784 by Jean-François Chalgrin, Saint-Philippe-du-Roule is an example of the contemporary taste for styles influenced by Classical Antiquity. Departing from plans based on the Greek and Latin cross, traditionally favored by 17th and 18th-c. architects, without returning to the centrally oriented plans of the Renaissance, Chalgrin based his design on the Roman basilica, with three parallel aisles separated by two rows of pillars. The broad central aisle has barrel vaulting ending in a half-domed apse. These innovations in church architecture were highly successful in the 19th c., as shown by the churches of Notre-Dame-de-Lorette, Saint-Denis-du-Saint-Sacrement, and Saint-Vincent-de-Paul. Both the façade, with its four-columned portico, and the interior are distinguished by an elegant design whose extraordinary delicacy of proportion saves it from any trace of academic dryness. The church has been enlarged twice. In 1845 Etienne Godde extended the side-aisles into an ambulatory ending in the Chapel of Our Lady. In 1853,

Victor Baltard added the Chapel des Catéchismes to the l. of the choir.

The pediment is decorated with a statue representing Religion by François-Joseph Duret. The interior contains a masterpiece of 19th c. religious paintings: *The Descent from the Cross** by Théodore Chassériau (1855), an inspired synthesis of the abstract design of the school of Ingres and a romantic warmth of coloring. In the Chapel of Our Lady are paintings by Claudius Jacquard (1857–60).

The Rue de la Boétie, built at the end of the 18th c., recalls Montaigne's great friend Etienne de La Boétie. Between the two World Wars it was very elegant. Picasso lived at no. 29 from 1918 to 1937, and his first wife, Olga Khoklova, occupied the first floor. Jean Cocteau, Erik Satie, Misia Sert, the Comte de Beaumont and others met there. There are numerous art galleries.

Rue du Faubourg Saint-Honoré, continued

At no. 114 an ultramodern building has been put up on the site of the old Porte du Roule, which once marked the limit of the Faubourg du Roule. Cross the Rue de Colisée. Formerly the Chaussée des Gourdes, this street took its name from the great coliseum built by Le Camus from 1669 to 1671. It was used for public celebrations and entertainments and was demolished in 1780. The present Rue du Colisée, Rue du Faubourg-Saint-Honoré, the Ave. Matignon and the Ave. des Champs-Elysées are sited on land once belonging to the Comte d'Artois. The Rue du Cirque, opened in 1847, originally led to the Cirque des Champs-Elysées.

Place Beauvau

In this fine square dating from 1836, the Ministry of the Interior, with its beautiful gilded entrance gates, has occupied since 1860 the former mansion built by Le Camus de Mézières around 1770 for a certain Comte de Beauvau. The main courtyard has a plaque to the memory of the minister George Mandel, assassinated in 1944. Take a few steps along the Rue des Saussaies. In this little street with its rustic name (it is also called Rue de la Coudraie) are the headquarters of the Sûreté Nationale, the French equivalent to the FBI. In the Cour Pierre-Brossolette, is a plaque to the memory of patriots tortured here by the Gestapo, among them Pierre Brossolette, who committed suicide by jumping from one of the windows. The street continues into the Rue d'Astorg, an exclusive and famous street during the Second Empire. During that period, at her *hôtel* at no. 8, Mélanie de Pourtalès entertained all Europe in splendid style, an apt symbol of the extravagence of the time.

☐ The Palais de l'Elysée*

55–57, Rue du Faubourg-Saint-Honoré

This mansion has been the official residence of the Presidents of the Republic since 1873. Behind it, vast English-style gardens stretch as far as the Ave. Gabriel with access through the Grille du Coq (1900).

History of the building

Constructed by Mollet in 1718 for the Comte d'Evreux, this palace has served every régime since. The ground floor retains paneling by J. M. Alexandre Hardouin, who extended the building. After it was bought in 1753 by Mme de Pompadour, the supervision of sumptuous new alterations was entrusted to Lassurance. Furthermore, to open up the view toward Les Invalides and to the fury of the riverside residents Mme de Pompadour obtained the King's sanction to create a clearing in the surrounding woodland, which is now the Carrée Marigny. The marquise bequeathed her mansion to Louis XV, who returned it to her brother, (Marigny, 1764). The financier Beaujon, a ubiquitous figure in the history of the Faubourg Saint-Honoré, acquired it in 1773, and eventually sold it to Louis XVI, who in turn handed it over to the Duchesse de Bourbon (1787).

The building housed the National Printing Press during the Revolution and became a dancing school during the Directoire. In 1805 the mansion became the residence of Murat and his wife Caroline, sister of Napoléon, who lived there until Murat was made King in Naples (1808). Two beautiful interiors, the Salon Murat and the Salon Argent, have been preserved from this period. Josephine stayed here for a time and, after their divorce, the Emperor himself lived here until the end of the Empire. In 1814 Czar Alexander took up residence. In the Salon Argent on June 22, 1815, Napoléon signed his abdication. Wellington (1815) and the Duc de Berry (1816–20) were the next to live there.

The *hôtel* continued as a temporary residence until the election of Prince Louis-Napoléon to the Presidency, December 20, 1851. It was here that with Morny, the President Prince, prepared the coup d'état of December 2, 1851. Subsequently under Napoléon III, radical changes were made both internally and externally by the addition of a ballroom and the heightening of the wings and rebuilding of the Faubourg Saint-Honoré entrance. In 1873 the palace became the official residence of the President, to be occupied in succession by 13 presidents of the Third Republic: Mac-Mahon (1874), Jules Grévy (1879), Sadi Carnot (1887), Casimir Perier (1894), Félix Faure (1895), Emile Loubet (1899), Armand Fallières (1906); Raymond Poincaré (1913), Paul Deschanel (1920), Alexandre Millerand (1920), Gaston Doumergue (1924), Paul Doumet (1931) and Albert Lebrun (1932–40). The next president, the first of the Fourth Republic, was Vincent Auriol (1947), who set about the restoration of the façades by removing the bay windows, canopies and metal veranda, additions much prized at the end of the 19th c. He was succeeded by René Coty (1954) and finally the presidents of the Fifth Republic, Charles de Gaulle (1959), Georges Pompidou (1969), Valéry Giscard d'Estaing (1974) and François Mitterrand (1981).

Tour of the Palace

The Palais de l'Elysée may be visited only under exceptional circumstances. (M Giscard d'Estaing personally guided visitors on July 14, 1978.) The Council of Ministers presently meets in the Salon Murat, while the offices of the President and his colleagues have since the time of General de Gaulle occupied an entire floor of former apartments in the main building. The interiors by Agam created during Georges Pompidou's presidency have been moved from their original wing to be rehoused in the Beaubourg Center at the request of President Giscard d'Estaing. The President's private apartments are on the first floor of the wing overlooking the Rue de l'Elysée. To some extent President Mitterrand has introduced more contemporary furnishings and decoration.

Rue de l'Elysée

The street runs along the gardens of the Presidential Palace. Constructed during the Second Empire, it is lined with *hôtels* homogeneous in design, and is the only example in Paris of architecture in the English style (small cast-iron columns flanking steps above basement areas, with access via a stairway and courtyard), influenced perhaps by Napoléon III and his London exile. Two of these mansions contain presidential departments, no. 2 having incorporated the former mansion built by the Empress Eugénie for her mother, which is decorated with paneling from the Château de Bercy.

Rue du Faubourg-Saint-Honoré, continued

From the Palais de l'Elysée to the Rue d'Anjou.

No. 26 was for many years the famous Galerie Charpentier. No. 41 was commissioned by the Baronne de Pontalba from Visconti in 1842. After her death this magnificent mansion was sold to Edmond de Rothschild, who had it razed to the ground, with the exception of the wing overlooking the Rue de Faubourg-Saint-Honoré. In its place he built a new mansion in the style of Louis XV (architect, F. Langlois). To his collections of paintings was added superb antique paneling. In 1948 the buildings were acquired by the United States government. While part of the collections had been given by the baron to the national museums (→the Trésor de Bosco Reale and the Louvre), the paneling was removed and replaced by plaster copies.

For more than 150 years the British Embassy has occupied the Hôtel de Charost* at no. 39, built by Mazin in 1720. Here Pauline Borghese reigned supreme from 1803 to 1814. Her bedroom still retains its Empire decoration and furnishings, as does the Salon Blanc, its bronzes attributed to Thomire. In 1815 Wellington took it over to set up the embassy where, among others, was celebrated the marriage of Berlioz to the unfortunate Harriet Smithson. It has also received the Austrian Emperor, Queen Victoria, the Prince of Wales and Queen Elizabeth II.

No. 35, adjoining the Hôtel de Charost, is another part of the British Embassy. Nos. 35, 33 and 31 were built together in 1713. The Hôtel Chevalier (no. 35) and the Hôtel Levieux (no. 33), constructed by Grandhomme, were designed by common consent to be identical. The financiers Isaac and Emile Pereire modified no. 35 during the Second Empire. Dieterle, Bouguereau, Jalabert and Cabanet contributed to the lavish interior decoration, which still exists. No. 33, the Hôtel Levieux, at one time the Russian Embassy, was bought by Baron Nathaniel de Rothschild. He installed late 18th-c. paneling from the Hôtel Tourolle. After 1917 the building was heightened and rooms were added to the basement to accommodate the rapidly expanding Cercle de l'Union Interalliée. In 1801 the Concordat was signed at no. 31. Formerly the Hôtel Marbeuf, renamed Hôtel Pillet-Will, the Japanese Government bought it in 1965 and it was demolished to make way for offices, built behind the original façade. At no. 29, the hôtel built by Lassurance for the Duchesse de Rohan-Montbazon is now disfigured.

Rue d'Anjou: this long street, known as the Rue des Morfondus In the 18th c., links the Faubourg Saint-Honoré to the Rue de la Pépinière, after crossing the Boul. Malesherbes and Boul. Haussmann. No. 8 was built by Mazin; La Fayette lived there from 1827 until his death in 1834. Benjamin Constant died on December 8, 1930, in a house on the site of the present no. 29.

Rue de la Ville l'Evêque

This street, built in 1652 on land in the little town of L'Evêque that belonged to the bishop of Paris, has retained its clerical connections. No. 8, a vast building, is now the archbishop's palace, previously in the Rue Barbet-de-Jouy. In 1805 Alexis de Tocqueville, the politican and writer, was born at no. 12. No. 16 is the Hôtel Suchet built by Boullée in the 18th c. Maréchal Suchet lived there (1802–18) and curious onlookers would crowd beneath his windows to hear his parrots chanting vespers. In the courtyard of no. 18 is a Louis-Philippe pavilion. No. 2 is the Hôtel d'Arenberg.

Rue Boissy-d'Anglas

This street was once a country lane leading to the watering place known as L'Evêque, on the Seine; it was then called the Rue de la Bonne-Morue. Few of the beautiful early 19th-c. houses remain. Since 1928 at the corner of the Place de la Concorde the American Embassy has occupied the mansion of the gastronome Grimod de la Reynière. Its construction was allowed on condition that it be designed symmetrically with the Hôtel Saint-Florentin so that the layout of the Place de la Concorde would remain unspoiled.

The Rue du Faubourg-Saint-Honoré (end), mecca for all the great couturiers, jewellers and goldsmiths in the capital, ends at the Rue Royale, which has equally sumptuous and varied shops selling luxury articles.

The Hôtel de Balzac

Balzac purchased this mansion on September 28, 1846 to create a fitting background for the woman he dreamed of marrying and his assorted collection of bric-a-brac and furniture. The writer channelled all the energy of his remaining years into fulfilling this task. He had bought part of the former Folie de Beaujon for Eve-Constance Hanska, his future wife. After four years of patient waiting, their union was blessed March 14, 1850 at Berditchew, in the Ukraine. His happiness was short-lived, however; he died a few months later on August 18.

The architect Santi made a series of watercolors of the decor to be sent to Mme Hanska in far-away Russia, so that she could appreciate Balzac's efforts. He had in fact restored the decoration remaining from the Beaujon period and created sumptuous apartments hung with damasks and leather from Cordoba. But literature entails responsibility and he wrote detailed genealogies of every curio, including a chest which had belonged to the Duchesse de Berry, a cabinet of Marie de' Medici and Mme de Pompadour's bed. Among this distinguished collection, even admirers were never allowed to handle Balzac's famous turquoise cane, inseparable from his legendary silhouette.

▷ The Chartreuse de Beaujon

Nicholas Beaujon (1708–86) had a certain talent for making money, and became one of the wealthiest men in the 18th c. through trading and the diversity of his business ventures. From 1781 to 1782 he bought about 30 acres/12ha of land between the Faubourg du Roule and the Etoile. At the intersection of the present Rue Balzac and Rue Beaujon the architect Girardin built him a *folie* in Dutch farmhouse style, following the then current pastoral fashion. But the little apartments were furnished romantically: a secret staircase and a hidden door led to a bedroom resembling a grove, where four trees gave shade to the bed, their branches hung with drapes stretching to the ceiling, painted like the sky. There the old widower Beaujon, in blissful lethargy, would while away his insomnia in a cradle rocked by two charming, scantily dressed girls.

On the other side of the street, Nicholas Beaujon, philanthropic when he felt like it, built a home for poor children, whose buildings still exist. Adjoining the living quarters he built the Chapel of Saint Nicholas.

▷ The 18th-c. *folies*

Folies were unusual, sophisticated, little houses intended for the pursuit of pleasure and amusement, scattered in quiet locations far away from the court, such as Chaussée d'Antin, Clichy, Neuilly, Sèvres and Monceau. Abandoning their family seats, such nobles as the Dukes of Orléans, Gesvres, Richelieu and Chaulnes sought more modest, intimate retreats surrounded by nature, where they could amuse themselves with their friends or mistresses, play games, gossip and pursue their hobbies. They wanted their retreat to be exotic, rugged or gently escapist, surrounded by gardens in the English style, with 'workshops', cloisters, ancient ruins, temples, pagodas, Dutch windmills, minarets ... Fashionable architects were commissioned to decorate these treasure-chests of greenery in the taste of the day, and Ledoux, Soufflot, Brongniard and Bélanger put their talents at the disposal of these frivolous, princely aesthetes. With the creation of Bagatelle, the Folie Beaujon and Monceau in 1778, the age of the folies reached its apogee.

The Faubourg Saint-Jacques*

14th arr./Map ref. 22–D 2
Métro and RER: Port-Royal
Bus: 38, 68, 83, 91
Parking: Boul. du Montparnasse; Place Denfert-Rochereau
Taxis: 172 Boul. du Montparnasse. Tel: 43-25-00-00

The sober, classical silhouette of the Observatoire, which was surrounded by the countryside when it was built, today dominates a district uneven in its development. A few typically suburban, one- or two-storey houses nestle against expensive apartment houses, public housing projects and residential studios.

The Faubourg Saint-Jacques is crossed by the great north-south axis which cuts through Paris, taking in the Avenue Denfert-Rochereau and the Avenue de l'Observatoire on its way. This latter avenue, which leads to the Observatoire, follows the line of the Paris meridian.

Neither this astronomical peculiarity nor the noise of traffic seem to bother the religious communities which still exist here, tucked away behind their gardens. The Abbaye de Port-Royal, once the most famous, is still here, but in a form very different from its original one because, like most of the monastic establishments of the Faubourg, it has been converted into a hospital. Only a few patches of green remain in the Square de l'Observatoire and in a few pleasantly rustic artists' colonies.

History of the district

In the days when Paris was still Lutetia, the Faubourg Saint-Jacques formed a suburb set back from the slopes of the Montagne Sainte-Geneviève. Later the Gallo-Roman town grew to extend southward on either side of the great north-south axis formed by the Paris-to-Orléans road, which was an extension of the old *cardo maximus* (literally, 'great hinge'—today Rue Saint-Jacques and Rue du Faubourg Saint-Jacques).

Well into the Middle Ages all commercial, military and religious activity centered around this ancient road. From the 11th c. on it became a pilgrimage route, first to Saint-Martin de Tours, then to Santiago de Compostela. All this important activity brought about the creation of a new road to the west on the line of the present Boul. Saint-Michel and the Rue Denfert-Rochereau.

Situated outside the perimeter wall of Philippe Auguste, the Faubourg Saint-Jacques, like other suburbs on the Left Bank, developed slowly; fields and vineyards scattered with windmills made it a quiet and spacious area, and religious communities began to settle here. The district developed during the second half of the 17th c. with the consecration of the convent of the Oratorians (1650) and the Abbaye de Port-Royal (1626–48) behind which Colbert founded the Observatoire in 1667. At the same time Louis XIV decided to create a boulevard to establish a link between the new district and the royal Hôtel des Invalides. The south road (the *Cours de Midi*) was only completed under the Second Empire with the creation of the Boul. de Port-Royal and the other boulevards that extend from it. At the beginning of the 19th c., this hitherto mostly unplanned district became the site of new architectural experiments. It was particularly during the 1930s that a wealthy clientele, open to new ideas, made possible the construction of a number of buildings considered avant-garde.

Tour of the district

1½ hrs.

Métro: Port-Royal

This beautiful station, the canopies of which form a harmonious alliance of iron and glass, was built in 1892 (O. Rougier, engineer).

Boulevard de Port-Royal

Though this street is, by virtue of its name, associated with Jansenism, the renovation of its even-numbered side has altered the serious character derived from its history and its many hospitals. No. 88 is the first apartment house with a bow window (architect, P. L. Alinot, 1884; registered as an historic monument). Enter the courtyard to admire the brick façade. At no. 111 stands the imposing portal, all that is left of the novices' quarters of the Capuchin nunnery that moved in 1779 to the Rue Caumartin. One year later, the parish priest of Saint-Jacques-du-Haut-Pas, the Abbé Cochin, founded a hospital on this site which has since been enlarged several times. The entrance of the present Cochin Hospital is at 47 Rue du Faubourg Saint-Jacques. At no. 113 is an old deserted house with some old-fashioned charm.

⚰ The former Abbey of Port-Royal of Paris

123–125 Boul. de Port-Royal Baudeloque and Port-Royal Maternity Hospital /Cloisters (open daily 10am–8pm; chapel open Sun. 11am–3pm; for guided tours by the Caisse des Monuments Historiques of the convent buildings, tel: 48-87-24-14).

The origins of the abbey lie in the 13th c. with the foundation in 1204 by Matthieu de Montmorency and his wife of Port-Royal-des-Champs, a Cistercian abbey not far from Chevreuse. At the beginning of the 17th c. the abbey was under the direction of Mère Angélique Arnauld, whose reformations gave it such widespread spiritual influence that the community soon out-grew the building. In 1625 the mother of the abbess, Catherine de Marion, acquired for the community the Hôtel de Clagny, on the Rue de la Bourbe, at the end of the Faubourg-Saint-Jacques. This house had been built in the 16th c. for Pierre Lescot, Seigneur de Clagny, whose only known surviving work is part of the square Court (Cour Carrée) of the Louvre. From 1626 the contemplative order lived in these old buildings; eventually the buildings were restored through the generosity of Marie de' Medici and Louis XIV, and new convent premises were constructed. This new abbey, Port-Royal de Paris, became almost a fief of the Arnauld family: the mother and sister of Mère Angélique were nuns there, while her brothers, Robert Arnauld d'Andilly, a translator of religious tracts, and Antoine Arnauld, 'Le

Grand Arnauld', who were known as the *solitaires* or the *messieurs* of Port-Royal, made Port-Royal des Champs famous. From 1627, Port-Royal ceased to be a dependency of the Cistercians and was attached to the archbishopric of Paris. Jean du Vergier du Haur-anne, Abbé of Saint-Cyran, made the Jansenist doctrine of predesti-nation so well known that the two abbeys of Port-Royal became the center of the philosophy. The great philosopher mathematician and doctor Pascal, whose sister Jacqueline was a nun in the community, completed his conversion there, and upheld the Jansenist side in their long, drawn-out quarrel with the Jesuits. The scholar Nicole was also a pupil of the *messieurs* of Port-Royal. The sermons of the Abbé Singlin were famous, as were the nuns' Petites Ecoles. James Duke of Monmouth, natural son of Charles II, attended one of them. Fearing that Jansenism was becoming too extreme, Louis XIV proceeded to expel the nuns in 1664, three years after the death of Mère Angélique; four years later the two abbeys were separated, and Port-Royal de Paris was permanently purged of Jansenist influence. In 1709 Port-Royal des Champs was suppressed in turn, when during the night of October 28 the abbey was surrounded by French and Swiss guards who gave the old nuns 15 minutes to pack before they were put into coaches and driven to far-off destinations. During the Revolution the former abbey was turned into a prison called Port-Libre, where the chemist Lavoisier was held, and then into a foundling hospital (1795); it finally became a maternity hospital (1818).

The old convent buildings (registered historical monuments), have only partially survived but, seen from outside, have preserved their austere dignity. The Hôtel d'Atry is at present occupied by the hospital administration. It is an elegant, L-shaped, one-storey building with a tiled roof pierced by five mansard windows and a triangular pediment. The chapel, refurbished in 1952, was built by Le Pautre for the nuns of Port-Royal; its unusual portal does not open, as in other parish churches, at the end of the nave, but in the N transept. It has kept its 17th-c. architecture and paneling carved with a wine jar of Cana motif. Unfortunately the pictures specially painted for the abbey by Philippe de Champaigne have been dispersed: an ex-voto of 1622 to the Louvre, a *Magdalene* to the Museé des Beaux Arts at Rennes. The beautiful communion table in wrought iron was a gift to Mère Angélique. To the r. of the little passage leading to the cloister and the nuns' choir, is the chapterhouse, which has kept its original dimensions and its carved paneling.* The cloister, with flattened arches on three sides, is surmounted by 17th-c. convent buildings reached by a staircase with wooden banisters in the SE corner, known as the Staircase of the Miracle; on the N side in front of the chapel is a little summer house that could be a vestige of the old Hôtel de Clagny. To the NW the former lodging of Mme de Sablé, the friend of Rochefoucauld, may still be seen and, in the E, the two-storey apartment of the Princesse de Guémenée. On the second floor, N side, the wrought-iron balconies are original. During a century and a half the cloister garden served as a cemetery for the Cistercian and Visitation nuns and, according to the records, it is thought that several people were buried in the chapel, notably Mère Angélique. To the l. the Rue Henri-Barbusse runs alongside the maternity hospital, coming out into Ave. de l'Observatoire.

☐ The Observatoire**

61 Ave. de l'Observatoire: visit by written request addressed to the Président de l'Observatoire, Sept.–June first Sat. of every month, 2:30pm; July–Aug. tours offered without prior request Mon., Wed. and Fri., 2:30pm.

This building stands at the end of lovely Ave. de l'Observatoire, shaded by chestnut trees. Designed in 1667 by Charles Perrault and built from 1668 to 1672, this is the oldest observatory still in use in the world. In 1926 the observatory at Meudon was built, then around 1950, the radio astronomy station at Nançay in the Cher. Today the three form one of the great world centers of astronomical research.

History of the Observatoire

Its creation was part of the general movement in which societies and academies were formed all over Europe for the exchange of ideas and results of research between scientists and scholars. After 1665 some members of the French scientific community developed plans for creating an association of Arts and Sciences, at the same time as the astronomer Auzour, in a dedication to the King, outlined the pressing need for the establishment of an astronomical observatory. Louis XIV and his minister Colbert responded: the Académie Royal des Sciences held its first session on December 22, 1666, and land was bought on March 7, 1667, for the Royal Observatory. Wider at one end than at the other and covering 2.5ha/6 acres, the Observatoire was situated just outside Paris at the place called Le Grand Regard: because the horizon was completely clear on all sides it was a good place for observation. The exact location of the building was determined scientifically, and the plans were drawn up by Claude Perrault, author brother of Charles Perrault, of the French *Mother Goose* stories. The edifice was finished in 1672, but the interior was not completed until 1683. The four Cassinis, a family of Italian origin, successively kept up the scientific activity of the Observatoire until the Revolution, although other scientists were also involved. Jean Cassini I calculated the true dimensions of the solar system (1672) and discovered the division of Saturn's ring; his son established the fact of stellar movement; his grandson, Cassini de Thury, called Cassini III, began a topographical map of France, which was completed by Cassini IV. The Observatoire then came under the control of the Bureau des Longitudes, formed in 1795, and participated in the definition of the metric system. Numerous astronomical and topographical observations became widely publicized discoveries, resulting most notably in a large map of the moon and a map of France. Observations in the field were necessary for some research: expeditions left the Observatoire for Denmark, Cape Verde and the Canary Islands to try to estimate the dimensions of the solar system. Picard organized 'walks' in the neigborhood to measure one degree of the meridian, which was indispensable in calculating the size of the earth. Research at the Observatoire became multidisciplinary: Arago and his followers discovered the speed of light here; Le Verrier described planetary motion by mathematical calculations, and founded the national institute of meteorology. Photography, still in its infancy, was soon used to make a map of the heavens. It was therefore natural that this institution, renowed for its strict precision, should be the seat of the Bureau International since its creation in 1919.

The exterior

The Observatoire is composed of a central rectangular block, the four sides of which face the cardinal points of the compass. It is flanked to the E and W by two octagonal towers on its S meridional side. There is a square tower on the N façade, while the S façade is decorated with bas-reliefs of globes and astronomical instruments by Temporiti. Underground quarries facilitated the construction of a vertical shaft 180ft./55m deep, used for the study of falling bodies and pendulums. A terrace runs round the top of the Observatoire giving a splendid view over Paris. The E tower, which houses the great equatorial telescope, 15in./38cm in aperture, has been crowned with a cupola since 1845.

The interior

In the main courtyard on the meridian line is a fine statue of Le Verrier by Chapu. The entrance is on the N façade; in the vestibule to one side is the telescope used by Léon Foucault in 1859 and, opposite, the mirror of the siderostat from the great telescope of the 1900 World Fair; before climbing the fine stone staircase, you pass in front of the original speaking clock (built by Esclangon, 1933) which gives Coordinated Universal Time exact to one millionth of a second. On the first floor on the r. is the Council Chamber where, under the gaze of the full-length portrait of Louis XIV, are hung the portraits of all the directors of the Observatoire from J.-D. Cassini to Danjon. The great vaulted gallery, dominated by statues of Cassini and of Laplace, houses a collection of old scientific instruments: the Gregorian telescope of James Short, made in London in 1750; J. Bird's wall quadrant; a sextant constructed by Langlois in 1780 which was used by the Abbé de La Caille at the Collège Mazarin and at the Cape of Good Hope; Napoléon's pocket telescope, signed Le Rebours; standard measures for the metric system; and prisms used in optical experiments by Fresnel and Arago. At the end of the gallery, a round room with its original decoration in which are displayed some beautiful pieces: the celestial globe by V. Coronelli (1693); the astronomical telescope built in 1774; on the mantlepiece, the clock operated by a genuine astronomical clockwork movement, built by Pierre Fardoil in 1720, with its cabinet designed by A. Coypel and made by Caffieri. Exhibited in a display cabinet is a small transit telescope by Brumer (1819) and a cross-staff, or Jacob's staff, used by sailors to measure the angular height of the stars; on the walls, old engravings and some portraits. On the second floor, the spacious Salle de la Méridienne where Cassini represented the Paris meridian by a line in copper sealed between the marble tiles, which were engraved with the 12 signs of the zodiac. This room houses ancient instruments of physics and astronomy as well as busts of French astronauts and navigators. The main staircase leads to the terrace which covers the entire Perrault building. The dome on the E tower, built in 1850 and made entirely in copper, houses the great equatorial telescope which is still used for observations; the dome on the W tower houses the Secrétan-Eichens equatorial telescope; on the flat roof of the main building is a chute which goes down as far as the catacombs (in that section underground which is not open to visitors, and where some pious person placed a statue of the Virgin, known as Notre-Dame-de-Dessous-Terre (Our Lady Underground). At 88ft./27m deep, the cellars maintain a constant temperature of 53.35°F/11.86°C, and house a collection of meteorological instruments, the speaking clock, and four sidereal clocks at a constant pressure and temperature whose purpose is to synchronize electrically the clocks in the various observation rooms.

For more information, the brochure *L'Observatoire de Paris. Son histoire*, 1667–1963 (The History of the Paris Observatory, 1667–1963); 1984, available in French at the museum. The entrance to the observatory gardens is on the Boul. Arago (open April–Sept., 1–7pm; Sept.–Oct. 15, 1–6pm).

Rue Cassini*

On leaving the observatory, turn r. and take the Rue Cassini, a pleasant street, peaceful and full of flowers. It is bordered on both sides by early 20th-c. houses built for artists or patrons of art. This modern-style complex is remarkable for its variety of shapes, diversity of materials and lavish decoration. At nos. 3, 5 and 7 are three private live-in-workshops built by Louis Süe and Paul Huillard from 1903 to 1906. The architects used the latest technologies for these eclectically styled buildings, as shown in the reinforced concrete structure of the Hôtel Lucien Simon (no. 3). Many famous people have lived in this street. At no. 5 the sculptor Laurens entertained artists and writers such as André Gide and Charles Péguy in his studio. Alain-Fournier, author of *Le Grand Meaulnes*, lived at no. 1, on the fourth floor; the present-day building replaces the house where Balzac lived from 1828 to 1835 and where he began writing *La Comédie Humaine*. At no. 12, built by Abella in the style of Mallet-Stevens, is the studio of the English painter, S. W. Hayter. No. 8 is the residence of Robert-Jean Longuet, great-grandson of Karl Marx. No. 6 is a former outbuilding of Port-Royal built in the 17th c.; it was occupied by the philosopher Alain, and has an enchanting courtyard.

Rue de Faubourg-Saint-Jacques

The Hôtel de Massa* (38 Rue du Faubourg-Saint-Jacques, group visits by arrangement. Tel: 43-54-18-66). This mansion owes its name to the Duc de Massa, its last owner in 1880. The Duc de Richelieu lived there in 1788 and the Comte Marescalchi, during the Empire, held many splendid parties there. Built by Leboursier in 1784 on the Champs-Elysées, at the corner of the Rue de la Boétie, this is a relic of the follies built during the 18th c. It was acquired in 1926 for an important real estate operation and the promoters, to free the land, gave the building to the State. E. Herriot, minister for Public Education and the Arts, decided to transport it, stone by stone, to the observatory gardens, where he installed the Société des Gens de Lettres (Writers Society). The society has a collection of many literary souvenirs in this house (portraits, busts, manuscripts, autographs), evoking 150 years of literature.

At no. 83 the independent Faculty of Protestant Theology was inaugurated by Jules Ferry in 1879. At no. 102 the former Society for Evangelical Missions has today been replaced by the DEFAP (French Department for Evangelical Action); the house is remarkable for its troubadour-style architecture (gable with a stained glass window, gargoyles and other decorative sculptures); a vast garden, originally designed by the architect-landscape gardener Buhler, stretches out at the back. Go back and take the Rue Méchain which commemorates astronomer Pierre Méchain. At no. 21 is the mother house and central noviciate of the Congregation of the Sisters of Saint-Joseph de Cluny, founded in 1805. At no. 7 pause in the courtyard to see the building by the architect Robert Mallet-Stevens, one of the principal supporters of the international style in Paris (*ca.* 1930).

Rue de la Santé

Between the Boul. de Port-Royal and Boul.Arago.

At no. 29, on the l., is the mother house of the Dames Augustines du

Sacré Coeur de Marie, a beautiful example of Restoration architecture: a large courtyard with a portico on the ground floor has a chapel with colonnade and pediment, built in 1840 by Chalut. Take the Rue de la Santé S to reach the Boul. Arago. In spite of its austere appearance, this boulevard inspired the poet Rainer Maria Rilke to write unforgettable pages in *The Notebooks of Malte Laurids Brigge*. The boulevard runs alongside the Santé Prison, at the junction with the Rue de la Santé, on the edge of the 13th and 14th arrondissements.

Cité Fleurie**

65 Boulevard Arago

If by chance the door is open here, you will discover a charming garden full of acacias, elder trees and wisterias. This artists' complex has 29 studios, more shacks than real homes, built over 100 years ago with materials recovered from the demolition of buildings of the World Fair. As well as J.-P. Laurens, who lived here for some years, Picasso and Modigliani also stayed here, and Rodin had a smelting workshop with Maillol. Painters, engravers and sculptors still work here today. Threatened with redevelopment in 1973, it became a registered monument In 1976. A plaque at the entrance commemorates the founding of a free Germanic library by anti-Nazi German writers with the aid of French writers between 1934 and 1939. On leaving the Cité Fleurie, take the Rue de la Glacière to the r. On the r. is the Rue Léon-Maurice-Nordmann, a very ancient road which has lost all its character. Even so, look at the Cité Verte (at no. 147) where there is a group of artists' studios, unfortunately dilapidated, in the middle of an untended garden. Note also the Cité des Vignes at no. 152.

Rue Jean-Dolent

The even-numbered side of the street runs parallel to the wall of the Santé Prison whose entrance is at 42 Rue de la Santé. The prison occupies the site of the 17th-c. Sainte-Anne farm, the forerunner of the Asile Sainte-Anne in the Rue Cabanis; it was the architect Vaudremer who erected the Santé prison from 1821 and 1867 in the shape of a star radiating from a central nucleus, the so-called canoptical design, in which all prisoners may be seen by a guard stationed at a central point. Opposite, at no. 23, a small country house dating from the 18th c. (once the property of the Maréchal Masséna) survives alongside a series of artists' studios; around 1875, Renoir painted several portraits in the house, and Blaise Cendrars died here. To the l. is the Place Saint-Jacques, where the Arcueil barrier used to be. The Church of Saint-Dominique is situated on the other side of the Boul. Saint-Jacques, on the Rue de la Tombe-Issoire. It was built in concrete in the Byzantine style by

Gaudibert, from 1913 to 1921, and is decorated with paintings by Jeanne Dauchez (1929).

▷ The markets

Rue d'Alésia (behind the Hôpital de Sainte-Anne): Wed. and Sat. 7am–1:30pm.

Beside the Hôpital de Val-de-Grâce, Boul. de Port-Royal: Tues., Thurs. and Sat 7am–1:30pm.

▷ The Paris Meridian and the Bureau International de l'Heure

On June 21, 1667, the day of the summer solstice, the mathematician of the Royal Academy of Sciences determined the axis of the Paris meridian line of longitude in order to orient the Observatoire. This line, the building's N–S axis, appears as a band of copper embedded in the paving of the Observatoire. The Paris meridian remained the original meridian of France until 1884 when the Greenwich mean was generally adopted (9′ 21″ further W). Time was synchronized in France in 1891, with the national adoption of the time at the Paris meridian. It became clear, however, that a universal harmonization of time was necessary for the purposes of international navigation; thus the Greenwich meridian was adopted as the basis for the international time zone system. The International Bureau of Time, created in 1919, is based at the Observatoire in Paris. As the earth's rate of rotation is not uniform, the bureau sometimes has to add a few seconds at the end of the year. Time is transmitted through the medium of the famous speaking clock, the first in the world, invented in 1933 by Ernest Esclangon, who applied the technique of the sound cinema to the transmission of time by telephone. The talking clock receives fourteen million calls a year; anyone may ask it the time by dialing 36–99–84–00. The original clock displayed in the vestibule of the Perrault building has now been replaced by quite different models.

▷ The Paris water supply and the Arcueil aqueduct

Even in Roman times, Lutetia got its supply of water from the springs at Rungis. The course of the Arcueil aqueduct, which once brought water to the Cluny baths, is well established and two piles of masonry of quarry stone and bricks can still be seen to the Médicis aqueduct, in the Arcueil valley. In order to supply the Left Bank with clean drinking water, Henry IV commissioned two

Parisian burghers to study the possibilities of rebuilding the aqueduct, the maintenance of which had been neglected in the Middle Ages; this project was taken over by Marie de' Medici. The contract for the new aqueduct was awarded to the master mason Jean Coing, and it came into service on May 19, 1623.

The aqueduct starts at the Rungis springs. The Pirouette inspection hole is the departure point for the main pipework toward Paris. A 8ml/13km gallery takes the water to the Faubourg Saint-Jacques. It is punctuated by carved stone inspection holes allowing easy access for the maintenance of the pipework and the filtration system. The aqueduct ends at the Grand Regard Royal in the Faubourg Saint-Jacques (Bon Pasteur Convent, Ave. Denfert-Rochereau). This Baroque pavilion, with its large flat-tiled roof, skylights and beautiful chimneys, was built by François Francine and Salomon de Brosse and housed, in its basement, the distribution basins which were used to allocate the water to its recipients. This equipment, which was used to supply water to Paris until approximately 1860, is still partially in service today.

The Saint-Lazare district*

9th and 8th arr./Map ref. 10–C1, D1
Métro: Saint-Lazare, Trinité
Bus: 20, 21, 24, 27, 28, 29, 32
Parking: Cour de Rome, Place du Havre opposite the station.
Taxis: Gare Saint-Lazare
Market: Rue Corvetto; Mon.–Sat. 8am–1:30pm, 4–7pm; Sun. 8am–1pm.

Although the land south of Rue Saint-Lazare was developed in the 1780s, the creation of the Quartier de L'Europe dates from the end of the Restoration. The development of the land close to the fashionable Rue de la Chaussée-d'Antin began around 1830, and with the construction of the train station from 1836 on, the character of the area was transformed. However, it is above all the developers of the 20th c. who have reduced residential areas to isolated pockets.

Today, few Parisian districts know such violent contrasts between night and day as Saint-Lazare and the Chaussée-d'Antin. During the day the pavements around the station and the department stores are invaded by hurrying shoppers, the streets are congested, and during Christmas and New Year traffic jams make life impossible. This district, which was residential during the Second Empire, is now essentially occupied by businesses from the service sector—banks, insurance companies, travel agencies—their many offices sucking in large crowds and disgorging them in a daily ebb and flow. One must wait for the end of the day before the Place de l'Europe regains its usual sleepy calm, by which time the Chaussée-d-Antin is so deserted that it seems unreal. Late into the night a few solitary prostitutes keep up some sporadic activity in Rue de Provence, Rue de Mogador, or Rue de Budapest.

Tour of the district

45 mins.

☐ The Gare Saint-Lazare*

The Gare Saint-Lazare, the world's third largest railway station, handles more travellers than any other Parisian station, between Paris and W and NW suburbs shuttling about 136 million travellers per year in 1984 and 1985. The service to Normany is only a small part of the station's operation. The buildings of the present station-the Saint-Germain railway has been in existence since 1832, and the first station stood in the Place de l'Europe – were erected by Juste Lisch between 1886 and 1889, when the original building was extended as far as the Rue de Rome. The buildings borrow elements from the vocabulary of 17th-c. French architecture, blending them with the bay windows and glass roofs of the Rationalist style. The station's symmetrical design, intended to link it stylistically with the old Hôtel Terminus, is a typical example of Beaux-Arts architecture. In 1985, two column-shaped assemblage sculptures by Arman were installed here: *L'heure de tous* (Everyone's Hour), in the Cour du Havre, is composed of clocks; *Consigne à vie* (Abandoned Luggage), of suitcases.

Rue Saint-Lazare

The Concorde Saint-Lazare stands on the corner of the Rue de Budapest and the Rue Saint-Lazare, on the site of the Folie Boutin of 1766, which, after the Revolution, became the first Tivoli, an amusement park, the land of which was acquired by the PLM in 1869 (the second Tivoli will eventually be installed in the Rue de Clichy). The former Hôtel Terminus, now the headquarters of the French National Railway (SNCF), was completed for the 1889 World Fair. The building, in the Louis XVI style characteristic of the second half of the 19th c., is reminiscent of the great town houses that then stood in the vicinity. The now disused footbridge that links it with the station was much admired in its day, as was the magnificent reading room (now the entrance hall) where the anarchist Emile Henry carried out an assassination attempt in 1894.

Opposite the station, at 115 Rue Saint-Lazare, stands the local temple of American *pâtisserie*, Mister Donut, next to the Brasserie Mollard (no. 113), the long-established Dubly detective agency (no. 121), and the Café Dupont.

Avenue de Coq: The name of this cul-de-sac, created in 1854, recalls the Château de Coq whose origins date back to the 14th c. Around 1750 it was the Folie Brancas, of which there remains only the fountain wall at the end of the avenue.

Rue de Mogador

This busy thoroughfare, whose N section was built between 1894 and 1900, takes the overflow of the traffic from the Chaussée-d'Antin and the large department stores. The Mogador Theater at no. 25 is unmistakably English in character. Its architecture mixes the Romanticism of such details as the crowning little tower-shaped skylight or belvedere with pragmatism (note the side staircases). Founded by Alfred Butt In 1919, it was modelled on the London Palladium. The Ballets Russes performed there, and it was a popular theater for operettas. Among its stars were Maurice Chevalier and Régine Flory. Today this beautiful high-ceilinged auditorium is the setting for a wide variety of shows, from music hall to the Kabuki theater. Further along on the corner of the Rue de la Victoire there is a wall painted by Amenard.

Rue Joubert

This street lies at the heart of one of the big speculative developments from the *Ancien Régime's* last years; it was planned around 1780 by the architect of the Bourse, Alexandre-Théodore Brongniart, with François-Joseph Bélanger, architect of Bagatelle. A completely new district, including a market, was built near the Capuchin monastery (now the Lycée Condorcet). Its central axis was the Rue Joubert, which retains traces of its more noble occupants: no. 33 is typical of the original buildings; there are remnants of a *hôtel* by Bélanger in the courtyard of no. 20. The *hôtel* at the corner of the Rue de Mogador deserves restoration. No. 1 (35 Rue de la Chaussée-d'Antin) is well preserved. The N side of the Rue de Provence has also kept its period façades. But this whole district is now overrun by prostitutes, taking advantage of the crowds who come to the department stores.

Continuation of the Rue de Provence → below.

Rue de la Chaussée d'Antin

Between the Boulevard Haussmann and Place de la Trinités.

This area is one of the shrines of affordable Parisian ready-to-wear clothing. There are many façades dating from the end of the 18th c. and vestiges of Cardinal Fesch's *hôtel* at no. 68 (now without the parts of the house built by Ledoux). Mirabeau died on April 2, 1791 in a house on the site of no. 42. Gambetta lived at no. 55. At no. 29 you can see the earliest parts of the Galeries Lafayette, designed by George Chedanne (1906–08).

Continuation of the Rue de la Chaussée-d'Antin → Opéra district.

Boulevard Haussmann

This street runs alongside the Place de l'Opéra to the N, where it is bordered by the façades of the biggest Parisian department stores, including Galeries Lafayette at no. 40. Beginning in 1895 as a small shop on the corner of the Rue La Fayette and Rue de la Chaussée-d'Antin, the store, built by G. Chedanne (1906–08) and enlarged by F. Chanut (1910–12), at present occupies 1.3 million sq. ft./ 120,000m^2. Unfortunately the main staircase has been taken down, but the building has kept a pretty façade on the Rue de la Chaussée-d'Antin, interior balustrades attributed to Majorelle and a fine stained-glass dome. At no. 64 the Printemps department store, founded in 1865, is by Paul Sedille (whose fine façade of 1889 looks crushed beneath a recent additional storey) and by R. Binet, who designed the beautiful dome (1911) which covered a magnificent hall, now vanished.

Rue Caumartin

Between Boul. Haussmann and Rue Saint-Lazare

This part of the street dates from 1780 and still has a few buildings from the Directoire period (notably no. 71). Its transformation into a pedestrian precinct has led to the usual dramatic changes in the tenants.

The Lycée Condorcet and the Church of Saint-Louis d'Antin**

63 Rue Caumartin

With this massive group of buildings (1780–82), Brongniart introduced the fashion for the Doric order without base or plinth inspired by the temples of Paestum. Behind the porch, supported by two columns, stands an austere courtyard surrounded by colonnades, fitting for its monastic purpose. The interior decoration of the chapel is 19th c. From 1804, the monastery became one of the Empire's four great Parisian *lycées* (then called the Lycée Bonaparte). The first director of the school was Lakanal. Among the eminent pupils were Ampère, Léon Blum, Alexandre Dumas the Younger, the Goncourt brothers, Henri Monnier, Nadar, Proust, Texier and Taine. The monastery garden is now covered over by the extension to the *lycée* built by Henri Duc in 1865. Close by at 124 Rue de Provence is the elegant façade of the former Majorelle store by H. Sauvage (1913).

The Passage du Havre: between 69 Rue Caumartin and 107 Rue Saint-Lazare: this covered passageway, 377 ft./115m in length, has become a paradise for lovers of model-making and electric trains. It was built in 1848 and is the only arcade left in the district.

Rue de la Pépinière: This street is named after the nearby *Pépinières du Roi* (king's nurseries) which once existed in the village of Roule. The street layout of 1782 is still perceptible in spite of the rather dull buildings (such as no. 25, by Charles Morice) that border the street leading to Saint-Augustin and the Square Bergson.

⚓ The Church of Saint-Augustin*

46 Boul. Malesherbes (Open 7am–7pm. Tel: 45–22–23–12)

The church was built from 1860 to 1871 by Victor Baltard, who personally supervised the decoration. The angle formed by the boulevard and the Ave. César-Caire presented an awkward triangle, which Baltard used to advantage with an ingenious design. The church widens from the porch to the chancel; a vast nave flanked by progressively larger chapels leads to a sanctuary crowned by a large cupola, which gives the building its distinctive silhouette. The structure is of iron, the walls merely an envelope; this is one of the earliest examples of the use of metal in church architecture. The dome is 164ft/50m high. François Jouffroy carved *Christ and the Twelve Apostles* above the porch.

The interior is characterized by the decorative use made by the steel girder construction. The nave's pillars are crowned with cast-iron angels by Schönewerk. In the sanctuary are four medallions of the Evangelists on a gold ground by Emile Signol; in the vault, 16 Fathers of the Church by Louis Bézard. The two half-domes that form the transept are decorated with paintings by William Bouguereau: on the r., scenes from *The Life of John the Baptist*; on the l., *St Peter and St Paul*. In the second chapel on the r. a memorial records the fact that Charles de Foucauld was converted to the faith in this church in 1886.

The Cercle Militaire (National Army and Air Force Officers' club)

This other distinguished building in the Place Saint-Augustin is Art Deco in style, from 1927, by Lemaresquier. Its establishment in the capital is similar to that of the Hôtel Lutetia at Sèvres-Babylone, but the club's image is less formal because the reception rooms can be hired for weddings and banquets. Military presence in this district goes back to the 18th c., when the Polish barracks stood on this site. In the 19th c. the square, at the heart of the *quartier* then called 'La Petite Pologne' (Little Poland), was nicknamed Place des Grésillons after the small bits of coal picked up by the tramps who gathered there. The quiet Square Bergson has a statue of Paul Déroulède by Landowski (1927). Rue Portalis: In the courtyard of no. 10 there is a natural rock.

Rue de Rocher

The street is interesting for the footbridge over the Rue de Madrid and because its layout disturbs somewhat the carefully planned star shape of the Quartier de l'Europe, founded in 1826. In the 18th c. there were mills here, as well as a few pleasure houses where Casanova is thought to have stayed. Of this country setting only a few old houses remain in the NW part of the street. At no. 64, the Théâtre Tristan-Bernard; Jules Renard died in 1910 at no. 44; and the painter P. P. Prud'hon died in 1823 at no. 32. The Lycée Racine for girls (1887) is at no. 22.

The Conservatoire National Supérieur de Musique

14 Rue de Madrid.

This public establishment was created under the Convention and, until 1911, lay in the Faubourg Poissonnière. Music, singing and dance are taught here. There is also an musical instrument museum and a music library with an manuscript of Mozart's *Don Giovanni* in the building, which comes under the administrative jurisdiction of the Bibliothèque Nationale (National Library) (→ Museums). In the next few years the academy will move to the *Cité de la Musique* at La Villette.

Place de l'Europe

The square forms the center of the district of the same name and was part of a speculative development of the Restoration period. The Pont de l'Europe with its metal structure is a consequence of the extension of Saint-Lazare station; the view of the bridge attracts many sightseers, and was celebrated by 19th-c. artists —Monet and

Tissot each painted pictures of the bridge. Manet lived in this then modern district in the Rue Leningrad, and later in Rue d'Amsterdam.

The Rue de Rome is the headquarters of many violin makers (→ inset); the Rue de Constantinople is where Apollinaire spent his childhood. At 28 Rue de Liège (formerly Rue de Berlin) is one of the four Paris buildings attributed to Viollet-le-Duc; this was built for M. Courmont (1848) when the architect was 34 years old.

Rue d'Amsterdam

At. no. 41, a beautiful Neo-Gothic shop houses the restaurant and shop of the cheesemonger Androuet (although M. Androuet has recently retired), where it is possible to enjoy meals composed entirely of cheeses. The doyen of Paris ice cream makers is at no. 38: the firm of Baggi, founded in 1850.

Rue de Londres

On the corner of the Rue de Budapest, the modern building of the SNCF commercial management has advantageously used the space formerly occupied by small shops. Of the series of private mansions built from 1828 by the architects Godde, Mangut and Van Cléemputte, only nos. 19, 22 and 26 remain. Berlioz lived here on the site of no. 34. At no. 13 the private passage (1840) of the Cité de Londres, recently restored, into the Rue Saint-Lazare (No. 84).

▣ Museum to visit

Musée Instrumental (Conservatoire National Supérieur de Musique, 14 Rue de Madrid): collection of ancient musical instruments.

▷ The violin-makers of Rue de Rome

When lovers of musical instruments come to Paris from abroad to pursue their passion, they ask a taxi driver to take them to the Rue de Rome. This street, laid out in the late 19th c. and swept by the wind from Normandy, has the greatest concentration of violin and bow makers in France—about 60 shops and *ateliers*, or almost half of all such establishments in Paris, owned by members of a profession who number only a few hundred in the whole of France. The best craftsmen are trained at the Mirecourt National Instrument School where the dukes of Lorraine first introduced the art of lute making. The respect for tradition prevalent in the trade is not surprising considering that the necessary three years of training are often doubled by periods of apprenticeship, and that a commendable *esprit de corps* controls the quality of the work. There are three main branches: the manufacture with maple wood, always of the highest quality; instrument restoring, crucially important because so many orchestra musicians play with centuries-old instruments; and finally expert evaluation, which is provided by only a few masters. Precious 18th-c. violins are sometimes restored here, as Maurice Reims tells with such sensitivity in his *Le Luthier de Mantoue* (The Violin Maker of Mantua); but most often the pressing daily needs are the supply of instruments to students at the Conservatoire, the reconstruction of extensively damaged instruments, or the provision of same-day repairs for concert artists.

The lute makers settled in the Rue de Rome after the Conservatoire moved from the Faubourg Poissonnière to the Rue de Madrid in 1911. The creation of the *Cité de la Musique* (Music City) at La Villette will by no means bring changes within a trade where skill alone counts.

▷ **The work of Viollet-le-Duc**

Eugène-Emmanuel Viollet-le-Duc (1814–79) rebelled against the architectural establishment, refusing to go to the Ecole des Beaux-Arts, and helping to build barricades in 1830. He was a supporter of *éclectisme raisonné* (B. Foucard), a scholar and, above all, a restorer. His meeting with Prosper Mérimée, author of *Carmen* and Inspector of the Commission des Monuments Historiques, marked the turning point in his career. In 1840 his first job was the Madeleine at Vézelay; he then restored Notre-Dame-de-Paris with Lassus, and the Sainte-Chapelle with Dauban; Coucy and Pierrefonds followed.

He developed new ideas on the Gothic style, which to him was one of rational construction, based on the rib vault, buttress and flying buttress. These highly influential ideas are set out in his *Dictionnaire raisonné de l'architecture française* (published 1854–68). In his *Entretiens* (2 vols., published 1863 and 1872) he compared the Gothic stone skeleton with the 19th-c. iron skeleton. He was very modern in his defense of new engineering techniques and new building materials, especially iron. Despite the daring and originality of his ideas, the detailing of his buildings were surprisingly commonplace and not very attractive as, for example, at Saint-Denys-de-l'Estrée.

He also built some modest dwellings, four of which survive on the Right Bank: 28 Rue de Liège for M. Courmont (1848), 15 Rue de Douai for M. Milon (1860–61), 68 Rue Condorcet for himself (1862–63) and 23 Rue Chauchat for M. Sauvage (1863–65). Looking at these houses it is possible to see how far his theories could be realized when applied in a real urban context. Only the details (brackets, cornices, doors and windows) distinguish these houses from typically Haussmannian buildings. Viollet-le-Duc used a simple medieval vocabulary, and if the compositions betray a looseness in the arrangement of the apartments, the subtlety of design (Rue de Liège, Rue Condorcet) gives a personal quality to these works.

The Ile Saint-Louis**

4th arr./18–C3
Métro: no station on the island; the nearest are Cité and Pont-Marie
Bus: three routes cross the island: 67, 86 and 87; three routes have a bus stop close to the island: 63, 47, 246
Taxis: Pont Sully, 23 Boul. Morland. Tel: 42-77-59-88.

If the Ile Saint-Louis has kept its special character intact, this has nothing to do with its insularity, because its larger neighbor, the Ile de la Cité, has long since given in to the sirens of police cars and ambulances from the Hôtel-Dieu, and hordes of tourists. Here, on the contrary, one has the impression of being on a boat, in a self-sufficient village with its own church, post office and small shopkeepers.

Of course, there are the inevitable tearooms and a few slightly overrated restaurants, but it is a long way from the noise of the city, especially on the downstream side of the island. Majestic porches and elegant façades have kept tourist bistros and souvenir shops at bay. Time has stopped, and the town seems asleep in the silent majesty of its stone. Whatever the season or time of day, the surroundings and the light have a special quality. Far from the noise and haste, in these streets on the banks of this island, timeless Paris can still be enjoyed.

History of the Ile Saint-Louis

Before 1614 there were two tiny islands, the Ile aux Vaches (Isle of Cows) and the Ile Notre-Dame; the second had belonged for centuries to the chapterhouse of Notre-Dame. St Louis came here to give judgment and Philippe le Bel (the Fair) to knight his three sons. The two islands stayed in their natural state until the contractor Christophe Marie, with two financiers, Lugles Poulletier and François Le Regrattier, received royal permission to join the islands and sell the land for development. The first stone of the future Pont Marie was laid in 1614, but the work advanced so slowly that Marie's team was replaced by Jean Chevrier and Jean de la Grange, who

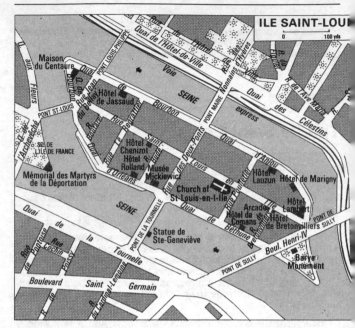

Ile Saint-Louis

hired the Le Vau family as architects. Stone embankments were built all round the island, streets were laid out on a rectilinear grid. By 1664 the work was completed. The first island inhabitants settled along the two main thoroughfares; they were craftsmen and shopkeepers. Later came people of higher rank, rich landowners who favored the embankments, which offered a view over the Seine and the city.

After the frenzied construction periods of the 17th and 18th c., the island was only slightly modified. In 1874 the building of the Pont Sully led to the cutting of the Boulevard Henri IV through the site of the splendid Hôtel de Bretonvilliers. In 1913 the Rue des Deux-Point was widened and lost many of its Louis XIII façades.

Tour of the Ile Saint-Louis

1½ hrs.

Rue Saint-Louis-en-L'Ile

From the Pont Saint-Louis to Rue Le-Regrattier.

This street is the backbone of the island and though it does not have the same charm as the embankments, it is still interesting. Laid out as soon as the first bridges were built, it bore the following names successively: Rue Palestine, Rue Carelle, Rue Marie, Rue Saint-Louis, Rue de la Fraternité (during the Revolution), Rue Blanche-de-Castille and, since 1814, its present name. Except for the Hôtel Lambert and the Hôtel Chenizot it does not have any mansions, but look upward, and you will notice many details from the past, especially on the even-numbered side of the street. Poulletier lived at no. 90. On the corner of the Rue Le-Regrattier, at no. 61, the 'Aux Anysetier de Roi' (anisette makers) cabaret (tavern) still has its old gates as well as a small carving, which was part of the sign for 'Au petit Bacchus' (Little Bacchus). In the Rue Le-Regrattier, opposite, a plaque marks the birthplace of Jules Guesde (1845–1922), one of the founders of French Socialism. (Continuation of the street → below). Cross the small Rue Budé which was long called simply Rue Guillaume (William). It was not a fashionable street but housed the ordinary, undistinguished people of the *quartier* (note the lack of portals on the houses). No. 58 dates from the 18th c.

The Hôtel de Chenizot*

51 Rue Saint-Louis en-l'Ile

This mansion was built in the 17th c. for Pierre de Verton. It consisted of two main buildings between a courtyard and a garden that stretched as far as the Quai d'Orléans. In 1719 the house became the property of the Collector-General of Taxes, Jean François de Chenizot, who commissioned the decoration of its façades. In 1726 the architect Pierre de Vigny carried out the decoration of the portal**, which is set at intervals with vermiculated masonry blocks; above, a majestic curving balcony supported on chimera-shaped brackets. This ensemble is one of the finest examples of *rocaille* decoration in Paris. In the courtyard the same exuberance is found on the façade of the second building in the fawn mask on the pediment. On the stairs at the far end of the courtyard chimeras decorate the banisters, which were forged by Nicholas Viennot. From 1788 to 1793 it was the residence of Teresa Cabarrus, the future wife of Tallien. In 1840, the house was rented by the State for use as the archbishop's place. In 1862, after having been a police station for a time, it lost its garden when an apartment building was built there.

Rue des Deux-Ponts

This street cuts across the Rue Saint-Louis-en-L'Ile. Most of the Louis XIII houses on the even-numbered side remain. At no. 25, on the attic storey, behind the gutters, are small canopied windows known as *fenêtres tabernacles*, typical of the 17th c. On the odd-numbered side, the Louis XIII houses were destroyed during the widening of the street at the beginning of the 20th c. All the buildings on that side date from that time. Beyond the intersection is an ice-cream parlor at 31 Rue Saint-Louis-en-l'Ile—tourists from the five continents seem to have crossed the seas only to taste one of the 116 flavors offered by the house. You will quickly be aware that the further you advance toward the upstream end of the island, the more aristocratic it becomes.

The Church of Saint-Louis-en-l'Ile*

19 bis Rue Saint-Louis-en-l'Ile (Open daily exc. Mon. and Sun. afternoon 9am–noon and 3–7pm. Tel: 46-34-41-30)

History of the church

At the beginning of the 17th c., the island's first inhabitants requested permission to build a chapel. With the growth in population this became too small and, from 1644, a new church was built with plans by Le Vau, who lived on the island.

After his death Le Duc continued to work, joining the chancel to the original chapel, which collapsed during a hurricane in February 1701. Jacques Doucet succeeded Le Duc, who died in 1704. The nave, communion chapel, transept and dome were completed in 1725 and the church consecrated in 1726. It is richly decorated in the Jesuit style with gilding and marble. In 1791 it was closed and its works of art dispersed.

After the Revolution some of these were returned. In the 19th c., while the City of Paris was commissioning 28 paintings to adorn the side chapels, the Abbé Bossuet, parish priest from 1864 to 1888, also contributed to the restoration and artistic enrichment of the church. A plaque in the N aisle, presented in 1926, is inscribed: 'In grateful memory of St Louis in whose honor the City of St Louis, Missouri, USA is named.'

The exterior

The church entrance is visible from the distance because of its unusual iron clock (1741), hanging like a sign, and its pierced spire. The need to build in an E-W direction while keeping the building aligned with the street means that the church does not have a W portal but, on its N side, has a side door* carved in oak by N. Legendre, and another door at the E end or apse decorated with fleurs-de-lis.

The interior

The Church of Saint-Louis-en-l'Ile is one of the best examples of 17th-c. French Baroque religious architecture. The church is light, with gold highlights shining on the white stone. The decorative sculptures were done under the direction of J.-B. de Champaigne, nephew of Philippe, and a churchwarden. On the l. as you enter is a holy water font which was in the Chapel of the Visitation in Chaillot at the time of Mlle de la Vallière (Louis XIV's mistress).

The nave has large arcades with semicircular arches separated by Corinthian pilasters and a barrel-vault supported by transverse ribs decorated with rosettes. The organ case was installed by the Abbé Bossuet at his own expense in 1888; the instrument was completed in 1923. Under the organ loft is a glazed terracotta statue of St Louis by Allar.

The r.-hand side-aisle and its chapels. On the back of the façade in the Chapelle du Calvaire is a Station of the Cross with a stucco crucifix by Jacques Sarrazin (17th c.). 2nd chapel (Communion) built as an annex at the beginning of the 18th c.: to the l. of the altar, *Resurrection* by Peyron (1748); above the altar, *Les Pèlerins d'Emmaüs* (Pilgrims of Emmaüs) by Coypel (1746) to the r. of the altar, *The Nativity* by Perrin (1784); above, *Donors*, a panel from the German or French school (15th c.). 3rd chapel: on the r., *Death of the Virgin*, a group in gilded and colored wood: Rhenish school (15th c.); opposite, panels showing figures of male and female saints, from the Italian school (15th c.); tomb and epitaph of the poet Quinault (d. 1688).

R. and L. arms of the transept, both of which end in a large concave recess holding a statute by Ladatte (18th c.): on the r., the Virgin, on the l., St Geneviève.

The choir. This has the same architectural arrangement as the nave. To the r. and l. of the altar are two plaster statues by Bra: St Paul (1819) and St Peter (1823). On the two first pillars, on either side of the choir: the *Apostles*, six 17th-c. paintings on copper from the same series as those in the nave. On the first chancel pillar: *The Entombment of Christ*, panel from the late 15th c., French school.

Periphery of the choir and its chapels beginning at the r. 1st chapel: Coutan's marble medallion (1890) of the Abbé Bossuet, parish priest (d. 1888) who helped in the restoration and decoration of the church; on the back wall, two 15th-c. alabaster reliefs, and paintings. (*Annunciation* after Fra Angelico). 2nd chapel: on the back wall: 15th-c. alabaster relief of the *Crucifixion*, marble bas-reliefs of *The Last Supper, The Entombment of Christ* (16th c.); on the altar, *The Deposition*, group is carved and gilded wood (16th c.). 4th and 6th chapels: the *Virtues*, murals in grisaille by Norblin (1843). Axial chapel: *Life of St Louis*, mural by Jollivet (1841); on either side of the entrance, two alabaster reliefs, *The Coronation of the Virgin* and

The Flagellation (15th c.). 7th chapel: above the altar, *St Francis de Sales giving the Constitution of her Order to St Jeanne de Chantal* by Noël Hallé (18th c.). 8th chapel: on the back wall, marble relief, *The Assumption* (15th c.); on the altar, *The Entombment of Christ*, carved wood (16th c.). 9th chapel: *The Martyrdom of St Denis*, by Leneupveu (1861), now unfortunately hidden by the organ.

The l. side-aisle and its chapels. 1st chapel: altar stone on which Pius VII celebrated Mass at Fontainebleau; *St John and St Peter Healing a Cripple* by Carle Van Loo (1742); below, *Pilgrims of Emmaüs*, Venetian school (16th c). Baptismal chapel: *The Baptism of Christ* by Stella (1675); all around the chapel, eight scenes from the *Life of Christ*, painted on wood, Flemish School (16th c.).

Rue Saint-Louis-en-l'Ile

From the church to the Pont Sully.

At no. 15 is a handsome 18th-c. portal. No. 12 was the birthplace of Philippe Lebon, chemical engineer, inventor of gas lighting. Note the series of town houses built for Claude le Ragois de Bretonvilliers about 1640 (nos. 13–3). The arcade, which is the ensemble's central motif, at that time gave access to the houses backing onto the Hôtel de Bretonvilliers. At no. 11, Marcel Schwob, journalist, essayist, Shakespearean translater, and husband of the actress Marguerite Moreno, who so often interpreted Giraudoux, lived in a beautiful 17th-c. house where he entertained the Comtesse de Noailles, Colette, Henri de Régnier, P. Fort and Léautaud.

The Hôtel Lambert

In 1641, the architect Louis le Vau was commissioned to build a house on land belonging to Jean-Baptiste Lambert, Seigneur (Lord) of Sucy and Thorigny, adviser and secretary to Louis XIII. In 1644, J.-B. Lambert died, leaving his house to his brother Nicolas who commissioned the extensive interior decoration from the painters Eustache le Sueur, Charles Le Brun and other artists in Paris. Having passed from hand to hand over the centuries, this residence, where the film actress Michèle Morgan once lived, now belongs to the Rothschild family and is unfortunately not open to the public.

The entrance in the Rue Saint-Louis-en-l'Ile is through a *porte-cochère*. The slanting of the walls allows horsedrawn carriages to stop before the front door. Coach ownership was by then no longer the prerogative of the aristocracy; everyone in Parisian social circles owned one. This *porte-cochère* is set in the main façade that gives onto the street. This is in fact just a simple enclosing wall topped by a balustrade that does nothing at all to detract attention from the main building on the far side of the courtyard. At the E end of the residence is a terraced garden on the same level as the first floor. It was necessary for Le Vau to create different ground levels to solve the difficulties presented by the uneven terrain. The house's originality lies in its oval gallery jutting onto the garden, which can be seen from the very beginning of the Quai d'Anjou. Modeled on royal constructions (the Petite Galerie and Grande Galerie of the Louvre), this kind of gallery was intended to house a library or an art collection. Here the painter Le Brun created the decoration, depicting the deeds of the mythological hero Hercules.

On the E tip of the island, which advances between the two Sully bridges, lies a small public garden containing the Bayre monument (by Bernier; 1884). There is a fine view of the ever-busy Seine.

Quai d'Anjou

From the Pont Sully to the Hôtel de Lauzun.

Follow the Quai d'Anjou on the river's N bank. No. 3 was built by Louis Le Vau for himself at the same time as the Hôtel Lambert. The two buildings are adjoining and the street façades are connected by the largest balcony on the island. At no. 3 note the handsome wrought-iron gate; the buildings at the far end of the courtyard were altered in the 18th c. by Louis Poisson de Marigny, brother of Mme de Pompadour. No. 7, built in 1642, has been the headquarters of the Guild of Paris master bakers since 1843. Cross the threshold to discover an entrance hall decorated with large reproductions of plates on the subject of the bakers' guild taken from Diderot and Alembert's *Encyclopédie*. Kneading troughs form an interesting arrangement up to the stairs leading to the library.

Nos. 9, 11, 13 and 15 belonged to the Lambert family. Honoré Daumier lived at no. 9 from 1846 to 1863. Pause to see the unusual types of staircase. At nos. 9 and 15 are staircases with two newel posts – the wooden posts supporting the staircase – and round wooden banisters. At no. 13, however, the staircase is built on four newels with square banisters, which allows for a central stairwell. This system, first used at the end of the 16th and the beginning of the 17th c., took over the previously predominant spiral staircase. The Barbizon painter Daubigny and the sculptor Geoffroy de Chaumefont lived in these houses.

The Hôtel de Lauzun***

Open Apr.–Oct., Sat.–Sun., 10am–5:40pm. Mon–Fri. (visits organized by the Caisse des Monuments Historiques. Tel: 48-87-24-14).

This house was built for Charles Gruyn des Bordes from 1656 to 1657. It is somewhat uncertainly attributed to Louis Le Vau. It was sold in 1682 to the Duc de Lauzun, a favorite of Louis XIV, and became the Hôtel de Pimodan when the marquess of that name bought it in 1779. In 1842 under its new owner, the famous bibliophile Jérôme Pichon, an interesting and lively period began when the residence was thrown open to the bohemian artistic and literary society of the time. The Baron kept a few rooms for himself and rented out the remainder—Charles Baudelaire and Théophile Gautier were among the many lodgers. The painter Fernand Boissard de Boisdenier organized evenings for the meetings of the Club des Haschinchins here. In 1889 the Ville de Paris bought the *hôtel* from Baron Pichon, but returned it in 1905 to Louis Pichon, who completely restored it. It was bought back by the City of Paris in 1928.

The exterior

The main decorative element of the façade is a wrought-iron balcony supported by three curved brackets. The façade is punctuated by rainwater pipes decorated with dolphins, with gilding added in 1910. A vaulted passage leads to the courtyard with a chequer-board layout characteristic of 17th-c. severity. The polygonal courtyards of the 16th c., surrounded by irregularly shaped buildings, were forgotten. The fashion was for perfect symmetry: the blind arcades of the l. wall balance the rounded arches of the other three façades. The gates are modern.

The interior

Almost all the wood paneling and painted ceilings have been preserved. It is an exuberant décor that contrasts with the simplicity of the mansion's exterior. The entrance is by the main staircase, restored to its former place in 1949 after being removed in the 19th c. The vaulted ceilings above this staircase is decorated with a painting attributed to Le Brun, representing *Time Discovering Truth*; its style is that of the 1660s. Two large niches hold statues of Minerva and Apollo. A tapestry illustrating the *Labors of Hercules* decorates the stairwell. On the first floor a large room contains Louis XIV and Napoléon III furniture; the ceiling has been completely restored; the chimneypiece (entirely original) bears a plaque displaying the escutcheon of the Marquis Gruyn des Bordes and his wife. Opposite hangs a tapestry of the *Chasses de Maximilien* (Maximilian's hunt) woven from a cartoon by Van Eckook. A small adjoining room has a ceiling painted with *Le Triomphe de Cérès* (Ceres' Triumph) attributed to Le Sueur. The portraits and the flower paintings date from the 18th c. The second floor rooms show the same taste for mythological subjects. Without any certainty these are attributed to Le Brun and Le Sueur. In the first drawing-room, a portrait of the Duc de Lauzun hangs opposite one of Mlle de Montpensier (*La Grande Mademoiselle*) by Mignard. The door of this salon opens onto a succession of rooms and anterooms arranged in the characteristic fashion of houses in the first half of the 17th c. As you advance into the main building the doorways narrow, creating an effect of perspective and making the space appear larger. The second room was made into a music room in the 17th c. by Baron Pichon, who also added the galleries. The ceiling is painted with *The Triumph of Venus*. The next room is dominated by an alcove with a ceiling painted with the God of Sleep. The main ceiling is decorated with Diana and Endymion. A little room ends this succession of salons. It has a superb arched ceiling decorated with *The Triumph of Flora* at its center.

Quai d'Anjou, continued

From the Hôtel de Lauzun to Rue Poulletier.

No. 19 belonged to Blaise de Méliand (1935–42), Seigneur of Bréviandes. Its entrance is at no 20 Rue Poulletier. It is now used by the City of Paris as a nursery school. Note the beautiful stone staircase.

Rue Poulletier

This street, which links the Quai d'Anjou to the Quai de Béthune, has replaced the broad ditch that divided the island in two from 1360 to 1614. No. 20, the Hôtel de Méliand, has a monumental 17th-c. portal, with a string-course decorated with two heads of Hercules covered by a lionskin. Across the street no. 9 was built (1637–38) by Le Vau for Melchior de Gillier, Seigneur of Lagny and master of the King's household. There are several old houses with doors studded with nails or with interesting keystones.

Quai d'Anjou, continued

From Rue Poulletier to the Quai de Bourbon.

Do not hesitate to open the doors of the 17th-c. houses along the street leading to the Pont Marie to see their pretty courtyards and beautiful staircases. After crossing the Rue des Deux-Ponts, follow the Quai de Bourbon.

Quai de Bourbon

No. 1 was the old Cabaret de Franc-Pinot, its wrought-iron gate decorated with vines and bunches of grapes. It was a favourite haunt of boatmen and barge operators. Wine was sold here as in many other merchants' houses on the island. No. 11 was built some time after 1637 for Philippe de Champaigne, painter and manservant of Marie de' Medici. The house still has its sculpted mascarons, a pretty façade overlooking the courtyard and a staircase.

The Hôtel le Charron

13 and 15 Quai de Bourbon.

This mansion was built by Sébastien Bruand from 1637 to 1640 for Jean Charron, Controller Extraordinary during the wars of Picardy. Like the large mansions on the island and contrary to current fashion, the architect chose a plan which set the façade of the main building on the street, and not at the far end of an inner courtyard. This choice is explained by the unusual character of the site, along the edge of which the houses were built. Thus, apartments on two or three floors had the benefit of light and views. A long arched passageway leads to the courtyard, surrounded by buildings, each one entered by an imposing wrought-iron staircase. Two arcades allow the stairs of the building on the r. to be seen, thereby defining a covered space. The wing onto the street is joined to the l. wing by a corner turret resting on a squinch, a widely used feature in architecture of the first half of the 17th c., which originated from the watchtowers of military architecture. A small town house stands at the far end of the courtyard: its façade has a mansard window with a pulley that was used to hoist up goods or furniture. To the l. of this *hôtel* a small passageway leads to an enclosed garden.

The Hôtel de Jassaud*

19–19 bis Quai de Bourbon.

This mansion was built around 1650 for Nicolas de Jassaud, former secretary of state. Its monumental façade with three curved pediments, elaborate balcony and portal is a registered monument. Go through the door to a large courtyard with a garden that gives access to a service yard behind the main building. In this type of plan, which appeared between 1620 and 1630, all the offices and outhouses were built around the service yard, which added an element of comfort to the whole building.

Rue Le-Regrattier

Between the Quai de Bourbon and Rue Saint Louis.

This very old street was once known as Rue de la Femme-sans-tête (Headless Woman) at the N end; the small mutilated statue at the corner of the quai represents St Nicholas. Go to see the S end of this street (→ see above) where most of the doors and windows, from the Quai d'Orléans onward, are interesting.

Quai de Bourbon

From Rue Le-Regrattier to Pont Saint-Louis.

The present mansion at no. 21 was built by Nicolas Gaillard on land he acquired in 1637. The paintings on the overdoors of the apartments date from the 17th c. Léon Blum lived at no. 25 during the time of the Popular Front. No. 27 was built in the 17th c. for a great-nephew of Mazarin. At no. 29 the Hôtel de Boisgelin was constructed in 1637 for Julius de Luynes. Aligned with the Pont Louis-Philippe, the Rue Jean-du-Bellay opens up a beautiful vista of the Panthéon and Saint-Etienne-du-Mont. Charles-Louis Philippe lived at 31 Quai de Bourbon. The beautiful *hôtels* on the tip of the island at nos. 45, 47 and 49 were built by and for the Le Vau family; at no. 45 the Maison du Centaure (Centaur's house), owes its name to the two round bas-reliefs representing Hercules killing the centaur Nessus. It was built after 1658 by François Le Vau, brother of Louis. This house has been the home of Princess Bibesco, André Billy, Dirue and La Rochelle; André Breton wrote *Les Champs magnétiques* (The Magnetic Fields) here. The Quai de Bourbon goes around the W tip of the island and ends at the Pont Saint-Louis. Finished in 1972, the bridge is closed to motor traffic and reserved for children. In the summer the island inhabitants stage several celebrations on this bridge.

Quai d'Orléans*

The very beautiful Hôtel Rolland* of 1639 is at nos. 18 and 20. No. 12 (fine balconies) was the birthplace of Félix Arvers (1806–50) whose name is still remembered because of the famous sonnet he wrote when inspired by Charles Nodier's daughter. Young Royer-Collard lived in the same house on the eve of the Revolution. Jean de la Ville de Mirmont, the 19th-c. Romantic poet, lived at no. 8.No. 6 was built in 1655 for Antoine Moreau, but has now been extensively restored. The Bibliothèque Polanaise* (Polish Library), founded in 1838, bought this building and was installed here in 1853. It is one of the largest specialized libraries in Paris. A few priceless items from its collections are exhibited on the first floor. A salon is entirely devoted to souvenirs of Chopin. The same building houses a museum founded in 1903, devoted to the poet Adam Mickiewicz (→ Museums).

Quai de Béthune*

Up to the Pont Sully.

Beyond the Pont de la Tournelle follow the Quai de Béthune. Because Louis Le Vau wanted all the houses on this side of the island to have balconies, the embankment was known in the 18th c. as the 'Quai des Balcons.'

No. 36 was built for President Violle in 1648, and was a meeting-place for the noble members of the Fronde. No. 34 was the home of Simon Huguet, head of the Audit Office; at the far end of the courtyard is a great wooden staircase with square banisters in the main building which, in the middle of the 18th c., belonged to Elizabeth de la Rochefoucault and her sister, Françoise de Biron. The house at no. 32 was built in 1642 by a master mason, the father of Louis Le Vau, for Philippe Gruyn. No. 30 was erected by Louis Le Vau and his father from 1640 to 1641, for Louis Potart. In the 18th c. the façade was decorated with emblems of musical instruments as a reminder of two previous tenants, one of whom was the composer Guy Cholet. At no. 28, the house built from 1640 to 1643 by Louis Le Vau's father was for Claude Aubert, Controller of Revenues for the Hôtel de Ville. The building was restored in 1770 by the president of the Audit Office, Pierre Perrot, who decorated the façade with three bas-reliefs representing Sculpture, Painting and Music. Louis Le Vau built no. 26 from 1639 to 1642 for Nicolas Sainctot, the King's majordomo. It was restored in the 19th c.

All that remains of the former Hotel Hesselin at no. 24, built by Le Vau in 1642, is the *porte-cochère* constructed by Etienne Le Hongre; it is in a style that was developed in the mid–17th c., with intricate designs inspired by the woodwork of the apartments: curving ornamental panels or cartouches, masks and garlands. The architect Louis Süe built the present building in 1935 for Helena Rubinstein, preserving the courtyard's semicircular wall backing onto the old garden facing the church. It is here that President Georges Pompidou died in April 1974.

The Hôtels Lefèvre de la Barre and Lefèvre de Malmaison at nos. 22 and 10 belonged to two brothers who bought the plots of land in 1643 and 1644 and had similar houses built on them. The two *portes-cochères* are very sober in design, and representative of the oldest and most common type on the island in which a string-course divides each leaf of the doors into two unequal panels. The decoration consists of small wood panels checked and fastened to the web of the door with round-headed nails. Each door is surmounted by a chimera with outspread wings. No. 22 was Baudelaire's first private home in 1842.

At nos. 18 and 16 is the Hôtel de Comans* or de Richelieu, after the field-marshal, who was its owner from 1729 to 1791. The date of construction of this *hôtel*, attributed to Louis Le Vau, is thought to be around 1647. At no. 18 the courtyard presents analogies with other Le Vau buildings, in the superimposition of Corinthian pilasters and composite pilasters on the rear façade, all resting on large bases, and the use of blind arcades. In the mid–17th c. there was no hesitation in using *trompe-l'oeil* painting to satisfy a keen taste for symmetry.

Rue de Bretonvilliers was cut through in 1642 by order of Claude Le Ragois, Seigneur of Bretonvilliers, principal tax collector. This street gave the financier access to the mansion that Jean Androvet du Cerceau had just built for him, on land situated at the very eastern tip of the island. There is nothing left of this house today.

> # Not to be missed

The Hôtel de Lauzun, one of the few Parisian 17th-c. mansions to have preserved all its rich interior decoration intact.

The Church of Saint-Louis-en-l'Ile, a rare example of Baroque religious architecture in Paris.

Many courtyards with admirable staircases in wood or wrought-iron (open Mon.-Fri. only): Rue Saint-Louis-en-l'Ile, no. 51 (courtyard, stairway); Quai d'Anjou, nos. 9, 13, 15, 37 (staircases), no. 17 (courtyard); Quai de Bourbon, no. 11 (staircase), nos. 13, 15 (courtyard, staircase); nos. 19-19 *bis* (courtyards); Quai de Béthune, nos. 18, 24 (courtyard).

> # Louis Le Vau

The island owes most of its architecture to Louis Le Vau. A speculator as much as an architect, he engaged extensively in land speculation. At the same time, he accepted a variety of commissions from landowners on the island, building up a private clientele of rich patrons, for whom he built such mansions as the Hôtel Hesselin and Hôtel Tambonneau (both early 1640s). He was also active in the Marais, where he designed, among others, the Hôtel d'Aumont. The *hôtel particulier* was not, however, the only type of building to which he turned his talents: He was also behind the construction of many châteaux, the most famous being that of Nicolas Fouquet, Superintendent of Finance, at Vaux-le-Vicomte (1643).

Appointed by Louis XIV as one of the royal architects, Le Vaux was commissioned in 1650 to renovate the Château de Vincennes; with the death of Lemercier in 1654, he became the King's chief architect and took charge of work on the Louvre, where he completed the Cour Carrée and began construction of the Pavillon de Flore. The last phase of his career was devoted to the construction of the Collège des Quatre-Nations (1661), now the Institut de France. At the same time, Louis XIV entrusted him with the renovation of the Château de Versailles. These two buildings are among the best examples of Le Vau's eclectic architectural style, which united elements of the curvilinear Italian Baroque with the severe grandeur of Colossal orders of Classical pillars (pillars rising through several storeys), as well as a decorative vocabulary derived from the tradition of Du Cerceau.

▷ Balconies and banisters

On the Ile Saint-Louis balconies and banisters illustrate the rise of an entirely new technique in Parisian houses during the 17th c. The transformation of the staircase, with its increasingly varied outlines, and the appearance of the first balconies in the early 17th c. gave Parisian ironsmiths little by little a new field of expression. Throughout Louis XIII's reign the projecting balcony, usually placed at the level of a building's *piano nobile* (main storey), had a stone balustrade. The same applied to the staircases, made of wood as well as stone, and whose banisters were cut around or square on the same model.

After Louis XIII's death these massive, heavy materials were replaced by wrought-iron, which lightened the façades and staircases. Ironsmiths then displayed tremendous virtuosity: interlacing, scrolls or twists of metal are gathered round a central motif for a balcony, while for a staircase they are repeated along the length of the handrail. For the first time luxurious craftsmanship in wrought-iron became commonplace and finally replaced both wood and stone in more modest houses.

▣ Museum to visit

Mickiewicz Museum (6 Quai D'Orleans): souvenirs from the Romantic period assembled by Polish poet Adam Mickiewicz.

▷ Wash-house on the Seine (*bateau-lavoir*)

When Christophe Marie undertook the development of the Ile Saint-Louis, Louis XIII granted him many privileges. One of the smallest of these was the ownership of a wash-house boat moored alongside the Quai Bourbon. It was a complex arrangement of three barges. The washerwomen, who were offered a 'washing site' for a consideration, would settle on benches arranged along the wicker shelters which were fitted with windows in winter. Each woman was provided with buckets of hot water to wash her laundry before rinsing it in the Seine. There were drying facilities on the roofs. The central barge was kept as the owner's apartment. In the second half of the 19th c. there were still about 20 such floating establishments along the Parisian embankments, though at the same time they were on the decline. The two main reasons for this were the nuisance they caused to the river traffic, and the appearance of the public wash-houses in the town. The Ile Saint-Louis wash-house was pulled down in 1942.

> The Ile Saint-Louis and Poland

After the Polish Insurrection of 1831 against the Russian occupation, the Ile Saint-Louis welcomed many Polish refugees. On the tip of the island Prince Adam Czartoryski, elected President of the Polish National Government in 1831, who was then condemned and became a refugee, acquired the Hôtel Lambert, where he created a fashionable circle for both Polish intellectuals and Polish high society. Frédéric Chopin was welcomed back to the privileged social circle he had known in his youth in the mansion's drawing-rooms, and became tutor to the Princess Marcelina.

During religious festivals, the *hôtel* was the setting for important ceremonies, and the magnificence of the Hôtel Lambert was much spoken of during the 'Bénits' (Easter festivities) organized by the prince. Princess Anna Czartoryska was equally influential and gave the immigrants much material assistance. She founded a Polish Ladies' Relief Committee and organized large charity bazaars. In 1845, she created the Polish Young Ladies' Institute, which aimed to teach to immigrants' daughters the language and literature of their native country. Finally, Adam Czartoryski set the seal on his cultural influence with the creation of the Polish Library in 1838.

The Saint-Marcel district

5th arr./Map ref. 23-B3
Métro: Gobelins
Bus: 27, 47, 83, 91
Parking: 4 Rue du Marchés-des-Patriarches, Gare d'Asterlitz
Taxis: 88 Boul. Saint-Marcel. Tel: 43-31-00-00.

Like the districts of Saint-Denis, Saint-Martin and Saint-Jacques, the name of Saint-Marcel is linked to a very old tradition of Parisian piety focused on a particular saint, in this case Marcellus, Archbishop of Paris, who was buried here in the middle of the 5th c. In the Middle Ages the wealthy bourgeoisie made their homes there, and until the 19th c. this peaceful *quartier*, guardian of centuries-old churches, still looked like a country village. Since the creation of the Boulevard Saint-Marcel and the Boulevard de l'Hôpital the district, which was built rapidly, has almost completely changed, although a few small back streets have kept the charm of this old countrified suburb, which once held a horse market on the banks of the Bièvre.

Today, due to the Faculté des Lettres in the Rue de Santeuil, the Ecole Supérieure de Chimie de Paris in the Rue Pirandello, the

Ecole Supérieure des Arts et Métiers in the Boulevard de l'Hôpital, but mostly to the largest University hospital group in France, La Pitié-Salpêtrière, this sector of the capital has revived the tradition of the student quarter comparable with that of the neighboring Latin Quarter, but without the tourists.

Tour of the district

1½ hrs.

Boulevard Saint-Marcel

From Ave. des Gobelins to Rue Scipion.

The laying of gas lines (1922–23) led to the discovery of 12 stone sarcophagi between nos. 73 and 83. Earlier work had also uncovered many other tombs in the area (over 500 from 1860 and 1873). Between the 3rd and 6th c., this was a large Christian burial ground, the most important one in the ancient city to judge by its size; it stretched from the Gobelins factory to the Rue du Petit-Moine and from the Rue Scipion to the Rue Pascal. It was close to three churches: Saint-Martin, Saint-Hippolyte, and the very old collegiate church of Saint-Marcel, situated somewhere near no. 79, named the *senior ecclesia* by Gregory of Tours. Rebuilt in the 11th c., it was demolished in 1806. Its memory lives on in the little Rue de la Collégiate: the present Church of Saint-Marcel is in the Boul. de l'Hôpital (→ see below). No. 75 is the Ecole Supérieure of the clothing industry, which comes under the jurisdiction of the chamber of commerce and industry.

Rue Le Brun starts on the r. It is a noble street both because of its name and because of the memory of the great collector and patron of the arts, Jean de Julienne, a friend of Watteau, who had a house at no. 20.

On the other side of the boulevard lies the Jardin des Plantes district.

Rue Scipion

This street took its name from the Italian Scipion Sardini, Comte de Chaumont, banker to Henri III and Catherine de' Medici. His father had been the bearer of the gonfalon (standard) of the Seigneurie of Lucques.

At no. 13, the Hôtel de Scipion Sardini was built in 1565 for Isabelle de Limeuil, who was notorious for her scandalous love life. It was the only example of Italian architecture at the time to mix stone and brick. In the same period the abbatial palace of the Saint-German-des-Prés was also built of stone and brick, but in a style that had less to do with the Renaissance than with the emerging Louis XIII style. The courtyard of the Hôtel Scipion is decorated with terracotta medallions. The gardens stretch as far as the Bièvre. From 1670 to 1974 the house was the bakery for Paris hospitals but now belongs to the hospitals' central pharmacy.

In the Square Scipion there is a large enamelled bas-relief.

Rue de Fer-à-Moulins (to the r.)

This street name is a corruption of Permoulin, owner of one of these plots, but between the 13th and 17th c. it was first called Rue Richebourg, because of the wealthy properties on either side of it; many rich people had settled on the banks of the Bièvre. In the 17th c. the street became the Rue des Morts (the Dead), then Rue de la Muette (the Dumb Woman), because of the neighboring cemetery for executed criminals.

Leave the Rue de la Clef, Rue de Santeuil and the Censier Faculty, to the l. (→ Jardin des Plantes district).

Rue Geoffroy-Saint-Hilaire

Between Rue du Fer-à-Moulin and Boul. Saint-Marcel.

The elegant *pavillon de police* still stands at no. 5, built in 1762 on the orders of the Chevalier Sartine, Lieutenant-General of the Paris police. On the opposite sidewalk there was the horse market which also sold pigs and dogs. Until Louis XVI's times, punishment of criminals by the *strappado* (a torture inflicted by hoisting the prisoner up to a height and then letting him fall to the end of the length of rope) was administered here.

For the remainder of the street, → Jardins des Plantes district. Take the Boul. Saint-Marcel on the l. At no. 35 is the group of buildings which form the private nursing home for the police. On the r. the Rue René-Panhard opens out and runs alongside the Institut de Paléontologie Humaine (Institute of Human Palaeontology), founded in 1912 by the generosity of Albert I of Monaco whose escutcheon adorns the main entrance. The institute is decorated with a sculptured frieze illustrating with considerable imagination the activities of early man, such as they were thought to be at the beginning of the 20th c.

Boulevard de l'Hôpital

From Boul. Saint-Marcel to the Salpêtrière.

Rejoin the boulevard via the Rue des Wallons. This broad thoroughfare, cut between 1760 and 1768, links the Place Valhubert, location of the Gare d'Austerlitz which dates from 1869, to the Place d'Italie. Almost in line with the Boul. Saint-Marcel, past the viaduct, and marking the end of the Pitié-Salpêtrière hospital complex, is the Square Marie-Curie with its statue of the alienist, Dr Pinel (1745–1826) to whom are credited improvements in the treatment of mental illness and the end of the custom of chaining the insane. The odd-numbered side of the boulevard is mostly taken up by the Pitié-Salpêtrière hospital complex.

☐ L'hôpital de la Salpêtrière**

Originally the Grand Arsénal, where powder was manufactured under Louis XIII (hence its name), this is now the largest hospital in Paris. It was intended by Louis XIV to become a 'general hospital for the homeless and the poor' (1654); a women's prison was added in 1694, not only for prostitutes but also for women whose fathers or husbands wanted to be rid of them. It was assigned to the care of the mentally ill in 1796 (alienists Pinel and Charcot were pioneers at this hospital). The architects Le Vau and Le Muet worked on it, but it is mostly linked to the name of Libéral Bruant. Standing in front of the huge main building it gives the same impression of severe grandeur as does the Invalides.

The Saint-Louis de la Salpêtrière* chapel, built on a Greek cross plan with an octagonal dome topped with a lantern-turret, was built by Libéral Bruant from 1657 to 1677. The slate roof and eight naves make an astonishing geometric composition. This chapel, where Bossuet and Bourdaloue preached, is curious for the arrangement of its interior (four naves separated by chapels and radiating from the high altar) meant to separate different categories of worshippers; it can accommodate 4000 people. Facing the chapel, the buildings on the l. date from the 17th c., those on the r. from the 18th c. These old buildings conjure up many historical and literary memories: Mme de Lamotte, for example, kept prisoner here following the affair of Marie-Antoinette's necklace, escaped, disguised as a man, in 1786.

Leave the chapel by the Cour Mazarin to reach the Pavillon de L'Enfant et de l'Adolescent (pediatric wards), which is opposite the central pharmacy. Completed in 1985 by the architects Vial, Costa and Bessirard, it is an excellent example of postmodern architecture. The garden façade, with its big arched bay and columns covered in white ceramic, does not look out of place opposite the work of Libéral Bruant. Inside is a panel painted by Hervé Télémaque. The Cour Saint-Vincent-de-Paul was one of the scenes of the September 1792 massacres, in which 45 women prisoners were murdered, though another 183 women were freed by the mob. The Bâtiment des Incurables (ward for the incurably ill), built by Viel, traditionally bears the name of Manon Lescaut whom the Abbé Prévost, in his famous novel, shows incarcerated in the Hôpital

Général to which Des Grieux comes to rescue her. Théroigne de Méricourt, said to have gone mad, was interned in La Salpêtrière, where she died in 1817. The library and the *cabinet de Charcot* (Charcot's study) have been preserved. The small building now used as a laundry is a remnant of the Louis XIII's arsenal. Behind stands the modern Pavillon Osiris which houses the surgical departments.

♁ The Church of Saint-Marcel

80 Boul. de l'Hôpital
Open Sun. Tel: 47–07–24–43

Leave the Salpêtrière and follow the Boul. de l'Hôpital toward the Place d'Italie.

In 1966 a sanctuary of highly contemporary conception with very simple lines was built (architect, D. Michelin) to replace the commonplace church built in 1856. The l. side, set back from the boulevard, is clad with roofing slates (as used in Savoy and Piedmont). The interior, with room for over 100 people, is vast and light and boasts a tapestry by Singier; the stained-glass windows are by Isabelle Rouault.

From here go along the Boul. de l'Hôpital to the Place d'Italie, or follow the Rue Jeanne d'Arc on the r., which offers a picturesque view of the Panthéon, and rejoin the Carrefour des Gobelins on the r. via the Boul. Saint-Marcel.

Boulevard de l'Hôpital

From Rue Jeanne d'Arc to the Place d'Italie.

At no. 151, the Ecole Nationale des Arts et Métiers (university level national engineering school) built by Roussi in 1912; an egg-shaped underground amphitheater, able to accommodate 1000 people, was added in 1960. At no. 165 is a big apartment building (cheap hygienic housing, as defined at the time), conceived in 1900 by the architect Sauvage; it has a concrete structure and a ceramic-tiled pavement.

▷ L'Hôpital de la Pitié

In 1612 Marie de' Medici had a refuge for beggars and homeless people built on the site of a tennis court (*jeu de paume*) near the Butte Copeau. To some this was a work of charity and in the interest of public sanitation; to others it was a repressive measure. The beggars were often forcibly brought here and indeed were referred to as *enfermés* (locked up). In 1656, on the advice of Bellièvre, speaker of the Paris Parlement, Louis XIV set up a large hospital organization, the Hôpital Général, which had several houses at its disposal, including the Salpêtrière and Bicêtre hospitals as well as the former Hôtel Scipion-Sardini. The Hôpital de la Pitié was attached to it and for a time became its administrative center. It was enlarged to take in abandoned children and orphans; the girls were placed in La Grande Pitié and the boys in La Petite Pitié. G. Cain wrote in his *Tableaux de Paris* that the bourgeoisie recruited the children they needed as servants from La Pitié and for funerals 'as officially appointed mourners at the rate of ten sous per child'. It was not until 1809 that La Pitié really became a medical care establishment, an annex of the Hôtel-Dieu (→ Ile de la Cité), then an independent hospital. It remained a hospital for the sick until its destruction (1912) and its replacement by the present Hôpital de la Pitié.

▷ **Markets**

Boulevard Vincent-Auriol, between the Rue Jenner and Rue Dunois: Wed. and Sat. 7am–1:30pm.

Boulevard de l'Hôpital, on the Place de la Salpêtrière: Tues. and Fri., 7am–1:30pm.

The Canal Saint-Martin district**

10th arr. Map ref. 12–D1
Métro: République
Bus: 70, 54, 56, 65, 75
Parking: 12 Rue Dieu
Taxis: 1 Ave. de la République. Tel:43–55–92–64

It is in the vicinity of the Place de la République that the Canal Saint-Martin, with its locks and iron footbridges, has remained at its most picturesque. A little further up, and somewhat in the background, stands the Hôpital Saint-Louis, one of the most remarkable Parisian examples of early 17th-c. architecture, in which Neo-Classical formulas already appear. Close by, the Hôtel du Nord still overlooks the canal bank, but the character of this poor industrial area is gradually changing.

The history of the Canal Saint-Martin

At the beginning of the 20th c., the approaches to the canal were occupied by factories and warehouses, and inhabited by a mainly working-class population, whose lively humor was immortalized on screen in the films of Marcel Carné. In 1963 the Canal Saint-Martin was threatened with extinction in favor of a new N-S highway crossing Paris to link the airports of Le Bourget and Orly. This was intended to carry traffic at the rate of 6000 vehicles per hour, in both directions. The abandonment of the project on December 15, 1971, marked the beginning of the renovation of the district and the development of the site.

Today a few workshops survive at the back of courtyards, but the big companies have moved out to the suburbs, leaving behind large empty spaces. These have been completely redeveloped as residential areas, thanks to coherent urban planning, that has made room for imaginative contemporary architecture. There is plenty here to satisfy the curiosity of students of pre-war Paris, industrial archeology, and contemporary architecture.

Tour of the district

1 hr.

Rue du Faubourg-du-Temple

Once a track leading to the village of Belleville, this is a working-class shopping street, still with picturesque fruit and vegetable sellers and their barrows. Where it crosses the canal two statues face one another across the street: on the r., *La Grisette*, erected in 1911, is a tribute to the working-class girls of easy virtue for whom the district was known; on the l. the bust of Frédérick Lemaître by Pierre Granet (1899), in memory of the popular actor of the 19th c. and his great performances in the boulevard theaters. At this point the street crosses the Canal Saint-Martin, which runs to the S beneath the Boul. Jules-Ferry.

The Canal Saint-Martin*

The Canal Saint-Martin, opened in 1825, is an extension of the Canal de l'Ourcq (→La Villette); with the Canal Saint-Denis it forms, to the N of the capital, a canal from one part of the Seine to another, saving barges 7 miles/12km of river travel. The length of the canal, between the Villette and Arsenal basins, is 2.8 miles/4.5km, with a drop of 82ft/25m via nine locks (numbered from upstream to downstream). The navigable width is 8ft/27m in the open part and 52-79ft/16-24m in the covered parts; the depth is 7.25ft/2.2m.

Originally the whole length of the canal was open, but the E part was covered over during the Second Empire, from 1861 onward, to provide the long Promenade de la Reine-Hortense, with its 17 squares, several of which survive. The justification for this was the need for a speedy crossing of the canal by the cavalry from the recently built Prince-Eugène barracks. The last section of the canal, the present Boul. Jules-Ferry, was also covered over in 1907.

Square Frédérick-Lemaître

This square offers a spectacular view over a lock basin (engineer, Freycinet). These are locks nos. 7 and 8, known as the Ecluses du Temple. The square, now renovated, has retained its oriental-style guard's kiosk and, at 36 Quai de Jemmapes, a curious chimney-street lamp, which comes originally from the Place de la Concorde. It now serves as an outlet for the smoke from the lockkeepers' quarters below. At the end of the square a footbridge, the Passerelle de la Douane, marks the beginning of the Bassin des Marais, a 1290ft/393m stretch of water, the banks of which have been cleared of parking areas to the benefit of fishermen and pedestrians. A number of companies, on either side of the basin, carry on the traditional activity of the district, the curing and selling of skins (64 and 72 Quai de Jemmapes and 51 Quay de Valmy). Follow the Quai de Jemmapes and take the Ave. Richerand to the r. towards the front of the Hôpital Saint-Louis, which can be seen from the quay.

☐ The Hôpital Saint-Louis*

Enter by the central pavilion in the Place du Docteur-Alfred-Pourinier, then cross the old quadrangle to the contemporary buildings.

Commissioned by Henri IV, the Hôpital Saint-Louis is one of the best examples of early 17th-c. Parisian architecture. Built in brick and stone from 1607 to 1611 by Claude Vellefaux, this is one of the first Neo-Classical designs, a large quadrilateral with central and corner pavilions. The decision to build it followed the plague epidemics at the end of the 16th c. A wide promenade runs around the main quadrilateral, separating it from the L-shaped buildings at the four corners of the promenade. One of these was reserved for the Augustinian nuns, another for the doctors, a third for a linen store and the fourth for paying patients, who enjoyed a private walkway. The buildings, registered as historical monuments, have been much restored. The gardens are now also being restored in their original form. The contemporary part, by the architects Badani and Roux Dorlut, show a care for harmony of composition and volumes, avoiding too large a disproportion relative to the old buildings. Erected in 1984, it is particularly noteworthy for its monumental entrance hall.

Return towards the Place du Docteur-Alfred-Fournier and make a detour to the r. to see the Chapelle Saint-Louis. Though in poor condition, the chapel can be visited (open Sun.–Fri. 2–5pm).

Quai de Jemmapes

From Ave. Richerand to Rue de la Grange-aux-Belles.

At no. 76, on the corner with the Ave. Richerand, is the Comptoir Général des Fontes, a marketing organization of the founding and casting industry, of which only the building and its imposing metal door remain as testimony of the importance of this industry in the 1930s. The Taillerie de Cristaux (Schweizer), at no. 84, perpetuates the tradition of the glass-cutting craft in the district. It is one of the few establishments of its kind in Paris, specializing in the restoration and repair of glass crystal. It retains its original equipment, dating from 1880, and functions today with three skilled craftsmen.

The Hôtel du Nord

102 Quai de Jemmapes

The surroundings of the fifth and sixth locks of the canal, known as the Ecluses des Récollets, are picturesque and romantic, and in particular contain the famous Hôtel du Nord. The son of the hotelkeepers, the writer Eugène Dabit (1898–1936) lived here during his youth. He was the author of the novel *Hôtel du Nord*, which was brought to the screen in 1938 by Marcel Carné, with Louis Jouvet and Arletty and is now considered a classic. The most celebrated scene, which brought the two actors together on the lock itself, was filmed not on the Canal Saint-Martin but in the Boulogne Studios, with Alexander Trauner's faithfully reproduced sets.

The *hôtel* was recently condemned for its state of dilapidation, but luckily the demolition permit was refused in 1983. It is now planned to conserve the façade and build new accommodation behind it, thereby preserving the image of the Hôtel du Nord as a landmark on the Parisian landscape. Nearby, at the corner of the Rue de la Grange-aux-Belles, two bistros add to the local atmosphere—the Café du Pont-Tournant and l'Ancre de la Marine. The second, at no. 96, is part of the building erected on the astonishingly narrow lot, which has a curious vertical roof.

Quai de Jemmapes, continued

As far as the Place du Colonel-Fabien.

Follow the canal to come to the curved Bassin des Récollets, 1400ft/ 430m in length.

To penetrate industrial Paris, make a small detour via the Rue de l'Hôpital-Saint-Louis and the Impasse Héron, where you will find a landscape of courtyards, warehouses and workshops characteristic of the early 20th c.

The former factory of the Compagnie Parisienne d'Air Comprimé (Paris Compressed Air Company) at no. 132 is a fine (and important) example of industrial architecture. For this imposing building, erected in 1903, Paul Friésé (a great architect of the 1900s) used contrasting materials: a metal framework, quarry stone and colored bricks. Note, on the side walls, the metal brick-filled buttresses and the steel St. Andrew's crosses. The factory has been converted into a printing works.

At the third and fourth locks (the Ecluses aux Morts) there is a group of dwellings, beginning at no. 148, which make up a whole new district, with a college, two nursery schools, a day-care center, swimming-pool, sports stadium and 1350 dwellings. This is the Zone d'Aménagement (development area) Jemmapes–Grange-aux-Belles. Built on about 14 acres/5.7ha, this development is noteworthy for its ochre and beige apartment buildings, the irregularity of its volume, its roofs and bow windows.

Place du Colonel-Fabien

Pétanque (bowls) players enliven the atmosphere of this vast square. The sinister Montfaucon gibbet (→ inset) once stood near here. The headquarters of the French Communist party (PCF) was built here from 1968 to 1971 by the architect Oscar Niemeyer. The façade of this S-shaped building is completely glazed, and 262ft/80m long and 66ft/20m high. Constants in the work of the architect recur here — an abundance of curves, the use of curtain walls in the façades and of V-shaped supporting pillars. The protruding sphere, in front of the façade, half-buried and in raw concrete, houses the Chamber of the Central Committee. From here, take the Ave. Mathurin-Moreau, which has become residential in recent years, and which leads directly to the Parc des Buttes-Chaumount.

▷ The road to Monfaucon

The name Montfaucon still has a sinister ring in the memory of Parisians. On an isolated hillock in the vicinity of the present-day 50 Rue de la Grange-aux-Belles, the gibbet of Monfaucon was erected in 1233, and served for almost four centuries to carry out executions ordained by royal justice. Of impressive size, it comprises 16 stone pillars arranged in a rectangle, linked to one another by two beams used as a gallows. Condemned prisoners were brought from the Châtelet to the gibbet along the Route de Meaux, an itinerary that can still be followed by taking the Rue Saint-Denis, Rue de Faubourg-Saint Denis, Rue des Récollets and finally the Rue de la Grange-aux-Belles. In 1627, at the request of the Hôpital Saint-

Louis, the gibbet was removed to the site of the present-day 46 Rue de Meaux for public health reasons. By then its value had become symbolic, and it was done away with in 1790.

The Financial Controllers to the King, Enguerrand de Marigny, Gérard de la Guette and the Baron de Sablancay, then Louis XI's favorite Olivier le Daim, were among the better-known of the victims of the gibbet, of which Villon wrote with such bitterness in his *Ballade des Perdus*.

The Saint-Sulpice district**

6th arr./Map ref. 16–C3, D2, D3
Métro: Saint-Sulpice, Mabillon
Bus: 58, 63, 70, 84, 86, 87, 89, 96
Parking: Place Saint-Sulpice, even numbers
Taxis: 1 Rue du Four. Tel: 43–29–00–00.

Superimposed during the 18th c. on an older street system, the Rue and the Place Saint-Sulpice are examples of projects undertaken but left unfinished in this period. All the houses surrounding the *place* were supposed to be constructed on the model of the one built by Servandoni at the corner of the Rue des Canettes. Standing before this house, it is easy to imagine what an extraordinary sight the *place* would have been, providing a harmonious frame for the sober façade of the Church of Saint-Sulpice.

Today it is one of the most elegant *places* in the capital. The interior decorators' boutiques, fashionable couturiers, bookshops and art galleries that give the Left Bank its atmosphere have progressively pushed out the shops selling religious items, the famous *saint-sulpiceries*. However, the charming, sleepy little back streets leading from the Luxembourg Gardens to the Place Saint-Sulpice have their air of provincial nobility.

⚓ The Church of Saint-Sulpice**

2 Rue Palatine. Tel: 46–33–21–75.
Open 7.30am–7pm

Saint-Sulpice, one of the largest and richest churches in Paris, bears witness to the changes of in architecture taste in the 18th c. Noble and majestic in its proportions and style, it is still one of the most frequented and lively parish churches in the capital.

The foundation of the church goes back at least to the 12th c., at which time it was run by the Abbey of Saint-Germain-des-Prés as a parish church for the abbey's peasant congregation. In the 17th c. the development of the area and its extension toward the W necessitated the construction of a new building. The first stone was laid in 1646; the master mason, Christophe Gamard, drew up the plans which were abandoned several years later in favor of those of Daniel Gittard. Work advanced slowly because of the cost and, in 1678, was halted after the choir alone had been built. Another forty years passed before work began again through the efforts of an active and tenacious priest, the curé Jean-Baptiste Languet de Gergy. The construction was carried out by Gilles-Marie Oppe-nordt, who scarcely altered Gittard's design except to add a tower above the transept crossing. This was demolished in 1731 because its weight threatened the vault. A competition was held in 1732 to select the design for the façade, in which Jean-Baptiste Servandoni was the winner. He built the majestic, two-storeyed colonnade to be seen today, as well as the towers which, after Servandoni's death in 1776, were completed by Oudot de Maclaurin. The N tower was built from 1778 to 1780 by Jean-François Chalgrin; the S tower has never been finished.

The exterior

The façade, which originally had a pediment, was destroyed by lightning in 1770, and today has an austere appearance, surprising for a work from the very middle of the 18th c. The porch is decorated with seven reliefs by the Slodtz brothers: the three theological Virtues, the four cardinal Virtues and, in medallions, the four Evangelists. The statues on the portals of the two transepts are by François Dumont (1725).

The nave

The vast interior is impressively tranquil and filled with light. The floor plan is based on the Latin cross; high arcades separate the nave from the side-aisles, which continue round the choir in a spacious ambulatory on to which opens the Chapel of Our Lady; the latter projects to the E and to the Rue Garancière. The great organ* by F. A. Clicquot (1781) has a monumental case designed by Chalgrin, decorated with carvings by Pierre-Joseph Duret showing King David and women holding musical instruments. The pulpit* (1788) was designed by Charles de Wailly. The pew for parish dignitaries dates from 1862; above is a fine *Christ on the Cross* by Hippolyte Maindron. The two enormous holy water fonts attached to the pillars on each side of the entrance are formed from two huge natural shells and were given by the Republic of Venice to François I; they rest on chunks of marble carved by J.-B. Pigalle who covered

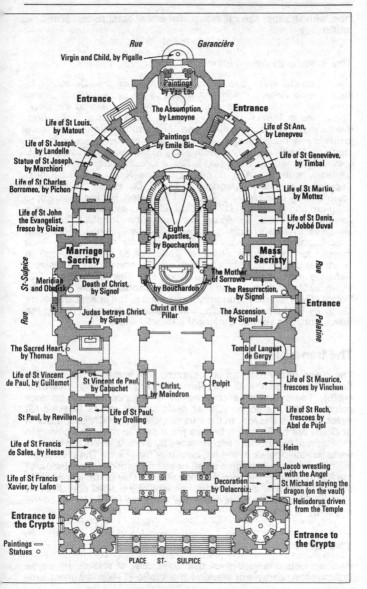

The Church of Saint-Sulpice

them with strange, naturalistic motifs: crabs, octopuses, corals and starfish.

The r. side-aisle

The 1st chapel is famous for its paintings by Eugène Delacroix: to the l., *Jacob Wrestling with the Angel*; to the r., *Heliodorus Driven From the Temple*; on the vault, *St Michael Vanquishing the Devil*. Completed in 1861, these works belong to the artist's final period; the daring of the composition and their strong colors make them justifiably famous masterpieces. A door at the r. leads to the mortuary chapel (usually closed; apply to the sacristan) under the S tower; designed by Chalgrin, it has a circular floor plan like the baptistry, with which it is paired, to the N. It contains *Christ Appearing to Mary Magdalene* by C.-G. Hallée (1705) and sculptures by L. P. Mouchy: Death of St Joseph, Resignation, Hope, Religion and Humility (1787). 2nd chapel: murals by François Joseph Heim (1845), *Religion Instructing the Christian Prayer for the Dead*; *Pietà with Angels* by Jean-Baptiste Clésinger (1868). 3rd chapel: paintings by Abel de Pujol, recently restored, *St Roch praying for the Plague Sufferers, Death of St Roch, St Roch in Glory*. 4th chapel: paintings by Auguste Vinchon (1821), *St Maurice Refusing the Sacrifice to False Gods* and *The Martyrdom of St Maurice*. 5th chapel: on the l., John the Baptist, marble by Simon Boizot (1785); on the r., funerary monument to the priest Languet de Gergy by Michelangelo Slodtz, which, though damaged during the Revolution, has kept its theatrical character intact.

The transept

The r. arm of the transept is decorated with immense paintings by Emile Signol: on the l., *The Resurrection* and r., *The Ascension* (1876). The transept is covered by a flat cupola framing four paintings by F. Lemoyne (*Christ, Melchizedek*) and C. G. Hallé (*St Peter, John the Baptist*). In the l. transept, *Arrest of Christ* and *Death of Christ* are by Signol. A bronze plate set into the stone paving in the S arm of the transept is connected by a bronze meridian line to a white marble obelisk at the NE corner of the N arm. The rays of the midday sun pass through a small opening pierced in the window of the S arm, striking the meridian line at a variable point according to the day of the year; these are the remains of a sundial completed in 1744 by Charles Langlois under the direction of Le Monier of the Academy of Sciences.

The choir

Backing onto the pillars of the choir are 10 statues by Edmé Bouchardon, partly the work of his studio (1740); the most outstanding are *Christ at the Pillar* and the *Mother of Sorrows* at the first pillars, to the l. and r. The present high altar has replaced that of the 18th c. designed by Oppenordt; the front of the altar in bronze gilt by Jean-Baptiste Debay shows *Jesus among the Doctors* (1829). The tabernacle and the altar furnishing have been removed to the marriage vestry. Some of the 18th-c. choir stalls come from Saint-Denis the remainder from the Abbey of Penthemont. The high windows are of 18th-c. stained glass, except the one representing the Sacred Heart (Charles Lameire; 1885).

The ambulatory

The stained-glass windows of the chapel were put in during the construction of the church. The sacristy is decorated with beautiful wood panels of liturgical vessels (early 18th c.). 1st chapel: paintings by Félix Jobbé Duval: *St Denis refusing to Sacrifice to Pagan Gods, St Denis and his Companions Led to Execution* (1859). 2nd chapel: frescoes by Victor Mottes: *St Martin Dividing his Cloak, St Martin Reviving a Catechumen* (1863). 3rd chapel: paintings by Charles Timbal, *St Geneviève during the Siege of Paris, The Miracle of the Fiery Furnace* (1864). 4th chapel: paintings by Jules Lenepveu, *Presentation of the Virgin in the Temple, Birth of the Virgin* (1864); over the door leading to the Rue Garancière, the *Assumption*, with its pendant, *Death of the Virgin*, by Emile Bin (1874).

The Chapel of the Assumption or the Germans' Chapel

The entrance opens into a passage where an elegant staircase leads to the roof. It was planned in the 18th c. and decorated with paintings, several of which still survive. On the ceiling, *Angels* by Noël Hallé who also painted *Christ and the Children* (1751); *The Flight into Egypt* by Jean-Baptiste Pierre (1751); there is also an *Annunciation* after Lemoyne and a *Deposition* most probably by Jean-Baptiste Decamps (late 18th c.); 18th-c. wood carvings.

The Chapel of Our Lady* owes its present appearance to the work of Charles de Wailly in 1774. It consisted originally of two orders of pillars surmounted by pilasters between which were large windows; the cupola, painted with frescoes by F. Lemoyne (1731–32) then had good natural light. The fire of the Saint-Germain fair in 1762 caused heavy damage to the chapel and the paintings, making restoration necessary. De Wailly added a false cupola under that painted by Lemoyne, which greatly diminished the light; the painting was restored in 1778 by Antoine Callet, who added below the painting of the curé *Languet de Gergy Surrounded by the Poor of his Parish*. Lemoyne's painting, famous in his time, has been restored several times during the 19th and 20th c. Nevertheless the skilful composition and elegant grouping of the figures still arouse admiration. The superb *Virgin** by Pigalle was set in place in 1774; it appears to spectacular effect in the niche lit by indirect light. It replaces a silver Virgin by Bouchardon destroyed during the Revolution. The lower part of the chapel is decorated with four canvases by Carle Van Loo (1746–51): from r. to l., *The Annunciation, The Visitation, The Presentation in the Temple* and *The Adoration of the Shepherds.* The bronze gilt bas-relief on the altar of *The Wedding at Cana* is by Michelangelo Stodtz.

6th chapel: the paintings are by Louis Matout: *St Louis dispensing Justice, St Louis Burying Plague Victims* (1870). 7th chapel: paintings by Charles Landelle, *Death of St Joseph, Dream of St Joseph* (1875). 8th chapel: paintings by Pierre-Auguste Pichon, *St Charles Borromeo at the bedside of Pope Pius IV* and *St Charles Borromeo and the Plague-stricken in Milan* (1867). 9th chapel: paintings by Auguste Glaize, the *Martyrdom of St John the Evangelist, St John teaching Brotherly Love* (1859). The marriage vestry (usually closed; apply to main vestry) contains, from r. to l., *The Marriage of the Virgin* by Antonio Pereda (1648), *Young Tobias and the Archangel Raphael* by Jean-Charles Renard, with its pendant on the other side of the window, *The Archangel Michael Vanquishing the Devil* (1827); *The Virgin Surrounded by Angels* (second half of the 18th c.) once in the Chapel of Our Lady; the stained-glass window representing the Marriage of the Virgin was made at Sèvres from a cartoon by Princes Marie d'Orléans.

The l. side-aisle

5th chapel: fine 18th-c. confessional; to the l., *The Establishment of Religion Among the Savages* by Jean-Simon Berthélemy (1785); at the far end, *The Sacred Heart* by Emile Thomas (1894). 4th chapel: much restored frescoes by Alexandre Guillemot (1824), *St Vincent de Paul and the Sisters of Charity, St Vincent de Paul at the Bedside of Louis XIII.* 3rd chapel, paintings by Michel Drolling (1850), *Conversion of St Paul, St Paul on the Areopagus.* 2nd chapel: paintings by Alexandre Hesse (1860), *St Francis de Sales preaching in the Valais, St Francis de Sales and St Jeanne de Chantal.* 1st chapel: painting by Emile Lafon (1959), *St Francis Xavier reviving a Dead Man, Translation of the Body of St Francis Xavier.*

A door in the wall at the l. leads to the baptistery (apply to the sacristan), work of Chalgrin, decorated with sculptures by Simon Boizot (1777–81): Baptism of Christ above the door and Grace, Innocence, Wisdom and Strength around the walls. The chapel contains several baptismal fonts; one from the 16th c., from Saint-Germain-l'Auxerrois, is ornamented with fine scrollwork.

Tour of the district

Place Saint-Sulpice

The architect Servandoni had planned to leave a harmonious and spacious square in front of the church, fine houses, of which only one was built, no. 6 at the corner of the Rue des Canettes. Houses and the seminary buildings piled up in front of the church and were only cleared away under the Empire. In the center is the Roman-style Fontaine des Quatres-Evêques (Fountain of the Four Bishops: Bossuet, Fénelon, Massiollon, Flechier), designed by Visconti. The last modification to the square has been the creation of an underground parking lot, with a pedestrian precinct in front of Saint-Sulpice, and the planting of new chestnut trees which, it is hoped, will eventually reach the height of those that were there previously. In June, the square is covered with the green-painted booths of a secondhand goods market that carries on the tradition of the Saint-Germain fair (→ Saint-Germain-des-Prés district). To the S, the Seminary of Saint-Sulpice, built by Godde (1820–40), where the religious historian Renan studied, was secularized in 1906; it is now under the direction of the Registry of the Ministry of Finance. The square is bordered on the W by the *mairie* (town hall) of the 6th arrondissement (1849). This houses the Library of Graphic Arts formed by the printer Edmond Morin (1859–1937), and left to the City of Paris on condition that it remained in the 6th arrondissement. The municipal library has been transferred to the former buildings of the Crédit Municipal at no. 78 Boul. Raspail. The festival room of the town hall was decorated by N. Levy and U. Bourgeois (1889).

Rue Saint-Sulpice

This is a busy and lively street full of shops selling religious objects. Many of the houses date back to the 18th c. (note the doors, ironwork, window ledges). At no. 27 note the fine portal of the Hôtel de Fougères and, from the courtyard, the view of the Hôtel de Brancas (6 Rue de Tournon → Odéon district). The façade on the N side of the church dominates the street with its majestic portal, placed picturesquely above a twisting flight of steps and the narrow pavement. The back of the apse is mounted on a squinch.

Rue Garancière

Our route takes you to the end of this street and back, alongside the apse of Saint-Sulpice. No. 8 is the Hôtel de Sourdéac*, later called Garancière. Built during the reign of Louis XIII, it has kept its admirable façade decorated with rams' heads and a fine flight of steps. It was one of its occupants, Françoise de Paris, wife of a

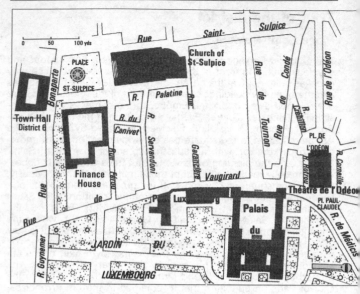

Saint-Sulpice district

president of parlement and an enthusiast for the theater, who discovered Adrienne Lecouvreur, who became a famous actress, and whose mother was a laundress in the Rue Servandoni. After having been the town hall of the 11th arrondissement (now the 6th), the *hôtel* has been since 1854 the office of the publishing firm Plon (now part of the Presses de la Cité group). Against its façade is a fountain, put there in 1715 by the Princess Palatine, wife of the Prince de Condé. Facing no. 10 is the little Hôtel de Nivernais, which communicates with the larger Hôtel de Nivernais (or Hôtel de Maréchal d'Ancre) on the Rue de Tournon. It once belonged to the family of the historian Thureau-Dangin. At no. 13 are the former outbuildings of the Hôtel d'Entragues. The end of the street is spanned by an arcade recently constructed by Christian Langlois, architect of the Senate. Take the Rue Palatine to the l., to see the S portal of Saint-Sulpice and the picturesque outbuildings near the apse; the Chapel of the Assumption, also called the Germans' Chapel, covered with a bulbous roof crowned with a pelican; there are charming windows in the upper part of the church. The street was created in 1846 and is named after the Princess Palatine, Anne-

Charlotte of Bavaria, widow of Henri-Jules de Bourbon, Prince de Condé.

Rue Servandoni

This quiet little street, lined mostly with old houses, is named after the Florentine architect of Saint-Sulpice, who died in 1766. There are several beautiful porches and some interesting houses (nos. 8, 9, 12, 14, 18, 23, 24). Condorcet, the philosopher, mathematician and politician, hid at no. 15 during the Revolution in 1793 and 1794, and it was there that he wrote his *Esquisse d'un tableau historique des progrès de l'esprit humain (Sketch for a Historical Picture of the Progress of the Human Mind)*. At no. 14, 18th-c. décor, with carved medallions and bas-reliefs; one of them is said to represent Servandoni, displaying his plans.

Take the short Rue de Canivet to the l. which dates from the 16th c. and contains several large townhouses of the period.

Rue Férou

No. 4 belonged at the time of its construction in 1750 to François Mahé de la Bouronnais, Governor General of the Ile de France and Ile de Bourbon. No. 6, which dates from the second half of the 18th c., was inhabited by the actress Mlle Luzy, whom Talleyrand visited while he was preparing his thesis at the Seminary of Saint-Sulpice. Note the two sphinxes above the entrance pillars and, over the first-floor windows, the bas reliefs attributed to Clodion.

Rue Vaugirard

Between Rue Servandoni and Rue Bonaparte.

At 2.7 miles/4.36km the longest street in the capital, it replaces the way which once led to the village of Val-Girard, later Vaugirard. On the odd-numbered side of this section, it borders the Luxembourg Gardens and the Senate buildings. No. 15, the Petit Luxembourg (→ Luxembourg Palace) is the residence of the president of the senate. No. 36 opposite served as the Princess Palatine's military household, built by Boffrand; and its fine portal remains, integrated into a recent unit of arcades (C. Langlois, architect). Here you may see the standard meter made of marble, fixed in 1799 at the request of the Department of Weights and Measures, to accustom the population to the metric system. At no. 19, the former Luxembourg Museum (→ the Luxembourg Palace). Opposite, at no. 48, the composer Massenet died in 1912. At no. 50 the parish priest of Saint-Sulpice lives in the house where the writer, Mme de La Fayette, lived from 1655 until her death in 1693.

Rue Bonaparte

Between Rue de Vaugirard and the Place Saint-Sulpice.

This stretch of the street does not have the charm of the section that forms part of Saint-Germain-des-Prés because it has been disfigured by new buildings. However, it has retained the magnificent 18th-c. Hôtel de Polignac (nos. 88–90), which belonged for some time to Cardinal de Polignac, an important personage during the end of Louis XIV's reign and the Regency. It was also occupied by the priest Henri Grégoire who, at the forming of the Convention, defended black and Jewish people and contributed to the formation of the Conservatoire of Arts and Crafts. No. 90 has a beautiful staircase and, at no. 88, the entrance should be noted. The Allée de Séminaire (r.) was laid down in 1936 over the site of the former Maison des Messieurs de Saint-Sulpice and is terraced down to the Rue Bonaparte. Here you may see the Fountain of Peace, one of the 15 fountains commissioned by Napoléon; bas-reliefs by Espercieux. This fountain was formerly in the Saint-Germain market (→ Saint-Germain district).

▷ The street names of Paris

It was only in 1729 that a royal decree required that street names should be shown. Together with the number of the *quartier* they had to be heavily engraved in hard stone and set into the wall of the first and last houses on every street. During the Revolution stonemasons were contracted to obliterate or conceal all references to royalty, nobility and superstition. When old façades are restored today, these uncovered inscriptions are left exposed beside the modern enamelled name plates. There are many examples of this in the old districts of the city. The names given to the streets stemmed originally from the names of buildings, shop signs, or corporations. Then, from the 17th c. on, certain streets took the names of princes, nobles and other notables. The First and Second Empires celebrated their victories by baptising the often new streets with the names of the battles involved but in the 19th c. streets named after famous people proliferated. The tendency to replace a traditional appellation with a name taken from a biographical dictionary resulted in the loss of many of the names and the folklore of the old Parisian neigborhoods.

For more information, consult *La Nomenclature des voies publiques et privées* (Nomenclature of Public and Private Streets); published by the City of Paris 8th edition, 1972, which gives the civil status of Parisian roadways, their measurements, the history and origin of the names and the dates of the by-laws concerning them.

The Sentier district*

2nd arr. Map ref. 11–A2, B2
Métro: Bourse Sentier
Bus: 20, 29, 39, 48, 67, 74, 85
Parking: Place de la Bourse

The district of Le Sentier is to the rag trade what the Place Vendôme is to fine jewelry. Here, however, there is no precise boundary defining the neighborhood. In the area loosely bounded by the Boulevard Poissonnière and Boulevard Bonne-Nouvelle (to the N), Rue Montmartre (to the W), Rue Réaumur (to the S) and the Boulevard Sébastopol (to the E), the maze of narrow streets, choked with traffic and milling crowds, indicate that you have arrived.

Le Sentier is a world of its own, where fortunes are made and lost with the seasonal changes of fashion. There is nothing of particular significance to see; there are no public monuments, and the façades of the few beautiful 18th-c. buildings are more often than not covered by advertisements. The cosmopolitan crowd that brings it to life — people with their arms filled with bales of cloth, or delivering clothes on hangers and racks — seem unaware of those who do not belong on their own strange planet. The simply curious, neither buying nor working, should let themselves be caught up in the mid-week chaos of this unique area and lose themselves in the labyrinth of its streets. This is the way to discover this tiny part of Paris, which is in many respects closed to the uninitiated.

History of the district

The name may come from the word *sentier* (path), referring to the path leading to the nearby ramparts, or maybe a distortion of the word *chantier* (building site). Until the beginning of the 19th c., Le Sentier was a green area, with open countryside lying immediately beyond a series of enclosing walls.

With gradual urbanization, from the 14th to the end of the 19th c., this suburb was progressively integrated into the centre of Paris, until it was absorbed completely, and its boundary walls gave way to boulevards. The construction of the perimeter wall of Charles V in 1350 determined the face of the district until it was demolished at the beginning of the 17th c. A new wall was built by Louis XIII, followed by yet another, built by Louis XIV. The radical transformation of the district was initially the work of the Revolution, which plundered, then nationalized and sold the churches and their extensive lands, long before Haussmann carved out the Rue Réaumur and the Boulevard Sébastopol, and finally determined the layout of the neighborhood's streets.

Le Sentier took on its present appearance at the end of the 19th c: a neighborhood devoted to the rag trade on the Bonne-Nouvelle side, and to the press and printing on the Montmartre side.

Tour of the district

1 hr.

Rue de Mail

This street was laid out in 1636 on the site of a playing field for the *jeu de mail* (a game, called pall-mall in English, played with a ball and a flexible mallet or *mail*) that lay along Charles V's old ramparts. The whole *quartier*, today's Sentier, was once named after the street. At no. 5, the Hôtel de Colbert, built by François Le Tellier (1650), a faun's mask framed by two cornucopias is carved above the door. No. 7, another mansion, was built in 1669 by the architect Thomas Gobert for himself, shortly before the nearby Place des Victoires. Note the arcades of windows on the ground floor and the Colossal order of pillars (two storeys high) with composite capitals.

Rue Montmartre

This street has borne its present name since 1200, when it was the route from Paris to the Abbey of Montmartre. Originally it went all the way to the Porte de Montmartre in the perimeter wall of Philippe Auguste (no. 30), but, in the course of time, the gates were pushed back toward the N. No. 82, at the intersection with the Rue d'Aboukir, is the site of the Montmartre gates of Charles V's wall, and at no. 156, the gates to the wall of Louis XIII. No. 112 is the *hôtel* where the young Mistral arrived from his native Provence one day in 1859, the manuscript of *Mireille* under his arm. A plaque to celebrate his centenary was put up in 1959. No. 136 is an attractive Restoration house decorated with statues and niches. No. 142, constructed in 1883, has allegorical sculptures by L. Lefèvre. No. 144 is by Ferdinand Bal (1882), on the site of the Saint-Joseph cemetery, where Molière was buried. The decoration of the façade is entirely comprised of motifs of the printing industry, and specifically the Presse d'Emile de Girardin. Various newspapers were produced here until 1914. At no. 146 is the café 'A la Chope du croissant', which was a haunt of journalists, editors and typographers of the great Parisian press of the 19th c. On July 31, 1914 Jean Jaurès, the socialist leader who founded the newspaper *L'Humanité*, was assassinated (see the inscription). Inside there is a table dating from the time of the assassination, a bust of Jaurès and a display case with mementoes and newspaper cuttings.

In the 17th c., between the Rue Montmartre and Rue Poissonnière, behind Louis XIII's new wall, stretched a previously little-known and infamous neighborhood that was just beginning to be developed. Many new streets were opened perpendicular to the Rue Montmartre: the Rue des Jeûneurs or des Jeux-Neuf, so called because *boules* (bowls) was played there; the Rue du Croissant, named after a local inn; and the Rue du Temps Perdu, which became Rue Saint-Joseph. Emile Zola was born at no. 10 in 1840. Take any one of these streets to reach the Rue du Sentier.

Rue du Sentier

No. 33 was the *hôtel* where Jeanne Poisson lived in 1741; she was to become the Marquise de Pompadour soon after her marriage to Le Normant d'Etioles. She was presented at court under the name and title of Madame la Marquise de Pompadour and, in the same year, suceeded the Duchesse de Châteauroux as the royal favorite of Louis XV. At no. 32 is an 18th-c. *hôtel*, redecorated in the 19th c. At nos. 22 and 24 is a 17th-c. *hôtel* lived in by the unfortunate Le Normant d'Etioles from 1745 until he was separated from his wife. At no. 8, Mme Vigée-Lebrun held her salon, famous among artists and writers at the end of the 18th c.

Rue de Cléry

The future Marquise de Pompadour was born in 1721 in the Rue de Cléry in the house next to no. 29. This street, the extension of the Rue du Mail, was created on the site of the path surrounding Charles V's wall just after it had been demolished. Its name comes from the Hôtel de Cléry which, in the 16th c., stretched as far as the moat of the court. From the second half of the 17th c. many writers and artists moved into houses in this street. Having left Rouen, Corneille lived here from 1665 to 1685, writing many of his works. The two houses that stand at nos. 19 and 21 today (only no. 19 is old) were, at the end of the 17th c., the property of Robert Poquelin, a brother of Molière, and a priest and doctor at the Sorbonne. In 1775 the house was rented to an art dealer, Jean-Baptiste Lebrun. The following year, he married the daughter of the painter Vigier, and in 1778 built a gallery for those young painters who exhibited outside the official salons, which also served as his sales room. Lebrun also built the house where Mme Vigée-Lebrun held her salon. The elegant inscription at no. 97 is wrong: the poet André Chenier never actually lived here, but in a house that was torn down when the Rue Réaumur was built.

Rue Beauregard

Dating from the early 16th c., this street, which crosses the top of the Butte aux Gravois, originally lay outside Charles V's ramparts. The street offers a panoramic view, hence the name; beautiful view. The area between the Rue Beauregard and Rue Poissonnière was called Villeneuve-en-Gravois. This district was built on a hill formed by enormous piles of refuse, mud and rubble that had been heaped up since the 10th. c. In the 17th c. a tax exemption was granted to shopkeepers and artisans, to encourage people to settle in this area, renamed Bonne-Nouvelle, after the local church. At the corner of the Rue Beauregard and Rue des Degrés (the shortest street in Paris, consisting entirely of a flight of steps), the Baron de Batz, with a handful of conspirators, tried to save Louis XVI on the morning of January 21, 1793.

Rue de la Lune

This street follows the line of the ramparts of Louis XIII's wall. The obtuse angle made by this street at the intersection with the Rue Notre-Dame-de-Bonne-Ville indicates the position of the old bastion.

🛎 The Church of Notre-Dame-de-Bonne-Nouvelle

25 Rue de la Lune. Closed noon–4pm. Tel: 42-33-65-74

The original church built on this site (1628–52) was demolished in 1797; all that was left was the steeple. A plaque, inside, to the l. of the choir, records that the first stone was laid by Anne of Austria. The present building was constructed between 1823 and 1830 by Hippolyte Godde. The barrel-vaulted nave is lined with columns with a continuous entablature like that at Saint-Philippe-du-Roule. The Chapel of Our Lady is not, as is usual, in line with the nave, but opens off the l. side-aisle. Without ostentation, the architecture impresses by the clarity and simplicity of its volumes.

Inside, among the numerous paintings adorning the church, note, in the 1st chapel to the r., *St. Geneviève Giving Food to the People of Paris* by Victor Schnetz, (1824); in the 3rd chapel: *St Peter of Alcántara* by Brother Luc (mid–17th c.). At the end of the r. side-aisle in the former sacristy, a small treasury is laid out (ask at the main vestry, last chapel on the l.), containing ornaments used by the Abbé Edgeworth de Firmont when he celebrated the last Mass for Louis XVI. The choir is decorated with paintings framed inside the paneling; in the center, *The Annunciation* by Giovanni Lanfranco (first half of the 17th c.); to the r., *Pope Sixtus IV Surrounded by Saints* by Ludovico Cardi, known as Cigoli (1610). To the far r., *St Isabelle of France* by Philippe de Champaigne (mid–17th c.). The Chapel of Our Lady is decorated with paintings by Auguste Hesse

(1840): *Annunciation, Nativity, Prophets and Saints*. In the 3rd chapel to the l., *Presentation of the Virgin in the Temple* by Nicolas Mignard (mid–17th c.). In the 2nd chapel, *St Louis Nursing Plague Victims* (anonymous, mid 17th c.)

Rue du Caire district

Situated on the other side of the Rue du Cléry, this *quartier* was created upon the return of Napoléon from his Egyptian campaign. The enterprise was cut short: the successes of Alexandria and of the Pyramids (July 1798) were followed by the naval defeat by Nelson at Aboukir (August 1799). The survival of the expedition, assured by the victory over the Turks at Aboukir (July 1799), enabled Bonaparte to return to France with a semblance of glory. Greatly impressed by the remains of the pharaonic civilization, Napoléon left his mark on the new district of the Rue de Caire with memorials commemorating his few victories and his nostalgia for Egypt.

The Rue d'Aboukir, which is built on the site of the moat and ramparts of Charles V's ramparts, took its name in 1807 from Napoléon's victory in Egypt.

At no. 1 (and nos. 2 and 4 Rue Vide-Gousset) is a *hôtel* built in 1634 for the banker Nicolas Rambouillet. The Rue du Caire (Cairo) was made in 1799, on the site of the convent of the Filles-Dieu. The Rue du Nil (the Nile) and Rue Damiette were opened in 1800 on the site of the former Cour des Miracles, which backed onto Charles V's ramparts. All three streets end in the Place du Caire, noteworthy for the façade of no. 2, built in 1799 and decorated with Egyptian motifs: sphinxes, a frieze with ancient Egyptian figures, lotuses and hieroglyphics.

The Passage du Caire dates from the same time. Like the Great Bazaar in Cairo, it has three covered shopping arcades (Sainte-Foy, Saint-Denis and du Caire), with Egyptian-style pilasters decorating the boutiques. Occupied originally by lithographers and printers the *passage* now has only one such workshop left, the main activity today being the ready-to-wear clothing industry.

▷ The fabric of the Church

Until December 19, 1905, the date when the church and State were separated by law, the administration of the temporal interests of parish churches was entrusted to the fabric, whose administrators were called *marguillers* (churchwardens). The Revolution, however, weakened their independence and put them under the control of the Cour des Comptes (audit office).

In addition to ordinary administrative tasks (overseeing the concessions for chapels, crypts, the renting of pews, galleries,etc.), the churchwardens had to maintain the churches and undertake renovation projects, essentially in the communal areas (the nave and choir). To the necessary work of construction and furnishing was added, less often, the commissioning of decorative works—stained glass, sculptures, tapestries, paintings. The fabric contributed widely to the embellishment of Parisian churches with commissions inspired by the devotion of private individuals or by religious orders and guilds of tradesmen. By choosing the artists, granting the commissions and supervising the execution of the works, the churchwardens were themselves, in effect, patrons of art.

☐ The Sorbonne**

5th arr./Map ref. 23–A1
Metro: Saint Michel, Odeon, Maubert-Mutualite
Bus: 21, 27, 38, 47, 63, 85, 86, 87
Parking: Rue Soufflot and opposite 37 Boul. Saint-Germain
Taxis: Place Maubert. Tel: 46–34–10–32.

The Sorbonne occupies a vast area bounded by the Rue des Ecoles, Rue Victor-Cousin and its continuation, the Rue de la Sorbonne, and Rue Cujas and Rue Saint-Jacques. Until recently it was the center for the Faculties of Literature and Sciences as well as the Ecole des Chartes. Today, in addition to the Ecole des Chartes, it accommodates the Université de Paris–IV and III (→Literature, French Civilization and the Humanities). The Gothic buildings of the Sorbonne were sumptuously rebuilt by the architect Le Mercier in 1629 at Richelieu's expense. But these buildings, which in their turn became too old and small, were rebuilt at the end of the last century in a severe, austere style by Nénot (1885–1900).

History of the Sorbonne

Robert de Sorbon, who came from Rethel in the Ardennes and was confessor to Louis IX (later St Louis) obtained from his master the use of a house in the Rue Coupe-Gueule (today Rue de la Sorbonne) and of the two neighboring houses, in order to found (1253) the College de Sorbon, which was to offer food and lodgings to 'poor teachers and students' who wished to study theology. The Sorbonne remained the seat of the Theological Faculty of the University of Paris until the Revolution. Throughout the centuries it has played an important political rôle; behind its walls the prelates of the Sorbonne formed, in the words of one of them, the permanent

Council of the Gauls and ruled the western church, debating the great questions that troubled the Pope or the King. During the Hundred Years War, the University, siding with the Burgundians, recognized Henry V of England as King of France and was the unrelenting adversary of Joan of Arc. Peace returned and the rector Olaus Magnus, a Finn, was chosen to take charge of matters at the Court of France. It was in the Sorbonne too, that in the '*librairie*' (the present 58 Rue Saint-Jacques) Guillaume Fichet, priest and then rector (director of education), installed three printers whom he had brought over from Mainz on Louis XI's orders, thus founding the first printing house in France. By 1472, they had already printed 30 works.

Over the centuries, the Sorbonne was virtually a state within the state. But during the dark days of the German occupation it was from the beginning an active headquarters of the Resistance, for which it paid heavily.

Tour of the Sorbonne

Entrances: 47 Rue des Ecoles, or Place de la Sorbonne
20 mins.

You may tour the courtyard and galleries freely, but you will require a pass (available from the Secrétariat de l'Académie) to visit the Grand Amphitéâtre (great lecture theater) and the main staircase. The Chapelle de la Sorbonne and the entrance on the Place de la Sorbonne are open to visitors only during temporary exhibitions; since the hours vary, consult newspaper or magazine listings.

The façade on the Rue des Ecoles is decorated with allegorical statues by Chapin and Mercie; behind it is a monumental vestibule with seated statues of Homer and Archimedes. From this vestibule stretched two parallel galleries that surround the great lecture theater, preceded by a spectacular staircase. The interior of the Sorbonne is decorated with important allegorical and historical murals.

The Grand Amphithéâtre

It is in the lecture hall, which seats 2700, that the university's great ceremonies take place. At the back is a huge allegorical mural, *Le Bois Sacré* (The Sacred Wood) by Puvis de Chavannes, the most important painting in the whole building. It shows, in the center, La Sorbonne, seated, Eloquence and Poetry standing; to the l., Philosophy and History; to the r., Science, Geology, Physiology, Physics and Geometry.

Cour d'honneur (The main courtyard)

From the vestibule the Galerie des Lettres, on the r., (in the entrance, a wall map of the Sorbonne) leads directly to the main courtyard, which occupies the same site as that of the early Sorbonne. In the square or *parvis* are statues of Victor Hugo and Pasteur by Hughes and Marqueste. This courtyard, which is entered from the Rue de la Sorbonne to the W (no. 17), is bordered to the E by the library building; and to the N by a gallery with seven arches, decorated with a huge two-panel composition by Weerts, showing the traditional Lendit Fair held at Saint-Denis in the 15th-c., and once a great university occasion. Above the gallery is an ancient sundial, restored, which comes originally from Le Mercier's building.

The University Library (first floor)

The library is decorated with various painting by Dubufe, J.-P. Laurens, and Baschet; the plaque on display is from the Old Sorbonne (1627). The library holds more than two million works. Below is the Richelieu Amphitheater, which holds nearly 2,000 people, and is used for certain official ceremonies.

✝ The Sorbonne Chapel*

The only surviving monument of Richelieu's Sorbonne, this chapel was built on the opulent Jesuit style from 1635 to 1642 by Le Mercier. Having worked in Rome, he was inspired by the Gesù and St Peter's, though his Sorbonne building is more elegant and narrow than these. The dome (1641–44) flanked by four bell-towers, was the fifth attempt at such a construction in Paris. On the side of the Place de la Sorbonne, the façade consists of two (instead of three) superposed orders: a Corinthian with engaged columns (with 19th c. statues) and a composite order. On the side of the main courtyard broad steps lead up to the façade, in front of which 10 freestanding columns support a pediment.

The interior

The chapel is rectangular (length 138ft/42m; width 79ft/24.5m; height 167ft/51m). The choir and the nave with three bays are of equal length. The side chapels of the nave and the choir do not communicate with one another. At the transept crossing the cupola, on pendentives, consists of a drum with eight windows separated by Corinthian pilasters. The pendentives were painted by Philippe de Champaigne and are decorated with Richelieu's arms, angels, and the Four Fathers of the Church. The floor of the choir is higher than that of the nave. The apse is vaulted with half domes.

The white marble tomb of Richelieu* was magnificently carved by Girardon (1694), and designed by Le Brun. When the chapel became the Temple of Reason in 1794, and the tomb and 27 caskets of the Richelieu family were violated, the cardinal's tomb was moved for protection to the Musée des Monuments Français. It was finally returned to its original home on December 4 1971. The death mask of the cardinal, stolen in 1794, is now set in the base of the monument. A religious service is traditionally celebrated on the anniversary of the cardinal's death (December 4 1642). Near the entrance, to the r., is the tomb of the Duc de Richelieu, minister to Louis XVIII.

In 1947, in the crypt, were laid the bodies of 12 faculty members, martyrs of the Resistance, and in 1952, an urn containing the ashes of four of the five students from the Lycée Buffon, shot by the Germans on February 8 1942. Leaving the courtyard of the Sorbonne to admire the façade of the chapel, you pass in front of the l'Ecole des Chartes.

The Ecole des Chartes

Founded by Louis XVIII on February 22, 1821, the Ecole des Chartes is responsible primarily for the teaching of history, but more specifically for the secondary sciences of history (paleography, Roman philology, archivism, bibliography, diplomatic history, sources of French history, legal history, archeology, etc.), and also for the recruitment of curators and librarians.

The Ternes district

17th arr.
Métro: Ternes
Bus: 30, 31, 43, 83, 92
Parking: FNAC, 22 Ave. de Wagram; Ave. des Ternes
Taxis: 272 Rue du Faubourg-Saint-Honoré. Tel. 47-63-00-00.
Markets: Rue Lebon, Rue Faraday, and Rue Torricelli, daily 8am-1pm/4-7.30pm; Sun. 8am-1pm.

Long before it became the quartier des Ternes, the district was for centuries the site of the country estate of the bishops of Paris, the Villa Externa (later corrupted to 'Ternes'), as opposed to the Villa Episcope or Ville l'Evêque, the bishops' urban estate. The villa lay amid fields and woods— the last vestiges of the once vast Rouvray forest—and the area remained essentially rural until the mid-19th c.

The nearby hamlet which had a mere 20 homes in the middle of the 18th c. and which became the village of Ternes, was first a dependency of the Abbey of Saint-Denis, then of the Abbey of Neuilly. It was incorporated into Paris in 1860 and immediately became the object of intense real estate speculation—especially when the circle-line railway was put through—as happened in the Monceau *quartier*. It was immediately inhabited by the secure and wealthy Parisian bourgeoisie. Several fine buildings by Haussmann can be seen, such as the one whose wonderful façade curves round the NW side of the Place des Ternes.

The avenue itself has kept the general appearance and liveliness that it had at the beginning of the 20th c. when the Magasins Réunis building, now a branch of Printemps, was built on the corner of the Avenue Niel. Here and there along this former road to Saint-

Germain pleasant streets can still be found, such as the Rue Poncelet and Rue Bayen with their markets, or the Rue Saint-Ferdinand with its charming little square.

Radiating out from the Place de l'Etoile, the airy and tree-lined Avenue Carnot and Avenue Mac-Mahon are quiet and rather dull, while the Avenue des Wagram and the Avenue de la Grande-Armée, the latter specializing in shops selling cycles and motor parts, are much more lively.

Tour of the district

1 hr.

Place des Ternes

This is a large intersection built on the site of the former rampart-walk round the Roule fortifications. The typically Art Nouveau entrance to the Métro, was designed by the architect Guimard. The center of the square bustles with one of the three Parisian flower markets (open Tues.–Sat. 8am–5.30pm).

Avenue des Ternes

The old route to Saint-Germain, this wide avenue, both commercial and residential is attractive for its many restaurants, some of which are very famous.

On the r., going toward the Place de la Porte des Ternes, is the Rue Poncelet, permanently filled with the activity of a picturesque open market. Then comes the former Magasins Réunis building, which recently became Printemps, with its interesting architecture in cast concrete, its dome and shop windows. It was built in 1912 by Oudin. The avenue then crosses the little Place Tristan-Bernard with a bust of this novelist and dramatist (1866–1947) outside nos. 63–65.

⚲ The Church of Saint-Ferdinand-des-Ternes

27 Rue d'Armaille.
Tel. 45-74-00-32.
Closed from noon to 3pm.

This church has replaced a building constructed in 1847, which in turn replaced the barn in which Mass was celebrated for the inhabitants of the hamlet of Ternes. The present church was itself reconstructed in 1937 in the Romano-Byzantine style.

The *église basse* (lower church), dedicated to St Teresa of the Infant

Jesus, decorated with a fresco by M. Zarraga, was consecrated in January 1941. The transept and the chancel of the *église haute* (upper church), opened for worship in 1944, are decorated with an important collection of frescoes: in the apse, *The Eucharist* by Pierre Dionisi; at the ends of the transept, the six other sacraments by H. Bezombes (on the r.) and P. Peugniez (on the l.); in the chancel, *The Resurrection* and *The Ascension* by Bouchaud. The frescoes in the four chapels giving onto the transept are by Delplanque (*Coronation of the Virgin*), by Mme Sornas (*Presentation of the Virgin in the Temple*), Guy-Loë (the *Curé d'Ars*), (St John Vianney and André Tondu (*Life of St Joseph*). The communion table was hewn *in situ* by Muguet. The wrought ironwork is by Poillerat, the stained-glass windows by Labouret.

The Rue Saint-Ferdinand leads to the square of the same name, which has a monument by Jean Boucher in honor of Léon Serpollet (1858–1907); this work, of great interest today, keeps alive the memory of this inventor of a precursor of the automobile, the first to attain the speed of 75mph/120kph in his steam-driven vehicle. Retrace your steps as far as the Place Tristan-Bernard.

Rue Pierre-Demours

The construction of the circle-line railway robbed this street of its cold sulfurous, ferruginous spring, which was considered to be one of the richest in France. At nos. 17 and 19 is the portal of the former Château des Ternes, built in 1740 on the site of the country residence of the bishops of Paris. The château, which had several different owners, was mutilated when the Rue Bayen was cut through the ground floor of the existing pavilion, which now forms an arcade. In front of it is a garden also cut in two by the Rue Bayen. Return to the Ave. des Ternes. On the other side of the Boul. Pereire at 96 Ave. des Ternes, the Ave. de Versy opens up, leading into the Villa des Ternes. It was here, in houses surrounded by greenery, that Rochegrosse, Chocarne-Moreau, Steinlen, Lotiron, and Luc-Albert Moreau worked. The Rue Aumont-Thieville is lined with artists' studios built at the beginning of the 20th c. Take the Rue Bayen.

The Boulevard Pereire

Opened in 1853 between the Porte Maillot and the Cardinet, bridge, the boulevard was formerly divided down its entire length by the railway cutting for the Pont Cardinet – Auteuil line. A section of this line is now in service again for the SNCF link from Vallée de Montmorency to Invalides, though the trench has been covered over between the Rue Alfred Roll and the Porte Maillot. The area has been partially landscaped and neighborhood amenities have been built (crèche, eating area, tennis courts, car park). The first sectors to be redesigned with gardens, between the Place du Maréchal Juin and the Rue Bayen, were opened early in 1989. On either side of the boulevard are a number of small town houses built by artists and actors at the beginning of this century. Sarah Bernhardt (d. 1923) lived at no. 56; no. 98 belonged to the lawyer and French Academician Henri-Robert (1863–1936) of the Académie Française. ▶ The Place du Maréchal-Juin has a little garden with a monument to the painter Albert Besnard (1849–1934). ▶ Continue by the Avenue de Villiers.

Avenue de Wagram

This avenue has two different faces: Between the Place de Brésil and the Place des Ternes it is quiet and elegant; farther on, up to the Place de l'Etoile, cafés and bars make it noisy and lively, especially at night. The Théâtre-Cinerama Empire is at no. 41, and no. 39 is the Salle Wagram (Wagram Hall) in the Neo-Classical style (entrance at 5 *bis*) Rue de Montenotte. Both belong to the Institut de France. At no. 43, the Céramic Hôtel is a typical example of Art Nouveau architecture (architect, J. Lavirotte) with a façade by Bigot completely covered in sandstone (1904). Next is the Place Charles-de-Gaulle (→ Arc de Triomphe). The Ave. Mac-Mahon and the Ave. Carnot, both streets laid out in 1957, lead back to the Ternes district.

Avenue de la Grandé-Armée

This long, broad avenue, which links the Etoile to the Porte Maillot, was opened in 1864. At no. 65 is the fine building of the Touring Club de France. You can reach, by way of this avenue, the Bois de Boulogne or Neuilly and La Défense. There are several fine contemporary buildings.

The Trinité district*

9th arr. Map ref. 4–C3, D3; 10–C1, C2, D1
Métro: Trinité-Estienne-d'Orves
Bus: 26, 32, 43, 49, 68, 81
Parking: Boul. Haussmann in front of the Galeries Lafayette Monoprix
Taxis: Place de la Trinité. Tel. 48-74-00-00.

This relatively new district, which sprang up a mere two centuries ago, is unjustly little appreciated. In its housing estates, its squares, and many of its streets, the 19th-c. architecture from the Restoration through the Second Empire, is still intact, from the pompous eclecticism of the Trinité Church to the Nouvelle Athènes development. During this era, the district in fact housed an elegant and fashionable bohemian community known for *les lorettes*, elegant young women of easy virtue, whose reputation was often exaggerated.

Today, around the Place de la Trinité, the *hôtels* that formerly housed actresses have been turned into offices or middle-class apartments, while the population of the district has become much more conventional than in the old days, except toward the Boulevard de Clichy, where an abundance of sex shops, bars, and erotic shows has sprung up. Nevertheless, a stroll through these quiet little streets lined with *hôtels particuliers* can be very pleasant.

Tour of the district

2 hrs.

☦ The Church of La Trinité

3 Rue de la Trinité (closed noon–2pm)
Tel: 48-74-12-77.

Built between 1861 and 1867 by Théodore Ballu, La Trinité is as characteristic of religious art under the Second Empire as Notre-Dame-de-Lorette is of the July Monarchy. Inspired by the architecture of the French Renaissance, it is original in form and in no way a pastiche. The church is elegantly linked to the square by a railing that ends in two curved stairways; its three fountains are topped by sculpted groups by Francisque Duret, symbolizing, from l. to r., Faith, Charity, and Hope.

The exterior

The exterior silhouette of the building features a high belfry, square at the base, octagonal above, which rises above a porch with three arcades; in niches in the pillars are statues of St Gregory of Nazianze, St Hilary, St Augustine, and St. Athanasius by Eugène Guillaume. The sculpted groups decorating the terrace above the first floor are copies made between the two World Wars; the originals were the work of Jacques Maillet, Pierre Cavelier, Jean-Baptiste Carpeaux and Adolphe Crauk.

The interior

The church has a very wide nave with a barrel-vaulted ceiling of four bays, with narrow side-aisles and side chapels; the deep chancel is raised by several steps and topped by a great arch painted with the Trinity and angels by Félix Barrias. The alternation of pillars and columns emphasizes the sense of space. Above the organ gallery is a great arch decorated by Félix Jobbé-Duval. For more than 40 years Olivier Messiaen (b.1904) has been the organist of La Trinité. Charles Gumery sculpted the holy-water fonts on either side of the entrance. The chapels are decorated with paintings by Pierre Brisset (1st chapel on the r.); Jean-Antoine Lecomte du Nouy (2nd chapel); Barrias (3rd chapel), and Désiré Laugée (4th chapel). In the chancel the original decorations by Emile Lévy (on the r.) and Elie Delaunay (on the l.) are now hidden in the lower section by two paintings by Morgan Snell (1966); the statue of the Virgin and Child is by Paul Dubois. The chapels on the l. are decorated by Eugène Thirion (4th chapel), Romain Cazes (3rd chapel), Michel Dumas (2nd chapel) and Louis Français (1st chapel).

Place d'Estienne-d'Orves

The development by Ballu of the square and its neighboring streets between 1860 and 1867 necessitated some extensive excavation involving the demolition of a *hôtel* by Ledoux (→ Hôtel du Cardinal Fesch, Rue de la Chaussée-d'Antin) and the Saint-Lazare barracks as well as the disreputable Les Porcherons Cabaret owned by the legendary Ramponeaux. He lowered the price of his white wine, which was most noted for making drinkers shudder—hence the name *ginguette* (an open-air café or dance hall). Today this square, surrounded by fine buildings by Haussmann, appears all the larger because most of the streets that lead into it follow an ancient layout (the S section of the Rue Saint-Lazare, the Rue Blanche, the Rue de Clichy, etc.). Since the liberation of Paris the square has borne the name of a hero of the Resistance who was shot by the Germans. At the bottom of the Rue Blanche, at no. 4, is a chocolate shop known for the fine quality of its merchandise.

Rue de Clichy

The lower part of this street was constructed in the 18th c. on the site of a very ancient road, which may have been a Roman road from Paris to Rouen. It marks a kind of boundary, namely that of the estate of the nuns called the Dames de Montmartre, which stretches away E of the street toward Montmartre. The aristocratic abbesses of this convent gave their names to the nearby streets—de Bellefonds, de Rochechouart, de La-Tour-d'Auvergne, and de La-Rochefoucauld. The Tour des Dames (Ladies' Tower) was a mill which stood where this street now lies. In 1730 the Richelieu *folie* or country pleasure-house was set up on the site of nos. 16–38, and Ruggieri created a second Tivoli here from 1811 to 1826. Rue de Clichy was essentially built after the division of this land into lots, and completed by 1870. There are few *hôtels particuliers* here apart from that of the De Wendel family of industrialists at no. 10 (now turned into offices). The Casino de Paris (1890) at no 15 occupies the site of the Tivoli and the first church of La Trinité. Its Art Déco façade is decorated with mosaics and magnificent stained-glass windows, recently restored after damage in 1985. This famous music-hall, where Josephine Baker performed, is still occasionally used for various entertainments. Victor Hugo lived at no. 21 in 1880. At no. 44 is a Neo-Classical pavilion. No. 39 was the scene for the second assassination attempt by the anarchist Ravachol in 1892.

No. 55 is the Théâtre de l'Oeuvre, dating from 1892 Cité Monthiers. There is a beautiful garden with a view of Square Moncey at the end of the Rue Cardinal-Mercier; this street was opened in 1879 on the site of the 1826 debtors' prison, for which the name of Rue de Clichy had become the synonym. Follow the Rue Moncey, a fine street with very homegeneous architecture, which has linked the Rue de Clichy with the Rue Blanche since 1843.

Rue Blanche

From the Rue Moncey to the Boul. de Clichy.

The white plaster which was transported along this street in carts from the Montmartre quarries gave this street its name. The Boursault *folie* was on the site of nos. 32–36 and 44–50. Ballu acquired some of this land. He himself lived in a Neo-Renaissance house decorated with beautiful stained-glass windows (no. 80 in this street) until his death in 1885 (→ inset). Farther up, the Rue Blanche becomes busier due to the proximity of the Boul. de Clichy. Return down the odd-numbered side of the street. At no. 71 there is a garage surviving from 1920. At the corner of the Rue de Calais is a watering trough for dogs, unique in Paris.

Rue Ballu

The architect Ballu's name has become synonymous with the Société des Auteurs et Compositeurs dramatiques (Society of Authors and Dramatists) which has its center at nos. 9 and II. The provincial side of the 9th arrondissement can be felt here in this street lined with detached houses from the second half of the 19th c. nos. 5, 11, and 22 for example where Ford Madox Brown, the French-born English friend of the Pre-Raphaelites, and Alexandre Dumas the Younger lived at no. 10 *bis*. Other artists moved into the adjacent streets, which are dotted with studios, among them Vuillard's Place Adolphe-Max and 4 Rue de Calais.

Rue Chaptal

This residential street, laid out during the Restoration, was the location of Maurice Magnier's Théâtre du Grand-Guignol (1896) at no. 20a, at the end of the cul-de-sac (on the site of the present Théâtre 347). The Société de Auteurs, Compositeurs et Editeurs de Musique (Society of Musical Authors, Composers and Editors) is at no. 10. Van Gogh worked in this street for the editor Goupil in 1875 on the site of no. 9. Its most charming building, a small Neo-Classical town house built for the painter Ary Scheffer at the end of the shady avenue, is now an annex of the Musée Carnavalet (→ Renan Scheffer Museum). As a whole—the outbuildings and adjacent workshops remain intact—it gives some idea of what the private gardens in this district were like.

Rue Henner

The *hôtel* at no. 13 is the most outstanding building in the street, and that at no. 6, by A. Feydeau (1854) is also very fine. The Rue Henner and the Rue Paul Escudier constitute the axes of a tiny, self-contained neighborhood, austere and uniform, the result of rapid speculation. Apollinaire met Marie Laurencin at no. 9; in 1908 she painted his portrait.

Rue La-Bruyère

Opened in several sections from 1924, this street crosses the land of the Boursault family's *folle* at no. 38, the façade is in a 1930s style. The building at the end of the courtyard of no. 43 is interesting for its *avant-corps*, which projects into the courtyard. The painter Henner died at no. 41, opposite the street which bears his name (1905). The most picturesque section of the street is found near the Place Saint-Georges near the Théâtre La Bruyère at no. 5, with many buildings from the 1830s and 40s. Berlioz lived at no. 45, Antonin Artaud at no. 28. This was also, in 1914, the writer Roland Dorgelès' street.

Rue Blanche, continued

From the Rue Moncey to Rue de la Tour-des-Dames.

This street is rather forbidding, even though the W side offers a series of remarkable buildings: No. 25 is the Neo-Byzantine Eglise Evangélique Allemande (German Evangelical Church) of 1899: note the stained-glass windows representing floral motifs and Le Warburg, the fief of Luther; the Neo-Palladian *Hôtel* at no. 21 by Girault, (1901), endowed with a remarkable porch roof, houses the Ecole Nationale Supérieure des Arts Techniques du Théâtre (National School of Technical Theater Arts); at no. 19 is the headquarters of the Sociéte des Ingénieurs Civils (Society of Civil Engineers), completed by the architect Delmas in 1897; no. 17 is a small building of the 1830s, the remains of the Chaptal College; no. 15 is the Théâtre de Paris. The sculptor Pigalle lived on the site of nos. 10 and 12.

Rue de la Tour-des-Dames**

By itself, this street makes up the Nouvelle Athènes development New Athens (→ inset). Nos. 16–20, the EDF (Electricité de France) with interesting architecture, has replaced the 19th-c. staging post on the same site. Several small *hôtels* were built from 1920 onwards. On the even-numbered side are no. 2 by Biet, for Baillot; and no. 4 by Gengembre, occupied by Etienne de Cambacérès, then by the banker Talabat. On the odd-numbered side are no. 1 by Visconti, where the actress Mlle Mars lived from 1824; and no. 3 by Constantin, acquired by Mlle Duchesnois in 1822. In his restrained design the architect has made full use of the sloping ground that extends to the Rue Saint-Lazare, the buildings on the odd-numbered side of which are reached by a picturesque passage (no. 54). No. 5, by Haudebourt, was occupied by the marine artist, Vernet and the historic painter, Delaroche; the architect Lelong built no. 9 for Napoléon's favorite actor, Talma.

Rue de La-Rochefoucault

This street was part of the Nouvelle Athènes development. No. 19 is a fine *hôtel* by Haudebourt (1827). No. 14 is the Gustave Moreau* Museum (→ Museums) housed in the painter's studio 1826–98, the master of Symbolism, who bequeathed his works to the State. The establishment was opened in 1902, façade by André Lafon. Rouault, the artist's pupil, more inclined toward Expressionism, was the curator. Take the Rue d'Aumale, opened in 1946, which still has some fine freestone buildings; Wagner lived at no. 3.

Rue Taitbout

The N part of the Rue Taitbout is the continuation of a street dating from the second half of the 18th c. where the painter Isabey and the writer Jouy, author of *L'Hermite de la Chaussée-d'Antin* (The Hermit of the Chaussée d'Antin) lived, near the Nouvelle Athènes. No. 80 is the entrance to the Square d'Orléans, a private estate of

1830–32. The English architect Cresy was inspired by the work of Nash in London in his conception of grouping façades around a central courtyard. George Sand and Chopin took up residence here in 1842. The garden of the square has lost its charm since the trees were cut down.

Rue Saint-Lazare

From the Rue Taitbout to the Church of Notre-Dame de-Lorette.

Here the layout has not changed since the second half of the 18th c. Anatole de Baudot, a pupil of Viollet-de-Duc and architect of Saint-Jean-de Montmartre, constructed no. 34 (1865–66). Two Empire façades from 1800 survive at nos. 30 and 31. An important group of Neo-Renaissance buildings can be found at nos. 27 and 29 (and Rue de Châteaudun). Nos. 16–18 were the site of the *folie* belonging to the firework manufacturers, the Ruggieri family, now occupied by a synagogue dating from the beginning of the 20th c.

☥ The Church of Notre-Dame-de-Lorette

18a, Rue de Châteaudun.
(Open Mon.–Sat. 8am–5.15pm, Sun. 8am–noon. Tel: 48-78-92-72.

Notre-Dame-de-Lorette was built from 1823 to 1836 by Hippolyte Lebas to serve the Nouvelle Athènes district then in the process of being developed. The area around the church was the neighborhood where the *lorettes* were to be found (→ inset).

The design is inspired by the Roman basilica, in particular Santa Maria Maggiore: five parallel naves, no transept, and a chancel ending in a hemicycle covered by a cul-de-four, or half-dome. The simple façade is ornamented with sculptures by Charles Nanteuil (Homage to the Virgin, in the tympanum), Jean Foyatier (Faith), Charles Laitié (Charity) and Phillipe Lemaire (Hope), all contemporary with the building. The interior was endowed with rich decorations, which are still almost all intact; it bears remarkable witness to the religious art of the July Monarchy. In the nave, eight large paintings recount the life of the Virgin; the four main ones are, on the r., the *Presentation of the Temple* (Auguste Vinchon) and the *Marriage of the Virgin* (Joseph Langlois) and on the l., the *Adoration of the Magi* (Jean-Pierre Granger) and the *Adoration of the Shepherds* (Auguste Hesse). The cupola of the chancel is by Pierre Delorme (*Transfer of the House of Lorette*, and four Evangelists) and the cul-de-four by François Picot (*Coronation of the Virgin*). In the 1st chapel on the r., Adolphe Roger has represented scenes relating to baptism; in the r. side-aisle are paintings by Alphonse Périn on the theme of the Eucharist. The symmetrical corresponding chapel on the l. is dedicated to the litanies of the Virgin; this is the principal work of the Lyon religious painter Victor Orsel, who died in 1850 without finishing it, (it was completed by Périn). Orsel was the leader of a movement with mystical and archaizing tendencies inspired by pre-Raphaelite models. The 1st chapel on the l., the Chapelle des Morts (Chapel of the Dead), is by Joseph Blondel; the paintings are badly damaged. In the 2nd chapel on the r. can be seen the door of the cell in which Father Sabatier, the parish priest taken hostage by the Commune and murdered in the Rue Haxo, was imprisoned.

Beside the church of Notre-Dame-de-Lorette, in the Rue Bourdaloue, is the *pâtissier* (pastry shop) of the same name at no. 7 renowned for its *puits d'amour* (wells of love), a kind of pastry. Rue Notre-Dame-de-Lorette up to the Place Saint-Georges. This first section, which leads to the Place Saint-Georges, is very quiet. At the corner by no. 18 (near the Ruggieri shop) the Rue Laferrière (1832) begins. Rue Laferrière is a remarkable piece of urban design that follows the circular layout of the Place Saint-Georges. No. 3 is a Greek Orthodox church; Mallarmé was born at no. 12 (1842).

Place Saint-Georges

This street is laid out in a circle (105ft/32.5m diameter) around the statue of the artist Gavarni erected in 1904 (sculptor, Denys Ruech, architect, Henri Guillaume). Two *hôtels particuliers* are prominent in the square. No 27, the Hôtel Thiers, rebuilt in 1873 by Aldrophe (designer of the synagogue in the Rue de la Victoire), today houses the Frédéric Masson Museum (→ Museums) and the Thiers library, annexe of the Institut dedicated to the Napoleonic area; the garden of the house is open to the public. The Hôtel le la Païva at no. 28, is a masterpiece of the Neo-Renaissance architecture from 1840, by E. Renaud. In comparison with the *hôtels* of the Nouvelle Athènes it is richly decorated, with sculptures by Garraud and Desboeufs, and pilasters, small columns, and panels.

Rue Saint-Georges

The houses here were built by Bélanger and Ledoux. The Goncourt brothers lived at no. 42 (1849–63). Renoir had a studio at no. 35, in the building formerly inhabited by General San Martin, liberator of Argentina, Chile, and Peru. The Théâtre Saint-Georges is at no. 51 (architect, C. Siclis, 1928).

Rue Notre-Dame-de-Lorette

From the Place Saint-Georges to Rue Pigalle.

This second section (→ above), beyond the Rue Henri-Monnier, leads to the Pigalle *quartier* where saunas and various dives lie in wait for their clientele. Over the last few years a small colony of Indian restaurants has grown up in the fork of the Rue Henri-Monnier, extending to the Place Gustave-Toudouze. Gauguin was born at 56 Rue Notre-Dame-de-Lorette; Delacroix had his studio at no. 58 from 1844 until 1857, before moving to the Rue du Fürstenberg. Cross again the Rue de La-Rochefoucauld where, at no. 66, at the far end of the courtyard, one of the district's rare 18th-c. residences still exists. Built in 1788 by Pierre Rousseau (1751–1810), architect of the Hôtel de Salm (→ Faubourg Saint-Germain), for his own use, this very simple house has kept part of its garden. Victor Hugo lived here.

Rue Pigalle

Cross this street, but do not follow it. The 18th-c sculptor Pigalle's name has unfortunately become synonymous with an area whose 'charms' become more pronounced as you near the square. Mass tourism has made it very artificial, but behind its outward appearance the district is in the process of returning to normal. In the 18th c. there were numerous small houses in this *quartier*; journalists, artists and writers lived here in the 19th c.: Baudelaire at no. 60; Victor Hugo at no. 55; Vuillard, Bonnard and Maurice Denis at no. 28; George Sand and Chopin at no. 16. More so even than the Rue Blanche, the Rue Pigalle has lost its architectural treasures. The Cité Pigalle at no. 43, where Van Gogh lived shortly before he committed suicide, is one of its rare attractive spots.

Rue Fontaine

This street, named after Napoleon's chief architect, is a continuation of the Rue Notre-Dame-de-Lorette up to the Place Blanche. Next to the nightclubs are several theaters, among them the Théâtre Fontaine, the cabarets on the corner of Rue Fromentin, site of the Academie Jullian in 1870, and a small music hall theater which was fashionable between the two World Wars, at no. 42 by G. H. Pingusson, (1930). Toulousé-Lautrec lived at no. 30 (1896); André Breton at no. 42. No. 15 Rue de Douai was built by Viollet-le-Duc from 1860 to 1861 (→ inset).

Rue Victor-Massé

Although it is always full of passing traffic, this street, which saw the opening of the Chat Noir (Black Cat), the first Montmartre cabaret. founded by Rodolphe Salis in 1881, seems a little secluded. Alfred Stevens had a studio at no. 12; Bonnard had his at no. 18 where, toward 1890, Maurice Denis and Vuillard came to work. The Ave. Frochot, the entrance to which is at the corner of the Rue Frochot and the Rue Victor-Massé, is a private estate in the heart of Pigalle. Built in 1830, it has some picturesque houses, among them Toulouse-Lautrec's last studio (no. 15). At no. 20 Rue Victor-Massé, the Cité Malesherbes is another important private street, with buildings dating from 1900; Degas had a studio at no. 37. The Ave. Trudaine, a wide thoroughfare that leads nowhere, is the remains of a development project from the Restoration, connected with the building of the Montmartre abattoir, a huge collection of detached buildings, then on the site of the Collège Rollin (N side). Rue Condorcet: No. 68 is the house that Viollet-le-Duc designed for himself (1862–63). A strange collection of beasts lurk on the façades and around the entrance to this house (→ Saint-Lazare district).

Rue des Martyrs

This commercial street, which serves the district as a market, climbs right up the hill of Montmartre, taking the same route that St Denis took himself. Its finest collection of buildings stretches from no. 41 to no. 47. The architect Alfred Normand, creator of a Pompeii-inspired house in the Ave. Montaigne (now demolished) lived at no. 51; Géricault at no. 49; Paul Léautaud at no 21; and the architect Hittorff, who designed Saint-Vincent-de-Paul and the Gare du Nord, at what was no. 12. Coming back down this street toward Notre-Dame-de-Lorette, cross the Rue Clauzel and the Rue de Navarin.

Rue Clauzel

This was Maupassant's street—he lived at no. 19 from 1878 to 1881—and that of Père Tanguy, who supplied colors to the artists who were soon to become known as the Impressionists, and others who would be the Nabis. He was kind enough to display in his window, at no. 14, paintings that nobody would buy.

Rue de Navarin

Note the astonishing façade at no. 9: Neo-Gothic and Romantic, it recalls the church architecture that flourished from 1830 to 1850. At no. 20, Théophile Gautier was host to Gérard de Nerval in 1840 and 1852.

▷ Théodore Ballu

The career of this architect (1817–85) who left his mark in many places in Paris, is characteristic of the 19th c. At the Ecole des Beaux-Arts (School of Fine Arts), where he studied under Lebas, architect of Notre-Dame-de-Lorette, he won the Grand Prix in 1840.

He left to study in Rome, then went to Greece until 1845. On returning to Paris he worked with the architect Gau, who was in the process of finishing the church of Sainte-Clotilde.

His vocation was thus mapped out—he was to work, essentially, on religious architecture. From 1860 onward he was head of the administrative body overseeing ecclesiastical architecture. In this capacity he restored the Saint-Jacques tower (1854–58); the tower of Saint-Germain-l'Auxerrois; Saint-Ambroise (1863–69); 71 *bis* Boul. Voltaire; Saint-Denis in Argenteuil (1866) and Saint-Joseph (1866–1875). His masterpiece in this field is still the church of La Trinité (1861–67) which illustrates not just his mastery of the use of historical styles, but also the wisdom of a good administrator. Despite its labor-intensive decoration, the church cost only 3890,000F. Moreover, the Trinité district became the architect's own neighborhood, as he bought various properties and built his house here. Ballu reached the summit of his career when he became Inspector General of Public Works in Paris, a post which he occupied from 1871 to 1876. He was elected to the Institut in 1872. In 1874 he won the competition to rebuild the town hall of Boccador, which had burnt down. The new town hall was inspired by the Reinaissance, but evokes too the optimism of the 19th c., for to architects such as Ballu, imitating historical styles while adding a dose of modernism was better than slavishly copying the past.

▷ The Théâtre de l'Oeuvre

Lugné-Poë (1869–1940) founded the Maison de l'Oeuvre in 1893. Here he introduced great foreign dramatists to the French public – in particular Ibsen and Strindberg, as well as young French authors, among them Claudel *L'Annonce Faite à Marie* (*Tidings Brought to Mary*, 1902). At first a travelling theater, l'Oeuvre took up residence in the Cité Monthiers (55 Rue de Clichy) in 1920.

▣ Museums to visit

Musée Gustave Moreau (14 Rue de La-Rochefoucauld): paintings by Gustave Moreau presented in his studio.

Foundation Dosne-Thiers (27 Place Saint-Georges): documents on the history of the 19th c.; temporary exhibitions.

Musée Renan Scheffer (16 Rue Chaptal): the life and times of George Sand.

▷ La Nouvelle Athènes (New Athens)

Beginning in the second half of the 18th c., and particularly with the first journeys to Greece (a country then occupied by the Turks) there was a certain infatuation with this 'homeland' of the arts. The War of Independence, which broke out in 1821 and in which foreign contingents took part, stimulated this fashion. Therefore the Collector General of Taxes for the Seine, Lapeyrière, in choosing the name La Nouvelle Athènes for the development being undertaken between the Rues Blanche, Saint-Lazare, de la Tour-des-Dames and de La-Rochefoucauld, hoped to attract a number of clients to it.

The unique feature of this development was its luxury: several small *hôtel particuliers* in a conventional style characteristic of the Percier school was built very quickly from 1820 on. Lapeyrière was in partnership with the architect Constantin, but Biet, Lelong, Visconti and Haudebourt also contributed. The name La Nouvelle Athènes has since come to include the whole of the Saint-George *quartier* where since the 18th c. many artists have resided: Mlle Raucourt, Pigalle, the architect Rousseau, Géricault; Mlle Duchesnois, Mlle Mars, Talma, Horace Vernet and Paul Delaroche chose to set up homes in the Rue de la Tour-des-Dames; George Sand, Delacroix, Chopin and Isabey also contributed to this district's fame. Today, this precious fragment of the Restoration seems to be safe.

▷ The Lorettes

The distinction between a kept woman and a prostitute posed a problem throughout the 19th c.—hence the necessity for euphemism. Nestor Roqueplan invented the name in 1841, taking it from the local church, to refer to a whole set of young women of poor origin who had moved into the district. Later, around 1854, they were also known as *biches* (does), but in artistic and literary circles, from Delacroix to Manet, Balzac, Flaubert and Baudelaire, the term *lorette* was preferred, as opposed to *grisette*, a term invented by Eugène Sue for a young woman working honorably. The portraitist of the *lorettes* was the engraver Gavarni.

A certain romantic idea of the *femme fatale*, popularized by 19th c. literature, should not be allowed to mask a rather sordid social reality. The *lorettes* were accepted in this new district because the owners wanted to realize a profit from their investments as quickly as possible. The women used it as a sort of dormitory estate from which they 'descended' on the Champs Elysées or the Grands Boulevards. The statistics given by Emile de Labédollière are pitiless: For every 100 girls, 42 became professional prostitutes, 17 died of disease, 6 committed suicide, 5 were locked up in the Salpêtrière, 4 emigrated to California or Australia, 4 married, 3 went away to the country, and the other 19 lived by odd jobs. Charitable institutions such as the Maison Eugène-Napoléon, founded in 1853, were created to remedy their situation.

The Tuileries district***

1st arr./Map ref. 10–C3
Métro: Concorde
Buses: 24, 42, 72, 73, 84, 94
Parking: Place de la Concorde, on the Tuileries side.
Taxis: 258 Rue de Rivoli. Tel: 42–61–67–70.

The heavy motor traffic along the Seine embankment and the Rue de Rivoli cannot lessen the sense of absolute tranquility you feel while strolling in the garden of the Tuileries. The broad vistas, pond, statues and greenery still transport us back to the age of the *fêtes galantes*. Planned in the 16th c., but redesigned in the late 17th c., the garden still has some of the twilight charm of the waning days of the Grand Siècle.

Behind the arcades of the Rue de Rivoli, the approaches to the Place Vendôme and the Church of Saint-Roch were built during the same period, but they differ greatly in feeling. The correctness of its proportions and simplicity of design make the Place Vendôme one of the most remarkable architectural features of Paris. Conceived as a harmonious whole, the area bears witness also to the rationalistic spirit of the age of Louis XIV. Its present occupants are almost as aristocratic as they were in the days when financiers and tax-collectors had their mansions here. Along with the Rue de la Paix and the Rue de Castiglione, the Place Vendôme has the greatest concentration of fine jewelry shops in the city. The international clientele of the great luxury hotels nearby, the many tourists and the business people who work in the neighborhood's offices have, however, altered the character of the district to some degree. Nevertheless, a more authentic, lively Paris can still be found in the Place du Marché Saint-Honoré and around the remarkable Church of Saint-Roch.

♣♠ The Jardin des Tuileries

Open daily at 6am or 6.30am; close Oct.–Apr. at 8pm, May at 10pm, June–Aug. 10.45pm, Sept. 1–15 at 10pm, Sept. 16–30 at 9pm.

The old part of the Tuileries, between the Place de la Concorde and the Avenue du Général-Lemonnier, is surrounded by railings. To the E of the Place de la Concorde the garden extends as far as the Place du Carrousel, between the Rue de Rivoli and the Quai des Tuileries. Covering an area of 63 acres/25.5ha, it is a veritable open-air museum, tracing the history of sculpture from Louis XIV to the present.

History of the garden

The Jardin des Tuileries is contemporary (1564) with the palace begun by Catherine de' Medici (for the history of the palace, demolished after the Commune, →Louvre). It marks the 'birth, in the city, of the fashionable public promenade in the Italian style' (M. Poëte). The garden originally boasted the famous grotto by Palissy, certain fragments of which can be seen in the Carnavalet Museum (→inset). In 1664, Le Nôtre redesigned it, creating a masterpiece of Neo-Classical art. The garden became a rendezvous for the fashionable people of the 18th c., who loved to promenade there; during the Directoire the 'Incroyables' and the 'Merveilleuses' revived the custom, parading about in their outrageous clothes and exaggeratedly tall wigs.

In August 1944, heavy fighting preceded the German surrender, seriously damaging many statues. Among these, the oldest were brought from Marly during the reigns of Louis XIV and Louis XV; they can be seen in that part of the park closest to the Place de la Concorde.

A great many statues, of varied quality, were installed under Louis-Philippe and Napoléon III. The Republic continued to populate the garden with sculptures, from W to E, and the process continues; in 1985 and 1986 several new works were placed to the W of the large round pond and on the terrace of the Jeu de Paume.

Tour of the garden

45 mins.

The main entrance to the garden opens onto the Place de la Concorde. On the l., before passing through the gates, note the plaque commemorating the first ascent in a gas-filled balloon by Charles and Robert, which took place here on December 1, 1783.

The equestrian statues by Coysevox*

1 and 2

These winged horses stand on the pillars at the gates. On the r. is *Fame*, on the l. *Mercury*, brought from Marly in 1719. Since 1986 the original works have been kept in the Louvre and replaced by copies (Guillaume Coustou's *Horses of Marly* on the other side of the Champs-Elysées, has suffered the same fate). Coysevox's horses were first commissioned for the watering-trough at Marly; they were replaced there by those of Coustou, brought to Paris in 1794.

The Terrasse du Jeu de Paume

(Between Rue de Rivoli and the garden).

The old Jeu de Paume which, from 1958 to August 1986, housed the Musée de l'Impressionnisme, stands here. The works it then contained are today in the Musée d'Orsay (→Museums). The building has been closed for renovation, but has reopened for temporary exhibitions.

In the blind arcade, under the ramp leading to the Jeu de Paume terrace, is the bust of Le Nôtre (1613–1700), a replica of the one in the Church of Saint-Roch, by Coysevox. On the terrace is a monument to Charles Perrault (1628–1703), author of the famous *Mother Goose Stories* who persuaded Colbert to open the gardens to the public, and not keep them for the royal family alone.

Three contemporary works by Alain Kirili, Sandro Chia, and Jean-Michel Alberola were placed here during the summer of 1986. Under the staircase leading to the terrace, *The Crowd* (12) by Raymond Mason was unveiled in 1985. Further on, also at the foot of the terrace, are the remains of the façade of the Château des Tuileries, burnt down in 1871. At the end of a large open space called the Allée des Orangers is a bronze, *Hercules Wrestling with Achelous* (13), by Bosio.

The Octagonal Pond

At the entrance of the garden are *The Seine* and *The Marne* by Nicolas Coustou (3), and *The Loire* and *The Loiret* by Corneille Van Clève (4), brought from Marly, as were the two groups, *The Nile* (6) and *The Tiber* (5), situated on the W side of the pond. To the E of the pond are four thermae symbolizing the seasons: *Spring* (8) and *Autumn* (9) by Barois, *Winter* by Raon (10) and *Summer* by Guillaume Coustou (11).

The garden's administration plan to remove these statues to protect them from pollution, and to replace them here with copies.

The garden is bordered along its entire length on both sides by two narrow terraces which can be reached by steps and gently sloping ramps. On these ramps stand the *Muses*, copies of antique statues that were formerly at Marly; *Calliope* has been placed on the Jeu de Paume terrace.

The Terrasse du Bord de l'Eau*

Running the length of the Quai des Tuileries, this charming promenade overlooks the Seine on one side and the garden on the other. At its W end, is the Orangerie,** enlarged in 1853, (→Museums) where the Walter-Guillaume collection has been installed, while two rooms contain Monet's *Water Lilies* series (1927).

1. *Mercury* (cast bronze), Antoine Coysevox (1640–1720)
2. *Fame* (cast), Antoine Coysevox (1640–1720)
3. *The Seine* and *The Marne,* Nicolas Coustou (1658–1733)
4. *The Loire* and *The Loiret,* Corneille Van Clève (1645–1732)
5. *The Tiber,* Pierre Bourdict (?–1711?)
6. *The Nile,* Lorenzo Ottoni (1648–1736)
7. *Lion Struggling with a Snake* (cast bronze), Antoine-Louis Barye (1796–1875)
8. *Spring,* François Barois (1656–1726)
9. *Autumn,* François Barois (1656–1726)
10. *Winter,* Jean Raon (1631–1707)
11. *Summer,* Guillaume Coustou (1677–1746)
12. *The Crowd,* Raymond Mason (1922)
13. *Hercules Wrestling with Achelous Transformed into a Serpent,* François-Joseph Bosio (1768–1845)
14,15. *Animals Fighting,* Auguste Cain (1821–94)
16. *The Good Samaritan,* François Sicard (1862–1934)
17. *Léon Blum,* Philippe Garel (1945)
18. *Standing Young Girl,* Marcel Gimond (1894–1961)
19. *Eve,* Charles Despiau (1874–1946)
20. *Rolande,* Robert Wlerick (1882–1944)
21. *Prometheus,* James Pradier (1790–1852)
22. *The Oath of Spartacus,* Louis-Ernest Barrias (1841–1905)
23. *Cincinnatus,* Denis Foyatier (1793–1863)
24. *Alexander in Battle,* Charles-Francois Leboeuf, known as Nanteuil (1792–1865)
25. *Nymph Seized by a Centaur,* Laurent-Honoré Marqueste (1848–1920)
26. *Pericles,* Jean-Baptiste Joseph Debay (1779–1863)
27. *Theseus and the Minotaur,* Etienne-Jules Ramey (1754–1838)
28. *Medea,* Paul Gase (1860–1944)
29. *Man and his Misery,* Jean-Baptiste Hugues (1849–1930)
30. *Monument to Jules Ferry,* Gustave Michel (1851–1924)
31. *Aeneas Carrying His Father Anchises,* Pierre Le Pautre (1660–1774)
32. *Arria and Poetus,* Pierre Le Pautre (1660–1744)
33. *Monument to Waldeck Rousseau,* L.-H. Marqueste
34. *Meditation,* Auguste Rodin (1840–1917)
35. *Great Shadow,* Auguste Rodin (1840–1917)
36. *Jean de Fiennes,* Auguste Rodin (1840–1917)
37. *Pierre de Wissant,* Auguste Rodin (1840–1917)
38. *The Sons of Cain,* Paul Landowski (1875–1961)

Level with this building, against the wall of the terrace overlooking the Quai des Tuileries, an inscription indicates where the portal of the Conférence building stood, erected in 1632, demolished in 1730. The Quai de la Conférence to which it gave access owed its name to the Suresnes conferences that put an end to the troubles of the Ligue (the Catholic League) in 1591.

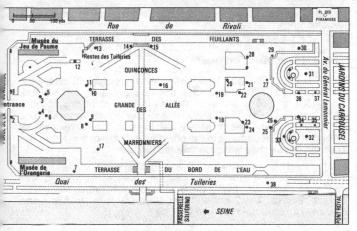

Statues of the Tuileries Garden

[*key opposite*]

The Terrasse des Feuillants

An extension of the Terasse du Jeu de Paume, the Terrasse des Feuillants runs the length of the Rue de Rivoli. Made famous during the Revolution, it owes its name to the Benedictine monastery that lay close by and which became, in 1791, the meeting-place for the club of Les Feuillants, a group of republican moderates, which included André Chénler. The celebrated riding school, the Manège, was also situated near this terrace. Louis XVI was condemned to death here.

The Quinconces des Marronniers*

A wide central avenue separates two vast orchards of chestnut and lime trees arranged in staggered rows (*en quinconce*) to provide open spaces and green arbors. Two kiosks sell coffee, drinks and food and provide an agreeable place for lunch or a snack. The last two of these arbors, formerly known as Les Jardins de Robespierre, have at their W end a white marble arch constructed under the Convention National.

The part of the garden that extends from the large round pond to the Ave. du Général-Lemonnier was formerly the private garden of the old palace. Louis-Philippe wanted to keep the garden as his own secluded retreat; it was converted into an English garden by Napoléon III.

The Jardins du Carrousel

These gardens, situated between the two wings of the Louvre, were created in 1889 on the site of the former French garden of Le Nôtre. From 1964 to 1965, a group of statues in bronze* by the sculptor Aristide Maillol (1861–1944) was installed. Since 1985, renovation on the Grand Louvre has necessitated the temporary removal of several of these sculptures to the chestnut orchard of the Jardin des Tuileries, where they will probably remain until 1990.

Among the N flowerbeds are: *Action Enchained, The River, Night, The Mediterranean, Homage to Cézanne, Venus, Pomona, The Ile de France, Draped Bather*. In the S flowerbeds: *Nymphs, Monument to Port-Vendres, Air, Summer, Flora, Swimmer with Uplifted Arms, Sorrow, The Mountain* (donated by Dina Vierny).

The Tuileries district

The Tuileries district, situated around the gardens of the same name, owes its development first to François I's decision to use the Louvre as his principal residence. Because the necessary remodeling continued for years, the King died in 1547 before the palace was complete. After the tragic death of Henri II in 1559, his widow Catherine de' Medici took the young king François II and went to live in the area known as the Tuileries, until then used as a rubbish dump, and whose clay soil, used for making tiles (*tuiles*), gave rise to the name, Les Tuileries. Catherine de' Medici decided to have a new place built with an Italian-style garden to remind her of her homeland.

Some religious orders established themselves N of the district, and the proximity of the Louvre, the Palais-Royal and the Tuileries Palace itself, added to the quarter's importance.

The Rue Saint-Honoré, which runs E–W, gave the district unity; until the opening of the Rue de Rivoli in the 19th c. it was the only main thoroughfare. The development of the Rue Saint-Honoré took place at the same time as the extension of the perimeter wall around Paris and the relocation of the Porte Saint-Honoré westward. Initially the *porte* was moved level with the Temple de l'Oratoire, then to the Place du Café de la Regénce (→Place du Théâtre Français), and finally in line with the Rue Royale, until 1773. In the 19th c. the cutting of the Rue des Pyramides, Rue du 29-Juillet, Rue d'Alger, Rue de Castiglione, Rue Cambon, Rue Danou and Rue Richepance resulted in the loss of many old houses.

Tour of the district

45 mins.

Place des Pyramides

This *place* is bordered by houses with uniform façades following the general arrangement of the Rue de Rivoli. At its center, the statue of Joan of Arc, by Frémiet, has long been a place of pilgrimage for the extreme Right, particularly the Royalists. At no. 2, the Hôtel Régina, its décor unchanged since 1900; in the entrance hall note the different clocks showing the times in the great capitals of the period, from New York to Peking. The Rue des Pyramides, opened in 1802, owes its name to Napoléon's victory in Egypt in 1798.

Rue de Rivoli

From the Place des Pyramides to the Place de la Concorde.

This street's name celebrates Napoléon's victory at Rivoli (1797). The section between the Rue de Rohan (E of the garden) and Rue Saint-Florentin (to the W), which was opened in 1800, is the oldest and most elegant. Farther on is the section opened in 1848, between the Louvre and the Rue de Sévigné, which is very commercial and has more commonplace architecture. The buildings facing the Jardin des Tuileries were constructed according to the plans of Napoléon's architects, Percier and Fontaine. The Emperor completed a project of the *Ancien Regime* to link the Louvre with the Place Louis-XV and the Champs-Elysées. The new thoroughfare, between the Tuileries and the Rue Saint-Honoré, ran through the gardens of the convents of L'Assomption and the Capucines and the monastery of the Feuillants. The architects' most notable innovation was the arcaded street where pedestrians can stroll sheltered from the weather and traffic. Under the Directoire, in 1795, private individuals had already constructed the Rue des Colonnes, close to the Bourse (Stock Exchange), which was the prototype of the Rue de Rivoli. But the scale and splendor of the new street as it developed, with its arcades and buildings, went well beyond the modest pretensions of the Rue des Colonnes. Restrictions on commercial activity and poster advertising forbade food shops and workmen using hammers (shoemakers, sheet-metal workers). Work must have proceeded slowly, since by the end of the Empire only the arcades and a few buildings had been built. The project was completed in 1835.

Follow the Rue de Rivoli towards the Place de la Concorde, and cross the Rue du 29-Juillet. Opened in 1826, this street received its present name in 1830 in memory of the third day of the Revolution of 1830. The Rue d'Alger and Rue du Mont-Thabor ran partly through the site of the Hôtel de Noailles (→211 Rue Saint-Honoré).

The Galignani bookshop (founded in 16th c. Padua) is at 224 Rue de Rivoli. In the 19th c. it was in the Rue Vivienne. At no. 226 is the Angelina tearoom, formerly the Maison Rumpelmeyer, famous for its 1900 décor and its speciality, a cake made with chestnut purée and whipped cream, called Mont-Blanc.

At no. 228 is the Hôtel Meurice, the German Military Headquarters for the Paris garrison during the Occupation. Level with no. 230 is the site of the Manège (riding school) constructed in 1726 for the young Louis XV, where the National Assembly met during the Revolution, and where Louis XVI was condemned to death.

Rue de Castiglione

Walk partway down this street. Opened in 1802, this street is named for Napoléon's victory over the Austrians in 1796. It was built over a thoroughfare between the monastery of the Feuillants and the convent of the Capucines. At no. 3 is the Hôtel Intercontinental, constructed in the 1880s on the site of the Foreign Office, which was burnt in 1871 by the Commune. No. 10 is the site of the cloister of the monastery of the Feuillants. During the Second Empire Napoléon III's mistress, the Comtesse de Castiglione, known as the *divina contessa*, lived here and received all of fashionable Europe. No. 14 was the monastery chapel of the Feuillants, where a well-known restaurant has been installed whose name honors the order. Return to the Rue de Rivoli.

Rue Cambon

Cut through the grounds of the Hôtel Piney-Luxembourg in 1719, whose name evokes the famous member of the National Convention, Cambon, creator of the National Debt Register. No. 13, the Hôtel de la Cour des Comptes, was built in 1900 on the site of the convent of the Dames de l'Assomption to replace the old Cour des Comptes at the Palais d'Orsay, and burned by the Commune. At no. 14 the half-crazed Comtesse de Castiglione, going out only at night so that no one should see the ruin of her beauty, but still very much a presence in the quarter, died alone and destitute in 1899. No. 31, the little apartment used by Coco Chanel to work and receive visitors (she slept at the Ritz Hotel) in 'three garrets overlooking the garden' remains as it was.

Return to the Rue de Rivoli where, at no. 248, is another famous bookshop, W. H. Smith and Son, and rejoin the Rue Saint-Florentin.

Rue Saint-Florentin

This street was created in the 17th c., and is named after the *hôtel* situated at no. 2, built in 1767 for the Comte de Saint-Florentin by

Chalgrin and designed by Gabriel, architect of the Place Louis-XV (now Place de la Concorde). In 1838 Talleyrand died there. Nos. 7 and 9 were constructed in 1761 by Louis Letellier.

Rue Saint-Honoré

From Rue Saint-Florentin to Rue de Castiglione.

Lying between the Rue Royale and the Place du Palais-Royal this thoroughfare is lined with 18th-c. mansions of the nobility. It is now devoted to luxury trades (expensive ready-to-wear, jewelry and antiques).

No. 442 (to the l. of the Rue Saint-Florentin) is on the site of the Porte Saint Honoré, part of Louis XIII's fortified wall. No. 382 is on the site of the convent of the Filles de la Conception, closed in 1790; it occupied the whole area between the Capuchin convent to the E (nos. 360–364), the Rue Saint-Honoré to the S, and Louis XIII's wall to the W and the N. The Rue Duphot and Rue Richepance, opened in 1807, were laid through this convent.

The Church of the Assomption* (263 *bis* Rue Saint-Honoré; open 7am–7.30pm. Tel: 42–60–07–69). This church was the chapel of the convent of the Dames de l'Assomption, founded in the 17th c. and suppressed during the Revolution. Only the church remains, built between 1670 and 1676 and designed by Charles Errard, better known as a painter and rival of Lebrun. The glaring disproportion between the dome and rest of the edifice earned it the nickname *sot dôme* (foolish dome), a pun on Sodome (malicious wits). Since 1850 the l'Assomption church has been the parish church for the Polish community in Paris. The interior comprises one circular space, covered by a cupola painted with a fresco of the *Assumption* (1676) by Charles de la Fosse. To the r., *The Adoration of the Magi* by Carle Van Loo (*ca.* 1740); at the high altar, *The Annunciation* by Joseph-Marie Vien (1763); on the l., *Birth of the Virgin* by Joseph-Benot Suvée (1779).

At 374 Rue Saint-Honoré is the mansion where Mme Geoffrin, nicknamed 'the Minister of High Society' held her famous literary salon, known as 'the kingdom of the Rue Saint-Honoré' (see the plaque). It was a meeting-place for such artists as Carle Van Loo, Boucher, Soufflot, Bouchardon, La Tour, Vernet and Vien, as well as for the *encyclopédistes* and other intellectuals of the Enlightenment. Chateaubriand also lived here. The house was much altered during the 19th c. The mansions at nos, 368 and 366 were built by Pierre Bullet (1705) and once belonged to the architect Robert de Cotte (1717).

Place Vendôme**

Dating from the final years of the reign of Louis XIV, contemporary with the Place des Victoires (→Bourse), this is, architecturally, one of the most attractive places in Paris. Louis XIV also envisaged the cutting of a street to link the two squares, but this costly project had to be abandoned. In 1686 at the proposal of Louvois, Superintendent of Buildings, Louis XIV signed a decree ordering the construction of a square to receive an equestrian statue of himself, to be surrounded by a National Library, academies and the residence of the Ambassador Extraordinary. The square was to be called Place des Conquêtes. It owes its present name to the mansion it replaced, which had been built by the Duc de Vendôme, son of Henry IV and Gabrielle d'Estrées. Construction of a four-sided square began in 1687, under the direction of Jules Hardouin-Mansart, but was abandoned in 1699 after the death of Louvois, although Louis's statue was unveiled. Work resumed in the same year with new plans by Mansart who gave the square its octagonal form, pierced through the middle of its N and S sides by two streets, one toward the church of the Capuchin Convent (built by François d'Orbay), the other toward the Rue Saint-Honoré and the main gate of the Feuillants. The Place Vendôme was conceived as a kind of enclosed salon, and balls were sometimes given here. The First Empire opened new perspectives from the square: the Feuillants' monastery was demolished to make way for the Rue de Castiglione, as was the convent of the Capuchin for the Rue de la Paix. However, the first sections of these streets have retained their very strict 17th c. layout.

At each corner of the square the buildings are placed obliquely and, in the middle of the longer sides, there are projecting sections, each with a triangular pediment supported by engaged columns. The arcades, with semi-circular arches, have mascarons at the ground-floor level, and are as crowded as those of the Place des Victoires, though more splendid. Corinthian pilasters rise up two floors, topped by steeply pitched roofs with dormer windows alternating with œil-de-boeuf windows (an arrangement that was modified in the 19th c. when many of the dormer windows were enlarged). All the decorative sculptures were made under the direction of J.-B. Poulletier.

▷ The Vendôme Column

Because it was intended as the site for the King's statue, the square was known as the Place Louis-le-Grand until the Revolution. Unveiled in 1699 during a magnificent fête, the statue, by Girardon, represented Louis XIV as a Roman Emperor on horseback. In 1792 it was destroyed and sent to the foundry, and soon after the body of Le Peletier de Saint-Fargeau, aristocrat and regicide, was exposed on its plinth. Napoléon chose this place to raise a monument to the glory of the victorious soldiers of Austerlitz. An admirer of ancient Rome, the Emperor took Trajan's column as his model. One thousand, two hundred bronze Austrian cannons were melted down to cover the stone core of the column of the Grande Armée (132ft/44m high), designed by Gondoin and Lepère in 1806. Spiralling bas-reliefs by Bergeret, a student of David, tell the story of the 1805 campaign. A statue of Napoléon as a Roman emperor by Chaudet was placed on the top in 1810. This statue did not survive the change of régime and was replaced by a statue of Henri IV in 1815. He was taken down for the 100 Days. Louis XVIII put up a gigantic fleur-de-lis; Louis-Philippe put up a new Napoléon in military uniform and finally Napoléon III erected a copy of the original statue of the Emperor, by Dumont, which is still in place.

The column itself was torn down in 1871 under the Commune, at the instigation of the painter Courbet. Restored, the column and its statue were re-erected at the artist's expense in 1873, which left him ruined financially.

▷ The mansions of the Place Vendôme

The creation of the Place Vendôme also provided an excellent opportunity for real estate speculation. The land behind Mansart's façades was sold to important Regency financiers such as John Law, Pennautier and Crozat. From 1702 to 1720, the construction of private *hôtels* was mainly the work of the architects Boffrand, Pierre Bullet and Bullet de Chamblain. It was said that Henri IV was on the Pont-Neuf with his people, Louis XIII in the Place Royale with his gentlemen (Place des Vosges) and Louis XIV in the Place des Conquêtes with his financiers. The Place Vendôme took over from the Place des Vosges and the Marais as the most sumptuous district in Paris. A few surviving houses testify to the splendor of these 18th c. mansions. John Law, the Scottish financier who became Con-trôleur Général des Finances, acquired several of those that lie toward Rue de la Paix.

No. 23 is the Hôtel de Montbreton, where Law narrowly escaped being lynched after his excessive speculation had led to the collapse of the banking system he had devised during the Regency, and the ruin of thousands of people, including himself.

At no. 19, the Hotel d'Evreux (guided tours available) which now belongs, like the neighboring mansion, to the Crédit Foncier, had as its first owner Antoine Crozat, a former clerk who became Fermier-Général (tax collector) and amassed a great fortune. A renowned and expert collector, he commissioned Bullet to build a mansion behind Mansart's façade; this he filled with works of art by Venetian painters, Van Dyck and Watteau. In 1707 he married his daughter to the Comte d'Evreux, whose name still appears on the entrance. The courtyard façade is decorated with columns, pilasters and large medallions. The mansion was renovated by Constant d'Ivry in 1747.

No. 17, built by Bullet, also belonged to Crozat. Next door, at no. 15, is the Ritz, one of the most famous Parisian hotels. It was founded in

1898 by César Ritz and preserves several interesting features, most of which date back to the late 18th c., notably a drawing-room painted with arabesques. At no. 13 is the former Hôtel Luillier, bought by the regent in 1717 for the purpose of housing the National Chancellery. After becoming the Ministry of Justice, it was restored under Napoléon III. On its facade is a standard meter in marble that was fixed there in 1795 to familiarize Parisians with the new unit of linear measurement. Nos. 11 and 9 were constructed by Mansart. The first was bought by the King in 1717 to enlarge the chancellery. The other was sold in 1750 to the Fermier-Général, Dangé, who had it decorated by Oudry (some of the panels are conserved in the Musée des Arts Décoratifs). The even-numbered side of the square was also occupied at first by tax collectors and financiers. Chopin died in 1849 at no. 12 (note the inscription). The greater part of the mansion was reconstructed in 1855. No. 20 is a beautiful Louis XVI *hôtel*. At no. 26 the jeweller Boucheron still occupies the Hôtel de Noce. He was the first to move here from the Palais-Royal at the end of the 19th c. The beautiful Comtesse de Castiglione was his tenant. At the end of her life, the 'madwoman of the Place Vendôme', as the 'divina contessa' was now known, lived there alone and in complete darkness, going out only at night, so as not to expose her ravaged beauty, as mentioned earlier.

Today the Place Vendôme continues to be home to luxury shops and, more recently, several international banks that have taken the place of the overly audacious financiers of the 18th c.

Rue de la Paix

Opened in 1806 under the name Rue Napoléon, this street was renamed in 1814 in honor of the Treaty of Paris of the same year. This street is world-famous for its jewelry shops. At no. 7 in 1858, Charles Frederick Worth, an Englishman, founded his famous fashion house. He was the first fashion designer to show his gowns on a living model – his own wife.

Rue des Capucines (to the r.)

This street is named for the old convent of the Capuchins, installed initially in the Rue du Faubourg-Saint-Honoré, and moved here to the site of a horse market in 1688. It is bordered on its odd-numbered side by imposing old mansions occupied by the *Crédit Foncier*. Nos. 15, 17 and 19 were constructed by the architect Tavenot; nos. 17–19 formed the mansion built in 1726 for de Casteignier, director of the Compagnie des Indes.

Rue Danielle-Casanova

Formerly part of the Rue des Petits-Champs, this street was renamed in 1944 after a Resistance heroine who was deported to a death camp by the Germans. There are numerous 18th-c. mansions here, one of which, no. 15, is the Hôtel de Coigny. No. 22 is the former Hôtel de Nantes, where Stendhal died of apoplexy on March 23 1842. On the top floor of no. 26 the Dadaist painter Francis Picabia had his studio. The Rue Louis-le-Grand dates from 1701 and has the same name that the Place Vendôme had at that time. The portraitist Hyacinthe Rigaud died at no. 1 (note the inscription).

Place du Marché-Saint-Honoré

The Rue du Marché-Saint-Honoré, to the r., leads to this square, created in 1807 on the site of the Jacobin monastery. The main gate of the monastery, installed in 1613 on the Rue Saint-Honoré, was situated at the intersection with the Rue du Marché-Saint-Honoré. During the Revolution the convent was occupied by the famous Jacobin Club, led by Robespierre. The market, opened in 1810, was demolished and unfortunately replaced in the late 1950s by a parking garage.

Rue Saint-Honore

From Rue de Castiglione to the Church of Saint-Roch.

From no. 229 to no. 235 is a group of houses built by Antoine for the Feuillants, who rented them out as apartments. It is all that survives of the famous monastery, whose church stood behind these buildings. In the courtyard of no. 229 the remains of the round apse of the old church can still be seen. The huge gate of the Feuillants' monastery, designed by Jules Hardouin-Mansart and completed in 1676, was exactly on the N–S axis of the Place Vendôme. It was in this building, closed in 1790, that the Feuillants Club was installed and where Louis XVI and the royal family found refuge after being forced to leave the Tuileries on August 10, 1792, before being imprisoned in the Temple. David painted *The Tennis Court Oath* in the deconsecrated church. In 1804 the monastery was demolished to make way for the Rue de Castiglione (1811) and Rue de Rivoli (1811–35). At no. 211 is the site of the famous Hôtel de Noailles, composed of several buildings and gardens extending S as far as the present Rue de Rivoli, and W to the Feuillants' monastery (no. 229). La Fayette was married there on April 11, 1774 to Adrienne de Noailles. The Hôtel de Noailles was renamed the Hôtel Saint-James and then the Hôtel d'Albany. The Louis XV façade of an outbuilding of the original *hôtel* can still be seen in the courtyard.

⚓ The Church of Saint-Roch***

296 Rue Saint-Honoré (open daily 8.30am to 7.15pm). Tel: 42–60–81–69.

Frequent concerts on weekday evenings and Sunday afternoons. Tel: 42–61–93–26.

As well as being one of the largest churches in Paris, Saint-Roch is also among the richest in paintings and sculptured monuments. In addition to the vestiges of its original decorations that escaped the Revolution, it contains a great number of works of art from religious establishments that have disappeared, among others the Feuillant and Jacobin monasteries, the Capuchin convent and the Church of Saint-Jean-en-Grève. It is a museum of 18th and 19th c. religious art.

Situated in the heart of one of the most elegant districts of old Paris, Saint-Roch has had many illustrious parishioners: François and Michel Anguier, Pierre Mignard, André Le Nôtre, Duguay-Trouin, Hevétius, Alexis Piron, Mme Geoffrin, Diderot, and the Abbé de l'Epée are all interred there. On September 5 1795 a bloody battle took place in front of the church between rebelling royalists and troops of the National Convention led by General Napoléon Bonaparte. A few marks from the 'whiff of grapeshot' that made his reputation can be seen on the façade.

The exterior

The design of the church dates it clearly to the second half of the 17th c. Its unusual N–S orientation was made necessary by the site on the Moulon's hill. Begun in 1653, designed by Jacques Lemercier, the church's construction was interrupted in 1660. The choir, the transept and the end bay of the nave had been built, but the nave had to wait until 1701 for completion. The Chapel of Our Lady was built at the same time, designed by Jules Hardouin-Mansart. Then, in 1719, a donation of 100,000 livres was made by the banker Law, newly converted to Catholicism and at the summit of his lightning career, which allowed the work to be completed. The elegant façade facing Rue Saint-Honoré, designed by Robert de Cotte, was begun in 1735. In 1760 another extension was built behind the Chapel of Our Lady, namely the Calvary Chapel, planned by Etienne-Louis-Boullée, but greatly modified in the 19th c. Zola refers to these renovations in his *Pot-Bouille*.

The interior

The church is 413ft/126m long. While the nave, its side-aisles and the short transept are Neo-Classical in conception, the plan of the apse is unusual. Behind the chancel is Hardouin-Mansart's vast,

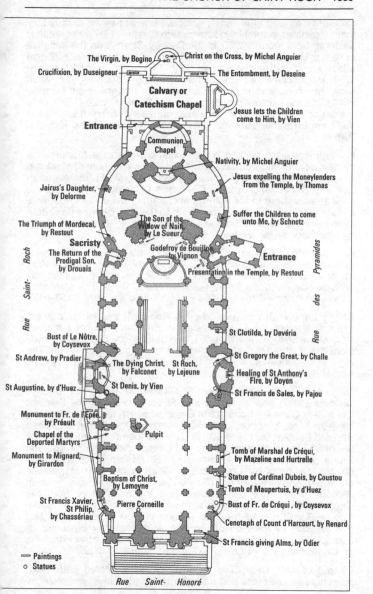

The Virgin, by Bogino
Christ on the Cross, by Michel Anguier
Crucifixion, by Duseigneur
The Entombment, by Deseine

Calvary or Catechism Chapel

Entrance

Jesus lets the Children come to Him, by Vien

Communion Chapel

Nativity, by Michel Anguier

Jesus expelling the Moneylenders from the Temple, by Thomas

Jairus's Daughter, by Delorme

Suffer the Children to come unto Me, by Schnetz

The Triumph of Mordecai, by Restout

The Son of the Widow of Naïn, by Le Sueur

Sacristy
The Return of the Prodigal Son, by Drouais

Godefroy de Bouillon, by Vignon

Entrance

Presentation in the Temple, by Restout

Rue Saint-Roch

Rue des Pyramides

Bust of Le Nôtre, by Coysevox

St Clotilda, by Devéria

St Andrew, by Pradier

St Gregory the Great, by Challe

The Dying Christ, by Falconet

St Roch, by Lejeune

Healing of St Anthony's Fire, by Doyen

St Augustine, by d'Huez

St Denis, by Vien

St Francis de Sales, by Pajou

Monument to Fr. de l'Epée, by Préault

Chapel of the Deported Martyrs

Pulpit

Tomb of Marshal de Créqui, by Mazeline and Hurtrelle

Monument to Mignard, by Girardon

Statue of Cardinal Dubois, by Coustou

Tomb of Maupertuis, by d'Huez

Baptism of Christ, by Lemoyne

Bust of Fr. de Créqui, by Coysevox

St Francis Xavier, St Philip, by Chassériau

Pierre Corneille

Cenotaph of Count d'Harcourt, by Renard

St Francis giving Alms, by Odier

— Paintings
○ Statues

Rue Saint-Honoré

St Roch Church

circular Chapel of Our Lady*, itself surrounded by an ambulatory that culminates in the Holy Communion Chapel (1717). Yet another addition, from around 1750, is the Calvary Chapel, on the initiative of Father Mazuel. The whole interior creates a remarkable theatrical effect, enhanced by the play of light. The organ case dates from 1752; the ancient instrument, made by the Clicquots, has been subjected to numerous renovations and restorations, most recently in 1927. Of the original pulpit, the work of Simon Challe (1760), only the canopy, in the form of a drapery representing Truth Lifting the Veil from Error, has survived; the rest was replaced in the 19th and 20th c.

R.-hand side-aisle: 1st and 2nd chapels, known as the Monuments, contain several important sculptures, including the bust of Maréchal François de Créqui* by Antoine Coysevox (1690–95), the statue of Cardinal Dubois at prayer by Guillaume I Coustou (1725) and the funeral monument to the astronomer, Maupertuis by Jean-Baptiste d'Huez (1766); 3rd chapel: monument to the Duc Charles de Créqui by Pierre Mazeline and Simon Hurtrelle (1688); 4th chapel: paintings by Louis Boulanger, *Souls in Purgatory*, 1850.

R.-hand side of transept: *The Three Hebrews in the Fiery Furnace* by Gabriel-François Doyen (1767), happily still in its original setting; on the l., *St Gregory the Great* by Simon Challe; on the r., St Francis de Sales by Augustin Pajou (plaster figure, 1766). The transept's cupola was painted by Adolphe Roger: *Christ in Glory* (1859–64).

Chancel: the vault was painted by A. Roger. At the entrance to the chancel against the l.-hand pillar, is Etienne Falconet's famous statue, *The Dying Christ*** (1757), part of a beautiful group commissioned by Father Mazuel, and dispersed during the Revolution. The high altar was decorated in the early 19th c. by the Thomire workshop.

1st chapel of the ambulatory: *St Clotilde at Prayer* by Charles Landelle (1847) and *Apotheosis of St Clotilde* by Achille Devéria; bas-reliefs of the *Stations of the Cross*, of which the 6th station can be seen here, by Louis Deseine, Constant Delaperche and Jean Bernard Duseigneur (1819–22); 2nd chapel: paintings relating to the life of St Teresa of Avila (1848); 3rd chapel: paintings by Adolphe Brune (*Martyrdom and Apotheosis of St Catherine*, 1848–50); 4th chapel: paintings by Louis Brisset relating to Mary Magdalene (1848–54); above the door, *The Purification of the Virgin* by Jean Restout (1759). The pillars separating the ambulatory from the Chapel of Our Lady are decorated with important pictures: *Godefroy de Bouillon in Victory**, by Claude Vignon (around 1620) and *Resurrection of the Son of the Widow of Naïm* by Eustache Le Sueur (1650); several epitaphs, among them those of the Princesse de Conti, daughter of Louis XIV, and of Duguay-Trouin.

Chapel of Our Lady: The ambulatory is decorated with large paintings, for the most part from the 19th c., the most important of which are *Suffer the Children* by Victor Schnetz (1855), *Jesus Expelling the Money Lenders from the Temple* by Antoine Thomas (1819), *Christ and the Centurion* by Michel-Ange Challe (1759) and *Christ Restoring to Life Jairus' Daughter* by Pierre Delorme (1817). The Chapel of Our Lady, an impressive area in the center of the church, has a tall dome decorated with an immense painting by Jean-Baptiste Pierre, *The Assumption*, finished in 1756, and now darkened and damaged. The altar is decorated with a group of three figures, representing the *Nativity** (1655) by the Anguier brothers, from Val-de-Grâce, where it was replaced by a copy; on the l., St Jerome by Lambert-Sigisbert Adam (1752); to the r., St Barbara (anonymous, 19th c.). The ambulatory of the Chapel of Our Lady was extended behind the altar by the Communion Chapel, with a curious piece of furniture that evokes the Temple of Jerusalem (early 19th c.) and beautiful stained-glass windows (1849). The great archway giving onto the Calvary Chapel (usually closed) contains a *Christ on the Cross* in marble by Michel Anguier (late 17th c.) and two large plaster groups in the niches: *Christ Being Nailed to the Cross*, by Duseigneur (1857–62) and the *Entombment*, by Deseine (1807); to the r. of the altar, *The Resurrection of Lazarus* by Vien (1759).

Main ambulatory, l.-hand side: above the door of the sacristy, the *Triumph of Mordecai*, by Restout (1755). The paneling of the sacristy is 18th c. Above a door opening onto the Rue Saint-Roch, *Return of the Prodigal Son* by Germain Drouais, a student of David. 3rd chapel, to the l. of the choir: a painting by Henry Scheffer and Auguste Loyer, episodes from the *Life of St Francis de Sales*; 1st chapel: nothing remains of Le Nôtre's tomb except the bust*, by Coysevox (1707), and a funerary inscription.

L. arm of transept: a large painting by Joseph-Marie Vien, *The Preaching of St Denis*, a pendant to the work by Doyen (1767); to the l., St Augustin, a plaster figure by d'Huez (1766); to the r., St Andrew, a plaster figure by James Pradier (1823).

L.-hand side-aisle, last chapel to the l. of the nave: monument of the Abbé de l'Epée, by Jean-Baptiste Lassus and Auguste Préault (1840); 3rd chapel: remains of the funerary bust of the painter: Pierre Mignard and his daughter, by Jean-Baptiste II Lemoyne (1744); 2nd chapel: *Baptism of Christ*, by Jean-Baptiste I and Jean-Baptiste II Lemoyne (1731); 1st chapel: paintings by Théodore Chassériau (1851–53): St *Philip Baptizing the Ethiopian Eunuch* and St *Francis Xavier Baptizing an Indian*.

Rue Saint-Honoré

From the Saint-Roch church to the Place André-Malraux.

Past the church of Saint-Roch at no. 161, is the site of the Porte Saint-Honoré, part of Charles V's wall. Joan of Arc tried to take this gateway into Paris on September 8, 1429, when she was fighting to recapture the town from the English who occupied it (see the medallion). In the 17th c. the same place was occupied by the famous Café de la Régence, a popular meeting-place for chess players. Voltaire, Franklin, Jean-Jacques Rousseau and Napoléon played there. Diderot set *Rameau's Nephew* there. Today, it is the headquarters of the Moroccan National Tourist Office. The Rue Saint-Honoré opens onto the Place André-Malraux, overlooked by the Palais-Royal, and with fountains designed by Davioud in 1874 (sculptures by Moreau and Carrier-Belleuse).

▷ The first Jardin des Tuileries

The symmetrical architecture of the Palais des Tuileries, designed by Philibert Delorme (1564), with later alterations by Jean Bullant, required an equally symmetrical design for the gardens commissioned by Catherine de' Medici. Separated from the palace itself by a road (now the Ave. du Général-Lemonnier), the gardens consisted of a vast enclosed trapezoidal area, with flower-beds designed to mirror one another exactly to the left and right of the garden's long E-W axis. Six large alleys lined with sycamores, elms, and evergreens, together with eight transversal alleys, divided the gardens into separate sections. Each of these was devoted to a different decorative motif; boxwood hedges, lawns, fruit trees, kitchen garden herbs and vegetables, or flowers were sculpted into arabesques and colorful patterns of extreme complexity that required constant maintenance. In one of these little gardens was a labyrinth, in another a fountain festooned with flowers, in still another a sundial and a moondial, and in one even a little enclosure with a crescent-shaped wall that gives back echoes of visitors' voices. The garden also boasted a menagerie, silkworm sheds, and many terracotta statues by Bernard Palissy. The most famous of the garden's attractions was the grotto, also designed by Palissy, the remains of which are preserved in the Musée de Sèvres and the Musée Carnavalet.

Every aspect of the garden's harmonious geometry – for the sake of which nature was aligned, corrected, leveled, shaped, even deformed – was designed to contribute to a single effect: to allow the essentially decorative architecture of the palace to stand out all the more brilliantly.

▣ Museums to visit

Musée de l'Orangerie, Jardin des Tuileries: paintings by the Impressionists and the school of Paris: *Les Nymphéas* (Water Lilies) by Claude Monet.

Musée des arts Décoratifs (Museum of Decorative Arts), 107 Rue de Rivoli: works of art and furniture from the Middle Ages to the present.

Musée des Arts de la Mode (Costume and Fashion Museum), 109 Rue de Rivoli: costumes and materials from the 16th to the 20th c.

▷ Religious art in the 18th c.

The 18th c., during which the Church had to defend itself – with varying degrees of success – against the attacks of philosophers and the progress of the Enlightenment, was not a great period for religious art. Nonetheless, parish churches, convents and monasteries did not cease to commission paintings and sculptures in great numbers to decorate new buildings such as Saint-Sulpice, Saint-Paul and Notre-Dame-des-Victoires, as well as old ones.

Among the painters specializing in religious painting, the most important was Jean Restout (1692–1768) who perpetuated, for the better part of a century, the tradition of his uncle Jean Jouvenet (1644–1711) who painted four colossal canvases for Saint-Martin-des-Champs (1706). François Lemoin or Lemoyne (1688–1737), who carried on the tradition of Lebrun, painted some large religious scenes preserved at Saint-Thomas d'Aquin and Saint-Sulpice. Carl Van Loo (1705–65) often worked for the churches, his masterpiece in the genre being the *Life of St Augustin*, still in place in Notre-Dame-des-Victoires.

The greatest sculptors of the 18th c. also contributed to the decoration of churches. Edmé Bouchardon (1698–1762) is the creator of the statue of Christ on a column at Saint-Sulpice; Jean-Baptiste II Lemoyne (1704–78) of *The Baptism of Christ* of Saint-Roch; Jean-Baptiste Pigalle (1714–85) of statues of the Virgin at Saint-Eustach and Saint-Sulpice; and Etienne Falconet (1716–81) of *Christ on the Mount of Olives* at Saint-Roch.

The mysticism and solemnity of the 17th c. was succeeded in the 18th c. by more human and less remote art, the expression of a religious spirit less given to austere meditations than to wonder and outpourings of sentiment.

The Val de Grâce district**

5th arr./Map ref. 22–D2, 23A1, A2
Metro and RER: Port-Royal.
Buses: 27, 83, 91
Parking: Rue Sufflot
Taxis: Place Edmond Rostand. Tel: 46–33–00–00
Market: Boul. de Port-Royal, in front of the Val-de-Grâce Hospital,
Tues., Thurs. and Sat., 7am–1.30pm

Beside the remarkable Church of Val-de-Grâce stands the former convent of the Feuillantines founded by Anne of Austria, mother of Louis XIV. Because it cannot be seen from the street this magnificent building, the façade of which has never been altered, is not well known to Parisians. In front, as far as the new military hospital and separated from the Boulevard de Port-Royal by a screen of trees, is a little-known garden containing a touching monument to the dead.

In the neighboring streets, the Institut National de Jeunes Sourds (Institute for Deaf Youth) with its enclosed garden and the church of Saint-Jacques-du-Haut-Pas keep alive the memory of those religious establishments that lined the old pilgrimage route to the shrine of St James of Compostela in Spain, and of which there is now little left. The atmosphere is different beyond the Rue Gay-Lussac, which marks the beginning of the Latin Quarter. A little away from the rowdiness of this district is the slope of the Montagne Sainte-Geneviève, crisscrossed by quiet, narrow streets bordered by the sober and imposing façades of large *écoles supérieures*. The old Rue Lhomond, which leads to a picturesque, almost provincial-looking square, retains a number of attractive old houses.

Tour of the district

2 hrs.

The Church of Val-de-Grâce***

1 Place Alphonse-Laveran (group tours by arrangement with the curator of the Musée Val-de-Grâce. Tel: 43-29-12-31, extension 4052).

Formerly a convent founded by Anne of Austria, the military hospital of Val-de-Grace (Valley of Grace), with its outbuildings and famous church, is one of the most remarkable pieces of 17th-c. architecture, as well as one of the best preserved to be seen in Paris today. Anne's son Louis XIV was seven years old when he laid the first stone of the church on April 1, 1645. He was 72 when it was consecrated in 1710. Begun by François Mansart, who worked too slowly to satisfy the Queen, the church was continued according to his design by his successors Le Mercier, Le Muet and Le Duc who, from 1654 to 1665, finished the construction, supervised the decoration and built the convent.

History of the building

An ancient fief of the Valois in the 13th c., this property of the Bourbons, called Petit Bourbon in the late 14th c., was confiscated and given to Louise of Savoy after the disgrace of the High Constable (1523). In 1611 it was rented by Cardinal Bérulle, who worked to establish there the seat of the Oratory's new congregation, which remained until 1616. In 1621 Anne of Austria installed the Benedictine Convent of Val-Profond, called Val-de-Grâce in the 16th c. (at Bièvres, Essonne), and laid the first stone of the bell tower. When, in 1638, after a wait of 21 years, the Queen gave birth to a son (the future Louis XIV) she fulfilled a vow she had made by building the church. An inscription recalls its origin: 'To the newborn Jesus and the Virgin Mother.' At the same time work began on the present convent in 1655. Secularized in 1790, transformed into a general military hospital in 1793 and then into an army teaching hospital by the Convention in 1795, it continues to be used for this purpose and has since 1850 housed the Ecole d'Application du Service de Santé (The Army Medical School). All the great military surgeons have studied here, from Larrey and Percy, doctors with Napoléon's Grande Armée, to Professor Hyacinthe Vincent (d.1950), for whom Vincent's infection of the respiratory tract is named.

The exterior

In the courtyard in front of the church is a statue of Baron Larrey (1766–1842), Napoléon's personal surgeon and surgeon-in-chief to the Grande Armée (bronze by David d'Angers, 1843), facing a plaque to the memory of medical officers who died in World War II. The church***, in the Jesuit style, is a monument of harmonious purity. The lead and gilt dome, one of the most famous in France, is, after those of the Panthéon and the Invalides, the highest in Paris (131ft/ 40.28m). The work of Pierre Le Muet and Gabriel Le Duc, who had been to Rome, it recalls in many ways that of St Peter's in the Vatican. With more buttresses than other domes, richer and more abundant sculpted ornamentation, and shadow effects caused by its projecting columns, the domed Val-de-Grâce has more affinity with the Roman Baroque than any other church in Paris. On the double triangular pediment are two angels sculpted by Michel Anguier.

The interior

Pierre Mignard's vast fresco in the cupola (1663, under restoration), *The Glory of the Blessed*, comprises more than 200 figures, each three times life-size. It inspired Molière to write his famous lines on the *Glory of Val-de-Grâce*. Above, the sculptures on the four pendentives and the bas-reliefs decorating the arcades of the nine chapels by Michel Anguier are allegories of the Virtues of the Virgin. The monumental baldachin* framing the altar (designed by Gabriel le Duc, decorated by the Anguiers) with its six huge wreathed columns of Barbançon marble, decorated with ornamental foliage and palms in gilded bronze was inspired by that of Bernini in St Peter's, Rome. Above is a marble group of the Nativity, an exact reproduction (made under the direction of Ruprich Robert) of Michel Anguier's work carried off during the Revolution and given to the Saint-Roch church under the First Empire. The sides of the chancel are occupied by two large chapels fronted by beautiful wrought iron gates. On the r. is the Saint Louis Chapel, formerly the nuns' choir, made smaller by a partition in the 19th c. On the l., the Sainte-Anne Chapel has an organ that was formerly in the Panthéon. In the 17th and 18th c., the hearts of members of the Orléans and royal families were kept in caskets here. Most of the 45 caskets desecrated during the Revolution, have disappeared. In the former chapel of the Saint-Sacrement behind the high altar (entrance on the r.; apply to the sacristan), is a fresco, *The Communion of the Angels*, by Jean-Baptiste de Champaigne, and sculptures by Michel Anguier.

The Cloisters

These are reached through the Saint-Louis chapel inside the church. Begun in 1624, the cloisters contain vestiges of the Petit

Bourbon. They comprise four groin-vault galleries, the semicircular arcades of which are surmounted by identical bays, separated by tall pillars. The convent buildings, mostly dating from 1655 to 1665 and almost intact, present a magnificent façade to the E, overlooking the gardens. At the N corner is the elegant pavilion** (built around 1624) named after Anne of Austria who used to stay there; it has a porch at ground level and is supported by banded Ionic columns; inside is a beautiful fireplace. The group is now listed as a historic monument. The former Petit Bourbon chapel served as a chapter-house and later as a kitchen. The Musée du Val-de-Grâce (→Museums) is in the W wing.

A new military hospital, visible from the Boul. de Port-Royal, has recently been built in the gardens. It comprises, on 12 floors, 13 specialist clinics, six operating theaters and 500 beds.

Rue du Val-de-Grâce

In order to admire the Val-de-Grâce from a suitable distance it should be seen from this street, which was cut in 1797 through the Carmelite convent and ends at the Boul. Saint-Michel. No. 6, a private *hôtel*, was decorated under the Directoire by its owner, a dealer in marble, with different kinds of marble throughout (under restoration).

Rue Saint-Jacques

From the Boul. de Port-Royal to Rue des Feuillantines.

Originally nothing but a Gallic track, this street became the principal N–S Gallo-Roman thoroughfare. Solidly paved and 30ft/9m wide, it ran from Genabum (Orléans) to the Boul. de Port-Royal. It is lined with apartment buildings, most of them recently built, which overlook here and there a house dating from the 18th c. Continuing in the direction of the Seine, it crosses many streets whose names recall famous convents now vanished.

No. 289, the Hôtel Du Barry, dates from 1702. At no. 284 is a gateway between two columns, integrated into the façade of a modern building. It was through here on April 21 1674, while hiding from the mob, that Louise de la Vallière, discarded favorite of Louis XIV, entered the Carmelite convent and lived there doing penance until her death (1710) under the name Sister Louise de la Miséricorde (Sister Louise of Pity). The old Carmelite convent, called the Grand Couvent de l'Incarnation, founded by the Duchesse de Longueville and Cardinal de Bérulle in 1603, extended as far as the present Rue Henri-Barbusse. At no. 25 there still exists a crypt closed to the public, uncovered in 1855 and repaired, which dates back to the 12th c. Notre-Dame-des-Champs chapel. Previously a Gallo-Roman catacomb, it served as a church for St Denis and his followers; over 200 tombs were excavated here in 1873. The Carmelite church, demolished in 1797, contained the tomb of Cardinal de Bérulle, by Pierre Sarrazin, now in the Louvre. Zola lived at 278 Rue Saint-Jacques.

The Schola Cantorum, at nos. 269–269 *bis*, is the academy of music founded privately in 1894 by three students or friends of César Franck: A. Guilmant, Charles Bordes and the composer Vincent d'Indy, to revive ancient and sacred music. It is an English property on French soil, having belonged to some English Benedictines, refugees in France after the Anglican schism of 1531. They established their community here in 1640 and constructed the building in 1674. Since the Revolution the property has belonged to the Catholic Bishops of England, under the control of the French State. The pretty courtyard is worth seeing. There is a beautiful 17th-c. drawing-room on the ground floor. The chapel (where the body of James II of England, who died in exile at Saint-Germain-en-Laye, rested until its desecration during the Revolution), has been converted into a music, drama and dancing school.

Rue des Feuillantines

Victor Hugo and Pasteur would not recognize the Impasse des Feuillantines of their boyhood, when it gave access to the convent of the Feuillantines founded by Anne of Austria in 1622. Its name is remembered thanks to the poet. Hugo retained a charming memory of the 'large, deep and mysterious garden' where he played with Adèle Foucher. It was, in fact, in an annex of the former convent (see the inscription at no. 8) that the poet's father, General Hugo, and his wife and children lived from 1808 to 1813. General Lahorie, implicated in Cadoudal's plot, found refuge at Mme Hugo's. Lamennais in 1815 and George Sand in 1886 also lived within these walls, which it is now difficult to imagine covered with wisteria and honeysuckle. Another outbuilding of the convent was the Barbet boarding school, one of whose pupils was Pasteur.

The Rue des Ursulines was opened in 1799 through the convent of the Ursulines, Daughters of the Christian Doctrine. Françoise d'Aubigné (the future Mme de Maintenon) left there to marry the writer Scarron, already crippled by rheumatism, who saved her from spending the rest of her life in the convent. At the corner of the street is a large modern-looking building by Labro (1900).

Rue Saint-Jacques, continued

From Rue des Ursulines to Rue Gay-Lussac.

The Institut National des Jeunes Sourds (National Institute for Deaf Youth) at no. 254, founded in 1760 by the Abbé de l'Epée and supported by the State since his death in 1790, occupies buildings reconstructed by Peyre in 1823, in the middle of a large garden. In the 14th c. this was a hospital run by the monks of Saint-Jacques-du-Haut-Pas, mainly a hospitaler order, which had its center in Italy at Altopascio, near Lucca. It was one in a chain of hospitals that lined the route to Santiago de Compostela. In 1572 the monastery was assigned to the monks of the Saint-Magloire, then in 1618, on the initiative of Henri de Gondi, Cardinal of Retz, to the Oratorians, who installed a seminary here in 1620, the permanent organization of which goes back at least as far as 1642, and which counted La Fontaine among its brothers (1641–42). In the courtyard is a statue of the Abbé de l'Epée (1712–89), by F. Martin (1879), himself a deaf-mute.

♟ Saint-Jacques-du-Haut-Pas

252 Rue Saint Jacques (open Tues.–Sun. 10am–12.30pm/4pm–7.30pm; closed January 1, July 14, December 25, and in August. Tel: 43–25–91–70).

This large Neo-Classical building, the plainness of which evokes the spirit of the Jansenist movement to which it is historically linked, takes its name from the hospital founded on the route to Compostela toward the end of the 12th c. by the Hospitalers of Altopascio, hence the name, St James of the High Pass. The first stone of the present building was laid in September 1630 by Gaston d'Orléans, the King's brother. Construction, however, proceeded slowly and it was only due to the generosity of the Duchesse de Longueville who is buried here that the project was revived in 1675. Daniel Gittard, who then worked at Saint-Sulpice, provided the plans for the nave and the façade; the r.-hand tower was never built. In 1688 work began on the Chapel of Our Lady, designed by Libéral Bruant. During the Revolution the church was taken over by the Theophilanthropists, who turned it into a Temple of Charity. A large Catechism Chapel was built in 1850; Norblin decorated it with paintings that are now hidden by a false ceiling.

The interior

The nave: the organ case from Saint-Benoît-le-Bétourné was installed here in 1792. It has undergone many modifications, and its oldest parts date back to the 15th c. (restored in 1790). R. side-aisle: 2nd chapel, plaque to the memory of the Duchesse de Longueville who laid the first stone of the nave in 1675, and plaques to the memory of former parishioners Branly and Pasteur. Against the wall next to the transept, *The Annunciation* by Le Nain. The r. arm of the transept contains the *Entombment*, by Degeorge (1819). The chancel: at the foot of the steps, the tombstones of Du Vergier de Hauranne, Jansenist Abbé of Saint-Cyran, the astronomer Jean-

Dominique Cassini (d.1712) and Charles de Sévigné, who was churchwarden here, and the priests Marcel and Cochin. Cochin was also a doctor at the Sorbonne and at the hospital that bears his name. Around the chancel: on the r., towards the apse, a beautiful carved oak door (17th c.) opening into the sacristy; *The Assumption of the Virgin* (1765), by Etienne Jeaurat; four 17th-c. paintings of the Fathers of the Church. The Apsidal Chapel is dedicated to the Virgin; it was designed by Libéral Bruant in the 17th c. and decorated with murals by Glaize in 1868. The l. side-aisle: 2nd chapel to the r. on going down again from the Chapel of Our Lady a confessional (17th c.). 4th chapel: above the altar, *Christ Healing St Peter's Step-mother* by Denis Calvaert (17th c.); at the far end, *St Peter* by Restout (1728), surrounded by four panels representing the *Four Virtues*, attributed to Le Sueur.

Rue Gay-Lussac

George Sand (at no. 5) and the tragedian Mounet-Sully, who died at no. 1, were the first famous residents of this uninteresting thoroughfare, which was only opened in 1859. After them, Paul Fort lived at no. 34, and the family of Simone Weil had an apartment there. During the construction of this street, at the level of no. 240 Rue Saint-Jacques, the remains of Roman baths were discovered, which turned out to be the Thermes du Midi from the Gallo-Roman city of Lutetia. Archeological finds are quite frequent in this quarter.

Rue Saint-Jacques, continued

From Rue Gay-Lussac to Rue des Fossés-Saint-Jacques.

No. 195 is the Institut d'Océanographie (Oceanographic Institute) founded by Prince Albert I of Monaco and built by Nérot in 1910. At no. 193, the Institut de Geographie ou de Physique du Globe (Institute of Geography and Geophysics) occupies the site of the Couvent de la Visitation known to St Jeanne de Chantal and her granddaughter, Mme de Sévigné. In 1978 the Institut Océanographique (Oceanographic Institute) opened its Centre de la Mar et des Eaux (Sea and Water Center) (open Tues.–Sun. 10am–12.30pm/ 1.15–5.30pm; tel: 46-33-08-61; frequent exhibitions).

On the site of the Gardens of the Visitation there now stands, between the Rue Saint-Jacques, Rue Pierre-Curie, Rue d'Ulm and Rue Gay-Lussac, a group of university buildings, the greater part of which was completed in 1931 and constitutes an important extension of the Science Faculty. The group comprises, in the Rue Pierre-et-Marie-Curie, the Institut de Biologie Physico-Chimique (Institute of Physiochemical Biology); (the Edmond de Rothschild Foundation); this brick building (architect, Germain Debré, 1930) should be viewed, above all, as an original interpretation of the

Cubic architecture of which Mallet Stevens is the most famous exponent.

Behind this is the Henri Poincaré Institute (mathematics and mathematical physics); the Institut du Radium and, to the l., a physical chemistry laboratory; farther on, the Institut de Chimie Appliquée (Institute of Applied Chemistry). Next several buildings belonging to the Curie Foundation. The Institut du Radium has several subdivisions: the faculty's radioactivity laboratory used by Mme Curie until her death in 1935 and then by her daughter and son-in-law, Irène Curie and Frédéric Joliot; the Curie building itself; technical services providing links with industry and measurements of radiation; a radiophysiology laboratory (Pasteur building), and outpatients' department for consultation on, and treatment of, cancer (the Fondation Curie). This radiophysiological department is in the process of expanding, with large modern laboratories along the Rue d'Ulm, and a hospital at 12 Rue Lhomond.

In the 13th c. at 218 Rue Saint-Jacques, stood the house of Jean Clopinel, known as Jean de Meung (1270–1305), author of the second part of the *Roman de la Rose* (the first half was begun around 1230 by Guillaume de Lorris). There are some pretty 17th-c. shops in this section of the Rue Saint-Jacques and, at the corner of the Rue Royer-Collard, a very interesting house. This street has retained its irregular 16th-c. layout and some of the façades are 17th c.; the political orator Royer-Collard lived there. Between 202 and 186 Rue Saint-Jacques part of the Gallo-Roman aqueduct of Arcueil (→Faubourg Saint-Jacques) that Marie de' Medici had restored to bring water to the Palais du Luxembourg and its gardens was uncovered. At no. 163 *bis*, note the old inscriptions on the tavern wall. Auguste Comte, founder of positivism, who really belonged to the Latin Quarter, lived at no. 159 from 1828 to 1834. A superb 18th-c. apartment building at 151 *bis* (architect, Lepas-Dubuisson, 1718), is unfortunately becoming dilapidated; there is a beautiful wrought-iron balcony; in the courtyard stands another 18th-c. mansion, with a balcony supported by four brackets. At no. 172 a plaque and a plan indicate the site of the Saint-Jacques Gate, demolished in 1684. This was one of the four principal gates of Philippe Auguste's fortified wall, during the 13th and 14th c. In 1306, at each of these gates, Philip le Bel (the Fair) hanged seven prominent citizens as a warning to those subjects who might have considered his taxes too heavy. Follow the Rue des Fossés-Saint-Jacques to the r. which replaced the old path that ran along the outer wall; note the 17th-c. houses.

Place de l'Estrapade

In the 16th c. this was known as the Carrefour de Braque (this is a large real or royal tennis court). It took its present name from the form of torture known in English by its Italian name, *strappado* meted out to soldiers as a punishment for desertion or other disciplinary problems. The men were hoisted up on the end of a rope and then allowed to drop its full length. Sometimes this was repeated several times. Here, at the end of the 18th c., was the Bureau Central des Falots (Central Lantern Office) where passersby could hire young boys with lanterns who would accompany them to their door (→inset). Today it is a peaceful square, prized by *boules* players.

Rue Lhomond

Follow this street to the l. Laid out in the 14th c., it was named in 1867 after almost forgotten Abbé Charles-François Lhomond, a grammarian and author of *De Viris Illustribus Urbis Romae (On the Illustrious Man of Rome)*.

Former Collège des Irlandais* (Irish College)

To the l.
Since World War II this institution has belonged to the Polish Catholic community. Karol Wojtyla (Pope John-Paul II), has stayed there. Until 1769 the Collège des Irlandais occupied the Collège des Lombards at 34 Rue de la Montagne-Sainte-Geneviève. At that date it was installed in the Rue du Cheval-Vert, renamed Rue des Irlandais in 1807, in the beautiful building erected by Bélanger (1755–69). The façade on Rue des Irlandais has 16 bays, the center three of which are partitioned; the middle one includes the arched portal surmounted by the arms of Ireland (a harp). The Saint Patrick-Chapel is in the wing in the Rue Lhomond. The altar is 18th c.; a two-tiered gallery bears the monogram of St Patrick. In the courtyard, below the gallery and beside the chapel door, is a bust of John Lee who, in 1578, gathered around him the scattered Irish community, and founded the Irish College.

Rue Lhomond, continued

No. 10 Rue Lhomond was the Hôtel de Flavacourt; the Marquis de Flavacourt married the only one of the five daughters of the Marquis de Nesle who had not been the mistress of Louis XV. Michelet lived here in 1839. The laboratories of the Fondation Curie at nos. 18–26 replaced the well-known, highly respected Jesuit College in the Rue des Postes, which itself had stood on the site of mansions and convents demolished during the Revolution. Cross the Rue Amyot, a provincial-looking little street that from 1588 to 1867 was called, for reasons still obscure, Rue du Puits-qui-Parle (Talking Well St.).

No. 27 Rue Lhomond is the Hôtel Le Menestrel de Hauguet de Luteaux, a vast, square mansion of seven bays with three floors, built in 1737. Note the unusual dormer windows, especially the one that overlooks the street. The garden façade (a registered monument) includes a central section with two large arcades reaching to the mezzanine level. Beyond no. 29 are some severe looking buildings, now converted into apartments, that once belonged to the Sainte-Aure institutes on the Rue Tournefort. At nos. 28–32 is the Congrégation du Saint-Esprit which, after being suppressed during the Revolution, and occupied by the Ecole Normale Supérieure from 1813 to 1822, was reinstalled here. The chapel (admission free), the first stone of which was laid by M. de Sartines, was constructed by Chalgrin (1769–80). But what was once a masterpiece of the Louis XVI style has been badly disfigured during the 19th c. An 18th-c. house is at no. 60. The painter Oudry had a large property at nos. 66–68, beyond the Place Lucien-Herr. Another painter, Chapelain-Midy, lives there now.

Place Lucien-Herr

This square forms a kind of frontier between two different neighborhoods: the tourist area around the Rue Mouffetard and the intellectual and residential areas in the streets around the Panthéon, where the Rue Pierre-Brossolette and Rue Vauquelin now bear no trace of the convents through whose grounds they were built. There is a small terraced restaurant here with a southern ambiance. Follow the Rue Vauquelin, which runs past the brick buildings of the Ecole de Physique et Chimie Industrielle (School of Industrial Physics and Chemistry) (entrance at no. 10), where the Curies discovered radium.

Rue Claude-Bernard

This street dates back only to the second half of the 19th c. No. 16 is the Institut National d'Argronomie (Agronomy), the major part of which has merged with the Ecole de Grignon on the outskirts of Paris. The street is on the site of the former Jardin des Apothicaires (Apothecaries' Garden), founded in the 16th c. to cultivate medicinal plants. Farther on, the mathematician Henri Poincaré lived at no. 63 from 1854 to 1912.

Rue d'Ulm

This street is the goal of many a young French scholar's dreams. Most of the street, which runs through the grounds of the former convents of the Visitation Sainte-Marie and the Ursulines, belongs to the Ecole Normale Supérieure (entrance at no. 45).

The Ecole Normale Supérieure, created by the Convention on October 30, 1794 and mainly organized by the decree of March 17, 1808 establishing the Université Impériale, provides post-secondary education for the nation's most gifted students who intend to become professors or researchers. Although, in the course of its existence, and recently in particular, the school has changed in character, its reputation remains as high as ever. Among the graduates are many famous people, notably: V. Cousin, Taine, Bergson in philosophy; A. Thierry, Duruy, Fustel de Coulanges, Lavisse, Jullien in history; Péguy, Romain Rolland, Giraudoux, Jérôme, Tharaud, Jules Romains, Léopold Sédar Senghor, Pierre-Henri Simon, Jean-Paul Sartre in literature; Jaurès, A. Tardieu, E. Herriot, Georges Pompidou in politics; and in the sciences, Darboux, Puiseux, Tannery, G. Bonnier, Appell, Painlevé, Emile Borel, Jean Perrin and, above all, Pasteur. On the ground floor of the central building (architect, A. de Gisors, 1841), a monument to the 239 students who died for France in World War I, by Landowski. In the Rue d'Ulm, beyond the entrance gate on the outer wall, a Pasteur medallion and a plaque recalling his principal discoveries, as well as the site of the corner of the attic that he used as a laboratory (1864–88). The school has been greatly enlarged with imposing buildings: vast modern physics, chemistry and biology laboratories (including fresh water and sea water aquariums) were built between 1933 to 1937 between Rue Erasme and Rue Lhomond (architects, A. and J. Guilbert). A main building has been constructed along Rue Rataud and another, opposite the oldest buildings, very contemporary in style.

At no. 31 stands the Ecole Supérieure des Arts Décoratifs (Decorative Arts), expanded in 1969 by the architect Joly. At no. 29 the Institut National de Recherches Pédagogiques (National Institute of Pedagogical Research), which comprises an information and research office, and a library with collections of historical interest (access is restricted to researchers).

No. 27 is the annex of the Institut Curie, built by Balladur in 1964. At no. 17 is the Maronite church of Notre-Dame-du-Liban (Our Lady of Lebanon): this was formerly the chapel of the famous Jesuits' College that stood in the Rue des Postes, now the Rue Lhomond (→see above). Since it was enclosed (1963) within the hall of the Franco-Lebanese Center the church can no longer be seen from the outside, but it can be visited by applying to the center. The Holy Week religious services held there are very beautiful.

Rue d'Ulm, whose last section is no longer part of the University, but is residential, ends at the Place du Panthéon.

▷ The Baroque in Paris

Paris is not a Baroque city, for in the 17th c. this style was resisted in France in favor of the Neo-Classical. The Italian innovations, however, were much appreciated, especially in religious architecture where a new kind of church appeared, with cupolas and façades with orders of columns deriving from, among others, the famous Gesú church in Rome. In civil architecture an extraordinary renewal occurred, as much in the arrangement of rooms within buildings, which became both more varied and more practical, as in the outward forms. By playing off symmetrical compositions against curvilinear elements Le Vau and Le Pautre sometimes arrived at very daring solutions. Decoration during this period was rich and fantastical but sometimes heavy.

The first Italian-inspired cupola constructed in Paris was that of the Petits Augustins (Ecole des Beaux-Arts) in 1608. The Carmelites of Saint-Joseph (Rue de Vaugirard) soon followed (1613-20); then the Church of Saint-Paul-St-Louis (1627-41); and the Church of Sainte-Marie-de-la-Visitation by François Mansart in 1632, like the preceding, in Rue Saint-Antoine. This last is one of the rare examples of a church with a circular floor plan. Then came the dome of the Sorbonne and that of Val-de-Grâce, which may be considered the culmination of these experiments. Finally, as late as 1661, Le Vau created the most 'Roman' design of all, at the Palais de l'Institut, with a dome flanked by curved wings.

Among the mansions, note the entrances or remarkable sculptures of the Hôtel d'Almeras, from the early 17th c. (30 Rue des Francs-Bourgeois); the Hôtel de Châlons-Luxembourg, 1612 (26 Rue Geoffroy-l'Asnier); the Hôtel Salé, 1656 (5 Rue de Thorigny); the elegant curved lines of the Hôtels Lambert by Le Vau, 1640 (2 Rue Saint-Louis-en-l'Ile), the Hôtel de Beauvais, by Le Pautre, 1655 (68 Rue François-Miron). In contrast, consider the monumental courtyard of Saint-Aignan. Le Muet, 1640 (71 Rue du Temple). For their interior decoration, see the magnificent galleries designed by François Mansart for Mazarin at the Bibliothèque Nationale (1640) and also the Hotel La Vrillière, now the Banque de France (1635); finally, the salons of the Arsenal and those of the Hôtel Lauzun (17 Quai d'Anjou).

▣ Museum to visit

Musée du Val-de-Grâce (1 Place Alphonse-Laveran). History of the Army Medical Health Service.

▷ Not to be missed

The Church of Val-de-Grâce, its gardens and the pavilion of Anne of Austria, mother of Louis XIV.

The Church of Saint-Jacques-du-Haut-Pas for its paintings.

Rue Lhomond, with its picturesque convents.

▷ **The first street lighting**

Before the 14th c. Parisians had never enjoyed the advantages of street lighting. At night the streets were plunged into darkness; the city authorities advised people not to leave home without a lantern. During the reign of Philip the Fair, Paris had only three public sources of light: one at the Tour de Nesle, one at the Cimetière des Innocents and one at the Porte du Châtelet, where the greffier (clerk of the court) was charged with keeping the lamps lit. It was not until 1558 that the parliament ordered citizens to place lanterns in front of their houses or light candles in their windows for the benefit of passersby – a measure that was largely ignored. In 1662 a royal charter authorized the Abbé Laudati Caraffe to organize a troupe of torchbearers, who could be hired to see people home. In 1667, thanks to the efforts of Lieutenant-General de la Reynie of the Paris police, 6000 lanterns were distributed to homeowners for their windows – Paris's first citywide lighting system. Street lamps were first installed experimentally in the Rue Dauphine in 1763, and in 1769 they were erected at 200ft/60m intervals throughout the city streets. There is an entertaining anecdote on the subject: at one point the nightly lighting of the Paris street lamps was entrusted to a contractor, with the stipulation that he receive no payment during the full moon. The money thus saved was deposited by the City in a bonus fund called the 'moonlight pension fund'; this practice was abolished in 1780, when permanent night-time street lighting was introduced. Although gas lighting was invented by Lebon in 1791, it did not become widespread in Paris until 1829.

▷ **The clay pits**

In Gallic times the S slope of the Montagne Sainte-Geneviève was well known for its numerous pits from which clay was extracted for making pottery. When work on the foundations for the Panthéon began, 69 such pits were uncovered, some of them descending to a depth of 82ft/25m. The clay pits also gave two of the district's main streets their original names: today's Rue d'Ulm and Rue Lhomond were originally called respectively Rue des Poteries-Saint-Séverin and Rue des Pots (later, Rue des Postes).

The Vaugirard district*

15th arr./Map ref. 20, C2, C3, D2; 21, A2, B2
This, the largest *quartier* in Paris, well away from the main tourist

centers and without any really outstanding monuments, is unjustly ignored by visitors passing through. This neglect on the part of tourists has had the effect of making the 15th arrondissement one of the capital's most authentically Parisian quarters.

Several extensive walks are required to appreciate fully the particular character of Vaugirard where one feels, in many places, close to its village origins. A series of narrow streets, markets and charming public gardens have survived the urban upheavals of the 19th and 20th centuries. But, like all genuinely living organisms, this neighborhood has adapted to the present day and offers numerous examples of interesting contemporary architecture. Close to shady squares where markets like those in provincial towns are held, hospital centers and ultra-modern administrative headquarters can also be found. The Pasteur institute and hospital are of particular interest in this sector, but don't miss the new Square Georges Brassens or the old workshops of La Ruche.

The history of the district

People began to move into this district in the 13th c. when, in 1256, Gérard de Moret, Abbé of Saint-Germain, built a convalescent home in the hamlet of Val Boitron, named Val Gérard in his honor; this name has since been transformed into Vaugirard. A church was built in 1340 and received the relics of St Lambert in 1451. As Vaugirard grew into a parish many aristocrats came here for the clean air and the hunting. Despite some excitement caused by the installation of the court at Versailles – for Vaugirard's main street was on the direct route – life went by peacefully in the town, with its windmills and *guingettes* (open air café–dancehalls), until the Revolution.

In the 18th c. large estates, summer resorts, country houses and rest homes were established. The villagers' houses themselves ran in serried rows along the Rue Blomet, Rue Lecourbe and Rue Vaugirard. To build the Ecole Militaire, Louis XV bought the plains of Grenelle from the Abbeye de Saint-Geneviève and the Vaugirard quarries from Saint-Germain-des-Prés, thereby bringing the village its first non-agricultural industry. The village expanded, eventually reaching the suburbs of Paris, and became the Commune de Vaugirard in 1790. With the construction of the Fermiers-Généraux's wall, however, the commune lost some of its territory.

In 1830 the hamlet of Grenelle, developed with a rectilinear street grid by Violet and Letellier, was separated from Vaugirard, which remained predominantly rural, with a population of older people of independent means, while Grenelle became industrialized. Nevertheless, the S and E of the *quartier* saw their empty space filled in by modest buildings with courtyards, devoted to crafts and cottage industries. In 1860 two *quartiers* were created: Necker in the N and Saint-Lambert, whose post-Haussmann apartment buildings soon attracted the middle classes. At the beginning of the 20th c. the S and the E saw the appearance of subsidized working-class housing (*Habitations à Bon Marche*, or HBM). During the course of the 20th c., Vaugirard has lost its working-class population, which has been replaced by the middle-classes, a process only accelerated by the vast development projects of the 1970s.

The traditional Vaugirard quarter

Métro: Sèvres-Lecourbe
Bus: 48, 89, 70, 39
Taxis: at the Métro Sèvres-Lecourbe (Square Pasteur). Tel: 47-34-00-00.
Parking: corner of Boul. Garibaldi and Rue de Suffren.
1 hr.
Market: Rue de la Convention, between Rue Alain-Chartier and Rue de l'Abbé-Groult (Tues., Thurs., Sun., 7am-1.30pm).

This walk between Necker and Saint-Lambert, takes us from very modern times back to the days of the village.

Follow the Boul. Garibaldi toward the Place Cambronne.

Rue Jean-Daudin

On the l. is an annex of the UNESCO Building (1975-78) by Bernard Zehrluss, with the collaboration of M. Faure (interior designer, Maldonado; engineer, Fruiter). Offices and conference rooms are spread through a series of buildings joined together to form an irregular mass. The metal framework is visible from the outside and the façades are entirely covered with reflective glass. At no. 20 is a building whose façade was sculpted by G. Petit (1926). Another interesting façade is the one at no. 32 by F. Vallois architect and sculptor.

Rue Lecourbe, formerly the Rue de Sèvres. At nos. 31-33 is a beautiful high building in brick and stone by the architect M. Gouverneur (1930), with stylized roses sculpted on the façade. At no. 11 are three-storey artists' studios. On the corner of the Rue François-Bonvin, to the r., a handsome house from 1900. Rue François-Bonvin. At no. 27 in this street is a small church situated within UNESCO territory. From no. 23 to no. 1 is an attractive collection of middle-class apartment buildings, 1900-03.

Rue Lecourbe, continued

Opposite no. 90 the Villa Poirier stands on the site of an old *folie* (pleasure house); also beautiful early 19th-c. buildings of brick and cut stone, and other handsome dwellings from the 1930s. At no. 91, at the rear of a courtyard, is the Russian Church of Saint-Seraphin-de-Satow, its roof pierced by a tree. Note the beautiful façade of the building (no. 116) situated at the intersection of the Rue Mademoiselle and Rue Cambronne, by the architect E. Delangle (1904) and those of nos. 118-120, 128, 130, 140 *bis* Rue Lecourbe.

Rue Cambronne

This is a busy and picturesque shopping street. The ground level food shops are often installed in low-roofed buildings, vestiges of the modest dwellings of the 19th c. The Rue Robert-Fleury has a certain unity, with buildings constructed by the architect J. Chartiau. In the Rue Mademoiselle at the corner of the Rue de l'Amiral-Roussin, on the r., is a pink-and-mauve nursery school with small courtyards like so many mini-amphitheaters. Klaus Schultze created an enclosure there in the form of a sculpture.

Rue de l'Amiral-Roussin

Go down on the l. side of this street. At nos. 63 and 65 is a beautiful group of houses built by the Societé Civile du Groupe des Maisons Ouvrières, recognized as a public utility in 1906, and made the homes of the Fondation Mme Lebaudy in 1917 (→ Rue de la Saïda, Rue de Constadt, Vaugirard Hospital). This building complex by the architect Labussière (1907) is grouped around a large courtyard used as a 'garden'. With its brick façades, extensive use of cut stone, bow windows and mansard roofs, this kind of dwelling was the prototype of the large residential development projects that would be built in the district between the two World Wars. Follow the Rue de Viroflay and the Rue Péclet.

Square Saint-Lambert

Here we are plunged back into the 1930s. This public garden was opened in 1935 on the site of the old gasworks and all the apartment buildings around it are of the same period. Rue Léon-Lhermitte consists of a group of buildings from 1934, by Heckly, made of cut stone, with bow-windows. Identical groups are in the Rue Formigé and Rue du Docteur-Jacquemart-Clemenceau. The Square, away from the main thoroughfares, is at the heart of a residential area. A large central lawn, bordered by a raised path creating different levels with terraces and sloping surfaces, presents a variety of landscapes. Although the famous Punch-and-Judy show recently moved away, the merry-go-round is still there. Cross the Rue Lecourbe; at nos. 190 and 181, old studios line paved alleys. Follow the Rue de l'Abbé-Groult; no. 52 *bis* is the Blomet Clinic.

Rue Blomet

The Blomet Clinic, at nos. 134 and 136 in this street, seems to radiate calm from its garden and the nursing home of the Sisters of Saint-Marie-de-la-Famille attached to it. One of Vaugirard's oldest streets, it has kept along its entire length an old-fashioned village charm. Stroll down the street to get some idea of the tranquility that attracted the leisured classes and religious communities in the days when the village was known for its healthy air. The Rue Ferdinand-Fabre on the l., which you pass, presents an attractive group of middle-class apartment buildings dating from the early 20th c. Follow, on the l., the Rue Alain-Chartier. At no. 14 is a Waterworks building dating from 1895 (architect unknown).

Place de la Convention

Cinemas and restaurants make this square very active, but it retains nonetheless a provincial air with its plane trees, benches, a market three times a week, a merry-go-round and a fortune-teller whose trailer is installed next to a shooting gallery.

Rue de Vaugirard

From the Place de la Convention to the Place Adolphe Chérioux.

Walk l. along the even-numbered side of the street. This is the village's first main street which led to Paris and became an essential thoroughfare when the court was installed at Versailles; it continues S as far as the village of Issy. The traditional village developed between this road and the Rue de Sèvres (now Rue Lecourbe). It is a very busy shopping street as far as the Place Adolphe-Chérioux and has some beautiful houses on its side-streets.

✝ The Church of Saint-Lambert

Off Rue Gerbert.

This church was constructed by Naissant from 1848 to 1853, with funds allocated by the Commune of Vaugirard on land donated by the Abbé Groult-d'Arcy, former municipal councillor of the village. Outside is a high octagonal stone bell-tower with a slate roof surmounted by the cross of the old church; inside, a statue of the Virgin, also from the old church. At no. 16 Rue Gerbert, a small mansion stands next to a fragmentary sign – a relic of 19th-c. commerce: 'coffee, wood, fuel oil'. Behind the Saint-Lambert church rejoin the Rue Blomet: at no. 128 the retreat house of Notre-Dame-du-Bon-Repos, founded in 1861 by the architect of Saint-Père. At the corner of the Rue Carcel is a building with its corners ornamented by sculptures in the form of heads by the architect Albert Preynaud (1919).

L'Impasse de Soleil d'Or

226 Rue de Vaugirard

Make a detour to visit this paved cul-de-sac, which resembles a village street. The sign 'Le Lavoir du soleil' is still in place. It belonged to an inn built at the beginning of the 18th c. In 1791 this was the meeting-place for royalist conspirators who hatched the 'Soleil d'Or' plot to exterminate the members of the Jacobin Club. Faithful accomplice to conspiracy, the inn was the scene, in 1796, of the 'Conspiracy of the Camp Grenelle' which aimed to overthrow the Directoire.

Rue Borromée: this paved street, narrow and quiet, is bordered by two- or three-storey buildings. No. 3 is one of the numerous examples of workers' houses built by private enterprise. Completed in 1897 by Torlet, this dwelling was awarded the silver medal at the first competition organized by the Habitations à Bon Marché committee for the Seine District in 1901. The façade on the street has bow windows and overlooks a small communal garden; the courtyard façade has iron panels with brickwork in between. The small Square Blomet replaced the artists' studios at no. 45 where Joan Miró and André Masson worked, as well as, later on, Robert Desnos; they were often visited by Max Jacob, André Breton, Michel Leiris and Georges Limbourg. In memory of that era Miró donated one of his most important sculptures, now in the gardens.

Cross the Rue des Volontaires on the l. The sculptor Carlo Sarrabezalles (1885–1971) lived and worked here from 1928 until his death, in a red brick studio on which there is a commemorative plaque. Farther up, the Rue Emile-Duclaux, rich in beautifully carved façades, leads towards the Rue de Vaugirard. Rue de Vaugirard. At no. 213 is the entrance of the Hôpital Pasteur, which specializes in infectious diseases. Return to the Pasteur Métro station, passing, on the l., the imposing outline of the Lycée Buffon (Buffon High School), constructed in 1889 by Vaudremer on the site of the old Vaugirard cemetery and a large amphitheater of natural history, decorated in 1925 by Roger Deboussin, who copied the technique of the Impressionists.

The Pasteur Institute quarter

Métro: Pasteur. Map ref. 21 A–2
Bus: 48, 89, 70, 39
Parking: Corner of Boul. de Vaugirard and Rue de Vaugirard
Taxis: Sèvres-Lecourbe Métro. Tel: 47–34–00–00.
Markets: Place Wassily Kandinsky, Wed. and Sat., 7am–1.30pm.

1 hr.
This second walk goes from the Pasteur Institute, in the S of Necker, to the streets of Saint-Lambert, still bearing the mark of its recent village days, but now modernized.

Leave the vast thoroughfare of the Boul. Pasteur, planted with chestnut trees.

Rue du Docteur-Roux

Dr Roux, a collaborator of Pasteur, was the institute's second director (1904–33) and gave the first course on microbiology and immunology in the world. On the l. of the street entrance, is Saint-Jean-Baptiste-de-la-Salle built by the architect Jacquemin from 1908 to 1910. The mosaic in the choir is by J. Gaudin (1935).

The Pasteur Institute

25 Rue du Docteur-Roux

Following the success of the first anti-rabies vaccination, Pasteur adopted a plan for a great international public subscription to found a center for research, vaccine production, and vaccination. The success of this fund-raising resulted in the inauguration of the Pasteur Institute's first building on November 4, 1888 (no. 25). In 1900 the Institute of Biological Chemistry was opened, thanks to a legacy of two million francs from the Baroness Hirsch, at no. 28 in this same street. The next facility to be opened was the Hôpital Pasteur, at 213 Rue de Vaugirard. The hospital was founded for the purpose of applying Pasteur's theories, and was the first medical institution to do so; it continues to concentrate on the treatment of infectious diseases, particularly through the Fondation Mme Lebaudy. Next to be built were the laboratories for tuberculosis research and for the preparation of the Bilié Calmette et Guérin (BCG) vaccine, at 96 Rue Falguière (architects, Duquesne and Bitterlin). The Metchnikoff building for immunological research, opened in 1981, is named after Elie Metchnikoff (1845–1916), one of the founders of immunology, a colleague of Pasteur and director of the institute from 1904 to 1916. New biotechnology laboratories are currently under construction on Rue Vigée-Lebrun.

The Pasteur Institute has three purposes: basic science and biomedical research, post-graduate instruction and the production of medicines and vaccines, which it markets commercially. Moreover, as a center for reference and consultation, the institute plays a leading role worldwide, particularly in the control of epidemic diseases.

At no. 25, in the institute's oldest building, is the library (open Mon.–Fri. 9.15am–5.45pm), closed except to medical students and researchers. Aside from the works of Pasteur and his followers, the library has a very extensive collection of material relating to microbial research; there are also portraits of Dr Roux and Elie Metchnikoff. The library also serves as the site for the institute's academic ceremonies.

For the Musée Pasteur (→Museums). After leaving the institute, proceed along the peaceful Rue Plumet and turn onto the Rue Mathurin-Régnier (note the artists' studios at nos. 32 and 34).

Rue Bargue

Note first the group of buildings (built 1910–13) by Provensal and Alter, which house the Rothschild foundation (founded by Alphonse, Gustave and Edmond de Rothschild). At nos. 11 and 13 are plaques for the 'Notre Village' development, created by the Hubert Montmarché and Rothschild foundations in 1904 to provide low-income working-class housing along the lines of that built by the Peabody Fund in the U.S. The little Square Necker is, like the whole neighborhood, very quiet.

Rue Tessier: The foyer of the Infirmières at no. 14 is typical of the architecture funded by philanthropic institutions at the turn of the century. The façade of the building at the corner of the Rue de la Procession and Rue Sainte-Félicité, by Théodore Lambert (1913), has fine bow windows and pretty ceramic decorations.

The Rue Sainte-Félicité crosses the Rue Paul-Barruel (note the buildings by Heckly from the 1930s) and ends before the immense Chèques Postaux de Paris building built in 1936 by Roux-Spitz.

Square de Vergennes

Opening onto the Rue de Vaugirard, this 'square' is really a private alley, yet another artists' colony. At no. 15 a plaque identifies the *hôtel particulier* built in 1931 by Robert Mallet-Stevens for the master glass artist Barillet. The building is a juxtaposition of simple volumes, completely bare of ornamentation. Barillet perfected the art of *vitrail blanc* (literally, clear stained glass), using special forms of glass more transparent than traditional stained glass, in response to a demand for increased natural light in architecture.

Rue d'Alleray

This whole area has many fine examples of post-Haussmannian architecture, especially no. 4 Rue d'Alleray (at the corner of the Rue François-Villon), no. 6 and nos. 14 and 14 *bis*. Farther along are two private alleys once threatened with destruction: the Hameau d'Alleray at no. 25, and the Villa Hersent at no. 27, where each private house has its own garden. Cross the Rue Corbon: no. 3 is a typical example of scholastic architecture from early in the century (1911). Opposite, at 41 Rue d'Alleray is an unusual millstone house covered with polychrome ceramic tiles.

Place d'Alleray

Note the nursery school at nos 121 and 15 Rue Aristide Maillol (1985) by Alexandre Ghiulamila.

Rue Falguière

This street, considerably altered in the last few years, leads back to the Boul. Pasteur. The *zone d'aménagement concerté* or ZAC (mixed public and private housing development), begun in 1982 on the site of some SNCF warehouses and just recently completed, occupies the entire area between the Rue de la Procession and Rue du Cotentin. These buildings, with their façades covered in white ceramic tiles, are thought to be very pleasing. At 36 Rue du Cotentin is another HBM (*habitations à bon marché:* low-income housing) built by the Anonymous Association for Housing Large Families, and designed by Beaudoin (1908–09).

Rue Falguière, continued

As far as Boul. Pasteur

At no. 106 on the other side of Rue Falguière, at the corner of Rue Vigée-Lebrun, is a building recently erected by the city, with *trompe-l'oeil* paintings in its interior courtyard. The l. side of the street is lined with more buildings belonging to the Pasteur Institute until you reach the Cité Falguière, another of the artists' colonies that proliferated at one time in the 15th arrondissement, today very much altered. Modigliani and Soutine frequented the place; Foujita lived here for a while; and Toda had a studio here. At the corner of Rue d'Arsonval and Rue Falguière is a related building by Léon Chesnay.

The Southeast of Saint-Lambert

Métro: Plaisance
Bus: 62, 48, 89
Taxi: Place Charles-Vallin. Tel: 48-28-45-98.
1 hr.

The following itinerary reveals a hardworking neighborhood that has nonetheless many fine façades and little gardens.

Immediately after the bridge, turn l. on the Rue Castagnary, then take the next r. down the charming Ruelle Charles-Weiss, a sort of private alley lined with trees and inaccessible to cars. At no. 10 is a successful piece of contemporary architecture consisting of three semi-detached triplexes, built by G.E.A. architects, G. André, G. Breton, G. Brzeckowski and J. M. Roques, 1979. The façade of smooth white tiles has a bay window three storeys high; the apartments overhang the street in an almost alarming way.

Rue Santos-Dumont

via Rue Franquet

This street, just a stone's throw from the much noisier Rue de Vouillé, is utterly enchanting to visit on foot – a trip through time back to a little village in the Ile-de-France. Brassens lived here and frequented the neighborhood's cafés and restaurants, which are still full of his photographs, personally signed and dedicated. This street, still relatively well preserved, is lined exclusively with little country style houses with tiled roofs, huddled in their gardens, with great trees overhanging the wrought-iron fences that guard their owners' privacy. This winding street still has a few old artisans' workshops. The Villa Santos-Dumont, with its artists' studios, consists of several fine millstone houses. At the exit from the villa, to the r., is a beautiful group of houses with slate roofs, all identical. At the end of the street, cross the Rue des Morillons, noting on the l. the school complex (nos. 66–82) built in 1935 by Pierre Sardou; the frieze depicting children was sculpted by H. Navarre. Turn into the Rue de Villafranca, gateway to the Village de l'Avenir (→inset). The original houses in the first section of the street were demolished in the 1970s, but the development's characteristically modest houses and little villas line the street toward the Rue Fizeau; now turn l. Rue de Bessin (via Rue du Lieuvin): At no. 5 is another example of early modernist architecture, the Centre d'Hémodialyse (Dialysis Center): Sartoli, architect, 1875.

Rue Castagnary

The whole neighborhood around this street is still marked by the presence of the abattoirs, which stood where the Parc Georges-Brassens lies today. The construction of the Abattoirs de Vaugirard, undertaken by the Municipal Council in 1887, was begun in May 1894, with plans by the architect Ernest Moreau. The hog abattoirs on the Rue de Dantzig were put into service in September 1894, those for cattle in late 1897. The horse abattoirs were not begun until 1904; nevertheless, it is horse butchering that has left the longest lasting traces in the district, as witnessed by numerous inscriptions, signs and sculptures. In 1966, the city decided to close the abattoirs, and began to demolish them in 1974. There are many *restaurants hippophagiues* in the neighborhood, with telltale names such as L'Ecurie or L'Etable (both mean The Stable), offering horse-meat on their menus.

At no. 136, on the corner of the Rue du Sommet-des-Alpes, is a two-storey building with an old plaque that advertises 'F. B—, horsemeat butchershop, wholesale and in bulk, sausages, saltmeat': note the wrought-iron grill and the sculpted horse. Old horsemeat butcher-shops still do business on the Rue de Chambéry. The numerous bistros, food-related businesses and horsemeat importers bear further witness to the era of the abattoirs.

Rue Brancion

At no. 106, near the entrance to the Carré Sylvia-Montford, is a brick building dating from 1904 by the architects G. Just and E. Denis. Next to the entrance, under the motto of Paris '*Fluctuat nec mergitur*' ('Though beaten by the waves, it does not sink'; the emblem of the city is a ship), is a bust of Emile Decroix (1821–1901), 'propagator of horsemeat'. The consumption of horsemeat was in fact not authorized in France until 1864. The façade overlooking Rue Brancion is decorated with medallions of Isidore Geoffroy Saint-Hilaire, Camille Leblanc, Armand-Charles Goubaux, Thomas-Eugène Renoult, and others. Inside, within the courtyard, close to the brick façade (1907) are the former stables. A sculpture of a horse's head keeps company with a bronze bust of François Barbaud (1862–1938) under which can be read: 'the grateful horsemeat industry.' Turn l. from the Rue Brancion to follow the Rue Chauvelot, still packed with shops, cafés, and restaurants, all dating from the 19th c. Stroll along the charming culs-de-sac of Montebello, the Rue Camulogène and the Impasse du Labrador, renovated in 1982. There are still many little houses with their garden and tree, their cats lounging in the middle of the street, grass growing between the paving stones. Return down the Rue Brancion, passing by the old covered horse market with its metal structure (1907). Horses destined for the slaughterhouse were sold here.

The Parc Georges-Brassens

Occupying over 20 acres/7ha, it was up until the present time the largest park created in Paris since the Second Empire, but it will be dethroned by the future Parc Citroën-Cévennes (→Javel) which will cover 33 to 40 acres/13 to 15ha. The Parc Georges-Brassens, named in honor of its celebrated neighbor, was baptized in November 1982 and completed in 1983.

To the l., entering from the market, the rose garden grows 27 varieties. On the r., along the Rue des Morillons, a school and a day nursery (architect, Ghiulmila and Milliex), give a cheerful note to this side of the street while respecting, despite their modernity, the architecture of the old slaughterhouses. Continuing in the direction of the auction-house belfry which has been preserved and now overlooks an ornamental lake fed by a stream cascading down an artificial hillock, you come to the Jardin des Senteurs (Scented Garden) which covers 4265 sq. ft/1300m². More than 80 varieties of fragrant plants grow there (jasmin, wistaria, lilac, lily of the valley, broom, honeysuckle, etc.) as well as numerous medicinal and aromatic plants (camomile, vervain, tarragon, thyme, laurel, sage, etc.). The labels indicating the names of each plant are translated into braille by courtesy of the Institut des Jeunes Aveugles (Institute for Blind Youth).

Behind the belvedere, on the wooded artificial hill, are 3281 sq. ft/1000m² of vines growing on the site of the old Clos de Morillons. This pinot noir vineyard is also planted with peach trees and harvested by schoolchildren. The Rucher-Ecole (Beehive School), run by the French Beekeeping Association, is close by. Return toward the lake, passing the heaps of stones, the remains of the old slaughterhouses that are being reused to create a rock-climbing course. On the l. a screen of trees conceals the brick-buildings of the Prefecture of Police. At the entrance to the park are two stone pavilions that have been restored. The two bulls on the esplanade are the work of the animal sculptor Nicolas Cain (1822–94).

Rue de Cronstadt (facing the Parc Georges-Brassens). To the l., a passage leads to the Church of Notre Dame-de-la-Salette, constructed in 1965 with a circular ground-plan of raw concrete. It has an interesting carved wood door, by J. M. Eaumel.

Rue de Dantzig. After crossing the Rue des Morillons, pass by the brick buildings housing the Centre des Objets Trouvés (Lost Property Office) (→inset).

La Ruche

2 Passage de Dantzig

This former wine pavilion from the 1900 Exhibition was re-erected on this site in 1902 by the official sculptor, Alfred Boucher, to accommodate young artists. The railings that screen La Ruche came from the Palais de la Femme (Women's Pavilion) and the bas-reliefs from the British India pavilion. The building narrowly escaped destruction by property developers before being listed as a historical monument in 1970. This was one of the most important centers of the School of Paris, with its studios arranged like the cells of a honeycomb where the *abeilles* (bees), Boucher's artists, could work in complete tranquility. The sculptors' studios occupied the ground floor, those of the painters the upper floor. Soutine and Fernand Léger, Kikoïne, Krémégne, Chapiro, Brancusi, Indenbaum, Archipenko, Henri Laurens, Zadkine and Gimond, among others, lived here. Modigliani made frequent visits and Chagall set up his studio in 1910. Writers also came, such as Blaise Cendrars, Max Jacob, as well as politicians. After 1945 a second generation of artists came to live around Rebeyrolle: Michel de Gallard, Thompson, Simone Dat, Elisabeth Dujarric de la Rivière, Tisserand, Biras and Aberlenc. The La Ruche school promoted a movement toward a new figurative style. Other well-known artists found refuge here, including Yankel, Mouy, Maunoir, Napper, Bertho, Ben-Dov, Rilov, Lino Melano, Dideron, Damboise and Michel Sima. It is still occupied by artists: the painter Michel Guérin, the Argentine sculptor Reynaldo, Tarabella, the *mosaiste* (worker in mosaic) Leonard Leoni, the sculptor Bonnard, Gertler and Arroyo. About 80 artists work here now, where there were once as many as 140 in Alfred Boucher's time. No. 6 Passage de Dantzig is an example of what an industrial district of the 19th c. could be; it is a private street entirely occupied by warehouses, with a garage and diverse craft workshops, still active.

Rue de la Saïda

The eye is immediately attracted by the impressive workers' housing of the Foundation Lebaudy, restored from 1982 to 1983. They have been registered as historic monuments in order to conserve the buildings for their value as a landmark in the history of social housing. The buildings (1912–13) of A. Labussière, who was virtually architect by appointment to the fondation, are at odds with the traditional design of urban apartment buildings. The complex consists of six apartment houses, nine storeys high, connected by exterior stairways of reinforced concrete in such a way that there are only four façades open to the outside. The framework is of reinforced concrete and Burgundy brick. The houses were reserved for 'large families of which the head had a low income.'

Rue Olivier de Serres. A large modern building hides the area of Canal Plus and the offices of the Secretary of State for Youth and Sport. Cross the square in front of these apartments and follow the Rue Vaugelas, with the Vaugirard Hospital on the l., and handsome dwellings dating back to the early years of the 20th c. on the r. (No. 11 has a beautiful arched gate). Be sure to walk through the Passage Olivier-de-Serres before rejoining the Place de la Convention.

The Southwest of Saint-Lambert

This sector of the Saint-Lambert quarter is a much less cohesive neighborhood, similar to Javel.

Note in particular here the apartment buildings dating back to the first quarter of the 20th c. on the Rue Desnouettes, Rue Auguste-Chabrières, Rue de Cadix, Rue Vasco-de-Gama, Rue Saint-Lambert and in the area around the Square du Clos Feuquières.

Vaugirard Cemetery

Rue Lecourbe

Opened in 1797, this cemetery was enlarged several times until 1853, particularly after the closure (in 1824) of the W Vaugirard cemetery, on the site of the Lycée Buffon. It has had family–plot interment rights in perpetuity since 1879. Since 1882 veterans who would previously have been interred at Montparnasse have been buried here. The graves of the Abbé Groult d'Arcy, the Fondary family, and the anonymous tombs of Vaugirard's religious communities can be seen. President Paul Doumer (assassinated on May 6 1932) and his three sons lie here.

▷ Le Village de l'Avenir (the village of the future)

At the turn of the 19th c. the developer Chauvelot, who was also behind the Hameau de Plaisance and La Nouvelle Californie à Malakoff developments, began to sell small lots in the E section of Vaugirard. The streets here have a more irregular layout than those in the Violet development in the Grenelle district, and the houses were designed for a clientele of more modest means. The Village de l'Avenir (or Village de Villafranca, as it was also called) became, after Javel, the second most popular neighborhood in the 15th arrondissement with members of the rag-and-bone trade. In honor of the Italian campaign of 1859, Chauvelot baptized his modest streets with grandiose names: Villafranca, Montebello, Chambéry, Nice la Frontière, Sommet-des-Alpes, and so on. It was only after the district's annexation to Paris in December 1859, that the village de l'Avenir became truly successful. It continued to be dominated by small artisanal businesses and by the middle classes until the construction of the abattoirs in 1894.

▷ Lost Property Office

The origin of this service goes back to a statute of December 10, 1804, under which the Prefect of Police, Dubois, organized the first centralization of lost property at the Paris Prefecture of Police. Another Royal decree regarding objects 'whose owners are not known', dates from May 23, 1830.

Today, it is the Service des Sèquestres of the Prefecture of Police

(5th Department of Traffic Control, Transport and Commerce), that is responsible. Valuable objects are kept for a total of three years; clothes and keys only three months. Unclaimed objects become the property of the State, which then sells them.

Some figures for 1988: around 137,000 items were turned in; there were 69,600 declarations of loss and approximately 29,000 items were claimed of which 2,600 were returned to finders. Sixty per cent of found items come from the RATP, which forwards them to this service. People lose many different things, but the umbrella takes first place among lost property, keeping company with the proverbial diamond necklace, wooden leg and many other unusual objects.

Open Oct.–June Mon. and Wed. 8.30am–5pm, Tues. and Thurs. 8.30am–8pm, Fri. 8.30am–5.30pm; July–Aug. Mon.–Fri. 8am–5pm.

The Villette district*

19th arr. 6–D3
Métro: Jaurès, Stalingrad
Buses: 150, 152, 250A and PC
Taxis: from the Métro Porte-de-la-Villette. Tel: 42-08-64-00

Soon after being annexed to Paris during the Second Empire, the old village of La Villette was devoted, for more than a century, to the sale and slaughter of livestock. At a time when the preservation of fresh meat was risky, animals had to be killed close to the place where their meat would be eaten. In 1867 the construction of the Paris livestock market and new slaughterhouses began. This distasteful industry, together with the port and industries around the Canal de l'Ourcq, made La Villette one of the poorest quarters of Paris. Stretching away from the admirable rotunda by Ledoux, the Bassin de La Villette, the Rue de Flandre and the Avenue Jean Jaurès formed nonetheless three great urban vistas; but the surrounding streets, poor and industrial, were naturally not very attractive.

For several years an ambitious development program has focused on the neighborhoods around the site of the old former slaughterhouses, which is now a place for strolling, leisure and cultural activities. In the new Parc de la Villette, the Cité des Sciences et de l'Industrie (Center for Science and Industry) with its Géode, Grande Halle (Great Hall), and the Zénith have already opened their doors. The Cité de la Musique (Music Centre) completes this exceptional group.

Tour of the district

2 hrs.

Rotonde de la Villette*

This sober, elegant building was formerly the tollhouse for the guards of the Fermiers-Generaux' enclosing wall, constructed by Claude-Nicolas Ledoux in 1784 to mark the entrance to the capital (→inset). This remarkable rotunda has a square-shaped ground floor on which stands the rotunda itself, a circular building adorned on the first floor with a round gallery entirely open to the outside. Following extensive structural and restorative work in 1966 by the architect Jean Trouvelot, the building was opened to the public for occasional temporary exhibitions. It houses the repository for archeological finds of the City of Paris and the Commission du Vieux-Paris, managed by Michel Fleury.

Part of the restructuring plan for the Place de Stalingrad in 1989 called for clearing the area around the rotunda, which was unfortunately surrounded by a bus station, parking lots and a public garden. The rotonda de la Villette has benefited today by the remarkable intervention of the architect Bernard Huet. The Neo-Classical facades of the rotunda are now visible in their new setting. The peristyle, which was destroyed at the of the 19th century to make way for some warehouses, has been reconstructed, restoring the original appearance of the building. A 7 acre/3ha triangular pedestrian precinct, bordered by poplars, now opens onto a wide expanse of water called the Bassin de la Villette.

Bassin de la Villette

Officially inaugurated by Napoléon on December 2, 1808, the basin was a place for strolling and relaxation, often called 'Paris's little Venice' or the 'Champs-Elysées of the East.' The basin connects the Canal de l'Ourcq, the Canal Saint-Denis and the Canal Saint-Martin. Today, with its boating and leisure activities, the basin has returned to its original use. Six stages of construction and restoration are planned, which will attempt to unify the disparate elements of the area, which range from old buildings in poor condition to sky scrapers, one of which reaches 328ft/100m. The height limit is now fixed at 85ft/26m.

Canal de l'Ourcq

Cruises leave from La Villette: Canauxrama, 13 Quai de la Lorre, Paris, tel: 46–24–86–16; Paris Canal, Paris Canal, 11 Quai de Loine Paris tel. 42–40–96–97, tel: 48–74–75–30.

The first engineering work to make the Ourcq river navigable began in 1632. In 1676 Manse and Riquet began work on building a canal. Their deaths (around 1680), and that of Colbert (in 1683), who had been keenly interested in the enterprise, interrupted the project. In 1790 Brulé failed in his efforts to resume the work. At last, in 1802, a Consular decree ordered the cutting of the canal de l'Ourcq. This canal, 67.5mls/108km long (only 1ml/1.6km of it in Paris) was intended initially to bring drinking water to Parisians and to establish a navigable waterway from one part of the Seine to another by means of the Saint-Martin and Saint-Denis canals, to be added later. The increased volume of commercial traffic in the middle of the 19th c., however, changed the commercial environment, bringing with it a proliferation of warehouses. It was Emile Pereire, and then the banker Dehaynin, who directed the important Compagnie des Entrepôts et des Magasins Généraux which stocked, among other things, coal, firewood, timber, fodder and sugar. Regenerated, in particular from 1867, by the presence of the slaughterhouses and their associated businesses (tanning, leather goods, etc.), the flow of merchandise increased greatly up to 1914. In the 20th c., the de-industrialization of Paris and the development of road transport brought about a decline in harbor activities and the warehouses fell into disuse.

The conversion of the canal and the surrounding area is now in the course of completion. It is especially pleasant to explore the canals on a short cruise.

The Quai de la Loire (to the r. of the basin)

This route skirts the water's edge, following the Quai de la Loire. Of the warehouses that once congested the banks, two have been preserved, at the S end of the basin. Their metal structures were taken from a pavilion at the 1878 Universal Exhibition and re-erected here. The metal bridge across the basin replaced, in 1963, an elegant curvilinear footbridge constructed by Gustave Eiffel in 1882. At no. 4 there is a contemporary complex of 111 dwellings, the materials, shapes and colors of which pay homage to Le Corbusier (architect, Edith Girard). At the far end of the basin stand two large, austere warehouses of the Magasins Généraux (built about 1896), with milled rubblestone façades, a fine example of industrial architecture. An imposing interior wooden structure of posts and massive beams provided space, on five floors, for the storage of sugar and cereal supplies destined for the capital. The vastness of the buildings gives some idea of the importance of this district's commercial activity in the 19th c.

Today these warehouses, no longer serving industry, provide 90 artists' studios for painters, architects, sculptors and master glassmakers. With their façades recently restored they are a natural focal point at the end of the view over the perspective of the Bassin de la Villette. Go round the warehouses of the Quai de la Loire and take, on the l., the lifting bridge that is a continuation of the Rue de Crimée.

The lifting bridge of the Rue de Crimée

This hydraulic bridge was erected in 1885 by the Societé Fives-Lille (which also constructed the hydraulic elevators of the E and W pillars of the Eiffel Tower). The ingenuity of its mechanism is obvious: 4 enormous pulleys frame the bridge roadway while the counterweights are contained inside cylinders. Just 9lb/4kg of hydraulic thrust is enough to operate the whole system. To the 'magic mechanism', that aroused everyone's curiosity at the time, was added the Egyptian-style decoration of the huge pulleys.

The Church of Saint-Jacques-Saint-Christophe, built in 1843, by the architect Lequeux, bears witness by the size of its nave to the rapid increase in La Villette's population during the 19th c. Restored in 1830, this church forms part of a pleasant provincial-style complex, along with the school, firefighters' barracks and public gardens: the Place de Bitche. After walking along part of the Rue de Crimée, which is one of the exotic parts of Paris, enlivened by a large Chinese population as well as Jewish and African communities, you come to the Rue de Flandre, which leads to the Cité des Sciences et de l'Industrie (Center of Sciences and Industry).

Rue de Flandre

Depart briefly from this itinerary to see no. 44 Rue de Flandre (to the l. off the Rue de Crimée), an unusual feature of the district; at the end of the entrance hall of a modern apartment building lies hidden a small Jewish cemetery dating from the late 18th c. It is permanently closed, but behind its walls some of the 30 headstones that it contains are just visible.

At the corner of the Rue de Crimée and Rue de Flandre stand several skyscrapers, survivors of a 1960s development project. The Orgues de Flandres complex at no. 67, built by the architect Martin Van Treeck and completed in 1976, constitutes, with its 2732 dwellings, park, day-care center, market and post office, a district in itself. The architectural interest of this estate, which consists mainly of low-income housing, lies in its use of volumes, the systematic use of ceramic tiles and the creation of grassed terraces. The apartment building at no. 27, by the architects Roger Anger and Pierre Puccinelli (1964), creates a sculptural and prismatic effect, a result of the arrangement of loggias to break up its verticality.

The Rue de Flandre has been enlarged. A two-way traffic system has improved access to the Parc de la Villette, and 550 trees have been planted along the thoroughfare. Among the houses demolished between Nos 147 and 177 to make way for the new system was the old sugar refinery (no. 159) owned by Lebaudy, one of La Villette's great industrialists of the 19th c. The façade of the '*chateau*' of the Roquelaire family at no. 152 is the only vestige of a once magnificent resident; the two bas-reliefs represent, to the r., *Painting* and to the l., *Architecture*.

Cross the Pont de Flandre (the railway bridge of the Petite Ceinture, built in 1867), to reach the beginning of the Ave. Corentin-Cariou near to the old slaughterhouses, which are recalled by the many businesses connected with butchery – curing, butchers' equipment and restaurants with evocative names (A La Pièce de Boeuf, Le Mouton Blanc, Le Cochon de Lait, Le Veau d'Or, etc).

🌲🌲 The Parc de La Villette*

Bounded to the N by the Rue de Flandre, and to the S by the Ave. Jean-Jaurès, and cut through the middle by the Canal de l'Ourcq, La Villette constitutes one of Paris's greatest inner-city development projects of the late 20th c., covering 136 acres/55ha (a surface area more than double that of the Parc des Buttes-Chaumont). This complex, completed in 1990, includes a 74 acre/30ha landscaped park (a public facility of the Parc de la Villette), the biggest museum in the world devoted to scientific, technical and industrial education, the Cité des Sciences et de l'Industrie (Center for Science and Industry), which includes a unique cinema with a hemispherical screen (La Géode), a museum devoted to the district's history (the Maison de la Villette), a multipurpose cultural center (the Grande Halle), a concert hall (the Zénith), a theater (the Théâtre Paris Villette), and a music center with a museum, conservatory and auditoriums. There are also 600 units of subsidized low-income housing integrated into the complex.

Several visits are required to get to know La Villette. As a first step begin at the N entrance (the Porte de la Villette) and study the scale model of the complex. Then head towards the Maison de la Villette to study the district's history. Cross the central hall of the Cité des Sciences (2nd bay of the building) then, crossing the canal, go through the park to the Porte de Pantin, the end of the itinerary.

The Maison de la Villette

The Rotonde des Vétérinaries (veterinary pavilion), is the only 19th-c. building still standing at the N end of the Villette. Since 1867 (the year of its construction) it has had diverse roles: tallow melting house, veterinarians' laboratory, wholesale butchers' association, as well as housing for those who worked there.

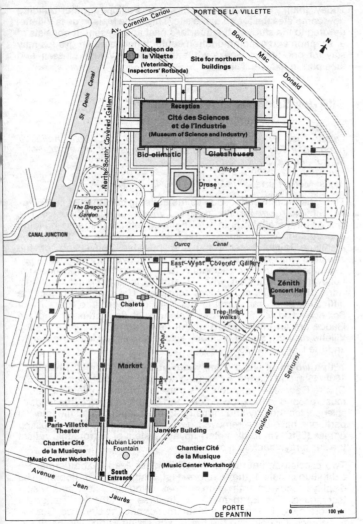

La Villette Park

Today, thanks to the historian Elisabeth Philipp, another building now completes the N end of the site. This is the Maison de la Villette, devoted to the study of the quarter's past and present. It consists of a reception and accommodation center where student groups may stay for one or two weeks while they attend 'Villette classes' and take part in local activities.

▣ Cité des Sciences et de l'Industrie**

19th arr.
Open: Tues.–Fri. 10am–6pm, on weekends and public holidays, noon–8pm; Tel: 40–05–72–72; group bookings. Tel: 40–05–70–70
Metro: Jaurés, Stalingrad
Bus: 150, 152, 250A and PC
Taxis: Métro Porte de la Villette. Tel. 42–08–64–00

This gigantic museum occupies the building constructed in 1969 as an auction room for the new La Villette slaughterhouses. The closure of the abattoirs in 1974 (→inset) left the immense building unoccupied. A preliminary survey was undertaken in 1977 by the architect Taillibert regarding the possible conversion of the structure into a museum, while the physicist Maurice Lévy developed exhibits for a scientific, technical and industrial museum. Following consultation with 27 architects, the French architect Adrien Fainsilber's project was accepted. This architect began the difficult task of transforming the 'City of Blood' into the 'City of Science'. Today the Cité des Sciences et de l'Industrie and the Geode are an integral part of the new Parc de la Villette (→ the Villette district), which includes also the Grande Halle, the Zénith and the Cité de la Musique.

With a length of 885ft/270m, width of 360ft/110m, and a height of 160ft/49m; and therefore a volume equivalent to 3½ times that of the Centre Georges-Pompidou, this museum of Pharaonic dimensions must respond to the growing demand for information in the fields of science, technology and industry. In the central hall all the internal partitions have been removed. Two computer-controlled revolving domes (55ft/17m in diameter) have a system of mirrors that reflect the sun's rays back into space.

Two escalators, entirely enclosed in glass, lead to the permanent exhibitions, called the *Explora* (1st, 2nd, and 3rd floors). The displays focus on four main themes using the latest audiovisual techniques. The Earth and the Universe – Paths for Tomorrow (Laboratory of the Universe, Mathematics and the Universe, Oceans and Space, Discovering the Earth, The Living Earth, The Earth – A Precious Vessel); The Adventure of Life (Secrets of Living Creatures, Water and Life, Humanity and the Environment); Matter and the Human Industry (The Heart of Matter, Sources and Producers of Energy, Extractions and Synthesis, The Robotic Garden, Electronic and Computer-assisted Work); Language and Communication (The World of Sound, Expression and Behavior, Light-Mirrors-Color, Space and Communication, Information and Society). Temporary exhibitions explain current events or the world of science, technology and industry and its economic, social, and artistic consequences. The Inventorium, main floor (Tues.-Sun., 2–6.30pm; weekends and public holidays, 12.30–6.30pm; tel 46–42-13-13). Areas reserved for children include a room for 3- to 7-year-olds and a discovery workshop for 8- to 11-year-olds. There they can make their first contact with the world of science through games and by handling the various exhibits.

The Mediatheque (Multimedia Library)

1st underground level Tues.-Sun. 12-8pm; Wed. and weekends 2-8.30pm Tel. 46-42-13-13.

This is a very modern documentation center, containing a book and videotape library and interactive study aids. The Planetarium (2nd floor). Astronomical and astrophysical images are projected onto a 69ft/21m diameter hemispherical screen. Louis-Lumière Hall (Tues.-Sun. 2.15pm-7pm, weekends and public holidays 1–7pm, tel: 40-35-79-40). Films of a scientific nature are shown continuously. The Maison de l'Industrie (House of Industry): information on France's industry and all aspects of its economy, in every region (1st underground level).

The Glasshouse façade

On leaving the hall you will see the S façade of the center, completely transparent, with its three glasshouses (104ft/32m high), which leads to the park. Glass-enclosed elevators pass over this expanse of plant life and offer access to the site. This futuristic building is surrounded by moats filled with 3ft/1m of water, which in fact surround the whole center.

The Géode

Open Wed. and Fri.-Sun. 10am-9pm, Tues. and Thurs. 11am-6pm. Tel: 46.42.13.13. Tickets sold in advance at the Géode, after 10am for the same day.

An integral part of the Science and Industry Center, and designed by the same architect, the Géode has been a veritable beacon of La Villette since May 1985. It is situated in the reception area where the museum and park meet on a 1½ft/40cm-deep stretch of water, and houses a cinema with a hemispherical screen.

The Géode is a silvery sphere (118ft/36m diameter), reflecting its surroundings on a mirrored surface of polished stainless steel. Its novelty lies in its construction, comprising two totally independent structures. A tree-like central pillar, clearly visible from inside, supports the tiers of seats in the hall, which can hold 357 spectators. The steel casing, created by the engineer-sculptor Gérard Chamayon (also known as Félix), is composed of 2580 steel tubes bolted together, supporting 6433 steel triangles. The Omnimax projection system, with its hemispherical screen (10,764 sq ft/ 1000m²) places the viewer in the very center of the image.

Parc de la Villette

Before crossing the Canal de l'Ourcq you catch sight of the Dragon of La Villette, a spectacular animal whose metal tongue serves as a tobogganing slope. This play area is destined to disappear, however. Bernard Tschumi has designed a 74 acre/30ha park which will connect the Science Center to the N with the Music Center to the S. Halfway between a park and a fun fair, the Parc de la Villette is being planned around the thoroughfare linking the different areas of activity.

Two covered walks, one N–S, the other E–W, will cross the site, and a narrow canal will run past the E wall of the Grande Halle while the tree-lined paths, preserving some of the old plane trees, will be laid out in a circular and triangular pattern with recreation grounds in between. A winding path will constitute a promenade through the 'theme' gardens: botanical, educational and landscaped. In this area, Tschumi's follies will be so many points of reference for visitors. The initial scheme envisages about 30 of these buildings, evenly spaced 393ft/120m apart. They will all be based on a cube, 35.4ft/10.5m on each side, with a concrete structure covered in a red-enamelled sheet steel, but each will vary the basic structure in an imaginative way according to its function. The first group includes: refreshment bar, belvedere, a Maison des Enfants (Children's House), restaurant, electronic games arcade, brasserie, garden center, and first-aid unit. Paved areas to the N and S will provide space for fairs, open-air exhibitions, and markets. The park's modular furniture will be by Philippe Starck (decorator of the Elysée's private apartments).

Le Zénith

A hall for pop and rock music, originally this vast area was only temporary, pending the construction of a building at the Porte de Bagnolet. When that project was abandoned, the Zénith became a public building in its own right within La Villette. The novelty of its construction (architect, P. Chaix and J. Morel) lies in its light, adjustable structure, which provides the cover and fixtures necessary for concerts and other shows. A space free of any supports, it allows for the free movement of scenery, and accommodates up to 6400 spectators.

A nearby concrete column is the only vestige of the new abattoirs' cattle sheds. It bears a red aeroplane pointed toward the earth. This, the well-known 'Zénith', has become the symbol of this concert hall.

The Grande Halle (Great Hall)*

This is one of the most beautiful iron structures of 19th-c. Paris. Built in 1867 by Jules de Métindol and inspired by a project of Hector Horeau, which was never realized for the 1862 Second Universal Exhibition of London, this work in cast and raw iron of astonishing dimensions (787ft/240m long, 269ft/82m wide and 62ft/19m high) was meant to house the cattle market. Originally built without side walls, it was only a simple, windswept shelter.

Transformed into a multicultural center by P. Robert and B. Reichen, this building can host large exhibitions, forums, festivals and concerts. The central area of the hall has been cleared and, with the use of canvas sheets, can be divided into two spaces. Stands at the sides enlarge the exhibition area. Portable ramps connect the stands, and mobile platforms adapt to varying requirements. Below the central aisle is the Salle Boris Vian, used for conferences and exhibitions.

The remains of the abattoirs

Two stone buildings, both constructed in 1867, stand on either side of the S wall of the Grande Halle: the Janvier (January) building, which contains the S reception hall and the former leather and skins exchange, and which is now occupied by the Théâtre Paris-Villette, and the Salle Arletty, where scientific, artistic, and experimental films are shown.

The Fontaine aux Lions de Nubie (Nubian Lion Fountain), strangely painted in blue, is a small structure originally located in the Place du Château-d'Eau (now the Place de la République) in 1811, and subsequently installed near the slaughterhouse in 1867, where it served as a watering-place for the animals.

La Cité de la Musique (Music Center)

This project was conceived by the architect Christian de Portzamparc. It will group together several musical facilities: a concert hall (seating 1200) intended for classical and contemporary music, the Conservatoire National de Musique (National Academy of Music), which will move here from Rue de Madrid, and the Galerie des Instruments (Musical Instruments Museum) which will hold exhibitions tracing the history of musical instruments. The W sections of the building are scheduled to be built first.

▷ Ledoux's city wall

By order of M. de Calonne, Contrôleur Général des Finances, Claude-Nicolas Ledoux (1736–1806), the royal architect, was instructed to erect a wall to enclose Paris, and to build, at each entrance to the city, tollgates where collectors could levy taxes on goods (the *octroi*). Four tollhouses survive today: the Rotonde d'Orléans or Barrière du Chartres (Place de la République-Domi-nicaine, Boul. de Courcelles), the Rotonde de la Villette or Bureau de Pantin (Place Stalingrad), the Bureaux du Trône (Place de la Nation) and the Bureaux de la Rue d'Orléans or Barrière Saint-Jacques (Place Denfert-Rochereau). The salient architectural features of these buildings are plainness, geometry, symmetry, absence of ornamentation and the almost systematic use of col-umns and plain, triangular pediments. With the circle, square and Greek cross as basic floor-plans, Claude-Nicolas Ledoux displayed the three volumes characteristic of his style, the cube, sphere and cylinder. He succeeded in designing, for the entrances to Paris, grandiose buildings whose outward appearance would impress the traveller.

▷ The abattoirs of La Villette

In the early years of the Second Empire, Haussmann undertook to combine the old Paris abattoirs and the livestock markets of Poissy and Sceaux, and relocate them away from the city center. The new Abattoirs Généraux were opened in La Villette on January 1, 1867. They were divided geographically between the slaughterhouses proper situated N of the Canal de l'Ourcq and the livestock markets to the S. A railway line connected to the Petite Ceinture network transported the animals from their regions of origin. The market comprised three metal structures: the central hall for cattle (now the Grande Halle), the E hall for calves (since demolished) and the W hall for sheep (demolished in 1987). The facilities included 23 sheds for slaughtering and 15 for skinning and butchering. A special abattoir for pigs was built in 1874. This 'City of Blood' was at its most active around 1900. Three thousand people worked there, forming a highly colorful community: blood collectors, gut dressers, tripe dressers, tallow melters, gland collectors, unloaders, drovers, whosesale mutton butchers, herders, milkers, carriers and veterin-ary surgeons. Little by little, however, new techniques rendered the enormous complex out of date. In 1969 the ministry of public works began modernizing the by now decayed slaughterhouses to turn them into ultra-modern buildings with the aim of establishing the largest abattoir in the world. Work started in 1969 on the immense concrete and steel structure destined to contain a huge livestock market with a ground-level surface area of 12½ acres/5ha.

In 1974 work came to an abrupt halt, an abattoir of such immense size at a major point of consumption having been made obsolete by new technologies that allowed animals to be slaughtered near the point of production and their meat to be transported in refrigerated trucks to urban markets. An abattoir at the gates of Paris had become a useless and uneconomical idea. The building became a 'temple of the absurd', a stillborn monument that had already cost 3120 thousand million francs. When the last bullock was felled on March 14, 1974, it marked the scandal-ridden end of a century of slaughter at La Villette.

The Bois de Vincennes*

12th arr.
Métro: Porte-Dorée
Buses: 46, 86; terminus for both at the Carrefour de la Demi-Lune – Parc Zoologique (entrance on Ave. Daumesnil), and PC.

The forest of Vincennes was acquired from the Abbey of Saint-Maur by the Crown in the 11th c. Annexed to the City of Paris in 1930, it lies entirely within the 12th arrondissement. With a surface area of 2658 acres/995ha it is the largest park in Paris. On weekends, especially on summer Sundays, it is literally invaded by hordes of people – a weekday visit is generally best.

History of the Bois de Vincennes

Since it has always been a royal hunting ground, one would have thought that this wood, remnant of the forest called Lanchonia Silva, would enjoy the same reputation for elegance as its counter-part to the W. The historian Joinville relates how Louis IX (St Louis), who enjoyed strolling there, would sit under an oak tree to dispense justice, and to receive his subjects without the interference of courtiers. In the 15th and 16th c. the kings, leaving behind the Louvre for the Hôtel Saint-Pol and the Tournelles, found themselves closer to Vincennes. Louis XIV, who had spent his honeymoon in the King's Pavilion, had the gates of the 12th-c. wall erected around the forest by Philippe Auguste, opened to the public. When the King moved back to Versailles, however, the nobility forsook this wood where for centuries hinds, stags, and fallow deer had roamed freely, to live in the monarch's shadow. Louis XV, however, liked to return here, and he revived the project started by Robert de Cotte in 1703, the aim of which was to restore the wood to its former glory. The obelisk in the polygon, called the Rond Pont de la Pyramide, which can be seen at the front of the floral garden on the site of the old artillery range, commemorates the total reforestation of the Bois de Vincennes in 1731, during Louis XV's reign. At that time the forest was magnificent, and suffered little harm during the Revolution; its troubles began in 1796 when the artillery range brought the presence of the military to the *Bois*. The château was turned into a barracks, its towers knocked down, and mounted with cannon, and the wood became an immense practice area for military maneuvers, with shooting ranges, redoubts, and strategic roads. Vincennes was nicknamed 'Cannonville'.

The depredations continued into the early years of the Second Empire until 1860, when Napoléon III concluded an agreement with the Ville de Paris under which the city took control of the wood and administered it as a public park. As in the case of the Bois de Boulogne, the Bois de Vincennes was planned by Alphand, according to the fashion of the time, as a landscaped park with plantations of exotic trees, ornamental lakes and artificial cascades; the Lac de Gravelle was created by Haussmann to supply the wood's other lakes with water from the Marne. The already large number of avenues was eventually doubled by the addition of bridle, walking and, later, cycling paths.

The 1931 Colonial Exhibition was organized by Maréchal Lyautey, who managed to avoid damaging a single tree.

The Bois de Vincennes today

While reforestation was in progress, military installations were replaced by sports facilities: 43 mls/27km of marked paths were opened for horse riders, cyclists, walkers, and gymnasts, and little by little the wood resumed the pattern outlined in Robert de Cotte's plan. Straight paths stretch from the Château's Esplanade, notably Route Dauphine, 1.2mls/2km long, which ends at the Carrefour la Patte d'Oie, and joins the château to the Gravelle plateau. Between this central path and the much wider Route de la Pyramide, the military training ground has been turned into stadiums and playing fields. The Route Dauphine was built through the old training grounds, while the site of the artillery range was occupied by the University Center of Vincennes. The most remarkable historical achievement was the recreation of the Alleé Royale, the broad path that played a part in the royal hunts of Louis XV. Its central section starts beyond the Cavalerie Carnot *quartier*, which separates it, unfortunately, from the château's esplanade, to where it should have continued. It runs for 136km over the sites of the former military grounds and the old University of Vincennes, in the form of a double row of plane trees hemmed in by dense woodland, mainly oaks, the most common trees of Vincennes.

Tour of the Bois de Vincennes

Coming from Paris, enter the Bois de Vincennes either through the Porte Dorée or the Porte de Vincennes, crossing Saint-Mandé. In the latter case, continue as far as the Carrefour de la Demi-Lune, facing the second entrance to the zoological garden, Avenue Daumesnil.

It is advisable to park here and continue on foot, as most of the roads that cross the wood are closed to traffic. Or, go round the wood following the Avenue Daumesnil, the Route de la Pyramide, the Avenue du Tremblay, the Route de la Ferme, Route de la Tourelle, and the Avenue de Gravelle.

The following 8ml/13km circular itinerary is suggested. Leave Paris by the Porte Dorée to reach the Place Edouard-Renard. Immediately behind and to the I., at the entrance to the wood, is situated the Musée National des Arts Africains et Océaniens (Museum of African and Oceanic Art: →Museums). Follow the Ave. Daumesnil past the museum, to reach the main entrance of the zoo (Porte de Paris), at the fork of the Ave. Daumesnil and the road that rings the Lac Daumesnil, now closed to traffic.

⚘ Parc Zoologigue de Vincennes* (Zoological Garden)

Open Mon.–Friday; Sat., Sun and public holidays 9–6.30 (1 April–30 Sept), 9–5pm (1 Oct.–30 March) 9am–6pm. Admission: half price for families with children, children aged 4–9, students and members of educational institutions, reduced rates for student groups and others. Tel: 43–43–84–95.

This zoo, part of the Musée National d'Histoire Naturelle (Museum of Natural History), which has some of the most attractive collections in Europe, is in a unique woodland setting close to the Lac Daumesnil. It has a surface area of 37 acres/15ha and replaced the previous, smaller park established nearby at the time of the 1931 Colonial Exhibition. It shelters a major collection of mammals and birds. On cold or wet days the animals remain in their cages among the rocks. Each rock has a built-in menagerie open to the public.

Toward the extreme N end of the garden rises the impressive mass of a huge artificial rock in moulded concrete on a metal structure housing mountain goats and chamois. It is 223ft/68m high and can be reached by two stairways or by an elevator; from the top there is

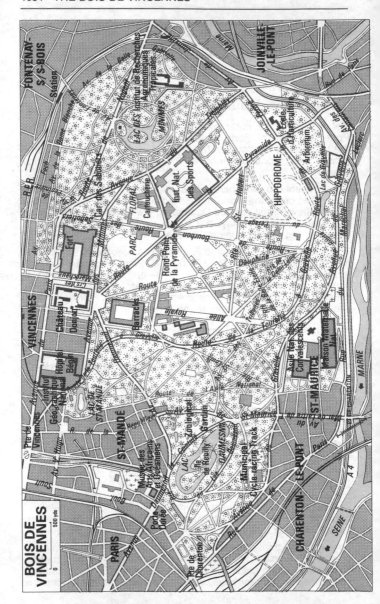

a wonderful view of the Bois de Vincennes and the adjacent districts.

The Lac Daumesnil

Immediately to the SW of the zoo is the Lac Daumesnil, also called Lac de Charenton, with an area of 29 acres/12ha. Each year, from Palm Sunday to the end of May, the Foire du Trône (Gingerbread fair) is held nearby on the Reuilly lawn. The lake has two islands linked to the shore and to each other by suspension bridges (rowboats and bicycles may be rented). The facilities on the islands are similar to, but more modest than, those in the Bois de Boulogne, with a refreshment room, a kiosk, and some small shops. A Swiss chalet on the Ile de Reuilly was bought by the City from the 1867 World Fair; it is now the Chalet des Iles restaurant, with miniature golf and games for the children. Close to the bridge, on the r., is a small temple in the form of a rotunda with monolithic Doric columns, rising above a grotto. It lends distinction to this popular promenade and recalls the *folies* of the 18th c. The architect was Davioud, who erected a similar structure in the Parc des Buttes-Chaumont.

L'Institut International Bouddhique* (International Buddhist Center)

40 Route de Ceinture du lac Daumesnil; tel. 43–41–54–48. (No visits.)

On the S bank, occupying the site of the old Musée de l'Industrie du Bois (Museum of Woodworking), is the Buddhist Center, housed in one of its four pavilions built for the 1931 Colonial Exhibition. Tens of thousands of Buddhists in the Paris region come here to practise their faith. Because of its international nature it is used by Buddhists of all sects and ethnic origins; its style is unusual. The main design motif is the leaf of the *bo* tree (Tree of Wisdom). The roof, made of 18,000 tiles of chestnut wood, incorporates an oblique leaf vein pattern symbolic of ultimate wisdom through spiritual perfection and reaches its highest point above a statue of the Buddha covered in goldleaf 29ft/9m tall. The temple is reached by crossing a stretch of water, the frontier between earthly turmoil and the spiritual life; some stairways and terraces are designed for open-air ceremonies. The monks also have their living quarters here, and the garden, with its statues and lanterns, attempts to evoke the atmosphere of Buddhist temples in Asia.

To the S is situated the Vélodrome Municipal, 1640ft/500m in circumference. Grand Prix cycle meetings are held there in June.

Now return to the car to make a tour of the wood. Beyond the zoo entrance the Ave. Daumesnil, after skirting the zoo, crosses the wood, passing the Lac Saint-Mandé 1640ft/500m to the l. (there is a café-restaurant house, too). It ends at the esplanade in front of the S side of the Château de Vincennes (→below). The Square Carnot, between the esplanade and the Cavalerie *quartier*, contains some beautiful specimens of trees, including a Virginia tulip that bursts into bright blossom from June to July, and a giant sequoia. Past the Cavalerie *quartier* the Allée Royale begins at the site of the old Université de Vincennes, recently replanted to look as it did in the reign of Louis XV.

Le Parc Floral (Floral Garden)**

The entrance to the garden is at the corner of the Route de la Pyramide and the Ave. des Minimes, which starts at the esplanade. Buses: 112, 115, 118, 124, 325.

Open Apr.–Sept. Wed., Sat., Sun. and public holiday afternoons. Open daily: 9.30am–7pm in spring, 9.30am–8pm in summer, 9.30am–9pm on Sat. June–Aug., 9.30am–6pm in autumn, 9.30am–5pm in winter.

This garden, a harmonious arrangement of flowerbeds and stretches of water, was created on the site of the former Ecole de Pyrotechnie for the 1969 International Flower Show. The gardens are in bloom five or six times each year, and three exhibitions are held annually, in spring, summer, and autumn. In the Jardin des Quatre-Saisons (Four Seasons Garden) are fine hyacinths, dahlias, and chrysanthemums. There is also a medicinal garden. Of particular interest are the valley of flowers, the pinewood, the children's playground and the dahlia garden (blossoms in autumn), which was originally in the Parc de Sceaux. In the water garden are water lilies and lotus flowers, at their best from August to October, and there are multicolored fish and reptiles in the exotarium.

There are also permanent exhibitions of houses and garden furniture; sculptures by Calder and Agam; and mobiles by Schoeffer and Van Thinen. The Hall de la Pinède (97,000sq ft/9,000m²), contains a beautiful exhibition room either for fragile plants (such as orchids) or for cultural and commercial exhibits, like the Biennale de Paris. Follow the Ave. des Minimes, then the Ave. de Tremblay.

The Cartoucherie de Vincennes

The former Cartoucherie (cartridge factory), S of the Floral Garden, received a new lease on life when Ariane Mnouchkine revived its theater with her acting company. She has put on several plays here dealing with particular years, such as '1789'. The Cartoucherie comprises the Théâtre de l'Aquarium, the Théâtre de la Tempête, and the Atelier (workshop) du Chaudron. There is a pony club for children. Continue on the same side of the forest to find the Institut

National des Sports (National Sports Center), which in 1952 replaced the old Ecole de Joinville, built in 1852 in the Faisanderie redoubt. The center possesses vast sports fields and a modern covered stadium, 453ft/138m long, with a wooden roof spanning 305ft/93m (1964). Finally, S of the Institut des Sports, is the old Pershing stadium and a large sports ground. On the other side of the Route de la Pyramide, the Saint-Hubert racecourse was converted into horseback riding grounds in 1986.

The Lac des Minimes*

By the Ave. de Tremblay (train station: Fontenary-sur-Bois, RER).

This lake (20 acres/8ha) is the most picturesque of the wood's four lakes. Created by Alphand, it contains three islands, on one of which stand the remains of the old Minimes monastery (of the Bonshommes order) founded around 1155 by Louis VII, the site of which was excavated for the lake in 1857. Nearby is the only tree remaining from the time of Louis XV, close to the two Minimes pavilions, which are made of red brick and date from 1816, and which served as lodges for the keepers of the wood and then, more recently, for policemen. Walk round the lake by the circular road (Route Circulaire), to reach the Porte Jaune at the N end, where a bridge gives access to the island of the same name, where small boats may be rented. To get there by car take the road to Nogent and follow it as far as the Ave. de la Belle-Gabrielle.

L'Institut de Recherches Argronomiques Tropicales (Institute of Tropical Agronomic Research)

45 bis Ave. de la Belle-Gabrielle. Tel: 43–94–43–000.

The entrance to the institute is notable for its red-lacquered Chinese gate. This institute, dedicated to research on agronomy in tropical countries, installed its offices in the pavilions of Morocco (in very poor condition), Indochina, the Congo, and Tunisia from the Marseilles Colonial Exhibition of 1906, after they were dismantled and transported here (→inset).

Le Centre Technique Forestier Tropicale (Tropical Forestry Center)

45 bis Rue de la Belle-Gabrielle,
94736 Codex Nogent-sur-Marne.
Visits arranged by written request. Open Sun.–Fri. Tel: 48–94–43–00.

Situated next to the Institut de Recherches Agronomiques Tropicales in a large, beautiful building designed by Roux-Spitz

(1951), this organization is concerned with everything involving the production, exploitation and use of tropical woods. The center offers information about its activities either by correspondence or by appointment. The collections of colonial woods are particularly fine.

If you do not wish to continue with the tour of the wood, follow the Ave. de la Belle-Gabrielle N towards the l. (pedestrians only); one-way for traffic going in the other direction as far as the main road from Vincennes to Nogent, where there is a bus stop. Bus no. 112 follows the circuit indicated and serves the sports fields and the arboretum. Also quite close is Nogent station (RER). To continue the tour of the wood, follow the Ave. de la Belle-Gabrielle in the opposite direction to the r. (S), then take the Route de la Ferme. On the l. it passes by the Faisanderie redoubt, then the Ecole d'Horticulture du Breuil, both built for the Empress Eugénie. After crossing the Route de la Pyramide you pass the Hippodrome to the r., with the Vincennes racecourse, renovated in 1955 (new stands with 3000 seats). To the l., the Arboretum of the Ecole du Breuil (open Mon., Wed., Fri., 1pm–4pm), is of great interest, containing 2000 species of tree. The Lac de Gravelle. This vast reservoir, created by Haussmann, surrounded by beautiful trees, is nearly 131ft/40m above the level of the Marne and takes all the water (about 26,140cu yd/20,000m^3) to feed the wood's lakes and streams. The lake is at the SW side of the Plateau de Gravelle; the highest point of the wood. The view, once very beautiful, is now obstructed by clumps of trees except toward the S and SE. From the plateau follow the Ave. de Gravelle along the S edge of the wood, overlooking to the l. the valley of the Marne (beautiful views), which slopes down to the Lac Daumesnil. Follow the Route du Bac and the Ave. de Saint-Maurice, then, to the l., the Ave. Daumesnil, which leads to the Porte Dorée and Paris; or go to the r., along the same avenue, to visit the château.

The jungle in Paris

One of the most popular attractions of the Colonial Exhibition of 1931 was unquestionably the Zoological Garden which, on the first Sunday after it opened, welcomed 50,000 visitors. The first of its kind, its originality lay in showing animals apparently at liberty, separated from the public by bars and deep ditches concealed by clumps of greenery, thus giving visitors the illusion of being in a completely natural environment. It was organized by a German expert, Hagenbeck, who had opened his own zoo in Hamburg in 1907. London Zoo had already been created on the same principle. Paris restricted itself to African wildlife; there were no tigers or panthers.

Giraffes, elephants, 20 lions, antelopes, buffalo, zebras, ostriches, 140 baboons from Abyssinia and even a rhinoceros, travelled for five days in 11 wagons from Hamburg. The unfavorable weather conditions caused considerable suffering for the animals, and some of the monkeys died. The biggest attraction was the lions' rock, where the beasts frightened the crowds with their roars and bloody fights. Visitors were yet to be educated; they fed the animals with the most ridiculous foods – such as tobacco packets for the giraffes, or candy wrappers for the monkeys.

▷ Asia in the Bois de Vincennes

The Tropical Forestry Center is situated on the site of the Colonial Garden of the 1899 Exhibition. Gathered here are several structures originating from exhibitions held in the early years of the 20th c. One such was the famous pagoda presented to the Colonial Exhibition of 1906 at Marseilles, which was unfortunately destroyed in a fire in 1984. It was an authentic *dinh* from S Vietnam, a communal house used for religious purposes and by village elders to debate matters of local importance. It was installed in Paris in 1917 as a memorial to the Indo-Chinese soldiers and construction engineers who were killed fighting in France in World War I. Each year, on November 2, there is a commemorative service in their honor. For visitors who happen to be in Paris in November, this is an opportunity to discover the garden and its monuments, now awaiting restoration. The temple's courtyard still exists, as does the bronze funeral urn. From here, an alley leads to the memorial to the dead troops from Laos and Cambodia (now Kampuchea); it is decorated with large reliefs copied from the famous avenue at Angkor Wat and presented to the Colonial Exhibition of 1931. Another path, lined with china elephants, leads to a red lacquer pontoon and the memorial to the Malagasay infantrymen. In the garden there are more monuments to the dead, to Colonial ex-servicemen and to Christian Indo-Chinese soldiers who died fighting for France. The Association Nationale des Anciens d'Indo-Chine, which has its headquarters here, was presented with a monument dedicated to the glory of colonialism by the City of Paris. This now embarrassing monument came from a Parisian square.

☐ The Château de Vincennes**

Métro: Château-de-Vincennes
Bus: 56, 112, 115, 118, 124, 325, 313
Entrance: Ave. de Paris. Tel: 43-28-15-48
Tours: accompanied by a guide-lecturer from Monuments Historiques (45 mins.). Open daily 10am–5pm in winter; 9.30am–6pm in summer (1 April–30 Sept).

Although the château is part of the municipality of Vincennes, it is included here in the visit to the Bois.

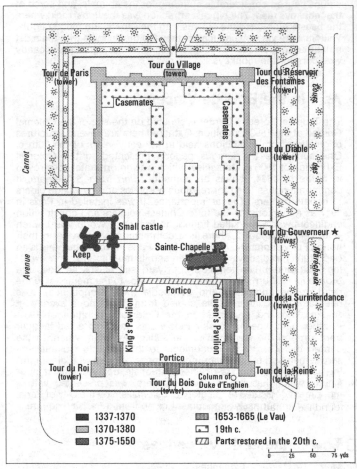

The Château de Vincennes

History of the Château de Vincennes

Vincennes and hunting

The Château de Vincennes was born of the French kings' passion for hunting. In the 9th c. the wood was bought by the Crown. Louis VII is said to have built a lodge for hunting parties on the site of the present château. There is definite historical evidence that his son, Philippe Auguste, built a royal manor house here, and the King signed several of his royal edicts at Vincennes. Philippe Auguste surrounded the wood with a high wall to protect any trees from being felled. From this time on, French kings stayed often at Vincennes. Louis IX (St Louis) in particular, loved the place, and Joinville's account of the monarch dispensing justice at the foot of an oak tree is a well-known story. He had a manor house built here, of which no trace now remains, and a Saint-Chapelle in the style of those in Paris and Saint-Germain, which was intended to house one of the thorns from Christ's crown, taken in 1239 from the relic in the Sainte-Chapelle in Paris. It was from Vincennes that St Louis left for the crusade to Tunis where he was to die.

The manor of Vincennes witnessed many great events: the marriage of Philippe III le Hardi (the Bold), 1274; the marriage of Philippe IV le Bel (the Fair), 1284, to Jeanne de Navarre, who was just 11 years old and who died at Vincennes in 1305; the court martial and execution by firing squad of the Duc d'Enguerrand de Marigny (1316); the deaths of Louis X le Hutin (the Headstrong), 1316, Philippe V le Long (the Tall), 1322 and of Charles IV le Bel (the Fair), 1328, the last of the direct line of Capetians.

The Windsor of the Valois

It was the Valois family who transformed the original manor into the immense fortress that Michelet compared with those of the kings of England. Philippe VI, first of the Valois, began the construction of the keep in 1334 and, by the time of his death in 1350, the foundations had been completed, but the Hundred Years War had begun and the treasury was empty. Work stopped until 1361, when Jean le Bon (the Good) ordered its resumption; three storeys were built. The keep was completed in 1370 by Philippe VI's grandson, Charles V (born at Vincennes in 1337) for whom it served as a retreat; he installed a part of his treasure and of his library there, as at the Louvre. A precious inventory lists the furniture and valuables, with their positions in the various rooms. The collection inspired the admiration of illustrious visitors such as Charles IV of Luxembourg, Emperor of Germany, who visited in 1378, the year of his death.

It is the château as it appeared under Charles V that is depicted in 'December' in the *Très Riches Heures du Duc de Berry*, perhaps the most famous medieval Book of Hours. The château is shown surrounded by a great rectangular outer wall bristling with nine towers. Christine de Pisan (1364–1430) tells us in her *Livres des faits et bonnes moeurs de Charles V* (a chronicle of the age of Charles V) that this wall was intended to contain a city where the King's best-loved nobles would build their palaces; the nobles, however, were reluctant to renounce their independence by living so close to the court, and the land within the château's walls remained unoccupied. The King demolished St Louis' Sainte-Chapelle and, in 1379, laid the first stone of a new chapel. Work had hardly begun when he died nearby, at the Château de Beauté-sur-Marne, in 1380.

Work stopped for a time when the château fell into the hands of the English. It was in the old bedchamber of Charles V that Henry V, King of England, died of dysentery in 1422, just as he was about to join forces with his Burgundian allies. After it was finally retaken from the English, the château was lovingly restored by Charles VII, who was especially fond of it because it lay close to by the Château de Beauté, which he had given to his mistress, Agnès Sorel, who gave birth to a daughter at Vincennes.

Although Louis XI preferred Plessis-les-Tours, he nonetheless built a lodge (now demolished) at Vincennes at the SW corner of the outer wall, which was completed by François I and decorated by Francesco Primatticio (or le Primatice, 1504–70). It was also François I who completed the new Sainte-Chapelle or Chapelle Royale consecrated by Henri II in 1552. Although Vincennes began to be neglected in favor of Fontainebleau, Saint-Germain-en-Laye, and the châteaux of the Loire, it still offered a safe haven during the Wars of Religion.

At the age of 24 Charles IX died in Charles V's bedchamber in 1574, tortured by remorse for having permitted the Massacre of St Bartholomew's Day. Henri III took refuge in the château from the Holy League, which captured him after a year-long siege.

Vincennes in the Age of Neo-Classicism

In the 17th c. the keep was finally abandoned as a royal residence and became a royal prison (→inset). The sovereigns preferred to lodge in one or other of the two vast wings facing each other across the Cour Royale (main courtyard), the plans for which had been drawn up by Catherine de' Medici in 1560, and the first stone laid by Marie de' Medici in 1610. The future Louis XIII lived there during the regency of his mother and, when he became king, continued with the construction of the two main buildings known as the Pavillon du Roi (King's Pavilion) and the Pavillon de la Reine (Queen's Pavilion). They were completed in 1659, by the architect Le Vau, commissioned by Mazarin who, advised by Colbert, took the title of Governor of Vincennes 'so as to have a safe place for his riches in the event of civil disorder.' He died in 1661 in the King's Pavilion while waiting for his apartments in the Queen's Pavilion to be completed. The interior was sumptuously decorated by the Flemish painter Philippe de Champaigne to welcome Louis XIV and Maria-Theresa on their return from the Ile des Faisans following their marriage in 1610. Mazarin died at Vincennes on March 9, 1661 and shortly afterward the King proclaimed his intention to govern for himself.

In 1715 after the death of Louis XIV, in accordance with his great-grandfather's wishes, the infant Louis XV left Versailles for the healthy air of Vincennes, where he spent 72 days.

Apart from this interlude the château was abandoned in favor of Versailles and was no longer used as a royal residence. While the keep held its distinguished prisoners, the castle was used for diverse purposes; from 1738 to 1756 it was the Royal Porcelain manufactory (→inset). In 1743 a cadet school was established at Vincennes, which was later developed into the Ecole Militaire. As an economy measure Louis XVI wanted to put his 'good-for-nothing château' up for sale, but he reckoned without the residents who had overrun it, as they had the Louvre, and who resisted his decision. The château narrowly escaped in 1791, when crowds from the Faubourg Saint-Antoine rushed the keep, a symbol of despotism, with the intention of demolishing it. La Fayette, however, arrived in time to stop them (→inset).

Vincennes as a military installation

Bonaparte began the château's military period, which was to last until recent times, with the execution of the Duc d'Enghien. Napoléon increased the military importance of Vincennes. The château became both an arsenal and a fortress, and all the towers except the Tour du Village were levelled to the height of the perimeter wall. The keep continued to receive prisoners such as the cardinals who supported Pius VII (one of them being Mgr de Boulogne).

From 1809 to 1814, during the Hundred Days, and from 1830 to 1832, the year of his death, Daumesnil was Governor of Vincennes. In 1814, when the Allies called for his surrender, he replied: 'The Austrians took one of my legs [he had lost it at Wagram]; let them give it back to me, or come and try to take the other one.' In 1815 he resisted both the enticements and the threats of Blücher. In 1830, when rioters invaded the fort to seize several ministers of Charles X who were held there, Daumesnil turned them away by threatening to blow himself and the castle up by setting fire to the powder magazine.

In *Servitude et Grandeur militaires*, Vigny recalled his stay at Vincennes in 1819.

After 1840 the château was systematically transformed into a fortress as part of Paris's defense system. All the exits to the outside were blocked up, and outer walls between the bastions reinforced by casements, the moat round the keep filled in and ramps raised all around the perimeter wall. Surviving parts of the original manor house, dating from before the 14th c., were totally demolished, as was the N portico connecting the King's Pavilion with the Queen's Pavilion, to make room for military structures. Most of Le Vau's decoration was destroyed. The Chapelle Royale was divided into several floors, the royal pavilions turned into barracks and the keep into an armory.

In 1840 the light infantry was formed at Vincennes; a museum dedicated to their memory is in the perimeter wall of the Vieux-Fort. From 1842 to 1848 the Duc de Montpensier, fifth son of Louis-Philippe, lived in the Queen's Pavilion as commandant of the fort. He resisted plans to demolish the Sainte Chapelle.

After the Revolution of 1848, Barbès and Blanqui were imprisoned in the keep as were, a little later, opponents of the Second Empire. In 1871 nine Fédérés (soldiers of the Commune) were shot in the N moat by troops of the Versailles government.

The resurrection of Vincennes

From 1854 to 1867, Viollet-le-Duc and his pupil Anatole de Baudot restored the Sainte-Chapelle. But it was not until 1930 that a fervent press campaign, launched by André Hurtret on behalf of the château, resulted in a general shift of public opinion in favor of restoration. The Chamber of Deputies voted for the staged evacuation of the château by the military. The construction of the Cours des Maréchaux was completed, as was the clearing of the W face of the ramparts. In 1934 the Musée Historique was inaugurated in the keep. During the World War II the château was occupied by the Germans. As they were on the point of retreating, Vincennes suffered the most tragic moment in its history. On August 20, 1944, about 30 hostages, students and members of the Resistance, were shot inside the ramparts and in the E moat. Then, on the night of August 24, the Germans blew up the casemates of the W and S façades, as well as a part of the King's Pavilion, while a fire devastated the Queen's Pavilion. The explosion uncovered the S portico and its triumphal arch by Le Vau, forgotten for 130 years.

Repair work revealed the whole of the entrance, and the reliefs of Van Obstal and Desjardins were restored. The reconstruction, set in motion in 1944 by the Service des Monuments Historiques, was entrusted to the architect Jean Trouvelot. Charles V's Sainte-Chapelle regained its stained-glass windows in 1952. The renovation of the King's and Queen's Pavilions was accompanied by the uncovering of the S portico and the reconstruction of the N portico. The demolition of casemates and clearance of the old moats, filled in since the 19th c., have restored the keep's original appearance (completed in 1972), while uncovering the 14th-c. drawbridge that gave access to it. Finally, the esplanade at the S entrance of the château has almost become, once again, the Y-shaped junction of three avenues: the Route de la Pyramide, the Ave. Daumesnil, and the Allée Royale, which still ends at the Carnot *quartier*. The Sainte-Chapelle is now entirely restored to its 17th-c. state, but the N part of the outer wall remains encumbered with military outbuildings.

Tour of the Château de Vincennes*

☐ The Château*

The site of the château is an immense rectangle, 1049ft/320m long by 584ft/178m wide, enclosed by a high defensive wall and a wide moat, no longer filled with water. The ramparts once included nine towers, with the keep forming an outwork to the W. With the exception of the Tour du Village, at the entrance, these towers were levelled to the height of the perimeter wall during the Empire. The tower is 157½ft/48m high from the bottom of the moats and has six floors; it is flanked at the rear corners by two turrets. From the Ave. de Paris side its façade shows the sober ornamentation of the 17th c. with, above the gate, two angels bearing the arms of France. The captain of the guard had his quarters here. In the Middle Ages it was the governor's apartment.

In the courtyard, to the l., a plaque indicates the site of St Louis's manor, destroyed in the 17th c. A little farther on, an engraved stone commemorates the execution of 11 hostages by the Nazis on August 20, 1944.

The Keep*

The exterior

The keep's strong, square tower has four turrets flanking each corner and a terrace 164ft/50m high. The chemise, or outer wall of the keep, was completely surrounded by a sentry path and a wide moat, which had been filled in from the courtyard side, but which has now been redug, work which led to the uncovering of the beautiful 14th-c. drawbridge. The casemates built onto the keep during the 19th c. have been demolished. This superb structure, which was at the same time both a palace and a fortress, has now been restored to its original state, isolated from the other buildings within the château's grounds.

The interior

The keep houses the Musée Historique (tel: 43-28-15-48). Collected in its various halls are documents tracing the château's history (facsimiles of miniatures, illuminated manuscripts), paintings, and engravings, casts of statues and seals in the splendor of the rooms themselves, with their magnificent carved ensembles of corbels and keystones, with more than 400 motifs. Above the ground floor, divided into two halls, each of the three floors is divided into a main chamber supported by vaults resting on a central pillar, with four small rooms in the turrets serving as oratories, attiring rooms, treasuries and waiting rooms. Later, these were converted into prison cells.

Ground level. One of the two 13th-c. gates comes from Louis XVI's prison in the tower of the Temple. The two great rooms on the ground floor were probably the center of activity. The old kitchens were here, in which the body of Henry V was boiled in 1422 to prepare it for transportation back to London. N Hall: documents on the history of the Capetian manor house, from its beginnings to Charles IV le Bel (the Fair). S Hall: the keep's early history, from Philippe VI to Jean Le Bon (the Good). There is a well in the kitchen, 56ft/17m deep. Also, Latude's cell, where he had time in over two years, concealed by the chimney place, to make a small hole in the wall over a meter thick, to communicate with the prisoners' yard. The first and second floors are reached by a wide spiral staircase.

First floor. The Great Hall* is where the King sat in Parlement or with his council, and received the Holy Roman Emperor. The oak-panelled, vaulted ceiling dates from the earliest construction (when the walls were completely covered by it). Here begins the superb series of corbels* depicting the four Evangelists and their attributes (the angel, the winged lion, the eagle, and the winged ox), which were discovered in the other two central halls. Also, souvenirs from the time of Charles V, and of Fouquet, who was incarcerated here. NW turret. Here is the cell in which Mirabeau and Barbès were imprisoned (documents and souvenirs). There are documents on the first prisoners of the château (15th and 16th c.). Go up the Royal staircase, constructed by Charles V, one of the widest remaining from the 14th c.; the steps are 7ft/2m deep.

Second floor. The King's Bedchamber*: This room is the most beautiful and the most evocative. Charles V lived here when he was visited by his maternal uncle, Emperor Charles IV of Germany, to whom he gave up this same chamber and bed to go and sleep in the Chambre aux Daims (Deer Room), not identified as a token of welcome. According to tradition it was here too, that Henry V of England died, as did Charles IX, and where Cardinal de Retz was imprisoned. As in the other main halls the vaulting rests on a central pillar; keystones, corbels and lintels, sculptures, mantelpiece, and walls bearing the traces of a decoration made by a prisoner in the

18th c. add to the room's beauty. Documents relating to the château's history, from Charles V to Louis XIV, are kept here. SW turret: reserved for the queens, princesses, and favorites who lived at Vincennes in the 15th and 16th c. NW turret: Former oratory of Charles V; souvenirs of the prisoners of the 17th c., one of whom was the Duc de Beaufort, famous for his escape; there are numerous graffiti. Chapel of Charles V: Note the exquisitely carved corbels and keystone (the Trinity). N-E turret: Raspail's cell.

3rd floor (not open to the public). Bedchamber of the royal children: the Duc de Beaufort, Condé, the Prince de Conti, the Duc de Longueville and Diderot were imprisoned in this room.

4th and 5th floors (not open to the public). This served as an annex. Four former ministers of Charles X were detained in the four corner rooms of the fourth floor in 1830.

 From the top of the keep there is a splendid panoramic view* of Paris and the Bois de Vincennes.

Le Châtelet (The Barbican)

Over the bridge to the E is the Châtelet or barbican, the generic name for an outer defensive structure, which guarded the drawbridge; a small building flanked by machicolated towers. Above the gate are the arms of Charles V, forged in 1791; note also the high window of *l'estude* (the study) where the King liked to work. Under the vault is a reconstruction of an old inscription of Philippe Ogier, relating to the construction of the keep and the château. On the other side of the barbican is the graceful staircase of Charles V (→above), which is the stair the King climbed to get to the keep; access to the keep from the barbican was, in effect, via the Entrée Royale on the first floor, which was connected to the barbican by a fixed bridge followed by a drawbridge. This entrance has been reconstructed, but without the drawbridge. In the courtyard, to the r., is an audiovisual projection room, whose show explains the history of the château.

The Sainte-Chapelle

The Sainte-Chapelle was built to the level of the sill of the stained-glass windows by around 1387. It was completed soon after 1520, under the direction of Philibert Delorme, and consecrated in 1552, in the reign of Henri II.

The exterior

Although finished during the Renaissance the building remains Gothic, only the stained-glass windows showing Italian influence. In

1661 after the death of Mazarin, it served as a mortuary chapel. The façade is in the Flamboyant Gothic style: There is a gable over the door and another, larger, one, filled with tracery above the beautiful stone rose window, while the gable end is framed by two turrets with belfries, decorated, like the pinnacles, with the monogram and salamander of François I. The spire vanished in the 18th c.

The interior

This chapel, 65ft/20m high, 108ft/33m wide, and 32ft/10m high, has a single aisle, and unlike the Sainte-Chapelle, only one storey. The ribbed vaults are surmounted with the monogram of Henri II, Catherine de' Medici, and Charles IX. The highly decorative consoles and the frieze below the windows are (15th c.) in the same style as the arch over the portal. In the seven windows of the apse, the 16th-c. stained glass shows scenes from the Apocalypse. They were commissioned by Philibert Delorme from Nicolas Beaurain, and may have been designed by Jean Cousin. They have been restored many times and the N bay, above the sacrarium, is entirely modern. At the base of the center stained-glass window is the figure of François I at prayer. To the r. and I. of the chancel are two small doors with carved 15th-c. tympanums (arms of France and Bavaria); each leads to an oratory. To the I. of the chancel is another door (15th c.) giving access to a large sacristy ornamented with beautiful consoles; above is the collection of relics. The oratory on the I. (to the I. a carved Flamboyant piscina or credence table) contains the tomb of the Duc d'Enghien (→inset) and four marble statues by Deseine (1825). Formerly in the chancel, it was placed in its present position by the future Napléon III. The rood screen, the stalls and the 16th c. altar disappeared during the Revolution.

☐ The Royal residence*

Generally not open to the public but there may be some temporary exhibitions.

This residence, built by Le Vau from 1654 to 1661, extends to S of the keep and the chapel, enclosed by the medieval exterior wall.

The exterior

On either side of the immense main courtyard, on two long pavilions lined with equally-spaced Doric pilasters in the classical manner: the King's Pavilion and the Queen's Pavilion. They are connected by two galleries that enclose the courtyard, embellished with niches between the arcades. The N portico, destroyed in the 19th c., has been reconstructed. The S portico, which had replaced the old façade facing the esplanade, was discovered almost intact under the casemate that had concealed it since 1840, after the latter was blown up by the Germans in 1944. It has now been restored. In the center, surrounding the base of the old Tour du Bois, the main entrance, formed by a triumphal arch. This beautiful work by Le Vau has lost the statues that once ornamented its alcoves and balustrade.

The two royal pavilions suffered badly in the explosion of 1944. The façades on the courtyard side have been wholly restored to their original state, but the interiors have had to be almost completely renovated, work which has brought to light some of the original stucco and paintings.

The interior

The King's Pavilion (to the W), built for Louis XIV and Maria-Theresa, is where Mazarin died before the completion of his apartments in the Queen's Pavilion; it now houses military archives. On the first floor the Queen's Antechamber has preserved intact all its original dóoor, painted in the 17th c. by Michel Dorigny (son-in-law of Simon Vouet), with winged figures and cupids carrying medallions with Marla-Theresa's emblem; the sculpted basket-of-flowers motifs are the work of J.-B. Monnoyer. At present this is all that remains of the château's interior decoration by Le Vau. The King's Apartment has been repanelled with woodwork by Gabriel, provided by the royal furniture repository in the Place de la Concorde.

The Queen's Pavilion (to the E)

Restoration of this pavilion, built for Anne of Austria and her lover Mazarin, is now completed. The decoration inside was unfortunately severely damaged by fire, but in the Louvre, you can see in the vestibule of the Salles de la Colonnade the ceiling and paneling of the Queen's Council Chamber (Chambre du Conseil de la Reine), which was taken there during Charles X's reign. Inside, nothing of the original décor remains except the magnificently restored staircase and a dressing room on the ceiling of which is a painting of *Fame* carrying the medallion of Monsieur, brother of Louis XIV. This wing contains the Naval Records Office, and the Musée de la Guerre de 1914–1918.

The outer wall of the Château

Leaving by the Tour du Village, follow the outer wall to the l. After passing the NW corner, flanked by the square Tour de Paris, which has preserved its 14th-c. tierce-pointed windows, continue past the

W façade as far as the Ave. Carnot. It is on this façade that the keep rises, projecting outward, surrounded by its square, fortified sentry paths, which are in turn surrounded by a wide moat. Observe, at the base, the enormous foundations and the berm separating them from the moat, designed to prevent sappers from digging under the walls. In the 15th c. the gallery or parapet walk, the machicolations of which are topped with battlements, was roofed over. It was through one of these openings that the Duc de Beaufort made his escape; the rope being too short he fell at the base of the tower and remained there unconscious for a few minutes, upon which his accomplices, posted on the counterscarp, came and pulled him from the moat with a rope. To the S of the keep, behind the King's Pavilion, the glacis has been levelled and the original terraces restored. Running along the S side is the Esplanade du Château, cleared in 1954, which extends to the entrance of the Bois de Vincennes. A bridge over the moat gives access to the principal gate of the Cour Royale (Main Courtyard), the foundation of the old Tour de Bois. The Tour du Roi is at the SW corner of the outer wall; the Tour de la Reine is at the SE corner. Near the foot of the Queen's Tower, in the moat, is a column erected in 1816 at the place where the Duc d'Enghien was executed.

The whole E façade of the château was cleared in 1931 by the creation of the Cours des Maréchaux. Following this promenade towards Vincennes one passes, successively, the Tour de la Sur-intendance, the Tour du Gouverneur in the center, and the Tour du Diable where the porcelain workers of Vincennes were installed in the 18th c., and through which the Duc d'Enghien descended into the moat to face his executioners; then the Tour du Réservoir at the NE corner. During this walk you will see, above the ramparts, the upper section of the Queen's Pavilion (note the beautiful Neo-Classical façade) and the apse of the Sainte-Chapelle.

▷ **The riot of February 28, 1791**

Having lost favor as a royal residence, the keep of the Château de Vincennes had been a State prison from the beginning of the 16th c. It was considered less disgraceful to be held there than at the Bastille. Jansenists, supporters of the Fronde, philosophers, aristo-crats and libertines were imprisoned in the small rooms in the corners of each floor. The Great Condé, Cardinal de Retz, Fouquet (guarded by d'Artagnan), the Prince de Conti, Diderot, Mirabeau, and the Duc de Lauzun were only a few of the famous people detained while awaiting trial. (→ inset).

In 1788 the prison was put up for sale but found no buyers. On November 20, 1790, the National Assembly placed the keep at the disposal of the commune of Paris to be used as an annex to the city's overcrowded prisons. The work of restoring and refurbishing the prison began on January 14, 1791.

This roused the Revolutionaries to a pitch of screaming fury. Their howls of rage stirred the inhabitants of the Faubourg Saint-Antoine, and armed bands including hysterical viragos and street urchins hurled themselves on Vincennes, destroying the statues, gates, and flooring of the keep and postern. The mayor of Vincennes called upon La Fayette for help. The revolt was quelled and 64 ringleaders were taken to the Conciergerie in Paris. However, with such violent public opposition to the idea of a preventive prison, work on the prison could not continue. The keep then became a house of detention for loose women but, badly supervised, they indulged in debauchery of the worst kind. Late in 1794 it was decided to transfer them to the Salpêtrière and Saint-Lazare.

Vincennes as a royal prison

After the 15th c. French monarchs rarely used the Vincennes keep as a residence and it became instead a royal prison. Catherine de' Medici imprisoned Henri of Navarre, the future Henri IV, there. The history of famous prisoners began during the Fronde: the Duc de Beaufort, the 'Roi des Halles', who escaped in 1648; the Cardinal de Retz; the Duc de Longueville, the Grand Conde and his brother and the Prince de Conti. In the 17th c. the keep was reserved for prisoners of 'distinguished quality': Louis XIV, displeased by the extravagant entertainment Foucquet put on for him, sent him there in 1662. La Voisin and her accomplices in the Poison Affair, Mme Guyon, founder of Quietism (1695) and finally the Jansenists, including the Abbé of Saint-Cyran in 1707, were all incarcerated there. Under Louis XV, Vincennes became the 'place of despair' evoked by Voltaire. The keep received Crébillon The Younger in 1734; Diderot, incarcerated in 1749 for his *Lettre sur les Avengles* (Letter on the Blind), was visited by Jean-Jacques Rousseau (on the way Rousseau had a revelation for the theme of his reply to the question posed by the Académie de Dijon: 'Has the re-establishment of the Arts and Sciences contributed to an (improved) public morality?'). Prince Charles Edward Stuart (Bonnie Prince Charlie) was briefly held after Culloden. Latude, who was imprisoned for 35 years without trial for having tried to extort money from Mme de Pompadour, escaped twice, in 1750 and in 1765. The first time he distracted the guards by demanding a priest to administer the last rites to an imaginary dying man. Sade, in 1777, had as a neighbor, Mirabeau, imprisoned from 1771 to 1780 for duelling; while there he wrote his scathing pamphlet against the *lettres de cachet* (private, sealed documents by means of which the King could order the imprisonment or exile of his personal or political enemies). Louis XVI closed the prison after it had, curiously enough, been reopened by the Revolution. It was used again during the two World Wars. Mata Hari, naked under her fur coat, was shot here in 1917.

▷ **The death of the Duc d'Enghien**

At 6pm on March 20, 1804, the Duke, seized five days previously at Ettenheim (opposite Strasbourg) on the territory of the Germanic Confederation, and indicated on a charge of conspiring with the emigrés against Napoléon, was imprisoned in the Pavillon du Roi (King's Pavilion) at Vincennes. At 1.45am the following morning he was condemned summarily in the Tour du Bois and shot at the foot of the Tour de la Reine (Queen's Tower) at 3am. His body, thrown into a pit close by, was exhumed by Louis XVIII in 1816 and placed in a funerary monument installed in the Chapelle Royale.

▷ **The Porcelain of Vincennes**

In 1738, Gilles and Robert Dubois, craftsmen from the Chantilly factory, were dismissed, and sought refuge at Vincennes. They were given permission to take over the unoccupied Tour du Diable. Enjoying highly placed protection they discovered, with their friend Gravant, the secret of *pâte tendre* (soft paste porcelain) and bought the secret technique of applying gold to china from a Benedictine monk in Saint-Martin-des-Champs. This enabled them to obtain a protective monopoly in 1745, the title of Manufacture Royale in 1753, and an unrivalled reputation. The use of gold was an exclusive prerogative of Vincennes, while rich background colors in the underglaze made the porcelain even more prized. The color 'Rose Pompadour' was perfected here, as was the superb *bleu céleste* (heavenly blue) or *gros bleu*, which became the famous 'Sèvres blue' in 1763. The adoption of the bisque technique in 1752 made possible the creation of many new forms. Outside artists such as Boucher, who contributed the models for the charming little groups called *enfants Boucher*, were brought in.

The factory's fortunes were at their height 1753 and 1756, when the Rococo style dominated. The most representative example of this period is a service sent to Louis XV, comprising 1744 pieces in *bleu céleste* with a pattern of polychrome flowers. In 1756 the factory moved to Sèvres where it earned the fame now associated with that name.

The Museums

The Museums of Paris

For a thousand years Paris has been the capital of a country with an extraordinarily rich and varied heritage, and the administrative center of a state whose centralizing tendency has long made itself felt as much in the cultural as in the political life of the nation. It is hardly surprising, then, that this city, over 2000 years old, favored so often and in so many ways over all other French cities, has over a hundred museums within its limits. Neither is it surprising that the collections housed in these establishments, taken as a whole, not only provide eloquent confirmation of the primacy of Paris, but also reflect all the spiritual and intellectual wealth of France itself.

The collections are as exceptional for their diversity as for their quality and abundance. Few cities in the world offer such a variety of objects and documents to both their citizens and their visitors in the fields of art, archeology, history, anthropology, literature, science, or technology – a wide range that is supplemented by the splendid museums to be found in the nearby châteaux of Versailles and the Trianons, Malmaison, Saint-Germain-en-Laye, Ecouen, Compiègne, and Fontainebleau, to name only a few. All in all, the museums of Paris present a stunning panorama of the knowledge, sensibility, and history of the people who through the centuries have created France and, with it, Paris, many of whose achievements have had repercussions throughout Europe and, indeed, worldwide.

From the beginnings to 1815

The first public museums in Paris were opened at the end of the 18th century, amid the turmoil of revolution. In conformity with the didactic aims and the historical and centralizing approach to knowledge of the Encyclopedists, these early museums organized their collections according to categories that have remained the guidelines in the development of the national collections to this day: art, archeology, natural history, science, and technology.

On May 26, 1791, the Louvre Palace was designated to house the monuments of art and science; in November 1792, the task of transferring to it works of art removed from royal residences was begun; founded on July 27, 1793, by decree of the Convention, the Museum of the Republic was inaugurated on August 10 of the following year, the anniversary of the fall of the monarchy.

In the western side of the Grande Galerie, 537 paintings and 124 *objets d'art* were put on display, partly for the benefit of the public, but first and foremost to serve as an inspiration to artists, for according to the educational ideas current at the time, the museums were intended primarily for the instruction of the latter. 'From that moment up to the time of Cézanne and Matisse, the Louvre was to be the great laboratory where modern art would be invented.' (G. Bazin).

Naturalists, engineers, and historians were not neglected. Created at the same time were the Musée d'Histoire Naturelle (Natural History Museum), inaugurated on June 10, 1793, in the old Royal Botanic Garden; the Musée des Arts et Métiers (Museum of Arts and Crafts), opened October 10, 1794, and soon installed in the old Priory of Saint-Martin-des-Champs; and, gathering up the scattered relics of the nationalized churches and chatêaux, the Musée des Monuments Français (Museum of French Monuments), opened on October 12, 1795, in the convent of the Petits-Augustins, where objects confiscated from Parisian churches and monasteries had been stored since October 1790.

The contribution of the royal collections

It would be inaccurate to think of the founding of these museums as some kind of spontaneous generation. They would have been, at least in the case of the first three, impossible or far less distinguished without the contributions made by the royal collections whose arrangement prefigured in many ways that of the museums created after the Revolution.

The Louvre museum grew from the collection of works created by François I, whose purchases of Italian paintings included the *Mona Lisa*, and were enriched by his successors up to the end of the Ancien Régime. Its present collection of drawings originated with the banker Jabach's collection of 5542 pieces, bought at the initiative of Colbert in 1671. The Département des Objets d'Art is also, in great part, a legacy from the Garde-Meuble de la Couronne (royal furniture collection), which can claim to be one of the first museums of France, since certain rooms were set aside in 1778 to be opened to the public on the second Tuesday of each month, in the mansion built by Gabriel for this purpose on the Place Louis XV (the present Admiralty) in which the museum was installed in 1774. And what better home could have been found for the Musée d'Histoire Naturelle (Natural History Museum) than the Jardin des Plantes (Botanical Garden), founded in 1626 by Louis XIII's physician, Guy de Labrosse, and expertly enlarged by Buffon between 1739 and 1788?

It is hard not to see a forerunner of the Musée des Techniques (Museum of Technology), at least in principle, in the 'storehouse of all the machines presented to the Academy', which was housed in the same building as the Paris Observatory, inaugurated on the summer solstice of 1667. At the very least this museum followed from the collection of machines and documents amassed by Vaucanson, opened to the public in 1760, and bequeathed to the King in 1782. Nor should the royal origins of some of the other collections be ignored. For example, the Bibliothèque Nationale (National Library) has a collection of medals begun by François I, reorganized by Henri IV, considerably enlarged by Louis XIV, and installed in 1741 in the mansion of the Marquise de Lambert. The Musée de l'Armée (Army Museum) dates from 1685 when the Maréchal Duc d'Humières, Grand Master of Artillery, obtained royal permission to install in the Bastille a group of models 'to serve for the instruction of young officers.' And the foundations of the Musée de la Marine (Naval Museum) were laid by Duhamel de Montceau, inspector general of the navy, when he presented his magnificent naval collection to the King in 1748, who had it installed in the Louvre, along with the collection of relief maps started in 1668 by Louvois to provide the sovereign and his military chiefs with a precise documentation of French and foreign fortifications. When these were moved to the Hôtel des Invalides in 1777, it was justified on museological grounds: the move freed the Louvre's Grande Galerie for the public display of the royal collection of paintings.

The idea of opening a museum in the Louvre, where the Royal Academy of Painting and Sculpture had been holding annual exhibitions of members' work in the Salon Carré, was already half a century old when the Convention made it a reality. First put forward in 1747 by the polemicist Lafont de Saint-Yenne in a pamphlet condemning the secrecy in which the King's collections were held, the idea was taken up and developed by Diderot in 1765 under the heading 'Louvre', (vol. IX). Three years later the Marquis de Marigny, the director of public works, brother of Mme de Pompadour and sympathetic to the Philosophers, drew up the first project and submitted it to Louis XV, to no effect. His successor, the Comte d'Angiviller, reopened the file under Louis XVI and, in spite of serious technical and financial obstacles, persevered with the plans; the work of refurbishing the Grande Galerie began in 1789.

It is sometimes claimed that, so far as museums are concerned, the Revolution was content to complete the projects started under the *Ancien Régime*, but this contention ignores both the passion for logic with which the old projects were rethought and extended, and the fervent conviction with which those still in the planning stages before the Revolution were realized in institutions governed by laws and regulations. Both the passion and the conviction were required to forge the museum effectively into the fundamental instrument of culture desired by the revolutionaries. At the same time French conquests abroad, which began as revolutionary evangelism and turned into an epic imperialism, provided the opportunity to seize the most famous works of art to enrich the Paris collections, with the justification that Paris would thereby become the showplace for the most complete and exalted demonstration of the superiority of human genius, to the profit of every citizen in Europe.

The Musée Napoléon

The Louvre was the main beneficiary of the influx of works of art confiscated after French victories in Belgium, Holland, Italy, Germany, and Austria. Under the watchful eye of Napoléon and thanks to the talents of Vivant Denon, appointed director in 1802, the Louvre became for several years after 1803, under the name Musée Napoléon, the most prestigious museum of all time, at least as regards painting and classical antiquities. This concentration of masterpieces in one place did not meet with unqualified approval. However weighty the arguments put forward, it was difficult to avoid the accusation of plunder. Still it should be recognized that the great Parisian collection served as a model for other European museums, which were established either by Imperial order, as in Milan and Venice, or, as in Boulogne and Antwerp, in response to the threat of confiscation. Also, and more importantly, entirely new museums were created by giving portions of the accumulated booty to some 15 provincial cities including Brussels, Mainz, and Geneva, which at that time were the capitals of French *départements*. It is also true that after Napoléon had departed for Elba and the French monarchy had been restored, the allies did not call into question the treaties by which the Louvre had so richly profited – proof, perhaps, at least to some extent, that this outrageous enterprise had succeeded.

It was not at all the same in 1815 after the Battle of Waterloo. This time the victors, on Wellington's recommendation, took care not to 'lose the chance to teach the French a great moral lesson.' All the plundered countries sent commissioners to reclaim their confiscated treasures; the loss in this way of 5000 works, including 2065 paintings, left the Louvre devastated.

The Louvre Museum, From 1815 to the present day

In spite of this 'disaster' there was no question of withdrawing the Louvre from service as a museum. Successive French governments since 1815 have made every effort to extend and diversify its collections. At first archeology made a huge contribution. The Musée des Antiquities (Museum of Ancient Art), which had opened in 1800 on the ground floor of the Petite Galerie, still consisted essentially of the original royal collection, consisting of bronze copies made at Fontainebleau for François I after ancient originals, and the original marbles assembled at Versailles by Louis XIV, as well as pieces from the Borghese collection acquired in 1807. Soon after 1815 the museum further enriched its collection of Greek and Roman antiquities with pieces brought back by French archeologists; through purchases made by French diplomats, such as the famous *Venus de Milo* (1821) and the *Winged Victory of Samothrace* (1863); through numerous and important purchases such as the Tochon (1818), Durand (1824), and Campana (1863) collections, which have made the Louvre a leader in Greek ceramics; and through many donations. There is no period in the history of Classical art, from the beginnings of Hellenism to the end of the Roman Empire, that is not illustrated, and often grandly so, in the collection now on view: marbles, bronzes, ceramics, precious metals, ivories, glass, frescoes, and mosaics vie for attention in this dazzling display.

Egyptian Antiquities

This department was created in 1826 as a result of the purchase of the British consul Salt's collection by Champollion, the first man to decipher Egyptian hieroglyphics. Soon afterward, part of the French consul Drovetti's collection was acquired, followed by that of Champollion himself, gathered in the course of his trip to Egypt. Later came the important addition of the 6000 objects found at the Serapeum by Mariette. These enabled the department to develop rapidly, with the aid of digs methodically undertaken from 1895 onward by its curators in close cooperation with the French Institute in Cairo; other valuable additions were the Curtis donation (1938) and the transfer to the Louvre in 1922 of the Egyptian collection from the Bibliothèque Nationale and in 1948 that of the Guimet Museum.

In the Louvre today, thanks to this world-famous collection, the civilization and art of the Nile Valley can be traced through every step of its evolution from the earliest beginnings to the Christian era.

Near and Middle Eastern Antiquities

Made into a separate department in 1881, this collection now offers an almost complete view of the ancient civilizations of the Near and Middle East. It is closely linked to the development of archeological research in Mesopotamia, Iran, Asia Minor, Cyprus, and the Carthaginian territories of North Africa, from Paul-Emile Botta's excavations at Khorsabad in 1843 – whose finds gave rise in 1847 to the first Assyrian Museum in the Louvre – to the contemporary work of Claude Schaeffer at Ras-Shamra and André Parrot at Mari. Other important finds came from the Renan expedition in Palestine and Syria (1860), from the expedition to Persia directed from 1897 by Jacques de Morgan and of the French archeologists who, exploring the Telloh site in lower Mesopotamia, brought to light for the first time the civilization of Sumeria. In 1945 a section of Islamic Art was added to this department.

Sculpture

When the Musée des Monuments Français, created in 1795 by Alexandre Lenoir, was closed in 1817, some of the remains from French châteaux and churches which it had contained were transferred from the former convent of the Petits-Augustins to the Louvre Palace, where they formed the basis of the future Department of Sculpture. Soon they were joined by sculptures brought from Versailles, Saint-Cloud, and Fontainebleau, thus completing a collection consisting almost exclusively of Renaissance and Classical works. From 1850 this was augmented by the hitherto undervalued sculpture of the Middle Ages, thanks to the efforts of the Marquis de Laborde and later of Courajod. They succeeded in adding pieces that had been piled up in the storerooms at Saint-Denis or left neglected in cathedral workshops. This department was first attached to the Department of Antiquities; it later formed a joint department with the Objets d'Art in 1871, and became autonomous in 1893.

It concentrates mainly on French sculpture from the Romanesque era to the end of the 19th c. but also contains sections of other European 15th-c. and 16th-c. work – Dutch, German, Spanish, and particularly Italian. The gems of the latter are two world-famous masterpieces: Michelangelo's *Slaves*, seized under the Revolution and added to the Louvre collection in 1794.

Objets d'Art

This department which, like the Department of Sculpture, became autonomous in 1893, is another that originated with the royal collections: gems, gold and silversmiths' work and enamels, to which were added the precious remnants of the treasures of the royal Abbey of Saint-Denis, the Sainte-Chapelle and the Ordre du Saint-Esprit. Under the Restoration came the acquisition of the superb Durand (1825) and Revoil (1828) collections, and the Louvre began to widen its scope in this field to cover objects from any source and in any technique, at first giving preference to the Middle Ages and the Renaissance. After the transfer in 1870 of the furniture from the royal residences at Saint-Cloud and the Tuileries, then in 1901 of the most important pieces of the royal furniture stored until then in the Garde-Meuble, a series of rooms devoted to French furniture was opened. Since then this department has continued to grow through important acquisitions and generous gifts (Sauvageot, Thiers, Arconati-Visconti, Adolphe and Salomon de Rothschild, Camondo, Schlichting, Martin-Leroy, David-Weill, and Niarchos, among others) and now offers one of the most complete displays anywhere of fine artistry in woodwork, metalwork, precious stones, textiles, ivory, ceramics, glass- and enamelware from medieval to modern times.

Paintings

After 1815 paintings continued to receive much attention, but it was above all after the Second Empire that the governments and curators actively sought to repair the irreparable.

Under the Restoration paintings such as Rubens' brilliant mural cycle of Marie de' Medici's life were brought from the Luxembourg Palace to redecorate the Grande Galerie. The Luxembourg, which since 1818 has been devoted to contemporary art, became a kind of antechamber to the Louvre. Under the July Monarchy, the creation of the historical museum at Versailles absorbed almost the whole of the purchase fund; and when Louis-Philippe installed his famous Spanish collection in the Colonnade wing in 1838, he did so only temporarily and the collection was dispersed at auction in London in 1853 after the exiled king's death. The development of the department took off again with renewed enthusiasm under the Second Republic, only to be held in abeyance during the Franco-Prussian war of 1870-71, and during the two World Wars. By enlarging the palace, the Second Empire happily created new, better-lit rooms of vast proportions where the paintings, by now much more numerous, could be hung. The purchase of the Campana collection (1861) introduced hitherto unrepresented artists such as Uccello and Tura to the Louvre but, in the main, benefited the provincial museums; recently the 14th-c. and 15th-c. works from the Campana collection have been rehung in the Petit Palais in Avignon, the most appropriate setting possible. On the other hand, the Dr. La Caze bequest of 1869 brought the Louvre 272 paintings – one of the finest gifts it ever received, including Rembrandt's *Bathsheba*, Franz Hals's *Gipsy Woman*, Ribera's *Lame Man*, Le Nain's *The Meal*, Watteau's *Pierrot*, and Fragonard's *The*

Bathers. Since then not a decade has passed without new acquisitions that have either filled a gap or been of outstanding quality, and these, combined with the talent of its curators, the wisdom of its directors, and the generosity of its donors, make the Louvre's collection of paintings the most complete, if not the largest, in the world.

Prints and Drawings

From 1870 onward the Department of Prints and Drawings, whose royal origin is discussed above, was greatly extended by purchase and by magnificent donations: His de la Salle (1878), Gatteaux (1881), Moreau-Nélaton (1907–27), Bonnat (1912–19), Walter-Gay (1913–38), Koechlin (1933), and David-Weill (1953–56), among others.

In all there are over 90,000 works of which 80,000 are drawings, an exceptional series of 18th- and 19th-c. pastels and miniatures: a most harmonious collection in which all European schools are represented since, here too, the golden rule of eclecticism has been followed, and especially so since the addition of the engravings, another collection of royal origin, and the gift in 1935 from Edmond de Rothschild of some 30,000 engravings and 3000 drawings, which are a museum in themselves.

At present the Louvre is going through drastic changes, first through the permanent transfer to the new Musée d'Orsay of post-1848 paintings, sculptures, drawings, and *objets d'art*; second because of the reorganization entailed in transferring the museum into the Grand Louvre as decreed by President Mitterrand in September 1981. The glass pyramid was opened to the public in the summer of 1989, and the wing occupied until then by the Ministry of Finance which has at last moved to Bersay, has been extended.

The other Paris museums, From 1815 to 1870

As the Louvre grew and diversified, step by step it took over for its collections three-fifths of the palace as it is today – the last extension was marked by the opening to the public, in 1968, of the Pavillon de Flore and the Aile de Flore – so the creation of other museums in Paris increased and accelerated, at a rate broadly following the development of the great national museum. This parallel development was to be expected, since the same intellectual, economic, and political driving forces underlay both movements, as they did the simultaneous proliferation of provincial museums.

During the First Empire, museological activity in Paris was concentrated almost entirely at the Louvre. It is true that on August 3, 1801, a naval museum was opened in the Place de la Concorde, in the former Garde-Meuble, bringing together the remnants of the Duhamel du Montceau collection, pillaged during the Revolution, and what remained of the collections of the *émigrés* and of the large corporations; but the psychological effect of the defeat at Trafalgar in 1805 quickly paralysed the initiative. Not until the Restoration did the capital see the creation of new, important museums.

The Restoration

Up to the end of the Second Empire the number of museums created was still small – six at the most. The first dates from April 24, 1818. On that day Louis XVIII inaugurated, in the Palais du Luxembourg, an institution that had long been called for: a museum devoted exclusively to the works of living artists which, in principle, were to remain there until the 100th anniversary of each artist's birth; after that the works would either be carried proudly to the Louvre, transferred to provincial museums or some public building, or consigned to the museum's reserves. Over the years the numbers of works exhibited increased: 74 in 1818, 149 in 1849, 240 in 1875, to mention only paintings. The museum occupied various parts of the palace until, in 1886, the Senate gave it the Orangerie, where it remained until 1939. It then vanished, to reappear after World War II in the form of the Musée National d'Art Moderne, while the Orangerie du Luxembourg is now devoted to temporary exhibitions.

By restoring France's naval prestige the victory over the Turks at Navarino rescued the Musée de la Marine from the oblivion into which it had fallen. A few months after the battle, on November 27, 1827, the Duc d'Angoulême, Grand Admiral of France, inaugurated at the Louvre the Musée Dauphin which, benefiting from the favor of the royal family, rapidly became rich in naval models, trophies, and mementoes of all kinds. Damaged during the riots of July 1830, and transferred from the ground floor of the Cour Carrée buildings to the first floor, then to the attics, the museum's fortunes revived only when the Ministère de la Marine (the Admiralty), to which it was attached in 1919, succeeded in installing it in the wing of the new Palais de Chaillot, where it has been open to the public since 1943.

It is also to the credit of Charles X's reign, that a decision was made in 1827 to house in the Hôtel des Monnaies (the Mint), built between 1771 and 1777, the museum inaugurated by Louis-Philippe on November 8, 1833; this now comprises, besides a fine collection of coins and medals from the Middle Ages to the present day, many stamps and dies, together with old instruments for the minting of coins.

The July Monarchy

From the July Monarchy, that golden age of antiquarians, Paris retains one especially precious heritage: the Musée des Thermes et de l'Hôtel de Cluny. This was born of the purchase by the State in 1843 of the collection of medieval and Renaissance objects of Alexandre Du Sommerard (1772–1842), at a time when these periods aroused little interest, and the acquisition of the former Paris residence of the Abbots of Cluny, which the collector had partially rented in 1833 to house the thousands of pieces he had already gathered together. To the *hôtel* were added the neighboring ruins of the Gallo-Roman baths, ceded by the City of Paris, where since 1819 the finds of local excavations had been on display. It is to Alexandre Du Sommerard's son, Edmond, who was appointed curator, that the museum owes its most famous acquisitions, such as the Basel altar and the tapestry called *The Lady with the Unicorn*.

Since the end of World War II the museum has been completely reorganized: the baths are reserved exclusively for the archeological collections, and the *hôtel* for the medieval works, the distribution of which is based on the *Livre des Métiers* (*Book of Trades*) in which Etienne Boileau, Provost of Paris, in 1270 registered the statutes of the various tradesmen's guilds of the city. The Renaissance objects have been transferred to the Château d'Ecouen, where the national museum devoted to this period was opened on October 25, 1977.

The Second Empire

Following the example of the First Empire, the Second Empire gave high priority to the Louvre among the museums of Paris. Nevertheless, 1864 saw the creation, following the acquisition by the State of the composer Louis Clapisson's collection, of the Musée Instrumental du Conservatoire National Supérieur de la Musique, and in 1867 the Musée de l'Histoire de France, founded in the fine setting of the palace of the Princes de Soubise by the Marquis de Laborde, curator of the imperial archives, to evoke, through documents drawn from the archives, the history of France from the Merovingian period onward. Just two years earlier, in 1865, the Cabinet des Médailles, augmented by the admirable collection of the Duc de Luynes (1862), had been transferred from the Hôtel Lambert to a large gallery in the Rue de Richelieu. It left there in 1917, further augmented by donations, for new premises in the Bibliothèque Nationale, where its former décor has been reconstituted.

From 1870 to 1918

It was during the Third Republic that the pace at which new museums in Paris were created, as in the rest of France, was to accelerate, and no longer only on State initiative.

The museums of the City of Paris

Out of a score of establishments founded between 1870 and 1918, five were created by the municipal authorities. The first was devoted to the history of the city, originally as a documentary section of the Bibliothèque Historique de la Ville de Paris, created by Jules Cousin after 1870. It was first set up in the Hôtel Carnavalet, then, as the collections grew, and especially after the donation by the Comte de Liesville in 1881 of numerous works of art and items from the Revolution, as a museum proper, to which the library gave way by moving to the nearby Hôtel Le Peletier de Saint-Fargeau. The flow of acquisitions necessitated the building of annexes in 1897, 1914, and 1945. Today the installation of the Bibliothèque Historique in the neighboring Hôtel de Lamoignon has allowed the conversion of the Hôtel Le Peletier for the presentation of the museum's collections.

The City of Paris opened another museum in the Hôtel de la Plaine Monceau, which was bequeathed to it in 1895 along with his Oriental collections by Henri Cernuschi, a Milanese financier who took refuge in Paris after the uprising of 1848. Under successive curators the museum came to specialize in the arts of ancient China.

A third large municipal museum was inaugurated on December 11, 1902, in the building commonly known as the Petit Palais, which had been erected initially to house a retrospective of French art in the World Fair of 1900, and to present subsequently the works of art owned by the City of Paris and to stage exhibitions exemplifying different civilizations. This policy has been scrupulously observed for three-quarters of a century.

Finally, before World War I, two great writers were honored by the municipality with museums: Victor Hugo in 1903, in the apartment he occupied from 1832 to 1848 on the second floor of the Hôtel de Rohan Guéméné in the Place des Vosges, and Honoré de Balzac in the house where he lived from 1840 to 1847 at no. 47 of what is now the Rue Raynouard.

The private museums

During the same period, certain associations fell into step with the municipality. In 1875, for instance, the Société de l'Histoire du

Protestantisme Français, created in 1852, began to gather together paintings, engravings, medals, and various mementoes in the building in the Rue des Saints-Pères where it was installing its library. Similarly, from its foundation in 1886, the Société du Vieux-Montmartre began putting together a collection that was to grow rapidly. In 1903 the Bibliothèque Polonaise (Polish Library), opened in Paris in 1833, was given an annex devoted to Poland's greatest poet, Adam Mickiewicz.

However, no establishment of this kind in Paris was to achieve the importance of the museum created in 1877 by a society founded for the purpose by the Union Centrale des Beaux-Arts Appliqués à l'Industrie (Central Union of the Fine Arts Applied to Industry). The two societies, dedicated to the struggle against visual mediocrity in the day-to-day environment and to the stimulation of public taste through displays of fine works of art from the past, merged in 1882 to become the Union Centrale des Arts Décoratifs. The Musée des Arts Décoratifs was originally set up in the Pavillon de Flore; it was then transferred to the Pavillon de l'Industrie and finally, in 1904, to the Pavillon de Marsan, following the signing of an agreement with the State. With more than 50,000 works, of which 45,000 have come from gifts and legacies, it also houses a most valuable library specializing in the history of the decorative arts, and for some three-quarters of a century its temporary exhibitions have been among the most successful Paris has seen.

Another museum worthy of particular attention may be added to this list, the Musée Jacquemart-André, created by the legacy to the Institut de France in 1912 of the mansion and collection of the banker Edouard André and his wife Nélie Jacquemart. This is a collection in the true sense of the word, formed by two great art patrons, lovers of 18th-c. French and Italian Renaissance art. The same is true, in the field of Asian art and religion, of the collection from the same period of the Lyons industrialist Emile Guimet which, after first creating a museum in Lyons itself in 1879, he installed in a building he erected in the Place d'Iéna between 1885 and 1888. Becoming a national museum in 1929, the Musée Guimet was expanded in 1945 by the addition of the collections of the Department of Asian Art that had been created at the Louvre in 1932. Many acquisitions have been made since then, to complete the brilliant display offered by the Museum of the Arts of Central and East Asia.

The national museums

But it was still to the State that, from the Third Republic to World War I, Paris owed most of its new museums. In the arts, four museums were created by the Direction des Musées Nationaux: from 1882, fulfilling one of Viollet-le-Duc's dreams, the Musée de Sculpture Comparée (Museum of Comparative Sculpture) presented, in the galleries of the Palais du Trocadéro, casts of the works of French sculptors of the Middle Ages, the Renaissance, and the modern age; the playwright d'Ennery (1811–99), in 1903, left to the State his interesting Far Eastern collections and the building that housed them; from the same benefactor two great artists, Gustave Moreau in 1902 and Auguste Rodin in 1916, each received a museum devoted exclusively to his work, the first in the building in the Rue de La Rochefoucauld that housed his works, the second in the Hôtel Biron, which he had occupied from 1908, and which was bought by the State in 1910.

History, sciences, and technology were also the basis for the creation of museums, of which various governing bodies and large public institutions were the instigators: the Opéra in 1878, the Observatoire in 1879, the Préfecture de Police in 1908, the present-ation of whose collections has recently been refurbished in the Hôtel de Police, Rue des Carmes, and the Val-de-Grâce in 1916. The Ministère de l'Instruction Publique (Ministry of Public Education) inaugurated its Institut Pédagogique by opening a museum in 1879, followed in 1880 by a Musée d'Ethnographie, and in 1911 by the Musée de la Parole (now the Musée Charles Cros), which in 1938 was attached to the Phonotèque Nationale. The Ministry of War in 1905 set up the Musée de l'Armée in the Hôtel des Invalides, combining the collection of the Musée Historique, founded by the ministry in 1896, with those of the old Musée de l'Artillerie, which had been added to many times during the 19th c. After 1945 it was augmented by the Musée des Deux Guerres Mondiales (Museum of the Two World Wars), which later became the Musée d'Histoire de la B.D.I.C., and by the Musée de l'Ordre de la Libération.

From 1918 to the present

Far from slowing down after World War I, the growth in the number of museums, in Paris as in the provinces, accelerated even further; the growth rate went from one museum every two years between 1870 and 1914 to one per year from 1918 to 1939.

The interwar period

During this period the idea of the museum finally became dominant in all areas, commemorating and honoring as much as educating and entertaining. The lives of famous figures were celebrated in small museums: Braille, in the Musée Valentin Haüy in the Institut des Jeunes Aveugles (Institute for Blind Young People); Clemenceau, in 1931, in his home in the Rue Franklin; Branly, in 1932, on the site of his former laboratory in the Rue d'Assas; Pasteur, in 1936, in the apartment where he lived from 1888 to 1895, at the institute that bears his name; Lenin, in 1955, in the lodgings he occupied in the Rue Marie-Rose during his exile. A Society of Friends did the same for the painter Eugène Delacroix in 1932 by organizing, at 6 Place de Fürstenberg, where the artist lived and worked from 1857 until his death in 1863, a museum that was handed over to the State in 1952. Again, in 1926, the State had accepted, from a nephew of Jean-Jacques Henner, the gift of the museum he had created in a building on the Avenue de Villiers, with a collection of paintings and drawings by this Alsatian artist.

In 1926 also the Fondation Dosne-Thiers was opened in the Hôtel de l'Homme d'Etat in the Place Saint-Georges, and houses the Musée Frédéric Masson, devoted to the Napoleonic period. This establishment has recently been renovated.

Similarly, great private art collections were retained in the mansions that housed them: the collection of the founder of the La Samaritaine department stores, Ernest Cognacq-Jay, given to the City of Paris in 1928; that which Paul Marmottan inherited from his father, the financier Jules Marmottan, and which he himself enriched before bequeathing it to the Institut de France in 1932; that of the Count Moïse de Camondo, ceded to the Union Centrale des Arts Décoratifs in 1935 in memory of his son Nissim, killed in action in 1917.

Still more museums were set up: in 1921, in the wings of the former Faculté de Médecine, the Musée de l'Histoire de la Médecine; in 1924, in a modern wing of the Hôtel de Salm, the Musée de la Légion d'Honneur; in 1934, in the former convent of the Filles de Sainte-Geneviève, the Musée de l'Assistance Publique, originally set up in 1670 in the Hôtel Martin (built in 1630) by one of Vincent de Paul's lady helpers.

Four great Parisian institutions are particularly representative of the museological orientation of this period: the museum set up in 1935 in a building erected for the Colonial Exhibition of 1931, devoted to the history and arts of the French colonies (the present Musée National des Arts Africains et Océaniens); the Palais de la Découverte, opened in 1937 in the Grand Palais des Champs-Elysées, and conceived as much as a museum for the popularization of science as a center of scientific education; the Musée National des Monuments Français, set up in the same year in the newly built Palais de Chaillot to replace the Musée de Sculpture Comparée at the Trocadéro, a change that encouraged the extension of the sections devoted to monumental art; finally, the Musée de l'Homme, a center of teaching and study which is part of the Museum of Natural History and which, since 1938, has brought together the Trocadéro's ethnographical collections and the osteological collections of the Natural History Museum.

After 1945

In the aftermath of World War II the pace of growth in the number of Parisian museums was only briefly maintained. The Musée de la

Pharmacie was opened in 1945, in the Pharmaceutical Faculty in the Avenue de l'Observatoire; 1946 saw the creation of the Musée de la Poste, now in the Maison de la Poste et de la Philatélie in the Boulevard de Vaugirard. In the following year came the opening of the Musée Arménien, later housed in the Musée d'Ennery, and the Musée National de l'Art Moderne, the successor to the Musée du Luxembourg, in a building erected in the Avenue Président-Wilson for the World Fair of 1937.

The Jeu de Paume in the Tuileries was given over to house the Louvre's collections of Impressionist paintings, and the contemporary works from outside France were transferred from the Jeu de Paume, their home since 1920, to the Musée National d'Art Moderne. The creation of the Musée d'Orsay for the Impressionists has meant a change of use for the Jeu de Paume, now devoted to temporary exhibitions. The Musée Bourdelle was opened in 1949, thanks to the gift to the City of Paris by the sculptor's widow and daughter of a collection of his works and the studios where he had worked all his life. In the same year the Musée d'Art Juif (Museum of Jewish Art) was founded, by a committee set up for the purpose, in the Rue des Saules; this is to be transferred to the Hôtel Saint-Aignan, which is now being restored, in the Rue Vieille-du-Temple.

After 1950 new museums suddenly became more rare. In 1956 the City of Paris opened the Musée du Costume in the twin of the Musée National de l'Art Moderne building in the Avenue Président-Wilson; this was based on the Carnavalet collections, to which had been added, in 1920, those of the Societé de l'Histoire du Costume, founded in 1907. The museum was transferred in 1977 to the Palais Galliera. In 1961 the municipality set up its own museum of modern art in the east end of the Palais de Tokyo, transferring to it the contemporary and Post-Fauvist works from the Petit Palais. In 1959 the Musée du Cinema was installed in the Palais de Chaillot with equipment, instruments, posters, models, and design projects tracing the history of film, further illustrated by the showing of old films. In 1962 the studio of Henri Bouchard, sculptor of the façade of Saint-Pierre-de-Chaillot, was opened to the public in the Rue de l'Yvette as the Musée-Atelier Henri-Bouchard, and was adopted by the Direction des Musées de France in 1985. Thanks to a foundation created for its preservation, the Hôtel Guénégaud, built by Mansart from 1648 to 1651 and remarkably well restored by M and Mme François Sommer, received in 1967 the Musée de la Chasse et de la Nature (Museum of Hunting). Finally, in the same period, the Réunion des Musées Nationaux in the Grand Palais in the Champs-Elysées, set up galleries suitably equipped for the pursuit of its policy of temporary exhibitions. Opened in November 1966 by André Malraux, the Minister of State for Cultural Affairs, a large Picasso retrospective, timed to coincide with the artist's eighty-fifth birthday, inaugurated the first stage of this important museum complex.

The last decade has seen the opening of the Musée de l'Affiche (Museum of Posters) in the 10th arrondissement (18 Rue du Paradis) by the Union Centrale des Arts Décoratifs and, in the fine Hôtel de Montmorency-Bours (85 Rue du Cherche-Midi) of a museum devoted to the academic painter Ernest Hébert (1817–1905) by his heir, René Patris d'Uckermann, who has recently presented it to the State. But the decade has been particularly marked by the inauguration of two museums of the highest order, the Musée National des Arts et Traditions Populaires, and the Musée National d'Art Moderne at the Pompidou Center. While both museums essentially provide only new homes for existing collections, it is unarguable that forethought and careful planning, coupled with appropriate financial and technical support, have resulted in the creation of two museums of international standing.

The Musée des Arts et Traditions Populaires. Created for the World Fair of 1937 and then installed in the basement and attics of the Palais de Chaillot, this museum from the start asserted its vocation as the nation's museum of ethnology. In association with the great social science laboratories at the Sorbonne, the Ecole Pratique des Hautes Etudes and the Collège de France, it was supported also by the Centre National de la Recherche Scientifique. Under the direction of Georges-Henri Rivière, over a period of 30 years it perfected its organization in terms of both research and museography, carrying out many research projects in the field, developing its relations with provincial museums devoted to local and regional history and ethnography, and participating in numerous national and international seminars and conferences. A grant of land from the Jardin d'Acclimatation in the Bois de Boulogne cleared the way for the creation of the new museum, designed by the architect Jean Dubuisson after long and detailed studies. The museum's departments were transferred to it in 1969; 1972 saw the opening of its *galerie d'étude*, where its collections are organized on typological principles, and 1974 the *galerie culturelle* which, from an anthropological standpoint, offers a global view of traditional French society of the 19th and early 20th centuries in all sectors that have not been affected by intensive industrialization. Halls for temporary exhibitions complete the section open to the public, which has in addition a library, a picture library and a record library. The museum archives will supply any information requested.

The Centre National d'Art et de Culture Georges-Pompidou. In 1969, President Georges Pompidou decided to launch the project for the cultural center that now bears his name, and which he wished to be 'both a museum and a center of creativity, where the plastic arts would be brought together with music, the cinema, books, audiovisual research, etc.' A project team, governed by the desire to end compartmentalization in the arts, began work in 1970; the site was acquired – the Plateau Beaubourg – in the exact center of Paris, and the architectural competition launched, leading to the choice of the proposals of Renzo Piano and Richard Rogers. The center was inaugurated on January 31, 1977, by President Valéry Giscard d'Estaing. It was the birth of the new Musée National d'Art Moderne, side by side in this vast metal and glass oblong block with the Center for Industrial Creation (CCI), the Public Information Library (BPI), and the Institute for Research and Acoustical-Musical Coordination (IRCAM). The new Modern Art Museum replaced the earlier one in the Avenue Président-Wilson for works later than 1905. An abundance of supporting information and constantly changing exhibitions add to the attraction of the easily accessible permanent collections.

The parts of the Palais de Tokyo freed by the transfer of the old museum's collections to the Pompidou Center were used to house various donated works, in accordance with the wishes of the artists (such as Georges Braque, Henri Laurens, Georges Rouault, Victor Brauner, and André Dunoyer de Segonzac), and to exhibit the Post-Impressionist works which, because they were painted earlier than 1905, could not be included in the collections of the Musée d'Art Moderne.

In 1972 the State tobacco organization, SEITA, set up the Musée du Tabac (12 Rue Surcouff), with a collection of pipes and an interesting collection of images of smoking and smokers. The historical collections of the Grand Orient de France have been on display since 1973 in the Rue Cadet, at the Musée de la Franc-Maçonnerie (Freemasonry Museum), presently being extended.

The 1980s

The past decade has been a fertile one for museological creativity. A number of museums were opened by the City of Paris: in the former district of Les Halles, the Pavillon des Arts, a gallery for temporary exhibitions; on the Quai Saint-Bernard, the Musée de Sculptures en Plein Air (Museum of Open-Air Sculpture), devoted to modern, Post-Brancusi sculptors; in 1982, the Musée Zadkine, including the sculptor's works bequeathed by his wife, Valentine Prax, in his studio and garden in the Rue d'Assas. The Musée Carnavalet, which doubled its floor area in 1989 by extending into the neighbouring Hôtel Le Peletier de Saint-Fargeau, had previously acquired an annex when in 1985, the municipality opened a museum in the house in the Rue Chaptal where Ernest Renan had lived, under the name Musée Renan-Scheffer. - The niece of the painter Scheffer married Renan in 1956. The collections of Renan and his wife will be exhibited in due course; meanwhile a series of mementoes of George Sand is on display.

The Musée des Arts de la Mode was opened in 1986, at the Musée des Arts Décoratifs in the Rue de Rivoli. In the near future its collections of costumes will be on permanent display, but until now it has presented only temporary exhibitions, mainly in honor of great *couturiers*.

Also worth noting is the private Musée Bricard, set up in Libéral Bruant's splendid mansion in the Rue de la Perle, where a precious collection of locks is displayed.

The national museums created were prestigious ones. In 1983 the Jean Walter-Paul Guillaume collection of 19th- and 20th-c. paintings found a permanent home in the Orangerie des Tuileries, which already housed Claude Monet's *Nymphéas* (*Water Lilies*) murals. In 1985, after lengthy refurbishment of the Hôtel Salé, in the Rue de Thorigny, the Musée Picasso was inaugurated. It comprises major works in all the techniques used by the master: painting, drawing, collage, engraving, sculpture, and ceramics, and his own collection of old master and contemporary paintings. This enrichment of the national heritage is owed to the gift made by Picasso's heirs in lieu of death duties. In March 1986 the Cité des Sciences et de l'Industrie was opened in the Parc de la Villette; a mixture of permanent and temporary exhibitions here present, in spectacular fashion, the history of modern science and its application.

Finally, another major undertaking, the Musée d'Orsay, was opened in December 1986 in the former Gare d'Orsay, following a masterly adaptation of the station building that has not detracted from its original character. It brings together the works of the 19th and the beginning of the 20th c., previously kept at the Louvre, the Jeu de Paume and the old Musée du Luxembourg. Specialized departments for the graphic arts, architecture, photography, cinema, opera and literary, musical and journalistic movements of the period complement, with temporary presentations, the permanent exhibitions of painting and sculpture. Lectures, symposiums, and concerts afford a deeper understanding of this period, a historical moment filled with contradictions – a museum concept unique in the world.

Pierre Quoniam

▣ Musée de l'Affiche et de la Publicité*
(Museum of Posters and Publicity)

18 Rue du Paradis, 10th arr. Tel: 42-26-13-09. Map ref. 12-C1, 10-D3
Curator: Yvonne Brunhammer
Open daily exc. Tues. noon-6pm
Métro: Gare de l'Est, Château d'Eau
Bus: 32

Set up in an old china shop of unusual architecture, the Musée de l'Affiche is part of the Union des Arts Décoratifs (for architecture → Gare du Nord, Rue du Paradis). It welcomes all those with an interest in commercial art, whether professionals or amateurs, researchers or the simply curious.

Tour of the museum

30 mins.

Opened in February 1978, following the transfer of the old poster collection of the Bibliothèque des Arts Décoratifs, the museum houses more than 50,000 French and foreign posters. It organizes exhibitions of old and contemporary posters and offers the public a consultation service, with a slide collection, card catalog, library and bookshop. It also has a film library, which shows publicity films concurrently with the exhibitions.

▣ Musée de l'Arc de Triomphe

Place de l'Etoile, 8th arr. Tel: 43-80-31-31. Map ref. 8-C1
Open daily Oct 1.-Nov. 12: 10am-5:00pm; Nov. 13-Jan 31: 10am-

4:30pm. Feb 1–Mar. 30: 10am–5pm
Métro: Charles de Gaulle-Etoile
Bus: 31, 30, 22, 52, 73, 92

Tour of the museum

30 mins.

Arranged discreetly at the top of the Arc de Triomphe, this little museum concentrates on local history. Engravings and drawings, including the working drawings of the architects of the arch, Chalgrin and Blouet, trace the construction of the monument from the laying of the first stone in 1806 to its completion under Louis-Philippe. Period documents and audiovisual recordings illustrate the historical events that the Arc de Triomphe has witnessed: the funeral ceremony for Victor Hugo, the interment of the Unknown Soldier in 1920, and the Liberation of Paris.

Musée de l'Armée**

Hôtel National des Invalides, 7th arr. Tel: 45–55–37–70. Map ref: 15–A2
Director: General Boisseau
Open daily Oct.–end Mar. 10am–5pm, Apr.–end Sept. 10am–6pm; closed Jan. 1, May 1, Dec. 25.

The entrance ticket gives access also to the Musée d'Histoire de la B.D.I.C., the Musée Mondial des Villes-Maquettes, and Napoléon's tomb (Invalides).

Métro: Invalides, Latour-Maubourg, Ecole Militaire, Varenne, Saint-François-Xavier

Bus: 28, 49, 63, 69, 82, 87, 92

The Musée de l'Armée is in the *hôtel* built by Libéral-Bruant, on Louis XIV's orders, for disabled soldiers (for the history of the building's architecture →Invalides). Toward the end of the 19th c. the administrative services of the Ministry of War gradually took over the premises and there are now only about 300 beds. The vast buildings are occupied by various prime ministerial services and those of the Ministère des Anciens Combattants (Ministry for Ex-Servicemen), and the ministries for the universities, cultural affairs, justice, and defense on the one hand, and, on the other, by the Musée de l'Armée, the Musée des Villes-Maquettes (models of towns), and the Musée d'Histoire de la B.D.I.C. (Bibliothèque de Documentation Internationale Contemporaine).

The Musée de l'Armée traces military history through documents, uniforms, arms, and historical artifacts. Several rooms show the evolution of certain types of armaments.

History of the museum

The museum was established in 1905 by the fusion of the Musée Historique de l'Armée (1896) and the Musée d'Artillerie (1871), which had already inherited the arms collection built up after 1685 at the Arsenal and transferred in 1793 to the Convent of the Feuillants before becoming settled in the Couvent de Saint-Thomas-d'Aquin (Monastery of St Thomas Aquinas). This original nucleus of the present army museum was added to over the years by private collections confiscated during the Revolution, by the collections of the Strasbourg Arsenal and by various donations (from the Duc de Bouillon, the Duc d'Aumale, the Prince de Condé, the Duc des Deux-Ponts, and others). The whole of this museum collection, though not yet officially recognized as such, was transferred to Brest during the war of 1870 and, on its return, the royal arms and armor were placed in the Invalides building, where they were joined by the collections that Napoléon III had assembled at Pierrefonds.

Under the German Occupation, a large part of the arms, armor, and other pieces were transferred to Berlin, to be recovered only after 1945. Since then there have been many important acquisitions, one of the largest being that of the Pauilhac collection in 1964, which comprises more than 3000 items dating from the Renaissance to the 18th c.

Tour of the museum

2 hrs.

The museum's collections are presented in two buildings, the Bâtiment Occidental and the Bâtiment Oriental (the W Wing and the E Wing), which flank the main courtyard.

Bâtiment Occidental* (The West Wing)

This building houses ancient collections of weapons and armor from the 11th to the 17th c.; Asian collections from the Near East, China and Japan; defensive weapons (16th–17th c.). The second floor is devoted to the history of both World Wars.

Ground floor

Salle de la Préhistoire au Moyen Age (Prehistory to the Middle Ages)

A few objects, from the Stone Age to the Carolingian era, evoke the first means of defense and attack. Displays trace the evolution of the

idea of the army and of armaments, and the history of arms
manufacture; hand-crafted by artisans and through mass production.

François I Room

This is one of the former refectories of the Hôtel des Invalides with
its original décor and paintings by Parrocel depicting the
campaigns of Louis XIV in the Netherlands. This room houses
armaments in use from the 11th c. (before the Norman conquest of
1066) up to about 1574, each display case exhibiting both suits of
armor and weapons.

Case 1 (on the l. as you enter): various types of sword (7th–13th c.);
a large iron hauberk of chain mail; a copper helmet of Scandinavian
origin; various pieces of harness. Case 2: 14th- and 15th-c. basinets*, the beak-like protective visors* which appear as the natural
progression of the helmets of the late Middle Ages; also exhibited is
one of the oldest firearms known: a 16in/40cm-long 'hand-gonne' as
well as the various pieces of a suite of armor and its fittings; a large
foot-soldier's shield (pavise) bearing the arms of the Requesens.
Case 3: relics from the battle of Crécy (1346); various swords from
the 14th c. Case 4: rapiers, daggers, and, most interesting, the back
part of a brigandine (mid-15th c.), a piece of armor worn by foot-
soldiers. Case 5: pieces of armor, gauntlets, vambraces (to protect
the forearm), different kinds of sallets (helmets), including the
Schalhem helmet (late 15th c.), from Germany. Case 6: various
sword pommels, one of which bears the arms of Eleanor of
Aquitaine; a long, decorated ivory hunting horn*. Case 7: early 15th-
c. assorted pieces of armor, suits of armor (during this period, a suit
of armor protected the entire body; the display shows the difference
between the cusped and pointed outlines of the German pieces and
the rounded form of the Italian). Case 9: armor used during the
Hundred Years War, a period that saw the necessary perfecting of
the art of war; a large archer's shield in use during the Hussite Wars
(Bohemia, 15th c.); pieces of English origin (a battle-axe from the
English court, end of the 15th c.); Swiss halberds; suits of armor
from the Italian Wars; examples of work by different European
armorers: those from Milan with elegant forms, those from
Augsburg, bulkier. Case 10: large shield bearing the arms of Prague;
various armors; two German sallets; rapiers and two-handed
swords. Case 11: swords from the early 16th c. – the cross-shaped
hilt of the medieval era has been further developed. Case 12:
harness comprising pieces of armor of different origins (Italy,
France, Germany). Case 13: a series of daggers; a helmet (top r.)
that bears the mark of the Constantinople arsenal. Case 14: North
Italian armor made in the German style. Case 15: a collection of
cinquedeas with artistically decorated blades. Case 16: magnificent
suits of armor** from the beginning of the 16th c. made by Nicolò

Silva (active in the first half of the century); suit of armor of Robert de la Mark, seigneur of Sedan; an impressive equestrian suit of armor* made by Hans Ringler of Nuremberg; sword belonging to a High Constable of France with a pommel decorated with fleur-de-lis (weapons and armor reflect all the decorative motifs of the period in their ornamentation). Case 17: *arbalète à pied de biche* (a type of crossbow drawn with a lever that has a cleft end to grip the string), which may have belonged to Maximilian I; piece from a parade armor (Augsburg, circa 1505); suit of armor, bearing the mark of W. Worms the Elder (Nuremberg, *ca.* 1510–20). Cases 18, 19, 20: mouldings of the bas-reliefs from François I's tomb, depicting the victories of Marignan and Cerisolles; collections of swords*, including that of François I, a true work of art with the guard decorated with acanthus leaves and gold-and-enamel foliage, bearing the motto *Fecit potentiam in brachio suo* ('He makes his arm powerful'); the blade bears the Jerusalem cross. Case 21: suit of armor for an infantry captain (Milan, 1510), very ornate. Near the case window, four *couleuvrines à main* (the oldest form of hand cannon; second half of the 16th c.). Case 22: suits of armor gilded in the Italian style; next to them five glaives or *fauchards* (a form of staff weapon) bearing the arms of Louis I of Bourbon, Prince de Condé. Case 23: Italian armor (1520–25). Case 24: suit of armor said to belong to Bayard; wheel-lock arquebus* of French origin, one of the first known portable firearms and probably one of the most important exhibits in the museum. Case 25: suits of armor and parts of armor of German origin; armor of the Elector Palatine Otto Henry bearing on the breastplate a Virgin in Majesty; suit of armor in the style of Helmschmied (Augsburg, 1525–30); very fine equestrian armor* made around 1540 for Ferdinand I to give to François I (since the war between the houses of France and Austria started up again, François never received it). Case 26: collection of daggers (1525–75). Case 27: very precious armor* from the royal workshop at Greenwich, founded by Henry VIII (*ca.* 1520). Case 28: note particularly an iron parade buckler*, embossed and gilded, the decoration based on a Raphael fresco. Case 29: the so-called Lion Armor; the engraved cross of Savoy makes it likely that it belonged to François I; collar of the Order of St Michael. Case 30: buckler with decoration representing the 'Judgment of Paris'; mace and saddle pommel (Italy, mid-16th c.). Case 31: French suits of armor of the mid-16th c.; they bear the stamp of that century's elegance. Cases 32, 33, 34, 35: suits of armor and pieces of armor enriched with historiated Mannerist decoration. Case 36: set of maces and *burgonets* (light helmets) made in various European workshops. Case 37: mementoes of Henri II; mace, *burgonet*, leather powder flask with decoration recalling the love affair between Henri II and Diane de Poitiers; rosewood crossbow. Case 40: the exceptional 'Dauphin's armor'*** which belonged to Henri II: each of its components bears the monogram H, intertwined with C for Catherine and D for Diane. Case 41: armor called *animes*, far more supple than plate armor. Case 42: armor of the Montmorency family, among which can be seen the helmet worn by the High Constable of France, Anne de Montmorency at Dreux when he was grievously wounded (1562).

Henri IV Room

This gallery, which continues the chronological presentation of the previous one, is mainly devoted to jousting and tournament armor from the 16th c., representative of its nobility and refinement. Armors in the so-called Maximilian style, made in Nuremberg and covered with a fine network of parallel lines worked in repoussé; two of these exhibits originate from the house of Christopher Radziwill; peytrals (armor protecting a horse's chest). Case 1: sallet (on the l.), made between 1558 and 1575 for Nicholas Radziwill, magnificently decorated; helmet 'à l'orientale'; German shield showing St George slaying the dragon; shield of Mathias Corvin bearing the arms of the king of Hungary and Bohemia (1460). Case 24 (opposite): decorative parade pieces of Venetian origin. Cases 2 and 23: pieces of armor decorated with scrolls, masks, grotesques, engraved or highlighted with gold; on the breastplate of the suit of armor on the r., collar of the Order of the Golden Fleece (mid-16th c.). Cases 3 and 22: three suits of armor from Maximilian I's court workshop, created by Lorenz Helmschmied of Augsburg, armorer to the emperor; tonlet armor from a Milanese workshop; armor for foot combat in the lists, one of which was given by Maximilian I to Giuliano de' Medici in 1515. Case 4: pieces of armor and decorative pieces in the very ornate Italian style; bucklers, burgonets. Cases 5 and 20: suits of armor and pieces from suits of armor made in Augsburg, made to the order of the court of Bavaria (*ca.* 1560); suit of armor for the tournaments of the court of Saxony; Polish helmet and vambrace 'a l'oriental'; pieces made on the occasion of the wedding of the Archduke Charles of Styria and Marie of Bavaria (1571). Cases 6 and 19: various pieces of armor belonging to Maximilian II and his sons Rudolph, Ernest and Mathias, made in Landshut; jousting *armets* (helmets), helmets with barred faceguards. Case 18: tournament suits of armor, made in Augsburg and Landshut. Case 7: suits of armor from Landshut and Augsburg; gilded saddle and shaffron belonging to Ferdinand I, made for the funeral parade of Charles V; collection of swords. Case 8: swords from France, Italy and Saxony (16th c.). Case 16: Italian and Spanish pieces of armor of the 16th c. Case 9: burgonet from the 'blued armor' of the Archduke Ferdinand of the Tyrol, breastplate bearing the arms of the Jagello (Poland) and Sforza families (made in Milan); suits of armor from Brunswick, Germany. In the central aisle extension: full armor for horseman and his mount (French, 1630–50). Case 10: suits of armor and shields from Louis XIII's time. Case 11: cavalry wheel-lock pistols; burgonets with the arms of Saxony (Nuremberg, beginning of the 17th c.); very beautiful sword, the creation of Gasparo Mola; daggers and swords. Case 12: German suit of *anime* armor, suit of infantryman's armor (Nuremberg, 1570). Case 13: *anime* armors from France and E Europe (16th c.); French and Flemish children's armors; two-handed swords. Case 14: collection of wheel-lock muskets and matchlock arquebuses. Case 15: *ensemble à la chimère***; set of arms decorated with a chimera comprising a burgonet, sword and buckler in the Mannerist style made for the French court.

Corridor de Marseille: saddle cloth from Istanbul (early 19th c.).

Salle Orientale (Asian Room)

This room contains several splendid exhibits given to the museum by Napoléon III.

The first case illustrates the exchange of techniques between Asia and the W: oriental forms and decorative motifs adopted in Europe; European firing mechanisms adopted in East Turkey: the offensive armament of the Ottoman army comprised the bow, the club, the sabre and the matchlock musket (the oldest exhibited helmets date from the 14th c.); the evolution of forms resulted in the Turban helmet (15th c.) and the Mameluke helmets**, bulb-shaped and with floral decorative motifs; in the center of the room, a Mameluke horseman, mounted on a horse protected by barding of mail, wears a coat of plates and mail complete with breastplate. Iran: the Iranian warrior, unlike the Turkish horseman, wore a suit of rigid armor-plate topped with a pointed helmet; conical helmets were adopted in central Europe: so-called voivode helmet (Russia, 16th c.). China: most of the Chinese protective armor now on display are state dress garments, used for military parade and called *habits de guerre* (war dress); they consist of thin plates of metal set into finely embroidered garments; the *habit de guerre en soie jaune* (yellow silk war costume) probably belonged to the Emperor K'ien Lung since yellow was the Imperial color. Japan: the art of armor making was at its best from the 7th to the 19th c.: suits of armor, supple and flexible, were made of small lacquered metal plates joined together by silk or hemp laces; four light Samurai armors are exhibited (1500), complete with helmets and shoulder plates (the samurai was armed with a sword, a spear, a bow and a matchlock musket).

Cour de la Victoire: French artillery from Louis XV's time up to the 1870 war; naval cannons from 1770 to 1870, and 1914.

Cour d'Angoulême: statue by Bartholdi de Gribeauval (1715–89) inventor of the artillery system in use from 1789 to 1828; artillery from the last two World Wars.

Salle Pauilhac: this collection, bought by the museum in 1964, allows the study of defensive armaments from the 13th to the 17th c. and the study of offensive weapons from the 7th to the 18th c.; two Burgundian basinets (15th c.), firearms from Louis XIII's gun room; *miquelet* gun of Philip V of Spain; gun *à chenapan* (Moscow, 1660);

pistol belonging to Charles V; Ripoll pistols; armor with polychrome decoration (the only one extant).

Salle Louis XIII: from the Valois to Louis XIV: weapons from the 15th c. to the end of the 17th c. (crossbows, pistols, muskets, swords); Louis XIII's arms cabinet; wheel-lock musket of James II of England; matchlock arquebus of Cardinal de Richelieu; sword of Louis I, Prince de Condé; sword with engraved hilt by Benvenuto Cellini and engraved steel arms by Lazarino Cominazzo; armor of Louis XIII, when a child and when king; armor given to Louis XIV by the Venetian Republic.

Corridor Tir et Chasse (shooting and hunting). In a long case in the passage which links the Louis XIII room to the Salle Louvois can be viewed hunting weapons which could also be used on occasion as fighting weapons: crossbows and wheel-lock arquebuses, one of which bears the arms of the Grand Dauphin; a collection of daggers and hunting knives; rifles and guns, one of which was made by the gunsmith at the court of the princes of Thurn Und Taxis.

Arsenal: very large collection of arms and armor (shafted weapons, sidearms and firearms) from the 16th and 17th c. To visit the military history rooms in chronological order, proceed straight to the second floor of the E wing.

Second floor

Vestibule: Exhibits from the two World Wars: armaments and uniforms of the combatants (1939–45); the batons of Field-Marshals Juin and Koënig.

Salles de Guerre (World War 1: 1914–18): equipment from both France and Germany. Mementoes of the first two casualties of the war. Scale model of Big Bertha. Animated talking maps. The three stages of the conflict. The battle of the Marne; scale model of a trench. The first planes (the first Taube shot down on September 11, 1914); the allied armies: Great Britain, Russia, Italy. French and German equipment of 1915. Scale model of the battle of Verdun, the offensives of 1917. The arrival of the Americans. Aviation (Guynemer's flying jacket). The German and Allied offensives (New Zealand, Australian, and American uniforms). Foch's ordnance map signed on the day of the Armistice. Uniforms of the three field-marshals: Joffre, Pétain, and Foch, who was also a field-marshal of Poland and Great Britain.

World War II. The causes of the war (maps); rise of National Socialism in Germany. The start of Germany's war against Poland. *La drôle de guerre* (the 'phoney war'). German offensive in Holland, Belgium and France (May 10, 1940). Life in France under the Occupation. Deportation. War beyond our frontiers: prisoners' camps, Free France, the African campaign. The start of Germany's war against Russia (June 21, 1941). The war in the Pacific. The war in Africa. Europe at war. The D-Day landing of June 6, 1944 (large-scale model). The French campaign, the German campaign. Final costs of the war.

Third floor

Joffre Room: This room retraces the military history of mainland France and its overseas territories from 1871 to 1914. **Salle Gribeauval**: the complete history of artillery from Roman ballistas up to the most recent models shown as small-scale replicas; numerous engravings.

The Bâtiment Oriental* (East Wing)

This building is devoted to the history of cavalry and cavalry standards and to French military history from the *Ancien Régime* to the war of 1870.

Ground floor

Vestibule. Monumental sculpted oak door, carved by M. Bourgaux from drawings by the architect Séville. Two large cases contain pikes captured from the enemy during the campaigns of the Revolution and the Empire and flags which were burned in 1814 in the courtyard of the Invalides by order of Field Marshal Sérurier. In one case is a continually changing display of the latest gifts to the museum and its latest purchases.

Salle Turenne (on the r. as you enter). This is the main exhibition hall in the museum and it houses a collection of different trophies, flags and standards from French regiments. It is the old dining hall of the disabled non-commissioned officers. On the walls are paintings by Van der Meulen, Martin des Batailles and Parrocel depicting the Dutch campaigns (1672–78). In the center of the room: relief plan of the Hôtel des Invalides, planned before 1690 and restored in 1838 and 1974; on the l. wall a portrait*** by Ingres depicts Napoleon on his Imperial throne.

Salle Vauban (opposite). This room houses an imposing row of lifesize models of horsemen from the First Empire to World War II and standard French arms from 1717 to 1979: naval weapons, hand weapons from various sources, and ammunition.

Second floor

Richelieu collection to the r. of the staircase. Paintings, weapons, and mementoes from the reign of Louis XIII (the Thirty Years War). **Salle Louis XIV**: uniforms and arms from the age of Louis XIV: remarkable historical exhibits are on view here, such as the cannonball that killed Turenne; original portrait of Turenne by Nanteuil; small gilded cannon presented to Louis XIV by the Francs-Comtois (people of the Franche-Comté) when Franche-Comté became part of France.

Grenoble Corridor: numerous engravings, plans, weapons (sabres, halberds), military flags; case devoted to Peter the Great and Charles XII of Sweden.

Salle Louis XV: royal orders, various orders, various paintings, portrait of the Duc de Choiseul, uniforms; relief plan of the battle of Dettingen (1743). **Besançon Corridor**: from Louis XV to the Empire, engravings, uniforms, weapons. **Salle Louis XVI**: paintings and engravings of the end of the old monarchy; weapons and uniforms; mementoes of the Comte d'Artois, of Louis-Philippe d'Orléans, Colonel-General of the Hussars; the French Guards.

Salle Rochambeau: bust of Suffren, portraits of the Comte de Vergennes and the Comte de Rochambeau; La Fayette's sword.

Salle La Fayette: various portraits; sappers artillery; the **National Guard**; in this room you can see the furniture of the lieutenant of artillery, Napoléon Bonaparte at Auxonne. First Republic (1793–1804): wars of the Republic; the princes' army; large relief plan of the battle of Lodi (May 10 1796). Egyptian campaign: mementoes of the Battle of the Pyramids; uniforms and weapons; trophies captured from the Mamelukes. The Consulate: Dragoons and Hussars from the opening years of the century; souvenirs of the First Consul.

Salle de Boulogne (1803–14): personal mementoes of the Emperor; **Coronation parade hall**: Napoléon's tent.
Tarascon Corridor: Napoléon and the Empire. The Legion of Honor display case.

A series of small side rooms depict high dignitaries (**Salle d'Austerlitz**), the Imperial Guard (**Salle d'Iéna**), the general officers (**Salle d'Eylau**), the Spanish and Portuguese War (**Salle de Somo Sierra**), the 1807 campaign (**Salle Friedland**), the infantry (**Salle Wagram**), the Russian campaign (**Salle de la Moskowa**) Moscow room, the German campaign, 1813 (**Salle de Lutzen**), the French campaign, 1814 (**Salle de Montmirail**); *Napoléon in Fontainebleau*, first abdication, painting by Paul Delaroche; toys that belonged to the King of Rome.

Grande galerie de la Restauration (1814–30): in addition to the large number of uniforms, the cloak of the Order of the Saint-Esprit (Holy Spirit), made for Louis XVIII and worn by Charles X (on loan from the Cluny museum), and apart from the numerous engravings and paintings devoted to this period, the main exhibits in this gallery are the personal souvenirs of Napoléon at St Helena and his death mask. Reconstruction of the Longwood House drawing-room where Napoléon died on May 5, 1821.

Salle Bugeaud: July Monarchy and Second Republic. Key of the citadel of Antwerp (1832). Mementoes of the Rome Expedition (1849); Algerian campaigns (1830–47): portrait of Bugeaud; mementoes of Bugeaud and the sons of Louis Philippe who fought in Algeria: Aumale, Joinville, Nemours, and Montpensier; mementoes of the Emir Abd-el-Kader and of General Yousouf. Paintings, military scenes, watercolors. Mementoes of the Duc de Reichstadt; the return of the Emperor's ashes.

Third floor

Salle Pélissier: recently renovated, this room retraces the military history of the Second Empire (1852–60), marked by the campaigns in the Crimea (1854–55) and Italy (1859). The center of the room is devoted to military equipment: ever more elegant uniforms and weapons; presentation of the Imperial Guard. In the side cases are displayed documents and mementoes from the various army corps. One section is devoted to Nadar's and Robertson's first photographic reports.

Salle Chanzy: retraces the end of the Second Empire and the Franco-Prussian War (1870–71). The side cases follow the evolution of the uniform as it became increasingly utilitarian and modern. The first half of the room recalls the overseas campaigns: Cochin-China, China, Lebanon, Africa, and Mexico. The end of the room concentrates on the Franco-Prussian war, and presents the military operations and the French armies under both the empire and the republic.

▷ Not to be missed

West Wing

Ground floor: 15th- and 17th-c. armor*, the Dauphin's armor and the collection of swords, including those of the Constable of France and François I (François I Room). The Asian Room: rare series of Turkish helmets, Chinese fighting costumes, and Samurai armor (Japanese, 16th c.).

East Wing

Ground floor: Turenne Room (or Salle des Emblèmes): flags, standards, and trophies from the *Ancien Régime* to the present day; portrait of Napoleon by Ingres.

▷ Additional information

Cinema (E side, ground floor): films and documentaries daily from 2pm; morning showings for groups by arrangement; program changes Wed. (tel. 45-55-37-70).

Introductory tour for the young: Wed. pm (tel. 45-55-37-70).
Library (E side, 2nd floor): documentation on military history, weapons and uniforms. Access only for members of the Society of Friends of the Museum and authorized researchers (Mon.-Fri., 10am-1pm/2pm-5pm; Sat. 10am-noon). Tel. 45-55-30-11, extension 5484.

Reception hall (entrance Place Vauban, entrée du Dôme).
Model soldiers, etc. on sale.

▷ History of the French flag

The flag as it is known today did not exist under the *Ancien Régime*. In that era, a regiment's standard took the colors of the coat of arms of its colonel, the *mestre de camp* (literally 'field marshal'). As a symbol of his authority, Louis XIV added a white *cravate* (bow) and tassels to these military flags. But it was La Fayette who created the three national colors by adding the white of the bow and tassels to the blue and red of the municipality of Paris's cockade. Napoléon officially established the *tricolore* in 1811. Replaced during the Restoration by the white flag, it reappeared in 1830 in conjunction with the figure of the national emblem, the cockerel - the *coq hardi* - mounted at the head of the flagstaff. The cockerel was replaced by the pike in 1848, then by the Imperial eagle in 1852. The Army flag has not changed since it was distributed by Jules Grévy on July 14, 1880.

▣ Musée Arménien (Armenian Museum)

(Foundation Nourhan Fringhian)
59 Ave. Foch, 16th arr. Tel: 45-56-15-88. Map ref: 7-A2
Curator: M. J.-P. Mahé
Open Thurs, Sat. and Sun. 2-10pm
Métro: Port Dauphine. Bus: 33, 82, PC

Armenia lies between the high plateaux of Asia Minor and Iran; its highest point is Mount Ararat (17,110ft/5215m) where, according to the Bible, Noah's ark came to rest. According to tradition, Armenia was founded by a descendent of Noah; however, modern scholars believe that the Armenians crossed the Euphrates into Asia Minor in the 8th c. BC. Conquered in succession by the Persians, Greeks, Syrians, and Romans, Armenia has enjoyed independence for only a few brief periods in its history. Armenia is the world's oldest

Christian state; its people were converted as early as AD 285, 15 years before Constantine issued the Edict of Tolerance and a century before Theodosius imposed Christianity on the empire.

Conquered by the Sassanid dynasty in the 3rd c. AD, the Armenians were persecuted for their faith; their martyrs inspired a nationalism that persists to this day. After the partition of the kingdom between Persia and Rome in 387, and before the present partition between the Armenian Soviet Socialist Republic, Turkey, and Iran in 1921, Armenia endured centuries of invasion, war, deportation, and bloody oppression. The kingdom fell prey to the Byzantines, Huns, Khazars, and Arabs; it was invaded by the Seljuk Turks, the Mongols, the Mamelukes, and the Ottoman Turks. The Armenians endured their greatest trial between 1894 and 1915 when the Ottomans attempted to exterminate them systematically; as many as two million were slaughtered, starved, or marched to death, a crime that Turkey still refuses to acknowledge.

Tour of the museum

30 mins.

This small museum, founded in 1943 by M. Achdjian, occupies two rooms on the ground floor of the mansion that houses the d'Ennery museum. It is run by the Nourahan Fringhian Association.

The Armenian museum houses great treasures, despite its small size: precious jewels and carpets, illuminated manuscripts, coins, and embroideries, but mostly church plate. One of the most important exhibits is the crown of Leo VI, which belonged to the the de Lusignan family of Poitou. Having taken refuge in the kingdom of France, Leo VI died in 1393 and was buried at Saint-Denis.

▣ Musée d'Art Juif* (Museum of Jewish Art)

42 Rue des Saules, 18th arr. Tel: 42–57–84–15. Map ref: 5–A1
Open Sun.–Thurs. 3–6pm
Métro: Lamarck-Caulincourt. Bus: 80

Established in 1948 in the heart of old Montmartre in the charming Rue des Saules, this museum aims to make known Jewish art, ancient and modern, sacred and secular. It occupies the third floor of a building in the Jewish Center of Montmartre (the Merkaz de Montmartre), where there is also a cultural center and an oratory.

Tour of the museum

30 mins.

Since its foundation the museum has constantly received gifts from artists; there are several lithographs by Chagall, drawings by Ryback, Benn, Pascin, Max Liebermann, Manet-Katz and, most important, Soutine; a copy of the Bible illustrated by Chagall; paintings by Alphonse Lévy, Pissarno, and artists of the Paris School; recent works by Tuszynsky. A number of engravings depict large European synagogues (Lisbon, Amsterdam, Prague, Toledo, etc.). Objects pertaining to rituals and worship; liturgical cloths; coins, the velvet covers that protect the scrolls of the Torah*, 18th-c. books from the community of Carpentras.

Sculpture: casts and life-size reproductions of tombstones from the Prague and Czernovitz Jewish cemeteries. An interesting room devoted to the architecture of synagogues displays scale models of the fortified synagogues of Poland and Lithuania in the 17th and 18th c. Scale models of ancient Jerusalem.

The museum organizes, about every two years, the Adolph Neuman art competition, which Neuman founded to encourage young Jewish artists.

▣ Musée d'Art Moderne de la Ville de Paris**

11 Ave. du Président-Wilson (postal address: 9 Rue Gaston-de-Saint-Paul), 16th arr. Tel: 47-23-61-27. Map ref: 14-C1
Head curator: Mme Bernadette Contensou
Open Tues. and Thurs.-Sun. 10am-5:30pm, Wed. 10am-8:30pm
Métro: Iéna, Alma Marceau
Bus: 32, 42, 63, 72, 80, 82, 92

The museum is housed in the eastern half of the Palais de Tokyo. Built for the Exhibition of Art and Technology to house the municipal contemporary art collections, which were too cramped in the Petit Palais, it has since been enriched through donations and acquisitions.

Since 1967 it has housed the ARC section (Animation, Research, Confrontation), devoted to the presentation of the latest trends in contemporary art. The museum runs the Children's Museum on the banks of the Seine; which aims to introduce young people to art.

Architecturally the building is modern, yet at the same time reminiscent of the classical style; it is the work of Dondel, Aubert, Viart, and Dastugue (description →Chaillot).

History of the museum

Completed in 1937, this building was widely admired for its lighting, provided by both windows and skylights, and for the fluid articulation of its masses, yet it was not opened until 1961. This long delay was due to the fact that the museum's first collections, acquired through purchases by Raymond Escholier and gifts from Vollard, Sarmiento, and Azaria, were not large enough to occupy all the available space. They therefore remained at the Petit Palais until the extraordinary legacy of Dr Girardin in 1961 of more than 500 pieces from his collection made opening the museum a practical reality. It has since been enriched by further large donations: 47 works of Raoul Dufy given by Mme Reisz; and the collection of Mme Germaine Henry and Professor Thomas, given jointly in 1976. Shown in its entirety, following the wishes of its donors, this collection is very rich in Fauvist paintings and in paintings by such great 20th-c. masters as Delaunay, Léger, and Kupka.

Today the museum acquires new works regularly in order to complete its basic collection, while remaining open to the latest movements as well as to new disciplines, such as photography. The museum has notable photographs by Charbonnier, Doisneau, Cartier-Bresson.

Tour of the museum

1½ hrs.

As well as the presentation of its permanent collections the museum organizes temporary exhibitions on the main 20th-c. artistic movements (basement, ground floor, and first floor).

Great works

Salle Dufy

This gallery is situated above the main entrance halfway up the stairs that lead to the ARC. There you can view *La Fée Electricité**** (The Spirit of Electricity), a vast work by Raoul Dufy (1877–1953) created for the Pavillon de la Lumière (Pavilion of Light) at the 1937 World Fair. Executed on 250 linked panels, with a huge steel turbine as its central motif, this huge composition 197ft/60m long and 33ft/10m high tells the story of electricity from Archimedes to the present day. While the lower half of the composition is reserved for the portraits of 100 or so scientists and philosophers who contributed to the discovery of electricity, the upper half is devoted to the benefits of its use.

Two floors directly below the Salle Dufy, five monumental wall paintings fill the space. On the back wall, *La Danse**** (1932) by Henri Matisse, is the first version of the composition now in the hall of the Barnes Foundation in Merion, Pennsylvania. This work, covering three arched panels, each 11½ft./3.5m by 10ft/3m, demonstrates the perfect mastery of the arabesque, characteristic of Matisse's female nudes. On the side walls are exhibited four abstract *Rythmes*** three by Robert Delaunay and one by Sonia

Delaunay, painted in 1938 for the Salon des Tuileries. Here color, freed from all figurative constraint, is developed dynamically in endless circular forms. On the floor below (lowest level in the building) in the hall, two paintings by Albert Gleizes and one by Jacques Villon, each 16½ft/5m by 13ft/4m, recall the rebirth of monumental painting at the end of the 1930s.

Permanent collections

Basement rooms

The museum offers a chronological tour which allows the stage-by-stage discovery of the evolution of modern art in the 20th c. However, the position of particular works varies according to the temporary exhibitions.

Fauvism

Dubbed *Les Fauves* (wild beasts) at the 1905 Autumn Salon, Matisse, Derain, and Vlaminck caused a scandal with their pure, violent colors, removed from any naturalistic concern. The movement is represented here by such masterworks as Matisse's *Pastorale* (1905), and Derain's *People Seated on the Grass*, 1906. The Henry Thomas collection, at the end of the tour, brings together fine paintings by Braque, Derain, and Vlaminck.

Rouault (1871–1958). Over 80 watercolors and about 12 paintings by Rouault are exhibited here thanks to the legacy of Girardin. Founder of the Autumn Salon, this extraordinary colorist exhibited a series of portraits of prostitutes, a theme which he was to explore constantly between 1903 and 1914 in masterly fashion: note his 1906 *Fille* (Prostitute).

Picasso's early works are represented by *L'Evocation* (1901), painted after the suicide of his young painter friend Casagemas, and his *Head of Fernando*, 1906, one of his first sculptures.

Cubism

Cubism was the first great innovative movement in 20th-c. painting, created by Braque, with his *Head of a Woman*, 1909, and Picasso, with his *Pigeon with Small Weights*, 1911. The term 'Cubist' was first used in 1908 by the critic Vauxcelles, for Braque's L'Estaque landscapes. Cubism was a rejection of anecdotal, historical, or emotional themes, and of the Impressionists' sensuous use of color and texture to create light and atmosphere. The representation of movement and, especially, the perspectival effects perfected in the 15th c. were abandoned, to be replaced by a new perspective of overlapping, interlocking, crystalline planes. Subjects, arranged in geometric planes, were shown simultaneously from many viewpoints, giving a fragmented two-dimensional effect. Rhythmic line was replaced by quasi-geometric forms. The preferred subject was still life with a narrow range of colors, sometimes almost monochrome. The interest of the collection lies partly in its major works by lesser-known artists, such as Auguste Herbin's *The Family* (1914), Jean Metzinger's *The Blue Bird* (1913), and André Lhote's *Port of Call* (1913). Also worth noting are Juan Gris's *The Book* (1913), Robert Delaunay's *La Ville de Paris* and *The Cardiff Team* (1912), as well as Cubist sculptures by Lipchitz and Laurens' *Spanish Dancer*, (1915).

The Paris School

This school includes artists who came to Paris at the beginning of the 20th c., in search of refuge and inspiration: Pascin; Soutine; Modigliani, *Woman with a Fan*, (1919); Foujita, *Nude Reclining on a Piece of Cotton*, (1922); Zadkine, *Orpheus* (1928–39); Chagall, *The Dream*, (1927).

The Post-World War I period

This period saw the birth of new movements: Dadaism, the international anti-rational, anti-aesthetic revolt to which Jean Crotti (*Portrait of Edison*, 1920) and Picabia (*Optophone III*, 1922–23) belonged. Surrealism is represented with works by Masson, Max Ernst, and Victor Brauner (→inset). Expressionist realism is illustrated by Jean Fautrier (*The Wild Boar*, 1926), and Marcel Gromaire (*War*, 1925), of whose paintings the museum has a unique collection bequeathed by Girardin. This artistic panorama of the interwar period would not be complete without such pioneers of Modernism as Léger, *Les Disques* (1918) and Ozenfant, *Large Still Life* (1926), nor without the champions of abstraction, Kupka and Hélion. A special place must be kept at the end of the 1930s for Bonnard, represented here by three masterpieces, notably the celebrated *Nude in the Bath* (1937), formerly in the Petit Palais.

Paintings of the war years

(in the rooms following)

Group of young painters in the French tradition included Estève, Bazaine, Lapicque, and Pignon, who set out to be deliberately provocative; beginnings of *Abstraction Gestuelle*, with Hans Hartung and Fautrier's series of anti-Nazi *Hostages*, exhibited immediately after the Liberation, and *The Jewess*, (1943).

The Post-World War II period

New currents emerged during this period. Lyrical abstraction took center stage in the 1950s, such as *Soulages* (16, 12, 59, executed in 1959). Then the New Realists in reaction against Abstract Expressionism; note the lacerated posters by Raymond Hains, and the *Blue Venus* by Yves Klein (1962). At the beginning of the 1970s narrative figuration triumphed with Adami, Arroyo, and Rancillac. Kinetic art blossomed at the same time and is well represented in the museum. On show are some even more recent works by the Support-Surface group: Viallat's *Cistern* (1977) and a tribute to Picasso by Wolf Vostell introducing the use of concrete in painting, (*Les Demoiselles d'Avignon*, 1983).

At the end of this circuit there is a whole range of admirable 1930s furniture in the Salle Art Déco, inaugurated in 1986, and the Henry Thomas collection, which comprises Fauvist paintings and works by Delaunay, Kupka, and Léger.

L'ARC (Animation, Recherche, Confrontation)

On the first floor

This section of the museum was created in 1967 to introduce the public to contemporary art. Through frequently changing exhibitions (once every six weeks) the sculpture, painting, music, and poetry of the last 15 or so years can be explored thematically, panoramically, individually, or collectively.

Today, the ARC enjoys an international reputation, and the publications that accompany each exhibition are regarded as authoritative in the current debates over contemporary art.

▷ Maurice Girardin, collector and patron of the Arts

Maurice Girardin (1884–1951) divided his life between his profession and his collector's vocation. A remarkable personality, this dentist 'fou de peinture' (mad about painting), struck up a friendship with Georges Rouault in 1916 and acquired over 80 of this artist's works. His second love at first sight was for Marcel Gromaire, just 28 years old, with whom he signed in 1920 an exclusive contract that allowed him to gather almost 200 of the artist's paintings. Today these form a collection unique in the world, owned by the museum, due to Dr Girardin's legacy. Having opened a gallery in 1921, La Licorne, Dr Girardin forsook it a few years later, claiming that it cost him too much to part from his favorite works of art. Art for him was certainly not a question of money; believing that masterpieces belonged first and foremost to the public, he donated to the City of Paris his priceless collections of Primitive Art and figurative art of the first half of the 20th c.

▷ Victor Brauner's 'Conglomeros'

In 1930, the arrival in Paris of Brauner, a Romanian painter born in 1903, coincided with his beginnings in the Surrealist adventure. From his first exhibition in the Gallery Pierre in 1934, he expressed through his painting a world born out of the depths of his unconscious and populated with obsessional creatures at once hybrid and polymorphous.

This approach, close to that of Tanguy, for example, took a more concrete form during the war years, when he created from a series of drawings a sculpture called *Conglomeros* (from *conglomerare*: to assemble in one mass). Made in 1944, the sculpture is composed of two male bodies intertwined with a central female body. One rounded head is common to all three bodies. The uneasiness it causes is compounded by the empty, globular eyes and by the material itself – white plaster, suggestive of a ghost-person. The museum is fortunate to be able to present together with this large-scale sculpture (5ft 3in×4ft 11in/160×120cm) another work by Brauner, a 1946 canvas entitled *Meeting at 2bis Rue Perrel*. In this painting, Brauner, who had just moved into the Douanier Rousseau's former studio, introduced his *Conglomeros* into the famous Rousseau canvas, *La Charmeuse de Serpents* (The Female Snake Charmer), producing an extremely eerie image.

▣ Le Musée des Enfants (Children's Museum)

16 Ave. de New-York

This museum is meant for everyone but gives a special welcome to the younger generation. Each exhibition approaches artworks through emotion and intuition, and offer meetings between the public and the creators, surrounded by their works. The organization of the gallery space is the prerogative of the artists involved. Numerous documents (films, catalogs) bear witness to the experiments conducted here over the last 15 years.

▷ Additional information . . .

Various activities are presented to illustrate the museum's collections: visits to exhibitions and series of lectures on 20th-c. art, organized by Paris-Musée (tel: 42-74-22-02); guided tour of the ARC (Thurs. 3pm); jazz concert and literary events in conjunction with exhibitions (tel: 47-23-61-27).

A special event is organized for young people: meetings with artists who present their own exhibits in the Children's Museum (by appointment, tel: 47-23-61-27). These are teaching workshops for teachers and their pupils: these offer teachers instruction to enable them to take charge of their pupils' visits; visiting schools take part in games, questionnaires, and workshops where the work is gone into more thoroughly.

The library (open Tues.–Sat. 10am–1pm and 2–6pm) has a large collection of information on modern art and many catalogs of exhibitions and shows. The library specializes in the art of the 19th and 20th c., follows closely all new French and foreign publications, and offers a very wide choice of books, reviews, catalogs, postcards, and posters.

The Friends of the Museum stall sells limited print editions (silk screen printings, engravings), scarves, jewelry, or objects designed by different artists.

Musée National d'Art Moderne

→Centre National d'Art et Culture Georges-Pompidou

Musée d'Art Naïf

→Halle Saint-Pierre

▣ Musée National des Arts Africains et Océaniens** (National Museum of African and Oceanic Art)

293 Ave. Daumesnil, 12th arr. Tel: 43–43–14–54.
Curator: Henri Marchal
Open daily exc. Tues. 10am–noon and 1:30–5:20pm. Sat.-Sun., 12.30–6pm. Free admission for school groups. tel: 43–43–14–54.
Lecture tours: tel: 45–44–40–41.
Métro: Porte Dorée. Bus: 46, PC

This museum occupies the vast building designed by the architects Jaussely and Laprade for the Colonial Exhibition in 1931, intended to serve as the permanent museum for the Colonies. The building, which marks the use of reinforced concrete, is a major example of the architecture of the 1930s. The huge bas-relief on the façade, 14,000sq.ft/1300m², executed by Janniot illustrates the overseas colonies in Asia, Africa and Oceania. By eliminating the third dimension, the sculptor has made the motifs appear an integral part of the wall: r., Asia; l., Africa, with Oceania between them. Inside are interesting frescoes and two beautiful Art Deco salons, one of which was designed by Rulhmann. The large gilt-bronze statue representing *Civilizing France* that stood on the steps is now in the Place de la Porte Dorée.

History of the museum

After the Colonial Exhibition closed, the building was altered to become an art and history museum showing French expansion into overseas territories. In 1960 the museum came under the Direction des Musées de France and soon after, André Malraux made it into a museum dedicated to the art of Africa and Oceania. Oceanic and African ethnography exhibits remains in the Musée de l'Homme (Museum of Mankind).

Tour of the museum

1½ hrs.

The museum is divided into four sections: the tropical aquarium, African arts, North African Arts, and Oceanic Arts. It also has two cultural activity workshops, a library, and an historical section that documents the collections of ancient artifacts.

The tropical aquarium

Installed in the lower ground floor, the tropical aquarium was built for the 1931 Colonial Exhibition. Originally, it was meant to house those species of aquatic animals found in the French colonies. In fact, it has specimens of all freshwater and saltwater fish, reptiles, in intertropical regions. The animals are grouped by themes – primitive fishes, *Cichlidae* family marine invertebrates, electric fish, feeding – or by geographical origins: Asia, Central America, Africa, Pacific Ocean, Red Sea, the Caribbean, and so on.

African Arts

Ground floor

On the l. side of the lobby the visitor is introduced to some of the main aspects of African arts: fertility and life of the fauna dominated by the Nimba*, a half-woman, half-animal goddess of the Baga people of Guinea; architectural elements are represented by sculpted pillars from the high plateaux of the Cameroons and the Dogon country in Mali. The tour continues upstairs.

First floor

On the landing are exhibited rock engravings from Tassili, described by Henri Lhote in his writings. Also exhibited are ceremonial and fighting weapons, honorary insignia, and tapas from Zaire.

West Gallery: West Africa

Among the peoples of the Sudanese savanna (Mali and the Upper Volta), now Burkina Faso, several factors have influenced sculptural tradition: Islam, the sculptor-blacksmith's personal position in the hierarchy, and the nature of the woods used (soft with long fibers).

The masks of the Bambara from Mali, worn in each of the six societies with initiation rituals, and especially those of the Tyiwara* (horizontal and vertical variations on the antelope theme), demonstrate with what ease their sculptors were able to make the synthesis between stylized geometrical forms and the more realistic sculpture in the round that prevails in the Guinea territories of the Atlantic coast.

The sculptures of the Dogon people, who migrated several centuries ago to the cliffs of the Niger bend, reflect the cosmogony and mythology of this people. The masks are often associated with funeral rites, and are intended to be ephemeral, discarded once they have served their purpose. The museum has a beautiful collection of ancestor statuettes* carved from very hard woods, characterized by its hieratic characters, with arms upraised and its parallel couples. Some of these statues, which the Dogon attribute to their predecessors, the Tellem, can be dated back to the 12th and 13th c.

In Burkina Faso, the Mossi, Gurun, Bwa, and Bobo people make or use masks with a high, flat latticed crest, decorated with polychrome and predominantly two-dimensional geometric motifs: 'butterfly' mask worn at the coming of the rainy season (Bwa); half-antelope, half-human mask of an association of blacksmiths (Bobo). Between the savanna and the forest, on the borders of Mali, the Ivory Coast, and Burkina Faso, Senufo sculpture makes a stylistic transition between the peoples of South Akau, and those of Bambara, Dogon, and Northern Volta. *La Portière*, Senufo statue of a woman; Bambara mother-forebear. In the west of the Ivory Coast, masks for official functions or for denoting rank are the only form of sculpture. Delicately naturalistic or violently expressionist, they demonstrate the artistic exuberance which, in the context of the regulating Poro society, characterizes the Dan, Guere, and Wobe peoples, and they are the pretext for an infinite variety of faces, materials, and accessories.

With the Baule, a people of Akan origin who have come from Ghana in successive waves since the 18th c., masks of gods testify to a very varied and refined art also applied to common and familiar objects:

pulleys, looms, ceremonial canes, musical instruments, hut doors. Together with the Ashanti, their Akan cousins from Ghana, they practised with a rare mastery the art of casting by the lost-wax method; they fashioned pendant masks** from gold and brass, images of Queen Mothers** or of conquered chiefs, also sacred vases, bracelets, cane pommels and, finally, figurines* and weights used to weigh gold powder. They also excelled in terracotta funeral sculpture modelled by the women: Agni heads raised to the sky, with half-closed eyes and thin-lipped mouths, Ashanti figures modelled on the lids of funerary pottery.

East Gallery: Central West Africa

The history of the arts of Benin (formerly Dahomey) and of Nigeria is linked to that of the royal dynasties and of the religious hegeomonies: the king of Abomey (18th c., 19th c.), the *obas* (divine rulers) of Benin (from the 14th to the 19th c.), Oni of Ife (from the 13th to the 15th c.). Court craftsmen, formed into trade corporations (smelters, wood sculptors, pearlers, embroiderers), were instructed to glorify the power and wealth of the kings: the *obas* of Benin are represented by mural plaques or bronze heads such as the Uhumwelao head** (18th c.); royal exploits are retraced on hanging tapestries with appliqué work from the palaces of Abomey, on fully carved ivory tusks** from Benin. Artists fashioned royal emblems and insignia, messengers' staffs, bell pendants, and pendant belt-masks.

From Nigeria to the Cameroon savanna a multitude of tribal styles revolve around the ancient centers of Igbo-Ukwu, Ife, and Benin. Among the Ibo and the Ekoi, naturalism is strongly permeated by borrowed European elements such as in the wooden Ekoi, carved, wooden, skin-covered heads, or the Ibo protective statues. The arts of chieftaincy are also found among the Bamum and Bamileke from the Cameroon high plateaux, where animal representations (buffalo, elephant, panther, trap-door spider) are the symbols of the power of the chief: ceremonial pipe with a 2yd/2m-long stem and a scabbard adorned with a head with puffed-up cheeks.

In Gabon, heads, figures or full-length statues surmount a bone shrine basket or box and are part of the cult of ancestors. The Fang and the Kota, peoples of Lower Ogowe, make the spirits take part in the life of the village through whitened, usually heart-shaped, face-masks: Lower Ogowe masks of dead women with somewhat Asian features, very elongated flat Fang masks and highly structured Kota helm-masks. From the 15th c., the kingdom of Kongo spread its power to the coastal region which stretched from Ogowe to present-day Angola; it formed, as early as 1842, close relations with the Portuguese. Kongo sculpture and that of its neighboring peoples draws its dual naturalistic and magical character from this origin. Here accessories (nails, iron, mirror, pouches of herbs and resin, a spear, or seeds) confer effectiveness, either benign or malign, upon a statue, itself often barely outlined.

In Zaire, the Kuba kingdom, influenced in the 17th c. by the Kong kingdom, perpetuated the memory of its kings through a series of idealized portrait-statues*, each distinguished by a particular attribute: a drum, an anvil, a game. Mythical heroes or kings of a divine nature are also represented by initiation masks to which a bulging forehead, a wide nose, enormous eyes, cowry-shell decoration, pearls, fabrics, or copper, confer great power.

Luba plastic arts (the Luba empire, from the 16th to the 19th c., stretched from the Sankura River to Lake Tanganyika) are characterized by their soft lines, taut rounded forms, and polished surfaces: Itombwa*, polished wood bowls*, divination crocodile.

Of the Yaka, Suku and Pende, to the east of the Kongo country, we know mostly the masks for initiation or circumcision rites: human portraits (old man, coquettish young woman, old woman) among the Pende people, masks with a small face, turned-up nose and multipointed headdress in varnished woven raffia; animal-topped bell-masks of the Suku.

The Lega arts form a link between the prolific Kuba and Luba styles and the spare, severe style of the Azande and Mangbetu to the NE of the state. Masks and statuettes in carefully smoothed and polished wood or ivory were personal badges of rank within the Bwame society. Some weapons (hatchets, sickles, bill-hooks, multi-bladed throwing knives) of the peoples from Upper Ubangi seem to function as emblems or insignia and replace statuary and masks.

North African Arts
Second floor
Morocco

In the arts of this country can be seen the influence of both Spain and Africa, expressed in plant and flower motifs, and geometrical elements of Berber origin.

The museum has gathered a small collection of architectural and decorative elements: window frames, monumental doors, sculpted wooden window bars of the 18th and 19th c.; a collection of blade weapons and firearms inlaid and decorated with copper studs; those from the Moroccan south are richly ornamented with enamels, ivories, and silver. There are many pieces of jewelry of gold and precious stones: the so-called town ones are elaborate, the rural ones more restrained. Note in particular gold pendants* and necklaces*, with pearls and precious stones originating from Fez and dating from the 17th c. The town pottery was made by men, and is mostly from Fez or Tetonan, Meknès, and Safi; it was for everyday use but also decorative (Zellij), with geometric or stylized floral motifs. The rural pottery is from the Rif, Zerhoun, T'soul, Upper and Middle Atlas regions: made by women, it is archaistic, both in its forms and in its decoration.

Collections of coins and bronzes: worth noting are an astrolabe and scientific instruments used to determine times of sunrise and sunset and prayer time. Very large collection of embroideries and costumes; each center of production had its own colors and motifs. One room is reserved for more ancient religious objects*.

Algeria

This country has assimilated trends from abroad, but has nevertheless preserved a cultural heritage in its mountain areas. Algerian art shows two tendencies, urban and provincial. There is more imagination and sensitivity in the former and more vigor and sense of historical tradition in the latter. Large jewel collection, mostly from Algiers, worked in gold and precious stones in a style that mixes arabesques, scrolls, and volutes. Headdresses imported from the Middle East by the Crusaders show much refinement. The best provincial jewels come from Kabylia and were made by the Beni-Yenni. Collections of arms, costumes, and embroidery. Ceramics are characterized by their affinities with antique art: large jars, very similar to Greek amphorae; peculiar jugs, in groups of two or three, very distinct from anything else in this field from North Africa.

Tunisia

This country had continuous contact with the brilliant Phoenician, Roman, Byzantine, and Arab civilizations, as also with the Moorish and Andalusian cultures. But Tunisian art, in assimilating all those influences, acquired its own personality: geometric lines, floral compositions with foliated scrolls and tracery, esoteric motifs in which the sign of Tanit, the Phoenician goddess, held an important place.

Painted or inlaid chests. Many cases displaying town jewelry (gold and precious stones): the technique of fitting together the gold and silver chains is remarkable. Provincial jewelry made of silver is decorated with motifs, either geometrical or naturalistic (flowerets, foliage, birds, and fish). Among the pottery and ceramics, often marked by Orientalism, a dish representing a lion with his tongue out and turning his head is worth noting. Extremely rich Tunisian embroidery, worked on silk with gold and silver threads; braid worked on wool or linen. Sumptuous costumes – those from cities show Turkish influence, those from the provinces a slight Classical influence.

Oceanic arts
West Gallery

Oceanic art occupies the refurbished ground-floor galleries. Oceania represents a third of the earth's surface. Art is represented by everyday objects made by the users themselves as well as by symbolic sculptures made for traditional ceremonies. These pieces, carved for the Vanuatu or to mark rises in rank, were sculpted in tree fern root or in wood, painted and decorated with motifs symbolizing the rank obtained.

Exhibited in the museum galleries are a great many common objects: spoons, a betel-crushing mortar, dishes, drums, shields; a beautiful set of masks in painted basketwork, such as those worn during the yam festivals among the Abelma people; several ceremonial headdresses made of tree fern root with a vegetable paste coating. A dance area for a rank-conferral ceremony has been recreated: each character occupies a precise position in it and plays a particular role. Many ornaments and characteristic objects, such as the very colorful giant combs.

East Gallery: Australia

The Australian art gallery is one of the most beautiful and interesting in the museum, because it houses a large series of paintings on bark*** from the Arnheim Land (Northern Australia).

▷ Paintings on bark

Australian paintings are done on panels of eucalyptus bark worked until smooth, scraped, and heated by fire. After this treatment, the original curve has mostly disappeared, and the bark is then weighed down with stones to make the surface completely flat. The artist uses natural colors, such as kaolin for white, charcoal for black, and ochers for red, brown, and yellow; the pigments are diluted in water. The paint thus obtained is applied with brushes made of chewed twigs, but first the artist will have coated the surface to be painted with wild orchid sap, which works as a fixing agent.

The artist works without preliminary sketch or retouching, and expresses an idea without concern for perspective or proportions, relying on the use of symbols. It is the act of painting that matters and not the finished work: however, many of these paintings evoke mythical or historical themes, in which each element bears a certain message depending on its position within the composition.

▣ Musée des Arts Décoratifs*** (Museum of Decorative Art)

107 Rue de Rivoli, 1st arr. Tel: 42–60–32–14. Map ref: 10–D3
Curator: Mme Yvonne Brunhammer
Open Wed.–Sat. 12:30–6pm; Sun. 11am–6pm
Métro: Palais-Royal, Tuileries
Bus: 21, 27, 48, 68, 72, 85

The objective of the Musée des Arts Décoratifs (Museum of Decorative Art) is to illustrate the links between artifacts and the society for which they were created.

The museum's collections run from the Middle Ages to our own day and include fine groups of 17th-, 18th-, and 19th-c. furniture, paintings, and *objets d'art*. It possesses an extensive collection of Art Nouveau and Art Deco, as well as a collection of Jean Dubuffet's work donated by the artist in 1967.

History of the museum

The Union Centrale des Beaux-Arts Appliqués à l'Industrie (Central Committee for the Application of the Fine Arts to Industry) was founded in 1863 with the avowed intent of 'encouraging in France the development of arts that seek to give beauty to the utilitarian'. The artists, industrialists, and patrons who were its founders sought to combat mediocrity in the objects and surroundings of everyday life. In 1887 the Musée des Arts Décoratifs was founded along the same lines by an association that aimed to stimulate contemporary design by public exhibition of fine work from the past, which they hoped would make the public more demanding.

The two associations merged in 1880. Thus the Union Centrale des Arts Décoratifs (Central Committee of the Decorative Arts, or UCAD) was formed in 1905 in the Pavillon de Marsan, Rue de Rivoli, and its constitution was underwritten by the government.

Although largely dependent upon government funding, the UCAD remains a fiercely independent autonomous body. It manages the following museums: Arts Décoratifs, Nissim de Camondo, Arts de la Mode and Publicité. In addition it runs three art schools – the Ecole de Camondo, the Institut de Communication Visuelle and the Centre des Arts du Livre.

Five years of renovations and reorganization have brought the Musée des Arts Décoratifs up-to-date and have enhanced the building itself, the work of H. Lefuel, the architect of Napoléon III's Louvre.

The museum's collections have been built primarily from bequests, by Peyre, Koechlin, Vever, Moreau-Nélaton, Martin-le-Roy, Perrin, Maciet, Duseigneur, Carnot, and David-Weill, to mention only the most substantial, which reflect the taste of these collectors who were proud to call themselves, not experts, but *connoisseurs*, lovers of the decorative arts.

Tour of the museum

2½ hrs.

The easiest way to tour the museum is to follow the route given below, though it does not go through the collections in chronological order.

First floor (garden side): Art Deco and Art Nouveau rooms

Turn r. at the cash desk and take staircase B on the l.-hand side of the vestibule.

Art Deco Galleries

In the first room, on an enormous carpet woven at the Aubusson factory from a cartoon by Benedictus, stand a Brazilian rosewood desk** by Pierre Chareau and an armchair called a *bergère*, upholstered in grey shagreen by André Groult. Both were made for the French section of the 1925 Exhibition and demonstrate the two trends of the period – Chareau's, modern and rationalist, opposed to the decorative and classical style of Groult and Ruhlmann. Ruhlmann's 'Etat Rect' cabinet* falls into this second category. The example on display is a 1922 version in kingwood veneer inlaid with ivory and Macassar ebony. The exhibits are complemented by a lacquer and porcelain eggshell table by Jean Dunand, a large glass cabinet* by Marcel Coard, and a daybed by Armand Rateau. On the wall hangs a *Composition* painted by Marie Laurencin, and Matisse's 1924 *Portrait of the Baronne Gourgaud**, a lavish benefactor of French museums.

Beyond the room stretches a gallery in which display cases alternate with reconstructions of specific interiors. The first is the office that the industrialist Pierre Levasseur commissioned in 1917 from André Fréchet, then the head of the Ecole Boulle. Next comes the bedroom in Brazilian rosewood and ebonized wood, again commissioned by Pierre Levasseur from Maurice Dufrène, and then M and Mme Pierre Girod's dining-room by Louis Sue and André Mare.

The next three rooms are devoted to the work of Armand Rateau, commissioned by Jeanne Lanvin (→inset) to decorate her private apartments*** at 16 Rue Barbet-de-Jouy from 1920 to 1922. In its use of animal shapes, his highly original and individual style is reminiscent of the decorative art of ancient Egypt. In the boudoir** there are a pair of bronze candelabra, a sofa, tea-table, and glass cabinet displaying fans and dolls dressed for Jeanne Lanvin. Next, the bedroom*** with its 'Lanvin blue' alcove, a pair of bronze standard lamps with antique patina, and the remarkable dressing-table, its black-and-white marble top supported by bronze legs topped with marguerites, a motif repeated on the furniture in the room in honor of Jeanne Lanvin's daughter Marguerite. The bathroom** contains a vast plain marble bath set into a stucco alcove designed by Paul Plumet; washbasin, table, and pedestal table.

The display cases in the gallery exhibit a full range of the applied arts. In the first there is a terracotta by Maillol and a vase by the Catalan potter, Artigas, decorated by Dufy. Next come various pieces of metalwork, pottery, and glass by Puiforcat*, Decœur, and Marinot**, including a notable pot with lid by the latter. In the fourth case there are two valuable pieces of furniture* by Clément Rousseau in Macassar ebony and green shagreen. The last two cases contain two vases which R. Lalique created by the *cire perdu* (lost-wax) method of casting, and a large example of Jean Dunand's hammered metalwork, which also belonged to Jeanne Lanvin. Roger de La Fresnaye's factory painting, *Usine à la Ferté-sous-Jouarre** (1911), which represented the Cubist Movement in the Salon d'Automne of 1912, proves his adherence to the Puteaux group along with Paul Vera, Duchamp-Villon, Metzinger, Gleizes, and Marie Laurencin. The l.-hand side of the gallery is hung with paintings by Valtat, Vera, Domergue, and the remarkable *Women Seated on a Terrace** (1891) by Maurice Denis, a member of the Nabis.

The jewelry room: technical development in the cutting of gemstones, new materials, the discovery of platinum, and the arrival of synthetics, the movement in the arts away from ornamentation and the taste for geometric forms all allowed the designers of Art Deco jewelry to make a clean break from their predecessors, the best of whom had still been subjected to Second Empire influences. Both styles are displayed together, the curves and plant shapes of Lalique's *Swallows** and Vever's *Alarm Clock** next to the strict severity of Templier's and Cartier's cigarette cases* and Fouquet's, Despres' and Dunand's pendants. The display cases at the far end of the room contain some fine pieces of plate by Guimard and Puiforcat, and a strange goblet-shaped vase** created by Lucien Falize from a design by the painter Luc-Olivier Merson.

Art Nouveau Galleries

The room devoted to the work of the architect Hector Guimard (1867–1942) displays some of the furniture** that he designed from 1903 to 1904 for the Hôtel Nozal in Paris. Made from polished pearwood, it is set apart from its predecessors by its architectural style and its use of highly stylized plant shapes as decorative motif. The most striking example of this is a three-legged pedestal table.

The room beyond is given over to the work of Emile Gallé (1846–1904) and displays a set of moulded and carved walnut furniture from the Hôtel Hannon in Brussels (1902–03). On a table stands a lamp by the American, Louis Comfort Tiffany, and on the walls, paintings by J. Béraud. Opposite is a piece of furniture decorated with umbels and in front of it a glass case containing some outstanding pieces from the Maison Gallé which show this artist's fresh approach to glass-making techniques.

In the end room Georges Hoentschell's panels* of Algerian platan, made for the UCAD pavilion at the 1900 World Fair, are on display together with Albert Besnard's panels (*The Happy Island* and *The Stars*). On the l. of the entrance hangs Gauguin's *Above the Abyss***, a small canvas painted at Pont-Aven in 1888. At the far end stands the Erard piano* designed and built by Louis Majorelle, its painted decorations by Victor Prouvé inspired by a poem by Jean Richepin. The verses are inscribed on the piano lid and illustrated in three scenes. To the r. is A. Charpentier's unique *meuble à quatuor**, a music stand for string quartet. The items exhibited in the display cases demonstrate the unbelievable burst of creativity in all fields during the 1900s. There are Henry Cros's *pâte de verre** (he was the first to rediscover this ancient technique of glass paste), glassware by Lalique, Dammouse, Decorchemont, Eugène Rousseau, and Gallé; pottery by Carriès (*Faun's Head**), Chaplet, Decœur, Delaherche, and Dalpayrat, and metalwork by Hirtz, Dunand*, and Gaillard.

Go back to staircase B for the second floor.

Second floor (garden side): 12th to 16th centuries

Gallery 1: a series of four tapestries from the Château de Canche in Brittany display scenes of courtly life against the green background drawn from the *Roman de la Rose*, typical of the Arras workshops in the first third of the 15th c. The 14th-c. strap-hinged chest, one of the oldest known French chests, served as both seat and cupboard. The late 15th-c. canopied bed from the Château de Villeneuve-Lembron (Puy-de-Dome) shows the lasting influence of Gothic architecture.

Gallery 2. You will find two chapel screens, also from Villeneuve-Lembron; a group of French polychrome wood and stone sculptures dating from the 13th c. to the last quarter of the 14th. On the wall, altarpieces, polyptychs and painted panels belonging to the International Gothic school, represented here mainly by Antonio de Carro, creator of the polyptych of the *Virgin and Child*, and Luis Borrassá who painted the altarpiece of *St John the Baptist*. On the r.-hand wall on entering, the altarpiece of the *Virgin Enthroned*

Between St Andrew and St James, attributed to the Master of the Magdalene (Florence, last quarter of the 13th c.); on the *épi* in the center of the room, a fragment of the altarpiece with architectural decoration painted by Jan van Eyck for the Charterhouse of Champol, and the ex-voto of *St Francis of Assisi* by the Master of the Triptych of Imola. On the far wall (r.) the figures of the tapestry *Couple under a Canopy* are reminiscent of the paintings of Rogier van der Weyden. In the showcase: Limousin champlevé enamel from the early 13th c.; a small diptych of the *Crucifixion* from the end of the 14th c., and a 15th-c. *Virgin of Malines* in gilded wood; above, the ivory diptych of the *Passion* is divided into eight registers illustrating eight scenes from the Life of Christ; to the side everyday items are displayed, a ladle and aquamaniles (basins to heat water at the fireside) in the form of a fantastic bird or the bust of a man. Two sculptures, a *Piéta* and a *Virgin of the Nativity* belonging to the entourage of the Master of Rimini, complete those display cases. The 3rd gallery is dominated by a *Crucifixion* more than 10ft/3m high from the School of Ferrara, surrounded by four German polychrome wooden sculptures (*ca.* 1520) that are of great interest; in the showcases opposite, small sculptures in oak and walnut of Netherlands and Brabant origin; in the 4th gallery, an interesting ensemble of transitional Gothic-Renaissance furniture, fine tapestries: *Le Festin* (The Banquet), Brussels, early 16th c.; scenes from the Life of Christ (Flanders, *ca.* 1550); on the first wall on the l., three Italian marquetry (*intarsia*) panels; in the second collection devoted to Spanish painted panels (Aragón, Catalonia, last half of the 15th c.); in the center of the room a beautiful panel from a *cassone* (type of chest) depicting *Jason Encountering Medea* (Tuscan School, *ca.* 1486); to the side, three important works from the Schools of Mantua, Milan and Northern Italy; at the back on the r., the chest called *The Labours of Hercules* decorated with mythological scenes, shows the influence of the Italian faïence, Pusaye stoneware, glasses. In the 5th gallery, a small portrait room housing the portraits of Marie Touchet, mistress of Charles IX; the Archduke Albert, viceroy of Portugal; Isabella d'Este shown standing, and Mary Tudor with the attributes of Mary Magdalene. The last gallery is devoted entirely to the Renaissance: two immense tapestries 17ft 5in/5.30m in length, one showing *Venus and Cupid*, the other called '*aux grotesques*' (France, mid-15th c.), which contains all the iconographic repertory of the French Renaissance. Two *armoires á deux corps* (double-fronted cupboards) characteristic of production in the Ile de France, have antique style decoration showing the influence of Italy and the School of Fontainebleau; in the display cases, a collection of glasses illustrating Venetian influence in Europe, bronzes including *Le Forgeron* attributed to Andrea Riccio and *La Bête Chiménique* attributed to Severo de Ravenna.

Go back down to the ground floor and take stairway C on the other side of the hall.

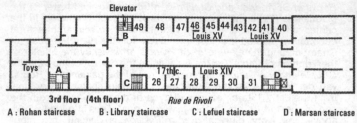

The Museum of Decorative Arts
(Le Musée des Arts décoratifs)

Paintings (Galleries 5 and 6)

Fragment of a panel with architectural motif** attributed to Jan Van Eyck, depicting the l. side of a canopy over a Virgin and Child. This painting was still intact in the Carthusian monastery at Champmol in the 18th c. On the r.-hand wall of Gallery 6 is a *Jason and Medea* attributed to Biagio d'Antonio (Tuscan School, *ca.* 1486); on the far wall, *The Virgin Enthroned Between St Andrew and St James* attributed to the Master of the Magdalene (Tuscan School, active *ca.* 1250–75), while on either side hang six scenes in all from the *Life of the Virgin*. On one side there is the *John the Baptist* altarpiece*, a rare example, surviving intact, of the altarpieces of the Catalan, Luis Borrassa, a representative of the international Gothic style. The central portion depicts John the Baptist and the Crucifixion, with scenes from his life and martyrdom on either side. On the l., *The Dream of Zacharias, The Visitation, The Birth of John the Baptist,* and his *Christening;* on the r., *St John the Baptist Preaching, The Baptism of Christ, Herod's Banquet,* and *The Martyrdom of John the Baptist.*

Go down to the ground floor and take staircase C on the opposite side of the vestibule.

Third floor: 17th to 18th centuries

17th century and Louis XIV Gallery (Rue de Rivoli side)

All along the passage which runs the length of the gallery fragments of panelling from the early 17th c. to the period of the Regency are displayed.

Gallery 26 is devoted to the Louis XIII period. A new type of furniture, a cabinet, built to hold collections of precious objects, made its appearance throughout Europe. On the leaves of ebony veneer on the doors of the cabinet attributed to Jean Macié, are carved two scenes from the *Life of the Virgin*, the *Presentation in the Temple* and her *Marriage*. A collection of Flemish and Dutch paintings hangs on the walls including a *Christ the Gardener*, in which Jan 'Velvet' Breughel painted the background landscape and Henrick van Balen the figures. The display cases contain Nevers majolica, the early examples very like Faenza and Urbino ware.

The four display cases in Gallery 27 exhibit Rouennais faience with high-colors, lambrequin decoration in the *rayonnante* style and majolica from Moustier* with stiff 'lacework' patterns (like those of the decorator Jean Bérain), Marseilles, and Strasbourg from the late 17th and 18th c.

The closed cabinet and the eight-footed bureau in Gallery 28 are covered with kingwood inlaid on a pewter base, a restrained version of Boulle marquetry – copper, pewter and tortoiseshell – of which a cupboard**, normally displayed in Gallery 29 but now being restored, is a fine example.

The carved and gilded console in Gallery 29 dates from the very end of the reign of Louis XIV but already shows signs of the Rococo style. The room is hung with portraits by Robert Tournières.

In Gallery 30 display cases exhibit Rouennnais high-fire polychrome faience**, and majolica from Sinceny, Marseilles, and Moustier.

Gallery 31: the *amoire*** (cupboard) inlaid with violetwood is the work of the Regent's cabinet maker, Charles Cressent. He is also responsible for the finely chased figures of children in the bronze arabesque medallions bearing the emblems of Geography and Commerce. The straight-backed armchair known as *à la reine*, with vigorously swirling lines in the Rococo style, rests on a removable frame with a new method of upholstery that allowed chair seats to be changed according to the time of year.

The large room, which links Gallery 31 with the Louis XV Gallery, displays very large decorative items. On the l. is a large gilded frame bearing the arms of the House of Lorraine and a large, double cupboard from the Midi; on the r., paneling** painted by Lancret for the Hôtel de Boulogne in the Place Vendôme, Paris.

Louis XV Gallery (garden side)

This gallery of ten rooms (40–49) provides a wide-ranging view of the decorative arts during the first half of the 18th c.

Gallery 40 is devoted to bronze work used in furnishings – the dial-case of clocks, fire irons, bronze decorations for furniture – from the Rococo to the Neo-Classical period. In the case in front of the window is a pair of window hasps shaped like the upper parts of a woman's torso* by C. Cressent and in the lower portion of the case on the l. of the doorway of the gallery is *The Hen*, an andiron by Jacques Caffieri, the most representative bronze sculptor of the Rococo style. The room also contains examples of decorative woodwork and furniture.

Gallery 41: Wall brackets and console tables; samples of paneling.

Gallery 42: The ceiling*, painted with grotesques and *singeries* (monkeys dressed as fashionable Parisians), attributed to Charles II Audran, comes from a mansion in the Rue Sévigné. In the center is a bowlegged, claw-footed convertible table for use in a carriage; the table pulls out to 6ft4in/1.93m, and the legs fold away. The display case contains a selection of Strasbourg low-fire faience. Until 1750 only high-fire colors had been used, but Strasbourg introduced low-fire overglaze enamels in the 18th c., after which this technique was widely used.

Gallery 43 displays sketches evoking the colossal paintings produced during the 18th c.; they are designs for ceilings by Lafosse, Lemoyne, and Tiepolo.

Gallery 44 houses a substantial display of Meissen porcelain**. This was the first pottery in Europe to manufacture successfully hard-paste porcelain with a kaolin base in 1710. Meissen figures, drawn from everyday life in both town and country, Commedia dell' arte and mythological figures, were very popular throughout Europe.

In Gallery 45 hang animal paintings by J. B. Oudry and his son J. C. Oudry and still-lifes by F. Desportes. The show case displays low-fire faience from potteries in eastern France.

The passage leading to Gallery 46 is paneled and lined with trophies of arms with, above, a pair of pistols that belonged to Louis XV.

A piece of furniture by Pierre II Migeon shares Gallery 46 with six armchairs signed by Lefèvre.

Gallery 47 is devoted to fine French faience** of the second half of the 18th c. The Pont-aux-Choux pottery was established in Paris close to the bridge of that name and produced items in white clay with a transparent glaze, their shapes inspired by silversmithing. Potteries in eastern France produced undecorated, fine 'creamware' pottery, first invented in Staffordshire.

The furniture in Gallery 48 provides a fine selection of the work of mid–18th-c. Parisian cabinetmakers. The commode signed R.V.L.C. and the corner cabinet (called an *encoignure*, signed C. Wolf) are inlaid with violetwood and satinwood, favorites with the cabinetmakers as was the rosewood and the kingwood used as inlays on the secretaire (signed Montigny). The small tables of so many different designs are real masterpieces, such as the *table de cabaret** (for serving tea or coffee, signed B.V.R.B.), inlaid with rosewood and with a Sèvres porcelain top. The chairs which the

Elevator

| 89 | 88 B | 60 | 61 | 62 | 63 | 64 | 65 | 66 | 67 | 68 | 69 | 70 |

End of Louis XV, and Louis XVI

| A | Second Empire | | 81 | 80 | 79 | 78 | Empire, and Restoration | | 77 | 76 | 75 | 74 | 73 | | | D |

4th floor   (5th floor)   *Rue de Rivoli*
A : Rohan staircase   B : Library staircase   D : Marsan staircase

The Museum of Decorative Arts
(Le Musée des Arts décoratifs)

cabinet makers produced are light and easy to handle. The *à la reine* chair between the windows, is Louis XV in the fluidity of its shape, but its ornamentation of acanthus leaves and bundles of rushes prefigure the Louis XVI style.

The exhibits housed in Gallery 49 demonstrate the 18th-c. infatuation with Chinoiserie. There are Chinese lacquer panels from the Hôtel du Châtelet in Paris; a commode by Pierre II Migeon, with French lacquer imitating the Japanese; a secretaire* with a sloping front varnished blue in imitation of lacquer, bearing the stamp of the Château de Bellevue; a commode in imitation Coromandel lacquer; porcelain from the English East India Company standing side by side with the Chinese and Japanese porcelain on which it was modeled.

Take staircase B (garden side).

Fourth floor: late 18th to 19th centuries

The cases in Gallery 88 follow the development of French soft paste porcelain, first made at Rouen (*ca.* 1673) and then at Saint-Cloud** (1675–1746). The porcelain is still inspired by Rouennais decoration and Far Eastern models (Chinese white and the Imari pattern).

In Gallery 89 there is now a permanent exhibition of one of the most substantial collections in the world of the work of 17th- and 18th-c. French goldsmiths. Particular notice should be given to a Parisian ewer* of 1603; to that masterpiece of *Rocaille*, the Duvivier chandelier** (1734–35: after Meissonier); to Mme de Pompadour's sauceboats** by Joubert (1754–55), and to the work of Guérin, E. P. Balzac, F. T. Germain, and R. J. Auguste.

Louis XVI Gallery (garden side)

The corridor displays sketches for ornamentation by Ranson, Cauvet, Pajou, Delafosse, Lalonde, Dugource, Pineau, Thomire, and Chalgrin.

Gallery 60 is devoted to the Chantilly porcelain* founded by the Prince de Condè in 1725. Its earliest products were free copies of Eastern models. Thereafter Chantilly developed a style of its own in which blue was the dominant color.

Gallery 61: Mennecy-Villeroy porcelain* (1734-73) was influenced by Far Eastern and by Meissen and Vincennes porcelain.

Galleries 62 and 63: the Vincennes factory was established in 1738, received the Royal warrant in 1752 and moved to Sèvres in 1756, and is still flourishing. You can follow the development of its style, originally influenced by Meissen and the Far East and then, at Sèvres, adopting a French *Rocaille* style**, typified by the use of gold and colored grounds – pink, sky blue, lapis lazuli, green, and yellow. The Neo-Classical style was borrowed for the dinner services made for Mme du Barry and for Marie-Antoinette's sister, Marie-Caroline-Louise of Austria, exhibited in Gallery 63. Opposite is displayed biscuitware, unglazed soft-paste porcelain made to models by the sculptor Falconnet.

Galleries 64-68 are reconstructions of Parisian interiors of the end of the 18th c. Pompeian-style wall-paintings inspired the decorated panels removed to Gallery 64. The fine pendulum clock*, decorated with Sèvres porcelain plaques and with Thomire's bronzes of the Vestal Virgins, once stood in Marie-Antoinette's boudoir in the Tuileries. In Gallery 65 there are two pieces of furniture by Reisener, great Parisian cabinetmaker to the French Crown; a chiffonier* dresser built on the same lines as the secretaire to which it was the companion piece, with an inlay of a basket of flowers and gilt bronze fittings to emphasize its lines; also a two-door commode of a type common at that date. The six decorative paintings* on the r. as you enter are fine examples of H. Robert's imaginary landscapes as is his *Feeding of the Five Thousand* in the Grande Galerie of the Louvre. Gallery 66 displays a landscape by Loutherbourg and *The Toilet of Amphitrite* by Lagrenée the Younger. The virtuosity of the sculptor Caffieri is seen in his bust of Doctor Borie* standing on the chimney-piece. The slightly curving lines, the solid mahogany sides and the discreet bronze fittings give Leleu's commode, in Gallery 68, a sober elegance. On the l.-hand wall hangs an important painting by Boilly, *The Gohin Family***, a perfect expression of the comfortable middle class of the late 18th c.

Galleries 69 and 70 display specimens of late 18th-c. paneling and a collection of terracottas* by Clodion, Rolan, and Marin. The portrait of Sophie Muller attributed to Tischben shows the interest of the period in children and in education.

The cases in the corridor display hard-paste porcelain from potteries in Paris, Bordeaux, and Orléans; snuff boxes; quizzing glasses; jewels and canes.

19th century (Rue de Rivoli side)

In the corridor hang architectural and ornamental sketches by David, Vaudoyer, Saint-Ange, and Bertrand the Younger, as well as collections of Paris and Sèvres porcelain, milk glass and miniatures.

Gallery 73: Lemarchand's small writing-desk, called a *bonheur du jour**, to the l. of the window is typical of the Empire style in its straight lines and simple structure. Its bronze fittings bring together Egyptian elements (palm trees, animal heads with pharaonic hairstyles and Classical motifs: women's heads, allegorical figures). The chairs are by the Jacob Brothers and Jacob Desmalter, a dynasty of cabinet makers who, with the painter David, created the Empire style. A painting of Houdon's studio in 1804, with the sculptor working on the plaster bust of Laplace, hangs close to the bust itself.

On the l.-hand wall of Gallery 74 one can admire one of the rare landscapes by Ingres, *The Casino of Raphael in Rome***, painted in 1807 when the artist was staying in the Villa Medici in Rome.

Gallery 75 is devoted to goldsmiths' work, including work by Genu, Biennais*, Odiot, and Froment-Meurice.

Galleries 76 and 77. Furniture: after the Bourbon Restoration light native woods competed with dark exotic woods. Roots, excrescences, and the knottiest parts of the tree were used for decorative effect, as the excrescences of elm and the ash-burrs on F. Rémond's cradle* in Gallery 76. The important Restoration cabinetmaker J. J. Werner used lengths of elm for his commode* and two secretaires. F. Beaudry's *lit bateau** in Gallery 77 is inlaid with burrs of ash and elm and Brazilian rosewood, and has elegant boat-shaped end-pieces. It was a popular design for beds at this time. The musical swing mirror with musical mechanism in the back of the plinth, which the Duchesse de Berry ordered from F. Rémond, is veneered in burred thuya and Amboyna wood with burred elm inlay, as is the dressing-table from the same source. Paintings: *The Emperor Justinian Drawing up his Institutes*** hanging in Gallery 76 is a study by Delacroix for his painting in a room of the Conseil d'Etat destroyed when the Palais-Royal was burned down in 1871. On the walls of Gallery 77 hang 'scenic' wallpapers* by Dufour and Leroy – landscapes with *Telemaque, The Incas* and *Rinaldo and Armida* (from *Jerusalem Liberated*) with strikingly fresh colors.

The next two rooms, as well as Gallery 80, which may be reached through the Second Empire Room, illustrate the period of Louis-

Philippe. In Gallery 78, the new Gothic Troubadour style is typified by the *objets à la cathédrale* in the display cases. In the r.-hand case the plaster, terracotta, and bronze statuettes demonstrate the growth of an art industry coupled with the appearance of a new middle-class market and new production techniques. On the walls of Gallery 79 hang the sketches and watercolors of the ornamentists, painters and architects who initiated this return to the past – Chenavard, Lami, Raffet, and Viollet-le-Duc. The paneling that Hope commissioned for the former Hôtel de Sagan has been set up in Gallery 80. It draws its inspiration from many styles, including the Renaissance and the Pompeian. The return to the past can also be seen in ceramics: corridor between Galleries 79 and 81, Avisseau's imitation of Bernard Palissy's plates. It is the same in jewelry, as exemplified by Alphonse Fouquet's Renaissance brooch exhibited further on in another case in this corridor. Item 92 in the same case is the admirable bracelet** by Froment-Meurice which shows the outstanding mastery of figure-chasing in the round possessed by this artist and the skill with which the sculptor Pradier used the female figure as a decorative element.

Gallery 81 houses some outstanding items from the Second Empire. The models** in terracotta in the case on the r. of the entrance are studies in movement and structure by the greatest sculptor of the period, J. B. Carpeaux. Second Empire furniture drew its inspiration from all styles. Christofle's dressing-table* in the middle of the room imitates a Louis XVI table, but the legs are pure Rococo. The double cabinet on the l., designed by architect Manguin for the Hôtel de la Païva in the Champs-Elysées, is a free interpretation of a Renaissance cabinet. The console table on the r., supported by two atlantes (male caryatids) carved by the sculptor Dalou, also comes from the Hôtel de la Païva. On it stands a silver nef* or ship by the Fannière Brothers, presented to F. de Lesseps by the Empress Eugénie to mark the opening of the Suez Canal. It is modeled in the classic shape of the 18th-c. nef, but with more movement and romanticism. The centerpiece*, comprising a bowl and pair of candelabra in which glass, silverplate, and gilt bronze are combined, is inspired by the Renaissance.

The scenic wallpaper on the staircase depicting the Garden of Armida was designed by E. Muller for its manufacturers, Defosse and Karth, not simply as a piece of decoration, but as a work of art on a grand scale to stand comparison with painting.

Third Floor: Toys

The museum houses a substantial collection of historical toys, which are displayed as a series of special exhibitions around a specific theme.

Go down the stairs at the end of these galleries. Entry to the

Dubuffet Bequest is via the staircase on the ground floor to the l. of the cashier.

First Floor: Dubuffet Donation

The museum accepted the Dubuffet donation in 1967 and has recently rehoused it in four rooms on the first floor in the Rohan wing. The donation comprises objects, paintings, drawings, and sculptures from 1942 to 1967.

Jean Dubuffet (1901–86) devoted himself totally to painting in 1942 after giving up the family wine business. A self-taught artist, he rejected the principles of 'fine art' in preference for graffiti, naïve figures, and the drawings of children and psychotics for whom he founded in 1949 the Compagnie de l'Art Brut (Raw Art Company), thus provoking public outrage.

His search for a personal means of expression led him to the study of natural textures, evidenced by his series, *Sols et Terrains* (Earths and Soils) and the psychotic landscapes of 1952 such as *Burning Landscape* (Gallery 1); the constructs he called *pâtes* in 1953; *Landscape with Car.* (Gallery 1) made of rope, glass, sand, etc.; of mixed media techniques (Galleries 2 and 3) and built-up compositions of asphalt, glue and plaster, such as *Coursegoules* (Gallery 2). Parallel with this search for expression ran his study of techniques. He used unusual materials, such as butterfly wings (*Pearl Garden*, 1955: Gallery 2) or garbage as in his *Little Statues of the Precarious Life* (Gallery 3). The formal arrangement of the *Cycle de l'Hourloupe* (Gallery 4) appears to be rational: a gaudy jigsaw puzzle bringing together commonplace motifs.

One of the greatest French 20th-c. painters, Dubuffet also wrote extensively about his own work, revealing the intelligence and sincerity that underlay his most unorthodox artistic strategies.

First Floor (Rue de Rivoli side): Contemporary Gallery

Entry on the ground floor to the r. of the cashier.

The Contemporary Gallery houses exhibits acquired over the past twenty or so years, from special exhibitions in the Musée des Arts Décoratifs, such as the Assises du Siège Contemporain (Contemporary Chair Design), 1968, and from loans from the Centre de Création Industrielle, (Center for Industrial Design), now a department of the Pompidou Center; from the CRNS and, in particular, from the Fonds National d'Art Contemporain which, since 1981, has included decorative art.

This gallery besides showing the way in which design has developed from the 1920s to the 1940s, presents a selection of furniture and other items loaned by the most eminent designers from 1945 to the present day. Techniques related to traditional materials and glass stand alongside fresh methods made possible by recently developed materials such as plastics, resins, and ultra-strong alloys. Charles Eames with his armchair of moulded ply-wood, aluminium and leather, 1956; Jean Royère, Jean Prouvé (desk of wood and bent and welded sheet metal), and Joe Colombo follow the tradition of functional furniture pioneered by Charlotte Perriand (chaise longue*), Mies Van der Rohe (armchair), and Marcel Breuer. Note the table* by Diego Giacometti and the armchair* by Niki de Saint-Phalle.

Mention should also be made of such contemporary designers as Philippe Stark, Nemo, Totem, Vilmotte and Memphis. The collection is complemented by objects both useful and beautiful, lamps, vases and dinner services.

▷ Jeanne Lanvin

By her enormous talent and sheer hard work, Jeanne Lanvin was able to raise herself from humble origins to the top of Paris high fashion. As she rose in the world of haute couture, she gained a deep appreciation of the arts and associated with many of the artists of the period. She entrusted the decoration of her mansion in the Rue Barbet-de-Jouy to her friend Armand Rateau, who was later to become head of Lanvin-Décoration. Here she housed her private collection of *objets d'art* and, above all, a series of paintings with women as their theme that included works by Renoir, Bonnard, Vuillard and Boudin.

This outstanding collection was bequeathed to the museum in 1965 by the Prince de Polignac in memory of Jeanne Lanvin's daughter, the Comtesse Jean de Polignac.

▷ Not to be missed

First floor:
Art Deco and Art Nouveau
Jeanne Lanvin's apartments
Gallé and Marinot glass
Lalique glass and jewelery
Nabis paintings by Gauguin and Maurice Denis
Second floor:
Medieval art
15th- and 16th-c. tapestries
Paintings by Van Eyck and Borassa
Fourth floor:
18th and 19th c.

Sèvres and Saint-Cloud porcelain
Collection of 17th- and 18th-c. plate
Bourbon Restoration wallpapers
Landscape by Ingres

▷ The Louis XIV style

A truly French style came into being during the reign of the Sun King. Enamored of grandeur and glory, Louis XIV determined to create a luxurious setting for himself and for his court, which would display his royal power to the world at large. Thus was undertaken the creation of the royal residences of Versailles, Trianon, Fontainebleau, Saint-Germain, and Marly.

Directed by Charles Le Brun, the king's First Painter, a team of ornamentalists was commissioned to engrave a series of designs to be used by craftsmen, cabinetmakers, tapestry weavers, goldsmiths, and potters in furnishing the royal residences. These ornamentalists were inspired by Classical Roman art to create an original and majestic style in which symmetry was the rule. In it may be found such classical motifs as lions' heads and paws, rams' heads and horns, stags' hoofs, acanthus leaves, fruit and flowers, arms and trophies of war. The mascarons and masks – especially the sun in its splendor, the symbol of the monarch – and particularly the cockleshell, recur most often in the decoration.

> Additional information . . .

Lectures:
Tour of one department of the museum (Sat. 2:30pm); lecture on furniture (Sun. at noon; entrance free upon request to the museum); course of lectures on furniture Mon. and Tues. (information and enrollment tel: 42-86-98-18).

The library contains substantial documentation on art history and specifically on the decorative arts, design, and architecture; it also houses the Maciet Collection of iconography comprising over 6000 volumes (entrance: 109 Rue de Rivoli; open Mon.-Sat. 10am-5:30pm; Mon. morning photographers only).

Documentation Centers (5th Floor):
Information center for the crafts (open Mon. and Wed.-Sat. 10:30am-5:30pm). Department of Wallpapers, National Glass Center and Toys: Documentation Center (Thurs. 2pm-6pm, or by appointment; tel: 42-60-32-14). Department of Drawings (by appointment).

Workshops:
These offer artistic activities:

Art-Déco Jeunes is for children under age 15 (tel: 42–60–32–14, extension 875); adult workshops (extension 933).

The Friends of UCAD organize a wide range of events.

The museum shop offers for sale items produced by ARCODIF; reproductions of museum exhibits and contemporary objects.

▷ The Regency and Louis XV styles

After the death of Louis XIV in 1715 the ideal of courtly life was no longer one of pomp and grandeur but of pleasure and comfort. Little by little the straight line fell into disuse until it was finally driven from the field of design. Furniture broke free from architectural patterns and developed sinuous and rounded lines; chairs followed the contours of the human body; the fronts and sides of furniture were curved.

Decoration followed the same path. The draughtsman Jean I Bérain took Le Brun's place. Symmetry was still the rule but it was given a lightness and a touch of fantasy: *singeries* – monkeys dressed like fashionable Parisians – and Chinoiserie appeared. Meissonier and Oppenordt introduced the Rocaille style to France, but avoided extravagance, and their rocks, tattered foliage, distorted shells and twisted scrolls conformed to coherent patterns. Floral decoration combined with geometric motifs in marquetry softened the exuberance of the bronze fittings and the shape of the furniture.

▷ The Louis XVI style

At the height of the fashion for Rococo, Mme de Pompadour sent her brother, the Marquis de Marigny, who was later to become the Superintendent of Public Works and Buildings, to receive his artistic education in Italy accompanied by the designer and engraver, Cochin (1715–90) and an architect named Soufflot. Their tour, the spectacular discoveries of the buried cities of Pompeii and Herculaneum, as well as the collections of drawings brought back by other travelers, all helped to popularize a fresh return to the Classical. The Louis XV style was more and more sharply criticized and a gradual but fundamental change could be seen in the range of decorative motifs: the column, the pilaster, the triglyph, fluting, Greek key patterns, the ovule and the pearl made their appearance. Lines became more restrained, shapes more simple and harmonious, surfaces flat. At the same time a return to nature, begun by such philosophers as Rousseau, inspired other decorative themes – flowers, foliage, fruits, and musical instruments – which moderated the severity of this revival of Classicism.

▣ Musée des Arts de la Mode**
(Museum of Fashion)

109 Rue de Rivoli, 1st arr. Tel: 40–67–90–00. Map ref: 10–D3
Curator: Pierre Provoyeur
Open Wed.–Sat. 12:30–6pm, Sun. 11am–6pm
Métro: Tuileries, Palais-Royal
Bus: 21, 48, 69, 72, 85

This brand-new museum opened its doors for the first time in 1986 in the attics of the Pavillon de Marsan at the far end of the Louvre. Founded in close cooperation with the heads of the French textile industry, this new temple of style aims to become the showcase for that distinctively French elegance that is both a part of the nation's artistic heritage and a major industry.

History of the museum

The Musée des Arts de la Mode comprises two separate collections. First, it displays the holdings of the Textiles Department of the Musée des Arts Décoratifs, with 1500 costumes from the 16th to the 20th c. as well as pictorial records and countless samples of material. Second, there are 9000 complete outfits and 32,000 individual items of clothing and accessories: the most important collections are those of Poiret and Madeleine Vionnet, followed by Schiaparelli's.

The new museum is run by the Musée des Arts Décoratifs; it has private status, but functions like a public museum.

Tour of the museum

1 hr.

The permanent collections are displayed in rotation to avoid damage to their exceedingly delicate fabrics. They are therefore rotated in thematic exhibitions changed every four months. These are augmented by loans from other French and foreign collections.

In association with the Union des Arts Décoratifs et du Grand Louvre, the museum is now planning its extension in the Pavillon de Marsan and in extra, modern, storage space beneath the garden.

The museum, whose collections are extraordinarily fine, also houses a library, a conservation department, and the Institut de la Mode at which future leaders of the industry receive advance training. These, now open to the public by arrangement, are also to be rehoused and enlarged.

Lastly there is a bookshop/boutique offering special reissues of fashion publications, clothes designed by the great fashion houses, exclusive accessories and jewelry.

▣ Musée National des Arts et Traditions Populaires**

6 Rue du Mahatma-Gandhi, Bois de Boulogne, 16th arr. Tel: 40–67–90–00.
Curator: Nicole Garnier
Open daily 9.45am–5:15pm except Tues.
Groups must apply for a permit 15 days in advance
Métro: Sablons
Bus: 73, 82, PC.

Located since 1969 in a modern building (specially constructed for it by the architect Jean Dubuisson) in the Bois de Boulogne the museum exhibits a broad panorama of the mostly rural and provincial way of life in traditional French society, illustrating its agricultural methods, customs and beliefs and costumes.

History of the museum

The museum was set up in 1937 to house the French collections and those connected with French culture from the former Musée d'Ethnographie du Trocadéro, whose foreign collections remained in the Musée de l'Homme. The Musée des Arts et Traditions Populaires was founded by Georges-Henri Rivière. Paul Rivet and Jean Cuisenier also figured prominently in its early years. Soon after World War II teams of researchers scoured the French countryside collecting tools and other items, making tape-recordings of explanations of their use, and amassing photographs. Under the guidance of Rivière, documents and testimonies were saved, restored, catalogued and preserved. In only 30 years the core collection of 7000 items from the Trocadéro had been supplemented by nearly 800,000 more objects.

The founding of the museum stimulated the observation of traditional French society and its transformation into an industrial one, and inspired the creation of some 800 regional and local ethnographical museums.

Tour of the museum

1½ hrs.

A third of the museum's space is devoted to the collections. The remainder is set aside for restoration, preservation, and study.

The exhibits are displayed in two galleries, the so-called 'Cultural' gallery (opened in 1975), and study gallery, offering the public two ways of exploring the collection. The casual visitor may be content to view the Cultural Gallery in which the exhibits are presented in their social context. The study gallery shows exhibits by an analytical method according to 17 aspects of study history, social structure, habitat, etc. An audiovisual presentation aims to make comprehension easier.

Cultural Gallery

The gallery's organization was inspired by Claude Lévi-Strauss's analysis of the structure of French society, and by his dictum 'All human civilization, however humble, can be presented under two major aspects: on the one hand it is in the universe; on the other it is itself a universe'.

First part: People and the environment

The first section evokes successively the environment, history, technology, customs, and beliefs of the French. The visitor can follow the circuit suggested by the museum or go straight to any section by following the passage called the Galerie de Circulation.

210 - Environment and history. This section relates the physical environment of France to its history. Note the parallel between a contemporary *sabotier's* adze and the image of the same tool engraved on a stele of the Gallo-Roman epoch. Presentation of the three main periods of French rural civilization.

220 - Technology. This section follows the technical achievements that gave people the means to survive. An important place is reserved for agriculture and animal husbandry. There are four reconstructed human dwellings with lighting and sound effects. An authentic ship from Berck (Pas-de-Calais) lies as if beached between tides for the crew to repair the hull. There is a reconstructed workshop of the woodworker Désiré Louvel who until 1863 made wooden bowls and spoons in Maine. There is also a reconstructed forge from Saint-Véran (Hautes-Alpes). The interior and activities of a communal workroom from about 1930 at Gaulien are also on display. 'From fleece to clothing' showcases display the tools used for working wool, from primitive shears to the loom from the village of Campan in the Hautes-Pyrénées.

240 - Customs and beliefs: Religious holidays and other rituals set the rhythm of social life and agricultural work in traditional society. Wedding casket (Queyras, 16th c.), crib (14th c.), clerical robes.

Second part: Society

The second part of the Cultural Gallery shows how culture is organized by customs, technology, and beliefs; this can be seen clearly in a sharply defined, relatively homogenous society such as France.

410 – Practices. Magic and predictive practices. Consulting room of a 1977 Parisian clairvoyant presented as an 'ecological unit'. Two packs of tarot cards that belonged to Edmond the clairvoyant consulted by Napoléon III, Victor Hugo, and Dumas the Younger. Representations of the principal magical arts: astrology, palmistry, etc.

420 – Institutions. Some, like the village, are limited in space; others, such as the family, are not. Two examples illustrate pastoral and agricultural organization in Aubrac and Savoy; reconstructed interior of a shepherd's hut where cheese is made, of Chavestas-Bas *ca*. 1913; interior of a high mountain pasture chalet (Savoy, early 20th c.). Painting of the school of the brothers Le Nain (storeroom of the Louvre) showing a peasant meal in the 17th c. Beautiful sign of a blacksmith called Bouquet de Saint-Eloi (Tours, late 19th c.); the center shows the items made in the workshop, and the decoration around the edge of the sign represents a tour of France made by the smith.

430 – Arts and Crafts. Collection of objects and works of art. A masterpiece of the *sabotier's* in the form of a tree covered with wooden shoes and birds opens the section (Saint-Amand-Montrond, Cher, 1931), made by J. F. Touzet. Puppets of the 19th and early 20th c.

Popular entertainments. In a showcase, gouaches from the first half of the 19th c. show a variety of Britanny's costumes. The arts section includes the study of the various materials and techniques used in the making of ordinary objects: pottery, wickerwork, horn, glassware. Problems of style in popular art are considered. Beautiful coats-of-arms decorated with geometric patterns.

Popular painting and sculpture. Handsome polychrome wood sculpture (early 18th c., Morbihan) representing St Isidore, the patron saint of ploughmen. Rotating flow showcases exhibit drawings, paintings, and engravings.

▷ Additional information

The visitor is offered many kinds of information:
Archive documentation room: open Mon. and Wed.–Fri. 10am–noon and 2–5pm.

Print room: open Mon.–Fri. 10am–noon and 2–5pm: popular prints, posters, and playing cards.

Examination of objects and record library (by appointment).
A public auditorium enables people to attend lectures, concerts and films, in connection with the museum's collections.

Some workshops for arts and crafts (weaving, embroidery) are organized for children. Tel: 40–67–90–00.

The bookshop has a large collection of useful literature for visitors.

▣ Musée de l'Assistance Publique*

47 Quai de la Tournelle, 5th arr. Tel: 46–33–01–43. Map ref: 17–B3, 18–C3
Curator: Mme Nadine Simon-Dhovailly
Open Wed.–Sun. 10am–5pm.
Métro: Maubert-Mutualité.
Bus: 86, 87, 63, 24

Set up in the beautiful, recently restored Hôtel de Miramion, this museum traces the history of Parisian hospitals. The displays illustrate the major stages of their development while evoking the atmosphere of a 17th-c. interior. This Neo-Classical mansion was built by Mansart or Le Vau in the first part of the 17th c. (see the garden façade); it was then turned into a convent by Mme de Miramion who enlarged it in 1675 to house the Filles de Sainte-Geneviève, nicknamed 'Miramionnes' after its founder.

Tour of the museum

45 mins.

First floor

Gallery 1 traces the history of the first hospitals and charitable institutions run by priests, monks, and nuns to look after the sick and needy, illustrated by various documents. The *Livre de Vie Active*** (*Book of the Active Life*) illuminated by Jean Henry, head of the Hôtel-Dieu (1482); portrait of St Vincent de Paul, founder of the order of the Filles de la Charité (Little Sisters of the Poor), a religious community that cared for the sick in free hospitals. The museum also possesses fine paintings from the chapels of these hospitals: *The Mocking of Christ*** by H. Terbrugghen (1588–1629), one of the most important masters of the Netherlands, greatly influenced by Caravaggio; *The Visitation** and *The Adoration of the Shepherds** by the French painter Noël Coypel (1626–1707). **Galleries 2, 3 and 4** are devoted to the great foundations of the 17th and 18th c. Foundation for Abandoned Children, created in 1638 by Vincent de Paul and established at Bicêtre; the General Hospital (1656) intended to shelter the homeless of Paris, beggars and prostitutes; the Necker Hospital (1776), forerunner of the modern hospital, conceived as a center for treatment and no longer as just a home for the needy. **Gallery 5** evokes a 19th-c. hospital: surgical kit of Dupuytren (1777–1835); electrocardiogram by Vaquez; feeding bottles in various shapes, for sick patients as well as children.

Ground floor

Gallery 6. The music room is furnished in 18th-c. style: Louis XV commodes; early 18th-c. Italian paintings. **Gallery 7** contains an amusing reconstruction of the Hôpital de la Pitié's porter's lodge, a true portrait gallery adorned with medical allegories. **Gallery 8**, the dispensary, contains very beautiful apothecary jars and vases collected from the bequest of the Assistance Publique. *Le cabinet de l'amateur*, **Gallery 9**, reconstructed from a 1660 description, is a beautiful example of the 17th-c. curio room in which the householder collected his treasures. Outstanding for its paneling and painted ceiling, it contains a collection of 17th-c-and 18th-c. faience. The visit ends with a reconstruction of a sick ward.

▣ Musée de l'Avocat (Lawyers' Museum)

25 Rue du jour, 1st arr. Tel: 47–83–50–03. Map ref. 17–A1
Open Mon.-Fri.
Appointments by telephone or write to François Gibault, 3 Rue Monsieur, 75006 Paris
Métro: Louvre, Halles
Bus: 67, 74, 85.

Tour of the museum

1 hr.

This beautiful mansion built by Antoine de La Porte (mid–17th c.), now at its best after recent refurbishing, has in its basements the legal collection of the Ordre des Avocats. A number of paintings and authentic documents recall certain periods of history and the famous cases that shook public opinion.

There is a bust of Gerbier, the lawyer nicknamed 'the eagle of the bar,' by Lemoyne; a defense speech and correspondence between Zola and the barrister Labori, Dreyfus' defense counsel; documents of the trial of Henriette Caillaux, who murdered the editor of the newspaper *Le Figaro*; a sketch by Belay during Stavisky's trial, and trial notes by Poincaré; writings by Gambetta.

Musée Baccarat

30 bis Rue du Paradis, 10th arr. Tel. 47-70-64-30. Map ref. 11-B1, 12-C1
Open Mon.-Fri., 9am-6pm; Sat., 10am-noon/2-5.30pm
Métro: Poissonnière, Gare de l'Est
Bus: 32

Tour of the museum

30 mins.

The former Musée du Cristal is a small private museum installed beside the Baccarat company's saleroom, in the heart of the Arts of the Table district. You can see the services created by the company (founded in 1764) for the royal and imperial courts of Europe, and the finest pieces from their workshops.

Maison de Balzac*

47 Rue Raynouard, 16th arr. Tel: 42-24-56-38. Map ref. 13-A2
Curator: Mme Judith Petit
Open Tues.-Sun. 10am-5:40pm
Library: open Tues.-Sun. 10am-5:40pm; closed public holidays
Métro: La Muette, Passy
Bus: 32, 72

Among the 11 Paris residences of the great writer it is here, in the only surviving one, that he was least happy. Balzac lived here from 1840 to 1847 and wrote his last novels, including *La Rabouilleuse*, *Une Ténébreuse Affaire*, *La Cousine Bette*, and *Le Cousin Pons*, and corrected the whole of the *Comédie Humaine*. Weighed down by debt, he worked like a madman.

Balzac's house is the headquarters of the Balzacian studies group (Etudes Balzaciennes) and of the Société des Amis de Balzac, which organizes various events, lectures, symposia, and the award ceremony of the Prix Balzac. Exhibitions are regularly organized.

History of the museum

This residence is one of the few relics of rural Passy. In the 18th c. the lodge was an outbuilding of a mansion, now disappeared, that Noël Halle, the king's painter, had built on the edge of the Rue Basse, now Rue Raynouard. Jean de Julienne, Watteau's patron, lived here, as did, later, two actresses from the Comédie-Française, Mlle Hus and Louise Contat.

In 1903 the *hôtel* housed a small private collection devoted to the writer. The Comtesse de Limur bequeathed it in 1948 to the city. The museum was officially opened in 1949.

Tour of the museum

30 mins.

Balzac's house

The study overlooks the Rue Berton and, further away, the Princess de Lamballe's former mansion, which is now the Turkish Embassy and was previously Dr Blanche's famous clinic, where Maupassant and Nerval were treated. Except for the study, of monastic austerity, the other rooms are decorated with numerous pastels, drawings and paintings portraying the writer, his family, his sister, his close friends and the woman who had a place in his life. Many documents relate to Laure de Berny who inspired the character of Henriette de Meursault in his *Lys dans la Vallée* and Zulma Carraud, Balzac's faithful friend and ancestor of the writer Philippe Hériat, who left his collection to the museum.

One room is devoted to Mme Hanska who, under the name 'L'Etrangère' (The Foreigner), corresponded with Balzac for 18 years, but became his wife for only five months before his death. Some precious personal objects as well as documents and portraits paintings and pastels by Gigoux illustrate his family and social life.

The Balzac Library

In 1965 the City of Paris opened a documentation and research center in the l. wing consisting of a library and a print room. The library, which is open to the public, offers readers the writer's entire works as well as the scholarly studies and theses devoted to him. It is surprising to see a collection of first editions from the Tsarskoe Selo Imperial Library.

Musée Bourdelle*

16 Rue Antoine Bourdelle, 15th arr. Tel: 45–48–67–27. Map ref. 21-B2
Curator: Mme Dufet Bourdelle
Open Tues.–Sun. 10am–5:40pm
Groups by appointment.
Library: Bourdelle's collection, open by appointment.
Métro: Falguière, Montparnasse-Bienvenue
Bus: 28, 48, 58, 91, 92, 94, 95, 96

The Musée Bourdelle is installed in the studio occupied by the sculptor Emile-Antoine Bourdelle from 1884 until his death in 1929. He began to work here just after starting at the École des Beaux-Arts, where he had taken second place in the entrance competition. One seldom sees such continuous use of one studio in an artist's career. Another sculptor, Jules Dalou, was his neighbor.

Mme Antoine Bourdelle bequeathed this studio to the City of Paris, which turned it into a museum, opened on July 4, 1949. It was enlarged by the Salle des Monuments in 1961, and new rooms were added in 1968. The museum makes it possible to follow Bourdelle's work from his sketches and studies through the finished sculpture.

Tour of the museum

45 mins.

The Bourdelle family house

Situated to the r. of the entrance, on the edge of the garden, this house was adapted for visits by the public in 1953. Gathered together in his own studio are Bourdelle's oil paintings, among others, several self-portraits at various ages, portraits of his parents, his children, his associates, as well as a curious portrait of Cécile Sorel at the age of 13. Only the cast of the Rheims cathedral *David* is on display – the original was destroyed. Other family portraits are displayed in the former workshop of Bourdelle's father, a cabinet maker, together with the old craftsman's bench and tools. Bourdelle's studio, kept in its original state, contains studies of statues, preliminary works, and the Gothic furniture of which he was fond.

Beethoven Room: The studies of Beethoven* are assembled here. From the musician's death mask Bourdelle produced 62 portraits, searching for increasingly monumental forms. Second studio: busts of Carpeaux, August Perret, Charles-Louis Philippe, and the model for the great monument of General Alvear commissioned by Argentina.

Garden: round the pond are statues of fauns and goats (the *Stubborn Ram*), screaming figures (1902), and the equestrian statue of Alvear, the cast of which is in the main hall.

The other rooms on the ground and first floors are reserved either for temporary exhibitions, or for repeat exhibitions of the most famous works chosen from among the 900 sculptures in the museum, among them busts of Ingres, Mécislas Goldberg, Rodin, Apollo, and a standing warrior.

The Great Hall

This hall contains the original plaster casts of Bourdelle's monumental sculptures. It was difficult to find suitably spacious settings for these works, planned as they were for wide public squares.

The décor of the Théâtre des Champs-Elysées*: these bas-reliefs cover the walls on each side of the hall; the elongated forms and large incised figures were inspired by American dancer Isadora Duncan. This group, executed in 1912, takes mythological subjects as its themes: *Apollo Musing, The Muses Running to Apollo*, and allegorical figures of Dance, Comedy, Music, Architecture and Tragedy. *The Birth of Venus* (1924), a frieze above the entrance, executed for the theater of Marseilles, was one of his last commissioned works.

The monument to General Alvear, liberator of Argentina, shows a horseman and four other figures: Victory, Strength, Liberty, and Eloquence. Bourdelle worked for over 10 years on this statue, erected in Buenos Aires in 1926. Next to this is the *Polish Epic* (1917). The statue of Mickiewicz unveiled in 1929 is a fragment of the monument dedicated to the great Polish poet, conceived in an original and modern spirit. First erected in the Place de l'Alma, this monument can now be seen in the Cours Albert 1er. Opposite: the *Offertory Virgin* (1923), *Sappho* (1885–1925), and *Hercules as an Archer** (1909), a large statue in which Bourdelle demonstrated a violent interpretation of Greek art, which made him famous. It was purchased in 1922 from the Luxembourg. *France Greeting America* (1923–25) was designed to stand on the Grave headland in gratitude for American intervention in World War I; *Penelope*, a monument to

Rodin (1910), whose assistant Bourdelle became in 1896. Collection of models and projects.

In the three following rooms some small studies are displayed: 49 sculpted heads for the four figures for the war memorial in Montauban where Bourdelle was born (1884–1902); bas-reliefs of the monument to Mickiewicz (1928); fragments of the war memorial at Montceau-les-Mines, commissioned in 1919.

Second Garden: a few bronze monumental works are exhibited, including the four figures surrounding the statue of Alvear, and portraits and studies for the monument to Beethoven.

Musée Branly

21 Rue d'Assas, 6th arr. Tel: 45-48-24-87. Map ref. 22 C1, C2
Entrance: ground floor of the Institut Supérieur d'Électronique (Higher Institute of Electronics)

Open Mon.–Fri., by appointment only. Closed July/Aug.
Métro: Saint-Placide, Rennes
Bus: 48, 68, 83, 94, 95, 96.

Tour of the museum

30 mins.

The museum is installed in the Catholic Institute: go into the hall, turn l., and continue under the archway to the Institut d'Électronique.

This is more a pilgrim's shrine than a museum, since it is installed in the small room where Professor Edouard Branly spent a great part of his life.

Edouard Branly (b. Amiens 1844, d. Paris 1940) was a professor of physics at the Paris Catholic Institute from 1875 and ended his career there. His discoveries on radioconduction are at the origin of wireless telegraphy. The first radioconductors and other scientific apparatus dating from 1890 are displayed in the museum.

▣ Musée Carnavalet***

23 Rue de Sévigné, 3rd arr. Tel: 42-71-21-13. Map ref. 18–C2, D2
Curator: M. B. de Montgolfier
Open Tues.–Sun. 10am–5:40pm; certain rooms are closed 12:30–
2:30pm; closed public holidays.
Métro: Hotel de Ville, Saint-Paul, Chemin-Vert
Bus: 29, 69, 76, 96

Devoted to the history of the capital, this is the most Parisian of all
the city's museums. Situated in the very center of the Marais
district since 1959, it occupies two former mansions adjoining one
another: the Hôtel Carnavalet, to which the museum owes its
name, and the Hôtel Le Peletier de Saint-Fargeau (29 Rue de
Sévigné). Before 1989 only the former was opened to the public. It
is a fine example of civic architecture from the Renaissance to the
17th c. In addition, it can boast of having been Mme de Sévigné's
favorite residence (for the history and architecture of the building
→Marais). The Hôtel Le Peletier de Saint-Fargeau is the family
mansion of Louis Michel Le Peletier de Saint-Fargeau, member of
the Convention, assassinated in 1793 for having voted for the
King's execution.

Tour of the museum

2 hrs.

The collection (about 500,000 items) illustrates the history of Paris
from its beginnings to the present day. The remote past, from
prehistory to the end of the Middle Ages, is evoked by objects found
during the demolition of buildings and other excavations made in
Paris. From the Renaissance to the present day, iconography is

dominant. Works of art, often of great quality, documents, a variety of memorabilia, show how Paris has developed through the centuries and bring to life the important people who lived there, and the great events that took place. In addition there are suites of decorative paneling, painted ceilings, furniture from various buildings in Paris, giving a marvelous account of the development of rich Parisian households since the Renaissance. All these help to give the Carnavalet tremendous atmosphere, and make a visit here as pleasant as it is enlightening.

Until the opening of the Hôtel Le Peletier de Saint-Fargeau the rooms open to the public exhibited only a selection of works of art dating from the early 16th c. to 1789, as well as a temporary exhibition of collections illustrating the French Revolution and the First Empire, together with shop signs and objects evoking Parisian 16th-c. and 19th-c. trades.

L'Hôtel Carnavalet

Ground floor (first section)

Rooms 4 to 7. This gallery generally houses temporary exhibitions.

Paris in the 16th c. and during the reign of Henri IV (Rooms 8 to 12).

These rooms occupy the ground floor of the Renaissance building. The vast fireplaces, exposed beams, tiled floors, together with a few pieces of furniture, illustrate an interior of the period. Room 8: in Tonnerre stone an altarpiece sculpted in 1542 by Pierre Berton for a chapel in the Church of Saint-Merri.

Room 9. In this room and in the two following can be found the oldest views of Paris; *The Prodigal Son in the Company of Courtesans** (Flemish school, mid-16th c.) depicts in fact an elegant musical gathering against a Parisian background with a view of the Seine and Notre-Dame. *St Geneviève Watching her Sheep* is a curiously anonymous painting in which a panorama of the city appears behind the figure of the patron saint of Paris; a painting of the cemetery and church of the Saints-Innocents (Flemish school) shows buildings demolished at the end of the 18th c., replaced today by the Square des Innocents. Note two portraits of the Renaissance monarchs François I (Flemish school) and Mary Stuart, Queen of France and then of Scotland, by the studio of François Clouet.

Paris at the time of the Holy Wars (Room 10).

Portraits of Catherine de' Medici, Queen of France, studio of F. Clouet; her second son Charles IX, by the same studio; Henri de Lorraine, Duc de Guise, called 'Le Balafré' (Scarface) attributed to François Quesnel. Head of the Roman Catholic party, the Duc de Guise led the League. An anonymous painting shows the procession

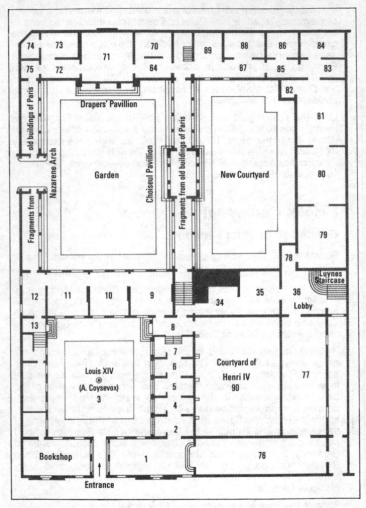

Carnavalet Museum/Ground Floor (First Floor)

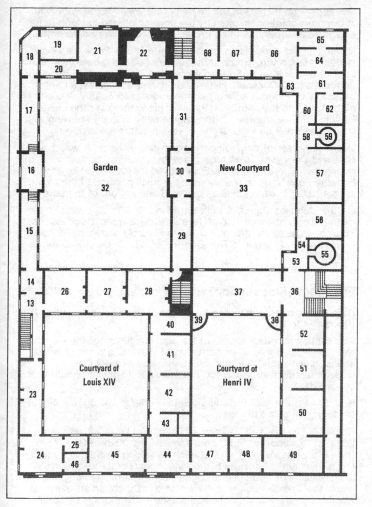

Carnavalet Museum/First Floor (Second Floor)

they organized in 1593 in the Île de la Cité. *Plan for the Pont-Neuf*, anonymous painting inspired by the drawing offered to Henri III for a large-scale urban planning project (carried out very differently).

Room 11. *The Procession of the League to the Place de Grève** (1590 or 1593, anonymous) shows another Catholic demonstration in front of the then unfinished Hôtel de Ville. Portrait of Henri III (attributed to F. Quesnel). Henri IV on horseback against a Parisian background (Flemish school) commemorates, probably, the entry of the king into the capital (1594) after his victory over the League. Painting of St Geneviève (anonymous, early 17th c.) showing the completed Hôtel de Ville; scene of Italian actors (anonymous).

Room 12. A set of engravings representing Paris as it was being built and the events that took place here during the 16th c. and during the reign of Henry IV. Four carved mascarons or keystones from the Pont-Neuf. In the showcase a small painting of the Dutch school (1606) showing skaters on the Seine in front of the Louvre.

On the staircase (no. 13), built partly in the 17th c., note (on the ground floor) the portrait of Adélaïde de Savoie, Duchesse de Bourgogne, a terracotta replica of the marble statue by Antoine Coysevox, and one of *The Charity of St Martin*, by Georges Lallemant.

First floor (first section) (*subject to rearrangement*)

Paris and its dwellings during the reigns of Louis XIII and Louis XIV (Rooms 14 to 25).

This section showing scenes of Parisian life illustrates the way the town developed into a modern capital. Several groups of decorations taken from various buildings and reassembled in the museum show the style of the most beautiful Parisian interiors of bygone days.

Room 14 (to the r. of the stairs). Small coffered ceiling, painted in the reign of Louis XIII.

Room 15. The views of Paris are of the time of Louis XIII and during Louis XIV's minority. First, note three views of the Place Royale (now Place des Vosges), an architectural setting unusual at the time for its symmetrical design, two of which represent the carousel on the occasion of Louis XIII's engagement in 1612. Other pictures show the Seine, usually by Flemish or Dutch artists such as Abraham de Verwer, a landscape painter known for his sensitivity.

Room 16. On the ceiling a working sketch by Bon Boullogne for a Rococo ceiling in the Palais de Justice (1688). A selection of engravings showing some 17th-c. monumental works.

Room 17. Recalls the Paris of Louis XIV. The Seine seen from the Pont-Neuf was the favorite theme of painters, often anonymous, of this period. Also worth noting is a view of the Observatoire presumed to be by Jean François called Francisque II Millet, and two paintings by Pierre-Denis Martin: *Visit by Louis XIV to the Hôtel Royal des Invalides** in 1709 and *The Seine viewed from the Quai de Bercy** (with the Hôpital de la Salpêtrière, the Jardin des Plantes, the numerous religious establishments of the Montagne Sainte-Geneviève, the Île Saint-Louis and the Cité) in 1716.

Room 18. Early 18th-c. paneling from the old Hôpital de la Pitié. A set of gouaches of Louis XIV's period, some of topographical interest; others showing popular aspects of Parisian life.

Room 19. Small room from the Hôtel Colbert de Villacerf* (23 Rue de Turenne). With its paneling painted with colored grotesques on a white ground, its wide curve with bays painted with *trompe-l'oeil*, and its ceiling painting of *Apollo and the Seasons*, this décor is an attractive example of the style favored in Paris from 1650 to 1660.

Room 20. In this passageway hang sketches by Pierre Mignard, the brothers Bon and Louis de Boullogne made for the decoration of Paris churches in the reigns of Louis XIII and Louis XIV.

Rooms 21 and 22. The large study*** and the great hall*** from the Hôtel de la Rivière (14 Place des Vosges) magnificently decorated between 1652 and 1655 for the Abbé de la Rivière, Bishop of Langres, by the architect François de Vau and the painter Charles Le Brun. The large study (*grand cabinet*) has kept its gilded stucco archway with motifs probably modelled by G. van Obstal framing the ceiling painting: *Aurora Awaking*. On the walls are tapestries made after Le Brun cartoons and a pair of paintings by René-Antoine Houasse representing the transport of the equestrian statue of Louis XIV to the Place Vendôme (1699).

The *grande chambre* (great hall) has retained only the broad arched ceiling with an important work by C. Le Brun, representing the story of Cupid and Psyche with eight beautiful Muses sitting in pairs at each corner. On the walls are 17th-c. portraits and views of Paris; two paintings by Adam-Frans van der Meulen depicting the royal residences around the capital: the *Château de Vincennes* and the *Château-Neuf de Saint-Germain-en-Laye*.

Room 23 (turn back and turn l. at the staircase): this gallery with its simple late 17th-c. paneling recalls Mme de Sévigné, who lived at the Hôtel Carnavalet for nearly 20 years; two portraits of the famous letter writer, an oil by Claude Lefebvre (1662 to 1665), and a pastel by Robert Nanteuil (*ca.* 1670); Mme de Sévigné's drop-leaf writing-desk with Chinese lacquer from her Château des Rochers; portraits of Mme de Grignan, Mme de Sevigné's daughter, attributed to Pierre Mignard, and of her husband the Comte de Grignan, attributed to Nicolas de Largillière.

Room 24. This corner room still has its late 17th-c. or early 18th-c. paneling; Regency furniture and pictures of that epoch: *Louis XV*

Leaving the Lit de Justice on September 12, 1715, gouache by P. D. Martin: note the Sainte-Chapelle in the Cour du Mai in the Palais de Justice's precincts; *The Retinue of the Turkish Ambassador Mehmet Effendi, coming from the Pont Royal 1721* by the same artist.

Room 25. In this small room is a display of faience (late 17th c., early 18th c.), from Nevers, Rouen and Delft.

The Municipality of Paris in the 17th and 18th c. (Rooms 26, 27, 28).

These three rooms, which are on the actual site occupied by Mme de Sévigné's suite, contain portraits of the members of the Bureau de la Ville de Paris including the Prévôt des Marchands, the four aldermen, the clerks of the court, the receiver, and the attorney. These dignitaries were represented in large paintings at the Hôtel de Ville at regular intervals before the Revolution. Here are some of the few that survive, with painted sketches for similar compositions.

Room 26 (opposite the staircase): fireplace from a mansion in the Rue Bernardins (Louis XIII). The picture dated 1611 is by Georges Lallemant; the one dated 1614 is anonymous. Sketch by Noël Coypel for the large painting dated 1674 of the Merchant Provost and the aldermen going to pay their respects at Notre-Dame after the victory at Senef.

Room 27. This room contains two fragments of a large picture by N. de Largillière commissioned in 1702 by the City of Paris to celebrate the accession of the Duc d'Anjou to the throne of Spain: a portrait of the *Prévôt des Marchands, Boucher d'Orsay; Two Aldermen**.

Room 28. A painting of the publications of the treaty of Aix-la-Chapelle commissioned in 1758 from Jacques Dumont, called 'Le Romain'. It shows the municipal officers in a richly allegorical setting. Among the sketches: *Inauguration of the Equestrian Statue of Louis XV* (1763) by Joseph-Marie Vien; this monument, destroyed during the Revolution, was erected in the center of the Place Louis-XV (Place de la Concorde). In the wall showcase: various objects bearing the coat-of-arms of the City of Paris.

Paris in the reign of Louis XV (Rooms 29 to 31):

(*Follow the little communicating passage at the end of Room 28*).

The pictures on display in the two galleries reveal in detail the general aspect of the town from 1720 to 1760. They show the architects to have been concerned with the construction of private dwellings (Faubourg Saint-Germain and Faubourg Saint-Honoré) to the detriment of large public works.

Room 29. This room contains nine views of Paris and the royal castles in the immediate vicinity of the city, painted in minute detail by Charles-Léopold de Grevenbroek, a landscape artist of Dutch origin.

Room 30. This room has *rocaille* paneling from a mansion in the Rue de Varenne. It is one of the several suites evoking a Parisian domestic interior of the 18th c. *The Triumph of Flora*, a ceiling painting on canvas, attributed to J. J. Lagrenée, comes from M. Vassal's folly in the Rue Blanche.

Room 31: Twenty views of Paris* painted by Nicholas J. B. Raguenet, who specialized in urban landscape. His close attention to detail makes this collection particularly precious as a record of the city in the time of Louis XV. Raguenet has portrayed the Seine as it crosses Paris, with its shipping, bridges, banks, quays, and its vast landscape. Notice particularly the view of the Pont Notre-Dame, whose arches still support a double row of houses; a jousting contest is taking place in front of the bridge.

Descend by the wooden staircase into the arched colonnade which separates the two parts of the garden.

Ground floor (second section) *(subject to rearrangement)*

The Parterre des Drapiers. This occupies the site of the former garden of the Hôtel Carnavalet, the main portion of which lies to the E. On the other three sides dating from the second half of the 19th c., but which incorporate three architectural features saved from the demolition of old Paris: to the S, the arch that spanned the Rue de Nazareth on the Ile de la Cité, 16th c.; to the W, the façade of the office of the Corporation des Drapiers, formerly central pavilion near Les Halles, the work of Jacques Bruant, 17th c; to the N, a projecting façade of the Hôtel des Marets, early 18th c.

The Parterre de la Victoire is also in the French style. The buildings date from the beginning of the 20th c. On the terrace is the original lead statue of *Victory* by François Boizot for the fountain in the Place du Châtelet (First Empire).

Interior decoration by C. N. Ledoux (Rooms 34, 35)

Two important interior design ensembles by the great architect Claude-Nicolas Ledoux one of the leaders of the Neo-Classical movement, have been provisionally mounted in these rooms.

Room 34. The Café Militaire* (1762) situated in the Rue Saint-Honoré, was the meeting place of Royalist army officers, which accounts for the military character of its décor. On one of the walls, a portrait of Ledoux and his daughter, attributed to François Callet.

Room 35: the Salon de Compagnie of the Hôtel d'Uzès* was created in 1761 by the sculptors Joseph Métrivier and J. B. Boiston from designs by Ledoux; the beautiful gold and white paneling comes from a mansion erected in the Rue Monmartre; the furniture is from the Louis XVI period.

The exit is in the stairwell by Luynes (no. 36), constructed early in the 20th c. but painted with large architectural *trompe l'oeil* murals* executed in 1750 by the Italian decorator, Paolo Antonio Brunetti, for the staircase of the Hôtel de Luynes in the Faubourg Saint-Germain.

First floor (second section)

The Parisian residence at the time of Louis XV*** (Rooms 37 to 52)

Paneling carved and painted in the *rocaille* style from old *hôtels* provides a background (except in Room 37) for the display of furniture collections and *objets d'art* of the same period, bequeathed in 1965, for the most part, by Mme H. Bouvier.

Rooms 37, 38, 39. The Grande Salle, decorated in the spirit of the *Régence* style, together with the two adjoining rooms, contains furniture and *objets d'art* from the Bouvier collection dating from the time of Louis XIV: two pairs of marquetry pedestal tables after Boulle; from the *Régence* period a pair of corner cupboards with tiered shelves and from the Louis XV period: commode bearing the name Migeon.

Room 40. Cabinet Doré. The blue-and-gold coffered ceiling (*ca* 1650) from the Hôtel Bouthiller de Chavigny (7–9 Rue de Sévigné).

Room 41. Salon Bleu. Paneling from the Hôtel de Broglie in the Faubourg Saint-Germain. Among the furniture and *objets d'art*: two desks marked Delorme; a two-piece chaise-lounge of the kind known as a *duchesse brisée*, which is inscribed Blanchard.

Room 42. Salle Grise: The paneling comes from the Hôtel de l'Aubespine (formerly on the Quai Malaquais).

Room 43. Chambre Polychrome: The paneling is from a mansion in Rue de Fleurus. Preliminary sketch for the portrait of Louis XV's Irish mistress, Mlle O'Murphy, pastel by François Boucher.

Room 44. Petit Salon. Paneling from the transitional period between Louis XV and Louis XVI, from a mansion in the Faubourg Saint-Germain.

Room 45. Paneling from various places. The Louis XV furniture is not part of the Bouvier collection. Portrait of the engraver Jean Mariette by Antoine Pesne. *The Billiard Game* is the work of the young Chardin. *Carnival in the Streets of Paris* and *Prostitutes Being Taken to the Salpêtrière Prison*, two paintings by Etienne Jeaurat, record the life of the people.

Room 46. Decorative paneling painted with polychrome scenes in the manner of Pillement.

Retrace your steps to continue the tour of the rooms containing the Bouvier collection (Louis XV period).

Room 47. Salon Turquoise. The paneling is from the Hôtel Brulart de Genlis (13 Quai Conti). Among the furniture and *objets d'art* are a chest of drawers* decorated in red lacquer with gilded motifs and a secretaire painted with polychrome motifs on a pale yellow background.

Room 48. Salon Jonquille. The paneling comes from the so-called Hôtel des Stuart d'Aubigny (demolished to make way for Rue Gay-Lussac). Among the furniture and *objets d'art*: two chests-of-drawers inscribed J. Dubois, decorated with Chinese lacquer. Here the suite of rooms containing the Bouvier collection is interrupted.

Room 50. The paneling comes from the Couvent des Premontées, Rue Hautefeuille. Two large commodes from the early 18th c. Oak console table carved in the *rocaille* style.

Room 51. The paneling is from the Hôtel Brulart de Genlis. The room is devoted to the theater. A series of four polychrome wooden figures representing the main characters of the Italian Commedia dell'arte.

Room 52. Writers, philosophers, and wits of the 18th c. Most plentiful is the memorabilia relating to Voltaire and Rousseau. Among the first: *Voltaire Awaking at Ferney*, a small humorous picture by Genevan artist Jean Huber noticed by Kafka during a stay in Paris; the philosopher's armchair has a reading stand and jointed writing-desk. *Herbier* by J. J. Rousseau. Portraits of Diderot by Barthélemy and of d'Alembert, by Catherine Lusurier.

Cross the landing of the great staircase.

Paris and the Parisian residence at the close of the reign of Louis XV and in the reign of Louis XVI (Rooms 53 to 68)

Thanks to its paneling and furniture (from the Bouvier bequest), this suite of rooms illustrates the flowering of the Neo-Classical style in Paris during the second half of the 18th c. Some portraits and historical artifacts of the period are also to be found here.

Rooms 53 and 54 (Passage). *Louis XVI Attired for His Coronation*, a painting by Joseph Silfred-Duplessis.

Room 55. Boudoir Rond. Paneling of the Louis XVI period originating, as in the case of rooms 56, 57, and 58, from the Hôtel de Breteuil, formerly in the Rue Matignon.

Room 56. Salon Jaune. Among the furniture and *objets d'art*: commode inscribed Reisener and Weisweiller.

Room 57. Salon Bleu. Note two scenes painted in the style of Michel Garnier: *The Interrupted Marriage Contract* and its pendant *The Volunteer's Departure*.

Room 58. Passage.

Room 59. Boudoir Ovale. Secretaire-cabinet inscribed J. H. Riesener. This marks the end of the Bouvier collection.

Rooms 60 and 61. Pictures recalling the urban planning and architectural schemes of the end of Louis XV's reign: *Laying of the First Stone of the Église Sainte-Geneviève** (today the Panthéon), September 6, 1764, by Pierre-Antoine de Machy, who painted the model of the façade in *trompe l'œil* for this ceremony; *The Chapelle du Calvaire in the l'Église Saint-Roch* by Nicolas-Bernard Lépicié; *Edmé Bouchardon* by François-Hubert Drouais is a portrait of the famous sculptor beside a wax model of the equestrian statue of Louis XV. Two architectural models: one for the façade of the Church of La Madeleine based on a plan (not carried out) by Constant d'Ivry, the other a reproduction of the façade of Saint-Sulpice, the work of Servandoni, with the N tower designed by Chalgrin. Three anonymous paintings showing the stages of development of the Place Louis-XV (today Place de la Concorde): the site of the square, construction work, and completed square.

Room 62. Salon of the engraver Demarteau***. This exceptional collection of decorative canvases, set into paneling that simulates a trellised summerhouse, by the famous painter François Boucher was commissioned in 1765 by Demarteau. Boucher carried out this work in collaboration with Fragonard: *Love Triumphant*, and animal painters, including J. B. Huet.

Room 63. Views of Paris in the same period showing some of the churches.

Room 64 and 65. Closed for renovation.

Room 66. This room, like the three following, is decorated with paneling dating from the time of Louis XVI from the Château de Conflans, formerly the residence of the bishops of Paris. Two models for the Pont Louis-XVI (today Pont de la Concorde), the work of Perronet, as is the Pont de Neuilly, whose *décintrement* (literally 'de-arching': the removal of the wooden arching used in the construction of the arches of the bridge) is the subject of a painting by Hubert Robert (1772). *Fire in the Opéra at the Palais Royal** (1781), by Hubert Robert. Bust of the actress Dorothée Luzy* by J. J. Cattieri (1776).

Room 67. Two paintings by H. Robert portraying *La Démolition des Maisons sur le Pont Notre-Dame** (1786) and *Sur le Pont au Change** (1788). Louis XVI furniture (gift of Mme Nelly Debray).

Room 68. Views of Paris painted by Alexander Noël and Genillon. Others (anonymous) demonstrate typical ideas of the second half of the 18th c.: the Hôtel de Salm under construction; the English garden of La folie Monceau (today Parc Monceau). *A Popular Festival at Les Halles to Celebrate the Birth of the Dauphin on January 21, 1781**, is depicted in a painting by Philibert-Louis Debucourt.

▣ The Hôtel Le Peletier de Saint-Fargeau

The Musée d'Histoire de Paris is divided between the Hôtel Carnavalet and the Hôtel Le Peletier de Saint-Fargeau. The former contains all the collections concerning Paris from its origins to the end of the *Ancien Régime* and continues to hold temporary exhibitions. The Hôtel Le Peletier de Saint-Fargeau shows all the collections relating to Paris from the French Revolution to the present day; it also contains the signboards and other objects concerning the trades of Paris (in the Orangerie), the print room, an auditorium, and the conservation offices. The two museums are linked by a gallery on the first floor.

A tour of the Hôtel Le Peletier de Saint-Fargeau begins on the second floor with the collections relating to the French Revolution.

The Revolution and the First Empire** (Rooms 101 to 112)

Louis Michel Le Peletier de Saint-Fargeau, French noble elected to the States General, would doubtless have been proud to welcome to his Paris home the most important collection of Revolutionary objects ever brought together.

In the first room (no. 101) Mirabeau, at the head of the Third Estate, is represented by a bust by Tessier, dated 1791. The popular orator, nicknamed 'The Hercules of Liberty', is caught in a lifelike pose and seems to turn towards the interlocutor who could be Bailly, the first mayor of Paris. These two men personified the early impulse of a revolution that sought to be peaceful and modern, guaranteeing the rights and liberty of all, the resolution of which is symbolized by the 'Tennis Court Oath'. This national aspiration was rudely ended by the Parisians who stormed the Bastille (no. 102), where there was a large stock of gunpowder and a prison. Among its famous prisoners was the Chevalier de Latude who remained imprisoned for more than thirty-five years. A few objects have survived from the 'Citadel of Despotism', as the Bastille was then called, like the studded chest and, especially, the interesting representation of the fortress* sculpted in one of its own stones. Finally, a precious memento of the time: the insurgents' crossed pikes beside the drums of the Republican army in the war room (no. 110).

The Constitution and the Declaration of the Rights of Man and the Citizen greet visitors to the room (no. 103) devoted to the Fête de la Fédération, that is, to the national oath of constitutional rights, sworn on July 14, 1790, on the Champ de Mars. The main protagonists of the Revolution are brought together in the painting by Charles Thévenin, which depicts in a sort of painted chronicle, step by step, the different stages of the ceremony. The following room (no. 104) illustrates the episode of the royal arrest with a bust of the 'constitutional king', sculpted by Deseine. Room 106 is a recreation of the royal prison in the Temple. This was installed in the apartments of the Temple's archivist. Busts of Le Peletier and Marat greet visitors to Room 108, given over to the Convention and especially rich in personal mementoes of the great figures of the Revolution. Danton's watch and dressing case are set beside Robespierre's shaving dish and Saint-Just's pistol. A little further on, beside the stove in the form of the Bastille that heated the Convention, the armchair of the paralyzed Couthon. He sat next to Robespierre in the Committee of Public Safety and went to the scaffold with him.

The room (no. 111) devoted to the Revolution is a homage to Alexandre Lenoir, creator of the first Musée des Monuments Français, opened on September 1, 1796. Finally, the last room (no. 112) contains the cut-out silhouettes painted by Lesueur, which illustrate certain revolutionary events in the manner of an illustrated and picturesque journal of the Revolution.

Ground floor

On the ground floor are the collections relating to the first half of the 19th c.

The Empire (Room 115)

Official portrait of Napoleon I, by R. Lefevre (1809). Portraits of the women of the Empire: *Juliette Récamier*, by F. Gerard.

The Restoration (Room 116)

Of the small paintings recalling the events and atmosphere of this period: *Entry of the Allies to Paris, Boulevard Saint-Denis* (1815) by Zippel; *Death of the Duc de Berry, Nephew of Louis XVIII* by Cibot. Memorabilia of the Duc de Bordeaux are collected together, including a gold and mother-of-pearl toy coach*; statue of the young duke by Lemaire.

Paris during the first half of the 19th c. (Rooms 117 and 118)

In the large collection of views of Paris on display here, certain detailed and precise works, faithful to the 18th-c. tradition, are worth attention. Others from England bear witness to a more romantic style: *The Boulevard des Capucines**, by Robert Stanley; *Landscape with Windmill* by Georges Michel. *The Pont Saint-Michel*** and *The Quai des Orfèvres***, by Camille Corot are also on display.

From 1830 to 1850 (Rooms 119 to 121)

Some small narrative pictures record the events of July 1830 called *Les Trois Glorieuses*. A large model by Foulley shows the arrival at the Hôtel de Ville of the Duc d'Orléans, proclaimed Lieutenant Général du Royaume before becoming King Louis-Philippe. The splendor and pomp of the July Monarchy can be seen in some of the small scenes: *Ladies Banquet at the Tuilieries**, a sketch by Viollet-le-Duc; *The Hôtel de Ville Lit Up for the King's Birthday*, by Roux. A series of portraits depicts the great figures of the Revolution of 1848: Ledru-Rollin, Eugène Blanqui, and Proudhon. Other pictures show the fighting: *Lemartine raising the Red Flag on the Steps of the Hôtel de Ville*, a sketch by Philippoteaux.

Parisian art and life during the Romantic period (Rooms 122 to 125)

Some small sculptures of the personalities of the era have been collected together in these rooms; some portraits and mementoes of writers, including Lamartine, and Alfred de Musset; portraits of actresses and musicians – *Mlle Mars*, *La Malibran*; *Franz Liszt and His Muse, Marie d'Agoult* by Lehmann. Scenes of Parisian life: *The Parade of Bobèche and Galimafré on the Boulevard du Temple*, by Jean Roller.

Go up to the first floor by the main staircase of the Hôtel Le Peletier de Saint-Fargeau, decorated with a gilded iron grille* dating from the late 17th c.

First floor

A series of views of early 19th-c. Paris are exhibited in Rooms 126 and 127.

From the Second Empire to the Third Republic (Rooms 128 to 132)

The State Cradle** given by the City of Paris for the birth of the Imperial Prince was designed by the architect, Ballard, and made by the goldsmith Froment Meurice; a collection of busts of the most beautiful women of the period by Carrier-Belleuse. Various architectural projects and urban planning schemes of the Second Empire are on display: the Opéra, the Cirque d'Hiver, the Gard du Nord. Large canvases recall the events of the war of 1870 and life in Paris during the siege: the departure of Gambetta by balloon from

Montmartre; *Le Rêve** or *Paris Burning* is a strange painting by Corot; *The Carrier Pigeon** by Puvis de Chavannes. Some other canvases show the Commune: portraits of the famous writer Jules Vallès* and of the revolutionary Louis Michel, by Gustave Courbet. The principal political figures of the Third Republic can also be seen: Waldeck-Rousseau; General Boulanger.

Paris at the close of the 19th and the beginning of the 20th c. (Rooms 133 to 135)

Paris as seen by the artists: works by S. Lépine, Johann-Bartold Jongkind, Guillaumin (*The Seine, Where it Enters Paris*) and Signac (*Windmills at Montmartre*). Room 136: Literary life is recalled by the memorabilia of various figures of the world of the arts; portraits of Alphonse Daudet and Edmond de Goncourt by Carrière; statue of Sarah Bernhardt; statuettes of Réjane and Yvette Guilbert by Capiello. Rooms 137, 138: Small scenes of Parisian life; *The Grand Staircase de l'Opéra* by Louis Beroud; *Boulevard Montmartre* by A. Gill.

Reconstruction of interiors from the early 20th c. (Rooms 141 to 146)

Room 141: Private dining-room from the famous Café de Paris. Rooms 142 and 143: The Fouquet jewelry boutique of Rue Royal, whose décor was created in 1900 with designs by Mucha. Room 146: Ballroom of the Hôtel de Wendel, Quai de New-York, whose interior with its painting of *The Procession of the Queen of Sheba* was designed by J. M. Sert y Badier. Room 147: three collections of memorabilia recall the life led by Marcel Proust, Anna de Noailles, and Paul Léautaud. Room 148: Impressions of 20th-c. Parisian life in a series of pictures.

▷ Not to be missed

First Floor (first section)

Grand Cabinet of the Hôtel de la Rivière (Room 21); ceiling painted by Charles Le Brun, with stucco surround by G. von. Obstal.

First Floor (second section)

Bouvier Collection (Rooms 37 to 48): furniture, *objets d'art* and paneling in the *Rocaille* style, Louis XV period.

Salon du Graveur Demarteau (room of the engraver Demarteau) by François Boucher and Fragonard (Room 62).

Ground floor (third section)

Portrait of Madame Récamier by F. Gérard (Room 75). (Another portrait, Room 115)

▷ **Additional information**

Print room (open Tues.-Fri. 2pm-5:15pm, Sat. 10am-12:15pm). Paris in pictures, from drawings, prints, and photographs.

Temporary exhibitions: detailed surveys of different aspects of Paris and its history.

Wednesdays at the Carnavalet: research, visits, lectures and presentation of Parisian life (16th-19th c.) for visitors aged 7 to 17. (Meet in the hall of the museum at 2:30pm on Wed. For groups, enrolments, tel: 42-72-21-13).

Musical Sundays (tel: 42-77-92-26): Organized concerts on Sundays at 3pm. Tickets at booking office 30 min. before the beginning of the concert.

Centre Pompidou

→*Centre national d'art et de culture Georges-Pompidou* → *Pompidou Center.*

▣ Musée Cernuschi*

7 Ave. Vélasquez, 8th arr. Tel: 45-63-50-75. Map ref: 3-A3
Curator: Mlle M. T. Bobot
Open daily except Mon. and public holidays 10am-5:40pm
Groups by appointment.
Métro: Monceau, Villiers
Bus: 39, 84, 94

The Cernuschi is a museum where amateurs and connoisseurs alike are able to admire and study the art of East Asia. The museum exists thanks to Henri Cernuschi, who in 1896 bequeathed his Parc Monceau residence and precious East Asian art collection to the City of Paris. Henri Cernuschi, a politician, economist and scholar, brought back the collection in 1873 after a two-year journey he had undertaken with the art connoisseur Théodore Duret.

Since it opened its doors in 1898 it has been considerably enriched and contains some rare pieces of archaic Chinese art.

Tour of the museum

45 mins.

In the entrance and hall are assembled Buddhist sculptures from China. The most important piece is the seated Bodhisattva from Yunkang (late 15th c.); next to it: a stele of the Northern Ch'i (dating from 560); a Bodhisattva, a column statue of the Sui (6th c.); and marble Buddha of the Liao (11th c.).

Ground floor

This floor is devoted to Chinese classical art from its beginnings to the 13th c. First section, Neolithic painted pottery and grey pottery (3000–1000 BC); divinatory bone objects and white ceramics of the Shang Dynasty (14th–11th c. BC). Archaic bronzes* of the Shang, Chou, and Warring States (481–221 BC) dynasties, including the famous vase called the Tigress** (12th–11th c. BC); nearby, mirrors, clasps, and jades. A collection of bronzes from Eurasia (Louristan, Siberia, Ordos) illustrates the art of the Asian steppes. The next section has ceramics from S China and the first celadon porcelain made at Ch'ang-cha (9th–10th c.). A unique group of terracotta funerary statuettes (1st–8th c.) is on display; these characters, figures of animals, and architectural models give an account of Chinese daily life from the Han to the T'ang dynasties. There are also some ancient paintings: fragments of frescoes from tombs, showing court ladies (8th–9th c.); the scroll of *Horses and Grooms**, an outstanding specimen of T'ang painting attributed to the era's greatest painter of horses, the court artist Han Kan (active *ca.* 720–780). Two birds (also on paper) illustrate the painting of signs from the early 13th c.

The first floor is used to show alternately temporary exhibitions and the collection of contemporary Chinese paintings given by Dr. Kuo Yu-Shou to the museum in 1953. The Japanese Buddha in bronze (18th c.) brought back by Cernuschi in 1873 is in the Grande Salle. On the landing are a bronze stag and doe (China, end of 17th c.).

Musée Charles-Cros** (Phonothèque Nationale)

Gallerie Colbert, Rue des Petits Champs, 1st arr. Tel: 47–03–88–23.
Map ref: 10–D3
Director: Dominique Villemot
For all information: Phonothèque Nationale Tel: 47–03–88–23.
Métro: Bourse, Palais-Royal
Bus: 21, 27, 29, 39, 48

The Charles-Cros museum is part of the Département de la Phonothèque Nationale et de l'Audiovisuel whose aim is to preserve all recorded sound and audiovisual material. This successor to the Musée de la Parole et du Gest (Museum of Speech and Gesture), opened in the spring of 1987, is devoted to the history of the invention of recording technology from the most outlandish theories, such as that dreamed up by a 17th-c. traveler who claimed that some populations used sponges to transmit messages and squeezed them out afterward to hear the words, to the most brilliant modern technical achievements.

Tour of the museum

30 mins.

Among the 350 pieces of equipment on display there are several mechanical musical instruments, a child's symphonion, a pianola, music boxes, and barrel organs. The museum possesses the earliest phonographs, among them the one conceived by Charles Cros (→inset) in 1877 but realized independently a few weeks later by Thomas Edison; also the enormous cylinder-machine that allowed 15 people to listen together to the same recording; several phonographs and their records from the smallest (4in/10cm) to the biggest, with flower-shaped horns made of wood, copper, brass, papier-mâché or crystal.

The museum also shows the many applications of sound recording from its first appearance: the dictation of letters, language instruction, and public entertainment.

Another section is reserved for temporary exhibitions connected with current events or devoted to certain kinds of equipment (for example, an exhibition on the child and the musical toy).

▷ Portrait of an inventor

Charles Cros (1842–88) was a brilliant jack-of-all-trades. A self-made man with a passion for Asian languages, he was engaged at the same time in important scientific research and an unusual literary work. In 1869 he described a three-color photographic process. A few years later he invented an apparatus called the *paléophone* a short time before Edison produced his famous phonograph in 1877.

This new museum and the Academy Charles-Cros honors his memory by awarding prizes for the best recordings. All this might make us forget that this brilliant inventor was an assiduous devotee of the *fin-de-siècle* Bohemian literary scene that included Villiers de l'Isle-Adam, F. Coppée, and Verlaine, who called Charles Cros's poems 'jewels alternately delicate, barbaric, multicolored, rich, and simple'. It is not surprising that this 'poet of the absurd', who excelled in comic monologues such as *The Kipper*, was extolled by the Surrealists.

▣ Musée de la Chasse et de la Nature**
(Museum of Hunting)

60 Rue des Archives, 3rd arr. Tel: 42-72-86-42. Map ref: 18-C1
Curator: Mme Chantal de Guilqueran-Beaujeu
Open Mon. and Wed.-Sat. 10am-5.40pm; closed public holidays.
Métro: Hôtel de Ville, Rambuteau
Bus: 29, 67, 69, 70, 72, 73, 75, 96

This museum occupies 12 rooms in the l. wing of the Hôtel de Guénégaud des Brosses. Its aim is paradoxically twofold: on the one hand it shows hunting through the ages, and on the other temporary exhibitions to illustrate the protection of nature. From the Rue des Quatre-Fils one can admire a model garden in the French style dominated by the beautiful rear façade of the museum.

History of the museum

The Hôtel de Guénégaud des Brosses was built by François Mansart in 1656 for Henri de Guénégaud des Brosses, who was secretary of state and keeper of the seals. It then became the property of the Thiroux d'Epersenne family up to the mid 19th c. The mansion was later divided up and partially demolished, and was so dilapidated that it was threatened with demolition. It was rescued at the last minute by the intervention of André Malraux, then the Minister of Culture. Acquired by the City of Paris in 1961 and registered as an historic monument, it was leased for 99 years to François and Jacqueline Sommer who had it completely restored (1964-66) by the architect André Saller to house the Maison de la Chasse et de la Nature, which comprises both a private club and a museum; the latter was officially opened on February 21, 1967 by André Malraux.

Tour of the museum

45 mins.

Ground floor

Prehistoric weapons, hunting spearheads, hunting lances, knives, and other weapons of the 14th, 15th, and 16th c., crossbows and arquebuses of the 16th and 17th c; Flemish tapestries; *The Vision of St Hubert*, a 15th-c. Burgundian sculpture; a recumbent lion, a drawing by Rembrandt; paintings by Lucas Cranach, Tiepolo, Jan 'Velvet' Breughel, and Rubens.

On the staircase, works by Desportes.

First floor

A magnificent collection of hunting weapons, mostly firearms, from the 16th to the 19th c. (the Sommer and Pauilhac collections, principally from Germany and Central Europe). Note the powder flask made from a wild ox's shoulderblade.

Second floor

Hunting trophies from Africa, America, and Asia (ceiling of the African room painted by Lorjou). Fine collection of stuffed animals: bear, caribou, and elk killed in Alaska; animals hunted in Kashmir, Nepal, and India; elephant tusks. A set of Mexican terracotta animal figures. Asian engravings of hunter scenes. Lady's hunting rifle given by Marie-Antoinette to her mother, Marie-Therese of Austria; the hunting rifle of Frederick I of Sweden; an important series of paintings and studies by François Desportes (1758–1836), among them a large *Wild Boar Hunt* painted in 1725 for the Château de Virginie; paintings by Chardin and Oudry; a set of paintings by Carl Vernet (1758–1836); hunting rifle given to General Rapp by Napoléon I; rifle offered by the Liège armorers to the First Consul (1803); a set of Sèvres porcelain known as the *Déjeuner des Chasses*, decorated with hunting scenes, given by Louis XVIII to his nephew, the Duc de Berry (1817); *The Beaters* by Claude Monet.

Beyond the landing are the temporary exhibition rooms, which can be rented for private functions.

▣ Musée du Cinéma*

Palais de Chaillot, E wing, Place du Trocadéro, 16th arr.
Tel: 45–53–21–86. Map ref: 13–B1
Open Tues.–Sun. 10am–5pm
Guided tours (50min.) at 10am, 11am, 2pm, 3pm and 4pm.
Group visits by arrangement
Cinémathèque (Film Library): Tel: 45–53–21–86
Métro: Trocadéro
Bus: 32, 63, 72

This could be called a museum born of an obsession, for it was due to Henry Langlois's passion for the cinema that the museum came into existence. He managed with the help of friends to assemble most of the documents connected with this 20th-c. art form, a task that took many years and was achieved with no outside financial help.

History of the museum

Le Cercle du Cinéma, which later became the Cinémathèque, existed from 1936 to 1940, thanks only to the subscriptions and donations of cinema enthusiasts. It was not granted an official subsidy until 1945. Its center, which was in the Ave. de Messine, could be called the birthplace of the Musée du Cinéma. In 1963 the museum was given a projection room in the Palais de Chaillot where the lack of space forced it to consider finding a larger place of its own. In June 1972 Jacques Duhamel, then the Minister of Culture, inaugurated the Musée du Cinéma in the former premises of the Musée des Arts et Traditions Populaires.

Tour of the museum

To visit the Musée du Cinéma is, in the words of Henry Langlois, to go from the prehistory of the cinema to the cinema of today, for film is not quite 100 years old. The exciting museum is full of the atmosphere of illusion, from the anamorphoses (distorting mirrors) of the 16th c. to the emergence of the first film in 1894, Robert Houdin's *théâtre d'illusions*, and Emile Raynaud's *pantomimes lumineuses*.

All along the 525ft/160m of winding galleries, with their little rooms and alcoves, the history of the cinema unfolds in chronological order: magic lanterns, Asian shadow theaters, and various attempts to capture movement. There are examples of the most important photographic apparatus invented since Etienne Marey and Edison; a reconstruction of Méliès's studio at Montreuil; the first productions by Pathé and Gaumont; displays on the first stars; the first art film, *L'Assassinat du Duc de Guise*, with Berthe Bovy and Le Bargy; and a rich collection of Charlie Chaplin material.

American cinema's great moments are recalled with a Broadway melody decor. The directors Murnau, Pabst, and Fritz Lang represent German expressionism. For the French cinema, there are works by Marcel L'Herbier and Louis Delluc. Memorabilia of the stars are on display, such as the dress worn by Françoise Rosay in *La Kermesse Héroïque*; Man Ray and *L'Etoile de la Mer*; Cocteau and *Le Sang d'un Poète*; the costumes from *Les Enfants du Paradis*; the boots and coat of mail of *Ivan the Terrible*. Material on the gods, goddesses and idols of the cinema; photograph stills and publicity shots, posters, and examples of early film projectors.

A small cinema that belongs to the Cinémathèque shows rare films

(entrance outside, at the corner of Ave. Albert-de-Mun and Ave. du Président-Wilson: Tel: 47–04–24–24)

Musée de Cire

→*Musée historial de Montmartre*

▣ Musée Clemenceau

8 Rue Franklin, 16th arr.
Tel: 45–20–53–41. Map ref: 13–B1
Curator: M. Wormser
Open Sept.–July Tues. and Thurs.–Sun. 2pm–5pm.
Guided tours by request
Métro: Passy, Trocadéro
Bus: 22, 32

This museum, at the end of the courtyard of a bourgeois building in a quiet street, is entirely devoted to statesman Georges Clemenceau (1841–1929). La Société des Amis de Georges Clemenceau is based here.

Tour of the museum

30 mins.

The museum is in two parts:

Ground floor

The small apartment in which Clemenceau passed 34 years of his life and where he died on November 24, 1929. Restored in 1985, it is just as it was in his lifetime.

First floor

A gallery, renovated in 1970, displays documents, letters, manuscripts, other writings and photographs, all bearing witness to Clemenceau's prodigious curious mind. He was not only a great statesman, but also a doctor, journalist, newspaper editor, writer, art collector, and friend of artists.

Musée de Cluny***

6 Place Paul-Painlevé, 5th arr. Tel: 43–25–62–00. Map ref: 17–A3
Chief Curator: Mme Joubert

Open daily exc. Tues. 9:45am–12:30pm and 2–5:15pm
Group visits by request
Métro: Saint-Michel, Odéon, Luxembourg, Maubert-Mutualité
Bus: 21, 27, 38, 63, 81, 85, 86, 87, 96

The Hôtel de Cluny, beyond doubt the finest example of Parisian medieval architecture, was built by Jacques d'Ambroise of the end of the 15th c. beside the ruins of the 2nd–3rd c. Gallo Roman baths. It houses a very rich collection of works of art from the Middle Ages.

History of the museum

Around 1330 Pierre de Chalus, Abbot of Cluny in Burgundy, bought the ruins and surrounding land and built a house for visiting abbots. Between 1485 and 1490 the Abbot of Jumièges in Normandy, Jacques d'Amboise, turned it into a palatial residence with mullioned windows, turrets, and a Flamboyant Gothic balustrade with gargoyles along the base of the roof. In the 17th century the house was the residence of the papal nuncios, including the greatest, Mazarin. The house was sold for the benefit of the State after the Revolution, and had many owners, including a surgeon who used the chapel as a dissecting room. The ruins were covered in earth and turned into a kitchen garden and an orchard. In 1832 the house was taken over by Alexandre Du Sommerard, a State official at the Cours des Comptes (State Audit Office), but also a great art collector, and author of several works on the Middle Ages. With the German and English Romantics' rediscovery of medievalism this private 'museum' soon became a place where visitors could recapture the atmosphere of those times.

After Sommerard's death in 1842 his heirs sold the mansion and its contents to the State. Supported by the Commission des Monuments Historiques, they opened the *hôtel* as a museum in 1844. In 1819 Louis XVIII, who was interested in Classical Antiquity, had already uncovered the baths and the City of Paris had collected material for an important stonework museum. The State proceeded to acquire the ruins, and on July 24, 1843, decreed the founding of the Musée des Thermes et de l'Hôtel de Cluny, which was inaugurated on March 17, 1844. Edmond Du Sommerard became director of this museum and, with exceptional skill, continued the work of his father. After 40 years of administration he left a rich museum containing more than 10,000 objects, including the tapestries of *Seigneurial Life, The Lady and the Unicorn, The Story of David* (now in Ecouen); the golden altar of Basel), some unique gold pieces and the crowns of the Visigoth kings.

In 1907 the museum came under the national museums administration. However, this beautiful museum has been suffering visibly from lack of space for a long time. The transfer in 1977 of some of the collections (8000 objects relating to the Renaissance) to the Château d'Ecouen allows the visitor to take full advantage of the wealth of objects now displayed to much better advantage. Finally, in June 1977, the Musée de Cluny received the heads of the Kings of Judah and the column-figures from the portals of Notre-Dame, found in April 1977 during construction work at 20 Rue de la Chaussée d'Antin.

▷ Not to be missed

Ground floor
Flemish tapestries of the 15th c. (Room II)
Seigneurial Life, 16th-c. tapestries (Room IV)

First floor
The Lady and the Unicorn, famous late 13th-c. series of six tapestries (Room XIII)
The Pietà of Tarascon, 1457 (Room XIV)
The precious metal and enamel collection, 7th–12th c. (Room XVI)
Golden altar of Basel Cathedral, 11th c. (Room XIX)
The courtyard is entered through a depressed arch surmounted by the Amboise coat-of-arms (description of the *hôtel* →Quartier Latin, Boul. Saint-Michel).

Tour of the museum

1½ hrs.

Ground floor

Room I. Medieval costume accessories: shoes, leather objects, trinkets, buckles, and clasps. Tapestries: *The Concert, l'Arithmetic, Auguste and Sibylle* (the southern Low Countries, early 16th c.); emblazoned wooden column (France, late 15th c.); stable casket shaped like a saddle holster (France, 14th c.).

Room II. Tapestries woven in the southern Low Countries: the *Offering of the Heart**** in wool (International Gothic, early 15th c.), showing a courtier paying homage to a lady, is the earliest tapestry in the museum; *Deliverance of St Peter, Miracle of St Quentin* (mid–15th c.); *The Grape Harvest*. Head of the funeral effigy of Jeanne of Toulouse (Paris, *ca.* 1285). The most interesting object in this room is a folding table* which is in fact an altarpiece with folding panels decorated with very old paintings (Germany, early 15th c.) bordered in quatrefoil with the arms of the cities of the Holy Roman Empire.

Room III. Textiles, of which the earliest are Coptic from Egypt and Byzantium (6th c.); medieval embroideries, altar cloth (Rhineland, 14th c.). Three mitres* of the 14th and 15th c.; the wash-painted one is from the Sainte-Chapelle. A bishop's shoe (Sicily, 12th c.). Two

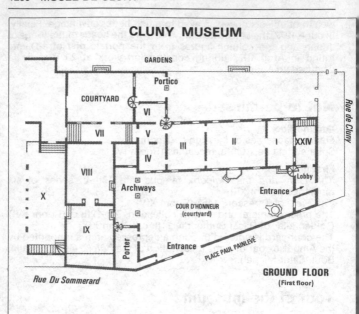

CLUNY MUSEUM

GARDENS

Portico

COURTYARD

VI

VII

V

IV

III

II

I

XXIV

Rue de Cluny

VIII

Archways

Lobby

X

Entrance

COUR D'HONNEUR
(courtyard)

IX

Porter

Entrance

PLACE PAUL PAINLEVÉ

Rue Du Sommerard

GROUND FLOOR
(First floor)

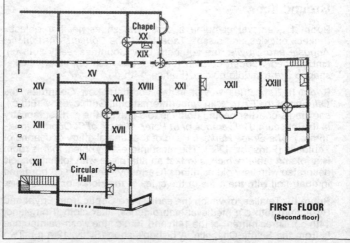

Chapel
XX

XIX

XV

XIV

XVIII

XXI

XXII

XXIII

XVI

XIII

XVII

XII

XI
Circular
Hall

FIRST FLOOR
(Second floor)

Musée de Cluny

precious embroideries**: *Les Léopards d'Angleterre* (The Lions of the Arms of England, England 14th c.) and a large embroidered panel from Grenjardarstad (Iceland), which depicts 12 scenes from the Life of St Martin (13th c.). Tapestry: sumptuous altar hanging, *The Resurrection*, woven in silk and metal thread (early 15th c.).

Room IV. Reconstruction of the furnishings and decor of a room in a typical manor of the late Middle Ages. The room is adorned with the famous tapestry *Seigneurial Life**** (early 16th c.) which consists of six hangings showing life in a noble household: *Embroidery, Reading, Strolling, The Departure for the Hunt, The Bath,* and *Scenes of Gallantry*. It has been noted that the halberdier in the scene showing the departure for the hunt, bears a strange resemblance to a character in the Dürer engraving *Six Warriors* (1495–96). He appears again in a tapestry in the Louvre, *The Miracle of Julian*, as well as in a tapestry with a rose background in the Art Institute of Chicago. Fireplace from a house in Le Mans.

Room V. Exhibition of 15th-c. English alabaster collection from Nottingham. A showcase contains fragments of Flemish and northern French altarpieces (15th and 16th c.). Window shutters, corbels, and woodworks of the 15th c.

Room VI. Display of stained-glass windows from Saint-Denis and Neuwiller-lès-Saverne (12th c.) and from Gercy, the Sainte-Chapelle in Paris and Rouen (13th c.).

Room VII. This room leads to the Roman section of the museum. Exhibition of engraved funerary slabs (13th–15th c.). Column-figures representing King David and a Prophet, undoubtedly originating from the Ile-de-France (second half 12th c.). The portal giving entry to Room VIII is from the Abbey of Saint-Germain-des-Prés. It leads to the chapel of Our Lady built by Pierre de Montreuil.

Room VIII. This room Is devoted to the sculpture of Notre-Dame de Paris and shows fragments of sculptures discovered in the Rue de la Chaussée-d'Antin in 1977. The 21 heads of the Kings of Judah** are the remains of the 28 kings carved about 1220 during the reign of Philippe Auguste, apparently by several different sculptors. The column-figures come from the portal of Sainte-Anne; until recently the Hôtel de Cluny fragments and those in the Metropolitan Museum in New York were the only known examples. The discoveries in April 1977 have enabled certain others to be reconstructed, due to the engraving published in the work of Dom Bernard de Montfaucon (of the Abbey of Saint-Germain-des-Prés) entitled *Monuments de la Monarchie Français* (1725). In addition to their interest as works of art, the discoveries in Rue de la Chaussée-d'Antin throw new light on the cathedral's statuary.

Room IX. Exhibition of Parisian Romanesque sculpture: extraordinary collection of capitals** from the nave of the Church of Saint-Germain-des-Prés (first half 11th c.) and from the nave of the Sainte-Geneviève church (early 12th c.), demolished in the 19th c.

Finally, head of an Old Testament queen from the central portal of the Church of Saint-Denis (before 1140).

Room X. Four statues** of the Apostles from the Sainte-Chapelle in Paris (before 1248), remarkable for their beauty and grandeur; altarpiece of Saint-Germer-de-Fly (13th c.), altarpiece of Saint-Denis (13th c.). Altarpiece portraying the Passion (14th c.), tombstones, mural paintings from Charlieu (later 12th c.). In the center: a group of decorated capitals (Catalonia, 12th c.); carved tombstones; capitals covered with carved animals and a Burgundian pilaster (12th c.). On the ceiling, 10 keystones from the vault of the chapel of the Collège de Cluny in Paris (13th c.). Very beautiful altarpiece representing the Passion from Plailly (Oise, early 14th c.); 13th- and 14th-c. ivories.

Room XI. Archeological room. Capitals from Notre-Dame at Corbeil (12th c.) adorned with foliage. Capitals with acanthus motif. Set of modillions (small brackets), formerly in the abbey of Saint-Martin-des-Champs (13th c.). Byzantine capital portraying three crusaders (13th c.). *Virgin and Child* from Notre-Dame in Paris.

Room XII. Grande Salle des Thermes Romains** (Great Hall of the Roman Baths). This room, constructed around AD 200, is of prime archeological interest since it forms part of the public baths adjoining the Hôtel de Cluny on its E extremity. This is the best-preserved part of the Roman site, which has the same layout as Trajan's Baths in Rome, which served as a model throughout the Empire. The ruins consist essentially of a large rectangular room 69ft/21m in length, 36ft/11.5m wide and 47ft/14m high, whose walls, 6ft/2m thick, are constructed of small unfinished stones alternating with red brick courses and covered with a thick coat of plaster from which the paint has disappeared. It is the only Roman room in France to preserve its vaults and it is from these that the hanging gardens of the abbots of Cluny were suspended and flourished until 1820. It is actually roofed with three barrel vaults; the ribbed vaulting rests on consoles carved in the form of ships' prows, which seem to show that the building could have been, at least in part, constructed with money put up by the powerful guild of Parisian *nautes* or boatmen. This room, lit on each side by wide semicircular arched windows, was formerly the frigidarium, the baths' cold room; to the N it contained a *piscina* or swimming-pool. The water serving the baths, which came from Rungis, 7.5 miles/12km from Lutetia, was fed to the room by conduits, the traces of which are still visible. Imposing drains encircle and cross the building. Around the main room are ranged several smaller rooms: five or six on the S side, two to the E, and two particularly large ones to the NE and NW. Below is a vast network of cellars. To the W below the level of the Boul. Saint-Michel is the tepidarium (warm bath), recently excavated, to the SW the caldarium (hot bath), where the hypocaust (underground furnace) was found in 1950. Also to be seen in this imposing room are four carved blocks from a pillar erected by the sailors in honor of Jupiter (reign of Tiberius, A.D. 14-37) found near Notre-Dame, and three other blocks from a pillar discovered near Saint-Landry and a statue of St Julian the Apostate.

The ruins were recently the subject of some important excavations that uncovered building foundations buried 6-17ft/2-5m deep in the rubble. At the same time restorations and later additions were removed, and windows, crudely blocked up in the 19th c., were reopened.

First floor

The first floor is reached from Room XI; on the staircase a number of epitaphs and tapestries telling the *Story of Lérian and Laureólle* (southern Low Countries, ca. 1525); altarpiece bearing the arms of Aragon.

Room XIII. Rotunda especially arranged for *The Lady and the Unicorn****, the celebrated, exquisite tapestries woven at the end of the 15th c. in the southern Netherlands, and rediscovered in the 19th c. in the Château de Boussac (Creuse). Five of these six hangings represent the five senses; the sixth, showing jewels being laid in a box, symbolizes the renunciation of worldly goods. The six scenes, on a flower-strewn red background, all depict the same blue-green islands of grass where one or sometimes two ladies appear, variously attired and framed by a lion symbolizing chivalric nobility and a unicorn (bourgeois nobility). All the tapestries bear the coat-of-arms of the Le Viste family from Lyons, who were officials of the royal family.

Room XIV** One of the principal rooms in the museum, it contains a large number of works (pictures, sculptures, tapestries) of the 14th and 15th c. Note the *Christ Bearing the Cross* in polychrome and gilded wood, doubtless Flemish, and dating from about 1400 (first showcase on l.); marble *Presentation in the Temple*, a work characteristic of the art of Charles V's reign attributed to either André Beauneveu or Jean de Liège. An early 16th-c. polychrome altarpiece from the Belgian Abbey of Averbode portraying the *Passion of Christ* and on the other side the *Mass of St Gregory* by Jan de Molder. A small altarpiece in the center of the room comes from the Duchy of Clèves and was carved by Arnt van Kalkar (*ca.* 1490). Religious pictures on display: *Scenes From the Life of the Virgin**, a rare example of English painting (*ca.* 1325) and finally the famous *Pietà* of Tarascon*** (before 1457) commissioned by Jeanne de Laval, wife of René I le Bon (the Good), King of Aragon and Sicily. The museum's imposing collection of Flemish and German sculptures is illustrated by Henrik Douvermann's *Virgin and Child* (early 16th c., Kalkar region), a Virgin and Saint John from a Bavarian Calvary (late 15th c.), the celebrated *Mary Magdalene*** from a Brussels workshop and a half-lifesize *Virgin* by the Master of the Madonna of Pietrebais (late 15th c.). Also a large collection of sections of altarpieces.

The tour of this room ends with a display of French sculpture of the same period from Champagne, Lorraine, and Normandy. Among the tapestries in the upper portions of the room note the *Departure of the Prodigal Son*, a fine example of Tournay work (early 16th c.).

Room XV. In the showcases, Alexandrian, Byzantine, Caraligan and Romanesque ivories from the 4th to 12th c., *Ariadne* (6th c.), diptych panel of the consul Areobindus (Constantinople, 506), objects related to various daily occupations: the table, the toilette, courtly life, war, the hunt, travel, the sciences, games (chessboard, ivory pawns), writing, books.

Room XVI. This room houses the museum's marvelous collection of precious works of art**. In the center of the room: crowns from Guarrazar, the golden crowns of the Visigoth kings, (7th c.); the Golden Rose of Basle, a tiny rose tree given by the pope at Easter, made by Minucchio of Sienna *ca*. 1330 for the first Avignon pope, Clement V; Gallic treasure. The exhibition then continues in chronological order: rock crystal lions' heads (4th–6th c.); censer (6th c.); casket reliquary (7th–8th c.); jewelry and other ornaments from the Roman era and late Middle Ages. Saxon portable altar (11th c.); cross from the Abbey of Clairvaux (late 12th c.); book cover from Novara (12th c.); Mosan and German enamel work, including the *Hildesheim Crucifixion* (*ca*. 1160–70). Southern French enamel work is represented by the magnificent *Christ* from the Spitzer collection. An example of Limoges enamel can be seen in the two plaques from the Grandmont altar: *Adoration of the Magi* and *Conversation between Etienne Muret and his Disciple Hugo Lacerta* (about 1189). The museum also has some beautiful precious metalwork: reliquary from the Treasure of the Sainte-Chapelle (1261): filigree crosses (13th c.); jewelry (13th–15th c.); cross from Barcelona (14th c.); Italian cross (second half 15th-c.); reliquary of Sainte-Anne by Hans Grieff, Ingolstadt, 1472).

Room XVI and XVII, in course of restoration.

Room XVIII. Choir stalls from Saint-Lucien in Beauvais (France, late 15th c.); statue of John the Baptist (Tuscany, 15th c.); altarpiece representing the *Crucifixion* (Germany, *ca*. 1500). Two *Books of Hours* are displayed on a pulpit. Their glass-encased pages can be turned to reveal the occupations proper to each month. Dresser (15th c.). Statue of St Anne with Mary and Jesus (Bavana, *ca*. 1510–20). Continuation and end of the hangings of St Stephen (below).

Room XIX** altarpiece origin Stavelot (Mosan art, *ca*. 1160). At the end of the room is the frontal of the Golden Altar of Basel Cathedral*** (*ca*. 1020), gift of the Holy Roman Emperor Henry II (represented with his wife, Kunigunde, at the feet of Christ, surrounded by three archangels and St Benedict). Only four of these 'golden tables' are left in the world. They are made of beaten gold on a core of wax and wood, with no other decoration. It was bought by the Cluny Museum in 1880.

Room XX** Chapel. This chapel, the old Oratory of the abbots of Cluny, is a jewel of the Flamboyant Gothic style, with its single central column from which the vaulting appears to fan out like palm leaves. The altar was situated in an apsidiole that projected into the garden. Spread across the walls is the famous tapestry the *Life of St Stephen*. The tapestry, woven around 1490 for the chancel of Auxerre Cathedral, at the expense of the Bishop Jean Baillet, comprises 12 panels divided into 23 scenes (→ Rooms XVIII and XIX for the continuation of the tapestry). In the clerestory, stone altar frontal and processional cross from the Grands Carmes of Paris (Carmelites, 15th c.). Bronze baptismal font (German 14th c.).

Room XXI***. Tapestry: *The Life of the Virgin*, donated by Léo Conseil to Bayeux Cathedral (late 15th c.), double lecturer for the presentation of illuminations (11th–15th c.).

Room XXII. Ironwork, locksmith. Wrought-iron objects. Kitchen utensils, grilles; lectern (15th c.), coffer, locks, casket. Arms and armor, swords and knives. Finally shields and *pavois* (shields with perpendicular indentation, Germany and Central Europe, 15th c.), bombards (stone-throwing cannon), and culverins (long cannon) (15th c.). Fireplace from a house in Le Mans. Tapestry depicting Tubalcaïn the inventor of metalwork (early 16th c.). Arms. At the end of the room is a remarkable picture showing the family of the magistrate and historian Jean II Jouvenal des Ursins (*ca.* 1445).

Room XXIII. Pewter and lead articles; children's toys, pilgrims' badges. *Méreaux* or Parisian corporation tokens, party badges, miniature toys. Misericords from choir seats from Saint-Lucien at Beauvais, showing artisans at work (late 15th c.). Baptismal font** (14th c.) from a priory in Saint-Sernin at Toulouse.

A staircase (statue of St Maurice, 15th c.) leads back to the ground floor.

▷ # The unfinished history of Notre-Dame

In April 1977, workers on a site in Rue de la Chaussée-d'Antin (no. 20) made a discovery that contributed significantly to medieval history in general and in particular to that of Notre-Dame. They uncovered 21 of the 28 heads of the Kings of Judah from the Gallery of Kings; 15 fragments of column-figures and more than 300 stones from various parts of the cathedral, some belonging to the portals of the N transept.

The royal heads had been torn down on October 23, 1793, and abandoned, with all the other fragments, in the cathedral yard, which had been turned into a vast public garbage dump. In 1796 Bertrand, a contractor from Rue de la Lanterne, bought all the stones at public auction. Meanwhile, Jean-Baptiste Lakanal, brother of the scholar and a member of the Convention who had voted for the death of Louis XVI, was building a mansion in Rue de la Chaussée-d'Antin, and thought of buying back some of the stones that Bertrand wanted to use in a large building project. Lakernal, a royalist and ardent Catholic, did this to preserve the stones and out of respect for the ancient law decreeing that sacred objects should not be destroyed, but buried or burned. So he buried them in his courtyard, face down, pointing south. Lakanal had serious business problems and was obliged to sell his mansion to General Moreau. Moreau, a fiercely anti-royalist atheist, had no suspicion that he lived in the neighborhood of the 21 royal heads, which were, in fact, not to see the light of day for another 170 years.

▣ Musée Cognacq-Jay*

Hôtel Donan, 8 Rue Elzévir, 3rd arr. Tel: 42–61–94–54. Map ref: 18–C2
Curator: M. P. de la Vaissière
Open Tues.–Sun. 10am–5:40pm
Métro: Saint-Paul. Bus: 29, 76, 69, 96

This intimate, elegant museum is entirely devoted to the 18th century. It was created by Ernest Cognacq and his wife, Louise Jay, founders of the Samaritaine chain of stores, to display their private collection. In 1929 it was bequeathed to the City of Paris by M Cognacq.

Installed until 1988 near the former Samaritaine de Luxe (see Grands Boulevards), the museum now occupies the Hôtel Donon, in the heart of the marais.

The Hôtel Donon was built in 1575 for Mérédac de Donon, Controller of the King's Buildings. The building is in the style of Phililert de l'Orne. Note the height of the roof, one of the finest roofs in Paris.

Tour of the museum

45 mins.

The museum contains an interesting collection of paintings, and other artworks, furniture, and trinkets that recreate the refined elegance of the 18th c.

Furniture and curios

Some marquetry work by Denizot and Topino; a desk in lemon tree wood* by Oeben; a pair of commodes by Carlin; an oval table stamped RVLC; armchairs by Tilliard; some fine paneling of the

Louis XV and Louis XV periods. Of particular interest is the museum's very rare collection** of porcelain beauty-spot boxes, scent bottles, various containers and other articles for the dressing-table in gold, enamel, agate, and so on. There is some delicate marble sculpture, including Falconet's *Nymph on a Rock*, and some Meissen porcelain*.

Paintings

The French school is represented by pastels by two great masters of the period: *La Présidente de Rieux*,* by La Tour, and a self-portrait** that shows the artist cutting an elegant figure; portraits of M du Coudry* and Mme d'Epremesnil** by J.-B. Perronneau. Interesting too, is a small picture by Chardin; *Queen Marie Leszczynska** by Nattier; some works by Boucher, including *Diana Returning from the Hunt*, (*ca.* 1745): *Perrette and the Milk Jug** by Fragonard; portrait of *La Camargo* by E. Vigée-Lebrun; children's heads by Greuze; genre scenes by Boilly; *La Coiffe Blanche* by Lépicié; and some drawings by Watteau.

There are also numerous other European paintings on display: *Balaam's Ass***, a work by the young Rembrandt; *The Feast of Cleopatra***, by Giambattista Tiepolo; sketch for the fresco of the Palazzo Labia at Venice; *San Marco* by F. Guardi; views of Venice by Canaletto. The Musée Cognacq-Jay is one of the few museums in Paris to possess 18th-c. English paintings: *Portrait of Mlle de Metternich** by Lawrence; *Miss Power*, pastel by J. Russell (1745–1806); some gouaches by Gardner; and Reynolds's masterpiece, *The End of Northington*.

▣ Musée de la Contrefaçon (Museum of Counterfeiting)

16 Rue de la Faisanderie, 16th arr. Tel: 45–01–51–11. Map ref: 7–A2
Open Wed. 9.30am–12.40pm; 2–5.30pm.
Groups by arrangement
Métro: Port Dauphine. Bus: 33, PC

In a handsome building in the Rue de la Faisanderie the Union des Fabricants has set up an unusual museum which shows how, from the Gauls who plagiarized the Romans onwards, creators and manufacturers have ever been the victims of imitators. Certain counterfeits are subtle, others less so.

Tour of the museum

30 mins.

The Union des Fabricants have got together an odd little museum in a beautiful building on the Rue de la Faisanderie. It shows how, since the Gauls imitated the Romans, inventors and manufacturers have always been the victims of imitators. Some forgeries are clever, others less so.

▣ Fondation Dapper

50 Ave. Victor-Hugo, 16th arr. Tel: 45-00-01-50. Map ref: 7-A2, B2
Open Mon.-Sat. 11am-7pm
General Secretary of the Dapper Foundation: Mme C. Falgayrettes
Métro: Victor-Hugo, Kléber, Boissière
Bus: 22, 52, 82

Tour of the museum

30 mins.

The Fondation Dapper, at the end of a courtyard in a bourgeois building built in 1910, organizes temporary exhibitions of traditional African art. Inaugurated in 1986, this museum is supported by the Dapper Foundation, which was created in 1983 in Amsterdam to bring together those who shared a love for African art and to honor Olfert Dapper, the Dutch historian and author of a famous description of Africa in 1686. The aim of the foundation is to promote the study of Black African civilizations by financing research, study visits and specialized publications. In 1986 two exhibitions were held: African Art in 17th-c. Europe and a survey of Kota Reliquaries. A library specializing in sculpture can be visited by appointment.

▣ Palais de la Découverte**

Ave. Franklin-Roosevelt, 8th arr. Tel: 40-74-80-00. Map ref: 9-A3
Director: M. E. Guyon
Open Tues.-Sun. 10am-6pm; closed Jan. 1, May 1, July 14, Aug. 15, and Dec 25. Groups by prior arrangement.

Métro: Franklin-Roosevelt, Champs Elysées-Clemenceau
Bus: 28, 42, 49, 53, 73, 80, 83

The Palais de la Découverte, situated in the west wing of the Grand Palais, is a science museum based on an original concept. It was created in 1937 by a group of scholars, including Jean Perrin, winner of the Nobel Prize for Physics, for the International Exhibition of Art and Technology. It was so successful that it became a permanent establishment under the direction of the national ministry of education.

The museum has remained faithful to its original aims: to illustrate the basic concepts of traditional scientific disciplines through live experiments. (On the history and architecture of the building, →Champs-Elysées).

Tour of the museum

1-2 hrs.

The aim of the museum is to stimulate visitors' interest by involving them in experiments. The principal fields dealt with are mathematics (including data processing and automation), astronomy, physics, chemistry, earth sciences, biology, and medicine. The museum is best visited in an unsystematic way; visitors should find the rooms and experiments that most interest them. In each department, museum assistants receive visitors at fixed times, in order to present the experiments and answer questions. Various audiovisual aids (illuminated diagrams, animated models, videos, and interactive computer programs) complete the exhibits.

Highlights

The Planetarium** (→inset) and the solar system gallery which bring together the latest information gathered on space probes.

▷ The Planetarium**

The Planetarium, which was completely renovated in 1979, has 270 seats. It can show the most beautiful star-studded summer night skies at any latitude and at any point in time. It is a poetic and thrilling 45-minute journey that carries the visitor to the very center of the universe. The projector in the center of the room, reveals all the astral bodies visible to the naked eye worldwide onto a hemispherical dome, 49ft/15m in diameter. By accelerating their movements it is possible to follow their trajectories. A special device also reconstructs a genuine lunar panorama. The visitor can admire the earth, sun and planets as seen from the moon, then journey beyond the solar system and observe each planet's orbit around the sun or follow the movements of Jupiter and its satellites.

(3–5 showings daily. Separate admission charge. Contact the museum for times. Tel: 40-74-80-00. Private performances for school groups.)

Electrostatics: Many astonishing experiments. Visitors' hair literally stands on end, and Saint Elmo's fire appears at their fingertips. **Electricity**: A section that includes a Tesla transformer of 1.5 million volts and a 7-ton electromagnet. **Nuclear physics**: Illustrated by a model of a PWR reactor (one third actual size); entry into the heart of a reactor; a particle accelerator enables materials to be irradiated and made radioactive. A **micro-computer room**, where you can bring your own software. **Chemistry**: high and low temperatures offer a wide range of demonstrations; the properties of liquid air; Moissan's electric furnace (1892). **Human and medical biology**: A room opened in 1985 (sponsored by the Fondation pour la Recherche Médicale) is one of the current gems of the Palais de la Découverte with, among other things, *L'Homme de Verre* (the Glass Man) and a show, *La Loterie de Hérédité* (the fundamentals of genetics) created by Jean Rostand using the latest modern techniques of control by computer. The youngest visitors will be attracted by the Salle Eureka exploratorium, with a series of experiments in which they themselves are the actors.

Temporary exhibitions, organized two or three times a year, explore such areas as topics in contemporary science, technical developments, and the history of the sciences.

▷ Additional information

Lectures every Sat., 3pm, by a specialist (for example, epidemics in history, quasi-crystals).

Cinema performances, Tues.–Sun (2:30pm and 4pm). Cinema Club, Sat.

Library, Tues.–Sun. (10am–6pm): scientific literature for the young and for specialists.

Photothèque photographic library, Mon.-Fri. 10–11.30 am and 1pm–6pm.

▣ Musée Delacroix*

6 Rue de Furstenberg, 6th arr. Tel: 39-48-63-95. Map ref: 16–D2
Curator: Mme Arlette Sérullaz
Open daily exc. Tue. and some holidays: 9:45am–5:15pm
Métro: Saint-Germain-des-Prés, Mabillon
Bus: 48, 63, 86, 87, 96

Eugène Delacroix, leader of the Romantic movement in painting, was born at Saint-Maurice on April 26, 1798. He moved into this pretty little house in the Rue de Fürstenberg on December 29, 1857 and remained there until his death on August 13, 1863. His previous principal residences in Paris were, in chronological order: 118 Rue de Grenelle, 20 Rue Jacob, 13 Quai Voltaire, 17 Rue Visconti, 58 Rue Notre-Dame-de-Lorette.

In 1952 the Société des Amis de Delacroix, founded in 1929 by the former tenants, was able, with State assistance, to acquire the apartment and studio where this small museum, now a national museum, is installed. Apart from personal mementoes of the artist (signed letters, documents, his palette) there are also temporary exhibitions of the work of the artist and of his followers.

Delacroix was, for Baudelaire, the 'true painter-poet'; with his ability to transfigure reality his work is versatile, complex, and astonishingly rich. Through passion and ardour his subjects are metamorphized in a very personal and subjective vision. A painter of the fantastic, he has sometimes been considered as a distant ancestor of Fauvism, since for him color is both a means of expression and an end in itself. His dynamic canvases paint terrible, glorious but always controlled passions.

Tour of the museum

45 mins.

The apartment

Delacroix's apartment is on the first floor between the courtyard and the garden. The room in which Delacroix died, the drawing-room and also the library overlook this charming garden. There are portraits of the Riesener family and of George Sand, several self-portraits, drawings, and watercolors, still lifes, animal paintings, as well as some studies whose strength gives them the beauty of accomplished work.

The studio

Set in the middle of Delacroix's romantic garden, the studio is also houses copies of the decorations by Delacroix for the ceiling of the Library of the Chambre des Deputés, a series of original lithographic stones for *Hamlet*. Throughout the year the exhibits are changed.

Musée des Deux Guerres Mondiales

→*Museé d'Histoire contemporaine de la BDIC*

▣ Fondation Dina-Vierny–Musée Maillol

59–61 Rue de Grenelle, 7th arr. Map ref. 16–C2
Métro: Rue du Bac
Bus: 63, 69, 83, 84, 94

This is a museum in the making, part of Dina Vierny's foundation. It will be installed in the beautiful *hôtel* in the Rue de Grenelle (where Alfred de Musset lived, 1824–30), in front of which is the *Four Seasons Fountain*, by Bouchardon.

The museum will show works by masters for whom Vierny was both friend and model, Maillol and Matisse, as well as the work of painters whose work she exhibited in her gallery in the Rue Jacob – Kandinsky, Pollakoff, Dufy, Russian avant-garde, and naïve art.

▣ Fondation Dosne-Thiers

27 Place Saint Georges, 9th arr. Tel: 48–78–14–33. Map ref: 5–A3
Library: open Thurs. and Fri. noon–6pm
Métro: Saint-Georges
Bus: 67, 74, 85

This private mansion in the Place Saint-Georges, where Thiers lived after his marriage to Elise Dosne, which was demolished during the Commune, was rebuilt in 1873. It was bequeathed to the Institut de France in 1905. The foundation organizes temporary exhibitions in the main ground-floor rooms and on the first floor. The library specializes in the history of France in the 19th c. (up to 1914). It has about 150,000 works. 1500 manuscripts and 120 titles of old periodicals. Access to the objects and pictures of the Masson collection (Napoleonic mementos) is possible on request.

▣ Musée Dupuytren

15 Rue de l'Ecole-de-Médecine, 6th arr. Tel. 43–29–28–60. Map ref: 17–A3
Bus: 63, 86, 87, 93
Open only to members of the medical profession: For an appointment apply to Professor Abelanet at the Hôpital Cochin or at the Centre Universitaire des Cordeliers, 15 Rue d l'École-de-Médecine
Métro: Odéon
Bus: 58, 63, 70, 86, 96

Tour of the museum

30 mins.

This museum is named after Guillaume Dupuytren (1777–1835) surgeon to both Louis XVIII and Charles X. He was also a pioneer of anatomical pathology.

An important collection of photographs and engravings are housed here, as well as parts of the anatomy that illustrate malformations and illnesses, preserved in jars; engravings, photographs.

▣ Musée Edith-Piaf

5 Rue Crespin du Gast, 9th arr. Tel: 43-55-52-72.
General Secretary: M. Marchois
Visits by appointment only, daily exc. Fri-Sun., in the afternoon
Métro: Saint-Maur, Ménilmontant
Bus: 96, 46, 69, 61

Tour of the museum

30 mins.

The association known as Les Amis d'Edith Piaf was formed in 1967. It has assembled an extensive collection of material relating to the singer – stage dresses, personal clothes, sculpture, paintings, and lithographs by Charles Kiffer, thanks to gifts by the parents of Théo Sarapo, Piaf's husband, and bequests from other singers.

These numerous mementoes have been on display since 1977 in two rooms of a private apartment. A true museum devoted to Edith Piaf and to the French *chanson* in general, it allows the public to see the stock of letters, photographs, films, books, records, tapes, and other treasures kept in the cupboards of this apartment.

▣ Musée d'Ennery*

59 Ave. Foch, 16th arr.Tel: 45-53-57-96. Map ref: 7-A2
Curator: M. J.-F. Jarrige
Open Sept.-July, Thurs. and Sun. 2-5pm
Métro: Porte Dauphine

Bus: 32, 82, PC

If one word could describe this museum it would be 'profusion'. The visitor is overwhelmed by the number of objects of greater or lesser value collected together in this mansion dating from the Second Empire.

Adolphe d'Ennery, 1811–99, a popular playwright author of *Les Deux Orphelines*, amassed here, under his real name, Eugène Philippe, these treasures which he wished should remain in their original surroundings. The exhibition has the charm of a private collection assembled by an enthusiastic amateur. It is a collection formed at a time when Far Eastern art was just beginning to attract the attention of collectors.

The collection of Far Eastern *objets d'art* reverted to the State in 1906. The museum came under the direction of the Musées Nationaux in 1943.

Tour of the museum

30 mins.

Most of the objects show daily life and popular beliefs of China and Japan from the 17th to the 19th c. They were fashioned by artisans according to tradition and with techniques that have now vanished.

The collections are housed on the first floor in four galleries: Chinese and Japanese statuettes representing real or mythological people and animals, classed by material, wood, clay, etc in the 1st gallery and by subject in the 2nd and 3rd (China) and 4th gallery (Japan). The 4th gallery has a display of netsukes, intricately carved ornamental buttons, used in Japan to fasten clothing and to hang medicine boxes, tobacco pouches, pipe holders and so forth from the belt; and kogos, small ceramic Japanese scent boxes.

There are also some large animal statues from Japan and China; dragons; wooden furniture inlaid with mother of pearl; Chinese and Japanese socles; and a copy on paper of a Japanese fresco of the 7th or 8th c. (ground floor).

▣ Musée de la Franc-Maçonnerie (Freemasonry Museum)

16 Rue Cadet, 9th arr. Tel: 45–23–20–92.
Open Mon.–Sat. 2–6pm; closed public holidays.
Métro: Cadet et Rue Montmartre
Bus: 39, 42, 48, 49

This museum, created in 1973, is installed in a very modern building of glass, aluminium and marble. It replaces the old pied-à-terre of the Monaco princes, which became first a concert hall, and was then bought in 1855 by Prince Murat to turn into the Grand Temple of French Freemasonry. The collections illustrate the history of one of the oldest European fellowships.

Tour of the museum

30 mins.

Some interesting documents are on display: the creation of Anderson's *Constitutions*, the arrival in France of the Order (engravings showing the Hôtel de Chaulnes in the Rue de Varenne, where the 1773 meetings were held); a showcase devoted to the highest ranks and the objects associated with them; the symbolic Freemason; portraits of personalities who have belonged to the Order since its creation in France (some of them unexpected); and finally, some letters (→ inset).

▷ An Ancient Order

Although Freemasonry was officially born in England at the beginning of the 17th c., its origins go back much further. The members of this secret order like to say that their ancestors were builders of cathedrals, and that the order stems from the medieval fraternities of stonemasons in England and Scotland.

It was in England that Freemasonry took a new and definitive direction. Religious and political persecutions gave rise to a deep desire for tolerance: Anderson's *Book of Constitutions* (1723) made Freemasonry a 'union between people of high moral standards and beliefs'. It was not a corporate association, like the medieval guilds, but a brotherhood united by philosophic principles and concerned with the enlightenment of society. In 1717 the first Grand Lodge was created in London. After the creation in 1725 of the first Continental Lodges, modeled on those in England, Freemasonry quickly spread through France and Europe.

In the second half of the 18th c. Freemasonry, the symbol of fraternity and liberty, encouraged the development of revolutionary thought. It was never again able to achieve this extraordinary influence, faithful as it was to its original principles.

Musée Frédéric-Masson

→*Fondation Dosne-Thiers*

Palais Galliera

→Musée de la Mode et du Costume

▣ Centre National d'Art et de Culture Georges-Pompidou*** (The Pompidou Center)

Rue Saint-Martin, 4th arr. Tel: 42–77–12–33. Map ref: 17–B1
Open: Daily, ex. Tues. noon–10pm. Closed Tues.
Métro: Hôtel-de-Ville, Rambuteau, Châtelet-les-Halles
Bus: 21, 29, 38, 47, 58, 67, 69, 70, 72, 74, 76, 81, 85, 96

The Pompidou Center's immense and unusual shape (for exterior description → Beaubourg) rises up in the heart of an area which has in the past been the setting for many great events in French history. Opened in February 1977, it had after one year counted over six million visitors – more than the Eiffel Tower.

The Centre Pompidou or Centre Beaubourg – its official name is shortened to one or the other of these – should be, according to Pontus Hultèn, the first director of the Department of Plastic Arts, 'an original and unique effort to unite and make accessible all elements of modern culture in one single place'. It aims to reduce, or completely end, the isolation in which until now every form of artistic expression has been, as it were, imprisoned. Striving to be accessible to everyone, it does not set out to offer a potted history of the art of our time, nor does it try to focus attention on a particular aesthetic point of view; on the contrary, it aims to present the art of today to the greatest number of people possible, and to show that art is concerned with the day-to-day life of everyone. The center also tries to establish a kind of personal relationship between the beholder and the beheld – while at the same time attracting a large number of people who seldom visit museums. Beaubourg is supposed to be a place for artists and the public to meet and exchange ideas, a platform for multiple activities. The Beaubourg Center aims to do in Paris something attempted in museums in Stockholm, New York, Amsterdam, and Copenhagen shortly after the 1960s, to bring to life things which, until now, have merely been preserved.

The departments and activities of the center are spread over five levels: the Musée National d'Art Moderne which, by law, is responsible for the State collections, the Centre de Création Industrielle (CCI), the Bibliothèque Publique d'Information (BPI) (Public Information Library), the Institut de Recherches et de Coordination Acoustique/Musique (IRCAM) (Institute for Acoustic/Musical Research and Coordination), and a department of graphic arts. No one facility in the center is given precedence over the others. A film library, an annex of the one at Chaillot, was opened in 1978.

Tour of the museum

2½ hrs.

Ground floor (square level)

This vast hall houses the reception area and bookshop; the BPI's current affairs room, which offers to the public a wide range of new books and records and a comprehensive range of the French and foreign newspapers and periodicals; the children's library; the Forum Gallery, which stages exhibitions of photographs, the cinema, and books in conjunction with the various departments of the center; and The Children's Workshop.

Le Centre de Création Industrielle (CCI) (Center for Industrial Creation). Set up in 1969 by the Union Centrale des Art Décoratifs, the CCI has become one of the departments of the Pompidou Center. On the one hand it deals with the relationships between individuals, spaces, objects, and signs and is thereby involved in the fields of architecture, urban design, product design, visual communication, and public works and spaces; on the other hand, it is the meeting point of industrial creation and the fine arts. In the Pompidou Center the CCI organizes temporary exhibitions in this gallery, in the mezzanine galleries, and sometimes in the Forum or in the galleries on the fifth floor.

The Children's Workshop. This is first and foremost an open space serving many functions, welcoming every year nearly 25,000 children between the ages of 6 and 13. The aim is to make the children aware of the most diverse forms of contemporary art through games, and other activities. The children are accepted either as part of a school group with their teachers, for courses in the fine arts, music, the environment, and audiovisual studies, or individually on Wednesdays and Saturdays and during the school holidays at workshops where they can make their own experiments, usually under the direction of an artist. The workshop also organizes exhibitions in which children are invited to actively explore some theme or material of the works of contemporary artists. Its work is extended beyond the Center by publications (books, games, catalogs), courses for teachers, educational exhibitions and portfolios which travel around the provinces and abroad.

Basement

The Forum: in the large space, which occupies the middle of the basement floor and the ground floor, the center's various departments organize spectacular events.

The Petit Foyer and the Grand Foyer, and the Petit Salle and the Grande Salle are multipurpose rooms used for all types of shows, films, conferences, debates, and meetings.

The Mezzanine

The Contemporary Galleries house exhibitions on current trends in art.

The CCI Galleries: temporary exhibitions (→ information room of the CCI on the ground floor). The Salle Garance is a cinema.

First floor

The Bibliothèque Publique d'Information (BPI) (Public Information Library).

The objective of the BPI is to promote access to information, and to welcome all visitors equally, favoring none, giving free, open, and informal access to its collections to everyone. Librarians and other personnel can be found throughout the library, as well as inventories of catalogs. The BPI can satisfy the encyclopedic curiosity of its users in many languages; its collections cover every conceivable subject. Using a variety of media, the library presents information in many different ways: books and periodicals, records, slides, video recordings, databases, microfilms, and microfiches. It also allows the study, in individual, self-operated booths, of 95 languages through 460 courses at several levels; it regularly organizes exhibitions, debates, conferences, as well as the Cinéma du Réel (Cinema of the Real) a famous international festival of ethnographical and sociological films which takes place in March each year.

The reading rooms on the first and third floors can be reached from this floor.

▣ Fourth floor: Musée National d'Art Moderne

The Musée National d'Art Moderne aims to bring together important examples in all media of the fine arts, both French and foreign, dating from the beginning of the 20th c. The display areas of the museum have been renovated by the Italian architect Gae Aulenti; the renovation was necessitated by the growth of the permanent collections and by an examination of the building itself, which showed the possibility of making better use of the space and lighting. The museum was completely reorganized; the historical collections (1095–1965) are now presented on the fourth floor, while contemporary art is displayed in the flexible gallery spaces on the third floor. The richness of the collections and limited hanging space give rise to frequent changes. You may find alterations to the foregoing.

History of the museum

The Musée National d'Art Moderne brings together the collections of the former Musée d'Art Moderne founded in 1937, set up in Ave. du Président Wilson in 1947 and directed by Jean Cassou, Bernard Dorival, and Jean Leymarie, and those of the Centre National d'Art Contemporaine or CNAC which was founded in 1967. Some important donors contributed to the creation of the former museum, including Paul Rosenberg, André Lefèvre, Eva Gourgaud, Marie Cutolli and Henri Laugier, Georges Salles, Raoul Laroche, Sonia Delaunay, and Brancusi; those who have enriched the new museum include Nina Kandinsky, the Mesnil Foundation, and Louise and Michel Leiris. A firm policy of acquisition has been followed since the museum opened in order to fill the gaps in its collections, especially with regard to non-French artists.

Fourth floor south: Fauvism, Pierre Bonnard, Henri Matisse, Fernand Léger, and Cubism

Fauvism .The term Fauves (wild animals) was used for the first time by a critic in 1905 to express his disapproval of the violent colors of these young artists, whose work upset the whole history of painting – 'Colors were becoming sticks of dynamite', as Derain said. *The Two Barges** by Derain: *Street in Marly-le-Roi* by Vlaminck: *Posters in Trouville* by Dufy, the l'Estaque landscapes* by Braque, pictures painted around 1905 and 1906, are typical examples.

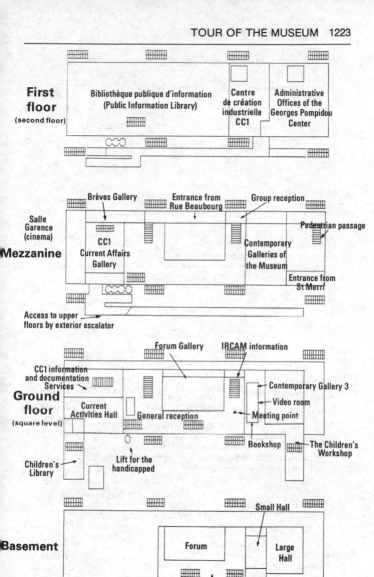

Georges Pompidou National Art and Culture Center

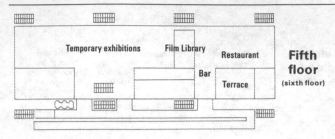

Fifth floor (sixth floor)

Temporary exhibitions — Film Library — Bar — Restaurant — Terrace

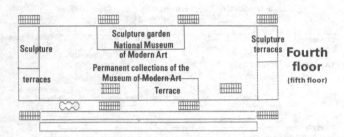

Fourth floor (fifth floor)

Sculpture terraces — Sculpture garden National Museum of Modern Art — Permanent collections of the Museum of Modern Art — Terrace — Sculpture terraces

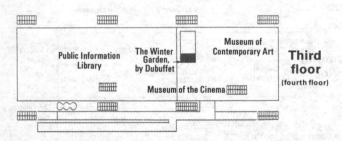

Third floor (fourth floor)

Public Information Library — The Winter Garden, by Dubuffet — Museum of the Cinema — Museum of Contemporary Art

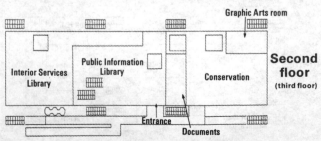

Second floor (third floor)

Interior Services Library — Public Information Library — Conservation — Graphic Arts room — Entrance — Documents

Georges Pompidou National Art and Culture Center

Pierre Bonnard (1867–1947). Bonnard's works are divided between the Musée d'Art Moderne and the Musée d'Orsay. On the fringe of all the trends, this painter was acutely aware of the endless variety of the effects of light on color; note his *The Bath Tub* and *Studio with Mimosas***. Sadness and anxiety are evident in the self-portrait* of the artist in a bathroom mirror.

Henri Matisse (1869–1954). The pictures in the first gallery bear witness to Matisse's everlasting search for expressive line and color: the *Dream*, from which there emanates a perfect serenity; *The Romanian Blouse** in which the process of simplification reaches a peak; the *Great Red Interior*. Matisse's plans for the chapel at Vence are on display in the next gallery. Then comes a collection of works from the years 1907 to 1917, including *Porte- Fenêtre à Collioure.** The very famous *Nude on a Decorative Ground* dates from 1925. In the following rooms is the *Sadness of the King*, a gigantic collage of cut paper with gouache. At the entrance to these galleries, the four powerful nudes known in English as *The Backs I–IV*, executed in bronze between 1909 and 1930, show the stages of Matisse's schematization of forms.

Cubism. The presentation of Cubism in this center, begins with the *Cheval Majeur***, a bronze by Duchamp-Villon that is a key piece of 20th-c. sculpture. In the following room, Cubism is represented by the works of its originators, Braque and Picasso, from 1909 to 1914. Braque's *Guéridon* (he did a series of table tops with still lifes) the first, so-called analytical phase of Cubism. Less austere, the *Man with a Guitar** by Braque and the *Portrait of a Young Girl*** by Picasso are masterpieces from the second phase of their works, so-called synthetic Cubism. Juan Gris's *Breakfast* also belongs to this period. At the side are works by Léger: *The Wedding*, Gleizes, Metzinger, La Fresnay, Duchamp, and Gris. On view in the cases In the corridor separating these rooms from the following, collages and sculptures in a somewhat Cubist manner by Gaudier-Brzeska, Brancusi (→ inset) and Laurens.

Gonzalez, Picasso and Braque after 1918
Metal sculptures including some in welded iron are displayed on the podium; here, the Catalan artist Julio Gonzalez, a friend of Picasso, has given free rein to his imagination. Picasso's still life with antique head is a synthesis between late Cubism and the classic style of his Harlequin pictures. *Confidences* with its distorting arabesques, is a tapestry cartoon. After 1918 Braque continued to pose the question of how to represent space by means of light.

Fernand Léger (1881–1955). The museum owns a rich and comprehensive collection of Léger's works. *Contrast of Forms** (1913) is a semi-abstract painting. After World War I Léger's interest turned to the representation of modern life, in such works as the *Pont du Remorqueur* and *Mechanical Elements***. He tended also toward monumental paintings, such as his *Large Composition With Two*

Parrots. His *Les Loisirs* is a homage to David, whose realism and classicism he admired.

Fourth floor North: the Great Movements from World War I to 1965

Kandinsky, Klee, avant-garde in Europe. Next to Kandinsky (1846–1944) are the paintings of Paul Klee (1897–1940) with musical associations, such as *In Rhythm** (1930) and views of Florentine villas. German Expressionism is illustrated by Kirchener (1880–1938); *La Toilette** is painted in an unnatural blue with broad, harsh brushstrokes and sharp lines in a flat space. Rayonism, a Russian abstract movement akin to Italian Futurism, is represented by its theoreticians Mikhail Larionov (1881–1964) and Natalya Goncharova (1881–1962). In the *Running Man* (1933–34) the avant-garde artist Kasimir Malevich (1878–1935) reverts to traditional representation.

The beginnings of Abstract art

The works presented here illustrate the various forms of abstract art: *New York City** by Mondrian, composed of syncopated visual rhythms; Malevich's *Black Cross*; Brancusi's *Sleeping Music*, a severe ovoid head. In Holland a new kind of abstract painting, Neo-Plasticism, was born under the influence of Mondrian (1872–1944) and the periodical he founded in 1917, *De Stijl*, in which he set out its aesthetic theory. It was a new geometrical abstract style, which did not use figurative elements even as points of departure. It is illustrated by Van Doesburg's *Composition* (1920), Vantongerloo, *SXR/3*, in iron and Rietveld's *Armchair in Painted Wood*. The German Bauhaus school (1919–31) wanted to unite art and industrial techniques as in Moholy-Nagy's *Composition AXX* (1924). In 1912–1913 Robert Delaunay (1885–1941) an exponent of the short-lived Orphism, painted brightly colored pictures such as *The Window**. His wife Sonia Delaunay followed the same path: *Electric Prisms* (1914). Kupka (1871–1957) quickly passed from Symbolism to compositions of planes, color and movement: *Vertical Planes* (1912–13). For the constructivist Pevsner (1886–1962), voids and transparent glass or plastic create the space of sculpture.

Figuration (1920 to 1930)

After his Fauvist period, Derain returned to classical tradition. The *Portrait of Iturrino** of 1914 stands out from a blue background reminiscent of those of David. After World War I, artists of all nationalities disputed the aesthetic prejudices of modern art. The portrait of the journalist *Sylvia Von Harden** by Otto Dix, with its extreme realism, is a legacy of the portraits by the ancient German masters. In all his work Chagall drew inspiration from the world of the small Russian town of Vitebsk, where he was born in 1887. He remained faithful to the brilliant tones already present in *To Russia, the Asses, and the Others**** and in the *Double Portrait with Glass of Wine**. The thick, nervous strokes and violent hues of the *Groom* and *Poultry* betray the anguish of Soutine. Rouault (1871–1958) searched for a new form of expression for the Christian message, as in his *Sainte Face* (1933). His early works, such as the *Girl at the Mirror*, with their realism and freedom of touch, are close to Expressionism. The corridor between these galleries and the following ones bring together Dadaist works of Picabia, another exponent of Orphism, such as *The Vitriolic Eyes*, Schwitters, Haussmann, *Spirit of our Times*, Grosz, Man Ray, and Duchamp. They question the conventional idea of the work of art with their humorous, provocative tone.

Surrealism

De Chirico (*Precursory Portrait of Guillaume Apollinaire*) was a forerunner of Surrealism. For the painters of this movement, traditional figuration allowed the creation of images that were unreal, unusual, dreamlike: *Partial Hallucination, Six Images of Lenin on a Piano** by Dali; Magritte's *Red Model*; Tanguy's *Summer at Hain* and *Hope*; Max Ernst's *Loplop Presents a Young Girl*. Miró and Calder: though deeply personal, Miró's work is strongly linked to Surrealism. Indeed, *Sunset Object* was owned by André Breton. The poetic *Bleu II* is a masterpiece. Calder's motives have the same poetic grace with the addition of a touch of humor (*Sharks and Whale*). In 1941 the emigration to the United States of Masson gave a new momentum to young New York artists such as Gorky and Pollock who familiarized themselves with the techniques of the Automatisms which Masson had been using since 1923: *Les Villageois* (1927).

Jean Dubuffet (1901 to 1985). By creating in 1948 the Compagnie de l'Art Brut (Raw Art Company) to show the works of psychotics, children and untrained amateurs, Dubuffet set himself against established cultural values. His paintings, crude portraits such as *Dhôtel* shaded in apricot or landscapes of *pâtes* (sand, earth, junk) such as *Traveller Without a Compass*, emphasize sensation and emotion.

COBRA (1948 to 1952). The COBRA group is represented by the works of Asger Jorn (*Woman of October 5*), Karel Appel (*Children Asking Questions*), Atlan and Alechinsky, distancing itself from any dogmatism. The name comes from the initials of the group members' homes: Copenhagen, Brussels and Amsterdam.

The Paris school. These two galleries, which show alternatively works by Fautrier, Bram van Velde, Staël (*The Roofs*), Poliakoff, Bazaine, Szenes, and Viera da Silva and Hélion show the originality of the Ecole de Paris, which was somewhat overshadowed by the vitality of American abstraction.

Figuration in the 1970s. Three independent artists are exhibited here. Alberto Giacometti produced Surrealist sculptures such as *Pointe à l'Oeil* and paintings such as the *Portrait of Jean Genet*, which shows the artist's obsession with the representation of the figure in space (*Standing Women*, bronze). Balthus is represented by *The Turkish Room* and *La Toilette de Cathy*; Francis Bacon by *Three People in a Room*.

Zoltan Kemeny room
Abstract Art in the 1950s and 1960s
American abstraction is dominant here: the colorful Abstract Expressionism of Sam Francis (*In a Lovely Blueness*), and the Canadian Riopelle; *Dripping* by Pollock; a monochrome by Rothko, a true modern icon (*Dark over Brown*). Alongside these can be seen works by the European artists Mathieu, Hartung, Soulages and Tapiès. Further on, the monochromes of Yves Klein are grouped together, as are the *Spatial Concepts* of the Italian Fontana.

The New Realism. This movement is a reaction against Abstract Expressionism and hard to describe precisely. Making use of objects from everyday life, the artists give them aesthetic value believing that art should partake of the world of things rather than merely reflecting it: accumulations by Arman (*Miaudulation de Fritance*); poster by Hains; machines constructed out of scrap metal by Tinguely (b. 1925); poetic assemblies of junk objects by Niki de Saint-Phalle (b. 1930); trapped objects by Spoérri, *The Flea Market*.

Pop Art. A term created to describe ironic works celebrating popular culture, pop artists introduced the consumer society into art, using collections of the most mundane objects (*Oracle* by Rauschenberg), transposing solid objects into soft forms (*Ghost Drum Set* by Claes Oldenburg, b. 1929), and enlargements of images taken from advertising or the mass media (*Electric Chair* by Warhol, 1928–1987). *Homogeneous Infiltration* by Joseph Beuys (b. 1921) is a cry of alarm: the piano, a symbol of spiritual life, has been enclosed before the public, in a felt skin, a symbol of isolation.

On the S side one room is reserved for temporary exhibitions of graphic art, of which the museum possesses a very fine collection kept in the Cabinet d'Art Graphique (Office of Graphic Art, 2nd floor). The terraces display (to the N) monumental sculptures by Calder (1898–1976) and Tinguely (to the S). Near the entrance, in the sculpture garden, are bronze works by Laurens (1885–1954), Ernst (1891–1976) and Miró (1893–1983).

Third floor

This floor is reserved for contemporary art. The arrangement of its shows, which are changed several times a year, does not allow for a comprehensive guide to the works on view. Only the *Winter Gardens* by Dubuffet and *The Shop* by Ben are on permanent display. The presentation focuses on certain important movements.

The geometric abstraction collection focuses on Herbin (1882-1960, founding member of the Abstraction-Creation group) with works by Vasarely, Soto, Dewasne, and Agam. Its American counterpart, Hard Edge Abstraction, in which the artists eliminated virtually every trace of painterliness, is illustrated by Ellsworth Kelly, Kenneth Holland, and Frank Stella. The second generation of Abstract Expressionism is illustrated by Joan Mitchell. Minimal sculptures by Carl André, whose works are emphatically horizontal, can be seen (*Assembly on the Ground*), and by Donald Judd, a conceptual artist (*Superimposed Boxes*), Don Flavin (*Fluorescent Lighting*), and Richard Serra (*Sheets of Steel*). In total contrast to this trend, which is wholly devoted to form, Conceptual Art questions the very content of art. Various forms are represented: writings on paper (Kosuth), and on an electronic screen (Jenny Holzer): striped canvas by Buren. The Support Surface group is represented here with works by Hantaï, Viallat, Buraglio, Rouan, and Jacquard. The tour ends with international figuration of the 1980s, with paintings by Baselitz, Cucchi, Gilbert and Georges, Kiefer, Alberola and Garouste.

The museum's cinema regularly shows films on modern art and films by artists.

Fifth floor

Large exhibitions dedicated to the most important artists and movements of the 20th c. are organized in the galleries. The film library (*cinémathèque*) is also on this floor as well as a restaurant and bar. There is a terrace which provides splendid views over Paris.

▷ The IRCAM

The Institut de Recherche et de Coordination Acoustique/Musique (Institute for Acoustic/Musical Research and Coordination) is housed beneath the Stravinsky fountain, between the Pompidou Center and the Church of Saint-Merri. It occupies an immense underground area of 43,000 sq. ft/4000m with soundproof studios, an information center, an electro-acoustic workshop, an anechoic chamber and workrooms. It is a vast center for research dedicated to developing, under the direction of its founder, the conductor and composer Pierre Boulez, new techniques for making music. The institute also has on site a unique multipurpose room with variable acoustics and volume: the Espace de Projection (Projection Space).

(For information tel: 42–77–12–33 ext. 4843).

▷ Daniel-Henri Kahnweiler (1884–1979)

Most of the works in the collection of Louise and Michel Leiris once belonged to the great art dealer, editor and writer Kahnweiler. From 1907 Kahnweiler was the advocate of Picasso, Braque, Derain, and later Gris and Léger. In 1914 he was forced into exile in Switzerland, his belongings were sequestered and his collection dispersed. In 1920 he opened another gallery displaying both pre-1914 painters and a second generation of artists such as Masson, Beaudin, Laurens, and Lascaux. As well as his activities as a dealer, he was also an editor. Before 1914 he published Apollinaire and Max Jacob and, after 1920, Artaud, Malraux, Bataille, and Leiris. Close ties were established then between Kahnweiler and Michel Leiris, who married Lucie Kahnweiler's sister Louise. Louise and Michel Leiris enlarged the collection with works by Miró, Asger Jorn, Giacometti, Bacon, and others.

▷ Brancusi's Studio

When Constantin Brancusi bequeathed his studio, containing his unfinished works, to the State, he asked that it be reconstructed in the Musée National d'Art Moderne. This was never satisfactorily achieved in the Palais de Tokyo, but in 1977 the studio from 11 Impasse Ronsin (now demolished) was reconstructed on the Beaubourg Piazza. Although the exterior is depressingly banal, at least the inside of Brancusi's home and studio can be seen. Coming to Paris in 1904 from his native Romania, Brancusi spent 32 years of his life between these walls – or what represents them – and died here in 1957. The studio apartment had become his living museum. Sketches, sculptures in bronze, stone, and marble and original casts, all enable the visitor to rediscover the closed and secret world, the pure forms, almost immaterial in their purity, of one of the greatest sculptors of our time. (Open Mon., Thurs., and Sat. 2:15pm–3:45pm, tel: 42–77–12–33, ext. 4727. Entrance in the Beaubourg Piazza).

▷ Wassily Kandinsky (1866–1944)

Born in Moscow, Kandinsky abandoned a legal career in order to dedicate himself to painting. After some Expressionist works (*Landscape with Tower*), in 1910 he painted what is believed to have been the first purely Abstract work. If his *Impressions* remained true to nature (*Impression V, Park*, 1911), his *Improvisations* (*Improvisation XIV*) and his *Compositions* (*Compositions with the Black Bow*, 1912) became constructions of forms and colors. He stayed in Moscow during World War I, but once Socialist Realism became the officially sanctioned style in the Soviet Union, he went back to Germany to teach at the Bauhaus (1922–33). During this period of his so-called 'lyrical geometry,' signs, colors, forms, and spaces acquired symbolic weight in his work. He fled the Nazis and settled in Neuilly-sur-Seine in 1933. Thanks to donations and the legacy of Nina Kandinsky, the National Museum of Modern Art has brought together one of the most complete collections of the works of this influential artist.

▷ Additional information

Guided tours
General tours of the center, Mon.–Fri. 3:30pm, Sat.–Sun. 11am.
Musée National d'Art Moderne: tours of the permanent collections by a museum guide, Mon.–Fri. 4pm and 7pm, Sat. 11am.

Free tours for unaccompanied children: Wed. 3pm.
Tours of the contemporary galleries by a museum guide Mon. and Thurs. 5pm.

Tours of the fifth-floor exhibitions by a museum guide: Mon. and Wed.–Sat. except 4pm and 8pm.

Tours of the BPI: Tel: 42–77–12–33, ext. 4426 and 4435.
Tours of the IRCAM: Tel: 42–77–12–33 ext. 4843.
Information on weekly activities:
Recorded message on the programs: tel: 42–77–11–12.
Museum information desk: tel: 42–77–12–33.

▣ Galeries Nationales du Grand Palais

Ave. du Général-Eisenhower, 8th arr. Map ref. 9–A3
Tel: 42–56–09–24. Map ref: 9–A3
Administrator: Mme Leboissetier
Open daily exc. Tues 10am–8pm, Wed. 10pm
Groups by prior arrangement. Tel: 42–96–58–30
Library: posters and works of art (catalogs) open Mon.–Fri. 10am–noon and 2pm–6pm; closed public holidays.
Métro: Champs-Elysées, Clemenceau
Bus: 49, 72

Since 1971 the Grand Palais has become a major cultural center thanks to the Galerie Nationales temporary exhibitions.

Between the two World Wars and up until 1963, the events

sponsored by the Grand Palais and the official Salons were extremely varied, but in 1959 the Ministère des Affaires Culturelles took over the responsibility of the Grand Palais. In 1964, André Malraux, having consented to the annexation of the Cours-la-Reine wing to the Faculté des Lettres et des Sciences Humaines as well as the school of architecture at the École des Beaux-Arts, gave Reynold Arnould the task of transforming the Grand Palais and developing the Galeries Nationales d'Expositions Temporaires. The work of creating this museum, was given to Pierre Vivien, chief architect for the Bâtiments Civils et Palais Nationaux, and completed in 1971.

The Galeries Nationales occupy the nave and the N, NE and NW galleries of the Grand Palais on various levels, including the basement. Their capacity is such that a number of exhibitions can be held simultaneously.

The Galeries Nationales plan to be a major international center for the presentation of original and exceptional works of art, and for exhibitions of different forms of creative expression.

Tour of the museum

In the reception hall (Door A; also open Tues.) visitors can find all the necessary information for the exhibitions (catalogs, slides, brochures) and various activities: access to Area 404 and Studio 84 (lectures, debates, history of art courses, exhibition of important cultural events, concerts; free daily film shows).

Over the last 12 years many important public exhibitions have been held, for example: Le Centenaire de l'Impressionisme (1974); L'Or des Scythes (The Gold of the Scythians 1975); Max Ernst (1975); Puvis de Chavannes (1976); L'Amérique Vue par les Peintres (America Through the Eyes of American Painters, 1976); Masson (1977); Courbet (1977–78); Le siècle de Rubens (Rubens' Century, The Age of Rubens 1977–78); Réalisme et Poésie dans la Peinture Russe (Realism and Poetry in Russian Painting, 1978); Claude Gellée, dit Le Lorrain (Claude Lorraine, 1983); Manet (1983); Watteau (1984); Renoir (1985); Estève (1986); Boucher (1986); Tanis, the Gold of the Pharaohs (1987); Treasure of the Celtic princes (1987–88), and so on.

▣ Musée Grévin*

10 Boul. Montmartre, 9th arr. Map ref. 17–B1
Tel: 47–70–85–05. Map ref. 17–B1
Open daily 1–7 pm, during school holidays; 10am–7pm
Métro: Rue Montmartre
Bus: 15, 24, 43, 48, 67, 74, 85

Visitors are advised to obtain, on entry, the guide brochure to the exhibits, available in several languages.

This is one of Paris's most famous and most visited museums. In its strange décor, enhanced with gold and marble, you will find wax models of the famous figures of French history and those of the present day.

Tour of the museum

1½ hrs.

Ground floor

The wax models follow one another through the centuries to arrive at Mitterrand, Reagan, McEnroe, Nureyev, and all the other outstanding personalities of our time.

The basement galleries

These retrace the history of France. Small scenes evoke Roland at Roncevaux, the assassination of the Duc de Guise, Louis XIV at Versailles, the arrest of Louis XVI, and so on.

The spectacles

30 mins.

On the first floor there are two shows to be seen: the Palais des Mirages, which takes you to the heart of the jungle, and the Cabinet Fantastique with its magician.

▣ Le Grévin du Forum des Halles

Forum des Halles, Level 01, Grand Balcony; Tel: 40-26-28-50. Map ref. 11-A3, B3

Open Mon.-Sat. 10.30am-7.30pm, Sun. and public holidays 1pm-8pm
Métro: Halles.
Bus: 38, 47, 67, 69, 75

This annex of the main museum on the Boul. Montmartre offers a guided tour of the *Belle Epoque* from 1885 to 1900.

Tour of the museum

40 mins. guided tour in French (English on request)

The museum was conceived as a *son et lumière* spectacle which brings to life the entertainments and personalities of Paris in the *Belle Epoque*. Victor Hugo and Verlaine greet visitors and take them on a tour of the world of Jules Verne, the Opéra, the Café Napolitain and even the Universal Exhibition.

▣ Musée Guimet***

6 Place d'Iéna, 16th arr. Tel: 47–23–61–65. Map ref: 8–C3
Keeper: M Jarrige
Open daily except Tues. 9:45pm–5:15pm
Groups by prior appointment
Métro: Iéna, Trocadéro
Bus: 32, 63, 82

Since 1945 the Musée Guimet, devoted to the arts of China, Japan, Central and Southeast Asia, India, Vietnam, and Indonesia, has been the Department of Asian Arts of the French National Museums. At that time its own collections, considerably enlarged since its foundation, were further enriched by the transfer of the Asian collections from the Louvre. The Musée Guimet has today undoubtedly one of the richest collections of Asian art and artifacts in the world.

Large-scale reorganization, completed in 1983, has made possible a more accessible and instructive presentation of its collections.

History of the museum

Founded in Lyons in 1879 by Emile Guimet (1836–1918), an industrialist, musician, and orientalist, under the name of Musée Guimet d'Histoire des Religions et des Civilisations de l'Orient, the museum was moved to Paris in 1884 when its collections were bequeathed to the nation. A huge building was then erected in the Place d'Iéna and the new museum opened in 1888. In the spirit of its founder, its purpose was to propagate the knowledge of Asian religions and civilizations, and Guimet further endowed it with a library which from the start comprised 13,000 volumes. In 1929 it was given the status of National Museum.

Before the end of the 19th c. the Musée Guimet had become the only institution in Europe to function both as a museum and as a research center for Asian studies, a dual vocation that Emile Guimet's successors have been anxious to preserve. This home of Asian scholarship owes its most distinguished collections (Grecco-Buddhist plasters and sculptures the Begram treasure, for examples, to the feats of archeological discovery achieved by Pelliot, Hackin, Foucher, Barthoux, and Schlumberger. The museum keeps in constant touch with expeditions in the field and with such Asian institutes as the Ecole Française d'Extrême-Orient. It is also the home of such learned societies as the Association Française des Amis de l'Orient (19 Ave. d'Iéna) and publishes two journals: the *Annales du Musée Guimet* and *Arts Asiatiques*.

Tour of the museum

1½ hrs.

Ground floor

Southeast Asian Arts (Cambodia, Indonesia, Thailand, Laos, and Burma) and Buddhist art from Tibet and Nepal.

Khmer Art (Cambodia). The Musée Guimet holds the finest collection of Khmer art outside Cambodia. Strongly influenced by Indian culture in its early stages, this art broke free early on and, after various stages of development which can be followed on this tour, reached its peak in the extraordinary carvings in the style of the Bayon.

Salle George-Coedès. Here is a large Hari-Hara** (the peaceful Vishnu and the terrible aspect of Shiva combined as a single being; 8th c. A.D.) and female statues whose accentuated thighs show Indian influence as do the Buddhas found in the province of Prei Krabas; 7th-c. lintels from Sambor Prei Kouk and Prei Khmeng; a Buddhist bronze (Maitreya, the Buddha of the future, 2nd half of the 8th c.).

Main hall. In the first half of the 9th c. the Koulen style shows the mastery of Khmer artists apparent in the fine statue of Vishnu, and in a male torso. The large Brahma shows the tendency of 10th-c. Koh Ker sculpture to stylize the expressions of the face and to thicken the limbs, while the late 10th-c. Banteay Srei and 11th-c. Baphuon styles, the latter with its apsaras (spirits of the sky), carved in high relief, display great delicacy and delightful realism. The hieratic pose of the statues is counterbalanced by the liveliness of the bas-relief figures, whose sensuousness and richness are the glory of the Khmer ornamentalists. Architectural ornament is represented by the Banteay Srei pediment** (2nd half of 10th c.), distinguished by the beauty of the modeling, and by fragments of architectural decoration and lintels.

Salle Louis-Delaporte. Architectural decoration in the styles of Angkor Wat (1st half 12th c.) and the Bayon (late 12th–early 13th c.), colonettes, acroteria, lintels, and stylized beasts (lions, elephants, divine serpents or *naga*); note especially a huge *naga*'s hood which, together with a lion rising on its hind legs and a *dvarapala* (gatekeeper), show the huge, ambitious sculptures of the late Khmer art. In the showcase: an erect divine serpent (*naga*), an elephant bell, the hook from a palanquin, a conch shell for ritual water purification, etc.

Salle Gilberte-de-Coral***. This display tries to re-create the atmosphere of the shrines and the forests that surrounded them. The Bayon style marks the peak of Khmer sculpture, in which faces are given that particular expression known as the 'Angkor smile', with eyes half-closed and the wide, curved mouth given a meditative expression. By the entrance there is what is presumed to be the portrait of the Javanese God-King Jayavarman VII, surrounded by Buddhist heads, and with a remarkable kneeling statue** in front, believed to be the posthumous portrait of his first wife, Jayarajadevi, depicted in the guise of Prajnaparamita, or Supreme Enlightenment. Other notable sculptures include a statue of the bodhisattva Avalokitesvara**, with eight arms and the body covered with small figures; a head with many faces, related to the figures decorating the towers of the Bayon at Angkor; a head wearing a crown; a head with small beard, perhaps of a follower of Shiva; fragments of a pediment, one decorated with a frieze of dancing *apsaras* (spirits of the sky), and a large standing Buddha, postdating the reign of Jayavarman VII.

Champan Art (ancient Central Vietnam). Although subject first to Indian, and then to other outside influences, the country had a very potent culture of its own. The earliest piece of sculpture is an 8th-c. figure of Vishnu riding Garúda, half giant, half eagle, 9th-c. The Dóng-duong style is represented by a large head of the Buddha** of a striking local type, by a bust of a *dvarapala* (gatekeeper), and a statuette of the bodhisattva Avalokitesvara. A male dancer and two baby elephants are typical of the grace and perfection of the 10th-c. Mi-so'n A 1 style. An impressive 12th-c. ten-armed seated Shiva of the Silver Towers and fantastic dragons from Thap Mam (12th- or early 13th-c.) reveal the trend of Champan art towards complete stylization.

Javanese Art is represented by Indo-Javanese heads, two of them (Buddhas) typical of the carvings at the famous 9th-c. shrine at Borobudhur; a 9th-c. lintel (Prambanam style); an Eastern Javanese bas-relief in which local influences predominate (13th–15th c.), and decorative carvings. The display cases contain bronzes, those of the 7th to the 9th c. being among the most important items in the museum's collections. There are the shapely yet hieratic lines of the standing statue of Avalokitesvara*** with 10 hands; Kuberá***, the god of treasure, set on a substantial base, and Wayang (shadow theater) puppets cut from leather.

Art of Thailand. The Stone Age is represented by fine painted pottery from Ban Chieng. There are stuccoes from P'ra Pathom (ca. 7th c.), while Buddhas' heads and a fragment of a stele display a facial type characteristic of the art of the Mon-Dvaravati kingdom (ca. 7th–11th c.). Khmer influences are paramount in the 11th to 12th-c. Lapburi school (multi-headed Avalokitesvara which may still be observed both in the U Thong and the first Ayudhya school; standing bronze Buddha. Nonetheless a purely Thai style is apparent in the Suk'ot'ai and Northern schools (Lan Na, 13th–14th c.): bronze Buddha. There is a large head of the Buddha (of a type also found in Bengal) adorned with jewels and a crown. Notable, too, are a cupboard** and a bookchest lacquered in black and gold by a method peculiar to Thailand, while on the walls hang traditional paintings and pierced leather panels.

Laotian Art. Thai influence is apparent in the large statue of the Buddha holding a begging bowl, and Burmese influence in the two standing wooden Buddhas, the one bejewelled (14th c.), the other lacquered, gilded and encrusted with jewels (18th c.), and in the 19th-c. manuscripts of religious texts and courtly literature with painted miniatures.

Art of the Himalayas (Nepalese and Tibetan). The Nepalese collections comprise very fine Buddhist paintings** from the 14th to the 19th c. with their warm harmonious blues and reds (Varjadhatu, mandala of the divinity Amoghapasa), wooden statues, and a small bronze statue of Queen Maya giving birth to the future Buddha). All the Tibetan work was executed (ca. 11th–19th c.) on the same traditional principles. The artworks are grouped according to their affinities within the pantheon of Tibetan Buddhism. First comes the benign or serene pantheon of Buddhas and bodhisattvas; in the display cases (gilt bronze statues) and on the walls (banners, embroidered or painted on cloth, called *thankas*). Narrative paintings depict the life of the Buddha Sakyamuni in a long roll or series of several scenes. In the Salle Jacques-Bacot (named after the generous donor of the bulk of the Tibetan collections) a large gilt bronze statue**, notable for its size, stands surrounded by paintings in harmonious, sombre colors depicting the demonic pantheon of tutelary and guardian divinities, the so-called 'angry deities', with their complicated iconography and fierce appearance, such as Hevajra, with eight faces and 16 arms, Lha-mo on her mule, and Yama, god of death; then a series of five paintings*** of the very highest quality depicting the Masters of Magic (Mahasiddha) and a series of ten richly decorative paintings of the Grand Lamas of the Trashi Lumpo Monastery. The next room displays paintings, sculptures, and various other objects connected with the cult of the Lamas and Holy Men (Padmasambhava, who introduced Buddhism into Tibet in the 8th c.; the poet and saint Milarepa, and the great reformer Tsong-kha-pa, d. 1419), as well as the cult of the book; jewels and personal ornaments, and musical instruments and such Lamaistic ritual objects as magical daggers (*phur-bu*), reliquaries, a bone 'apron,' prayer wheels, and libation cups.

First floor

Chinese Art (proto-historic and archaic periods); Vietnamese Art, the arts of ancient Afghanistan and Pakistan; Indian Art.

Chinese Art (Salle Gieseler): Exhibits include a collection of Late Neolithic pottery of the Yang-cho culture in Northwest China (2500–2000 BC) and a splendid group of jade, bone, and carved ivory*** objects from the 17th to the 3rd c. B.C., including ritual objects, ceremonial armor, and items of personal adornment, coming for the most part from the Gieseler and Michel Calmann Bequests.

Salle David-Weill. A substantial collection of archaic bronzes, including ritual vases and weapons, going back to the Shang Dynasty and coming from its capital An-yang on the Yellow River. A *Kou* vase shaped like a calyx; pieces of harness from the Shang and Chou Dynasties (11th–3rd c. BC); the Camondo Collection elephant**; a *p'an* bowl; a *li* vase with feet decorated with rams; a monumental *huo* vase of the Chou Dynasty. The Li Yu Treasure**, a notable collection comprising a sword decorated with jade, and inlaid with turquoise and gold, and ritual vases, goes back to the period of the Warring States (5th–3rd c. BC). In addition there are mirrors, pins, weapons, *huo* vases inlaid with red copper, vases decorated with hunting scenes, a collection of coins (5th c. BC – 2nd c. AD). A display case built into an extension of this room exhibits bronzes (the gift of Mme Vladimir Golschmann) which come from the Eurasian steppes, from northern Iran to Mongolia.

Salle Han. Items from the Han Dynasty (3rd c. BC–3rd c. AD) have been grouped together in a single room. They comprise ornamental and funerary jades, painted lacquer, carved stones from graves (lion, inscribed slabs), tomb furniture, and the decorative end-tiles from roofs.

The next room displays a range of large stone statues, notably a Buddha from Yun-kang; the head of the Buddha's disciple Kasyapa**, from Long-men; a meditating Buddha from Kong-hien (Wei Dynasty: late 5th–early 6th c.); the Buddha's two disciples, Ananda and Kasyapa dressed as monks (Sui Dynasty: 561–618); a *dvarapala* (temple guardian) of the T'ang Dynasty (618–906). In the display case terracotta tomb figures (*ming-k'i*) and a series of small gilt bronzes of the Northern Wei, Sui, and T'ang dynasties of which the most notable is a stele dated 518, depicting two Buddhas in mystic conversation; T'ang goldwork. The lacquer collection is one of the most comprehensive in the world and includes, most notably, furniture (cupboards, a traveling chest, an armchair, a screen), cups and boxes that exhibit all the techniques of lacquerwork (painting, carving, incising, incrustation). The same room displays jades, gemstones, and personal ornaments made of kingfisher feathers (10th–19th c.).

Ancient Vietnamese Art. The Vietnamese collections have been reorganized in a room near the Chinese Bronzes room. They comprise a large bronze drum** (2nd–1st c. BC), bronzes and pottery from the end of the Bronze Age to the beginning of the period of Chinese colonization and stoneware from the 11th–17th c.

Indian Art. Seals and and terracotta figurines from the Indus Valley civilization (ca. 2500–1500 BC). A terracotta sarcophagus standing on 15 feet, pottery and jewelry from a megalithic tomb near Pondicherry (2nd c. BC). From the Early Classic period (2nd c. BC–1st c. AD), during which the principles of Indian art were evolved, note the base of a Buddhist pilaster and the statue of a *yakshi* (female tree spirit). Among the exhibits representative of Mathura art is an item of prime importance, a very large torso*** in pink sandstone, full of exuberance, executed with great vigor; the Serpent King who brings the rains (2nd c.). The art of the Amaravati region is transitional between the early naturalism and Indian classical art and is represented by three elaborately carved, large bas-reliefs: *Sleeping Women* has a multitude of subjects in supple poses, the stone still stained by the red soil; a large bas-relief of the 'wounder' Mara (one form of Kamadeva, the love god) tempting the Buddha who, in accordance with the ancient rules of iconography, is represented by an empty chair; the *Great Renunciation* (the Buddha leaving his father's palace), in which the same rule applies and where the sculptors have simply carved his horse. Many other bas-reliefs are displayed in this room. Note the scale models of a stupa (a round tomb, reliquary, or memorial) and of a building showing the different methods of timber construction in ancient India. Two Buddhas show the ancient form of the Master when, soon after the beginning of Christianity, artists dared to depict him. One is a Buddha of the Mathura School (1st c. AD) against a pillar, the back of which is decorated with a lotus; it once formed part of the balustrade of a small stupa. The other is an Amaravati Buddha with his robe falling straight to the ground. From the Gupta period (4th–6th c.), held to be the classic period in Indian art, comes a headless standing Buddha, the supple lines of the body resting its weight on one hip, its robe so light and transparent that it seems to cling to the flesh; a head of Buddha with a calm, serene expression; and the head of the bodhisattva of compassion, Avalokitesvara. The large 9th-c. reliefs in the Gupta tradition came originally from a monastery in Orissa; a standing Buddha; the bust and head of a bodhisattva. Notice, too, a Hindu relief from South India of the Pallava Dynasty (ca. 7th c.) portraying the divine couple Shiva and Parvati; sculptures that decorated temples of different regions (note especially the god holding a child and the Buddhist steles of the Pala Dynasty, 8th–12th c.). Dravidian art from South India (10th c.) is displayed in two rooms. The first contains stone sculptures (female demons or Yogini, Vishnu, Shiva), the second, bronzes: the most outstanding, the Cosmic Dance of Shiva; Shiva as protector of the arts, etc.

Miniatures. The last room exhibits miniatures from the 16th–19th c.

In the center are those of the Mughal school, around them those from provincial schools (Deccan, Rajasthan) and Pahari painting (Punjab, Himalayas, Garhwal). A painting by the Dutch artist Schellinks shows the direct influence of the Mughal miniature upon European painting in the 17th c.

Afghan Art. The Foucher and Hackin Rooms are devoted to objects brought back by the Foucher mission (1895–97) and to finds made by French archeological expeditions from 1922 onward. The country stands at the crossroads of trade routes running from the Near East to India and China and its ancient art mirrors the aesthetic traditions of the Greco-Roman West, Iran, and India. Invasions opened the way to foreign influence and its continuance is explained by trade relations. The term Greco-Buddhist art is applied to those works inspired by Indian Buddhism and realized in what are very close to Hellenistic artistic terms. This art developed most strongly at Gandhara (Pakistan) from about the 1st to the 5th c. Gandhara sculpture is represented by items in blue-grey schist. Buddha is portrayed with a nimbus or halo and the face of Apollo, dressed in a heavy Classical toga. Later, as in the Sharbazgarhi bodhisattva, Indianization creeps in. The show-case contains narrative bas-reliefs portraying incidents from the life of Buddha and his previous incarnations; decorative bas-reliefs with themes borrowed from the catalog of Hellenistic motifs (children bearing garlands, Dionysiac revels, atlantes, acanthus capitals, etc.). There is a 2nd-c. AD pilaster and capitals from the fire-worshippers' temple discovered at Surkh Kotal in Bactria.

Salle Hackin.*** The excavations at Begram are of major importance both artistically and historically. The objects unearthed by Joseph and Ria Hackin provide striking confirmation of the regular trading relations between East and West. In the same room the Hackins found Greco-Roman, Syrian, Indian, and Chinese objects of the 1st and 2nd c. AD lying side by side. Greco-Roman items: bronze dishes and receptacles, plaster medallions in low relief, glassware classically shaped, blown in the forms of fish, decorated in relief or painted in the Hellenistic style, items of Indian origin: ivory plaques from furniture. These are of extraordinary interest, since the realistic shapes of the plants and animals and the sensuous grace of the female figures carved in relief or incised on them link them firmly with Indian art. Delicate white plaster figurines from the Buddhist monasteries of Hadda, although still influenced by Hellenistic art, show great skill and originality. One of the most outstanding exhibits is *The Genie with Flowers*, purely Classical in style, *The Great Renunciation*, a group of great charm and feeling, and the intensely powerful *Demon in a Furred Cloak*. Fragments of painting also show Hellenistic inspiration. In the 3rd c. AD Sassanid influences from Iran were found side by side with Greco-Roman influences, before succeeding them. Irano-Buddhist art is apparent in fragments of frescoes (boar's head) and blackened fragments of plaster reliefs from the Buddhist monastery at Bamiyan and in fragments of the frescoes which decorated the dome of the Buddhist monastery at Kakrak (ca. 5th c.) In the monastery at Fondukistan Iranian influences mingled with those of India (ca. 7th c.) as seen in clay statues whose rich ornamentation and elegant swirling poses have something of the Baroque.

Second floor

Japanese, Korean, and Central Asian Art; the Michel Calmann and Grandidier Collections (Chinese pottery and porcelain).

Japanese Art. The Japanese collections contain a substantial group of pre- and proto-historic items: Jomon (10th–1st c. BC) and Yayoi pottery (1st c. BC–3rd c. AD); bronze bells (*dotaku*), mirrors and weapons; the large glazed earthenware coffin of Kyushu (3rd–4th c.); *magatama* (jade and gemstone ornaments); *haniwa* (terracotta figures, often on a cylindrical base, which encircled the edges of funeral mounds) from the period (5th–6th c.) of the great tomb builders. The masks of polychrome wood and the dry lacquer bust belong to the resplendent Nara period (8th c.). Sculpture from later periods is most notably represented by two wooden statues of the Buddha, one standing (8th–9th c.), the other seated (Fujiwara period, 11th c.), and by 16th to 18th-c. Noh theater masks. Painting is represented by two fine portraits of priests of the Kamakura period (14th c.) and by paintings and painted screens of the Tosa and Kano schools (16th–17th c.). An early 17th-c. screen belongs to the category known in Europe as Portuguese Screens*** and humorously depicts the arrival of a European ship in Japan. The decorative arts which were so important in Japan complete this collection: lacquers deriving in part from Marie-Antoinette's collection; sword-hilts, netsukes, pottery; a fine set of pieces for the tea ceremony (*cha-no-yu*), and Imari, Kakiemon, and Satsuma porcelain.

Korean Art. Although the Korean section is somewhat scanty it does contain an item of major importance: a bronze gilt funerary crown** and plate from the Silla kingdom (3rd–5th c.), and jewels and sword-hilts from the same period. From the Koryo period (918–1392) some lacquer encrusted with mother-of-pearl, and pottery, most notably celadon ware, produced by a method peculiar to Korea (late 12th c.) called Sanggam. White and black ships were used in engraved patterns, willow trees, ducks, etc. and the celadon glaze was applied on top.

Central Asian Art. The Pelliot Room. Buddhist paintings discovered by Paul Pelliot in a cave in the Tuen-huang shrines which had been walled up since the 11th c., as well as banners and ex-votos on silk, coarse cloth, and paper, the most outstanding being the 8th-c. gouache on paper of a knight and his attendant: a picture of the Buddha's disciple Kasyapa, dated 729; depictions of the bodhisattva

Avalokitesvara (Kuanyin) dated 943 and 981 and of the bodhisattva Ksitigarbha as Judge of the Underworld (note the portraits of Chinese donors at the foot of all these paintings); a large painting of the Paradise of Amitabha** and of Mara and his demons attacking the Buddha. All these paintings show the persistence of Indian and Persian elements and the way in which figures and landscapes are gradually influenced by China.

The Michel Calmann Collection*. This is a magnificent collection of Chinese pottery from the Neolithic period to the Sung Dynasty with pottery and stoneware of the Han Dynasty (206 B.C.–A.D. 220), white porcelain, green-glazed pottery and black stoneware from the Sui (581–618) and T'ang (618–906) dynasties. Also from the T'ang Dynasty comes a fine collection of 'three-colors' pottery, the designs outlined in raised clay; statuettes, plates and containers. From the Sung Dynasty (960–1278) a long series of the green celadons, ivory-toned porcelain, Honan vases in the so-called Northern celadons, and black glazed bowls and *temmoku* bowls from Fukien province and Ki-chou.

Grandidier Collection. A very fine collection of Chinese porcelain: Han enamelled pottery; 3rd to 6th-c. proto-porcelain; polychrome enamels and early porcelain; Sung Dynasty celadon ware including the famous 11th-c. pot with the phoenix-head spout***; ornamental vases with bold designs painted in brownish-black on a creamy slip in the Tz'u Chou style; *kien* and *temmoku* tea-bowls, white porcelain from Fukien province and King-totchen, among the latter the 13th-c. Camondo Kuanyin**; Yüan Dynasty (1260–1368) blue-and-white china, including the outstanding Mei-p'ing vase***, decorated with dragons; Ming Dynasty (1368–1644) 'three-colors' pottery** and blue-and-white china from the Ming and Ch'in Dynasties. There is a substantial series of *famille verte* (from the reign of K'ang Hsi: 1662–1722), unglazed biscuitware, a large *famille noire* vase, a group of *famille rose* (from the reigns of Yung Cheng, 1723–35, and Ch'ien Lung, 1736–96), *millefiore* (thousand flower) vase, 17th- and 18th-c. monochromes, and trade porcelain.

▷ # Buddhism

Buddha: a prince of the Sakya tribe, for which reason he is called Sakyamuni, 'sage of the Sakyas', named Siddhartha Gautama who renounced his wealth and birthright to search for the way of truth. After extensive experiments with the asceticism common in his era, Siddhartha achieved enlightenment by simply sitting beneath a tree and meditating. He understood all life to be *dukkha*, usually translated as 'suffering', and taught that the goal of the spiritual life was nirvana (enlightenment, the elimination of all desire). The Buddhist religion developed from the lay and monastic communities inspired by the Buddha's teaching before his death in 483 BC

Bodhisattva: a sage who has halted along the path toward enlightenment before becoming a Buddha in order to help all sentient beings to achieve their own enlightenment.

Brahma, Shiva, Vishnu: the three main deities of the Hindu pantheon, forming three different aspects of the same godhead. Brahma is the creator of the universe. Shiva is both destroyer and builder of the universe, Lord of the Cosmic Dance; under either his terrifying, or his benevolent aspects, he rules the world. Vishnu, often depicted with dark blue skin, and often placed opposite to Shiva; his task is to preserve the world.

Not to be missed

Ground floor:
Khmer Art Collection: carvings from the temple of Banteay Srei (Main Hall); sculptures from the Bayon, noted for their famous 'Angkor smile' (Gilberte-de-Coral Room)
Javanese bronzes
First floor:
Chinese lacquer
The large pink sandstone Buddha from Mathura (India)
The finds excavated at Begram in Afghanmistan (Hackin Room)
Second floor:
The collection of Chinese porcelain (4th–18th c.)

▷ Additional Information . . .

Musée Guimet Annex (19 Ave. d'Iéna; for opening times contact the museum): iconography of Japanese Buddhism.

Lectures (tel: museum extension 321): special series (free) Wed. and Sat. 1:45pm.

Workshops for Young People from 12 to 18 years old (enrolment and information, tel: museum extension 321): introductory course in Asiatic alphabets and Indian dances (free) Wed. and Sat. 3–5pm.

Library (1st Floor: open Mon. and Wed.–Sat. 10am–noon and 2–5pm): Asian arts, archeology and religions; books in Asian languages; Tibetan books collected by the famous traveler Alexandra David-Neel.

Picture Library (3rd Floor: open Wed. 10am–noon and 2–5pm Mon., Thurs., and Fri., 2–5pm.

Record Library: (3rd Floor: by appointment): recordings of Asian music.

◼ Musée Gustave-Moreau*

14 Rue de La-Rochefoucauld, 9th arr.
Tel: 48-74-38-50. Map ref. 10-D1
Keeper: Mme Geneviève Lacambre
Open daily exc. Tues. 10am-12:45pm and 2-5pm; groups by
appointment
Métro: Trinité
Bus: 26, 32, 43, 49, 68

This town house in Rue de La-Rochefoucauld was bequeathed to the State by one of the leading Symbolist painters, Gustave Moreau (1826-98), with the wish that the apartment where he spent his last years in almost total seclusion, might retain its private character. The artist died on April 18, 1898; the museum was founded on March 30, 1902.

Tour of the museum

45 mins.

It would not be too great an exaggeration to call the Musée Gustave-Moreau a temple of Symbolism, in which with meticulous skill the artist created his obsessional fantasies. His imagination was a strange, romantic world peopled by biblical and mythological figures, visions, ghosts, gods, women in the artist's mind, the embodiment of evil, men, unicorns, and chimera – a world seen by some as typically *fin de siècle*, but in which others have seen the seeds of Surrealism. Moreau was an outstanding painter and a tolerant, intelligent teacher; it is no accident that his pupils at the Ecole des Beaux-Arts included Rouault (the museum's first curator), Matisse, Marquet, and Manguin. The Fauves, the Surrealists, and the abstract painters have always been considered the heirs of Moreau, whose rich, impasto paintings in jewel-like colors, and breathtaking non-figurative watercolors are housed in the museum. It is rare to encounter a painter whose work is so little known yet whose influence was so great.

The museum holds some 1000 paintings and watercolors of all kinds (mostly studies, sketches, or preliminary drawings), over 7000 drawings and tracings, and 23 more boxes of various tracings.

The most outstanding of these works are: *Evening and Grief* (ca. 1870; inspired by Baudelaire's poem); *The Ghost* (1874-76); *Dead Poet Carried by a Centaur* (ca. 1870); *Mystic Flower* (1880); *Salome Dancing* (1874-76); *Galatea* (1880-81); *Orpheus on the Tomb of Eurydice* (1890); *Jupiter and Semele*** (1895); *Dead Lyres* (1897).

Opposite the spiral staircase on the third floor note *The Triumph of Alexander the Great* (1890), in which the countries crossed by the conqueror are painted in black.

▣ Musée de la Halle Saint-Pierre

2 Rue Ronsard, 18th arr.
Tel: 42–58–74–12. Map ref. 5–A2, B2
Open daily 10am–6pm. Groups by arrangement.
Métro: Anvers
Bus: 30, 54, 85

The Halle Saint-Pierre, built in 1868 in a style similar to Baltard's, contains two museums (architecture → Montmartre): the Museé d'Art Naïf Max Fourny and the Museé Herbert.

Tour of the museum

1 hr.

▣ Musée d'Art Naïf Max Fourny*

First floor

This museum consists of the collection of M and Mme Max Fourny. They assembled a collection of naive or folk art, comprising 500 pictures and 80 sculptures by contemporary artists from all over the world. Max Fourny's work as a publisher enabled him to meet numerous artists whose work is on display.

A wide variety of media is represented in the collection: oil painting, watercolors, painting on glass, fabric, sculpture. The works on display are examples of 'naive' art according to the contemporary definition of the term. The elements of this style are clearly defined today: a simplification of reality; the expression of dream or fantasy;

bright, flat areas of color without modeling; a disregard for perspective; techniques inherited from folk art; and, unusually, a lack of professional training. Two famous exponents of this art are Rousseau in France and Grandma Moses in the United States.

The rotating exhibitions focus on selected themes, which means that the visitor's attention is drawn to paintings rarely seen in museums.

▣ Musée en Herbe

Ground Floor

(see also pp. 1249)

The Musée en Herbe in the Jardin d'Acclimation has no permanent collection, acting instead as a center for educative activities. Visitors are led through temporary exhibitions by means of film shows and guided routes. The museum's activities are of interest to people who live in the neighborhood, Parisians and tourists of every age. The community program organizes workshops relating to the exhibitions and the life of the *arrondissement*. Contemporary artists are invited to the museum to create works reflecting the theme of the exhibtions.

▣ Musée Hébert*

85 Rue du Cherche-Midi, 6th arr.
Tel: 42–22–23–82 Map ref. 21–B1, C1
Open daily except Tues and public holidays 2pm–6pm
Métro: Sèvres-Babylone, Saint-Placide, Vanneau, Duroc
Bus: 39, 48, 70, 82, 84, 89, 92, 94, 96

This delightful museum has been arranged in the fine Hôtel de Montmorency-Bours, built in 1743 and recently restored. The nobly proportioned town house with its original marble flooring, oak paneling, and elegant, pearl-grey silk wall hangings has a slightly antiquated but aristocratic atmosphere. Marshal Lefèvre was among those who lived here before the heir of the society painter Ernest Hébert (1817–1908), the Baron Uckermann, turned the house into a museum and donated it to the state.

Like his cousin, the novelist Stendhal, Hébert came from the Dauphiné. A pupil of David d'Angers and of Delaroche, he spent many years in Rome, which he first visited at the age of 22. In the many landscapes that he executed at this time the painter caught the luminous glow of the Roman Campagna in broad sweeps of light and shade. After a period as court painter under the Second Empire, Hébert returned to Italy as the director of the Villa Medics. Long before it became fashionable, he turned his back on the sophistication of Venice and Florence, the majesty of Rome, the mandolins of Naples, and went to live among the mountaineers of the Abruzzi.

The Musée Hébert has one of the very few collections of Italian landscapes in Paris. Note, too, that there is a very substantial body of the painter's work in the Musée Départemental de La Tronche (Isère), where Hébert died.

Tour of the museum

45 mins.

Ground floor

The first two rooms are devoted to portraits, including a whole series depicting 'La Donna Romantica', Maria Pucci, and a fine picture of Catherine de Bouchage as a child (1879).

First floor

Herbert's very fine and delicate watercolors of the Roman Campagna are displayed here. Other rooms, opened only in 1978, are devoted to the poetic and mystical side of Hébert's art, mainly large canvases influenced by the Symbolist movement.

▣ Musée National J. J. Henner

43 Ave. de Villiers, 17th arr.
Tel: 47–63–42–73 Map ref: 2–D2
Curator: M. Cheyssial
Open Tues.–Sun. 10am–noon and 2–5pm
Métro: Malesherbes
Buses: 30, 94

This small museum, devoted to the Alsatian painter Jean-Jacques Henner (1829–1905), is installed in the townhouse built in 1840 for the portrait painter Dubufe. It was converted into a gallery by Henner's nephews in 1920.

A monument to the taste of its period, the house preserves its exotic atmosphere and old-world charm.

Tour of the museum

30 mins.

Ground floor

The room provides a complete conspectus of the work of Henner, from his *Self-Portrait in a Cap* painted at the age of 18 to his last unfinished canvas of *Atala*. Famous for the golden flesh tints of the nymphs who inhabited his landscapes, the painter's public commissions were rewarded by numerous medals. In addition to such paintings as *Susannah and the Elders* and *The Spring*, exhibited in the Salons of 1865 and 1881 respectively, he was an accomplished portrait painter, as his portraits of children, such as *Paul Henner* and *The Italian Girl*, show.

First floor

The drawing-room, of which the main feature is a curious *machrabiyah* (Islamic balcony), displays the paintings of his maturity (*The Dead Christ, Madame Henner Reading*) which reveal the influence of Holbein upon this artist, who stood a little outside the mainstream of late 19th-c. painting. In the small anterooms are copies of paintings by Correggio and Proudhon, who both influenced Henner's work.

The second floor is devoted to Henner's residence in Rome (where he won the Prix de Rome in 1858) with small landscapes in the style of Corot.

On the third floor an exhibition of sketches show the painter's techniques.

▣ Musée Henri-Bouchard

25 Rue de l'Yvette, 16th arr. Tel: 46–47–63–46.
Curator: Mme Marie Bouchard
Open: Wed.-Sat. 2-7pm (closed the last 15 days of each quarter)
Guided tours the first Sat. of every month at 3pm
Métro: Jasmin
Bus: 52

Tour of the museum

1½ hrs.

In 1942 the sculpture Henri Bouchard (1875–1960) built this studio, where he lived until his death.

The artist's works are on display, and traditional sculpture techniques are explained by examples.

▣ Musée en Herbe*

Jardin d'Acclimatation, Bois de Boulogne, 16th arr.
Tel: 40–67–97–66.
Open daily 10am–6pm
Métro: Sablons
Bus: 73

Tour of the museum

45 mins.

The Musée en Herbe was founded in the early 1970s by three archeologists, Sylvie Girardet, Claire Merleau-Ponty, and Anne Tardy, with the aim of introducing children to the riches that museums had too often reserved for a cultural elite. Each year 160,000 adults and children come to discover art and archeology through reconstructions, games, and a whole range of temporary exhibitions: Egg and Feather (1983), a Gaulish village of the time of Astérix (1984–86), or Eléphantillages, which explored the world of mastodons, mammoths, and elephants (1987–88); Uluru, the aborigines of Australia (1988–1989); On the Pavements of Paris (1989). A second Musée en Herbe has been opened at the Halle St-Pierre.

Special routes through the museum have been mapped out to help children get the most out of the exhibitions.

Individual visitors: each child receives clues to a 'treasure hunt' on arrival, according to age.

For group visits, a tour of the museum, with the school curriculum in mind, is arranged, with hour-long slide shows and a supervised studio where children can draw and paint.

All reservations tel: 40–67–97–66 and 42–58–74–12, Mon. and Wed. 10am–5pm.

Games and other activities are arranged on Wednesday, Saturday and Sunday afternoons and during school holidays. (Tel. 40–67–97–66 and 42–58–74–12 Monday or Wednesday from 10am–5pm.)

The museum can also provide teas for groups of between eight and fifteen children. (Tel. 40–67–9766 and 42–58–74–12 every day from 10am–5pm.)

▣ Musée d'Histoire Contemporaine (BDIC)

(Bibliothèque de Documentation Internationale et Contemporaine:
Library of International and Contemporary Documentation)

7th arr.
Hôtel National des Invalides. Tel: 45–51–93–02. Map ref: 15–A2
Entrance: 3rd floor of Musée de l'Armée
Curator: Mlle Cécile Coutin
Group visits only. Temporary exhibitions.
*Métro: Invalides, Latour-Maubourg, Ecole Militaire, Varenne, Saint-
François-Xavier*
Bus: 28, 49, 63, 69, 82, 83, 87, 92

Tour of the museum

30 mins.

This museum houses the iconographic collections of the Bibliothèque de Documentation Internationale et Contemporaine (under the
aegis of the Universities of Paris) and was transferred from the
Château de Vincennes to the Invalides in 1973.

Its collections spring from the Leblanc donation (1917) and comprise works of art as well as thousands of posters, prints, medals,
badges, ceramics, and other items, reflecting the artistic, social, and
political history of the 20th c.

▣ Musée de l'Histoire de France**

60 Rue des Francs-Bourgeois, 3rd arr. Tel: 40–27–60–00 (ext. 2178).
Map ref. 18–C1
Open daily exc. Tues. 2.30–5.30pm.
*Groups by appointment. (Tel: Museum ext. 2297 two weeks before
date of visit.)*
*Appartement Soubise: groups by appointment. (Tel: Museum ext.
2340).*
Métro: Rambuteau, Hôtel-de-Ville
Buses: 29, 69, 75, 76

Founded in 1867 and constantly brought up to date, the Musée de
l'Histoire de France allows visitors to admire some of the most
beautiful documents in the history of France in a magnificent
setting. The museum occupies the former apartments of the
Princesse de Soubise on the first floor of the *hôtel* built for the

Prince de Soubise from 1705 to 1708 by the architect Delamair. He had the brilliant idea of preserving within the building what remained of the old Hôtel de Clisson (14th c.) and the Hôtel de Guise (16th c.).

Napoléon acquired the mansion in 1808 for the National Archives which had been organized during the Revolution (1790). Original documents from the central governmental agencies are preserved here, from Merovingian times to the present day.

Tour of the museum

45 mins.

Ground floor

The apartments (visits by appointment) retain in their entirety the matchless interior decoration** completed under Boffrand from 1735 to 1740 for the marriage of Prince Hercule-Mériadec de Soubise and the young Marie-Sophie de Courcillon, who was 40 years his junior.

The bedroom, with an alcove supported by two lofty columns, was painted by Trémolières, Van Loo, Restout, and Boucher. The oval drawing-room is decorated with eight stucco figures in high relief by Adam and J.-B. Lemoyne representing Astronomy, Epic Poetry, History, Justice, Music, Painting, Fable, and Arithmetic. The Prince's study has painted decorations by Restout and Van Loo.

The staircase leading to the first floor dates from 1844. Unfortunately it replaced the 18th-c. original, which the painter Brunetti had decorated with *trompe-l'oeil*. On the landing hangs a portrait of the Maréchal de Soubise attributed to Van Loo.

First floor

The chapel. Immediately opposite the entrance to the museum is the former chapel of the Hôtel de Clisson, built in 1375. When, in 1555, ownership of the mansion passed to the Guises, Primaticcio remodelled it (two arched bays and the opening of a third survive in the thickness of the walls). Niccolò Dell'Abate painted the walls and vaulted ceiling with a celebrated series of frescoes, which unfortunately disappeared in the 19th c.

The old guardroom of the Hôtel de Guise became the main antechamber of the Hôtel de Soubise. Here again none of the original decoration survives. Two tapestries, depicting the Emperor

Maximilian [or the Duc de Guise] hunting and woven from cartoons at the Gobelins factory under Louis XIV, recall the famous series which once hung here and now hangs in the Louvre. A large canvas at the far end of the room, *Typus Religionis* (*The Allegory of Religion*), painted in the 16th c. for the Jesuit Collège de Billom in the Auvergne, depicts the Jesuits steering the Ship of the Church toward the Harbor of Salvation. It was confiscated by the Parlement of Paris in 1762, during the suppression of the Jesuits, and came to the *hôtel* along with the archives of the Parlement. The room houses a permanent exhibition of key documents in the history of France from the Merovingians (Dagobert papyrus, 7th-c.) to World War II (Jean Moulin's report on the Resistance, 1940). In addition to autographs of famous people (Colbert's report on Versailles, the wills of Louis XIV and Napoléon, a letter from Voltaire on the Calais Affair, a poem by Louise Michel), are crucial documents from French history, such as the *Edict of Nantes*, the *Treaty of Westphalia*, the *Declaration of the Rights of Man*, and the *Walloon Amendment* which set the seal on the Third Republic in 1875. Others illustrate economic, social, and cultural developments (a document in Provençal, a table of river tolls on the Seine, a report by Sully on the exchequer, laws governing child labor and paid holidays). Photographs, maps, family trees, and explanatory notes set all these original documents in their historical context.

The state reception room still has the original overdoors painted by Van Loo (*The Toilette of Venus*), Boucher (*Venus Bathing*) and Restout. It is used for temporary exhibitions.

The princess's state bedroom*** retains the decoration of 1735 to 1737, with white-and-gilt paneling, and four matt-gilt, oval medallions depicting the loves of Jupiter. The two overdoors are by Boucher (*Cupid and the Three Graces*) and Trémolières. At the far end, the state bed is framed by two paintings by Boucher.

The oval drawing room*** (1735–39) is one of the wonders of Rococo art, a masterpiece of both Boffrand's architecture and Natoire's painting (*The Story of Cupid and Psyche*). Terrestial and celestial globes from the 17th c., gilded copper late-18th-c. orrery.

The princess's ordinary bedroom has overdoors by Boucher (*Mercury Teaching Cupid*), Trémolières (*Sincerity*), Restout (*The Secret* and *Prudence*) and Van Loo (*Castor and Pollux*). On the wall are two paintings, Restout's *Apollon enseigment à l'Amour à jouer de la lyre* (Apollo Teaching Cupid to Play the Lyre) and Trémolières' *Diana Disarming Cupid*. This room and the room beyond are currently devoted to an exhibition of 450 archival and iconographic items from the French Revolution recalling (in the first room) the course of events and, in the second, the achievements of the Revolution from 1789 to 1799. Included are such famous documents as the text of the Oath of the Jeu de Paume [Tennis

Court], Louis XVI's diary, the list of names of the deputies who voted to condemn the King to death, and the order for Robespierre's arrest; autographs (Louis XVI's will and the last letters written by Marie-Antoinette and Charlotte Corday); and the important decrees by which the country was reorganized, the *départements* formed, the metric system imposed, and primary education made compulsory; as well as contemporary newspapers, posters, engravings, songs, and caricatures.

▣ Musée d'Histoire de la Médecine

12 Rue de L'Ecole-de-Médecine, 6th arr. Tel: 40-46-16-93 (ext. 448). Map ref: 17-A3
Curator: Mme M-V. Clin
Open Tues. and Fri. 2-6pm; Sat. 2-5pm; closed Christmas and Easter holidays and July-Sept
Métro: Odéon
Bus: 58, 63, 70, 86, 87, 96

Housed in the former Faculty of Medicine building, the museum is mainly devoted to the history of the teaching of medicine and surgery in the 18th and 19th c.

Tour of the museum

30 mins.

On the staircase note the dummy in rot-proof wood created in Florence in 1799 by the famous Fontana. The museum displays a collection of surgical instruments: an amputation saw of the 18th c.; a lancet called the *bistouri de Félix*, designed by Louis XIV's surgeon at the time of the King's sinus operation; the case of instruments of Dr Antomarchi, used for Napoleon I's autopsy. Old medical treatises are displayed in cabinets, among them Ambroise Paré's treatise and Dürer's *Anatomical Treatise**. Portrait of Pourfour du Petit by Restout (1692-1768). Contemporary medicine is not forgotten: the culture of penicillin by Fleming; double cardiac catheter of Professor Cournand, Nobel Prize winner in 1955; the first gastroscopes.

▣ Museé National d'Histoire Naturelle**

57 Rue Cuvier, 5th arr. Tel: 40-79-30-00. Map ref: 24-C2
Director: Philippe Taquet
Open: Mineralogy and Geology, Mon. and Wed.-Sun. 1:30-5pm
Sun. 10:30am-5pm; Comparative Anatomy, Paleontology, and Special Exhibitions, daily exc. Tues. 10am-5pm. Ticket of admission

to the galleries not valid for the menageries, the vivarium, the winter garden, or the alpine garden.
Métro: Monge, Jussieu, Gare d'Austerlitz, Censier
Bus: 24, 47, 57, 61, 63, 65, 67, 89

In a setting of beautiful gardens (→Jardin des Plantes) and in a *quartier* of Paris that retains its distinctive character, these galleries provide their visitors with an inexhaustible fund of wonderful discoveries. Apart from the permanent displays, the museum mounts special exhibitions on specific themes.

History of the museum

The distant ancestor of the museum was the botanic garden planned by Henri IV and Sully, realized in 1626 as the Jardin Royal des Plantes Médicinales (Royal Physic Garden) thanks to the efforts of two of Louis XIII's physicians, Jean Héroard and Guy de La Brosse. Some 50 years later Colbert drew up the regulations by which it was administered, but it was not until the Enlightenment that what had meanwhile become known as the Jardin de Roi (King's Garden) received its richest endowments, thanks to Buffon. For 49 years (1739–88) Buffon was Superintendent of the Royal Garden; during this long career, assisted by Daubenton, he expanded and coordinated all branches of the natural sciences, considerably enlarging their scope through a worldwide network of correspondents, in the process gaining extraordinary fame. His work was enshrined by the Convention which, on June 10, 1793, turned the royal gardens into the national museum of natural history and endowed 12 professorships.

The galleries are open to the public, but the museum laboratories are reserved for researchers. Since Daubenton's day all the great French naturalists have worked in them: Jussieu, Fourcroy, Brongniart, Portal, Geoffroy Saint-Hilaire, Lamarck, Thouin, Haüy, Vauquelin, Lacépède, Cuvier, Chevreul, Milne Edwards, Quatrefages, and many others. At present there are 25 professorships as well as free public courses in drawing and photography applied to the natural sciences. The Musée de l'Homme and the Zoo at Vincennes are branches of the museum.

▷ Not to be missed

The Comparative Anatomy Gallery, which shows the evolution of the verebrate skeleton, and its collection of mounted skeletons of major mammals.

Mineralogy Gallery: the treasure house of the museum, with Louis XIV's collection of precious stones: the giant-crystal room.

Tour of the museum

2 hrs.

Comparative Anatomy and Paleontology Galleries

These are housed in a large building decorated with bas-reliefs in bronze and marble. Above the windows stand bronze busts of famous naturalists.

Ground floor

Beyond the entrance hall is the lecture theater, decorated with 10 panels painted by Cormon, depicting scenes in prehistoric times.

Comparative Anatomy Gallery (at the far end of the entrance hall)

36,000 specimens of vertebrates to illustrate the theme 'From Amphibian to Humans'. To the l. and r. of the entrance stand busts of Duvernoy and Gervais. Opposite are two views of the coelacanth (*Latimeria chalumnae***), the sole survivor of the group of crossopterygian fishes, some of which in the Devonian period made a decisive shift toward the evolution of vertebrates. On the l. is the only example in the world of a complete prepared skeleton: on the r. a lifesize cast of the fish. The gallery is lined with display cases, those on the r. devoted to the digestive systems of vertebrates, those to the l. to the comparative osteology of fish, amphibians, reptiles, birds, and mammals. The middle portion is occupied by a notable collection of mounted skeletons of the great mammals**, split into two groups by a central aisle. In it a bust of G. Cuvier, first holder of the professorship in anatomy, stands in front of the skeletons of marine mammals. The aisle also contains the display case used for special exhibitions, whose theme is advertised at the entrance.

Paleontology Gallery

The museum's collection of about a million fossils comprises specimens of all groups known to paleontology.

In the entrance hall is displayed the skeleton of the Siberian mammoth* presented to France in 1912 by Count Stenbock-Fermor and found in the Lyakhov Islands at the mouth of the river Lena. Although both flesh and skin had been preserved, only the head could be stuffed, and this stands on a small plinth to the l. Next to it is the skeleton of a giant stag from Les Tourbières* with the typical enormous antlers. Still in the hall, on the far wall, is the fine skeleton of an ichthyosaurus, a marine reptile of the Mesozoic era and the cast of the head of a crocodilian of the Cretaceous period from the Niger. This was the largest living crocodile; the original is in the museum at Niamey.

On the walls of the main staircase can be seen: footprints of the cheirotherium, a vertebrate of the Triassic period; a stratigraphical table demonstrating the vast range of geological time (the Cambrian period, when fossils first appear, beginning 570 million years ago); a large ichthyosaurus skeleton; a wall-chart showing how animal life developed (open to argument from several points of view); Mesozoic echinoderms (their modern descendants are the sea urchins and starfish); the echinoderms on the staircase are crinoids, which anchored themselves to the seabed by a peduncle, a characteristic nowadays found only among crinoids in the ocean depths.

First floor

On the first-floor landing note the skeleton of the paleotherium from Vitry-sur-Seine, a remote relative of the horse, first described by Cuvier from remains found in Montmartre; dinotherium heads (these elephant-like creatures strangely enough had their tusks growing from the lower jaw); and the skeleton of a chalicotherium, a peculiar animal with ungulate teeth and clawed feet.

The small room from which the main gallery leads, is devoted to the history of paleontology. Notable exhibits include the small oppossum found by Cuvier in the Montmartre gypsum beds and identified as such from the two special pelvic bones that supported the marsupial pouch; a mastodon's tooth described by Buffon; a fragment of bone from a proboscidian* (elephant family), found during the reign of Louis XIII and then thought to be the bone of a giant, and, more specifically, of the gigantic king of the Cimbri, Teutobocchus, who fought with Marius; various mastodon bones presented to France by Thomas Jefferson. A bust of Gaudry, the eminent 19th-c. French paleontologist and one of the earliest Darwinians, looks down on the gallery that he founded.

In the gallery itself the large exhibits occupy the center, with the earliest at the entrance and the more recent geological specimens at the far end. Notable among these large exhibits are the head- and shoulder-plates of armored fish (arthrodires, titanichthys); the cast of a stegocephalus (unlike this gigantic fossil, today such amphibians as newts and frogs are small sized); from Morocco the huge heads of metoposaurus (Stegocephalia); from South Africa the skeleton of a lystrosaurus, a large reptile with some features foreshadowing the mammals; from the United States, a gift to France in 1912, the cast of a diplodocus, a reptile some 82ft/25m long from the Cretaceous period and apparently warm-blooded; from the Sahara the gigantic vertebra of a dinosaur (even larger than that of diplodocus); a large marine reptile of the Mesozoic era with limbs ending in paddles; the plesiosaurus; the cast of the skeleton of an iguanodon (a mass of these huge reptiles was discovered near Mons in Belgium and the skeletons of a regular herd of the creatures are exhibited in the museum in Brussels); the head of a tyrannosaurus, a Mesozoic reptile with numerous large teeth and, at its feet on the diplodocus stand, its Mongolian counterpart, the tarbosaurus; the head of a huge lizard, found near Maastricht at the end of the 18th c., looted by Napoléon's troops, and named mosasaurus (Meuse-lizard); various ichthyosaurus skeletons, some containing the skeletons of smaller specimens, doubtless their young, for the ichthyosaurus was viviparous; the skeleton of a mastodon, animals differing from present-day elephants by their flatter, elongated skulls, their simpler tooth forms and the fact, too, that they often had tusks growing from both upper and lower jaws (*Mastodon angustidens*); giant South American mammals, zoologically related to present-day armadillos; the huge shells of the glyptodon and a gigantic megatherium skeleton (both creatures being comparatively recent in geological time and only extinct within the last few thousand years; the Megatherium already described by Cuvier, was discovered in 1789; the skeleton of the now extinct giant elephant (*Elephas meridionalis*, not the mammoth) found at Durfort (Gard); the skeleton of a woolly rhinoceros with an engraving copied from a prehistoric cave drawing; a small case containing the head of a sabre-toothed tiger with the characteristically elongated canines used like daggers when attacking its prey; skeletons of the giant stag from Les Tourbières with its enormous spread of antlers, and of its unantlered mate; skeletons of the fossil remains of the aepyornis from Madagascar and the diornis from New Zealand, giant birds something like ostriches. A small case contains the egg of the aepyornis, a bird only extinct within the last 2000 years and contemporary with the earliest inhabitants of Madagascar.

The cases along the walls to the r. of the gallery and on the far wall facing the entrance, are devoted to the evolution of the animal kingdom; note especially cases 70 (dinosaur's egg), 104 (evolution of the horse), 109 and 111 (casts of skull cavities which to some extent allow one to reconstruct the brains of extinct animals). To the l. of the entrance stand cases containing recent acquisitions and displays of fossil vertebrates from the principal fossil beds. Of these the museum holds important collections: Autun (case 27), Montmartre including the specimens originally discovered by Cuvier (case 59), phosphorites from the Quercy, including a naturally mummified frog (case 43), from Sansan (case 59), Pikermi in Greece (case 73), Montpellier (case 70), and so on.

Second floor

The entrance hall is devoted to the paleontology of the Paris Basin; the fossils are classified in cases both zoologically and by the beds from which they were taken. The cases contain: a giant cerithium; models of the Paris Basin during the Tertiary era with a wall chart of the flora at its start. There are geological maps, including a relief map of the basin with cutaways to show the main geological strata to be found there. On the balcony there is an exhibition of the paleontology of invertebrate fossils, containing some of the oldest known specimens, with explanations of fossilization and the classification of the main groups. Particularly noteworthy is the giant dragonfly (meganeura) from the Commentry Basin.

Paleobotanical Gallery (plant fossils)

The purpose of this gallery is to recreate the vegetable kingdom from the first appearance of plants on earth.

The most beautiful fossils discovered in sedimentary rocks from every geological era have been selected as specimens of each of the groups that comprise the vegetable kingdom. It is thus possible to follow the changes and the evolutionary stages in plant life over the ages. Here, for example, can be seen the earliest forerunners of living algae stromatolites* from about 2000 million years ago. There are fossil specimens of wood and impressions of foliage, of fern and other extinct trees (sigillaria, lepidodendron). A score of models faithfully reconstruct the types of tree extant in the Paleozoic and Mesozoic eras, while a series of dioramas shows the plant life of each geological period by depicting a landscape most typical of it.

This permanent exhibition is designed to satisfy everyone from the expert in plant paleontology to the novice on a weekend excursion to the Jardin des Plantes.

Botanic Gallery

Built in 1935 by the architect Chaussemiche, the collections that the gallery houses stem from the gifts of Adolphe-Théodore Brongniart (1832) supplemented by that of Robillard d'Argentelle, with other collections that swelled the historic herbals of Adanson, Jussieu, and Lamarck. At the far end of the botanic gallery is the massive trunk of the old Robinia or false acacia, the first to be planted in Europe, by Vespasien Robin in 1601. Beside it stands the Table de Plaisanterie, two tonnes of shell-encrusted limestone, found 6ft/2m down in the forest of Chantilly thanks to the brood mare whose name it bears.

Mineralogical and Geological Galleries

These galleries occupy a building flanked by beds of iris and roses erected in 1841, with two rows of Doric columns and pediments sculpted by Pradier. In the middle of the rose garden in front of the building stands Charles Depaty's marble statue of Venus Genetrix (1810). Beyond it may be seen the first Pagoda tree (sophora) planted in France (1747). The entrance is under the r. pediment, where some fine mineral specimens are on display.

The galleries were reopened to the public in July 1967 after restoration and reorganization.

Main Gallery (l.)

At either end oil paintings by Rémond depict the wonders of nature. In the center of the gallery stand marble statues of Cuvier by David d'Angers (1788–1856 r.) and (l.) of Haüy by Brion. On the r. is a collection of minerals from Madagascar. The enormous piece of Swiss quartz presented by Napoléon and Romé de l'Isle's historic collection of specimens of crystal formations (1772). On the l. is the collection of American minerals presented in 1903 by Pierpont Morgan and two petrified tree trunks from Arizona.

Great hall or vestibule

Frescoes depicting polar scenes by Biard. In the center is a Carrara marble table inlaid with semiprecious stones (16th c., Florentine).

The mineralogical collection of some 251,000 specimens is displayed in cases round and against the walls of the main gallery. The first set of these cases is devoted to the history of mineralogy in an instructional display; beyond them the specimens are arranged by crystalographic classification. The museum's notable Treasury*** contains 1000 precious stones along with the gems and numerous jeweled *objets d'art* from Louis XIV's collections, together with the gold and platinum nuggets presented by the Russian Czars.

The extraordinary Giant Crystal Room*** (to the r. of the main entrance) was opened in 1987. It is the only collection of its kind in the world.

The collection of meteorites is displayed in the central area of the main gallery and comprises 2500 specimens from 650 strikes, in particular those at La Caille (Alpes-Maritimes), Tamenit (Sahara), and Cohahuila and Charcas (Mexico). In the aisle are two cases crowned by veined marble vases with gilt-bronze mounts, containing collections of cut gems and in particular the collection of precious stones that belonged to R. J. Haüy.

The cases along the central and the upper transverse aisles are devoted to geology and contain what is perhaps the most complete collection in Europe of classified stratigraphy, with about 10,000 specimens. Starting from the r. by the library the strata are classified as follows: Precambrian, Cambrian, Silurian, Devonian, Carboniferous, Permian, Triassic, Jurassic, Cretaceous, Tertiary, Quaternary, and Recent. There is a collection of rock specimens and another important geographical and paleontological collection covering the Paris Basin and the former French colonies.

At the far end of the mineralogical galleries there is an exit under the archway which brings the visitor out at the SW edge of the museum complex into a small court with Buffon's house on the l. Buffon bought the property in 1772, for use when he stayed in Paris, and died there in 1788. There is an entrance to the gardens themselves at the junction of the Rue Buffon and the Rue Geoffroy-Saint-Hilaire.

The Evolution Gallery

This gallery is in a large building whose façade is decorated with medallion portraits of famous scientists and, in the center, a statue of *Science*.

Inaugurated by Armand Fallières in 1889, just two and a half months after the Eiffel Tower, the Galerie de Zoologie presented to the public the first zoological museum in the world, a true model of its kind.

Today, a large-scale renovation project (by P. Chernetov and B. Huidobro) is in hand; this will make of the gallery a modern museum of natural science objects and ideas that will allow the visitor to discover the diversity of the living world since life began. Without loss of its period architectural character, the Muséum National d'Histoire Naturelle will present through its priceless collections and the work of its researchers and museographers, a scientific spectacle in four acts on the theme of Evolution. A zoological library (Zoothèque) for researchers is installed in the basement in front of the gallery.

▣ Musée d'Histoire de la Préfecture de Police

1bis Rue des Carmes, 5th arr.
Tel: 43-29-21-57 (ext. 336). Map ref: 17-B3
Open Mon.-Thurs. 9am-5pm; Fri. 9am-4.30pm; closed public holidays.
Métro: Maubert-Mutualité
Bus: 24, 47, 63, 86, 87

Since leaving the Quai des Orfèvres this museum has been housed in the ultramodern building of the Commissariat de Police of the 5th arrondissement, almost at the point where the Rue des Carmes runs into the Place Maubert.

Tour of the museum

½ hr.

Here are displayed all the documents relating to famous trials: those of the Maréchal de Brion, Eléonora Galligaï, Théophile de Viau, de la Brinvilliers, Damiens, de Calas, the Chevalier de la Barre, Cartouche, Cadoudal, Malet, Gorguloff, Petiot, Landru. Also the committal and release registers of many prisons: La Tournelle (1667–1743), Bicêtre (1780–96), La Force (1790–1800), Saint-Lazare (Year II), Sainte-Pélagie (1743–Year VII), Les Carmes (1793–Year II), Le Temple (Year IV–1806), Vincennes (1808–14).

There is a large collection of pictures dealing with famous criminals and prisoners, and with the uniforms of the marshalsea and of the police from the constables of the watch onward. There is also a collection of *lettres de cachet*, secret orders under the King's private seal that condemned people to exile, prison, or death – one of the most hated instruments of royal absolutism under the Ancien Régime.

One room is devoted to the Resistance and the Liberation of Paris. A new section evokes early scientific police work (municipal laboratory, toxicology laboratory, Bertillon).

▣ Musée de l'Histoire du Protestantisme Français

54 Rue des Saints-Pères, 6th arr. Tel: 45–48–62–07. Map ref: 16–C2, D2
Visits by appointment on Sun., Mon., and mornings.
Métro: Saint-Germain-des-Prés
Bus: 39, 48, 63, 70, 87, 95

The museum is integrated with the Bibliothèque de l'Histoire du Protestantisme in the courtyard of the rather austere building that replaces the house of Salomon de Brosse.

Tour of the museum

½ hr.

The museum has a large collection of pictures relating to historically important Protestant figures. Besides the most famous, such as Ambroise Paré, Sully, Henri IV, Agrippa d'Aubigné, and Bernard Palissy, you will also find Jean Cousin, the Androuet Du Cerceau dynasty, Cujas, Théodore de Bèze, Renée de France (daughter of Louis XII and Anne de Bretagne), and Pastor Monod.

Miniatures, engravings, and various mementoes such as religious objects from the days when the sect was clandestine. Handwritten letters, one of which is signed 'Antoine de Bourbon, Roi de Navarre.'

▣ Musée de l'Holographie

Forum des Halles, level 1, Grand Balcon, 1st arr. Tel: 40–39–96–83.
Map ref: 17–B1
Open Mon.–Sat. 10am–7pm, Sun. and public holidays 1pm–7pm
Métro: Châtelet, Les Halles
Bus: 38, 47, 67, 69, 75

Tour of the museum

30mins.

Holography was only invented in 1947 by Denis Gabar. It is the sole means available of creating a three-dimensional image. This small museum displays different sorts of holograms, some produced by the museum's own research laboratory, from the simplest reproductions of an object to the stereogram, which provides the illusion of movement if the spectator moves, and holographic film that gives the same three-dimensional effect in motion.

Holography operates on a simple principle. Unlike photography, it is not the object itself that is recorded, but the light reflected from it when it is lit by a laser. The hologram looks like a cloudy plate, but if it is lit by a lamp or a laser, the subject stands out as if in three dimensions.

The museum runs courses in holography and travelling exhibitions.

▣ Musée de l'Homme** (Museum of Anthropology and Ethnography)

W wing of the Palais de Chaillot, 17 Place du Trocadéro, 16th arr.
Tel: 45–53–70–60. Map ref: 13–B1
Open daily exc. Tues., 9:45am–5:15pm. Groups by appointment
Métro: Trocadéro
Buses: 22, 30, 32, 63, 72, 82

The museum was formed in 1938 to provide a new setting for the collections from the Musée d'Ethnographie du Trocadéro and the anthropological gallery of the Musée d'Histoire Naturelle. It is housed in the W wing of the Palais de Chaillot, built for the 1937 World Fair in a Neo-Classical style combining the monumental with the modern. Reorganization, started in 1986, will involve the rearrangement of a number of galleries (History and Architecture →Chaillot).

The museum provides a wide-ranging synthesis of human studies – anthropology, prehistoric archeology, and ethnology. It examines the history of the human race back from its very origins, in Africa and Madagascar, Europe, Asia, Oceania, the Arctic, and America, whose peoples are represented by their arts, crafts and customs. The Musée de l'Homme is administered by the Ministry of Education and also houses research and teaching facilities as well as several branches of the CNRS (Centre National de la Recherche Scientifique) and various learned societies.

Tour of the museum

2 hrs.

The entrance hall contains a gigantic stone head brought back from Easter Island by Pierre Loti in 1872, and several North American totem poles.

The staircase on the l. leads to the first floor.

First floor

A gallery, opened in 1988, illustrates the development from hominids to *Homo sapiens*, from nature to culture.

Anthropology Gallery (*on the l. at the head of the stairs*)

The purpose of the gallery is to demonstrate the biological diversity of humankind and of the groups that comprise the species, as well as the process of human evolution.

Exhibits are displayed in two concentric circles; it is best to make both circuits, taking the inner circle first (the central cases and panels devoted to individual genetic variation), and then the outer cases and panels describing the different human populations. In order fully to understand the exhibits and the explanatory texts that accompany them, follow the directions on the notices posted at the entrance to the gallery.

A brief review of the fundamentals of human biology (genetics, fetal development, growth) and demography preface the theme of the gallery: to show by means of selected examples the physical and biochemical characteristics that vary in humankind (height, pigmentation, blood group, etc.) and current theories on human genetic diversity. Another, and somewhat more technical section, is devoted to the mechanics of human evolution (mutation, natural selection, the genetic code, and the role of environmental factors in biological diversity). One gallery is devoted to deliberate alteration of the human body, living or dead (tattooing, ritual scarification and other mutilation, ornamentation of the face and head, shrunken heads and other trophies, Egyptian and Amerindian mummies). Current research methods on mummified bodies are explained on a large display panel.

Paleontology Gallery (r. of staircase)

This gallery traces human physical and cultural evolution from its origins to the earliest use of metals. It starts with the order of primates and the central place human beings hold in it. The first series of cases is devoted to the evolution of *Homo sapiens* with emphasis upon such major human characteristics as upright posture, bipedal locomotion, cranial and brain development, teeth, jaws and facial structure, articulate language, the origins of human behavior, and the relatively slow rate of growth and maturation. The next set of cases displays the most recently discovered human fossils, and details the evolution from the Austropithecines to the Neanderthals and to the Neolithic communities.

Prehistory

The final exhibit reconstructs a dig on a prehistoric site and shows the means and methods employed by archeologists. The third part is devoted to prehistoric tool making: chipping and polishing stone, carving antler and bone, and Neolithic pottery. A wide range of tools illustrates these developments, including flints at all stages of working, Mousterian scrapers, Upper Paleolithic scrapers and carved bones, spear points, arrowheads, needles, and harpoons. The exhibition leads up to Neolithic tools and the earliest metal objects. The last section is devoted to paleolithic art: originals**, such as the Venus of Lespugnes and casts of other steatopygous female statuettes (so-called 'Venuses') and tracings of cave paintings, among which the copies by Abbé Breuil are noteworthy.

Sub-Saharan Africa Gallery***

This gallery remains much as it was when the museum was opened in 1936. The texts accompanying the exhibits are consequently out of date, but the gallery is scheduled to be renovated soon. Each display case is devoted to one striking characteristic of either the region's material culture or of its social or religious life. The first section displays a small sample of the art of the region with the finest pieces in a variety of materials – ivory, wood, terracotta, stone, and gold. Some of the exhibits, such as the large white Fang mask** from Gabon, have exerted considerable influence upon early 20th-c. European art. Other sections are devoted to the Dogon art of Mali: many of the statues, masks* and other ritual objects were brought back by the famous Dakar-Djibouti expedition, and to the former kingdom of Dahomey, located in what is now the Republic of Benin. These include *récades* or staffs held by chieftains, bas-reliefs from the royal palace**, thrones, and symbolic figures of the kings*. Also worth seeing is the collection of Sao archeological items from Chad**, comprising bronzes, terracottas, and funerary urns, and the bronze panels and ivory carvings from the former kingdom of Benin, now part of Nigeria. Other key items of West African art, past and present, include the wrought-iron figure of the war god Gu** from ancient Dahomey, a masterpiece of African art; a gigantic Nimba mask* from Guinea, a fertility symbol made of wood and raffia. Central Africa comes next: masks, nail-studded magical figures, and ceremonial objects*: carved cups, boxes for face paints, ceremonial axes, and grass robes. Noteworthy are the Fang and Kota figures* from Gabon and the Congo, protectors of the bones of the ancestors, and exquisite sculptures in their own right. Note too, the musical instruments: the Mzakara harp* and the large Yangeri slotted drum shaped like an ox (Central African Republic).

Madagascar is treated as part of Sub-Saharan Africa though its dominant cultural influences have been Indonesian, especially in glass- and ironwork and in the use of flooded paddies for rice growing. From the Island come carved funerary posts, one of which is decorated with buffalo heads. From the church of Antonioz in the province of Gondar come paintings on cloth, unique in Ethiopian art both for their scale and their age, dating from the early 18th c.

North Africa and the Near East

After an introduction to Islam, whose faith and law have deeply affected North Africa and the Near East, are display cases devoted to different ways of life in this part of the world: the nomadic Bedouin of Syria and Arabia (a noblewoman's palanquin) in contrast with the settled agricultural communities of the Near East, where methods and implements of agriculture remained unchanged until the middle of the 20th c.; the Saharan nomads are unlike the settled tribes of the oases; the tribes of the Atlas Mountains differ from the artisans and townsfolk of North Africa. The use of the swing-plough in agriculture and the use of draught and pack animals marks the difference between North and Sub-Saharan Africa. The museum houses unique Touareg and Teda collections. Recent expeditions to Yemen have also produced some notable exhibits.

European Gallery

A tour of the first floor ends with Europe. (France is treated as a separate entity, in the Musée National des Arts et Traditions Populáires.) On the window side of the gallery, display cases provide background information on the peoples of Europe, classified linguistically: Basque, Celtic, Latin, German and Scandinavian, Slavic, Romanian, Finno-Ugric, Greeks, Albanian and Baltic. The exhibits attempt to show typical activities among each of these main groups (Swiss dairy farming, agriculture among the Western Slavs), or to re-create a home environment (interior of a Romanian house in the Carpathians). Most of these exhibits come from a bygone age. A series of cases displays examples of folk art: pottery, tools used for spinning, a Sicilian farm cart, even a collection of pipes* of all shapes, sizes and materials. A place is kept for seasonal festivals and carnivals with masks and fancy dress from Central Europe, Switzerland and, from Belgium, that of the famous Gilles* of the town of Binche. There are also some fine examples in the collection of folk dress**. From the Europe Gallery a staircase leads straight up into the Arctic Peoples Gallery.

Second floor

Arctic Peoples Gallery**

Here the collections relative to the native peoples of northern Scandinavia, Canada, Greenland, Alaska, and eastern Siberia are displayed. Eskimo society is examined according to the division of labor: men's and women's work and by seasonal activities such as seal hunting. There are archeological exhibits in ivory and bone from Canada, a kayak and an umiak from Greenland, masks, and ritual objects. The Lapps are shown to be first-class herders and their reindeer sledge is contrasted with the dog sledge of the Eskimo. There is an almost complete set of Chawchu clothes from Siberia.

Asia Gallery

First comes a case displaying different aspects of the use of tree bark in Asia and then a small room devoted to the prehistory of Asia (Vietnam, Cambodia, China, Japan, Siberia, and Malaysia). In the gallery proper each section displays a unified collection devoted to the Siberian, the Finno-Ugric, Turco-Mongol, Afghan, and Iranian peoples, as well as the peoples of India and Pakistan, Nepal, China, Japan, Malaysia, and Southeast Asia. The cases on the window side contain exhibits related to a specific theme within a given civilization (weapons, cult objects, clothes, crafts) or else they summarize an entire group (such as the Nagas of Assam). The most notable exhibits include the robes of a Siberian shaman with accessories, fish-skin Ghiliak robes*, Ainu cloaks** from Japan, the Turkish and Iranian collections, the collection of musical instruments from Rajasthan, Chinese theater costumes*, shadow puppets from India*, Thailand*, and Malaysia*, and Japanese armor. The wealth of the Asia Gallery is to be found on the one hand in its costumes and on the other in its presentation of the ethnography of the minority peoples of Southeast Asia. Three new sections are devoted to Laos and Cambodia: habitation (reconstruction of a house interior) clothing and silks; religion; and agriculture. Especially noteworthy are the costumes of the ethnic minorities and a tableau of offerings being made to the masks of the Cambodian court theater.

Oceania Gallery

The first section of the gallery retraces the successive migrations from Southeast Asia toward Australasia between 40,000 B.C. and AD 600 which peopled Oceania. Indonesia and the Philippines mark the boundaries of Asia. While the main emphasis is placed upon Indian, Chinese, and Islamic influences, the western influences on the peoples of these island chains is not neglected. The display cases take full account of the region's diversity while stressing its cultural unity. A Barong mask* from Bali is displayed opposite a painting of the forecourt of a Balinese temple.

Beyond, the gallery splits Oceania into Melanesia, Polynesia, and Micronesia for the purposes of study, although in reality the ethnic distinctions corresponding to these geographical divisions are not at all clearly marked. The section devoted to Papua New Guinea is in the course of reorganization; the exhibits are being redesigned to show the interrelationship between daily life and creative art by stressing that in Papuan society objects are conceived with functional as well as aesthetic aims. Beyond, cases will display Australasia in the light of the current renaissance of its aboriginal cultures. The Oceania Gallery next displays the remainder of its exhibits from Melanesia (the Admiralty and Solomon Islands, Vanuatu and New Caledonia) and Polynesia (bounded by Fiji, Hawaii, Easter Island, and New Zealand), stressing again through religion and social customs both the differences and the similarities among the various cultures. There is a round hut from New Caledonia; whalebone ornaments* from the Marquesas Islands; and the figure of a war god* from Hawaii brought back by Captain Cook. A gigantic head from Easter Island demonstrates what some of these societies could achieve with carved megaliths. Micronesia is represented by a Tino**, a very rare anthropomorphic statue, among other exhibits.

Americas Gallery

A recently rearranged portion of this gallery displays the collections relating to North America, with reconstructions of living quarters; model of a 19th-c. village from the south-western United States. In the older portions of the gallery are the somewhat overcrowded exhibits of artifacts from Pre-Columbian civilizations. There is a cast of the monumental Gateway of the Sun from Tiahuanaco, a considerable collection of Chimu and Nazca pottery, and objects in wood and stone from the civilizations antedating the Spanish conquest. Death is illustrated by impressive mummies from Peru and the shrunken heads, trophies of the present-day Jivaro hunters of Ecuador. Maya, Totonac, Zapotec, Toltec, and Aztec civilizations are amply represented. Particularly memorable are the stone funerary masks, and the statues of the god Quetzalcoatl, the 'Plumed Serpent,' while, from the West Indies, comes a superb carved wooden chair. The present way of life of different groups of Native Americans, as well as the ethnography of Mexico, fittingly widens the scope of the gallery.

Finally, there is the Arts and Technology Gallery which shows how, despite variations in style, the efforts made by these different civilizations to master their materials and use their natural environment are common to all human beings.

Music Room

Here over 400 instruments are displayed with a wealth of photographs. There are three live music programs. The collection shows both the variety and the importance of musical expression on a worldwide scale. There are two outstanding exhibits, now for the first time in full working order. The early 19th-c. Slendro gamelan* came from the princely court of Ciberon. It comprises 16 instruments, bronze gongs and plates, drums and xylophones with wooden stands painted red and gold, decorated in a style derived from the Chinese. Silenced for a century, this historic orchestra can now be heard thanks to a group of musicians who practise regularly under the direction of an Indonesian master. Another attraction of the live music program is provided by the prehistoric lithophone discovered in Vietnam in 1949. Its glassy chimes are struck from 10 large pieces of hewn stone, the biggest of which is over 3ft/1m long.

▷ Additional information

Lectures: information from Action Culturelle (tel: 45–53–09–16) and the Amis du Musée de l'Homme (tel: 47–04–62–10).

Cinema (1st floor) shows films on the traditional lifestyles of peoples throughout the world.

Picture Library (3rd floor) and Library (4th floor). Open Mon., Wed.-Fri. and Sun. 10am–5pm. Tel: 47–04–53–94.

Archive of ethnology, Pre-Columbian archeology, prehistory and anthropology.

Bookshop (ground floor): pictorial travel books, *Objets et Mondes*, the museum's own review; the publications of the Institute d'Ethnologies; discs and tapes of traditional music recorded by the CNRS.

Special exhibitions (1st floor) displaying the results of current research.

Concerts and music workshops for children in the Music Room (1st floor). Tel: 45-53-09-16.

▷ Not to be missed

First floor
The arts of Sub-Saharan Africa: masks and ritual objects, bas-relief panels from the royal palace of the former Kingdom of Dahomey, statues of gods and ancestors.

Second floor
Arctic Peoples Gallery: archeological items from Canada, a Greenland kayak.

Americas Gallery: Homes and environment of North American peoples, Aztec and Maya art collections.

Music Room: Indonesian gamelan orchestra, prehistoric lithophone from Vietnam.

▣ Maison de Victor Hugo*

6 Place des Vosges, 4th arr. Tel: 42-72-10-16.
Map ref: 18-D2
Curator: Henri Cazaumayou
Open daily Tues.–Sun. 10am–5:40pm. Guided tours by request.
Library open by appointment. Works of Victor Hugo and critical studies.
Métro: Chemin-Vert, Bastille, Saint-Paul
Bus: 20, 29, 65, 69, 76, 96

It was in the beautiful Hôtel de Lavardin, better known as the Hôtel de Rohan-Guéménée, that Victor Hugo lived between two revolutionary upheavals from 1832 to 1848. He left the Rue Jean-Goujon to set up house on the second floor of the *hôtel*, among what Juliette Drouet fondly called his 'bric-a-brac'. Here life went on for 16 years, filled with everyday family affairs, with society gatherings, with literature and politics. Here the poet saw his daughter Léopoldine married, and here he lived through the tragedy of Villequier. In the study he wrote his great dramas: *Les Burgraves, Ruy Blas, Marie Tudor, Les Chants du Crépuscule, Les Rayons et les Ombres, Les Voix Intérieures,* a large part of *Les Misérables,* and the first parts of *La Légende des Siècles* and *Les Contemplations.* In the drawing-room he entertained his friends Vigny, Lamartine, Béranger, Sainte-Beuve, Dumas, Balzac, Mérimée, the Devérias, Célestin Nanteuil, and David d'Angers. It was while he was living in the Place des Vosges that he was elected to the Academy, was made a peer of France, and became a deputy.

The heart of the collection is the books, drawings, and other items donated to the City of Paris in the year of the museum's creation, 1902, by Paul Meurice, an intimate friend of the poet and executor of his will.

Tour of the museum

45 mins.

The apartment, 2nd floor

The apartment was occupied by Victor Hugo from 1832 to 1848. The rooms, completely refurbished in 1983, contain much memorabilia but do not give an exact idea of what the poet's home was like, since the auction of Hugo's furniture in 1852 and the numerous changes that the rooms underwent after the family left, make its reconstruction impossible.

Youth. Beyond the antechamber, where documents are displayed illustrating Hugo's childhood and youth and the early years of his marriage to Adèle Foucher, up to their arrival in the Place Royale (family portraits, drawings by Achille Devéria), the red drawing-room reconstructs the poet's time here. Several paintings are on display (Victor Hugo and his son François-Victor, *Léopoldine with the Book of Hours*, *Léopoldine's first Communion at Fourqueux*, by Auguste de Châtillon, a portrait of Adèle by Louis Boulanger), along with drawings by Adèle Hugo, the bust of Victor Hugo by David d'Angers and that of Adèle by Nicolas-Victor Vilain.

Exile. The Chinese diningroom and the next room commemorate the years of exile (1852 to 1870). Hugo's passion for ornament shows in the panels which he decorated with pyrography and the furniture he created for Hauteville Fairy, Juliette Drouet's house on the isle of Guernsey. A small room displays an outstanding collection of photographs of Hugo and his family during their exile on Jersey (1852–55). The collection is by Charles Hugo and Auguste Vacquerie. Hauteville House, the poet's home in Guernsey, and its inhabitants, are commemorated in this room.

On September 5, 1870, Victor Hugo returned to France. After living in several different homes in Paris, he moved in 1878, with Juliette Drouet, into a private mansion on the Ave. d'Eylau (no. 124 of the present Ave. Victor Hugo), since demolished. The penultimate room, with its original furniture, conjures up the final years of his life (*Georges and Jeanne in 1879* by Charles Voillemot; a copy of a portrait of Victor Hugo painted by Léon Bonnat in 1879; a bust by Rodin; photographs by Nadar). The tour ends with a reconstruction of the room in the Ave. d'Eylau in which Hugo died (1885).

Exhibits and drawings, first floor

Apart from temporary exhibitions, drawings by Victor Hugo are displayed in rotation, chosen from among the 550 drawings owned by the museum out of a total of 3000 executed by the writer. Victor Hugo was particularly fond of these sketches. In a letter to Baudelaire he wrote 'I am delighted and most honored that you think well of those things I call my ink drawings. I've ended up adding pencil, charcoal, sepia and all sorts of strange mixtures to them which more or less manage to convey what I see, and more important, what I feel. It keeps me amused between verses.' It is impossible in a few lines to examine this activity, which was essential to the poet. Suffice it to say that in his graphic work examples of both visionary and photographic styles can be seen; important themes include architecture (walled cities, keeps, ruins, battlements, flying buttresses), and things oceanic – as Gaétan Picon put it (waves, storms, jetties, breakwaters, boats in distress, and dunes). The striking thing about these hundreds of drawings is 'their absolute spontaneity'. Everywhere Hugo drew, no matter where, no matter what. Also noteworthy is the cruelty of some of the caricatures, and the obsession with death. The print room and the library, which contains a more or less complete collection of all the editions of the writer's works, along with the majority of the works and studies devoted to him, are open to researchers by appointment.

▣ Musée de l'Institut du Monde Arabe*

1 Rue des Fossés Saint-Bernard. Tel. 40–51–38–38. 5th arr. Map ref: 18–C3
Open daily ex. Mon. 1–8pm.
Métro: Jussieu
Bus: 24, 63, 67, 86, 87, 89
Parking: Forecourt of IMA

Inaugurated in 1987, this museum is part of the Institut du Monde Arabe (→), an organization formed with the aim of making Arab-Islamic civilization better known in France and of fostering cultural exchanges between Islam and the West.

Tour of the museum

45 mins.

The museum presents, on three floors, the full extent of Arab-Muslim civilization from the 7th to the 19th c., illustrated by more than 500 objects, the product of widely varying techniques – ceramics, metalwork, woodwork, textiles, ivory, glass and so on.

The tour begins with a brief presentation of pre-Islamic civilizations. The next level presents Islam and its historical development. There is an audiovisual account of the foundations of the religion and culture; 150 objects from the first two dynasties, Ommiad (661–750) and Abbasid (750–1258), including a very fine collection of astrolabes.

The last level, arranged around the patio, stressed the unity and variety of the Muslim world, from Spain to India, through Persia (Iran) and Anatolia from the 9th to the 19th c.

Contemporary Arab creativity in the plastic arts is widely represented: painting, sculpture, graphic arts. There are frequent exhibitions.

Art and Society Section: (2nd floor) introduction to contemporary (19th- and 20th-c.) Arab societies urban, rural, and nomadic Bedouin, by careful juxtaposition of pictorial elements with objects of everyday life.

Contemporary Arts Section: (1st floor) contemporary Arabic artistic achievements in such media as painting, sculpture, graphic design, architecture, and film. Espace-Jeunes (for 5 to 15-year-olds).

▣ Musée Instrumental de Paris*

Conservatoire National Supérieur de Musique, 14 Rue de Madrid,
8th arr. Tel: 42-93-15-20. Map ref: 9-B1
Curator: Mme Bran-Ricci
Open Wed.-Sat. 2-6pm; closed public holidays.
Métro: Europe
Bus: 53, 66, 80, 95

This museum, which is an annex of the Conservatoire National Supérieur de Musique de Paris, displays an important collection of mainly European musical instruments from the Renaissance to the present. Some of the items are quite outstanding.

Tour of the museum

30 mins.

The Musée Instrumental has grown from the original Clapisson Collection acquired by the State under Napoléon III and now numbers over 4000 individual exhibits.

Notable among these are a series of Renaissance lutes and archlutes, some of them works of art in their own right, and an important collection of French stringed instruments: viols, violins, guitars, harps, and hurdy-gurdies. The museum owns such valuable violins as the Stradivarius* that once belonged to the famous Spanish virtuoso, Sarasate (1844-1908), and Delphin Alard's 18th-c. Guarneri*. There is a remarkable group of Flemish, French, and Italian harpsichords as well as fortepianos. Among the historical items are clavichords* that belonged to Beethoven and to Grétry, Mme de Lamballe's harp, a guitar that Vuillaume lent to Paganini, who then gave it to Berlioz, and pianos owned by Boïeldieu, Paër, and Gabriel Fauré.

▣ Musée Jacquemart-André**

158 Boul. Haussmann, 8th arr. Tel: 45-89-04-91/42-62-39-94. Map ref: 9–A1
Director: M Huyghe
Open Wed.–Sun. 1.30–6.30pm
Métro: Saint-Philippe-du-Roule
Bus: 22, 43, 52, 83

The Hôtel Jacquemart-André is far more than a museum in the usual sense – rather it is a delightful and luxurious town house which its owners have filled with artistic treasures. The Neo-Classical mansion was built by the architect Henri Parent from 1860 to 1875 for Edouard André who, in 1881, married the portraitist Nélie Jacquemart. After the death of her husband in 1894, Mme André carried on the work which they had started together, and when she died in 1912 she bequeathed her wealth, her art collections, and the house to the Institut de France.

Today the Musée Jacquemart-André is famous for its Italian Renaissance and 18th-c. French works of art. The collections are arranged by the artists' nationality: paintings and furniture from France, Flemish paintings, Italian and English paintings. However, since the rooms are often used for special exhibitions, it is not always possible to view all the exhibits.

Tour of the museum

45 mins.

Interior decoration

On the ground floor, recently restored, one fine reception room leads to the next. Louis XV paneling, Gobelins tapestries, and overdoors in the style of Watteau decorate Room 2 (the Round Drawing Room). Room 3 contains three Beauvais tapestries entitled *Russian Games**, designed by Le Prince, commissioned by Louis XVI just before the outbreak of the French Revolution and never displayed until after their purchase by Edouard André. The overdoors from the reign of Louis XVI depict the *Four Elements*; the ceiling is painted with *Vulcan presenting Aeneas with his armor*, (Louis XV). Unique among French museums is a collection of paintings by Giambattista Tiepolo from the Villa Contarini in Venice: they include the Baroque ceilings in Room 4 (the *Apotheosis of a Hero*) and *Peace and Justice* (Room 5) and the fresco on the staircase which shows Federigo Contarini greeting Henri III; this fresco mingles the theatrical with stunning perspectives and those details of natural scenery so dear to Tiepolo.

The first floor: the decor here is Renaissance. The architraves of the doors are 15th- and 16th-c. stonework and the first room has an encyclopedic ceiling in blue grisaille with gold by Mocetto, covered in figures and objects dealing with the arts and sciences.

French art

Furniture, carpets, and *objets d'art* recreate the atmosphere of 18th-c. France. There is an especially fine collection of Louis XV chairs* upholstered in Beauvais tapestry with the *Fables* of La Fontaine designed by Oudry, and some small Louis XVI sofas from the Royal Workshops at Beauvais.

Sculptures include a collection of portrait busts among which is that of the architect, J. A. Gabriel*, by one of Louis XIV's court sculptors, Coysevox (1640–1720), conveys an almost Baroque exuberance; also notable are the portrait of Chancellor Maupéou, Mme de Pompadour's brother, the Marquis de Marigny, by Jean-Baptiste Lemoyne (1704–78); Lefebvre de Caumartin* by Houdon (1741–1828), famous for his masterly hand and eye; and Richelieu* by Jean Warin (1604–72), the sculptor from Liège.

Paintings: the collection includes such key works as the two paintings by Fragonard, *Les Débuts du Modèle***, delicate treatment of an erotic subject, and the lively, naturalistic *Portrait d'un Viellard*** (Portrait of an Old Man**); *Venus and Cupid** and *Sleeping Venus**, decorative canvases by François Boucher (1703–70); and the still life by Chardin (1699–1779), *The Attributes of the Arts and Sciences**. A large and varied collection of portraits illustrates the different styles of the 18th c.: the formal portrait of the *Marquise d'Antin** by that favorite of the French royal family, Nattier, and a *Portrait of a Gentleman* by Largillière (1656–1746); the domesticity of Drouais and Perronneau (1715–83); portraits of artists, including a fine psychological study by Greuze of the engraver George Wille* and the *Self-Portrait** by the Swede, Roslin

(1718–93); a portrait of *Catherine Skavronska** by E. Vigée-Lebrun, painted in exile during the Revolution. Late 18th-c. art is represented by drawings by Watteau; *Comte François de Nantes** by David; and Prud'hon's sketch for his large-scale portrait of the *Empress Josephine** at Malmaison.

Flemish paintings

The museum houses a number of very interesting canvases of the 17th-c. Flemish school. There are three paintings by Rembrandt, a youthful work from around 1630, *The Pilgrims at Emmaus****, highly original in its simplicity of composition and its Caravaggesque use of chiaroscuro; the portrait of *Amalia von Solms*** (1632) where the frame is painted in *trompe-l'œil*, and which shows Baroque influences; and the portrait of *Dr. Tholinx** showing Rembrandt more deeply engaged in psychological study. The *Portrait of an Old Man* by Van Dyck has the typically rich Flemish impasto while the same artist's *Time Clipping Cupid's Wings* shows the influence of Italian art. There is a lively and expressive touch to Frans Hals' (1581–1666) *Head of a Man**: There are landscapes* by Ruysdael and Van Goyen, while Quentin Metsys's *Portrait of a Man* is inspired by Leonardo da Vinci's sketches of old men.

Italian Art

Italian Renaissance painting is represented by some extraordinarily fine canvases, most of which were acquired by M and Mme André during their visits to Florence. They include: by Mantegna (1430–1506) *The Making of Christ**, and his *Madonna with Three Saints***, a painting of great gravity, with its cold palette and strong lines; by Carpaccio (1465–1525) *The Mission of Hippolytus***, which displays the world of legend and story typical of this highly original Venetian artist; and by Uccello (1397–1475) the small but magnificent *Saint George Slaying the Dragon****, one of the few paintings by the artist to be found in a French museum, and which displays Uccello's delight in tricks of perspective. The collection also contains works by Alessandro Baldovinetti (*ca.* 1426–99) and a traditional Florentine late 15th-c. gilded wood altarpiece by Botticini (*ca.* 1446–97); a *St Bonaventure* by Crivelli (active 1457–93) in which late Gothic and early Renaissance influences mingle; the *Portrait of an Old Woman* (1494–1557) by Pontormo with the Mannerist elongation of the figure, and a painting by Cima da Conegliano* (1459/60–1517/18). The museum also houses a collection of *cassoni**, wooden coffers with painted panels – popular in the 15th and 16th c. There is a Siennese processional banner* painted on one side with *St Catherine in Glory* and with a *Crucifixion* on the reverse.

Sculptures and *objets d'art* include a polychrome wooden

Madonna, well preserved, and expressive bas-reliefs by Donatello of the *Martyrdom of St Sebastian***, and two cherubs carrying flaming torches. There are massive andirons by Riccio and a portrait bust of the Duke of Gonzaga by the famous Florentine architect Alberti (1404–72). There are panels from choir stalls with religious subjects in marquetry (Urbi region) and a rare and high-quality stained-glass *Madonna and Child* by Cosimo Tura, the first major artist of the Ferrarese school.

British paintings

18th-c. portraits by Reynolds, Gainsborough, Hoppner, and Romney.

Manuscripts shown on special request.
For reasons of conservation two very fine illuminated manuscripts are not on display. They are the *Book of Hours of the Duke of Savoy*** (13th c.) and the *Boucicault Book of Hours*** (late 15th c.) which belonged to Diane de Poitiers.

▣ Musée du Jeu de Paume

Place de la Concorde, 1st arr. Tel: 42–06–12–07. Map ref. 9–B3, 10–C3
Métro: Concorde
Bus: 14, 72, 73, 84, 94

Once the sanctuary of Impressionism, this museum has recently been reorganized for use as a showplace for exhibitions of art and design.

The Jeu de Paume (*Réal* Tennis Court) was built by Napoléon III on the site of Henri IV's orangery for the recreation of the Prince Imperial. When *réal* (royal) tennis was replaced by lawn tennis, the court was used for art exhibitions; later the Musée du Luxembourg housed its collection of foreign paintings there. During World War II the Germans used it to store works of art looted in France before shipping them back to Germany. Then, in 1947, René Huyghe decided to transfer the collections of Impressionist paintings to 'the setting predestined for them', and there they remained until they were transferred in 1986 to the new museum of 19th-c. art set up in the former Gare d'Orsay (→Musée d'Orsay).

◪ Musée Kwok On* (Museum of Asian Theater)

41 Rue des Francs-Bourgeois, 4th arr. Tel: 42–72–99–42. Map ref: 17–C1, C2
Open Mon.–Fri. 10am–5.30pm. Closed public holidays.
Métro: Saint-Paul
Bus: 75, 67, 69

The core collection of this museum consists of the unusually fine group of objects relating to the Asian theater arts donated by the Chinese collector Kwok On.

The City of Paris arranges introductory courses on Asian art here.

Tour of the museum

½ hr.

The collection is displayed as a series of special temporary exhibitions, built around some specific legend or set of characters and conveyed through a display of masks and costumes. These include costumes* from the Chinese opera, and the Kabuki and Noh theaters of Japan, masks* from the Indian theater, string puppets* from Japan, and glove, string, and shadow puppets*.

Puppet shows

In Asia the puppet theater is far more than a simple piece of children's entertainment. Its repertory draws from that of the classical theater and some master puppeteers are as famous as leading stage actors. Nor is their task an easy one. For example, each puppet in the famous Japanese Bunraku theater needs at least three people to manipulate it: one for the head and right arm, another for the left arm and a third for the legs. Nor does the wizardry end there, since a series of strings behind the head enable the lips, eyes and eyebrows to move.

Every Asian country has its own special brand of puppet. Vietnam has its water puppets while the Chinese shadow-puppet theater uses puppets cut from goatskin and operated by rods.

▣ Fondation Le Corbusier

8-10 Square du Docteur-Blanche, 16th arr. Tel: 42-88-41-53.
Open Mon.-Thurs. 10am-12:30pm and 1-6pm, Fri. 10am-12:30pm
and 1-5pm.
Library and Archives open Mon.-Thurs. 1-6pm, Fri. 1-5pm.
Métro: Jasmín. Bus: 52

The villas La Roche and Jeanneret, headquarters of the Fondation Le Corbusier, were built in this quiet corner of Passy in 1923 and are among the earliest of the famous series of 14 projects completed by the architects Le Corbusier (1887-1966) and Pierre Jeanneret from 1922 to 1929. They mark the perfect application in practice of the theories of modern architecture developed by Le Corbusier in books and in articles published in the review *L'Espirit Nouveau*. In the Villa Roche the play of light and volume and the handling of internal and external space are 50 years ahead of their time and show Le Corbusier's architectural mastery.

The villa was owned by the banker and art patron Raoul La Roche, who was advised by Le Corbusier when forming his collection, the bulk of which was acquired from the sales of the property con-fiscated from the collector D. H. Kahnweiller. These treasures of modern painting may now be seen in the Musée des Beaux-Arts in Basel and in the Musée National d'Art Moderne to which La Roche presented them. The foundation arranges meetings and exhibitions in the Villa La Roche on the work of the architect.

▣ Musée de la Légion d'Honneur et des Ordres de Chevalerie*

2 Rue de Bellechasse, 7th arr. Tel: 45-55-95-16. Map ref: 15-C1
Curator: Mme Isabelle du Pasquier

Open Tues.–Sun. 2–5pm. Closed on public holidays.
Métro: Solférino, Chambre des Députés
Bus: 24, 63, 68, 69, 73, 83, 84, 94

In the elegant setting of the Hôtel de Salm, the Musée de la Légion d'Honneur et des Ordres de Chevalerie displays a significant collection of decorations, insignia, and medals to illustrate the history of the orders of chivalry. These exhibits are complemented by paintings, tapestries, and *objets d'art*.

The *hôtel* was built in a Palladian style similar to that of the White House in Washington, for the Prince de Salm-Kyrbourg in 1782, burned down in 1871 during the Commune, and was heavily restored later (for history →Faubourg Saint-Germain).

Tour of the museum

45 mins.

The Classical peristyle is decorated with busts of Henri IV, Bonaparte, Lacépède who was Grand Chancellor of the Legion of Honor, and General Dubail, who founded the museum.

First room, (on l. of entrance)

This room is devoted to French royal orders. There is an 18th-c. collar, cross, and patent of the Order of St Michael and related portraits of Louis XI and Charles IX (studio of Clouet). The Order of the Saint-Esprit (Holy Ghost) is represented by a collar and ceremonial mantle of the French Restoration period (on loan from the Musée de Cluny), the blue ribbons of the order worn by Louis XVI and the Dauphin when they were prisoners in the Temple, dozens of stars from mantles, and different robes of the order.

Two large-scale paintings illustrate its ceremonies, the *Foundation of the Order of the Saint-Esprit by Henri III* by J. B. Van Loo (on loan from the Louvre) and Subleyras' painting of *The Duc de Saint-Aignan admitting Prince Vaïni to the Order*. The military Order of St Louis was founded by Louis XIV and awarded without distinction of birth; crosses, portraits of *chevaliers* (knights) and a court dress of the order with its embroidered star. There are the collar and cross of the Order of St Lazarus and Our Lady of Mount Carmel, and a painting of Mme Labille-Guiard; decorations of the Restoration period, a portrait of General Foy by Horace Vernet; and Gobelins and Beauvais tapestries with the arms of France.

Second room, (to the r. of the entrance hall)

These exhibits retrace the history of the Order of the Legion of Honor (→inset). Muskets and Sabers of Honor awarded under the consulate and from whose recipients the first awards of the Legion of Honor were made. There were maces of honor of the little drum of Arcola. The history of the building of the Hôtel de Salm, including a portrait of Prince Frederick III of Salm-Kyrbourg. In the showcase devoted to Napoléon are the sword made for him by Biennais, the case of pistols presented to the Czar in 1807, the emperor's own breastplate and Legion of Honor, and a model of the inaugurural ceremony at the Camp at Boulogne. The history of the Maisons d'Education de la Légion d'Honneur is illustrated by Isabey's portrait of Mme Campan. There is a portrait of Napoléon as First Consul by Gross; the collar of the Legion of Honour made for Napoléon by Biennais (also worn by Napoléon III), collars of the Legion of Honor from the Third and Fifth Republics. Next comes a collection of other Imperial orders, such as the Iron Crown, then orders founded by Napoléon's brothers. There is a portrait of Napoléon in his coronation robes by Robert Lefèbvre. A drawing by Boilly of Napoleon decorating Cartellier recalls the ceremony of the order. There is an exceptionally rare collection of decorations awarded to Cambacérès*.

Third room

The theme here is women and decorations. The exhibits for the period of the Second Empire include the St Helena Medal, the Médaille Militaire and the campaign medals issued by Napoléon III. Next comes a series of small display panels illustrating certain periods of French history. World War I: uniforms and decorations, Croix de Guerre. From the French colonies comes Marshal Lyautey's uniform. World War II: photographs, portraits, and decorations. The Ordre National du Mérite and the decorations awarded by the different government ministries.

Three preliminary sketches by Moitte for the statues round the dome of the mansion.

Cases devoted to the religious knightly orders include the Knights Hospitaller of St John of Jerusalem, known after 1530 as the Knights of Malta; portrait of the Grand Master Rohan. View of the harbor of Valetta, some old crosses. There are robes, insignia and documents of the Order of the Holy Sepulchre.

First floor

The exhibits here are devoted to foreign orders.
Great Britain: Victoria Cross, Order of Bath, Order of the Garter with its insignia, the collar and the blue velvet garter worn on the left leg. There is a reproduction of the mantle and collar of the Order of the Golden Fleece, founded by the Duke of Burgundy. Imperial Russia: Orders of St Andrew, St Anne and St George. The Soviet Union: the

Hero of the Soviet Union star, the Order of Lenin. Denmark: Orders of the Elephant and of Dannebrog. Spain: orders of Charles III and of Isabella the Catholic. The former Italian States: the collar of the Order of the Annunciation of the royal House of Savoy. There are decorations from Africa, East Asia, and from Central and South America. United States of America: the Eagle of Cincinnatus, Distinguished Service Cross, Purple Heart and the NASA Medal.

▷ French Orders of Chivalry

The orders of chivalry comprised a force of crack troops drawn exclusively from the nobility and the royal household and surrounded by an aura of prestige and elaborate ceremony. The Order of the Saint-Esprit (Holy Ghost), the most famous French order, numbered scarcely a hundred. In 1781 all these orders were swept away by the Revolution, until Napoléon founded the Legion of Honour to enroll all those 'who by their talents contribute to the safety and the prosperity of the nation.' When the First Empire fell the order numbered 30,000, divided into the following five classes: *chevalier, officier, commandeur, grand officier* and *grand croix*. With nearly 250,000 members today, the Legion of Honour still remains the most prized French national decoration. However, it is the Ordre de la Libération that most closely resembles the old orders of chivalry. This order was founded in 1940 by General de Gaulle to enroll the worthiest of his companions, and it will disappear when the last of its holders dies.

▣ Musée Lénine [Lenin]

4 Rue Marie-Rose, 14th arr. Tel: 43–22–83–38 (afternoon only).
Open: 9.30am–5pm.
Visitors by appointment
Métro: Alésia
Bus: 28, 38, 68

Tour of the museum

30 mins.

The apartment where Lenin lived during his exile in Paris between 1909 and 1912 has been turned into a museum with copies of its original modest furnishings. A display of documents enables the visitor to follow the various stages of his career.

▣ Musée National du Louvre*** (The Louvre Palace Museum)

Palais du Louvre, Cour Napoléon, 1st arr. Tel. 40-20-51-51. Map ref: 17–A1
Open daily except Tues. 9.am–6pm, Mon. and Wed. evenings till 9.45pm. Access to auditorium, library, restaurants until 10pm daily. Main entrance: Pyramid (Cour Napoléon). Other entrance: Porte Jaujard (Pavillon de Flore)
Métro: Louvre, Palais-Royal, Tuileries
Bus: 21, 24, 27, 67, 69, 72, 81, 85, 95

NB All the arrangements in this museum are subject to change until 1993. Visitors should consult a current catalogue floor plan before touring the galleries.

By a strange irony this old, fortified castle, as elaborate and forbidding today as it appears in the *Le Parlement de Paris* retable, built originally to keep the world at bay as part of the defenses of Philippe Auguste's Paris in the 13th c., is now a huge museum, open to the world. It has survived massacres, revolutions, the rise and fall of regimes, and withstood the rigors of time. Charles V's fondness for silence may have led him to prefer Saint-Pol as his retreat, but it was at the Louvre that he lodged his most precious collections. Ever since, kings, emperors and presidents have continued to amass treasures in this palace, one of the world's largest (for descriptions of both the interior and exterior of the palace and for the history of the Pyramid → Louvre district).

The museum's origins

What was to become the Louvre museum can be traced back to François I and his royal collection. Primaticcio (who also worked on the gallery of François I at Fontainebleau) and Andrea del Sarto were commanded to seek out the greatest works of art in Italy, and to make bronze reproductions of the most beautiful sculptures of the ancient world. By the time of François' death, the collection included many statues: *Diana the Huntress,* and 12 of today's museum's most beautiful paintings, among them four by Raphael, four by Leonardo da Vinci, and Titian's portrait of the king.

At Louis XIV's accession the king's collection consisted of barely 200 paintings, but Colbert, taking advantage of the financial difficulties in which the banker Jabach found himself, bought for some 220,000 *livres* not only his collection of 5542 drawings admired by Bernini, but also 101 paintings acquired by Jabach when the Parlement sold off Charles I's immensely valuable collection. This included the collection of the Dukes of Mantua, considered the most beautiful in Italy. Prior to this, on Cardinal Mazarin's death, Colbert had bought back the paintings sold to the cardinal by Jabach, among which was Correggio's *Antiope*. This constitutes the nucleus of today's collection, and the inventory of 1709 to 1710 records the royal collection as comprising 1500 paintings.

Under Louis XV it was further enriched by the purchase of the Prince de Carignan's collection, and by royal commissions from such painters as Le Brun, Mignard, Coypel, and other French masters. Louis XVI added many Flemish and Dutch paintings. Some masterpieces from the king's collection were exhibited from 1750 to 1785 at the Luxembourg palace, while from 1737 to 1848 there were regular exhibitions of paintings in the Salon Carré (Square Room).

From palace to museum

(*See also pages 435–57.*)

In May 1791 the National Assembly ordered 'The creation of a museum at the Louvre Palace'. On July 27, 1793, a decree establishing a Muséum Central des Arts was adopted, and the museum opened its doors to the public.

Since the Convention had decided to transfer all the remaining paintings at Versailles to the Louvre, the Grande Galerie proved before long to be too small and had to be reorganized. Between 1791 and 1801 the Salon Carré, the Galerie d'Apollon and the Grande Galerie were reopened. By the time it became the Musée Napoléon, enriched with the fruits of imperial conquest, it could lay claim to being the most magnificent collection of modern times; in 1815, however, restitution of these treasures was one of the conditions imposed by the victorious allies, and many were dispersed throughout Europe.

Louis XVIII shared out approximately 300 paintings (which at the time were allocated to the royal family) among provincial museums and churches. It was his decision that the newly discovered *Venus de Milo* be displayed at the Louvre in the condition in which it had been found. In 1824 the first pieces of what was to become the modern museum of sculpture were gathered together in the open ground floor rooms of the Louvre. The beautiful Greek and Roman rooms were opened during the reign of Charles X. It was at this time too that the State acquired the priceless Revoil and Durand collections. The Assyrian museum was set up under Louis-Philippe.

In 1848 the Louvre museum became State property, which proved a great stimulus to its organization. The Salon Carré, the Salle des Sept-Cheminées (Room of the Seven Chimneys or Fireplaces), the Galerie d'Apollon and the Grande Galerie were all decorated and refurbished. Under the Second Empire the museum was further enriched by some important canvases and ancient statuary, and the Campana collection was purchased. Sauvageot donated his collection in 1856, and in 1869 Dr La Caze bequeathed his picture gallery. From 1870 the museum benefited from many important legacies: in 1874 the snuff-boxes and miniatures of M and Mme Lenoir; M His de la Salle's bronzes and drawings; in 1878 five very valuable canvases from Mme Duchâtel; in 1881 the collection of A. Thiers; in 1885 Baron C. Davillier's rich collection; in 1889 Mme Boucicaut's bequest; in 1890 those of Picot and Caillebotte although the latter did not arrive until 1929; in 1901, 1904, and 1906 the bequests of the Baron Nathaniel, and the Barons Arthur and Alphonse de Roths-child; in 1902 the Thomy-Thierry bequest; in 1906 the Moreau-Nélaton donation; in 1909, the Chauchard bequest; in 1911, the Camondo bequest; in 1914 a legacy from Arconati-Visconti and the Martin le Roy donation; in 1915 the Schlichting bequest; in 1919 the bequest of Chassériau; in 1927 the magnificent Etienne Moreau-Nélaton bequest, in 1930 the Princesse Louis de Croy's donation; the Gustave Schlumberger bequest, the Carrière and Devillez collection; in 1931 the Raymond Koechlin bequest; in 1936 the distinguished collection of engravings and drawings from the Baron Edmond de Rothschild; in 1937 the David-Weil donation; between 1939 and 1945 the important Carlos de Beistegui collection, the Paul Jamot collection of paintings, and the donations of the Princesse de Polignac, Nanteuil de la Norville, Edmé Sommier, and Seymour de Ricci; in 1952 the Paul Gacher bequest; in 1955 the Niarchos donation (the Puiforcat collection, with 373 pieces of jewelry and goldsmiths' work); in 1961 the Mège and Côte donations, together with the important Lung collection of modern paintings; in 1962 a considerable collection of Raoul Dufy paintings from his widow; and a number of acquisitions made possible by the Friends of the Louvre, including Le Brun's group portrait, *Chancellor Séguier on Horseback with his Attendants.* Finally, the Antiquities Department acquired some 3500 new pieces from the Clercq-de-Boisgelin collection.

French artistic and scientific expeditions (many of which were subsidized by the Council of Museums) have continued to build up these treasures for some 50 years. Meanwhile the Council of Museums (set up in 1895 to administer the funding of artistic acquisitions) was responsible for many important Louvre pur-chases, often with the help of the Friends of the Louvre, such as the Laborde head, the Li-Yu treasure, Barberini's *Suppliante,* Courbet's *Interior of My Studio,* the *Portrait of a Gentleman* by Watteau, an unusual *Allegory* by Louis (?) Le Nain; Bellini's *Calvary,* Barnaba de Modena's *Madonna,* Goya's *Marquesa de Santa-Cruz,* and Piero Della Francesca's portrait of Malatesta.

Currently under the directorship of Michel Laclotte, the Louvre has divided into seven main sections: Oriental Antiquities; Egyptian Antiquities; Greek and Roman Antiquities; Paintings and Drawings; Sculpture; Objets d'Art, Decorative Arts, Furniture. The recent opening of the Pyramid has facilitated access to all the Louvre's departments. The planned extension of the museum is already under way and, after 1993, the N wing (Richelieu wing) vacated by the Ministry of Finance, will be rearranged.

The Hall Napoléon

Beneath the glass superstructure of the Pyramid, this space contains the reception and information services, and gives direct access to the various museum departments. Open daily except Tues. 9am–10pm.

The auditorium: concerts, audiovisual presentations, discussions and lectures, the program for which is displayed on the museum's video screens. For information, tel. 40–20–52–99 (2–5.30 pm).

The bookshop and boutiques: sales of books, periodicals, engravings, postcards and reproductions, casts and jewelry.

Reception: in addition to the three-monthly programs prepared by the museum, and the diaporama presenting the Louvre's great works, there is an information system for visitors. Fifteen video monitors tell you what it is possible to do day by day (auditorium program, guided tours, exhibitions, workshops, collections open to the public, etc.).

Restaurant and other facilities (bureau de change, post office, public telephones, etc.).

The Louvre's history and the medieval moats

From the Hall Napoléon the Sully entrance leads to 2 new rooms presenting a permanent exhibition on the architectural history of the palace. It has relief plans of the Louvre itself and the district, archeological finds from recent digs, paintings of sovereigns and of views of the palace, and sculptures related to the external decoration. The visitor can then see remains of the ancient royal residence, the first Louvre, the foundations of which were rediscovered during works carried out in the Cour Carrée in 1977. These are parts of the defensive wall built by Louis-Philippe (1165–1223), of the keep, and one of the rooms dating from the reign of St Louis (1214–1270). Various objects discovered during the dig are displayed, including a gilded-copper helmet belonging to Charles V (1368–1422).

▷ Additional information

Guided tours: rendezvous under the Pyramid 15 mins before the start of the tour, in the space reserved for *Acceuil des groupes*.

General tour: 11am daily exc. Tues.; 3pm daily exc. Sun. and Tues.; 7.45pm Wed. In English, 10am, 11.30am, 2pm daily exc. Sun. and Tues.

Architectural tour: 10.30am daily exc. Tues.; 3.30pm daily exc. Sun. and Tues.; 6.30pm Wed.

Tour of a collection: 2 per day (consult video screens or programs). Tour in depth (of part of a collection): 2.30pm daily exc. Sun. and Tues.; 10.15am and 2.30pm Sat.

One work: daily on weekdays (not Tues.) from 12.30pm to 1.30pm. Note: for visiting groups (max. 30 people) wanting a guide-lecturer (daily exc. Sun. am and Tues.) it is necessary to book 2 months in advance. Tel. 40–20–51–77.

Oriental Antiquities

Chief Curator: Mlle Annie Caubert
Entrance: from the Pyramid and the Hall Napoléon, head toward the Pavillon Sully or the Pavillon de l'Horloge, and turn l. near the Charles V moat to reach the department.

The Louvre museum has one of the world's finest collections of ancient Near-Eastern monuments. The department dates back to May 1, 1847 when it was inaugurated as the Assyrian Museum to house the discoveries made by P. E. Botta at Khorsabad in Northern Mesopotamia. Thereafter throughout the 19th c. the French excavations under V. Place at Khorsabad, under E. de Sarzec at Telloh in Southern Mesopotamia (Sumeria), and under M and Mme Dieulafoy and, later, J. de Morgan, at Susa in Iran, gradually revealed the Assyrian, Sumerian, and Elamite civilizations to the world. From the beginning of the 20th c. to the present, various French expeditions have provided monuments for the Louvre: the work at Telloh by Cros, H. de Genouillac and André Parrot; by J. de Morgan, R. de Mecquenem and R. Ghirshman in Iran, but especially at Susa; by C. Schaeffer at Ras Shamra, and A. Parrot at Mari in Syria. The Department owes part of its display to donations and acquisitions, the most important of which was part of the De Clercq collection donated in 1967 by the Comte de Boisgelin.

These collections, which occupy the entire northern half of the ground floor of the Cour Carrée are divided into three main geographical sections: Mesopotamia, Iran and the Levant.

Mesopotamia

Gallery 1: general presentations of civilizations of the ancient Near East; the origins of Mesopotamian civilization.

Maps and tables of the civilizations of the ancient Near East.

Two major works: the obelisk of Manishtusu, king of Akkad, and the Colossal statue of Gudea, the Neo-Sumerian prince of Lagash.

Showcase on Neolithic era.

Showcase on the birth of writing.

Gallery 2: Archaic Mesopotamian civilization (2850-2000 BC).

Most of the objects on display come from the excavations at Telloh*** (ancient Girsu, capital of the state of Lagash) in Lower Mesopotamia, by E. de Sarzec, G. Cros, H. de Genouillac and A. Parrot. They allow us to rediscover the last century of the civilization of Sumeria. In the showcases: ceremonial mace of Mesilium, king of Kish; perforated marble slabs of King Ur-Nanshe, founder of the Lagash dynasty; marble slab of the priest Dudu; stone statuettes. The Stela of Eannatum** (known as the Vulture Stele) illustrating the victory of King Eannatum over the town of Umma is the oldest known historical document (2450 BC); this story of the capturing of enemies in a net can be found in the Bible. Showcase 8: the great silver vase of King Entemena shows the metalworkers' artistry; statue of Saturn, and praying votive statuettes.

Mari was a town on the middle Euphrates whose civilization bordered that of Sumeria. To the r., in the center, an alabaster statue of the Intendant Ebih-II*** (provincial administrator) of Mari in 2400 BC, dressed in a leather skirt known as a *kaunakès*. Man in the 2nd millennium.

The kings of Akkad supplanted the Sumerian civilization, and imposed their culture throughout the whole of Mesopotamia creating a veritable empire. The principal remains of this civilization were found at Susa (Iran), whence they had been transported as war booty.

The stele of Naram-Sin** in rose-colored sandstone, which narrates the victory of this king of Akkad over a mountain people. Statue of King Manishtusu (2300 BC). Fragments of stelae of Sargon, founder of the dynasty.

With the fall of the Akkadian Empire the Sumerians took power again. Their capital cities were Lagash (where Prince Gudea reigned) and Ur. The Neo-Sumerian objects on display here are all from the Telloh excavations. At the end to the l., intact diorite statue of the *ensi* Gudea*** holding a vase with life-giving water gushing out; black diorite statues; several statues of Gudea: one small, with him seated; another, with damaged shoulder; another depicting him as architect. All these were offerings in the town's temples. Showcases 7 and 8: fragments of stelae. Showcase on the l. (Cour Napoléon side) woman with scarf; diorite heads. Showcase 10: a libation vase depicting the head of Gudea wearing a turban***. In the window recess showcases to the r. (Cour Carrée side): history of cuneiform writing and literature from its beginnings to the first half of the 2nd millennium BC (inset). Showcase 14: one of Gudea's cylinders, narrating the construction of the temple to the god Ningirsu at Lagash. Showcases 11 and 12: the Telloh excavations**, bronze and terracotta figurines; folk art from the Neo-Sumerian era.

Gallery 3: Mari and Larsa (A. Parrot's excavations)

Zimrilim Palace murals* (early 2nd millennium); sacrificial scene; king's investiture. Foundation stone from the Temple of Dagan, and the forequarters of the bronze lion that stood guard over the Temple's entrance (18th c. BC); pottery made for the royal table.

Larsa, the S Mesopotamian royal town, also played a large rôle in this era: large cult vase dedicated to the goddess Ishtar, depicting her in relief, together with various animals. Cylinder seals, jewels, lapis lazuli and mother-of-pearl amulets.

Gallery 4: The Babylonian civilization

At the end of the 3rd millennium BC the Amorites descended on Mesopotamia, creating several small rival kingdoms. Among these, at the time of Hammurabi (1797–1750 BC), the most dominant was Babylon.

The Babylonian dynasty was later interrupted when overthrown by the foreign Kassites, only to be re-established during the 1st millennium. Nebuchadnezzar (604–562 BC) was the greatest king of the Babylonian Empire.

Most of the Babylonian monuments in this room were found at Susa (J. de Morgan's excavations): they had been taken there in the 12th c. BC as booty by an Elamite king. In the center the Code of Hammurabi***, King of Babylon (1792–1750 BC): this cylindrical black basalt stele some 8ft/2.25m high bears the cuneiform text of 282 laws revealed to the king by Shamash, the god of justice. This is depicted in the relief at the head of the stele. Showcase 2 and 4: a royal head**, perhaps of Hammurabi in old age; terracotta figurines from Eshunna, dating from the beginning of the 3rd millennium, depicting various gods, chariots and amusing genre scenes: musicians, cabinetmakers, a showman with monkeys, lute players. On the wall, mural panel in enameled brickwork of a lion, taken from the Babylonian processional mall built by Nebuchadnezzar in the 6th c. BC. Showcase 5: cuneiform stone tablet depicting the Tower of Babel, and Babylonian objects from the 1st c. BC. To the l. of the room, *kudduru* (boundary stone which marked the gifts of land by the king to favored persons) from the Kassite era (2nd half of the 2nd millennium BC); it bears the symbol of the god under whose protection the gift was placed. Showcase 1: Babylonian and Assyrian cylinder seals (2nd and 1st millennia BC).

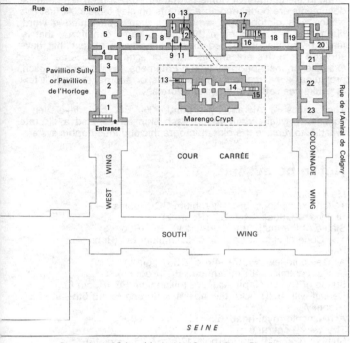

Department of Oriental Antiquities/Ground Floor (First Floor)
This arrangement is subject to change

1. The origins of Mesopotamian civilization
2. Archaic Mesopotamian civilization
3. Mari and Larsa
4. The Babylonian civilization
5. Iranian prehistory and metalwork
6. Elam 3rd – 2nd c. BC
7. Elam and the Persians
8. Susa
9. Susa, Urartu
10. Parthians and Sassanids
11. Luristan bronzes
12. Parthian, Sassanian, Christian and Islamic Iran
13. Phoenicia
14. Palmyra
15. Punic antiquities
16. Phoenician and Aramaean Levant
17. Palestine and Transjordania
18. Levant 3rd – 2nd millennium BC
19. Cyprus
20. Islam
21. Assyria
22. Assyria: Nimrod and Khorsabad
23. Nineveh

▷ The birth of writing

The oldest example of writing dates from around 3300 BC, found at Uruk, in the country of Sumeria (modern-day S Iran). The earliest documents are bookkeeping accounts on clay tablets. At first this writing was pictographic, whereby a sign represented a word; during the 2nd millennium this then became cuneiform, that is, made up of wedge-shaped dashes. The types of text that have survived from this era are historical or economic documents: for example, an inscription by which Entemena, the prince of Lagash, promulgates the freedom of his subjects; or, another example, a text of Urukagina setting out social reforms.

The scribes of Akkad, by around 2300 BC, had developed a cuneiform syllabery, in which each sign represented a discrete syllable, to replace the older pictographic and ideographic system.

▷ Not to be missed

Mesopotamia
Telloh excavations, 3rd millennium BC (Rooms 1-2).
Statues of Gudea, 2150 BC (Room 2).
Statue of the Intendant Ebih II, 2400 BC (Room 3).
The Code of Hammurabi, 2nd millennium BC (Room 4).
Iran
Achaemenid jewelry, 6th-4th c. BC (Room 5).
Susian ceramics, 4th millennium BC (Room 5).
Statue of Queen Napir Asu, 3rd millennium BC (Room 6).
Capital with bulls from the *Apadana* (throne room) 6th-4th c. BC (Room 7).
Achaemenid royal head, 6th c. BC (Room 9).
The Levant countries:
Stele of Baal with thunderbolt, 17th c. BC (Room 18).
Bas-reliefs from the palace at Khorsabad, 8th c. BC, and at Nineveh, 7th c. BC (Rooms 22-23).

Iran

Galleries 5 to 12 are dedicated to the Susa excavations and monuments from Iran.

Gallery 5: Iranian pre-history and metalwork

The city of Susa, capital of the Elamite kingdom (modern-day Iran) was a long time rival of Sumer and Babylon. The dig revealed not only Elamite antiquities going back to the dawn of this mountain people's civilization, but also Babylonian treasure (carried there as booty). There are many items from some of the more distant sites such as Tepe Sialk, and Tepe Giyan.

Central showcase, Iranian precious metalwork: jewelry of the Achaemenid period*** – necklaces, bracelets, and pendant earrings of gold with colored encrustations, arched handle of a vase in the shape of a mountain goat (in silver and electrum). Iranian metalwork from the end of the 2nd and early 1st millennia: goblets in electrum and silver overlaid with gold appliqué. To the l., showcase with vases from Susa***, outstanding for the quality of their decoration and the delicacy of the ware (4000 BC). To the r., showcase 2: ceramics and objects from Tepe Giyan (the Contenau and Ghirshman excavations) and Tepe Sialk (R. Ghirshman's excavations). Rue de Rivoli side, very early ceramics, various dishes and small sculptures from Susa (2nd half of the 4th millennium); prints from seals from (4th millennium); and early Elamite stone tablets (ca. 2900 BC). On the walls, panels of Achaemenid enameled brick. Showcase 12: N Iranian ceramics from Ismailabad (end of 5th millennium); ceramics from Tepe Hissar (3rd millennium); ceramics, jewelry, and various objects from Tureng Tepe (late 3rd–early 2nd millennium BC), the Marlik civilization (10th–9th c.), the necropolis at Khurvin (10th–7th c.); Tomadjan (9th–8th c.); Hasanlu IV (10th–9th C.), Kaluraz (7th c.) and Ardebil (7th c.).

Passageway from Gallery 5 to Gallery 6: showcase displaying Bactrian antiquities (N Afghanistan) with strong Elamite affinities. A composite statue of a woman dressed as an Elamite princess. Ceremonial axes.

Gallery 6: Elam 3rd–2nd c. BC

In the mid-3rd c. BC Susa was a fairly important city, not unlike those of Mesopotamia, under whose influence it came. Showcase 1: furnishings from mid-3rd c. tombs; painted vases. Showcase 2: Trans-Elamite (S.E. Iran) antiquities: chlorite vases; plates with central decoration. Showcase 3: items discovered at Susa, but brought in from the Trans-Elamite area, India and the Persian Gulf. Showcase 4: furniture from temples at Susa; sculptures in Mesopotamian and local styles. Showcase 5: Vase a la Cachette**, the treasure found hidden in two vases** (ca. 2400 BC).

Showcases 6, 7 and 8: Susa, late 3rd to early 2nd millennia. High-quality vases in bitumen. Copper statuette of a smiling Sumerian god. Showcase 9 (center): painted terracotta funerary portraits (15th c. BC). Showcase 10: items found at the 13th c. BC royal Elamite city Tchoga Zanbil (18 mls/30km from Susa); to the side can be seen a model of the ziggurat built by King Untash Napirisha in the city center. In the center of the room: bronze statue of Queen Napir Asu***, wife of Untash Napirisha, an outstanding example of Elamite metalwork, weighing some 3850 lb./1740kg. Opposite, statue of an Elamite goddess*, on a throne decorated with lions (ca.

1200 BC). Bronze votive salver* with cult scene in an outdoor sanctuary (12th c. BC). Showcase 11: items laid in the 12th-c. royal tombs at Susa; bronze praying figures; toys. Enameled brick frieze showing a goddess in the act of blessing and a bull-man, guardian of the palm grove. Four-tiered stele of King Untash Napirisha: lower down, the guardian spirits of the domain of the king's patron-god.

Gallery 7: Elam and the Persians

In the showcases: vases and Neo-Elamite objects. Bricks with inscriptions from temples at Susa. Silver mask and hands from a statuette. Stele of the last king of Elam, Adda Hamiti, wearing a helmet.

Medio-Elamite enameled terracotta lion (13th–12th c. BC). In the 6th c. BC the Medes and then later the Persians overran the Near and Middle East, establishing a so-called universal empire. Darius I set up his administrative capital at Susa, where he built a sumptuous palace.Capitals with bulls***, in limestone from the *apadana* (throne room) of Darius' palace (6th–4th c. BC). Along the walls the celebrated enameled brick friezes that decorated the palace walls: archers, lion, winged bull, floral and geometric motifs. A bronze lion, used as a weight. Bone-shaped bronze weights, brought to Susa as booty from the Temple of Apollo at Milet (5th c. BC). Showcases 2, 5, and 7: vases and other Neo-Elamite objects. Central showcase: Pre-Achaemenid and Achaemenid jewelry; various animal-shaped drinking cups *(rhytons)*. Fragments of bilingual stele of Darius I (recovered from the Nile Canal at the Red Sea).

Gallery 8: Susa Palace décor and cylinder seals

Enameled brick friezes from Darius' palace, including the celebrated Frieze of the *Archers of the Guard* (from Dieulafoy's excavations); griffins; a sphinx bearing the winged disc, symbol of the Persian monarchy. Bas-reliefs from Persepolis. Large showcase, tracing the evolution of small carved seals and cylinder seals in Elam and Iran.

Gallery 9: Enameled decoration from Susa; Urartu

On the walls a series of enameled brick friezes from the Achaemenid palace at Susa. Showcase dedicated to the Kingdom of Urartu (Lake Van region): bronze helmet (8th–7th c. BC); bronze votive plaques; small carved seals. Bronze bulls' heads; a god carried by a monster (Toprak-Kale).

Gallery 10: Parthians and Sassanids (3rd c. BC–AD 7th c.)

Alexander the Great's conquest brought with it a new culture: Hellenism. The subsequent seizure of power by the Sassanid Persians in AD 224 unleashed a nationalistic reaction which found an echo in very original artistic work.

Jewelry showcase: scabbard and handle of a sword in gold; ewer in gilded silver (AD 6th–7th c.), decorated with dancing girls; horse's head in silver and gold; parts from a belt in gold; large royal hunting cup in gilded silver; royal bronze bust. Various Parthian and Sassanid terracotta items.

Gallery 11: Luristan bronzes

The bronze items on show in this room represent the funerary furnishings of the nomadic mountain people of the province of Luristan, which is in the Zagros hills, N of Elam.

Showcase 1: ancient era (2500–1800 BC). Showcase with Elamite-style axes decorated with circular insignia.* Central showcase: classical era (12th–8th c. BC); swords, hatchets, funerary insignia, equine death plaques** placed in cavalrymen's tombs, decorated with winged bulls in the distinctive nomadic style. Showcase 4: circular votive brooches decorated with mythological scenes.

Gallery 12: Parthian, Sassanid, Christian, and Islamic Iran

Parthian sculpture from R. Ghirshman's excavations at Bard-e-Nechandeh and Majid-i Soleiman (AD 1st–3rd c.). Mosaics and moulding from a stucco niche from the palace at Bichapu (AD 3rd c., R. Ghirshman's excavations). Sassanid stucco motifs (AD 4th–6th c.) In the showcases, Christian antiquities found at Susa, Islamic vases. Khatchkar**, a large stele with a cross from the cemetery of Arindj in Soviet Armenia (given by the Armenian Soviet Republic).

Pre-Islamic Arab world.
Showcase: Hauran, Petra, Arabia.
Showcase: kingdoms of the Yemen.

Countries of the Levant

Gallery 13: Phoenicia

The sarcophagi presented in this room show clearly the extent of both Greek and Egyptian influence on Phoenicia.

Sarcophagi and reliefs from around Sidon, discovered by the Renan expedition in 1861. In the central bay, the sarcophagus of King Eshmunazar**, in the shape of an Egyptian mummy (5th c. BC). Anthropoid sarcophagi or with a two-part hinged lid; a lead sarcophagus. On the walls, bas-reliefs from Um el Awamid (3rd–2nd c. BC). In the last bay to the l., a reconstruction of the Mithreum at Sidon, with marble statues relating to the cult of Mithra, depicting the sacrifice which symbolizes the creation of the world (AD 4th c., formerly part of the De Clercq collection).

Gallery 14: Palmyra

The oasis of Palmyra (literally, 'the palm groves'), a stopping place for caravans in the heart of the Syrian desert, was at its most prosperous from AD 1st to the 3rd c. It is illustrated here by funerary reliefs which would have covered the niches containing the bodies: busts of men and women, their names inscribed on the base; relief of a dead man laid out on a bed, with his wife seated on a footstool at his feet. Note, to the l., a beautiful bust of a woman wearing a disillusioned expression. Facing her, a relief of three Palmyran divinities in military attire. At the far end of the room there is a well shaft that predates the construction of the Louvre.

Gallery 15: Punic antiquities

(Staircase leading back out of the crypt.)
Carthage lay at the crossroads of several great civilizations, in particular the Libyan (N Africa), the Eastern and the Greek cultures.

Votive and funerary stelae from Carthage. Stele of Gorfa (AD 1st–2nd c.) with the sign of Tani. Sarcophagus of a Punic priest, which shows marked Hellenic influence (300 BC).

Gallery 16: Phoenician and Aramaic Levant

At the end of the 2nd millennium BC, the Aramaean people, who had been nomads in the Syrian desert, began to settle and establish various warrior kingdoms in the Levant. The Phoenicians were the only ones to remain on the coast; they were the first people to develop an alphabet which they passed on to inland Aramaean settlers. Phoenician monuments are arranged in the first part of the room.

The bust of the pharaoh Osorkon I (924–895 BC) with a Phoenician dedication, shows the close links established between Phoenicia and Egypt. Stelae of a warrior god from Amrit, and stele of Yehawmilk, king of Byblos, modern day Jubail (from the De Clercq collection). Throne of Astarte (2nd c. BC). Along the wall at the end of the room are Aramean monuments from inner Syria. Aramaean and Phoenician ivories (Showcase 1); ivories from Hadatu, modern day Arslan Tash** (Showcase 2), Aramaean stelae; stelae of Zakir; stele of Tell Ahmar, an Aramaean warrior; three stelae of Halaf; two stelae of Neirah. Rivoli side: bronzes from Roman times; from Baalbek, Roman era statuettes in honor of Jupiter of Heliopolis (Showcase 6). Several items from Dura Europos, a Parthian era (3rd

c. BC–AD 3rd c.) Roman citadel in the Middle Euphrates, are on display. Statue of Aphrodite with a tortoise. A fresco depicting a huntsman on horseback* pursuing wild asses (194 BC).

Gallery 17: Palestine and Transjordania

During the Aramaean period, many small kingdoms came into being: the first Israelite kingdom and the kingdoms of Moab and Edom in Transjordan.

The stele of King Moab** otherwise known as the stele of Mesna, drawn up to commemorate the king's triumph over the Israelites in 840 BC. Ceramics and everyday items discovered at Tell el Far'ah (formerly Tirsa) the first capital of the Northern Israeli kingdom.

Gallery 18: The Levant 3rd–2nd millennium BC

The many countries that go to make up the Levant saw a whole succession of kingdoms blossom, each one different from the others.

Items from several French excavation sites have been gathered into this room: from Byblos, which was home to the Egyptians from the 3rd millennium (Montet and Dunand excavations); from the once prosperous Amorite royal kingdom of Mishrite Qatna (Dumesnil and Buisson excavations); and most notably from Ras Shamra (C. Schaeffer excavations) in ancient Ugarit. This last, whose harbor was discovered at Minet el Beida, was extremely prosperous in the 2nd c. BC, due to the trade that the city enjoyed with Egypt, Cyprus, Aegeus, and the entire Middle East.

Note the stele of Baal with a thunderbolt***, where the god is shown brandishing a spear decorated with foliage, as a sign of his beneficent power. A hunting cup, the *Patère de la Chasse*** depicting a prince at full gallop in his chariot, has traces of Egyptian stylistic influence. Bronzes, pottery, alabaster vases from Ras Shamter. The Ugaritic tablets** are particularly note-worthy, since they show the earliest examples of cuneiform alphabet, which was to find its fixed form subsequently with the Phoenicians. Mycenaean lid in ivory depicting a goddess of fecundity breast-feeding two rearing bucks; ivory cosmetics boxes. Cypriot and Mycenaean ceramic work. A gold breastplate from Byblos (*ca.* 1800 BC). 2nd millennium bronzes from various places; head of the god Djab-bul in basalt. On the walls, reliefs from the most recent Renan expedition.

Gallery 19: Cyprus

Cyprus was renowned for copper deposits. Its artistic culture, though very original, clearly owes a lot both to its geographical position between the Greek world and the East, and to its trading relationships with the Phoenicians. These influences are most obvious in its ceramic work and jewelry.

In the center, the huge Vase of Amathonte** , carved from a block of limestone, used to hold lustral water in some cult sanctuary (5th c. BC). Around the room, Cypriot statues (6th–3rd c. BC): large statue of a woman, from Tricomo; a winged sphinx with a woman's head, from Marion; statue of a man, from Dali. Rue de Rivoli side, a collection of red glazed ceramic vases from Vounous (late 3rd millennium: Schaeffer-Dikaios excavations). In the showcases, ceramics and terracotta figurines dating from the Bronze Age to the 4th c. BC, flat dishes *(paterae)* in gilded silver from Dali, decorated with Egyptian stylistic characters. Showcase 7: from the C. Schaeffer excavations at Enkomi; golden ornaments; bronze statuette of an enthroned person; a Cyprio-Minoan writing tablet, whose message is as yet undeciphered (end of 2nd millennium).

Gallery 20: Islam

Islamic art from the 7th to the 17th c. is well represented at the Louvre, and features, amongst other things, ceramics, glasswork, carpets and woodwork. Though directly descended from Hellenic art and influenced by both the Far and the Near East, Islamic art gradually evolved its own distinctive features. It is primarily decorative, concerned with color and surface; and features arabesques, stylized flowers, and foliage, as well as geometric and epigraphic motifs. Occasionally, despite the constraints of the Koran and tradition, which forbade the representation of living creatures, animal and even human figures appear as decoration.

There is a collection of pottery from Nishapur (8th–11th c.), from Persia (9th–13 c.) glazed pottery tinted with metallic oxides (Persia, Mesopotamis and Egypt), vases from Asia Minor richly decorated with beautiful colored floral and ornamental motifs.

Jewelry is represented by bronze and copper work from Persia, Syria, and Egypt (13th–15th c); candelabra with animal ornamentation (13th c.); copper ewers; Persian and Afghan arms (16th–17th c.); the Barberini vase** , made for the sultan of Alep and Damas; the baptistery of St Louis** , the large basin which served as baptismal font for the royal children in the chapel of the Château de Vincennes (Syria, 14th c.).

There is also the shroud of St Josse* , a precious silken fragment decorated with camels and elephants (Persia, 10th c.); the magnificent 16th-c. Persian wall-hanging from the collegiate church of Mantes*** , worked *à haute laine* (thick pile) and in the contemporaneous style of miniatures. Mosque lamps, jewels, and wooden panels carved with bas-reliefs.

Gallery 21: Assyria

Eventually (by 1993) the Assyrian exhibits, currently in Rooms 21, 22, 23 will be moved to the Richlieu wing (now occupied by the Ministère de Finances). This space will then be allocated to the Egyptian Antiquities department.

From the 9th to the 10th c. BC, the Assyrian kings undertook a number of evermore far-reaching conquests, which lasted until their crushing defeat by the Medes and the Babylonians in 612 BC. They set up great governmental palaces at Nineveh and Nimrod, which were adorned with bas-reliefs showing royal power. The palace entrances were guarded by stone colossi to defend the palace and to stand as symbols of the world's stability.

To the l., bas-reliefs from the palace of Sargon at Khorsabad, depicting the transport of wood from the Lebanon to Assyria by land and sea. On a plinth, the door sill from the palace of Ashurbanipal at Nineveh. Assyrian writing tablets. Showcase in the entrance: bronze relief of the Assyrian King Asarhaddon and his mother (6th c. BC); bronze head of a bull from Khorsabad; vases, amulets, bronze statuette. Bronze plaque with an inscription to ward off Lamashtu, a demon who tormented the sick (formerly part of the De Clercq collection). On the wall, to the r., main axle from Sargon's chariot, and the stele of Ishtar of Arbela from Til Barsip. Central showcase: frescoes from the palace at Til Barsip; bronze wall plaques.

Gallery 22: Assyria (Palaces of Nimrod and Khorsabad)

This gallery is lined with huge bas-reliefs, some of them from the palace of Ashurbanipal II at Nimrod (formerly Kalakh; 9th c. BC), but most of which are from the palace of Sargon at Khorsabad (formerly Dar-Sharrukin; 8th c. BC). Seven larger bas-reliefs depict life at the palace. At the gallery doors, the winged bulls with human heads wearing tiaras symbolizing their divinity, used to defend the palace. They were associated with the epic hero Gilgamesh, who is himself represented by two high-reliefs in the center of the room; to symbolize his strength, he is shown strangling a small lion. Stele from Arslan-Tash, Hadad on a bull.

Relief depicting court officials from the palace of Sargon. Sargon's son, Sennacherib, built a palace at Nineveh, later destroyed by his grandson Ashurbanipal (668–627 BC) to make way for another, even more sumptuous.

The stairway is adorned with bas-reliefs from Ashurbanipal's palace at Nineveh (7th c. BC); royal hunting and war scenes. Flanking the foot of the staircase are two bulls from the portals of the temple of Ishtar at Arslan-Tash (8th c. BC: Thureau-Dangin excavations).

▷ **Chronological chart of the civilizations represented in the Department of Oriental Antiquities**

Ca. 8000 BC	Neolithic villages in Syria and in Kurdistan.
Ca. 6000 BC	Later Neolithic period: the spread of painted ceramics.
Ca. 4200 BC	The establishment of Susa (SW Iran).
Ca. 3500–3200 BC	Civilization of Uruk: birth of writing.
Ca. 2800–2340 BC	The era of the archaic Sumerian dynasties.
2340–2190 BC	Semitic empire of Akkad.
2190–2000 BC	Neo-Sumerian renaissance
1894–1595 BC	First Babylonian dynasty. Hammurabi (1792-1750 BC).
1595–1155 BC	Kassite dynasty in Babylon.
13th–12th c. BC	Zenith of Elam.
9th–7th c. BC	Assyrian Empire (612 BC): fall of Nineveh.
6th–4th c. BC	Achaemenid Persian Empire.
305–65 BC	Seleucid Empire: Hellenic civilization.
250 BC–AD 226	Parthian Empire in Iran and Mesopotamia.
AD 226–641	Sassanid Empire in Iran and Mesopotamia.

Egyptian Antiquities

Chief Curator: Jean Louis de Cenival
Entrance: from the Pyramid and the Hall Napoleon, head for the Pavillon Sully (or Horloge). This leads from the Sully crypt to the dry moats of Philippe-Auguste and Charles V. A stairway leads to the Sphinx crypt; the best place from which to follow the chronological layout of the exhibits.

The study of Egyptian civilization began with the expedition that accompanied Bonaparte to Egypt in 1798. Champollion was the first curator of the Egyptian Museum (also known as the Musée Charles X), founded in 1826 to house the huge collections acquired by the State. Since then the department has been constantly enriched by acquisition, gifts, and excavation expeditions, such as those of François Mariette at Serapeum (1851), or those of the Louvre, or those of the Institut Français d'Archéologie Orientale in Cairo at Abu Roach, Tod, Medamud, Assiut, and Deir el-Medineh.

Visiting this collection starts on the ground floor (S wing of the Cour Carrée), and then continues on the first floor.

Ground floor

Gallery 1: Sphinx Crypt

An underground corridor (the Passage des Arts) between the Greek and Roman Antiquities and the Oriental Antiquities.

The colossal sphinx*** in pink granite, from the site of Tanis in Lower Egypt, may be a likeness of King Snefru (4th dynasty), later usurped by the kings Mineptha (19th dynasty) and Chechonq (22nd dynasty). On either side of the sphinx is a bas-relief showing Rameses II offering incense to the sphinx-god Harmakhis (Hore makhet). These form the walls of a chapel, framing the stele of the 'Dream of Tutmosis IV' (18th dynasty), which stands between the paws of the great sphinx of Giza.

Gallery 2: The mastaba (tomb) of Akhut-Hetep

The funerary chapel of the mastaba of Akhut-Hetep*** (→ inset), a high official of the 5th dynasty (*ca.* 2350 BC) has been rebuilt (the unpainted flagstones are modern; the painted stones are original). This came from Sakhara, the necropolis of Memphis, the one-time capital, which remained one of Egypt's most important cities.

In the door recess, to the l., weavers are seen presenting bales of fabric to the landowner, and being rewarded with necklaces and diadems; to the r., statues of Akhut-Hetep are hauled toward the tomb. Inside, on the front partition wall to the l., are scenes of cattle raising, harvesting, catching birds with nets, and goat rearing; to the r., jostling competitors on papyrus boats, hunting in the marshes, fishing, and the preparation of fish. The two sides, below, depict the deceased's last journey by boat. On the l., gift-bearers pass in procession before Akhut-Hetep, who is seated at a banquet below the slit in the *serdab* (the *serdab* was a concealed room within the *mastaba* connected to the public chamber only by a narrow slit in the masonry). On the r. Akhut-Hetep can be seen taking part in the funerary banquet, complete with music and dancing.

Gallery 3: End of the Thinite Archaic Period, and the 3rd dynasty.

The culture of Nagada evolved during the 4th dynasty in two phases, called Nagada I (4000–3500 BC) and Nagada II (3500–1300 BC). Originally confined to Upper Egypt, after 3500 BC this culture spread across the whole country. It is the work of a sedentary, formerly hunting, people, who had roamed across a vast area; and who had contact with Mesopotamia.

There is no doubting their outstanding ability in pottery, represented here by black-bordered red vases* (the border is achieved in the firing). They excelled in the dressing of hard stone, out of which they fashioned vases* and make-up palettes. Relief work was another of their skills: the dagger of Gebel-el-Arak** has a flint blade and a beautiful carved ivory handle with one of the oldest extant Egyptian reliefs (around 3400-3300 BC). The handle, of Mesopotamian inspiration, is decorated on one side with a sea-and-land battle scene; on the other side there are two tamed lions under the mastery of a man. Around this time there appears what was to become the principal feature of the Egyptian style up to the Roman era: the rendering of the human figure with the face, legs, and arms in profile, with the torso shown from the front or back. Cosmetic palettes were used for grinding eye makeup; they could be geometric or animal in shape. The larger ones with relief decoration probably had only a votive function: the collection includes examples commemorating a hunt, a victory, a bull motif, and others simply depicting animals, such as jackals. These objects, all found in tombs, testify to the belief in life after death; the dead person is accompanied by whatever may be necessary for the Afterlife. The culture of Nagada puts art at the service of religion. Its artistic evolution was to make a major leap forward with the unification of Egypt and the establishment of the 1st dynasty.

Thinite (Archaic) era. The Serpent King's stele (King Djet)** recovered from his tomb at Abydos; portrays a falcon symbolizing the god Horus above an inscription of the king's name, which is framed by an image of a palace. This is a masterpiece of reliefwork, whose perfection shows in the smallest detail. The falcon and the serpent acquire here their definitive form, but it was not until the 4th dynasty that the complete set of hieroglyphic symbols was fixed.

Galleries 4, 5 and 6: the Old Kingdom

The passage from the Thinite era to the 3rd dynasty was marked by the advent of stone architecture, and the building of the Old Kingdom's first pyramid.

The god-king of Ancient Egypt, surrounded by a court of high dignitaries, ruled over a strongly centralized state with its capital at Memphis. Under the 4th dynasty Cheops and Chepren built their gigantic pyramids at Giza; the dimensions of their successor's tombs were less overwhelming. Around these pyramids stood the *mastabas* of the State's civil servants. From this evidence a clear picture of life in the Ancient Kingdom can be pieced together. Art at Memphis was in full flower; provincial art, however, was rather more mediocre.

Gallery 4

The two statues of Sepa and his wife Nesa are depicted in a hieratic pose that was copied throughout succeeding centuries; although static, it did not prevent the artist from creating truly individual

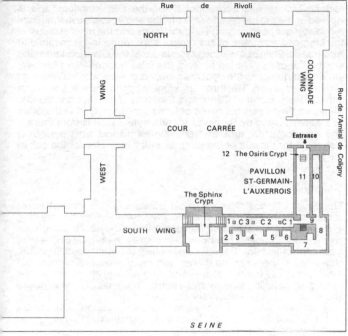

Department of Egyptian Antiquities/Ground Floor (First Floor)
This arrangement is subject to change

1. The Sphinx Crypt
2. The Mastaba of Akhut-Hetep
3. Thinite (Archaic) era
4,5,6. Old Kingdom 2700–200 BC
7,8. Middle Kingdom, 2060–1785 BC

9. New Kingdom
10. The Galerie d'Alger
11. Galerie Henry IV
12. The Osiris Crypt
C1,C2,C3. The Coptic Era

portraits. This style of sculpture, though still a little clumsy in this archaic era, reached its peak in the 4th dynasty.

At the entrance of the gallery, the stele of Princess Nefertiabet*** depicts the dead princess at a meal, a key theme in funerary art. The well-preserved colors serve to underline the delicacy of the relief and highlight the balanced arrangement of the symbols.

In the center of the gallery stands a vat-shaped limestone sarcophagus from Abu Roadh (the necropolis near Memphis). It is rectangular, as was conventional for the Old Kingdom, and is worked in the palace-façade style. In the showcase is a magnificent red sandstone head of King Didoufri**; this and the other statuary of the king and members of his family were found in his pyramid at Abu Roach. Statues of various dignitaries of the Old Kingdom stand around the gallery. At the far end, the false door of Meri (Sakhara, 4th dynasty) depicts the deceased seated at table with his offerings laid out before him. The three large granite columns with palmiform capitals were found at Tanis and Sakhara, and date from the Old Kingdom. One bears the name of Unas (5th dynasty), but the other two were usurped by Rameses II (19th dynasty). It is from this era Old Kingdom) that funerary temples (as distinct from pyramids) were built for the cult of the king, as well as temples for the cult of the gods.

Gallery 5

The *Seated Scribe**** is the most outstanding of the statues of scribes from the Old Kingdom. The artist has succeeded in creating a strikingly realistic portrait, accentuating the eyes by using rock crystal set in copper. The showcases display the typical contents of a tomb from this era. Food was obviously the chief preoccupation. Not only are there serving dishes and representations of food, but there are stone models of servants to attend to the needs of the deceased, including a baker and a miller. Dummies of trussed goose and of cuts of meat effectively replace the real offerings the living may not have brought. Other aspects of the deceased's afterlife are also provided for: comfort (headrest), appearance (jewelry), and work (writing materials, weapons).

Between Galleries 5 and 6, a bas-relief depicting the Libyans weakened by famine.

▷ The mastaba

The mastaba is the tomb of the nobles of the Old Kingdom. A rectangular mass with sloping walls, it recalls the form of a bench (Arabic: *mastaba*). It is built of brick and limestone in two parts, the burial vault and the chapel. The vault is the underground part of the tomb, with the sarcophagus and funerary material.

Access to it was via a well, refilled after the burial ceremony. The chapel was intended for worship of the deceased, and the living came to place their offerings in it. The dead person was supposed to communicate with the chapel by means of its false door, and through his or her statue placed in the *serdab* (a small windowless room sometimes provided with a narrow slit). The walls of the chapel were decorated with scenes of everyday life and of offerings. By virtue of the statue and the funerary equipment the deceased was thought to be able to continue the familiar pattern of everyday life, and survival in the afterlife was assured.

▷ # Ancient Egypt: chronological table

4000–3100BC	End of prehistory: Nagada I, Nagada II
3100–2700 BC	Thinite era: 1st–2nd dynasties
2700–2200 BC	Old Kingdom: 3rd–6th dynasties
2200–2060 BC	First Intermediate Period: 7th–10th dynasties
2060–1785 BC	Middle Kingdom: 11th–12th dynasties
1785–1555 BC	Second Intermediate Period: 13th–17th dynasties
1555–1080 BC	New Kingdom: 18th–20th dynasties
1080–525 BC	Late period: 27th dynasty (Persian domination). Third Intermediate Period: 21st dynasty (Tanite dynasty), 22nd–24th dynasty (Libyan era), 25th dynasty (Ethiopian dynasty), 26th dynasty (Saitic dynasty)
525–332 BC	28th–30th dynasties (last indigenous dynasties)
332–30 BC	Greek era: Lagide dynasty
30 BC–AD 392	Roman era
AD 397–641	Coptic or Byzantine era
AD 641 Arab conquest.	

Gallery 6

To the r. of the entrance, a very realistic bas-relief of Libyans weakened by famine. A moving statue of a couple conveys the emotional bond that unites the spouses (end of 5th dynasty and 6th dynasty): in painted wood, an anonymous couple hold hands tenderly. Painting on limewood from the mastaba of Metheti, with scenes from everyday life.

Galleries 7 and 8:
Middle Kingdom (11th–12th dynasties)

The Middle Kingdom dates from the reunification of Egypt by Montuhotep, the founder of the 11th dynasty, thus ending two centuries of social and economic troubles (1st Intermediate Period). The 12th dynasty, under which the country was reorganized and began to prosper, was to end in the collapse of royal power, which led to another troubled period. The kings of this period elevated the Theban god Amun into the first rank of Egyptian deities. As the civilization developed, so did its art. Reliefwork in stone was more finely chiselled. Private statuary, often small, became more popular, and evolved a new form the so-called cube-statue. Royal statuary moved away from an idealized portrait of the rulers, so that they are no longer fixed in an eternal youth, but show the ravages of age, worry and obesity.

Gallery 7

Senkhare Montuhotep* granite block (11th dynasty, Tod), with two beautiful portraits of the god Montu and the goddess Tanent, enhanced by headdress and adornments. Dog-headed statue* with delicately worked coat. Door lintel* bearing an image of Sesostris III (13th dynasty, Medamud) worshipping the god Montu. The two statues of Sesostris III in diorite (Medamud) are reminiscent of the same king's portrait on the lintel. The showcase contains a collection of Middle Kingdom royal heads, among which those of Sesostris II and Amenemhet III (13th dynasty) stand out. The coffins of Sopi, both the inner and outer cases, are rectangular, made of wood, and decorated with a painted frieze based on objects and religious texts taken from royal funerary texts of the Old Kingdom. To the side stands the wooden statue of Hapydjefai, one of the Middle Kingdom's largest and most important funerary statues. There is also some smaller statuary from the Middle Kingdom, including the statuette of Ihay, son of Hathor. The treasure of Tod* consisted of the foundation offerings made in the name of King Amenemhat II for a new temple. A whole series of ceremonies preceded the building of a temple, including the burying of certain items including, finally, the tools used in its construction, in a corner of the building. At Tod the treasure comprised four bronze coffers of gold and silver bullion, pieces of lapis lazuli, and most importantly silver cups with Aegean decoration indicating the foreign origin of the treasure.

Gallery 8

State-chapel of Senusret (12th dynasty), a veritable miniature funerary chapel decorated with scenes of everyday life and of the journey to death. The torso of Queen Neferusebek, last ruler of the 12th dynasty, wearing the *nemes*, the triangular headdress of the king with the lappets hanging down over the breast.

Gallery 9: Second Intermediate Period and the New Kingdom.

Note also the great sphinx of the Middle Empire, which Rameses II and Mineptah had rededicated to themselves in the 19th dynasty.

Gallery 10: The Galerie d'Alger.

This hall is given over to the children's workshop. A number of activities are offered, such as building models of Egyptian temples, boats, and so forth, by way of introducing the children to the culture of the pharaohs (for further information and reservations, telephone the *Service d'action culturelle*, 40-20-51-77).

▷ The Royal Dynasties

3100–2850 BC	1st dynasty
2850–2700 BC	2nd dynasty
2700–2620 BC	3rd dynasty
2620–2500 BC	4th dynasty
2500–2350 BC	5th dynasty
2350–2200 BC	6th dynasty
2200–2060 BC	6th – 10th dynasties
2060–1990 BC	11th dynasty
1990–1785 BC	12th dynasty
1785–1555 BC	13th–17th dynasties
1555–1305 BC	18th dynasty
1305–1185 BC	19th dynasty
1185–1080 BC	20th dynasty
1080–946 BC	21st dynasty
946–820 BC	22nd dynasty
820–740 BC	23rd dynasty
740–730 BC	24th dynasty
730–664 BC	25th dynasty
664–525 BC	26th dynasty
525–404 BC	27th dynasty
404–380 BC	28th–29th dynasties
380–342 BC	30th dynasty.

Gallery 11: Galerie Henri IV, New Kingdom and the Third Intermediate Period

This display is set out in the Galerie Henri IV, designed by Louis Le Vau. The entrance to this gallery has been set up to evoke the courtyard of an Egyptian temple. So where the entry door would have been that led from the pylon (the monumental gateway building of Egyptian temples, usually comprised of two vast truncated pyramidal forms) into the temple, the museum displays a door stile from Coptos (Upper Egypt), dedicated to Tuthmosis III (18th dynasty) who is depicted making an offering of flowers and ducks. The courtyard was sometimes closed by a second pylon, represented here farther down the gallery by a door stile of Rameses II, which portrays the king making an offering of lettuce to the sky god Min. In front of the pylons would have stood royal colossi, such as that of Amenophis III (18th dynasty) whose head** and feet ** are preserved here. Leaning against the base are statues of the Vizier Montuhotep (12th dynasty), which used to stand in the courtyard of the temple of Karnak. Often there was a colonnade between the two pylons, and statues were placed between the tightly spaced columns. Here this is represented by several column pieces, as well as eight statues of the formidable lion-headed goddess Sekhmet**, a diorite statue of the goddess Nephthys*, and a group of statues of 26th-dynasty dignitaries (cube-statue of Uahibre, and kneeling statue of Nakhorteb). At the end of the courtyard to the r., near the array of Sekhmet figures, is the Tutankhamen*** group, protected by the god Amon. Despite the damage, this statue of the young king is one of the best surviving pieces of late 18th-dynasty art.

Apart from the display of earthenware tiles, dedicated to Sethi I, which adorned one of the Nile delta palaces (to the l., in the window recess showcase) the remainder of the gallery is given over to large monuments from temples and tombs. The capital of the goddess Hathor*, with her head as decoration on two sides, comes from Bubastis and may date from the New Kingdom. The sarcophagus of Rameses III** (20th dynasty), whose lid is in Cambridge, is in the shape of an oval cartouche, decorated with images of the goddess Isis (at the foot), Nephthys (at the head), and religious texts about the sun's journey through the night. To the r., the group of four baboons worshipping the sun is in fact the base of the obelisk of Rameses II which still stands at Luxor, and whose twin can be seen in the Place de la Concorde. To the r., on the wall, a painted bas-relief of Sethi I*** receiving the magic necklace from the hands of Hathor, represented here as goddess of the Theban necropolis. This once decorated a pillar in the king's tomb in the Valley of the Kings. To the l., Theban funerary chapels surmounted by pyramidions, inscribed with hymns to the sun. A bas-relief from Karnak depicting the enthronement of Nitocris (26th dynasty) as a 'divine worshipper'; also of Chapenupet as a 'divine worshipper', pictured here as the goddess Isis fanning Horus with her wings, from the temple at Medinet Habu (25th–26th dynasty). The 'divine worshippers' were the wives of the god Amon. Invested with this cultic function, under the 25th–26th dynasty they took on the attributes of the pharaohs, without having any political power. These divine worshippers were virgins, but the custom was for them to adopt a child to succeed them. Note the very beautiful head of Hathor*, which once graced a capital (3rd c. BC).

At the end of the gallery there are two examples of a naos. The naos was the sanctuary, deep within the temple, which housed a statue of the divinity to whom the temple was dedicated. On the r. is the naos dedicated to Osiris* by King Amasis, whose decoration presents most of the Egyptian pantheon. The naos on the l. was dedicated to Isis by Cleopatra.

Gallery 12: Osiris crypt: Late Period

This room houses funerary works, including three fine Ptolemaic sarcophagi: of these, the sarcophagus of Djedhor* features (at the foot) the sun traveling from one boat to another. In a niche, a cult statue of Osiris, god of death and rebirth, which faces a statue of his wife Isis, weeping.

Part of the showcases are given over to sacred animals. They were considered to be divine, they were the object of a cult that was taken to extremes in late dynastic Egypt. The number of cemeteries for animals increased, and were filled with their mummies. In the center of the room is the mummy of a ram, and the limestone sarcophagus of an ibis; to the l., mummies of a cat, a dog, a fish, and a crocodile.

The zodiac on the ceiling is from the temple at Denderah*, and dates from the Roman period. In this era, the signs of the zodiac were added to the traditional Egyptian constellations and decans (each zodiacal sign had three decans, or 10° segments).

Go back through Gallery 9, to reach the rooms displaying Egyptian Antiquities.

▷ Not to be missed

Ground floor
Tanis Sphinx, 4th or 12th dyn. (crypt).
Mastaba of Akhut-Hetep, 5th dyn. (Gallery 2).
Stele of Nefertiabet (Gallery 3 and 4).
Seated scribe, 5th dyn. (Gallery 5).
Sculpted group of Tutankhamun and the god Amun, 18th dyn. (Henri IV Gallery).
Bas-relief of Sethi I, 19th dyn. (Henri IV Gallery).
Icon from the monastery of Baoit, 6th–9th c. (Gallery 3 of Coptic Art).

First floor
Colossal bust of Amenophis IV–Akhenaton, 18th dyn. (landing of the Egyptian staircase).
Female statuettes from the reign of Amenophis III (Gallery B).
Salt head and head of Amarnian princess, from Tel el Amarna 18th dyn. (Gallery D).
Display cabinet of jewels and gold- and silver-ware, 12th–22nd dyn. (Gallery E).
Statue of Queen Karomama, 22nd dyn. (Gallery F).
Display cabinet of small bronzes, 3rd Intermediate Period (Gallery F).

Galleries C1, C2, C3: The Coptic era (4th–12th c. AD)

The word 'Copt' comes from the same root as 'Egypt', the Greek word *aigyptios* (Egyptian). The term 'Coptic' designates both the period of Egyptian history from the 4th to the 12th c. AD, as well as the native Egyptian Christian minority (an autonomous Monophysite sect that survived the Arab conquest in AD 641). In the history of Egypt – which was the cradle of Christian monasticism – Coptic art immediately succeeds the Roman era. It evolved from pagan origins, gradually becoming more Christian through the 12th c. Its roots lay in the Mediterranean world, but occasionally it looked to the tradition of the pharaohs for inspiration. Its masterpieces are in weaving, painting, and sculpture. Three galleries at the Louvre are dedicated to Coptic art.

Gallery C1: The Roman era and the birth of Coptic art

Entry wall: two shrouds, with painting in a wax encaustic medium of the deceased. On one of them, the deceased is being guided by the jackal-headed god Anubis. To the r., well-preserved mummy of an elegant woman. Note the naturalistic Fayum portrait, inserted into the bandaging at face level, and painted in the same wax medium. To the l., the veil of Antinoös**, a cloth with bacchic scenes. In the showcase, a fine collection of Alexandrian ivories. On the far wall, tapestries show the early beginnings of Coptic weaving: the Shawl of Sabina decorated with scenes of the Nile, and wall-hangings of wine-harvesting cherubs (end of 3rd c. AD). To the l., there is a statue of Horus dressed as a Roman legionary on horseback, impaling a crocodile with his lance (5th c. AD).

Gallery C2: The blossoming of Coptic art (5th–7th c. AD)

To the l. is a great collection of tapestries in astonishingly vivid colors, with scenes of the Nile, hunting, an eagle, or a dancer. They all feature the Christian cross as a decorative motif. One showcase relates to the techniques of Coptic weaving; another, reconstructions of Coptic costumes. The sculptures are on the theme of Aphrodite Anodyomena (she who emerges) and various Christian subjects. The mural paintings are from the site of the monastery at Kellia (SW of Alexandria).

Gallery C3: Coptic art from the Arab conquest to the 12th c.

This room is devoted to a reconstruction of the nave of the monastery church of Baouit (Middle Egypt, 6th–9th c.). It has been reconstructed on the same scale as, and using elements of, the original. Both the interior and exterior are decorated with friezes sculpted in wood and stone. Note the fine basket capitals** on display inside. In the chancel there is the magnificent icon*** depicting the Abbot Mena protected by Christ.

The Egyptian stairway

Turn back up the Egyptian stairway, to reach the Egyptian rooms on the first floor.

On the partition wall to the l., blocks from the temple at Karnak which constitute part of the Annals of Tutmosis III* (18th dynasty). Here the king describes some of his campaigns into Asia.

Mid-landing: beautiful statue of Bes*, divine protectress, from Serapeum. Upper landing: magnificent, colossal bust of Amenophis IV*** (Akhenaton), 18th dynasty (→ inset) in the form of Osiris. This was presented to France by Egypt in recognition of her part in saving the great monuments of Nubia. The funerary chapel* of the scribe Unsu and his wife Imenhétep (18th dynasty). The paintings, on limewood, are mainly agricultural scenes. The chapel houses a sandstone statue of the couple. The colossal pink sandstone statue of King Seti II (19th dynasty) was found in the courtyard of the temple at Kernak. The items on display at the side of this room relate to various aspects of everyday life, such as cooking and drinking. It is clear that bread was the staple of the Egyptian diet, followed by roast meat and stews, with vegetables and fruit, all washed down with quantities of beer and wine. In the neighboring showcase, notice the unusual wooden statue of a pig, and a terracotta statue of a weeping girl. Though this last theme is common enough in reliefwork, it is rare to find it as the subject for a statue.

The Serapeum: A number of items displayed on this stairway are from the temple of Serapeum at Sakkara. These are: a fine statue of Apis** (→ inset) in painted limestone; several blue *shawabti* (funerary statuettes of servants placed in the sacred bulls' tombs); six sphinxes which used to border the pathway to the underground necropolis; four canopic vases (urns for the entrails) of a bull who died in the reign of Tutankhamun; and the stelae which commemorated the burial of the sacred bulls, giving the name and date of the king in whose reign the burial took place. This documentary evidence has proved very important in establishing our knowledge of Egyptian chronology.

▷ Apis, the sacred bull

Apis, the bull (Hapi in Egyptian) was thought to be the living incarnation of Ptah, the great god of Memphis. Not all bulls could be thus considered; to be declared Apis a bull had to display certain key markings on its hide and tongue. When it died, the Apis was mummified, placed in a large sarcophagus, and buried along with its *shawabti* in a special tomb at Serapeum. This underground necropolis for Apis bulls was discovered in 1851 by François Mariette. Though this cult of Apis may well go back to earliest times, the oldest monuments discovered at Serapeum date only from the time of Amenophis II (18th dynasty); the most recent are no later than Caesarion, son of Cleopatra and, according to tradition, of Caesar.

First floor

Currently the first floor space allocated to the Egyptian Department is restricted to the southern wing of the Cour Carrée. Once the Objets d'Arts Department is rehoused in the Richelieu wing, the colonnade wing of the Cour Carrée will be given over to the Egyptian Department. The wall showcases are numbered starting on the l. and working clockwise round the room: B4, for example, is the 4th showcase in Gallery B.

Gallery A: Middle Kingdom (continued)

The items on display here from private tombs show Egyptian art diversifying into other materials. The stone models typical of the Old Kingdom are replaced by wooden ones, often simply made, but with a great variety and liveliness of style.

The tomb of Nakhti (12th dynasty): the wooden statue of Chancellor Nakhti** must rate as one of the most beautiful statues from a private tomb of this era. His coffin in painted wood is decorated (as is that of Sopi – Gallery 7) with funerary texts known as the *Sarcophagus Texts.* Showcases A3, A4, the neighboring showcase and the desk under the window all contain items from this tomb: small wooden statues, reminiscent of his bigger statue; clothing; toiletry objects (razor, mirror); wooden scepter, symbol of his authority; weapons and tools. Note the interesting model of a granary and statuettes of peasants garnering the corn under the watchful eye of the scribe.

In the showcase to the l., the famous *Woman Bearing Offerings** in painted wood. Elegant and slender, she carries a duck in one hand, while with the other she balances on her head a small box and a piece of meat. The purpose of the blue glazed terracotta hippopotamuses**, whose bodies are decorated with lotus and papyrus leaves, was to keep alive for the deceased the pleasure of hunting and of fishing in the marshes. They reveal the superb style of Egyptian artists in rendering animals. At the far end of the room are models of boats designed for the journey of death. The deceased was thought of as a pilgrim making his way to the holy city of Abydos, dedicated to the cult of Osiris, so that he might benefit from the Osirian rites of rebirth.

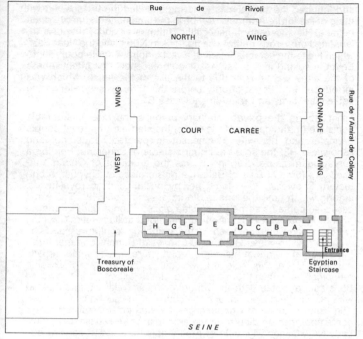

Department of Egyptian Antiquities/ First Floor (Second Floor)
This arrangement is subject to change

A Middle Kingdom (continued)
B, C, D, E New Kingdom

F Third Intermediate Period
G Late Period
H Ptolemaic and Roman Periods

Galleries B, C, D, E: The New Kingdom

Gallery B: from the 18th dynasty to the end of the reign of Amenophis III.

The Theban kings of the 17th dynasty struggled against the invading Hyksos, a Semite dynasty, who ruled Egypt for almost a century. The Louvre has several items from this dynasty, including two wooden coffins that belonged to two kings named Antef (Showcase B6). The sarcophagus in this period was no longer rectangular in shape, but mummiform. It was Ahmosis, a descendent of the Antefs, who re-established the unity of Egypt, and founded the 18th dynasty, having expelled the Hyksos. Something of the future Ahmosis may be in the limestone statue of Prince Iahmes. His successors, especially Thutmosis I and Thutmosis III, launched numerous military campaigns in Nubia and the Near East, which led to the establishment of a vast empire. Tribute poured into Egypt, resulting in a great artistic efflorescence. The effectiveness of the army was mostly due to the use of the horse, which was introduced into Egypt shortly before the 17th dynasty. Hence the equestrian items and relief in showcase B1.

From among the private statuary perhaps the most memorable items are (in the center of the room) the statue of the royal couple Sennefer and his wife Hatshepsut in painted sandstone, and (Showcase B3) the small red quartz statue of Senenmut holding a surveying measure. Senenmut was the architect of Queen Hatshepsut's tomb at Deir el-Bahari, a masterpiece of Egyptian architecture. Showcase B3 is dominated by the 18th dynasty royal heads, among which note the one in diorite of Amenophis III*. The same case also contains some lovely blue glazed faience cups*. Amenophis III (1402–1364 BC) inherited an empire at its zenith. The king (whose image can be seen in the paintings, sculptures and the *shawabti* in showcase B4) issued a series of scarabs commemorating the great events of his reign. Architecture was his major artistic concern. Under his rule art was characterized by an extreme refinement, of which there are several classic examples in showcase B5: statue of Setau with the vulture goddess Nekhbet, Imennakhet with his wife and his son, and the statue of the scribe Neferrenpet. The same refinement characterizes the statuettes*** of the king's contemporaries on display in the neighboring showcase: Lady Tuy, Lady Nay, Queen Tiy, wife of Amenophis III, a naked servant girl, and two groups in alabaster and slate of the scribe Nebmertuf writing under the protection of the god Thoth. This careful relief work extended to trivial items such as the three exquisite cosmetics spoons* in the form of swimming girls (cosmetics showcase). Showcase B7 contains a very good example of a funerary stele*, dedicated by Paser, head of the harem, to the god Osiris.

Gallery C: Everyday life

Through sculpture, paintings, and stelae, Showcase C2 traces the evolution of fashion from the Old Kingdom onward. Note the beautiful couple Raherka and Mersankh*. This reached great heights of studied elegance with wigs and costumes in the time of the New Kingdom as seen in the statue of Piay**, from the temple of Amon. Although available only to the favored few, there was a wide range of toiletries, such as mirrors, razors, combs, and tweezers. Some of the best examples are displayed in the neighboring showcase. Particularly worth noting is an unguent jar**, decorated with a young woman carrying a bunch of water lilies and a vase.

Since the Egyptian notion of death implied rebuilding the

deceased's ordinary life within the tomb, the discovery of tombs and their contents has given an accurate insight into the contents of an Egyptian house. The deceased was made to feel at home not just with the most ordinary of domestic items (terracotta lamps, brooms, rush matting, wicker work baskets), but with the very best of his or her furniture (wooden chests, chairs, footstools, and a headrest for sleeping). Note the very fine wooden chair* inlaid with ivory in the next showcase. Alongside, models of houses in earthenware or limestone give an idea of how Egyptian houses were laid out. Showcase C7 contains a display of weapons from different periods: bows, arrows, hatchets, daggers, as well as reliefs and paintings depicting hunting and fishing. Though these were essentially food-gathering activities for the peasants who used nets to catch birds and fish, for the nobility hunting (with throwing sticks and fishing with harpoons) was a favorite pastime. The Egyptians were very fond of sports and games, as is demonstrated in a showcase on the r. of the room. Another case is devoted to women, with a pretty blue glazed faience figurine* of a concubine for the deceased. The group of showcases to the r. of the entrance provide explanations of Egyptian artistic techniques for working glass and faience with opaque glazes, stone and wood.

Music accompanied all Egyptian feasts, sacred or secular. The favorite instrument was the harp (Showcase C6), and its neighbor, which houses the world's only example of a trigonal harp* (Saïte Period, 7th–6th c. BC). After the harp, the most widely used instruments were the flute and the hautbois or oboe (Showcase C6). The lute and the lyre were imports, not reaching Egypt until the time of the New Kingdom (Showcase C5 shows seductive lute players as decoration on cosmetics spoons, faience cups, and wooden chests). Drums and small two-headed drums supplied the rhythm, together with castanets and clackers (Showcases C5 and C6). Sistra metal frame rattles, crotals (small round metal rattles), and cymbals complete the panoply of instruments in the desk below the window. It is impossible to be sure what Egyptian music sounded like, but it must have had elements of both Asian and African music.

Gallery D: The Amarnian revolution and the end of the 18th dynasty

Toward the end of the 18th dynasty, under Amenophis IV Akhenaton (→inset), a religious and artistic evolution took place which had already begun under Amenophis III. Academism, with its fixed forms of representation, was abandoned in favor of a greater sense of movement together with a more realistic treatment of the face and body. Under Akhenaton, who encouraged reliefs and sculptures of the members of his court, artists invented a new canon of proportions for depicting the human body. The artistic style of the decoration for the palaces at Tel el Amarna was closer to nature.

To the r. of the entrance is the majestic head of a princess*** of the royal family, in painted limestone. To the l. of the entrance are fragments of a seated group in gypsum, of which only the figure of Akhenaton has survived, and a fine bust of Akhenaton in painted limestone. In Showcase D2: fragments of a sandstone relief depicting Akhenaton and members of his family worshipping Aton. The beneficent rays of the sun end in hands, bestowing life and prosperity on the king. At the end of the room in the showcase to the l., a splendid Amarnian female torso, perhaps of Nefertiti, in red quartz and a statuette** in painted limestone of Akhenaton and his wife, the beautiful Nefertiti, holding hands. The other items on display relate to the end of the 18th dynasty and its kings, Tutankhamen and Horemheb.

At the far end of the gallery, under glass, is a small plaque in sculpted and painted ivory, showing a young prince (Tutankhamen perhaps) picking grapes. Showcase D3: delicate head** in blue glass paste, which may have been part of a statue of Tutankhamen. At the end of the room, near the window, two diorite statues of Amun, one of which was dedicated to the god by Tutankhamen. The reliefs of General Horemheb* come from his tomb at Sakhara. Once he became king, Horemheb had a hypogeum hollowed out for himself in the Valley of the Kings at Thebes. On one of the reliefs, Libyans, Syro-Palestinians and Nubians are depicted marching past Horemheb in homage. On the other, the general's funeral is portrayed, dominated by the doleful lamentations of weeping women (Showcase D5). Equally illustrative of art at the end of the 18th dynasty are the reliefs from the tomb of Chief General Imeneminet* (Showcase D6). This period's statuary is exceptionally well represented in the Salt Head*** from the collection of Henry Salt, the British Consul in Cairo. The artist has caught the strong but quiet character that lies hidden behind a faint smile. The statue is in red painted limestone, but his close-cropped hair is black.

Gallery E: The Ramesside Era: 19th and 20th dynasties

Horemheb named one of his generals, as heir, Rameses, who founded the 19th dynasty. His son Sethi and grandson Rameses II were its most brilliant kings. They gave themselves unstintingly to the defense of the empire against the Hittites. Egypt's last great national sovereign, Rameses III, belonged to the 20th dynasty. Subsequent successors from Rameses IV through Rameses IX could do nothing to prevent the decline of the empire and its partitioning anew. Under Sethi I, art rediscovered the high standards it had achieved under Amenophis III. Rameses introduced a new style which developed alongside phenomenal architectural activity, whose keynote was colossal size. Technically this art may have been less refined, but it managed to respect, without being constrained by, artistic conventions. This greater sense of freedom was especially noticeable in bas-relief, which replaced to a degree high relief.

Showcase E1 contains portraits of the rulers of the 19th and 20th dynasties. The village of Deir el-Medineh was where the artisans of the Theban necropolis lived. This community is well known through the archaeological remains that have survived: houses, rare examples of Egyptian domestic architecture; the contents of tombs; and hundreds of *ostraca,* or potsherds, on which artists made sketches and notes. Papyrus, being much more costly, was rarely used for such informal uses. The showcase that stretches the length of the wall to the l. is full of *ostraca* drawings in which the artists have given full rein to their inspiration and their fantasies. Showcase E2 presents the goddess Hathor and her divine aspects. With the goddess Mertseger she was worshipped in the form of a serpent at Deir el-Medineh, although she is usually shown with a cow's head. Prayer is the theme of showcase E3, where ear-shaped votive stelae are on display; these were meant to help the divinities hear the prayers of the artisans. Near the window are three admirable Ramesside stelae: the stele of Dedia* making offerings to the Osirian triad (Osiris, Isis, and their son Horus); the stele of Hormin* to whom Sethi I is offering gold as a reward for his services: and the stele of Ruru, the king's chief intendant.

Private statuary, in stone, is displayed in several showcases; including the interesting limestone cube-statue* of the scribe Turoi. Wooden statues of this era are gathered together into one showcase. Note especially that of a man carrying the insignia of Amun* with a ram's head, and a statue of Queen Ahmes Nefertari (18th dynasty) dedicated by an artist from Deir el-Medineh. Showcase E4 contains the golden mask of Prince Khamuaset and the amulets laid on his mummy. His tomb was discovered by Mariette at the Serapeum of Memphis because as well as being the son of Rameses II he was the high priest of Ptah, and so was buried near the Apis.

The best of the Louvre's collection of jewelry and metalwork from every era of Egypt's history is gathered together into a gold- and silverwork showcase***: a mirror handle (12th dynasty) in faience or possibly amazonite and gold; jewelry with the name of King Ahmosis (18th dynasty); flat dishes (patera) in gold and silver, offered by Thutmosis III to General Djehuti (18th dynasty) and an 18th-dynasty 'fish' necklace; jewelry of the Vizier Paser; 'horse' breastplate and ring of Rameses II; necklace of Pinedjem I, a 21st dynasty king, and a triad depicting Osiris, Isis and Horus in solid gold and lapis lazuli; gold and silver jewelry from the Greek and Roman eras.

Gallery F: Third Intermediate Period (11th–7th c. BC; 21st–25th dynasties)

At Thebes, the high priests of Amun took power, but their influence extended only over the southern part of the country. The north was under the control of a parallel dynasty, established at Tanis. The Tanite kings were succeeded by the 22nd and 23rd dynasties, which were Libyan. The 24th dynasty briefly had its capital at Saïs on the Nile Delta, before Egypt was conquered by the Ethiopians, who set up the 25th dynasty.

During this period, metalworking, especially in bronze, reached extremely high standards. This showed itself not only in statuary, but also in smaller objects. Examples of the former are the statue of Queen Karomama*** the divine worshipper, a masterpiece encrusted with silver, copper, gold, and platinum; statues of the dignitaries Pachasu (22nd dynasty) and Padiimen (25th dynasty); and statues of the falcon god Horus. Examples of the latter are in a showcase***, as well as a gold-encrusted sistrum belonging to Henuttway, one of the Amun's musicians; a box with the name of the divine worshipper Chapenupet II; a sphinx of King Siamon, presenting a table laden with offerings (21st dynasty); shield bearing a lion's head in electrum (22nd dynasty); King Taharqa (25th dynasty) offering wine to the god Hemen.

At this time everyday objects and furniture were no longer placed in the tomb, but the deceased was surrounded instead only with things needed for rebirth. The faience *shawabti* were still there, the funerary servants whose task was to fulfil on the deceased's behalf any work that he might have to do (in the showcase to l., near the entrance). Funerary art now included stelae with stucco and painted decoration depicting the deceased before the sun god Rae-Horakhty – for example, the stele of the harpist* (Showcase F1), the stele of Lady Taperet* (Showcase in the center of the gallery) – and carefully executed coffins – for example, the mummy's protective plate* and coffin of Sutymes (Showcase F6 and window recess). At the side, a statuette of a female nude*, a masterpiece of ivory carving.

Gallery G: Late Period (7th–4th c. BC; 26th–30th dynasties)

The 26th Saite dynasty expelled the Ethiopians and reunited the kingdom. Art twined back resolutely to the antecedent periods, which it copied faithfully. In statuary, some extremely detailed faces are true portraits of the individual, even if unflattering. In the middle of the gallery, bust of an old man* in schist, and a statue of Yahmessaneith*.

The Saite renaissance was brutally cut short by the Persian invasion and the subsequent annexation of Egypt, which established the 27th dynasty. However, Egyptian artists resisted Persian influence of which there are, consequently, few traces: the Louvre has only an Apis stele dating from the year 34 of Darius, and the head of a Persian dignitary (Showcase G7).

The country recovered its independence for some 60 years from the 28th to the 30th dynasties, only to fall a second time under Persian dominance, which itself was to end with Alexander the Great's conquest of Egypt. In the 30th dynasty, sculptors worked statues in very hard stone in which they could achieve an unequalled polish: the heads of old men* in quartzite and schist (showcase to the r., far end of the gallery). Showcase G5 has some interesting examples of 4th-c. sculpture, including a torso of Nectanebo I (30th dynasty) which can be compared to the large torso of the same king near the window.

The art of bas-relief in the 7th–6th c BC (Showcase G6): a relief from the tomb of Pairkep (600 BC) in limestone showing the manufacture of perfume from lilies, and a relief depicting the grape harvest and grape pressing (4th c. BC). The artists looked to the Old Kingdom in their portrayal of pose and costume, but they were less sure and precise in their presentation. Their forms are more rounded, which manages to suggest gentleness.

The dictionary of the gods (Showcases G1 to G3): Above, the gods are presented in alphabetical order in their most usual aspects. Below, animals with explanations of the divinities they represent. The cat, sacred to the cat goddess Bastet, is the theme of a fine collection of bronzes* (showcase to the l., center of gallery).

Showcase G4 and its neighbor are dedicated to magic (→inset). A statue** whose body is engraved with magic texts and carrying a stele in its arms marked 'Horus on the crocodiles', would have been set up in some public place; the statue was believed to have the power to transform any water poured over it into a remedy against scorpion and snake bites.

Gallery H: Ptolemaic and Roman eras

From 332 BC to AD 392 Alexander the Great set up Alexandria as the new capital of Egypt, and the administration of the newly conquered country was entrusted to Ptolemy, son of Lagos. Ptolemy took upon himself the attributes of pharaoh, and gave his name to the Ptolemaic or Lagide dynasty. Three hundred years later the last Lagide ruler, Cleopatra VII, seduced first Caesar, then Mark Antony, before being overthrown in AD 30 by Augustus. So began the Roman occupation. From this period art was a mixture of Egyptian, Greek and Roman styles, techniques, and iconographic themes.

Showcase H1: the Greek and Roman rulers are represented here principally by a stele showing Cleopatra dressed as a pharaoh, making an offering to the goddess Isis, who is fanning her son Horus with her wings (dated July 2 AD 51); and by a bust of a Roman emperor (perhaps Nero, 1st c. AD), dressed in pharaonic insignia. Showcase near the entrance: sculptures from the Ptolemaic era; note the fine torso of the goddess Isis to the side. Showcase H2: faience said to be of Mit Rahineh,* with Greek decoration, and Roman pottery; some terracotta figurines, produced in vast quantities in the Roman era. One development in funerary art was the introduction of stucco masks, decorated with a portrait of the deceased's face, and also portraits on wood, painted in a wax encaustic medium, which covered the mummy's face, called *Fayum* after the place of their principal discovery.

The l. side of the room is dedicated to writing: the scribe (present here in the form of a 5th-dynasty statue) was a permanent feature of every echelon of Egyptian society. Here he is surrounded by the tools of his trade: wooden palette, faience bowl, and the coffer for his papyri (in the showcase before Showcase H3). Scribes were under divine protection: Thoth, god of knowledge and many forms of writing; Sechat, goddess of certain forms of writing; Imhotep the sage Djeser's architect in the 3rd dynasty, he was deified in the Late Period considered as patron of the sciences. Writing materials varied greatly: papyrus for important documents, but also wooden tablets, potsherds, flakes of stone, even pebbles.

There are also instruments used in measuring and calculating (Showcase H3). The large desk nearby traces the evolution of writing, including an explanation of the rudiments of grammar.

Embalming and interment (r. side of the gallery): the preservation of the body, essential for survival in the after life, was entrusted to embalmers, whose patron was the jackal-headed god of the dead, Anubis (Showcase H5). The body was dipped in natron hydrated sodium carbonate, anointed with various oils and perfumes, and then wrapped in bandages. Between the layers of bandaging the embalmers slipped protective amulets and a heart scarab (Showcases H5 and H6, and the mummy in the next showcase). The mummy was then returned to the family for interment. This process has been reconstructed (showcase opposite H7) based on illustrations from the *Book of the Dead*** of Nebqued (Showcase H7). The sarcophagus and funerary material were taken in procession at the head of the cortège. Before the mummy was placed in its tomb, the priests completed the ritual opening of the mummy's eyes and mouth, so that the deceased would be ready to take in a fresh breath of new life (showcase to the r. of the entrance).

▷ The Revolution of Amarna

Amenophis IV (Akhenaton), son of Amenophis III and Queen Tiy, and husband of Nefertiti, started a religious revolution which was to last only as long as his reign (*ca.* 1372–*ca.* 1354 BC). He renounced Amun and the many gods of Egypt, in favor of the monotheistic worship of the sun god Aton (Ra). He erased Amun's name from monuments – only to have his own name in turn erased from monuments after his death. He left Thebes to establish a new capital in Middle Egypt, which he called Akhetaton (the modern Amarna), and took the name Akhenaton himself. The king's successors regarded him as a heretic; his city was destroyed and his daughters imprisoned. During his reign, however, art underwent an important transformation in both form and iconography. Some scholars believe Akhenaton to be the origin of the Oedipus legend.

▷ Magic

Throughout their history, the Egyptians always had recourse to magic whether as a defence against their enemies or for protection against sickness or disease. Bes and Tueris, for example, were protective divinities who could be called upon to help with childbirth; people would wear amulets that allegedly had beneficial effects; a letter would be written to a dead person who was troubling the living.

In the Late Period, magic was very widely practised. The divinities of the pantheon were attributed with more and more efficacious powers to intercede in human affairs. Enchantment or charming by means of wax effigies was very popular for a while.

The Louvre has a particularly fine basalt example of the healing statues that began to be sculpted around this time.

Greek, Etruscan and Roman Antiquities

Chief Curator: Alain Pasquier
Entrance: from the Pyramid.
A few statues from the former royal collections formed the first Musée des Antiquités, opened in 1800, but the department took its present shape in 1849. Quite recently Anne of Austria's summer apartments have been opened to the public to display Roman and Etruscan exhibits. A tour of the Graeco-Roman collections starts with sculpture on the ground floor and goes on to vases, terracottas and bronzes on the first floor.

▷ Not to be missed

Greece
Ground floor, Gallery 1: the so-called *Dame d'Auxerre* (7th c. BC) a small figure of Cretan origin; the *Hera of Samos* (6th c. BC); the

Rampin Head (6th c. BC). Gallery 3: sculptures from the Temple of Zeus at Olympia (5th c. BC). Gallery 5: Fragments from the Parthenon (5th c. BC). Gallery 9: head of the *Cnidian Aphrodite* (2nd c. BC); the *Venus de Milo* (2nd c. BC). First-floor landing of the Escalier Daru: the *Victory of Samothrace.*

Rome
Ground floor, Gallery 1: Bronze bust of Hadrian (1st c. AD). Gallery 23: mosaic from Kabr Hiram (575 AD). Gallery 27: *Four Seasons* mosaic.

First floor, Gallery I: the Treasure of Boscoreale (near Pompeii, 1st c. AD).

Ground floor

Go towards the Aile Denon by the Denon staircase; this leads to the Salle du Manège which houses the colored marbles: *Dying Seneca* and the *Barbarian Prisoners* (Borghese Collection), the Albani fountains, the Manzarin *Minerva* etc.; cross the Denon vestibule which contains the Farnese Candelabrum, the Richelieu *Bacchus* and the Manzarin *Adnois.* The Denon Gallery is on the r.

Denon Gallery

Sarcophagi (2nd-and 3rd-c.) depicting Demeter and Triptolemus, Phaedra and Hippolytus, Apollo and Marsyas*, Achilles at the court of Lycomedes, the Legend of Actaeon, and a few 1st- and 2nd-c. Roman statues, Antinous as Aristaeus, Tiridates, King of Armenia and Sabina.

Skirt the Daru staircase and go down a few steps to enter the Archaic Greece room in what was the old Vestibule des Prisonniers Barbares (Hall of the Barbarian Prisoners).

Gallery 1: Archaic Greece (Orientalizing and Archaic Periods: 7th and 6th c. BC)

The Archaic period runs from the end of the 7th c. to the beginning of the 6th c. BC. Sculpture of the period falls predominantly into two types: the *kouros,* a standing nude male figure, with arms hanging straight by his sides and the left foot slightly forward; and the *kore,* a draped standing female figure, her feet close together. Their development shows a continuous and growing mastery of sculpted drapery and the nude. In addition to the *kouroi* and *korai* are to be found such other categories as the seated statue and, most important of all, that essentially Greek creation, the equestrian statue. At the same time bas-reliefs, too, struggled to achieve accuracy of expression and of anatomy. Three stylistic currents inspired this young and lively art – the Ionian, the Dorian, and the Attic.

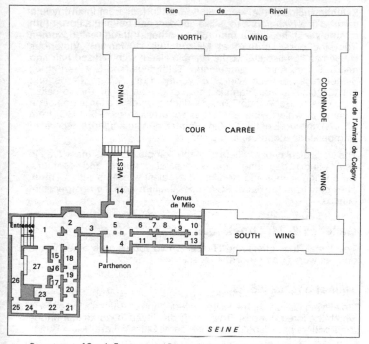

Department of Greek, Etruscan, and Roman Antiquities / Ground Floor (First Floor)
This arrangement is subject to change

Greek Antiquities
1. Orientalizing and Archaic periods
2. Early 5th c. BC
3. Olympia
4, 5. Original works from the second half of the 5th and early 4th c. BC
6, 7. Original works from the 4th c. BC
8. Original works from the 3rd c. BC
9. Original works from the 2nd c. BC
10. Original works from the 2nd and 1st c. BC
11. Replicas of 5th-c. BC originals
12. Replicas of 5th and 4th-c. BC originals
13. Replicas of 4th-c. BC originals
14. Salle des Caryatides, replicas of 4th-c. BC and Hellenistic originals

Galleries 15, 16 17, Etruscan Antiquities

Roman Antiquities
18. Republican and Julio-Claudian periods
19. Julio-Claudian period
20. Julio-Claudian, Flavian and Antonine periods
21. The Age of the Antonines and the Severi
22. 3rd and 4th c. AD
23. Late Antiquity
24. Christian Antiquities from North Africa
25. Christian Antiquities from Syria
26. Salle des Mosaiques or Roman Civilization Room
27. Cour du Sphinx

Exhibits include: the Hera of Samos*** (6th c., Ionian); youth dressed in a *himation*, a toga like garment and holding a flower (6th c. Attic stele); head of a man (6th c., Athens); three seated women from the burial ground at Miletus (6th c., Ionian); Victorious Horseman*** (also called the Rampin Head; with stylized hair and beard, 6th c., Attic); Agamemnon, Talthybius, and Epeius (6th-c., Samothrace); archaic *kouroi,* or youths, from Actium, Paros, and Miletus; small draped female figure of Cretan origin, the so-called Dame d'Auxerre*** (late 7th c., Dorian); a *dinos***, a large goblet on a stand in which wine and water were mixed (600–590 BC, from Etruria), the work of the Gorgon Painter, and an amphora decorated with dancers, a chorus, and a sphinx.

The walls display bas-reliefs from the Temple of Assos (near Troy in Asia Minor) depicting processions of animals and centaurs, banqueting scenes and Herakles (Hercules) wrestling with a Triton. They date from the 6th c. BC as does the lion from the necropolis of Miletus.

Galleries 2–14: Greek tour

The Greek tour offers the choice of two routes: one takes in the original works, the other the replicas.

Tour of original works

On leaving Gallery 1., the visitor enters Anne of Austria's Rotonda in which the foreground of Greek art is displayed in works that bridge the frontiers between Archaic and early Classical art.

Gallery 2 (early 5th c. BC)

The visitor is greeted by the *Apollo of Piombino**, invaluable evidence of progress in bronze statuary in which the conventions of Archaic art are retained but softened in the modeling, where the harmony of line presages the Classical style. The late 5th-c. Pharsalus Relief** (upper part of stele), also called the *Exaltation of the Flower,* retains the freshness of Archaic art but mingles it with a Classical suppleness and ease of movement. Next come the Thasos Reliefs** which decorated the processional way of the Ambassadors leading to the Agora of Thasos. The figures are set in hieratic poses, but there is wide variety in the folds of their garments, and their gestures are full of life. The torso of Apollo** (Miletus); note how the rigidly vertical pose is relaxed and the median line is gently curved.

Gallery 3: Olympia***

This gallery was reopened late in 1987, to house sculptures from Olympia. These comprise the two metopes unearthed by A. Blouet during the 1829 expedition to the Morea, with other fragments from the Temple of Zeus (470–460 BC). The metopes show two of the Labors of Herakles (Hercules) – Herakles taming the Cretan Bull, and presenting Athena with one of the Stymphalian Birds. Bronzes and pottery accompany these splendid examples of the Severe style. It should be remembered that the fragments of sculpture from Olympia, unearthed by the French archeologist Blouet in 1829, were presented by the Greek senate as a token of gratitude for French support during the War of Independence.

From the Olympia Room the visitor gains the Corridor de Pan. Turn r. to reach the Parthenon Gallery.

Gallery 4 and 5: The Parthenon Gallery and the Corridor de Pan

Original sculptures of the second half of the 5th c. and early 4th c. BC. The first room bears the name of the temple dedicated to the goddess Athena, on the Acropolis at Athens, erected by Phidias between 447 and 432 BC, on the orders of Pericles. A number of fragments of the Parthenon's decorations are on display including a substantial fragment of the frieze of the Panathenaic Procession***, which dominates the entire room from its place on the r. wall; to its l. a metope – no. 10 from the S side – shows a centaur carrying off a Lapith woman; to its r. the head of a rider*** from the N frieze, a Lapith's head from one of the S side metopes, and the superb *Laborde Head*** of a woman from the W pediment of the Parthenon. Facing these fragments stand two graceful figures, undoubtedly from the *acroterion* * of the temple at Bassae, near Phigaleia, designed by Ictinus who, with Callicrates, built the Parthenon.

Along the wall that separates this room from the Corridor de Pan a series of stelae show the revival in Attica of the use of stelae toward the mid-5th. c. BC and the influence of the Parthenon sculptures upon Thasos or Crete.

If you wish to continue the tour of original works, return to the Corridor de Pan and then walk through the gallery leading to the *Venus de Milo.*

▷ Greek chronology

3200–1050 BC	Bronze Age *ca.* 3200 BC: birth of Cycladic civilization; *ca.* 2000 BC: birth of Cretan civilization; *ca.* 1400 BC: decline of Crete and rise of Mycenae
End of 2nd millennium BC	Dorian Invasions
1050–720 BC	Geometric Period

720–620 BC	Orientalizing Period
620–480 BC	Archaic Period
480–450 BC	Transitional style from the Archaic to the Classical: the Severe style.
Mid-5th c.–early 4th c.BC	First Classical Age: Athens at the height of her power. Pericles. Phidias and the Parthenon.
4th c. BC	Second Classical Age: Philip of Macedon conquers Greece. Alexander the Great (336–323 BC) carries Hellenism to the ends of the Near Eastern world. Praxiteles, Scopas, Lysippus.
3rd c.–1st c. BC	Hellenistic Age. Greece becomes a mere province of the vast Hellenic world.

Galleries 6 and 7: Original works of art from the 4th c. BC.

Note the classic shapes of the funerary urn – the lekythoi (oil jars) and loutrophoroi (water jars); a fine lion presented to Charles X by Admiral Halgan (symbolic animals sometimes marked the site of a grave). There are numerous stelae carved in ever higher relief until the figures are almost cut in the round; among the exhibits are small heads and statues that have become detached from their grave-stones.

Gallery 8

Among the 3rd-c. BC originals on display are likenesses of the descendants of Lagos, whose reputed son, Ptolemy, one of Alexander's generals, seized Egypt when the empire of Alexander the Great broke up. There is a particularly fine portrait* of the founder of the Ptolemaic dynasty.

Gallery 9

Original works from the 2nd c. BC, when the Hellenistic Age revived the arts inherited from the great Classical masters. The so-called *Kaufmann Head****, long considered the finest copy of Praxiteles' head of the Cnidian Aphrodite, is now acknowledged to be an original work executed by a major 2nd-c. sculptor inspired by the Cnidian Aphrodite. The Guimet *Alexander** is a reworking of a piece by Leochares. The *Inopos**, perhaps a portrait of Mithridates IV Eupator idealized to resemble Alexander the Great, has sometimes been attributed to the sculptor of the *Venus de Milo,* one of the most famous statues in the world.

The figure known as the *Venus de Milo****, which is one of the greatest masterpieces of ancient sculpture, was unearthed in 1820 by a peasant near the village of Castro on the island of Melos (Milo).

The Marquis de Rivière, French Ambassador to Constantinople (Istanbul), purchased it and presented it to Louis XVIII in 1821. The statue dates from the end of the 2nd c. BC and in its majesty and perfection recalls the great Classical period. However, its creator is unknown. The arms, missing at the time of its discovery, were unearthed in 1987, but have not been restored to the statue.

Gallery 10: 2nd and 1st c. BC.

Originals among which the *Borghese Warrior***, signed by Agasias of Ephesus (*ca.* 100 BC), recalls the work of Lysippus and his school and obeys the same stylistic rules: the result of this liking for the past gives the art of the period an eclectic character. Note the volute krater signed by Sosibius of Athens (*ca.* 50 BC).

Tour of the replicas

To tour the replicas, return to the Corridor de Pan. The replicas are more or less faithful copies made in Roman times, imitating or adapting the most renowned items of Classical Greek sculpture, of which most of the originals are no longer extant.

Gallery 11: Replicas of 5th c. BC.

Sculptures include the so-called Barberini *Supplicant,* which stands on the borderline between the replica and the original work of art. For long classified among the latter, it is now considered to be the copy of an original carved shortly after the completion of the Parthenon. Since the vast majority of Greek sculptures of the Classical period are now lost, our only knowledge of them derives from copies of the most celebrated, mostly made during the Roman period. The torso of a *Discobolus* (discus thrower)** – the original is attributed to Pythagoras of Rhegium – marks a definite step forward in spatial control. The *Apollo with Lyre** reminds us of the Severe style that preceded Polyclitus (*ca.* 460 BC). There is a *Head of Apollo* reminiscent of the *Apollo of Delphi* carved by Calamis. Of the two groups by Myron which were set up (*ca.* 460 BC) on the Acropolis at Athens – his *Athena and Marsyas* and his *Theseus and the Minotaur* – only an infinitely graceful *Athena*** remains. The goddess seems to be practising a dance step, together with a small torso of the *Minotaur* (in a glass case). The *Diadumenus* youth winding a band round his head belongs to a type of statue created by Polyclitus around 430 BC and recaptures the rhythmic balance in the pose of his athletes. The same sculptor is credited with the original (*ca.* 430 BC) of the wounded Amazon, traditionally supposed to have been displayed at the shrine of Artemis at Ephesus with the *Amazons* of Phidias, Cresilas, and Phradmon. The replica in the Louvre was clumsily restored in the 17th c. Phidias imbued his Olympians with the serenity of Polyclitus' athletes. His *Apollo,* known as the *Bonus Eventus* of the type of the Kassel

Apollo, presages the works of his maturity, his *Zeus* at Olympia and his *Athena Promachos*. Echoes of the latter are to be found in the *Minerva with Necklace* and in a small head. The relief depicting *Orpheus, Eurydice and Hermes* is one of the best copies of an Attic original, which postdates the Parthenon frieze (end 5th. c. BC). Its inscription is later than the work itself.

Gallery 12

Replicas of 5th- and 4th-c. BC originals. We come back to Phidias again; the originals (*ca.* 440 BC) are attributed to him of the superb *Torso of Persephone** of the Albani *kore* type and of the Athena known as the *Ingres Minerve**. The original (*ca.* 450 BC) of a head of the lyric poet Anacreon may also be attributed to him, while the bronze original of the *Farnese Athena* is attributed to one of his pupils. The originals (*ca.* 330 – 430 BC) of the *Diomedes*, companion of Odysseus, and of the *Velletri Pallas* are attributed to the Cretan sculptor Cresilas. However, the replicas are eclectic in style and bear traces of the influences of Phidias and of Polyclitus. Callimachus carved the original of the graceful *Naples Aphrodite* known as the *Venus Genetrix*. The way in which the dampened draperies reveal the statue's feminine contours presages the works of Praxiteles. Alcamenes is the sculptor to whom is attributed the original of the head of Ares**, known as the *Borghese Mars*, in which the majestic calm of Phidias mingles with the harmonious poise of Polyclitus. Alcamenes himself contributes a warmer humanity and a refined elegance. There is the same elegance in the two *Aphrodites** leaning against a pillar. The original, attributed to the same sculptor, may well have stood in the sanctuary of Aphrodite at Daphni unless, indeed, this is the *Aphrodite of the Gardens* so greatly admired by Lucian of Samosata. Lastly, to Alcamenes again is attributed the original of the charming Athena at the Cist, making a maternal gesture, in which, once more, the divine becomes humanized (second half 5th c. BC). Two works from the very beginning of the 4th c. mark a clear break with strict Classical tradition: the replicas of the *Discophores*, attributed to Naucydes, a pupil of Polyclitus, and of Athena as goddess of Peace. The bronze original of the latter was discovered some years ago in Piraeus and is now in the National Museum in Athens; it is as yet unattributed. Both statues clearly show avowed realism and a quest for truth to nature.

Gallery 13

Replicas after works of the 7th c. BC. The room is dominated by the larger-than-lifesize statue of Melpomene (1st c. BC) from Pompey's Theater in Rome, which is part of the decoration and has nothing whatever to do with the exhibits, which consist of some of the finest replicas of 4th-c. sculptures by Praxiteles (*ca.* 370–330 BC). This Athenian, the son of Cephisodotus the Elder, is the sculptor of youthful grace. His *Satyr Pouring Wine* and his *Apollo Sauroktonas* ('slaying a lizard') are full of the flowing rhythm inherited from Polyclitus but heightened and applied to adolescent figures whose supple lines exude an easy mastery. It is, however, in his statues of Aphrodite that Praxiteles triumphs. The *Venus of Arles** altered by Girardon, perhaps a copy of his *Aphrodite of Thespiae,* presages his *Aphrodite of Cnidos***, which shows the goddess leaving her ritual bath; it was one of the most famous and most copied statues of Antiquity and the first important female nude. The Artemis**, known as the *Diana of Gabii,* is doubtless a copy of the statue carved by Praxiteles toward the end of his career, for the sanctuary of Artemis Brauronia on the Acropolis of Athens, dedicated in about 345 BC. The striving for monumental effect and for pathos in his Lycian Apollo, sets the original, so famous in Athens, again among the last years of his artistic life.

Now return to the Corridor de Pan in order to reach the Salle des Caryatides on the r.

Gallery 14: The Salle des Caryatides

Contains copies of works of the 4th c. BC and of the Hellenistic period. This gallery was opened at the same time as Pei's glass pyramid. In the first half of the room are replicas of the works of Lysippus, an artist of the first rank and a key figure in the transition from the Classical to the Hellenistic Age. Temperamentally the antithesis of Praxiteles, he returned to the study of movement and muscular structure of the athlete and is believed to have made a complete revision of the Polyclitan canon of proportions for the human body. His *Hermes Fastening his Sandal** operates within real three-dimensional space. Lysippus was court sculptor to Alexander the Great and the *Azara Head** is a very fine copy of his *Alexander with a Lance.*

The Artemis known as the *Diana of Versailles**, copied from an original allegedly by Leochares, shows how artists in the late 4th c. BC strove for decorative effect. The goddess, who has decorated many royal residences since the 16th c., has that peculiar attraction that makes her akin with the *Apollo Belvedere.*

There is an Aphrodite of the Capitoline type which was long considered to be the replica of an original by Scopas, but is now judged to belong to the Hellenistic period. There was a change in iconography, preference now being given to the old man or to such subjects as the child with the goose rather than to the athlete in his prime. The female nude lost her religious aura – witness the *Crouching Aphrodite of Vienne*, while the sleeping Hermaphrodite breathes an ambiguous sensuality quite foreign to the works of Praxiteles. Sculptors are now drawn to psychological truth rather than to frigid beauty. *The Dying Gaul* and the *Marsyas* are good examples of this trend towards realistic pathos. The large bacchic krater, known as the *Borghese Vase,* demonstrates the application of the Neo-Attic style to traditional subjects, and the harmoniously linked figures and realistic detail make this a work allied to all that is best in Hellenistic inspiration.

Galleries 15-17: Etruscan tour

Retrace your steps and return via the rooms that run along the E side of the Cour du Sphinx to the Archaic Greece Room, where the Etruscan tour begins.

By the 9th c. BC the Villanovan culture had become established in Central Italy and the Po Valley to be succeeded by the Etruscans. Soon they had become an important center of civilization of which the remains have come down to us in the rich furnishings of their monumental tombs, often decorated with frescoes.

Around the end of the 8th c. BC they made contact with the Greek colonies in S Italy, and although their art was influenced by Greek techniques, it retained the stamp of their imaginative temperament and mythology.

Gallery 15

Objects of Villanovan culture (9th–8th-c. BC) are displayed on the l. immediately before those belonging to the Etruscan civilization. Exhibits include biconical cinerary urns with raised slip decoration, vases of laminated bronze, bronze ornaments for clothing, and weapons with repoussé or incised decoration – all representative of a culture that practised cremation of the dead, and used bronze and iron worked by its own native craftsmen in their own geometric decorative style. In the center of the room stands the *Married Couple's Sarcophagus**** (*ca.* 510 BC) from Caere (Cerveteri). This masterpiece of Etruscan art renders in terracotta and in the round a motif – that of a husband and wife conversing as though still alive – often found on stelae or funerary reliefs, and shows marked Ionian influence. On the r. the development of pottery from the 8th to the 6th c. BC is illustrated: pottery painted with geometric designs and heavily glazed incised designs; Orientalizing pottery and, around 650 BC, the first appearance of thin-bodied Bucchero ware, black pottery made from iron-bearing clay, surface-polished to a metallic gloss; Etrusco-Corinthian pottery (*ca.* 625–575 BC).

Gallery 16

The Etruscans were outstanding jewelers, past masters in the techniques of graining precious metals and in filigree work, as seen in the cases of jewelry here; note the pendant* with a head of the river god Achelous. On the r. is a case with a collection of canopic vases from Clusium (Chiusi) and on the l. another case displaying heavy Bucchero vases (6th c. BC), with thicker bodies, coarser shapes, and relief decoration.

Gallery 17

Etruscan art of the Classical and Hellenistic periods (4th-1st c. BC).Note the cinerary group in pietra fetida (a form of limestone) dating from the 4th c. BC, from Clusium (Chiusi), together with sarcophagi carved from local marble, and terracotta cinerary urns dating from the end of the 2nd c. to the beginning of the 1st c. BC. From Volterra come alabaster cinerary urns (late 2nd-1st c. BC), while from Tuscania there are terracotta sarcophagi (late 3rd-2nd c. BC). A case displays a whole series of engraved bronze mirrors** (4th-3rd c. BC), while another is filled with terracotta portraits. Last, don't miss the fine bronze head of a man from Faesulae (Fiesole).

Galleries 18-27: Roman tour

On leaving Gallery 17 turn r. to enter the former apartments of Anne of Austria in which the Roman collections are exhibited.

▷ Roman chronology

8th-6th c. BC	Rule of the Kings
753 BC	Founding of Rome
6th c. BC	Etruscan dominance
509 BC	Expulsion of the Kings
5th-3rd c. BC	Rome widens its dominion
6th-1st BC	Rome dominated Latium, Central Italy, and then the whole Peninsula
3rd-2nd c. BC	The Punic Wars. Defeat of Carthage
2nd c. BC	Victories in Greece, the Near East, N Africa, and Spain
1st c. BC	Battle of Actium. Rome controls the entire Mediterranean Basin
27 BC	Octavian takes the title of Augustus
27 BC-AD 69	The Julio-Claudian Emperors
1st c. BC-3rd c. AD	The Empire (Augustus, Tiberius, Caligula, Claudius, Nero)
69-96 AD	The Flavian Emperors (Vespasian, Titus, Domitian)
96-192 AD	The Antonine Emperors (Nerva, Trajan, Hadrian, Antoninus Pius, Marcus Aurelius, Commodus)
193-235 AD	The Severi (Septimius Severus, Caracalla)
3rd-5th c. AD	Late Antiquity
235-284	Military anarchy
284-305	Reign of Diocletian
306-337	Reign of Constantine the Great

379–395	Reign of Theodosius. Division of the Eastern and Western Empires
410	Sack of Rome by Alaric
476	Fall of the Western Empire.

Gallery 18: Republican and Julio-Claudian Periods (27 BC–69 AD)

Two modes of sculptural expression were highly esteemed during this period: the portrait and the historical relief. Official portrait busts include the likenesses of the kings of Numidia, Juba I, Juba II, and Ptolemy, and of Augustus and of members of the Imperial family. The unofficial side of the art is exemplified by a number of Republican portraits with their heavy emphasis on realism. Note the portrait said to be of Aulus Postumius Albinus, the fine bust of Agrippa*, and the heroic statue of Marcellus** as Hermes (late 1st c. BC) signed by Cleomenes the Athenian and inspired by a style originating in 5th-c. Greece. The so-called *Relief of Domitius Ahenobarbus* is one of the earliest examples of the Roman historical relief. It must have decorated one side of the massive pedestal set in the Temple of Neptune in the Campus Martius (the other three reliefs are preserved in Munich). The fragment from the Ara Pacis (Altar of Peace) dedicated by Augustus on his triumphal return from Spain in 9 BC, is clearly inspired by the Panathenaic frieze. Good examples of unofficial art are the frescoes from the Tomb of Patronus, near the Porta Capena in Rome, which show his family gathered at his tomb.

Gallery 19: the Julio-Claudian Period (continued)

Several portraits of members of the Imperial family are on view, above all the superb basalt bust of Livia*, wife of Augustus and mother of Tiberius. Two *cippi* exemplify unofficial funerary art, those of Amemptus and of Julia Victorina. The funerary *cippus*, a short column, was designed to receive libations and also to house the urn containing the ashes of the dead.

Gallery 20: The Julio-Claudian, Flavian (AD 69–96), and Antonine (AD 96–112) Periods

Julio-Claudian portraits include Caligula wearing a beard in sign of mourning; Nero, of whom there are few portraits, since his memory was condemned by the Senate, and Claudius' second wife, Messalina, carrying their son Britannicus, inspired by a 4th-c. BC group of Irene holding Plutus (Peace holding Wealth) in her arms by Cephisodotus. Several Antonine portraits including Trajan, *Hadrian**** – the bronze recently acquired by the Louvre is outstanding – Antoninus Pius, Marcus Aurelius, and his friend, Herodes

Atticus**, the last two by Greek sculptors. There is the affecting portrait of a child** – perhaps Marcus Aurelius' son, Annius Verus, who died at the age of seven – one of the masterpieces of Roman portrait sculpture in which the treatment of the hair enhances the expressive and delicate handling of the face. Do not overlook the *Sarcophagus of the Muses**, one of the finest in the Louvre, dating from the reign of Antoninus Pius (mid 2nd c. AD). Lastly there is a Mithraic relief, one side depicting the sacrifice of the bull and the other Mithras and the Sun feasting on the sacrificial remains of the bull. Mithras, a Persian sun god, was known and worshipped in Rome from the 1st c. BC.

Gallery 21: Age of the Antonines and of the Severi (AD 193–235).

The large portraits of Marcus Aurelius and of his adoptive brother, Lucius Verus, seem to dominate the room. They are posthumous portraits of these emperors, deified during the principate of Commodus. There is a lifelike simplicity in the statue of Melitina*, a priestess of Cybele, who herself dedicated this statue to the goddess during the high priesthood of Philemon, son of Praxiteles.

From the reigns of the Severi there are two sarcophagi from Saint-Médard d'Eyrand, near Bordeaux, decorated with mythological stories of Dionysus and Ariadne and of Endymion and Selena. From the same period come two portraits of Septimius Severus and three of Caracalla. The statue of Caracalla as a child* is stylistically akin to Antonine portraits and in marked contrast to the brutal expression found in portrait statues of Caracalla as emperor.

▷ The Roman bas-relief

The Romans were precise and practical people who seldom indulged in fantasy. The favorite subjects for their sculptures were religious ceremonies, feats of arms, and important events in local history. Unlike the Greek relief, which always idealizes the events it seeks to depict and willingly chooses mythological subjects, the Roman relief is in general the work of annalists seeking to record contemporary events. It therefore provides valuable historical evidence. It often also provides genuine portraits of the principal personages in an accurately observed setting with careful attention to detail.

▷ The Roman portrait

The characteristic realism of the Romans lent overwhelming importance to portrait busts or statues. While the Greeks always sought a more or less idealized likeness within a range of conventional types, the Romans on the contrary looked to a realistic likeness that expressed individual character. During the Republican period statues of honor and busts preserved the likenesses of rich and important personages in what was generally a lifelike manner. The foundation of the Empire and the establishment of emperor worship could only promote the development of this genre. While many of the subjects of these portraits remain unknown to us, their coins have enabled us to identify emperors and members of their families.

Just as these statues reflect the changes in fashion (hair styles for example), so their own style changes. The somewhat spare if forceful style of the early sculptors gives way, under Hadrian, to something more cosmetic, only to return to a cruder realism soon to be replaced by the hieratic style of Byzantium.

Gallery 22: (3rd and 4th c. AD)

In the center of the room stand four 3rd-c. pillars** decorated in relief with figures borrowed from the Dionysus cycle. They came from the attic storey of a Corinthian portico from Thessalonika. In the Middle Ages they were believed to be the remains of some enchanted palace, hence their name Incantada. Among the 3rd-c. portraits note those of the Emperor Pupienus who reigned for a few months in 238, and of a charioteer** in a leather hat; the modeling of both is outstanding. During the 4th c. portraits regain a static and hieratic quality, which gives them a degree of majesty but makes identification difficult. Thus a personage wearing a crown and dressed in the narrow toga of the 4th c. may or may not be Julian the Apostate. A fine portrait of Theodosius II completes this series, which stands on the borders of the worlds of Byzantium and of Medieval Christendom. The *Borghese Sarcophagus* (4th c.) depicts Christ surrounded by his Apostles; other fragments from this sarcophagus are preserved in the Capitoline Museum in Rome. Pass the *Borghese Sarcophagus* to enter the room immediately behind it.

Gallery 23: Late Antiquity

On the W wall of this room is the splendid mosaic*** from Kabr Hiram near Tyre in the Lebanon, on which vine tendrils enclose hunting scenes and scenes of animals fighting. Four cases are worth examining: the first contains small pottery figures; the second a collection of glassware; the third a collection of jewelry including a medallion* of Constantine. The case on the E wall displays ivories and silverware. Among the latter, note the Emesa Vase*, from what is now Homs in Syria, a large amphora decorated with busts of Christ and his Apostles, and as an illustration of the survival of decorative motifs inspired by mythology during the development of a Christian iconography, the 6th-c. Cherchel patera, its handle decorated with a Poseidon.

Next, enter the small rooms behind the statue of Theodosius II.

Gallery 24: (Christian antiquities from N Africa)

Besides some clumsily decorated architectural fragments from the basilica of Tigzirt in Algeria, there are sarcophagi ornamented with vine tendrils and, predominantly, with the Sacred Monogram – the *chi-rho,* the first two letters of Christ's name in Greek – which is also found in floor mosaics in churches or on the sides and tops of tombs. One frequently recurrent theme is that of the Good Shepherd guarding his flock, while the ram and the ewe can be seen in a mosaic from Rusguniae on Cape Matifou near Algiers. The center of one sarcophagus is decorated with a Good Shepherd within strigil-shaped fluting. Another case displays terracotta lamps and flasks and a votive tablet from Kherbet-um-el-Ahdam (Algeria) decorated with the Sacred Monogram in the center.

Gallery 25 (Christian antiquities from Syria)

Mosaics were as common in Syria as in N Africa. Two views of churches* provide interesting evidence of Early Christian architecture. A motif often used for the floors of sanctuaries or baptisteries is the *kantharos* flanked by animals, in this case by gazelles. There are some basalt gravestones and two pillars* on which St Simeon the Stylite, the hermit whose cult was popular in 5th- and 6th-c. Syria, is depicted. There are two basalt tomb doors (6th–8th c.) decorated with leaf and geometric patterns, crosses and the Sacred Monogram, and, also in basalt, a reliquary in the form of a sarcophagus decorated with peacocks, tendrils and with the cross enclosed by alpha, omega, the sun, and the moon.

Gallery 26: known as the Mosaic, or Roman Civilization Room

Here are gathered together the paintings and mosaics that decorated the walls and floors of Roman houses. Some are inspired by lost masterpieces of Greek painting. The mosaics come from N Africa (Carthage, Utica, Sousse, and Constantine) and from Syria (Antioch), and range from the 1st to the 6th c. AD. The paintings come from Italy (Rome, Pompeii, and Boscoreale) and date from the 1st c. AD. The same motifs are common both to paintings and to mosaics: mythological (the Muses, reclining river gods, the Judgement of Paris, the Triumph of Neptune) or decorative tendrils. From Antioch comes a remarkable mosaic, *The Judgement of Paris***, directly inspired by a Greek painting. From the 3rd to the 5th c. mosaics gradually become more decorative, and symbolism appeared, seeming to anticipate Byzantine art. The mosaic of a Phoenix has something of the visual effect of a Persian carpet. In the middle of the room on stands and in cases are exhibited objects that evoke Roman civilization, or rather its day-to-day life – childhood, games, pastimes, and the rituals of death.

In the E wall of the Mosaics Room a passage leads to the Cour du Sphinx.

Gallery 27: Cour du Sphinx

From the steps leading down from Gallery 26 there is a view of the whole of Le Vau's fine façade, cleared of later accretions in 1933 and forming the E side of the court. In the center is the mosaic of the *Four Seasons****, which decorated the floor of a villa in Daphne, near Antioch, in the age of Constantine; it shows such rustic scenes as a shepherd with his flock, another milking a she-goat, and peasants wreathing garlands of flowers; the seasons are depicted as four female figures separated by hunting scenes.

Here there is a collection of monumental and architectural sculptures grouped without regard to chronology, Greek statues next to Roman.

On the W wall are displayed the 2nd-c. BC friezes** from the Temple of Artemis at Magnesia on the Meander in Asia Minor. They were brought to France in 1843 by Victor Texier and depict battles of Greeks and Amazons. Below them are fragments from the celebrated Temple of Apollo the Deliverer at Miletus in Asia Minor. A capital and the bases of two columns from this temple may be seen on the S side of the court. Apart from the *Four Seasons* mosaic, Roman oriental art is represented by a colossal group symbolizing the Tiber* (imitation of an Alexandrian model) and by the Pergamon Vase* with its beautiful frieze of galloping horsemen, presented by the Sultan Muhammad II.

Go back to the Escalier Daru to reach the first floor.

First floor

On the landing stands the Nike or *Winged Victory of Samothrace****, a masterpiece of 2nd-c. BC Hellenistic art. An original Greek marble, this winged figure commemorates a naval victory and antedates slightly the Altar of Pergamon. It was discovered in fragments by Champoiseau in 1863. To the r. of the statue one of its hands, unearthed in 1950, is displayed in a small case.

Turn l. on the landing, cross the Rotonde d'Apollon to reach the Salle de Boscoreale.

Gallery 1: the Boscoreale Gallery – ancient jewelry

The walls of the room are embellished by some fragments of Greco-Roman painting. In its center and against the W wall two cases display the incomparable collection of silverware found at Boscoreale near Pompeii, in the cistern of a villa destroyed in AD 79 by the eruption of Vesuvius. Almost the whole of the hoard is here (106 items) presented to the Louvre in 1895 by Baron Edmond de Rothschild, along with some gold jewelry. The Boscoreale Treasure*** is in the Hellenistic tradition, particularly noteworthy items being two *patera* (shallow dishes), one decorated with the bust of a female figure symbolizing Africa, the other with the figure of an old man; *oinochoe* (wine jugs) ornamented with Victories sacrificing animals to Athene; *kantharoi* (drinking cups) decorated with cranes feeding their young, with plane leaves, or with olive branches.

A third case against the E wall, displays silverware found in France, notably the Gallo-Roman hoard, the Treasure of Notre-Dame d'Alençon, with its two masks dedicated to Athena. There is also the silver-plated bronze figure of Fortune, bearing traces of gilding, found at Saint-Puits in the Yonne (2nd c.).

Next cross the Salle des Sept-Cheminées, and then an antechamber (the former Cabinet du Roi), to reach the Salle Clarac, once the Queen's bedchamber.

Gallery 2: Salle Clarac Pre-Hellenic civilization (3rd and 2nd millennia BC)

In the 3rd millennium BC,when the island chain of the Cyclades was the center of what is known as Aegean civilization, simultaneously in Crete a brilliant indigenous civilization was coming into being centered at Knossos and the palace of the legendary King Minos. In the room to the r. are displayed two *pithoi* (large storage jars: 17th – 10th c. BC) from Knossos. During the second millennium BC, the Achaeans diffused throughout the Balkan peninsula and the Aegean Islands their civilization, deeply imbued with Cretan influence, but bringing the spontaneity and naturalism of Crete into a more stylized and formalistic frame.

As the room is presently being rearranged only one showcase is on view, to the r., with a temporary display of pre-Hellenic objects: figurines in bronze or terracotta, Minoan and Mycenean vases (2nd millennium).

On leaving the Salle Clarac turn r. to enter the Campana Gallery.

Campana Gallery: Galleries 3–11

The nine rooms running parallel with the Seine display one of the most substantial collections of Greek vases and terracotta figures in the world, all due to the initial acquisition in 1863 of the Campana Bequest, after which the galleries are named.

Gallery 3: (8th–4th c. BC) Geometric and Orientalizing ceramics

Following the Dorian invasions, an artistic style gradually spread across Greece, which was enamored of tauter shapes and more precise decoration. At Athens this Geometric style was more evident in the vases found in the cemetery of the Dipylon (*ca.* 750 BC), often large, and decorated with scenes of battle and funerals. The Boeotians copied Attic art and soon showed their taste for modeling figures (animals, bell-shaped cult idols). The Geometric style was strongly represented in the islands. Toward the end of the 8th c. BC contact was re-established with Asia Minor and Egypt, giving rise to the Orientalizing style which appeared in Corinth, characterized by bright colors and by decorative motifs: – palmettes, lotus flowers plants and animals (groups or files of bulls, lions) and by the division of the whole decorative pattern into smaller separate areas. Almost the sole representation of the human figure is to be found in vases moulded to human shapes. Note, among the exhibits, a sarcophagus decorated with warriors and animals. A case in the center contains examples of the Orientalizing style (Rhodes) and another of Proto-Corinthian vases and vases of the late 8th and 7th c. BC in the earlier Corinthian style.

Gallery 4: Archaic black-figure pottery

From the early 7th to the mid 6th c., maritime Corinth produced a style inspired by Anatolian models. The black-figure technique of incising (engraving) the details on a full silhouette painted in black glaze on the red body of the vase, with dashes of white added was soon preferred to the decoratively conventional Orientalizing style.

It was applied to small and delicate pieces, including perfume flasks, (*aryballoi*), oil jugs (*olpe*), perfume jars (*alabastra*), small boxes or vases in human or animal shapes (*pyxes*), or broad, wide-bellied *kraters* and *hydriae*. Decorative patterns persisted, but the human figure was depicted more and more, used in narrative scenes of battles and banquets. During the 6th c. BC throughout Greece the number of active kilns increased, each with its distinctive style. Wine cups from Naucratis and amphorae from Chalcis are distinguished by their perfect proportions. The Laconians painted over a white slip ground, while black figure reigned supreme in the school of Chalcis and was known in Ionia. Greek *hydriae* (still somewhat clumsy) from the Etruscan cemetery at Caere (Cerveteri) are brightly painted with mythological scenes, sometimes treated humorously. Figurines and vases with human or animal shapes were popular in Ionia and especially in Boeotia. The Attic style continued to evolve, for example, in Tyrrhenian amphorae with their banded friezes.

Gallery 5: Attic black-figure pottery of the Archaic period

From the end of the 7th c. BC the Attic style evolved under the influence of Corinthian incised black-figure painting. Attic potters fashioned ever more elegant amphorae with banded friezes, *lekythoi* and cups. Their creators, potters or painters, begin to emerge as individual personalities. Execias and his school decorated large vases with epic scenes, while the Painter of Amasis preferred Dionysiac scenes. A mannered elegance characterizes the work of the so-called Little Masters.

Gallery 6: Attic red-figure pottery of the Archaic period: (*ca.* 530–500 BC)

Traditional black-figure pottery still had its adherents, but other artists experimented with new methods. Andocides is perhaps the artist who invented the most interesting technique of reversing the black-figure color-values. This was a draftsman's technique, the details being drawn in thin lines of black glaze; either the relief line which stood out like fine wire, or the flush line which varied in density of color. The background was filled in with black. Nicosthenes imitated metal vases. There are a superb cup attributed to Oltos and masterworks by Euphronios, notably his *Herakles Wrestling with Antaeus***. In the passage between galleries there are cases with statuettes from Boeotia, Ionia, and Sicily of the second half of the 6th c. BC.

Gallery 7: Attic red-figure pottery of the Archaic period: (500–480 BC)

This period marks the high point of Greek pottery and the undisputed predominance of Athens as a producer. The cup was now of great importance and reached perfection, being frequently decorated with youths, banquets, the gymnasium. Artists of high quality were numerous. The center case brings together superlative pieces by the Cleophrades Painter, by the Attic vase painter Douris, his cup representing Eos and Memnon** and the Brygos painter's *Fall of Troy***.

Gallery 8: Attic red-figure pottery of the Classical period; second quarter of the 5th c. BC

Until the end of the century Athens remained the center of pottery manufacture, but a more classic style succeeded the archaic freshness of the earlier period. A krater, *The Death of the Children of Niobe***, illustrates the way in which a more realistic style was evolved in an attempt to set individual figures in three-dimensional space. Side by side with traditional subjects, there was a search for more rarefied themes, and yet domestic scenes in which women played an important part were popular, too. Figure drawing evolved under the influence of Pre-Classical sculpture, as did that of the small clay plaque, the Melos *plaquette,* produced to be fixed on to furniture.

Gallery 9: red-figure pottery of the Classical period, second half of the 5th c. BC

This was the age of the Parthenon. A new note is struck of serenity and sublimity and this purified style is exemplified in the white-ground funerary oil jars *(lekythoi).* Simultaneously there is a refinement of sensitivity and the infusion of charm into the work of the artists. Besides the Dionysiac subjects treated in a new, more mystical spirit, scenes of dancing and of music emphasize this taste for contemplation, balanced by the increasing occurrence of scenes of everyday life depicting both the daily round and recreations of Athenian women such as a lady and her servants.

By the end of the century large vases, such as the *Melos Amphora,* display a romantic exuberance of decoration. Note the Canosa vases in the central case.

Gallery 10: 4th-c. BC Italiot pottery

Although the pottery displayed here is temporarily inaccessible, the visitor may go through this room in order to reach Gallery 11. The room will be reopened when the Grand Louvre is opened to the public.

In the 4th c. BC, pottery moved away from classical sublimity toward grace and elegance. There was more freedom of shape, a greater delicacy of design and a more frequent use of pink, blue, and white highlights. The subjects chosen underline the preoccupation of the age with mysticism and, at the same time, with ever stronger emphasis, the pre-eminent place of women in art. At the same time, the kilns of S Italy, established in the previous century by Athenian colonists, were evolving a sometimes exuberant richness of color and decoration, to be seen in the large vases in the center of the room. Here also are examples of the potters' activities in the Hellenistic Age.

Gallery 11: the Salle de Myrina

Except in S Italy vase production was in decline from the beginning of the 4th c. BC; however, that of terracotta figurines expanded. A number of Attic or Boeotian Tanagra figurines, full of delicacy and grace, are displayed in Gallery 10; Gallery 11 is wholly devoted to the work of these modelers of clay. Their studios increased throughout the whole Greek world – in Boeotia, Asia Minor, where

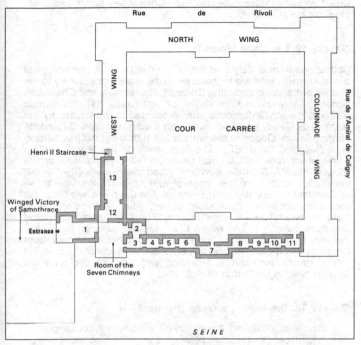

Department of Greek, Etruscan, and Roman Antiquities/ First Floor (Second Floor)
This arrangement is subject to change

1. Ancient jewelry
2. Pre-Hellenic Civilization
3. Geometric and Orientalizing pottery
4. 5. Archaic black-figure pottery
6. 7. Archaic red-figure pottery

8. 9. Classical red-figure pottery
10. Italist pottery
11. Salle de Myrina
12. Salle Henri-II: S Italy
13. Salle La-Caze: Antique bronzes

Myrina was the leading center — in Italy, in Cyrenaica, and elsewhere. The most notable specimens – the *Myrina Eros**, the *Aphrodite with Scallop Shell** – are displayed in the center of the room.

Now turn back to the Salle des Sept-Cheminées, turn r. and enter the Salle Henri II.

Gallery 12: the Salle Henri II

Collections from S Italy and Sicily are displayed in chronological order. Archaic items are in the case on the S wall immediately to the r. of the entrance, comprising Daunian, Campanian, and Chalcidian pottery. There is a fine series of antefixes, and the *Aurula Siciliana***, a small domestic altar presented to the Louvre by the Marquis de Ganay and decorated with a representation of Herakles fighting Triton. Opposite the entrance, a pithos in the Orientalizing style (Megara, 7th c. BC). The two cases on the N wall contain works of art from the Classical period: a few bronzes, such as the (*Capua Rider***, *Samnite warriors***, and the *Sybaris Stag***), but above all, pottery from the Lucanian and Apulian kilns, from those of Campania and lastly from Paestum. On the r. the late Classical period is represented by Apulian pottery which evolved an ornate style of decoration of large *kraters*. There are some charming pisciform dishes*. Going round the room, the case on the S wall displays Hellenistic ware, pottery from Gnathia and vases from Centuripae and Canosa. The last case in the middle of the S wall is for Hellenistic terracottas, including two plaques depicting the Nereids bearing the armor of Achilles.

Gallery 13: the Salle La-Caze (bronzes)

The statuettes exhibited here provide a complete conspectus of Greek, Etruscan, and Roman plastic art from the Geometric period to the Decline of the Roman Empire (8th and 7th c. BC to the 4th c. AD). Unlike their marbles, most of which are copies of Greek originals, many Roman bronzes are original works of high quality. Meanwhile, the utensils trace the changes of taste and custom in the Ancient World. The richest collections are those of lamps and candelabra and especially of mirrors, among which are to be numbered some of the most delicate masterpieces of Greek and Etruscan art.

A number of large cases display these small bronzes – mirrors and statuettes. The most notable 7th- and 6th-c. BC Archaic Greek bronzes include a 7th-c. BC basket-bearer; a warrior wearing a Homeric helmet; Corinthian mirrors; a number of statuettes of Athene; a 6th-c. BC head of a goddess with a high-standing hair-style from Cyprus; a boy standing on a tortoise, and a quantity of

Sileni. From the Classical 5th c. BC come a superb early 5th-c. BC athlete; an Olympian Dionysus (460 BC); Herakles Resting; Herakles Fighting; Herakles holding the Golden Apples from the Garden of the Hesperides, in the style of Lysippos, a Dodonian Zeus; another statue of Zeus in the style of a lost archetype of Phidias, and two boys from the school of Polyclitus. Among the Hellenistic bronzes are a large *cistus;* Dionysus holding a Cup; an Apollo in a deliberately Archaic style; two wrestlers; statuettes of Aphrodite and Eros; a Priest of Isis, and grotesque figurines. Notable Etruscan bronzes include two *cistus;* an outstanding Archaic warrior; a 6th-c. BC Archaic Aphrodite; Ares dancing; Hermes; and several statuettes of Herakles. Nearby there is an isolated group of Eros and Psyche as children, from Asia Minor. The *Lillebonne Apollo** is a gilt bronze, larger-than-life-size statue found in 1823 near the Roman theater at Lillebonne in the Seine Maritime. There is a magnificent collection of 6th- and 5th-c. BC Etruscan mirrors engraved with mythological subjects.

The museum also has a substantial holding of Greek, Etruscan, and Roman bronze utensils. There is a charming group*, in the Alexandrian style from Lower Egypt, of Dionysus with a Satyr playing the flute and two Maenads. The *Sleeping Eros* was unearthed in the Ile-de-France. There are bronzes of the Roman period from the Hellenic E, and Greco-Roman bronzes from Egypt. The cult of foreign deities intermingles with the gods of Greco-Roman mythology and a Greek Aphrodite bears the attributes of an Egyptian Hathor. Then there is the so-called *Beneventum Head** of an Athlete, a notable Roman interpretation of a 5th-c. BC masterpiece representing the youthful head of a victorious athlete. There are silver figurines, representing Greek art exported to the Near East; Gallo-Roman bronzes that express a strong feeling for nature in the many figures of animals and a great sensitivity, the *Seated Girl* and the *Sick Woman.* Bronzes from Italy show a greater naturalism. the *Courrière Apollo* was found in Gaul, but probably originated in Italy; there are household utensils and decorations for vases; a cockerel from the Roman period; a bronze bed, and a fine series of Greek mirrors decorated in relief. Cases contain small Roman bronzes, including a Hermes from Herculaneum. Among the lamps and candelabra is a Roman marble candelabrum restored by Piranesi. There are a gladiator's armor and chariot fittings. Other cases contain small Greek and Etruscan bronzes and Greek, Italiot and Roman weapons.

The Louvre's collection of ancient jewelry* follows its development from the Archaic Greek and Etruscan period (8th and 7th c. BC) down to the art of the Dark Ages. There is a wide selection of gold-working techniques – repoussé, incised, grained or filigree. The setting of precious stones and, later, of fine pearls did not begin until the 4th c. BC, after the era of Alexander the Great's conquests.

▷ **Not to be missed**

French School
Gallery 2: Column-figures from Notre-Dame at Corbeil (12th c.).
The Carrières-Saint-Denis altarpiece (12th c.)

Gallery 3: The so-called *Vierge de la Celle* (14th c.). Charles V and
Jeanne de Bourbon (14th c.)

Gallery 4 and 5: The rood screen from Bourges Cathedral (15th c.).
The effigy of Philippe Pot (15th c.)

Gallery 7: Germain Pilon's *Three Graces* (16th c.). Nymphs from the
Fountain of the Innocents by Jean Goujon (16th c.). *The Diana of
Anet* (16th c.)

Gallery 8: *Virgin of the Annunciation* (Javernant: 14th c.)

Gallery 11: The *Marly Horses* by G. Coustou (17th c.)

Gallery 15: *Milo of Cotrona* by Pierre Puget (17th c.)

Gallery 17: *Marie-Adélaïde, Duchesse de Savoy as Diana* by
Coysevox (18th c.)

Gallery 18: Groups from Marly by A. Coysevox (18th c.)

Gallery 20: *Cupid Carving his Bow from the Club of Hercules* by
Bouchardon (18th c.)

Gallery 21: *Madame de Pompadour as Friendship,* and *Voltaire* by
Pigalle (18th c.)

Gallery 22: Portraits by Houdon (18th c.)

Gallery 24: *Psyche Revived by Cupid's Kiss* by Canova (First
Empire)

Gallery 26: *The Lion and the Serpent* by Barye (19th c.)

German School
Gallery 10: The *Virgin of Isenheim* (15th c.). The Coligny *Retable of
the Passion* (16th c.)

Italian School
Gallery 12: *Descent from the Cross* (Tuscan: 13th c.); *Seated Virgin*
by Jacopo della Quercia (15th c.); *Virgin and Child* attributed to
Donatello (15th c.)

Sculpture

Chief Curator: Jean René Gaborit
*Entrance by the Porte Denon: to see the exhibits in their chrono-
logical order, first walk through the entire department to reach*

Gallery 1. There is direct access to Gallery 23 through the Porte de Flore or Porte Jaujard.

Since 1934 the collections have filled the ground floors cf the Galerie du Bord de l'Eau and the Pavillon des Etats, restored by Lefuel toward the end of the Second Empire. A suite of beautiful, spacious well-lit rooms show to advantage the sculpture collection of, which the principal items are listed below.

The original items came together haphazardly, following the dictates of fashion and historical events, and included neglected royal commissions, gifts from ambassadors, works presented by sculptors on election to the Académie Royale, and works of art confiscated from Royalist emigrés who fled from the Revolution. The bulk of the medieval exhibits come from churches either deconsecrated, destroyed, or converted into secular buildings. Since the 1930s a consistent acquisition policy has enabled gaps to be filled and for the French School to be displayed in an almost unbroken chronological line. However, 19th-c. works are now in the Musée d'Orsay.

The Middle Ages

Gallery 1: Romanesque art

A series of capitals* shows the development of the French style and its regional variations. The capitals come from Sainte-Geneviève in Paris: – *Daniel in the Lions' Den** (11th-c. recutting of 6th-c. original); from Flavigny (11th c.); from Saint-Pons-de-Thomières (Hérault, late 11th and late 12th c.); and Moutiers-Saint-Jean (Côte-d'Or, 12th c.). Polychrome wood sculptures: a 12th-c. *Head of Christ*** from Lavaudieu (Haute-Loire); a *Descent from the Cross* (Burgundy: first half 12th c.); early 12th-c. *Crucifixion* (German style); a *Virgin in Majesty*** (Forez, late 12th c.). A glass case contains the *Head of St Peter*** from the tomb of St Lazarus in Autun Cathedral (12th c.) and other heads from the abbey church of Saint-Denis. Lastly, from the Gard, the doorway (first half 12th c.) of the former Priory of Estagel frames the entrance to the Gothic sculpture rooms.

Galleries 2 and 3: Gothic art

Gallery 2: Notable exhibits include: a capital and a column with the statue of a prophet (late 12th c.) from the cloister of the Cathedral of Notre-Dame-des-Doms in Avignon; column-figures*** of King Solomon and the Queen of Sheba from the doorway of the former Church of Notre-Dame in Corbeil (1180–90); retable*** from Carrières-Saint-Denis, depicting the *Annunciation, The Virgin in Majesty* and *The Baptism of Christ* (late 12th c.); fragments of a

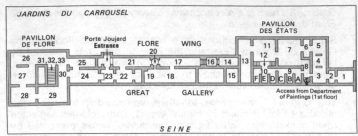

Department of Sculptures/Ground Floor (First Floor)

This arrangement is subject to change

1. Romanesque Art
2, 3, 4. Gothic Galleries
5. Salle Paul-Vitry (15th c.)
6. French Renaissance (1st Period)
7. Salle Jean-Goujon
8. Corridor
9. Galerie Haute (Upper Gallery), small French Gothic statuary
10. Galerie Haute (Upper Gallery), Germany and the Low Countries: 15th and 16th c.
11, 12. Italian Rooms (13th–16th c.)
13, 14. 17th-c French Sculpture
15. Salle Puget
16. Crypt
17. Galerie Rocaille
18. Salle Marly
19. Salle Verte
20. Rotonde de l'Amour (18th-c. French)
21. Galerie du Vase
22. Salle Houdon
23. Vestibule de Flore
24. Neo-Classical Room
25. Romantic Room
26. Salle Barye

frieze (legendary animals and people) from Notre-Dame-en-Vaux in Châlons-sur-Marne; two historiated columns from the Abbey of Coulombs.

Gallery 3: The art of the great 13th-c. cathedrals is represented by a certain number of items: the statue of St Geneviève, which embellished the doorway of the Church of Sainte-Geneviève in Paris (first half 13th c.); a relief showing an angel dictating while St Matthew writes his Gospel, from the rood screen of Chartres Cathedral (mid–13th c.); magnificent heads from Rheims (mid–13th c.), and a statue of Childebert from the doorway of the refectory of Saint-Germain-des-Pres. From Notre-Dame in Paris comes a group depicting the *Harrowing of Hell* from the mid–13th c. rood screen, and the relief showing Pierre de Fayel, Canon of Paris, carved in the 14th c. by Jean Ravy for the chancel tower. There is a beautiful *Head of Christ** (ca. 1300) from the Hôtel-Dieu in Tonnère, and statues of the Madonna and Child**, notably from the Ile-de-France – the exquisite *Vierge de la Celle* — and others from Lorraine and Normandy. There are recumbent effigies of Charles IV and of the queen, Jeanne d'Evreux, sculpted by Jean de Liège for the Abbey of Maubuisson; a recumbent statue of Charles V* from the same abbey, or of Jean de Dormans*, Canon of Paris, interred in the Collège de Beauvais (late 14th c.). The statues of Charles V** and

Jeanne de Bourbon** from the Louvre Palace show the great development in the art of portrait sculpture in the 14th c. with faces bearing very individual characteristics. In the same room is the early 15th-c. retable which once belonged to the church of Nolay (Côte-d'Or). It shows the Virgin and Child surrounded by the Twelve Apostles.

Two passages lead to Gallery 4 (Salle Gothique) and Gallery 5, known as the Salle Paul-Vitry. In the first passage is a recumbent statue of Guillaume de Chanac, Bishop of Paris, from the Church of Saint-Victor (mid 14th c.); a polychrome stone Virgin and Child from Cîteaux (first half 14th c.); a Provençal head of the Virgin (14th c.), and an early 14th-c. statue in painted wood of a woman at prayer. The second passage contains the head of an apostle* attributed to André Beauneveu, from the Château de Mehun-sur-Yèvres (Cher, late 14th c.); an early 15th-c. black and white marble statue of Marie de Bourbon, Prioress of Saint-Louis at Poissy.

Between the two passages are the tomb of Pierre d'Evreux-Navarre and Catherine of Alençon, striking portraits; two bases from Bourges decorated with angels, and Our Lady of Mercy from Montmorot (Burgundy, 15th c.).

Gallery 8

The vestibule from which an internal staircase leads up to the Galérie Medicis and in which may be seen a large early 16th-c. altarpiece from Champagne and the *Calvaire de Nivelles* (Southern Low Countries, late 15th-c).

Gallery 9: sculptures from the 13th to the 16th c.

The room comprises a series of three bays devoted to small-scale works from the 13th to the 16th c.

A (1st alcove): the other art of the 14th c. used the attractive combination of black and white marble* embellished with gold. Retables* from the Sainte-Chapelle, Paris, showing scenes from the Passion, and from the Abbey of Maubuisson, the gift of Jeanne d'Evreux; fragments of altarpieces; remains of funeral monuments: masks from recumbent statues or from wall tombs, and small statues of Our Lady, such as the exquisite *Virgin of the Annunciation*** from Javernant (Aube).

B (2nd alcove): 13th and 14th-c. works in wood include angels* carved as altar decorations inspired by the art of Rheims, among them the famous Sachs Angel. Several images of the Madonna and Child, including the famous Virgin of Abbeville in a typically late 13th-c. pose, a 14th-c. Virgin from Beauvais.

C (3rd alcove): Late medieval sculpture in stone, marble and wood.

There is a case devoted to funeral sculptures with a series of *pleurants* or 'weepers'*; a *pleurante* dressed as an abbess (stone by Juan de La Huerta); two mid-15th c. weepers from the tomb of the Duc Jean de Berry (Burges): 15th-c. weepers from the royal tombs at Poblet (Spain). Burgundian art is exemplified by a statuette of St Stephen (Etienne), from Champagne others: a female saint holding a palm branch, a Virgin and Child.

Gallery 4: Gothic art (continued)

Until a special exhibition site has been built for it in its native town, the mid-13th-c. rood screen*** from Bourges Cathedral is housed here. Mutilated scenes from the Passion are carved in high relief in polychrome stone, in which fragments of glass have been found. The center of the room is dominated by the imposing tomb of Philippe Pot***, Grand Seneschal of Burgundy, from the Abbey of Citeaux. In conception it is extremely original: eight hooded figures support the slab on which lies the recumbent statue of Pot.

Gallery 5 (Salle Paul-Vitry): 15th-c. sculpture

Burgundian works* include a painted and gilded stone *Virgin and Child* from a house in Dijon; John the Baptist, St James as a pilgrim (from Semur-en-Auxois). The evolution of the Parisian funeral monument is illustrated by the recumbent statues of Philippe de Morvillers, Président of the Parlement, interred in the Abbey of Saint-Martin-des-Champs, and of Anne of Burgundy, Duchess of Bedford, carved by Guillaume Vluten from the church of the Celestines in Paris. A *Mary Magdalene* from Champagne, *St George and the Dragon* from a studio in the Nivernais.

Late medieval works include a Calvary from Saint-Léger-les-Troyes and early 16th-c. statues of *St Anne Teaching Our Lady,* of St Peter and of St Susanna carved by Michel Colombe's pupil, Jean de Chartres, for Anne de Beaujeu.

Renaissance and medieval Italian sculpture

Gallery 6: French Renaissance (first stage)

Exhibits include portrait busts of Chancellor Duprat and of Louise de Savoie from a studio in Tours (early 16th-c.); a lion's head and pilasters from the chapel of the Château de Gaillon; from the same chapel, the altarpiece carved in low-relief of *St George Slaying the Dragon*** by Michel Colombe (1430–1511); the powerfully affecting tomb from the church of the Celestines, of Renée d'Orléans-Longueville; the Virgins of Olivet and of Ecouen (early 16th c.); from Saint-Germain-l'Auxerrois; the recumbent statues of Louis de Poncher and his wife (early 16th c.) by Michel Colombe's nephew, Guillaume Regnault.

Gallery 7 (the Salle Jean-Goujon): French Renaissance

In the center stands a marble fountain from Gaillon, at one end a chimney-piece from Villeroy by Mathieu Jacquet; at the other, from the Capitole in Toulouse, the Porte du Grand Consistoire from the studio of Guiraud Millot. Fremyn Roussel's *Genius of History* sculpted for the tomb of François I. The great French 16th-c. sculptor was Germain Pilon (1528–90) who created the funerary monument for Henri II's heart (representing the *Three Graces****), erected in the church of the Celestines in Paris from 1560 to 1566; the *Risen Christ*, flanked by the two soldiers guarding the sepulchre, a marble group (*ca.* 1583) sculpted for Henri II's funerary rotunda in Saint-Denis; a terracotta of Our Lady of Sorrows, a preparatory model for the marble statue designed for the same rotunda; a preparatory model of the recumbent statue of Henri II for the tomb in Saint-Denis; the tomb of Valentine Balbiani from Saint Catherine-du-Val-des-Ecoliers, with the bronze figure of her husband, Chancellor, later Cardinal, de Birague, kneeling at prayer; three reliefs from the Church of Saint-Etienne-du-Mont: the *Agony in the Garden, Melchizedech* and *St Paul*; a bronze *Descent from the Cross* from the Birague Chapel; two reliefs from the pulpit of the church of the Grands-Augustins: *John the Baptist preaching, St Paul preaching*; the marble bust of a child; finally, Pilon's works include busts of Henri II, Henri III, and the four funerary figures in wood which supported the reliquary of St Geneviève. Pierre Bontemps (*ca.* 1505–68): funeral statues of Charles de Maigny, Captain of the King's Guards, shown seated at his post and asleep (1557); recumbent statues propped on one elbow of Jean d'Humlères and of Admiral Chabot, which display great vigour, are also attributed to the same sculptor from the court of François I. Jean Goujon (*ca.* 1510–*ca.* 1565) exemplifies Classical Antiquity in French Renaissance sculpture: the *Deposition*** and a relief of the Four Evangelists** from the rood screen of Saint-Germain-l'Aux-errois (1544–45); three large elongated reliefs*** of nymphs and *putti* from the Fontaine des Innocents (Paris, 1547–49). Barthélemy Prieur continued the Pilon tradition by combining realism with Classicism: elegant polychrome marble funerary monument to Anne I, Duc de Montmorency, Constable of France; recumbent marble statues of the duke and his widow, Madeleine of Savoy; tomb of Christophe de Thou with a colored marble portrait bust and two bronze geniuses (guardian spirits) in the style of Michelangelo.

1st alcove: François Marchand, four bas-reliefs for the rood screen of Saint-Père in Chartres (1543); Domenico del Barbiere also called Dominique Florentin (*ca.* 1506–*ca.* 1565/75): reliefs illustrating the life of the Duc de Guise from his tomb at Joinville. 2nd alcove: preparatory funerary statue for the tomb of Catherine de' Medici by

Girolamo Della Robbia; the recumbent bronze figure, propped on one elbow, of Albert Pius of Savoy, Prince of Carpi; a cast, perhaps by Clouet, of the face of Henri II. 3rd alcove: bronze reliefs by Blondel de Rocquencourt; terracotta by Henri II's court sculptor, Ponce Jacquiot, of a girl drawing a thorn from her foot; two angels in the Lorraine style from the school of Ligier Richier; terracotta typical of Maine of the Virgin suckling the Child. In the center stands *The Diana of Anet****, from the Château d'Anet, home of Diane de Poitiers, mistress of Henri II, a marble fountain, an influential example combining the sensitivity of Classical Antiquity with the elegance of the French Mannerist school.

Gallery 11

Above the doorway, also from the Château d'Anet, the bronze bas-relief, the *Nymph of Fontainebleau***, made for François I by the famous Italian goldsmith and sculptor, Benvenuto Cellini. This room was once devoted to Italian sculpture and substantial examples still remain: the door from the Palazzo Stanga in Cremona; two retables by Della Robbia, and a *Mercury* by Giovanni da Bologna (1524–1608).

For reasons of conservation, four large marble equestrian groups from the Tuileries gardens and the Place de la Concorde were brought here in 1984 and 1986 and are provisionally on display: *Mercury and Fame riding Pegasus*** by Antoine Coysevox and the *Marly Horses**** by Guillaume Coustou. The Winged Horses were originally erected in the park at Marly in 1702, before being transferred to Paris: the Marly Horses were set on their original site in 1745. Casts have replaced them in the Place de la Concorde.

Gallery 10: Germany and the Low Countries (15th and 16th c.)

D (1st alcove): German 15th-c. sculpture: a Bavarian St Wolfgang; a *Virgin and Child* from Uzgorod (Hungary); a Virgin from the Salzburg region in the new *Beau style* or *weicher stil*, showing the tender grace of the early 15th c. The Virgin of the Abbey of Eberbach (Middle Rhine) and the Rhenish (?) alabaster statue of Our Lady of Mercy are somewhat later. Other statues bear witness to the stylistic revival at the end of the 15th c.: a deacon, attributed to the Master of the Kefermarkt Altarpiece (Upper Austria); a bust of a bishop (Tyrol); a flying angel (Nuremberg); the monumental Virgin of Isenheim*** (near Colmar) showing the spirituality of the Middle Ages; St Anne carrying the Virgin of Wasserburg, the relief of the *Nativity* (Colmar).

E (2nd alcove): late 15th- and 16th-c. German sculpture: the delicate statue of the *Virgin of the Annunciation* in painted and gilded marble, from St Peter's (Erfurt), by the celebrated Tilman Riemenschneider (b. *ca.* 1460, d. Wurzburg 1531). Most of the Swabian works of around 1500 come from Ulm studios, among them a *St Mary Magdalene*** by Gregor Ehrant (b. Ulm–d. Augsburg, 1540); a group of prelates from the workshop of Daniel Mauch (b. Ulm 1477–d. Liège, 1540); a praying Christ from a group depicting the *Agony in the Garden;* a Doctor of the Church, and a Holy Kindred. Two cases display Renaissance works, notably the *Holy Family* in stone from Solnhofen, after an engraving by Dürer, attributed to Viktor Kayser (active from 1516, Augsburg, d. 1552); a small delicate alabaster bust of Ottheinrich, Elector Palatine, attributed to Dietrich Schro (active 1545–68), and a *Calvary* by the Flemish sculptor Willem van den Broek, known as Guilielmus Paludanus (b. Malines 1530–d. Antwerp 1579/80) who also worked in Augsburg.

F (3rd alcove): 15th- and 16th-c. Flemish and Dutch sculpture. Different production centers of the South (modern Belgium) are represented by a fragment of gravestone from Tournal depicting *St Christopher with the Donor and his Sons;* a Flemish St Sebastian; several small statues bearing the stamp of Malines (3 pales); a stone Virgin of the Annunciation from Brabant; a pretty seated *Madonna and Child,* bearing the stamp of the Brussels workshops (a mallet), and a significant series of statues with the Antwerp mark (a hand), scattered fragments and altarpieces, most notably the great altarpiece of the *Passion****, in painted and gilded wood, made in an Antwerp workshop for the parish church of Coligny (Marne).

From the North (modern Netherlands), a *Nativity* from the school of Adriaen van Wesel (Utrecht *ca.* 1417–*ca.* 1490); a *Virgin and Child* attributed to Jan van Nude (active 1450–90 Utrecht), and several statues from the Lower Rhine, notably a St Leonard and a St Anthony.

Gallery 12 (Galerie basse/Lower Gallery): 11th to 15th c. Italian sculpture

On either side of the staircase are two figures from the demolished façade of Florence Cathedral; at the foot on the r. stands the graceful 14th-c. *Virgin of the Annunciation*** by Nino Pisano (d. *ca.* 1368), immediately in front a polychrome wood group, the *Descent from the Cross****, the work of a studio active in Umbria and Lazio during the second quarter of the 13th c.; to the l. an early 12th-c. pulpit from Pomposa.

In the alcove to the r. is a 13th-c. seated *Madonna and Child*** from the cloisters of San Francesco in Ravenna, where it is supposed to have marked the site of Dante's grave; *Faith* (studio of Nicola Pisano, active *ca.* 1258–78) allegedly from the tomb of St Dominic at Bologna; the *Four Virtues* (caryatids) from a Neapolitan tomb.

To the l. of the staircase works from the 15th-c. studio of the Della Robbias: they specialized in great enameled terracottas*, white on a blue ground for the earliest examples, polychrome for the later.

In the alcoves beyond, to the r.: *Madonna and Child***, a painted and gilded terracotta by Donatello and another, in colored stucco, in the style of the Pazzi Madonna, from his studio; Desiderio de Settignano: marble relief of *Julius Caesar*, and his large but very delicate marble medallion of *John the Baptist with the Infant Christ*, from the Medici collections; *La Belle Florentine,* gilded bust of a woman in wood (3rd alcove); Luca Della Robbia's original terracotta of the Virgin and Child surrounded by six angels; a bust of Beatrice d'Este, Duchess of Milan by Gian Cristoforo Romano; works from the studio of the Mantegazza, sculptors active in the Charterhouse of Pavia, late 15th c.; Francesco Laurana, bust of a Princess of Aragón (4th alcove).

At the far end of the gallery is a large polychrome wood seated *Madonna**** attributed to Jacopo Della Quercia, and on either side two fragments from the tomb of Pope Paul II in St Peter's, Rome (Mino da Fiesole and Giovanni Dalmata).

On the r. wall returning to the staircase, a bust of Alfonso of Aragón, King of Naples, by Pietro da Milano; the so-called *Madonna of Auvillers**, a relief by Agostino di Duccio, perhaps for Pietro de' Medici; Benedetto da Mariano's bust of Filippo Strozzi; a St Christopher by the Sienese sculptor, Francesco di Giorgio Martini. Backing onto the central pillar is a bust of Diotisalvi Neroni* by Mino da Fiesole dated 1464.

The seventeenth century

Gallery 13 (first half of the 17th c.) from Henri IV to Louis XIV

Alcoves to the r. display secular subjects. Works from the Second School of Fontainebleau under Henri IV include Mathieu Jacquet's relief taken from the marble embellishments of La Belle Cheminée de Fontainebleau (1598–1602), bronze head of Henri IV, bronze bust of Jean d'Alesson, medallion of the poet, Philippe Desportes. Pierre Francheville studied under Giovanni da Bologna in Florence; a number of his works, the allegorical figure of *Geometry*, a sketch for the statue of the Grand Duke of Tuscany, emphasize the Florentine background of this sculptor of Henri IV. His four bronze *Slaves***, for the statue of Henri IV on the Pont Neuf, his marbles of Orpheus and of David are examples of French Mannerism. The subtle sophistication of the European Mannerists is seen in the fine group *Psyche Abducted by Mercury**, commissioned by the Emperor Rudolph II from the Dutch sculptor, Adriaen de Vries. The most important influence in French sculpture in the mid–17th c. was

Jacques Sarrazin, with his personal mixture of the Classical and the Baroque; note his group of *Children with a Goat* (the pedestal was added when the work was set up at Marly early in the 18th c.). Marble reliefs by Gerard van Opstal of satyrs and putti, graces, tritons, nereids, and centaurs typify the *bacchandia* and child subjects of early French Neo-Classicism.

To the r. of the entrance royal commissions are typified by the monument from the Pont-au-Change erected by Simon Guillain (*ca.* 1647), incorporating bronze statues of Louis XIII, the young Louis XIV and his mother, Marie de' Medici, entrusted with the Regency during her son's minority. A bronze bust of Louis XIII shows the realism of the art of the French portrait. It is set off by the Baroque grand manner of Bernini's busts of Richelieu and Pope Urban VIII.

Examples of funerary art include the swirling Mannerist bronze of *Fame** which its sculptor Pierre I Biard set on the top of the tomb of the Duc d'Epernon at Cadillac. The development of the sculpture of tomb figures at prayer can be traced from the rigidity of the figure of Marie de Barbanson-Cani by Barthélemy Prieur (the de Thou monument) or again in Michel II Bourdin's *Amador de la Porte,* through the flexible style of Simon Guillain's *Princesse de Condé,* to the stronger emphasis on movement on Jacques-Auguste de Thou's tomb on which François Anguier (1604–1669) sculpted young Gasparde de la Châtre leaning towards the spectator, or in the kneeling figure of Charles de Vieuville, which Gilles Guérin (1611–1678) carved for the Minims, or again in the mystical offering of self expressed in Jacques Sarrazin's sculpture of Cardinal de Berulle**. There are the monuments for the hearts of the Duc de Longueville by François Anguier, and of the Duc de Brissac by Etienne Le Hongre, which make use of highly abstruse allegories. Jacques Sarrazin (1592–1660) stands out as the great sculptor of the beginning of Louis XIV's reign. After long residence in Rome he created the reliefs for the monument for Louis XIII's heart, originating from the Jesuit Church of Saint-Louis; a charming bust of Louis XIV; statuettes of St Peter and of St Mary Magdalen, and a sensitive terracotta Virgin and Child.

Staircase: the four reliefs displayed here were carved by their sculptors – François Girardon and Gaspard Marsy among them – for their election to the French Academy of Painting and Sculpture

▷ **The teaching of sculpture**

The Academy was founded in 1648 and became the main center for training in the fine arts. The future sculptor was taken into his master's studio around the age of 14 and then, at the end of several competitive examinations, became a scholarship student at the French Academy in Rome. The culmination of all official careers was election to the French Academy of which membership was unrestricted in point of numbers. In order to be elected, the intending Academician had to surmount two obstacles. He had first to submit one or more works to demonstrate his abilities and, provided that these were accepted, he then would have to submit a further work on a set subject – his election piece. During the 18th century this was generally a statuette in the ronde-basse, in marble, of a subject taken from Classical mythology or from ancient history, less frequently from the Bible or the martyrology. This series of masterpieces in the full sense of the word was transferred from the Academy to the Louvre after the French Revolution.

Gallery 14: Galerie des Enlèvements (Gallery of abductions)

On the r., the series of 'election pieces' continues with reliefs by Desjardins, Rousselet, Hardy, Prou, and Nicolas Coustou, glorifying Louis XIV. Girardon's lifelike *Boileau,* the *Grand Condé** by Coysevox and the pomp of office in Lemoyne's *J. Hardouin Mansart* exemplify three strands of sensibility in the art of the portrait statue. The four terms (pedestals supporting busts) of *The Seasons* from Saint-Cloud are reminiscent of the formal garden, but even more so are the objects from Versailles such as the urns by Girardon and the two abductions: *Saturn abducting Cybele* (symbolizing *Earth*) and *Boreas abducting Orithyia (Air)* by Thomas Regnaudin and Gaspard Marsy respectively.

Gallery 15: Salle Puget

This room is devoted to the work of three sculptors: Pierre Puget, Martin Desjardins, and Michel Anguier.

The great Baroque sculptor Pierre Puget (1620–94) was born in Marseilles, trained in Rome, Genoa and Florence and was the all-round artist – architect, painter and sculptor. Because his work did not conform to the Classical ideals of Colbert it was only after the latter's death that Puget carved three major marbles for Louis XIV: *Perseus Liberating Andromeda*, the great relief of *Alexander and Diogenes** and the *Milo of Crotona***, which took him 12 years to complete and which was erected in Versailles in 1682. It is a work that expresses his sense of human drama and in which emotion, strength, and the control of mass predominate. A youthful work, *Hercules Resting*, and a fine *Crucifixion* in the display case give the finishing touches to this exhibition of a distinctive French Baroque style of which he may be regarded as the founder.

The work of another major sculptor, the Dutchman Martin Desjardins, subsists in the fine bust of Colbert from Villacerf, the bronze decoration for the base of the statue of Louis XIV for the

Place des Victoires, consisting of four reliefs of historical subjects and four medallions. These embellishments are completed by other bronze medallions by Arnoul and Le Nègre from designs by the painter Mignard, mounted on the columns at the corners of the square: three are on display in this room.

Lastly the elegant Classicism of Michel Anguier (1612–86) which imposed itself on his early Baroque style is represented by the terracotta *Hercules and Atlas* which he presented to the French Academy, and by the marble *Amphitrite* which he carved for the park at Versailles.

Gallery 16: the Crypt

In the center is a reduced scale model of the equestrian statue of Louis XIV in the Place Vendôme, by François Girardon. On the walls four examples of Neo-Classical busts: Martin Desjardin's *Pierre Mignard* shows fine-drawn tension; the other three: *Le Brun, Colbert,* and *Marie Serre*, illustrate the development of Antoine Coysevox (1640–1720) from the lifeless formality of his election piece to the psychological penetration of the ornate female portrait.

On the r. cases display terracottas of religious subjects by Jean Dubois, Paillet and Goullons.

The eighteenth century

The development of French sculpture from the closing years of the reign of Louis XIV to the end of that of Louis XV can be seen in the works on display. They are a representative selection mounted in a low key setting.

Gallery 17: Galerie Rocaille

This room houses the most significant examples extant of early 18th-c. garden statuary. From the gardens of the Duc d'Antin at Petit-Bourg come Coysevox's *Marie-Adélaïde, Duchesse de Savoie as Diana****, N. Coustou's *Louis XV as Jupiter* and G. Coustou's *Marie Leczczynska* as *Juno*. From Marly there are N. Coustou's *Julius Caesar,* S. Slodtz's *Hannibal* and Frémin's *Flora and Diana*. Imbedded in the far wall of the gallery is a monumental dragon from a house near Saint-Germain-des-Prés, an example of *rocaille* decoration as applied to private houses. Also on display are a number of Academy election pieces** of which the Louvre possesses a nearly-complete set for the 18th c. Because each item can be dated precisely, they are invaluable for following the developments of style and taste: G. Coustou, 1704; Cayot, 1711; Coudray, 1712; Dumont, 1713; J. B. Lemoyne the Elder, 1715; Bousseau, 1715;

Thierry, 1717; A. Slodtz, 1743; Hutin, 1747. In two showcases are works by N. Coustou, Le Lorraine and M. A. Slodtz.

Gallery 18: Salle Marly

Once again the emphasis here is upon garden statuary, in particular the statues from Marly. The four groups*** by Coysevox (*The Seine, The Marne, Neptune, Amphitrite*), and a single figure (*Faun Playing a Flute*) were created for the wonderful Grande Cascade, also called La Rivière, as were the three groups by N. Coustou (*Sleeping Huntsman, Nymph with Quiver, Nymph with Scallop Shell*). Also from Marly, but from different groups, are Prou's *Amphitrite* and A *Nymph of Diana* by Flamen. The two copies by Coysevox of Neo-Classical statues: *Crouching Venus* and *Nymph with the Scallop-Shell* come from the gardens of Versailles.

Gallery 19: Salle Verte

This little room is devoted to a further series of election pieces: L.-S. Adam, 1737; Ladatte, 1741; Pigalle***, 1744; Bouchardon, 1745; N.-S. Adam, 1762; exquisite small marbles (Caffieri, particularly the memorial to Madame Favart; Falconet, *Baigneuse*) and four terracotta busts: *N. Coustou* by G. Coustou; *Louis XV as a Child*** by Coysevox; *N. N. Coypel* by J.-B. Lemoyne; *Madame Favart* by Defernex; *Self-portrait*** by Pigalle. Funerary art is reflected in the wax maquettes: Bouchardon, projected tomb for Cardinal Fleury; Pigalle, mausoleum for Marshal de Saxe and a reduced scale model in bronze (J.-B. Lemoyne), monument to Louis XV in Rouen.

Gallery 20: called the Rotonde de l'Amour, is devoted to Bouchardon: *Cupid Carving his Bow from the Club of Hercules* ***, sketch for *The Marne* for the fountain in the Rue de Grenelle.

Gallery 21: Galerie du Vase

This gallery is devoted to Louis XV's sculptors, where the patronage of Mme de Pompadour is emphasized by the presence of the statues of *Lyric Poetry* by L.-S. Adam and *Music* by Falconet, executed for the Château de Bellevue, and by a number of works by Falconnet**: *The Threatening Cupid, Pygmalion*, and by Pigalle: *Love and Friendship, Madame de Pompadour as Friendship***. Also by Pigalle is his nude statue of *Voltaire**** which shocked contemporary sensibilities, and his famous *Boy with a Cage,* and *Boy with a Bird.*

On the other hand, Allegrain's *La Baigneuse* or *Venus Bathing,* and *Diana Surprised* come from Mme Du Barry's collections, as do the Cupids of Boizot and of Vassé*, and *Comedy* by the latter. The royal mistress protected the career of Pajou; *Marie Leczszynska*, an early work, and the masterpiece of his maturity, *Psyche Abandoned***, are among the exhibits.

The series of election pieces continues (Vassé, 1751; Falconet, 1754; Gillet, 1757; Caffieri, 1759; Pajou, 1760; Mouchy, 1768).

In the center of the room stands a vase by Verberckt for the Château Choisy, and a reduced scale model in bronze by Bouchardon of his equestrian statue of Louis XV. A case displays medallions in wax (J.-B. Nini) and terracotta (D. Chassel).

▷ The *Eminent Frenchmen series*

During the reign of Louis XVI, the majority of royal commissions were designed to embellish the museum and especially the Grande Galerie of the Louvre. In line with this project is the series of *Grands Hommes,* begun in 1776.

Every two years four sculptors were asked to provide a group of four statues. Thus 17 artists, among them Pajou, Caffieri, Julien, Clodion and Houdon, carved 30 statues. The series, started in the Middle Ages with Du Guesclin, showed a strong bias towards philosophers and soldiers in the 17th c. and ended in the 18th c. with Montesquieu and d'Alembert, the statue of the latter not being finished until 1808. The scheme aroused an interest in history which increased in the following century.

Gallery 23: Vestibule de Flore

This intermediate room is embellished by a large vase with decorative plaques and by four of the *Hommes Illustres (Eminent Frenchmen)* from the series commissioned by the Comte d'Angiviller for the Grande Galerie of the Louvre (→inset). By Julien, *La Fontaine writing 'The Fox and the Grapes'* and the painter Nicolas Poussin; by Pajon, the writer Blaise Pascal, with his *Pensées* and his *Provinciales* at his feet, and by Caffieri, Pierre Corneille with a list of his plays.

In the passage leading to Gallery 22 are two cases containing terracotta children (Houdon's masterpieces: *Louise and Alexandre Brongniart****; *Couasnon*), and others in plaster (Houdon: *Sabine Houdon*; J.-B. Lemoyne).

Gallery 22: Salle Houdon

It is advisable to go straight to the far l. corner of the room, which houses an impressive collection of the works of Houdon*** (1741–1828). Arranged round a bronze *Diana the Huntress* and a marble mausoleum (signed and dated 1781) for the heart of the Comte d'Ennery are an exceptionally fine series of portraits ranging from Louis XV's daughter Madame Adélaïde and the famous singer, Sophie Arnould, to statesmen such as Washington and Benjamin Franklin, philosophers such as Rousseau, Voltaire, and Diderot, and intimates such as Mme Houdon (original plaster).

Go back to see two busts by Pajou: the marble of Mme Du Barry** from Louveciennes – a haughty likeness, that became the subject of pastiche and the trade-mark of a certain attitude towards the 18th c. – and of the engraver, Bassan**, in his working clothes. J. -L. Vassé's *Grief,* from the tomb of Feydeau de Brou, exemplifies the somewhat affected grace which infused funerary art at the dawn of Neo-Classicism. By their realism and restraint, and the clear influence of a taste for Antiquity, two works of Julien, *Ganymede with Jove's Eagle** and his election piece of 1779, *The Dying Gladiator**,* foreshadow the 19th c., as does Stouf's *Death of Abel* (1785). Two medium-size terracottas by Pajou: *Anacreon Clipping Cupid's Wings* and *The Stream* balance the two cases of small terracottas by Clodion, Moitte, Gois, Guiart, and Sergel. Busts by provincial sculptors Attiret and Breton stand in contrast with those by academicians from Paris such as Pigalle: the *'Compère' Diderot* and Caffieri: *Canon Pingré**.*

The nineteenth century

Following removal of the works of the second half of the 19th c. to the Musée d'Orsay, Galleries 27–30 have been reorganized around Michelangelo's *Slaves,* to present Italian sculpture of the 16th c. (Rustici, Pierino da Vinci, Mosca, Vittoria, Antico); of the 17th c. (Bernini, Foggini, Mazzuoli) and of the 18th c. (Corradini), and also Dutch Baroque sculpture (Quellin, Pompe, Delvaux).

Gallery 24: the First Empire

This room might well be called the Salle Psyché since this myth-ological character takes first place here with the tender group *Psyche Revived by Cupid's Kiss***,* and *Cupid and Psyche**,* both by Antonio Canova (1757–1822). François Nicolas Delaistre (1746–1832): *Cupid and Psyche.* Denis Antoine Chaudet (1763–1810): *Cupid,* a monumental silver *Peace** and, in more forceful style, *Oedipus and Phorbas.* J.-C. Marin: *Woman Bathing.* James Pradier (1790–1852): *Wounded Son of Niobe**. Napoleon in his Coronation Robes* by Claude Ramey (1754–1838). Pierre Chinard (1756–1813): *Madame de Vernirac as Diana the Huntress* and several small clay maquettes. Henri-Joseph Ruxthiel (1775–1837): *Zephyr Abducting Psyche.* Bertel Thorwaldsen (1770–1844) *Venus with the Apple**;* and *Charity.* Jacques Edmé Dumont (1761–1844): bust of Marceau.

Charles Louis Corbet (1758–1808): bust of La Tour d'Auvergne; Claude Michallon (1751–99): bust of Alexandre Lenoir. Philippe Laurent Roland (1746–1816): marble bust of Mlle Roland. François Milhomme (1758–1823): plaster bust of *Andromache*.

Gallery 25: Salle Romantique

In this first room works from the years 1820–1840 are exhibited which, although by contemporaries, show how very differently each was affected by the spirit of Romanticism. The sculptors still faithful to Classical Antiquity were François Joseph Bosio (1768–1845) with his recumbent statue of *Hyacynthus,* Apollo's favorite; The *Nymph Salmacis; Henri IV as a Child***, carved in silver; *Marie-Amélie, Queen of the French* (preparatory study in plaster). Jaley (1802–66): *La Prière;* J.-P. Cortot (1787–1843): *Daphnis and Chloë.*

Although his subjects are Neo-Classical, the female figures carved by Jean-Jacques [James] Pradier (1792–1852) have a sensuousness far removed from the art of Canova: for example: *Psyche, The Three Graces***, Satyr and Bacchante*,* and a terracotta preliminary study for *Diana and Endymion.*

Hippolyte Maindron (1801–86): *Velléda,* the Druid priestess in Chateaubriand's *Les Martyrs.*

François Rude (1784–1855): his dash and vigor make him one of the greatest sculptors of the Romantic era. *Mercury Tying his Sandal* is closer to Renaissance Mannerism than to Classical Antiquity. Other sculptures include his *Young Neapolitan Fisherman*,* exhibited at the first Salon de la Sculpture Romantique (1831), and two preparatory models** for the figure of *La Marsaillaise* on the Arc de l'Etoile. Displayed in a case are a number of Rude's small, energetic maquettes in wax and terracotta, as well as bronzes by Feuchère, David d'Angers, Gechter and Pradler. A few medallions exemplify the substantial output in this genre of David d'Angers (1788–1856); he executed portraits of all the celebrities of his day.

In the corridor there is a portrait statue of his son by David d'Angers, *The Boy with the Grapes;* also *Orlando Furioso* by Duseigneur (1808–66), inspired by Ariosto's poem. A few portrait statues typical of the July Monarchy: Barre (1811–96), *Rachel** and *Madame Paul Delaroche,* both in ivory; Carle Elshoect (1797–1856), the dancer Thérèse Elsslet.

Gallery 26: Salle Barye

Some of the later works of this artist and particularly all the commissions he undertook for Napoléon III's embellishment of the Louvre, have been removed to the Musée d'Orsay, where they are currently exhibited. The intention is that they will be brought back to the Louvre and displayed in a room devoted to the decoration of the palace. The originality of Antoine-Louis Barye (1795–1875) lies in his lively, accurate observation of the animal world, which he displays in scenes filled with Romantic ardor and great realism. Generally speaking, his bronzes are of the highest quality. The plaster model of his *Lion and Serpent**** was shown at the first Salon de la Sculpture Romantique in 1831 and the bronze was cast by the *cire perdue* (lost wax) method by Honoré Gonon, who cast for Barye such other important bronzes as *Tiger and Gavial** and *Roger Carrying off Angelica on the Hippogriff*, from Ariosto's *Orlando Furioso*. A number of plasters* retouched with wax are displayed, among them three dining-table centerpieces later cast in silver for the Duc d'Orléans in 1838 – *Lion Hunt, Wild Bull Hunt*, and *Indian Riding an Elephant*.

In the cases are more wax models by Barye: (*Tigre en Sphinx*) or plasters retouched with wax: *The Three Graces, Minerva,* and *Apollo* and especially *Lion Hunt*** and *Wild Bull Hunt***, the plaster models for the dining-table centerpieces for the son of Louis Philippe.

Paintings

Head Curator: Pierre Rosenberg.
Access from the pyramid and the Hall Napoléon: Head towards the Pavillon Sully and take the recently-restored Henri II and Henri IV staircases, which lead to the first galleries of French painting, on the 2nd floor.

The arrangement of exhibits is subject to change.

The collections of French paintings (from the 14th c. to the end of the reign of Louis XIV) are arranged in chronological order in an area of 31,200sq.ft/2900m², in 12 new rooms in the north and north-west wings of the Cour Carrée. The itinerary continues on the 1st floor within the Grande Galerie and the Aile Mollien (18th and 19th c.), in the Salle Mollien, the Salle Denon and the Salle Daru (large works).

Italian painting is displayed in the Grande Galerie (13th–15th c.), the Salle des Etats (16th c.), the Salon Carré (17th c.), and the Aile de Flore (17th and 18th c.). The Beistegui Collection is presented at the end of the Aile de Flore.

The Northern Schools – Flemish, Dutch and German – are arranged chronologically in the Louvre (15th and 16th c.: Petits Cabinets, Seine side; 17th c.: Petits Cabinets, Tuileries side, Salle Van Dyck, Salle Medicis and Salle des Sept-Mètres (Rembrandt).

The Spanish School is presented in the Pavillon de Flore, and the English School, together with the Croy and Victor Lyon donations, in the zenithally-lit gallery on the 2nd floor of the Aile de Flore.

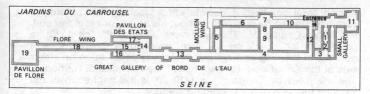

JARDINS DU CARROUSEL

PAVILLON DES ÉTATS

FLORE WING

MOLLIEN WING

Entrance

GREAT GALLERY OF BORD DE L'EAU

PAVILLON DE FLORE

SMALL GALLERY

SEINE

Department of Paintings/ First Floor (Second Floor)
This arrangement is subject to change

[see page 1367]

1. Salle Percier et Fontaine
2. Salle Duchâtel (French School: 14th c.)
3. Salon Carré (French School: 15th and 16th c.)
4. Grande Galerie, 1st Section (French School: 17th and 18th c.)
5. Aile Mollien (French School: 18th c.)
6. Salle Mollien (French School: 19th c.)
7. Salle Denon (French School: 19th c.)
8. Vestibule of the Salle des Etats (Italian School: 16th c.)
9. Salle des Etats (Italian School: 16th c.)
10. Salle Daru (French School: 19th c.)
11. Salle des Sept Cheminées (Italian School: 17th c.)
12. Salle des Sept Mètres (Dutch School: 17th c.)
13. Grande Galerie, 2nd Part (Italian School: 14th and 15th c.)
14. Salle Van Dyck (Flemish School: 17th c.)
15. Galerie Médicis
16. Petits Cabinets, overlooking the Seine (Northern European Schools: 15th and 16th c.)
17. Petits Cabinets, overlooking the Jardin des Tuileries (Flemish and Dutch Schools: 17th c.)
18. Aile de Flore (Italian School, 17th and 18th c; Collection Beistegui.)
19. Pavillon de Flore, 1st floor (Spanish School; Schools of Valencia, Catalonia and Castile, 15; Schools of Toledo and of Madrid, 16th and 17thc; the great religious works of the Siecle d'Or (Golden Age), 18th c.)

French Painting, Cour Carrée, 2nd floor

The first room is devoted to current events in the department (acquisitions, restorations, paintings on loan abroad, forthcoming temporary exhibitions, and so forth).

A large adjoining room (Salle Sully), used as a public rest room and information center, has a magnificent view over the Pyramid, the Carrousel and the Place de l'Etoile to La Défense. There is an official to answer visitors' questions. A bookshop sells works on painting, and postcards. The furniture in this room is by Jean-Michel Wilmotte.

Gallery 1: the 14th c.

In the 14th c. easel painting developed considerably: *Portrait of Jean le Bon, King of France**** (1319–1364), the oldest surviving

French easel painting; it depicts either Jean le Bon before his coronation, since he is shown without his crown, or his eldest son, the future Charles V. The Narbonne *Parement*** (*ca* 1375), a painting in Indian ink on silk commissioned by Charles V, with portraits of the king and his queen Jeanne de Bourbon on either side of the *Crucifixion*, for the altar of the cathedral of Narbonne. The altarpiece by Thouzon, *ca* 1410–20, is a distant echo of the Avignon frescoes of the preceding century.

Gallery 2: the 15th c.

Charles V and his three brothers, Louis d'Anjou (d. 1384), Jean, Duke of Berry (d. 1416), and Philip the Bold, Duke of Burgundy (d. 1404), shared a taste for the arts, and their commissions gave rise to many artistic creations. From Henri de Bellechose, painter to the Duke of Burgundy from 1415 to 1440–44, there is a *Last Communion* and *The Martydom of St Denis***, a large altarpiece painted in 1415–16 for the Carthusian monastery at Champmol, near Dijon; Jean de Beaumetz, the duke's painter from 1375 to 1396, was the creator of the Charteux *Cavalry**, for the same monastery: the large, round *Pietà*** is attributed to Jean Malouel, painter to the duke from 1397 to 1415; this painting was probably commissioned by Philip the Bold, whose arms are painted on the back of the picture; a small round *Pietà* and *The Entombment of Christ*, from a Dijon or Paris studio; Jacquemart de Hesdin, painter to the Duke of Berry from 1384 to 1409, was the creator of the *Carrying of the Cross*.

Declining from about 1420 with the collapse of government, French painting was reborn in the middle of the 15th c. in the Midi and along the River Loire. This was the generation of the greatest artists (Fouquet, the Master of the Aix Annunciation, Enguerrand Quarton), who founded a new, distinctive art based on a sensitive, yet stylized, observation of reality, which was particularly successful in portraiture, in which their concern was with simple grandeur and balance. Jean Fouquet (*ca.* 1420–*ca.* 1480): portraits* of Charles V, an individualistic work wholly in the Gothic tradition, and of Guillaume Juvénal des Ursins. At the end of the century, Jean Hey, (who may have been the Master of Moulins), was at the frontiers of late Gothic and Northern Renaissance: *Child at Prayer*, who could be Suzanne de Bourbon, granddaughter on his mother's side of Louis XI; fragments of the *Bourbon Triptych***; portrait of Pierre de Beaujeu, son-in-law of Louis XI, with St Peter, and of Anne of France presented by John the Evangelist; portrait of a donor with St Mary Magdalene. Nicolas Froment: the *Matheron Diptych* representing King René, and his wife Jeanne de Laval. *Pietà* of Avignon***: the beauty of this work, its balance, nobility and its incomparable pathos, make this *Pietà*, attributed to Engeurrand Quarton, one of the highest achievements of Christian art. From the Avignon school: Boulbon Altarpiece (*ca* 1457). Josse Lieferinxe (a native of

Hainaut, but who worked in Provence): *Calvary* and *Adoration of the Infant Jesus*, surviving parts of a lost altarpiece. Paintings of Flemish origin: altarpiece of the Paris Parlement (*ca.* 1455). Amiens studio: *Mass of St Gregory* and *Coronation of the Virgin*.

Gallery 3: the 14th c., First School of Fontainebleau

On his return from captivity in 1530 François I decided to set up his court in the newly-constructed Château de Fontainebleau, and called many French, Italian and Flemish artists to decorate it. They painted large fresco compositions, interpreting mythological and allegorical themes which, through engravings, were to enjoy enormous popularity. Erotic subjects, elongated proportions of the figures and linear contours in light, acid, tones were the characteristics of this style.

Jean Cousin the Elder (*ca* 1430–1561): *Eva Prima Pandora**, one of the first French nude paintings; Jean de Gourmont (*ca.* 1483–*ca* 1551): *Adoration of the Shepherds*, from the Château d'Ecouen; Luca Penni (?), a pupil of Raphael, who worked at Fontainebleau from 1537 to 1540: *La Justice d'Othon* (gift of the Société des Amis du Louvre, 1973). First School of Fontainebleau (*ca* 1530): *Diana the Huntress** (an idealized portrait of Diane de Poltiers, mistress of Henri II?), *Diana and Actaeon, Charity*. With the Renaissance, which diverted to human beings the attention that for centuries had been focused on the divinities, France saw the flowering of a magnificent school of portraiture. Most of the portraits from this school kept at the Louvre come from the total of 1096 works collected by Roger de Gaignières (1642–1715). Jean Clouet (1485/90–1541):*Portrait of François I**. François Clouet (*ca* 1505–72), son of Jean, from whom he inherited the office of king's painter, but better known for his portrait drawings: *Pierre Outhe***. A double portrait attributed to Daniel Dubmonstier. François Quesnel: *Portrait of Henri III***. Works of the French School: *Portrait of a One-eyed Flautist**.

Gallery 4: Cabinet des portraits

True portrait galleries were a 16th-c. invention. Catherine de' Medici, for example, collected several hundred portraits in her Paris mansion. Roger de Gaignières collected 1096, which he bequeathed to Louis XIV. These portraits are generally busts, full- or three-quarter-face, against a neutral background. Note the portrait of Elisabeth of Austria, by François Clouet (active *ca* 1536–72), those of Jean de Bourbon-Vendôme, Charles de la Rochefoucauld and Jacques Bertaut, by Corneille de Lyon (*ca* 1505–*ca* 1575), the anonymous portraits of Jean de l'Hospital and Jean Baboues de la Bourdaisière, and the portrait presumed to be of Clément Marot.

Gallery 5: The Second School of Fontainebleau

This covers the end of the 16th c. *Gabrielle d'Estrées and her sister the Duchesse de Villars****, a famous painting, variously interpreted: it is often seen as an allusion to the birth of César, Duke of Vendôme, son of Henri IV and his mistress Gabrielle d'Estrées; it could equally be a satirical allusion to the moral frivolity of the court. Antoine Caron (1521–99): *The Massacre of the Triumvirate*, 1566, during the Wars of Religion, *Sybille de Tibur*. Toussaint Dubreuil (1561–1602): *La Toilette et le Lever d'une Dame* and *Sacrifice Antique*, both formerly part of the decoration of the Château de Saint-Germain-en-Laye.

Galleries 6 to 12 (Aile Nord) – the 17th c

Painting in the 17th c. presented many aspects, especially before the coronation of Louis XIV (1661). With the coming of absolute monarchy, royal power made itself felt in every field. Charles Le Brun operated as a veritable superintendent of the fine arts, and his influence was considerable, both in painting and in the decorative arts. But this century also saw the flowering of the genius of Poussin, Le Nain, La Tour, Champaigne, Claude Gellée, and others.

Gallery 6: painting under Louis XIII; the Caravagesques

These painters were so named because Simon Vouet and his school of French artists were influenced by Caravaggio and Italy in general. Valentin de Bourgogne (1591–1634): *The Judgement of Solomon, Recognition of the Innocence of Susannah, Cabaret Scene**, *The Fortune-Teller*, the bas-relief *Concert*. Claude Vignon (1593–1670): *The Young Singer**. Nicolas Régner (1590–1667): *The Fortune Teller*. Nicholas Tournier (1590–1639): *Crucifixion*.

Simon Vouet (1590–1649): *La Présentation au Temple*, donated in 1641 by Cardinal Richelieu to the Jesuit church in the Rue Saint-Antoine in Paris, now the Church of Saint-Pierre-Saint-Louis; portrait of Marcantonio Doria, painted in Italy before his return to France in 1627; *Allegory of Wealth*; portrait of Gaucher de Châtillon, possibly, like Phillipe de Champaigne's *Louis XIII*, from the Galerie des Hommes Illustres set up by Richelieu in the Palais-Cardinal (now the Palais-Royal) between 1630 and 1637. Vouet's painting, lyrical, light-toned and sweeping in execution, was widely spread through engravings and by the many pupils who passed through his studio.

Eustache Le Sueur (1616–55): *Meeting of Friends*; Jacques Blanchard (1600–38), Vouet's rival: *Venus and the Graces surprised by a mortal*; *Charity*.

Laurent de La Hyre (1606–56), who went neither to Italy nor into Vouet's studio, but developed an analogous painting style in more peaceful compositions: *Pope Nicolas V in 1149 having the Tomb of St Francis of Assissi opened, The Assumption of the Virgin*.

Gallery 7: Nicolas Poussin

Nicolas Poussin (1594–1665) is generally considered the greatest French painter of the 17th c. Although spending most of his life in Rome, he was not an Italianizing painter, but the painter of the Roman countryside and of Antiquity, treating his subjects with both rigour and poetry. The Louvre has a large collection of Poussin's works, showing his great diversity. Working for cultivated Italian and French art lovers, he painted subjects drawn from Antiquity: *The Rape of the Sabines**, *The Inspiration of the Poet*, *Echo and Narcissus***, *The Triumph of Flora*, *The Arcadian Shepherds****; from the Bible: *The Plague of Asdod*, *Manna*; and from religion: *Apparition of the Virgin to St James the Greater*, *St John the Baptist baptizing the people*, and numerous versions of the Holy Family. His landscapes are hung in Gallery 9.

Gallery 8: realistic painters

These painters were rehabilitated by the taste for realistic painting in the 19th c. Georges de La Tour (1593–1652): *St Joseph the Carpenter***, *Adoration of the Shepherds***, *The Vigil of St Mary Magdalene****, all typical of his characteristic method of treating light and shade. *The Cardsharper with the Ace of Diamonds**, on the other hand, is one of his works known as diurnal, as is *St Thomas**, acquired in 1988 by public subscription. Louis Le Nain (1593–1648): *The Cart****, of which the harmony of grey and yellow is unique in painting of the period; *Peasants' Meal***; *Family of Peasants*; *The Forge* (there is a very similar variant at Rheims); *Return from the Baptism*; *Meeting of Musicians*; *Victory*, one of the rare nude studies in this painter's production. Mathieu Le Nain (1607–1677): *Le Corps de garde*. Lubin Baugin (1612–1663): two still lifes*, *Gaufrettes* and *Chess-board*, the latter being an illustration of the five senses; symbolic still lifes were popular at this time. Still lifes by Pierre Dupuis and Jacques Linard.

Gallery 9: landscape (Le Lorrain) and decorative painting

While Claude Gellée and Nicolas Poussin were in Italy inaugurating the tradition of the Classical landscape, the Parisian painters were developing an original formula, which found its outlet in the decoration of the many mansions built by rich Parisians.

Claude Gellée, called Le Lorrain (1600–82), worked in Rome for Roman dignitaries, but also for French and other ambassadors and nobles. He made a speciality of views of imaginary ports, using either real architectural elements or recreating Classical buildings, with luminous and atmospheric effects: *The Village Fête*, *View of the Campo Vaccino in Rome*, *Harbour at Sunset***, *Ulysses returning Chryseis to her Father*, *Cleopatra Landing*.

Nicolas Poussin (1594–1665) in the last years of his life painted landscapes dominated by a feeling of the grandeur and the mysterious forces of nature. *The Four Seasons** were painted for Richelieu between 1610 and 1664; they take their subjects from episodes in the Bible, and are a meditation on the different ages of life. Sébastien Bourdon (1616–71): *Augustus before the Tomb of Alexander*, *The Meeting of Antony and Cleopatra*; Laurent de La Hyre (1606–56): *Laban looking for his Household Gods in Jacob's Baggage*; Eustache Le Sueur (1617–55): *Melpomene, Erato and Polymia*, painted for the Cabinet des Muses of the Hôtel Lambert, as was *Aeneas driving off the Harpies*, by François Perrier (*ca.* 1590–1650). Jacques Stella (1596–1657): *Minerva with the Muses*, *Cloelia swimming across the Tiber*.

Gallery 10: Religious painting

This room houses the great religious paintings commissioned by churches and religious orders, including those painted for Port-Royal.

Sébastien Bourdon (1616–61): *Deposition*; Laurent de La Hyre (1606–56): *Christ appearing to the Three Marys*. Eustache Le Sueur (1617–55): *The Annunciation, Deposition, St Paul preaching at Ephesus**, a painting donated by the goldsmiths' corporation of Paris to the Cathedral of Notre-Dame de Paris in 1649. Each year, from 1630 to 1707, during May, whence the name of May offerings given to this series of works, the corporation gave the cathedral a large painting on a subject drawn from the Acts of the Apostles.

Of the large cartoons for tapestries commissioned by the churchwardens of the Church of Saint-Gervais in Paris in 1654, to recount the story of St Gervase and St Protase, the Louvre has Le Sueur's *St Gervase and St Protase, brought before Astasius, refuse to sacrifice to Jupiter* and *St Gervase and St Protase appearing to St Ambrose*, and *The Translation of the Earthly Remains of St Gervase and St Protase*, by Philippe de Champaigne. This collection gives an idea of the former richness of decoration of Parisian churches.

A native of Brussels, Philippe de Champaigne (1602–74) came to Paris in 1621, and worked here to the end of his life. From him may be seen: *Portrait of a Man***, formerly called *Robert Arnauld d'Andilly, Prévost des Marchands*, and the *Magistrates of Paris*, and *Christ on the Cross*. He was also the painter of the Abbaye de Port-Royal: *Dead Christ lying on his Shroud*; *Portrait of Robert Arnauld d'Andilly*; *Ex-Voto****, one of the Louvre's masterpieces, painted on the occasion of the miraculous cure of his daughter, who was the Abbess of Port-Royal, showing not the moment of recovery, but the moment when Mère Angélique had a vision of her cure. It is charged with contained emotion, and the austerity and spirituality that characterize the work of this great artist. Also in this gallery are two of the four landscapes he painted for Anne of Austria at Val-de-

Grâce: *The Miracles of St Mary Repentant*, and *Paphnutius freeing Thais*.

Gallery 11: the Battles of Le Brun

Charles Le Brun (1619–90) was the *maître d'oeuvre* of Versailles and Louis XIV's official painter. The portrait of him by his pupil Nicolas Largillière shows him in his studio, surrounded by the attributes of his office, and before a small-scale reduction of one of the compartments of the Hall of Mirrors at Versailles.

He painted a sumptuous *Portrait of Chancellor Séguier*, in which he presents his protector in all the pomp of his office. He received commissions for cartoons for tapestries to illustrate *The Story of Meleager* (the *Hunt of Meleager and Atalanta* and the *Death of Meleager*) and *The Story of Alexander*; of these, four only were executed: *Crossing the Granicus*, *The Battle of Arbela*, *Alexander and Porus*, and *The Entry of Alexander into Babylon*. These four immense canvases were inspired by Raphael's frescoes in the Vatican. Their subject flatters the young Louis XIV, who is compared in them to the emperor Alexander. Displayed in the King's study, which was used for meetings of the Académie, they played a considerable part in forming academic doctrine.

Gallery 12: Jouvenet and religious painting at the end of the 18th c.

Jean Jouvenet (1644–1717) devoted himself above all to religious painting: *Deposition*, painted in 1697 for the church of the Capuchins in Paris. *The Miraculous Draught of Fishes* and *The Resurrection of Lazarus*, from 1700–06, were part of the series of immense canvases painted for the nave of Saint Martin-des-Champs.

The tour of French painting of the 17th c. ends with the famous *Portrait of Louis XIV*, by Hyacinthe Rigaud, in which the King is shown with the coronation paraphernalia displayed in the Galerie d'Apollon.

Grande Galerie, French Painting of the 18th and 19th centuries (First Floor)

In the eastern part of the Grande Galerie there is a temporary display of French painting of the 18th and 19th centuries, pending completion of rearrangement of the rooms of the 2nd floor of the Cour Carrée. French painting of this period comprises many portraits and genre and mythological scenes. A new social class — the bourgeoisie — had become important through its wealth; away from the court, art was now no longer concerned only with pomp. Distancing himself from the monarchy, the painter was ceasing to see the large and ceremonious to look instead at the agreeable, comfortable, attractive aspects of life; in particular, his work was becoming more individualistic. As the influence of Louis XIV formality waned, portraits became more intimate, more simple.

Watteau (1684–1721), the painter of *scènes galantes*, used the effects of diffused light to melt his figure into his landscapes. His work, engraved in *Le Recueil Julienne*, was distributed throughout Europe, and was influential in deflecting painting towards intimacy and grace. Of that admirable work, the *Pélerinage à l'île de Cythère**** (known all through the 19th c. by the name of *Embraquement pour Cythère* [Embarkation for Cythera] and regaining with its true title all its meaning) there is another version in Berlin, but the Louvre painting, with its sixteen completely self-engrossed, pleasure-seeking characters, is undoubtedly the finer. *Gilles****, that mysterious and ambiguous character, is one of the strangest figures in French painting, and while differing from all other Watteau figures (to the point where the identity of the artist has been challenged) it is, through its very strangeness, clearly from the hand of this painter, one of the greatest in French painting. He had a genius for the moving composition as well as, more than any other, a sense of fragility and of the fleetingness of time. The *Portrait de Gentilhomme*** (acquired in 1973) may be Jean de Julienne, for although Watteau never accepted commissions, nor agreed to paint formal portraits, Julienne was a friend. *Diane au Bain*** is one of the latest acquisitions. There are eight other undisputed Watteau paintings in the Louvre, and some of the small ones hang in the Aile Mollien.

Boucher (1703–70), painter of mythological subjects, *scènes galantes* and landscapes very typical of the Louis XV style: *Diana Resting**** (1742); *The Rape of Europa* (1747); *Cephalus and Aurora*, *Vertumnus and Pomona* (1763), two models for Gobelins tapestries; *Rinaldo and Armida* (1763), his admission piece for the Académie; *The Mill* and *The Bridge*, from the decoration of the bedchamber of the Cardinal de Soubise at the Hôtel de Rohan (now the Archives Nationales); *Vulcan presenting Venus with arms for Aeneas***; and a small genre scene that gives an insight into a bourgeois interior of the first half of the 18th c.: *Le Déjeuner**.

Genre scenes and mythological allegories by Noël Hallé (1711–81): *Minerva and Neptune disputing over a name for Athena*; by Nicolas Lancret (1690–1743): *The Music Lesson*; *Innocence*.

Portraits of *Madame de Sorquainville** and of the painter Oudry, by Jean-Baptiste Perroneau (1715–83).

Various aspects of the work of Jean-Baptiste Siméon Chardin (1699–1779) are presented: the painter of still lifes with *The Rayfish*, *Le Buffet*, admission pieces for the Académie (1728), *The Attributes of the Arts*, *The Attributes of Music*, overdoors from the Château de Choisy, *Menu de Gras* and the *Menu de Maigre*, *The Jar of Olives*,

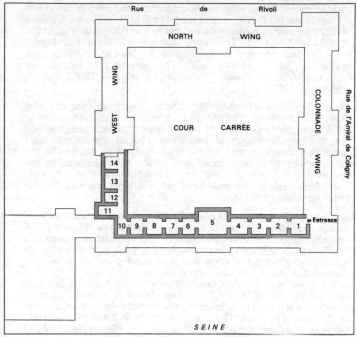

Department of Paintings / Second Floor (Third Floor)
This arrangement is subject to change

[see page 1361]

1 14th-c. French painting
2 15th-c. French painting
3 First School of
   Fontainbleau (14th-c.)
4 Cabinet des Portraits
5 Second School of
   Fontainbleau (end 16th-c.)
6–12 (Aile Nord) – the 17th c.:
6 The Caravagesques

7 Nicolas Poussin
8 Realistic painters (16th–17th c)
9 Landscape: Claude Lorrain,
   Poussin
10 Religious painting (17th c.)
11 Le Brun
12 Religious painting (end 18th c.)

Dead Hare with Game-bag and Powder-flask, acquired by gift in lieu of inheritance tax (1979), one of the last still lifes by the artist before devoting himself to painting genre scenes and the human figure; the painter of children with *The Young Man with a Violin* and *Child with a Top****, two portraits of the son of the jeweler Godefroy; the painter of genre scenes with *The Industrious Mother*, *La Pouvoveuse* (Saying Grace)*** and *La Serinette* (The Bird Organ)**, acquired in 1985.

Pierre Subleyras (1699–1749): *L'Abbé César Benvenuti** and *Giuseppe Baretti* (gift of the Foundation Bella et André Meyer, 1981), two intense portraits of well-balanced composition, handled in an extraordinary range of colors, heavy black, powder-grey, pale pinks, very characteristic of the art of Subleyras: *Supper at the House of Simon**, a wide, horizontal canvas commissioned by the canons of Latran for the refectory of the monastery of Asti, near Turin. Subeyras painted essentially in Rome, where he was director of the Académie Française.

Jean-Honoré Fragonard (1732–1806), an artist very representative of the second half of the 18th c., famous for his scenes of frivolity, but who also painted superb landscapes. The contrast of values, his vivacious brushwork and freedom of style, led him sometimes into bold and very modern endeavours, as in the *Figures de fantaisie***, of which the Louvre has eight examples; one of the figures, *Music*, is said to have been painted in less than an hour. You will see also *Coresus sacrificing himself to save Callirhoe*, a large painting intended as a model of a tapestry; *The Bathers*; *Portrait of Diderot*; *La Guimard*; *Le Verrou* (The Bolt), acquired in 1984; *Mercury and Argus*, or *The Sleeping Shepherd**, acquired in 1981 as belonging to the 18th-c. French school and recently attributed to Fragonard; *Le Songe du mendiant* (Beggar's Dream)*, acquired only in 1987. Jean Barbault (1718–66); *La Sultane* and *Le Prêtre de la Loi*, portray two *pensionnaires* of the Académie Française in Rome in fancy dress for the Carnival of 1748 (donated to the Louvre in 1971).

Joseph Vernet (1714–89): *La Nuit* (1765), one of a series of paintings representing different times of the day commissioned by Louis XV for his library in the Château de Choisy; *Le Ponte Roto*; *Le Château Saint-Ange*; *Le Port de Toulon** (1757), one of fifteen views of French ports commissioned by Louis XV.

Hubert Robert (1733–1808), the painter of ruins: *Le Pont du Gard*, *Interior of the Temple of Diana at Nîmes*, *La Maison Carrée*, *The Triumphal Arch and Amphitheater in Orange*, four paintings commissioned for a drawing-room of the Château de Fontainebleau; *Imaginary View of the Grande Galerie in Ruins*; *Project for alteration of the Grande Galerie*.

Jean-Baptiste Greuze (1725–1808), painter of moral sentiments, whose edifying paintings were so much admired by Diderot: *A Father's Curse** and its pendant *The Prodigal Son*; *The Village*

Bride*, *The Milkmaid*, *The Broken Jug*, two oval compositions much admired in their time; *Portrait of Watelet* (acquired by gift in lieu of death duties).

Elisabeth Vigée-Lebrun (1755-1842), wife of the art dealer Lebrun and painter to Marie Antoinette, of whom she made many portraits: *Péace restoring Abundance*, reception piece for the Académié (1783), portraits of Hubert Molé and of Madame Molé Raymond; *Madame Vigée-Lebrun and her daughter**.

Genre scenes by Louis Boilly (1761-1845): *Arrival of a Coach*, *Artists meeting in the Studio of Isabey*, *Entrance of the Théâtre de l'Ambigu-Comique for a free performance*.

Neo-Classical School

Jacques-Louis David (1748-1825): *Monsieur et Madame Monguez*, *Madame Trudaine**, an unfinished portrait, probably intentionally so, earlier taken to be of Mme Chalgrin, wife of the architect; Louis-Eugéne Larivière (1801-23): *Portrait of Eugénie-Paméla Larivière*, daughter of the artist; Antoine Berjon (1754-1843): *Vase of Flowers*. Antoine, baron Gros (1771-1835): *Portrait of Madeleine Pasteur*. Martin Drollin (1752-1817): *Interior of Kitchen*. Léon Gauffier (1762-1801): *Jacob and the Daughters of Laban*. François Gérard (1770-1837): portraits of Madame Barbier Walbonne and the Comtesse Regnault de Saint-Jean-d'Angély. Jean-Baptiste Regnault (1754-1829): *The Flood*. Pierre-Paul Prud'hon (1758-1823): *Young Zephyr hovering above the Water**; *The Bath of Venus*; *Diana beseeching Jupiter*, a sketch for a ceiling of the galleries of Greek Antiquities; *The Marriage of Hebe and Heracles*, sketch for a ceiling of the Hôtel de Ville de Paris (1810), alluding to the marriage of Napoleon I and Marie-Louise; *The King of Rome, heir to the Imperial Throne, born 20 March 1811* (acquired 1982). Léon-Mathieu Cochereau (1793-1817): *The Studio of David*, painted by a pupil of Cochereau in 1814. Madame Benoît (1768-1826): *Portrait of a Negress**. Girodet-Trioson (1767-1824): *The Shades of French Heroes received by Ossian in the Garden of Odin*, a copy of the composition painted in 1801 for the state drawing-room at Malmaison. Guérin: *Aeneas and Dido*; *Phaedra and Hippolytus* (acquired 1982). David: *The Oath of the Horatii*, three sketches for the large compositions presented in the Salle Mollien, on the first floor.

Jean Auguste Dominique Ingres (1780-1867), eminently Classical painter and draughtsman of genius: portraits of M Boschet, M Cordier, M Cortot (from the Musée des Beaux-Arts d'Algerie), Mme *Marcotte de Sainte-Marie**, *Pius VII in the Sistine Chapel* (1820), a subject often painted by Ingres, who had been greatly impressed by the ceremonies of Holy Week in the Vatican; *Angélique*, a study for the painting presented in the Salle Denon; *The Turkish Bath****. Théodore Chassériau (1819-56): *The Toilet of Esther** (1846), *Apollo and Daphne* (1846), *Venus* (1836), three paintings that owe much to his master, Ingres; *Portrait of Adèle Chassériau*. Constance Mayer-Lamartinière (1778–1821): *The Dream of Happiness*. Pierre Narcisse Guérin (1774–1833): *The Shepherds at the Tomb of Amynats*. Léon Bénouville (1821–59): *The Mystic Communion of St Catherine*. Hippolyte Flandrin (1809–64): *Jeune Homme nu au bord de la mer* (Young Nude Male on the Seashore).

Géricault and Delacroix

Théodore Géricault (1791–1824): *The Derby at Epsom*; *Le Vendéen**; sketches for *The Wounded Cuirassier*, *Cavalry Officer Charging*, *The Raft of the 'Medusa'*, *The Madwoman****, which is part of the dozen works executed for a friend of the artist, Dr Georget, who laid down the first basis for the scientific study of psychiatry; a number of horse paintings, which reveal Géricault's passion for this animal.

Eugéne Delacroix (1793–1863): *Assassination of the Bishop of Liège*; *Hamlet and Horatio*; *Jewish Wedding in Morocco*; *Tiger Hunt*; *Mlle Rose*; *Nude*; *Self-portrait****; *Portrait of Chopin***, the pendant to which, *George Sand*, is in Ordrupgard (Denmark). Works by Ary Scheffer (1795–1858) and Chassériau.

Aile Mollien

Gallery 1

This gallery displays all Boucher's small-scale paintings: *The Painter in his Studio*. Watteau: *L'Indifférent**** and *La Finette****, *Le Faux Pas*, *The Judgement of Paris*; Chardin: *The Copper Cistern*. Hubert Robert: *Fountain below a Portico*, *Spiral Staircase at the Farnese Palace at Caprarola*. Boilly: *Cabaret Scene**, *The Shower*, Ingres: *Don Pedro of Toledo**.

Gallery 2: Moreau-Nélaton donation

This is made up of works of the Romantic School, a number of landscapes by Corot, and by paintings from the Barbizon School, which marked the beginning of a new way of observing nature. Prud'hon: *The Spirit of Peace*. Delacroix: *The Prisoner of Chillon* (Byron), *Combat of Horsemen in the Country*, *Young Orphan in a Cemetery*, *Turk smoking on a Divan*, *The Entry of the Crusaders into Constantinople* (another version of this large canvas hangs in the first floor). Works by Nino Diaz de la Peña, Thomas Couture and de Daubigny.

Gallery 3: Thomy-Thierry donation

This comprises a large selection of 19th-c. French works. Delacroix: *Rebecca*** (1858); *Medea*, the second version of a work painted in 1838, now in the Lille Museum; *Lion devouring a Rabbit*; *Lion and Alligator*; *St George and the Dragon*; *The Betrothed of Abydos*; *Hamlet and Horatio at the Cemetery*. Corot: *The Valley*; *The Road to Sin-le-Noble**. Barye: *Lions near their Den*. Alexandre Decamps (1803–60): *The Knife-grinder* and *The Bellringers*, two of many scenes painted by the artist during his time in Turkey. Eugène Fromentin: *Falcon-hunting in Algeria**. Théodore Rousseau (1812–1867), the master of the Barbizon School: *Groups of Oaks*, *Apremont*, *The Plain before the Pyrenees*, *Spring*. Jules Dupré (1811–78): *The Big Oak*, *The Watering Place*. Charles Daubigny (1817–78): *The Sluicegate at Optevoz*.

Gallery 4: Corot

Landscapes and portraits by Jean-Baptiste Camille Corot (1796–1875): *Countryside at Naples*, *View of Tivoli*, *Windmills at Etretat*, *Interior of the Cathedral of Sens*, *The Road to Sin-le-Noble*, *Woman with a Pearl***, *Young Girl at her Toilette*, *Women in Blue***; also works by Delacroix, Géricault, and others.

Salle Mollien (6): 19th century

David: portraits of M and Mme Sériziat** and of their son. Gérard: *Cupid and Psyche*, *The Painter Isabey and his Daughter*. Girdoet-Trioson (really Girodet de Roucy): *The Sleep of Endymion*, *The Deluge*, *The Entombment of Atala*. Guérin: *Hippolytus accused by Phaedra*, *The Return of Marcus Sextus*. David: *The Sabines stopping the Battle***, *Leonidas at Thermopylae**, *Andromache by the Body of Hector*, *The Oath of the Horatii**** (→ inset), *Paris and Helen*, *The Lictors returning the Bodies of his sons to Brutus**. These are large compositions on subjects drawn from Antiquity, an inexhaustible source for the artist – only the epic of Napoleon was able to arouse comparable feelings, as in *The Coronation of Napoleon at Notre-Dame***, executed from 1804 to 1807; this very official and imposing canvas is truly an historical document. Among his portraits, *Mme Récamier****, *Mme d'Orvillers*, *Pope Pius VI** and the *Self-portrait* further reveal David's sensitivity and attention to the psychology of his models. Prud'hon: portrait of *The Empress Josephine at Malmaison*; *Justice and Divine Vengeance Pursuing Crime*, *Psyche Carried Off*, the last two works showing the influence of Romanticism. Baron Gros: portrait of Christine Boyer, the first wife of Lucien Bonaparte. Ingres, of whom it has been said that he was the leader of the French Classical School, and of whom characteristic works are seen here: the *Grande Odalisque****, of great purity of design; the portraits of M and Mme Rivière and of their daughter***; *The Apotheosis of Homer* and *Oedipus and the*

Sphynx, which testify to his talent for expressing the truth about his model, and his addiiction to Antiquity.

Salle Denon (7): 19th century

Ingres: *La Baigneuse de Valpincon****, *Ruggiero rescuing Angelica***, *Joan of Arc at the Coronation of Charles VII***, portraits of Cherubini* and of Monsieur Bertin***. Théodore Aligny (1798–1871): *Prometheus*. Archille Michallon (1796–1822): *The Death of Roland*. Marc Gleyre (1806–74): *Lost Illusions*. Louis-Léopold Robert (1794–1835), Swiss painter, a pupil of David who worked in Italy after 1818: *The Return from the Pilgrimage to the Madonna of Arc* (1827), *L'Arrivée des Moissonneurs dans les marais Pontins* (The Arrival of the Harvesters at the Pontins Marshes) (*ca* 1830). Paul Delaroche (1797–1856): *The Young Martyr*. Auguste Hesse (1795–1869): *The Death of Titian at Venice* (gift of the Société des Amis du Louvre, 1985).

Salle Daru (10): 19th century

In this room are grouped works highly-coloured and visionary in style, taking their themes largely from legend, the Orient, and allegory, as also paintings illustrating contemporary events with pathos and realism. Baron Gros: portrait of Lieutenant-général Comte Fournier-Sarlovèse* refusing to surrender at Vigo (Spain), painted in 1813; equestrian portrait of Joachim Murat, King of Naples (1812), acquired by gift in lieu of death duties (1913); *Bonaparte visiting the Plague-stricken at Jaffa*** (1804) *Napoleon on the battlefield at Eylau***. Géricault: *Wounded Cuirassier, Cavalry Officer Charging, Raft of the 'Medusa'****. Delacroix: *Barque of Dante** (1821), *Massacre at Chios*** (1824), *Liberty on the Barricades**** (on 28 July, 1830) (1831), *Death of Sardanapalus**** (1827), *The Shipwreck of Don Juan, Women of Algiers in their Apartment*** (1834), *The Entry of the Crusaders into Constantinople*** (1840), *Young Tiger and its Mother*. Chassériau: *The Bath of Susannah**; *The two Sisters**; *Portrait of Lacordiare**; *Commerce* and *Peace*, two large fresco compositions from the Cour des Comptes de Paris. Paul Delaroche: *The Children of Edward* (1830), *Bonaparte Crossing the Alps* (gift of M and Mme Birkhauser, through the Lutéce Foundation, 1982). Alexandre Decamps: *Battle of the Cimbrians*. Ary Scheffer: *Paola and Francesca, Les Femmes souliotes*. Victor Schnetz (1787–1870): *The Vow to the Virgin* (1831).

▷ Not to be missed

The numbers in brackets refer to the numbers indicated on the plan, page 1361.

First floor

Salon Carré (3): *Pietà* of Avignon, Enguerrand Quarton, (15th c.) *Portrait of Gabrielle d'Estrées and her sister* (16th c.).

Grande Galerie (4); *The Arcadian Shepherds* and *Self-portrait*, by Poussin (17th c.). *The Vigil of St Mary Magdalene*, by G. de La Tour (17th c.). *The Cart* and *Family of Peasants*, by L. Le Nain (17th c.). *Ex Voto*, by Philippe de Champaigne (17th c.). *Pèlerinage a l'Ile de Cythère* and *Giles*, by Watteau (18th c.). Portraits of Diderot and La Guimard, by Fragonard (18th c.).

Aile Mollien (5): *Le Buffet*, *Le Bénédicité* and *Child with a Top*, by Chardin (18th c.) *Diana Resting*, by Boucher (18th c.) Salle Mollien (6): *The Oath of the Horatii* and *Portrait of Mme Récamier*, by David (early 19th c.).

Salle Denon (7): *Grande Odalisque*, *La Baigneuse de Valpincon* and portraits of M and Mlle Bertin and their daughter, by Ingres (19th c.). Salle Daru (10): *The Raft of the 'Medusa'*, by Géricault (19th c.). *Liberty on the Barracades* and *Death of Sardanapalus*, by Delacroix (19th c.).

Second floor (Aile Mollien)

Gallery 2: *The Turkish Bath*, by Ingres (19th c.).
Gallery 3: *View of Tivoli* and *Woman with a Pearl*, by Corot (19th c.).
Gallery 4: *The Madwoman*, by Géricault (19th c.). *Self-portrait*, by Delacroix (19th c.).

▷ The age of Neo-Classicism

The period of reaction against the Rococo style of the reign of Louis XV began towards the middle of the 18th c., when the excavations at Herculaneum and Pompeii made fashionable a whole new range of ornamental motifs. The Comte d'Angiviller, the King's Superintendant of Buildings, the thinkers of the Enlightenment, especially Diderot, whose art criticism covered the Salons, all preached the need for moral and heroics subjects to elevate the mind and refine the emotions. Painters were drawn to these new theories and one, Jacques-Louis David (1748–1825), was to revolutionize and overshadow French painting for the next 30 years and more. *The Oath of the Horatii*, painted and exhibited first in Rome in 1784, and then in Paris at the Salon of 1785, embodies the aspirations of the period – patriotism and spiritual vigor – in a heroic if static composition, with an unobtrusive but absolute mastery of technique. David's authority was undisputed, but he was never a dictator. His rivals Peyron, Regnault, Prud'hon and Guérin, as much as his pupils Drouais, Girodet, Gérard, Gros and Ingres, each demonstrate their individual genius whether, like Ingres and Guérin, they remained adherents to the teachings of his school or, like Prud'hon, Girodet and, especially, Gros, they turned away from it to originate the Romantic movement.

Italian Painting

Current plans for general reorganization envisage that this section will fill the Salle Duchâtel, the Salon Carré (13th, 14th and 15th c.), the first part of the Grande Galerie, the Salle des Etats (16th and 17th c.) and the Salle des Sept-Cheminées (17th c.)

Best represented of all the foreign schools in the Louvre, the Italian School was a prime favorite with the kings of France beginning with Louis XII, who had always shown a marked preference for Italian art. François I, a great figure in the French Renaissance, brought back several masterpieces from Italy. After him Richelieu founded in his Palais-Cardinal (the future Palais-Royal) an important collection, demonstrating a sureness of taste for those painters who were the forerunners of the Renaissance masters. It is thanks to him that the Louvre has canvases by, for example, Perugino and Mantegna. Paintings came into the Louvre, too, from the collections of Charles I of England, of the financier Jabach, of Cardinal Mazarin, and from the treasures of the Duke of Mantua. (→History of the collections). The loot of the Revolutionary and later the Napoleonic Armies and purchases, such as that of the Campana Collection, during the 19th and 20th c. completed this magnificent collection.

Grande Galerie (13): Italian Painting of the 13th, 14th and 15th c.

An example of the work of Cimabue (Cenno di Pepi, active *ca.* 1240–1302) is his *Madonna with Angels****. If the stance of the figures remains hieratical and if the stiff parallel folds of the robes and the golden highlights still show a persistent Byzantine influence, the fact that the practice of giving the figures a heavy outline has been consciously abandoned and that modeling has been employed to express mass shows new developments in painting that put Cimabue at the head of the line of great Italian painters. Giotto (b. Colle di Vespignano *ca.* 1267–d. Florence 1337) is represented by *St Francis Receiving the Stigmata****, early 14th c. in which, despite the gilded background, the canons of Byzantine painting have been replaced by a fuller pictorial representation of the human figure. There is also a large *Christ* after Giotto.

From these two painters Italian painting was to take wing in its two great centers of 14th-c. Siena and Florence. The Florentines were quicker to break away from Byzantine tradition than the Sienese. It was only later that the Venetian School gained a reputation and because of its trading links it remained far longer under Byzantine influence than the others.

A *Crucifix* by the Master of San Francesco (active in Hungary in the second half of the 13th c.) is an example of painted crucifixes, common in Umbria, where they began to be produced at the start of the 13th c.; recent restoration has revealed its brilliant coloring, reds, lavender, and lilac blues (purchased 1984). Lippo Memmi, Simone Martini's brother-in-law, active in Siena 1317-47: *St Peter,* a panel from a triptych of which the center panel was probably a *Madonna and Child* now in the Berlin museum; Master of San Pietro d'Ovile (Siena, 14th-c.): *Crucifixion.* Anonymous Florentine painter (14th-c.): *Calvary.* Giovanni da Milano, Florentine painter active 1346-69: *Francis of Assisi.* Bernardo Daddi (Florence *ca.* 1290-*ca.* 1353), pupil of Giotto: *The Annunciation.* Bartolo di Maestro Fredi (*ca.* 1353- *ca.* 1410), Sienese School; *The Presentation in the Temple.* Lorenzo Monaco, called Lorenzo di Giovanni (1370-*ca.* 1422), was born in Siena but worked largely in Florence, and was important as a miniaturist: *Seated Virgin and Child, Crucifixion; Scenes from the Lives of St John the Baptist and of James the Greater.* Anonymous Bolognese painter: a triptych of the Crucifixion. Barnaba de Modena, (active at Genoa, 1361-83): *Madonna and Child* (purchased 1968). Paolo Veneziano (active in Venice 1324-58): *Virgin and Child Between Four Saints**; part of a polyptych of which some wings were in the Campana Collection and others in museums in Toulouse and Ajaccio; they were reunited in 1956. Lorenzo Veneziano (active in Venice, 1356-79): *Virgin Enthroned.* Rimini School: twelve *Scenes From the Life of the Virgin.*

First case on the r. is *The Carrying of the Cross**, a wing of a polyptych of *The Passion* by Simone Martini (b. Siena 1284-d. Avignon 1344), a painter of the Sienese school. The vast range of his technical abilities and the extraordinary freshness of his talent can be seen at its best in the miraculous *Annunciation* in the Uffizi in Florence. Attributed to Lippo Memmi: *Crucifixion* purchased, 1984. The Master of the St George Codex (Sienese School): *Madonna.* The Master of the Rebel Angels (Sienese School, *ca.* 1440-50): *The Fall of the Rebel Angels* and *St Martin as a Beggar.* Pietro da Rimini (end of the 14th c.): *Deposition.* Guido da Siena (active 1260-70); although little is known about this painter, his influence may be traced in many of the works of the Sienese School: *Nativity; Presentation.*

In the case on the l., Pisanello (b. Verona before 1395-d. 1455): *Portrait of a Princess of the House of Este****, which shows the incisive style of the enamelist, which the artist also was; this is one of the earliest known portraits of an individual painted in Italy. Gentile da Fabriano (b. *ca.* 1370-d. Rome 1427): *Presentation**.

Jacopo Bellini (Venice, 1400-71): *Virgin and Child Adored by Lionel d'Este**. Lorenzo Monaco: *Christ on the Mount of Olives; The Holy Women at the Tomb.*

Fra Angelico (Florentine School: ca. 1387-1455) stands alone as undoubtedly the greatest painter of the first half of the Quattrocento: *The Coronation of the Virgin****, the great pyramidal composition from the Church of San Domenico in Fiesole: *The Martyrdom of SS Cosmas and Damian*. The Master of the Observance (Sienese School: first half of the 15th c.): *St Anthony*, the central wing of a now dispersed polyptych. Sano di Pietro Siena 1405/06–81: *Five Incidents in the Life of St Jerome*.

Sassetta (Sienese School, 1400–50): *St Anthony of Padua; Virgin and Child with Angels**; *St John the Evangelist; The Blessed Ranieri Freeing the Poor from Prison*, from the predella and wings of a polyptych from the church of San Francesco in Borgo San Sepolcro. Nerrocio di Landi (Siena 1447–1500): *Virgin and Child Between St John the Baptist and St Anthony*. Attributed to Liberale da Verona (1445–1525): *The Rape of Europa*. Benozzo Gozzoli (b. Florence 1420–d. Pistoia 1487): *The Triumph of Thomas Aquinas**; Fra Lippo Lippi (Florence 1406–69): *Virgin and Child between St Fedriano and St Augustine**. Alessio Baldovinetti (Florence, 1425–99): *The Virgin Adoring the Infant Jesus*. Piero Della Francesca: *Portrait of Sigismondo Malatesta****, recently acquired and apparently one of the earliest oil paintings to be executed in Italy.

Paolo Uccello: *The Battle of San Romano**** (1437) is part of a series of paintings which survive in the Uffizi in Florence and the National Gallery, London. This work is outstanding for its extraordinary boldness of composition with an equally daring conception of perspective. Uccello was an intellectual painter who typifies the concern with geometrical construction common to Florentine painters of the 15th c.

School of Fillipo Lippi: *Nativity*. The Master of the Nativity of Castello: *Virgin and Child with Angels. Virgin and Child with John the Baptist*** represents the work of Sandro Botticelli (Florence, 1445–1510): the most important painter of the second half of the Quattrocento, his fame has been overshadowed by the dazzling glory of the Renaissance masters, yet his great humanity and the technical strength of his drawing keep the grace and lightness of his work from degenerating into languid vapidity: *Virgin and Child with Five Angels****; *Portrait of a Young Man***; *The Virgin and Child with John the Baptist***. Giovanni Boticcini (Florence, 1446–97): *The Virgin Adoring the Infant Jesus with John the Baptist and Two Angels*. Filippino Lippi: *Scenes from the Story of Virginie; Madonna with a Pomegranate; The Story of Esther and Ahasuerus*. Luca Signorelli (Cortona, 1450–1523): *The Birth of John the Baptist* (in a case). Andrea Mantegna (b. Padua 1431–d. Mantua 1506): this great painter, a lover of Classical Antiquity, nevertheless endeavored to depict what he saw with great realism and precision in drawing and perspective. *St Sebastian**** which, until 1910, hung in the parish church of Aigueperse, was brought to the Auvergne on the marriage of Clara de Gongaza with a member of the Montpensier family; *The Crucifixion***; *The Madonna of Victory*. Antonello da Messina (Venetian school, 1430–79): *The Condottiere*** is notable for the transparency of the flesh tints which bring to life the harsh, commanding, and intelligent face. Giovanni Bellini: *Portrait of a Man**. Cosimo da Tura (Ferrarese School, 1430–95): *Pietà***. Carlo Crivelli (Venetian school, 1430–1516): *St James of the Marche*. Bartolomeo Vivarini (Venice, 1430–91): *St John of Capistrano*.

Display case to the l.: Vincenzo Catena (1480/85–1531): *Portrait of Guilio Mellino*. School of Roberti (Ferrara, 1450–96): *SS Apollonia and Michael*. Cosimo da Tura: *St Anthony of Padua Reading*, one wing of a polyptych of which others are in the Uffizi, Florence (St Dominic) and the Caen museum (St James). School of Padua (second half of the 15th c.): *Virgin and Child*. Bernardo Parentino (1437–1531): *Adoration of the Magi*. Carlo Crivelli: *Dead Christ**.

Display case to the r.: Fra Angelico: *Angel in Adoration*. School of Fra Angelico: *Herod's Banquet*. Francesco Pesellino (1422–57): *St Francis of Assisi Receiving the Stigmata; SS Cosmas and Damian Healing the Sick*. Attributed to Leonardo da Vinci: *Annunciation*. Luca Signorelli (1450–1523): *Birth of John the Baptist*. Raphael: *Angel*, fragment of an altarpiece from San Nicolò of Tolentino (1500–01), painted for the Church of San Agostino at Citta di Castello; the recent acquisition (1981) of this first dated work by the master allows the visitor to the Louvre to follow the painter's development from these beginnings to the great works from the end of his career hung in the Salle des Etats. Zoppo (1433–78): *Virgin and Child Surrounded by Angels*, typifies the Paduan enthusiasm for archeology (acquired 1980). Giovanni Bellini (Venetian school, 1430–1516): *Sacra Conversazione; Crucifixion; Christ Giving His Blessing**; The Virgin Between SS Peter and Sebastian;* portraits of two men. Vittore Carpaccio (Venice, 1437–1525): remarkable for his sense of color which looked forward to the great Venetians (Canaletto, Guardi), as well as his feeling for architectural construction: *St Stephen Preaching in Jerusalem***, one of a series of five paintings devoted to the life of the saint. Bartolomeo Montagna (1450–1523): *Ecce Homo*. Cima da Conegliano (1459–1517/18): *Virgin and Child with John the Baptist and Mary Magdalene*. Jacopo de' Barbari (1440–1516): *Virgin at the Fountain*. Marco Palmezzano (1445–1539): *Dead Christ* (1510). Lorenzo di Credi (Florence, 1456–1537): *Virgin Between SS Julian and Nicholas*. Mantegna, several allegorical canvases: *Parnassus**. Perugino (Pietro Vannucci, 1445/50–1523): prolific painter who worked in Florence with Verrocchio and Leonardo da Vinci and who possessed a feeling, rare at that time, for space and perspective: *Virgin and Child Between St Catherine and John the Baptist***; Virgin Surrounded by Saints and Angels**. Piero di Cosimo (Florence, ca. 1462–1521?): *Virgin of the Dove*. Domenico Ghirlandaio (Florence, 1449–94): *The Visitation**; Virgin and Child;* portraits of an old man and of a child**, said to have been painted in the Flemish style. Bartolomeo di Giovanni (active at the end of the 15th c.): *The Marriage of Thetis and Peleus; The Bridal Procession of Thetis*. Sebastiano Mainardi (1460–1513): *Virgin and Child and John the Baptist*.

▷ **Not to be missed**

The numbers within brackets refer to the galleries marked on the map.

Grande Galerie (4) Cimabue: *Madonna with Angels* (13th c.); Giotto: *St Francis Receiving the Stigmata* (14th c.); Pisanello: *Portrait of a Princess of the House of Este* (15th c.); Fra Angelico: *Coronation of the Virgin* (15th c.); Piero Della Francesca: *Portrait of Sigismondo Malatesta* (15th c.); Paolo Uccello: *Battle of San Romano* (15th c.); Botticelli: *Madonna and Child with Five Angels* (15th c.); Mantegna: *St Sebastian* (15th c.).

Salle des Etats (9)
This gallery is devoted to masterpieces by the greatest painters of the 16th c. and is where *The Mona Lisa (La Gioconda)* is displayed.

Salle Duchatel
Caravaggio: *Death of the Virgin* (17th c.)
Aile de Flore (18)
Caravaggio: *Fortuneteller* (17th c.); Magnasco: *St Jerome* (early 17th c.; Guardi: series of *Venetian Festivals* (18th c.); G. B. Tiepolo: *Last Supper* (18th c.)

Salle des Etats (9): Italian Painting of the 16th c.

Throughout the 15th c. Florence was the center where that new world was born that in the 16th c. would spread far beyond the confines of Italy. Inspired by the spirit of the age, 16th-c. painting was to become one of the glories of European art.

Titian (Tiziano Vecelli *ca.* 1485 or 1488/89–1576), pupil of the Bellini brothers and then of Giorgione, was a magnificent colorist and a passionate lover of beauty. His handling of the darker colors in a painting – as in his *Man with a Glove* – enabled him to stress his interpretation of the sitter's character: *Entombment* (1525); *Madonna of the Rabbit; St Jerome in the Desert**; *Man with a Glove****; *Portrait of a Man***; *Portrait of François I* (after a medal); *Woman at her Toilette; Virgin and Child; Allegory;* the so-called *Madonna of the Pardo; The Supper at Emmaus; The Crowning with Thorns**; *Musicians in a Landscape****, long attributed to Giorgione but now considered to be one of Titian's earliest works.

Veronese (called Paolo Calliari 1528–88): painter of luxury, wealth and pleasure, he had a keen feeling for the theater and his paintings are imaginary stage sets for his characters, heroes of mythology or of religion: *Jupiter Destroying Crime with his Thunderbolts: La Belle Nani***; *Susannah and the Elders***; *Christ Carrying the Cross; Virgin and Child with St Catherine and a Benedictine Monk; Crucifixion; Esther Fainting; The Supper at Emmaus*** (part of the collection bequeathed by Cardinal Richelieu to Louis XIII); *The*

Marriage Feast at Cana**. Painted for the Benedictines of San Giorgio Maggiore, this work came to the Louvre in 1799 and, although it is an unusually large composition, it is regarded as one of the most successful of its kind. Among the 132 people depicted on the canvas may be recognized the Sultan Suleiman I, Elizabeth of Austria, François I, and the Emperor Charles V, while, among the musicians, are Titian (double-bass), Veronese himself (viola), Tintoretto (violin), and Jacopo Bassano (flute). Its inspiration is less that of the New Testament than of Plato's *Symposium*.

Tintoretto (Jacopo di Robusti, 1518–94). Very different from the other two Venetians, he had an extraordinary ease and unceasingly strove to perfect his art: *Self-Portrait* (dating from the end of his life); *Paradise*** a study for the far wall of the Council Chamber in the Doges' Palace; *Portrait of a Man; Susannah and the Elders***.

Raphael (Raffaello Sanzio, 1483–1520): *St Margaret; St Michael Slaying the Dragon**; large *Holy Family***, the last two works were brought to France by François I and hung in Fontainbleau; *SS George and Michael; La Belle Jardinière**** also called *The Holy Family* (1507); *Madonna of the Blue Turban*.

Correggio (Antonio Allegri: *ca.* 1489–1534). *Antiope Sleeping*** is daringly composed on the diagonal plane of Antiope's body; *The Mystic Marriage of St Catharine of Alexandria* (1520); these two canvases were brought by Louis XIV from the heirs of Cardinal Mazarin who had himself purchased them from Jabach.

Sebastiano del Piombo (properly Sebastiano Luciani, *ca.* 1485–1547): *The Visitation*. Andrea del Sarto (1486–1531): *Holy Family; Charity**. Giovanni Battista Rosso Fiorentino (1494–1540), active in Florence (1513–23). Fiorentino was brought to Fontainebleau by François I with Primaticcio: *The Deposition* was painted for Montmorency, Constable of France, and preserved in the Château d'Ecouen for a long time. Raphael: portrait of *Baldassare Castiglione****, Italian courtier, diplomat, humanist, and author of *Il Libro del Cortegiano* (The Book of the Courtier) which challenged Machiavelli's *The Prince*, 1513.

Leonardo da Vinci (1452–1519): one of the most outstanding artists of all time. The Louvre houses a collection of his world-famous paintings. The *Mona Lisa****, purchased by François I for 4000 écus, is the portrait of 24-year-old Mona Lisa Gherardini del Gioconda, wife of a Florentine patrician; *Bacchus**** may originally have been a John the Baptist; *Virgin and Child with St Anne****, commissioned for the Annunziata in Florence; the composition uniquely suggesting the continuity of one generation to another and symbolizing the union of the spirit and the flesh in motherhood. The painting, which had belonged to the Royal Collections, was given away and bought back from its unknown owner by Cardinal Richelieu. Another version, *The Virgin of the Rocks**** is in the National Gallery in London, notable for the subtlety of the light, its mysterious blue-green colors and cave setting, and the ambiguous atmosphere common to Leonardo's work; *John the Baptist**, painted in France; *La Belle Ferronière***.

Vestibule of the Salle des Etats (8)

In the corridor on the l., behind Veronese's *Marriage Feast of Cana,* are displayed paintings by Northern Italian artists of the early 16th c. strongly influenced by Leonardo da Vinci. Andrea Solario (*ca.* 1470–1514), who worked in France for Cardinal Georges d'Amboise at the Château de Gaillon: *Crucifixion* (1503); *Annunciation* (1506) to which the background landscape was added in the 17th c. by a Northern European painter; *Portrait of Charles d'Amboise,* Governor of Milan and the Cardinal's nephew who, in 1500, recommended the painter to his uncle; *Madonna of the Green Cushion,* a famous painting which Catherine de' Medici purchased from the Cordeliers of Blois. Giovanni Boltraffio (*ca.* 1467/71–1516): *The Virgin of the Casio Family,* commissioned by them in 1500 for the Church of the Misericordia in Bologna. Lorenzo Lotto (1480–1556): *Christ Carrying His Cross* (1526), found in a church in Le Puy and purchased by the Louvre in 1982; *The Woman Taken in Adultery.* Savoldo (1480–1548): *Portrait of a Man in Armour,* may depict Gaston de Foix, who directed the siege against Brescia, Savoldo's native city; the interplay of the three mirrors in the background makes this a highly original painting. Correggio: *Allegory of the Virtues and Vices.*

Returning towards the Salle des Etats, there are Florentine Mannerist portraits: Bronzino (1503–72), *Portrait of a Sculptor;* Franciabigio (1482–1525): *Portrait of a Man;* Pontormo (1494–1556): *Portrait of a Goldsmith.*

Salle Duchatel

Major 17th-c. paintings are temporarily hung in this vast room. Here can be seen Caravaggio's *Death of the Virgin***, painted for the church of Santa Maria in Trastevere in Rome. The ecclesiastical authorities rejected it as indecorous, but it excited the enthusiasm of other painters. Its creator, Michelangelo Merisi, known after his birthplace as Carravaggio (1573–1610), depicting the subjects of his religious paintings as ordinary people and by strongly accentuating his shadows, set himself against the prevailing humanist and Mannerist trends in art. Its realism and the earthy beauty of the Virgin give this technically brilliant scene of everyday life a moving quality. Jabach purchased this painting at the sale of the English king Charles I's collections, and it was resold to Louis XIV. Annibale Carracci (1560–1609): *The Virgin Appearing to SS Luke and Catherine; The Hunt; Fishing.* Ludovico Carracci (1555–1619): *The*

Madonna of St Hyacinth. Guido Reni (1575–1642): *Deianira and the Centaur Nessus; Hercules on his Funeral Pyre; David Slaying Goliath; Hercules Slaying the Hydra of Lerna; Hercules and Achelous.* Antonio Carracci (1583–1618): *The Flood.* Domenico Fetti (1589–1623): *The Guardian Angel.* Guercino (Giovanni Francesco Barbieri, 1591–1666): *The Raising of Lazarus.* Luca Giordano (1634–1705), nicknamed 'Fa Presto' because of his speed of execution: two *Portraits of Philosophers**. Serodine (1600–30): *Jesus Among the Doctors of the Law* (acquired in 1983).

Aile de Flore (18): Italian Painting of the 17th and 18th c.

There is direct access through the Porte de Flore (1st floor), or through the Grande Galerie and the room devoted to Northern European painting. The majority of the works were acquired by Louis XIV. Their wide variety allows the viewer to range from the strict academism of the Carracci to the lively realism of Caravaggio. A number of paintings have been taken out of storage to provide a representative selection of several of the Italian schools. There is a substantial collection of works by Domenichino, one of the earliest of the great classical landscape painters, and a large number of Venetian canvases typical of the age and, above all, of the city itself, where unbridled licentiousness flourished in a tragic atmosphere of social disintegration.

Annibale Carracci: *The Resurrection.* Orazio Gentileschi (Pisa, 1561– London, 1647): *The Rest on the Flight into Egypt.* Caravaggio (Gallery 11): *Adolf de Vignacourt**; *The Fortune Teller***, the latter differing from other works on the same subject and itself the center of an exhibition mounted by the Dossiers du Louvre (1977). Bartolomeo Schedone (1578–1615): *The Entombment.* Guido Reni (1575–1642): *Ecco Homo**; *St Sebastian**. Domenichino (Domenico Zampieri, 1581–1641), Bolognese painter, favorite pupil of Annibale Carracci: *Landscape with the Flight into Egypt; Herminia with the Shepherds; St Cecilia; Hercules Fighting; Hercules and Cacus.* Agostino Carracci (1557–1602): *The Annunciation.* Annibale Carracci: *Abraham's Sacrifice.* Francesco Mola (1612–66): *The Barbary Pirate; John the Baptist Preaching in the Wilderness.* Pietro da Cortona (1596–1669): *Venus as a Huntress Appearing to Aeneas.* Carlo Maratta (1625–1713), the leading painter in Rome in the second half of the 17th c.: *Maria Maddalena Rospigliosi.* Guercino: *SS Francis of Assisi and Benedict.* Lionello Spade (1576–1622): *The Return of the Prodigal Son.* Domenico Fetti (1589–1624): *Melancholy; The Emperor Nero.* Bernardo Strozzi (1581–1644): *The Holy Family; Virgin and Child with an Angel.* Giovanni Castiglione (1610–65): *Abraham and Melchisedech; Christ Driving the Moneylenders from the Temple; Adoration of the Shepherds.* Gregorio da Ferrari (1644–1726): *Juno and Argus* (gift of the Société des Amis du

Louvre, 1981). These last two painters represent the Genoese school. Il Baciccio (Giovanni Battista Gaulli, 1639–59): *Moses Striking the Rock*. Salvatore Rosa (1615–1705): *The Marriage of the Virgin; The Adoration of the Shepherds*. Neapolitan School, 17th c.: *The Concert*. Paolo Porpora (1617–73): *Still Life*. Aniello Falcone (1607–56): *Battle Scene*. Francesco Solimena (1657–1747) unchallenged leader of the Neapolitan school in the first half of the 18th c.: *Heliodorus Expelled from the Temple*. Giuseppe Angeli (1709–98): *The Soldier and the Drummerboy*. Giuseppe Crespi (Bolognese school, 1665–1747): *Woman With a Flea; St Anselm Writing at the Dictation of the Virgin*. Alessandro Magnasco (1667–1749): *St Jerome**, Seascape; The Gypsies' Meal*. Sebastiano Ricci (1660–1734): *Satyr and Peasant*.

Francesco Guardi (Venice, 1712–93) was a painter of originality who left views of his native city which are both extremely accurate and highly evocative: 10 of the series of a dozen *Venetian Festivals***, held on the occasion of the election of Alv Mocegino IV as Doge of Venice in May 1763, the other two are in Grenoble and Brussels; *View of the Church of SS John and Paul; The Church of San Zanipolo and the Confraternity of San Marco at Venice; Scenes in Honor of the Doge Mocegino*. Pietro Longhi (1702–1785): *The Presentation*. Giovanni Paolo Pannini (1692–1766), painter of large town scenes, and the first to make a speciality of ruins: *Concert and Preparation for the Fête Held on the Piazza Navone for the Birth of the Dauphin, Son of Louis XV, in 1729*. Michele Marieschi (1710–43): *View of the Salute, Venice*. Giovanni Battista (or Giambattista) Tiepolo (1696–1770): *The Last Supper**; Apollo and Daphne; Alexander and Campaspe at the House of Apelles*. Giandomenico Tiepolo (1727–1804), son of Giambattista: *Carnival Scene*; The Charlatan; The Triumph of Religion*. Giovanni Antonio Pellegrini (1675–1747): *Triumphal Entry of Prince Johann Wilhelm von Pfalz*. Giovanni Battista Pittoni (1687–1767): *The Chastity of Scipio; Polyxena Sacrificed to the Shade of Achilles; Christ Giving the Keys to St Peter*. Pompeo Batoni (1708–87), the most successful painter and portraitist in 18th-c. Rome; every Englishman making the Grand Tour had to sit for him: *Charles John Crawle*.

The Beistegui Collection

The remaining part of the Galerie Flore is reserved for the Bestegui Collection, presented to the Louvre in 1953. Franco-Flemish school (late 14th c.): *Virgin and Child*. The Master of Moulins (active *ca*. 1480–1500): *Portrait of the Dauphin Charles Orland***. Nicolas de Largillière (1656–1746): the *Duchesse de Bouillon*. Jean Honoré Fragonard (1732–1806): *Firing the Train; Portrait of a Young Artist*. Jean Marc Nattier (1685–1766): The *Duchesse de Chaulnes as Hebe***. François Hubert Drouai (1727–1775): *The Artist's Wife*. Peter Paul Rubens (1577–640): *The Death of Dido*. Anthony van

Dyck (1599–1641): *Portrait of an unknown man*. Thomas Lawrence (1769–1830): portrait of *Mrs Cuthbert*. Ignacio Zuloaga y Zabaleta (1870–1945): portrait of *Carlos de Beistegui* (1911). Meissonnier (1815–1825): *Mme de Verninac**; portrait of *General Bonaparte***; portrait of *M. Meyer*. François Gérard (1770–1837): portrait of *Mme Lecerf*. Jean Auguste Dominique Ingres (1780–1867): portrait of *Bartolini*, the sculptor from Lucca (1820); portrait of *Mme Panckoucke**.

Francisco Goya (1746–1828): the *Condesa del Carpio, Marquesa de Solano****. This painting, considered the jewel of the collection with its play of black, white and pinks, brings the visitor to the Spanish paintings in the Pavillon de Flore.

Spanish Paintings

Direct access through the Porte Jaujard.

The collection of Spanish paintings was only formed comparatively recently and has, since 1969, been on display in the first-floor galleries of the Pavillon de Flore (19). Although their numbers may not be as substantial as those of other Schools, they are of very high quality individually.

To view the paintings in their chronological order turn l. when coming from the Beistegui Collection.

▷ Not to be missed

Crucifixion by El Greco (16th c.); *Adoration of the Shepherds* by J. de Ribera (17th c.); *Two Scenes from the Life of St Bonaventura* by F. de Zurbarán (17th c.); *Portrait of Marie-Anne of Austria* by Velasquez (17th c.); *The Young Beggar* by Murillo (17th c.); portraits of the *Marquesa de Santa Cruz* and of the *Marquesa de la Solana* by Goya (18th c.).

The Aile de Flore (19) 1st floor

The Master of Burgo de Osma (Valencia, early 15th c.): altarpiece of the Virgin and Child with John the Baptist and St Ambrose. Barnardo Martorell (active in Barcelona from *ca.* 1443, d. 1453): panels from a *St George* altarpiece. Jaime Huguet (1415–92): *The Flagellation; The Entombment*. The Master of St Ildefonso (active in Castile late 15th c.): *St Ildefonso receiving the Chasuble;* Anonymous Portuguese master (mid-15th c.): *Man With a Glass of Wine;* this fine portrait was once attributed to a French master, but the art historian Charles Sterling has recently identified it as being by Nunŏ Gonçalves (active 1450–71). Francisco Herrera the Elder (*ca.* 1590–*ca.* 1656): *St Basil Dictating his Dogma.* Luis Tristan (active Toledo *ca.* 1586–1624): *St Francis of Assisi.* El Greco (1541–1614): *Crucifixion with Two Donors***; this Christ is very close to the artist's first religious works in Toledo, but at the same time anticipates *The Burial of Count Orgaz; St. Louis, King of France;* portrait of *Covarrubias.* José de Ribera (1591–1652): *Adoration of the Shepherds***; *The Clubfooted Boy; Christ in the Tomb; St Paul the Hermit.* Juan Carreño de Miranda (1614–85): *Foundation Mass of the Trinitarian Order.* Francisco Zurbarán (1598–1664): *St Bonaventura at the Council of Lyons**; *Exposition of the Body of Saint Bonaventura.* Francisco Collantes (1599–1656): *The Burning Bush.* Diego Velazquez (1599–1660): *Queen Maria Anna of Austria***; the *Infanta Margherita* (*ca.* 1653). Attributed to Velazquez, the *Infanta Maria Teresa.* Esteban Murillo (1618–82): *The Angels' Kitchen***; *The Birth of the Virgin***; *The Young Beggar****; *The Immaculate Conception.* Francisco Goya (1746–1828): portrait of *Ferdinand Guillemardet* (*ca.* 1798); *The Unequal Marriage,* a genre painting acquired in 1970; *Woman with a Fan,* the sitter is unknown but to judge from the greys and blacks of the artist's palette it must have been painted after 1810; portrait of the *Marquesa de Santa Cruz***, acquired 1976. Luiz Melandez (1716–80): *Self-Portrait: Still Life.*

Second floor (Rooms 11–14 West Wing)

NB. These rooms may be in the course of rearrangement.

Salles zenithales: the Helene and Victor Lyon Bequest

This collection passed to the Louvre in 1971 and includes Impressionist paintings by Renoir, Sisley, Monet, Cezanne, and Degas and a varied collection of paintings from the 15th to the 19th c., notably works by Jan van Goyen (1596–1656); *Landscape* (1632); *The Skaters* (1637), and one of his masterpieces, the almost monochrome *View of the Rhine* (1647). Bernardo Strozzi (1581–1644): *Portrait of a Man,* often attributed to Velasquez. Canaletto (1686–1768): *The Rialto; Santa Maria della Salute.* Gian Domenico Tiepolo (1727–1804): *Christ with the Woman Taken in Adultery; Christ Healing the Paralytic.*

The Princesse de Croy Bequest

This collection was given to the Louvre in 1930 and 1932 by the Princesse de Croy who inherited it from her father, the Comte de l'Espine. It comprises 3700 landscape paintings and drawings of Valenciennes – some of which are exhibited in Gallery 3 on this floor – and a number of Dutch paintings: *The Slippers** long attributed to a follower of Vermeer, but recently assigned to Samuel van Hoogstraten; *The Tooth-Drawer** by Gerard van Honthorst; marine paintings by Salomon Ruysdael and Abraham van Bayeuren, and *The Five Senses* by Antoine Palamédes.

English and German Paintings of the 18th and 19th c.

Portraits by Johan Zoffany (1733–1810): *Reverend Burroughs and his Son* (1769), purchased in 1974. Allan Ramsey (1713–84); Thomas Gainsborough (1727–88): *Lady Alston: Conversation in a Park*, a youthful work which shows the painter with his wife. Sir Joshua Reynolds (1723–92): *Master Hare*; George Romney (1734–1802); John Hamilton Mortimer (1740–79); Sir Henry Raeburn (1756–1823). Sir Thomas Lawrence (1769–1830): *Sir Thomas Bell*; *Mr and Mrs Angerstein**. Joseph Wright of Derby (1734–97): *Portrait of a Gentleman*, purchased in 1985. Giovanni Batista Lampi (1751–1830). Burne-Jones (1833–98).

Paintings of the Northern European Schools

Entrance via the Porte Jaujard or Porte Denon, 1st floor (Galleries 12, 14, 15, 16, and 17).

Until all the schools of painting are displayed in the Grand Louvre, the Flemish, Dutch, and German Schools are housed chronologically in the Louvre: 15th and 16th c. in the small rooms on the S side overlooking the Seine, 17th c. in those on the N side overlooking the Tuileries, in the Salle Van Dyck, the Galerie Médicis, and the Salle des Sept-Mètres.

Petits Cabinets (South) 1–5 (16): Flemish and Dutch Paintings of the 15th and 16th c.

The 15th-c. was the golden age of the Flemish primitives; the differences between Flemish and Dutch art only appear in the 17th c. The area comprising modern Belgium and the Netherlands was cloaked with enormous artistic wealth. The prosperity of trade centers such as Bruges, Ghent, and Brussels attracted painters in search of clients and to further their own training. Van Eyck at Bruges and Van der Weyden at Brussels were the two most important artists to revive the fundamentals of painterly technique and to exercise a profound influence upon their contemporaries and successors. During the 16th c. Antwerp became the clearing house of European trade, the nursery of the Protestant Reformation and the major artistic center of the Northern European art. The influences of the Italian Renaissance, of Erasmus and the humanists, and of Luther and the Reformation, combined to engender those new forms of easel-painting which were to be the glories of

Flemish and Dutch painting – still-life, landscape, and genre painting.

The Master of the St Bartholomew Altarpiece (active Cologne, 1450–1510): *Descent From the Cross;* Joos van Cleve (*ca.* 1490–1541): *Virgin and Child Adored by St Bernard; Christ Taken Down From the Cross; The Last Supper,* altarpiece from the church of Santa Maria della Pace in Genoa.

Cabinet no. 1. Dieric Bouts (d.1475): fragment of a *Nativity* from an altarpiece; *The Deposition,* directly inspired by the work of Rogier van der Weyden; *Virgin and Child.* Jan van Eyck (1390–1441): *The Madonna of Chancellor Rolin***,* from the collegiate church of Autun; known also as the *Virgin of Autun,* it depicts the donor kneeling before the Virgin. He is Nicolas Rolin, Chancellor of the Duchy of Burgundy and father of Jean Rolin, Bishop of Autun. This is one of the Louvre's masterpieces which has survived in an exceptionally fine state of preservation. Rogier van der Weyden (1399–1464): *The Annunciation**,* the center panel of a triptych of which the side panels are in the museum at Autun; *The Braque Family Triptych**,* probably painted around 1450 after the artist's return from Italy and before the Beaune altarpiece of the *Last Judgement,* in which the same hieratic figure of Christ in blessing appears. On the back of the side panels are painted a skull, a cross, and the arms of Jean Braque and those of his wife, Catherine de Brabant, for whom this little portable altar had been created. Master of the View of St Gudule (active *ca.* 1470–*ca.* 1500): *Pastoral Instruction with a view of the façade of the Cathedral of St Gudule at Brussels, then under construction,* shown in the background of this panel. Petrus Christus (1415–72/3): *The Lamentation,* directly inspired by Van Eyck's *Pietà.* Dieric Bouts (d.1475): *The Lamentation,* directly inspired by Van der Weyden's triptych, *The Madonna of the Pomegranate.* Geertgen tot Sint Jans (*ca.* 1460–*ca.* 1488/90): *The Raising of Lazarus,* a composition identical with that on the same subject by Ouwater in the painting in the Berlin Dahlem Museum.

Cabinet no. 2. Hans Memling (*ca.* 1430–1494): *Portrait of an Old Woman** (its pendant, *Portrait of an Old Man,* is in the Berlin Dahlem museum); *The Mystic Marriage of St Catherine**; The Martyrdom of St Sebastian;* from his final years a late triptych of the Resurrection and Ascension of Christ; the so-called *Virgin of Jacques Floreins**;* study for a head; *John the Baptist, St Mary Magdalene* and *The Flight into Egypt,* panels from a dispersed triptych presented by Mme Bethsabée de Rothschild, 1874. Gerard David (*ca.* 1460–1523): *The Marriage at Cana; Virgin and Child Between the Donor Jean de Sedano and His Wife with Their Patron Saints.* Jean de Flandres (active in Spain 1496–1504): *Christ and the Woman of Samaria,* one of the 47 panels which he painted for Isabella the Catholic, Queen of Castile, from 1496 to 1504 in collaboration with Michel Sittow (*ca.* 1496–1525). In 1965 the Louvre purchased the latter's *Coronation of* *the Virgin* from the same series. Hieronymus Bosch (*ca.* 1450–1516) is represented by *The Ship of Fools***. One of the strangest figures in the world of painting, he was endowed with unbridled powers of imagination, a faculty for grotesque, even shocking fantasies whose details are nonetheless utterly clear. A mystic steeped in the world of demons, witches, magic, signs and symbols, Bosch belongs to the twilight of the Middle Ages and the dawn of the Renaissance.

Cabinet no. 3. Quentin Metsys or Massys (1465–1530): *The Moneylender and His Wife****, one of the most famous paintings of the period in which may be seen links between the vision of Van Eyck and that of Vermeer; *Pietà* (1515); *Virgin and Child* (1529). Jan Gossaert, known as Mabuse (1472–1536): *Jean Carondelet Diptych**; *Portrait of a Benedictine Monk*. Bernard van Orley (*ca.* 1492–1552): *Portrait of a Man*. Cornelis van Dalem (1535–73/75): *Farmyard on a Winter Morning*. Gilles Mostaert (1534–98): genre painting. Aergten van Leyden: *The Nativity; The Sacrifice of Abraham* by the 16th-c. Master of the Brunswick Monogram. Pieter Bruegel the Elder (1525–69): *The Beggars**. Joachim Patenier (1475/80–1524): *St Jerome in the Desert***. (16th-c. Leyden or Antwerp School): *Lot and His Daughters*. Lucas van Leyden (*ca.* 1489–1533): *Woman Playing Cards*, bequeathed in 1962 by Mme Pierre Lebaudy; Joos van Cleve (*ca.* 1490–1540): *St Bernard and the Virgin; Christ in Blessing*. The Master of the Martyrdom of St John the Evangelist. Jean Bellegambe (b. *ca.* 1467, d. before 1536): *Pietà* (inspired by Bouts); *Virgin and Child*.

Cabinet no. 4: Jan Sanders van Hemessen (*ca.* 1500–*ca.* 1565): *Tobias and the Angel*. Frans Floris (1516–70): *The Holy Trinity*, which, before the Revolution, hung in the church of Saint-Sulpice in Paris. Otto van Veen or Venius (1566–1629): *The Lamentation*, a monumental composition by Rubens' master, from the church of Villeneuve-sur-Yonne, long attributed to a pupil of Andrea del Sarto (*ca.* 1500–89): Vincent Sellaer (ca1500–1589): *Jupiter as a Satyr with his Twins*, a painting reminiscent of *Charity* by Andrea del Sarto and of the School of Fontainebleau. Giovanni Stradarus (1523–1605): *Vanity, Moderation and Death,* an allegorical painting (bequeathed in 1980), executed in Florence in 1569 when the artist was collaborating with Vasari on the decoration of the Palazzo Vecchio. Antonio Moro (1519–76/7), leading portrait painter of the Spanish-Burgundian Court, under the patronage of the Cardinal, who was chief minister to the Emperor Charles V: *Cardinal Granvella's Dwarf**.

Flemish, Dutch, and German Paintings

Galerie Médicis (15): The 21 canvases by Rubens devoted to the *Story of Marie de' Medici* (17th c.).

Salle des Sept-Mètres (12): 17th c. portraits by Frans Hals (1st bay);

Bathsheba; Pilgrims at Emmaus; Slaughtered Ox and self-portraits by Rembrandt van Rijn (3rd bay).

▷ Not to be missed

Numbers in parenthesis refer to the galleries shown on the map.
Petits cabinets, S Side (16): 15th and 16th centuries *The Virgin and Chancellor Rolin* by Van Eyck (1st cabinet); *The Annunciation* and a triptych by Rogier Van der Weyden (1st cabinet); *The Mystic Marriage of St Catherine* by Hans Memling (2nd cabinet); *The Ship of Fools* by Hieronymus Bosch (2nd cabinet); *The Moneylender and his Wife* by Quentin Metsys (3rd cabinet); *St Jerome Preaching in the Desert* by Joachim Patenier (3rd cabinet); *Self Portrait* by Dürer (7th cabinet); *Erasmus* by H. Holbein (7th cabinet).

Petits cabinets, N side (7) 17th c. *The Lacemaker* and *The Astronomer* by J. Vermeer of Delft (2nd cabinet); sketches by Rubens (3rd cabinet); *The Battle of Arbela* by Jan (Velvet) Breughel (7th cabinet).

Salle Van Dyck (14): 17th c. *The Kermesse, The Adoration of the Magi* and *Portrait of Hélène Fourment and her Children* by P. P. Rubens (17th c.); *Charles I* by A. Van Dyck (17th c.); *The Four Evangelists* by Jacob Jordaens.

Cabinet no. 5. houses a replica of the *studiolo* which Federigo III da Montefeltro, Duke of Urbino, had built in 1476 in his palace. This small room was decorated with *trompe-l'oeil* marquetry and the portraits of 28 famous men. The Louvre owns 14 of these paintings attributed to the Flemish artist, Joos van Wassenhove called Justins of Ghent, (ca. 1435–ca. 1485), and to the Spaniard, Pedro Berruguete ('Pietro Spagnnolo', d.1503), and here they can be seen in an appropriate setting.

Petits Cabinets (South) 6–8 (16): German Painting of the 15th and 16th Centuries

Exemplified by works of the highest quality.
Cabinet no. 6. The Master of the Holy Family (active in Cologne, 1480–1520): fragments from an altarpiece of the *Seven Joys of Mary: The Presentation***, *The Adoration of the Magi*, the *Virgin Enthroned at the Side of the Risen Christ*. The Master of St Severin (Cologne School, 1500–15): *The Presentation*. The Master of the St Bartholomew Altarpiece (Cologne, ca. 1470–510): *Descent from the Cross*.

Cabinet no. 7 and 8. Albrecht Dürer (1471–1528): *Self-Portrait* (1493), probably painted for the artist's fiancée since the thistle Dürer holds signifies marital fidelity in German folklore. Even in this youthful work, the painter shows the same clarity of expression and firmness of line which were to become his hallmarks. There are a number of portraits by Hans Holbein (1497–1543): *Anne of Cleves* (ca. 1539); *Archbishop William Warham (ca.* 1527); *Nicolas Kratzer** (ca. 1528); *Erasmus***, undoubtedly one of the most famous and true portraits of the learned humanist ever painted. It was purchased from Jabach by Louis XIV. Hans Baldung Grein (1484–1536): *Death, the Knight and the Lady.* Lucas Cranach the Elder (1472–1553): *Portrait of a Girl** (perhaps Magdalena Luther); *Venus in a Landscape.*

Petits Cabinets, (North) (17): Flemish and Dutch Painting of the 17th c.

These rooms house small or medium-scale paintings (Vermeer).

Cabinet no. 1 contains work by genre painters influenced by Rembrandt; Gerrit Dou (1613–75), head of the so-called 'Precise' School: *Woman with Dropsy** (1663); *The Silver Ewer; The Trumpet Player.* Adran Coorte (active 1685–1725): *Shells.* Nicolaes Maes (1634–93): *Bathing Scene,* an unusual subject for the period. Gerard Ter Borch (1617–81): *The Gallant Officer.* Pieter de Hooch (1629–84): *The Cardplayers* (former Pereire Coll.). Michael Sweerts (1624–64): *The Go-Between and the Young Man* (once attributed to Ter Borch).

Cabinet no. 2. Jan Vermeer of Delft (1632–75). This painter was only rediscovered in the 19th c. His output was restricted; there are only about 35 authenticated canvases extant. His paintings are on a small scale, their subject matter commonplace, with no picturesque or anecdotal details. The setting is enclosed, the atmosphere low-key, silent, and peaceful and yet the play of light and color turns everyday things into poetry. The Louvre has two of his paintings, *The Lacemaker***, purchased by Napoléon III in 1870, and *The Astronomer****, accepted in settlement of death duties in 1983. Gerard Ter Borch (or Terborch): *The Duet; The Concert; Reading Lesson.* Caspar Netscher (1639–84): *The Viol Lesson.* Jan van der Heyden (1637–1712): the *Herengracht* (Amsterdam); *The Palace of the Dukes of Burgundy* (Brussels). Nicolaes Pietersz Berchem (1620–83): *The Ford.* Adriaen van Ostade (1610–85): *Family Portrait* (another is at the Hague). Gabriel Metsu (1629–67): *Still Life with Herring; The Tipsy Woman; The Apple Peeler; Amsterdam Herb Market.* Gerrit Adriaensz Berckheyde (1638–98): *Place du Dam* (Amsterdam).

Cabinet no. 3. Studies by Rubens. *Abraham's Sacrifice**, *Abraham and Melchisedech** and *Christ Carrying the Cross**, were made for the ceiling of the Jesuit church in Antwerp, gutted by fire in 1718; *The Raising of the Cross** is a study for the great triptych in Antwerp Cathedral (1610); *Genius Crowning Religion.* For the ceiling of the Banqueting Hall, Whitehall, London (ca. 1630), and *The Raising of Lazarus,* a study for a painting which hung in the

Kaiser Friedrich Museum, Berlin, destroyed in 1945. *Philopomena Recognized by an Old Woman* was a study for the painting once in the Regent's gallery in Paris. Two studies on the same panel show the first and last scenes in the series depicting the life of Maria de'Medici (Salle Médicis): *The Fates Weaving the Thread of the Life of Maria de'Medici* and *The Triumph of Truth*. Other studies for this series are preserved in the Alte Pinakothek, Munich, and the Hermitage Museum, Leningrad. *Landscape with Mill*** is one of the few examples of Rubens' work in this genre. *Mars and Venus* is on permanent loan from the Salavin-Fournier Bequest of the Fondation de France.

Cabinet no. 4. Cornelis van Poelenburgh (*ca.* 1590–1667), who lived in Italy from 1617 to 1625, and grew to love the Roman Campagna and its ruins: *Women Bathing; The Pasture; Ruins of Ancient Rome with the Castel Sant' Angelo; View of the Campo Vaccino*. Bartolomeus Breenberg (*ca.* 1599–1657): *Jesus Curing a Deaf-Mute*, painted on his return from Italy (1633), the setting is the Villa of Maecenas at Tivoli. Willem Claesz Heda (1599–1680/82): *Still Life with Silver Goblet*. Jacob van Velsen (*ca.* 1600–56): *The Fortune-teller*. Willem Cornelisz Duyster (1599–1635): *The Looters*. Pieter Codde (1559–1638): *The Dancing Lesson; Woman at her Toilette*. Hendrik Gerritsz Pot (*ca.* 1585–1657): *Charles I of England**, a copy of Daniel Mytens' portrait at Buckingham Palace. Frans Post (1612–80): who, from 1637 to 1664, accompanied Prince John Maurice of Nassau on the Dutch West India Company's voyage of colonization to Brazil. He returned with several landscapes: *Fort Maurice and the São Francisco River; View of the Outskirts of Porto Calvo*. Pieter Saenredam (1597–1665), renowned painter of church interiors, a painting by whom was purchased by the Louvre 1983: *Interior of the Church of St Bavo in Haarlem**.

Cabinet no. 5. Teniers the Younger, genre scenes. David Teniers the Elder (1582–1649): *Crucifixion,* inspired by Rubens' painting at Rotterdam. David Teniers the Younger (1610–90), his son, painted *Smoker on a Barrel**; *The Tavern; The Bowls Players, Hoquet Players; The Prodigal Son; The Seven Works of Mercy; Dead Christ,* a small copy of the now lost painting by Lotto then in the collection of the Archduke Leopold Wilhelm at Brussels, of which Teniers, whose painting of the *Archduke in His Gallery* is in the Louvre, was curator. Adriaen Brouwer (1605–1638): *Twilit Landscape; Interior of a Tavern*. Joos van Craesbeck (1608–60): *Man Smoking,* possibly a self-portrait painted under the influence of Brouwer to whom the canvas was attributed. Adriaen van Ostade (1610–85): *Reading the Gazette; Slaughtering a Pig*. Simon de Vos (1604–76): *The Works of Mercy,* purchased 1982, notable for the architectural setting based upon memories of Italian paintings.

Cabinet no. 6. Joos de Momper (1564–1635): Landscape. Paul Bril (1554–1626): *Market in the Campo Vaccino, Rome; The Fisher*. Denis van Alsloot (*ca.* 1570–*ca.* 1627), considered by some to be the founder of the Brussels school of landscape painting: *Winter Landscape.* Georg Flegel (1563-1638): *Still Life with Flask of Wine and Small Fishes* (acquired 1981), German work showing Flemish influence, as does the still life by Gothard de Wedig (1583-1641). Roelandt Savery (1576-1639), Flemish painter in the service of Henri IV in France, Rudolf II in Prague and the Emperor Matthias in Vienna: *Hungarian Troopers on the March; Orpheus Charming the Beasts.* Joachim Wttewael (1566-1638): *Jupiter and Diana* (acquired 1179). Ambrosius Bosschaert the Elder (1573-1621): *Bunch of Flowers in an Arch* (acquired with the help of the Friends of the Louvre, 1984).

Cabinet no. 7. Adriaen Pietersz van der Venne (1589-1662): *The Truce of 1609,* allegorical depiction of the banquet given for the Twelve Year Peace, which united the northern and southern states of Holland. Jan 'Velvet' Breughel (like the rest of his father's descendants he retained the *h* in his name although his father had dropped it), second son of Breugel the Elder: *The Battle of Arbela***; The Banquet of the Gods; Earth or the Earthly Paradise,* the last two paintings are part of the *Four Elements* commissioned by Cardinal Federigo Borromeo (the other two are in the Biblioteca Ambrosiana, Milan); the figures are attributed to Hendrick van Balen. *Virgin and Child in a Garland of Flowers* (1621), the figures painted by Rubens, the flowers by Breugel.

Cabinet no. 8. Hendrick van Steenwyck the Younger (*ca.* 1580–*ca.* 1649); *Christ Appearing to Mary and Martha.* Frans Francken II the Younger (1581-1642): *Ulysses Recognizing Achilles Disguised as a Woman Among the Daughters of Lycomenes; Solomon in the Temple Treasury; The Prodigal Son.* Bartholomeus Spranger (1546-1611); a Mannerist painter: *Justice,* an allegorical painting.

Salle Van Dyck (14): 17th-century Flemish Painting

In the 17th c. Flemish painting was dominated by the mighty figure of Peter Paul Rubens (1577-1640), the most strongly Baroque painter of his day. His extraordinary, highly civilized personality and his employment on several occasions in the most delicate of diplomatic negotiations undoubtedly make of him that ideal of the 17th c., the *honnête homme.* He undertook many commissions for Maria de'Médici and so the Louvre has inherited from the Royal Collections a substantial number of his paintings: *The Adoration of the Magi*** from the chapel of the Dames de l'Annonciation at Brussels; a *Tournament;* the dazzling, flashing, whirling *Kermesse***; The Flight of Lot** (see Delacroix's copy on the second floor of the Cour Carrée, Gallery 4); a portrait of his second wife, *Hélène Fourment with their Two Children**; Hélène Fourment in a Coach* (acquired 1977 in settlement of death duties); *Virgin of the Holy Innocents.* Anthony van Dyck (1599-1641), court portraitist to Charles I of England, was a master of the genre as seen in his

*Portrait of Charles I*** (The King in riding habit with no emblems of royalty in this, his best-known portrait, is remarkable); the *Marchesa Geronima Spinola Doria**; *Charles Louis, Elector Palatine and his Brother Prince Rupert* (later Duke of Cumberland); *Gentleman with a Sword; Man with His Son; Lady with her Daughter;* Isabella of Austria; the *Conde d'Osuna; Venus asking Vulcan for the Armour of Aeneas**; *Rinaldo and Armida**; *Virgin with Donors.* Jacob Jordaens (1593–1678), lavish master of the Baroque: *The King Drinks; Jupiter and Amalthea**; *Diana Sleeping* presented, 1982, by the Société des Amis du Louvre; *Jesus Driving the Moneylenders From the Temple; The Four Evanglists***; *The Adoration of the Shepherds* (purchased, 1981). The room also contains still lifes by Snyders (1579–1667) and Jan Fyt (1611–61).

Galerie Médicis (15)

This vast room, 148ft/45m long, 49ft/15m wide and 43ft/13m high, is devoted to Rubens' *Story of Marie de' Medici****. Commissioned from the painter in 1621 for the Luxembourg Palace, in 1625 he applied the finishing touches in Paris to the great series of paintings he and his pupils had executed in Antwerp. These 21 paintings with three additional portraits (Marie de' Medici, and her father and mother) hung originally in the W gallery on the first floor of the palace until 1778. In 1803 they were rehung in the E gallery of the Luxembourg until after 1815, when they were moved to the Louvre and hung in a row in the Grande Galerie. From 1900 to 1939, 18 of the 21 paintings were hung out of order in the room redecorated by G. Redon in the over-elaborate style of the period. Since 1953, this splendid series has been rearranged in its original chronological order in a completely refurbished room, in black and gold frames specially designed to match frames of 17th-c. paintings in Antwerp churches. The 19 large compositions are enhanced by their red velvet backing with inscriptions carved and gilded on a grey marble base below. Only the two narrow panels have been hung outside the room, on either side of the entrance: on the l., *The Fates Spinning the Thread of Marie de' Medici's Life;* on the r., *The Triumph of Truth.* The large paintings are set in the following order: 1. *The Birth of Marie de'Medici,* April 26 1575; 2. *The Education of Marie de' Medici;* 3. *Henri IV Presented with the Portrait of Marie de' Medici;* 4. *The Marriage by Proxy in Florence, October 5 1600;* 5. *The Arrival of Marie de' Medici at Marseilles, November 3 1600;* 6. *First Meeting of the King and Marie de' Medici at Lyons, December 9 1600;* 7. *The Birth of Louis XIII at Fontainebleau, September 27 1601;* 8. *Henri IV Entrusts the Regency to Marie de' Medici;* 9. *Coronation of the Queen at Saint-Denis, May 13, 1610;* 10. *The Apotheosis of Henri IV and of the Regency* (at far end of room); 11. *The Queen's Government;* 12. *The Capture of Juliers, 1610;* 13. *The Exchange of the Princesses at Hendaye, November 9 1615;* 14. *The Joys of the Regency;* 15. *Louis XIII Celebrates his Coming of Age, October 20*

1614; 16. *The Queen Escapes from the Château de Blois, February 21 1619;* 17. *Peace Terms are Submitted to the Queen;* 18. *The Treaty of Peace is Concluded, April 30 1619;* 19. *Marie de'Medici is Reconciled with her Son, September 5 1619.*

Salle des Sept Mètres (12): Dutch paintings of the 17th century

The Dutch School is displayed in all its variety. For most of the 17th c. artists from the Low Countries and Northern Europe reached perfection in all genres of painting. They could give an infinite variety to the monotonous Dutch landscape by depicting the subtle interplay of sky and water, while their genre paintings and portraits encapsulate the daily lives of a people who were patient, frugal, and industrious and yet had a keen enjoyment of music, entertainment, and the pleasures of the table. Still lifes demonstrate this taste for the good things of this world, and a deep knowledge of pictorial values. Rembrandt's handling of chiaroscuro, his feeling for both the human and the divine, and his intimate knowledge of human nature make him the dominant figure of the age.

1st alcove. Cornelis van Haarlem (1562–1638): *The Baptism of Christ;* an example of the Dutch Mannerist style, as is the later *Perseus and Andromeda* by Joachim Wttewael (1566–1638), both paintings donated by the Société des Amis du Louvre in 1983 and 1982. Frans Hals (1580–1666): portraits of Paulus van Berensteyn and of his wife Catherine Both van der Eem**; *Gipsy Girl**, Clown** (acquired 1984), two paintings with a freedom of technique, a vitality and spontaneity that make them not only masterpieces of Dutch painting but treasures of the Louvre. Salomon van Ruysdael (1600–70): *The Ferry; The Landing-Stage.* Jan van Goyen (1596–1656): *View of Dordrecht; The Coast of Egmont.*

2nd alcove. Gerrit van Honthorst (1590–1656): *The Concert;* Jan Davidsz de Heem (1600–84): *The Dessert.* Both these large paintings are examples of Flemish Baroque.

3rd alcove. Rembrandt van Rijn (1606–69). The Louvre has an outstanding collection of 15 authentic paintings including some of the most famous by this artist. The development of his style may be traced in the Louvre collection, which includes all genres explored by the painter: portraits of Albert Cuypers and his wife Cornelia Pronck, of the artist's son Titus, and of his second wife, Hendrijke Stoffels; self-portraits: with a golden chain***, bareheaded, in front of an easel**. Old Testament subjects: *Bathsheba**** (1654) for which Hendrijke Stoffels posed; *Tobias and the Archangel Raphael* (1637). New Testament subjects: *The Holy Family* or *The House of the Carpenter (*1640); *Pilgrims at Emmaus*** (1648); *St Matthew and the Angel* (1661). Genre painting: *The Philosopher** (1631); Still life: *Slaughtered Ox*** (1655). Landscape: *The Twilit Castle*.*

4th alcove. Govaert Flinck (1615–60): *The Annunciation to the Shepherds*, its composition inspired by an etching by Rembrandt. Batholomeus van der Helst (1613–70): *The Reepmaker Family; Young Woman Revealed Raising a Curtain* (1658), donated in 1984 by the Société des Amis du Louvre.

5th alcove. Landscapes by Jacob van Ruysdael (1628–82), nephew and pupil of Salomon: *The Thicket; Sunbeam*. Philip Wouwermans (1619–68): *Landscape with Farmcart; Horseman Resting*. Adam Pynacker (1622–73): *Landscape at Sunset; Mountain Landscape with Goat and Birds* (acquired 1980). Karel Dujardin (1662–78) *Italian Mountebanks*. Jan van der Heyden (1637–1712): *Town Hall, Amsterdam*. Nicolaes Berchem (1620–83): *Landscape with Animals. Woman Drinking; Interior of a Dutch House***, genre paintings by Pieter de Hooch (1629–84). Gerrit Dou (1613–75): *Reading the Bible; The Money Changer; Dutch Housewife; The Village Grocer's Wife*. Works by Frans van Mieris (1635–81) and Gabriel Metsu (1630–80). *Still Life with Turkey*** (1661) by Salomon van Ruysdael, one of his finest still lifes painted at the end of his career, purchased 1965.

Cabinet des Dessins (Department of Drawings)

Chief Curator: Mme Roseline Bacou
Aile de Flore: Entrance by the Porte de Flore or the Porte Jaujard.

With its 105,000 drawings, the Department of Drawings at the Louvre is, with the Albertina in Vienna, the richest collection in the world. It originates from Colbert's purchase of the Jabach Collection and was enriched by the king's earliest court painters (Le Brun, Mignard, A. Coypel) whose collections reverted by rights to the Crown, as well as by purchases and by substantial bequests. Apart from the Italians, whose earliest works go back to the 14th c., the Louvre collections aim at completeness from the 17th c. onwards and there are few major gaps.

The Edmond Rothschild Collection. In 1960 this department was set up in the Aile de Flore. It comprises 30,000 prints and 3000 drawings presented to the nation by Baron Edmond de Rothschild. Accommodation includes a Students' Room, accessible only to specialists approved by the Curator, and a gallery for temporary exhibitions open to the public.

Département des Objets d'art

Chief Curator: Daniel Alcouffe
Entrance: Porte Denon

In addition to the Galerie d'Apollon and the former private chapel between the Henri II and Henri IV staircases, this department is accommodated on the first floor in the E and N Wings of the Cour Carrée and in half the W Wing. The rooms are arranged in chronological order, the Escalier Percier being the starting point.

Rooms 1–7 in the Aile de la Colonnade are to become part of the Egyptian Antiquities Department. The Art Objects Department will have considerable new display space in the Richelieu block. Late 17th- and 18th-century exhibits will be displayed in the N wing and the northern end of the W wing of the Cour Carrée; everything else in the Richelieu block.

The Department of Objets d'art houses a collection of furniture and of *objets d'art* of all descriptions from Antiquity to the middle of the 19th c. Its nucleus is provided by the former royal collections. Those assembled by Charles V (1360–80) and by François I were dispersed by their successors and it was Louis XIV who revived the royal collections by the purchase of Cardinal Mazarin's collection almost in its entirety. His son the Grand Dauphin, collected ornamental jewels and, on his death, part of his collection went to his second son, the new king of Spain, Philip V, while the remainder was absorbed into the royal collections. These remained intact until the Revolution, when the jewels were stolen in 1792, the *objets d'art* scattered, and the tapestries and plate sold off by the Directory to pay the army contractors. The core of the Department was formed from the former royal collections, the Treasures of Saint-Denis including the French Crown Jewels, and of the Order of the Saint-Esprit. This was increased by gifts and bequests from Durand (1825), Revoil (1828), and Sauvageot (1856), and by the purchase by Napoléon III in 1861 of the Campana Collection.

Not to be missed

Salles de la Colonnades:
Early Christian and Carolingian carved ivories (Gallery 4); the so-called statuette of Charlemagne (Gallery 4); *Virgin and Child* from the Sainte-Chapelle (Gallery 5); arm-reliquary of St Louis of Toulouse and St Luke (Gallery 5); tapestries of the *Hunts of Maximilian* (Gallery 7); Italian enamels and majolica ware (Gallery 7); 16th- and 17th-c. gold and silver pieces (Gallery 15); furniture by A.-C. Boulle (Galleries 13 and 14); furniture by Cressant (Gallery 16); 18th-c. porcelain (Gallery 20).

Galerie d'Apollon:
French Royal Gem Collection; French Crown Jewels, including the 136 carat Regent diamond, 5th-c. porphyry vase from the Treasure of the Abbey of Saint-Denis.

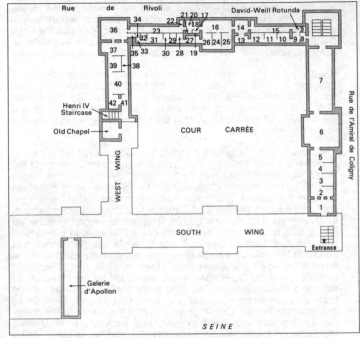

Department of Objets d'Art and Furniture/Colonnade Galleries

This arrangement is subject to change

1, 2, 3, Paneling
4 Salle Romane
5 Salle Gothique
6 Renaissance bronzes
7 Majolica
8 Salle Sauvageot
9 Salle Henri IV
10 Watches
11 Bronzes by Giovanni da Bologna
12 Salle d'Effiat
13, 14, Salles André-Charles Boulle
15 Rotonde David-Weill and Niarchos Gallery
16 Salle Cressent
17 Rotonde des Saisons
18, 19, Faience

20 Cabinet des Porcelaines
21 Salle Bérain
22 Salle Landau
23 Galerie des Tabatières
24, 25, 26, Salles Louis XV
27 Salle Schlichting
28 Salle Oeben
29 Salle Condé
30 Cabinet Louis XVI
31 Salle Lebaudy
32 Cabinet Chinois
33, 34, 35, Cabinets Marie-Antoinette
36 Salle Camondo
37 Salle Claude Ott
38 Salle Restauration
39 Salle Louis-Philippe
40, 41, Collection Thiers

Salles de la Colonnade

Gallery 1

The ancient paneling* and the coffered ceiling* come from the Council Chamber of the Pavillon de La Reine at Vincennes (1654–58). The four cloaks and other ceremonial items displayed in the case relate to the Order of the Saint-Esprit, founded by Henri III in 1578.

Gallery 2

The paneling from the Kings of France Bedchamber* in the Louvre has been mounted here, the oldest pieces dating from the reigns of Henri II and Henri IV. The current condition – but not the arrangement – of the panels is that of 1654, when Le Vau drew up the plans for the refurbishment of the Bedchamber for Louis XIV. Cases display jousting arms and armor including some mid–16th-c. North Italian round shields (*rondaches*) decorated by members of the architect and painter Giulio Romano's circle, and the mid–16th-c. armor of Henri II.

Gallery 3

The ceilings, paneling, and doors come from the State Bedchamber of the Kings of France in the Pavillon du Roi. The ceilings were painted by Scibec de Carpi (1558) from P. Lescot's designs. The gilded wood pedestal table* with porphyry top comes from the former royal collections, as does *Jupiter Hurling his Thunderbolts at the Titans*, attributed to L'Algarde (first half of the 17th c.); the Gobelins tapestries (late 17th or early 18th c.) depict the *Subjects of Fable Themes* after Raphael and Giulio Romano.

Salle Romane (4)

The two porphyry columns (4th c.) come from the old basilica of St Peter in Rome.

Case 1. Early Christian art: jewelry, ivory carvings, pyxes (round boxes), the Imperial so-called *Barberini Diptych**, the *Areobindus Diptych** (6th c.)

Case 2. Byzantine art: the *Harbaville Triptych** (mid–10th c.), casket with scenes from the story of Hercules (10th c.), lid of the Reliquary of the Holy Sepulchre 12th c.

Case 3. Carolingian art: casket with scenes from the Life of Christ (9th c.).

Case 4. Mosan and Rhenish Art: reliquary of St Henry (Saxon, 2nd half of the 12th c.), the portable Ipplendorf Altar (late 11th c.) and examples of 12th-c. Mosan enamelwork such as the *armilla** (bracelet) attributed to Nicolas of Verdun, the last great Romanesque goldsmith.

Case 5. S Italian art of the 10th and 11th c.: ivory horn from an elephant's tusk.

Case 6. Limoges enamels and ivory carvings: crosses and applied figures. The central case contains the famous bronze equestrian statuette, said to be Charlemagne (9th-c.); carved ivory panels, 12th-c. Mosan enamelwork and the reliquary of Charlemagne's arm* from Aachen (Liège, *ca.* 1166–70). Another case contains the reliquary of St Potentin (13th c.), and a double-fronted case containing the ciborium of the master enameller Alpais (Limoges, 12th c.) stands at the entrance to the Gothic Room.

Salle Gothique (5)

Here is a substantial number of masterpieces of gold- and silver-smith art and enamelwork.

▷ The techniques of enameling

Cloisonné: This is one of the oldest techniques, used in Byzantine jewelry. Cells (cloisons) are built up on a thin sheet of metal by fixing fine strips of the same metal or metal wire, edgewise. These cells are filled with colored, finely powdered glass paste. As the enamel shrinks in the furnace when it fuses to the metal, more powder has to be added, and the process repeated until the surface is level, and can be smoothed and polished.

Champlevé: A metal plate is cut out in a predetermined pattern of small compartments into which powdered enamel is placed. When fired the enamels vitrify. The plate is then polished and the exposed metal gilded. This is the technique of 12th and 13th-c. Limoges enamels.

Painted: The technique used in the 16th c. involved painting a copper plate with oxides which vitrified when fired.

In the wall cases are many examples of 13th-c. Limoges enamels: panels for book-bindings, crosses, the reliquary of Saint Valerie, the casket of St Louis (Limoges, late 13th c.), ivory carvings: the *Coronation of the Virgin* (13th c.), 14th-c. ivory diptychs. There are two translucent enamel mirrorbacks (Paris, before 1379). Various items of medieval gold- and silver-plate: the chalice from the Gaillon Treasure and silver goblets. Examples of medieval lapidary work, such as the jasper cups of Lorenzo de' Medici, 14th-c. rock-crystal ewer. In the center of the room there stands one of the most important ivory carvings, the 14th-c. *Virgin and Child***, full of Gothic spirituality, from the Treasure of the Sainte-Chapelle; *Descent From the Cross,* and a *Prophet* (13th c). Other Gothic masterpieces include a crown-reliquary (*ca.* 1260), the Floreffe Triptych (13th c.); the arm-reliquaries of St Louis of Toulouse and St Luke (14th c.). The large wood-and-ivory Embriachi altarpiece from Poissy depicts the lives of Christ, John the Baptist, and St John the Evangelist (Italy, *ca.* 1400). The wall tapestries include the hanging from Saint-Anatole de Salins (Bruges, 1501–1506).

Gallery 6: Renaissance bronzes**

Window side: two bronze bas-reliefs by Andrea Riccio (Padua, 1470–1532); bronze human and animal figures (Italy, 16th c.); two large Renaissance linen cupboards (France: 16th c.); a bronze *Gnome with a Snail* (Padua, late 15th c.); eight bronze bas-reliefs by Riccio, from the tomb of Marcantonio della Torre; French and Italian medals (Chancellor de Birague attributed to G. Pilon). In the center: *Boy Drawing a Thorn from His Foot** (Rome, 1540) cast after an ancient original by Fancelli and Sansovino. In the case to the r.; Paduan and Florentine 15th-c and 16th-c. bronzes: *St Jerome* and *David* by Bellano; a *Weeping Cupid* attributed to Verrochio; *St John the Baptist* by a pupil of Donatello; *St John the Baptist as a Child* and *Cupid Playing an Instrument* attributed to Donatello; Italian 15th- and 16th-c. medals and small plaques. The case on the l. contains bronzes by Riccio* (Padua, early 16 c.); medals and small plaques from N Italy, France, Burgundy, Germany and Flanders, including the seal of Cardinal Innocenzo Cibo attributed to Cellini (Rome, *ca.* 1525), and 15th- and 16th-c. bronzes from Padua and N Italy.

The furniture is French and Italian, 15th and 16th c., and includes a cypress-wood chest embellished with scenes of courtly life (N Italy, 15th c.); a linen-press decorated with three terms (half-columns with busts), attributed to Hugues Sambin (Burgundy, 2nd half of the 16th c.); a door with the salamander emblem of François I; a coffer ornamented with medallion portraits in profile (1st half of the 16th c.) and the throne of the archbishops of Vienne (late 16th c.).

Tapestries: *The Death of Phaeton* after Battista Dosso (Ferrara, *ca.* 1545); two hangings depicting Scipio after Giulio Romano (Gobelins, 17th c.) and a fragment of the *Life of St Mammes* (Paris, 1544).

In the corridor are examples of 15th- and 16th-c. stained glass.

Gallery 7: Majolica

The tapestries depict the *Hunts of Maximilian**** of which the cartoons are attributed to Bernard van Orley (woven for Charles V in *ca.* 1530), from the collections of Cardinal Mazarin and Louis XIV.

S wall: three marquetry panels attributed to Fra Vicenzo da Verona (*ca.* 1500); four pottery medallions attributed to Girolamo della Robbia from the Château of Saint-Germain-en-Laye (mid–16th c.); in the center, a coffer with large carved busts (France: *ca.* 1530) on two steps (as protection from the damp floor) decorated with paving tiles from Isabella d'Este's palace in Mantua (*ca.* 1500), from the Palazzo Petrucci in Siena (*ca.* 1509) and from San Giovanni at Carbonara, Naples (*ca.* 1450).

The central cases house a matchless collection of Italian and especially of Limoges portraits on enamel**, by the School of Pénicaud, the Master of the Aeneid, Léonard Limousin (1st half of the 16th c.), Pierre Reymond, Pierre Courteys, Suzanne de Court, and the Noailher family.

N wall: on the l. a coffer on a step decorated with paving tiles by Masséot Abasquesne (Rouen, mid–16th c.), from the Bâtie d'Urfé (1557). On the r. a case containing statuettes by the School of Avon (1st half of the 17th c.).

The wall cases house a collection of Hispano-Moresque, Italian, and French majolica***. On the Cour Carrée side: Tuscan and Orvietan (14th and 15th c.); Spanish (Andalusian, Aragonese, Valencian, 14th and 15th c.); French, including the work of Bernard Palissy and his school, decorated with frogs, fruit, etc. cast from life, majolica from Lyons (16th c.) and from Nevers (16th and 17th c.). Colonnade side: a notable collection of Italian majolica from Faenza, Caffaggiolo, Casteldurante, Deruta, Gubbio, Urbino, Venice (15th and 16th c.) and Castelli (17th c.). It includes items from services made for such rulers as Isabella d'Este (Casteldurante: *ca.* 1520), and Alfonso II d'Este (Urbino, *ca.* 1580). In the center of the gallery are two rare and costly collections: items of Saint-Porchaire earthenware* (mid–16th c.) and of Medici porcelain, the first soft-paste porcelain to be manufactured in Europe, at Florence in 1580.

Landing: at the entrance to the N wing of the Cour Carrée: 17th- to 19th-c. furniture and *objets d'art* are displayed.

▷ **Faience and porcelain**

Faience: earthenware covered with opaque white glaze containing tin, which preserves the painted designs when fired. A clear lead glaze is added before firing. Faience can be painted blue (cobalt oxide) or polychrome. Faience was first made in France in the 15th c. Majolica: Hispano-Moresque (14th and 15th c.) and Italian Renaissance: 16th-c. tin-glazed faiences from Lyons and Nevers are also called majolica.

Soft-paste porcelain: translucent, ivory-white pottery, the clay of which comprises a mixture (*frit*) of earths, clay, quartz, glass that is beaten, crushed, and purified to produce the porcelain paste; the clay is soft enough to cut with steel blades. This is then coated with translucent lead varnish. The late 16th-c. Medici porcelains were of this variety, as were the French porcelains of the first half of the 18th c., especially Vincennes and Sèvres.

Hard-paste porcelain: white translucent pottery invented at Meissen, its components are kaolin, feldspar, and quartz too hard to cut with steel. Meissen, Paris, and Limoges porcelains are all hard-paste. Hard-paste porcelain was invented in Meissen, in Saxony, from 1709 to 1710, and was difficult and costly to make. Factories opened in Vienna (1719) and Venice (1720, Vezzi factory).

Salle Sauvageot (8)

Collection of glassware from the 16th to the 18th c. from France, Italy, Germany and Bohemia.

Salle Henri IV (9)

Furniture from the first half of the 17th c. including *caquetoire* ('gossips') chairs with bowed arms, wide enough for voluminous skirts, and choir stalls from Saint-Etienne in Toulouse. Parisian tapestries: *The Story of Rinaldo and Armida* after Simon Vouet, and *placets* (stools covered in tapestry) with *The Story of Artemisia* after Antoine Caron (early 17th c.). Bronzes: *Monkey* attributed to Giovanni da Bologna (Florence, *ca.* 1570), and *Henri IV and Marie de' Medici as Jupiter and Juno** by Barthlémy Prieur (*ca.* 1608).

Take the door leading to the collection of gold and silver plate.

Rotonde David-Weill and Niarchos Gallery*** (15)

These rooms bear the names of the two benefactors who have made the Louvre's collections of gold and silver plate among the finest in the world.

The Rotunda houses a princely collection of 16th- and 17th-c. goldsmiths': silver-gilt dish (Paris, 16th c.); a gold coffer** said to have belonged to Anne of Austria (mid–17th c.); a mirror that belonged to Anne Hyde, Duchess of York (1600); Charles IX's shield and helmet (*ca.* 1570). A silver-gilt basin decorated with animals and plants by Wenzel Jammitzer (Nuremberg, *ca.* 1550).

The Gallery presents a lavish display of the art of French goldsmiths of the 17th and 18th c.: centerpiece** (1736) by J. Röettiers for the Princes of Condé; the centerpiece for Joseph I King of Portugal by F. -T. Germain (1758) and the church plate which he made for the Duc de Bourgogne; Marie Leczczynska's silver-gilt dressing case*

(1729); pieces from the dinner service ordered by the Empress Catherine II of Russia (late 18th c.); Sèvres biscuitware statuettes (18th c.) include *Pygmalion and Galatea* after Falconet 1763.

Return now to the Henri IV (9).

Gallery 10: Watches

The collections of jewels and watches are housed in a room hung with Gobelins tapestries (late 17th c.) depicting the *Story of Moses* after Nicolas Poussin. The jewelry and medals are in the case on the l. The collection of watches (17th–19th c.) in gold, enamel, and precious stones comes mainly from the Garnier and Olivier bequests. Two cases are dedicated to German 16th-c. gold- and silverwork. The wallcase houses 16th-and 17th-c. table clocks.

Gallery 11: Bronzes by Giovanni da Bologna

The tapestries are after Simon Vouet: *Moses in the Bulrushes* (Paris, 1630); *Rinaldo in the Arms of Armida* and *Mars and Venus* (Paris or Amiens, 17th c.). The collection of 16th- and 17th-c. French and Italian bronzes**: Pulci's ferocious giant *Morgante* (Florence, 16th c.); works by Giovanni da Bologna: *The Rape of Dejanira*** (Florence: late 16th c.) and by his studio: (*The Rape of Dejanira, The Labors of Hercules*); reduced copies of Michelangelo's statues: *Night and Day, Dawn and Dusk* (Italy, late 16th c.). *Apollo and Daphne* by Foggini (late 17th or early 18th c.). Susini's *Venus Chastising Cupid* (17th c.).

Salle d'Effiat (12)

Wall hangings comprising late 17th-c. Gobelins tapestries (*The Life of Scipio* after Giulio Romano) and a Savonnerie carpet (1668). In the case: collection of 17th-c. Nevers faience and a Delft tulip vase (2nd half 17th c.). A bed and armchairs from the Château d'Effiat*; an eight-legged pewter-inlaid bureau (mid–17th c.); a pair of Japanese lacquer cabinets; an ebony cabinet (Paris: 1st half 17th c.) and a Boulle bureau (early 17th c.).

Salles André-Charles Boulle (13 and 14)

These two rooms are devoted to the art of the age of Louis XIV. Presses, cabinets, and small bookcases*** illustrate the luxurious art of the royal cabinetmaker André-Charles Boulle (1642–1732) (→inset).

Gallery 13: Arabesque tapestries of the *Months* (Apollon, Gobelins:

1697) and French 17th-c. bronzes. Gallery 14: 17th- and early 18th-c. tapestries and a Savonnerie carpet made for the Galerie d'Apollon in the Louvre (1667). Writing-table, Max-Emmanuel of Bavaria's bureau*** and presses attributed to Boulle; and gilt-wood consoles (*ca.* 1715).

Salle Cressent (16)

Work** by the cabinetmaker Charles Cressent including a flat-topped bureau, presses, and the *Monkey Commode* in bronze. A suite of 18th-c. chairs; mounted Asian porcelain and large French East India Company vases with the arms of the Duke of Orléans.

Rotonde des Saisons (17): four terms depicting the *Four Seasons,* Rouen faience (mid–18th c.).

Galleries 18 and 19

Collections of faience from Rouen (18) and Marseilles, Niderviller, Moustiers, Sinceny and Sceaux (19).

Cabinet des Porcelaines (20)

Surrounded by 18th-c. paneling, a collection of 18th-c. Vincennes and Sèvres porcelain; an ornamental ship with mast and a pair of sconces which once belonged to Mme de Pompadour.

Salle Bérain (21)

Beauvais tapestries after Bérain (*ca.* 1730), grotesque designs on a snuff-colored ground: imitation Chinese lacquer (*vernis Martin*) tables (18th c.).

Salle Landau (22)

This gallery is devoted to the scientific instruments* bequeathed to the Louvre in 1979 by the collector, Nicolas Landau.

Galerie des Tabatières (23)*

This gallery, which once housed a collection of snuff- and other small boxes, now contains ivories (including portions of an 18th-c. frieze by Van Obstal), fragments of tortoiseshell piqued with amber, gems, and ornamental stones; cutlery and tazzas (shallow cups for wine) from the 16th to the 18th c.

Retrace your steps to reach Gallery 24.

Grande Salle Louis XV (24)

A table from the Hôtel des Invalides; chairs by Boucault, and a Coromandel lacquer commode.

Deuxième Salle Louis XV (25)

Furniture*: a writing-table made by Joubert for Marie-Antoinette, when she was Dauphine (1770); a lacquer commode (1737) made for Marie Leczczynska at Fontainebleau, and a lady's small writing-table, both by B.V.R.B. (*ca.* 1750). Gobelins tapestries.

Troisième Salle Louis XV (26)

Gobelins tapestry: *Alceste and Rodogunde* after Charles Coypel and J. -B. Oudry; furniture: the so-called Choiseul lacquer bureau by J. Dubois; a corner cupboard in blue and white imitation Chinese lacquer (*vernis Martin*) with silver-bronze mounts (1743). Reduced-scale copy of the statue of Louis XV at Rennes after J. -B. Lemoyne.

Salle Schlichting (27)**

Armchairs by Louis Delanois; rosewood bureau by J. Dubois and Pierre II Migeon (*ca.* 1750); a perfume burner by François-Thomas Germain (1757); Gobelins tapestries (Mois Lucas, 18th c.).

Salle Oeben (28)**

This room is devoted to the famous cabinetmaker Jean-François Oeben, responsible for Louis XV's bureau the (*bureau du roi*), now at Versailles, and contains a selection of his work, a desk and chiffonier (dresser), a writing-table, a mechanical table, and a piece of mechanical furniture known as the *table à la Bourgogne** (the mechanical fittings fulfilled several functions). There is also the screen which Delanois may have made for Mme du Bourg (*ca.* 1770). Gobelins tapestries: scenes from opera, comedy, and tragedy.

Salon Condé (29)

This room houses a collection of furniture in the Transitional Style with princely provenances (Comte d'Artois, Prince de Condé): a commode by Leleu (1772); a sofa and armchairs by N. Hertaut. A collection of marble vases on gilt-bronze mounts (late 18th c.). Sèvres vases* in a wall case.

Cabinet Louis XVI (30)

The different pieces of furniture* from the royal apartments were created by major representatives of the elegant and majestic Louis XVI style: Riesener, Benneman, Boulard Sené (cabinet-makers).

Salle Lebaudy (31)

In a room lined with paneling from the Hôtel de Luynes (*ca.* 1770–75) is housed furniture** which once belonged to Louis XVI (a commode by Benneman) and to Marie-Antoinette (armchairs by Sené for the Queen's Bedchamber at Saint-Cloud, and a roll-top desk used by Napoléon, by Reisener). Sèvres porcelain vases are displayed in a wall case.

Cabinet Chinois (32)

On the walls, 18th-c. wallpaper with Chinese designs. The furniture, formerly of royal ownership, demonstrates the 18th-c. taste for chinoiserie and lacquerwork. Furniture by Martin Carlin for Madame, Louis XV's daughter, at Bellevue; a writing-table for Marie-Antoinette by Weisweiler (1784). There are Sèvres porcelain vases in the wall case.

Cabinets Marie-Antoinette (33–35)

1st cabinet: contains *moiré* mahogany furniture; in a case, late 18th-c. dinner service* for George III of England by R. -J. Auguste. 2nd cabinet: bust of the Queen in Sèvres biscuitware, 3rd cabinet: items which once belonged to the Queen, such as her traveling case and her collection of bibelots**.

Salle Camondo (36)

Around a monumental Sèvres porcelain vase (with bronze mounts by Thomire: 1784) is a collection of furniture and clocks from the reign of Louis XVI, among them a Louis XVI Sèvres porcelain vase stand (*guéridon*)** which belonged to Mme du Barry. In an alcove there is Napoléon's gold and silver plate, his throne and the King of Rome's cradle.

Salle Claude Ott (37)

Empire furniture, gold- and silver-plate and porcelain, which includes the *armoire à bijoux* (jewelry cupboard) of the Empress Josephine*** by Jacob Desmalter (1809), the tea-set (Biennais) and the coffee-set (Sèvres) of Napoleon; the Duchesse de Berry's dressing-table set in crystal and gilded bronze (1819).

Salle Restauration (38)

Charles X's bed from the Tuileries is in this gallery (1825).

Salle Louis-Philippe (39)

Displays Louis-Philippe (1830–48) furniture and *objets d'art*: chairs and library steps made for the Tuileries. The cases house a substantial collection of gold and silver plate**: a tea urn by Odiot, a vase by Vechte and a cup by Froment-Meurice.

Collection Thiers (40–41)

Renaissance bronzes and 18th-c. porcelain.

Galerie d'Apollon

The Gallery is situated on the first floor and entered by the Escalier Daru, the museum's main staircase. These stairs divide at the intermediate landing on which stands the *Nike of Samothrace* or *Winged Victory,* one flight leading to the Department of Painting (r.), the other to the antechamber of the Galerie d'Apollon (l.) The paintings in the dome are by Blondel, Mauzaisse, and Couder: the mosaic pavement by Belloni.

Its dimensions (length 201ft/61.39m, height 36ft/11m, breadth 31ft/9.46m) as much as its decoration make the Galerie d'Apollon one of the noblest of its kind in the world. It occupies the first floor of the Petite Galerie. It was built in the reign of Henri IV, gutted by fire in 1661, restored under Louis XIV by Lebrun, and now houses part of the Department of Objets d'Art. (decoration → Palais du Louvre).

At the entrance the iron grille was forged *ca.* 1650 for the Château de Maisons-Laffite. Collections: a mosaic table* from Richelieu's château, made in Florence in the 17th c.; carved 19th-c. pedestal Louis XIV style.

Display cases

These house the extraordinary Royal Gem Collection*** inaugurated by Louis XIV.

Case 1: agate and sardonyx, some ancient.

Case 2: Medieval gems (rock crystal, jasper).

Case 3: rock crystal from the Royal Collections, including a 10th- or 11th-c. Islamic chalice; most of the pieces were carved in North Italian workshops in the 16th c. Note a vase depicting Noah working in his vineyard (valued at 100,000 livres in 1791) and an urn depicting Judith and Susanna; a 14th-c. chessboard.

Case 4: The so-called Crown of Charlemagne, made for the coronation of Napoleon I by the jeweller Nitot, ornamented with very ancient cameos; the sword and dagger of the Grand Master of the Knights of Malta (16th c.).

Case 5: jasper, lapis lazuli, amethyst and other ornamental and semi-precious stones. Particularly noteworthy are a *Scourging of Christ** and a large *nef* or boat of lapis lazuli surmounted by a silver-gilt Neptune.

Case 6: The French Crown Jewels***, the gems exhibited being the remains of the treasure first amassed by François I, added to by his successors, partly looted during the Revolution and sold off in 1887; the most valuable items were retained. These are: the Regent diamond, a very pure gem of 137 carats, bought by the Regent in 1717 for 2,500,000 livres and valued at 12 million livres in 1791; the Côte-de-Bretagne ruby which once belonged to Marguerite de Foix and passed to the French Crown on the marriage of her daughter, Anne de Bretagne, with Charles VIII, originally weighing 200 carats, (It was reduced to 105 when Jacques Guay cut it into the shape of a dragon for Louis XIV's insignia of the Order of the Golden Fleece in the 18th c.); the Hortensia diamond, a 20-carat, five-faceted gem purchased by Louis XIV; the Le Sancy diamond, sold by the State in 1792 and bought back in 1976; the brooch-reliquary made by Alfred Bapst in 1855 for the Empress Eugénie; the diamond-studded insignia of the Order of the Saint-Esprit presented by Louis XV to his son-in-law, the Duke of Parma (*ca.* 1750: purchased 1951); the Bey of Algiers' watch; Queen Hortense's diamond and sapphire parure; a pair of bracelets in ruby and brilliants made for the Duchesse d'Angoulême in 1816: a pair of earrings belonging to the Empress Josephine; crown of the Empress Eugénie.

In the center stands a marble mosaic table made at the Gobelins around 1680, bearing the monogram of Louis XIV, the pedestal dates from 1873; another marble mosaic table from the Gobelins also *ca.* 1680, stands between the windows.

Wall cases (numbered from the far end of the gallery).

Case 1: jewels of Queen Arnegunda (*ca.* 570) discovered at Saint-Denis; items from the Treasure of the Abbey of Saint-Denis including an antique porphyry vase*** on a 12th-c. silver mount in the shape of an eagle presented by the Abbot Suger; antique sardonyx vase mounted as ewer; antique serpentine green porphyry patena with 12th-c. gold mounts; rock-crystal ewer (Egypt 10th c.).

Case 2: (further items from the Treasure of Saint-Denis): scepter (14th c.); sword (11th c.); a *main-de-justice*, a scepter terminating in a hand, (10th and 19th c.) of the kings of France; the so-called ring of St Louis (14th c.); clasp (13th or 14th c); reliquary statuette of the *Virgin and Child*** given to the Abbey of Saint-Denis in 1339 by the queen, Jeanne d'Evreux, daughter of Louis X.

Case 3: contains a selection of the most important snuff- and small boxes in the Louvre.

Case 4: ancient items from the Treasure of the Order of the Saint-Esprit**: a ciborium and pair of rock-crystal candlesticks mounted on gold (France, 16th c.); reliquary angels (Collection of Anne de Bretagne, France, 14th c.); osculatorium (pax) a cross used during Mass, (Italy, *ca.* 1500); holy-water stoup and sprinkler (Italy, early 16th c.).

Case 5: Further items from the Treasure of the Order of the Saint-Esprit*: censer; incense-boat; covered cups; bottle; a pair of basins and ewers; the silver-gilt mace (Paris, 1579-85) with the arms of Henri III, King of France and Poland.

▣ Musée des Lunettes et des Lorgnettes* (Eyeglass Museum)

2 Ave, Mozart (the optician Pierre Marly), 16th arr. Tel. 45-27-21-05.
Open Tues.–Sat. 10am-7pm.
Métro: La Muette
Bus: 22, 32, 52.

This is one of those curious Parisian museums that is a joy for both amateurs and connoisseurs. It was created by a lover of rare and unusual things and good workmanship, named Pierre Marly, a well-known optician, who set up his museum in the basement of his shop.

Tour of the museum

30 mins.

The museum consists of a series of display-cases showing about 2500 pieces selected from the 3000 owned by the collector.

Basement

You can follow the evolution of spectacles from the 13th-c. *bésicles clouantes* (held on the bridge of the nose with a finger while writing with the other hand) found in a German monastery, to the improvements brought about during the 18th c.; lattice-work fans known as *jalousies;* riding crops, canes, and fans with magnifying glasses. Notice particularly a superb cane* with a knob containing a spyglass and a lorgnette, also the gold knob decorated with Vernis-Martin, of a cane (Louis XV) concealing a telescope* by Gregori. English models are oval. Venetian spectacles* with two-toned lenses for protection from the sun (18th c.).

Large collection of glasses from the Directoire era (1795), worn by people whose exaggeratedly fashionable clothes, with wigs 3ft/1m high, were known as the Incroyables (in England called by the Italian name, Macaroni): *lorgnettes incroyables** in the shape of scissors with a handle more than 3ft/1m long. The glasses* come in all shapes: pinces-nez with blue lenses in a gilded silver frame; in silver and shell; and with lenses of rock crystal. There is a cabinet of charming romantic snuff boxes, bonbon boxes, bottles for smelling salts, fans, dance cards, all equipped with spy glasses. There is also a collection of spectacle cases ranging from plain boxwood to silver and gold, and some studded with precious stones.

The cabinet in the center contains historical or famous pieces such as the glasses belonging to Mme Victoire*, Louis XV's daughter, adorned with the *fleur de lis*; the Princesse de Lamballe's lorgnettes; the Comte d'Artois' glasses, made in London; Sarah Bernhardt's lorgnettes* (one pair of which is decorated with rubies). Also on display, from the time of Louis XVI, is a *loupe à automates*** (magnifying glass with spring handle) in gold. The collection also includes contemporary creations such as glasses belonging to Sophia Loren and to Michel Polnareff.

Ground floor

Chinese cabinet: glasses cut from rock crystal (tea stone) to ward off evil spirits. Tibetan cabinet: spectacles that belonged to a brother of a Dalai Lama. Lapp and Eskimo goggles to prevent snow-blindness, with a very narrow slit.

▷ **The history of spectacles**

Around the year 1000 an Arab scholar discovered that a half sphere of glass made letters bigger, but it was as much as three centuries later that Salvino d'Armati invented glasses for the farsighted.

These first glasses, called *bésicles clouantes* in French, had round lenses and no side pieces. During that period they were made in wood, copper, lead, iron; they were heavy and awkward, falling incessantly from the nose and, in fact, usually had to be kept in place with a finger. In the 15th c. spectacles were invented that attached to the ears with a ribbon or cord, or were hooked onto a cap. It was only in the 18th c. that short side-pieces were fixed to the spectacles; these ended in large rings often covered in velvet, and stayed in place by exerting pressure on the temples. In certain countries, such as Spain, glasses in the 18th c. were a sign of intelligence and nobility: 'the more one increases one's wealth, the more one increases the size of the glass of the spectacles to the point that certain Spanish nobles wear glasses as large as their hands.' The shapes gradually changed: by the end of the 18th c. telescopes, spy-glasses, and monocles were being used; in the 19th c. pinces-nez became fashionable for men, whereas women preferred lorgnettes or small opera glasses. The most recent invention dates back to 1888 with the advent of contact lenses.

◘ Musée de la Marine** (Maritime Museum)

West wing of the Palais de Chaillot, Place du Trocadéro, 16th arr.
Tel. 45-53-31-70.
Map ref. 13–B1
Curator: Captain François Bellec
Open daily except Tues. and public holidays 10am–6pm.
Métro: Trocadéro
Bus: 22, 30, 32, 63, 72, 82

The Musée de la Marine is situated beside the Musée de l'Homme in the W wing of the Palais de Chaillot, built for the 1937 World Fair in a Neo-Roman style, at the same time modern and monumental (for the history and architecture →Chaillot).

The museum houses a collection of models of world-famous ships, illustrating important stages in French naval history and the history of French naval dockyards since the end of the 18th c.

History of the museum

Sketches and models of ships under construction in French naval dockyards were brought to Paris in 1748 by an inspector-general of the Navy, Louis-Henri Duhamel du Monceau. These scattered flotillas, instead of being dispersed in the storm of the Revolution, came to anchor at the Louvre, which became the home port for these ships of the high seas. The Duc d'Angoulême, eldest son of Charles X, created in 1827, the first Maritime Museum, the Musée Dauphin, which suffered somewhat during the uprising in July 1830 but which, a few years later, was opened to the public.

The long-debated decision to move the museum was taken only in 1937, when the Palais de Chaillot replaced the Palais du Trocadéro.

It reopened its doors in 1943 as it now stands, and in 1971 the Musée de la Marine was given the status of a national public establishment. The renovations of 1982 allow for modern presentation, leaving the historical objects within to tell their story.

Tour of the museum

1½ hrs.

Entrance hall

Some archeological models are grouped around a large model of *L'Océan*, a first-class vessel (1810); cast of the costly nef (or bon-bon dish) from the silversmith, Jacques Coeur's, mansion in Bourges (15th c. made by himself); model of a long ship. Some of the figureheads which line the museum include: the *Poursuivante*, *La Couronne*, the *Duquesne*, the *Henri IV*, the *Amphitrite* and the decoration from the bow of a corvette from the early 19th c.

Grande galerie

From the 16th to the 17th c.
In the entrance two 17th-c. atlantes frame *The Embarkation of de Ruyter at Texel* (1 June 1667), by Eugène Isabey. Note the impressive period model of the *Louis le Grand*, model on the scale of 1:12 of a vessel with two bridges built in 1678 for training the Gardes de la Marine at Rochefort.

Some paintings illustrate episodes of maritime history. The *Departure of Henry VIII of England for the Field of the Cloth of Gold*, a 19th-c. copy after Hans Holbein; the meeting between the French squadron commanded by d'Estrées with that of the Duke of York in 1672, and Duquesne at Chios (1680) depicted in two paintings after Van Beecq; *View of Amsterdam* by Ludolf Bakhuysen (1631–1708); episode from *The Four Day Battle* (1666) by Stork. Various models of ships, including a reconstitution of *La Couronne*, the first large French warship built at La Roche-Bernard.

Terrestial globe made *ca.* 1799 by J.-B. Poirson for the study of Louis XVIII. It is surrounded by four wooden statues representing the Continents, by Victor Aimone (*ca.* 1820).

In the following section is the *Royal,* model (scale 1:12) of a second-class vessel built at Rochefort in 1720 for training purposes.

On the r. are portraits of Tourville and Marshal de Coëtlogon. The *Louis XV* is an educational toy made around 1720 for the young king. Among the models are some unrigged hulls: the *Soleil Royal,* built in 1669, which bore the ensign of Tourville on July 9, 1690 at

Bévéziers (scale model 1:40.) built at the Musée de la Marine in 1839); two vessels, one from the time of Louis XV (signed 'Pic', 1755) and the other from Louis XVI's reign.

Other models of boats fully rigged: the *Sans Pareil,* with 108 cannons, model to the scale of 1:30 (end 18th c.); the *Protecteur,* period model with 64 cannon to the scale of 1:20 (mid-18th c.); the *Dédaigneux* (1766) which took part in the American War of Independence. Two paintings of the *Battle of Texel* (June 29, 1694) and Jean Bart reclaiming a convoy of over 100 ships carrying wheat captured by the Dutch by Isabey (1803–86).

To the l., a small adjoining room is devoted to models of the world's first boats. It has a collection (19th c.) of models of primitive craft, and a kuf, a circular boat of pitch-covered rushes used on the Tigris.

The next aisle is devoted to the Mediterranean. It opens on to two rostral columns from the Château de Richelieu. Crockery from an ancient wreck, Roman anchor stocks and the model of an Egyptian boat from the Richelieu's Château. Crockery from an ancient wreck, Roman anchor stocks and the model of an Egyptian boat from the necropolis of Asyut (2200 B.C.) lead on to Venice, the Mediterranean tradition, galleys and, on the r., the Arab tradition.

A large boat lamp from a Venetian galley (17th c.) marks the center of the aisle.

Among many period models note the *Singe,* model with 24 cannon and 24 swivel guns; the *Bretonne,* ordinary galley, early 18th c.; the *Minerve;* the *Réale,* admiral's flagship (its decoration attributed to Puget). Some works of art are on show beneath an arch in the gallery, thereby making it a hall of honor. There is a bronze bust of Colbert, after a work by Coysevox, and a group of sculptures attributed to Pierre Puget (1622–94), director of the workshop for naval decoration in Toulon: 15 pieces in gilded wood, original sculptures** from the stern of the *Réale;* paneling from galleys and carriages. Audiovisual presentation.

The *Ports de France***, a series of paintings (18th c.) by Joseph Vernet, are displayed around a rare training model, the *Royal Louis,* a rare model built in 1770 to plans for a first-class vessel with 124 cannon built in 1759. The museum owns 13 of the 24 paintings of France's ports commissioned by the Court in 1752 from Vernet. Only 15 paintings were executed between 1754 and 1765; painted with painstaking topographical precision, today they are of great documentary interest.

Next, the remains of *Le Juste,* lost on November 22, 1759, the day after the battle of the Cardinals; two cannon bearing the arms of the Duc de Beaufort and the Comte de Vermandois, salvaged from a shipwreck in the Mediterranean.

The American War of Independence

This room contains the stern and the prow of Marie-Antoinette's barge from Versailles (1669). A series of paintings by Rossel and contemporary objects displayed in the cabinets evoke the American War of Independence: the *Flore*, an American armed commercial ship (*ca.* 1770); the lugger, the *Coureur*, privateer of the Channel; documents and a statuette commemorate France's role in the American War of Independence. *The Artésien*, period model (1:30) made in 1765. *The Battle of Ouessant* (July 1778) painted by Gudin.

The Revolution and the Empire

Views of the ports of Brest (1794) and Saint-Malo by Jean-François Hue complete the series by Vernet. One showcase is devoted to the Boulogne flotilla, built for Napoléon's departure for England planned in 1805. *The Bayonnaise Grappling the English frigate Ambuscade* (1798), painted by Crépin; *The Lion*, model of a vessel with 64 cannon (under construction in 1779). Two models of the *Océan,* begun in 1790, fitted in 1840, first ship to bear the tricolour flag at the battles of Prairial. Naval battles of Trafalgar, by Crépin and Auguste Mayer. Period model of the *Rivoli*, 74 cannon, constructed in Venice in 1812; *Achille,* 74 cannon, period scale model 1:33; *Triomphant,* 82 cannon; *Battle Between the Canonnière and the Tremendous* (1806), by Crépin; *Naval Combat at Grand-Port Led by Duperré,* the only one depicted on the Arc de Triomphe, painted by Gilbert. *La Foudroyante* and *Le Muiron,* ships of the Empire. Various eagles in gilded wood. In the center of the room, the Emperor's ceremonial barge (56ft/17m), built in three weeks in 1811 for Napoléon's visit to Antwerp. It was later used for Napoléon III's visit to Brest in 1858, and again for President Loubet in 1903. Scale model (scale 1:48) of the frigate *La Flore* (of the *Méduse* type); and of the *Cygne,* a period model. Memorabilia of the Prince de Joinville, displayed in a Dauphin cabinet signed by François Honoré Jacob. Scale model 1:40 of *La Belle Poule* – which carried Napoléon's body back from St Helena (1840), four cannon taken in battle at San Juan de'Ulloa (1838) and at Obligado (1845).

The Restoration

Scale model (1:40) of the last large sailing ships; launched 12 years after construction began in the shipyard, they were out-moded after the lessons of the Crimean War (1854–55): the *Hercule, Algésiras, Tage* and *Valmy* (modelled in silver, ebony and ivory), and from the naval school at Brest harbor (1863–90) the *Borda, Alceste,* and *Neptune.* Representations of naval operations in Algeria (1830), by Théodore Gudin; *Evening of the Battle at Navarin* (October 20,

1827), by A. Meyer; view of Mers-el-Kebir; *The Bombardment of Mogador (August 15, 1844) by the Prince de Joinville's squadron,* painted by Durand Brayer.

From the Second Empire to the end of 19th c.

View of Brest Port (1854); *Queen Victoria Visiting Cherbourg* (1858) by Morel-Fation, curator of the Musée de la Marine from 1852 to 1871. Scale models (1:33) of the frigate *Audacieuse,* of composite construction with propellor; armoured frigates, *Gloire, Solférino,* built according to Dupuy de Lôme's plans; scale models (1:25) of the *Bouvet* (1866). One of the showcases contains a collection of memorabilia from Dupuy de Lôme, Barbotin, Admiral Hamelin; the Imperial Prince's toy cannon; case of monitors and armored coastguard ships.

On display are three busts* by Carpeaux: Vice-Admiral Bergasse, Petit-Thouars, and Admiral Tréhouart, who distinguished himself at Navarin in 1827 and won the battle of Obligado on the River Plate in 1845; a sculpture by Hirou representing Admiral Courbet, famous for his campaigns in Tonkin and China, 'model expeditions wisely and bravely led'. Paintings showing a sailor's life: *Queen Victoria Visiting the French Fleet* by Isabey (1844); the *French Squadron in Cherbourg in 1863,* by T. Gudin, and various scenes aboard large vessels by Léon Couturier, Le Blant, P. Jazet. One case contains mementoes of Duboc, Rivière and Courbet and is devoted to the events which marked French intervention in the Far East at the end of the 19th c. The bronze gun-muzzle representing a dragon comes from a gun that armed the citadel of Chaudoc and was retrieved by La Grandière. A diorama represents the uprooting of the Louqsor obelisk and its journey to Luxor (August 14, 1831 to April 1, 1833). Mementoes of Ferdinand de Lesseps and the building of the Suez Canal are arranged in cabinets and on picture rails; model of the *Aigle;* section devoted to the explorer Charcot, with paintings of the *Pourquoi-Pas* among the ice floes where he died (1936); the colonizer Savorgnan de Brazza and the sailor and novelist Farrère, called Claude (d.1957). Some great ships were launched at the end of the 19th c.; the cruiser *Sfax,* scale model 1:60 (1882); the battleship *Hoche* (1886); the battleship *Redoutable* which had an exceptionally long career (1878–1910): in 1904 this ship was rebuilt and its sail, and the wood used in its construction, removed.

World Wars I and II: Salle d'About

This room houses a collection of contemporary fleet warships. The *Surcouf,* the largest submarine of the inter-war period (1929–42); ships of today: aircraft carriers *Foch, Clemenceau;* helicopter carrier *Jeanne d'Arc* (formerly the *Résolue);* the frigate *Tourville;*

the corvette *Aconit;* the sloop of *Estienne d'Orves;* model of the *Redoubtable,* a missile-launching nuclear submarine, and the *Rubis,* a nuclear attack submarine. French presence in Indochina, 1945 to 1954. Works by the official marine painters: Paguenaud, Chapelet, Brenet, Delpech, Rigaud, Hauterives.

Collection of optical instruments used by Fresnel in his experiments, and of ship's optics themes.

Side gallery, Trocadéro garden side

This reconverted gallery, which runs from the Salle d'About toward the entrance hall, presents various technical, scientific, and traditional maritime themes.

Underwater exploration. A collection of diving suits: that of Denayroux, used around 1880; those of the Carmagnole brothers, with *coquilles articulées* (jointed shells like metal rhinoceros skin), 1882; rigid suits, such as the *'Neufeldt Kuhnke'* used for greater depths (394ft/120m), made in Kiel around 1940; the Autonome, for very great depths (1,312ft/400m); a diving suit of the *Spirotechnique;* aqualungs. The FNRS III bathyscaphs scale model 1:20, which reached depths of 13,288ft/4050m in 1954, already out of date in 1963, and the *Archimède,* which in 1961 dived to 30,317ft/9545m in the deeps of the Kouriles. The *Triton* and *Térebel,* ships for underwater training and experimentation.

Fishing. Cases displaying different types of boats and rigging. Models of Newfoundland fishing-boats, whalers, and tuna boats. A harpoon rigged on the bow of a boat. Audiovisual presentation.

Sea rescue. Models of ships used by the National Society for Sea Rescue and related items. The shipwreck of the *Sémillante. The Burning of the Kent* by Gudin.

Tour of a workshop for restoring models. Pleasure cruising; lighthouses; the principles of naval propulsion; demonstration model of the *Jouffroy d'Abbans* steamship, made to show the Académie des Sciences the reality of the steamship *Pyroscaphe's* successful attempts to navigate the Rhône upstream to Lyons on July 15, 1783; model of the *Sphinx;* a 160-h.p. steamship and the first steam vessel of the French military fleet. Opposite, the paddle-wheel mechanism of this ship.

Commercial vessels; maritime commerce. One cabinet displays a large collection of cargo boats and liners, a mixture of ships dating from 1850 to the present. A collection of engravings, sections of hulls, and hulls: *Normandie* and *France.* Presentation of some commercial objects; porcelain from the Compagnie des Indes; a plate with squirrel motif from Fouquet's service. The Deschima and Nagaski trading posts. A map of the Canton region and models of junks; *Bombarde* (1816); 18th-c. documents on maritime commerce;

three Dutch masts; slave-trading brig; tankers; four masts from the barque *La Gloire.*

Wooden boats. The concept and building of these ships is illustrated: the woods used in shipbuilding; diorama showing the setting of a shipbuilding yard; the *Juste* on its launching slipway; models of bows and sterns; sections of boats; ships under construction on cradles and in dock; tools, models of port machinery and naval dockyard. In the adjoining room, an exhibition of ship's ornaments; engravings and sculptures. Diorama of the careening of the *Artémise;* frigate with 22 cannon. Audiovisual presentation.

Lapérouse's voyage. Illustrated in showcases is the tragic expedition of Lapérouse, commander of the sloop *The Astrolabe,* and of Fleuriot de Langle, commander of *La Boussole.* The story of their shipwreck and massacre at Vanikoro in 1788 is told by the pieces of wreckage brought back many years later by Peter Dillon, Dumont d'Urville (1790–1842) and by contemporary and recent contributions (1962–85).

Navigational instruments. Methods of dead-reckoning and astro-navigation are explained; marine charts; navispheres for identifying stars after measuring their height by sextant; measurement of angles at sea; the devices used to observe the height of the sun, the stars, or the planets: astrolabes from the 15th to 18th c., Davis' back staff (1594), octants and sextants, angled compasses and compasses; logs, gyrocompasses; cartography and geometric devices: graphometers, reflection circles, theodolites. The visit ends with an exhibition of astronomical instruments: planetaries, meridian circles, telescopes. In the side room: portulans, longitude, and weather gauge; modern quartz copy of the longitudinal watch no. 65 belonging to F. Berthoud (1817).

Temporary exhibitions hall. The last section of this gallery is reserved for temporary exhibitions which are announced in the Parisian entertainments-and-events guide and in daily papers. A second room in the basement is kept free for extra exhibitions and for the biennial Marine Shows.

▷ Ancient ships

The king's vessels constituted the nucleus of the fighting fleets, some of them also being used for long-haul commercial voyages. They were classified according to their size: in 1716, a first-class vessel of the first rank would carry 80 cannon, whereas fourth-class would carry only 40. The fleet was completed by heavy boats with oars, called galleys; the largest of these, sumptuously decorated, were called *réales.* These were difficult to maneuver and were abandoned in the 18th c. in favor of brigs, which were lighter in tonnage and had many sails. The slender, streamlined frigates were used as scouts while cutters, small ships with only one mast, were responsible for the liaison between the ports and the squadrons and also for keeping watch on the shores.

In general, pirates sailed on xebecs, very fast and maneuverable boats, and effective for pillaging commercial boats. Toward the end of the 18th c. they used luggers, English smuggling boats.

Schooners appeared in the United States around 1780; they were fast yachts rigged with several masts (the largest yacht had seven masts). Some are still used today for pleasure cruises.

Musée Marmottan**

2 Rue Louis-Boilly, 16th arr. Tel: 42–24–07–02.
Curator: Arnaud de'Hauterives
Open: Tues.–Sun. 10am–5:30pm
Métro: La Muette
Bus: 32, 63, PC

This museum, situated opposite the Jardin du Ranelagh, is famous for its collections of Empire style furniture and for its collection of Impressionist paintings, which ranks second only to the Musée d'Orsay.

History of the museum

Created in 1934 this museum is housed in a beautiful 19th-century mansion, which was bequeathed together with the collections it already contained, to the Institut de France by Paul Marmottan (1856–1932), an art historian and collector. A devotee of the Napoleon era, he built up an exceptional collection of paintings, furniture, and *objets d'art* illustrating the style of the First Empire, which he, Marmottan, had been among the first to discover. There is also a small section devoted to Flemish and Italian Primitive paintings that had been collected by his father, Jules Marmottan (1829–83). Subsequently, the Donop de Monchy donation to the museum, including seven paintings by Claude Monet, and the very important legacy from Michel Monet (the painter's youngest son) changed the initial vocation of the museum, which has now become a mecca of Impressionism in Paris.

Tour of the museum

45 mins.

Ground Floor

The tapestries. The large gallery on the ground floor is decorated with magnificent tapestries, including *La Chaste Suzanne***

(*Susanna and the Elders*), a series woven in Burgundy for Benigne de Cirey (16th c.)

The Empire collections. This suite of rooms has been used to show to advantage the splendid Empire furniture. In the first room are two objects of great value: Prince Lucien Bonaparte's *Surtout de table* (table centrepiece), sculpted in bronze and gilded by Thomire (approximately 1803); and a 'geographic' clock commissioned by the Emperor, a most remarkable example of Sèvres manufacture. In the grand salon is a collection of very fine pieces: a monumental desk in carved mahogany signed by P. A. Bellangé; drawing-room furniture* stamped Jacob; and a beautiful portrait of Desirée Clary** by Baron Gérard. In the following rooms there is much evidence of the Egyptian Campaign's influence on decoration and furniture: firedogs in chiselled bronze and the legs of console table modelled in the forms of Egyptian women. The entrance hall is decorated with sculptures: marble busts of Napoléon's wives, Josephine and Marie-Louise by Bosio.

Basement and ground floor

The Impressionist works are housed in the basement of the museum and on the first floor when the latter is not being used for temporary exhibitions.

Claude Monet. Some of Claude Monet's most famous paintings are in this collection: *Le Pont de l'Europe à la Gare Saint-Lazare*** (1877), a work from the *Rouen Cathedrals*** series (1894) and the view of *Parliament*** (1905). Apparent in these three works is Monet's tireless effort to convey the transience of objects under the effect of smoke, sun, or the reflection of water on stone. Another of the great treasures of this collection are the works less known to the public from the artist's own collection: a series of caricatures of theater personalities; a dazzling *Suite des Nymphéas*** (*Water Lilies*) as well as the *views** of Giverny, where the artist lived. Monet's personal collection also includes works by Caillebotte, Pissarro*, Berthe Morisot*, Jongkind, Boudin, and especially Renoir, whose works on display include *Claude Monet Reading*** and *Madame Claude Monet***, both dated 1872.

The Primitives. Added to the initial collection of works by Rogier van der Weyden and Martin Schongauer is the extraordinary Wildenstein donation of medieval illuminations, representative of various 13th- and 14th-c. European schools.

▣ Musée des Materiaux (Research Center of Historic Monuments)

9 Ave. Albert-de-Mun (entrance through the Musée des Monuments Français), 16th arr. Tel: 47-27-84-64. Map ref: 13-B1

Open Mon.–Fri. noon–6pm
(appointments by telephone preferred)
Métro: Trocadéro
Bus: 22, 30, 32, 63

Tour of the museum

30 mins.

Because the museum was specially designed as a documentation center it unites architectural elements used in several old buildings: tiles, bricks, ornamental tiling, tools, cut stone, parts of locks. It also has a series of models depicting the evolution of Romanesque and Gothic buildings and a large collection of drawings of which a section is devoted to Viollet-le-Duc*. There is also a department of geology which analyses building materials and lists the stone quarries in use today.

▣ Cabinet des Médailles et des Antiques**

(Medals and Antiques Gallery)
58 Rue de Richelieu, 2nd arr. Tel: 47-03-81-26. Map ref. 10–D3, 11–A3
Open daily 1–5pm
Numismatic documentation center open Mon.–Sat. 9am–5pm.
Métro: Bourse, Palais-Royal
Bus: 21, 27, 29, 39, 48

The collection of the Kings of France is the nucleus of this museum, which houses a rare display of coins and medals, from antiquity to the present, jewels, gold and silver plate, Greek vases and Roman bronzes.

History of the museum

The royal collection, begun in the time of Philippe Auguste, originally comprised jewels, medals, and precious curios. Pillaged several times, the Cabinet de Médailles began to take shape only under François I and Henri IV. Louis XIV enriched it substantially with the collection of his uncle, Gaston d'Orléans. This was followed by the collections of scholars such as Caylus, by the treasures of Saint-Denis and the Sainte-Chapelle expropriated during the Revolution, and other fine collections, such as that of the Duc de Luynes in 1862, famous for its Greek vases and coins. The Cabinet was kept in the Louvre, then in the Rue Vivienne, but Louis XIV, who liked to have his collection where he could see it, removed it to Versailles.

Known under Louis XV as the finest collection of antiques in Europe, it was returned to the capital in 1741 and, during the

Revolution, became the property of the State. Installed since 1917 in a wing of the Bibliothèque Nationale, the Cabinet de Médailles has its own library, a documentation center, and exhibition rooms.

Tour of the museum

45 mins.

Ground floor

The 1st room is devoted to Classical Antiquity and its first showcases to Gaul. These contain gold coins and jewels (4th–1st c. B.C.). Gold *parisis** found at Levallois in 1954 and, most notably, the Berthouville Treasure***, an exceptional collection of Gallo-Roman silverware (1st–2nd c. AD), discovered in 1830 that probably belonged to a temple dedicated to Mercury: vials with the effigy of the god, ewers decorated with scenes of the Trojan Wars. The following case contains a few Greek and Roman jewels, among which are some beautiful cameos. Much admired in Antiquity, these cameos are delicate stones, engraved to take advantage of their different colors, a technique used to perfection by Greek and Roman artists. The Sainte-Chapelle cameo***, the largest Classical cameo, carved in sardonyx with five colors, shows the Emperor Tiberius receiving Germanicus, his adopted son; on the upper part Germanicus is shown with the gods. The *Ptolemy Cup****, a Hellenistic work in sardonyx decorated with bacchanalian scenes, once belonged to the Abbey of Saint-Denis. Next comes a collection of Greek and Etruscan jewels** (7th–3rd c. B.C.), and of Greek vases, including the amphora of the famous painter Amasis, depicting Dionysus and Athena (540 B.C.)

The 2nd room houses the Near and East Asian antiquities. In the center of the room are rare Persian objects of the Sassanid period (5th–8th c.): the goblet***, in rock crystal, set with gold and decorated with garnets, whose central medallion depicts the triumph of Khrosu, the famous Persian warrior-king. Splendid pieces of silver chased with gold, decorated with animal scenes. Another case presents a series of Chinese and Vietnamese coins*; the sword of the Moorish King Boabdil**, a true masterpiece; the cameo of Shah Jehan**, on which the Mogol emperor is seen slaying a lion (17th c.).

First floor

The 3rd room brings together the medieval and Renaissance exhibits. In the center, the Childeric Treasure** (5th c.; belonging to the father of Clovis), among the oldest treasures of the French monarchy, found in a tomb in the 17th c.; coins, arms, gold jewelry encrusted with garnets. Dagobert's Throne*: a Merovingian work altered in the Middle Ages, its last official function goes back to Napoléon, who used it for the first award ceremony for the Legion of Honor. German and Italian medals (14th–16th c.), including a series by Pisanello*.

The 4th room evokes Europe from the beginning of the modern era to the present, and brings together Renaissance jewelry, royal medals and tokens, and foreign and commemorative medals. It also contains fine furniture: a medal cabinet** made by Cressent for the son of the Regent (18th c,); the collector Joseph Pellerin's lacquered cupboard (18th c.).

Not to be missed

Ground floor
Room I: the Berthouville Treasure, Gallo-Roman silver; antique cameos: the Sainte-Chapelle cameo, the Goblet of the Ptolomies.

Room 2: the Sassanid antiquities: precious objects and precious metalwork.

First floor
Room 3: Childeric's Treasure (5th c.); Dagobert's Throne.

▣ Musée Adam Mickiewicz

6 Quai d'Orléans, 4th arr. Tel: 43–54–35–61. Map ref. 18–C3
Open Oct.–June Thurs., 2–6pm; July-Aug. Tues. and Thurs. 3–6pm;
closed 15 days at Christmas and Easter
Métro: Pont-Marie
Bus: 24, 63, 67

The Musée Mickiewicz has been arranged within the Polish Library in Paris and was founded in 1903 by Ladislas Mickiewicz, eldest son of the poet and patriot Adam Mickiewicz (1798-1855). The latter was a major force in Polish cultural and political life. His writings introduced Romanticism to Polish literature; he strove constantly to heighten patriotic sentiment, and much of his writing was devoted to Poles oppressed at home or in exile. Mickiewicz was Professor of Slavonic Literature at the Collège de France from 1841 to 1844.

Tour of the museum

45 mins.

First floor

Items relating to Frederic Chopin are displayed here, including musical and other autographs; his death mask by Clésinger, etc.

Second Floor

The museum contains autographs (including those of Michelet, Quinet, George Sand, Vigny and Hugo), portraits, memorabilia and extensive documentation of the Romantic period and in particular of Adam Mickiewicz, his family and his friends. Among the exhibits are such important items as the bust of Adam Mickiewicz by David d'Angers (1835) and medallions by that sculptor; Antoine Bourdelle's first sketch for the head of the poet's statue in the Cours Albert-I[er]; an appeal by Victor Hugo dated from Hauteville House May 17, 1867 expressing his admiration for Adam Mickiewicz; a pastel portrait of the museum's founder by Stanislas Wyspianski (1904); the medallion portraying Michelet, Quinet, and Mickiewicz by Borel (1845); the autograph of a poem by Goethe, dedicated to the famous Polish musician Marie Szymanowska, after their meeting at Marienbad in 1823.

▣ Musée de Mineralogie*

*Ecole des Mines, 60 Boul. Saint-Michel, 6th arr. Tel: 42–34–91–00.
Map ref. 17–A3
Curator: M. Guillemin
Open Wed.–Fri. 2–5pm, Tues. and Sat. 10am–12.30pm/2–5pm
Métro: Luxembourg, Saint-Michel
Bus: 21, 27, 38, 82, 84, 85, 89*

Tour of the museum

1 hr.

The Musée de Minéralogie is housed on the first floor of the Ecole Nationale Supérieure des Mines.

This mineralogical and geological museum houses the French national reference collection of utilizable minerals, a collection of large-scale mineral specimens and meteorites, a collection of synthetic minerals and the Adam and Delessert Collections.

The library (closed to the public) contains some 150,000 volumes.

▣ Collection des Minéraux de Jussieu* (Mineralogical Museum)

*(Collection de l'Université P. et M. Curie)
4 Place Jussieu, Tower 25, ground floor level (1st basement).
Tel: 43–36–25–25. Map ref. 24–C1
Open Wed., Sat. 2–6pm; Groups by telephone appointment.
Métro: Jussieu*

Bus: 67, 89, 91

Tour of the museum

2 hrs.

Located in the basement of the university, this small museum surprises the visitor by the beauty of the minerals, which are advantageously displayed along the lines of the Teheran Jewel Room and lit so as to avoid the destructive effects of light.

In 1809 the Faculty of Sciences created a mineral collection and this has been handed down and expanded by such important acquisitions as the Vésigné Collection (1953) and by discoveries made by scientific expeditions.

The museum exhibits 700 different species of minerals including rare specimens of uranium (case 15), quartz (case (16), silicates from Zaire (case 18), and fabulous azurites and malachites from Katanga weighing over 220lb. (100kg) in case 12.

Musée de la Mode

→*Musée des Arts de la Mode*

▣ Musée de la Mode et du Costume*

Palais Galliera, 10 Ave. Pierre-Iᵉʳ-de-Serbie, 16th arr. Tel: 47–20–85–23. Map ref. 8–C3
Curator: Mme C. Jovin-Dieterle
Open during exhibitions only Tues.–Sun. 10am–5:40pm.
Library and Print Room: open by appointment Tues–Sun. 9am–1pm.
Métro: Alma-Marceau, Iéna
Bus: 32, 63, 82, 92

Devoted to fashion and costume from the 18th c. to the present day, the museum is housed in a building originally designed for the collection of 17th-c. Italian pictures that the Duchessa Maria de Ferrari Galliera subsequently bequeathed to the city of Genoa. The Duchess was anxious that the style of the building should match that of the paintings and insisted that the architect, Louis Ginan, take the Italian Renaissance as his inspiration. The building was completed in 1892 and is a perfect example of the way in which the late 19th c. absorbed different styles, with its graceful stone peristyle, its cupolas decorated with ornamental painting, their metal framework – which is in any case rather fine – camouflaged by decorations of foliage.

Finally the Duchessa de Galliera left Paris an empty palace which was to house successively collections of decorative art, exhibitions of contemporary painting and, since 1977, the Musée de la Mode et du Costume (Museum of Costume and Fashion).

History of the collections

These collections, from the costume section of the Musée Carnavalet, comprise over 10,000 outfits from diverse donations, must importantly from one made in 1920 by the Société de l'Histoire du Costume founded by Maurice Leloir. Since 1956 the museum's holdings have been continually augmented by such splendid contributions as those from Mme Edmond de Galea, the Comtesse Greffulhe, the Princesse Murat, Anna Gould, the Comtesse de Castellane and, more recently, by the donations of Lady Deterding, the Baronne Guy de Rothschild, and Princess Grace of Monaco.

Among the most complete and most interesting sets of clothes are the haute couture collections of Lanvin, Balenciaga, Balmain and Worth, the Englishman who was the first couturier in Paris; contemporary ready-to-wear clothes, civil service uniforms, dolls in costume, and collections of lingerie and fans.

Tour of the museum

45 mins.

Lack of space as well as the need to conserve fragile fabrics means that items are displayed in rotation during two or three annual exhibitions which may either trace the progress of a major couturier (Schiaparelli, Castillo, Balmain, Poiret) or be based upon a specific historical theme (such as prints in fashion from the 18th c. to the present; Fashion and Literature; or Fans, Mirrors of the *Belle Epoque*). The expensive materials and the elegance of their design make these dresses and fashion accessories objects of genuine beauty. They are also very special witnesses of the age in which they were made. Because the museum is so conscious of the sociological interest of its collections it provides (by telephone appointment) educational facilities staffed by lecturers and backed by a specialist library and a print room housing fashion prints and photographs.

Musée de la Monnaie*

Hôtel de la Monnaie, 11 Quai de Conti, 6th arr. Tel: 40-46-55-26.
Map ref. 16–D2
Curator: M. Jean Belaubre
Open Tues.-Sun. 1–6pm. Wed. 9pm. Closed on public holidays.
Métro: Pont-Neuf, Odéon, Saint-Michel
Bus: 24, 27, 58, 70

The Musée de la Monnaie is housed in the luxurious setting of the Hôtel de la Monnaie (the Mint), erected between 1771 and 1777 by D.-J. Antoine and where the minting and rolling presses operated until 1973. Founded by Charles X in 1827, it offers a notable collection of coins, medals and dies from the Renaissance to the present day, presented always in their social, political, economic, and cultural context.

As its subtitle, History of a People, indicates, the primary aim of the museum is to tell in a lively way of the relationship between Frenchmen and money, the practical instrument of daily life and economic development. The history is shown also of medals, privileged vehicles of propaganda as well as being art objects. The story is richly illustrated with paintings, engravings, stained-glass windows, and sculptures. The tour ends with a production cycle with machines of end-19th c. early-20th c.

▣ Historial de Montmartre (War Museum)

11 Rue Poulbot, 18th arr. Tel: 46-06-78-92. Map ref. 5-A1
Curator: M. Patrick Piquemal
Open Mon.-Sat. 10.30-12.30; 2.30-6pm; Sat. 11am-6pm.
Métro: Lamarck-Caulaincourt
Bus: 30, 54

The exhibits in this little museum, on the heights of Montmartre with the broad sweep of Paris lying below, its skyscrapers piercing the haze, are set out in cellars far below the ground and commemorate important events in the history of the Commune of Montmartre. Although the architectural reconstructions are the work of the Compagnons du Devoir, much of the furniture is genuinely period and has historic associations, such as a desk that belonged to Lafayette.

Tour of the museum

Guided tour 25 mins.

A succession of dioramas with life-size figures recreates the story of the hill of Montmartre from the martyrdom of St Denis and the foundation of the Society of Jesus by Ignatius of Loyola to the Bateau-Lavoir, including Henri IV's famous remark 'Paris is worth a Mass!' uttered as he stood and gazed over the superb scene spread out at his feet, and the loves of the young Louis XIV.

Other historic moments represented include the Mayor of Montmartre supported by Danton and Lafayette in his refusal to allow Bailly, Mayor of Paris, to absorb the Commune into the city; the gatherings in Berlioz's rooms in the district of such famous Romantics as Chopin, Delacroix, Liszt, and George Sand; Paris besieged in 1814 by the Allies and in 1870 by the Prussians; Victor Hugo looking on while Gambetta prepares to escape to join the Army of the Loire; the most famous mayor of Montmartre, Clemenceau, with Louise Michel and Jean-Baptiste Clément, composer of the charming song, 'Le Temps des Cerises' ('Cherry-time'); reconstructions of such famous cabarets as Le Chat Noir, with Jane Avril and Toulouse-Lautrec, and Le Lapin Agile, with Frédé, Mac Orlan, and Dorgèlés. There is a new diorama depicting Le Cabinet du Néant, a cabaret in the Boul. Clichy from 1892 to 1975, where you drank at tables shaped like coffin lids, while the light fixtures were made of 'genuine' human bones. The museum is next door to an art school which may also be visited.

▣ Musée de Montmartre*

12 Rue Cortot, 18th arr. Tel: 46–06–61–11. Map ref. 5–A1
Curator: Claude Charpentier
Open Mon. and Wed.–Sat. 2:30–5:30pm, Sun. 11am–5:30pm
Métro: Lamarck-Caulaincourt
Bus: 80

Standing in a terraced garden which drops down to the Rue Saint-Vincent, the Musée de Montmartre has the peaceful atmosphere of a middle-class home. It tells the eventful story of the hilltop from the days of the abbesses of Montmartre to the present, including those of the art students and café singers right up to the dawn of modern art with Picasso, Gris, and Braque. This big white house, a real gentleman's residence, is undoubtedly the finest in Montmartre and belonged, 300 years ago, to Claude de la Rose (Rosimond), an actor in Molière's Illustre-Théâtre and his successor, who died, like the great playwright, during a performance of *Le Malade Imaginaire*.

The house belongs to the City of Paris and the museum, which Paul Yaki created in 1960, is the property of the Société d'Histoire et d'Archéologie du Vieux-Montmartre, founded in 1886.

Tour of the museum

30 mins.

Archives and a substantial iconography retrace the history of Montmartre. Exhibits include Paul Delmet's piano, and reconstructions of the Café de l'Abreuvoir, where Utrillo was undoubtedly the most regular customer, and of the workroom of Gustave Charpentier (1860–1956), composer of the opera *Louise*. There are mementoes of Aristide Bruant, who wrote *Les Escaliers de la Butte*, and photographs of its café singers – Noël-Noël, Jean Rieux, Raymond Souplex, Jean Rigaux, and Dorin – as well as of Pagnol and Malraux. A small room is devoted to Emile Bernard of the Pont-

Aven group, who lived in the house for 10 years. There are drawings and caricatures by that observer of everyday life in Montmartre, Steinlen (1859–1923); an extensive collection of posters of Yvette Cuilbert, Dranem, and Félix Mayol; a poster designed by Steinlen for Le Chat Noir and mementoes of Poulbot and Willette. In the Louise-Michel Room there are mementoes of Georges Clemenceau dating from 1870 when he was mayor of Montmartre.

Note the collection of porcelain from the Clignancourt pottery founded in 1870 by the Comte de Provence. There is also a model of the district as it was in 1956.

Occasional exhibitions are mounted centered upon painters and writers (Foukita, Marcel Aymé) who lived on the hilltop.

▣ Musée des Monuments Français** (Museum of French Monuments)

E Wing of the Palais de Chaillot, Place du Trocadéro, 16th arr. Tel: 47–27–35–74. Map ref: 13–B1

Curator: M. Philippe Chapu
Open daily except Tues., 9am–6pm
Métro: Trocadéro
Bus 22, 32, 63

Set up through the efforts of Viollet-le-Duc in 1879, this museum was opened to the public in 1882 in the former Palais du Trocadéro as the Musée de Sculpture Comparée (Museum of Comparative Sculpture). When the Palais du Trocadéro was converted, becoming the Palais de Chaillot in 1937, the museum was completely renovated (for the architect →Chaillot).

Devoted to French monumental art, the collection consists mainly of casts for sculptures and reproductions of mural paintings, through which the visitor is able to follow the whole evolution of monumental sculpture and statuary from the Romanesque period to the 19th c.

Tour of the museum

1½ hrs.

Sculpture section

The chronological evolution of sculpture shown in both galleries simultaneously; the route laid out below passes alternately from one to the other entrance hall.

Ground floor galleries

Gallery 1, Pre-Romanesque period (on the r. in the r.-hand gallery)

Casts of Merovingian and Carolingian works decorated with imported ornamental elements, the oldest dating from the 7th c. Note a sarcophagus from Moissac; tomb of St Leonian in Vienne (Isère); sarcophagi from Jouarra Abbey (Seine-et-Marne); panels from the chancel of the Church of Saint-Pierre in the stronghold of Metz; Carolingian interlacing motifs: pillar from Falvigny (Côte-d'Or); altars from Saint-Polycarpe (Aude); Crucifixion from Saint-Mexme at Chinon (Indre-et-Loire); sarcophagus from Bourg-Saint-Andéol (Ardèche); from the 11th c. there is a lintel from Saint-Genis-des-Fontaines (Pyrénées-Orientales, 1019–20).

Galleries 2 to 6, Romanesque period

It was not until the 12th c. that regional sculpture workshops appeared, distinguishable by the quality of the stone they used, the temperament and skill of the artists and the models they copied: antique or Franco-Roman sculptures, pieces in ivory or gold, miniatures, embroidered cloths from Asia.

Languedoc workshops: these began to develop from the end of the 11th c., the two centers being Toulouse and Moissac: altarpiece from the high altar of Saint-Sernin, Toulouse, signed Bernard Gilduin (ca. 1096); three bas-reliefs from the same church and bas-reliefs from the cloisters of the Abbey of Moissac. The sculpture developed with decorations on tympani, great iconographic ensembles, and ornamental elements on buttresses: Miègeville door from Saint-Sernin, Toulouse; portal from the Abbey church of Saint-Pierre, Moissac (ca. 1115–30), portal from Carennac; tympanum from the portal of the Church of Saint-Foy de Conques which still has traces of the original polychrome.

Bourgogne workshops: capitals from the former Abbey church of Cluny; tympanum from the W portal of the cathedral of Saint-Lazare, Autun, signed Gislebertus, and capitals from the nave of the same cathedral; magnificent figure of Eve picking the forbidden fruit; fragment from the lintel of a side door; portal from the narthex of the Church of the Magdalen in Vézelay; portal of the Church of Saint-Lazare, Avallon; portal from the ancient Priory of Charlieu; portal from the Church of Monceaux-l'Etoile; capital from the Church of Plaimpied; tympanum from the Church of Neuilly-en-Donjon.

Western workshops: this decorative sculpture is seen above the arches of portals which have no tympani, around windows and on outside walls; the great iconographic ensembles of the preceding schools are no longer evident: portal from the Church of Saint-

Marie-des-Dames des Saintes; portal of the church of Saint-Pierre, Aulnay; lintel from Angoulême Cathedral; gryphon from Angoulême; small tympanum from the portal of Saint-Michel-d'Entraigues (Charente); cornerstone from the nave of Bayeux Cathedral with a decorative motif inspired by Far Eastern art.

Auvergne workshops: this sculpture is found inside churches, on capitals of imported limestone, which is easier to work than the local stone, granite or arkose: capitals from Notre-Dame du Port, Clermont-Ferrand, from the Church of Saint-Nectaire, and from the church of Mozat. Apparition of the Virgin in Majesty, carved in wood: examples from Notre-Dame, Mont Cornadore, and Saint-Nectaire.

Provence workshops: this sculpture began to develop only in the last third of the 12th-c. and took its inspiration from the antique monuments left in the area by the Romans: façades from the Church of Saint-Gilles and Saint-Trophime, Arles. In this room a map shows the routes taken by pilgrims to Santiago de Compostela in Spain, which had a great influence on Romanesque art.

Gallery 7, Art of the Crusades

Models of castles built by the Crusaders in the Holy Land in the 12th and 13th c.; Château de Saône, Crac des Chevaliers; sculptures executed in the Holy Land by French artists in the same period, notably the capitals of the basilica of Nazareth; inscriptions, tombstones, photographs, plans and maps showing the French settlements in Syria and Palestine in the 12th and 13th c.

Galley 8, Gothic art in the 12th century

The artists of the Ile-de-France, seeking their inspiration in nature, created a new style, inappropriately called Gothic, which began to appear in Saint-Denis from 1140 onward: central door of the royal portal of Chartres Cathedral; column-figures from the Church of Saint-Loup-de-Naud, from Notre-Dame, Corbeil and from Notre-Dame, Senlis, Virgin in Majesty from the portal of Saint-Anne-de-Notre-Dame, Paris, executed around 1165; lintel from the great portal of Senlis Cathedral (the casts from Senlis were taken before restoration).

Galleries 9 to 13, sculpture in the 13th century

This sculpture is seen at its best on the portals of the great cathedrals, on which the evolution of style and technique can be followed as it became more graceful and lifelike in its interpretation of nature.

Chartres: tympanum and statues of the Confessors from the S façade (1205–30); statues of St Theodore; statues from the N façade (about 1230); four bas-reliefs from the ancient rood screen (1240–50). **Paris**: tympanum from the Portal of the Virgin (1210–20); S portal, scenes from the life of St Etienne and from the life of novices (1258–70); the so-called 'Virgin of the Door to the Cloister' (ca. 1255–60); two tablets show the dates of various building projects. **Amiens** (1225–35): Christ conferring blessings from the central portal, the so-called 'Beau Dieu'; Virgin from the S portal, the so-called Golden Virgin (ca. 1280), and the lintel with the Apostles; the tombs of Evrard de Fouilloy (d. 1222) and Gaudefroy d'Eu (d. 1236). **Rheims**: the Smiling Angel, cast from the original before 1914; group of the Visitation, notable for its attention to the flowing drapery inspired by antiquity; groups from the back of the W façade.

Strasbourg: pillar with Angels; the Synagogue; tympanum from the S façade: the Dormition of the Virgin; two Wise Virgins; the Tempter and a Mad Virgin (late 13th c.). **Rouen**: portal with St John (mid–13th c.). **Bourges**: part of the tympanum from the central portal of the W façade: the Last Judgement. Tympanum from the W portal from Saint-Urbain of Troyes; bas-reliefs from the ancient rood screen of the church of Bourget-du-Lac; funerary statues from the Abbey of Fontevrault and the Abbey of Saint-Denis; tomb in the form of a reliquary, of the bishop St Etienne at Aubazine; ornament from the House of the Musicians at Rheims; three statues from the tomb of Isabella of Aragon, Queen of France, who was the wife of Philip III the Bold, and died in 1271 at Cosenza (Cosenza Cathedral in Calabria; French art, ca. 1275).

Gallery 14, 14th-century sculpture

The great religious compositions came to an end, and artists carved bas-reliefs and statues that were usually placed inside the churches: sculptures from the base of the portals of the Church of Saint-Etienne, Auxerre; bas-reliefs from the apse and choir screen of Notre-Dame, Paris; statues from the Collegiate Church of Ecouis; Virgin from Magny-en-Vexin (c 1340). During this period the art of portraiture developed: statue of St Louis, King of France, from the Church of Mainneville (Eure), which has kept its original polychrome (statue made from a portrait of the king painted in his lifetime); mask from the funerary statue of Philippe III the Bold, taken from a cast made immediately after his death (1285); funerary statues of Bishop Guillaume de Chanac (from the old Church of Saint-Victor, Paris), Bishop Bernard Brun (Limoges Cathedral), and Charles V at Saint-Denis (by André Beauneveu, from Valenciennes, 1364); statues from the N tower of Amiens Cathedral; funerary statue of the High Constable of France, Bertrand Du Guesclin, by Thomas Prive and Robert Loisel; statues from the great hall of the Palais de Justice (Law Courts) at Poitiers.

Gallery 15

Workshops of the dukes of Burgundy at the Carthusian Monastery of Champmol, first under the direction of Jean de Marville (1383–89), then of Claus Sluter: statues of Philippe le Hardi (the Bold) (1363–1404), and Marguerite of Flanders kneeling at the feet of the Virgin; Moses' Well. Weeping figure (*Pleurant*) from the tomb of Philippe Pot, originally from Cîteaux.

Galleries 16 to 18, 15th-century sculpture

Under the influence of religious drama new themes appeared; decoration took a more prominent part: *recevresse* chapel of Avioth, a tiny shrine annexed to the church in which only 1 or 2 pilgrims could make vows to the Virgin or saint whose statue was kept there; Coronation of the Virgin on the tympanum of the entrance to the Château de la Ferté-Milon; the Virgin of Marthuret, Riom; Angel from Le Lude, signed Jehan Barbet (called de Lyon, 1475); figures from the choir screen of Albi Cathedral; tombs from Souvigny; funerary statue of the Duc Jean de Berry by Jean de Cambrai. Family of donors being presented to the Christ of Pity by St Michael and St William of Aquitaine (Church of Ecos, Eure, 15th c.). Virgin of Pity from Montluçon (Allier); *Ecce Homo* from Ecouis; Breton calvary from Pencran (Finistère, 1521); Saint Sepulcher from the hospital of Tonnerre, by Jean Michel and Georges de la Sonnette (1453); sepulcher from Solesmes (1496); altarpiece from Aix-en-Provence; windows and entrance of the chapel of the Hôtel Jacques-Coeur, Bourges (1443–53); window of a house at Villefranche-de-Rouergue (Aveyron).

Galleries 19 to 21, sculpture from the first third of the 16th c.

Italo-Antique decoration gradually gave way to Gothic, while statues remained in the tradition of French art: choir stalls from Amiens Cathedral (1508–22); leaves from the portal of Aix-en-Provence Cathedral (1508–10); tomb of Duc François II of Brittany and Duchesse Marguerite de Foix in Nantes Cathedral, executed between 1502 and 1507 by the workshop of Michel Colombe; tomb of the children of Charles VIII and Anne of Brittany in Tours Cathedral; Anne of Brittany's private chapel from the Royal Residence at Loches; fountain of Beaune-Semblançay, Tours (1510); altarpiece from the chapel of the Château de Gaillon (Louvre), by Michel Colombe (1510), with decorations by Jérôme de Fiesole; Virgin of Olivet (Louvre); statue of St Martha from the Church of the Magdalen, Troyes (Aube); *Entombment of Christ* from Villeneuve-l'Archevêque; portico from the courtyard of the Hôtel Bernuy, Toulouse (1530–35); rood screen from Limoges

Cathedral; vault of the Great Clock from Rouen (1528); ridge ornament and coping from a window in the apse of the Church of Saint-Pierre, Caen, by Hector Sohier (1518–45); S door of Beauvais Cathedral.

Staircase: medallions from the Château de Montal; bas-relief from the Hôtel du Bourgtheroulde, Rouen, showing episodes from the meeting at the Field of the Cloth of Gold in 1520; skylight from the Château de Puyguilhem (Dordogne).

Galerie Haute, upper gallery first floor

On the r. by the entrance to the Galerie Haute is a room containing architectural models which can be visited only with permission: models of Notre-Dame, Paris; of the Merveille de Mont-Saint-Michel; models of basic constructions and exhibition of materials used in the building and decoration of French monuments.

Gallery 22 or the Salle Jean Goujon

Toward the middle of the 16th c., works imported from Italy or executed in France by Italian artists had a profound influence on French artists: François Marchand worked on the tomb of François I in Saint-Denis; Jean Goujon was greatly influenced by Antiquity. *Deposition* from the ancient rood screen of Saint-Germain-l'Auxerrois; decoration from the Fountain of the Innocents, Paris (1549); bas-reliefs from the Zodiac Room in the former Hôtel de Ville, Paris, destroyed by fire in 1871; funerary urn containing the heart of François I by Pierre Bontemps; tomb of François I and Claude de France in the basilica of Saint-Denis, also by Bontemps; statues decorating the courtyard of the Hôtel d'Escoville, Caen; bust of the poet Pierre de Ronsard who died in 1585 (Blois Museum).

Gallery 23 or the Salle Ligier-Richier

Ligier Richier (1500–67) was born in Lorraine, where he worked. Recumbent figure of Philippa de Gueldre, Duchess of Lorraine (d. 1547, aged 87), Chapelle des Cordeliers, Nancy: the effigy from the tomb of René de Châlons (Prince of Orange, killed at Saint-Dizier, 1544), in the form of a standing skeleton (Church of Saint-Pierre, Bar-le-Duc); sepulcher from Saint-Mihiel (1554–64).

Gallery 24 or the Salle Germain-Pilon

Working from 1560 to 1590, Germain Pilon successfully combined the French tradition with the influence of Antiquity: three Graces carrying an urn intended for the heart of Henri II; recumbent effigies of Henri II and Catherine de' Medici; Henri II and Catherine de' Medici in coronation robes on their tomb in the basilica of Saint-Denis; Virgin and Child from the church of la Couture (largest church in the town) in Le Mans; Mater Dolorosa from the Valois rotunda, Saint-Denis.

Sculptures from the first half of the 17th c.: busts of Louis XIII and Louis XIV by Jean Warin: group of children sitting on the cornice of a staircase from the Château de Maisons-Laffite, from the studio of Jacques Sarrazin (1642–51); statue of Sully kneeling on his tomb at Nogent-le-Rotrou, by Barthélemy Boudin (1642).

Gallery 25, 17th-c. sculpture

While finding inspiration in the Antique, genre artists were also producing original works: Pierre Puget, atlantes (carved male caryatids) from the door of the old Town Hall of Toulon (1656); Coysevox, *Vase de la Guerre* and symbolic figure of the *Garonne* from Versailles; Girardon, group, *The Rape of Persephone* and bas-relief of Nymphs bathing from a grotto in the gardens of Versailles; *The Vow of Louis XIII* in the choir of Notre-Dame, Paris, by Coysevox, Nicolas and Guillaume I Coustou (1713–15).

Galleries 26 and 27, 18th-c. sculpture

Next to works of a truly decorative character such as the *Horses of the Sun* by Robert Le Lorrain, the fountain of the Gros Horloge (Great Clock) at Rouen, the bas-reliefs from the Fountain of the Seasons in the Rue de Grenelle by Bouchardon, and the fountain of Neptune in the Place Stanislas in Nancy by Guibal, there are some excellent portraits by Pigalle, Pajou, Caffieri and, in particular, Houdon, whose *L'Ecorché (Flayed Man)* and *St Bruno* from the Church of Sta Maria degli Angeli in Rome, can also be seen. Spectacular tomb of the Maréchal de Saxe by Pigalle, in the Church of Saint Thomas in Strasbourg (1753–56).

Gallery 28 or the Salle Rude

Atlanta by Pradier; the *Hound* by Grégoire Giraud; bas-relief from the tomb of Maréchal Suchet and busts by David d'Angers. Some 19th-c. works including Rude's *The Little Neapolitan Fisherboy* (1831), allegorical figure of Victory, the high-relief of the so-called *Marseillaise* on the Arc de Triomphe, at the Etoile, Paris, (1838–36).

Gallery 29, architectural models room

These models illustrate the various solutions Romanesque and Gothic builders found for the problems of balance, stress and vaulting. Romanesque and early Gothic arches (Saint-Pierre in Chauvigny, Paray le Monial, Cluny, Le Puy, Conques, Saint-Etienne in Caen, Sens Cathedral, Saint-Serge at Angers). The statue of Watteau at Valenciennes.

Mural painting section

The mural painting museum is dedicated to preserving and presenting copies of decorations painted on the walls of French churches; the originals, which have been left in place, are gradually fading and disappearing.

The most important compositions of the Romanesque period have been reproduced and displayed in the first floor galleries, which were opened in 1945. Gothic painting occupies the second and third floors. The reproductions were painted from the originals on canvas which has been remounted here on replicas of the buildings' interiors. Besides these, the museum has a collection of around 2000 watercolor copies on paper of reduced dimensions 3ft. 5ins./ 1.05m×2ft./0.75m), a collection begun on the initiative of Prosper Merimée.

Ground floor (back of entrance hall).

Carolingian paintings. Paintings from the crypt of Saint-Germain d'Auxerre, 11th c., showing episodes from the *Life and the Stoning of St Etienne*; paintings from Saint-Pierre-les-Eglises, Vienne, and others.

First floor, (l.h. staircase)

Romanesque era, gallery overlooking the gardens. S apse of the Chapel of Saint-Gilles, Montoire (Loire-et-Cher): *Christ in Majesty Giving the Keys to St Peter*, 12th c.; traces of paintings added in the 13th to 14th c.: *Martyrdom of St Lawrence*. Half-columns from Saint-Savin with roughly hewn capitals and *trompe-l'oeil* painting. Two fragments of paintings from the gallery of Saint-Julien-de-Brioude (Haute-Loire): opposite the windows, choir of angels; above the door at the end of the gallery, *Hell*; these sombre paintings, from the end of the Romanesque period, show a Byzantine influence in certain details as well as a Persian influence. At r. angles to the windows: *Christ Driving the Moneylenders from the Temple*, from the Church of Chalivoy-Milon; *The Magi* from the church of Brinay; figures from the crypt of Notre-Dame-la-Grande,

Poitiers. *Crucifixion* from Saint-André-des-Faux. Church of Saint-Pierre, Vienne (Isère): large seated figure of St John, the face of which shows it has been based on an Antique model. Chapel of Saint-Martin-de-Fenollar, Maureillas: *Christ in Glory* surrounded by the symbols of the Evangelists carried by angels; *Annunciation, Nativity, Adoration of the Magi*: the stiffness of the postures and decorative elements are characteristic of the Catalan school of the 12th c. At the far end of the gallery, paintings from the choir and the nave of the Church of Saint-Jacques-des-Guérets: *Christ in Glory* surrounded by the symbols of the Evangelists, *Last Supper, Calvary* and *Resurrection of the Dead, Raising of Lazarus* and the *Legend of St Nicholas, Descent of Jesus into Limbo, Martyrdom of St James the Greater*; note the harmony and beauty of the coloring which can also be seen in the fresco from the Church of Saint-Genest, Lavardin, showing the *Baptism of Christ*. Model of the baptistry of Saint-Jean, Poitiers, built in the 4th c. and decorated with frescoes in the 12th-c., three of them are related to the sculpted figures of the Languedoc school and reproduced here: the *Crowned Horseman*, said to be Constantine; *St Maurice between the peacock and the dragon*, inspired by primitive Christian art; group of apostles from an *Ascension*. On leaving this room retrace your steps and turn r.

Painting from the gallery of the Church of Ebreuil: *Beheading of St Pancras, St Austremoine and St Clement*; this work from the second quarter of the 12th c. forms the link between the schools of the Loire, Auvergne, and Limousin. Apse of the church of the Cluniac Priory of Berzé-la-Ville: Figures of saints of the Greek Church, *Christ in Majesty* surrounded by figures probably representing the glorification of the Cluniac Order, *Life of St Blaise, Martyrdom of St Lawrence*; the blue backgrounds and the figures are reminiscent of the art of Ravenna and make this 12th-c. work an exceptional example of decoration in the French school. Crypt of Chartres Cathedral: Saints in arcades. Crypt of the Church of Notre-Dame-de-Montmorillon: *Virgin Holding the Infant Jesus Crowning a Saint* (St Catherine of Alexandria or the Church), scenes from the life and the martyrdom of St Catherine (end 12th c. or beginning 13th c.). Paintings decorating the crypt of the Abbey of Château-Landon representing two episodes from the life of St Séverin: *The Healing of Clovis* and the *Thanksgiving Mass* celebrated by St Séverin in the presence of Clovis and Clotilda (the originals have been removed). Choir of the Church of Saint-Martin-de-Vic: these compositions of an anecdotal character, reminiscent of certain works of the Catalan school, were executed by a single artist. They show: in the half-dome of the apse, *Christ in Glory* supported by two angels and surrounded by the symbols of the Evangelists; below, the *Visitation*, the *Crucifixion of St Peter, Jesus Before Herod*, the *Fallen Angels*; in the upper section, the *Purification of the Lips of the Prophet Isaiah*, the *Entry of Jesus into Jerusalem*; on the W wall, the prophets Daniel and Moses, continuation of the *Entry into Jerusalem*, the *Last Supper*, the *Story of Lazarus*, the *Washing of Feet*, the *Arrest of Christ in the Garden of Olives*, *Simon the Cyrene Carrying the Cross*, *The Funeral of St Martin*, *Virtues and Vices*; at the side of the nave, *Presentation of Jesus at the Temple and Descent from the Cross*, the *Arrival of the Magi*, the *Adoration of the Magi*, the *Virgin Accused by Annas the Scribe*, the *Annunciation*, and ten Apostles. These paintings of a uniform color must date from the beginning of the 12th-c. Church of Saint-Aignan, Brinay: scenes from the *Childhood and Life of Christ* (note in the gallery facing the garden, two other scenes from the same church, the arrival and departure of the Magi): 12th c., clear, bold tones. Puy Cathedral: below the staircase, *Crucifixion* (13th c.).

Retracing your steps, on the l. is the great figure of *St Michael Slaying the Dragon* (gallery of the N arm of the transept), Byzantine in character, appearing to belong to the second half of the 11th c. S chapel of the crypt of the Church of Saint-Aignan-sur-Cher: *Lamb of God* in a nimbus and scenes from the *Life of St Giles* (end 12th or early 13th c.). S door of the Church of Saint-Pierre, Vienne (Isère): St Peter carved in relief, flanked by two painted figures. This combination of painting and sculpture is also to be found on the arches of the cloister of the Abbey of Saint-Aubin, Angers: in the center, seated Virgin holding the Child in a nimbus of light, supported by two angels, sculpted archivolt (12th c.); small paintings representing the *Magi*, the *Massacre of the Innocents*, the Holy City, *Jerusalem*, which appear to date from the beginning of the 13th c. Chapel of Liget at Chemillé-sur-Indrois: *Descent from the Cross*, *Death of the Virgin*, *Tree of Jesse*, *St Benedict*, *St Giles*, *St Nicholas* and *St Hilary*. These paintings, from around 1200, with their clear, pure colors, and their supple and graceful postures, show a deep sense of harmony. Souday Church: *Annunciation* and *Visitation* (paintings no longer visible in the church). A saint and two horsemen ornamenting the splays of the choir windows in Areines Church (certainly from the second half of the 12th c.), show the same qualities.

Galleries on the side of the Place du Trocadéro: Reconstruction of the crypt of the church at Tavant: the vault is decorated with figures: *Adam and Eve*, *Saul and David*, the *Libertine*, *Sagittarius*, the *Descent from the Cross*, *Christ in Limbo*, the *Crucifixion of St Peter*, *Cain and Abel*, *Christ in Majesty*. As the architecture and sculpture date from the early 12th c., it is likely that the paintings were executed at the same time. High chapel of the Abbey Church of Saint-Chef: the entire painting represents the *Heavenly Court Surrounding Christ in Glory* and can be dated to the second half of the 11th c. Rocamadour: the *Annunciation and the Visitation*; this painting, executed on the rock, in the open air, relates to the Limousin shrines, echoing their enamel colors and their unfaceted precious stones, represented here by stucco reliefs. Palluau: *Virgin in Majesty* between two saints, a particularly beautiful example of Berry painting (first half 12th c., discovered in 1949). Opposite the staircase; E apse of Saint-Gilles in Montoire: *Christ as Judge of the*

Apocalypse (end 11th c. or early 12th c.). The Church of Saint-Savin-sur-Gartempe: the greatest collection of Romanesque paintings to have survived is largely reproduced here: *Virgin in Majesty between two angels and two kneeling abbots*, at the entrance to the nave; a piece of the vault for which there was no room in the *parvis* gallery: *Jacob Blessing Joseph*; four pieces from the crypt: *Judgment and Martyrdom of St Savin and St Cyprian*; two half columns decorated with animals. In the *parvis* gallery: upper half of the gallery decorated with paintings designed to be seen from below, without stepping back (hence the attenuation of the figures): *Descent from the Cross*, the *Holy Women at the Tomb*, the *Hanging of Judas*, *St Denis*, the *Kiss of Judas*, the *Entombment*; the same gallery displays the whole of the famous barrel-vault of the nave, although at a much lower height than the original so that it can be better seen. It is decorated with panels representing, in four bands, scenes from Genesis and Exodus: the *Creation of the World*, *Eve Spinning Wool*, *Cain and Abel*, *Life of Noah*, *Life of Abraham*, *Life of Joseph*, Moses and the *Exodus*. The porch is painted with scenes from the *Apocalypse*. There seems to be no doubt today that all these paintings were executed by a single studio toward the end of the 11th c. or the beginning of the 12th c.

Second floor

Gothic period (13th–14th c.). Gallery overlooking the gardens: scenes of Hell from Asnières-sur-Vègre (Sarthe, 13th c.). Vault from the choir of Petit-Quevilly, *Childhood and Baptism of Christ* (end 13th c.). *Martyrdom of St Etienne*, at Saint-Dié (Vosges, 14th c.). *Life of St Blaise*, at Vic-le-Comte (14th c.). *Presentation of the Keys to St Peter*, from Ferrières-en-Gâtinais (end 13th c.). *Procession of Horsemen*, from Saint-Jacques-des-Guérets (13th c.). etc.

Gallery facing the *parvis*: this gallery is reserved for exhibitions. At either end, the *Transfiguration* and the *Virgin Mother*, porch of Puy Cathedral (beginning 13th c.). In the center, *Christ in Majesty* from the crypt of Saint-Aignan (end 12th c.), surrounded by ex-votos (end 14th c.). Decorated tomb, at Neuvillette-en-Charnie (13th c.). etc.

Gallery opposite the Place du Trocadéro, partly used for exhibitions. On the ceiling, at the top of the staircase: *Choir of Angels*, from the Château de La Clayette (14th c.). Episodes from the romance of *Tristan and Iseult*, from the Château de Saint-Floret (second half 14th c.). Hunting scenes from the Palais des Papes (Palace of the Popes) at Avignon (14th c.). *Life of St John the Baptist*, from the Carthusian monastery of Villeneuve-lès-Avignon (Gard, 14th c.).

In the center of the floor. Prophets from the dome of Cahors Cathedral (Lot), 52ft/16m diameter (early 14th c.). Either side of the entrance: *Holy Women at the Tomb* and *Martyrdom of St Catherine*,

Puy Cathedral (13th c.). *Scenes from the Childhood of Christ*, Saint-Amant-de-Boixe (end 13th c.). *Coronation of the Virgin*, Vernais (end 13th c.). *Life of St Martin*, Etigny (13th c.). *Life of St Andrew*, Frétigny (Eure-et-Loir, 13th c.). *Legend of St Martial*, Saint-Junien (end 14th c.). *Sermon on the Mount* and *Feeding of the Five Thousand*, Clermont-Ferrand Cathedral (13th c.). *Life of St John the Baptist*, from the baptistry of Poitiers (13th c.). Funeral scene, Sainte-Croix-en-Jarez (1327).

At the foot of the stairs: *Choir of Angels* from the church of Auzon (14th c.).

Second floor, I.-hand staircase

Gothic period (15th and 16th c.). (Numerical order being at the I. of the staircase.)

New decorative styles, close to secular art and tapestry, are apparent in the *Tree of Jesse* from the Church of Saint-Bris (1500, no.1); the vault of the Church of Kernascléden (ca. 1465, no. 2) is more traditional; anecdotal painting in the cloister of the Abbey of Abondance (1480–90, no. 5); experiments in expression in the vault of Savigny-les-Beaune (1470–78, no. 6) and in Nuits-Saint-Georges (15th c., no. 8).

Take the gallery which begins with a macabre scene very much in the taste of the period (Church of Saint-Maurice, Annecy, 1458, no. 11) and continues with interesting scenes showing the customs and dress of the time (Chaource, 1548, no. 15). On the other side of the stairs is the famous *Danse Macabre* cycle from La Chaise-Dieu in the Auvergne, one of the most important compositions on this theme (ca. 1460–70, no. 17); at the far end of the gallery, the famous fresco of the *Liberal Arts* from Puy Cathedral (ca. 1500, no. 23) shows a new spirit of secular inspiration. The paintings from La Brigue (1492, no. 26) have an affinity with the art of the miniature, while the vault of the Château de Pimpéan (1460–70, no. 28) is almost archaistic. The morbid and dramatic imagination of the 15th c. is rarely shown with such force as in the paintings from Albi Cathedral (1496–1500, no. 29); those from the Château de Dissay (1493–1505, no. 30) blend secular and religious themes with a remarkable attention to detail; interesting hunting scenes from the Château de Rochechouart (1510–13, no. 35); last appearance of medieval monsters from the Château de Villeneuve-Lembron (1515–17, no. 36).

▷ Mural paintings

The term *fresco*, often wrongly used, is properly applied only to murals executed in water-based pigments applied to a wet, freshly laid lime plaster ground. This paint penetrates the surface as it dries and becomes fixed, keeping its brightness as time passes. Very common in the Middle Ages, fresco painting is a delicate operation: the colors brighten as they dry and the artist must work quickly, within a period of 36 hours, without retouching. Another technique, know as tempera painting, allows the painter to work more freely. The colors are prepared with an emulsion of egg yolk or white glue or size, and applied to dry mortar. In the Romanesque period this technique was used in conjunction with that of fresco to paint certain details. Painting executed entirely in tempera became increasingly common from the 14th c. onward. Painting on remounted canvas is a very different procedure: the work is executed on a flexible canvas which is fixed to the wall using a very strong glue containing special remounting paste (resin, wax, and red ochre). The paintings on display in the museum are remounted canvases.

▷ Additional information

The library (open Mon., Wed. and Thurs. 10am–noon and 2–5pm) allows research into certain subjects arising from a tour of the museum.

Guided tours are organized regularly (tel: 47–27–35–74).
Young people can discover the museum by following the exploration tour, either on their own or with a guide available daily, 9:45am and 2pm; ask at the cash desk). There are also workshops providing artistic activities for young patrons. Sessions last 2 hours on Wed. and Sat. afternoons (by arrangement for groups). Subjects deal with: architecture (1 session); sculpture and fresco (2 sessions); modeling (3 sessions).

For all information write or telephone 47–27–35–74.

▣ Musée de Musique Mécanique*

Impasse Berthaud, 28 Rue Beaubourg, 3rd arr. Map ref. 18–C1
Tel. 42–71–99–54
Open Sat., Sun., and public holidays, 2pm–7pm
Métro: Rambuteau, Hôtel de Ville
Bus: 58, 67, 69, 70, 72, 74

Tour of the museum

30 mins.

This small museum, which is subsidized by the City of Paris, is the work of an enthusiastic collector, Henri Trinquet, and houses his extraordinary collection of barrel organs, mechanical and pneumatic pianos, automatons, music boxes, and gramophones. All the instruments are demonstrated during the tour of the museum.

Do not miss the automatic violin and banjo, the robotic accordionist and drummer, several fairground and merry-go-round organs, and a piano by the firm of Parisian instrument makers, Gaveau, that plays music by Cortot, Gershwin, Prokofiev, Saint-Saëns, and others.

▷ Mechanical music

The quest for means of recording music began long before the invention of gramophones and cassette-players. Carillons first appeared in the Middle Ages, followed later by hand-operated bird-organs that 'taught' songbirds to sing tunes. The music box with vibrating metal strips came out in 1796, and the 19th c. saw the invention of the pianola – self-playing pianos, from the lowly bar-room instrument to the concert grand. However, it is the barrel organ and the merry-go-round organ (the Limonaire), worked by cylinders with protruding pins or by perforated cards, that have enlivened streets and fun fairs from the 19th c. to the present day.

Musée Nissim de Camondo**

63 Rue de Monceau, 8th arr. Tel: 45-63-26-32. Map ref. 9-A1
Curator: Mme Yvonne Brunhammer
Open Wed.-Sun. 10am-noon and 2-5pm; closed Christmas and
Jan. 1.
Métro: Villiers, Monceau
Bus: 84, 94

The Nissim de Camondo Museum is housed in a mansion on the edge of the Parc Monceau. It was built by Sergent at the beginning of the 20th century, based on the plans of the Petit Trianon. It is a recreation of an aristocratic Parisian home of Louis XVI's time with its magnificent collection of furniture, pictures, tapestries, porcelain, and silverware from the 18th c. Much of the furniture bears the stamps of the greatest cabinetmakers of the era, and some pieces came from the Châteaux of Bellevue, Montreuil, Saint-Cloud, and Versailles.

Count Moïse de Camondo formed this collection with as much intelligence as taste. He came from a family of financiers and collectors, established in France during the Second Empire. He bequeathed his large town house to the Union des Arts Décoratifs in 1935 in memory of his son Nissim who was killed in World War I. Looking at the past in this house is made more poignant by the knowledge that the remaining members of the family were exterminated at Auschwitz.

Tour of the museum

45 mins.

Ground floor vestibule: flat-topped bureau by Riesener; fountain in red marble from the Château de Saint-Prix, Montmorency; two paintings of the school of Hubert Robert.

Main staircase: pair of lacquered Louis XV Chinoiserie corner cupboards attributed to RVLC; two perfume burners known as 'Athenians'; pair of large Regency armchairs covered in Savonnerie tapestry.

First floor

Grand bureau. White marble fireplace inlaid with bronze (ca. 1775, from a large house in Bordeaux); pair of low cabinets by Leleu; low bookcase, secretaire and cylindrical writing-desk in bird's-eye mahogany by Saunier; rectangular table (from the Château de Bellevue) and circular stand by Carlin; bedside table by Topino; eight chairs by N.-Q. Foliot covered in Aubusson tapestry; (scenes from La Fontaine); six large Aubusson tapestries with fables from La Fontaine after Oudry, and a screen in Beauvais tapestry two low chairs by Sené (from Madame Elizabeth's set at Montreuil); *Bacchante*, painting on wood (1785) by Mme Vigée-Lebrun; two Savonnerie carpets made at Aubusson.

Grand salon: white-and-gilt paneling (from 11 Rue Royale, Paris, ca. 1775); low marquetry cabinet and rectangular table by Riesener; pair of low cabinets by Weisweiler with elaborate gilt-bronze mounts and a Japanese lacquer panel in the center; lady's writing desk (formerly in the collection of General the Baron de Charette) and a round table, both decorated by Carlin with Sèvres porcelain plaques; pedestal table in chased bronze attributed to Thomire; suite of furniture including two sofas and an armchair covered in fine Aubusson tapestry (formerly in the collection of Sir Richard Wallace) by Georges Jacob; desk armchair attributed to Nadal the Elder; six-paneled Savonnerie screen; marble bust of his daughter (*L'Eté*) by Houdon; portrait of Mme Le Coulteux de Molay by Vigée Lebrun; Beauvais tapestry after Boucher's cartoon (1736) for *The Fisher-girl*; two Savonnerie carpets: *L'Air*, made for the Grande Galerie of the Louvre (1678), and another with garlands of flowers on a grey-blue ground (1660).

Salon des Huet. Seven panels and three overdoors showing pastoral scenes (one signed, dated 1776) painted by J.-B. Huet; pair of *meubles d'appui* (low cabinets) by Carlin, once owned by the Duc de Penthièvre; pair of japanned cabinets by Garnier; marquetry rolltop desk by J.-F. Oeben; painted chiffonnier table, the top decorated with Sèvres *pâte tendre* (soft-paste porcelain), stamped RVLC; sofa, two chairs, and two armchairs by Sené (once in the collection of the Baron de Charette); Savonnerie carpet made from Perrot's designs for the king's residence (*ca.* 1740).

Dining room. Pair of small cabinets by Leleu; sideboard and two tables in ebony and chased bronze by Weisweiler; oval soup tureen, two tureens, and four wine coolers (1770–71) in silver by Roettiers (commissioned by Catherine II, Empress of Russia, for Prince

Orlov); round soup tureen with boar's head (1784–85) and four dish plate covers (1782–83) by R.-J. Auguste; bronze bust after Houdon: the *Negress*; Beauvais tapestry, *Fishing with a Net*, after the cartoon by Casanova (1772); four early 18th-c. tapestries; four still lifes, two in Savonnerie and two in Beauvais tapestry after paintings by Mme Vallayer-Coster; two Savonnerie carpets made at Aubusson.

Cabinet des Porcelaines. Note view of the Parc Monceau dinner services* in Sèvres by Buffon; services in Chantilly and Meissen porcelain.

Gallery: two Aubusson tapestries showing Chinese scenes after Boucher. Chinese vases and porcelain in showcases.

Petit Bureau. Low cabinet and pair of glass-fronted cabinets stamped RVLC; commode stamped RVLC; bedside table by Topino; snuff boxes, Chinese porcelain, watches, statuettes; marble bust of Mme Le Comte by Coustou (1748); terracotta medallions by J.-B. Nini; four views of Venice by Guardi; three paintings by Hubert Robert: *Porte Saint-Denis*, *Porte Saint-Martin*, and *Monument Antique*; portrait of Necker by Duplessis (1781); eight colored sketches by Oudry for Gobelins tapestries of *The Royal Hunts of Louis XV*; knotted pile Aubusson carpet (*ca*. 1790).

Staircase. Banquette marked HF; terracotta bas-relief by Clodion: *The Triumph of Amphitrite*; two Aubusson tapestries with Chinese scenes after Boucher.

Second floor

Gallery. Sofa and 14 armchairs by Nogaret; 32 engravings after Chardin.

Blue drawing-room (on r.). Furniture (ca. 1750–90), notably by Macret and J. Dubois; seats (*ca*. 1740–80) by J. Avisse, A.-P. Dupain and Nogaret; red morocco casket embossed with the arms of Marie-Antoinette; portrait of a family by Gautier Dagoty; views of Paris painted by Bouhot, Canella, De Machy and Raguenet; picture of *The Duc d'Orléans' Gentlemen* by Philippoteaux (1839); landscapes and seascapes in watercolor by Jongkind (1877–84); Aubusson carpet (early 19th c.).

Library. Paneling (*ca*. 1775); bookcase in ebony and chased bronze attributed to Weisweiler; writing-desk by Leleu; two bronze and Sèvres biscuitware candelabras by Blondeau after Boucher; plaster bust by Houdon: (*L'Eté*); two views of the park, one by Hubert Robert; two still lifes in Savonnerie tapestry; Beauvais tapestry after the cartoon by Casanova (1777); knotted-pile carpet made at Aubusson (ca. 1765–75); Japanese vases.

Bedroom. Paneling (from a mansion in Bordeaux, 1780); marquetry commode by G. Cramer; console by C. Topino; two armchairs by

Georges Jacob; Sèvres biscuitware centerpieces in hard-paste porcelain by Boizot; *Sabine Houdon* (?), plaster bust by J.-A. Houdon; *Rosalie Duthé*, painting by Danloux (1792); Alexandre de Beauharnais as a child, by Drouais; *Les Rémois (Citizens of Rheims)*, painting on copper by Lancret; *The Singing Lesson*, gouache by Lavreince; Savonnerie carpet, delivered on March 4, 1760 for the use of the 'Mesdames de France on feast days and Sundays in the chapel of Versailles'.

Second bedroom. Secrétaire attributed to Riesener; screen by G. Jacob; folding screen by Canebas; bed in steel and chased bronze; hunting scenes painted by Demay, A. de Dreux, Schayer, Sweback, H. Vernet; Aubusson carpet (*ca.* 1800).

▣ Musée de Notre-Dame de Paris*

10 Rue du Cloître-Notre-Dame, 4th arr. Tel: 43–25–42–92. Map ref: 17–B2
Curator: Mlle Anne-Marie Joly
Open Sept.–July 15, Wed. and Sat.–Sun. 2:30–6pm.
Métro: Cité, Hotel de Ville
Bus: 21, 38, 47, 96

This small cathedral museum, founded in 1951 by the Société des Amis de Notre-Dame (Society of Friends of Notre-Dame), commemorates the great events in the cathedral's history.

Tour of the museum

30 mins.

Several engravings show how the ancient *parvis* looked before Haussmann's alterations in the 19th c.: occupying a sixth of the present space, it was bounded by a small wall, to the south of which was the Hôtel-Dieu on the bank of the Seine. Paintings show the interior of the church with its golden rood-screen, its furnishings, and the standards taken from its foes. The transformation of the choir, instigated by Louis XIII following his vow to put France under the protection of the Virgin (1638), gave rise to several projects that are united here: a replica of the medal of J.-H. Mansart that was placed in the altar in 1699; drawing by R. de Cotte (1708). Plans for a new vestry by Soufflot (1756). A showcase contains the Gallo-Roman objects discovered during the excavation of the *parvis* (1965–70). A 4th-c. glass cup, decorated with a chrisma* is the oldest Christian relic in Paris and marks the beginning of the story which culminated in the present church, built from 1160 to 1270.

The parish church of the Kings of France, Notre-Dame was the scene of solemn celebrations (Notre-Dame), such as the *Te Deum* of 1594 that marked the conversion of Henry IV, or the funeral of

Mary of Spain in 1746, the catafalque was designed by Slodtz, not to mention the coronation of Napoléon on December 2, 1804, shown in detail by some amusing engravings.

The case of the great organ by Cavaillé-Coll (1863) was installed in 1962. Interesting watercolor drawings* by Viollet-le-Duc illustrate the restoration project carried out between 1845 and 1864 at the instigation of the Romantic poets, including Hugo and Vigny.

Musée de l'Observatoire (Observatory museum)

→Faubourg Saint-Jacques

▣ Musée de l'Opéra* (Museum of Opera)

1 Place Charles-Garnier, entrance: in the side of the Opera House, Place de l'Opéra, 9th arr. Tel: 47–42–07–02. Map ref: 10–C2, D2
Curator: Mlle Kahane
Open 10am–5pm Mon.–Sat. 11am–5pm, and during intermissions, closed public holidays.
Métro: Opéra
Bus: 21, 27, 42, 48, 66, 68, 81, 95

Almost as old as the Opera House itself, with its charming, if slightly outdated décor, this small museum is connected with a very fine library, and is dedicated to the memory of the great artists who have brought glory to the Opéra throughout its history.

Tour of the museum

30 mins.

The collections, which are frequently brought up to date, are spread over the library gallery and the museum gallery.

Rotunda (ground floor). On the r., model of the Mystery Play of Valenciennes, from 1547; on the l., reconstruction of the stage of the Théâtre d'Orange by M. Darvan and Charles Garnier.

Vestibule (1st floor). Busts of Lully, Rameau, Gluck, Wagner, Debussy, Chabrier, Saint-Saëns, and G. Enesco; medallion of Ravel.

At the far end, on the r., Ida Rubinstein in the role of Shéhérezade, by J.-E. Blanche.

Library gallery

The library, which is connected to the Bibliothèque Nationale, is open to the public. It is devoted to the history of the theater and of music and contains the first editions or manuscripts of all the scores performed at the Opéra since its inception (1669); more than 80,000 volumes relating to music, dance, or the theater; the archives of the Opéra since 1900, with over 100,000 drawings, models of stage sets, costumes, portraits, and photographs of performers; a collection of posters, programs, and books from the Opéra and other theaters; and a newspaper library (1000 titles).

On the r., the Rotunda room is reserved for readers (catalogue).

Museum gallery

Two pictures showing the fire at the Opéra in 1781, by Hubert Robert; old lighting systems; souvenirs of the Opéra in the Rue Le Peletier; Orsini's bombs (1858) with which he tried to assassinate Napoléon III outside the Opéra in 1858. Busts of composers, singers, and dancers: *Eugénie Fiocre**, *Gounod*, by Carpeaux; *Madeleine Guimard* by Merchi; *Pauline Viardot* by Aimé Millet. Portraits of famous musicians and performers, including *Wagner** by Renoir and *Johanssen* by Van Dongen. Objects once belonging to composers and artists or used by them in their principal roles: Massenet's table-piano, Spontini's piano, souvenirs of Diaghilev given to the museum by Serge Lifar, and others. Theatrical masks. Four scaled-down panels which decorate the dance foyer by Boulanger, dedicated to Charles Garnier, who designed the Opera House in 1861.

▣ Musée de l'Orangerie***

Jardin des Tuileries, on the edge of the Place de la Concorde, 1st arr, Tel: 42-97-48-16. Map ref: 9–B3
Open daily except Tues. and public holidays, 9.45am–5:15pm.
Métro: Concorde
Bus: 24, 42, 52, 72, 73, 84, 94

At the side of the Seine, an extension of the Musée du Jeu de Paume, the Orangerie des Tuileries was for many years a gallery for temporary exhibitions. It is now an autonomous museum.

Reorganized in 1984, the museum houses the famous Walter Guillaume collection and Claude Monet's *Nymphéas (Water Lilies)* which, since 1927, have been arranged in two rooms on the ground floor. This outstanding collection consists of 144 masterpieces by the artists of the Ecole de Paris, from Impressionism to the 1930s. The collection was assembled by the art dealer Paul Guillaume (→inset) and enlarged after his death by the acquisitions of his widow Domenica and her second husband Jean Walter, the architect and patron of the arts; Mme Walter donated the collection to the Louvre in 1977. In accordance with her wishes the intimate character of the collection has been preserved by its presentation in comparatively small rooms and by the quality of the lighting, which comes from above through a glass roof and from the sides through large bays windows overlooking the Tuileries gardens.

Although the number of artists represented is small this collection is the envy of museums the world over because of the quality of the works on display.

Tour of the museum

1 hr.

First floor

The first room***, situated in the round stairwell, is devoted to Chaim Soutine. Born in 1893 in Lithuania, he died in Paris in 1943. An artist of unclassifiable genius – somewhere between Van Gogh and German Expressionism – he, with Picasso and Modigliani, contributed most to the Ecole de Paris. This outstanding collection brings together 22 works: a series of poignant and touching portraits, the sitters wearing cheap garments or their work clothes, such as the *Little Pastry Cook*, and *The Bride* of 1922; the series of southern landscapes with their tumultuous, unnatural colors and distorted perspectives; still lifes of dead animals, whose bloody corpses are rendered with vivid color in thick impasto, such as the *Plucked Chicken*, 1925.

The second room, assigned to Paul Cézanne (1839–1906), invites more peaceful contemplation, in contrast to Soutine's tense imbalance and expressive violence. The destroyer of traditional perspective as it had been known since the Renaissance, Cézanne is represented by some admirable still lifes including *Fruit, Napkin, and Milk Can**** (1880), an outstanding work in which a glass is seen from the side and from above at the same time. This flouting of the rules of perspective influenced the whole of the next generation, in particular the Cubists, but should not be allowed to obscure the moving solemnity of such portraits as *The Artist's Son*** or *Madame*

*Cézanne*** (1885), nor the lyricism of color of the great mature landscapes, *In the Grounds of the Château Noir**** (1900).

The two following rooms bring together the works of Pierre Auguste Renoir (1841–1919), that other great master of Impressionism. Walter's favorite artist, he is represented by some major works such as *Young Girls at the Piano**** (1890) and various portraits** of his sons: Jean, the future film director, as a baby playing with his governess; Claude in a wonderful clown's costume (1909).

After the splendid colors of the Impressionists come the great artists of the 20th century. Some beautiful early works by Pablo Picasso (1881–1973) are on display: *The Embrace*** (1903), the strange composition of the *Peasants**, a sketch on cardboard (1906). André Derain (1880–1954), is represented by *The Kitchen Table* (1922), and *Harlequin and Pierrot*** (1924). Note also the various portraits of Paul Guillaume, the art dealer, by Modigliani* (1915), Derain** (1919), and Van Dongen* (1930). Such a panorama of French painting from between the wars would be incomplete without Henri Matisse (1869–1954), whose beautiful series of *Odalisques**, dating from 1924 to 1925, can be admired here.

The next room presents the works of the two great self-taught painters of the 20th c., Henri Rousseau, known as 'Le Douanier' because he was a customs official (1844–1910), and Maurice Utrillo (1883–1955). The visitor will recognize two of 'Le Douanier' Rousseau's most famous paintings *The Wedding*** (1908) and *Old Man Junier's Cart*** (1910) which so excited the Surrealists. Some of Utrillo's Parisian landscapes, stark and dismal, but with a rare beauty of composition, look as though they were painted in whitewash, typical of what is known as his 'white period' (1909–14): *Berlioz's House*** (1914).

The tour of the collection ends with the works of Picasso, in particular two monumental *Bathers*** of 1921 and 1923, and the *Young Apprentice*** (1917) by Amedeo Modigliani, of whom Paul Guillaume was one of the few supporters in Paris.

Ground floor

Discovering the *Water Lilies***, an astonishing set of murals, is still an incomparably moving experience. Painted by Claude Monet in his garden at Giverny during World War I, the series continues the exploration of the *Haystacks* and *Rouen Cathedral* series. The quintessence of his experiments into the ways in which matter dissolves under varying conditions of light, the Orangerie's great paintings were given by Monet to the State because of his friendship with Clemenceau and were arranged in their present place according to the artist's own directions.

▷ Paul Guillaume, the unknown man

Born in 1891, Paul Guillaume belonged to that line of outstanding art dealers which also included Durand-Ruel, Vollard, and Kahnweiler. At the age of 23 he opened a gallery in the Rue La Boétie with an exhibition of Russian avant-garde painters, Mikhail Larionov and Natalya Goncharova. In future years he never abandoned his courageous attitude toward the new either in the art review he published, *Les Arts à Paris*, or in entrusting the prefaces to his exhibitions to the poet and art critic Guillaume Apollinaire, or in helping unknown artists such as Soutine or Utrillo, whose works he was the first to sell. Until his premature death in a car accident in 1934, he remained a pioneer collector and dealer in modern art, in particular helping to assemble one of the most fabulous American collections, that of Dr Albert C. Barnes. His widow commissioned the sculptor Zadkine to create his tomb near the entrance to the cemetery at Passy.

▷ The Nymphéas at Giverny

After living in Giverny for seven years, Monet bought a house there in 1890, in which he lived until his death. Bequeathed to the Institut by his son, the house has recently been renovated, and is one of the most attractive museums in the vicinity of Paris. Thanks to the perfect restoration of the garden, the famous ornamental pond can still be seen, just as Monet specially created it to grow the variety of water lily to which he gave the poetic name of *nymphéas*. Having thus invented his own theme, Monet dedicated his work from then on to the tireless effort of capturing the light and the shifting colors of his garden as it moved through the course of the hours and the seasons.

(Musée Claude-Monet, Giverny, 27200 Vernon. Tel: 32-51-28-11.)

▣ Musée de l'Ordre de la Libération

51 bis Boul de Latour-Maubourg, 7th arr. Tel: 47-05-04-10. Map ref: 15-A2
Curator: Mme Michèle Michel
Open Mon.-Sat. 2pm-5pm. Closed on public holidays.
Métro: Latour-Maubourg, Invalides, Varenne
Bus: 28, 49, 63, 69, 82, 83, 92

The Musée de l'Ordre de la Libération occupies the beautiful building erected in 1747, designed by Robert de Cotte for the officers of the king and which, by its elegant simplicity, contrasts with the majestic proportions of the nearby Invalides.

The Ordre de la Libération was created in 1940 by General de

Gaulle to 'reward those civil and military individuals and groups who have distinguished themselves in the struggle to liberate France and her Empire'. The list was closed in 1946.

The museum, which was originally intended as a memorial to the comrades-in-arms of the Liberation, has gradually become the museum of the Resistance, the Free French and the Deportations.

Tour of the museum

45 mins.

The museum contains nearly 200 showcases in five rooms and three galleries. On display are many souvenirs of the five years of fighting to free French territory: Free French uniforms as well as the rags worn by prisoners in the camps; letters, memorabilia, and all kinds of evidence bearing witness to the *drôle de guerre* (phoney war), the Armistice, the war in France and in the overseas territories, the expeditionary corps from the *Appel de Londres* to May 8, 1945, by way of Chad, Tobruk, Tunisia, Libya, Italy, the liberation of Paris, of France, the war in Germany, the French Resistance, and the concentration camps.

The museum also has General de Gaulle's private papers as well as the names of the 1036 civilians and military personnel, the 18 units, and the five towns to have received the Ordre de la Libération.

▣ Musée Orfila

Faculté de Médecine, 45 Rue des Saints-Pères, 6th arr.
Tel: 42-86-20-47., ext. 4201. Map ref: 16-C2, D2
Open Fri. by request to Prof. Delmas, Laboratoire d'Anatomie,
Faculté de Médecine, 45 Rue des Saints-Pères.
Métro: Saint-Germain-des-Prés
Bus: 39, 48, 95

Tour of the museum

30 mins.

Created in 1844 by the physician and chemist Mateo Orfila (b. Minorca 1787–d. Paris 1853), this museum has been handed down to the Department of Anatomy of the Faculty of Medicine. Its collections, which appeal mainly to specialists in anatomy and to anthropologists, bring together over 400 specimens, including the curious flayed monkey that belonged to the anatomist Fragonard.

▣ Musée d'Orsay***

62 Rue de Lille, 7th arr. Tel: 45-49-48-14. Map ref.: 15-B1, C1
Main entrance: 1 Rue de Bellechasse
Entrance for the museum's great exhibitions: Quai Anatole-France
Entrance to restaurant after the museum closes: Rue de Lille.
Chief curator: Mme Françoise Cachin
Open Tues.–Sat., 10.am – 6pm (in summer opens at 9am); Sun. 9am
–6pm; Thurs. 10.30am –9.45pm; Closed Mon.
Métro: Solférino; RER (line C): Quai d'Orsay
Bus: 24, 63, 68, 69, 73, 83, 84, 94

The Musée d'Orsay, one of the most beautiful museums in the world, is dedicated to the art of the second half of the 19th c. Presenting art in every medium (painting, sculpture, graphic arts, decorative arts, architecture, photography, cinema), it illustrates their connection with literature, music, and the society of the era. Works by the Barbizon painters, large Courbets, a very beautiful collection of Impressionists and Post-Impressionists, some lovely collections of sculptures by Daumier and Carpeaux, as well as Art Nouveau pieces, are found alongside works that were for a long time relegated to museum storage: paintings, sculptures, and official or academic décors of the Second Empire and the Third Republic. Photography and the graphic arts are illustrated by temporary exhibitions. Architecture, too, is represented by drawings, plans, and models created specially for the museum. Informative exhibitions, integrated into the permanent displays and frequently renewed, serve to emphasize the connections between the various modes of artistic creation and the social, economic and historic contexts. Other temporary exhibitions are directly accessible through an entrance on the embankment.

Besides these, the museum has an auditorium in the basement, a shop selling books and postcards on the ground floor, and a reference room on the upper level. The restaurant on the middle floor, in the dining room of the former hôtel. From the café on the top floor there is a magnificent view over the Seine.

History of the museum

Designed by Victor Laloux (1850–1937), the Gare d'Orsay (Orsay railway station) and the hotel beside it were opened on July 14, 1900, for the Universal Exhibition. The station was reserved for the use of passengers of the Paris-Orléans Company. The gradual change in the building's function began in 1939, after which the station was used only for suburban trains, and was completed in 1973 with the closure of the hotel. The Gare d'Orsay housed the Drouot-Rive Gauche auction room, the Orsay-Renaud-Barrault Theater, and served as a backdrop for a film (Kafka's *The Trial*, directed by Orson Welles).

The decision not to destroy these buildings was made shortly after the controversy surrounding the destruction of the great Baltard market. In 1971 the station was registered in the supplement to the list of historic monuments; in 1977 it was proposed that the buildings be turned into a museum devoted to the art of the latter half of the 19th c. and, in 1978, a public foundation was created to carry this out.

The great difficulty of the program was to set up a modern museum, requiring a great deal of display space, inside the enormous station hall (105ft./32m high, 131ft./40m wide, 452ft./138m long), a masterpiece of turn-of-the-century architecture. The plans of the ACT team (made up of three associated architects: Colboc, Bardon, and Philippon), chosen after consulting six architects, allowed for the preservation of much of the architecture intact. The great nave was entirely preserved, its impressive dimensions accentuated by the creation of a longitudinal axis, reinforced again by placing the entrance in the Rue de Bellechasse. The interior design was entrusted, in 1980, to the Italian architect Gae Aulenti. Her austere style contrasts with the exuberance of Laloux's architecture.

History of the collections

The collections of the Musée d'Orsay originated mainly from the Louvre. The works from the period 1848 to 1900 that were exhibited at the Louvre are now on display at the Orsay. The Musée du Jeu de Paume, an annex of the Louvre which was closed in 1986, used to house the Impressionist masterpieces which can now be seen at the Musée d'Orsay, such as *Olympia* by Manet, *Le Moulin de la Galette* by Renoir, *The Bellelli Family* by Degas and *The Cathedrals of Rouen* (a series of views) by Monet. The small scale and extreme discomfort of the Jeu de Paume, faced with an increasing influx of visitors, were the chief arguments for the creation of a larger museum devoted to the 19th c. The former Musée du Luxembourg once housed the works of many academic artists of the period considered to be great painters in their own time. Tastes having changed, many of these works had been placed in storage at the Louvre or put in provincial museums or government offices. Some of these canvases have now reappeared on the walls of the Musée d'Orsay. Thus *The Birth of Venus* by Cabanel, and *The Sons of Cain* by Cormon (rolled up for 50 years), have come out of the storerooms of the Louvre; *The Recall of the Gleaners* by Jules Breton has come from the museum of Arras and *The Birth of Venus* by Bouguereau from Nantes museum. The Post-Impressionist collections of the Musée National d'Art Moderne which had remained at the Palais de Tokyo after the transfer of this museum's collections in 1976 to the Pompidou Center, have now joined the collections of the Musée d'Orsay.

The new museum benefited from many legacies and donations

Orsay Museum, ground floor (first floor)

(Redon, Signac, de Ménil, Boutaric, the Guilleminault collections and the Kodak-Pathé Foundation) and from several payments in lieu of inheritance taxes (*La Rue Montorgueil* by Monet, *Dance in the City* by Renoir, and more recently, the second part of Monet's *Déjeuner sur l'Herbe*). Finally, an intensive policy of acquisition was undertaken in order to fill the gaps, to enrich certain resources, especially in foreign painting (Klimt, Munch, Mondrian, Hodler, etc.), and, indeed, even to create new departments, in such fields as architecture and photography.

Tour of the museum

3 hrs.

Information displayed in five languages allows visitors to find out quickly what they are likely to see in each gallery. Instead of adopting an arbitrary numbering system each room is listed in our itinerary by its title as displayed in the museum. The systematic route outlined below allows everything to be seen.

The parvis

The tour of the museum begins outside on the *parvis* where some bronzes executed for the Trocadéro gardens at the time of the World Fair of 1878 have been placed.

On the l.: *Young Elephant* by Frémiet, *Horse* by Durenne, *Rhinoceros* by Jacquemart. On the r.: *Australia* by Durenne, *South America* by Aimé Millet, *North America* by Durenne, *Africa* by Delaplanche, *Asia* by Falguière and *Europe* by Schoenwerk.

Ground floor

In the entrance to the museum one can admire *Le Génie de la Patrie*** (part of *La Marseillaise*) by Rude, a detail moulded in plaster from the relief of the Arc de Triomphe at the Etoile, a masterpiece of Romantic sculpture.

Central aisle: sculpture 1850 to 1870

The great movements of the period are evoked. Romanticism is represented by the superb *Lion** by Barye and by *Napoléon Awakening to Immortality** by Rude, commissioned from the sculptor by a former commander of grenadiers at Elba. *Sappho* by James Pradier is Neo-Classical, but the subject and the melancholy pose of the poetess are influenced by Romanticism. *Napoléon the First as a Roman Emperor* by Barye, a model one-third the size of the monument at Ajaccio, illustrates the archaizing Neo-Classical trend, as does *Cornelia, Mother of the Gracchi* by Eugène Guillaume, which is inspired by Roman funerary monuments. *David* by Antonin Mercié bears witness to certain sculptors' passion for Florentine Renaissance sculpture. They were known as the Florentins. The *Bacchante** by Ernest Carrier-Belleuse, which comes from the Tuileries Garden, is closer in style to the 18th c. The bust of a *Negro from Sudan* by Charles Cordier, with its quest for realism and above all its use of color, bears witness to the taste for luxury and for the Orient which appeared under the Second Empire. Jean-Baptiste Carpeaux is represented by *Ugoline*** , *The Four Quarters of the Earth*, reliefs from the Pavillon de Flore, *The Dance**** and busts*** (→inset).

First group of rooms on the l.

This comprises the first three rooms opening on to the central passage and the gallery behind them.

Honoré Daumier (1808–79). The 36 small busts*** (in colored unfired clay) on display served this satirist as models for the official portraits of the Juste Milieu (middle-of-the-road) parliamentarians, published in the anti-government weekly *Caricature*, then in *Charivari* during the July Monarchy. Daumier could bring out each person's character by their physical peculiarities and in this comes close to the Romantic trend, but the power of his modelling, his sense of movement and the breadth of inspiration in his other sculptures – such as one of the busts, *Ratapoil*** , a satirical political type he created, the bas-relief *The Emigrants*** and in his paintings such as *The Washerwoman**** –made him one of the greatest artists of his time.

Salle Chauchard I (→inset):

Millet, Rousseau, Corot. The Musée d'Orsay presents works from the second half of Corot's (1796–1875) career: poetical, misty landscapes: *Memory of Mortefontaine**, *Une Matinée*, *Dance of the Nymphs*; and figures: *My Studio*, *Woman with a Mandolin*, *Woman in Blue***. Barbizon, a hamlet in the forest of Fontainebleau, became a center of attraction for painters who, away from industrial civilization, painted landscapes from nature. Those of Théodore Rousseau (1812–67), one of the main thinkers behind the Barbizon school, bear witness to an almost mystical love of nature. His friend Jean-François Millet (1814–75) began his career with portraits (*Madame Lecourtois*) and ended it at Barbizon with landscapes (*Spring***). *The Gleaners***, an image of the labor and the poverty of the countryside, attracted much criticism at the Salon of 1857.

Salle Chauchard 2: Realism.

This gallery is reached by the staircase in the small central room.The works on display show that a certain realism was appreciated, so long as it did not question the values of the bourgeoisie. In this way Jules Breton was successful with his pictures of peasant subjects (*The Recall of the Gleaners*, 1859). Paintings of domestic animals by Rosa Bonheur (*Ploughing in Nivernais*) and Constant Troyon (*Oxen Going to Plough*), were also popular. Daubigny exhibited at the Salon with moderately Realist paintings, such as *The Harvest*, 1851, and *The Wine Harvest*, 1863, and reserved the pictures he painted in the open air for true art lovers.

Salle Courbet

The gallery gives onto the large space situated on the l. of the central pasage, reserved for this painter, the foremost exponent of Realism.

The new display of the works of Courbet (1819–77) at the Musée d'Orsay allows the visitor to admire in daylight the splendor of his technique with its free and sensual touch. A champion of Realism, Courbet scandalized the Salon of 1850 with *A Burial at Ornans***. Opposite, the massive allegory *The Artist's Studio****; he tried to symbolize his philosophical and artistic ideals in terms of personalities from the political world (Napoléon III, Garibaldi) or the artistic world (Champfleury, Baudelaire) and his friends. Beside these two masterly canvases one can see the portraits of P.-J. Prudhon* and his wife*; paintings of animals in the forests of Doubs, Courbet's native region: *The Mating Season in Spring; Stags Fighting**, *Covert of Roe deer*; a superb nude (*The Spring**); the expressive *Trout**. *Cliffs at Etretat after a storm*** is a subject also painted by Monet (the Moreau-Nélaton collection) and its limpidity and atmosphere bring to mind Impressionist landscapes.

Opposite, on the r. of the central passage, the vast canvas *Les Romains de la Décadence* (known as his 'orgy' picture) by Thomas Couture (Manet's teacher) recalls Antiquity, Veronese, Rubens, Tiepolo, and Titian all at the same time. The height of eclecticism, it won its painter a first-class medal at the Salon of 1847.

First group of rooms on the r.

This consists of three rooms opening into the central passage and the gallery behind them. Return to the start of the central passage in order to enter the first of these rooms.

Ingres and the Ingres school. Most of the works of Ingres (1780–1867), whose career spanned most of the first half of the 19th c. are displayed at the Louvre. Only a few pictures evoke the great master, who had considerable influence on the official painting of the second half of the century. *The Spring***, (1856) goes back to an idea that Ingres sketched in 1825. Its simplified relief, full curves, precise contours and muted harmonies are characteristic of the style of the master. It inspired the Neo-Classicists such as Gérôme in his Neo-Hellenistic picture *The Cock Fight*. The four models* in polished plaster by Barye for the decoration of the Denon and Richelieu pavilions of the Louvre illustrate the Neo-Classical trend in sculpture.

Delacroix and Chassériau. Another outstanding figure of the 19th century, the master of Romanticism, Delacroix (1798–1863), is represented at the Orsay by only a few canvases, the most important part of his work having remained in the Louvre. The ardor and the explosion of colors of one his masterpieces, *The Lion Hunt***, contrasts with Ingres. One of Ingres' most gifted pupils, Théodore Chassériau (1819–56) had an artistic vocation early in life and preserved the legacy of his master, as seen in *The Tepidarium*. *Arab Chiefs Challenging One Another** reveals the Romantic influence of Delacroix, whom Chassériau admired passionately. The bronze bas-relief *Ophelia** by Auguste Préault (1809–79) is a major piece of Romantic sculpture.

Historical painting and portraiture (1850–70)
The works are displayed in the third room and in the gallery behind. Throughout the 19th c. historical painting, which takes its subjects not just from history, but also from mythology and allegory, remained the ultimately noble art, the genre that attracted the highest rewards from the Salon and gave artists the opportunity to enjoy glorious careers. *The Birth of Venus**, a mythological, idealized nude by Cabanel, was a great success at the Salon of 1863. The voluptuous pose of Venus is similar to that of the *Woman Bitten by a Snake*, a marble by Clésinger that caused a scandal at

the Salon of 1847 because everybody recognized the model: Madame Sabatier, Baudelaire's 'muse'.

In the gallery (access via the staircase to the r. of the canvas by Thomas Couture, *Les Romains de la Décadence*), are hung the works of Henri Regnault, a promising young painter of historical scenes who was killed in action in the Franco-Prussian War in 1871; *Execution Without Trial Under the Moorish Kings of Grenada**, with its macabre subject and vivid colors, was his last picture. The portraits of *Madame F.* by Edouard Dubufe and of *Charles Garnier* by Baudry, painted against dark backgrounds, are in the tradition of classical portraits, restrained and full of insight.

Galleries on the r.: Decorative Arts (1850–80)

These galleries can be reached by going behind the huge painting by Thomas Couture, *Les Romains de la Décadence*.

The eclecticism which drew on styles from the past became the universal language of the applied arts. *The Toilette of the Duchess of Parma*** combines the influences of Islam, the Middle Ages, the Renaissance, and the Baroque. The vase of the *Education of Achilles* (also in a showcase in the gallery), an exceptional piece by the House of Christofle, combines new naturalist motifs with others borrowed from Mannerism. The great medal case** executed by Dielh (in the first room opening on to the gallery), is a unique work. It takes its subject from France's Merovingian past, which was being discovered at the time, and includes a relief by Frémiet, the plaster model of which is on view. As a reaction against the Industrial Revolution some artists wanted to return to the Renaissance ideal of the artist as artisan. Avisseau rediscovered Bernard Palissy (cup and basin in a showcase in the gallery); Popelin, the Limousin enamelers.

The crafts of Asia also came into favor and Japan soon made its impression: Félix Bracquemond took his subjects from Japanese illustrated books and woodblock prints for the service* that E. Rousseau commissioned from him (showcase in the second room opening onto the gallery). Later, the cabinet by Duvinage and the wardrobe* designed by Lièvre, which includes a portrait of a Japanese warrior by Detaille, were inspired by an imaginary vision of 'the Orient'.

Paintings, sculptures, and wallpapers of eclectic taste complete this presentation: *La Dévideuse*, a marble by Jules Salmson, and *The Sea's Gifts* and *The Earth's Gifts* by Hans Mackaedt.

Second group of rooms on the r.

After coming back down the central passage, enter the first of the three rooms that open onto the second part of the passage.

Puvis de Chavannes (1824–98). *Meditation, History* and *Vigilance**
are some of the decorative works among the very great number of
commissions this painter executed as part of his total renewal of the
genre of mural painting as much for public buildings (museums in
Lyons and Rouen, the Sorbonne, the Panthéon) as for private
homes. His easel paintings are counted among the first Symbolist
works: *Hope,* 1871; *Young Girls at the Seaside,* 1879. After *The Poor
Fisherman***, 1881, Puvis de Chavannes had a growing influence
among the Symbolists.

Gustave Moreau. Another precursor of Symbolism, Gustave Moreau (1826–98) admired Delacroix and Chassériau. His iconography,
drawn from the Bible and from mythology, was very complex.
*Jason** and *Orpheus*** are typical examples of the two images of
women as they appear in the work of Moreau: women dominant,
tempting and infernal as betrayed in the look Medea casts on Jason,
and women suffering and melancholic, close to the soul of the poet,
who carries the head of Orpheus. Works lent by the Gustave
Moreau Museum complete this display. (→Gustave Moreau
Museum.)

Degas before 1870. Born into a banking family, Edgar Degas
worked under the direction of Lamothe, a pupil of Ingres and
Chassériau, and completed his studies with a long stay in Italy,
where he discovered the Primitives of the 14th and 15th c. A
passionate admirer of Ingres, Degas remained, faithful to the Neo-
Classical tradition until 1870. As early as his *The Bellelli Family***,
however, the characteristic traits appear which were to make him
one of the representatives of modernity in the following decade.
Also on display are portraits of the artist*, of Marguerite de Gas*,
Thérèse de Gas*, the cellist Pillet* and a painting of the *Orchestra of
the Opéra**** one of the first pictures in which dancers appear (in
the middle ground).

Second group of rooms on the l.

Return down the central passage to enter the Manet room.
Manet before 1870: *Les Parents de l'Artist**, *Olympia****, portrait of
Zola***, *The Piper, The Balcony****.

Monet, Bazille, and Renoir before 1870. Return to the central
passage and into this room next to the preceding one.

Monet, Bazille, and Renoir had met in the studio of Gleyre in Paris
and went together to paint in the forest of Fontainebleau, developing a new interest in painting outdoors. Bazille, who died prematur-
ely in the Franco-Prussian War of 1870, painted his family in the
open air under the sun of the south of France: *The Artist's Family.*
*Women in the Garden*** by Monet is a more modern work; there is
already in the landscapes he painted before 1870 an incomparable
freshness: *Garden in Bloom; Country Railway*; *The Magpie**, a

recent acquisition; *L'Hôtel des Roches Noires à Trouville*** in which the influence of Boudin shows through.

In the gallery behind these two rooms can be seen, opposite the *Déjeuner sur l'herbe*** (Luncheon on the Grass) by Manet, *The Pink Dress*; an al fresco painting by Bazille, and a superb early portrait by Monet: *Madame Gaudibert**. Further along on the r. are works by the southern painter Paul Guigou: *La Route de la Gineste* (1854); *The Laundress**. On the l. in *A Studio at Batignolles** by Fantin-Latour, all the models represented around Manet are either his or Fantin-Latour's friends.

Galleries on the l.

Fantin-Latour and Whistler. *Hommage à Delacroix* (1864), the first of the great group portraits by Fantin-Latour, is a true manifesto; it assembles around the self-portrait of the great master those perso-nalities who represent the new school of painting: painters (Manet, Whistler), writers (Baudelaire), and critics (Champfleury). Less austere, the still lifes and portraits of women (*Mademoiselle Charlotte Dubourg***), display more clearly the sensibility of Fantin-Latour, who sought a path between the academic and the new painting. A friend of the artist, the American James Abbot McNeill Whistler, is represented with *The Artist's Mother* and *Arrangement in Grey and Black*.

Boudin, Jongkind, and Lépine. In this room landscapes by the precursors of Impressionism are collected together: Eugène Boudin (1824–8), Johan Barthold Jongkind (1819–91) and Stanislas Lépine (1836–92). The Mollard collection has some superb examples: *The Beach at Trouville*, 1864, by Boudin; *La Rue de l'Abbé de l'Epée* by Jongkind; *Montmartre, Rue Saint-Vincent* by Lépine. Alongside these are landscapes by painters of the Hague School: *Seaweed Gathering* by Mauve; *Sunset* by Mesdag.

Moreau-Nélaton Collection (→inset): *Red Poppies* by Monet, *Blonde Woman With Bare Breasts* by Manet.

Mollard Collection: *White Frost***, 1873, representative of the work of Camille Pissarro, a painter who loved the earth and the coun-tryside. This painting belongs, along with others by Boudin, Lépine, Jongkind (→above), Sisley (*The Bridge of Moret*), Théodore Rousseau, Stevens, and Renoir, to the 1961 donation which was completed in 1972 by the legacy of Dr Eduardo Mollard to the Louvre.

Photography and graphic arts (Rooms 1 and 2). In these two small rooms situated on either side of the space reserved for the Moreau-Nélaton Collection, as well as in a third on the upper floor, the museum's collections of photographs and graphic arts are presented in temporary exhibitions. The fragility of works on paper, which deteriorate when exposed to light, explains the relative dimness of these rooms.

Realism. The Spanish school played a determining role among the Realist painters: in *Amende Honorable* Legros was inspired by a picture by Zurbarán, in the Louvre, while the *The Martyrdom of St Sebastian* by Théodore Ribot recalls the style of Ribera. Alongside these works, which were contemporary with the beginnings of Impressionism, are paintings* by Monticelli, landscapes* by Ravier and, in a showcase, Meissonnier's famous wax sculpture *The Traveller****.

Orientalism. Under the Second Empire, Orientalism remained an important aesthetic movement. *The Desert* by Guillaumet and *The Country of Thirst* by Fromentin are close to Realism, while Barrias' sculpture, *Young Girl from Megara*, who sits and spins, inhabits a more picturesque Orient.

Salle de l'Opéra***

At the end, in the middle of the central passage, this room presents the Opéra from a variety of perspectives. Inaugurated in 1875 after 13 years of construction, the new Opéra de Paris symbolized the triumph of Second Empire architecture, and made its architect, Charles Garnier, famous. The relief map (scale 1:100) of the Opéra district in 1914 is displayed on the floor under glass. It shows the problems encountered in trying to integrate the building into the Haussmannian architecture surrounding it and the deliberate contrast of the highly decorative exterior with the austerity of the district. The large model*, a lengthwise cross section of the building, emphasizes the contrast between the rigorous logic of the interior layout and the exuberance of the exterior. In addition, the Musée d'Orsay presents sketches, maquettes, models, and originals (including a relief of *La Danse**** by J. B. Carpeaux) of the sculpted decoration. Numerous documents on loan from the Bureau of Architecture and the Opéra Museum accompany in rotation the great model of the stage made for the Universal Exhibition of 1900.

If time is short, take the escalators at the end of the central passage and go straight to the upper level where the Impressionist collections are on display.

Le Pavillon Amont on the l. of the Salle de l'Opéra

Architecture 1850 to 1900. The structure of the Gare d'Orsay is completely revealed here. Colored reliefs based on elements taken from those buildings that are most representative of the era trace the history of 19th-c. architectural grammar, its decorative vocabulary, and materials. They are displayed on a tower invented by the

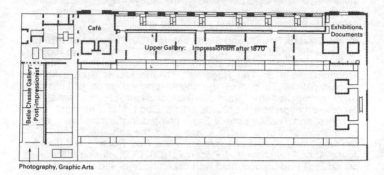

Orsay Museum, upper level

decorator Richard Peduzzi. The great picture by Victor Navlet representing Paris in 1855,* before Haussmann's transformations, shows just how extensive was the modernization carried out during the Second Empire and the Third Republic.

The revival of the Decorative Arts: Pugin, Morris, Webb, Mackmurdo, Jeckyll, Godwin, Sullivan. Going up the pavilion staircase you first reach a level where several areas are devoted to the Arts and Crafts Movement. Around William Morris a group of artists and architects was formed; champions of a total art, they laid the foundations for a revival of the decorative arts. The painted woodwork* by the decorating film of Morris, Marshall, Faulkner & Co., the sideboard* by Philip Speakman Webb and *The King's Daughter*, both painting and frame by Burne-Jones, illustrate the diversity of their quests.

Viollet-le-Duc. In a room on the same level, the theories of Viollet-le Duc on décor and interior design are displayed by means of mural paintings. Continue to the upper level and the areas reserved for informative displays on architecture.

Upper level

The Galerie des Hauteurs

This gallery is devoted to works from the post-1870 period when Impressionism had reached its peak. The museum possesses one of the world's richest collections (→inset). The natural overhead lighting, thanks to the glass roof, is eminently suited to the works of these artists, who were obsessed by the study of light. At this point our tour abandons strict chronological order, reserving the intermediate level for the last part of the visit.

Monet, Pissaro, Renoir, and Sisley before 1880. The decade 1870 to 1880 saw the development of Impressionism. These first two rooms follow its evolution through the works of its founders. In his views of Argenteuil such as *The Regattas**, Claude Monet used a light-colored palette. To convey the shimmering reflection of light on water he applied the short, broken brushstrokes that were to become an Impressionist characteristic. Don't miss *Zaandam**, *Les Barques*, and *The Argenteuil Basin* painted in the same vein, and more 'Intimist' works where Monet used the same technique: *Le Déjeuner** and *Apartment Interior**. *The Red Roofs*** and *Landscape After Rain* show that Pissarro (1830–1903), during the same period, was also preoccupied with depicting light and the changing aspects of sun, sky, and weather. While Monet painted water, Pissarro had a deep affection for earth, as shown in *Hillside at the Hermitage, Pontoise** or *Harvest at Montfoucault***. Sisley was similarly occupied at Port-Marly: *The Flood at Port-Marly*** is one of his masterpieces. Like Monet, Renoir (1841–1919) adopted the Impressionist technique which he was soon to apply to his portraits, such as those of *Claude Monet** and *Alphonsine Fournaise**. In his masterly *Moulin de la Galette*** and *The Swing** he made a study of the colored reflections and blue-tinted shadows of the sun through foliage. The Impressionists also took their subjects from urban life, as in Monet's *Gare Saint-Lazare*** or *La Rue Montorgueil***.

Manet and Degas after 1870. Like Monet after the Franco-Prussian War of 1870, Manet (1832–83) was drawn to Impressionism and painting outdoor scenes: *On the Beach*** (1873) is an example. In his *Portrait of Nina de Callais**, *The Lady with the Fans** or the *Portrait of Mallarmé** the nervous brushstroke of the Impressionist is evident. New subjects taken from Parisian daily life appear in his work: *La Serveuse de Bocks** (The Waitress). Next to Manet's works are the paintings of his sister-in-law Berthe Morisot (1841–95): *The Cradle**; *Young Woman Dressed for a Ball*. Degas (1834–1917) exhibited alongside the Impressionists, but his method deviated from theirs, for he painted his open-air subjects from memory in the studio: *Racehorses before the Judges*. Degas' paintings are striking in their originality: the strongly vertical composition of *Woman with Vase** or *At the Stock Exchange***; the diagonal composition inspired by Japanese prints in *L'Absinthe*** and *Women Ironing*** and the composition relegating the characters to the middle distance in *Au Café*. The paintings of ballerinas, a favorite theme of Degas, allowed for studies in group arrangements in a confined space, and for studies in movement: *Ballet Rehearsal on the Stage* (1874); *Ballet Class**, (1874); *Blue Dancers*** (1886–90). The bronzes on view in the center showcases complement the paintings: a series of horses, dancers (including *Prima Ballerina in Costume*), and women at their toilette. Degas' sculpture was ignored for a long time but today it is regarded as some of the most interesting artists of the period.

Monet and Renoir after 1880. Based at Vétheuil in 1878, then at Giverny in 1883, Monet pursued his studies of light and atmosphere: *Church at Vétheuil, Snow, The Seine at Vétheuil, Accident on the Seine, Rocks at Belle-Ile, Fields of Tulips in Holland, Woman with a Parasol,* two decorative panels. He embarked upon several series of canvases based on the same subject seen at different times of day: *Haystacks**, Rouen Cathedral***, five of which are owned by the museum; *London and the Houses of Parliament*, which are part of the Thames series. Finally, his garden at Giverny claimed all Monet's attention for studies of light, plants, water, and weather: *Water Lily Pond**; Blue Water Lilies*** (→*Nymphéas*, Musée de l'Orangerie).

Renoir brought back some magnificent landscapes from a trip to Algeria: *Algerian Landscape**; Arab Festival at Algiers**; Banana Plantation.* His style then went through a critical period when line took precedence over color. *Dance in the City*** and *Dance in the Country*** were painted during this time. He went on to the so-called *style nacré* (pearly style), a more supple technique: *Young Girls at the Piano** and *The Bathers****, which Renoir considered his greatest painting. This last painting, with its brilliant palette, where red predominates, bears witness to the vitality of this artist in his old age, crippled with rheumatism, paralysed, yet still devoted to the female form.

On the central dais late works by Pissarro are exhibited: *The Wheelbarrow**, Jeune Fille à la Baguette*, 1881, and Sisley's *The Loing Canal*, 1892.

The next room contains a display of sculptures by Renoir executed with the assistance of Guino: *Madame Renoir, The Judgement of Paris.*

Personnaz Collection. The collection bequeathed to the national museums by Antonin Personnaz (1854–1936) is on view in this room. A native of Bayonne, he was connected with Pissarro, Degas, and Armand Guillaumin (1841–1927). The 14 canvases by Pissarro show the painter's development during the second part of his career: *The Louveciennes Road* (1870), *Landscape at Chaponval** (1880); *Women in an Enclosure** (1887). There are also works by Monet: *The Bridge at Argenteuil** (1874), Sisley: *Fog;* Guillaumin, Berthe Morisot: *In the Corn** (1875): and the only painting in the museum by the American artist Mary Cassatt (1844–1926): *Woman Sewing.* Works from the collection of Dr Gachet (→inset) complete the exhibition: *Chrysanthèmus** by Monet, *Margot*** by Renoir.

Van Gogh. After wavering for several years between theology and painting, Vincent van Gogh chose the latter in 1880. Arriving in Paris in 1886 he joined his brother Theo, who remained until Vincent's death his source of both financial and moral support. Van Gogh abandoned his dark palette with its broad, thick brushstrokes (*Head of Dutch Peasant Woman*, 1884). Through contact with the Impressionists his palette lightened and his brushstroke became more fragmented: *La Guinguette*, 1886, *The Mermaid Restaurant*, 1886, *Self-Portrait**, 1887. Japanese prints provided him with new ideas of composition: *L'Italienne* (The Italian Woman, 1887). At Arles, in 1888, he concentrated on color: *Dance Hall at Arles* and *L'Arlésienne* (Madame Ginoux) show an affinity with the style of Gauguin, with whom he was working. The moving *Van Gogh's Bedroom at Arles* and the magnificent *Self-Portrait** (1889) were painted after Van Gogh's tragic bout of insanity at Arles in December 1888. Taken in by his patron and friend, Dr Paul Gachet, at Auvers-sur-Oise, he continued to paint frenetically. With their broad, feverish brushstrokes, strangely clashing colors and distorted perspective, certain pictures, such as *The Church at Auvers-sur-Oise*, express the spiritual anguish of the artist, who shot himself on July 27, 1890, and died on the 29th.

Cézanne. Every stage in the career of Paul Cézanne (1839–1906) is represented here. From his *couillard* 'butch' manner, with its heavy, thick black paint, the museum possesses *The Magdalen or Grief*, the amazingly intense *Portrait of Achille Emperaire** and *Still Life With Kettle**. In 1872 he settled at Auvers-sur-Oise near Pissarro and adopted the Impressionists' bright palette and broken brushstrokes: *House of the Hanged Man*, *A Modern Olympia* (a reworking of Manet's painting), *Dahlias* and *Still Life With Soup Tureen*. Cézanne exhibited unsuccessfully with the Impressionists, but was publicly defended by Zola. He soon distanced himself from the movement, as is evident from *Farmyard at Auvers* with its almost abstract rigidity; *Poplars* and *The Bridge at Maincy**, in which Cézanne used a mosaic-like brushstroke and a quasi-geometric structure, as in *L'Estaque***. Cézanne spent his last years in Aix-en-Provence. He tried to 'do Poussin from life' by treating nature 'by means of the cylinder and the sphere'. Accordingly his last works were broad in scope and had considerable impact on the painting and art of the 20th c.: *Bathers***, *The Card Players***, the monumental *Woman With Coffee Pot****, *Still Life With Onions*, and the masterly still life *Apples and Oranges***.

Pastels by Degas***. These are on view in a small room at the far l. of the gallery. Throughout his career Degas made use of pastel: the study for *Semiramis Building Babylon* dates from 1861. When his eyesight began to fail he gradually had to give up drawing and engraving and worked more extensively in pastel. Degas contributed to the revival of this technique by exploiting all its possibilities, from the light, hazy strokes of his landscapes, created from 1869 to 1870, to the complex system of cross-hatching evident in such fine works as *Dancer With Bouquet Taking a Bow on Stage*, *Fin d'Arabesque*, *After the Bath*, or *Woman Drying her Neck*. Degas' assertion: 'my art is in no way spontaneous, it is entirely reflective', is particularly appropriate to these pastels. Their harmonious colors show great refinement, notably in *At the Milliner's* or in the series of women at their toilette: *The Tub, Woman Combing Her Hair, After the Bath*.

To the r. is the upper-level café, which offers a fine view over the Seine and Paris. The café gives access to the outside terrace overlooking the Seine.

The reference room, with its modern computer resources, is situated on the mezzanine floor of the upper-level café.

Les Salles d'angles (the corner rooms)

Seurat and Neo-Impressionism. *The Circus*, an unfinished painting by Georges Seurat (1859–91) was his final composition. Seurat applied to it his theories on the scientific division of the brushstroke, substituting an optical mingling of discrete dots of pure hues for the actual mixing of pigments to achieve a greater luminosity [a technique called pointillism]. He also attempted to apply Charles Henry's theories on the emotive effects and psychological expressiveness of lines, according to which diagonals suggest movement and cheerfulness. Notice the frame, also painted by Seurat. The studies for his large canvases allow a clearer insight regarding his technique. The use of short broken brushstrokes, in accordance with Seurat's theories, is characteristic of Neo-Impressionist paintings: *The Red Buoy*, The Green Sail, Women at the Well* by Paul Signac; *The Golden Isles, Evening Air* by Cross; *Couple in the Street** by Angrand; *The Marne at Dawn** by Dubois-Pillet; *On the Boat* by Van Rysselberghe; *The Seine and Notre-Dame* by Maximilien Luce.

Salle Redon***. Access is via the first room, devoted to Neo-Impressionism. Do not miss the mysterious *Portrait of Gauguin* by Odilon Redon (1840–1916), the portrait of *Madame Redon*, and the series of pastels which show the particularly brilliant talent of this great colorist. Thanks to the donation by Ari and Suzanne Redon, the artist's son and daughter-in-law, the museum possesses a unique collection of drawings and a series of luminous little landscapes in oils. They show every side of this great artist, secret, sensitive, independent of any movement or theory.

The pastels. Three rooms on either side of the Redon room show in rotation the museum's collection of pastels. The second half of the 19th c. saw the revival of the pastel technique used by the Impressionists (Manet, Bracquemond, Berthe Morisot) and their contemporaries (Helleu), but especially by the Symbolists, such as Levy-Dhurmer or Degouve de Nuncques.

Salle Toulouse-Lautrec***. *Woman Dressing* shows how greatly Degas influenced Henri de Toulouse-Lautrec (1864–1901) in both his themes and the boldness of his composition, though Toulouse-

Lautrec's rapid, tense, and simplifying stroke remained very personal. His portraits of cabaret artistes such as *La Goulue*, *Jane Avril Dancing*, and *La Clownesse Cha-U-Kao*, and his portrayals of prostitutes (*The Bed*, *Blonde Prostitute*) show his psychological perception and also the tenderness he felt toward his models.

The Gallerie Bellechasse

Henri Rousseau. *War** (hung on the l.) in its primitive, naïve style, shows the richness of Rousseau's imagination. As mentioned earlier, Henri Rousseau (1844–1910) was nicknamed 'Le Douanier' (the Customs Officer), for he was an employee of the Customs Service of Paris. Opposite, the monumental *Portrait of a Woman* illustrates another side of this enigmatic painter's work.

Gauguin (→inset), Emile Bernard, and Sérusier. *Washerwomen at Pont-Aven*** dates from Gauguin's first stay in Brittany and still shows the influence of Impressionism. Gauguin painted the view of *Les Alyscamps** when staying with Van Gogh at Arles. *La Belle Angèle****, *La Famille Schuffenecker**, and *Yellow Haystacks** represent the Synthetism perfected at Pont-Aven. You can follow the parallel evolution of Emile Bernard. On the back of his picture *Stoneware Pot and Apples* is written 'first attempt at Synthetism and simplication.' *Madeleine au Bois d'Amour*** 1888, a Symbolist work portraying the painter's sister, is Emile Bernard's Synthetic masterpiece. Thanks to the Mlle Boutaric donation the museum has a fine collection of works by Sérusier: *Gate with Flowers*, *Eve Bretonne or Melancholy*, *The Shower*.

Gauguin. To the l. of the gallery are canvases painted by Gauguin after his first departure from Paris. *Le Moulin David*, 1894 is similar to his Pont-Aven landscapes. Painted during his first stay in Tahiti, *Tahitian Women****, *The Meal***, and *Arearea**, combine sensuality, warm, exotic colors, and Symbolism. *And the Gold of Their Bodies****, *Vairumati** and *The White Horse*** are three masterpieces from his second stay in the West Indies. Opposite are objects and sculptures by Gauguin: ceramics produced with Chapelet; the fantastic relief *Soyez Mystieuses***, 1890; the superb sculpture *Oviri***, a recent acquisition; *Native Curios* inspired by Tahitian mythology, idols in shell or pearl, and finally the carved wooden panels** from his hut at Atuana in the Marquesas Islands. Beside Gauguin's carvings are those of the Nabi sculptor Georges Lacombe, with strange, symbolic themes: *Isis* and the bed panels based on the theme of *Human Life* show a primitive style.

The Nabis. All these paintings are in the two end rooms of the gallery. The Nabis (a term coined by the poet Cazalis, from the Hebrew word for 'prophets') bought together artists determined to 'regenerate' painting: Maurice Denis, Pierre Bonnard, Ranson; later Vuillard and Roussel, and finally Verkade, Lacombe, Rippl Ronai,

Maillol, and Vallotton. Near Sérusier's *Talisman*** are hung two works by the group's theorist Maurice Denis, *Taches de Soleil sur la Terrasse** (Splashes of Sunlight on the Terrace) and the *Ascent to Calvary*, for which it is appropriate to quote Denis well-known formulation: 'Remember that a painting – before being a war horse or a nude woman or an anecdote – is essentially a flat surface covered with colors assembled in a certain order' (Maurice Denis, *Art et Critique*, August 2, 1890). To the r., the painting *In Bed*** by Edouard Vuillard typifies the Nabis' style. Intimist subjects, simplification of form, and flat planes of color, partitioned by marked contours. The Nabis were interested in decorative art, as shown by the Vuillard panels, *The Public Gardens*, or *Women in the Garden*** by Bonnard, four works acquired recently. Particularly admirable are the canvases by Bonnard, nicknamed the 'Japonard Nabi': *Child with Sand-Castle**, *Le Peignor*** and, in the last room, *By Lamplight*; and *Woman with Parasol*** by Aristide Maillol. Félix Vallotton's paintings are distinguished by the originality of their compositions: *The Ball***, *The Third Gallery at the Théâtre du Châtelet*. Maurice Denis showed a more marked preference for Symbolism: *The Muses*** is one of his masterpieces.

Max and Rosy Kaganovitch Donation. This collection is housed in the gallery after the one reserved for temporary exhibitions of graphic art and photography, and brings together Impressionist, Post-Impressionist and Fauvist works. It includes the masterpieces *A Corner of the Garden at the Hermitage* by Pissarro, *L'Hôpital Saint-Jean*** by Van Gogh (1889), *Breton Peasant Woman* by Gauguin (1894), *Intérieur* by Bonnard (1920) and *Charing Cross Bridge* by Derain.

Leave this room and go down to the middle level for the last part of the tour.

Passage de la Presse. An escalator leads to this area where significant stages in the history of the press and the illustrated book are represented with the aid of information panels.

Off this corridor is an area where there are documented exhibitions on the same theme.

Passage des Dates. A second escalator leads to a series of audiovisual consoles that give year-by-year information on the main political, social, and cultural events of the 19th c.

Middle level

Art and decoration during the Third Republic

The ballroom of the former Hôtel d'Orsay. Official paintings and sculptures of the Third Republic are assembled here (→inset). Allegorical subjects introduced the idealized, female nude. Most

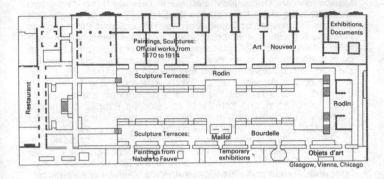

Orsay Museum, middle level

famous are *Birth of Venus* by Bouguereau, *Nature Unveiling Herself before Science*, in polychrome marble and Algerian onyx by Barrias, and a marble statue by Gérôme, *Tanagra*. In another gallery behind the ballroom, overlooking the Seine, is Gervex's painting *Le Jury de Peinture du Salon*, representing the men who hallowed this official art.

Leaving the ballroom, cross the footbridge. On the r. is the restaurant entrance. On the l., overhanging the central aisle, are the sculpture terraces, with works arranged chronologically from 1870 to 1914.

The first terrace is devoted to official sculpture of the Third Republic, rich in monumental works such as the *Monument to Gérôme*, representing the sculptor working on his group of *Gladiators*, *St Michael Slaying the Dragon** by Frémiet, a replica of the statue on the summit of Mont Saint-Michel.

First group of rooms opening onto the sculpture terraces: Naturalism and Symbolism

Naturalism. The first of these six rooms houses the great Naturalist canvases. After its rejection in academic circles during the Second Empire, Naturalism was adopted by the most highly regarded official painters of the Third Republic, such as Cormon in his enormous canvas *The Sons of Cain*, Bonnat in *Madame Pasca*, or Cazin in *Close of Day*. Equally noteworthy are more modest, but interesting works by Bastien-Lepage, *Hay*, and again Cormon, *The Smithy*.

Dalou, Meunier. This gallery, like all those overlooking the Seine, has a splendid view. Naturalism was a vehicle for the republican views of the sculptors Dalou and Meunier. *The Blacksmith***, a plaster cast by Dalou (1838–1902), was the model for one statue of the *Triumph of the Republic* (cast in bronze in 1886 and erected on the Place de la Nation in 1899) while his bronze *Tall Peasant* was sculpted for his project for a *Monument to Labor*.

Blanche, Boldini, Helleu, Troubetskoy. The frivolous, brilliant, witty Parisian society at the turn of the century is represented by the artists on display here. Robert de Montesquiou, a worldly character if ever there was one, is presented at the Orsay Museum thanks to the superb bronze* by Paul Troubetskoy and the painting by Boldini. Sarah Bernhardt is present in the tinted marble bust by Gérôme.

Naturalism (continued). This second hall shows the international growth of Naturalism at the end of the 19th c. *Country Brasserie* by the German artist, Liebermann; *Madame Lwoff*, by the Russian, Valentine Serov; *Two White Horses Carting Piles at Amsterdam* by the Dutchman, Breitner; *Fishing Boats* by the Dane, Kroyer; *The Disciples Peter and John Running to the Sepulchre* by the Swiss, Burnand and *The Ages of the Laborer* by the Belgian, Léon Frédéric.

Symbolism. These two rooms are reached via the sculpture terrace. The first, containing the large works, opens before Frémiet's *St Michael*. Symbolism, seeking to interpret the inner world of dreams, was a reaction against civilization, industrialism and materialism. Several artists, painters, sculptors, poets, and musicians were Symbolists, such as the academic painters Henri Martin (*Sérénité*) and René Ménard, whose enormous canvases destined for the Paris Faculty of Law are worthy of admiration. Equally noteworthy are the smaller, more evocative works: *Summer Night* by the American, Winslow Homer, and the works of Eugène Carrière.

Several Symbolist masterpieces are on view in the room overlooking the Seine: *The Dream* by Puvis de Chavannes, *With Closed Eyes*** by Redon, *The Wheel of Fortune* by Burne-Jones.

Second sculpture terrace

The second sculpture terrace, following after the great void above the Courbet room, is devoted to Auguste Rodin (1840–1917), the artist who dominated the sculpture of the period. A few majestic statues – *Walking Man, The Age of Bronze** – represent this great genius, although most of his works are in the Rodin museums in Paris and Meudon. Unique plaster casts from these museums are: *Ugolino***, *Balzac****, *The Muse*** from the *Monument to Whistler*, and the *Gates of Hell****. A major work by Camille Claudel, *Maturity*, a bronze, has been placed near Rodin's works at the entrance.

Second group of rooms opening into the sculpture terraces: Art Nouveau

These six rooms are devoted to Art Nouveau which appeared simultaneously in France and Belgium at the end of the 19th c., shortly after its English precursor, the Arts and Crafts movement.

France, Belgium. Situated at the head of the concourse this room shows works of the Belgian architects Victor Horta (paneling and furniture from the Hôtel Aubecq in Brussels) and Henry Van de Velde (armchair made in 1896 for the banker Biard), with a cabinet displaying jewelry (Lalique: pendant and chain) and costume accessories (Bastard: barley-ear fan).

Guimard. From the start the architect Hector Guimard (1867–1942) obtained numerous public and private commissions (apartment buildings, Métro stations) and left an abundant output featuring stylized vegetal motifs. The stained-glass window, chimneypiece and the banquette with display cabinet** come from the same property in the Loiret, built from 1897 to 1898. Another stained-glass window, *At the New Circus****, produced by the American glass artist, Louis Comfort Tiffany, from a sketch by Toulouse-Lautrec, comes from a series of 12 commissioned from the Nabis in 1894 by the merchant Siegfried Bing. The display case with ceramics and glassware* (Dalpayrat, Bigot and Dammouse) shows the Japanese influence on ceramics at that time.

Gallé. Emile Gallé (1846–1904), a glassmaker and furniture designer, was variously inspired to transform the decoration and shape of his objects: ornamental dish* with Japanese-style decoration, jardinière* in the shape of an Egyptian falcon. The numerous techniques applicable to glass that he went on to use resulted in a wide range of objects: *October Convolvulus*, a two-layer crystal vase; *Onion Flowers*, glass marquetry made for the 1900 World Fair. A perfectionist, he next created a collection of furniture to harmonize with his decorative pieces, like the display cabinet *Winter Flora**, presented at the 1889 Universal Exhibition, or the monumental *Dragonfly Cabinet**, Emile Gallé's final creation in 1904. The stained-glass window is the work of Henri Carot, designed by Albert Besnard.

Nancy School. Around Emile Gallé in Nancy, artists, artisans and manufacturers gathered with a common loyalty to the principle of decoration inspired by nature. The cabinetmakers built furniture with designs of plant motifs: a bureau and bookcase with orchids, a bed with waterlilies (in mahogany and gilded bronze) by Majorelle, a bed and mirror-front wardrobe by Eugène Vallin. The glass fountain by Henri Cros was commissioned by the State for the Luxembourg museum in 1892.

Carabin, Charpentier, Dampt. Relegated to the rank of minor arts, the decorative arts found a new dimension at the turn of the century.

The bookcase by Rupert Carabin, made for the engineer Montaudon, depicts the triumph of the mind over ignorance with lavish symbolism. Jean Dampt created paneling in oak, ash and elm for the Comtesse de Béarn's drawing-room, complemented by matching furniture and an overmantel surmounted by a bas-relief, *The Knight of the Ideal*. From the villa of the banker Benard at Champrosay, Charpentier's *grande boiserie*** with his monumental table, corner silver cabinets, and Bigot's great basin make up one of the rare Art Nouveau collections that exists in its entirety. The last cabinet contains ceramics by Carriès, Delaherche, Valombreuse and Massié.

Guimard Tower and Art Nouveau international tower

Guimard Tower. Access is through the sculpture terrace as far as Rodin's plaster cast of Balzac. Decorative casts by Guimard are displayed on the landings and staircase going up. From the tops of the towers, which are linked by a footbridge, the view stretches the length of the building: below is the central aisle, bordered by the sculpture terraces, and above are the glass roof and the ornamental bays of the ceiling.

Art Nouveau International. The simultaneous presentation of architect-designed furniture** from different countries makes clear the contrast existing at the turn of the century between the decorative conception of Gaudi and Bugatti, related to French Art Nouveau, and the bare, severe, Modernist trend (→inset) anticipating 20th-c. design with Hoffman, Wagner and Mackintosh.

Vienna, Glasgow and Chicago. These three rooms at the end of the museum, open onto the sculpture terraces overlooking Rue de Lille.

Third and fourth sculpture terraces

The sculpture terraces on the Rue de Lille side present works by sculptors contemporary with or later than Rodin: Desbois, Rosso, Bartholomé (*Portrait of Anatole France**), akin to Symbolism; and *Hercules the Archer** by one of Rodin's assistants, Bourdelle. Finally Joseph Bernard's *Effort Toward Nature** and Maillol's *Mediterranean* end the chronological display.

The first group of rooms opening onto the sculpture terraces is reserved for archival exhibitions.

Last group of rooms opening onto the sculpture terraces: 20th-c. art

Bonnard, Denis, Vallotton, Vuillard. After 1900 the painters of the Nabis group went their separate ways. In the first room are portraits by Vuillard: *Thadée Natanson**, *Coolus***, *Claude Bonheim de Villers**; works by Bonnard, *La Toilette*, *Woman With Cat*. Further on is *Battledore and Shuttlecock* by Maurice Denis, still close to the Nabi style.

In the second room are several large canvases: by Ker Xavier Roussel (1867–1944), *Rape of the Daughters of Leucippus and Polyphemus**, *Acis and Galatea**; by Vuillard, *La Bibliothèque***, and Bonnard's masterpiece, *The Yacht****.

The 20th c. In this little room are several international masterpieces from the early years of the 20th c.: *The Wave* by Strindberg; *Roses under the Trees** by Klimt; *Summer Night at Aasgaarstrand* by Munch; *Luxe, Calme, et Volupté*** by Matisse; *The Beach at Fécamp*** by Marquet and *The Snake Charmer**** by Henri Rousseau.

At the end of the terrace in a little room is a display tracing the history of the cinema.

▷ Jean-Baptiste Carpeaux

Despite his modest background, Jean-Baptiste Carpeaux (1827–75) had a brilliant, though brief, career as the leading sculptor of the Second Empire. He was introduced to the court by Princess Mathilde, the cousin of Napoléon III, and became the latter's protégé, painting portraits of members of the imperial family (*The Imperial Prince and his dog Nero*, 1865). He also participated in the decoration of the great constructions of the Second Empire, the Louvre and the Opéra. In his groups Carpeaux made great use of the circular compositions, which allowed him to reconcile balance with movement. As early as his *Ugolin* whose subject, inspired by Dante's *Divine Comedy*, was later used by Rodin – the children form a lifeless circle around their father. This circle is again outlined by the high-relief of the putti on the façade of the Pavillon de Flore (Louvre), who turn around the goddess. In *The Dance* (1869), a relief executed for the Opéra, the movement is more frenetic. This work caused a scandal both for the nudity of the dancing girls and the ambiguity of the masculine figure and the general turmoil of the sculpture's composition. In fact Carpeaux took up this ensemble again for *The Four Quarters of the World* on the Observatory fountain, which circles a globe.

Carpeaux left many portraits which overflow with life (*Mademoiselle Fiocre, Charles Garnier*), and in which grace joins with a powerful realism, and expression with movement. Though Carpeaux's work is intimately connected with the Second Empire, it can also be counted among that of the greatest sculpture of the European tradition.

▷ The Alfred Chauchard Collection

Alfred Chauchard (1821–1909) was one of the founders of the Grands Magasins du Louvre (Louvre chainstores). From 1885 he dedicated his fortune to charitable work and to amassing a collection of paintings which he left in its entirety to the Louvre Museum in 1906. The most famous work in the collection is Millet's *Angelus* for which Chauchard bid against American collectors and bought at an exceptionally high price. He also purchased several pictures by the Barbizon painters. Thus around the *Angelus* one can admire *An Avenue, Forêt de l'Isle-Adam* by Théodore Rousseau, *Les Hauteurs de Jean de Paris* by Narcisse Diaz de la Peña; *La Mare aux Chênes* by Jules Dupré. The rest of the Chauchard Collection (exhibited in the gallery behind this group of rooms, on the partition wall between the Chauchard Room 1 and the gallery) shows works by Delacroix (*The Tiger Hunt*), Decamps, Meissonnier, including the famous *The French Campaign* (1815), *Ziem*, and *Atlas*.

▷ Not to be missed

Ground Floor
Central passage: *The Dance* and *The Four Quarters of the World* from the Observatory fountain by Carpeaux.

Salle de l'Opéra: the relief map of the Opéra district.

Rooms on the l.: the busts of the parliamentarians by Daumier; the *Angelus, The Gleaners* and *Spring* by Millet; *The Burial at Ornans* and *The Artist's Studio* by Courbet; *Le Dejeuner sur l'herbe, Olympia,* and *The Balcony* by Manet; *Women in the Garden, L'Hôtel des Roches Noires à Trouville, Red Poppies* by Monet.

Rooms on the r.: *The Toilette of the Duchesse de Parme, The Poor Fisherman* by Puvis de Chavannes; *Orpheus* by Gustave Moreau; *The Bellelli Family* by Degas.

▷ Manet and the beginnings of Impressionism

Edouard Manet (1832–93) worked for a short time in the studio of Thomas Couture but soon rebelled against this academic instruction. It was by copying Velázquez and Delacroix that he achieved his artistic education. After a few small successes at the Salon (notably with the portrait of his parents, 1861), *Le Dejeuner sur l'herbe* (*Luncheon on the Grass*), presented at the Salon des Refusés (salon for rejected painters) in 1863, created a scandal. More than the subject matter, it was the technique with its broad brushstrokes, his handling of pigment, and the perspectiveless drawing that shocked. Two years later *Olympia* was laughed at for the same reasons. In 1866 *The Piper* was rejected by the Salon. In 1869 the modernity of *The Balcony* was met with incomprehension. Although the critics unleashed their fury, those artists who were fighting against the academic approach, saw in Manet their leader: Zola took up his pen to defend the young artist (Manet painted his portrait by way of thanks); Fantin-Latour showed him in his *Homage to Delacroix* as the representative of young painters and in the *Studio at Batignolles* as an undisputed master. Finally, in *The Studio* by Bazille he appears side by side with Monet and Renoir as an influential friend. Thus Manet played, a little reluctantly, a determining role in the history of Impressionism, though it was not until after 1870, in some pictures influenced by Monet, that his painting could be said to be Impressionist.

▷ The Moreau-Nélaton Collection

Painter, art historian and collector, Etienne Moreau-Nélaton (1859–1927) gave to the Louvre in 1906 a collection of paintings and drawings that make up the finest donation of 19th-c. works ever made to the museum. The Impressionist works are exhibited at the Musée d'Orsay, while the remainder of the collection is at the Louvre. Among the masterpieces to be seen are the famous *Déjeuner sur l'herbe* and *Blonde Woman with Bare Breasts* by Manet; *Red Poppies*, (1873), *Rust Under the Lilacs* and *The Bridge at Argenteuil* (1873) by Monet; *The Butterfly Hunt* by Berthe Morisot (1874); *The Stagecoach at Louveciennes* by Pissarro; *The Footbridge at Argenteuil* and *Rest Beside the Stream* by Sisley.

▷ Gustave Caillebotte

Gustave Caillebotte (1848–1894), after working as a naval architect with the fortune left to him by his father, was able to devote himself to painting and to supporting the Impressionists. After working with Bonnat and entering the Ecole des Beaux-Arts in 1873, he abandoned formal education to join the Impressionist group. His long unrecognized great talent is revealed in *Les Raboteurs du Parquet* (*The Parquet Planers*), an astonishing composition. The presence of Caillebotte at the Musée d'Orsay is felt, above all, through his magnificent collection of Impressionist paintings. In 1897, after three years of negotiating, the Louvre accepted only part of his bequest of 67 works. Among them were *Regattas at Argenteuil* and *La Gare Saint-Lazare* by Monet. *The Red Roofs* by Pissarro, *The Balcony* by Manet, *Le Moulin de la Galette* by Renoir, *L'Estaque* by Cézanne and *Regattas at Molesey* by Sisley are among the museum's greatest masterpieces.

▷ Not to be missed

Upper level
La Galerie des Hauteurs (Upper gallery)
Monet: *Régates* (Regattas) *The Luncheon, La Gare Saint-Lazare, Haystacks, Series of Views; Rouen Cathedral, Water Lilies.*
Pissarro: *The Red Roofs, La Jeune Fille à la Baguette*
Renoir: *Le Moulin de la Galette, The Swing, Young Girls at the Piano, The Bathers.*
Manet: *On the Beach, The Lady with the Fans, Clemenceau.*
Degas: *Women Ironing, L'Absinthe, The Ballet Class, Blue Dancers.*
Van Gogh: *L'Arlésienne, Self-Portrait* (1889), *The Church at Auvers-sur-Oise.*
Cézanne: *The Card Players, L'Estaque, Woman with Coffee Pot.*

The corner rooms
Degas: pastels and bronzes, in particular *Ballerina in Costume,*
Seurat: *The Circus.*

The Redon and Toulouse-Lautrec rooms
The Galerie Bellechasse
Henri Rousseau: *War.*
Emile Bernard: *Madeleine au Bois d'Amour* (Madeleine in the Wood of Love).
Gauguin: *Tahitian Women, The White Horse, And the Gold of Their Bodies, Washerwomen at Pont-Aven, La Belle Angèle,* and his wood carvings.
Georges Lacombe: *Isis.*
Sérusier: *The Talisman.*
Vuillard: *In Bed.*
Bonnard: Four panels of *Women in the Garden; Le Peignoir.*
Aristide Maillol: *Woman with Parasol.*
Vallotton: *The Ball.*
Maurice Denis: *The Muses.*

In the Kaganovitch collection: *L'Hôpital Saint-Jean* by Van Gogh.

▷ Paul Gachet

From his youth onwards, Dr Paul Gachet (1828–1909) became friends with such artists as Courbet, Bresdin and Bonvin and also painted himself. In 1872 he bought a house in Auvers-sur-Oise where he received Guillaumin, Pissarro and Cézanne, whose first client he became, and finally Van Gogh whom he looked after in the asylum, and who is buried in the village cemetery there. A large part of Dr Gachet's collection was given to the Louvre by his children, notably his *Portrait;* the *Self-Portrait* of 1889 and the *Church at Auvers-sur-Oise* by Van Gogh.

▷ Additional information

Guided tours

General guided tours of the museum are available Mon. to Sat. at 11am Thurs. also at 7pm. For more detailed visits and itineraries consult the brochure *Les Nouvelles du Musée d'Orsay*, available at the reception counters, or the Point-clef ('key-point') information screens in the museum. 'Une oeuvre à voir' (a work to be viewed): presentation of a specific work, Mon. to Sat. at 12.30pm.

Groups

Groups of not more than 30 are admitted to the museum Tues.–Sat. 9am–1.30pm (9am–2.15pm for school groups), and Thurs. 6.30pm and 8pm for lecture tours. Booking required three weeks in advance. (Tel: 45–49–45–46).

Children

Aged 5–15: studios, general visits, exploration visits, computer games, film. Information leaflet *Jeunes Visiteurs* (Young Visitors) available at reception counter.

Cultural events

Concerts, films, lectures, discussions and history of art classes in the auditorium (basement) and, for certain concerts, in the *Salle des fêtes*. For details, consult brochure, *Les Nouvelles du Musée d'Orsay*, or ask at reception.

Publications

The opening of the Musée d'Orsay was accompanied by numerous publications by the Réunion des Musées Nationaux. These are on sale in the ground-floor bookshop and include a fully illustrated guide written by Caroline Mathieu, a curator at the Musée d'Orsay.

▷ Paul Gauguin

Gauguin (b. Paris 1848, d. Dominica 1903), a precursor of 20th-c. painting together with Cézanne and Van Gogh, was the guiding light of the two movements represented at the Bellechasse gallery – Synthetism or Choisonnism and the Nabis.

After a childhood spent in Lima (his mother was a Peruvian Creole), to which he dreamed of escaping throughout the rest of his life, a dream intensified by a trip to Martinique in 1887, Gauguin worked first as a successful stockbroker, while painting as an amateur under Pissarro's guidance. In his thirties, a financial crisis made him decide to devote himself exclusively to art, which he did, to the detriment of his physical, moral, financial and familial stability. As a result of reflection, reading, experimentation and discussion, the broad outline of his style evolved. In 1888 at Arles, while staying with Van Gogh, he discovered a new way to use color. In Brittany, at

Pont-Aven, the little village where he stayed in 1886, 1888, and 1889, his forceful personality inspired the young painters working near him. With Emile Bernard he perfected Synthetism, reacting against Realism and Impressionism, rejecting perspective and advocating the use of pure color applied in broad, flat tints within marked outlines. From Gauguin's 'dictation', Paul Sérusier painted *The Talisman*, a small Synthetic landscape in dazzling colors. It was the point of departure for the research of the Nabis. In 1891 Gauguin left for Tahiti to fulfil his dream of primitive life far from civilization. Sick and penniless, he was forced to return to Paris. It was three years later that he left again for Tahiti, supported by a regular stipend paid by the dealer Vallard, in return for paintings. Having decided to pursue still further this return to the primitive, he lived in a hut in the village of Atuana on the Marquesas Islands, where he died in 1903.

▷ The Official Salon during the Third Republic

The official Salon, which got its name from the Salon Carré (the Square Salon) of the Louvre, where it took place for many years, was a cultural event. It was indeed one of the few places where painters and sculptors could exhibit and be appraised by the public. The admissions panel, abolished in 1848 and reinstated in 1894, was composed of the most accepted award-winning artists, and favored academic art, neglecting the paintings of Courbet, Manet, Monet and Pissarro. During the Third Republic it became more intransigent than ever, and the official view triumphed. Therefore in 1884 the salon of independent artists was created, with the principle 'no panel, no awards'. There the public could view works by such artists as Seurat, Signac, Cross, Van Gogh, Lautrec.

▷ Not to be missed

Middle level
The restaurant and the ballroom of the former station hotel (Hôtel d'Orsay).

Naturalist and Symbolist rooms: *The Dream* by Puvis de Chavannes; *With Closed Eyes* by Odilon Redon; *The Wheel of Fortune* by Burne-Jones.

Second sculpture terrace: *Balzac* and *The Gate of Hell* by Rodin; *Maturity* by Camille Claudel.

Art Nouveau rooms: collection of furniture by Guimard; *At the New Circus*, a stained-glass window by Tiffany designed by Toulouse-Lautrec; glassware by Gallé; bookcase by Rupert Carabin; dining-room furniture by Charpentier.

The international Art Nouveau tower.

20th-c. rooms: *Coolus*, by Vuillard; *En Barque* by Bonnard; *Luxe, Calme, et Volupté* by Matisse and *The Snake Charmer* by Henri Rousseau.

▷ Modernism

Steeped in the ethos of the 19th c. Art Nouveau did not survive to integrate itself with the Modernist movements that heralded the 20th c. simultaneously – the Glasgow School in Great Britain, the Sezession in Austria, the Chicago school in America. Charles Rennie Mackintosh, rejecting exaggerated floral ornamentation, created a range of furniture and objects which were austere in form, showing the characteristic Mannerist calligraphic quality of Art Nouveau, as in the bedroom at Hill House near Glasgow. In Vienna, Otto Wagner, Joseph Hoffman and Koloman Moser founded the Weiner Werkstätte (Vienna Workshop) which, from 1898, produced furniture and articles intended for mass production (such as an armchair with adjustable back manufactured by Kohn). They laid the foundations of a sober, austere, graphic style, as illustrated in *Paradise*, the sketch for a stained-glass window in the Church of St Leopold of Steinhof near Vienna. In Chicago, Frank Lloyd Wright was designing furniture along architectural lines, the high-backed chair for the Roberts' residence in River Forest and the stained-glass window of Avery Coonley's house show him to be one of the pioneers of pure abstraction.

▣ The Musée Pasteur*

25 Rue du Dr.-Roux, 15th arr. Tel: 44–68–82–22. Map ref. 21–B2
Curator: Mme Perrot
Open Sept.–July Mon. to Fri. 2pm–5pm; groups by appointment.
Métro: Pasteur
Bus: 45, 68, 82, 82

This is one of the most interesting of the small museums of Paris. Set out in the apartment where the famous scientist lived from 1888 to 1895, it has been preserved down to the smallest detail as it was when Pasteur lived in it with his family – and this is not the least of its charms.

History of the museum

When the laboratory in the Rue d'Ulm where Professor Pasteur (1822–95) worked became too small for the flood of rabies patients, a new institute was built and inaugurated on November 14, 1888, with an apartment set aside for the scientist's family. His daughter and son-in-law, René Valléry-Radot, made a gift of everything in the apartment to the institute. Later, Professor Louis Pasteur-Valléry-Radot was authorized to reconstitute his grandparents' home as it originally was. This museum, opened in 1936, forms part of the Institut Pasteur.

Tour of the museum

45 mins.

The museum organizes exhibitions illustrating the lives and work of other 'Pasteurians', such as Charles Nicole; Edouard de Pomiane, a former Pasteurian who became a chef; Jacques Monod (1910–76),

Nobel prize-winner and director of the institute; Elie Metchnikoff, Emile Roux; Albert Calmette and the centenary of the first rabies vaccination. Every day scientists and researchers, professors and students, come from all over the world, in particular from China and other Asian countries, to visit these rooms that still seem to await the scientist's return, and which reveal the multiplicity of Pasteur's activities, from his pastel drawings to his fundamental biological discoveries.

Numerous portraits of Pasteur and his family, including the official one by Bonnat, and several others by Albert Edelfelt, a Finnish painter and close friend of the family.

The scientific room

This room brings together the apparatus used daily by Pasteur; the labels are in his hand; the categorization, case by case, is chronological.

The tomb

Contrary to the wishes of the French government, who wanted Pasteur's body to lie in the Panthéon, the family wished to keep the scientist in the place where he had worked. His tomb is exactly below the cupola, in a crypt constructed by Charles Girault in the Neo-Byzantine style and decorated with precious marble and Art Nouveau mosaics (by G. Martin) which retrace his career. The tomb is a simple block of Swedish granite; Mme Pasteur's body lies beneath a white marble flagstone in the choir.

▣ Musée du Petit-Palais**

Ave. Winston Churchill, 8th arr. Tel: 42-65-12-72. Map ref: 9-B3
Curator: Mlle Thérèse Burollet
Open Tues.-Sun. 10am-5.40pm; for a guided tour telephone the museum's education service.
Métro: Champs Elysées-Clemenceau
Bus: 28, 42, 49, 52, 63, 72, 73, 83, 93

The Petit Palais (Little Palace) was built at the beginning of the 20th century by the architect Charles Giraud to house the retrospective of French art presented as part of the World Fair of 1900 (for the exterior architecture → Champs-Elysées). The City inherited it for exhibitions of its art collections and on December 11, 1902, the new museum opened its doors. Due to its regular acquisitions and some important donations and legacies, it soon acquired prestige. Since 1983 the museum has been changing progressively. Around 1991 the floor currently open to the public will be reserved exclusively for temporary exhibitions and for French art of the 19th c.; the ground floor will be kept for ancient art and reception services.

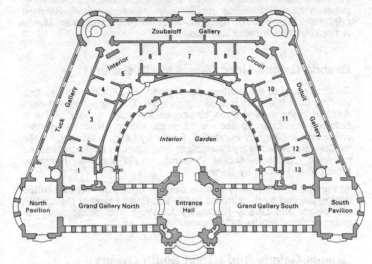

Petit Palais Museum

The museum, which owns an interesting collection of works from Antiquity to the 19th c., organizes internationally renowned exhibitions two or three times a year. Among the most famous have been the Homage to Pablo Picasso (1966), Tutankhamen and his Times (1967), Rembrandt's Century (1970), Pompeii (1973), The Golden Age of Spanish Painting (1976), and The Thyssen Collection (1982). Since 1983 the exhibitions have concentrated more and more on presenting European art of the 19th c. (Bouguereau, Tissot), but not to the exclusion of earlier art from all over the world (Rembrandt, etchings). They are presented in galleries 1 to 10 of the inner circle, such that the placing of pictures is subject to change.

Tour of the museum

2 hrs.

The interior décor

The galleries and rooms of the Petit Palais present a panorama of official art around 1900. The tour is centered around a charming indoor garden with ornamental ponds.

Entrance hall. The dome over the entrance porch is decorated, between beautiful stucco motifs, with paintings by A. Besnard (1903–10): *Plastic Art* or *Antique Art*, on its *Substance*, then *Mystic Art* or *Christian Art* and last *Thought*.

Grande Galerie Nord (Great North Gallery)

On the ceiling of the gallery opening on the l., F. Cormon painted, starting from the entrance, *Modern Times*, *The French Revolution*, *Ancient History* as well as 10 scenes from the history of Paris; between these can be seen eight busts: starting from the garden entrance, Le Sueur by Pendaries, Boulle by Laporte-Blairsy, Pigalle by Convers, Boucher by Champigny and, coming back towards the entrance, Cochin by Malric, Delacroix by Fix-Masseau, Barye by Mengue, and Dalou by Berthet.

At the end of this gallery a large pavilion opens up, with a vaulted ceiling painted by F. Humbert (1909–13): *Paris, Heart of Civilization and Peace and Liberty Necessary for Work and Intellectual Progress* or *Paris, Intellectual Capital*.

Grande Galerie Sud (Great South Gallery)

The décor in the other great gallery is by A. Roll (1906–14); *Fantastic Music* or *Glorification of Berlioz*, *Apotheosis*, (showing the Republic surrounded by busts of famous French citizens), *Poetic Drama*. The busts are those of Corot by Michelet, Goujon by Plé, Lescot by Jacquot, Mansart by Block, Gabriel by Pècle, Viollet-le-Duc by Fagel, Le Nôtre by Dejean, and Ballin by Waast. The pavilion is decorated with *The Triumph of Woman* and an allegory (1906–20) by G. Picard. The dome of the Corner Pavilion, between the Galerie Dutuit and the Galerie Zoubaloff, was painted by Maurice Denis between 1919 and 1925 and constitutes an amazing synthesis of the history of French art. The indoor garden is surrounded by a charming peristyle with a vaulted ceiling painted by P. A. Baudoin (commissioned in 1906, finished in 1910): it shows the *Four Seasons*, the *Months of the Revolutionary Calendar*, the *Hours of the Day and of Night*. Sculptures can be seen in the upper parts: two figures of *Fame* by Peynot, groups of young musicians by Ferrary and Convers, groups of children and flowers by Hercule.

The permanent collections

The collections divide into two: 19th-c. art and earlier art from Antiquity onwards. The museum's originality consists in presenting all the works from one period together in order to evoke the spirit of each period.

The older art collection

The collection of art other than 19th-c. French, i.e. Pharaonic Egypt up to 18th-c. Europe, comes mainly from the bequest made in 1902 to the City of Paris by the brothers Eugène and Auguste Dutuit. The two brothers from Rouen had dedicated their lives to the search for rare and fine pieces at the time of the famous sales of the second half of the 19th c., in order to 'create a useful public institution'. Principal additions to this legacy have been those of Edmond and Julia Tuck in 1929, Charles Vincent Ocampo in 1931, and Pierre Marie in 1930.

The very rich collection of Egyptian, Greek and Roman antiquities, and the medieval collection, will be presented only after the reopening of the museum in 1991.

Grande Galerie Sud. Beside some pieces from ancient Egypt, the main interest of this first room consists in the astounding collection from the excavations at Sala Consilina, a Greek colony in ancient Lucania, in southern Italy: amber jewel brooches, bronze or terracotta vases (6th and 5th c. B.C.). A series of Greek and Etruscan bronzes leads into the following room which contains Roman bronzes. Of particular interest are two fine statuettes: an athlete** and Bacchus**. Note also the amazing ivory tragic actor. The third room presents some fine quality Greek vases: early black-figure vases and *Athenian* lecythoi covered in white slip (6th c. B.C.), later red-figure vases (5th c.).

Galerie Dutuit. In the small entrance rotunda are some French, Flemish, and Spanish primitives and two 15th-c. German sculptures. Then come the busts of the brothers Eugène and Auguste Dutuit, leading into a room dedicated to the Northern Renaissance: Limousin enamels* by the great artisans of the 16th c. (J. de Court, P. Reymond, L. Limousin), very rare collection of ceramics* from the school of Bernard Palissy, lead-glazed pottery from Saint-Porchaire*, French and German clocks of the 16th and 17th c., outstanding French *epi de faîtage*** decoration for a roof ridge from the 17th c.. The next room is reserved, apart from a few pieces of Moorish earthenware, for the Italian Renaissance: an important collection of majolica typical of all the great centers (Faenza, Urbino, Gubbio, Deruta, Castel Durante), Venetian glass and some furniture, along with paintings by Mantegna, Botticelli and Cima da Conegliano. In the last room of this gallery some of the Flemish and Dutch paintings of the Dutuit collection are displayed (the whole collection will be one exhibition in a few years' time on the ground floor). These paintings are representative of the various genres of the art of the Low Countries, history (Jordaens, Rubens**), portraiture (Rembrandt)**, rustic scenes (Brouwer, Teniers), bourgeois genre scenes (Metsu, Ter Borch*), realist landscapes (Van Goyen, Ruysdael, Hobbema), Italianate landscapes (Wouverman), architectural views (Berckhedye), seascapes

(Van de Velde), animals (Weenix, Cuyp), archaic still lifes (Soreau) and decorative still lifes (Huysum).

Dutuit Rotunda. This serves as a setting for some of the medieval exhibits. Ivory pieces: carved Evangelical plaques and Byzantine caskets, processional effigy of the Virgin from the Abbey of Ourscamps, diptychs illustrating the Life of Christ; enamels: reliquary triptyches* attributed to Godefroy de Hy, the master enameller of Limoges.

Tuck Rotunda. The decorative paintings* by Pillement and by Hubert Robert, and the Rouen and Moustiers faience, introduce the Tuck Gallery's display of 18th-c. art.

Tuck Gallery. Among a wealth of panels and Beauvais tapestries (cartoons by Boucher, Huet, Leprince), a beautiful collection of paintings, sculptures and works of art of the 18th c. can be admired. In the first room paintings by Boucher, Largillière and David (early works) may be seen as well as fine marquetry furniture. The following room presents landscapes by Vernet and Hubert Robert beside cases displaying the famous *rose Pompadour* or *gros bleu* Sèvres porcelain, pieces of superb furniture and sculpture, in particular two busts* by Houdon of Voltaire and Franklin. The latter appears again in the next room in a painting by Duplessis. Around the room are portraits by Nattier, Fragonard, Roslin, an exceptional display of Meissen porcelain**, a collection of painted English enamels, and watches in gold and enamel; among the furniture, is a finely decorated sedan chair. At the far end of the gallery, past the two busts of Julia and Edmond Tuck, a modest but significant collection of 17th-c. French art with, most notably, *The Massacre of the Innocents*** by Poussin; *Landscape with the Port of Santa Marinella* by Claude Lorrain and *St Sebastian** by Puget.

The collection of 19th-c. French art

This collection of 19th-c. French art was originally started by contemporary acquisitions and commissions made by the City of Paris, and was then added to by the purchases of studios, collections, donations, and legacies at the beginning of the 20th c.: 1904, Hoentschel Donation (Carriès Studio); 1905, Henner, Ziem, and Vierge legacies, and purchase of the Dalou Studio; Juliette Courbet donation (1906–09); 1916, Zoubaloff donation (Redon). Since then the generosity of donors has never ceased: 1938, Clément Carpeaux donation; 1945, Ambroise Vollard legacy (Cézanne); 1972, Zagorowski donation (Lévy-Dhurmer); 1979, Brokman donation; 1982, Guéniot donations and, especially since 1983, an active policy of acquisition has allowed the rapid development of the collection: religious paintings of Gustave Doré (1984): Baron Gros' *Clovis and Clotilda* (1985): *Bacchante* by Jean Baptiste Carpeaux (1986), *The

Prodigal Son, by Tissot, *Blanche of Castile succouring the Prisoners* by Granet and others.

Zoubaloff Gallery: For a chronological approach to this collection it is best to begin a tour of the gallery from the Dutuit Rotunda.

First comes historical painting of the kind that the Neo-Classicists tried to bring back into vogue after the frivolities of the Rococo in the first half of the 18th c., a genre that was practised throughout the 19th c. – a solemn and meditative art form inspired by Antiquity (pictures by Monsiau, Gros, Couture, Scheffer, Barrias). Then a more anecdotal tendency appeared within this genre of historical painting, inspired by the history of France: the Troubadour style of Granet and Ingres. Next came Romanticism, which sought a further outward expression of the passions with all their irrationality, and which can be seen in the works of Delacroix and later Carpeaux. Note also, nearby, two fine studies: *Brown Horse** by Géricault and *Marietta** by Corot.

A great change came about with the advent of Realism, which turned to the candid study of the banal, everyday life of the bourgeoisie and the peasants. This trend is shown by Millet's *Portrait of a Man*, in several works by Daumier and an outstanding collection of paintings by Courbet which includes *Young Women Beside* the Seine**, *Portrait of Proudhon and his Children***. Note, in the middle of the room, a collection of sketches by Dalou for a monument to Labor, which was never executed. The last room recreates the history of landscape painting in the 19th c., from the little, detailed pictures in the Flemish style (Leprince, Demarne) up to the brilliant luminosity of Impressionism (Monet, Pissarro, Sisley, Guillaumin), by way of Romanticism (Huet, Isabey), New classicism mixed with Realism (Corot) and true Realism (Rousseau, Harpignies, Breton). It is impossible to miss the fine collection of works by Cézanne, including the *Three Bathing Women*** and *Portrait of Ambroise Vollard.** To end, there is a splendid collection of Impressionist portraits by Monet, Cézanne, Pissarro, Renoir, Cassatt, Morisot, and Toulouse-Lautrec.

Grande Galerie Nord (Great North Gallery). Portraits predating or contemporary with Impressionism are on display amid this sumptuous architecture: from the followers of Ingres (Scheffer, Mottez) and the Realists (Millet, Couture) up to the large works of the Third Republic (Baudry, Bonnat, Roll). As an accompaniment to these paintings there are busts by Carpeaux as well as other sculptures by this artist, who captivated the Second Empire: (→ inset) *Fisherman with a Shell*, sketch for the Watteau preliminary models by Dalou, notably for the monument to Victor Hugo.

The Pavillon Nord houses several large original plaster casts of Paris monuments: *République* by Morice, *Denton* by Paris and *Condercet* by Perrin.

Grande Galerie Sud (Great South Gallery). Devoted to monumental art. It displays, after decades hidden from view, the paintings commissioned for the Hôtel de Ville after the revolution (of Schnetz, Delaroche), *Lamartine in front of the Hôtel de Ville in 1848*, by Philippoteaux, and models of sculptures for the Hôtel de Ville rebuilt after the fire during the Commune in 1870 (Chapu, Coutan, Morice). These are also large landscapes (Géricault, Jongkind, Sisley) and Courbet's *Les Pompiers****.

The Pavillon Sud is also devoted to monumental art, religious rather than secular: works from the churches of Paris which were dismissed for a long time and are at last esteemed (Scheffer, Gleyre, Lazerges) as well as the grotesque paintings of the Doré Gallery. (→ inset).

Inner Circle, Rooms 11 and 13. Room 11 contains late 19th-c. Symbolist landscape paintings (Lévy-Dhurmer, Osbert, Ménard, Brokman), historical painting (G. Moreau, Fantin-Latour, Henner), sculpture (Alaphilippe) and *objets d'art* (A. Point, Feuillatre, Lemaire). Room 12 is the setting for the celebration of womanhood under the Third Republic (*Sarah Bernhardt* by Clairin, Gervex, Carolus-Duran, Fantin-Latour). Finally, decorative art of 1900 is presented in Room 13: glass case by Carabin, dining-room furniture by Guimard, decorative panels by Vuillard, vases by Gallé and Decorchemont, jewelry by Lalique and Fouquet. These rooms are sometimes closed during large exhibitions.

Indoor garden. In the garden itself or under the peristyle which surrounds it: sculptures by Maillol, Renoir, Bourdelle and Pompon.

▷ The Galerie Doré

Gustave Doré (1832–83) is best known today for his illustrations of Rabelais (*Oeuvres*, 1854), Dante (*Inferno*, 1861), Cervantes (*Don Quixote*, 1863), Chateaubriand (*Atala, 1863*), Milton (*Paradise Lost*, 1866), Hugo (*Travailleurs de la Mer*, 1867). His widely known engravings swarm with figures, often grotesque, and seethe with a tragic or burlesque zeal through the artist's skill use of black and white.

The success of his illustrated Bible (1866) in England was such that two London financiers commissioned him to produce large-scale religious pictures for a Doré Gallery, for which there would be an entrance fee. During this exhibition's 24 years in existence, the 20 canvases (1866–83) received about 2½ million visitors. His depiction of London's slums (1872) was used as evidence in a government inquiry.

After a tour in the United States, the collection was dispersed. In 1984 the Petit Palais was able to acquire three of these paintings and show the French public that Gustave Doré was also a great painter, a link between Romanticism and Symbolism.

▷ Gustave Courbet (1819–77)

'The term of Realist has been imposed on me just as the term of Romanticism was imposed on the men of 1830 . . . I simply wanted to draw from the whole knowledge of tradition that rational and independent feeling of my own personality. To be able to translate the customs, the ideas, the whole appearance of my era as I see them; to be not only a painter, but also a man; in a word, to make living art, that is my aim.'

In this manifesto of 1855, Courbet summarized perfectly his life and his art: a passion for life, however banal, celebrated freely in the manner of historical painting.

Hence the long series of genre scenes, portraits, landscapes and still lifes, of which the Petit Palais owns an exceptional collection due mainly to the generosity of Juliette Courbet, the artist's sister.

▷ The Carpeaux Donation

Supported by Princess Mathilde, Jean-Baptiste Carpeaux (1827–1875) was the sculptor of the Second Empire and of the carefree life of the aristocracy. Best known for his group *La Danse*, for the Paris Opéra (→ Musée d'Orsay), he strove to capture the personality of some of his contemporaries in an unforgettable series of busts (Princess Mathilde, Charles Garnier, Gérôme).

In contrast to the optimism of his sculptures, Carpeaux also created pictures of a Romantic and tragic nature. These works, full of emotional expressiveness, were not intended for public display and are of uncompromising craft. Thanks to the donation, in 1938, by Louise Clément-Carpeaux, the artist's daughter, the Petit Palais has at its disposal a unique collection of sculptures, sketches and paintings by this artist yet to be displayed.

Musée du Phonographe (Gramophone Museum)

→ *Musée Charles-Cros (Charles Cros Museum)*

▣ Musée Picasso**

Hôtel Salé, 5 Rue de Thorigny, 3rd arr. Tel: 42–71–25–21. Map ref: 18–C1, D2
Head Curator: M. Regnier
Open daily except Tues. 9.15am–5.15pm, Wed., 8pm
Group visits by arrangement
Tel. 42–71–70–84.
Métro: Saint-Sébastien-Froissart, Saint-Paul

Bus: 29, 96
This museum traces the prodigious career of Pablo Picasso (1881–1973). The collection was recently moved to a sumptuous mansion in the Marais, the Hôtel Salé, built in 1656 by Jean Boullier, known as Jean de Bourges, for Aubert de Fontenay, the Fermier des Gabelles (salt-tax collector), hence the nickname given to it by the Parisians, *Salé*, salty. After the restoration of the Hôtel, the organization of the museum, which was entrusted to Roland Simounet, had to reconcile two principles: respect for the authenticity of the surroundings and the adaptation of the building to its new function as a modern museum meant to receive large numbers of visitors.

History of the museum

An exceptional law allowing the donation of works in lieu of inheritance tax has led to the enrichment of the national collections by 203 paintings, 158 sculptures, 16 collages, 29 welded *tableaux reliefs* (relief constructions), 183 ceramics pieces, more than 3000 drawings and prints, along with other works and manuscripts – a coup that no other means of acquisition would have allowed. Thanks to the generosity of the heirs the State was able to have priority of choice before the estate was divided up. The selection was made with regard to the works of Picasso already in the national collections. Picasso's personal collection donated by the artist's family and exhibited in 1978 in the Louvre, is now on permanent display in the Hôtel Salé.

Tour of the museum

1½ hrs.

The marvelous sculpted decoration of the vestibule, staircase, and Jupiter drawing-room is the work of the Marsy brothers, who also worked at Versailles, and of the young Martin Desjardin. The magnificent flight of stairs in wrought iron contrasts harmoniously with the delicate bronze by Diego Giacometti.

First floor

The tour of the permanent collections begins on the first floor. It is arranged in chronological order.

Room 1. *The Girl with Bare Feet* and *Man in a Cap* show the artist's precocious talent at the age of 14. The *Self-Portrait** of 1901 heralds the Blue Period: using only tones of blue, Picasso, who was just 21 at the time, paints himself grown old, with thin features.

Room 2. The *Two Brothers* belongs to the Rose Period. The *Self-Portrait** of 1906 shows a desire for simplification. The famous picture in the Museum of Modern Art, New York, *Les Demoiselles d'Avignon* is represented here by numerous studies. Already in this picture Picasso was trying to resolve the great problem of Cubism: the abandonment of naturalistic perspective in favor of the two-dimensional representation of overlapping, interlocking planes, eschewing that transformation of the two-dimensional picture plane into an illusionistic three-dimensional pictorial space. In his 1907 wood carvings the influence of Gauguin and the Primitives can be seen.

Room 3. The *Landscape with Two Figures* of 1908 is a reference to the *Bathers* by Cézanne, but it is also an application of the latter's motto: 'To treat nature with the cylinder, the sphere, and cone, the whole put into perspective', written in a letter of 1904.

Room 4. Picasso's Cubist works are brought together here. He was with Braque the founder of the movement, between 1910 and 1917. The many facets of *Man with a Mandolin*, and *Man with a Guitar* are characteristic of 'analytical' Cubism. In the *Still Life with Wicker Chair** (1912), the introduction of a piece of oilcloth resolves the problem of how to represent the chair and achieve a new organization of space. This picture marks the start of the *papiers collés* (collages) of which the museum has a fine collection. The relief constructions in which found objects are incorporated, of this period follow the same principles. From the 'synthetic' phase of Cubism there are the *Man with a Pipe** and *Man at the Fireplace*. *The Painter and His Model* and the *Portrait of Olga*.** The figuration is traditional but the space, made up of superimposed, interlocking planes, is still Cubist.

Room 5. It was Picasso's wish, carried out by his heirs, that a part of his personal collection be added to the national collections. This collection reveals the painter's admiration for certain great masters: Chardin, Corot, and Cézanne, and also for his contemporaries Matisse and Derain. The works displayed in this room have some connection with the first 20 years of Picasso's career. The remainder of the donation is exhibited on the second floor.

Room 6. After World War I there began a fertile period when Picasso followed several paths. First there was the continuation of Cubism, represented here by *The Lovers*. This time also marked the beginning of his Neo-Classical style (1918–24), when Picasso rediscovered the harmony of Ingres and Antiquity. *Pan's Pipe**** is the masterpiece of the series (1923).

Room 6 bis. Designs for the theater for the ballets *Parade*, *The Three-Cornered Hat*, and *Pulcinella*.

Room 7. Picasso was never a Surrealist, but Surrealism perhaps helped the development of his work. In fact, a complete disruption took place in his art. In *The Kiss**, of 1925 the strident colors, sharp lines and extreme contortions express the tensions between the artist and his wife Olga.

Ground floor

Coming downstairs, you arrive at Room 8. It displays the incomparably rich engravings and lithographs, more than 200 catalogued prints.

Room 9. The naked bodies of bathers are metamorphosed into phallic shapes in the *Figures by the Sea*, 1931, or into angular forms in the vast *Baigneuse*. The series of relief constructions***, made up of assorted objects covered in sand, is unique.

Room 10. In May 1931 Picasso took possession of the Château de Boisgeloup and built a studio there where he worked in clay and plaster and continued to weld his reliefs. His model, 17-year-old Marie-Thérèse Walter, gave him a new formal language made up of spherical volumes that can be seen in the enormous plaster works and in *Reading*.

Room 11. *Crucifixion, Bullfight, Minotaurs.*

Room 12. *Women at their Toilette** (1938), a monumental collage, is a tapestry cartoon.

The sculpture garden. This covered garden brings together several of Picasso's sculptures, of which the museum owns the world's most complete collection.

Basement

Room 13. The portrait of Marie-Thérèse, 1937, (who, in 1935, gave birth to Picasso's child Maïa) with its undulating lines and cold tones contrasts with that of Dora Maar**, a young photographer Picasso met in 1936, later his mistress, with its sharp lines and warm tones.

Room 14. Ceramics created at Vallauris from 1946 onward.

Room 15. Even if Picasso did not actually paint the war, his works, such as the *Cat Catching a Bird* or the *Young Boy with a Lobster*, are steeped in its anguish.

Room 16. The *Bust of a Woman in a Hat*, with its impossible distortion, is a portrait of Dora Maar.

Room 17. Here can be seen the works of several poets illustrated by Picasso: Max Jacob, René Char, Tristan Tzara, Pierre Reverdy.

Room 18. *Claude Drawing Françoise and Paloma* (1954) is a portrait of Françoise Gillot with her two children by Picasso, Claude and Paloma; *Massacre in Korea* expresses the artist's outrage at the American intervention in Korea. Ground floor (end of tour).

Room 19. *The California Studio*, painted in Cannes in the villa to which Picasso moved in 1955, is reminiscent of Matisse in its theme and in its great arabesques.

Room 20. Half a century after *The Kiss* of 1925 (Room 7), that of 1969 is just as violent.

On the second floor, next to the Picasso donation, temporary exhibitions of the artist's drawings and engravings are held.

▷ Diego Giacometti

Diego Giacometti, who disappeared in 1985, was born in 1902 in a small village in the Italian region of Switzerland. In 1925 he came to Paris and in 1928 joined, with his brother, the sculptor Alberto Giacometti, the team of the designer Jean-Michel Frank. From 1940 on he created his own models and specialized in the creation of metal furniture with simple lines, decorated with plants and animals that make up a little world full of humor and poetry.

Works by this artist to be seen in the Picasso Museum are the two bronze *torchères* in the Jupiter drawing-room, the white resin (type of plaster) chandeliers in the four salons on the garden side of the first floor, as well as the seats, chairs and tables in bronze which have been placed there for visitors to rest on.

▣ Musée des Plans-Reliefs* (Museum of Relief Maps and Plans)

Hôtel National des Invalides, 7th arr. Tel: 45–51–95–05.
Map ref. 15–A2
Entrance on the 4th floor, by the W. wing of the Musée de l'Armée
Open daily 10am–5.45pm, 1 Apr.–30 Sept.; 10am–4.45pm.; 1 Oct.–31 Mar.; closed 1 Jan., 1 May, 1 Nov., 11 Nov., 25 Dec.
Métro: Invalides, Latour-Maubourg, Ecole Militaire, Varenne
Bus: 28, 63, 69, 82, 83, 87, 92

This museum is being completely reorganized; however, the new gallery foreshadows, in 1/5th of the space, the future museum, which will open in 1992. The relief maps come from the collection of Louis XIV (formed on the advice of Louvois, one of the king's chief ministers from 1668), from the collection of Louis XV, and from the works commissioned in the 19th c. by Napoléon, Louis-Philippe and Napoléon III. The collection, which was kept until 1776 in the Bord de l'Eau (Seine side) Gallery of the Louvre and considered a military secret, has been classified as a historical monument since 1927 and was opened to the public in the 1950s. As well as models of towns and fortified sites (generally 1600) of France and the neighboring countries, the museum also houses ancient maps and engravings relating to these towns.

In the new gallery two areas, distinguished by the height of their ceilings, give an informative overview of the collection. The careful presentation, which emphasizes the beauty of the 18 models on show, and the numerous documents which guide visitors through the collections, allow you to appreciate the history of the collection and the research carried out by the engineers into methods of representing relief, and the production of these models.

Entrance hall

A round window allows a view of the superb main courtyard of the Hôtel des Invalides. This room, in which the tour begins, combines two ancient relief maps with two contemporary sculptures representing fortified towns by J. Perreaut and H. Damian. Projections on the walls show the beauty of some of the relief maps when lit directly from the side.

Room 2

History of the collection. The presentation shows that since the 18th c. relief maps have been both a tool to aid urban and military planning and make decisions, and a symbol of the prestige of the French state in foreign eyes. The model of La Kenoque, which has preserved its corner scrolls and original mount, dates from the golden age of the collection (1730–50).

Room 3

History of cartography. The art of mapmaking was known in Antiquity. In France it was not until the end of the 18th c. (1782) that the use of contour lines allowed cartographers to go beyond bird's-eye views and elevations.

Room 4

Production of models. Various documents illustrate the stages leading up to their production: a book containing town surveys and a color chart; the depth of water was indicated by the contour lines in different colors – useful for military purposes. Example of a traditional model (Wesel) in wood, silk and paper; relief map of Constantine (Algeria) in cork.

Room 5

Models of Antwerp (1833), Metz (1825), and an imaginary one by Martin Boitard (1805) illustrating the evolution of military architecture in response to the progress in attack techniques (15th–19th c.), as well as the basic principles of bastioned fortifications.

Room 6

A six-minute film shows the originators of the collection, the techniques by which relief maps are produced, and presents the entire collection before ending with the role of relief maps in military strategy.

Rooms 7 and 8

These rooms concern the relief maps of six towns which differ in their origins, their relationships to their sites and their fortified walls (*enceintes*). Metz* is an example of a town of Roman origin, Berg-op-zoom (Netherlands) is a town of Celtic origin that grew up on branch of the Scheldt expanded haphazardly. By contrast, Landrecies in Northern France shows a plan that radiates from the church and the square. Gravelines (Nord) is a town that grew up spontaneously, with irregular street pattern, created by the clustering of the houses around an abbey. The plan of Brest (Finistère), divided up in the 17th c. into grids in the Greco-Roman tradition, demonstrates the appearance of the first industrial landscape outside fortifications. The fortifications of Marsal (Moselle) are by the great military architect Vauban.

Room 9

The landscape is shown as it appeared in relief maps at the time of traditional farming methods before mechanization and the compulsory consolidation of small holdings.

Room 11

This gallery is devoted to the town of Perpignan*, of which the relief map, made in 1686, is one of the oldest in the collection. Constructed in Perpignan itself by Jacques Laurens, it recreates the ambience of the town at the end of 17th c. and shows in great detail the extent of Vauban's works. The restorations made in 1757 bear witness to the work of teams from the surrounding countryside in the 18th c.

Room 12

Here may be seen the enormous relief map of Strasbourg* (36ft/10.86m × 22ft/6.65m), constructed in 1830 to replace the one which the Prussian took to Berlin in 1815 (currently in the Historical Museum in Strasbourg). A series of reproductions allow the visitor to compare the first model (1727) with that of the town as it appeared in 1863, the last time the relief map saw the light of day.

Room 13

This room presents the models built in 1705 and updated in 1811 of the former citadel of Bordeaux, the Château Trompette, demolished in 1785. A truly princely toy, this plan is made up of hundreds of pieces which come apart: roofs, frameworks, floors to interiors and substructure.

Room 14

This room is devoted to the relief map at Briançon, the highest fortified town in Europe, at the junction of the Durance and Guisane valleys. Briançon, built like an amphitheater, is encompassed by the impressive tiers of Vauban's fortified *enceinte*: the architect had to abandon his famous dug-in fortifications because of the steep contours of the site. Note that Vauban has placed the collegiate church on the most exposed bastion, on the principle that a Christian assailant would feel compunction at bombarding the house of God.

▣ Musée de la Poste (Postal Museum)

34 Boul. de Vaugirard, 15th arr. Tel. 43-20-15-30. Map ref. 21-B2
Director: M. Bruzeau
Open Mon.-Sat. 10am-5pm; closed Sundays and public holidays.
Métro: Montparnasse, Pasteur, Falguière
Bus: 28, 48, 89, 91, 92, 94.

Since 1974 the newly renovated postal museum has been housed in part of the Centre Maine-Montparnasse, a building designed to display its collections. Going back to the beginnings of writing, it traces the history of postal communication and its various methods of transport: deliveries on foot and the horse post invented by Louis XI, postal boats and trains, airmail and the telegraph, not omitting the immediate transmission of the spoken word by telephone. French postage stamps have an important place, since the State-owned philatelic collections are kept here.

Tour of the museum

1 hr.

The tour begins on the fifth floor; the rooms follow in sequence going down, each room developing a specific theme.

Room 1. A filmshow of all the works by great artists created for stamps (paintings, sculptures, and the corresponding stamps).

Room 2. The birth and development of writing. The Roman Way. Parchments carried by monks between villages in the 15th c.

Room 3. Uniforms and bits of equipment from the horse post and early postmen: horse bells and harness accessories; postillions' boots; mail-coach plates from the *Ancien Régime* to the end of the 19th c.; an old safe and signs from coaching inns.

Room 4. Models of mail steamers, stagecoaches, and traveling post offices (from the earliest to those of today's high-speed trains: the TGV).

Room 5. The epic story of the mail and '*la ligne*': evocation of the airplanes of the 'Postale'.

Room 6. Dispatch of the mail in times of war from the time of Louis XV: during the Prussian blockade (1870–1871) messages were placed in lightweight metal balls called *boules de Moulins*, which were tossed into the Seine to be picked up downstream; carrier pigeons with postmarks stamped on their wings; message balloons; memorabilia from the two World Wars.

Room 7. La Lettre: French mailboxes; postmen (19th and 20th c.); scales and letter scales; calendars. A representation of the first postmasters and superintendents of the mail.

Room 8. The history of the Abbé Chappe's aerial telegraph (18th c.); the electrical telegraph, the telephone and the pneumatic underground postal delivery fondly known as *le pneu*, and taken out of service recently; collection of early apparatus.

Rooms 9–10. Stamp production (typography, copperplate engraving and photo-engraving); postmarks.

Rooms 11–12. A complete set of French postage stamps and temporary thematic exhibitions.

Room 13. Mail boxes and uniforms of foreign postal services. Treaties of postal exchange (Louvois).

Room 14. Post office counters from 1900 to the electronic age. Mail and toys since the 1930s.

Room 15. Automated sorting and coding of letters; technical installations at the major sorting centers.

The library is on the sixth floor.

Musée de la Publicité

→*Musée de l'Affiche et de la Publicité*

▣ Musée de Radio-France*

116 Ave. President Kennedy, 16 arr. Tel: 42–30–21–80 (Sat.-Sun., Tel. 42–30–33–84) Map ref: 13–A3
Technical adviser: Roger Herbaut
Guided tours daily exc. Sun. and public holidays, 10.30am, 11.30am, 3.30pm, 4.30pm: for groups, write to Service Acceuil-Animation.
Metro: Ranelagh, Passy, Mirabeau.
Bus: 22, 52, 70, 72.

This museum can be said to be 'on the job' as the tour of the Maison de la Radio takes place simultaneously with a visit to the museum. The visitor alternates between the pioneering days of radio, and the modern recording studio, which can be seen through wide double-glazed windows.

The 'House of Radio', home of the Société Nationale de Radiodiffusion (National Broadcasting Company), is housed in a vast building, opened in 1963, designed by Henry Bertrand. The building comprises three incomplete concentric circular structures with a rectangular tower 223ft/68m tall, partially set in the innermost circle, covering 5 acres/2ha, for the Maison Radio-France. It is the largest single construction in France.

The museum, created in 1966, relates the prehistory and the history of radio while, at the same time, affording a glimpse of the everyday life of La Maison. A small room is set aside for television.

Tour of the museum

30 mins.

Large model of the Maison de la Radio

This model shows the three 'crowns' and the vertical tower. The largest exterior crown which contains 1000 offices and small studios, a cafeteria, a restaurant, and the museum. The second crown houses the large studios, such as the auditorium: Studio 104, (936 seats). Studio 102 and Studio 103 (812 seats); Studio 105, which is for concerts (256 seats) and Studio 106 (180 seats).The third small crown contains all the technical installations, seven studios, the transmitting center, a record library, and a library of music and drama. The 23-storey tower is reserved for the sound and document archives.

Some statistics: about 60 broadcasting studios, two television studios; approximately 1000 offices where 3000 employees use 3000 telephones – and 300 clocks.

The museum

The history of the transmission of sound is examined from its beginnings (there is a cast of Trajan's white marble column, erected in Rome in A.D. 114 to commemorate the Emperor's conquest of Dacia), up to the latest transistor models; the Chappe brothers' optical telegraph (1793); crystal sets; the electric telegraph of the American inventor and painter, Samuel Morse (1832), who invented Morse code, and the Bell telephone, also an American invention (1876). Wireless telephony with the works of Maxwell, Hertz, Branly, Popov, Marconi, Ducretet (showcase 4: original ribbon of the telegram sent from the Eiffel Tower to the Panthéon in 1898), Forest (showcase 5; three-electrode lamp).

Reconstruction (showcase 8) of the first Radiola (broadcasting) studio built in 1923. Various types of receiver, their development, their improvement from the crystal set to the transistor.

Prehistory of animation: works of Paul Nipkow, Baird, René Barthélemy (who, on April 14, 1931, first demonstrated television in France). Reconstruction of a television studio from Rue de Grenelle in 1935.

Musée Renan-Scheffer

(→Musée de la vie Romantique.)

▣ Musée Rodin**

77 Rue de Varenne, 7th arr. Tel: 47–05–01–34
Map ref. 15–B2
Curator: Jacques Vilain
Open daily except Mon, 10am–6pm,1 Oct–31 Nov, 10am–5.15pm, 1 Apr.–30 Sept; 10am–6pm.

Métro: Varenne
Bus: 69, 82, 92

The Rodin Museum, in the magnificent 18th-c. Hôtel Biron (for history of the hôtel → Faubourg Saint-Germain, Rue Varenne), brings together the definitive works, and their preliminary sketches, with Auguste Rodin's private collections, bequeathed to the nation by the artist himself (1840–1917). The Meudon annex houses most of the rough sketches, models, and drafts.

Tour of the museum

1 hr.

Restoration has given back some of its former atmosphere to the Hôtel Biron: the 18th-c. wood paneling has been put back in place and the rooms are now organized around a defined theme.

Entrance hall: portraits of Rodin by Bourdelle and Desbois, collaborators of the artist; *Walking Man*, enlargement of a cast executed from 1877 to 1878.

Small vestibule. Youthful works and some dating from his apprenticeship in the Carrier-Belleuse studio: bust of J. -B. Rodin, the artist's father, showing his stern features; *The Titans*, terracotta from 1876.

Ground floor

Room 1. Busts showing masterly realism: youthful work; the R. P. Eymard, *Man with a Broken Nose*; works influenced by Carpeaux: *Young Woman in a Flowery Hat* (1865–70); *Dosia* (*ca.* 1875); Rodin's portraits of his family.

Room 2. These works date from the time when Rodin was working in the Carrier-Belleuse studio in Brussels: portraits of A. Van Beckelaer, Paul de Vigne (Belgian sculptor); decorative figures such as *The Spring* and *The Bacchante*; domestic subjects: *Children Kissing*.

Room 3. This is the former oval drawing-room of the Duchesse de Maine, in which the unpainted natural wood paneling has been restored. Exhibited here is *Age of Bronze*** (1875–1876), which shows Michelangelo's influence: Rodin traveled in Italy, where he discovered Renaissance sculpture. *The Call to Arms* and *L'Alsacienne* show the historical context of his work after the Franco-Prussian War of 1870. Numerous portraits painted between 1874 and 1884 as well as an expressive bust of Mme Cruchet.

Room 4. *The Hand of God****, also called *The Creation* (1898), shows Rodin's artistic evolution; breaking with academic tradition, it appeals directly to the imagination. The subject of *Eternal Spring* and *Eternal Idol* is the human couple; various portraits.

Room 5. The main drawing-room houses some of Rodin's masterpieces: the beautiful nude *St John the Baptist Preaching** (1878); *The Kiss*** which, in miniature, was to become part of *The Gate of Hell*, (described below); it illustrates the passion of Paolo and Francesca da Rimini and is still breathtaking. Rodin has transformed cold marble into an embodiment of the tenderness of human love. *The Earth and the Moon*; several paintings by the Symbolist artist E. Carrière, friend of the sculptor.

Room 6. The former *chambre de parade* (state drawing-room) focuses on Camille Claudel, sister of Paul Claudel, who was Rodin's pupil and companion from 1882 to 1898. She was the model for some of Rodin's works: *France, Aurora*, but some of her own works are also on view, revealing her strong personality.

Room 7. The second oval drawing-room, at the far end of the gallery, has also had its original décor restored. Most of the works on display were studies carried out during the creation of *The Gate of Hell*: some, like *La Centauresse* and *Eve*, are found in the finished work; others such as *Orpheus and the Maenads*, *The Toilette of Venus* and *Kneeling Female Faun*, are not.

Room 8. Here is a collection of portraits of women, some of whom played a romantic role in the sculptor's life, others who were simply friends or gave their social support: the Duchesse de Choiseul, Mme M. Fenaille, Lady Sackville-West, M. Potter-Palmer, Mme Elisseieff, a Slav woman of whom little is known.

On the staircase: *The Three Shades* from *The Gate of Hell*; large bust of Rose Beurret. On the landing: *La Martyre*, who heralds *The Gate of Hell*.

First floor

Rooms 9 and 10: These are reserved for preparatory works and sketches for *Gate of Hell*.

Room 11. This is the *Burghers of Calais* room, with several sketches, the first cast (1884), and the second cast (1885) for this monument which was commissioned by the town of Calais in honor of its liberation from the besieging English during the Hundred Years War in the 14th c. The figures are all placed on the same level, to emphasize the notion of their shared ordeals.

Room 12. These works date from 1890 to 1905, the period when the sculptor reached his peak: *Christ and Mary Magdalene* (1894); *The Tempest* (1898), also known by other titles, and *Before the Sea*.

Room 13. Rodin and his time, or Rodin and his friends. Here is a display of some of the famous works which the sculptor had bought and which made up part of his donation; sculptures of the eminent personalities who were his friends are also on view. From Van Gogh, *Père Tanguy****, *The Harvesters****; from Renoir, *Nude*; from Claude Monet, *Landscape of Belle-Isle****. Portraits of Roger Marx, Henri Becque, Bernard Shaw, Clemenceau, Nijinsky, Gustav Mahler, and Pope Benedict XV.

Room 14. This room contains what are known as 'projects', in differing versions, for the great monuments: *Victor Hugo*, a project illustrating him with the *Sirenes* for *The Voices of the Sea*; Balzac; plans for monuments of Claude Lorrain for the town of Nancy, of Bastien-Lepage, Whistler, and others.

Room 15. Decorative sculpture, to which Rodin was to return towards the end of his life: plans for chimneypieces, fountains, and jardinières. *The Cathedral**, where the pair of hands which evoke piety and meditation in an ogival arch were to be part of a fountain. In the display case: *Dance Movements* (1910), which evokes the early modern dance forms brought from America.

Room 16. Sculpted groups or drawings of mythical or legendary subjects, illustrating the theme of the couple.

Main courtyard

The courtyard and gardens contain some of Rodin's monumental casts. On the l. on entering, *The Burghers of Calais**** and *The Gate of Hell****; to the r., *The Thinker****, formerly (in 1906) in front of the Pantheon and, lastly, *Balzac***.

▲▲ The garden

Renovated In 1927. In front of the S façade of the *hôtel*: two fallen caryatids by Rodin. The garden pond, formerly filled in by the nuns, has been cleared: in the center, the Ugolin group. At the end, the *Call to Arms*, a group by Rodin. Fragments of antique sculptures. On the r. of the entrance, a pseudo-Gothic chapel of the former Sacré Coeur (Sacred Heart) convent, built in 1875 and converted in 1967 as a home for temporary exhibitions and lecture sessions.

▷ Not to be missed

Ground floor: *The Kiss* (Room 5).
First floor: preliminary sketches for *The Gate of Hell*: *The Thinker* (Rooms 9 and 10); the collection of paintings owned by Rodin: works by Van Gogh and Claude Monet (Room 13).

Garden: *The Burghers of Calais* (1886–68); *The Gate of Hell*, the monumental gate that was to be positioned in the future Musée des Arts Décoratifs (1880–1917).

▷ The Gate of Hell

The Gate of Hell, illustrating Dante's *Inferno*, was a monumental doorway commissioned for the proposed museum of decorative arts, which was never built. The first, made in 1926, is now in the Rodin Museum in Philadelphia; but Rodin was to continue working on this project. This unfinished work appears as the sum of all the single or grouped figures that recur many times in the sculptor's repertoire: *The Thinker, Caryatid with an Urn, Caryatid with Stone, Fugit Amor, La Douleur, Youth Triumphant, Falling Man, Crouching Woman, La Danaïde*. These collections of casts, bronzes, sketches, and small preliminary models facilitate a deeper understanding of Rodin's work.

Musée des Sciences et de l'Industrie (Science and Industry Museum)

→ District of La Villette, Cité des Sciences

▣ Musée de la Sculpture en plein air de la Ville de Paris (Open-Air Sculpture Museum of Paris)

Quai Saint-Bernard, 5th arr.
Address all enquiries to the curator of the Musée Zadkine, 100 bis Rue d'Assas, 6th arr.
Tel. 43–26–91–90. Map ref. 18–C3, 24–C1
Open 24 hours daily, admission free
Métro: Jussieu, Gare d'Austerlitz
Bus: 24, 63

Tour of the museum

30 mins.

Opened in 1980 in the Square Saint-Bernard, on the banks of the Seine, this museum offers a wide range of sculpture from the second half of the 20th c. Badly affected by weather and vandalism, the museum is due for a complete refurbishment shortly.

Among the sculpture on show the oldest is *The Table of Silence* (1920–1948), by Constantin Brancusi, one of the founders of modern sculpture. Next to this can be seen *Dwelling-place no. 1* (1954–1958), by Etienne Martin, composed of four bronze elements; *Marseilles*, created by César in 1960 at the time when he was producing his first crushed cars. Further on: *Large Window* (1974) by Augustin Cardenas, sculpted from a single block of Carrara marble; *Espirit, Eau et Sang* by Emile Gilioli (1973); *Hydrorrhage*, a sculpted form by Ipousteguy (1975).

▣ Musée de la Seita* (The State Tobacco and Matches Monopoly)

12 Rue Surcourf, 7th arr. Tel: 45-56-60-17. Map ref. 15-A1
Curator: Mme Adès
Open Mon.-Sat. 11am-6pm; closed Sun. and public holidays.
Information center open by appointment.
Métro: Invalides, Latour-Maubourg
Bus: 28, 49, 63, 69, 83.

The tobacco factory in Gros-Caillou, where the first French cigarettes were produced in 1845, was built at the beginning of the 19th c. on the corner of the Rue Surcourf and the Quai d'Orsay, and was later enlarged towards the Rue de l'Université and Jean-Nicot, incorporating a former farm called La Grenouillère, once owned by the playwright Beaumarchais. In 1905, as the Gros-Caillou district became residential, the factory was demolished, apart from the management building, which was replaced in 1937 by the present-day Hôtel des Tabacs. The museum, renovated and reorganized, was opened in January 1979 in a building erected in 1963 at the corner of the Rue Surcouf and de l'Université.

Tour of the museum

30 mins.

The museum's collections, brought together by Seita since 1937 (the year of the World Fair), are presented in such a way as to illustrate the social role of tobacco in France and throughout the world. Some 500 objects are currently on display.

The collections

The introduction of tobacco to Europe. Among the foods and plants brought back to Europe by Christopher Columbus was tobacco, a plant whose origins are wholly American. On display are pre-Columbian objects, and a model of a caravel.

A discovery among others. From the Old World (Europe, Africa, Asia) the Americas received crops such as wheat, coffee, cotton, and sugarcane, while from the Americas to Europe and Asia came the tomato, maize, potatoes, and tobacco, as well as quinine from cichona bark, called *quinapuria* in Quechua, coca, cannabis and coffee. Only tobacco was universally distributed, and with it spread a number of its applications: pipe-smoking, snuff-taking, tobacco-chewing and, later, the smoking of cigars and cigarettes. Tobacco-related objects from all over the world: snuff boxes, pipes, etc., decorated plates from the 18th and 19th c., and various objects linked to the use of tobacco, stimulants, and drugs.

Tobacco – the plant. In modern classification – *Nicotiana* is a genus belonging to the *Solaneceae* family, and comprises at least 60 species divided into three subgenus groups: *Nicotiana tabacum*, *Nicotiana rustica*, and *Nicotiana petunoides*. Herbariums, engravings, specimens of cultivated tobaccos, and so forth.

From the plant to the product. The industrial processes of today were long performed by tobacco consumers themselves. Models of dryers and choppers from different periods.

Medical ventures. Originally used by the medical profession as a sneezing powder, snuff and its taking gradually became a widespread social practice in France (→ inset).

Books and engravings from the 17th c. to the present day. Tobacco graters made from ivory, enamel, boxwood, and so on; snuff boxes in every shape and size and in every kind of material from the 17th to the 19th c.: a quite outstanding collection.

The pipe. This was the basic technique that ensured the popularity of tobacco before the appearance of the cigar and the cigarette. Introduced from America along with tobacco, the pipe underwent its first modification when the simple tube used by Native Americans was replaced by an angled form. The pipe was rapidly adapted to the uses of different nations, and found its definitive form in the 17th c., except in Europe, where it continued to evolve until the start of the 20th c.. A collection of pipes from all over the world and from every period.

The cigar and the cigarette. Cigars and cigarettes existed in America before the arrival of Columbus and the Europeans, albeit in rudimentary form. They took the place of snuff and the pipe from the 18th c. (cigars) and 19th c. (cigarettes) onwards, giving rise to methods of packing and presentation that were often very refined. Cigar cases and boxes, *vistas*, cigar-bands, cigar and cigarette holders, and other related objects.

Distribution. A collection of items that lent their charm to old tobacconist's shops: jars, scales, posters, shop signs, and the like.

The smoker's artifacts. Tobacco has given rise to the production of objects of a diversity that makes classification difficult: things for storing tobacco and others for use in its consumption, cleaning tools, individualized tobacco jars, cigar clippers, tobacco pouches, pipe racks – an endless list.

The smoker's study, or how a 19th-c. gentleman indulged his secret passion. Here can be seen, notably, a *cabinet à cigares* specially made for Napoléon III.

A gallery adjoining the museum (Galerie de la Seita) houses temporary exhibitions of the plastic arts.

Various audiovisual programs complete the presentation of the museum and its collections.

▷ Snuff

Made popular by the court, where it had been introduced by Jean Nicot, snuff found great favor with the nobility. At first simple, it was eventually developed into many refined forms. In the 17th c. it was mixed with all kinds of flavors, while in the meantime craftsmen and artists pitted their wits against one another to find ingenious designs for graters and snuff boxes. But there was also fraud, to an extent that an association was formed of *Râpeurs jurés*, who alone had the right to grind tobacco into powder.

The passion for snuff died out in Europe in the 19th c., but its use is still considerable in certain parts of the world, such as North Africa.

▣ Musée de la Serrure* (Museum of Locksmiths)

1 Rue de la Perle, 3rd arr. Tel: 42–77–79–62.
Map ref: 18–C2, D2
Curator: Mme Prade
Open daily Tues. to Sat. 10am–noon and 2–5pm; closed public holidays and Aug.
Métro: Saint-Paul, Chemin-Vert
Bus: 29

This beautiful museum, in the heart of the Marais district, tells the history of locks through the ages. The collection has been displayed with great taste and refinement in the Hôtel Libéral Bruant (for history and architecture → Marais, Rue de la Perle). The Bricard Company, which specializes in decorative locks, has restored the hôtel in order to house the museum.

Tour of the museum

45 mins.

The collections

From Gallo-Roman times to the present day: numerous bronze and iron Gallo-Roman keys; Gothic door knockers; bolts with the cipher of François I, the arms of Anne de Montmorency, High Constable of France, and Diane de Poitiers' emblem, pendant door-knockers*; 15th-c. German pieces. Lock with hasp in chased bronze (Milan, 1550); in showcase 3, Renaissance keys in the shape of chimeras.

From the 16th to the 18th c.: locks with the arms of Nicolas Fouquet; iron bolt with the arms of Henri IV and Marie de' Medici; flat bolt shaped like a parsley leaf*. Door-knocker from Venice (16th c.); lock with night bolt. A remarkable collection of locks that are real masterpieces.

18th to early 19th c. In the center showcase a *vase de rampe*, a small decorative feature found on hinges, from the Château de Saint-Cloud; keys for cases and portfolios, mounts for bracket clocks. Elaborate long hasp, called an *espagnolette*, from a French-window, made by the famous chaser and gilder Gouthière (1732–1814). Locks for coffers and chests.

A collection of early 20th-c. door handles.
One room is devoted to the work of Bricard, dating from 1900.

Anterooms: provostal lock (*ca.* 1780); small coffer for carrying packages. Bolts with Napoléon's monogram, formerly in the Louvre. Chamberlains' keys bearing the arms of Nicholas I; a lock** from the Marshals' salon at the Tuileries, and a window catch also from the Tuileries, with the monogram of Napoléon III and the Empress Eugénie. Many original items from royal residences.

There is a reconstruction of a locksmith's workshop in the courtyard.

Musée du Service de Santé

→*Musée du Val-de-Grâce*

▣ Musée de la Table

15 Quai de la Tournelle, entrance: ground floor of La Tour d'Argent restaurant, 5th arr. Tel: 43-54-23-31. Map ref: 17-B3, 18-C3
Tours: restaurant clientele only.
Métro: Cardinal-Lemoine.
Bus: 24, 47, 63.

Tour of the museum

On the ground floor of the very famous, very exclusive restaurant La Tour d'Argent, Claude Terrail has set up a small museum of the table and gastronomy.

The table at the Café Anglais round which the three emperors (Tsar Alexander II – with the Tsarevich, later Alexander III, William I of Prussia, and the Prince von Bismarck) met on June 7, 1867, has been recreated in all its sumptuous brilliance. There are several superb dinner services; East India Company dishes; Sèvres china from the Château d'Eu; as well as a collection of menus and famous autographs, and books on the culinary arts.

▣ Musée National des Techniques**

270 Rue Saint-Martin, 3rd arr. Tel: 40-27-22-20.
Map ref: 12-C3
Open Tues.-Sat., 10am-5.30pm
Groups must make reservations 15 days in advance.
Métro: Réaumur-Sebastopol, Strasbourg-Saint-Denis.
Buses: 38, 47,

Within the National Conservatory of Arts and Crafts, which

occupies the old Priory of Saint-Martin-des-Champs, the Musée National des Techniques possesses a collection of 80,000 objects and documents from the 17th c. to the present day: 8000 objects are on permanent display, illustrating the stages of technical history and the origins of technical invention. The permanent exhibitions are of interest to all, and are supplemented by temporary exhibitions changed annually.

History of the museum

The Priory of Saint-Martin-des-Champs, often called 'the third daughter of Cluny,' was for centuries one of the most important religious establishments of Paris until it was expropriated under the Revolution. Various users were suggested for the building until, in 1798, it became the home of the Conservatoire des Arts et Métiers, founded on October 10, 1794.

The Musée des Techniques, opened to the public in 1802, occupies the large quadrangle between the main courtyard and the Rue Vaucanson, built partly by Antoine in the 18th c. It is the oldest museum of its kind in the world. The personal collection of Jacques Vaucanson, who had acquired a certain celebrity for his invention of certain mechanical figures, called *automates* – most famous among them a flute player and a duck. Vaucanson presented all his inventions to the king; the collection formed the basis of the museum, with the later addition of objects relating to science and technology confiscated from the migrés. Since then the collection has been further enriched by numerous bequests and donations.

In 1836 Léon Vaudoyer had the buildings considerably enlarged; the church was completely restored in the second half of the 19th c. and an extensive program of renovation was undertaken after 1958. Since 1978 considerable changes have taken place in the organization of the museum.

Tour of the museum

1½ hrs.

The current reorganization renders a room-by-room description impossible, so the collection is presented below thematically.

Entrance: the Salle de l'Echo (Hall of the Echo) is so called because words whispered in one corner can be heard clearly in the diagonally opposite corner. The instruments of Lavoisier's laboratory are kept here.

Energy

Model windmills and scale models of machines, some of which are very beautiful, dating from the 18th c. Water wheels and turbines, including Fourneyron's (1832). The famous 'Marly machine.' Water pump by Montgolfier. Newcommen's atmospheric machine (1705); machine by Watt (1781). Electric motors by Pierret and Froment; epicycloid electric motor; electromagnetic motor by Froment; Electricity generating apparatus. The first internal combustion engine made by Lenoir (1860), and Planté's first accumulators (1859).

Uses of electric energy in everyday life: elevators, municipal heating, Edison's inventions. Domestic technology; domestic electrical appliances.

Old electricity machines, some dating from the 18th c. (machines by van Marum, Nairne); large electric machine from the Duc de Chaulnes' study. Electric motors by Ampère and Deprez.

▷ Not to be missed

Stephenson's locomotive (transport section).
The collection of 18th- and 19th-c. planetarium clocks.
Girl playing a dulcimer, musical automaton that belonged to Marie-Antoinette.

The outstanding collection of microscopes (optics section).

Mechanics and mechanical tools

Numerous models of mechanical tools; a drawing picture device for portraits used by Louis XVI; towers made by Vaucanson before 1750 and by Senot (1795). Models of cogwheels and mechanisms for the transmission of movement.

Metallurgy and iron and steel manufacture

Extraction and conversion of ores; Thomas convertors; different types of furnace. Pudding furnace in use in 1867, 18th-c. forge-hammer; Bessemer convertors; blast furnaces.

The old church of Saint-Martin-des-Champs

In the nave various locomotion engines are arranged. Esnault-Pelterie airplane (1906); the airplane in which Blériot crossed the Channel on July 25, 1909; Bréguet airplane (1910) in which Henri Brégi flew from Fez to Casablanca in 2 hours and 50 minutes; steam motor of Atar's airplane *Eole*; Cugnot's steam '*fardier*' dray (1770), forerunner of the heavy truck; steam-driven carriages made by Amédée Bollée (1873) and Serpollet (1888); gasoline-powered cars by Panhard, Peugeot, and Dion (1893–96); gearboxes worked by electric motors which visitors can set in motion; Millet's first tricycle (1878) with rotary motor and electric light; collection of cycles from the *draisienne*, ancestor of the bicycle invented by the Baron Drais onward. Display of trams, trolleys. Stephenson's locomotive and tender**; machine by Marc Seguin; complete collection of models** (scale 1:43) of French locomotives and train cars from their beginnings.

Chronometry

Foucault's clock (1855) demonstrating the earth's rotation. Astronomical, electric, and atomic clocks. Calendar clocks.

Early clock-making***: celestial globes by Burgi and Reinhold, with perpetual calendar (16th c.); Thomas Heath's planetarium (mid-18th c.); astronomical clock by Mathieu Kriegseissen (1726); regulator by Lepaute in a Louis XV case (1775); earth-and-moon planetarium clock by Raingo and Garnier (1830); calendar clock by Brocot (1839); 15th-c. iron clocks; clock by Thurel in a case attributed to Boulle (1712). Marble clock with mobile dial by Lepaute (1770); planetarium clock, solar systems; clock with carillon and pipe music by Van Hoof (Antwerp, 1790); clock by Lepaute with planetarium (1795); calendar clock showing the days of the month by Charles Bertrand (1785); clock with winder regulator, by Bourdier (1880); clock that can also serve as a metronome, by Bréguet (1800); celestial globe with clockwork movement by Desnos (1775). Naval clocks and tools by Berthoud. Japanese clock by Nori Yoshi (early 18th c.); clock with night-light (1670); universal clocks by Pierre Fardoil (1710); Dutch clock with mechanical figures and organ music (1700); Louis XV wall clock with case in green shell; collection of watch movements with balance wheels (18th c.); decimal and sexagesimal time clock by Lepaute; astronomical regulators by Gallonde, Berthoud, Gudin, Lepaute.

Astronomy and Geodesy. A number of old instruments. Collections of astrolabes: the astrolabe was the most widely used astronomical instrument of ancient times, reaching its peak during the Renaissance. Octants and sextants; astronomical rings; telescopes.

Early automatons

Moving tableau with the arms of Marie-Antoinette (1770); moving tableau with the arms of Mme de Pompadour (view of Saint-Ouen); mechanical singing birds (1785); *Girl playing a Dulcimer*** by Kintzing (1785), an automaton once belonging to Marie-Antoinette that plays tunes taken from Gluck's *Armide*, arranged by the composer.

Mathematics: various calculating and writing machines; arithmetical machines. From the abacus to the Bull machine. Machines by Pascal (1652) and Bollé (1889).

Communications and telecommunications

Images and sounds. History of photography. Reconstruction of a photographer's darkroom. Second Empire itinerant photographer's carriage. Display case devoted to Marey and his research on movement. Important dates in photography since 1822: the work of Niepce and Daguerre (1829); the daguerrotype (1840). From photography to cinematography: the Lumière brothers' first camera (1895), professional and amateur cinema. The phonograph: past and present models. Television. Radio astronomy: radar detection: a satellite; goniometry angular measure. Telegraphy: the work of Branly; the birth of radio broadcasting (it is interesting to follow this visit by one to the Radio Museum).

Physics

Mechanical physics: weight, falling bodies (General Morin's apparatus); center of gravity, colliding bodies; parallelogram of forces, levers. Display case with Foucault's experiments. Various items from royal houses and from the Abbé Nollet's study. Apparatus of the physicist Charles, and of Regnault for the study of steam pressure; refrigerating apparatus of Thilorier, Carré and Cailletet. Apparatus for demonstrating the laws of the dynamics and statics of solids and of hydrostatics. Undulatory mechanics. Electricity: 18th-c. static electricity apparatus; works by Volta; works by Planté, inventor of electrical accumulators.

La Salle d'honneur

Situated at the top of Antoine's spiral staircase, this hall contains a group of scale models illustrating various crafts based on the plates in the *Encyclopédia* commissioned by Mme de Genlis for the children of the Duc d'Orléans, to whom she was governess.

Glass: various uses of glass both artistic and practical. Pieces by the Nancy glassmaker Gallé, characteristic of his style and period. Pieces by Lalique and Daum; crystal from Venice, Saint-Louis and Baccarat.

Metrology: collection of weights and measures. Optics: microscopes from the Nachel collection**, the most important in the world; Foucault's apparatus for measuring the speed of light.

Agricultural Technology: evolution of machines from the medieval peasant's hand-plough to the tractor; agriculture in general.

▣ L'Institut Tessin* (Swedish Cultural Center)

11, Rue Payenne, 3rd arr. Tel: 42–71–82–20.
Map ref: 18–D2
Open Thurs–Fri Sept—July 2pm–6pm. Closed August
Library: open Tues.–Fri. 2pm–5pm
Métro: Saint-Paul, Chemin-Vert.
Bus: 29, 69, 76, 96

The Tessin Institute was founded in 1933 by Gunnar W. Lundberg, then Cultural Attaché at the Swedish Embassy in Paris, and since 1971 has occupied the Hôtel de Marle, built at the end of the 16th c. On show is a collection of 17th to 20th-c. paintings recalling the close links between France and Sweden. The foundation is named in honor of Count Carl Gustav Tessin, Swedish Ambassador to France from 1739 to 1742 and a great art collector. An important part of his collection is now in the Department of Drawings at the National Museum, Stockholm.

The Hôtel de Marle also houses the Swedish Cultural Center, which accommodates Swedish artists and researchers staying in Paris and organizes exhibitions of contemporary art, concerts, film shows, and lectures. The library has an extensive collection of books on Swedish art.

Tour of the museum

30 mins.

The institute's collection is on view on the first floor in an 18th-c. setting, with a Rouen faience stove, beneath the original ceiling with painted beams.

Among the works on view are a portrait of Count Tessin by Martin Meytens (1695–1770); Academy diploma piece, by Wertmüller (1751–1811), a portrait of the artist Bachelier; the exquisite portrait of Suzanne Giroust* by her husband Alexander Roslin (1718–93), famous for his portraits in late 18th-c. Paris; some important pastels by Gustaf Lundberg (1695–1786), including a portrait of Guillaume de Taraval, first Professor at the Stockholm Academy of Fine Arts, and a little-known portrait of King Gustav III*. Also works by 19th-c. and 20th-c. Swedish artists, notably landscapes by the great mystic Carl Kylberg (1878–1952).

▣ Palais de Tokyo

13 Ave. du Président-Wilson, 16th arr. Tel: 47–23–36–53. Map ref: 14–C1
Métro: Alma-Marceau, Iena.

Bus: 32, 42, 63, 82, 92.

The Palais de Tokyo no longer houses the collections of the National Museum of Modern Art, which are now divided between the Centre Georges-Pompidou (1977) and the Musée d'Orsay (1986). However, the building, erected in 1937 for the World Fair (→ Chaillot), is to become the Palais de l'Image and the home for several organizations connected with the cinema and photography.

The Centre National de la Photographie (open daily except Tues., 9:45am–5:15pm), mounts temporary exhibitions of a thematic or retrospective nature in conjunction with the Mission du Patrimoine Photographique and the photographic service of the Délégation aux Arts Plastiques (for information on programs, tel: 45. 35. 43. 03).

FEMIS (Fondation Européene des Métiers de l'Image et du Son) is not open to the public, but it trains students in the cinematic and audiovisual arts. Current plans include the installation of the Cinemathèque Française and Musée du Cinema (→Museums), at present in the Palais de Chaillot, in the Palais de Tokyo, as well as a joint library which would bring together the existing resources of the three organisations.

The Musée du Val-de-Grâce (Museum of the Army Medical Service)

1 Place Alphonse-Laveran, 5th arr. Tel: 43-29-12-31. Map ref: 22-A2
Métro: Port-Royal, Saint-Jacques
Bus: 27, 83, 91

The Val-de-Grâce museum was created during World War II to house the ever-increasing number of documents relating to the history of the military medical service and medical supplies. It is run by the army medical service itself.

The museum is situated on the first floor of the W Wing of the old monastic buildings, which have remained more or less as they were when they were built by order of Anne of Austria to celebrate the birth of the dauphin. Begun by F. Mansart, the construction was completed (1645-57) by the architects Le Mercier, Le Duc, and Le Muet. The Val-de-Grâce became a military hospital in 1795 and, since the medical service's school of instruction was added to it, all military doctors of Paris have studied within these imposing walls.

Tour of the museum

30 mins.

The first rooms

The first rooms are devoted to the history of the medical service since it was institutionalized by Baron Dominique Larrey, surgeon-in-chief of the Grande Armée. Here are housed busts and portraits of doctors of lasting repute, various memorabilia, insignia, decorations (such as the ribbon of the Order of St Anne of Russia), as well as a number of scientific reports and compilations of clinical observations made in military hospitals. Summary of medical history from the 14th to the 19th c.

The gallery

In the large horseshoe-shaped gallery are actual specimens or small-scale models of equipment used in World War I to administer first aid to the wounded and for their evacuation behind the lines. In the glass cases, surgical instruments, from the most primitive to the most highly perfected; various artificial limbs; military doctors' instrument kits. Reconstructed field hospitals; hospital aircraft.

The uniform rooms: watercolors and dummies illustrating the history of military surgeons' uniforms from their creation in 1757 to the present day. Manuscript room: souvenirs of the Drs Larrey, father and son.

▣ The Musée Valentin-Haüy

5 Rue Duroc, 7th arr. Tel: 47–34–07–90. Map ref: 21–A1, B1
Open Tues.-Wed., 2:30pm–5pm; closed public holidays and July-Aug.
Métro: Duroc
Bus: 28, 39, 70, 82, 72

The Musée Valentin-Haüy is a private museum belonging to the Valentin-Haüy Association for the Blind, founded in 1889. It is a historical and teaching museum which presents, in a bright and attractive room, everything that has contributed to the teaching of the blind and allowed them access to all the intellectual disciplines and to many activities, from the first books produced with raised characters by Valentin Haüy (1745–1822) to the script of raised dots invented by Louis Braille (1809–52), the only one now in general use.

Among other objects of interest here are machines and typewriters with keys cast in relief, maps, world globes, objects made by blind artisans, various moving and precious mementoes and documents, and bronzes by the blind sculptor Vidal (1832–92).

▣ Musée de la vie Romantique

16 Rue Chaptal, 9th arr. Tel. 48–74–95–38. Map ref: 4–D3
Curator: Mme Á. M. de Brem
Open Tues.-Sun. 10am–5.40pm.; Closed on public holidays.

Métro: Saint-Georges, Pigalle
Bus: 67, 74

The Musée Renan-Scheffer (also known as Musée de la Vie Romantique) was passed to the City of Paris in 1982. It is now an annex of the Carnavalet Museum. The ground floor houses a permanent collection of memorabilia associated with George Sand. The first floor is used for temporary exhibitions associated with the literary and artistic life of the 19th c.

Tour of the museum

30 mins.

The museum is in a beautiful Restoration mansion which, from 1830, was the home of the painter and engraver Ary Scheffer (→ inset), and where he held his Friday salons. Here, for almost 30 years, he entertained the most brilliant names in the world of the arts, including Ingres, Delacroix, Chopin, Liszt, Lamartine, George Sand, Turgenev, and Ernest Renan, who married his niece. Later, she continued to hold the weekly salons.

Four rooms on the ground floor contain memorabilia of the writer George Sand, who lived close by in the Square d'Orléans from 1842 to 1847. Portraits, drawings, and jewelry, given by her granddaughter, Aurore Lauth-Sand, have been collected together in these rooms. Exhibitions on the other occupants of the house – and on the 19th c. are presented each year.

▷ Ary Scheffer

Of Dutch origin, Ary Scheffer (1795–1858) settled in Paris in 1811. As a painter he embraced many genres: historical, religious and classical paintings, portraits, illustrations for the works of Byron, Dante and the Germans, Goethe and Schiller. As drawing master to the children of the Duc d'Orléans (the future Louis-Philippe) he had considerable success. Favored by the king whose portrait he painted (Musée Condé, Chantilly), he received many commissions. He participated in the decoration of the historical museum at Versailles: *Entry of Philippe Auguste into Paris*, *Death of Gaston de Foix*, *Entry of Louis XII into Genoa*. In his day he was considered to be one of the most representative painters of the Romantic movement, and his sentimental pictures were very fashionable throughout Europe and America in the 19th c.

Cité de la Villette (The Villette Museum)

→La Villette district

▣ Musée du Vin (The Wine Museum)

Rue des Eaux. Entrance: 5 Square Charles-Dickens, 16th arr. Tel:
45-25-63-26.
Map ref: 13–A2, B2
Open daily except Mon. noon–6pm.
Métro: Passy (down the stairs and turn r.)
Bus: 72

Tour of the museum

30 mins.

Situated among quarries in use since the Middle Ages and used as a
cellar by the monks of the Abbey of Passy (15th c.), this museum
brings together, in its vaulted galleries, numerous objects and
documents relating to the cultivation of the vine and wine-making
(harvesting, cooperage, glassworking, oenology). A dozen scenes,
brought to life by wax figures, show the history of the place and the
principal French wine regions. The wine museum is the seat of the
council of the Echansons de France (Cup bearers of France).

Food is served in a bistro-like reconstruction, where rooms may be
hired for the evening and wine-tasting and purchase of some wines
are available.

▣ The Musée Zadkine*

100 bis Rue d'Assas, at far end of courtyard, door on the r., 6th arr.
Tel: 43–26–91–90. Map ref. 22–D2
Curator: M. Sylvain Lecombre
Open Tues.–Sun. 10am–5:30pm
Library: open by appointment. Documents relating to Zadkine's works.
Métro: Notre-Dame-des-Champs, Vavin, Port-Royal
Bus: 38, 58, 82, 83, 91

This municipal museum is situated in the studio that Zadkine occupied from 1928 until his death in 1967. The little house, an unexpected find in the very heart of Paris, captivated the artist, who wrote to a friend 'Come and see my folly in Assas and you will understand how much a man's life can be changed by a dovecote or a tree'.

The museum possesses some 300 works by Zadkine, bequeathed by his widow, the painter Valentine Prax. It allows the visitor to follow the career of this sculptor who, beginning from Cubist theories, went on to develop towards Expressionism and Abstraction.

Tour of the museum

45 mins.

Room 1

This room brings together the artist's first sculptures, under the influence of Cubism: *Woman with a Fan* (1923); *The Accordion Player* (1924).

Room 2

Works from the years 1928 to 1945, inspired by Antique models: *The Maenads* (1929); *The Counsellors* (1930).

In the middle of the room is displayed the model for *The Destroyed City* (1947), Zadkine's most famous work, erected in Rotterdam after World War II.

Room 3

Post-war works: *Prometheus*, the original wood carving of the sculpture which stands in front of the Pompidou Center (1955); a series of studies for two monuments to Van Gogh erected at Auvers-sur-Oise and in Holland.

The garden

Monumental works: *The Human Forest* (1945), in which Zadkine plays with solid and hollow shapes; *The Poet*, a homage to Eluard (1954) *The Home*, (1959) and *The Portico* (1965), tending toward abstraction.

Select Bibliography

For further reading, consult BRITISH BOOKS IN PRINT, published by J. Whitaker and available in most reference libraries, which lists all the titles currently in print on France in general and Paris in particular. Most of the works of the great French writers are available in translation. Consult your librarian or a good bookshop.

General
Ardagh, J. *France Today*, Penguin, 1982, rep. 1970.
Arnold, W., *A Select Guide to Historic Hotels of Paris*, Thames & Hudson, 1990.
Baville, K. and Salmon, T., *The Rough Guide to Paris*, Harrap-Columbus, 1989, rep. 1990.
Bond, M., *Pleasures of Paris*, Pavilion Books, 1987
Cobb, R., *Streets of Paris*, Duckworth, 1980
Cooper, M., *French Music from the Death of Berlioz to the Death of Fauré*, Oxford University Press, 1970.
Crow, T., *Painters and Public Life in the 18th-century, Paris*, Yale, 1985.
Gallant, M., *Paris Notebooks*, Bloomsbury, 1988
Haigh, *Walks in Gertrude Stein's Paris: 5 tours for the literary traveller*, G. M. Smith (U.S.), 1988
Landes, S. & Landes, A., *Paris Walks*, Robson, 1986
Mehling, F. N. (ed), *Paris and the Ile de France*, Phaidon Press, 1987
Pita (ed), *An Encyclopaedia of Paris Opera*, Greenwood Press, London, 1985
Miller, R., (trs.), *Secret Paris of the Thirties* (by 'Brassai'), Thames & Hudson, 1978
Moore, C., *Paris for all Seasons*, Venton, 1975

Post, L., *A Shopper's Guide to Paris*, Michael Joseph, 1987

Slide, A., *Fifty Classic French Films: 1912–1982*, Dover Publications, 1988

Steele, V., *Paris Fashion: A Cultural History*, Oxford University Press, NY, 1988

Stein, Gertrude, *Paris, Personal Recollections*, Brilliance Books, 1982

Trollope, F., *Paris and the Parisians*, Sutton Publications, 1985

Wells, P., *The Food Lover's Guide to Paris*, Methuen, 1984

White, S., *Sam White's Paris*, New English Library, 1983

Wiser, W., *Crazy Years: Paris in the Twenties*, Thames & Hudson, 1983

Wright, J. B., *Paris as it Was*, Hendon Publishing Co., 1985

Art and Architecture

Blunt, A., *Art and Architecture in France 1500–1700* (Pelican History of Art), Penguin Books, 1957

Boinet, A., *Les Eglises parisiennes*, Paris: Ed de Minuit, 1958–1964.

Clark, T. J., *Paris in the Art of Manet and his Followers*, Thames & Hudson, 1985

Dacier, Emile, *L'Art au XVIII siecle en France: Epoques Regence, Louis XV, 1715–1760*, Paris: Le Prat, 1951

Dumolin, M., *Les Eglises de France; Paris et la Seine*, Paris: Letouzey, 1936

Dunlop, F. (ed), *Paris Art Guide*, Art Guide Publications, 1983

De Goncourt, F. & J., *French XVIII-century Painters* (trans. by R. Ironside), Phaidon, 1981

Friedlander, W. F., *From David to Delacroix*, Harvard University Press, Cambridge, Mass., 1952

Honour, H., *Neo-Classicism*, Harmondsworth: Penguin, 1968

James, J., *The Traveller's Key to Medieval France. A Guide to the Sacred Architecture of Medieval France*, Harrap Columbus, 1987

Kalnein, Wendy Graf and Levey, M., *Art and Architecture of the Eighteenth Century in France*, Penguin, Baltimore, 1972

Lavedan, P., *L'architecture française*, Paris, 1944; English ed., Penguin Books, 1956

Martin, H., *Guide de l'architecture moderne à Paris 1900–1990*, Paris: Alternatives, 1986

Milner, J., *Studios of Paris – Capital of Art in the Late Nineteenth Century*, Yale, 1988

Reau, L., *L'Art au XVIII siecle en France: style Louis XVI*, Paris: Le Prat, 1952.

Rewald, J., *The History of Impressionism*, 4th ed., New York Graphic Society, Greenwich, Conn., 1973

Savage, G., *French Decorative Art 1638–1793*, London: Penguin; NY: Praegar, 1969

Thomson, D. & J. (trans. S. Gilbert), *Renaissance Paris: Architecture and Growth from 1475–1600*, Zwemmer, 1984

Thuillier, J. & C., *French Painting from Le Nain to Fragonard*, Skira, Geneva, 1964

Violle, B., *Paris, son église et ses églises,* Paris: Le Cerf, 1982
Wakefield, D., *French 18th-century Paintings,* Gordon Fraser, 1984
Whelpton, B., *Painters' Paris,* Johnson Publications, 1970

Economics
Carre, J. J., *French Economic Growth* (trans. from the French), Oxford University Press, 1975
Holmes, G. & Fawcett, P., *Contemporary French Economy,* Macmillan, 1983
Lewis, H. D., *French Economic System,* Croom Helm, 1985

History and Politics
Anderson, R. D., *France 1870-1914 – Politics and Society,* Routledge, 1984
Berlanstein, L., *The Working People of Paris,* 1871-1914, John Hopkins University Press, 1988
Cazelles, R., *De la fin du régne de Philippe Auguste à la mort de Charles V (1123-1380),* Paris: Hachette, 1972
Doyle, W., *Origins of the French Revolution,* Oxford University Press, 1981
Elwitt, S., *Making of the Third Reich: Class and Politics in France, 1900-04,* Louisiana University Press, 1975
Evenson, N., *Paris: A Century of Change 1878-1978,* Yale University Press, 1979
Fawtier (trs.), *Capetian Kings of France, Monarchy and Nation 987-1328,* Papermac 1963
Garioch, *Neighbourhood and Community in Paris,* 1740-90, Cambridge University Press, 1986
Gibson, V. P., *Paris During the Commune,* 1895 (new ed), Haskell House Publishers (U.S.), 1982
Hibbert, C., *The French Revolution,* Penguin, 1982
Horne, A., *The Fall of Paris; the Siege and Commune 1870 71,* Macmillan, 1965; Papermac, 1990
Jones, D. P., *Paris in the 3rd Reich,* Collins, 1918
Kranzberg, M., *Siege of Paris, 1870-71: Political and Social History,* Greenwood Press, London (n/e of 1950)
Leveque, J. J., *Guide de la Revolution Francaise,* Paris: Horay, 1986
Lissagareay, H., *History of the Paris Commune of 1871,* New Park, 1976
Millet, M., *Histoire de l'Ile de France et de Paris,* Toulouse, Privat, 1971
Ouston, P., *France in the 20th Century,* Macmillan, 1972
Paxton, J., *The French Revolution,* Facts on File (U.S.), 1988
Randell, K., *The Third Republic, 1970-1914,* Edward Arnold, 1986
Salmon, J., *Society in Crisis: France in the 16th century,* Methuen, 1979
Sauvigny, G. De, (ed. Pinkney), *History of France,* Forum Press (U.S.), 1983
Slater, M., *Contemporary French Politics,* Macmillan Educ., 1985

Sutherland, D., *France, 1789–1815. Revolution and Counter-Revolution*, Collins, 1985/Fontana p/b, 1985
Tulard, J., *Paris Pendant la Revolution*, Paris: Hachette
Villefosse, Heron de, *Histoire de Paris*, Ed. Parus, 1950

Literature and Philosophy
Brereton, G., *A Short History of French Dramatic Literature in the 17th century.* Lancaster, n.d.
Brereton, G., *French Comic Drama from the 16th to the 18th c.*, Methuen, 1977
Brereton, G., *French Tragic Drama in the 16th and 17th c.*, Methuen, 1973
Carpenter, H., *Geniuses Together: American Writers in Paris in the 1920s*, Unwin Paperbacks, 1989
Cazamian, L.: *A History of French Literature*, Clarendon Press, Oxford, 1955; rep. 1960
Charvet, P. E. (Gen. Ed.): *A Literary History of France, 1967–70* (6 vols) Ernest Benn, n.d.
Cruickshank, K. (ed): *French Literature and its Background* (6 vols), Oxford University Press
Dictionary of Literary Biography (DLB), ed. K. L. Rood: vol. 4: Gale Research Company, 1980
Fitch: *Literary History of Paris in the Twenties and Thirties: Sylvia Beach and the lost Generation*, Souvenir Press, 1984
Gregory, A., *The French Revolution and the English Novel*, Haskell House Publishers, (U.S.), 1982
Jones, D. P., *Paris in the 3rd Reich.* Collins, 1918
Haig, S., *Pursuit of Illusion in 19th-century French Fiction*, Louisiana State University Press, 1988
Lancaster, H. C., *Sunset: History of Parisian Drama in the last years of Louis XIV, 1701–15*, Greenwood Press, 1977
Littlewood, I., *Paris, a Literary Companion*, John Murray, 1987
Maurice, A. B., *Paris of the Novelists*, Kennikat Press, 1973
Oxford Companion to French Literature (ed. Sir Paul Harvey), Oxford University Press, 1959
Penguin Book of French Verse (ed. B. Woledge), Penguin, 1975
Peyre, H., *French Literary Imagination*, University of Alabama Press, 1976
Rees, W. C., (ed.), *French Poetry 1820–1950* (trans. from the French.), Penguin, 1989

The following list has been reproduced from the French edition of this book in case it will be of interest to readers of this volume. Most of the works listed below are available in English translations Consult your librarian or a good bookshop.

Bibliographie littéraire

French Literature – a select list (includes a few titles set in by American authors)

15th c.
Villon (François), *La Ballade des pendus* (1463).

18th c.
Marivaux (Pierre de), *La Vie de Marianne* (1731–1741); *Le Paysan de Paris* (1734–1735)
Mercier (Louis-Sébastien), *Tableau de Paris* (1782–1788), Marseille, Slatkine Reprints, 1979
Montesquieu (Charles de), *Lettres persanes* (1721).
Prevost (Abbé), *Manon Lescaut (1731).*
Restlf de la Bretonne (N.-E), *Le Paysan perverti ou les dangers de la ville* (1777); *Les Nuits de Paris ou le spectateur nocturne* (1788–1793).

19th c.
Balzac (Honoré de), *La Comedie Humaine* (1838–1848), *scènes de la vie parisienne,* 23 vol.
Beaudelaire (Charles), *Les Fleurs du mal* (1857); *Spleen de Paris* (1869).
Daudet (Alphonse), *Fromont jeune et Risler aîné* (1874); *Les Rois en exil* (1879).
Dumas (Alexandre), *Les Trois Mousquetaires* (1843–1870); *Les Mohicans de Paris* (1845–1855).
Flaubert (Gustave), *L'Education sentimentale* (1869).
France (Anatole), *la Rôtisserie de la Reine Pédauque* (1893); *Le Lys rouge* (1894); *M. Bergeret à Paris* (1901).
Gautier (Théophile), *Tableaux de siège* Paris (1870–1871).

Concourt (Edmond et Jules de), *Journal. Mémoires littéraires* (1887-1888), Paris, Laffont, 1989
Hugo (Victor), *Choses vues* (1830-1885); *Notre-Dame-de-Paris* (1832); *Les Misérables* (1862).
Maupassant (Guy de), *Bel Ami* (1885).
Nerval (Gérard de), *Promenades et souvenirs* (1852-1854); *La Main enchantée* (1885), nouvelle
Sue (Eugène), *Les Mystères de Paris* (1842-1843), Paris, Laffont, 1989.
Zola (Emile), *Les Rougon-Macquart*, 1871-1893; *Les Trois Villes. Paris* (1897).

20th c.
Apollinaire (Guillaume), *Le Flâneur des deux rives* (1918).
Aragon (Louis), *Le Paysan de Paris* (1926); *Les Beaux quartiers* (1936).
Beauvoir (Simone), *Les Mandarins* (1954); *La Force de l'âge* (1954).
Benjamin (Walter), *Paris, capitale du XIXᵉ s. Passages,* Paris, ed. du Cerf, 1989.
Breton (André), *Nadja.*
Brink (André), *L'Ambassadeur,* Paris, Stock, 1986.
Carco (Francis), *Jésus-la-Caille* (1914), Paris, Albin Michel; *Envoûtement de Paris* (1938), Paris, Nathan Image.
Carpentier (Alejo), *Le Recours de la méthode,* Paris, Gallimard, 1975.
Cortazar (Julio), *62 maquettes à monter,* Paris, Gallimard. 1971.
Dabit (Eugène), *Hôtel du Nord* (1929), Paris, Denoël.
Fallet (rené), *Paris au mois d'août* (1964).
Fargue (Léon-Paul), *D'après Paris* (1932); *Le Piéton de Paris* (1939).
Hemingway (Ernest), *Le Soleil se leve aussi* (1926); *Paris est une fête* (published posthumously, 1964) – [*The Sun Also Rises* and *A Moveable Feast*].
Lepidis (Clément), *L'Arménien,* Paris ed. du Seuil, 1973.
Leroux (Gaston), *Le Fantôme de l'Opéra* (1920), Paris, Laffont.
Mac Orlan (Pierre), *Quai des Brumes* (1927).
Malet (Léo), *Les Nouveaux mystères de Paris,* Paris, Laffont.
Miller (Henry), *Tropic of Cancer* (1934), *Tropic of Capricorn* (1939), *Quiet Days in Clichy* (1956).
Modiano (Patrick), *Les Boulevards de ceinture,* Paris, Gallimard, 1972; *La Place de l'Etoile,* Paris, Gallimard, 1968.
Perec (Georges), *Tentative d'épuisement d'un lieu parisien* (1975), Paris, Bourgeois, 1983.
Proust (Marcel), *A la Recherche du Temps perdu* (1913-1922).
Queneau (Raymond), *La Saint-Glin-glin* (1948); *Zazie dans le métro* (1959).
Reda (Jacques), *Les Ruines de Paris,* Gallimard, 1977; *Le Château des courants d'air,* Paris, Gallimard, 1986; le Piétron de Paris.
Rhys (Jean), *Quai des Grands Augustins,* Paris, Denoël, 1979.
Rolland (Romain), *Jean-Christophe* (1903), Paris, Albin Michel; *L'Ame enchantée,* (1922-1934), Paris, Albin Michel.

Romains (Jules), *Les hommes de bonne volonté* (1931–1946).
Roubaud (Jacques), *Le Belle Hortense,* Paris, Ramsay, 1985.
Sabatier (Robert), *Les Sucettes à la menthe.*
Sartre (Jean-Paul), *Les Chemins de la Liberté,* 3 vol. (1944–1949).
Simenon (Georges), Les histoires du commissaire *Maigret* (1930–1979).
Simonin (Albert), *Confession d'un enfant de la Chapelle* (1977).
Soupault (Philippe), *Les Dernières nuits de Paris* (1928), Paris, Seghers.
Vilar (Jean-François), *Bastille-Tango,* Paris, Presses de la Renaissance, 1986; *Passage des Singes,* Paris, Presse de la Renaissance, 1984.

What to see in the Paris Museums

Ancient Civilizations: Art and History

Architecture

Astronomy

Ceramics: Porcelain and Pottery
Middle Ages and Renaissance

17th, 18th and 19th c.

1262   Musée de l'Homme

Industrial Design
1076   Centre de Création
       Industrielle
1280   Fondation Le
       Corbusier

Institutions
1169   Musée de l'Assistance
       Publique
1170   Musée de l'Avocat
       (Law)
1217   Musée de la Franc-
       Maconnerie
1250   Musée de l'Histoire de
       France
1260   Musée d'Histoire de la
       Préfecture de Police

Locks
1510   Musée de la Serrure

Maritime
1413   Musée de la Marine

Medicine
1169   Musée de l'Assistance
       Publique
1209   Palais de la
       Découverte
1213   Musée Dupuytren
1253   Musée de l'Histoire de
       la Médecine
1454   Musée Orfila
1519   Musée du Val-de-
       Grâce

Military Art and History
1124   Musée de l'Armée
1142   Musée National des
       Arts Africains et
       Océaniens
1194   Musée de la Chasse
       et de la Nature
1250   Musée d'Histoire
       Contemporaine
       (BDIC)

1280   Musée de la Légion
       d'Honneur et des
       Ordres de Chevalerie
1413   Musée de la Marine
1453   Musée de l'Ordre de
       la Libération
1495   Musée des Plans-
       Reliefs

Models and Statuettes
1413   Musée de la Marine
1495   Musée des Plans-
       Reliefs
1512   Musée National des
       Techniques

Music
1166   Musée National des
       Arts et Traditions
       Populaires
1192   Musée Charles-Cros
1262   Musée de l'Homme
1273   Musée Instrumental
       de Paris
1442   Musée de Musique
       Mécanique
1449   Musée de l'Opéra

National History
1124   Musée de l'Armée
1197   Musée Clemenceau
1213   Fondation Dosne-
       Thiers
1232   Musée Grévin
1250   Musée d'Histoire
       Contemporaine
       (BDIC)
1261   Musée de l'Histoire du
       Protestantisme
       Français
1280   Musée de la Légion
       d'Honneur et des
       Ordres de Chevalerie
1413   Musée de la Marine
1453   Musée de l'Ordre de
       la Libération

Natural Sciences
1253   Musée National
       d'Histoire Naturelle

1209 Palais de la
Découverte
1501 Musée de Radio-
France
1512 Musée National des
Techniques

Religious Art and History
1135 Musée d'Art Juif
1261 Musée de l'Histoire du
Protestantisme
Français
1447 Musée de Notre-Dame

Sculpture
Middle Ages
1197 Musée de Cluny
1344 Musée de Louvre
1430 Musée des
Monuments Français
1484 Musée du Petit Palais

16th, 17th and 18th century
1206 Musée Cognacq-Jay
1274 Musée Jacquemart-
André
1344 Musée du Louvre
1430 Musée des
Monuments Français
1484 Musée du Petit Palais

19th and 20th century
1136 Musée d'Art Moderne
de la Ville de Paris
1173 Musée Bourdelle
1219 Centre National d'Art
et de Culture
Georges-Pompidou
1245 Musée de la Halle
Saint-Pierre: naïve art.
1344 Musée du Louvre
1430 Musée des
Monuments Français
1484 Musée du Petit Palais
1455 Musée d'Orsay
1502 Musée Rodin
1507 Musée de Sculpture

en plein air (outdoor
sculpture) de la Ville
de Paris.

Sciences
1209 Palais de la
Découverte:
chemistry, electricity,
mathematics,
industrial mechanics,
optics, physics.
1253 Muséum d'Histoire
Naturelle: sciences of
the earth.
1262 Musée de
l'Holographie
1449 Musée de
l'Observatoire
1076 Cité des Sciences et
de l'Industrie:
electronics,
mathematics, robots.
1512 Musée National des
Techniques:
electricity, energy,
mathematics,
industrial mechanics,
optics, physics.

Tapestries
1149 Musée des Arts
Décoratifs
1176 Musée Carnavalet
1197 Musée de Cluny
1274 Musée Jacquemart-
André
1284 Musée du Louvre

Telecommunications, Television
1209 Palais de la
Découverte
1498 Musée de la Poste
1501 Musée de Radio-
France
1412 Musée National des
Techniques
1076 Cité des Sciences et
de l'Industrie

Terrestial and Extraterrestial Explorations
1413   Musée de la Marine
1076   Cité des Sciences et de l'Industrie

Textiles
1142   Musée National des Arts Africains et Océaniens
1166   Musée National des Arts et Traditions Populaires
1262   Musée de l'Homme
1512   Musée National des Techniques

Theatre
1166   Musée National des Arts et Traditions Populaires
1262   Musée de l'Homme
1278   Musée Kwok Ou: Far East.

Tobacco
1508   Musée de la SEITA

Toys and Games
1149   Musée des Arts Décoratifs
1166   Musée National des Arts et Traditions Populaires

Transport
1262   Musée de l'Homme
1413   Musée de la Marine
1498   Musée de la Poste
1512   Musée National des Techniques

Wine
1522   Musée du Vin

Zoology
1142   Musée National des Arts Africains et Océaniens: vivarium.
1194   Musée de la Chasse et de la Nature
1253   Muséum d'Histoire Naturelle

Thematic Index of Insets
(*Marked in the text with the symbol ▷*)

Architecture and Styles

History

Housing and Urban Planning

Populations of Paris

Public Highways, Street Furniture and Lighting

Science and Techniques

Scientific personalities, Inventors

Sculpture and Sculptors

Index of People

General Index